Nikolai Leskov
The Man and His Art

Nikolai Leskov
The Man and His Art

Hugh McLean

Harvard University Press
Cambridge, Massachusetts
London, England
1977

Library of Congress Cataloging in Publication Data

McLean, Hugh, 1925-
  Nikolai Leskov: the man and his art.

  Bibliography: p.
  Includes index.
  1. Leskov, Nikolai Semenovich, 1831-1895. 2. Authors,
Russian—19th century—Biography.
PG3337.L5Z77   891.7'3'3 [B]   77-647
ISBN 0-674-62471-8

Publication of this book has been aided by a grant from the
Andrew W. Mellon Foundation

To the memory of
Michael Karpovich

ᯓᯖ Preface ᯘᯖ

Leskov was a deeply embittered man. From the beginning of his career
to the end he made the same complaint over and over again, in almost
the same words and with the same emphasis: "In print I have received
only abuse." During thirty years of creative effort he waited vainly for
critical recognition. In the 1890s, as a sick old man, he said irritably
when an article or two did at last appear about him, "Now I am much
more interested in my illness than in articles about me." But he hardly
meant it. At the same time he was pitifully grateful to a now forgotten
critic who had written a patronizing article about him called "A Sick
Talent." Leskov wrote an uncharacteristically humble letter to the
author of this pompous misestimate, only objecting mildly to being
called a "sick talent" and offering "difficult growth" as a substitute
epigraph for his career. But humility is only an occasional counter-
point to the basic theme of Leskov's resentment and self-pity. The
quotation he was fondest of applying to himself was from Pushkin's
"The Hussar": "Here the care a man gets is like being caught in
Turkish crossfire."

Leskov was justified in his sense of injury. Russian criticism had
been badly mistaken about him. Long after he had earned the epaulets
of a literary general, the critics kept failing to endorse his promotion.
In the end he had to promote himself: "I only know," he said in the
1890s, "that in fifty years' time [of all the present-day writers] people
will read Tolstoy, Turgenev, and me." The list is a bit short, and the
reason Leskov gives for his expectation of literary longevity (his ideas,
not his art) has proved largely mistaken. But his confidence was legitimate. Leskov was indeed a great, if uneven, writer, and his persistent
survival of countless would-be burials has at last forced historians of
literature to admit the fact.

The reasons for the underestimation of Leskov by Russian critics are
many, but they fall into two general categories, ideological and liter-

ary. The ideological reasons are the more familiar. Since the days of Belinsky, Russian critics had been predominantly radical in politics, positivistic in philosophy, and "civic" in their demands on literature. Leskov stubbornly refused to produce according to these specifications. Although he toyed briefly with radicalism in the early 1860s, he remained basically a liberal and gradualist, who believed in working for reforms within the existing system rather than pulling it to pieces and starting afresh. Philosophically, his quest for a viable Weltanschauung took him not to Western secularism and socialism, as it did so many of his contemporaries, but back to a Christianity originally more or less in harmony with official Eastern Orthodoxy, but later developing into a thoroughgoing "Protestant" moralism that eventually merged with Tolstoy's. Leskov ardently believed in the didactic powers of literature, and he was also convinced that lasting improvements in the human condition could only be achieved by raising the moral standards of individuals, not by tinkering with social forms. He undertook to use his literary powers to promote that end. Reform must begin in the individual heart. On these and other ideological grounds Leskov's position was sharply divergent from that of the leading spokesmen of the Russian intelligentsia from the 1860s onward. There was a partial rapprochement in the 1890s, when Leskov's moral radicalism had brought him into sharp conflict with church and state; but there was never real agreement. In the eyes of the Russian intelligentsia, the label of religious conservative pasted on Leskov at the outset of his career had made him an object of suspicion forever.

This same label has made Leskov's position tenuous in postrevolutionary Russia, where, particularly but not exclusively in the Stalin period, there has been a tendency to revive and rigidify the civic tradition of nineteenth-century criticism in its worst features and to enforce its canons with the power of censorship and police. Leskov was too popular a writer to be discarded altogether, especially by a regime that claimed to represent the fulfillment of all that was best in the old culture. But he had to be passed through a filter: his religion and his political ideas had to be strained out and an essence of latent social protest distilled for the Soviet reader. This is the burden of the many editions of Leskov's selected works published since the Revolution, with their safely orthodox introductions designed to protect the faithful against any remnants of Leskovian error remaining after the selection. Leskov's antinihilism and his God were both deemed subversive to the good order of Communist society. A multivolume, though by no means complete, Soviet edition of Leskov became possible only in the "thaw" years, 1956-1958.

The literary explanation for the neglect of Leskov is not so well known, but equally important. Side by side with his belief in literature as a vehicle of social criticism, the typical nineteenth-century reader acknowledged a hierarchy of genres according to which the major form, indeed the only serious literary medium, was the realistic novel. By this he meant a fairly long piece of narrative prose fabricated on the assumption that literature faithfully reflects life, organized according to some unified structural plan, and preferably written in clear language that does not interfere with one's perception of contents. Serious novelists like Tolstoy, Turgenev, or Dostoevsky might also try their hands at the smaller genres, the short story or the novella, but their reputations rested on their novels.

Again Leskov was at odds with this stereotype. His best work was done in the very lesser genres traditionally regarded as mere pastimes or exercises. Moreover, even his stories and novellas do not conform to type. They are as a rule not organized around a central plot line, but made up of a series of episodes, often anecdotal in character, merely attached to one another within a loose framework. Worst of all, with Leskov, style becomes an aggressively independent aesthetic value demanding attention for its own sake. Readers deadly serious about content, including the supermoralist Tolstoy, regarded Leskov's floridity of language as an irritating and frivolous mannerism, evidence that he was fundamentally not a serious artist. It was only decades later, after Chekhov, Bunin, Remizov, Zamyatin, and others had shown that one could be a first-class prose writer without being primarily a novelist, and the Symbolists, especially Andrei Bely and his imitators, had accustomed people to so-called ornamental prose, that the average Russian reader was ready to admit Leskov to the ranks of the great. Before this process had reached its culmination, however, it was cut short by the Revolution and its aftermath.

Outside of Russia other factors have affected Leskov's reputation. Foreigners were obviously less likely to be dominated by Russian ideological stereotypes and taboos, either pre- or postrevolutionary. Nevertheless, some of these attitudes have been carried across Russia's borders, as if by a kind of inertia: we naturally expect a country to export its best cultural products, and we tend to rely on the natives to make the appropriate selection. Since nineteenth-century Russians did not, on the whole, regard Leskov as a major figure, there was not much inclination to promote his reputation abroad. Furthermore, in his case the problem of translation is severe. He is a very style-conscious writer with a varied and broad linguistic range, who manipulates his Russian—and even some other languages—for diverse artistic purposes; and it is extremely difficult to transpose these effects into another linguistic medium.

In France, Italy, England, and the United States, translations of Leskov have appeared from time to time—up to now some eleven volumes have appeared in English. But in spite of this accumulation and a discerning article by such a distinguished critic as V. S. Pritchett, Leskov's name still remains virtually unknown to the English-speaking public, even among people otherwise well-read. Germany, however, has been the exception among the Western countries. There much more of Leskov has been translated than elsewhere, and even before the Second World War Leskov's name had become a household word among German lovers of good literature, ranked alongside Turgenev, Tolstoy, and Dostoevsky. Perhaps the time has come for English-speaking readers to do the same.

I have worked on Leskov off and on for many years, and the institutions and people to whom I owe debts of gratitude are many, too many for me to mention them all here. The Guggenheim Foundation provided me with a fellowship, kindly supplemented by the University of Chicago, which granted a year's leave of absence during which most of the first half of this book was written. Later the Humanities Research Committee of the University of California made possible part of another year free from teaching and administrative duties, when most of the remainder was completed.

I must thank Mouton and Co., The Hague, the Division of the Humanities of the University of Chicago, Fink Verlag, Munich, the University of Chicago Press, and the University of California Press for permission to reprint portions of this work that appeared in books or magazines to which they hold copyright. The illustrations showing Leskov in the 1880s (frontispiece), in the 1860s (parts I and II), around 1890 (part III), and later in the 1890s (part IV; portrait by Valentin Serov) are from Lidia G. Chudnova, *Leskov v Peterburge* (Leningrad, 1975). The lithograph of Leskov's study is from N. S. Leskov, *Polnoe sobranie sočinenij*, 2nd ed., vol. 12 (St. Petersburg, 1897).

Important bibliographical assistance has been rendered by Thomas Aman, Irina Corten, and, in the Soviet Union, by K. P. Bogaevskaya and V. G. Zimina. A succession of research assistants at the University of California have provided help and stimulation: David Brodsky, Stephen Grad, and Barry Jordan, the last of whom both prepared the index and, with amazing accuracy, typed large portions of the long and difficult manuscript. Valued assistance with typing was also rendered by Nina Shebeko. Most of all, I want to record my unbounded appreciation for the help I have received over many years from William B. Edgerton of Indiana University, whose many painstaking and illuminating studies of Leskov have been an inspiration to me.

Berkeley, California   HMcL
December 1976

Note on Transliteration

Russian words and names forming integral parts of English sentences are spelled so as to facilitate pronunciation by readers who know no Russian. Russian words and sentences quoted in parentheses and bibliographical references in the notes are spelled according to the "international scholarly" system.

�☾☞ Contents ☜☽

Contents

⨳ Part I ⨳

⨳ Packing the Trunk ⨳
(1831-1859)

1

Class, Family, and Mr. Fear

The literary explosion in nineteenth-century Russia must remain one of the mysteries of human history; available explanations only nibble at its edges. Who could have predicted, looking forward from the year 1801, when Alexander "the Blessed" ascended the bloodstained throne of his murdered father, that the literature of his laggard country, then virtually unknown beyond Russia's borders and consisting mostly of pupilary imitations of European models, was soon to produce a succession of giants who would outdo their European masters at their craft and before the century was out would make their country loom as large on the literary as on the geographic map? Who can even explain the fact retrospectively?

Certainly the society that gave birth to these giants was anything but a healthy and "integrated" parent. It was riven by the deepest of class divisions. Its dominant elite was the numerically tiny landed gentry, for the time being the chief purveyor and consumer of this new, European-style literature, a class that in the course of the century was energetically to spend itself into bankruptcy. This self-destructive gentry was foolishly favored and at the same time oppressed by the cumbersome bureaucracy of the autocratic state, which assisted it in controlling and exploiting a vast population of agricultural peasants, impoverished, enslaved, and intermittently rebellious, as yet untouched by their proprietors' cultural importations from the West. Sandwiched in between these major estates were the medieval-style merchantry, fanatically conservative in mentality, and the benighted clergy, chronically underpaid, undereducated, and treated with contempt by gentry and peasantry alike. Each of these disparate classes was thus amply supplied with woes of its own, and their interaction engendered antagonisms in abundance. In the course of the nineteenth century all these groups were to spin off dissidents and drop-outs who coalesced to form that famous intelligentsia (the word itself is a Russian contribution to the world's vocabulary) that led the revolutionary movements that in turn ultimately succeeded in bringing the whole teetering structure down in ruins. Was this the formula for the social ambiance of a great literature?

In any event, if one was born in Russia in 1831, as was Nikolai Leskov, it made a great deal of difference just where one landed in the social hierarchy. Not only economic well-being, but culture, life-style, even language depended on it. For a future writer who undertook to depict this society in all its diversity, Leskov may be said to have chosen well. His father was a priest's son who had achieved technical nobility through government service; his mother was the daughter of a civil servant who claimed aristocratic descent but had married a merchant's daughter. Such a mixed-up ancestry was not so rare in Chekhov's time, but in 1831 it was highly unusual.

To start life from such a social crossroads had many psychological disadvantages: it was hard to establish a clear identity, to know just who you were and where you belonged. But it proved enormously useful to Leskov as a writer. It gave him a splendid view of the inner worlds of the three social classes to which he was genetically related, and of the peasantry as well, since his early years were spent on a small country estate where he was in constant contact with peasants. Furthermore, since he belonged securely to none of these worlds, he was a spokesman of none. He could compare and judge them. His literary creations in their entirety probably offer a better cross section of nineteenth-century Russian society than the work of any other writer of his time. In social range Leskov has no rival until Chekhov— not the aristocrats Turgenev and Tolstoy, nor the gentleman-clerk-professor-Bohemian Gogol, nor the doctor's son Dostoevsky, technically a nobleman but without any experience of country life. On their own territory they may perceive more keenly than Leskov, but none of them equals him in breadth.

Legally, Leskov belonged to the gentry, and it is evident that he would have liked to be more of a nobleman than he was. In most of the autobiographical summaries that he compiled from time to time, Leskov lists himself simply as stemming from the "nobility of Oryol province" (11:18), and he often refers to himself as a *barchuk* ("lord-ling"; 9:219) or *dvoryanskoe ditya* ("nobleman's child").[1] In the free territory of fiction, particularly in his early work, Leskov sometimes creates for himself an even more impressive genealogy. In one characteristic first-person story the narrator, clearly an alter ego of the author, comes from a "very ancient Russian noble line," one included in the "sixth section of the genealogy book" (3:384), that is, a family, rare among nineteenth-century Russian gentry, that had held estates before 1685.[2] But as he grew older, in moments of frankness Leskov was more willing to spell out the truth about his ancestry:

> By origin I belong to the hereditary nobility of Oryol province, but our nobility is recent and insignificant, acquired by my father on achieving the rank of collegiate assessor. Actually our family stems from the clergy, and it is there that we have an honorable sort of family tree. My grandfather, the priest Dimitry Leskov, and his father, grandfather, and great-grandfather were all priests in the village of Leski . . . Our family name comes from this village of "Leski." (11:7)

Even his mother, whom he describes in a letter as a "pure-blooded aristocrat,"[3] in fact had an ancestry almost as questionable as his father's. Not only was her mother a merchant's daughter—which Leskov knew very well when he called her "pure-blooded"—but her father's proud family name, Alferiev, which optimistic family tradition had derived from a romantic itinerant Italian named Alfieri, (supposedly a relative of the poet and dramatist), was of purely Russian, peasant origin, as Leskov eventually pointed out in print a few months after his mother's death (11:117-120).

Legal nobility, then, Leskov had on his father's side, and yet a long line of ecclesiastical ancestors; on his mother's side, a merchant grandmother married into a family of impoverished gentry ultimately of peasant origin. It was hard to know which part of this background to accept and which to repudiate, which to take pride in and which to be ashamed of. This very uncertainty created an inner tension, a struggle to achieve a clearer definition of himself, that provided the dynamic force behind much of Leskov's writing. Many of his literary works appear to be experiments in identification with different parts of his ultra-heterogeneous background.

Of the primary emotional influences that shaped Leskov's personality in his early years we know very little. Not one of his close relations in his parents' generation or his own wrote a single line of reminiscence about him, and practically nothing survives in the form of letters, diaries, or family papers. Leskov's son Andrei, who seems to have felt his vocation as his father's biographer early, tried even in his father's lifetime to collect what information he could about Leskov's early life, but he ran up against insurmountable barriers, some created by his father's secretiveness, some by the forgetfulness and distortions of others, and some simply by the corrosive effects of time—he was trying, in the 1880s and 1890s, to find out about people who had lived and events that had occurred forty or fifty years before. But from the scraps he managed to preserve, and from information scattered through Leskov's own writings, some notion can be formed of the character of Leskov's parents and of the atmosphere in which he spent his early years.

Semyon Dmitrievich Leskov and Marya Petrovna Alferieva were married in 1830; he was then forty-one and she seventeen. The difference in age seems enormous by our standards, but such marriages were not uncommon among the Russian gentry of that period. It was a frequent practice for young noblemen to spend twenty years in the army or civil service, after which they retired to the country, settled down on their estates, and only then looked about for an attractive girl of marriageable age, perhaps with a sizable dowry to add to her charms. It may be recalled that Tolstoy was thirty-four when he married the eighteen-year-old Sofya Bers; and one of Leskov's aunts was fifteen when she married a man nearly fifty—an extreme gap even by Russian standards.

Leskov's father, Semyon Dmitrievich, is a difficult figure to assess. His total literary heritage, preserved in the archives of his grandson Andrei Leskov, consisted of two letters and an official curriculum vitae.[4] Born nearly twenty years after Semyon Leskov's death, Andrei Leskov knew little about him except what he found in his father's writings, and no one else took the trouble to record his image for posterity. There are, however, scattered through Nikolai Leskov's letters, stories, and memoir pieces, a good many fleeting reflections of his father's image. They may not exactly correspond to the original, but they can perhaps be made to reveal what is after all the major concern here, Leskov's "internal father"—the composite of experience, emotion, and imagination that he created in his childhood and bore within him all his life.

The personality that comes through to us is a complicated one—at times stern and forbidding, at times pathetic and quixotic. Semyon Leskov seems to have been torn by a powerful rebelliousness struggling with a harsh ethical sense that could tolerate few rebellious acts. But the few he permitted himself are revealing. The most important was his refusal, on completing the seminary in 1808, to enter the priesthood. At that time this was a tremendous defiance of accepted social behavior, so flagrant that old Dimitry Leskov, the priest, felt justified in forcibly ejecting his son from the house and forbidding him to cross its threshold again. Leskov describes this scene briefly, but with meaningful detail: "Driven by my grandfather from the house for his refusal to enter the clerical calling, my father fled to Oryol with forty copecks in copper which his late mother gave him 'over the back gate.' Grandfather's anger was so great that he cast my father out with literally nothing at all to his name, even without a piece of bread beneath the fold of his cloak" (11:8).

Semyon Leskov managed nevertheless to make a creditable career. At first he supported himself by giving lessons to the children of local landowners and officials in Oryol.[5] In 1811 he entered the civil service as a minor official in the Oryol district court, later serving briefly in Petersburg, and in 1825 got himself transferred to the Caucasus, where promotions came faster. There he worked in the government vodka monopoly. Two years later he returned to Oryol, having achieved his aim, the rank of collegiate assessor, which gave legal nobility to him and all his descendants. While in the Caucasus, according to his son, he passed up innumerable opportunities to enrich himself by accepting bribes—such uprightness being extremely unusual among Russian officials at that time.[6]

After his marriage in 1830 he reentered government service in Oryol, working first as crown representative in the local court, later as an elected representative of the local nobility in the criminal court. In these jobs he distinguished himself, his son writes, for the outstanding qualities of "his whole long-suffering life"—"intelligence and honesty" (11:8). Although these qualities earned him the reputation of a redoubtable investigator and a respected man of principle, quixotic rebelliousness once more prevented him from reaping the rewards of virtue and ability. After seven years of service, in 1839, when Nikolai was eight, Semyon Leskov somehow incurred the displeasure of the governor of the province. The situation apparently could have been rectified by a little diplomacy: "Father was asked to make some concession to the governor, which he could have made under the guise of politeness, simply by paying a call on him. I remember how several noblemen came and tried to persuade father to do this, but he kept his reputation of a 'stiffnecked man' and did not go" (11:10). The nobility could not reelect a man at odds with the governor, and Semyon Leskov was left without a post. It was the end of his career.

With his savings he bought a tiny farm called Panino in the Kromy district, consisting of "a water mill with a grindstone, a garden, two families of peasants, and about forty *desyatiny* of land" (a *desyatina* was equivalent to 2.7 acres). It was not a successful move. At the most the farm could bring in two or three hundred rubles a year, and with

7

this "father and mother had to live and educate us children, of which there were by this time seven, of whom I was the oldest [. . .] Father used himself to go out sowing in the fields, looked after the garden and the mill, and was always reading; but the farming went badly, because it was not at all his forte. He was a man of intellect, and he needed a vital intellectual life, and not a tiny one-horse farm" (11:10-11). Poverty, boredom, and a sense of futility seem to have overcome the elder Leskov, and he fell into despondency, letting things slip from his hands. He spent his time translating Horace and Juvenal, relics of his seminary Latin, and left his wife to run the farm and the household. In 1848 he died.

The image of his father that Leskov retained was not an integrated one; it was composed of disparate and often contradictory elements, some remembered, some reconstructed, some imagined. The father that Leskov probably remembered best was the father of the Panino years—a deteriorated, depressed, defeated man, who sat dozing over his books and let the major responsibility for his farm and his family pass to his wife. Children were hardly congenial company for this melancholy old man, and Leskov's writings contain scarcely any recollections of vital contact between him and his father. The only letter from Semyon Leskov to his son that has survived is an example of noncommunicative communication, more of a spiritual testament than a letter—a series of moral precepts and warnings addressed in 1836, from what he professed to believe his deathbed, to his eldest son, then only five years old.[7] It is a strangely empty, bombastic compendium of copy-book maxims, obviously written more in a spirit of sickbed self-dramatization than genuine feeling about the boy or his future. The fact that the father lived another twelve years only underscores its absurdity. He seems to have made little use of his remaining time to instruct his son in a less pompous way.

There is a notable lack of warmth in Leskov's reminiscences about his father, where matter-of-factness is mixed with irony; and we are perhaps entitled to speculate that he interpreted his father's increasing withdrawal from the world as a personal rejection. This feeling may have been one of the causes of the marked instability of Leskov's emotional relationships through all of his life. If his father did not love him, who would? He could never feel sure of being accepted as he was; and so, in every relationship, he would always be looking for, and in fact bringing about, the rejection he felt was inevitable. Hypercritical and impossibly demanding, he would strain a relationship to the breaking point, and then, when it did break, he would conclude that his worst suspicions had been confirmed. He could then feel justified in violent repudiation, hurling accusations at the person he had once loved or admired. For his close relatives, as his son reports, he was a veritable "organizer of unhappinesses."[8] Not only joy, but even the semblance of peace was impossible in his vicinity. It takes a great many unhappinesses to produce a character like that, but perhaps not the least of them was caused by this father who died emotionally for his son long before he died in fact.

Besides the pain of this rejection, the psychological causes of which he could only dimly comprehend, there was probably also a good deal of straightforward shame mixed with Leskov's memories of his father's last years. The broken and bitter old man was certainly not a figure to admire and dream of emulating; the son must have felt to some extent humiliated by his father's defeat and have hated him for allowing it to happen.

Imagination mixed with history provided the son with a remedy. He could resurrect from the past his true, original father, the father of the period before 1839, the strong, vigorous, active official, the famous detective, fearless and incorruptible, the terror of bribe-taking bureaucrats and guilty landowners for miles around Oryol. "Father was a superb investigator" (11:10), "a detective well known in his time" (7:260), Leskov wrote several times. He went about on commissions from high officials, including one from the emperor himself. Once offered thirty thousand rubles as a bribe, he turned it down and went on to uncover a particularly revolting crime (11:10). Thus romance and glory could be found in his father's past—more, indeed, than Leskov ever made use of in his works. And there was passion too. Leskov remembered with pleasure his father's "terrible rage" against a bishop who had had Leskov's cousin, his father's sister's son, sent into the army as a recruit.

If memory proved insufficient for building up a more satisfactory father, sheer fantasy could create a still more romantic one, a father who had been a Decembrist and had been banished to the Caucasus for his revolutionary activities. As late as 1871 Leskov wrote such an account, not in a work of fiction or semifiction, but in a letter to a friend who was considering a move to the country:

> My father was close to Ryleev and Bestuzhev; he was sent to the Caucasus, then came to Oryol, married, and because of his incredible powers of observation and penetration, acquired the reputation of such an outstanding criminal investigator that his

supposedly supernatural qualities of perspicacity brought him honor, respect, and everything you like except money, with which they passed him by. He became angry and, like you, began to rave about fields and gardens, bought a farm and began to dig vegetable beds, but—bad harvests, fights among the peasants, storms, cattle disease, and other delights that we forget about when we surrender to these bucolic dreams, flattened him out to the extent that in five years he had become a piece of rubbish [*drjazga*], and then he died, leaving a pile of papers consisting of his translations of Quintus Horatius Flaccus and Juvenal, which he had made during the years when mother had nothing to pay for our schooling with nor to buy shoes for our feet (literally). (10:310)

The story about the elder Leskov's association with the Decembrist leaders Ryleev and Bestuzhev (executed in 1826) has apparently not a grain of truth in it.[9] It was a myth that Leskov needed to help erase the painful memories of the "piece of rubbish."

Of the more conscious and palpable influences that Leskov's father exerted on his son, the most important seems to have been his effect on Nikolai's religious development. Here too there was conflict. Semyon Dmitrievich had felt an "insuperable revulsion" for the priest's cassock worn by his father and had stubbornly refused to don it, despite great pressures brought to bear on him. Yet, Leskov says, "he was a man well trained in theology and sincerely religious" (11:8), and in the spiritual testament he addressed to his five-year-old son he sternly admonished him: "Never for anything in the world betray the faith of thy fathers."[10] Eventually that son, as he began to work out his own religious philosophy, had to try to make sense of the contradiction between such conservative precepts and the manifest anticlericalism of his father's example. Part of the solution he seems to have perceived early: that genuine piety, sincere religious feeling, might be compatible with repudiation of ecclesiastical rites. But the issue was complicated by his mother's (and his grandmother's) contrary example of purely Orthodox piety, so that even as a child Leskov had in effect to compare and choose between his father's and his mother's God:

Religiosity had been in me since my childhood, and moreover of a rather fortunate kind, that is, one which began early in me to reconcile faith with reason. I think that in this I am in many ways indebted to my father. Mother was also religious, but in a purely ecclesiastical way—she read acathisti [eulogistic hymns] at home and the first of every month had *molebny* [prayer services] held and watched to see what the consequences of this would be in the circumstances of her life. Father did not try to hinder her from believing as she liked, but he himself went to church rarely and did not perform any rites except confession and Holy Communion, about which, however, I know what he thought. It seems that he "did this in His (Christ's) memory." [He regarded the Eucharist as a commemorative observance only.] He was impatient with all other ceremonies, and when he was dying, asked that no funeral mass be said for him. In general, he did not believe in the intercession of living or dead, and when mother wanted to take a trip to venerate wonder-working icons and relics, he spoke disparagingly about all this. He did not like miracles and considered discussions about them futile and harmful, but he used to spend much time at night praying before a thaumaturgic Greek icon of the Savior, and when he was walking, he liked to sing [the hymns] "Helper and Protector" and "Through Ocean Wave." He was unquestionably a believing Christian, but if he were to have been examined according to Philaret's catechism, he could hardly have been considered Orthodox, and I do not think he would have been frightened by this or have tried to dispute it. (11:11)

Leskov was thus confronted with two opposing religious mentalities: his mother's, ritualistic and magical, Orthodox; and his father's, rationalistic, moralistic, incipiently Protestant. The conflict between these fundamental attitudes he had to work out within himself, and it took him most of his life.

Both attitudes found reinforcement in many outside influences, both in childhood and in later years. The father's incipient Protestantism was made overt and explicit in the example of Leskov's uncle by marriage, Alexander Scott, the son of a British nonconformist who had settled in Russia. There were many visits with the Scott family during Leskov's childhood, and in his early manhood Leskov worked for some time in his uncle's business. This direct experience of British Protestantism, most unusual for a nineteenth-century Russian, left a deep impression on Leskov. On the other hand, the example of his "very God-fearing and pious mother" (6:125), the wonderful trips with his grandmother to monasteries and holy places, so poetically invoked in "The Musk-ox," the many warm and pleasant childhood memories associated with local priests—Father Aleksei Lvov, for example, who "married my father and mother, baptised me and taught

11

me the Commandments,"[11] and especially Father Yevfimy Ostromyslensky, the beloved teacher of religion in the Oryol gymnasium, for
whose "good lessons" (6:125) Leskov remained eternally grateful—all
left very positive associations, and an almost equally powerful pull in
the direction of Orthodoxy.[12]

No wonder the religious question was such a difficult one for Leskov, and no wonder, therefore, that his struggles with it were so interesting and so important. Throughout most of his adult life he wrestled
with it, oscillating between the two rival principles originally represented by his father and mother. In the 1870s, for instance, he could
truthfully describe himself as a "humble and devoted son" of the
Orthodox church.[13] It was at this time that he became famous for his
Cathedral Folk, often acclaimed as the warmest evocation of that
church in Russian literature. Yet even then, in his most Orthodox
period, Leskov was searching for some sort of compromise, for a more
rational, nonmystical Orthodoxy, one that would place its primary
emphasis on charity, moral enlightenment, and good works in this
world rather than on sacramental rites, asceticism, and contemplation
of the next. Eventually it was the "Protestant" principle that won the
day. Toward the end of his life Leskov concluded that Orthodoxy
bore "no resemblance to the teachings of Christ" and indeed was *"not*
Christianity at all."[14] By that time Leskov had discovered the last and
the greatest of his ideal fathers, Lev Tolstoy, and had become his
"humble and devoted" disciple.

Although in his adult life Leskov was able to create in his writings
the imaginary figure of a stronger father, as a boy he must have
yearned for a real one, a vigorous man who would make his presence
felt, take charge of the household and the farm, and provide for his
wife and children—and, perhaps an even stronger wish at that age,
not permit his wife to rule the family as autocratically as she appears
to have done.

Under circumstances like these a boy may come to contemplate in
fantasy a more desperate remedy for the problem. He may wish he
could replace his father altogether, substitute for him a different sort
of man, strong, powerful, and dominant. But such a wish necessarily
brings with it powerful feelings of guilt: it is, after all, mental murder.
In order to mitigate these feelings, a compensatory development may
take place. The internal father is split in two, each half acquiring a
strongly marked moral quality. The real, genuine father, originally
rejected for his weakness, becomes the good half, duly accepted and

loved, while the much-desired strong father is labeled bad and ostensibly rejected with vehemence.

Such a hypothetical reconstruction of Leskov's feelings would help to account for his attitude toward the long series of good and bad fathers he encountered during his life and for his prolonged effort to reunite the two halves, to find a father who would be both powerful and good.

Leskov's childhood certainly did provide him with a striking prototype of the bad father, in the person of his uncle by marriage, Mikhail Strakhov, the fifty-year-old bachelor who had married a girl of fifteen. Strakhov (whose very name means "fear") had all the qualities Leskov's father lacked. He was rich and powerful, a born nobleman possessed of large estates; he enjoyed an influential position among the gentry of Oryol province, at one time serving as their elected marshal. In the lives of both of Leskov's parents he played an almost godlike role, and for their son he was a towering figure, greatly admired and at the same time passionately feared and hated.

Leskov's maternal grandfather, Pyotr Sergeyevich Alferiev, had fled to Oryol from Moscow before the French invaders in 1812. When he returned to Moscow after the war his house was burned to the ground and all his possessions gone. He was unable to find even the valuables he had buried. It meant complete ruin for him and his family. He went back to Oryol and eventually was hired as estate manager by Mikhail Strakhov, who settled Alferiev, his wife, and their two baby girls in a wing of the huge Strakhov house at Gorokhovo, where they lived for many years. Two more children were born to them there, Marya (Leskov's mother), in 1813, and Sergei, in 1816. In 1824, when the eldest daughter, Natalia, was fifteen, the family benefactor, Strakhov, announced that he would like to marry her. Under the circumstances there could be no question of refusal, whatever the girl's or her parents' feelings about the union. Becoming in-laws, the Alferievs moved into the main part of the manor house at Gorokhovo. Before long the other daughters were married off—Aleksandra to Aleksandr Yakovlevich Shkott, as he was known in his adopted country, Marya to Semyon Dmitrievich Leskov, who had once been a tutor in the family.[15]

Although they lived in Oryol, where Semyon Dmitrievich's job was, the Leskovs visited frequently at Gorokhovo, and it was there that Nikolai was born—Marya Petrovna evidently wanted to be with her mother during her confinement. Later Nikolai was often left at

Gorokhovo even when his parents were absent. His aunt Natalia, in order to help out her much less affluent sister, allowed him to be taught together with her own children by their tutors and governess.

Mikhail Strakhov died in 1836, leaving a considerable estate to his youthful wife, who before long married a man much nearer her own age. Leskov was thus only five years old when Strakhov died, yet the impression "Mr. Fear" had left on his nephew remained with him, carrying a strong emotional charge, for the rest of his life. An early memory of Strakhov is presented in "The Wild Beast," where Strakhov appears in somewhat fictionalized form, a "rich, old, and cruel" man whose character is dominated by "malice and implacability." He does not regret these qualities in the least, but regards them as manifestations of his manliness: "Everyone was afraid of my uncle, and I most of all, because in me too [as well as in his own children] he wanted to 'develop manliness,' and once when I was three years old and there was a terrible thunderstorm, which scared me, he put me alone out on a balcony and locked the door in order to teach me by such a lesson not to be afraid of thunderstorms" (7:260-261). Such sadistic lessons would hardly develop manliness in the way they were intended to do. But they might have another effect, namely, to convince their victim that there is a necessary connection between manliness and cruelty. To be a man endowed with "manly strength and unbending firmness of spirit" (7:260), Leskov may have felt, meant to become like Strakhov himself.

A passage in one of Leskov's purely autobiographical sketches points to another aspect of the conflicting feelings aroused by Strakhov:

My mother's sister, Natalia Petrovna, was married to M. A. Strakhov. She was a great beauty, and her old husband suspected her in the most monstrous and indecent way of relations with anyone in sight. He was an uneducated, despotic, and, I think, slightly insane man: he was some forty years older than my aunt and slept with her first tying her by the leg to the foot of his double bed. My aunt's sufferings were a subject of general commiseration, but neither her father nor mother nor anyone else dared intercede for her. These were my first childhood impressions, and terrible impressions they were—I think that they began to develop in me that agonizing nervousness from which I have suffered all my life and under the influence of which I have committed many stupid and vulgar acts. (11:12)

It is not unlikely that the boy Nikolai felt that such behavior as Strakhov's was the only alternative to the flabbiness of his father and the increasingly irksome matriarchy he knew in his own family. He wished his father to be strong and powerful, yet the strongest and most powerful man he knew was a despot and a brute. No wonder the result was "agonizing nervousness."

Although Leskov tended to focus his jealousy and fear on Strakhov (which left him free to admire his own father by contrast), not far under the surface there was great admiration, or perhaps it should be called envy or awe, of this mighty ruler of an "excellent and at that time very well organized and rich estate," where "people lived in the grand style, even in luxury" (11:9). Strakhov had in fact been a true benefactor to all of Leskov's mother's family; he had maintained her mother and father for more than twenty years; he had helped to start Leskov's father on his official career. He was a fountainhead of power, authority, and wealth, respected and feared by everyone around him. Yet for Leskov to acknowledge his admiration would have seemed to require a repudiation of his own father, as unacceptable an alternative as Strakhov's cruelty.

It was not until fifty years later that Leskov was able to bring this conflict to an end, at least in fiction. Within the confines of "The Wild Beast" Strakhov can at last be reconciled with his nephew. Like Scrooge ("The Wild Beast" is also a Christmas story), Strakhov is morally transfigured by an overpowering experience, miraculously transformed from the "rich, old, and cruel" man he had always been into a saintly benefactor of mankind, known throughout the slums of Moscow for his charity. Such a reformed bad father could at last be forgiven his past cruelties and unreservedly loved. The reform, however, was only the artistic realization of Leskov's deep wish; in life Strakhov died as he had lived, an unregenerate inspirer of fear.

Leskov's mother is a more straightforward and accessible figure than his father; at any rate her life seems a more predictable series of adjustments to external circumstances. Born in 1813, she received the kind of education usually given in those days to girls with aristocratic pretensions: she learned to speak French passably, do needlework, and behave acceptably in society. At seventeen she married her former teacher, the ex-seminarian Semyon Leskov—not a brilliant match by any means, but her parents could not be choosy, since they could offer no dowry and she was evidently no beauty. Eighteen years later, in 1848, she was left a widow, having borne her husband seven children who lived beyond infancy, four sons and three daughters. She brought them up on the little farm her husband had left her, and after they were grown (one of the daughters died in adolescence), she sold the farm and went to live in Kiev with her son Aleksei and his family. There she died in 1886.

Education had not prepared Marya Petrovna for the life she was to lead as a married woman, especially after her husband's enforced retirement and their move to Panino, but luckily temperament had. At Panino there was little need for drawing-room French or for Italian love songs accompanied at the piano, but there was a great need for efficient management. As her husband sank into lethargic melancholy, Marya Petrovna had to manage not only the household, but the farm as well. It was hard, anxious, incessant work, struggling to make ends meet. Yet she did make the tiny farm feed all those hungry mouths and later gave her children at least enough education so that they could move up instead of down the social ladder.

Marya Petrovna had many solid virtues to her credit: good management, thrift, sound judgment, and, above all, perseverance in the face of adversity, but they are not qualities readily appreciated by children, though they may suffer from a lack of them. From her children's point of view there was something missing. She lacked warmth, softness, tenderness. She was too preoccupied with practical affairs to have much time for sentiment. Leskov says that she had a "quick and impatient character" (9:221), and seems to have associated her with sharp words, commands, and cuffs rather than caresses and sweets.

References to his mother are scanty in Leskov's literary work, and what evocations there are seem chilly and businesslike, if not openly resentful. In one nonfictional article she is given recognition for her administrative talents, but the admiration is social and external; there is not a drop of filial love in it. Furthermore, Leskov stresses that such ability was essentially a masculine, not a feminine trait:

> Among the nobility the entire male sex was exterminated [in the cholera epidemic of 1848]. My late father was the first to die [. . .] Estates were left without men, and we found ourselves in a "women's kingdom," which went so far that the parishioners elected my mother (who, thank God, is alive and well to this day) "elderess," i.e., disburser and treasurer of funds for the repair of our Dobrynya church. It was quite out of order to elect women for such jobs, but people wanted it that way, and so it was done.

Without knowing the law very well, they simply said, "Either Leschikha manages things, or we won't give anything."[16]

Evidently "Leschikha" was indeed an efficient manager; but what her son longed for was not a treasurer, but a loving mother.

Marya Petrovna's methods of childrearing may be judged from a letter she wrote to Leskov toward the end of her life, commenting on the way his daughter Vera was bringing up *her* children, Marya Petrovna's great-grandchildren: "I think I wrote you that I visited Verochka on the fourteenth of July. Everything is in order in her house. She is a careful housekeeper and is bringing up her children in our good, old-fashioned way: the child eats everything, caprices are not permitted, and if they appear, he gets a smack for them and becomes like silk."[17] But a child does not feel silky inside after one of these smacks; and if he feels an overall deficiency of love, he may develop a deep and lasting resentment. Something like this seems to have been true in Leskov's case. As his son Andrei puts it, quoting one of his father's favorite expressions, Leskov's experience with his mother had left him with a "residue in his liver," a bilious rancor from which he never recovered.[18]

When literature gives him free rein, Leskov's memories of his mother's well-intentioned punishments are transformed into scenes of thoroughgoing sadism:

In our neighborhood from Bobovo all the way to Pipikhino the mothers used to boast to one another about which one of them spanked her children the most coolly; and to spank just as the child was being put to bed was considered a lofty pedagogical device. The child was made to say its evening prayers, then undressed, put in bed, and there spanked. Then one bashi-bazouk [*židomor*] of a landowner, Andrei Mikhailovich his name was, thought up another fashion, known as spanking your child in a bag. This is what he did to his children: he would lift the child's shirt over his head, tie the hems together, and then turn the child loose, whipping him as he ran, without holding him. This appealed to many people, and many of them still spank their children in this way. Forgiveness was granted only in an insignificant number of cases, and for that the child, sentenced by its father or mother to an unspecified amount of corporal punishment with birch rods, had to throw itself at their feet, beg for forgiveness, and then sniff the rods and in the presence of everyone kiss them. Very young children will usually not consent to kiss the rods, and only with

17

years and education do they attain realization of the necessity of putting their lips to the twigs destined for their bodies. Masha was still young; feeling in her prevailed over calculation. They spanked her, and long after midnight she was still pitifully whimpering in her sleep and convulsively shuddering, pressing against the side of her bed. (1:297)

The autobiographical character of this episode is considerably disguised, but there are clues that this is not wholly the realm of fiction. Masha's mother, the woman who inflicts this flogging, is a small landowner in the very district where Leskov's mother lived ("Gostomlya," from the name of a river that ran by Panino); furthermore, her husband is "Mitry Semyonych" to his peasants—Dmitry Semyonovich in more literary Russian, reversing the first name and patronymic of Semyon Dmitrievich Leskov. By the same logic, it may not be going too far to suggest that the sadistic "Andrei Mikhailovich" may likewise represent Mikhail Andreevich Strakhov—the bad father thus joining the bad mother in refined cruelty to their children.

There can be no doubt of the deep ambivalence in Leskov's feelings about his mother, the instinctive love being counterbalanced by an acquired bitterness. He seems to have coped with these conflicting feelings the way he did with the feelings aroused by his father: he divided womankind into two categories, one consisting of the true women, soft, tender, warm, and loving, the other of the pseudowomen, "quick and impatient," and armed with a whip. The term "coachmen in skirts" occurs several times in Leskov's writings—in the novel *No Way Out* (2:22), for instance, and most explicitly in a letter to his brother Aleksei, then a widower, when Aleksei was contemplating remarriage:

Your first wife, dear Lenushka, brought into your life something new, fresh, vital, and delicate; but she was not long for this world, and afterward your household again became entwined in ennui and egotism. Now once again you have found a kind and apparently a healthier and even more experienced person than Lena. God grant something live, simple, warm, and passionate; God grant a tender woman for that circle, where the lack of this quality is so great and so painful. It is grief and general misery with the coachmen in skirts, and there are so many of them that it is terrible to say it.[19]

Behind the passion, one can sense Leskov's conviction that God had not granted him such a woman—neither in his mother nor in either of his wives.

In later life, time healed some of these wounds, superficially at any rate, and Leskov's relations with his mother were for the most part at least filially correct. But he kept his distance from her and allowed the entire responsibility for her care to fall on his brother. She spent all her later life with Aleksei in Kiev, except for occasional visits with her daughter Olga, who after her marriage in 1873 lived nearby in Kanev. There is no evidence that Marya Petrovna ever came to St. Petersburg to visit Nikolai, possibly because she felt the journey too arduous, but possibly because she felt herself unwanted. Nikolai did make occasional trips to Kiev, and he and his mother kept up a regular correspondence, but one senses in their relationship an ominous rumbling, constantly threatening to burst out in stormy scenes of recrimination.

Only one of Leskov's letters to his mother has been preserved, and her letters to him, though extant, have not been published. In the letter that we have, Leskov is advising his mother, who is opposed to Aleksei's second marriage, to leave Aleksei's house for the time being without making a fuss and stay with Olga. He evidently hopes that in time she will be reconciled to the situation and won over by the charm and consideration of her new daughter-in-law (as indeed she eventually was). The letter ends:

> My brother is leaving here [Aleksei and his bride had been visiting in Petersburg] in a fine, gay mood, and you will do well if you do not meet him with a downcast face. Everything that you did not desire has already happened, and it can't be helped. There is no use now in moaning and groaning, and you should look cheerfully ahead and teach your sorrow to be proud. Don't say anything unnecessary to him about your love for him. What mother does not love her son, and especially such a good one as Aleksei? Who is he, anyway, some Sergei Petrovich who had such pity on his mother that he threw her out of the house without any cause? He took care of you and found a husband for his sister in a brotherly way. How could you help loving him? You are a good mother, but even a bad mother would love such a son. Why talk about it? Part with him as calmly and peacefully as possible. That is all that your best friend can wish for you. Time, which is more inventive than we are, will reveal the rest.
>
> Your devoted son, Nikolai[20]

It is a strange document, with its reversal of roles—the son admonishing the mother in this peremptory and rather condescending way, with much hostility showing through the ostensibly helpful judiciousness— the schadenfreude over the thwarting of the mother's wishes, the uncalled-for thrust at her brother, Sergei Alferiev, who, like Marya Petrovna herself, was spending his old age in Aleksei's house, and the praise of Aleksei used as a means of belittling the mother's love for him.

In sum, it would probably not be wrong to conclude from the evidence we have about Leskov's relations with his mother, both in childhood and later, that he was left not only with a "residue in his liver" but with a profound malaise that affected his relations with women all his life, no doubt contributing to the instability of both his marriages. This malaise is very likely the fundamental reason for the difficulty Leskov always had in his literary work with the theme of love—a difficulty that eventually led him to renounce it altogether as a fit subject for fiction. This renunciation encompassed not only the love of man and woman but also that of parents and children. In fact, it is astonishing that in his works of fiction Leskov was able to avoid almost entirely the central human subject, the emotional constellation of the family circle. It was not, as Leskov professed to believe, that the theme of love was hackneyed and overworked, for his contemporary Tolstoy was producing among the most profound and brilliant representations of love, marriage, and family life that literature possesses. It was rather that Leskov himself, because of the peculiar relationship between his personality and his artistic inspiration, was unable to maintain artistic control when he tried to represent these experiences; after a few startlingly unsuccessful attempts, he preferred to abandon the effort altogether.

There are in Leskov's writings, however, not only bitterness and resentment but also many warm feelings associated with the women of his childhood. He seems to have consolidated into an ideal image the impressions left in him by various surrogate mothers—his grandmother, his nurse, aunts—plus, no doubt, the positive feelings he had about his real mother.

Leskov's maternal grandmother, Akilina Vasilievna Alferieva, earned a favored place in her grandson's heart. He was with her a good deal: during his childhood she was living with her husband on the Strakhov estate at Gorokhovo, where Leskov was placed for a while in order to be taught by the Strakhovs' tutors. She also, as Leskov reports in one of his stories, sometimes visited with his parents in Oryol (6:352). Akilina Vasilievna represents Leskov's ancestral connection with the merchant class:

> She stemmed from the Kolobovs, a Moscow merchant family, and had been taken in marriage into the nobility "not for her riches, but for her beauty." But her best qualities were her spiritual beauty and her clear intelligence, which always retained a certain plebeian cast. When she entered the world of the gentry, she yielded to many of its demands and even allowed herself to be called Aleksandra Vasilievna, although her real name was Akilina; but she went on thinking like a commoner and even retained, unintentionally, of course, a certain common flavor in her speech [. . .] She did not permit any pressures of fashion to shake her faith in the good sense of the common people, and she herself never lost this good sense. She was a fine woman and a real Russian lady; she managed her household very well and knew how to play hostess to anyone from the Emperor Alexander I to Ivan Ivanovich Androsov [an Oryol merchant, a friend of Leskov's father]. She never read anything at all except her children's letters, but she loved to refresh her mind in discussions, and for this purpose she used to "summon serfs for conversation." (6:393)

Certain distortions in this account may be taken as tokens of Leskov's esteem for his grandmother. She certainly never received the emperor, nor—according to her great-grandson, at least—had she any valid claims to beauty: "She was well formed, tall, with an unpretentious comeliness. There were no fine features in her good-natured, rather common face."[21] Furthermore, the substitution of the name Aleksandra for Akilina was not actually a symbol of the change in class status; her parents had intended to name her Aleksandra, but the uneuphonious name Akilina was given her by the priest who baptized her, apparently to spite her father, with whom he had quarreled.

In this encomium of Akilina Vasilievna there is a note of condescension, a subtle effort to bring out the fact that her grandson, the author, has passed far beyond her stage of social and mental development and can now look back—and down—at her; benevolently, to be sure, but with a sense of his superiority. He spells this out a few sentences later when discussing the subjects of the conversations Akilina Vasilievna used to have with her serfs:

> These discussions were never idle, but useful and to the point. They went into such topics as why tales were being told about the

maid Feklushka or why the boy Grishka was unhappy with his
stepmother. . . . For her all this was full of vivid interest, perhaps
quite incomprehensible to her granddaughters. For this reason she
could possess the keys to many secrets which may seem petty to
us, but are most significant for people in that sphere. (6:393)

A certain amount of condescension is present in many kinds of love,
and Leskov's feelings toward his grandmother are not unusual in
themselves. But this kind of detached and patronizing affection
proved to be the only form of love Leskov could be at ease with in his
own life, and the only one he could successfully represent in his art.

Akilina Alferieva was a vital link for Leskov with Orthodox
religion—the "magic" religion of his mother, regarded with skepticism
by his father. Through his grandmother Orthodoxy was associated
with many joyful memories. These may have been poeticized in the
telling, but there seems to have been genuine experience and feeling at
the root of them.

In our province there are quite a good many monasteries, which
are situated in the woods and are called hermitages. My grandmother was a very religious old lady. A woman of the old school,
she felt an uncontrollable passion for visiting these hermitages.
She knew by heart not only the history of every one of these isolated monasteries, but she knew all the monastic legends, the histories of the icons, the miracles attributed to them, she knew how
rich each monastery was, its treasures, and all the rest. She was a
decrepit but lively guide to the holy places of our region. . . . I
was the old lady's adjutant from the very earliest age. When I was
only six, I set out with her and her roan-colored mares for the first
time to the hermitage of L——, and from that time on I accompanied her every time until at the age of nine I was taken to the
provincial gymnasium. To journey around these monasteries had
much that was attractive for me. Grandmother had an unusual
ability for poeticizing her travels. (1:53-55)

Left a widow around 1840, Akilina Vasilievna lived on until about
1860, dying when she was somewhere near seventy. (She was thus by
no means as "decrepit" during those monastic excursions as Leskov
makes her sound.) Two years later, in one of a series of travel pieces
written for the newspaper *Northern Bee*, Leskov casually refers to his
grandmother Akilina Vasilievna, "who lived to be nearly one hundred
and had twenty-seven grandchildren."[22] The number of grandchildren

may not be wrong, but the age can only be regarded as part of the halo that Leskov apparently wished to create around his grandmother.

Leskov had two aunts on his mother's side, whom he saw frequently, and one on his father's, whom he saw rarely. They all seem to have been dear to him, to have collected some of the latent love that he felt had been rebuffed by his mother. Perhaps it was not so much his real aunts that Leskov loved as the creature of his imagination who might be called the good mother. At times his grandmother might do duty for her, at times an aunt; but she was much less firmly attached to any real person than the bad father was to Strakhov. The literary apotheosis of all these good mothers is Aunt Polly in "Vale of Tears," a true woman endowed with softness, warmth, and solicitude. But Aunt Polly is a product of Leskov's late, Tolstoyan period, and she therefore must also represent his ideal of Tolstoyan sainthood. She is an angel of goodness, courage, and self-sacrifice, succoring the peasants in the terrible famine of 1840. And, what is most important for Leskov, she is a practical angel, enterprising and efficient, who knows how to make her charity effective. Though she is purely a fictional creation and her character so nearly a perfect incarnation of Tolstoyan virtues, it is curious that Leskov named Aunt Polly for a real person, his father's sister, Pelageya Dmitrievna. There seems to have been little resemblance, however. Pelageya Dmitrievna, the wife of the priest who succeeded old Dimitry Leskov in the parish of Leski, is a shadowy figure whom Leskov hardly knew. The closest model for Aunt Polly's personality was probably his mother's Anglicized sister, Aleksandra Petrovna Scott. But this backhanded use of real names in a fictional story (which hardly meant anything to Leskov's readers and has confused many of his biographers) may be taken as an indication that Aunt Polly does have some links to real life. She is the last product of Leskov's lifelong search for a more satisfactory mother than life had granted him.

Leskov's brothers and sisters appear to have been of little importance in his early development. Nikolai was the oldest; his sister Natalia was five and his brother Aleksei six years younger (there were probably other children born in the interval who did not live beyond infancy). His other brothers and sisters were between ten and sixteen years younger, and thus did not enter his early world at all. Furthermore, Leskov did not spend many of his later childhood years at home. He was first taken off to be educated with the Strakhov children at Gorokhovo, and at the age of ten he entered the gymnasium at Oryol.

Difficult as it is to reconstruct the emotional relationships of Leskov's early life, we can arrive at a reasonably plausible hypothesis of what they must have been. The central fact of Leskov's childhood is the deep emotional ache left by what seemed to him the insufficiency of love bestowed upon him by his parents—the deterioration, withdrawal, and death of his father, and the harshness of his mother. He tried to compensate for these losses in various ways, by seeking substitute parents among his near relations and endowing them with, or recognizing in them, qualities he felt his parents lacked. But the compensations never made up for the original loss; the ache remained in him for life, reappearing in many guises both in reality and in art.

One of these guises, which some of his friends later considered the central trait of his character, was a suspiciousness bordering on paranoia that bedeviled all his relationships. Leskov seems to have felt that no love could be trusted, that one could never rely on the affection or benevolence of others. Therefore they must be bound to one not by the tenuous ties of affection but by the more reliable ones of duty and obligation. These at least are to some extent enforceable. If obligations are not met, one can blame and perhaps punish the guilty party; one can demand and exact one's due. But who can be blamed if one is not loved? Who can be punished? The only explanation—too depressing to accept—is that one is unlovable, unacceptable, deficient as a human being. Much better to shift the whole ground of human relations to a legal or a moral one. One can insist on justice, if not on love.

Such a formula must lie at the root of Leskov's lifelong difficulties with close relationships, and it may also account for his preoccupation with questions of abstract morality. Since no friendship could be trusted, he made every effort to turn it into a moral or legal relationship. Then immediately he was on the lookout for infractions, failures of the other person to fulfill his obligations toward him. His friends never measured up for long to the exacting standards set for them by Leskov; they soon began receiving reproaches and often long and detailed indictments, listing their many sins of omission and commission against him. Small wonder that few people could stand this sort of thing for long. For a while they remonstrated, pleaded, tried to justify themselves; but the time eventually came when they would have no more of it, and they broke off the relationship, sometimes violently, sometimes quietly. This was the outcome of every relationship with man or woman that Leskov formed, except those that were too new at the time of his death to have reached the point of rupture. Decade after decade it went on: all his ties of blood, two marriages, innumerable friends, causes, and allegiances—all passed through the same cycle: an attachment formed, often a passionate one, with protestations of eternal devotion; then a period of mutual esteem and satisfaction; then discoveries of "flaws" in the other person's conduct; charges and countercharges; and in the end the inevitable break.

A single illustration will suffice at this point. In 1883 Leskov wrote to S. N. Shubinsky, editor of the magazine *Historical Messenger* (where he published frequently) and at that time one of the best friends he had. Shubinsky had expressed misgivings about the length of an article Leskov had submitted for publication and had rejected another outright. Leskov replied:

> It is not for you, sir, to issue any reminders to me about friendship, devotion, and favor. I have had all these and demonstrated them. Whatever else I may be, I am a plainspoken man. If I love, I love, and if I don't like someone, I don't conceal it; but I won't talk behind his back about anyone I don't like. There are, of course, people who do not like me, but there are those who do . . . . I think that this is the case with everyone, even with you [. . .] I loved you very much, with a warm love, and I was therefore painfully hurt, to the point of aches in body and soul, when once, twice, and finally three times I became convinced of the amazing strangeness of your actions [. . .] I was surprised myself: what desire was this in you to humiliate a person devoted to you, useful to you, I hope, and one who had never spoken against you by word or hint. Amazing! It is as if you were fulfilling some inexorable need to complain. First I "placed you in difficulties" by the length of the article; then many people "didn't like" "Personalities of the Synod" (among them the blockhead Maikov, who understands as much about literature as a pig about oranges); then there was something wrong in the way I took money from you. Ugh! What sort of nonsense is this! I am always precise and businesslike, and in business matters I do not tolerate any complaints against me. I do not deserve them. Further: how could you, as historian, say that twenty-four pages about the remote period of the 1830s is "too much"? It is offensive to hear, because it is an absurdity without measure [. . .] Insofar as personal feelings are concerned, I too am not so young as to fail to appreciate them or to sacrifice them frivolously. Without affectation I have the right to call myself
>
> Devotedly yours,
> N. Leskov[23]

The Ineducable
Autodidact

Leskov's education began, he writes in his autobiography, at the Strakhovs', where there were a resident French governess and a German tutor as well as a visiting preceptor of Russian spelling and grammar. "I lived at the Strakhovs' almost until the age of eight, and this benefited me in that I was well brought up, that is, I knew how to behave properly in society, was not shy with people, and had decent manners —I answered politely, bowed decently, and quite early learned to chatter away in French" (11:12-13). These were achievements not to be despised, and they might have led further had not the whole process been interrupted. Like so many of his later relationships, Leskov's primary education at the Strakhovs' broke off suddenly, an event which he as usual ascribed to the unfairness and cruelty of others. According to his account, he was a better student than his cousins, and a tutor's tactless remark to this effect was not to the liking of their mother. A neighboring landowner serving as the widow's guardian organized a little comedy: at a family gathering Leskov was to be presented with a certificate commending his scholastic successes. When he marched up and undid the ribbon on his "certificate," it proved to be an advertisement of an ointment for rheumatism. Leskov was so humiliated by this joke, he claims, that he cried all night and begged his father to take him away from the Strakhovs' forever. His wish was granted—apparently without demur from anyone.

Implausible as it may seem, some such episode must have occurred; and very likely Leskov was occasionally treated at the Strakhovs' like the poor relation he was. Yet surely there must have been more to the incident than this. Why, for instance, were all the adults so ready to gratify an eight-year-old's injured self-esteem as to whisk him triumphantly away from the scene of his humiliation? Was Natalia Strakhova, who had originally been kind enough to take him in, really so callous that she made no attempt to assuage her nephew's hurt feelings after this ill-advised joke or to keep him on in her house afterward?

And why was Leskov's father so ready to fly to his rescue, without making any attempt to smooth over the situation?

Whatever the explanation for Leskov's departure from the Strakhovs' (which would seem more plausible as the consequence of an adult quarrel or of some change in the Strakhovs' circumstances, such as Natalia Petrovna's impending remarriage), the abrupt termination of his early education is a significant fact, both literally and symbolically. When Leskov induced his seminarian father to take him away from the aristocratic Strakhovs, he thereby removed himself from the kind of culture the Strakhovs represented and thus defined his future cultural identity as different from theirs. For it was the Strakhov type of education—private tutors, gymnasium, university, and foreign travel—that produced the typical aristocratic Russian men of letters, the Herzens, Turgenevs, and Tolstoys. They all had German tutors, French governesses, and English nannies; ill-qualified as these often were, their pupils nevertheless acquired from them a fluent command of their languages and at least a rudimentary acquaintance with their cultures. This early exposure to foreign languages was one of the bases for the easy familiarity with European culture that is one of the hallmarks of the aristocratic Russians, so much more international in outlook than most English, French, or German writers of their time. Their knowledge of other cultures was not always deep. But since the initial contact had come easily and naturally in childhood, their adult cosmopolitanism was unforced and unlabored.

By his departure from the Strakhovs', Leskov severed his tenuous connection with this class and thereby assumed a degree of kinship with another, the "plebeian" intellectuals of the 1860s, most of whom were, like Leskov's father, ex-seminarians. Unlike their aristocratic contemporaries, any knowledge they possessed of Western languages and culture had to be laboriously acquired by reading and study in their adult years. Try as they might, they could never obtain the sense of comfortable belonging, of feeling at ease in the languages and cultures of the West that is such a striking attribute of their gentry contemporaries.

It is difficult to ascertain how well Leskov knew French and German. He says that he learned at the Strakhovs' to "chatter away" in French and that, in preparation for the gymnasium, he formed a nodding acquaintance with the grammar-book of Lomonde (8:23). Although his marks in French at the gymnasium were mediocre,[1] he seems either to have retained, or in his later life to have developed, some facility in French, though it is not likely that he ever spoke or read it with real ease. He made two trips to France, one in 1862-63 and another in 1875. On the first occasion he established himself in the Latin Quarter with an attractive and good-humored grisette, who doubtless helped him improve his fluency, but his intellectual contacts and cultural interests at that time seem to have been almost wholly concentrated among émigré Russians and other Slavs living in Paris.[2] Leskov's writings during this period show little concern with French cultural values; he met no French writers and made no effort to do so. In 1875 he did attend a performance at the Comédie française and went once to Versailles to hear the debates in the National Assembly[3] —which indicates that he had some understanding of the spoken language. He had one important interview with a French-speaking Swiss Protestant theologian named Naville, which was probably conducted in French.[4] But in 1875, as in 1862, he seems to have clung mainly to Russian circles in Paris; his principal enterprise on this visit was to seek out some old Russian Jesuits living there.[5] Finally, although Leskov knew French literature reasonably well, he had probably read most of it in Russian translation. He could, however, and sometimes did, read French books.[6]

Leskov had some knowledge of German, but probably less than of French. He remembered the German tutor at the Strakhovs', Kohlberg, with affection—it was Kohlberg's praise that had induced his relatives to present him with that ill-starred "prize" (11:14). But at the Oryol gymnasium the German teacher was an absolute monster, and Leskov's progress in German came to a halt. In his later life he spent little time in German-speaking countries: in 1875 and in 1884 a few weeks in Marienbad; in 1875 a week or so in Dresden and the surrounding country; and in 1884 Dresden again and a brief visit to Vienna. From Marienbad he reported with pleasure that half the visitors and even some of the doctors—probably Czechs—spoke Russian,[7] and in the other cities he was merely a passing tourist. Leskov knew German literature largely through translations, but in a pinch he could read a German book in the original.[8]

There is no evidence that Leskov ever studied English, although his interest in England and in English literature and thought was great, perhaps inspired by his Russian-speaking British relatives, the Scotts. His extensive reading in English literature and English social and religious philosophy seems to have been limited to translations.[9] Likewise, Leskov retained enough of his schoolboy Latin to "puzzle out an epigraph," like Yevgeny Onegin, and even to make use of a few, but he was no classical scholar, and apparently knew no Greek.

In his youth Leskov did acquire two languages known by few Russian intellectuals of his day, Ukrainian and Polish, in both of which he attained considerable mastery and also literary connoisseurship—another feature that set him apart from other Russian writers of his generation, whose European culture generally skipped over the territory lying between Russia and the Oder.[10]

Leskov's formal, institutional education was of astonishingly short duration: the five years, from 1841 to 1846, that he spent in the Oryol gymnasium, beginning at the age of ten. What he learned there and what the gymnasium experience meant to him must be deduced from very fragmentary evidence. Leskov touches on his gymnasium years rarely in his writings, even then usually dealing with secondary aspects of his life there, anecdotes about other pupils and teachers, not about himself. In one article he discusses the inadequacy of the school's privies. His projected autobiography breaks off just as he is beginning his account of the gymnasium period (although a lost part of this work may have gone further), and an autobiographical piece entitled "How I Learned to Celebrate" comes to an even earlier end—it never gets beyond a description of the landlady in whose house he lived while attending the gymnasium.[11]

Two facts we do know: that at fifteen Leskov, much against his parents' wishes, dropped out of the gymnasium without completing the course and that the record he had made there was far from brilliant. In five years he had completed only two years' work; he left without taking the examinations for the third-year courses, and in the courses he had completed his marks were only average.[12]

It is not surprising, especially in a person of Leskov's temperament, so profoundly unable to bear any burden of self-blame, to find him eager to ascribe his failure to the institution. The picture of the Oryol gymnasium he gives in his autobiography is a dark one:

I was terribly bored, but studied well, although the gymnasium, which was at that time under the directorship of Al[eksandr] Yak [ovlevich] Kroneberg, was conducted in the worst possible way. Who our teachers were and how they taught it is laughable to recollect. Among our teachers there was one, Vas[ily] Al[eksandrovich] Funkendorf, who often appeared in a state of drunken madness and at one minute would go off to sleep, leaning his head

29

on his desk, and the next minute would jump up with a ruler in his hands and run around the classroom, slashing with it at whichever one of us happened to cross his path and at whichever part happened to be nearest. One student, Yakovlev I think his name was, had his ear cut off by this ruler, like a certain servant Malchus, and this aroused neither surprise nor indignation. (11:14-15)

The story of the amputated ear seems a little too heady to be believed, and we know from the school records that "studied well," as a characterization of Leskov's scholastic performance, is a hyperbole. No doubt the Oryol gymnasium was in reality a grim place, in which both brutality and ignorance were present in abundance; yet on one occasion, at least, when writing an obituary of one of his classmates, the physicist K. D. Kraevich, Leskov gives a different picture: "[Kraevich's education took place] at a time when teachers in secondary schools had a *moral influence* on their pupils, and in the Oryol gymnasium at that time among the other teachers there was a man of extraordinary honesty and purity, Valerian Varfolomeyevich Bernatovich, whom his pupils recollected with gratitude their whole lives for having known how to give a certain firmness to their characters."[13] Leskov does not mention Bernatovich elsewhere, and presumably he influenced Leskov less than he did Kraevich, although firmness of character, of a kind, Leskov managed to acquire somewhere.

This early abandonment of formal schooling plagued Leskov all his life. In spite of educating himself, by vast and incessant reading, enough for at least ten university degrees, he could not rid himself of that gnawing feeling of inferiority: not the conviction that he was really inferior in learning or culture (he knew he was not), but the fear that people with university diplomas might dare look down on him, a man who had not finished the gymnasium and yet presumed to class himself as a writer. This idea was so unbearable that Leskov took pains to conceal the facts of his educational past. When the truth had to be told, he always implied that the responsibility was not his.

Two reasons invented for this purpose were the death of his father and the Oryol fires. As late as 1890, when success and old age had taken some of the edge off this ancient shame and his Tolstoyanism should have taught him the virtues of honesty and humility, Leskov was still unable to give anything approaching a truthful account of his education and its termination. In a "Note on Myself" he writes: "Studied in the Oryol gymnasium. Left an orphan in my sixteenth year and entirely without means. The insignificant amount of property left by my father was lost in a fire. This was the time of the famous Oryol fires. This put an end to the proper continuation of my studies. After that—an autodidact" (11:18). This ostensibly factual protocol is mostly sheer fabrication.[14] In reality Leskov's father died in 1848, two years *after* his son had voluntarily dropped out of the gymnasium.[15] The great Oryol fire also took place in 1848; moreover, the Leskovs had no property in Oryol at that time, having sold their town house when they moved to Panino in 1839.

What is surprising about Leskov's sudden exit from the gymnasium, like his departure from the Strakhovs', is that his parents, who had staked a good deal on their son's education, should have acquiesced in it with so little resistance. Apparently they did not feel able to stop him. His father, who in a letter of 1848 described him as a "youth with a strong character,"[16] was probably too far gone in his melancholic decline to grapple with his obstreperous son; and Marya Petrovna had enough on her hands with the farm and, at that time, five other children, including a newborn baby. Furthermore, it was a considerable journey in those days from Panino to Oryol, and Leskov saw his family only on long vacations; the reins of parental control were therefore loose. Finally, for a family as financially hard-pressed as the Leskovs, it must have been tempting to let the eldest son at least support himself, if not contribute to the family exchequer.

Later Leskov more than made up for his lack of schooling, and few people suspected that he had no university degree. His general culture was broad, and his detailed knowledge of such recondite subjects as church history was such that he would have been qualified to teach them in a university. Like many autodidacts, however, he tended to educate himself in pockets, acquiring specialized information on a great variety of subjects, many of them out of the way from the point of view of his more conventional contemporaries—icons, Old Believers, Jewish rituals, Protestant theology and ethics, jewelry, clocks, rare editions, even spiritualism—in fact, the range of his competences is astonishing. And it is not even that he lacked general knowledge for these specialties to rest upon; what he missed was the confidence in dealing with cultural matters usually exhibited by people with university degrees.

This lack of confidence may help to account for some of Leskov's peculiarities as a writer. Feeling somewhat out of his depth in the mainstream of nineteenth-century European literature, he tried to find some lesser streams, a bit shallower perhaps, where his feet could touch bottom. He knew that there were areas of Russian life with which he was better acquainted than Turgenev, Tolstoy, and Dostoevsky—for instance, the world of the Russian clergy;[17] and after some unhappy early attempts, he learned to avoid their patented genre, the novel. Instead, he became a master of all sorts of other forms—short story, novella, reminiscence, "chronicle," "potpourri," "story apropos," "picture from nature"—and he developed a particular fondness for the spoken inner narrative, or *skaz*, in which he could exhibit and exploit his ultra-Russian Russian, a Russian no one could learn in a university. Perhaps part of the explanation for the *samobytnost*, the peculiar "self-nature" that Tolstoy perceived in Leskov,[18] stemmed from his fateful abandonment of the Oryol gymnasium at the age of fifteen.

After he had become an established writer, Leskov felt he had something valuable to offer that better-educated writers could not—a range of experience that few intellectuals could boast of, an intimate knowledge of the rough-and-tumble life of the provinces, the kind of life lived by petty officials, peasants, and priests, but not St. Petersburg poets or journalists. The years from 1846 to 1861 were spent acquiring this experience, first as an official in Oryol and then in Kiev and subsequently as a private businessman in the employ of his uncle Alexander Scott. This experience formed a trunk, as he once put it, pointing to his forehead, in which he stored the materials for his later literary creations.[19] It should be noted, however, that Leskov was thinking primarily of *external* experience, of what he saw, heard, and observed, rather than what he felt or lived through himself.

At the age of fifteen, no doubt through his father's influence, Leskov managed to get a position as a clerk in the office of the criminal court in Oryol. At first he was merely a hired employee, but a year later he was granted what amounted to civil service status of the second class, and in another year, in July 1848, taking advantage of the hereditary nobility achieved by his father, he qualified as a civil servant of the first class. The work cannot have been very interesting in itself—it mainly consisted in copying documents. In his adolescence Leskov thus enlisted in that army of human typewriters, like Akaky Akakievich Bashmachkin, who became such dominant figures in Russian literature of the Gogolian period. But even such a second-hand exposure to the annals of crime provided Leskov with many vivid demonstrations of varied human behavior, some of which found expression in his later stories.

Leskov's self-education proceeded apace during this period; indeed, its beginning doubtless antedated his exit from the gymnasium. In the government office his immediate superior was a former gymnasium teacher named Illarion Srebnitsky, and partly under Srebnitsky's guidance Leskov seems to have begun an intensive reading program in contemporary literature. Leskov remembered Srebnitsky with affection, and long afterward, hearing that Srebnitsky was destitute in his old age, contributed money to his support.[20] Andrei Leskov's surmise that "M. Stebnitsky," the pseudonym Leskov used in the early part of his literary career, is a variation on Srebnitsky's name, is entirely plausible—a tribute to the teacher's importance in the writer's intellectual development.[21]

A boy with Leskov's native gifts, and especially one with his extraordinary verbal facility, would probably develop his mind by extensive reading even if he refused to read the books prescribed by school authorities. The habit of continuous reading, which he retained all his life, began in the Oryol years, even before he had finally disallowed all attempts to educate him formally. Many times in his later writings Leskov refers to the library of a wealthy Oryol landowner, the niece of a minor and now forgotten writer named Masalsky, where he was allowed to browse at will; and he says that during his years in Oryol he managed to read nearly every book it contained. The most vivid account of this reading is found in an interview he gave a few months before he died. Asked to explain how he had become a writer, he responded:

> I think that I prepared for it gradually from my very earliest years. It began with the reading of the most various books and especially belles lettres during my sojourn in the Oryol gymnasium. In that city I frequented the house of A. N. Zinovieva, the niece of the well-known writer Prince Masalsky. Mme Zinovieva had a rich library, providing a mass of material for reading, and I read it through almost entirely. Thus began my intellectual development, which then continued to progress swiftly, thanks to my close acquaintance with such personalities as, for example, A. V. Markovich, the husband of the writer Marko Vovchok, and S. S. Gromeka.[22]

A. V. Markovich was a Ukrainian ethnographer and writer who had been banished to Oryol from his native Kiev for membership in the Cyrillo-Methodian Society, an idealistic brotherhood of young Kievan intellectuals dedicated to the principles of civil liberty and pan-Slavic solidarity. Although it was little more than a discussion club, when the spy reports were brought to his desk it stirred up in Nicholas I alarming memories of the Decembrist societies of twenty-five years before. According to a curious tenet of Nicholas's political science, the best way to keep track of persons suspected of sedition in one place was to make them civil servants in another; and so Afanasy Markovich, deemed a dangerous subversive in Kiev, became a clerk in the governor's office in Oryol.

Markovich was about ten years older than Leskov, much better educated, and with memories from Kiev of a cultivated society that did not exist in Oryol. Though Leskov was then only sixteen years old, an insignificant scribbler in the criminal court office, there must have been something about him capable of arousing the interest of a man like Markovich. He gave the impression of a youngster with promise, and it must have appealed to the older man to provide some guidance for a mind obviously strong, but utterly undisciplined and largely ignorant. Although they were in the same city for less than two years, Markovich left an impression on Leskov that he remembered for life: "Besides his interesting political position Afanasy Vasilievich possessed in concentration many splendid spiritual qualities, which attracted to him the hearts of people sensitive to goodness, and won for him the love and admiration of everyone who came to know his fine and noble spirit. His literary education was very vast, and he had the ability to make people interested in literature. In a general sense he brought benefit to many people in Oryol."[23] Markovich's chief claim to historical recognition is that while in Oryol he married Marya Vilinskaya, who under the pen name of Marko Vovchok later became a noted writer in Russian and even more so in Ukrainian, although she was herself a Russian. But for Leskov the important person was "Pan Opanas," as he liked to call Markovich, using the Ukrainian form of his name, and he deplored the extent to which Markovich's reputation was eclipsed by his talented wife's. Markovich died in 1867, and as late as 1883, when the above lines were written, Leskov says even more forcefully in a private letter that Marko Vovchok's "development is entirely due to her splendid husband, whom I knew very well and loved, and indeed am indebted to him for my whole [ideological] tendency and for my passion for literature. He is long since dead, killed by grief, and, perhaps, by lack of fame."[24]

Besides his direct intellectual influence on the young Leskov, this wife-eclipsed Markovich became an archetypal figure for the writer, the live ancestor of a long line of his most vivid and successful fictional characterizations, the *pravedniki* (righteous ones)—eccentric, a bit ludicrous, usually the victims of ridicule or outright persecution, often lonely and isolated, yet warm and generous and charitable, and with a latent moral courage that sometimes leads them to defy the mighty for the sake of justice and truth. It is indeed a potent and attractive image, and Markovich could hardly have asked for a more gratifying form of immortality.

My Universities

In 1849 Leskov's uncle Sergei Alferiev, a doctor and professor of medicine at Kiev University, invited his eighteen-year-old nephew for a visit. On September 7 Leskov obtained a leave of absence from his position in the Oryol criminal court and set off for the south. Kiev was the largest and most cosmopolitan city Leskov had seen, and it impressed and attracted him. He evidently determined, soon after his arrival, to stay there if he possibly could. Uncle Sergei, no doubt largely out of pity for his widowed sister with her many burdens, agreed to take Nikolai in as a permanent boarder, provided he could obtain a suitable post in the civil service in Kiev. On September 28 Leskov submitted a petition asking to be transferred from Oryol to Kiev, and by the following February a favorable reply had been received. He was assigned the post of assistant clerk in the army recruiting bureau in Kiev, where he was to work for more than seven years.[1]

Leskov's duties in the recruiting office were arduous and time-consuming, and often painful as well. In the reign of Nicholas I army service in the ranks was for twenty-five years, an entire lifetime for a young peasant, and it meant permanent separation from wife, children, and parents, who lamented the departing recruit as if he were a dead man. Selection of conscripts for a given village was made by the landowner, often as a punishment, or by the mir (the peasant council); both were frequently susceptible to bribery. As one of the officials in charge of recruiting, Leskov witnessed many scenes of grief and despair and saw the power of the rich to make the poor suffer for them. A helpless cog in the giant bureaucratic machine, he could only sympathize—and observe.

Leskov seems to have been an unusually responsible and competent official. In seven years he received two promotions, a letter of commendation, and a medal—a good showing for a young clerk without diplomas or influential connections.[2] Whatever the roughnesses of his private life, in his public roles Leskov was always very much the solid citizen: dutiful, responsible, hard-working, honest, and dependable, and this in a culture where such qualities were far from common.

As time went on, the moral ambiguities of his position must have troubled Leskov more and more, as similar ambiguities have troubled other conscientious officials assigned to carry out policies that violate their basic moral sense. True, compliance and conformity generally prove stronger than conscience. Not only do position and promotion depend on the obedient execution of policies handed down from above, but these policies, issued in the name of law (*pravo, Recht*) with all the solemnity of governmental authority, seem "right" by definition. If this "right" is questioned in the name of some higher law or human value, if the possibility is admitted that laws themselves may be immoral, then the official's whole moral order collapses. He must himself decide whether the acts his government calls on him to perform are consistent with his humanity. If they are not, he is faced with a choice between his conscience and his career. And one of the chief functions of the human intellect seems to be to find justifications for evading this choice, for keeping one's advantages while quieting one's conscience.

Such a conscience-quieting process appears to underlie the retrospective story "Episcopal Justice," which reflects, although in somewhat distorted form, the moral conflicts Leskov experienced in his days as a recruiting clerk. The story deals with an extreme case of official inhumanity: the Russian government's policy of forcibly inducting Jewish boys, some of them less than twelve years old, into the army as a means of Russifying them and converting them to Orthodox Christianity.[3] These children were torn away from their homes and parents and shipped off, in uniforms ridiculously too big for them, to army camps hundreds of miles away, where their enlightened government endeavored to root out their past, destroy their identity as Jews, and remold them to fit its notion of loyal Christian subjects.

From his own account, despite the numbing force of habit, prejudice, and self-interest, and despite the seemingly inexorable machinery of the law and the uselessness of opposing it, Collegiate Registrar Leskov was deeply disturbed by this bureaucratically manufactured human misery he was forced to witness. The poignant cry of "Rachel weeping for her children and being not comforted" (6:90)[4] sounded louder than the rustle of official papers. But disturbed or not, what could a mere clerk do? Open criticism or protest would have led only to arrest and exile; and although quixotic "righteousness" later became one of his favorite literary subjects, Leskov had little thirst for personal martyrdom, least of all on behalf of the Jews. He could perhaps have quietly resigned, refused to collaborate in the evil. Eventually he did; but not yet, and not in response to this moral predicament. Instead, like most people under like circumstances, he looked for excuses, of which the most convenient was the standard formula: I am only a clerk; I don't issue the orders or make policy; I am powerless (and therefore innocent). But the guilt and the pain continue to gnaw.

Besides this standard defense, in "Episcopal Justice" Leskov absolves himself of moral responsibility in other ingenious ways. First, he debases the victims—not the children (he assiduously avoids describing the miseries of the child recruits, since children tend to appeal even across the barriers of prejudice), but the parents, or rather the father, who is the central figure. If the victim is debased, represented as ridiculous, subhuman, and grotesque, the reader's identification with him is blocked, and his sufferings seem less terrible, less immediate. Although Leskov plays up the pathos of the father's agony, his anguish over the loss of his son, and describes in detail his frenzied efforts to save his child, at the same time he stresses the father's ridiculous, offensive, and even contemptible qualities. The wretched Jew squeals, grovels, cringes, sleeps on the floor like a dog, jabbers incoherently, and—worst crime of all for a language lover like Leskov—writes an absurd mixture of Russian, Ukrainian, and Yiddish, though he claims to be a learned man. He is ready for any self-abasement in order to gain his end. Symbolically, even the blood he supposedly sweats in his anguish has a disgusting odor.

Second, Leskov tries to shift the responsibility for this suffering from the Russian government, which in fact caused it, to the Jewish community. Apart from the stern requirements of the Russian law— now abrogated, Leskov piously intones, thanks to God and the new sovereign—the sufferings of the Jews were greatly aggravated by "the boundless cruelty of Jewish deceit and chicanery, practiced in all possible forms" (6:90). Thus Leskov's retrospective stance is one of respectful dissent from an official policy already safely and officially abolished, but the vehemence of his indignation is directed against the one element from which he was completely dissociated, the Jewish community. No doubt he was right to deplore the unscrupulousness with which the more affluent Jews rescued their children from conscription, managing by various tricks and bribes to substitute the names of less fortunate Jewish boys, even those under the minimum legal age of twelve. But he fails to acknowledge that such behavior was part of a desperate effort to survive in an inhumanly discriminatory environment.

Effective as it is as a specimen of Leskov's narrative art, "Episcopal Justice" is clearly an effort on the author's part to assuage the lingering feelings of guilt he still felt, as a Russian and in particular as a Russian official, for his part in the persecutions he had witnessed in his youth.

The Crimean War was a shattering experience for most Russians, including the emperor. A painful and humiliating military defeat had been inflicted on a nation that since 1812 had prided itself on its military prowess. In bewilderment people sought an explanation. Looking behind the once imposing facade of Nicholas's military regime, Russians discovered an administration both corrupt and inefficient, incapable of successfully conducting even this relatively small war on its own territory. Moreover, the country was suffering from an accumulation of social, economic, and moral ills that Nicholas's regime had tried to hide rather than remedy. The death in 1855 of that august and implacable tsar and the accession of his son were the signal for an outpouring of pent-up indignation at the gross inequities and inefficiencies of the old order.

During the Crimean War Kiev was an ideal site for viewing the underside of the conflict. Kiev was the funnel through which the endless convoys of troops and supplies passed, and it was the center for the gigantic and well-organized peculation that made millionaires of many officers in the Russian supply services. As an official on the scene, directly involved in army recruiting, Leskov must have observed all this. As a Russian, he doubtless supported his country's flag, obscure as the war's causes and objectives were, for there were foreign troops on Russian soil. But not only was Russia clearly losing the war, she was losing it not because her soldiers were fighting badly but because the government could not cope with the problems of supply. Leskov saw how widespread among the officials was the attitude that government service in wartime was a golden opportunity for plunder. Toward this there were only two possible moral reactions: cynicism or indignation. Clearly, the latter was Leskov's response. Perhaps for the first time in his life he felt acutely the classic moral dilemma: how to reconcile one's patriotism, one's love for his country, with sharply critical and antagonistic feelings toward its government.

The year 1877 seems to have been a time for resurrecting these memories with all the emotional conflicts associated with them. In that year Leskov wrote, in addition to "Episcopal Justice," one of his neatest short memoir pieces, "The Cynic,"[5] in which he recreates, with characteristic irony, a Kievan view of the Crimean War. As he tells the story, soon after the end of the war a dramatic confrontation took place at a Petersburg party between representatives of the two Russian sides, so to speak, of the war: a nobly upright and honest naval officer, a hero of Sevastopol, and a noncombatant supply officer who had enriched himself at the country's expense, obese, smug, and imperturbable, with a wallet as fat as his paunch, both of which he stuffs with satisfaction. In such a confrontation the reader's moral choice would seem predetermined. But Leskov craftily avoids the obvious solution. The former supply officer, Anemodist Petrovich, turns out to be intelligent, adroit, and even wise, and Leskov gives him the last word. His opponent, the hero of Sevastopol, Anemodist Petrovich asserts, has insulted the Russian people by claiming that half of them are thieves:

> It is unjust, sir! We are all Russians, and as our heritage, as part of our rich nature, we have the ability appropriate to all things. We Russians are like cats: wherever you throw us, we'll never land with our faces in the mud, but will land right on our feet [. . .] If it's dying that's called for, we'll die; and if it's thieving, we'll rob. You were assigned to fight, and you did it extremely well. You fought and died as heroes, and you won distinction through all of Europe; and we were put in a position where we could steal, and we also distinguished ourselves and stole so well that we also became famous far and wide. And if, for example, things had turned out in such a way that our positions were reversed, and we, for example, had been sent to the trenches and you to the supply services, we thieves would have fought and died, and you . . . would have stolen. (6:157-158)

Throughout his literary career Leskov was fond of taking such sly jabs at the Russian ego. From an artistic point of view, this moral twist transforms the story, which would otherwise be an obvious and familiar denunciation of obvious and familiar crimes. The irony was then, and still is, too bitter for many Russians to swallow.[6]

This ironic view of the moral conflicts of the war is an artistic construct elaborated twenty years after the fact. During the war itself and its aftermath Leskov's attitude was doubtless more patriotically correct. He was indignant at those who took advantage of their country's peril in order to pad their purses, and like many others he began to wonder whether something profound might not be wrong with Russian society. The general moral upheaval of the late 1850s must have been both exhilarating and unsettling for him. There was much that was amiss in Russia's past and in her present, that was clear; but where was the line to be drawn? How much was to be repudiated? From the left, cries were heard to the effect that everything must be rooted out, the whole system—governmental, social, and economic—dismantled. Nothing could be accomplished with the ruling elite; it must be annihilated. A just society had to be made from scratch, with institutional materials supplied by the lower orders alone, especially the peasants. More moderate voices averred that whatever their faults, the upper class and the government were the only instrumentalities of civilization and enlightenment in the country; that the just society could not be built on peasant barbarism and ignorance; and that therefore what was needed was a progressive reform of the existing system rather than its destruction. Of course, the further question of what institutions had to be reformed, and in what ways, allowed for an almost infinite spectrum of opinion.

In the end Leskov sided vigorously with the gradualist position and took a strong stand against the extremists. It was a choice for which he suffered much in his lifetime and for which he has frequently been excoriated by latter-day critics. Yet in the light of history this decision has much to be said for it, for we have before us too many lamentable consequences of the first alternative. Whether valid or not, the gradualist solution must have felt much more comfortable for a person like Leskov. It did not involve so total a repudiation of one's own position, such deep questioning of one's identity; it admitted that there might be such a thing as a good Russian gentleman and a good Russian official. The bad old tsar was dead; a good new tsar was on the throne; Russian men of good will should rally round to help him carry through the necessary reforms rather than senselessly hurl bombs in the name of utopia.

This basically was Leskov's position throughout his life, despite his brief, early flirtation with radicalism. In his later years, although embittered and caustic about the reactionary regime of Alexander III, presided over by "Lampadonostsev" (Pobedonostsev), Leskov looked back on the government of Alexander II as the most practical progressive instrument Russia had possessed since Peter's time, and he steadfastly condemned the radicals for refusing to cooperate with it. For Leskov the greatest irony, and a symbol of a basic Russian ineptness, a

41

lack of historical judgment and sense of reality, was the fact that of all the Russian tsars of the nineteenth century, it was this one, the "Tsar Liberator," the most intelligent and progressive, who was murdered by revolutionaries.

Leskov's intellectual horizons notably expanded during the years he spent as an official in Kiev. Most of the stimuli for his intellectual growth came from living in his uncle's house, where many of the leading intellectuals in Kiev gathered. The level of conversation, the range of topics discussed, and the knowledge displayed by these people undoubtedly exceeded anything Leskov had experienced in Oryol. Here and there in his writings he mentions the names of some of these academics: a "gifted young scholar" named Nikolai Pilyan-kevich, a professor of the encyclopedia of jurisprudence, as his subject was officially called; Savva Bogorodsky, another professor, a specialist in criminal law; Ignaty Yakubovsky, a professor of agriculture and forestry; and Ivan Vigura, a professor of state law, a relative of whom was the model for Figura, the hero of one of Leskov's tales of Ukrainian goodheartedness.[7] The most important of these for Leskov seems to have been Yakubovsky, who is described in an autobiographical note almost as his private tutor: "Here [in Kiev] N[ikolai] S[emyonovich] continued his education under the particularly friendly supervision of Ignaty Fyod[orovich] Yakubovsky, who was stimulated by the giftedness of his pupil and worked with him with great affection" (11:16). Another important figure was Dmitry Petrovich Zhuravsky, an independent economist who was devoting his life to the abolition of serfdom, not only by advocating it, to the tiny extent that it was possible to do so publicly, but by using what money he had to buy peasants from their owners and set them free.[8]

Even more impressive than the intellect of these young professors was their living example of idealism and altruism, of a life devoted to something more than the pursuit of power and pleasure. Of Zhuravsky Leskov wrote, "He was very nearly the first living person who in the days of my youth in Kiev taught me to understand that virtue exists not only in abstractions."[9] They remained surrounded in Leskov's memory with a halo of reverential admiration, the kind of admiration felt by a youth of eighteen who had emerged from the self-seeking and cynical world of Oryol officialdom to enter their cultivated society. These high-minded young men, about ten years older than he was, treated him with kindness and offered to help him educate himself. People of such moral and intellectual quality were a revelation to Leskov, and the gratitude he felt toward them remained to inspire many of his portraits of *pravedniki*, those men of righteousness and true virtue who abound in his pages. True goodness is difficult to depict without sentimentality or priggishness, and Leskov's ability to accomplish this feat is one of the remarkable features of his talent. Perhaps one reason for his success was the power of the revelation of goodness he had received in his youth. He had discovered in Kiev, to his surprise, that generosity, kindness, and intelligent effort to help others are realities, not myths.

In Leskov's writings there are a few echoes, though perhaps not wholly reliable ones, of these conversations and readings of the Kiev years. "I was taught in a gymnasium," he writes in a quasi-autobiographical story, "and then sent 600 versts away to a university town where I learned to sing one Latin song [no doubt *Gaudeamus igitur*] and read a bit of Strauss, Feuerbach, Büchner, and Babeuf" (1:64). In this passage there is a curious legalistic compromise between *Dichtung* and *Wahrheit*: Leskov does not actually say that he went to the university town to attend the university, which would have been untrue, but that is what he wants the reader to believe. And in the list of authors there is some anachronism. Writing in 1862-63, Leskov, at least in part, was projecting backward to his alleged university life readings and discussions that probably belong to a period about ten years later, the era of radicalism and nihilism. In fact, it is odd that Leskov, an ardent antinihilist at the time this story was written, allowed such a list of nihilist ideologues to stand beside his name in this work, ascribed to the philosophical delectations of his youth.

For this is almost a nihilist quadrinity. David-Friedrich Strauss was one of the first nineteenth-century scholars to set out in quest of the historical Jesus, applying the developing techniques of *Quellenforschung*, though still strongly influenced by Hegelian dialectics, to the problem of the authenticity of the Gospels. His *Life of Jesus* (1835), though not denying the existence of a historical person called Jesus, concludes that the Gospel accounts of him consist almost entirely of implausible myths of later origin. The book created an uproar, led to Strauss's dismissal from his university post at Tübingen, and made him a martyr of the radical cause. It could not be published in Russian translation until 1907, but it was widely known and discussed long before that, particularly in the age of nihilism, when his books were linked with those of Feuerbach, Büchner, Buckle, and Moleschott as canonical components of the radical scriptures. Ludwig Feuerbach, the celebrated Left Hegelian and anti-Christian rationalist, had become known in Russia somewhat earlier, in the age of Belinsky and the young Herzen, and his influence might have reached the intellectuals of Kiev by the time Leskov was there.[10] But Friedrich Büchner published his famous *Force and Matter*, the Bible of what is nowadays called vulgar materialism, only in 1855, and it was two or three years before it became widely known in Russia, popularized in articles in the radical monthlies and sometimes piously distributed in the German original to those in need of such enlightenment, like Arkady Kirsanov's father in Turgenev's *Father and Sons*. As for Gracchus Babeuf, the martyred leader of a radical conspiracy against the Directoire, he seems out of place in this array of German philosophers, and one suspects that his name found its way into this list more for its alliteration with Büchner's than for any other reason. Moreover, Babeuf was not a writer, although a few of his papers had been published in a French monograph on early socialist thinkers.[11]

A more likely list of Kievan readings is given in "Pechersk Eccentrics," where Leskov speaks nostalgically of the "quiet slopes of the upper garden where we had our lyceum. There we young lads used to spend whole nights, until daybreak, listening to whoever seemed cleverest to us, whoever had more information than the rest of us, and could tell us about Kant and Hegel, about 'feelings of the lofty and the beautiful,' and about a great deal else that is never talked about in the gardens of present-day Kiev" (8:135). Kant and Hegel were more likely subjects than Büchner and Babeuf for Kievan philosophizing in the early 1850s, and Schelling, the principal source of ideas about the lofty and beautiful, should no doubt have been included as well. These were the names and the ideas that intellectuals conjured with in the age of Belinsky, and whatever knowledge of them Leskov possessed, he acquired at this time, mostly secondhand.

Despite Leskov's rather pathetic effort to construct for himself a romantic philosophical youth in the style of Herzen or Turgenev, these intellectual experiences were necessarily rather shallow. Leskov's connections with the generation of the forties, the age when philosophy had been discussed with such passion and dedication by Belinsky, Bakunin, Herzen, and Ogaryov, were tenuous. Regardless of his statement in "Pechersk Eccentrics," Leskov never drank deep at the fountainhead of German philosophy, and in fact the whole mentality of Dostoevsky's generation, with its fondness for abstract idealism and theoretical speculations, remained alien to him. He had a more practical cast of mind, and all his life he retained a certain abhorrence for theory, for the sake of which, he felt, human realities were crammed into artificial molds. This may help to explain why Leskov's books are by and large less philosophical than those of Dostoevsky or Tolstoy, or even Turgenev. Leskov was a little afraid to venture into the regions where the "accursed questions," as Russians are fond of calling them, were discussed. Probably the deepest question aired in Leskov's writings is the choice between Orthodoxy and various forms of Protestantism, whereas for Dostoevsky it is the confrontation of Christianity and atheism.

To return to Leskov's intellectual environment in the Kievan period, there is one more older-brother figure who looms large, one even more important than the young professors or the fellow students of the upper garden. This is Stepan Gromeka, whom in 1894 Leskov linked with Opanas Markovich as among the greatest intellectual influences of his youth. Born in 1823, Gromeka was nearer to Leskov's age than the professors, yet old enough to command his respect. He could be a comrade and a teacher at the same time. Gromeka was also more practical and experienced than the professors, and moreover immensely stimulating, but not so threatening to Leskov's self-esteem as those unattainably well-educated academics. Gromeka seems to have taken Leskov under his wing, probably at the beginning of the 1850s, and they remained close friends for more than a decade—not a bad score for one of Leskov's friendships.

After 1852 Gromeka was on the staff of the new governor-general of Kiev, Prince Illarion Vasilchikov;[12] and it was through him that Leskov was brought into the circle of the governor-general's wife— quite a social ascent for the former inky-fingered copyist of the Oryol criminal court. Princess Vasilchikova had a passion for amateur theatricals, and Leskov was enlisted as a performer, apparently showing considerable histrionic talent.

Besides aiding his ascent to the top of the social pinnacle, Gromeka provided Leskov with example and encouragement in two of the major decisions of his life: to leave government service in 1856 for private business and, subsequently, to try his hand at writing. As Leskov recounts it in a protocol-style autobiography of 1890:

> Served a short time [actually more than seven years] in the civil service, where his position brought Leskov into contact with the late St[epan] St[epanovich] Gromeka. This contact had a decisive significance in Leskov's later fate. The example of Gromeka, who left his government post and went over to the Russian Society for Shipping and Trade, induced Leskov to do the same; he entered

commercial service, which demanded constant travels and sometimes kept him in the most remote provincial backwaters. He
traveled up and down Russia in the most various directions, and
this gave him a great fund of impressions and a supply of information about how people live. (11:18)

In the late 1850s, in the muckraking period preceding the great reforms, Gromeka became a sensational figure. A former officer in the
gendarmes, he wrote a series of articles on abuses in the Russian
police, some legally published in Katkov's *Russian Messenger*, then an
organ of the liberals, others sent clandestinely to London for Herzen's
Bell. Gromeka was thus in a position, in the early 1860s, to introduce
his young friend from the provinces to leading journalists and writers
in Petersburg. In his autobiographical sketches, Leskov repeatedly
lists Gromeka as one who "ensnared" him for literature by introducing
him to Kraevsky and Dudyshkin, the publisher and editor of *Notes of
the Fatherland*, one of the leading literary monthlies (11:17, 19, 459).

Gromeka seems to have become disillusioned with the radicals at
about the same time Leskov did, but despite their similar ideological
positions, they quarreled in this period, and their friendship ended in
rupture. As early as 1863 Leskov was making jibes at Gromeka in
print, [13] and these continued for years, even after Gromeka's death. In
the late 1860s, while Leskov pursued his own thorny literary path,
Gromeka drifted back into the service of the tsar's government and at
the end of his life, as vice-governor of Siedlce in Poland, distinguished
himself chiefly for his persecutions of the Uniate church, earning for
himself the ironic epithet "Stephen the Baptist," as Leskov maliciously
pointed out, long after Gromeka was dead. (11:97)

The time Leskov spent in Kiev was one of emotional growth, a time
for exploring the potentialities of sexual experience and emotional relationships with women. Unfortunately, this aspect of his private life
is a subject about which extraordinarily little is known, considering
how recently he lived and how prominent he was. To be sure, he
belonged to the post-Romantic generation, which did not consider an
artist's life an integral part of his oeuvre. But if the realists tended to be
more reticent, less exhibitionistic, the insatiable voyeurism of the
literary public, catered to by the inexhaustible zeal of literary scholarship, has long since lifted any veils they may have tried to draw over
their lives. Every skirmish in Tolstoy's long battle with his wife has
been diagrammed and refought, the diaries of each published and

footnoted at length. Whole books, however tasteless and trivial, have been devoted to the "three loves" of Dostoevsky, and at least one to the history of Turgenev's one pseudolove.[14] But until 1954, with the publication of his son's biography, even professional Russian literary scholars could hardly have said whether Leskov was ever married, let alone have given any details about his erotic experiences.

There are many reasons for this ignorance. In the nineteenth century Leskov was generally considered both a minor writer and politically a somewhat tarnished figure, in stature far below Turgenev, Tolstoy, or Dostoevsky, and therefore the public demand for gossip about him was considerably weaker. By the time his literary reputation had grown, Leskov was long since dead, and the trails that might have led to his secrets were cold. Furthermore, even when memoirists did write about him, the Leskov most of them recalled was the Leskov of the 1880s and 1890s—a crotchety, solitary oldster who must have had some sort of family past (he had a son living with him during most of this period), but as far as anyone could tell had a purely celibate present. The writer Lidia Veselitskaya (V. Mikulich), who became friendly with Leskov in the 1890s, visiting and corresponding with him frequently, had only the vaguest notion of his blood relatives, about whom he seldom spoke, preferring to talk about literature.[15] And those who had known him in the fifties and sixties were either gone or uninterested in recording their recollections of Leskov's life.

Leskov himself is of little help. He was a secretive man, and although in his fiction he unconsciously revealed a great deal about his feelings and attitudes, he avoided giving much direct, factual information about himself. He kept no diaries. There was much he was ashamed of in his relations with others, particularly the people who had been close to him, and he was not the kind of man to admit his sins, even to himself. His surviving correspondence therefore tells little about his intimate life. Here and there a few hints do leak through his censorship, however, and a few others have been cast up by the researches of scholars, especially his son.

Of Leskov's premarital experiences with women next to nothing is known. There is no trace of any romance serious enough for the lady's name to be linked with his in any record left from the past. At that time, and in that class, romances were carefully supervised, and the connection between romance and marriage quite rigidly enforced. In the meantime, for men, there were other diversions. In one late memoir-type story that seeks to recapture the spirit of Kiev in the early 1850s, Leskov paints a vivid picture of the cozy form of prostitution practiced in those prereform days, a picture so convincing that one feels it must have been drawn from experience. He tells of ramshackle houses at Kresty, along the Dnepr, where those "shameless girls lived [*meškaly bessoromnye divčata*, in Ukrainian] who represented a curious combination of urban, civilized prostitution with Cossack homespunness and hospitality. These ladies, who wore not European clothes, but the Ukrainian national costume, the so-called 'simple dress,' were visited by good citizens bearing 'vodka, sausages, lard, and fish,' and from these imported provisions the girls from Kresty would artfully prepare tasty repasts and spend their hours of pleasure with their visitors in good family style." (7:134)

Agreeable as these encounters were, after some years Leskov evidently yearned for something more permanent. In April 1853, much to the surprise of his relatives, he suddenly married one Olga Vasilievna Smirnova, the daughter of a well-to-do Kiev businessman. Again, our information about this marriage, and about the personality of Leskov's wife, is exceedingly scanty. Not a single person who knew Leskov at this time left memoirs or preserved any letters giving a contemporary outsider's view of Olga Vasilievna or of their relationship; nor is there anything from Olga herself. Except for a few elusive references in the writings of her husband, certainly fictionalized and probably distorted, we are limited to a modicum of secondhand and contradictory evidence passed on by Leskov's son and granddaughter. Andrei Leskov, Olga Vasilievna's stepson (who probably never saw her), reports that "according to the collective judgment passed down in our family, she had neither mind nor heart nor self-control nor beauty. A pile of unredeemed 'not's'."[16] Leskov's (and Olga's) granddaughter, on the contrary, claims that she was "tall, beautiful, and unusually feminine."[17]

Whatever the truth about Olga Vasilievna's mind, heart, and physique, there is no doubt that in Leskov's life the marriage was a catastrophe. Fights, scenes (scandals, as the Russians call them) began even before the honeymoon was over. Before long Olga became, for Leskov, the epitome of female evil: scheming, unscrupulous, shrill, hysterical, disloyal, shallow, ignorant, and pretentious, she was alternatively a millstone around his neck or a fury sent by heaven to torment him.

How he had managed to select such a harridan is hard to say. His granddaughter reports that Olga's father had promised her a dowry of 200,000 rubles, a promise apparently never kept because of business reverses.[18] Such a shortcut to comfort and position might well have appealed to Leskov, after the hardships of his early life and the seeming hopelessness of making headway in his official career without connections. But the muffled echoes of the marriage in his writings seem to indicate another motive, for which the financial one may have been only a reinforcement and a rationalization: a sudden outburst of passion.

A travelogue Leskov wrote in 1862 contains a digression in which he tells of lying alone, musing on his past, in a hotel in Grodno, a dreary Polono-Jewish town in western Russia. Two Polish women in the next room were carrying on a long discussion about dowries, and Leskov's thoughts turned to the same subject and to the many images associated with it in his own life.

> I recollected another half-Polish city, not in cold Lithuania, but in luxuriant Ukraine; I recollected masquerades, a yellow house, a little room beneath the gate, blond curls on a pretty little face and a brown dress on a well-proportioned figure. Then came other recollections; the roses were mixed with thorns; then the roses themselves vanished altogether, and there were left only sharp prongs, prongs, prongs; and here was I, alone and broken, lying in a cold room in a Lithuanian inn and obliged to listen to the conversation of two Polish ladies, talking about a dowry. Dowry! What a strange word that is, I thought, and once again began to doze off.[19]

In the novel *No Way Out*, which contains Leskov's most fully elaborated fictional picture of his marital experience, the autobiographical hero, trapped in a wretched marriage, speculates on the strange play of motives "uniting couples by chance, calculation, or their own wayward passions" (2:486). Earlier in the novel, as if to absolve the hero of any responsibility for his mistake, Leskov presents the matter as if his hero, in marrying, had been merely the helpless and passive victim of a female conspiracy: "This weak-nerved maiden [whose name is Olga Aleksandrovna in the novel] in the first year after the doctor's arrival in town had put the crown of matrimony on his head" (2:169). Much later Leskov again speculated in print on the subject of marriage, reaching much the same conclusion: "How do people sometimes marry? Careful observers maintain that in no other area does human folly appear to such a frightening degree as in the formation of conjugal unions. They say that the most intelligent people buy their boots with much more care than they select their wives. And they are right: people frequently seem to be governed in their selection by nothing but blind, mocking chance" (5:244-245).

There is no doubt that Leskov's marriage was a miserable failure, and it is surprising that it lasted as long as it did. Besides the remnants of passion and the inertia of habit, perhaps a sense of obligation to their children helped to keep the couple together: a son, Dmitry, was born in December 1854, and a daughter, Vera, in March 1856.[20] (Little Dmitry died, apparently of cholera, during a family visit to Leskov's mother in Oryol in 1856 or 1857.) But the disharmony at home must have contributed to Leskov's restlessness, and thus, in a negative way, to his willingness to give up his official career and launch into private business; and later, after his business career had dissolved, his resolve to become a professional writer. The nature of his business obliged Leskov to travel a great deal. One of the ancillary benefits of these journeys was that they kept him away from Olga, thus indirectly prolonging his marriage. Later, in 1860, after his commercial position had collapsed, Leskov's attempt to resume his career in the government service in Kiev was abandoned partly because settling down again in one place meant the constant proximity of Olga Vasilievna. After three months of this life he was ready to take the exceedingly bold and perilous step, for a man of thirty without formal education or literary experience, of setting off for Petersburg with the intention of becoming a professional journalist.[21]

During his first years as a writer, Olga made several attempts to pursue him. She turned up, much to Leskov's chagrin, in Moscow in the summer of 1861, just when he was reveling in his freedom and in his sudden, amazingly successful ascent into a scintillating world of intellectuals, journalists, and political activists. There she succeeded in poisoning his relations with his employer, Countess Yevgenia Salias de Tournemire. By the end of the year Leskov had not only broken all ties with the countess, who had taken Olga's part, but carried in his heart a bitterness against her that rankled for years. At least one more time Olga attempted to assert her conjugal claims to Leskov. She appeared in Petersburg, possibly early in 1862, and again regaled Leskov's new friends with lurid tales of his mistreatment of her.[22]

By this time Olga Vasilievna must have been exhibiting, more and more obviously, symptoms of serious mental illness. Many years later, in a letter to Aleksei Suvorin—one of the few people Leskov then associated with who had known Olga Vasilievna—Leskov claims that he "was regarded as a beast [by Countess Salias and her friends] because [he] did not let a mentally ill woman do everything that may enter the head of a madwoman."[23] According to Andrei Leskov, the failure of the Kiev bank where most of her money was deposited served to trigger, or at least intensify, these symptoms.[24] But not for nearly twenty years was she finally committed to a mental hospital. In the meantime, with her daughter Vera in tow, she spent years wandering around in pursuit of various chimeras, now begging help and protection from all and sundry, now rejecting offers of assistance and rushing away. At last, in 1878, she was permanently incarcerated in the Hospital of St. Nicholas in Petersburg. The diagnosis, characteristic of the nineteenth-century genetic fallacy, was "acute schizophrenia resulting from the alcoholism of her father."[25] She was to live there for more than thirty years, until her death in 1909.[26] In the beginning Leskov used to visit her often; later he virtually gave it up, since by then she hardly knew who he was or cared, except for the delicacies he brought her. It was easier and less painful simply to arrange for the nurses to give her the fruit and fried *koryushka* (smelt) she loved.

Leskov never confided his feelings about this marriage to anyone, as far as can be determined. Only in his letters to Suvorin does he, very occasionally, refer to it; and he invariably assumes his typical defensive stance: "But I suffered so much. Marriage with a mad woman, marriage with a leper, marriage with a slanderer who tried to ruin me."[27] But a defensive stance implies a fear of attack, and the fear would hardly be so strong if he did not believe himself vulnerable. Deep down, beneath all the self-pity and the accusations leveled at others, including his wife, Leskov must have felt an agonizing sense of his own guilt. Only on the rarest occasions were others allowed glimpses of this guilt. Leskov's son caught one of them. As he tells the story,

> Once one of Leskov's latter-day visitors, looking hard at his early photographs, said "Yes, Nikolai Semyonovich, what a fellow you must have been when you were young!"
> "Ugh! I was a demon, a demon," with a nervous twitch of the shoulders and an abrupt movement of his hand, as if brushing away an image keenly palpable and even frightening.[28]

In the spring of 1857, inspired by the example of his friend Gromeka, and doubtless not unwilling to be away from his wife, Leskov took a leave of absence from his government position and set off to investigate the possibilities of private employment. The most accessible and amenable potential employer was his British uncle, Alexander Scott, who from headquarters near Penza, in northeastern

Russia, operated a firm engaged in a variety of agricultural and commercial operations, including, at one time, the management of the vast estates of the Perovsky and Naryshkin families. Scott offered his nephew a regular position with the firm, and Leskov formally resigned from the service and moved with his wife and family to Penza.

Leskov's duties as a commercial agent obliged him to travel across European Russia "from the White Sea to the Black and from Brody to Krasny Yar."[29] Reminiscing about this period in later years, he always depicts it not only as one of the most interesting and exciting epochs in his life but as an inexhaustible source of literary materials, which he continued to mine throughout his literary career. "I was obliged to travel all over Russia on business [. . .] This was the best time of my life, when I saw much and lived easily," Leskov said to an interviewer shortly before he died.[30] Twenty years earlier he presented an almost identical image of this period: "Before being a writer, I was a businessman [*čelovek kommerčeskij*]—I worked for Scott and Wilkens [sic]. I was in charge of an independent enterprise, receiving about 6,000 rubles a year; I was always well regarded and may say that I know Russia like the palm of my hand."[31] From these and other remarks it is clear that the three years "on Scott's barges" made it possible for Leskov to assume one of his basic literary postures, one he exploited throughout his career: the man of experience, the widely traveled connoisseur of Russian life, intimately acquainted with its picturesque byways and backwaters, its characters and its color.

But there is much that remains unclear about Leskov's business life, including the nature of the business. According to Leskov's scattered, and sometimes contradictory, statements about it, an "Englishman" or Scotsman (Leskov never distinguishes them) named James Scott, the father of Leskov's uncle, had been hired during the reign of Nicholas I as the manager of the estates of Count L. A. Perovsky, a wealthy grandee who served as minister of the interior and as minister of crown property under Nicholas, and probably also those of L. A. Naryshkin, another high magnate at Nicholas's court. After James's death, the position was passed on, according to one of Leskov's statements, to James's four sons and held by them jointly.[32] In another source, however, he says that James Scott had managed the "enormous estates of the Naryshkins and Perovskys [not further identified] together with his three sons" and that his successors were the great abolitionist Dmitry Zhuravsky and his associate N. V. Verigin (9:357).

At the time of Leskov's employment the active head of the firm seems to have been Alexander Scott, now in partnership with another Englishman named Wilkins. As for the nature of the business, Leskov states that at the time he worked for him, Alexander Scott was the manager of the Perovsky and Naryshkin estates and received a salary of up to 40,000 rubles a year. One of Scott's undertakings was to supervise the transference of peasant serfs from the region of Oryol and Kursk in central Russia to newly acquired steppe lands in the southeast. The only fact we know for certain about Leskov's own duties in his uncle's firm is that he was once assigned to accompany one of these shipments of human cattle, transported by barge down the Oka and Volga to their owners' new estates in the steppe. Besides the agony of being torn from their homes and familiar surroundings and herded off into the unknown, on the journey itself the people were driven to a veritable frenzy by lice. For Leskov this trip was a searing experience of human misery, vividly described in "A Product of Nature," its poignancy intensified by the memory of the author's own mistaken liberalism in dealing with his unhappy peasant cargo.

Scott's arrangement with the Perovskys and the Naryshkins does not seem to have continued after the resettlement was completed. Subsequently the firm devoted itself chiefly to managing an estate in the Penza area owned by Scott himself and in such subsidiary operations as milling grain and distilling vodka.[33] In these activities Leskov apparently served as his uncle's general executive assistant.

The business did not prosper. The withdrawal of the Wilkins partner—if Andrei Leskov's account is to be trusted—left the firm financially shaken, and Scott was no longer able to afford his nephew's services. In 1860, feeling considerable bitterness toward his uncle, Leskov was obliged to return to Kiev, his commercial service at an end.

Leskov soon drew an unflattering fictional portrait of Scott in "The Mocker," showing him, despite his high principles and basic decency, insufficiently attuned to the peculiarities of Russian conditions and to the psychology of the Russian peasants. Despite his good will, therefore, he comes to grief in his dealings with *homo russicus in terra russica.* The theme of the flounderings of the foreigner in Russia is taken up again in "Iron Will," where the hero is an obtuse German who, like Scott, finds his plans frustrated and his enterprise dissolved in the fluid chaos of Russian life. Before beginning the main narrative, Leskov refers, in his favorite autobiographical vein, to his own experiences in working for foreigners in Russia—not Germans, but Englishmen. "They were very kind people," he says, "and both rather practical. The latter I conclude from the fact that after the total collapse of their enterprises, they understood that Russia had its own peculiarities which it was fatal to ignore. They then set about their business in a purely Russian way and soon got rich again in good English style" (6:8). While the first of these statements may be true, the alleged financial apotheosis of the chastened and Russified Scotts is pure fiction.

Though their personal relations were permanently damaged, Leskov ultimately revived a positive image of Scott, and he made use of it several times in his writings to contrast with what seemed to him the conscienceless opportunism and flabby sycophancy of the Russian character. Whatever his tactical mistakes, Scott was a man of principle who tried to lead a virtuous life. He assumed moral responsiblity for the people and things committed to his charge and systematically worked to make their lot better. As a moral type, he exemplified more vividly and more successfully precisely those qualities of sturdy independence, self-reliance, practicality, enterprise, and ethical uprightness Leskov had admired in his father. Among other things, Scott had a strong sense of his own dignity—something Leskov felt too many Russians lacked—and would not demean himself before the high and mighty (in this too he resembles Leskov's father). Leskov recounts with gusto how Scott wrote an insulting letter to a governor who had offended him, challenged a marshal of nobility to a duel, and called a bishop to order for addressing him rudely (6:419; 9:364). Indeed, by the end of his life, with his resentment dissolved by time, Leskov was ready to reverse totally the judgment he had pronounced in "The Mocker."

In his sharply critical and antinationalist mood of the 1890s, Leskov now maintained that it was not Scott who was to blame for his impracticality in building snug stone houses for his peasants and then feeling embittered when they insisted on living in wooden shanties they put up alongside, using the stone houses as privies. It was rather the Russian peasants themselves, long objects of self-immolating worship by generations of Russian intellectuals. Scott is allowed to pronounce a terrible judgment, a judgment the author had come to share:

"Nothing good is of any use here, because the people who live here are savage and bad."
"Not bad, uncle!"

"No, bad. You are a Russian, and for you it may be unpleasant, but I am an outsider and I can judge freely: these people are bad. But that in itself is not so terrible. What is much worse is that these people are being lied to and taught that the bad is good and the good bad. Mark my words: the retribution for this will come when it is least expected." (9:368-369)

Part II

From Left to Right
(1860-1874)

4

Journalist, Revolutionary, and Pariah

During the year 1860, probably after he left Scott's employ and before he resumed working in the office of the governor-general of Kiev, Leskov at last ventured to write for publication. He still had no idea of trying to earn his living by writing; he was simply adding his voice to the chorus of amateur journalists who were making Russia reverberate with their discordant harmonies. Since the accession of Alexander II, the educated classes had been enthusiastically playing this newly authorized game of exposé journalism, calling attention in print to multifarious social and economic problems formerly kept hidden under the censor's bushel.

Leskov's career as a publishing writer was launched with two tiny such articles.[1] On June 18, 1860, an unsigned note written by Leskov appeared in the *Economic Index*, a specialized magazine edited in Petersburg by a former Kiev professor named Ivan Vernadsky. The author complained that a Kiev bookshop was selling the newly authorized translation of the Gospels into modern Russian (hitherto only the Slavonic Gospel had been permitted) for 40 copecks instead of the 20 indicated on the wrapper. Apparently in an effort to gain a wider audience for this momentous protest, on June 21 an unsigned "Correspondence" registering the same complaint appeared in the *Saint Petersburg News*, a big newspaper with a liberal reputation.

Such is Leskov's entrance into "literature": hardly a burst of inaugural glory. Nevertheless, these two articles, seemingly inconsequential, are interesting as indicators of Leskov's mentality and intellectual concerns. The Gospels and prices, the spirit and the pocketbook— these two fundamental polarities were to confront one another throughout his career, for all his life he was to grapple with the question of how spiritual values could be realized in the actual world of economic relationships. In making his point, besides venting rather more fury than the cause would seem to warrant, Leskov provides a survey of the bookstores of Voronezh as well as of Kiev, showing that he was both well acquainted with their stock and adept at estimating their profit margins. These two articles provide a striking portrait of the artist as a shrewd and keen-eyed businessman engaged in the endless process of self-education. Leskov mentions in passing some of his particular interests as a bookstore browser: religion (not only the Gospels, but the history of the Russian schism, which was to remain one of his specialties); economics (a book entitled *On the Productive Forces of Russia*); and literature, specifically Belinsky, the great critic of the previous generation, who was then being claimed as patron saint by both liberals and radicals.

One of Leskov's acquaintances in Kiev, a colleague and friend of his uncle, was a Russian doctor with a German surname, Aleksandr Petrovich Valter, professor of anatomy at the university, whose lectures Leskov had attended as an unregistered auditor. Valter was the editor of a professional magazine called *Contemporary Medicine*, and he prevailed upon Leskov to write for it a series of articles. During the summer and fall of 1860 Leskov wrote five of them. Despite the magazine's specialized audience and limited circulation, these articles, written with vigor and literary flair, anticipate in form and content some of Leskov's later works. They also provide evidence of his ideological position at the outset of his career, before he plunged into the Petersburg melee.

"A Note on Buildings," the first, is a protest against poor design in Russian public edifices, with their striving for monumentality at the expense of comfort.[2] With the freedom possible in a medical journal, Leskov deals with the problem of toilet facilities. Using what later became a favorite literary device, the illustrative memoir, he reminisces about his own experiences in the Oryol gymnasium, seen from the vantage point of its privy. The picture is a satiric microcosm of Nicholas's empire: every school, every classroom, is a harsh and capricious despotism, callous to human needs, where children early learn from their elders that you can tyrannize over your inferiors only at the price of unlimited sycophancy toward your superiors. Leskov recalls that the younger boys were obliged to beg and even to bribe the older ones for a chance to use the tiny privy during the absurdly brief time allowed for the purpose.

In the next article, "On the Working Class," the topic of unhygienic buildings is extended to dwellings of urban workers, and the medical profession is taken to task for failing to protest more energetically against the squalor in which these "lesser brethren" live.[3] "We wait for the government to do everything and don't want to undertake anything ourselves," Leskov laments. His ideal seems to be a society of self-sufficient, socially responsible capitalists voluntarily allocating resources to improve the living conditions of their employees, something like the New Lanark of Robert Owen, of whom Leskov was a great admirer. And in his enthusiasm for such a society, he tended to view it as already realized, not only at New Lanark, but in England as a whole.[4]

Leskov's other articles in *Contemporary Medicine* are in much the same spirit—exposing social and economic ills and exhorting the educated classes to set about remedying them.[5] His vehemence is directed at the doctors themselves, and most of all he denounces physicians who hold posts in the civil service, both those employed in the army recruiting stations, which Leskov knew so well, and those who serve as medical inspectors in the police.

Although it was not published until April, 1861, after several other pieces had appeared in print, the first article Leskov wrote was a much more ambitious work, "A Sketch of the Distilling Industry (Penza Province)," which came out in *Notes of the Fatherland*.[6] To have an article printed in this prestigious liberal magazine must have provided a big boost to Leskov's literary ego, doubtless influencing his decision to become a professional writer. *Notes of the Fatherland* was a national magazine, one of the *tolstye zhurnaly*, or "fat monthlies," that served as media for much of the country's intellectual life. The article is a painstaking survey of the vodka-distilling industry in Penza Province (where Scott's headquarters were), treating in detail such matters as the size of stills, types of distilling apparatus, disposal of waste products, use of these as cattle fodder, as well as problems of finance and credit. Showing beneath the economic factualism is the denunciatory bias of the ex-businessman. Leskov particularly deplores the government's policy of restricting licenses for distilleries to the gentry, for whom special credits and privileges were made available, while prohibiting merchants and peasants from engaging in this profitable business. The government, he maintains, should treat the classes equally and stop meddling in the private sector. Though solidly competent, the essay is hardly one that would have much appeal for the general readers of a literary magazine. Nowadays such articles would be found only in journals for specialists, but at that time the "fat monthlies" accommodated a good deal of such ballast, which helped maintain their stance of high seriousness.

Toward the end of 1860 Leskov made his great decision. His business career had long since collapsed and, after the freedom and adventure he had enjoyed in it, government service in Kiev was confining. And most unbearable of all was the constant proximity of Olga Vasilievna. He had succeeded in publishing several articles; people had discerned in him a talent for writing; and he felt he had much to say about the world and its problems. A God-sent opportunity appeared in the form of a letter to some friends of his in Kiev from a Russian lady with the unlikely name of Countess Salias de Tournemire (née Sukhovo-Kobylina, she was the sister of the playwright and had been briefly married to an itinerant French aristocrat). Countess Salias had undertaken to promote the liberal cause, and likewise recoup her depleted fortunes, by publishing a magazine of current affairs to be called *Russian Speech*. She asked her friends in Kiev if they knew of any promising young writers, and they recommended Leskov.

At the same time Professor Vernadsky, the editor of the *Economic Index*, also wrote to Leskov, perhaps in reply to an inquiry, and encouraged him to come to Petersburg, promising to provide him with introductions in the journalistic world. In addition, Leskov's friend Stepan Gromeka had already thrown over his commercial service and joined the fraternity of Petersburg journalists, and he urged Leskov to come do the same.[7] Leskov needed no further encouragement. On his way to Petersburg he stopped off in Moscow to negotiate with Countess Salias, and she agreed to engage him as a Petersburg correspondent.

Once in Petersburg, Leskov plunged into his new profession with gusto, reading, writing, talking, learning as much and as fast as he could. Vernadsky and his wife welcomed him almost as a relative, taking him in as a boarder in their apartment. In addition to introducing him widely among his acquaintances, Vernadsky invited Leskov to accompany him to meetings of several learned societies, including the Economic Committee of the Imperial Geographical Society and the Free Economic Society. These gatherings were attended by such august personages as Grand Duke Konstantin Nikolaevich, the emperor's brother, noted for his liberalism, and Count Nikolai Muravyov-Amursky, the former governor-general of Eastern Siberia. To hear so many intelligent, well-informed, important people discussing so freely so many fascinating questions was thrilling for such a raw provincial as Leskov. Even more exciting was the opportunity to speak out at such meetings oneself, to be taken seriously, recognized as a man of experience with practical ideas. What a spectacular leap upward in the world! An ex-clerk with little education and no position suddenly speaking authoritatively in a learned society and listened to by the tsar's brother—whatever Leskov's "bourgeois-democratic" views may have been at this time, they did not hinder his ecstacy at such a vertiginous experience: "The words of His Highness, spoken in a society which engages in public debates, enraptured everyone present. This feeling was especially warm and joyful in those who were hearing a grand duke speak for the first time in their lives and who had themselves for the first time spoken in the presence of a member of the royal family."[8]

During the spring of 1861 Leskov wrote articles on a variety of subjects. In some of them he simply indulged in speculation on topics of general interest, but in many he exploited his unusual experience and hard-won expertise: the resettling of peasants on virgin lands[9] (as he had done for Scott); employment of former officials in commercial business;[10] peasant land ownership following the Emancipation;[11] and the labor market in town and country.[12] Though no expert, he also spoke out on such questions as the emancipation of women,[13] taking a strong profeminist stand (perhaps calculated to please Countess Salias), and adult education for workers and peasants.[14] (Like many idealistic intellectuals in this period, Leskov served as a teacher in one of the Sunday schools for workers until they were closed by the police as nuclei of subversion.) The only remotely literary piece is a moving account of the death and funeral of the Ukrainian poet Taras Shevchenko.[15]

Taken together, these articles present a clear picture of Leskov's social philosophy at the outset of his career as a writer. He is a reformist, acutely aware of the unfavorable comparison between his country and the more advanced nations to the west, particularly England. He is gratified by the Emancipation but wishes that the equalization of classes before the law had been carried much further. He is sarcastic about reactionaries opposing reforms, calling them "Chinese Europeans."[16] He is against the government's protection of gentry privileges; he thinks the market should be allowed to operate freely, without state interference. About political institutions he has little to say, partly, no doubt, because of censorship, but one surmises that he favors some form of representative government. He is no republican, however, and feels an attachment to the royal family and especially to Alexander II.

Leskov's attitude toward the radicals is more complicated. As late as 1861 the distinction between liberal and radical was not well defined, at least on concrete issues. Russian society still had so many feudal survivals, and the government, even under Alexander II, was so conservative and so intolerant of criticism, and the mass of the population so backward, that all the members of the cultural elite who advocated change, whether sweeping or not, tended to be lumped together in one progressive camp. On the greatest social issue of all, the abolition of serfdom, all progressives had been united, although they may have disagreed about its specific terms; and they were essentially in agreement on many subsidiary issues, such as civil liberties, the atrocious state of the judicial and penal systems, abolition of corporal punishment, and equitable treatment of minorities. Finally, there was, at least tacitly, a common spirit of criticism of the autocracy as a system of government and of hostility to autocracy's servant, the corrupt and overweening bureaucracy.

But after 1861, with the Emancipation achieved, this coalition began to break up. Most liberals, essentially loyal in their opposition, felt that a great step forward had been taken, and they were ready to applaud the "Tsar Liberator," hoping that in time he would vouchsafe them additional reforms. The radicals, on the other hand, generally more theoretical as well as more alienated than the liberals, cherished a whole system of goals they wished to impose on Russian society; it was not so much specific reforms they wanted as an entire new way of life. The Emancipation Act did not satisfy them, not because its provisions were ungenerous toward the peasantry, but because by definition no reforms carried out by the imperial government could ever satisfy them: they sought to annihilate that government and the gentry class from which it drew its primary support. They hoped that the peasants' disappointment with the terms of the act would be the impetus for a revolutionary uprising, which they looked for in the immediate future, and they began to take steps to promote such a revolt. On secret presses they began printing incendiary proclamations and distributing them to an astonished and apprehensive public, sending emissaries to the villages to incite the peasants to violence, and endeavoring to promote active rebellion among the persecuted religious sectarians.

On arriving in Petersburg Leskov was confronted with the necessity of choosing between these rival factions, which from the distance of Kiev had sounded like a single voice of progress. In later years he averred that he had from the beginning sided surely and firmly with the gradualists, the *postepenovtsy*, in opposition to the *neterpelivtsy* or "impatient ones." This latter-day image of gradualist consistency was not entirely valid: Leskov did have, at the very outset of his career, a brief flirtation with revolutionary radicalism. But whatever his temporary enthusiasms and extravagances in 1861 and early 1862, the revolutionary mentality was in a fundamental way alien to Leskov, and in some sense his war with the nihilists can be said to have begun in 1861.

First, there was a profound difference in background, in ethos, in intellectual makeup. In relation to the plebeian, radical intellectuals of Petersburg Leskov felt jealous and defensive. He was a former provincial official and businessman who had not completed the gymnasium; they were mostly graduates of universities or at least of seminaries. To compensate for his educational inferiority, he had to stress the value of his practical experience, his close contact with real Russian conditions. Their ideas about "what to do," he felt, came largely from theories of Western provenance; his came from an informed assessment of concrete realities. He therefore developed a basic antitheoreticism, a cult of practicality, which remained with him all his life; and it set him apart, both in his eyes and theirs, from the more bookish radicals.

Second, Leskov's alienation from Russian society and Russian institutions was never as deep as the revolutionary's. The revolutionary was convinced of the hopelessness of the existing social system. He maintained that the imperial government and the ruling classes had a vested interest in opposing progress and that therefore the just society could be achieved only by destroying them. It was not only useless but harmful to speak of reforming a system evil and incorrigible by nature. Emotionally, the revolutionary had to sever all the ties that bound him to the past, such as patriotism, religion, and family, and be ready to hurl himself against the old order even at the risk of his life. At no time did Leskov fit this image. What he desired was simply the Westernization of Russia: the adoption of certain fundamental economic, social, and perhaps political institutions and practices already prevalent in western Europe, especially in England: civil liberties, equality of the classes before the law, a decently paid and therefore relatively honest civil service, and economic freedom, by which he meant freedom from government interference in economic life. These goals, basically products of "enlightenment," he believed, could only by achieved by the educated classes. If the imperial government and the conservative section of educated society opposed the changes those goals required, an effort should be made to persuade them of their error; if they persisted in their opposition, perhaps in his exasperation the gradualist might be willing to condone such illegal methods of persuasion as underground printing presses. But to wipe out the enlightened elite would be to plunge the country back into peasant barbarism.

For Leskov did not share the revolutionary's optimistic view of the peasants, with their famous communes, as natural socialists who would move directly into a just society if only their exploiters were removed. He saw the "people" as primitive and backward, stubbornly resistant to any change, even when actually beneficial to them; only through long, patient efforts at education could their cultural level be raised to the point where they would correctly perceive their own interests.

Furthermore, he did not really believe in the feasibility of the revolutionary program. The radicals could not accomplish their ends without the support of the classes they aimed to destroy, since they themselves were ridiculously few in number, and he was convinced that any hopes for effective participation of the peasant masses were illusory. The peasants as Leskov knew them, however hostile they might feel toward their masters, remained loyal subjects of the tsar, and, moreover, they were too dispersed and backward to be susceptible to mass organization for any purpose.

Even as early as 1861, Leskov, like many other educated Russians, had begun to be repelled by the radicals' style. As in other periods, indignation was as much aroused by the radicals' dirty hands, long (or short) hair, and alleged sexual promiscuity as by their ideas. To this day readers of *Fathers and Sons* find it hard to forgive the rudeness of Bazarov, although they may admire his intelligence and courage; and in its own day the book was considered by some as a lampoon on the "younger generation"—the accepted euphemism for the radical Left.[17] In the summer of 1861, in an article in *Russian Speech*, Leskov took the radicals to task for their wholesale negativism and especially for their unmannerly behavior both in society and in print. He discerned in the radical journalists a whole cluster of repellent qualities, such as "clownishness, mountebankery, buffoonery, and unblushing insolence hand in hand with impenetrable ignorance," and in their literary products he found "abuse accompanied by expressions of readiness 'to speak in nonliterary language.' " He especially deplored the tendency of radical polemicists to resort to ad hominem arguments rather than deal with the issues, and even more the offhand arrogance with which they dimissed whole areas of knowledge: "Among the radicals authorities are scorned; almost nobody knows history or studies it; certain sciences, like political economy for instance, have, as a certain Petersburg 'fat' magazine has it, been 'digested and discarded'; no one knows any law or cares to. What's the use of it? Out with everything; trample on authorities; throw out learning; ridicule the fruits of the thought and the labor of thinkers in whom peoples more advanced than we take pride."[18]

Nevertheless, in 1861 and early 1862 Leskov had numerous friends and acquaintances among the "impatient ones," many of them close, and despite his irritation over their frequent ignorance and bad manners, he maintained for a time a stance of solidarity with the radicals, in the name of progressive unity against stagnation and reaction.

In Petersburg he revived an old acquaintance, dating back to Oryol gymnasium days, with Pavel Yakushkin, the "muzhik in glasses"[19] who served as the principal model for the hero of "The Musk-ox." In 1884, after Yakushkin's death, Leskov wrote a warm, if somewhat patronizing, memoir on him (11:71-89). Both "The Musk-ox" and the memoir show that Leskov was impressed by the ideas and especially the spiritual qualities of this quixotic peasantophile, even though he later felt obliged to depreciate Yakushkin's ideas as unrealistic and the man as hopelessly impractical and ineffectual, however selfless in his dedication.

Leskov also formed a close association with the Kurochkin brothers, Nikolai and Vasily. Nikolai was a doctor turned journalist, editor of a satirical magazine; Vasily, also an editor, was the founder of the humor magazine *Spark* and well known as a poet and translator, especially for his versions of Béranger. The Kurochkins also shared Ukrainian connections with Leskov: Leskov mentions Nikolai Kurochkin as one of the orators at Shevchenko's funeral, so choked up with tears that he was almost unable to speak (10:11). Both the Kurochkin brothers were members of the revolutionary circle Land and Freedom in 1861-1863[20] and later belonged to the entourage of Nekrasov and Shchedrin, the extreme left wing of Russian journalism. They were bitter enemies of Leskov in subsequent years; but in February 1862, when Nikolai Kurochkin became involved in a conflict with the owner of his magazine *Illustration* and decided to resign the editorship, Leskov's name was prominent on a list of writers who publicly proclaimed their solidarity with Kurochkin and vowed to boycott the magazine until the owner came to terms with him.[21]

While teaching in the workers' Sunday schools, Leskov's immediate supervisor was a former Kiev professor, whom he had doubtless met much earlier, Platon Pavlov. Pavlov, a historian, had moved to Petersburg in 1859 to serve on the Imperial Archeographic Commission, the principal state-sponsored research institute for the study of Russian history. He was an associate and admirer of both Herzen and Chernyshevsky and was already under police surveillance. At a public meeting in Petersburg in March 1862 he departed from the previously approved text of his speech, evoking an enormous outburst of enthusiasm from the crowd. Alarmed, the authorities promptly arrested him, and without the semblance of a trial he was banished to the provinces for an indefinite period.[22]

At meetings of the Economic Committee of the Imperial Geographical Society in 1861 Leskov met Nikolai Serno-Solovevich, one of Herzen's young disciples. True to the principles of his master, at the meeting of April 8, which Leskov attended, Serno-Solovevich spoke out in defense of the Russian peasant commune against the attacks of the classical liberal economists, like Leskov's mentor Vernadsky, who considered it an obstacle to the entrepreneurial initiative of individual peasants.[23] Leskov was more inclined to agree with Vernadsky, but he could hardly help being impressed with Serno-Solovevich, who was a man of outstanding qualities, both intellectual and personal. Serno-Solovevich ran a bookstore in Petersburg that served as a distribution point for Herzen's *Bell* and other clandestine literature, and Leskov, who could never resist a bookstore, undoubtedly frequented it. Later that year, during the government's first large-scale crackdown on Herzen's followers in Russia, Serno-Solovevich was arrested and eventually sentenced to twelve years' penal servitude in Siberia, which he did not survive. Like Bazarov, he died of typhus, in 1866.[24]

In the spring of 1862 Leskov joined Serno-Solovevich, Yakushkin, the Kurochkin brothers, and other leading Petersburg radicals, including G. Z. Yeliseyev, N. V. Shelgunov, and A. P. Shchapov, in taking control, on a cooperative basis, of the weekly magazine *The Age*, which promptly moved as far to the left as the censors would permit. Before long, however, there was disagreement among the cooperators over the policies of the chief editor, Yeliseyev, and the ultra-Left wing, led by Serno-Solovevich, withdrew from the magazine. Leskov sided with Yeliseyev and the majority. Suffering from the effects of this rupture and also from financial difficulties, *The Age* gave up the ghost with the number for April 29, 1862.[25]

Probably Leskov's closest radical connection in Petersburg was Andrei Nichiporenko, a young Ukrainian official, also one of the cooperators on *The Age*. In 1861 Nichiporenko had taken a room in Professor Vernadsky's apartment while Leskov was living there (Nichiporenko was hired as a tutor for Vernadsky's son), and with

Leskov he accompanied Vernadsky to the meetings of the Economic Committee. Like the Kurochkins and Serno-Solovevich, Nichiporenko was a member of Land and Freedom, and he had already made the pilgrimage to Herzen's headquarters in London, where he had left a favorable impression—hardly justified as it turned out. In the summer of 1862 he was sent by Herzen and Bakunin as a courier to Garibaldi. At a frontier station he allowed to fall into the hands of the Austrian police a large packet of revolutionary correspondence, of which they obligingly made copies for their Russian confreres. Partly with this evidence, the Russian authorities decided to prosecute as many as they could round up of Herzen's agents, including Nichiporenko. While imprisoned in the fortress, he displayed great zeal in cooperating with the police, dredging his memory for names and information about his quondam revolutionary comrades; but his efforts as a stool pigeon availed him little, since he died in 1863, before the investigation was completed.[26]

Although Leskov had by that time become much more conservative in his views, he was named by Nichiporenko and called to testify. No charges were brought against him, but he never forgave his erstwhile friend for this scare. Under the name of Parkhomenko, Nichiporenko is vigorously caricatured in *No Way Out*; he appears again, under his own name, in "An Enigmatic Man," where he is represented as the epitome of radical boorishness and moral turpitude—unattractive, dirty, ill mannered, ignorant, irresponsible, and cowardly. It should be remembered, however, that this is an image of later construction; all the evidence indicates that in 1861-62 he and Leskov were good friends. For some time they harmoniously shared the hospitality of Vernadsky, and their social circles tended to merge. In his testimony before the Investigating Commission Nichiporenko stated that it was through Leskov that he had met the Kurochkins as well as several other radicals;[27] and about this time a photgraph was taken of Leskov with his arm around Nichiporenko.[28] Later they both collaborated on the *Northern Bee*.

Early in the summer of 1861 there arrived in Petersburg from London a young man named Artur Benni, who was to have a lasting influence on Leskov. Benni was the cosmopolite incarnate, being of mixed Polish, Scottish, German, Italian, and Jewish descent. He had been brought up as a Protestant in Poland and had received his higher education in England. While in England he met Herzen, and he not only embraced Herzen's socialism, but determined to go to Russia to propagate it. He brought with him to Petersburg a petition addressed to the emperor of all the Russias, asking him to grant his country a constitution and to establish a parliamentary government.[29]

Through his London Russian connections Benni met Nichiporenko and through Nichiporenko Leskov, and the three became close friends. Benni impressed Leskov not so much by his socialist ideas as by the extraordinary purity of his character. He was a man of culture and refinement, widely read, gifted at languages, with an unusual background, who would have aroused Leskov's interest and admiration in purely intellectual terms. But the attraction was heightened by Benni's moral qualities. Here was a highly educated, capable young man, a naturalized British subject, who had given up a well-paid civil service position at the Woolwich Arsenal and voluntarily come to Russia to work for the socialist cause. Altruistic and devoted, gentle and considerate, fastidious and pure—Leskov makes much of Benni's virginity—he was a secular saint. All his life Leskov was a seeker after saints, and Artur Benni, first in life and later in art, was to occupy a prominent place in his gallery of virtue.

When the Petersburg winter season was over, Leskov moved to Moscow to be near the editorial headquarters of *Russian Speech*. Countess Salias had evidently formed a high opinion of his abilities; she received him warmly, gave him a place to live in a wing of her house, and assigned him to write a regular column, the "Internal Survey," at a salary of 1,200 rubles a year. The countess, who fancied herself a Russian Mme Roland, had her house filled with disputatious political people, particularly young men with liberal or socialist convictions. Defining herself as a "Girondiste," the countess espoused a liberal-democratic and reformist ideology; her deities were the recently deceased liberal professors of the previous reign, Timofei Granovsky and Pyotr Kudryavtsev. But her house was frequented by "Jacobins" as well, and the atmosphere was one of excitement, controversy, and the fever of political martyrdom.

During this brief stay in Moscow Leskov became acquainted with two writers of note, members of the generation of plebeian novelists who came to the fore in the late 1850s and early 1860s, Aleksandr Levitov and Vasily Sleptsov. Levitov, a priest's son who had refused to don the cassock, was one of many ex-seminarians, including N. G. Pomyalovsky, Nikolai V. Uspensky, and F. M. Reshetnikov, whose stars flashed briefly across the Russian literary sky in the early 1860s. Sleptsov was of gentry rather than clerical origin, but in other respects he fits the pattern: all these writers were born between 1835 and 1841;

all became minor literary celebrities at an early age; all faded out rapidly, led wretchedly unhappy lives, took to drink, and died young.

In 1861 these plebeian writers and their naturalistic ethnography were in vogue. Their harsh pictures of life in the villages or the provincial seminaries represented the aesthetic expression—in a form believed to be consciously unaesthetic—of the age of the great reforms, when to expose social evils in all their horror seemed not only an act of civic virtue but a liberation of literature from falsity, pretense, and aristocratic narcissism.

What Leskov's personal relations with Sleptsov and Levitov were in 1861 we do not know. After his violent break with the Left the following year, he regarded them both, along with many others, as bitter enemies, and he satirized them mercilessly in *No Way Out*; but in 1861 his feelings may have been friendlier. In any case, it was partly through contact and conflict with these writers that Leskov worked out his position in relation to the diverse literary and ideological currents of his time. He was four years older than the oldest of the plebeians, but since he had started at a comparatively advanced age he was at the same stage of his literary career as they. Despite his threadbare claims to a gentry background, he too was removed from the seminary by only one generation. Like them, he carried none of the burden of guilt that made the "penitent" gentleman prone to idealize the peasant. He knew the peasants to be ignorant, superstitious, backward, and brutish, and he saw no reason to conceal it. He too was caught up in the muckraking spirit; he too was an enthusiastic advocate of reform. And the plebeians were not without their literary influence on Leskov: one of his early experiments in fiction, "The Life of a Peasant Martyress," was in their favorite genre and style.

There was one radical Leskov encountered in Moscow in 1861 for whom he retained affection and admiration even after his break with the others. This was Ivan Kelsiev, the younger brother of Herzen's disciple Vasily Kelsiev.[30] Ivan had just finished the Petersburg Commercial School, where he had been a friend of Nichiporenko. Upon graduation he had settled in Moscow as a government clerk, attending lectures at the university as an auditor. He made contacts with radical student groups, including the revolutionary circle led by P. G. Zaichnevsky and P. E. Argiropulo. Zaichnevsky and Argiropulo were arrested in July 1861, and Kelsiev succeeded them as one of the leaders of the revolutionary underground in Moscow. Leskov, who had met him through Nichiporenko, introduced Kelsiev to the Salias circle.

71

Kelsiev became particularly friendly with the countess's son Yevgeny, then a student at Moscow University, and the two played a prominent part in the student disorders that broke out in the fall.[31]

During the summer, while Leskov was working for *Russian Speech*, Benni and Nichiporenko set off from Petersburg on a tour of the provinces with the aim of collecting signatures on the constitutional petition. This expedition was a fiasco. Educated Russians might be full of talk about reforms; they might occasionally be bold enough to send clandestine reports for publication in the *Bell*; but to put one's signature on a formal document that would inevitably be thoroughly scrutinized by the police was another matter. By the time they reached Nizhni Novgorod the two constitutionalists' funds were running low and they had begun to quarrel. After a visit with Turgenev at Spasskoe in August, they arrived crestfallen in Moscow with their petition still almost devoid of signatures. Nichiporenko soon departed for Petersburg and subsequently went abroad on a mission to Herzen. Benni remained in Moscow, living with Leskov.[32]

Leskov's wife and daughter arrived from Kiev and moved in with him toward the end of the summer. The results were disastrous for his social life. With the exception of Benni and Kelsiev, practically every friend he had made in Moscow was rapidly transformed into a bitter enemy. Olga Vasilievna managed to engage the sympathies of Countess Salias and her relatives, the Novosiltsev sisters; the countess evidently made some remark to Leskov about his behavior toward his wife that he interpreted as a reproach. The consequence, no doubt brought on by Leskov's unacknowledged feelings of guilt about abandoning his family, was a violent defensive reaction, ending eventually in a complete break with the countess and her entourage.

Three years later, his anger still smouldering, Leskov would wreak vengeance with a roman à clef, ridiculing and disparaging Countess Salias and her associates through many long pages of *No Way Out*. By deciphering this peculiar novel, rich in thinly disguised autobiographical material, we can obtain some interesting, if hypothetical, glimpses of Leskov's activities in Moscow during the fall of 1861. To be sure, much of this fiction-based history must remain conjectural, since one of the advantages of the roman à clef is precisely the freedom with which its practitioner may spice truth with invention. Moreover, *No Way Out* is sloppily written, as the author admitted, with many loose ends, unexplained references, and unmotivated exits and entrances. It was also severely mutilated by the censorship, leaving yawning gaps and blurs in the text which Leskov never tried to repair. Nevertheless, the confirming evidence we possess, scanty as it is, lends considerable credence to the hypothesis that in the fall of 1861 the sober gradualist Leskov committed several notably unsober political acts. He engaged in revolutionary agitation among the Old Believers; he had something to do with an underground printing press; he participated in a student demonstration and march to the grave of Granovsky; he was present during a student riot and may have been struck by a policeman's club. Let us examine these episodes in turn, comparing the fictional account with what historical evidence we can adduce.

In later years Leskov never tired of repeating how wrong radicals like Vasily Kelsiev and A. P. Shchapov had been in regarding the Old Believers as a potential revolutionary element. According to his later accounts, Melnikov-Pechersky, his teacher in matters concerning the sectarians, had understood from the beginning that however much the Old Believers resented persecution and yearned for religious freedom, they were deeply conservative politically and remained loyal subjects of the tsar. The notion of their revolutionary potential was sheer illusion.[33] But in 1861 Leskov seems to have thought otherwise.

Ivan Kelsiev appears in *No Way Out* under the name of Persiantsev.[34] The account of Persiantsev's activities would appear to confirm the supposition, for which there is confirming evidence, that in 1861 Ivan Kelsiev was engaged in revolutionary activity among the Old Believers in Moscow.[35] And in the novel Dr. Rozanov, the author's alter ego, is very much a participant in this activity. Unfortunately, the picture of their enterprise is blurred by the censor's excisions. Occasionally, however, we get fleeting glimpses of a murky underground. For no apparent reason, in the middle of the central section, which takes place in Moscow, Rozanov visits a family of Old Believers, which enables the author to paint one of his characteristic genre pictures of odd corners of Russian life. The visit is ostensibly motivated by mere ethnographic curiosity. Yet a political note can be detected in a passage in which Rozanov is talking with an "awakening" young Old Believer named Adrian Nikolaev.

Adrian Nikolaev frequently forgot himself and shouted, "We are very grateful for that, very grateful. He writes richly, richly."

"Not so loud," Rozanov warned.

"Never mind [. . .] We're all friends here [. . .] Rich, rich is his every word; honor to this man. I get these things quite regularly," he added with a significant smile. "I have a friend who is a naval officer, a skipper in a flotilla: we get everything through him." (2:347-348)

The "things" this Old Believer has been getting from his naval friend are surely copies of the *Bell* and other revolutionary publications printed abroad, and the man of honor is Herzen, but one has to decipher this through the censor's pencil marks. The passage as it stands in the novel is scarcely intelligible.

Several chapters later Persiantsev pays a visit to the same house. He has delivered to Nikolaev three hundred copies of something—presumably more issues of the *Bell*. Later we learn that this dangerous literature was placed safely at the bottom of the Moskva River by the white-bearded chieftain of the Old Believers. Rozanov learns of this event from wise old General Strepetov, a "stern but just" paternal figure who perhaps represents Leskov-Rozanov's return, as of 1864, to political sobriety. The general lectures Rozanov on the subject of the schismatics: "You have to be out of your mind yourself not to see that this is all madness. Out of the Old Believers, who are the most peaceful people in the world and only want to be granted the right to pray freely and believe as they choose, you have concocted revolutionaries. In the same way you transform the peasant community [*obščina*] into a *commune* [*kommuna*, that is, a nucleus of socialism]: it's madness, that's all." (2:400-401)

Rozanov is somewhat chastened by this tirade and seems convinced; at any rate General Strepetov's is the position on the Old Believers Leskov held for the rest of his life. This position, it must be admitted, was reasonably consistent, realistic, and humane: the efforts of the revolutionaries to make allies out of the Old Believers did come to nothing, and Leskov always maintained, even in his most conservative period, that the problem of the schism could be surmounted only if the schismatics were first granted complete freedom of worship. The older Leskov was anxious for people to believe that this had always been his position, that he had never shared the youthful illusions of Shchapov and Kelsiev; but perhaps the "fictional" experience of Dr. Rozanov is closer to the truth about the real Leskov.

There is another episode in which Rozanov and Persiantsev are linked in revolutionary enterprise—although Rozanov eventually does what he can to sabotage it. This is the case of the underground lithographing plant—it is literally hidden in a cellar—operated by Persiantsev and a friend named Arapov. One night Rozanov finds Persiantsev desperately working there to produce five hundred copies of some text. Persiantsev is exhausted, and Rozanov offers to finish the job for him. Persiantsev goes off to sleep. After meditating for some time—and presumably reading the text—Rozanov burns all the printed literature and dumps the lithograph stone into the river. He thus saves the revolutionaries from dire consequences, except for Persiantsev, who is soon arrested and sent into exile.

The historical Ivan Kelsiev was arrested after the student uprising of October 1861, but he was not charged with illegal publishing, nor does he mention underground lithographing in the letters he wrote after leaving Russia.[36] However, it is known that the Zaichnevsky-Argiropulo circle, with which Kelsiev was connected, had engaged in underground lithographing on a considerable scale;[37] and it seems plausible that Kelsiev would have tried to carry on this tradition after the arrest of the two leaders. But the tantalizing question remains: did Leskov ever offer to help with an underground lithographing operation? If so, did he really destroy the equipment or is this a revision of history imposed by the safely conservative Leskov of 1864? The answer lies hidden under the veil Leskov carefully laid over much of his past.[38]

Although not officially a student, Ivan Kelsiev was one of the leaders of the student disorders that broke out in the fall of 1861, in protest against the new restrictive regulations imposed on university students by the Ministry of Education. Another leader was Count Yevgeny Salias de Tournemire, the countess's son, whom Leskov had introduced to Kelsiev. From the account of the student uprising given in *No Way Out*, garbled as it is, we can get some idea of the attitude toward these events, not only of Kelsiev and Salias, but of the author himself, in his guise as Dr. Rozanov.

History: on October 4, 1861, a group of students held a memorial service at the grave of Granovsky. About three hundred persons assembled at the outskirts of the city, marched to the cemetery, had a requiem said, and made several speeches. Salias was the bearer of the wreath laid on Granovsky's grave. The police observed these goings-on carefully, but on the express order of the governor-general did not interfere with them.

No Way Out: this incident is recounted in some detail, but without the mention of Granovsky's name; it is a requiem "for the most peaceful and honest of citizens," as Dr. Rozanov characterizes him. (Granovsky had, however, been mentioned by name earlier in the novel, when, in a grandiloquent gesture, the marquise de Baral, that is, Countess Salias, ordered Parkhomenko, or Nichiporenko, out of her house for taking Granovsky's sacred name in vain.) The marquise is excited by the requiem, and especially by her son's heroic role in this event; and in her thirst for martyrdom, in which she generously includes her son, she seems to expect the police to round up the admirers of Granovsky and ship them off to Siberia without further ado. Rozanov, also a great admirer of Granovsky (as Leskov was in life),[39] participates in the parade to the cemetery, pooh-poohing the marquise's excessive anxieties.

History: after the Granovsky requiem, a group of students drew up a petition and list of grievances and tried to present them to the university authorities, who refused to accept any collective petition. The authorities asked the governor-general to provide them with police protection and to have the ringleaders arrested. Although he felt they should have treated with the students, the governor-general acceded to this request, and several students were arrested on the night of October 12. The next morning a large throng of students gathered outside the governor's palace to demand the release of their comrades. A delegation of four representatives, including Ivan Kelsiev, entered the palace to present their demands directly to the governor-general; they were promptly arrested. The crowd outside was surrounded by infantry troops and mounted gendarmes. A clash took place; most of the students were forced into the courtyard of the nearby police station, where they were held for questioning, the majority subsequently released without charge. In Russian revolutionary historiography this event became known as the Battle of Dresden, since there was a Hotel Dresden facing the governor-general's mansion.

No Way Out: the traces of censorship are again apparent. Here is the entire passage in which the "battle" is referred to:

> With unbelievable speed the news of what happened to the students in the city flew through Moscow, and Rozanov in a state of the most furious indignation rushed off to see the marquise. He was all atremble from impotent rage.
>
> The marquise was sitting on a chair in the vestibule and twisting pieces of straw for cigarette holders. In front of her were standing Bryukhachev and Mareichka [a young architect and his wife who lived in the marquise's house; they represent the apolitical Philistine]. Bryukhachev was arguing that the students were acting stupidly, and the marquise was listening: she could not for the life

of her decide what role Madame Roland would have assumed in such a case.

Rozanov roared at Bryukhachev and said, "That is all nonsense. One has to stand up when people are being beaten and not make speeches."

It was four o'clock in the afternoon.

Lobachevsky [Rozanov's friend, a dedicated and apolitical doctor who never visited the marquise; the scene has evidently shifted to the room Rozanov shares with Lobachevsky] laughed at Rozanov's smashed nose and said, "Serves you right."

"For what?" asked Rozanov.

"So you won't spend your time in idle chatter." (2:373)

The text has obviously been garbled here. There is no transition from the marquise's house to the Rozanov-Lobachevsky apartment, and no explanation of Rozanov's battered nose. Something has been excised that must have had to do with the activities of Rozanov between the time he left the marquise's house and the time he turns up at home with a bruised physiognomy. It seems probable that in the interval before four o'clock in the afternoon Rozanov had participated in the Battle of Dresden on the side of the insurgent students and had received his bruises at the hands of the police. Could it be that in reality his creator stood on the Tverskaya Ploshchad on October 12, 1861, and received an equally palpable testimonial to his martyrdom in the cause of progress? If so, he kept it a dark secret.

What makes it seem not unlikely is that in recounting Rozanov's reactions to the student disorder, Leskov no longer represents the doctor, as he does through most of the novel, as a detached and ironic observer of the antics of the revolutionaries. He is filled with indignation against the brutality of the police, and the first place this indignation carries him is to the house of the marquise de Baral, whose shallow fears and enthusiasms he so mercilessly ridiculed a few days before. In narrating these events from his viewpoint of 1864, Leskov has a tendentious motive for representing his alter ego as detached and ironic in relation to the revolutionaries. But there is no tendentious motive for showing Rozanov enthusiastically caught up in the radical ferment. May not one therefore infer that Rozanov's enthusiasms are not literary constructions, but reflect the actual, unreconstructed experience of Leskov?

Leskov remained in Moscow until the end of November, continuing to edit the "Internal Survey" for *Russian Speech*. He was then replaced by Aleksei Suvorin, at that time, like Leskov, a young man from the provinces on the threshold of a great career. Leskov's final rupture with Countess Salias must have occurred at about the same time, triggered by the scenes and intrigues of Olga Vasilievna and by the countess's imprudent meddling in Leskov's marital troubles.[40] After a final explosion, Olga Vasilievna at last departed for Kiev with little Vera, and shortly thereafter Leskov returned to Petersburg alone to undertake a second launching of his career as a journalist.

When Leskov returned to Petersburg toward the end of 1861 there was no chance of continuing as the correspondent of *Russian Speech*, in view of his break with Countess Salias; and in fact the magazine was moribund.[41] Leskov's relations with Vernadsky seem likewise to have deteriorated. At any rate, he published nothing more in the *Economic Index*, and the following year he made several hostile sallies against Vernadsky in print. He therefore had to find a new outlet.

A prominent daily newspaper called the *Northern Bee*, which the previous year had been taken over by a liberally oriented editorial staff, promptly hired him as one of its major editorial writers—a tribute to his rapidly rising reputation. In the 1840s this paper had been the organ of the notorious Faddei Bulgarin, who had operated it on a subsidy from the secret police. Such tainted connections had long since been terminated, but under the peculiar rules of the Russian censorship, it was much easier to obtain permission to continue an existing publication, even if its editorial staff, content, and orientation were to be completely changed, than to start a new one. Thus the new editor, Pavel Usov, had been forced to retain the odoriferous name. Despite this handicap, by 1862 he had transformed it into one of the leading liberal dailies in Petersburg.

Leskov was already acquainted with several members of the staff. He had met the economist Nikolai Perozio and the historian Pavel Nebolsin the previous year at meetings of the Free Economic Society.[42] The most distinguished man on the staff was Pavel Melnikov, who under the pseudonym of Andrei Pechersky had become eminent as a writer of ethnographical fiction and a connoisseur of the Old Believers. In matters concerning the Old Believers, Leskov ever after acknowledged Melnikov as his teacher (11:36), and the older man doubtless also influenced his political and literary opinions. Leskov lists Perozio, Nebolsin, Melnikov, and several other members of the *Northern Bee* staff in a footnote to "An Enigmatic Man" (3:340n; written in 1868), but he notably avoids mentioning there Andrei

Nichiporenko, who in 1862 was actually his closest collaborator and friend on the paper. (Nichiporenko is mercilessly lampooned elsewhere in that work.) The two, and later Artur Benni as well, were assigned to write the unsigned editorials on all sorts of current issues.[43]

The *Northern Bee* was trying to articulate a position somewhere between radicalism and conservatism. Under the influence of his new colleagues Leskov naturally gravitated away from the radical aberrations he had allowed himself in Moscow back to a gradualist philosophy more in harmony with his mentality and experience. Unfortunately his centerward movement took place at a time when the government, frightened by a few revolutionary proclamations and scattered peasant disturbances, was beginning to persecute radicals more actively that it had done since Nicholas's reign. Angered by the persecutions, the radicals directed much of their bitterness not against the seemingly impervious citadel of the state, but against the more accessible and vulnerable moderates, who now seemed turncoats. The old popular front of the late 1850s was on the verge of dissolving in recriminations and antagonism.

The first sign of the troubles ahead was the charge spread in revolutionary circles in Petersburg at the end of 1861 that Benni was an agent of the Third Section, the Russian secret police. Benni was a particularly mysterious, and therefore suspicious, figure—a Polish Protestant with an Italian name, apparently of Jewish descent, who was a naturalized British subject, claimed to be an emissary of Herzen, and was for some reason circulating a petition for constitutional government in Russia. When confronted with this charge, Benni attempted to obtain from Herzen a testimonial to his revolutionary virtue, first by letter and then by a special trip to London. But Herzen had not approved of Benni's constitutional petition in the first place, did not regard him as a serious disciple, and, though he did not suspect him of being a spy, felt no inclination to issue him a revolutionary passport. When Benni returned to Petersburg, his radical friends avoided him, and he was forced to take refuge in the arms of the liberals, including Nichiporenko and Leskov, who got him a job on the *Northern Bee*. But a friend of a "spy" is inevitably suspected of being a spy himself, and so Leskov now became suspect in the eyes of many radicals.

Nevertheless, some leftist solidarity remained through the spring of 1862. In February Leskov and several of his liberal colleagues joined a large group of radicals in support of Nikolai Kurochkin against his publisher; and a month later Leskov was one of the group of left-wing writers who took over the magazine *The Age*. However, the tensions between the liberals and the radicals on the staff proved explosive, and after three months the magazine folded, a victim in equal measure of its internal disorders and public indifference.[44]

In the meantime, in the unsigned editorial columns of the *Bee*, Leskov was obliged to follow the *Bee's* official line, which was to maintain its distance from both extremes, criticizing the Right for obtusely resisting progress and the Left for nihilistic negativism. This middle ground was exposed to heavy fire from both directions, especially from the Left, which was always sensitive to liberal criticism. Before the radical hostility became total, however, there was at least one attempt to win Leskov back to the radical cause. In April 1862, Yeliseyev, the embattled editor of *The Age*, who apparently liked Leskov and admired his talent, published an anonymous editorial in the radical organ *Contemporary* advising the author of the *Bee's* editorials to reconsider his position before it was too late:

> A force is being vainly wasted there [in the *Bee*] which has not only not expressed or exhausted itself, but which perhaps has not yet even found its true path. We think that with more concentration and consistency of activity and with greater attention to its labors it will find its true path and will sometime become a notable force, perhaps of a quite different kind from that to which it now belongs. And then it will blush for its leading articles and for its wholesale condemnations *de omnibus et quibusdam*. The tendencies of our own circle and our interests of the moment will often influence our views in a strange way. People say one only needs a change of climate, to go abroad, especially to London, and perhaps in a month or less one assimilates a quite different mood and different views. People say there have been such cases.[45]

In this murky Aesopian language, reflecting the constraints under which Russian journalism was obliged to operate, Yeliseyev was urging Leskov to go to London and drink deep at the fountainhead of Herzen's socialism; the dose, Yeliseyev hoped, would immunize him against the noxious microbes of liberal compromise and corruption with which he was being infected at the *Bee*. The tone, for the *Contemporary*, was unusually mild.

Leskov seems to have been moved by Yeliseyev's gentle admonition. He replied in the same vein, thanking the *Contemporary* for its kind attentions but averring that he had nothing to blush for, that the views expressed in the *Bee's* editorials were identical with views he had held personally for a long time. He looked forward to trips to London, but doubted that they would change his fundamental convictions.[46]

By the time his reply to Yeliseyev appeared in print, however, an event occurred that put an end forever to courteous interchange between Leskov and the radicals. In the afternoon of May 28, 1862, a fire broke out in the Apraksin and Shchukin markets in Petersburg. These were congeries of little shops and booths filled with all manner of new and secondhand articles: clothes, furniture, household wares. The fire spread rapidly and devastated a whole district of the city. These markets were as inflammable as tinder, and it is surprising that fires had not occurred there more often. Nevertheless, a rumor spread that the fire was the work of arsonists. Only a few days before, the peace of the capital had been disturbed by the distribution of a fire-breathing revolutionary proclamation entitled *Young Russia*, urging the populace to take up arms and engage the imperial government in bloody battle. The popular mind linked these two events together: clearly it was the revolutionaries—and, by extension, the students, from whose ranks most revolutionaries were drawn—who had set Petersburg afire.[47] Some students were assaulted on the streets and barely rescued by the police from serious bodily harm.

Leskov perceived a unique opportunity: he would defend the mass of students against this vicious calumny and at the same time strike a blow at irresponsible revolutionaries, who, he believed, might have set the fires. In an editorial that appeared in the *Northern Bee* on May 30, 1862,[48] Leskov writes that in view of the rumors circulating through the city, rumors that threaten the life and limb of anyone identifiable as a university student, the police, if they have any evidence that arson has been committed, should come out with it and make charges; then guilt will be fastened on the individuals responsible, and not on a large body of blameless persons.

Although he genuinely meant to defend the students as a body, Leskov's editorial was bound to provoke violent radical hostility, for he did not dismiss the notion that the fires had been caused by arsonists, and specifically by revolutionary arsonists. On the contrary, he left open the question of "how much validity all these popular suspicions have and how appropriate are the people's fears that acts of arson are connected with the recent vile and seditious proclamation calling for the overthrow of the entire civil order of our society," adding that "to pronounce such a judgment is a task so terrible that the tongue turns mute and horror grips the soul." Thus Leskov not only admitted the possibility of a connection between the revolutionaries and the

fires, but he adopted the same tone of horrified indignation in referring to the authors of the real proclamation as that he used for the
hypothetical arsonists. Moreover, since the authors of the proclamation were themselves students, Leskov's defense of the innocent majority of the student body was at the expense of its activist minority; it
was thus an attempt to divide the students and ostracize the student
revolutionaries.

Leskov always professed surprise at the violence of the radicals'
reaction. If we can believe Leskov's account, a few days later two men
appeared in the editorial offices of the *Northern Bee*, describing themselves as a "deputation of the young generation." Mistaking Benni for
the editor of the paper, they demanded that he announce to the entire
staff that the accusation of arson the paper had made against the
"young generation" would not go unpunished. Leskov received two
anonymous letters informing him that he would shortly be "killed
near the Egyptian Bridge," which he used to cross frequently alone at
night, returning from the house of some friends (3:347). (Why he was
informed so precisely of the geographical setting of his intended murder is not explained, but the evocation of the Egyptian Bridge seems to
give the threat a certain basis in reality.)

Benni tried to rectify the situation by organizing volunteer fire bri-
gades made up of students, the idea being that when people saw students engaged in fire fighting they would cease to believe they were
arsonists. The project required the authorization of the police; Benni
visited, and then wrote a long memorandum for, the Petersburg police
chief, General Annenkov, urging him to give his blessing to Benni's
student firemen. Annenkov delayed in replying, saying that the proposal required study, and the radical press began to mock the idea,
publishing cartoons of the staff of the *Northern Bee* dashing heroically
alongside a fire engine. The plan came to nothing, leaving Benni and
Leskov infuriated far more by the mockery of their former radical
friends than by the suspicions and inaction of the government.

In the eyes of the intelligentsia, the *Northern Bee* was now hopelessly beyond the moral pale. Not only radicals, but even many gradualists were critical of what Leskov and his fellow editors had done.
They had dignified and lent credence to the arson rumors by publicizing them; and by advocating police action against revolutionaries
they had violated an unwritten, but fundamental and strongly held
ethic. For a Russian progressive intellectual of the nineteenth century,
this was the ultimate mark of Cain; you became a *donoschik*, a stool
pigeon.

The desperate *Northern Bee* printed editorial after editorial, trying to explain and justify its conduct, to erase this indelible stain on its progressive honor. But feeling that its cause was already lost in the eyes of the Left, it more and more began to edge to the Right, toward a menacing identification with the state:

> Our paper is not a government paper, but it is not a demagogic one either [. . .] We write and will continue to write solely in the name of the law. As servants of society, in its name we demand legality and humanity, truth and order. We demand them filled with a sense of absolute assurance that in so doing we will not draw on ourselves the wrath of the SOVEREIGN, Whose tears at the calamity of May 28th the Russian people will never forget. Let others rage at us—we care not for that. For us: only the Sovereign, the Law, and the People![49]

With reference to the "calamity of May 28th" the *Northern Bee* at first tried to maintain its original position: the fire might have been caused by arsonists from the revolutionary group that produced the proclamation *Young Russia*, but students in general should not be held responsible.[50] By June 13, although not repudiating the idea of arson altogether and still futilely begging the police to make public the names of the suspects it had arrested (it had never arrested any), the *Bee* began to retreat, debasing the arson idea with a typically Leskovian folk anecdote:

> The stories about arsonists are absurd to the point of monstrosity, and it is hardly possible to credit many of them. But the people are eager to believe them, and the more absurd and improbable the rumor, the more rapidly it spreads. For instance, it was said that the arsonists were Poles, then students; then the "masters" [*gospoda*] in general, who wanted to destroy the peasants' liberty and Him who had granted it. Then it was said that the arsonist was a general whose back was smeared with some incendiary substance so that he only needed to scratch his back against a wall and the wall would burst into flames.[51]

Argue as they might, even with some concessions to their opponents' point of view, the *Bee* and its staff never succeeded in clearing their name or winning public recognition of their honest and good intentions. Their separation from the radicals had become absolute and permanent. A line had been drawn, a real battle line; and in this battle

Leskov found himself fighting alongside Alexander II and the government against his radical allies of a few months before.

Again and again in his later years Leskov returned to his editorial on the fire, reliving, rearguing the case, trying to justify himself and to pin the guilt on his opponents. His methods of argumentation were by no means completely scrupulous. He resurrected the fire event in the second version of "Russian Society in Paris" (1867) and in his biography of Benni, "An Enigmatic Man," written early in 1868, and in both he engaged in doctoring the evidence. In this reconstruction of the story, the revolutionaries and the revolutionary proclamation are eliminated entirely, and with them, of course, the editorial's horror-stricken description of them as "vile and seditious," possibly guilty of the arson of which they were accused. The editorial in the *Northern Bee*, Leskov now asserts, was written solely to refute the rumors that the fires were the work of students and to induce the police to publish the names of their real suspects. To interpret it as "accusing the students of arson" or "inciting the police against the students" is malicious nonsense. To prove his point Leskov claims to cite "word for word" his original *Northern Bee* editorial: "During the fire among the crowds of the populace there were heard absurd accusations of arson directed against people of a certain corporate body [the students]. Without admitting that there is the slightest basis for such rumors, we believe that in order to put an end to them, the police of the capital should name the real arsonists, if it knows them."[52] This arson-denying "quotation" is actually a forgery, designed to shift the gist of the controversy and to make his opponents appear blind and ridiculous in their inability to read plain Russian.

Even toward the end of his life, when questioned about the fire affair, Leskov was capable of exploding in self-justifying indignation: "Read more carefully what I wrote in the *Northern Bee* and stop repeating to this day the nonsense that I incited the police against the young students. If you will read my article, you will see that I was defending the students, not accusing them."[53] By a familiar psychological process, the version consciously falsified for tactical reasons in the late 1860s had by the 1890s been adopted—and firmly believed—as historical truth.

For a person of Leskov's temperament, with its paranoid tendencies, the fire episode of 1862 was bound to have violent psychological repercussions. It seemed to confirm his worst nightmares. He had always tended to see the world around him as bristling with aggression and unfair criticism directed against him. Most of this hostility, of course, was imaginary, an attribution to others of his own antagonistic feelings. At some level, however, the paranoid secretly knows that there is a good deal of exaggeration in the animosity he ascribes to others, though for tactical reasons he will not admit it publicly. Exaggeration gives him room to maneuver. By deliberately magnifying the faults of others, he can represent himself as their innocent victim, bask in self-pity, and perhaps induce his antagonists to pity him and feel remorse for their unjust behavior. But when the paranoid encounters real aggression in others, the self-pitying image, always half acknowledged as a fantasy, of the innocent, dutiful self surrounded by mean, unfair adversaries, is suddenly transformed into reality. There are actual murderers afoot; the fake terror beomes genuine.

Whether he was really afraid of being murdered we do not know, but Leskov's response to radical aggression was extreme. He undertakes to magnify his defenses to dimensions which seem to him proportionate to the danger. Trying desperately to justify himself, he eventually works himself into an absolute frenzy of shrill, screaming rage, hurling imprecations and calling down the wrath of the gods on his enemies. Nor does his rage subside with time, as one would expect it to do. On the contrary, for a long period it seems to get more violent with each passing year, as the hopeless attempt to "get even" goes on, provoking an endless series of reactions and counter-reactions.

From this time forward, *the* enemy in Leskov's life, the embodiment of all the hostile forces he saw besetting him on all sides, was these former friends, the radicals of the sixties. Leskov felt positively haunted by these "nihilists," as they had been baptized in Turgenev's *Fathers and Sons* and were thereafter commonly called, especially by their antagonists. Feeling unbearably slandered, mocked, abused, and dishonored, for the next ten years he devoted the major part of his energies, literary and otherwise, to an all-out war on nihilism, which in his mind came to be almost synonymous with demonism. Though some of its literary products have value apart from their function as campaigns in the war, this period in Leskov's career presents a sorry spectacle of futility, of fantastically exaggerated charges and countercharges, of wasted talent and energy.

The controversy over the Petersburg fire left Leskov "morally and physically shattered," and he announced his intention to "abandon journalism and get out of Russia."[54] The latter aim was easily accom-

plished—by arranging a trip to Paris. But the idea of giving up journalism was hardly serious. In fact, the trip was to be financed with a
series of travel articles commissioned by the *Northern Bee*.

After the completion of the railroad between Petersburg, Warsaw,
and Berlin most Russian vacationers took the train to Paris and in
sixty hours or less rolled comfortably into the Gare du Nord. Leskov,
however, chose to avoid that easy and conventional route. In later life
he was fond of quoting a dictum of Pisemsky's to the effect that the
greatest enemy of literature was the railroad (too fast and smooth, it
left no impressions; 7:432-433), and in 1862, as if prophetically aware
of Pisemsky's law, Leskov dutifully rode that eminently literary
vehicle, the stagecoach. More practically, the *Northern Bee* would
never have underwritten a travelogue describing an ordinary railway
journey to Paris. Leskov therefore spent three months wandering in
eastern Europe, visiting such places as Grodno, Pinsk, Lvov, Cracow,
and Prague, little known to the average Russian tourist. In Russian
Lithuania and Poland the rumbles of national discontent were always
audible, and open revolt was less than a year away. Austrian Poland
offered an opportunity for investigating how the same nationality was
dealt with by another oppressor, and Bohemia offered another example for comparison—a Slavic nation oppressed only by Germans
rather than other Slavs and therefore ready to regard "Slavic
solidarity" as its means of liberation.[55]

Leskov was unusually well qualified for this journey. With his
Kievan background, he spoke both Ukrainian and Polish fluently, and
he had not adopted a chauvinistic attitude toward either culture. He
had been a personal friend of Shevchenko and an admirer of his
poetry, though he was not ready to admit, as some Ukrainian
nationalists insisted, that Shevchenko should be ranked alongside
Homer and Shakespeare. Leskov, citing what he claimed would have
been Shevchenko's own estimate of his literary status, placed him beside Syrokomla, Havliček, and Koltsov, definitely below Pushkin,
Mickiewicz, and Lermontov.[56] And from readings in the original that
were impressively wide, if spotty and oddly chosen, Leskov had
formed a deep respect for Polish literature, of which most Russians
were ignorant. In one of his travelogues Leskov deplored the fact that
few Russians could recite two lines from Mickiewicz and had never
heard of Korzeniowski, Kraszewski, Odyniec, or Syrokomla[57]—an
odd selection of marks for a Polish literary measuring stick, but an
indication of a fairly wide-ranging familiarity.

Leskov's impressions from this trip are detailed in his "From a Travel Diary," published serially in the *Northern Bee*, beginning in December 1862. This series contains much interesting topical and ethnographic material as well as many scenes and experiences recounted with verve, for instance the picture of the bison preserve in the Belovezha forest, where the few remaining specimens of that rare beast, the European aurochs, were preserved so that the tsar could personally destroy them with his rifle. This was a ticklish subject (there was hardly any sport at all: the animals stood placidly while His Majesty took aim and dispatched them), and Leskov treats it with irony bolder than might be expected in a censored publication.

Leskov was a keen and surprisingly tactful observer of human beings as well. Having spent half his youth in a Polish environment, as he tells us,[58] he was adept at playing down national antagonisms in his conversations. Even in his most chauvinistic period, after the Polish uprising of 1863, Leskov consistently advocated freedom of language and culture for the Poles within the Russian Empire, and he deplored the Russians' ruthless treatment of the Poles, including religious and political persecution. In 1862 he probably advocated some kind of political autonomy for the Poles in Russia. At the same time, he perceived the moral as well as political weakness of the Polish cause in a large part of the "Polish" territory occupied by Russia since the partitions of the eighteenth century, namely, that only the ruling class was ethnically Polish and shared Polish nationalist ambitions. The mass of the Belorussian and Ukrainian peasantry, and sometimes the Lithuanians too, were often more hostile to their Polish landlords than they were to the Russian government, which they not infrequently regarded as their protector and, in 1861, their liberator.

In Galician Poland, in the Austrian Empire, Leskov was favorably impressed by the freedom of speech accorded to the Slavic nationalities. In Lvov he witnessed a loud argument in a coffee house between Poles and Ukrainians about how they could best resist the German rule, while two Austrian soldiers were calmly playing billiards a few steps away. Polish newspapers there were free to attack the anti-Polish policies of the Russian and Prussian governments.

In Lvov (or Lviv, as Ukrainians would insist) Leskov encountered a Ukrainian nationalism more vehement and more articulate than anything he had known in Russia, and on a higher cultural and intellectual level. He was impressed by the Ukrainian intellectuals he met in Austria. Many of them were Uniate priests and presented a striking contrast with the benighted Orthodox clergy of Russia. Not only did they lack beards and wear Western dress, but they were men with university educations and broad interests. One of them, Volodymyr Terletsky, was a doctor as well as a priest; the directors of the Ukrainian gymnasium in Lvov and the professor of Russian literature at the university were all Ukrainian Uniate priests. Leskov was dismayed, however, at the virulence of national antagonisms, and since he spent most of his time among Ukrainians, he found most offensive the universal Polish contempt for Ukrainian culture. In Cracow, in a more homogeneously Polish region, the atmosphere was comparatively tolerant, and less anti-Russian sentiment was directed against him.

From Cracow Leskov went on to Prague, accompanied by Bronisław Zaleski, a Polish writer and artist recently released from twelve years' exile in Siberia. Zaleski introduced him to various Czech writers and journalists, with some of whom Leskov formed firm friendships. Leskov remained in Prague nearly two months. He made an effort to learn Czech, which he later described as a "soft, birdlike language."[59] He translated two specimens of Czech literature. One is an atrociously sentimental story by Martin Brodsky (pen name of Jozef Frič) called "From You It Doesn't Hurt." The other, "On the Twelve Months," is a trivial and prettified transcription of folklore by Božena Nemcova, who deserved a better choice than this.[60] However superficial his acquaintance with Czech language and culture was, Leskov conceived a great liking for the Czech character. Basically a plebeian, a democrat, and a businessman himself, he appreciated particularly the tolerance, unassuming behavior, and practicality of the Czechs—qualities he more and more found wanting among the Poles. These impressions were confirmed by his later experiences among Slavic exiles in Paris.

Leskov arrived in Paris early in December 1862 for a visit that lasted nearly four months. Unfortunately, none of Leskov's private correspondence during this Paris sojourn has been preserved. Our information is therefore limited to what he reported in published articles, particularly the voluminous treatise entitled "Russian Society in Paris," the original version of which appeared early in 1863 in the magazine *Library for Reading*. Although the topics covered in that article are considerably broader than the title might suggest, especially with regard to the non-Russian Slavic "societies" of Paris (which are discussed in copious detail), comparatively little is said about the author's impressions of the city itself or his French contacts and experiences.

Leskov established himself in the Latin Quarter and before long found himself an agreeable companion, entertainer, and French tutor in the form of a genial grisette, a species that impressed him, like the homespun Cossack prostitutes of his youth in Kiev, by their cheerful good humor and practical domesticity.[61] Despite this valuable opportunity for linguistic exercise, it is doubtful that Leskov's oral command of French ever became sufficient for extended intellectual contacts with Frenchmen. Like any foreign tourist in Paris without native command of the language or any special entrées, he remained an outsider to French life. He did, however, manage to get two glimpses of Napoleon III, one a close-up, which left him with a very unfavorable impression: "I did not take my eyes from his face and must confess that I have never seen anything more terrible than the face of that monarch. It was the face of a cadaver, with open eyes which looked wearily and at the same time penetratingly. There was no motion in a single feature of that face; not a muscle moved."[62]

The Louvre provided Leskov with an opportunity to expand an acquaintance with Western art already well founded during frequent visits to the Hermitage. All his life Leskov kept up a keen, if untutored and idiosyncratic, interest in the graphic arts, though with respect to contemporary art his taste did not rise much above the average level of his time.[63] Especially in view of his tendency, more pronounced later in his life, to judge art by didactic and moral standards—"I do not acknowledge the art of drawing naked women," he said in 1894[64]—it is doubtful that Leskov admired, if he was exposed to it, the revolutionary school of French painting then gathering forces for its epochmaking assault on the Academy and the bourgeoisie. There is no evidence that Leskov had the slightest idea what was going on in Montmartre or Montparnasse, either in 1862 or on his second visit to Paris in 1875.

Most of Leskov's exploratory energies were concentrated among the Slavic exiles in Paris. He had letters of introduction from his recent acquaintances in Prague and made many friends in Czech circles in Paris, notably Jozef Frič. Frič was a journalist, poet, and historian as well as a revolutionary who had served time in Austrian prisons. He had attempted to involve Herzen and Bakunin in a pan-Slavic revolutionary movement, but he became convinced that Herzen, at least, was not seriously interested in the fate of the smaller Slavic nations. It was thus partly under Frič's influence that Leskov decided to cancel his planned trip to London.

The Polish rebellion broke out in January 1863, while Leskov was in Paris. Vainly hoping for diplomatic and military support from the Western powers and with their quixotic romanticism, the Polish nationalists once again, as in 1831, hopelessly took up arms against the Russian state and once again were ruthlessly put down by the tsar's armies. These events confronted Russian liberals and radicals with a severe test of their convictions. A few of the more consistent radicals, such as Herzen and Bakunin, stood firm by the libertarian principles they had always preached. The Russian government, they said, had no right to occupy Polish territory in the first place, and therefore a true Russian democrat had no choice but to support the Polish uprising and oppose by every means he could his government's work of repression. Bakunin even undertook to lead an expedition of Russian radicals to fight the tsar side by side with the Poles. But the nationalism of most Russian liberals turned out to have deeper roots than their liberalism. When they heard the drums beating, saw Russian armies on the march, and knew there were Russian boys dying in combat with a people that had always regarded them and their compatriots with hostility and disdain, their hearts stirred again with patriotic fervor, and they were ready to follow their tsar into battle. They might advocate civil liberties for the Poles as individuals and even autonomy for the Polish nation within the Russian Empire, but they could not support an armed rebellion that might be secretly instigated by Russia's enemies in the West and that aimed to deprive Russia of a large slice of territory. During 1863 the circulation within Russia of Herzen's *Bell* dropped catastrophically, and Herzen's effective influence in Russia, except in a very narrow circle on the extreme Left, was essentially at an end. As Herzen's star waned there rose that of Mikhail Katkov, the erstwhile Anglophile and liberal who now rapidly transformed himself into a rabble-rousing Polonophobe, nationalist, and imperialist.

The Polish revolt brought on a moral crisis even more difficult and painful for Leskov than it was for most Russian liberals. Of all the Russian writers of the nineteenth century, he was the only one for whom Poland was much more than an abstraction. He knew Polish, was well read in Polish literature, appreciated Polish art and architecture, and had innumerable Polish friends of long standing. Furthermore, he had never been a chauvinist or a worshipper of imperial power, and he not only opposed attempts to Russify Poland but believed that Poland should be liberated from all foreign rule. He was a Russian, however, and the primitive allegiance to home, hearth, fatherland, and tsar still had a firm grip on his heart.

In Paris Leskov found that his liberal views about Poland did not prevent him from being regarded like any other Russian by the Parisian

Poles and therefore treated with rudeness and hostility. He had formed the habit of dining frequently at a Polish restaurant. After the uprising broke out, a group of husky young Poles there menacingly told him they did not care to have Russian spies in their midst. A pro-Polish Frenchman spattered Leskov with flour. Such episodes tended to evoke in Leskov a generalized feeling of injury and resentment against all Poles, especially since he was still smarting from the rough handling he had received from the Russian revolutionaries. The only pro-Polish Russians were socialists and revolutionaries, and for them Leskov felt only hatred and rage, which was easily transferred to the Poles. As Leskov put it later, his "sentimentality" in relation to Poland, which he claimed to have imbibed only in Petersburg, not in Kiev, had been greatly weakened in Lvov. Now, in Paris, its last remains were obliterated.[66]

This retrospective view was an oversimplification. Leskov's Polonophobia took somewhat longer to develop. During his stay in Paris, he continued to maintain friendly contacts with his Polish neighbors in the Latin Quarter, taught them to read Lermontov, read and discussed with them Mikhail Pogodin's book on Russia's relations with the other Slavs, *Lettres et mémoires sur la politique de la Russie vis à vis les peuples slaves de l'Europe occidentale.*[67] He also paid a visit to the venerable Alexander Chodźko, Mickiewicz's successor as professor of Slavic literatures at the Collège de France, who impressed him both by his learning and his friendliness. Even in 1867, in his most anti-Polish period, Leskov sent public greetings to Chodźko and proclaimed his respect for his "honest gray hairs."[68]

Thus in 1863, in the relatively neutral environment of Paris, Leskov's old admiration for Polish culture and his relations with individual Poles did not immediately give way to national antagonism, despite the effects of the rebellion. It was only later, after years of warfare with Russian radicals and of increasingly close association with the Russian Right, that Leskov, for a time, came to speak of the Poles almost with the voice of Katkov. In 1867, when he substantially revised his Paris letters for a volume of his stories, Leskov greatly intensified their anti-Polish tone, introducing such phrases as "Poland, which has spat upon us for our kind feelings."[69] Recalling his experiences among the Ukrainians in Lvov, he now claimed to have "trembled with indignation and resentment" at the Poles' "insolent contempt for everything Russian in Lvov,"[70] though he had said nothing about such feelings in his writings of 1862 and 1863.

Polonophobia proved a temporary aberration. Leskov later re-

turned to a position of greater fairness, and his interest in Polish literature also revived.[71] But in general, after the 1860s the Polish question
was as quiescent in Leskov's mind as it was in history. It belonged to
the past. Leskov's life in the present lay not in Polono-Ukrainian Kiev
and not in Paris, but in Petersburg.

In March, 1863, he headed for home.

Home, however, could not hold him for long in that hyperactive
year in which he somehow managed not only to produce several major works of fiction but to keep up a lively career as a traveling journalist, specializing in national and religious minorities. The next minority on his docket was one with which he had already been involved
in Moscow, the Old Believers.

Under the new, liberal minister of education, A. V. Golovnin, the
government was considering some revision, particularly with regard
to education, of its rigid and ineffective policy of persecuting the Old
Believers. Instruction in religion by Orthodox priests was part of the
required curriculum in all Russian schools. Members of other recognized Christian sects, such as Roman Catholics, Lutherans, and Cal-
vinists, were permitted to organize independent private schools; if
their children did go to the state schools, they were not required to attend the classes in "God's Law." This tolerance, however, did not extend to the Old Believers, whose religion was illegal. For generations
the government had tried to bring to an end the schism in Orthodoxy
by indoctrinating the schismatics' children in the official faith. In defense of their "ancient piety," the Old Believers preferred not to send
their children to school at all rather than have them exposed to the
ministrations of the heretical Nikonians. The more prosperous schismatic communities organized secret schools, where the intellectual
standards might be low, but the faith was pure.

To bolster his position in the higher councils of state, Golovnin
wanted an independent investigation of the whole educational system
as it applied to the Old Believers, particularly their underground
schools. To save money it was decided to limit the investigation to
two important Old Believer communities, Riga and Pskov, where
secret schools were known to exist. The assignment as school investigator was first offered to Pavel Melnikov and then to Nikolai Subbotin, a Moscow seminary professor who specialized in the schism,
but neither was able to serve.[72] Probably at Melnikov's suggestion,
Golovnin's choice then fell upon Leskov. Melnikov had already introduced Leskov among the Petersburg Old Believers, and Leskov was

delighted at the opportunity to expand his knowledge of the schismatics through an interesting trip at government expense. He left Petersburg on July 12, 1863, returning in late August. His report was delivered to Golovnin on September 23.

This report, published in an edition of sixty copies for distribution to high officials, is a soberly presented and well grounded plea for tolerance.[73] The intellectual level of the schismatic children Leskov found deplorable: they needed schools desperately. The effort to force them into the official schools had failed and was bound to fail, in view of the Old Believers' passionate resistance to exposing their children to Orthodox indoctrination. Education was the only realistic means of overcoming the schism, and to maintain the schismatics in a state of ignorance was to defeat the government's own purpose. Therefore, Leskov urged, let them operate their own schools, but openly, legally, and under official supervision. Open schools, supervised by the Ministry of Education, even without classes in Orthodox God's Law, would be better than the wretched secret ones. Unfortunately, the forces of conservatism, led by the notorious minister of internal affairs, Count Pyotr Valuev, proved stronger than Golovnin, and Leskov's recommendations were not carried out. The government continued to persecute the Old Believers until the Revolution.

Leskov published a version of his report in *Library for Reading*, somewhat simplified and enlivened for popular consumption.[74] Many times in later years he returned to the subject of his Riga expedition, apparently hoping to receive more recognition of his expertise than he ever did. In 1869 he rehashed the material in a series of newspaper articles; in 1874 he again tried to stir up interest in his "lost book on schools"; and as late as 1883 he was still trying to have his report reprinted in the *Historical Messenger*.[75] He ought to have realized that there was little point now in so insistently exhibiting this old sample of sociological raw material. It had already been successfully transmuted into a higher form—his own wonderful evocations of the Old Believers in such stories as "The Sealed Angel" and "Pechersk Eccentrics."

✥ 5 ✥

The Leap into Fiction

The beginning of Leskov's career as a writer of fiction differs markedly from that of other Russian authors of the nineteenth century, such as Pushkin, Lermontov, Gogol, Turgenev, and Tolstoy. Their collected works commence with a body of juvenilia, interesting primarily for the picture they give of the artist's growth, for the evidence they provide of the prevailing ideals, models, and fashions in whose image the young talent shaped itself. In Leskov's case, however, no such pattern of literary adolescence is discernible. In all the biographical documents on his early life, including his own testimonies, there is next to nothing about literature, no remnants of a literary apprenticeship. It is clear that in his youth it did not occur to him that he might become a writer; such a goal would have seemed unattainable for a young man as poorly educated as Leskov was. The only flicker suggesting a literary propensity was his apparent fondness for reading, as attested by his claim to have read almost all the books in Mme Zinovieva's library.[1] But even in asserting his youthful bibliophilia, Leskov says nothing about what particular books or writers impressed him. In Kiev his primary intellectual interests were apparently not literary but rather in philosophy, economics, and what we would now call sociology. Although he must have read and reread the Russian classics (his works and letters, even in the earliest period, are studded with quotations from Pushkin, Griboedov, Gogol, and Turgenev), he does not seem to have considered them professionally, from the standpoint of form or style. He judged them by their ideas. Indeed, throughout his career, despite his reputation as a stylist and verbal acrobat, and despite the beauty of many of his stories, Leskov was not an aesthete. His articulated view of literature, like that of most of his contemporaries, was aggressively utilitarian and didactic. "I love literature as a means which enables me to express what I consider true and good," he said not long before he died. "If I cannot do that, I no longer value literature. To regard it as art is not my point of view."[2]

Leskov's first trial of the pen was not an attempt at belles lettres and certainly not juvenile. When he was nearly thirty, working as a commercial agent for his uncle, he sent back to Scott's headquarters in Penza letters that were more entertaining than would be expected of either business reports or family correspondence. "When a little blue envelope arrived in Scott's house," Leskov recalled with pride, "everyone who lived there as well as neighbors who habitually visited him would say 'From Leskov,' and then make Scott read the letter aloud."[3] A literary neighbor of Scott's praised these letters so highly that their author conceived the idea that he might even make writing his profession.[4] Those travel letters, though written privately and never published, did more than demonstrate a natural literary gift: they pointed the way to what became one of Leskov's favorite genres, the travelogue. The typical narrator of many of his travel stories bears a close resemblance to the real Leskov of these early letters: the man of experience who has "been around" and seen a great deal of life, not on the circuit customary among young Russian gentlemen, including Berlin, Paris, and the Riviera, but on the back roads of remote Russian provinces. For him the country and its inhabitants are never mere socioeconomic categories to be theorized about in magazine articles. They are an endlessly fascinating and varied human museum, exhibiting all sorts of unexpected and colorful human types, innumerable varieties of status, occupation, and religious belief.

The fact that Leskov began as a writer of travelogues brings out another significant aspect of his art: its ambiguous fictionality. In genres like the memoir, the letter, and the travelogue, especially when utilized by a writer who is known to have had at least some of the experiences he describes, who can tell where the borderline lies between fiction and fact, where imagination or artistic requirements have stretched or twisted the truth? In thus confounding truth and fiction Leskov managed to deceive even many scholars; the literature on him is full of biographical nonfacts painstakingly culled from his putative "memoirs."

In 1860-61, when he began to write professionally, Leskov still did not consider himself a literary artist. He was a journalist, a purveyor of truth about conditions that really existed, events that really happened. Later, when he did try his hand at literary art, he instinctively chose forms close to journalism—quasi reports, letters, stories "apropos."

Like a journalist's. Leskov's is primarily a *narrative* talent, in the most restrictive sense. His major gift is not dramatic, or psychological, or philosophical, or even moralistic. Apart from his virtuosity as a stylist, he is essentially, as Walter Benjamin perceived, a storyteller.[5] The basic element linking the storyteller to the journalist is interest in the unusual. Newspaper stories must deal with exceptional, "interesting" events; their readers would tolerate nothing else. At a different level of sophistication and insight, as Gogol understood, the ordinary may become acceptable material for literature; but for Leskov this possibility never had much appeal. His instinct as an artist was essentially the instinct of a reporter. He always had an eye for a story.

In the spring of 1862, before the Petersburg fires, Leskov published three pieces that mark the beginning of his career as a writer of fiction. The first, "A Case That Was Dropped (From the Notes of My Grandfather)," displays the typically Leskovian balancing between fact and fiction.[6] We would normally assume, on encountering such a title, that both "grandfather" and "notes" are imaginary creations; eighteenth- and nineteenth-century novels and stories abound in "letters," "diaries," and apologetic tracts written by fictional characters, designed to enhance the illusion of their supposed authors' reality. But in this instance our normal suspicion may well be unfounded. It is quite likely that Leskov is reporting an actual "case," an episode that really occurred, however improbable it may sound to the modern reader. It is even possible that Leskov's paternal grandfather, the priest Dimitry Leskov, was the source of the story. (Although this grandfather died before Leskov was born, Leskov could have heard the tale from his father.) Or the story may have come from Semyon Leskov's long experience as a court official; or perhaps Leskov himself learned about it while a court scribe in Oryol.[7] Whether the episode is literally true or not, Leskov preferred to represent it that way, not only as an illusionistic device, but as a means of validating it, even to himself, qualifying it to be told at all.

The central character is a priest like Leskov's grandfather, and Leskov thus makes his entrance into Russian literature arm in arm, as it were, with a bearded *batyushka* (priest), a figure with whom he remained linked, at least in the popular mind, throughout his career. Father Iliodor has much in common with Savely Tuberozov, Leskov's archetypal archpriest from *Cathedral Folk*. Both represent the kind, benevolent pope, fatherly and understanding with his flock, tolerant of their ignorance and waywardness, long-suffering but not cowed in dealings with secular and ecclesiastical authority. It is an attractive and potent image, although it does not entirely succeed in avoiding the perils of sentimentality. Juxtaposed with this admirable priest are his peasant parishioners, depicted in the starkly naturalistic manner made popular by the plebeian ethnographers of the 1860s, such as Sleptsov or Levitov.

The action of the story takes place "about fifteen years ago," that is, about 1847, during the reign of Nicholas I. Despite his moral aversion to this period, Leskov, like Turgenev, preferred it above all others for his fiction. It was the time of his own youth, when his deepest impressions had been formed. Though ethically repellent, it seems to have appealed to him on aesthetic grounds as well: it presented scenes more colorful, more "interesting" than the more homogeneous, Europeanized, and humane Russia of the later nineteenth century. Regional and class differences had not yet been blurred by industrialism, railroads, and social leveling, and life itself, if often painful, seemed somehow larger, less petty and frivolous. Perhaps the prevalence of violence has something to do with it: in this "barbarous" age, human passions tended to be acted out more unrestrainedly and therefore more vividly.

Desperate after a prolonged drought, some peasants ask their village priest to celebrate in the fields the prayer service prescribed by the church as the means of beseeching God for rain. Father Iliodor complies, but the drought continues. A stranger wanders into the village, a peddler or ex-soldier; widely traveled and literate, he is regarded by the peasants as a fountainhead of wisdom. He amuses himself by "explaining" to them the reason for the drought. The body of a drunken sexton, recently deceased, has just been buried in the church cemetery; the more virtuous inhabitants of the graveyard, offended by his presence, have persuaded God not to hear the villagers' prayers for rain. Therefore the body must be exhumed, and to notify God of its removal, a candle must be made of the corpse's fat and burned at night. Although the priest tries to dissuade them, the peasants carry out this gruesome rite; and as if to spite both Christians and rationalists, it begins to rain just as the candle is burning out.

Leskov seems to take delight in painting the spiritual darkness of the peasants as black as possible. Not only has the severity and totality of their benightedness a certain aesthetic shock value of its own, but it serves as an antidote to the romantic idealization of *le paysan russe* popularized a generation earlier in the stories of Grigorovich, and even to the more sober appreciation of peasant talent and virtue in Turgenev's *A Sportsman's Sketches*.

In Russian society cultural light might reach the peasants from two sources, the clergy and the landowners; Leskov's story illustrates the inadequacy of both, especially the gentry. Father Iliodor does his best to prevent the peasants from carrying out their impious project, but when they do, committing not only a mortal sin but a civil crime, he tries to cover up for them. After its disinterment, the sexton's body was deposited in a swamp, but the torrential rains wash it away, and the peasants cannot find it. If the corpse were to be discovered and brought to the attention of the authorities, there would be a police investigation and eventually a criminal prosecution.

To avert this disaster, Father Iliodor journeys to the nearest town, hoping to induce the authorities to let the "case" drop. Fearing to accost the civil officials, he approaches first his ecclesiastical superiors. Even to gain an audience with the bishop's secretary he must bribe the doorman. Pocketing the bribe, the doorman says there is no use in seeing the secretary, who has not recovered from his latest encounter with the bishop. Following his customary procedure in dealing with erring subordinates, that dignitary had taken hold of his secretary by the hair and banged his face against his desk.[8] Recounting such an episcopal outrage in his earliest story, Leskov anticipated a favorite later stance. If he was, at least for the first half of his literary career, the leading champion in Russian literature of the village priest, he was equally the sworn enemy of the church hierarchy, the bishops, the Synod, and the Ober-Procurator, determined to expose their arrogance and callousness.

Despairing of help from the church, Father Iliodor goes to the peasants' owner. This appeal involves the risk of humiliation: priests were generally snubbed by the gentry. Custom requires Father Iliodor to apply to the servants' entrance. He is kept waiting in the kitchen, and when he is at last ushered into the master's study, the gentleman does not rise to greet him, nor does he kiss the priest's hand or ask his blessing. (He is probably not a believer himself, although he may consider religion a useful anodyne for his peasants.) However, he shows a "liberalism," for which he takes great credit, by asking the priest to be seated. To show his awareness that he must not presume too much on such graciousness, Father Iliodor perches on the edge of the chair.

The landowner succeeds in quashing the affair of the corpse at the cost of a thousand rubles in bribes, and he insists that the peasants reimburse him in full, as well as take his word for the amount. For Father Iliodor's benefit, he philosophizes on the difficulties of the village clergy: "They send a priest into a village without a penny to his name, without books, and then expect him to be a Fénelon or a Bourdaloue [. . .] Among the Germans or the English [. . .] a pastor is a man, a member of society, but in Russia—I ask you: you are a priest; tell me, please: can a teacher who is intellectually beneath his pupil have any influence?"[9]

The story ends with a dream that Father Iliodor has as he returns to his village: "Father Iliodor [. . .] imagines himself a ship perishing in the waves. No matter how much he wants to save himself, how much he tries to escape, he is quite unable to do so; a wretched peasant with a torn collar, heavy as a load of earth, has grabbed him by the legs and is pulling him down; and on his head is sitting His quondam Regal Oxcellency [*korolevskoe eruslanie*, a meaningless title used that day by Father Iliodor's peasant driver in addressing the landowner] and stuffing a red cork into his mouth."[10] Despised and often thwarted by the gentry, wretchedly poor, living in terror of an arbitrary and rapacious ecclesiastical bureaucracy, the village priest, with only a rudimentary education, could do little to illuminate the spiritual darkness of his peasant parishioners, even if one accepts the view, as Leskov was inclined to do at this stage in his career, that Christianity in its official Orthodox version was any improvement over the largely pre-Christian peasant culture of superstitious magic. In any case, the priest was a frustrated, forgotten, and often tragic figure in Russian society, and in him Leskov had found one of his greatest themes.

Thirty years later Leskov utilized the same incident as one of the main episodes in "Vale of Tears."[11] In that story, apropos of the terrible famine of 1891, he brings forth what purport to be reminiscences of a worse but less well known famine that had taken place in his boyhood, in 1840. In "Vale of Tears" an unknown outsider comes to a village during a drought. He advises the peasants that the only effective way of bringing rain is to burn a candle made of the body fat of a drunkard. He happens to have such a candle, and for a fee calculated in eggs and money he obligingly carries out the rite that night. A good rain cloud appears, but it stops in the sky a little way off and releases no water. The peasants explain this failure by the strange antics of a drunken harnessmaker named Leathery, who frequently has hallucinations of being chased by a bull. Leathery has been seen running about in the field, waving his arms in the direction of the cloud, and shouting "Whoa, whoa!" To eliminate this intolerable interference and to intensify the effect of the original magic, the peasants murder Leathery and make candles of his fat. While burning one, they accidentally set fire to an old shed and thus attract the attention of their owner, who extracts their secret. Without dealing with any officials, he and his neighbor agree to keep the matter quiet (the murderers are among their ablest and most prosperous serfs). Then, to "freshen" the spirits of the peasants and to provide some diversion, they arrange to have three priests try once again to get the message to heaven by celebrating three services, in the garden, in the meadow, and in the wheat field. During the service a retired major entertains everyone by loudly joining the clergy in singing "Vouchsafe rain to the thirsting earth, O Savior" (*Dažd' dožd' zemle alčuščej, Spase*). When refreshments are served later he sings the line several times solo. His performance appeals so much to the gentry children that they devise a game of dressing up as priests and chanting "Vouchsafe rain to the thirsting earth." At last their nurse tells them that it is too late for any prayers: the crops are ruined, and famine is imminent.

A comparison of the two stories, one from 1862 and the other from 1892, brings out what are probably the two most fundamental facts about Leskov's artistic career: the marked stability of his technique and the overwhelming change in his religious convictions. In both tales the narrative method is basically the same: a gruesome event is described in a matter-of-fact tone, with an undercurrent of irony but without pathos and even with grim humor. Not the slightest expression of indignation is allowed to appear in the text; any such reaction is left to the reader. Thus in his very first story Leskov discovered the effectiveness of tension beteen the stated fact and the unstated reaction. The stark contrast between Leathery's ludicrous terrors of the imaginary bull and the atrocious murder that follows is more extreme than anything in "A Case That Was Dropped," where the horror lies only in the grisliness of the exhumation and candlemaking, but the technique is essentially the same. Laughter and grief, to use the title of one of Leskov's stories, follow each other in close succession in life; in literature juxtaposition of the absurd and the revolting can deliver a powerful jolt.

In the realm of ideology the difference between 1862 and 1892 is immediately apparent. Leskov's attitude toward the peasantry has not changed: they remain as ignorant and brutal as ever. But in 1892 the admirable priest hero has disappeared. In "Vale of Tears" the priests' incantations and prayers for rain are regarded as no great improvement on burning candles made of human fat: their services are merely a more decorous form of superstitious sorcery. True Christianity is now represented by the narrator's Aunt Polly and her Nonconformist English friend, Hildegard, whose religion, during that terrible famine year, is expressed not in ecclesiastical mumbo-jumbo, but in sustained and practical works of mercy.

Leskov's second short story, "The Robber," is an account of a journey narrated in the first person.[12] We find ourselves in a stagecoach, traveling to the famous fair at Nizhni Novgorod. A sense of movement is evoked by the first word in the opening sentence. *"Exali my k Makar'ju na jarmarku* ("We were on our way to see Makary at the fair"), the verb *exali* given pride of place by the inverted word order ("riding we were"). The narrator then tells us his destination—an ultra-Russian, provincial one, not with the flat locution of ordinary speech ("We were on our way to the fair at Nizhni") but with a picturesque and somewhat arcane folk equivalent, "to see Makary at the fair"—which harks back to the time before 1817 when the great fair had been regularly held in a town called Makarievo; in the saying the town's name is transformed into a personal one, Makary. This locution was retained in popular speech long after the fair had moved to Nizhni. Short as it is, the sentence conveys the movement and excitement of travel as well as the destination, and it shows that the narrator is no gentleman tourist or sportsman but a man of experience, linguistically in the know.

Except by such stylistic clues, the narrator says practically nothing about himself, his age, social status, or occupation; nor does he play any part in the action. His responses to events tend to be dissolved in those of his fellow travelers: he always says "We thought," "We felt," "We believed," never "I." He is, however, a superb observer. First, by way of sociological survey, he scans the other occupants of the tarantass, singling out their peculiarities of dress and language. He immediately perceives the religious identity of two of his companions, and he records precisely the linguistic emblems of their faith. Like the narrator of "The Sealed Angel," they are Old Believers who live "according to the ancient piety."

Despite the detailed description of these travelers, none of them takes part in the main action—from a structural point of view a diseconomy of means somewhat reminiscent of Gogol, although the motive is not playfulness, as it often is with Gogol, but rather the pictorial and ethnographic value of the material. We scrutinize the travelers as an interesting and varied collection of people, even though for the principal narrative they serve only as audience. To be sure, the travelogue, as a genre, does not require the concentration or narrative symmetry necessary in the short story proper, but here Leskov pushes structural looseness perilously close to chaos.

The coach rolls into a peasant's courtyard, where a new driver and horses are supposed to be waiting. This driver, who is also the proprietor of the house, is reluctant to venture on the roads at that late hour because of rumors that robbers are afoot in the neighborhood. The travelers, obliged to spend the night, listen to a story related by their peasant host before they go to sleep. This story constitutes the main narrative, for which the travelogue is structurally the frame. The peasant's tale is a grim one. Once, when walking in the woods, he had been terrified of robbers, and in his fright he had beaten with a cudgel, probably to death, a wretched beggar, apparently a deserter from the army, whom he took for a brigand. After this tale the travelers retire for the night, and the story ends, without ever reaching the fair.

Thus in this early attempt at fiction Leskov employed for the first time the form for which he is most celebrated in Russian literature, the skaz, or oral story-within-a-story, narrated by a character with a distinct voice or style of his own. By an unspoken convention, the frame narrator functions as a human tape recorder, providing an exact transcription of the peasant's words. It is not a conventionalized literary reproduction of the peasant's language but a real attempt to convey in print the peculiar diction, cadence, and intonation of oral speech. For instance, at the climax of his tale the peasant narrator reports: "A deathly fear gripped me. No time to think, I see, and I lifted up the stick and I swished it down along his backbone, as hard, you know, as ever I could. He just flopped right down, with his arms stuck out to the sides."[13] This is the climax of the action, and at this point, for purposes of structural punctuation and commentary, the skaz is broken off so that the frame narrator can convey the reaction of the audience: "We looked at our host's athletic build and exchanged glances."[14] The reader's impression of the frame setting, and thus of the orality of the narrative, is reinforced by this evocation of its auditors; more important, the vital fact is elliptically conveyed, over the head, as it were, of the skaz narrator, that his strength was such that the blow was probably a mortal one.

"The Robber" offers some clues to Leskov's ideological position before his break with the radicals. The picture he paints of Russian life is anything but idyllic. The countryside is a lawless domain where freebooters roam almost unhindered. The population lives in terror, caught between their fear of robbers and of the inept and rapacious police. The authorities cannot maintain order; the cossacks posted along the road are more interested in chasing skirts than in apprehending thieves and are suspected of conniving with the bandits. There can be no normal economic life in a country where merchants and their goods are as unsafe on the roads as this tale implies.

Leskov's peasants are no dignified rustics à la Turgenev; their manners are atrocious, the hut is smelly, the food revolting. The senseless murder of the beggar, an act committed because hostility and fear had paralyzed judgment and made communication impossible, seems to symbolize the arbitrariness of human fate, especially in Russia—an idea that remained a favorite of Leskov. Russia (perhaps standing for the world at large) is a place where the unexpected may happen at any moment; and the unexpected is almost always unpleasant, often disastrous. Man's efforts to construct a meaningful existence are pitiful in view of the ever-present danger that some malicious act of man or fate will leave him and his hopes in ruins.

In "The Robber" facts are allowed to speak for themselves; neither social sermon nor philosophical conclusion is directly expressed. Only in the last sentences, when the frame narrator recounts a ghastly dream he had about the murdered man's corpse, does emotion break through his objective manner. He speculates about the victim's relatives, his parents, perhaps his widow, waiting for him and wondering where he is and whether he will return; and the frame narrator concludes the story with an ironic apostrophe to them: "Keep on waiting, my friends," more striking in its bitter flavor than any expression of sympathy or pathos.

"The Robber" was followed by a sequel, "In a Coach," in which the same travelers are taken further along their way toward Nizhni Novgorod.[15] After their night in the hay, the travelers move on the next morning in their coach, which provides the setting for another skaz, brought in to illustrate a point in a discussion. The travelers have been arguing about the traits of various nations, and to make his opinion clear, Yellow-Eye, one of the Old Believers, relates a legend he has heard "from trustworthy people." "You see," he begins, "in very ancient times, soon after the Ascension of Christ, when the ancient faith [the faith of the Old Believers] still flourished throughout the world, a pilgrim walked the earth." Leskov manages to capture the naive charm of his speech. The pilgrim is a saint, a missionary, carrying the gospel of Jesus to many nations. At last he is arrested in a "catch-all country," made up of people of various nationalities, and condemned to be crucified as a seditious element. He is nailed to a board, but the arrows shot at him are miraculously turned aside, and the people perceive that he must be freed. Each nationality then makes a proposal. The English offer to buy him from the king; thus they are destined for all time to be shopkeepers. The French (in 1862 still the leading soldiers of Europe) offer to win him in battle. Finally, the Russians offer to steal him; and the pilgrim replies to them: "Go forth and steal your whole lives."

The anecdote shows Leskov's curious ambivalence about the Russian national character, his fondness for delivering deflationary blows to the national ego. In Russia, robbery is no mere by-product of misgovernment and poverty; it is the hallmark of the nation's soul. Leskov liked this parable so much that he incorporated it into the fourth act of *The Spendthrift;* its basic idea is also the essence of "The Cynic." At the same time he derived pleasure from exhibiting his knowledge and indeed his love of Russia, its types, its atmosphere, and especially its language. As a result such stories as "In a Coach" have an ultranational flavor scarcely matched by any other Russian writer.

This first skaz in the story is followed by a less successful one, telling how Moses, returning from Sinai, was so shocked at the sight of the people sinning that he dropped the tablets with the law. They were shattered into pieces; people picked up the fragments and fled with them in all directions. Some of these broken pieces, having lost their "not's," bore such inscriptions as "kill" or "steal"; and it was thus that crime came into the world.

The faults of "In a Coach," like those of "The Robber," anticipate defects found in many of Leskov's later works. Both stories lack concentration and focus. In "The Robber," the frame narrative, including the elaborate introduction of all the occupants of the coach, takes up more than half the text, throwing the skaz out of balance. On the contrary, the frame situation of "In a Coach" is hardly maintained, and we tend to forget where it is we are traveling to. Furthermore, the two inner narratives are related to each other (and to "The Robber") only by the abstract idea of thievery and violence. "In a Coach" would have been a more satisfactory work if Leskov could have disciplined himself to omit the second skaz, thus enhancing the shock of the first one's ending, the revelation of the thievish essence of the Russian character.[16]

The year 1863 marks Leskov's emergence as a major figure in Russian belles lettres. In that year he published six works of fiction, and three of them—"The Musk-ox," "The Mocker," and "The Life of a

Peasant Martyress"—belong to the permanent corpus not only of Leskov's best writings but of Russian literature as a whole.

At the end of "The Musk-ox" appears the legend "Paris, November
28, 1862."[17] Leskov was not in the habit of dating his works, especially
in collections; he evidently attached significance to this inscription
and wished it to influence the reader's perception of the story. The action takes place somewhat earlier, in the late 1850s, and the inscription
may be intended to underscore the perspective in time and space from
which Leskov views the action. In 1862-63, from the vantage point of
Paris and through the medium of his newly discovered art, Leskov undertook to recapitulate his experiences during the past ten tumultuous
years. He wanted to make a considered statement about Russian society and its future—not Russian society in Paris but Russian society in
Russia. Although he had been shaken by the controversy over the
Petersburg fires and was embittered against the radicals who had criticized him, Leskov's rage against the Left was not so violent as it became a year or two later. In 1862-63 he wanted to demonstrate his renewed conviction that the radicals' dream of a peasant uprising in
Russia was illusory, that meaningful progress could come only through
the sustained efforts of practical people, homegrown entrepreneurs
who understood the country and within its institutions and customs
would work for concrete improvements, especially economic ones. At
the same time—perhaps guided by an artistic instinct for balance, perhaps by historical insight—Leskov sought to portray the radical cause
as at least generous in its impulse, if misguided in its judgments.

For a human symbol of this position Leskov needed a radical Quixote, a man admirable and even noble but slightly ludicrous, essentially impractical, and out of touch with reality. Life had provided
Leskov with an ideal specimen. In the Oryol gymnasium he had been a
classmate of Viktor Yakushkin, the son of a local landowner who had
married a serf girl. Viktor's older brother, Pavel, had graduated from
the gymnasium in 1840, the year Leskov entered it. Pavel Yakushkin
studied at Moscow University but withdrew without completing the
course in order to devote himself to collecting Russian folklore.[18] The
product of a marriage between a gentleman and a serf, he apparently
decided to serve as a cultural intermediary between the two classes—
rescuing from oblivion, for the benefit of educated society, some of
the magnificent products of the oral tradition, and likewise giving the
peasants various useful ideas of upper-class or Western origin, including, perhaps, the idea of revolution. A picturesque and incongruous
figure, wearing a belted red peasant shirt in summer and a sheepskin

jacket in winter, with a pair of spectacles (something no peasant possessed) on his nose, he wandered on foot over a vast territory from
Novgorod to Astrakhan, collecting songs, proverbs, and folktales.

In 1858, at the height of the muckraking era, Yakushkin suddenly
became nationally famous. An overzealous police chief in Pskov became suspicious of this "muzhik in glasses" and arrested him as a possible subversive. The police had no evidence against him, and he was
soon released. Characteristically, he even made friends with the police
chief who had arrested him; unlike most revolutionaries, Yakushkin
was free of self-righteous vindictiveness. But he did publish a vivid account of his experiences in the Pskov jail, and overnight he was a hero
of the liberal cause.[19]

In 1858 or 1859, soon after Yakushkin's sojourn in the Pskov jail,
Leskov ran into him in Petersburg, and they reestablished their long-
broken connection. Later, when Leskov had settled permanently in
the capital, Yakushkin sometimes stayed in the writer's apartment. At
that time their social and professional circles partially overlapped, although Yakushkin was much more of a radical and had close ties with
the *Contemporary*. After the split between the gradualists and the
radicals Yakushkin refused to sever his connections with the moderates, and he and Leskov remained on good terms. The relationship
was never intimate, but Leskov evidently enjoyed contact with this
good-natured peasantophile, who was too bizarre and childlike to be
threatening.

Yakushkin had exactly the quixotic qualities Leskov required for his
hero: intelligence combined with naiveté, selfless generosity and moral
courage together with utter impracticality, and a picturesque, somewhat absurd exterior. Certain alterations were necessary, however.
Leskov's specimen had to be more representative, less idiosyncratic
than Yakushkin; the typical radical of the 1850s and 1860s was not a
déclassé gentleman but a secularized priest's son. Vasily Bogoslovsky,
the hero of "The Musk-ox," is therefore given the social provenance
not of Yakushkin but of Chernyshevsky, Dobrolyubov, Pomyalovsky, Reshetnikov, and the Uspenskys: with a surname meaning "theologian," he is the son of a poor village subdeacon and has attended a
provincial seminary, not a gymnasium. Since he is the epitome of inef-
fectiveness, he is also stripped of Yakushkin's serious achievements,
his writing and his ethnography. Thus despite his high principles and
selflessness, Bogoslovsky seeks but never finds; and nothing he does
produces any lasting good.

Yakushkin's external characteristics, especially the ludicrous ones, are lavishly bestowed on Bogoslovsky. In the Oryol gymnasium, according to legend, Yakushkin had been famous for the unruly tufts of hair that protruded from his forehead, giving him the look of a porcupine. Bogoslovsky is correspondingly endowed with two long curls on either side of his forehead, which he constantly twists; they look like the horns of a musk-ox as pictured in a zoology textbook. Yakushkin had a habit of turning up unexpectedly at Leskov's house and expecting to be fed and sheltered for as long as he chose to remain. He would even help himself to his friend's extra pair of boots if his own happened to be worn out. He was aware that his standards of personal hygiene were not those of his host and especially of his host's female servant, a German, and therefore "out of delicacy" he preferred to sleep on the floor, no matter how energetically his host tried to persuade him to use the sofa. Leskov relates these details with gusto in his memoir on Yakushkin, written in 1883 (11:71-89); twenty years earlier virtually the same details had been used in "The Musk-ox." Though such a man's character may be noble and his fate tragic, we are held at a distance by his absurdity. We cannot feel full community of spirit with a "musk-ox."

Bogoslovsky is also endowed with some interests that are more Leskov's than Yakushkin's, especially religion. There is no evidence that Yakushkin was particularly concerned with Christianity except as an aspect of peasant culture. His religion, like that of many upper-class radicals, was peasant-worship: he cherished the myth of the beautiful kingdom to come, when the "people" would cast aside their oppressors and corrupters and create the just society according to their natural wisdom. In his memoir on Yakushkin, Leskov says that on one of his visits Yakushkin made much of Matvei, a former serf of the Leskovs at Panino who had accompanied Leskov's brother Aleksei to Petersburg. Yakushkin and Matvei got drunk together. Later, during an argument about populism among Leskov's guests, Yakushkin dragged Matvei from the kitchen out in front of the company, embraced him, and proclaimed, "Everything you say is nonsense; but if you want to talk sense, study from him!" Leskov comments ironically, "What there was to study from Matvei, we didn't understand." To underscore the point he adds that Matvei later became an alcoholic and committed suicide (11:81).[20]

Perhaps because he felt it was more appropriate to his character's plebeian origin, Leskov ascribed to Bogoslovsky his own skepticism about the "people." Bogoslovsky has no inclination to idealize the muzhiks or to prostrate himself before them, although he deplores the injustice of their lot. With his clerical background, Bogoslovsky, like Leskov and unlike Yakushkin, has a built-in involvement with formal religion. Upon graduating from the seminary, Bogoslovsky, like the typical emancipated priest's son of the fifties and sixties, had refused to enter the clergy, but he did not become a nihilist and atheist. He even for a time attended the Kazan spiritual academy, an advanced seminary for the higher, "black" clergy, though, disillusioned, he eventually left it.[21] Later he joined a village of Old Believers, in which he briefly had a wife, but again he was frustrated in his search for a spiritual haven, finding only formalistic nit-picking where he had sought inner light and a genuine concern with social justice.

In his life of religious seeking Bogoslovsky resembles Leskov—and Leskov's father—rather than Yakushkin. Like Semyon Leskov he reads only the Gospels and the Greek and Roman classics, scornfully dismissing modern literature, including the populist stories in the radical magazines. Whether he continues to believe in God is not entirely clear; it seems that he does. He feels only hostility toward heathen radicals from among the intelligentsia; and at the end of his life he regrets that he never became a village priest. As a priest he would at least have had a niche, a definite role to play and a chance to exert a moral influence. As a wanderer, a secular truth seeker, he has no place in Russian life and no influence.

The plot of "The Musk-ox" consists of a reconstruction of Bogoslovsky's life experience, pieced together from the narrator's observations, reminiscences told him by the Musk-ox himself, and the testimony of others. It is the story of a lifelong quest for meaning, both metaphysical and social, ending in defeat and despair. For all his intelligence and sincere desire to be of use, Bogoslovsky is everywhere a misfit; and each failure chips away at his self-esteem and his hope, until at last both are quite gone.

One of Bogoslovsky's quixotic undertakings is his attempt to use the Orthodox monastery in which he lives for a time as a base for spreading revolutionary propaganda among novices and pilgrims. He is soon discovered at this oddly directed subversion and expelled. His friends then get him a job as a foreman on a commercial farm operated by one Aleksandr Ivanovich Sviridov. Sviridov is Leskov's personified antidote to radicalism and revolution, standing for true practical progress. Through intelligence, shrewdness, and immense perseverance Sviridov, an ex-serf, has enriched himself and become a landowner (but not a gentleman). Like Alexander Scott and other landowners Leskov knew in Penza, Sviridov is involved in many operations besides agriculture, especially vodka distilling. He has been to Germany and understands the importance of machinery and efficiency. Unlike the Russian gentry, who tend to be extravagant and unrealistic, and unlike foreign businessmen in Russia, who often come to grief out of failure to understand the Russian mentality, Sviridov knows how to get the most out of his employees and how to introduce changes without arousing their resistance. He makes his land produce far more than it ever had and thus provides jobs and increases the wealth of the whole area.

Bogoslovsky tries to instill in Sviridov's workers a sense of class solidarity and class antagonism to their boss. But the workers take him for a clown, and the lesson is lost on them. As a revolutionary agitator, Bogoslovsky is hopeless; he has no common language with the people. As the monks had done before, Sviridov calls him "touched": he may have the character of a saint, but he is useless in the real world.

Bogoslovsky's dilemma eventually crystallizes in his mind as a head-on confrontation between himself and Sviridov. "I see," he writes to the narrator, "that this Aleksandr Ivanov [Sviridov] had been blocking my way in everything, even before I knew him. Here is the real popular enemy—this type of well-fed lout, this lout who feeds with his crumbs the poor vagabonds so that they should not die out but work for him [. . .] With my ideas we two cannot live on the same earth. I will get out of his way, for he is their beloved one." Bogoslovsky hangs himself in the woods. As his body is being cut down, an old peasant sounds the refrain of the story, speaking ingratiatingly and in rhyme to Sviridov: "It's for him to rot and you to live" (*"Emu gnit', a vam žit', batjuška Liksandra Ivanyč"*; 1:95).

This image of the folk capitalist—perhaps a descendant of Gogol's Kostonzhoglo from the second volume of *Dead Souls*—seems to be a less mythical figure for Leskov that he was for Gogol. Under another name he reappears abruptly at the very end of *No Way Out*, where again he represents the true "way out," in contrast with the paper utopias of the radicals. But neither there nor in "The Musk-ox" is he an artistic success (nor in Gogol either, for that matter). In Bogoslovsky, however, Leskov created a character whose significance is not merely local and historical. His is the universal tragic destiny of the man who despite unusual intelligence, courage, and will is doomed to failure and perishes from his inability to make effective contact with the world.

The narrative system Leskov uses for his exposition of Bogoslovsky's character might almost be considered a separate genre: the "history of my discovery of a character." An enigmatic personality is exhibited to the reader at the outset as a picturesque but puzzling phenomenon. The narrative reproduces not the dynamic sequence of the events themselves but the excitement of their discovery by the narrator. The narrator tells of his encounters with the central character, each one adding something to his information about the hero and his understanding of his personality. Besides introducing evidence as he learns it, the narrator may include his own analyses and speculations, but without being obliged, as an omniscient author would be, to guarantee their truth. Furthermore, by placing the angle of vision on the same plane as the hero (the narrator is a character in the story), the discovery of the hero is given the air of incompleteness, of relative uncertainty, that haunts all our "discoveries" of other human beings in real life.

The naive reaction to any such story told in the first person is that the narrator and the author are one, unless the narrator is clearly given a separate identity or exists on a geographical, temporal, or social plane that could not possibly be the author's. In "The Musk-ox" no attempt is made to confute this identification. The history of character discovery thus appears at the same time as an author's memoir: it is a presentation of what purport to be the author's own experiences with the central character. And "The Musk-ox" to some extent really is a memoir, an account of Leskov's discovery of Yakushkin. Thus Leskov perches his story neither solidly in the realm of reality nor in that of fiction, even realistic fiction, but in the no-man's-land between them. He introduces a wealth of presumed autobiographical material, including a long reminiscence by the narrator about his experiences as a small boy, when he accompanied his grandmother on expeditions to holy places in the central Russian provinces. The narrator's grandmother is given the Christian name and patronymic of Leskov's own maternal grandmother, Aleksandra Vasilievna Alferieva. Partly on the strength of this real name, Leskov's biographers, trying to eke out their scanty material on the writer's childhood, generally treat this and similar passages in "The Musk-ox" as authentic biographical documents.[22] Yet the narrator cannot be wholly equated with Leskov; several details about him do not fit the facts. For instance, in May 1854 the narrator "had business to conduct in connection with a trial being held in the government offices in Kursk"; at that time Leskov was working in the recruiting bureau in Kiev.[23]

In general, the portrayal of the narrator bears marks of authorial wish fulfillment. One is struck by the exceptional affection all the characters feel for him. His relative Chelnovsky, through whom he meets the Musk-ox, feels "extraordinary joy" at the narrator's arrival (1:34). A monk is as glad to see the narrator "as a country miss is to hear the sound of sleigh bells" (1:67). Another old monk, Father Vavila, when he realizes who the narrator is, embraces and kisses him, and they both burst into tears (1:69). The Sviridovs too are unusually fond of him, spend six months with him in Petersburg, and then persuade him to accompany them back to the provinces. Even the dour Musk-ox seems to consider the narrator the only person on earth who understands him. The narrator is everybody's best friend. These friendships, however, notably lack reciprocity and balance. The narrator maintains a clear emotional distance from other people, especially Bogoslovsky, and there is an air of condescension in his friendliness. His involvement with Bogoslovsky is founded more on curiosity than on affection. And although he likes and admires the Sviridovs, he makes it clear that they are plebeians, while he is a man of culture.

There are, to be sure, artistic reasons as well as personal ones for bathing the narrator in such a warm light. A gatherer of information must remain on good terms with his sources if they are to keep confiding in him. Moreover, the narrator's mood—soft, melancholy, nostalgic—makes the reader more tolerant of the unattractive Musk-ox. To establish this mood, the narrator ranges far from his ostensible subject, all the way back to his excursions with his grandmother, long before he had heard of Bogoslovsky. This chapter of purported reminiscences is one of the most poetic that Leskov ever wrote, but its only connection with the Musk-ox is that one of the monasteries the narrator visited as a boy was later used by Bogoslovsky as a center for revolutionary propaganda. The narrator even calls attention to the irrelevance of these memories ("these reminiscences of mine, which, perhaps, have very little to do with the grim fate of the Musk-ox"; 1:64). One of the advantages of the memoir genre is its comfortable looseness and informality. Such irrelevant but natural associations have a psychological validity that increases both the charm of the story and its impression of authenticity.

In 1863 Leskov produced another putative memoir, "The Mocker," published in Apollon Grigoriev's magazine *Anchor* in May.[24] "The Mocker" is also related in the first person by a narrator who is to some degree a reflection of the author. It is not, however, a history of character discovery. It is a disquisition, with illustrations, on the subject of national types and their interactions.

111

The central character is an Englishman known to Russians as Stuart Yakovlevich Dane, the manager of the large estates of Prince Kulagin —a not very heavily camouflaged image of Leskov's uncle and former boss, Alexander Yakovlevich Scott, who managed the estates of Count Perovsky. To qualify himself as a detached and unbiased observer, the narrator is represented not as Dane's employee or relative but as an up-and-coming young "official for special assignments" on the staff of the local governor—a position analogous to the one Leskov held briefly in Kiev in 1860, after he had left Scott's employ. The locale of the story is Oryol Province. The narrator's mother is said to live, as Leskov's mother did, on a small farm on the Gostomlya River.[25] Dane's headquarters are nearby. Since Scott's headquarters were in Penza Province, we can observe here a fictional fusing of three distinct periods in Leskov's life: his Oryol childhood, his commercial career, and the climax of his government service.

From the psychobiographical point of view, the most striking feature of "The Mocker" is the hostility with which Leskov treats his English uncle, a man who had influenced him deeply and whom he later professed to admire as a model of Christian virtue. We can only guess at the reasons for Leskov's grudge. Perhaps he had chafed at his subordinate position and found his uncle less agreeable as a boss than as a relative. There may have been something self-righteous about Scott's rectitude, and possibly Leskov's Russian pride had been offended by the Englishman's assumption of national superiority. Leskov may have especially resented the fact that in 1859 Scott's financial reverses had made it necessary for him to leave the firm, bringing to an abrupt end his much-enjoyed career as a commercial agent.

In 1863 Leskov apparently still harbored a good deal of resentment against his uncle, and in "The Mocker" he vented it creatively, using a favorite idea of his, namely, that the attempts of foreigners to impose order on the jumble of Russian life, however nobly motivated, are doomed to defeat. Equally futile is Dane's attempt to substitute gentler ways of disciplining his peasants than the time-honored violence customarily employed by Russian masters against their serfs. The muzhiks, stubbornly attached to their barbarous ways, cannot bear a master who tries to induce them to work on a regular schedule and who refuses to flog them for their offenses.

In the central episode of "The Mocker," told retrospectively by the burly victim, a runaway peasant is brought back to Dane by the police. Instead of giving him the customary dose of the birch and sending him back to work, Dane has him pinned by his shirt to an armchair and compels him to sit all day watching his colleagues at their labors and bearing the brunt of their ridicule. This mocking chastisement and others like it are considered so offensive that the peasants eventually revolt, burn down the manor house, and oblige Dane to flee for his life.

From the point of view of the Russian ego, this anecdote has a wryness characteristic of Leskov. The narrator makes it clear that Dane had done nothing wrong, that his administration of Kulagin's estate was far more humane than the way most Russian gentlemen managed their lands. Moreover, the Russian peasants as he portrays them are devious, stubborn, ignorant, and unreasonable. If "The Mocker" is to be regarded as a confrontation between national types, the Russians do not come out the moral victors. The defeat they inflict on the Englishman is gained only by clinging to their own backwardness. But at the same time Leskov exults in the downfall of this outsider who came to Russia like a colonial administrator, with an assumption of moral and intellectual superiority, and is in the end vanquished by the immobility and brutishness of the Russian peasantry.

To his narrator Leskov gives a particularly satisfying role. Unlike the author, the narrator is not encumbered by any business or family connections with Dane. As an official on the governor's staff, he is simply introduced to Dane when Dane comes to pay his respects to the local authorities. Later, when news of trouble on Prince Kulagin's estates reaches the governor's ears, the governor dispatches the narrator, who had grown up in the district, to investigate the nature of the peasants' dissatisfaction. Thus the narrator is able to play a part that Leskov was especially fond of: the man of experience and practical sense who is called on for advice and asked to help extricate someone from a seemingly impossible difficulty.

The narrator finds the local landowners, including his mother, unanimous in their praise of Dane; only a cagey old merchant, who interviews one of Dane's peasants in the narrator's presence, perceives the precariousness of Dane's position and foresees the trouble to come.[26] When the revolt breaks out, the narrator, again sent by the governor to investigate, is in a position to display his wisdom and humanitarianism in action. He refuses to take a military escort, preferring to rely on his ability to reason with the peasants. He finds them pacific enough but steadfast in their refusal to identify the arsonists in their midst. The narrator promises to do what he can to help them and persuades the governor to intercede for them with Prince Kulagin. The prince agrees not to prosecute them on the condition that they ask

Dane's forgiveness and promise to obey him henceforth. This proposal, however, is utterly unacceptable to the peasants, and they elect to let the law take its course. As Leskov grimly ends the story, "a criminal proceeding was instituted, as a result of which three men were sent to penal servitude, twelve to punitive military companies, and all the rest flogged under the supervision of the local court and returned to their place of residence" (1:30).

There is thus a contradictory relationship between the moral point of "The Mocker" and its emotional underpinnings. Intellectually, Leskov is on the side of Dane, who represents progress, a more rational organization of labor, and civilized methods of discipline. But emotionally, and, as it were, nationally, Leskov cannot help gloating over Dane's catastrophe. It might be thought that the story would founder on such a contradiction, but the laws of art are not the laws of logic.[27]

"The Life of a Peasant Martyress" appeared in the July and August 1863 numbers of *Library for Reading*.[28] The editor of this undistinguished middle-of-the-road magazine was Pyotr Boborykin, later famous as a novelist of astounding productivity if mediocre quality. Boborykin was trying to steer a middle course between the uncompromising radicalism of the *Contemporary* and *Russian Word* on the one hand and the strident chauvinism and social conservatism of the *Russian Messenger* on the other. In 1863 this was approximately Leskov's position as well. Though still smarting from the charges leveled at him by the radicals, Leskov was not yet ready to align himself wholeheartedly with the Right.

"The Life of a Peasant Martyress" never appeared in book form during Leskov's lifetime, even in his collected works. Except for the few bookworms who cared to rummage through old numbers of *Library for Reading*, it remained unknown to the latter-day Russian reading public until after the Revolution. Probably in the late 1860s, Leskov revised it thoroughly, giving it the title *Amour in Bast Shoes*, but this version was not published in his lifetime.[29] The reasons for suppressing it may have been aesthetic, but it seems more likely that they were ideological. By 1869, when *Amour in Bast Shoes* was to have appeared in the second volume of his collected stories, Leskov had taken up an entrenched battle position on the Right. In view of his more extreme political orientation, he may have felt that "The Life of a Peasant Martyress" was inconsistent with his current allegiance. Indeed, in its theme and even style, the story has affinities with the work of the radical peasantophiles of the sixties, such as Sleptsov, Levitov,

and the Uspenskys, with whom Leskov was now "at daggers drawn."
He decided to scrap it.

"The Life of a Peasant Martyress" is Leskov's attempt as of 1863 to
make a major statement on the peasant question, then the most crucial
question in Russian life. His central conviction on this subject had
been voiced in "The Robber," "The Musk-ox," and "The Mocker": the
peasants were impoverished mentally and spiritually as well as economically. This was a fact, Leskov insisted, that had to be faced without evasion or idealization. In his uncompromising naturalism concerning the peasantry, Leskov was thus close to the position of his
worst enemies, the plebeian purveyors of semifictional ethnography.
For unlike their spiritual successors, the populists of the seventies and
eighties, these radical ethnographers of the sixties did not represent the
peasants as noble savages. Their strategy was just the opposite: to describe peasant life as grimly and starkly as they could. The more horrifying the conditions depicted, the more powerful the impression on
the reader would be, and therefore the more effective the message.

Although in general Leskov adopted the same strategy, he felt himself in competition with the ethnographic naturalists, and he was even
more antagonistic toward their admirers, the young radicals of
Petersburg. What right had these radicals to claim a monopoly of
knowledge of peasant life? He could outdo them in experience if not in
book learning. "I studied the people," he wrote in 1863, "in the
meadows of the Gostomlya, eating from a common pot, on the dewy
grass of a night pasture, beneath a warm sheepskin coat, and in the
mill of Panino, behind circles of dusty chaff; so it is indecent for me
either to place the peasants on a pedestal or to trample them beneath
my feet. The peasants thought of me as one of themselves, and among
them I have many friends and god-cousins, especially on the
Gostomlya, where there live bearded men for whom I knelt down
before my guardian and benefactor and begged him to spare them
from the birch and the stick."[30]

In a later version of this passage, published in 1867, Leskov goes on
to picture himself, the son of a poor gentleman, as closer to the peasants than the popovichi, the priests' children, "who used to catch the
peasants' chickens and baby pigs while their fathers were making the
rounds of the parish to collect offerings." Such children had grown up
to become the Uspenskys and Levitovs, who now represented
themselves as the unique champions of the people and had tried to
brand Leskov as the peasants' enemy. Therefore, although he essentially still agreed with them, he tried to dissociate himself from them

and their literary production: "I do not understand why the *paysan* stories of Grigorovich [the prototype of the sentimental idealizations of the 1840s] are subjected to ridicule, while the stories of a whole crowd of latter-day *narodniki* [peasantophiles], published in the most enormous quantities and leaving no trace whatever, are for some reason considered useful."[31] But to set himself apart from the literary popovichi, and at the same time engage in the very kind of village muckraking which they had mainly developed and even to do so in the same form—this contradiction proved too hard for Leskov to live with. Small wonder that by the end of the 1860s "The Life of a Peasant Martyress" had to be swept under the rug.

"A little runt of a peasant was Kostik of Ryumino, but so nasty mean that Lord save us!"[32] Without any introduction, without a frame situation to identify the narrator, this opening sentence of "A Peasant Martyress" conveys through stylistic means alone, with its emotionally charged nonliterary language, that we are in the presence of an oral narrator, either a peasant or someone close to the peasantry. No attempt is made to specify oral narration, and no explanation is given for the existence of a written text. We must conclude either that the written form is original and that the narrator, because of the nature of his subject or his own linguistic predilections, has chosen to render his account in this unusual style; or else that an oral narrative has somehow been magically transcribed for us. Whether written or oral, however, the stylization is not consistently maintained. Very dense at the beginning, it becomes diluted as the story progresses, more or less merging into literary Russian toward the end.

We never find out who this narrator is, and he does not participate in the action. During the main part of the story he uses the first-person singular, much in the way Gogol's Rudy Panko does in *Evenings on a Farm near Dikanka*, only for remarks appropriate to his role as narrator ("Another time I will relate how all this got started and developed"; 1:266). The first-person plural is used more frequently. It has the effect of identifying the narrator with the environment he describes, giving the impression that his report is based on first-hand knowledge. The narrator's information, though it may have implications for the Russian peasantry as a whole, is always presented as local: "Where we live on the Gostomlya, there are many people who are so crowded in their huts that the whole winter long they sleep in outbuildings, hay barns, or cellars." The words used to identify these places are technical terms of peasant architecture; one is a dialectism probably incomprehensible to the average educated Russian.[33] The narrator therefore provides a definition: "Such little outbuildings, like village prayer shrines, are put together out of plaited twigs, [and placed] either right in the yard or behind the barn, and they call them *punki*" (1:265-266). The folksy language is thus emphasized, and the reader concludes that the narrator is himself a countryman, steeped in local lore, custom, and manners of speech. Furthermore, he appears to be personally acquainted with all the main characters, not as an outsider, but as part of their world.

Only in the epilogue does the narrator provide any information about himself. It seems that although born and brought up on the Gostomlya, he now has a higher station in life. He has returned to his birthplace after a long interval, particularly interested to observe the changes brought about by the Emancipation: "Last summer I was on the Gostomlya. It was almost five years since I had seen my native places. Before that I had lived for five years without leaving the capital and had heard my fill of stories of peasant life. I began to imagine that I, who had grown up on the meadows of the Gostomlya among barefooted peasant boys my own age, had lost touch with peasant life. 'I'll go to the Gostomlya and find out what has died out and what has grown up in place of it' " (1:379). After five years in Petersburg, the narrator not only has acquired a perspective from which to view the people and events on the Gostomlya but can approach his educated readers on an equal plane. He is no Rudy Panko; he will not be condescended to. At the same time, he can get in digs at his rivals: their stories of peasant life are fakes, Petersburg concoctions of half ideology and half imagination; his are reality itself.

In order to score this point Leskov sacrifices a consistent identity for his narrator. The ultraprovincial countryman who writes (or speaks) as he does at the beginning of "A Peasant Martyress" is hardly a man who has spent the last five years in Petersburg. The angle of vision from which we view the action is also affected. Just as the language gravitates from stylized dialect back toward literary Russian, so the point of view shifts from that of a narrator belonging to the same world as the characters to that of an omniscient author. In the second version of the story, *Amour in Bast Shoes*, Leskov eliminated the epilogue, probably hoping to remedy this defect, especially since he was no longer interested in commenting topically on the effects of the Emancipation. But he did not undertake the wholesale revision that would have been necessary to give the story complete stylistic and narrative consistency.

In its main outlines, the figure of Leskov's narrator in "A Peasant

Martyress"—the country boy come home after years in the capital—was traditional in Russian literature, effectively utilized, for instance, by Gogol in "Old World Landowners" and by Turgenev in *A Sportsman's Sketches*. It has the advantage of providing an explanation for the alienated and critical view the narrator takes of a familiar environment, yet without forcing him to give up his rights of membership in local society.

In many respects the bits of the narrator's history given in the epilogue coincide with Leskov's, even his official rank in the service, collegiate secretary. Furthermore, among the characters there is a gentry family, not identified as the narrator's, which coincides fairly closely with Leskov's. The father's name, Mitry Semyonych, is a reversal of Semyon Dmitrievich. Leskov's sister Masha appears under that name, together with the (historically true) fact that she died of scarlet fever at the age of twelve. There is also a Misha (the name of Leskov's younger brother), said to be fourteen and a student in the Oryol gymnasium,[34] which affords Leskov an opportunity to comment on the improvements that had taken place since he had studied there. The real name of the inspector of the gymnasium, Pyotr Andreevich Az[buki]n, is also introduced, with only a few letters deleted from his last name; and the Father Larion of the story suggests Father Illarion, the priest at Panino during Leskov's childhood. Another family name, that of Leskov's aunt Pelageya Dmitrievna, is used for a servant. These semiautobiographical reminiscences, like the precise geographical names (many of which would have been unknown to readers from outside the Oryol region), serve to hold the story down to the real world of precise ethnography. In the revised version, however, apparently in order to give the story a more general relevance, the epilogue was eliminated, leaving the narrator without social or personal identity; the family names taken out; and most references to Oryol and the Gostomlya changed to "the city" and "the river." The folksiness of language is also considerably toned down. As a result, *Amour in Bast Shoes* is a more conventional literary story.[35]

"A Peasant Martyress" bore the subtitle "From My Gostomlya Reminiscences"; *Amour in Bast Shoes* was subtitled *A Peasant Novel* (*krest'janskij roman*). In later years Leskov conceived a dislike for the novel as a genre, partly because a love story was considered an obligatory ingredient, perhaps because the Russian word *roman*, "novel," also means "romance" in all its senses. All "romances," Leskov decided, boil down to one of two tiresome formulas: *vljubilsja— ženilsja* (he fell in love and got married) or *vljubilsja— zastrelilsja* (he

118

fell in love and shot himself). In view of his aversion to "romance" and the failures of his two major attempts at writing *romany*, critics have concluded that he lacked the insight or the talent to deal successfully with the theme of sexual love. What Leskov lacked was rather the ability to deal with the theme of sexual love among members of the Russian upper classes, that is, among characters like himself. He always found it easier to maintain artistic control if his characters were separated from himself by clear-cut social boundaries. In this early peasant romance, where the author-narrator's social and psychological distance from his peasant heroes is clearly marked off, the theme of sexual love is handled with power.

The martyress-heroine, Nastya, represents natural goodness ultimately crushed by the cruel and inhuman environment in which she lives. A quiet, responsible girl, neither flamboyant nor unusually pretty, she is affectionate with her mother and sister-in-law and with the little daughter of her owners, whom for a time she serves as a nursemaid. But her brother, who is making his way in the world by the most hard-fisted means, forces her, in order to cement a business alliance, to marry a half-wit for whom she feels extreme disgust. Since her father is dead, her brother is lord of the household, and his word is law. Nastya marries, but for a long time manages to resist the consummation of the marriage, despite enormous pressure; later, sexual relations with her despised husband drive her to madness.

After the failure of a peasant sorcerer's spells and the exorcism of a priest to cast out Nastya's "devil" (the linking of pre-Christian and Christian medical magic recalls the rainmaking in "A Case That Was Dropped" and "Vale of Tears") she is cured by the ministrations of Sila Krylushkin, a natural healer, who restores her to health by the excellent therapeutic technique of providing her with a tranquil environment and the opportunity to talk about her troubles with a sympathetic but neutral person.[36]

After considerable resistance, she drifts into a love affair with an attractive young peasant named Stepan, whose marriage—his shrewish wife bears a notable resemblance to Olga Vasilievna—is almost as wretched as Nastya's own. One of the means for bringing them together is their skill at performing folk music, which symbolizes, as it does in Turgenev's "Singers," the high degree of aesthetic refinement in the peasant milieu. Leskov skillfully selects the folk-song texts to harmonize with, and in part anticipate, the plot of the story. Deeply in love, Stepan and Nastya struggle to find a way of making a life together, but their society provides no more leeway for such romances than Anna Karenina's afforded her. At last they run away together, are caught, and (according to the standard procedure for runaway serfs) flogged by the police and returned to their owners. While in prison Nastya gives birth to a premature child, which soon dies; Stepan dies of typhus as they are being shipped home. Nastya again loses her mind and is taken to Krylushkin. Her health is improving when Krylushkin's establishment is broken up by a police raid: he is engaged in practicing medicine without a license. Nastya is now incarcerated in an official mental hospital, and there her mind snaps for the last time. She is released to her family without treatment, and that winter, wandering in the forest, she freezes to death.

With such a load of pathetic incidents "The Life of a Peasant Martyress" veers perilously close to sentimentality. It is rescued from disaster, however, partly by the detailed and convincing evocation of peasant life, its psychology, economics, ceremonials, artistic interests, and language, and also by its evocation of the power of sexual passion. The story is a harsh indictment of social conditions in the Russian countryside. Although not the main target, the landowners are not spared: Mitry Semyonych is portrayed as an ineffectual fuddy-duddy, and his wife as insensitive and cruel; they fail to exert any good influence over their serfs. The civil authorities are shown to be heedless of human values and needs; bureaucratic callousness reigns supreme. But as Chekhov later noted, the greatest oppressors of the peasants are the peasants themselves. This oppression is manifested not only in the rapacity and ruthlessness of well-to-do peasants or "kulaks" like Nastya's brother, but in the whole fabric of human relationships, in which affection and even reasonable cooperation often give way to irrational subordination based on custom and, all too frequently, on violence.

Leskov's literary output for 1863 includes three short stories, all inferior in quality to the three major works of that year, yet not without interest as examples of the author's experimentation with different literary modes: "The Mind Takes Its Own and the Devil His Own," "A Short History of a Case of Private Madness," and a story with a Polish title (a quotation from Mickiewicz), "Kochanko moja! Na co nam rozmowa?" ("My darling! What's the use of talking?").[37]

"The Mind Takes Its Own" is clearly a preliminary sketch for "The Life of a Peasant Martyress." Both bear the subtitle "From Reminiscences of the Gostomlya," and both lead off with highly stylized country speech, loaded with unexplained local references (from Oryol

Province) and emotional expressions: "Not only out our way, on the farms of the Gostomlya, but through the whole district, all the way to Rybnitsa there wasn't such a beauty as Pasha. What a delight she was! Tall, well built, with a white complexion, eyes blue as the sky, sable eyebrows, thick hair, and a bosom—why, if you took a long look at that bosom in the daytime, your head started spinning like a top, and there was no use going to bed, you just couldn't get to sleep." This image of an overpowering peasant Venus was eventually discarded in favor of the "martyress," Nastya; but Pasha remains an interesting specimen of Leskovian erotica. As usual, he is unable to tolerate the intoxicating power of female sexuality and must "punish" it. Pasha is a Russian Barbara Allen, driving a succession of young men to untimely graves from unrequited love, but herself remaining untouched and unmoved. In the central episode, a young gentleman, after two years of pining for Pasha, in despair gets himself betrothed to another girl. Only now are Pasha's desires awakened, and she finds her way to the gentleman's bedroom. It is too late, however, to stop the march of fate. The gentleman must marry his betrothed, who predictably turns out to be a shrew; and Pasha eventually marries another man. Their love affair, however, is later resumed, in a bucolic sylvan setting. At this point the story strangely trails off—into a discussion of the notion of the ideal woman in various countries and then into cookery, oddly ending with a eulogy of *krupenya*, a local delicacy.

Leskov revised the story later, but remained dissatisfied with it. His friend P. V. Bykov, who was given the manuscript of the revised version (still unpublished), recounts in his memoirs: "When I praised the story highly in its revised form, he [Leskov] shook his head and made a familiar motion with his neck (it was as if he were bothered by a starched collar that was too tight) and said, not without irritation, 'Don't flatter me. It is written truthfully and not without feeling, but you can't see me, the author, in the story. And in my other works you can recognize me at once, in every line.' "[38] Leskov's strictures, if accurately reported, are only partly true: the story is his, all right, and it is not hard to see him in it. But it is true that together with "The Life of a Peasant Martyress," it was an experiment in provincial stylization he subsequently deemed excessive, overloaded with local language and associations, and never repeated.

In "A Short History of a Case of Private Madness" Leskov attempted to expand his literary range to include straight humor. As a raconteur

Leskov had a natural affinity for humor, and later in his life he was to produce some of Russian literature's funniest pages. You would never guess it, however, from this crude early effort.

The story is a grossly overextended joke on animal surnames. An announcement appears in a newspaper that General Zherebtsov (Stallion) from Kharkov and Mme Kobylina (Mare) from Tobolsk have arrived in Petersburg and are staying in Konyushennaya (Stable) Street. Essentially that is all. Gogol might perhaps have tossed off such an anecdotal tidbit on the margin of one of his tales, but Leskov tries to construct a whole story around it and in so doing manages to crush out of it whatever feeble life it had. The revision of the story he unwisely attempted in 1869 only made matters worse,[39] since even more narrative weight is piled onto the thin joke about horsey names.

"My Darling! What's the use of Talking?" is one of many indications that Leskov's taste was far from dependable. In particular, it appears that the "coldness" with which he treats many intrinsically pathetic events—such as the suicide of the Musk-ox—was a vital ingredient of his art, a necessary defense against sentimentality. If he took a potentially sentimental theme, as he does in "My Darling!" and treated it without irony, the results were disastrous. This story is a dreadful nineteenth-century cliché from beginning to end: a poor pregnant girl, abandoned by her lover, is driven to prostitution; the baby dies; she becomes ill but is eventually rescued by a noble-hearted youth, who (chastely) nurses her back to health. Under the shelter of his altruism, true love at last blossoms between them, and so on.

Only three years later, in "The Battle-axe," Leskov took up the same theme, the unlucky girl in the hands of a procuress, and treated it with refreshing realism and even humor. It shows, if nothing else, how dangerous it is to jump to conclusions about an artist's potentialities.

⚜ 6 ⚜

No Way Out

Although his literary career seemed well launched with several suc- cessful short stories and novellas, Leskov realized that in view of the widely held prejudice in favor of the big form he would have to write a novel if he hoped to earn a major reputation. Furthermore, he now felt the need to reassess his own kaleidoscopic experiences of the past three years or so, since he had first come the Petersburg as correspon- dent for *Russian Speech*. He had been through many intensely interesting, if often painful, experiences in his effort to establish his identity, to find his way among the complicated cross-currents of the early 1860s. He had been involved in many sharp conflicts, especially with the radicals. With his paranoid and unforgiving temperament, he was still smarting from the charges made against him over the fire affair in 1862 and the rumors linking him and Artur Benni to the secret police. Ironically, at the very time the radicals were accusing him of collusion with the police, Leskov learned that he had been denounced to the police as a radical in the testimony of his former friend Nichi- porenko, who had been arrested the previous summer on charges of conspiracy with the "London propagandists," the Herzen-Ogaryov- Bakunin circle.

It was thus a time of great tension; and undoubtedly, as Leskov more and more broke his ties with the Left, ideological differences developed into personal antagonisms. There must have been many sharp clashes about which we can only guess. One of these, and that not a political one, has left a written record, testifying, if nothing else, to Leskov's extreme irascibility and the exacerbated state of his nerves. In May, 1863, angered by a delay in receiving payment for "The Musk-ox," Leskov wrote a furious letter to A. A. Kraevsky, the pub- lisher of *Notes of the Fatherland*, threatening to assault him physically in the streets if the money were not forthcoming within twenty-four hours.[1] And with his ideological opponents, there must have been even more bitter quarrels. Leskov could not bear to be accused of the slightest moral fault, and this was precisely what his former radical friends charged him with: he was a traitor who had betrayed their cause.

So Leskov had a literary career to make, a political "line" to expound, and many, many scores to settle. He decided to combine all these purposes in one novel. The result was *No Way Out*. It was not a happy combination, and the results in Leskov's career were more disastrous than he could have predicted.

Leskov obtained a contract to publish his novel serially in *Library for Reading*, and the first installment appeared in the January 1864 issue. The early chapters augured a roman-fleuve flowing gently through familiar scenes of rural life on gentry estates in the familiar Turgenev tradition. The editor of the magazine, and perhaps the author, who was barely keeping up with the installments as they fell due, had no clear idea of what was coming. The editor later recalled that Leskov

> began to familiarize me with his plan for a big novel called *No Way Out* and loved to recount in detail the contents of certain chapters. I saw that it was a broad picture of the revolutionary upheaval of that time, which would include provincial life and the Petersburg of the radical youth and even the Polish uprising. The plan looked very attractive to a young editor in search of interesting contributions for his magazine. And in the first—very lengthy—section of the novel there was as yet nothing that might become ticklish from the point of view of the liberal orientation of the magazine.[2]

At the beginning of book 2 the scene shifts from the country to the Moscow of 1861. To anyone who knew the Moscow journalists of that time, the prototypes of Leskov's characters were all too obvious. It was increasingly evident that *No Way Out* was a roman à clef and that its spirit was not just antiradical but personally vindictive. As early as June 1864 the well-known radical publicist Varfolomei Zaitsev was describing the novel as "a monstrosity which is simply dumbfounding: you read, and you can't believe your eyes, it's simply pitch dark. Actually this is simply a collection of poorly overheard gossip carried over into literature."[3] Zaitsev goes on to offer the first recorded key to the novel's real-life prototypes, stating—though obliquely—that the marquise de Baral, who plays a prominent part in the Moscow section of the novel, is a portrait of Leskov's erstwhile patroness, Countess Salias de Tournemire.

In fact, the whole Salias circle is there, much as Leskov remembered it from the summer and autumn of 1861. The countess's son Yevgeny Salias (Orest or "Onicha" de Baral in the novel), later a well-known historical novelist, but then a university student; the countess's factotum on *Russian Speech*, Yevgeny Feoktistov (Sakharov in the novel), who later rose to be chief censor under Alexander III, a position which gave him the opportunity, in 1889, to take belated vengeance on Leskov by "arresting" the sixth volume of his collected works; Leskov's mysterious friend Artur Benni (Wilhelm Reiner in the novel); Benni's sweetheart Marya Kopteva (Liza Bakhareva); Leskov's quondam friend, the ill-starred Andrei Nichiporenko (Prokhor Parkhomenko); the countess's close friends, the Novosiltsev (Yaroslavtsev) sisters, who had so angered Leskov by taking his wife's part in her dispute with him; Yevgeny Salias's friend, the pure-hearted young revolutionary Ivan Kelsiev (Persiantsev); and many others not identifiable at this distance in time.[4]

Leskov's picture of the Salias world emphasizes its futility, the emptiness of its inhabitants' claim to represent a force for progress. The radicals Parkhomenko and Bychkov are boorish and bloodthirsty, the liberal marquise a windbag and a posturer, her son a milksop, her assistant Sakharov a hypocrite. There are, however, exceptions. At this point in the novel Wilhelm Reiner perhaps remains too "enigmatic" to be judged, but Persiantsev is different. Unlike the others, Persiantsev is generous in his private life and courageous in his actions, however mistaken in his ideas, which inevitably lead to frustration and defeat. Likewise Liza Bakhareva, intelligent and sincere though a bit acerbic, achieves nothing except emancipation from her family, and even that at tremendous emotional cost. Dr. Rozanov, the author's alter ego, also accomplishes little in the outside world, but he does learn from experience. The lesson he learns is that with such people as the Salias entourage, liberals and radicals alike, there is no way out: nothing but vanity of vanities and striving after wind.

Some of the activities of that circle—the student revolt of October 1861, the underground printing press of Ivan Kelsiev, and the agitation among the Old Believers—have already been treated as biographical facts in the life of Leskov, recorded in the novel as the deeds of Dr. Rozanov. But *No Way Out* is not only a compendium of historical facts, even camouflaged ones. Writing in the aftermath of the Polish rebellion of 1863 and feeling an upsurge of patriotism, reinforced by his unpleasant experiences among Poles in Paris, and furious with the radicals, whom he considered allies of the Poles, Leskov did not stick at using his novel for the propagation of crude anti-Polish myths. He invoked the specter, conjured up by Katkov, of a huge plot against the Russian people and the Orthodox God engineered by Jesuit manipulators of their Polish puppets. In the Moscow section of *No Way Out* we are led into the inner sanctum of Jesuit intrigue in Russia, a room equipped with false doors and invisible speaking tubes. There we meet Canon Krakówka, a latter-day disguise for the veteran Polish officer Władysław Jaroszyński, and his slavish lieutenant Kazimerz Racyborski. These nefarious plotters hold the naive Russian revolutionaries in the palms of their hands: "There is nothing more useful than fools and enthusiasts," says Pan Kazimerz. "They can be made to do anything" (2:317). The scene reeks of artificiality, weakening the artistic integrity of the book and showing Leskov's unfortunate willingness to cater to vulgar prejudice.

In the third part the scene shifts to Petersburg in 1863. Leskov now undertakes a hatchet job on the Znamensky Commune, organized by Vasily Sleptsov, who appears in the novel under the name of Pyotr Beloyartsev. Inspired by Fourier and by Chernyshevsky's novel *What Is to Be Done?* Sleptsov had organized this phalanstery as a microcosm of socialism, a demonstration of how people of good will, even in an acquisitive and corrupt society, might live together in harmony. A group of single young people, especially women, who had difficulty finding suitable accommodations, by pooling resources and sharing expenses, could make much more pleasant living arrangements than they could obtain as individuals. One might think that the project would have appealed to the practical Leskov, since Sleptsov was not merely theorizing but attempting to "do" something to effect a concrete improvement in at least a few people's lives.

In fact, in that very year Leskov had written a rather favorable review of Chernyshevsky's novel.[5] Rightly denying that it is in any sense a work of art, Leskov recognizes that *What Is to Be Done?* must be regarded as a disguised treatise, its fictional form necessitated by the author's situation (Chernyshevsky wrote the book in prison). Leskov is pleased to discover that Chernyshevsky is not a "beyond-the-clouds dreamer" or a "desperate theoretician who . . . wants to create all at once a new heaven and a new earth"; he understands that "il faut prendre le monde comme il est, pas comme il doit être," and he advises his readers to engage in constructive work without exploiting others. Chernyshevsky's "new people" are in Leskov's view simply *good* people—industrious, generous, willing to respect the rights of others. But good people, Leskov points out, are always in a minority. Genuine nihilists, like Turgenev's Bazarov, have knowledge and strength of character, but there are very few Bazarovs. What exist in plenty are self-styled nihilists, capable only of mouthing fashionable phrases, verbally repudiating all existing institutions and customs, but in practice lazy, ignorant, cowardly, and untrustworthy.

Sleptsov was not likely, whatever he accomplished, to qualify in Leskov's eyes as a "genuine" nihilist: of all his radical enemies, Sleptsov was one of the most hated. The reasons for his animosity can only be guessed at. The two men had met in the Salias circle in Moscow in 1861, and they encountered each other in Petersburg the following year.[6] Probably there were many other meetings; the world of Russian literati was small. After the Petersburg fires and the Polish revolt Leskov had become sharply critical of the revolutionaries, and his new position involved a partial repudiation of his own former associations. In a sense Leskov was indeed a traitor to the radicals' cause, and this fact must have troubled him. Even if Sleptsov did not personally charge Leskov with treason, Sleptsov became a living symbol of Leskov's guilt. For Sleptsov had been confronted with essentially the same choices and had made the opposite decisions. A nobleman, Sleptsov had openly thrown in his lot with the ex-seminarians and had never gone back on that decision. Leskov needed to reassure himself that his decision had been right. Sleptsov, who made the opposite one, had therefore to be punished for it and his most ambitious social undertaking, the Znamensky Commune, heavily doused with satirical venom.

Beloyartsev (that is, Sleptsov), an artist by profession, is described in the Moscow section of the novel as caring nothing for social ideals, interested only in art and women. But in book 3, though still an aesthete and a libertine, he has become a *civic* artist. Having painted a social content picture entitled *The Father of a Family*, he "began to exhibit himself as a Citizen, lowered his eyebrows and began to sigh civic sighs" (2:547). He is, in short, like all the false nihilists, a poseur.

Beloyartsev has organized a Domus Concordiae, which purports to be a demonstration of practical idealism. Its high-sounding platform proclaims as its aim "to protect the working proletariat from arbitrary abuse of power, from the insults and acts of violence perpetrated by fattening capital and to open the eyes of a blind society by means of a living example to the possibility of a correct organization of labor, without capitalist entrepreneurs" (2:549). In brief, the commune was to be a lever with which to move society and transform the world. But what was it in fact, as Leskov portrays it? An unattractive apartment in a distant quarter of Petersburg, inconvenient, expensive, possible only because a loan has been treated as a subsidy, inhabited by seven or eight quarrelsome young people, led by a pretentious and irresponsible windbag. It is not merely an "absurd and stupid house" (2:646), as Liza Bakhareva calls it when she leaves it forever; it is a profanation of the ideals of the martyr Chernyshevsky.

Leskov has been much criticized for his "slander" of the Sleptsov commune.[7] It is argued that although objectively the Znamensky Commune was not a success—it soon disintegrated because of financial difficulties as well as discord among its members[8]—it should be given credit as an admirable attempt to put into practice some of the ideas of the pre-Marxian socialists. (Such an argument, of course, depends partly on a prior commitment to socialist values.) Whether one shares this admiration or not, however, it does seem probable that Sleptsov's motives were more idealistic than Leskov gives him credit for. It is certainly clear that Leskov's own motives in fictionally belittling the commune were hardly as immaculate as he later claimed. Although such a notorious fiasco may well have been, as Leskov believed, harmful rather than helpful to the socialist cause, his aim in publicizing an exaggerated and one-sided version of it was not that of an objective historian seeking only to record the truth about his time.

In Leskov's view, such buffoons and scoundrels as Sleptsov and his cohorts contaminated the ideals they professed to serve. With such people there was indeed no way out. But they were not quite the whole story: for a hundred Sleptsovs there was one Chernyshevsky. Although even Chernyshevsky could accomplish little with such followers, at least one could admire his moral grandeur. And Leskov always had an eye for moral beauty. Among the revolutionaries he found it in Benni and Ivan Kelsiev, and he places them in his novel as symbols of the incorruptibility of true virtue. "The strong characters and spiritual idealism of the heroes of *No Way Out* have always been dear to me," Leskov said in the 1890s. "I did not share in their practical activities, but I knew how to distinguish the genuine radicals from the imitation ones."[9]

This was invariably Leskov's second defense when he was criticized for *No Way Out* (the first being censorship): "In *No Way Out* I showed the attractive type of Russian revolutionaries: Reiner, Liza, and Pomada. Let them show me another work in Russian literature in which genuine, and not self-styled nihilists are so dispassionately and sympathetically treated. For there are attractive and noble people in every party. I found them in the persons of Reiner, Liza Bakhareva, and Pomada."[10]

In 1871 Leskov took pride in the fact (at least he claims it for a fact) that two prominent radicals had given Liza their endorsement: "To this day Shelgunov and Tsebrikova praise Liza, saying that although I 'sought to debase' this type, I had not done so, but *alone* had depicted the 'new woman' better than the friends of their party. In truth I never sought to debase her, but wrote only the *truth of the day*, and if she came out better than with other masters, it is because in her I gave room for the great strength of tradition and the practices of a Christian, or at least a good family."[11] Liza Bakhareva is indeed one of the most successful characterizations in the book, although not exactly in the way Leskov means. A self-willed, mettlesome, capricious young lady who fights herself free from her family, endures her father's curse, and flees to the House of Harmony, where she constitutes the major opposition to Beloyartsev—the portrait is hardly an ideal, but it is thoroughly believable. In later years Leskov spoke of her as if she were one of his saints, but the image in the novel is far from saintly. Perhaps Leskov forgot that he had Rozanov denounce her for her cruelty to the feckless Pomada, or that he had her turn yellow after breaking with Rozanov and telling him he was "an alien person and a pitiful mediocrity who vexed her" (2:417). She does preserve her independence of mind and spirit, however, and her ends, if not her means, are irreproachable. Furthermore, she eventually makes up with Rozanov. In short, she is a believably complex character: basically decent, but a bit prickly.

If it were not for the old chestnut that her hair turns gray overnight after she sees Reiner executed, Leskov's characterization of Liza would have been a notable artistic success. Perhaps her subsequent death from pneumonia is also too hasty—Leskov seems anxious to kill off all the "genuine nihilists" he professes to admire. (Perhaps their death is a necessary ingredient of their genuineness.) Her last words bring out both the courage behind her negativism and its futility. After refusing to allow a priest to confess her, she pronounces her own last judgment: "With them [the nihilists] I have at least hatred in common, at least the inability to make peace with this society with which you have all made your peace. But with you—nothing" (2:694). With the word "nothing" she expires.

Though Liza Bakhareva is more important within the framework of *No Way Out*, her devoted friend Reiner (Benni) looms larger as a permanent symbol in Leskov's mind, one that haunted him to the end of his life.[12] In his biography of Benni, "An Enigmatic Man," written in 1869, at a time when Leskov's rage against the radicals was at its very highest pitch, he was to treat his late friend rather satirically, as an "honest maniac," purehearted but ineffectual. Correspondingly, the early 1860s, the classic era in Russia of social idealism, is described in "An Enigmatic Man" as a "comic time," a period typified by the absurd antics of nihilist buffoons. In *No Way Out*, however, the very same period is called a "great, poetic epoch" (2:135). A great, poetic epoch requires heroic characters, and Wilhelm Reiner is Leskov's attempt to transform Benni into an unambiguous revolutionary hero. The original Benni is still apparent, but it is a Benni cleansed of his quixoticism and blown up to titanic dimensions.

First of all, he is given a more impressive revolutionary genealogy. Reiner descends not, like Benni, from Polish Protestants but from a glorious line of Swiss republicans. With a Swiss father and a Russian mother, he had been brought up on stories of William Tell and the fiery verses of Ferdinand Freiligrath, the poet of German liberty and friend of Marx. During his boyhood the family had been visited in Switzerland by a wonderful Russian, a "sensitive, soft, and talented man," who, "pushing his rebellious mane back behind his ears, in a trembling and nervous voice and with sparkling eyes unfolded to the old man [Reiner's father] his youthful hopes and passionate longings" (2:276-277). The Russian reader of 1864 recognized here a portrait of the young Herzen, whose name could not be mentioned in print. Herzen left a deep imprint on Reiner's heart, and at the age of twenty-two he set off for London to seek out the great revolutionist, also bearing letters to Freiligrath and Marx. From this point on, although he is better supplied with introductions to famous revolutionaries, Reiner's life resembles that of Benni. In London he becomes a full-fledged socialist of the Herzen school, believing in the Russian peasant commune as the prototype of the social forms toward which humanity should be striving. Before long he sets off for Russia to work in the revolutionary underground.

Reiner appears in the Moscow salon of the marquise de Baral and in the secret headquarters of the Jesuits masquerading as revolutionaries. In both places he holds himself aloof from the buffoonery of his pseudo-revolutionary comrades. The discerning eye of the Jesuit sees him as an "enthusiast and Neoplatonist" and "not a fool" (2:316). But no one seems sure who he is and what he is doing, and his mysteriousness gives rise to rumors that he may be an agent of the police.

In book 3, the Petersburg section, Reiner wanders in and out of the action. He is an interested observer of the infamies of Beloyartsev's House of Harmony, where Liza lives. Their love affair develops in chaste Victorian fashion, Liza being given the traditional opportunity to show her devotion by nursing Reiner when he comes down with pneumonia. By 1863, Reiner, who had come to Russia believing that "a revolution might break out at any moment" (2:287), is forced to recognize that "with such gentlemen as Krasin, as Beloyartsev, as the multitude of their kind there is absolutely *no way out*."[13] Though a socialist and an internationalist, Reiner decides to throw in his lot with that of the insurgent Poles, hoping that their revolution will create a Poland "repentant in the face of the people" and will grant land to the peasants (2:658). Reiner has none of Benni's genuine Polish background, but he somewhere has miraculously acquired a perfect knowledge of Polish; as Pan Kula he leads an armed band of Polish revolutionaries in the Belovezha Forest against Russian troops. He is captured and eventually executed. This martyr's death does not bring any nearer the ideals Reiner sought to serve, but it is at least unambiguously tragic. It lacks the absurd pointlessness of the real Benni's death as described in "An Enigmatic Man": while serving as a correspondent at the Battle of Mentana in 1867, Benni was accidentally wounded in the hand and subsequently died of gangrene.

In his characterization of Reiner, Leskov could justly claim that in a novel written against the nihilists he had presented one of them as a hero, indeed a saint. All the elements of traditional sainthood are present: early sense of vocation; undeviating purposefulness in pursuit of an ideal; selfless generosity; perseverance in the face of false accusations; rigid sexual purity; and the death of a martyr. While the sainthood of Benni in "An Enigmatic Man" is that of a holy innocent, a fool in Christ, the sainthood of Reiner is of a higher moral order: it is the conscious and total dedication of self by a man of great intelligence, energy, and inner strength.

Although all his life he remained proud of *No Way Out*, Leskov was aware that as a novel it had serious defects. In the "Explanation" attached to the last installment in *Library for Reading* he admitted that it was "a hasty, journalistic job. This novel was not subjected to any careful revising and very probably will prove unsatisfactory even to the most favorably disposed critic."[14] Later he wrote privately that "the novel was written all in haste and was printed directly from

131

scraps of paper not infrequently written in pencil at the printer's [. . .] The novel bears the marks of my haste and my inexperience. I consider it the most honorable deed of my life, but its success I attribute not to my art, but to the accuracy with which I understood the time and the people of this 'comic epoch' " (10:168-169). Leskov never tired of describing the severe censorwhip to which *No Way Out* was subjected: three regular censors went over the text, each making excisions or requiring revisions, and then the manuscript was sent to the Third Section (the secret police) for another going over. *No Way Out* does show the marks of the censors' ruthlessness; but the fact remains that Leskov never made any effort to restore the novel to its original form, although it was reprinted several times, and in periods when the censors would have been less concerned about the sensitive political topics of 1864. In 1871 Leskov claimed that he had proof sheets for the precensorship text but had not tried to reintroduce the excised portions because his publisher, Mavriky Volf, a Pole, was afraid of including even more scenes offensive both to Poles and to radicals (10:168-169). Yet further unaltered editions were brought out in 1879 and 1887 with an ultra-Russian publisher, A. S. Suvorin. In 1891 Leskov wrote that Volf had lost or "perhaps hidden from me" the single proof-sheet copy containing the lost chapters.[15] Whatever the truth of these assertions, at a deeper level it seems clear that the lamentations about censorship were largely excuses. Leskov's instinct told him that the artistic faults of *No Way Out* were beyond his power to remedy. He did not care to engage himself with it again.

Perhaps the greatest weakness of *No Way Out* is lack of structure. Characters wander in and out without any explanation; incidents are introduced that have nothing to do with the plot or with any of the major charcters; elaborate background is provided for certain minor characters, while several major ones are left without formative experiences. Great pains are initially lavished, for example, on the characterization of Jenny Glavatskaya, a schoolmate of Liza Bakhareva, but by the end of the first part she has dropped out of sight. In book 3 she abruptly reappears in Petersburg—apparently so that her house can provide a meeting place for more important characters. A whole chapter is expended on the heroic Swiss forebears of Reiner, going back to the Napoleonic wars, but on Rozanov's childhood there is scarcely a line, though he is a more central character. (This fact has more than literary significance, since Rozanov is an image of the author himself.) The wretched informer and murderer Soloveychik is likewise unexpectedly resurrected, in the shape of the prosperous Baron Alterson, married to Liza Bakhareva's sister Sofia. Not only are both the resurrection and the metamorphosis implausible, but the novel's moral quality, by which Leskov professed to set so much store, is badly tarnished by the obvious anti-Semitism of this characterization. Finally, in the last chapter people appear who have not been mentioned for hundreds of pages, to the extent that Leskov feels obliged to make an apology: "On the ninth of May, on the occasion of Nikolai Stepanovich's nameday, there was a party at the Vyazmitinovs'. Besides the usual guests at this house, we will encounter a number of guests here whom we don't know at all and several individuals who scarcely flashed before the reader's eyes at the very beginning of the novel and whom the reader has had every right to forget by this time."[16]

Despite its weaknesses, *No Way Out* shows marks of talent. Certain characterizations, especially the positive ones, have vitality. Leskov reported that "the late Apollon Grigoriev was delighted by three of the characters: 1) Abbess Agniya; 2) old Bakharev; and 3) the student Pomada" (10:169). The secret of these characters' success is that they are relatively minor figures on whom neither the plot nor the message of the novel depends. They can therefore be given a more plausible mixture of good and bad traits than the "loaded" major characters. The abbess is a wise if rather despotic ruler of her cenobitic domain; Bakharev, Liza's father, is a despot and a blusterer but has a kind heart (like Leskov and Rozanov, he too is afflicted with a shrewish wife named Olga); and Pomada is everyone's doormat, never so happy as when he is being trod upon.

Of the satirical characterizations, the most successful are those in which some humor is mixed with the venom. In Bertoldi, for example, characteristically known only by her last name, Leskov combines ridicule with good will. She is the epitome of the female nihilist, with her cropped hair, her naive faith in Beloyartsev, her refusal to shake hands on the grounds that the handshake is a symbol of social hypocrisy, her feeling "insulted as a woman and as a human being" when a man picks up her handkerchief for her, and her futile but somehow touching projects in revolutionary self-education ("I am working on Proudhon").[17]

The success of such balanced characterizations only underscored the failure of the onesided caricatures. By the end of his life Leskov was able to recognize the problem:

In my *No Way Out* Bertoldi, for all her severities and extravagances, is a simple and honest child. Her nihilist peculiarities are
recorded, but her human character is not forgotten. This is true of
Reiner, Liza Bakhareva, Pomada, and Bertoldi; and they are all
live people. But when I forgot this inexorable requirement of artistic creation and portrayed only nihilist features, ignoring the
whole human being, the result was one-sided denunciatory
figures, marionettes, and not living types from the nihilist mold.
These were pieces of patchwork, and very annoying and notice-
able ones.[18]

The trouble with much of *No Way Out* is that Leskov is too close to
his material. Art does not give the illusion of life; it is confused with
life. The emotions Leskov feels about the prototypes of the characters
are directed at the characters themselves. The novel thus becomes an
imaginary reenactment of a real past in the course of which an omnipotent author, whose alter ego is a character in the action, metes out
rewards and punishments to himself, his enemies, and his friends.
Such lack of detachment may explain why Leskov never became a
successful novelist. The novel as he conceived it, and as he tried to
write it in *No Way Out* and *At Daggers Drawn*, deals with the lives of
characters who belong to the author's own social sphere, who live
more or less the kind of life he himself lived, that is, the life of a
Russian intellectual. In both cases a novel about intellectuals turns
into a novel against particular intellectuals. Later Leskov seems to
have recognized, perhaps subconsciously, that since for him inner
detachment was impossible he had to stop writing about people like
himself. He substituted difference in social class for the emotional
distance he was unable to achieve otherwise. This stratagem had
worked well in "The Musk-ox," "The Life of a Peasant Martyress,"
and "The Mocker," where the settings are remote from the battles and
bitternesses of Leskov's real world. After *Cathedral Folk* (written
1867-1871), in which he tried to bring together in one book the
squabbles of Petersburg intellectuals and the tranquillity of the provincial clergy, Leskov finally gave up the attempt. He became a great
writer only by refusing to write about his own milieu, except in the
form of reminiscences. And even the reminiscences are almost always
memories of times and places as remote as possible from the Petersburg present.

Even before the serial publication of *No Way Out* had been completed, articles began appearing in the radical press reviling the traitor

and informer Stebnitsky (Leskov). There was an insidious piece by A. S. Suvorin, then still a radical, ominously entitled "Omitted Chapters from the Novel *No Way Out*," and filled with "police" innuendoes: "Stebnitsky is a man not without talent, and, moreover, an original one [. . .] Not only can he make up novels with descriptions of the features of certain persons, but he might even serve with success in the investigating line, for instance, as a police inspector's clerk, or supervisor, or some kind of expert."[19] Stooping to the same tactics he professes to deplore in *No Way Out*, Suvorin hints darkly at the skeletons in Leskov's personal closet, some of which he had viewed at Countess Salias's in 1861, in particular suggesting that in his quarrels with his wife Leskov had sometimes resorted to physical violence. An artist as libel-prone as Leskov, Suvorin writes, might paint a picture of him picking someone's pocket or with one hand writing a liberal treatise about women's rights "and with the other dragging his wife about by the hair."[20]

Infuriated by the taunts of the radical critics, Leskov felt obliged to defend himself in an "Explanation" attached to the last installment of *No Way Out*—in fact more a shrill scream of rage than a reasoned argument. First he makes, though ambiguously, the patently false denial that any real people are portrayed in *No Way Out*:

> They [the radical critics] could not forgive me for this political tendency, and they seized upon an *external* correspondence dug up by someone between certain characters of the novel and living persons from the literary world, and off they went [. . .] I affirm positively that in the entire novel *No Way Out* there is not a single word which could violate the privacy of anyone's family secrets. All the characters of this novel and all their actions are pure invention, and the apparent resemblances (if anyone imagines such to exist) can neither offend nor compromise anyone.

But then, after denying any resemblances, he goes on to assert that even if there were some, such things had happened in the case of other writers, such as Pisemsky, Turgenev, and Sukhovo-Kobylin, and nobody had waxed indignant against *them*. Having thus indirectly denied his own denial, Leskov makes himself look even worse by vulgar mud-slinging. The gradualist journalists do not, he avers, engage in personal talebearing, but if they did, they could tell such stories as "how a certain poet [Kurochkin?] comes to a meeting, gets drunk, and cannot refrain from trying to test whether the crinolines of the ladies who pass by are fastened on tightly."[21]

The counterattack was not long in coming. For this operation the radicals brought forward Dmitry Pisarev, who after Dobrolyubov's demise and Chernyshevsky's exile had become the chief radical ideologue—obliged, because of the peculiarities of the censorship system, to masquerade as a literary critic. Though only twenty-five years old, from his prison cell in the Fortress of Peter and Paul, Pisarev had taken on more formidable antagonists than Leskov. He was engaged in a duel with the entire Russian establishment, its tsar, its church, and even its aesthetic deity, Pushkin, whom Pisarev had just knocked off his hitherto solid pedestal. To demolish a mere Leskov was child's play. He was disposed of along with Apollon Grigoriev (treated with some restraint, since he had only just died), Pisemsky (for *Stormy Sea*, another antinihilist novel), Ostrovsky (whose *Commander* showed that he had written himself out), and several others—all in the course of a "Stroll through the Gardens of Russian Literature" in the March 1865 issue of *Russian Word*.

Pisarev is quick to seize upon the contradiction in Leskov's "Explanation" between his blanket denial that there are any portraits of real persons and his obscure references to "external" correspondences:

Note in the first place that he always speaks about an *external*, a purely external resemblance, and that not once does he use the word "accidental resemblance"—the only word that would completely vindicate him at once. If Stebnitsky had said "What are you after me for? I have never in my life seen the people you profess to recognize in my novel; an accidental resemblance has occurred." If he had said that, I say, his critics could do nothing but shake their heads in perplexity. But he did not say that; therefore, in all probability he *could not* say that [. . .] Thus for us it is no longer a matter of doubt that Stebnitsky did portray his acquaintances [. . .] If he had copied his good-for-nothings from living models who behaved like good-for-nothings in real life, he would only have been treating them according to their deserts. But just imagine the following situation. Stebnitsky notes down your characteristics, the peculiarities of your attire and your walk, your habits, your way of speaking. He studies you in every detail and then creates in his novel a notorious swindler who is an much like you in all his *external* attributes as two drops of water. Yet in the meantime you are the most honorable of men and are guilty only of having admitted to your house this eavesdropping and spying gentleman. At the same time all your acquaintances recognize *you* in the portrait of the swindler and with amazement question one another as to whether there might not be some measure of truth in what was written about you [. . .] Furthermore, in Stebnitsky's novel it is not swindlers that are portrayed, but "something still worse" [revolutionaries]; so that to find oneself among the ranks of people who are "something still worse" may even be more dangerous than being regarded as a swindler.

Pisarev prolongs the agony for another page. Then, suddenly turning serious, he pronounces his famous sentence:

I am very much interested in the following two questions: 1) Can there be found in Russia a single magazine—other than *Russian Messenger*—which would dare print in its pages anything emanating from the pen of Stebnitsky and signed with his name? 2) Can there be found in Russia a single honest writer who is so careless and indifferent to his reputation that he would agree to work for a magazine which adorns itself with the novels and stories of Stebnitsky? These questions are very interesting for a psychological test of our literary world.[22]

This was a real excommunication. By the highest priest of Russian radicalism Leskov had been read out, not only from Russian literature, but from the very company of honest men. From that time forth, in the eyes of most Russian intellectuals Leskov was a pariah, a man who had sold out to reaction. Rumors circulated that *No Way Out* had been written on order from the Third Section, which was supposed to have paid Leskov 10,000 rubles for it.[23] "When I appeared in society," Leskov recounted much later, "people picked up their hats and went away; in restaurants in my hearing people deliberately berated the author of *No Way Out*."[24]

Pisarev's admonition to magazines not to besmirch their pages with the name of Stebnitsky was quite effective. For many years Leskov indeed had great difficulty finding outlets for his works. There was, as Pisarev predicted, Katkov's *Russian Messenger*; Pisarev's excommunication undoubtedly helped to drive Leskov into Katkov's camp. By 1875, however, Leskov had virtually broken with the Moscow conservatives, yet this break still did not bring forgiveness from the radicals or even the liberals. It was not until nearly 1890 that he began to find his way back into liberal organs like *Messenger of Europe*. In the meantime, he was reduced, as he told Suvorin in 1888 (with a good deal of exaggeration), to "twisting out little articles in a monks' barbershop for the *Orthodox Review* at thirty rubles apiece while suffering need and unemployment, at a time when my energy was bursting at the seams."[25]

Leskov's ostracism by the radical critics and their followers provided an ideal foundation for the self-righteous rationalizations by means of which he deflected his own feelings of guilt. Persecuted by the censors for a novel rumored to have been paid for by the police, damned by the radicals as a traitor, and called dishonest by Pisarev— Leskov had good reason to feel hounded, harassed, and hated from all sides. Once again he, and even his publisher, received threats of murder and arson.[26] In the face of such outrageous aggression from his enemies, Leskov could once again cast himself in the comfortable role of innocent victim. He was then free to escalate the war even further.

Although he occasionally admitted to a few errors of taste or judgment in the "photographs" he had incorporated into *No Way Out*,[27] in later years Leskov retained a protective affection for this first novel, glossing over its faults and constructing a gratifying image of his motives and accomplishments in writing it. Like David against Goliath, he had attacked the nihilists in the heyday of their power, regardless of the consequences to himself; he had called attention to the impracticality of their program, the corruption of their spirit, and the contamination of their ranks. *No Way Out*, Leskov maintained, was both a prophetic book and an accurate record of its time; someday historians would have to turn to this novel to learn the truth about the 1860s.[28]

Unfortunately, like most such self-flattering reconstructions, this gratifying picture, although it does have some elements of truth, is hardly justified by the historical reality of *No Way Out*.

7

Katerina Bubnova

After his final separation in 1862 from Olga Vasilievna, Leskov was left in the anomalous state of a "wifeless husband." Russian law did not recognize insanity as grounds for divorce; the Orthodox clergy, which had jurisdiction over such matters, interpreted the Slavonic equivalent of "in sickness and in health, until death us do part" with rigid literalism. Among his many other irritations, resentment of this inflexibility may have been one of the causes of Leskov's gradual disillusionment with the church.

Certainly the subject of divorce was much on Leskov's mind. In an article written in 1866, for instance, he manages both to deplore the "free love" advocated by the nihilists and to propose a reform of the legal code to permit every citizen just one divorce so that unfortunate mistakes could be corrected. He disapproves, however, of the king of Denmark for setting a bad example by contracting a third marriage.[1] In several articles in the 1880s Leskov shows himself exceptionally well informed, even a specialist, on this subject. In the course of a vehement argument in favor of transferring jurisdiction over divorce cases from the ecclesiastical to the civil courts, he injects what sounds like a personal note: "Among the [suggested] grounds for divorce, insanity has frequently been mentioned, and even sharp incompatibility of character, when conjugal life becomes a real hellish torment, about which only a married man can have any idea, and not a monk who has never known domestic life."[2] Later Leskov wrote a long, substantial article on Russian divorce law that was suppressed by ecclesiastical censorship.[3]

Divorce on grounds of insanity would certainly have made Leskov's personal life much easier. But even if this solution had been possible, his wife was not certified as insane until 1878. In the meantime, he formed other attachments. We know next to nothing about them, however, for the years before 1864. One memoirist who met Leskov in the early 1860s says simply that he had "many romances" and "had success with women"—the latter is a conventional phrase in Russian and does not necessarily imply that he was an arrant Don Juan. Leskov himself, in a letter to Suvorin twenty-five years later, recalls the "Petersburg period of the Sleptsov communes" as a time of "bed-hopping" (*ložeperemennoe span'e*) and of "morning tea à trois." "You," he continues, "were never depraved; but I immersed myself in those depths and took fright of the abyss."[4]

Sometime in 1864, during a visit to his relatives in Kiev, Leskov met the woman who was to be the great love of his life. At twenty-five, Katerina Stepanovna Bubnova was by all accounts a remarkable woman, combining beauty with intelligence, intellectuality, and an independent spirit. An early marriage to a ne'er-do-well had left her with four children and a good deal of bitter experience. Leskov's intelligence and vigor must have attracted her, and she was bold enough not only to enter into a love affair with him but in 1865 to move to Petersburg to live with him. Her oldest son, seven-year-old Nikolai, she took with her and placed in a German boarding school near Leskov's apartment; the other children stayed in Kiev with their father and a governess. In July 1866 a son, Andrei, was born to Leskov and Katerina Stepanovna. From financial necessity, he was apparently boarded in an orphanage for the first two years of his life.[5]

Leskov's surviving letters from before 1868 are practically all pleas for money from editors and publishers, and it seems likely that Katerina Stepanovna was obliged to work to help maintain their household. (Leskov was keenly interested in the problem of gainful employment for upper-class women, and *Bypassed*, the novella he wrote in 1865, deals extensively with this topic.) The couple's circumstances considerably improved, however, in 1868, when Bubnov unexpectedly died and Katerina Stepanovna—or her children—inherited his property. She then brought her three other children to Petersburg, rescued little Andrei from the orphanage, and set up with Leskov a sizable household on Furstadt Street, near the Tauride Garden laid out by Potyomkin.[6]

Leskov seemed to have learned something from his unhappy marriage. This time he had not made a thoughtless selection of a mate under the influence of "the moon, a sweater, and a brooch" (9:340), as he wrote later, referring to the sexual lures so indignantly described by Tolstoy in "The Kreutzer Sonata," but had found a thoroughly suitable match: an attractive and intelligent woman willing to flout convention in her pursuit of happiness. Having found her, Leskov was not frightened off by anxiety about taking responsibility for her numerous family. To all appearances, it was a strong and mature attachment, one made to last.

It is possible that Leskov's romance with Katerina Bubnova is described in *No Way Out*, probably the most personal of all his works. There she appears, if the identification is correct, under the name of Polinka Kalistratova.[7] Certainly a juxtaposition of the fictional Kalistratova with the real Bubnova shows considerable similarity between them, if we make some allowances for intentional camouflage and perhaps unconscious idealization. Here is Polinka, as she first appears in *No Way Out*: "This person was young and not so much pretty as elegant in her graceful simplicity. She was tall and very thin, blonde with black eyes, a translucent pink face, a supple figure, and extraordinarily soft, white hands . . . She spoke in a soft, broken voice, such a voice as people begin to use when they are recovering from a severe case of pneumonia" (2:433). And this is Katerina Bubnova, as her son describes her: "A tall, well-built brunette, with light blue eyes, who knew how to smile in the Ukrainian style, without using her lips; thin, so-called 'classical' features, businesslike, original in conversation, well read, modest in her personal requirements, and quite alien to what in later days came to be called by the foreign word 'flirt.' "[8] To this may be added another description by a woman friend: "Katerina Stepanovna was a striking beauty: a brunette, above average in height, with large, expressive gray eyes, very graceful and elegant."[9] Despite the different coloration of eyes and hair—changes an author might make for purposes of camouflage —the two physical images are similar.

Both women came from well-off provincial families. Katerina Stepanovna, however, was one of six children, while Polinka, an only child, was left an orphan early in life and was exploited by callous uncles—a change perhaps dictated by the wish to make Polinka more pitiable and her illicit love affair with Dr. Rozanov thus pardonable. Both women had been separated from their husbands after very unhappy marriages. But whereas Bubnov was merely irresponsible, Kalistratov is a thoroughgoing scoundrel who extorts money from his wife by threatening to kill their child and is eventually arrested for forgery. The transformation serves to free her from moral responsibility for abandoning her husband and taking a lover. A similar guilt-minimizing purpose may be discerned in the changes Leskov introduces in Polinka's family situation. Katerina Bubnova had four reasonably healthy children by her husband; Polinka has only one, and in the course of the novel he dies of hydrocephalus—another pathetic detail designed to arouse sympathy for Polinka. (Perhaps it may also be an indication that Leskov secretly wished he might have his lady without the other man's children.) Finally, Polinka gives birth to a child by Rozanov a year and a half before Katerina Bubnova gave birth to Andrei.

Whether or not Polinka is a portrait of Katerina Bubnova, there can be no doubt that she represents Leskov's feminine ideal. What he seems to admire most is her softness, symbolized by her hands. She is unaggressive, noncritical, undemanding, gentle, accepting—the very antithesis of the "coachmen in skirts" for whom Leskov felt such an aversion, and who reminded him of his "quick and impatient" mother and of his accusing, hysterical wife. Polinka is not inquisitive about Rozanov's past, but when he confides his marital troubles to her, she listens sympathetically and takes his part. Even when he indulges in a bout of heavy drinking (rationalized as a permissible escape from the constant warfare with his wife), she nurses him tenderly, if a little didactically, back to sobriety, risking her reputation by (chastely) spending the night in his hotel room. As soon as he has arranged a separation from his wife, she is willing for their love to become a full one, though they cannot be legally married.

Yet this fictional romance, apparently so ideal from Rozanov's point of view, displays some psychological danger signals. Since Rozanov is so closely related to Leskov, and since Polinka may be a retouched portrait of Katerina Bubnova, we may perhaps be justified in drawing some inferences about Leskov's life from *No Way Out*. One of the principal emotions excited by Polinka in her truly miserable state is pity, pity for an inexperienced orphan girl treated with indifference by her uncles and with cruelty by her husband. Filled with protective feelings, Rozanov can take comfort in the notion that in having a love affair he is at the same time nobly rescuing a lady in distress. Polinka's feelings about the doctor are almost a mirror image of his about her. He too is an eminently pitiable figure: a decent, intelligent, and capable man whose life was being ruined by his wife. Her warm heart overflowing, Polinka not only commiserates with Rozanov and comforts him but manages gently to wean him from the bottle to which he had resorted in his despair. Thus these two wronged and unfortunate people join together in the mutually satisfying pastime of pitying and "helping" each other. Yet mutual pity is not a good foundation for a marriage. For one thing, the marriage itself eliminates the only realistic grounds for pity, the bad spouses having been discarded. It may develop that no firmer emotional basis for the relationship is ever built, especially if in one or both of the partners the desire to be pitied is stronger than the desire to love.

The outcome of the relationship between Rozanov and Polinka is not indicated in *No Way Out*. On the next to last page, Rozanov's evil wife is relegated to a convent, and presumably he and Polinka are destined to live happily ever after. Leskov's relationship with Katerina Bubnova had a less pleasant future. Although the early years seem to have passed agreeably enough, eventually the demon in Leskov's character began to assert itself. Demanding and fault-finding, he faced the world around him, and especially those close to him, with a petulant, accusing glare, always eager to point out failings in others and to excuse or deny his own. Apparently, in Leskov's emotional scale of values, more than anything else he cherished the feeling of being wronged. For the sake of that inner glow of self-pity, of regarding himself as the helpless and innocent victim of the sins and shortcomings of others, Leskov in the end was ready to sacrifice just about everything—the satisfactions of family life for himself, and the happiness and well-being of his wives and children.

But for a good many years, as long as the fires of their passion burned bright, the union was a reasonably satisfactory one. Leskov grew fond of the Bubnov children, and they of him: their mutual affection survived even after he had separated from their mother. He set great store by "Dronushka" (Andrei), the only child he and Katerina Stepanovna had together. Officially at least, Leskov cherished an ideal of family *Gemütlichkeit*, a cozy picture of two large and many little heads grouped "around the evening lamp." In fact, however, as his son slyly observes, Leskov himself would quickly get bored in the midst of such idylls and often actually pick a fight in order to have an excuse to stalk off to his study. There were faithfully awaiting him those manuscripts and books with which his relations were in many ways deeper and more satisfying than any he ever had with live human beings.

8

Lady Macbeth

During the fall of 1864, while visiting his relatives in Kiev, working up the final installments of *No Way Out*, and pursuing his love affair with Katerina Bubnova, Leskov somehow found time to complete a novella called *Bypassed* and the famous short story "Lady Macbeth of the Mtsensk District," two works about as far removed in quality as can be imagined. *Bypassed* is banal, derivative, and ridiculous, while "Lady Macbeth of the Mtsensk District" is an acknowledged masterpiece, and after *Cathedral Folk* probably Leskov's best-known work.

Bypassed shares most of the faults, and even some of the characters, of *No Way Out*, but it lacks the immediacy which makes that novel so interesting as a personal document.[1] In *Bypassed* Leskov fails to integrate his perennial antiradical sermon with the love story that provides the framework for the plot; and the love story itself is sentimental and lacking in psychological validity. Again there are gross implausibilities of plot and again there are semidigested autobiographical references. As in *No Way Out*, the hero is an alter ego of the author, a Russian with a Ukrainian background who at the outset of the action is working as a correspondent in Paris. The battered image of poor Olga Vasilievna is given another thorough going-over: she is fictionally incarnated as the wife of the spineless hero, Nestor Dolinsky, who somehow finds himself married to her, even though she is, as the author describes her with a volley of adjectives fired at her like bullets, "sly, traitorously vicious, vain, greedy, vengeful, demanding, and cruel." Again the hero is permitted to console himself with other women.

In so doing, however, Dolinsky must choose between two half-sisters, the elder of whom, Anna, appeals to his "higher nature," rather as a mother, while the other, Dora, is a little spicier and manages to stir him as a male. For the sake of novelistic interest, if nothing else, the victory must go to Dora. But Dora soon sickens with consumption and at last expires ecstatically, like a true Bohèmienne, in her lover's arms. Wracked by grief, Dolinsky ends his days, of all things, as a Jesuit missionary in Paraguay. To a widely traveled friend, who just happens to run into him there, his only words are "Memento mori."

In the midst of all this sentimental balderdash, perhaps partly adapted from Turgenev's *Nest of Gentlefolk* (the basically good, but passive male married to an unscrupulous and dissolute woman, who tries to wreck his last chance for happiness; the monastic ending), Leskov injects his inevitable denunciation of the nihilists. This time he tries to substitute scorn for the indignation of *No Way Out:* the sinister evil-doers of the past have now become simply stupid and dull. As he introduces them to his novel, Leskov comments—only too truthfully—that such people "nowadays are of no interest whatever." Instead of "new people," as Chernyshevsky had called them, Dora rebaptizes them "tiresome people." Unfortunately, this quality infects the novel itself, with its long arguments about materialism, morality, and especially women's rights, which was Leskov's favorite hobbyhorse in those days.[2]

As distinct from the nihilists, who spend all their time merely talking about the disabilities of women, Leskov's heroines are designed to demonstrate in practice what can really be done, even within the existing system, by two intelligent, industrious, and responsible women. Their dressmaking shop, run on ordinary capitalist principles and without pretentious ideological claims, is both successful as an enterprise and, in its small way, a progressive social force: a group of seamstresses, with whom Anna and Dora maintain excellent relations, are provided with secure employment and humane conditions of work. One such shop, Leskov insists, is worth a hundred Utopian dreams about socialistic sewing circles, like the one in Chernyshevsky's *What Is to Be Done?*.

In "Lady Macbeth of the Mtsensk District" Leskov reverted to the method that had worked well in "The Musk-ox" and "The Life of a Peasant Martyress," with the central characters safely "distanced" from him in class and culture.[3] Mtsensk is a small town about thirty-five miles northeast of Oryol; the very name, with its impossible consonant clusters, suggests some quintessentially Slavic backwoods. The author again assumes the congenial pose of the ex-provincial storyteller who regales his sophisticated readers with revelations of life as it is lived by un-Europeanized, ultra-Russian Russians, in an environment to which the author once belonged but has left behind.

Although the narrator's identity is thus essentially the same as in

145

"The Life of a Peasant Martyress," the technique he uses is very different. In "Lady Macbeth" there is no folksy language (except in the speech of lower-class characters), no personal digressions or anecdotes, no chumminess between the narrator and his characters, no obtrusion of the narrator's personality between the reader and the events and characters described. The only specific indication of the narrator's presence is the occasional use of the first-person plural, as in the original title ("Lady Macbeth of Our District"), announcing that the narrator is an insider. Otherwise, Leskov employs in this story, as successfully as he ever did, the more typical nineteenth-century narrative system of the omniscient author who tries to dissolve his personality in the story, making it appear as uncontrived as life itself.

Leskov originally intended "Lady Macbeth" to be the first item in an extended survey of his backwoods domain, a sociology of Oryol Province, presented through sketches of representative female types. In the letter that accompanied the manuscript to the editorial offices of Dostoevsky's *Epoch*, Leskov described his plan: " 'Lady Macbeth of Our District' is the first of a series of sketches of typical characters, female only, of our locality (along the Oka and partly the Volga). I propose to write twelve of these sketches, each one between one and two signatures long, eight from the peasant and merchant milieus and four from the gentry."[4] This project was never carried beyond the first number, although some of the female types were presented in later stories, such as "The Battle-axe" and "Boyarinya Marfa Andreyevna."

The title and the underlying idea for "Lady Macbeth of Our District" were obviously derived from Turgenev's "Hamlet of the Shchigry District," one of the component stories in *A Sportsman's Sketches*. The point of such titles is to juxtapose a Shakespearean archetype at a high level of psychological universalization with a specific, local, utterly Russian, and contemporary milieu. The effect on a Russian reader of that time was almost oxymoronic: how could there be a "Lady Macbeth," especially nowadays, in such a mudhole as Mtsensk? The truth to be demonstrated is that Shakespeare's universals know no boundaries of time or place or class.

The germ of the story goes back to a memory from Leskov's gymnasium days in Oryol, if we can trust the authenticity of an autobiographical fragment of uncertain date. Entitled "How I Learned to Celebrate," it recounts an episode in a neighbor's back garden, seen from the house where Leskov boarded as a gymnasium pupil: "Once one of the neighbors, an old man who had stubbornly kept on living past the age of seventy and who went one summer's day to take a nap under a blackberry bush, had boiling wax poured in his ear by his impatient daughter-in-law. I remember how they buried him. His ear had broken off. Later, on the Ilinka [the public square], she was flogged by the hangman. She was young, and everyone was surprised at how white she was."[5] As he did in speaking of the candles made of human fat in "A Case That Was Dropped," Leskov writes both of the murder and the public flagellation as if they were commonplace events. The writer appears to function as a cinematic camera, neutrally and without emotion recording the movements, shapes, and colors of these gruesome scenes.

In "Lady Macbeth of the Mtsensk District" Leskov supplies the crime with an erotic motivation, which may not have been present in the event he remembered from his youth. As he developed the theme, besides a crime story, it became the most evocative treatment of pure sexuality Leskov ever wrote, and one of the most powerful in all Russian literature. In the most profound of antitheses, murder and sex, love and death, are bound together in an inexorable sequence. In this sense Leskov's heroine is perhaps even more archetypal than her Shakespearean namesake. The original Lady Macbeth, more forceful, willful, and ruthless than her husband, murders out of a lust for power, not so much for his sake as for her own. She wants to be a queen, and since the queen would rule the king, she would rule the country and thus, in effect, be king. The essence of her character is the paradoxical combination of extreme masculine aggressiveness with a female body. The murders of Leskov's heroine, on the contrary, are directly linked to her female sexuality. She murders as a woman in order to achieve a woman's ends: so that she can live and be loved.

The movement of the story follows logically the development of feeling and interaction among the characters. There is nothing here of the additive, string-of-beads system Leskov more frequently employs, no superfluities likely to detract from the emotional intensity of the narrative. "Lady Macbeth" is one of the most condensed and highly charged pieces in Leskov's whole corpus.

The opening chapter provides just enough background for the events that follow. We get an acute sense of the heroine's emotional vacuum, the emptiness of a potentially strong and passionate character never yet aroused to feeling. Katerina Izmailova is a young woman of twenty-four, married for five years to a man past fifty who does not love her and reproaches her constantly, as does his father, for her infertility—even though he had also had no children by his first wife. Father and son are well-to-do merchants, absorbed in their business, in which Katerina has no part. The house is full of servants, and there is little for her to do. Unloved, alone, and most of all bored, she conceals explosive forces beneath her calm and somnolent exterior.

Life comes to her in the form of Sergei, a handsome young employee of her husband. Leskov successfully conveys his physical charm and the sexual electricity that passes between them at their first meeting. Hearing laughter, Katerina wanders into a granary where she finds Sergei teasing the fat cook Aksinya by catching her and weighing her like a sack of flour. Caught up by their frolicsome spirit, Katerina asks to be weighed. She is pleasantly stirred by the clerk's blarney. "I'm surprised," he says, "that you weigh as much as that, Katerina Lvovna. As I see it, somebody ought to carry you around in his arms the whole day long, and even then he wouldn't get tired, but would only feel it a pleasure for himself." Katerina boasts of her strength, for which she used to be famous in her girlhood, and offers to try it against his. Before she knows what is happening, he lifts her high in the air, first pressing her hard against him; then he gently sets her down again. That night Sergei appears at her bedroom door—her husband is away visiting one of his mills—and without much difficulty her marital scruples are overcome.

After this an overpowering passion for Sergei fills Katerina's heart; nothing else matters. When her father-in-law catches the young man climbing down her balcony, he flogs him, locks him up, and then threatens, when his son returns, to flog Katerina and send Sergei to prison. In response Katerina coolly doses his mushrooms with rat poison. His death is easily passed off as an unfortunate mistake with a toxic mushroom. Leskov follows the account of the father-in-law's demise with a potent description of a sultry summer night in the merchant's garden, as Katerina lies with Sergei beneath a flowering apple tree: "The moonlight, penetrating through the leaves and flowers of the apple tree, played in the most fantastic spots of light over the face and the whole figure of Katerina Lvovna, who was lying on her back; the air was calm, only the lightest of warm breezes barely agitated the sleepy leaves and broadcast the delicate aroma of the flowering grasses and trees. There was something oppressive in the air, something conducive to languor, voluptuousness, and dark desires."

Reality, in the form of the husband, returns to shatter this erotic idyll, but Katerina struggles to preserve it. Another murder is necessary. In this crime Sergei assists her: it marks the climax of the action, binding the two protagonists together in blood as in love. The murder scene is described with intensity.

Having received a warning from his father, Katerina's husband comes home alone in the dead of night in order to trap his wife. Katerina, sleeping with Sergei in her conjugal bed, has just had a guilty and prophetic dream: her murdered father-in-law appears to her in the shape of a cat, mocking and threatening her. Awakening from her dream, she hears her husband listening at the door. A tense conversation follows, the husband cold, accusing, confident of his power and authority, Katerina indignantly denying his charges. At last, infuriated by his threats to have her tortured in order to extract the truth, she defiantly brings Sergei into the open. There is now no way out but murder. Katerina employs her vaunted strength to throw her husband to the floor. While Sergei holds him down, she bashes his head with a candlestick holder, and then the two join hands in choking him. They bury him secretly under the house. Since none of the servants knew that the master had returned, no foul play is suspected; he seems to have disappeared on his journey.

Up to this point the line of the action has followed a perfect ascending curve. With the possible exception of the husband's unobserved return—the servants seem singularly heavy sleepers, since they are aroused neither by his entry, during which the dogs bark loudly until they recognize him, nor by the noise of the murder itself—psychological and sequential plausibility has been maintained. But in moving from this climax toward the dénouement, Leskov encounters difficulties, partly inherent in the nature of the action as he has presented it. The resolution of the action requires that the murders be discovered and punished; morality demands that the reader be made to accept, indeed insist on, this retribution. At this point, however, the reader is not ready to do so. Katerina and Sergei are young, they are good-looking, and they are lovers; their two victims are old, ugly, and mean, obstacles to their love. We find ourselves siding with the lovers, despite all indoctrinations of "Thou shalt not kill." One of the reasons why "Lady Macbeth" affects us so strongly is that the story evokes these powerful, presocial emotions, forcing us not only to condone but vicariously to share in two murders.

The author must find some way out of this moral dilemma. So that we can demand justice, our identification with the lovers must be broken. To accomplish this, Leskov suddenly introduces a sickly boy who is a nephew of Katerina's husband and an heir to part of his property. He is thus in some sense an economic rival of Katerina's. Sergei, previously depicted as a carefree and lighthearted Don Juan, now suddenly burns with avaricious jealousy of this unfortunate boy, who will take away part of the money Katerina and Sergei consider theirs. So they decide to murder him, and while they are stifling him with a pillow, they happen to be observed through a crack in the shutters by a group of young men who happen to be passing the house just at that moment on their way home from church and take it into their heads to spy on the amours of Sergei and Katerina.

Thus at one stroke Leskov appears to have accomplished two important ends: the murderers have been caught red-handed, and in a crime we are not likely to condone, the slaughter of a child from pecuniary motives. The lovers have been stripped of their glamour, and we are ready to move to the retribution section of the story. But Leskov paid dearly for this solution. Apart from the grossly implausible witnessing of the murder, the pile of corpses is growing too high for credibility; furthermore, the motivation for the third murder is unconvincing. Nothing has prepared us for the appearance of such overpowering avarice in the two lovers. If Leskov had brought out this trait earlier, we might be more willing to believe the third murder, but the powerful effect of our identification with the first two would have been lost.[6]

Fortunately Leskov recovers himself, and the dénouement is handled with undiminished power. The glamour, at least of the first two crimes, is ironically demolished by their outcome, a pathetic commentary on human inconstancy. Katerina has committed three murders, and will kill yet again, in order to secure Sergei's love, but in the end the object for which she has paid such a terrible price evaporates before her eyes. After their public flogging and his branding (in Leskov's day capital punishment was inflicted only for political crimes), Katerina and Sergei are marched off in shackles to Siberia. Katerina's passion remains unabated, but Sergei, tired of her and repelled by her excessive demands and possessiveness, begins to have affairs with other convict women. At last, driven to fury by jealousy and a rival's mockery, Katerina commits her fourth murder, wrestling her rival, and herself, off the deck of a ferry into the icy Volga, where they disappear beneath the waves. The ironic circle is complete: Katerina has lost not only the love for which she killed but life itself.

Even without the murder of the boy, the action of "Lady Macbeth" might seem overloaded with horror for a story less than fifty pages long. Leskov's achievement was to infuse this narrative with such tension that one's disbelief is not so much suspended as hypnotized away. Leskov himself experienced this hypnotic intensity while "Lady Macbeth" was being created. According to his son, he wrote the story in the *kartser* of Kiev University, a jail cell for misbehaving students.

Because of his uncle's position in the university, Leskov was able to use this place as a study.[7] A year or so later he described the composition of "Lady Macbeth" to his friend Vsevolod Krestovsky, whose secretary transcribed his account as follows:

"You cannot imagine [Leskov said] what I sometimes go through when staying up late at night. My nerves get so strained that I begin to feel scared at being alone. Then it suddenly seems to me that I have been abandoned by everyone, that I am in danger that my end is near. Sometimes I even have hallucinations. You sit there writing about all sorts of horrible things, murders and so forth. Your nerves must be in good order if you can do this at night without losing control of yourself. While I was writing my 'Lady Macbeth,' the effect of overstrained nerves and isolation almost drove me to delirium. At times the horror became unbearable; my hair stood on end; I froze at the tiniest sound I myself had made by a movement of my foot or by turning my neck. Those were painful moments, and I shall never forget them. Since then I have avoided describing horrors," he added, laughing.[8]

Although the last statement is not entirely accurate—there are horrors aplenty in *At Daggers Drawn*, for example, and in the play *The Spendthrift*—it is true that "Lady Macbeth of the Mtsensk District" stands apart in Leskov's work. This particular quasi dramatic mode, with its focus on hyperbolized action and psychological intensity, proved ultimately less congenial to Leskov's talent than a looser, "unrolling scroll" kind of narrative, which offers greater freedom for subsidiary episodes, anecdotes, digressive discussions, and exhibitions of the author's verbal virtuosity. But "Lady Macbeth" remains unsurpassed in its kind.

"The Battle-axe"
and *The Islanders*

During 1865 and 1866 Leskov's artistic production continues the same
roller-coaster pattern of 1864. Again there are two contrasting works,
one showing the writer at his best, an original, independent master;
the other exhibiting him at his worst, a third-rate imitator, a purveyor
of sentimental clichés. It is surely one of the bumpiest beginnings in
world literature. Looking back on this period five years later, Leskov
himself had an inkling of the extraordinary unevenness of his early
work. As he wrote a friend, a critic who was planning to do a survey
of his career up to that time, "some [artistic] powers I must have, but
they are somehow unevenly put together and slow to grow. I feel that
up to "Dwellers in God's House" [an early title of *Cathedral Folk*] I
kept staggering."[1]

Leskov at his best appears in the novella "The Battle-axe"[2]—a virtuoso display of skaz, which he had experimented with three years
earlier in "The Robber" and "In the Coach." The true skaz is a stylistically individualized inner narrative placed in the mouth of a fictional
character and related in such a way as to maintain the illusion of oral
speech; it is to be distinguished from other types of frame story in
which the narrator, although represented as speaking, uses language
indistinguishable from the author's literary prose, or is himself not a
genuine character, but only an impersonal mechanism for restricting
the point of view. The first and most difficult problem in skaz is what
Leskov called the "pitching of the voice," that is, contriving to produce, by means of a careful selection of characteristic phonetic, mor-
phological, syntactic, and lexical features of the narrator's language, a
vivid impression of its "orality" and its individuality. As Leskov put it
many years later, speaking of his late story "Night Owls" (1891),
which has many other links with "The Battle-axe":

> In order to "think in images" [a phrase from Belinsky] and write
> that way a writer must make each one of his heroes use the lan-

guage appropriate to his position. If these heroes use inappropriate language, only the devil can tell who they are and what their
social position is. This pitching of the voice consists in the writer's
ability to master the voice and language of his hero and not to slip
from the alto to the bass. In myself I have tried to develop this
ability and have achieved, I think, the result that my priests talk
like priests, my nihilists like nihilists, my peasants like peasants,
upstarts from their ranks and mountebanks talk a deformed jargon, and so on . . . All of us, my heroes and I myself, have our
own voices. In each of us they are pitched correctly or at least
carefully. When I write, I am afraid of losing control: therefore
my petty bourgeois talk like petty bourgeois and lisping aristocrats in their own way. This is a sure indication of talent in a
writer. But working it out is not only a matter of talent, but of
enormous labor. Man lives by words, and one must know what
words each of us will use and at what moments in his psychological life [. . .] This colloquial, vulgar, florid language in which
many pages of my works are written was not invented by me, but
overheard from the peasant, the semi-intellectual, the fine talkers,
the holy fools, and the pious souls. People reproach me for this
"mannered" language, especially in "Night Owls." But don't we
have plenty of "mannered" people?[3]

"Pitching of the voice" is obviously required for all forms of direct
speech in literature, not only inner narratives. In skaz, however, the
narrator's pitched voice becomes the chief medium of discourse. After
the frame is completed and the inner narrative begins, the author
obliterates himself, as it were, surrenders the right to speak for himself.

In order to serve such an important structural function, the narrative voice must be a distinctive one. Leskov's success in creating such
voices came as corollary to the solution he evolved for the "distancing" problem in his novels. He had difficulty writing about intellectuals like himself? Very well, intellectuals make very poor skaz narrators. Their language is too bookish, too hard to "oralize." It is easier
and also more colorful to select, as the narrator of a skaz, a character
who is set apart from the cultural elite by geography or class and who
therefore speaks a language with socially distinct features. Leskov was
a master at catching the "pitch" of such voices, displaying to perfection their quality, variety, and color without overburdening his text
with obscurities or pedantic transcriptions of linguistic oddities.

The narrative voice in "The Battle-axe" belongs to a highly original female character. Domna Platonovna—we never discover her last name—was evidently one of the female personages originally intended for the series initiated by "Lady Macbeth." Although by the time we meet her she is very much an old inhabitant of Petersburg, she is a native of Mtsensk; and her friendship with the "author" is based on the fact that they are *zemlyaki*, fellow-Orlovians. Domna Platonovna's speech retains, beneath superimposed layers of linguistic features, remnants of Oryol dialect, though Leskov avoids making the text irritatingly obscure to the nonlocal reader.

Domna Platonovna belongs to that amorphous class, the so-called *meshchanstvo* or petite bourgeoisie. The *meshchane*—a term usually translated as "artisans"—were a legal category of free townspeople, mostly engaged in petty trade or crafts. They were not substantial enough to qualify as "merchants," but considered themselves superior in status to both peasants and factory workers. In the parlance of educated Russians, however, the word became a virtual synonym for "philistinism," used not only to denote a social category, but to convey a pejorative judgment of its ignorance, vulgarity, smallness of mind and soul. Already alienated from folk culture, the *meshchane* existed on the fringes of educated society, generally despised and ridiculed, especially by intellectuals.

Domna Platonovna is a Mtsensk *meshchanka* who has moved to Petersburg after her husband's death. There she takes up the trade of a lace-peddler, serving as an intermediary between the lower-class producers of the goods and their upper-class consumers. It is her upper-class customers' language she admires and tries to imitate, but without understanding it completely or being able to reproduce it correctly. As a result her speech is essentially comic, an incongruous jumble, with absurd juxtapositions of ultra-colloquial dialectisms and bookish literary terms or loan-words of Western origin, often distorted and misused. Leskov exploits the humorous potential of this language with great skill.

It is virtually impossible to translate these comic incongruities, which is one reason why Leskov's popularity has never extended much beyond the boundaries of Russia. A few expressions, such as "Harem drops" for "Haarlem drops" (a popular nineteenth-century nostrum), are intelligible without footnotes; but the reader who knows no Russian must take the general effect on faith. Perhaps the following paragraph, in which the frame narrator comments directly on his heroine's linguistic artistry, will convey some idea of her style:

Moreover, Domna Platonovna's mode of address was a subtle one. In a drawing room she would never say like other people that she had "been to the public baths," but would rather say, "I had, sir, the good fortune yesterday to attend a noncorporeal masquerade" [*byt' v bestelesnom maskerade*]; about a pregnant woman she would never blurt out that she was simply pregnant, but would say, "She is in a maritally interesting condition" [*ona v svoem mar'jažnom interese:* the effect is odder in Russian than in this English rendition]; and so forth. (1:152)

Domna Platonovna's speech is thus individualized by specific regional and class features that place her in a geographic and social context, anchor her in a specific linguistic environment. But Leskov goes a step further. Domna Platonovna's idiosyncratic oddities of speech take on an independent aesthetic value, irresistibly attracting attention to themselves. The reader is forced to change the focus of his eye: he no longer merely perceives the characters and the action through the glass of language, but finds himself admiring the patterns and colors of the glass itself.

In making stylistic texture an end in itself Leskov ran counter to prevailing fashions and violated accepted canons of realism. The classic practitioners of high realism, like Tolstoy or the later Turgenev, strove for an optimum transparency of style, ultimately designed to make the reader forget he was reading, to give him the illusion that he was experiencing the events described. A mannered or ornamental style spoils this effect: it calls attention to itself, underscoring the literariness of the work. In this respect Leskov may be regarded as an artistic "reactionary," harking back to stylistic exhibitionists like Gogol and, as Boris Eikhenbaum has pointed out, that half-forgotten "other line" of Gogol's descendants, such as Dahl, Weltman, and Baron Brambeus, who stood apart from the procession of high realists.[4] Nineteenth-century critics could not forgive Leskov for this stylistic reactionism any more than they could forget his ideological "betrayal"; all his life they berated him for "verbal exuberance" and "lack of stylistic restraint," and they continued doing so after his death. Only in the early twentieth century, when the Symbolists had swung the pendulum of literary fashion back toward aggressive style-consciousness, did Leskov's verbal pyrotechnics receive the recognition they deserved and find admiring imitators, such as Remizov, Zamyatin, and Zoshchenko. The Battle-axe ultimately had her descendants, but their birth was almost half a century delayed.[5]

There is more to "The Battle-axe" than verbal texture, impressive as that is. Domna Platonovna—or Domna Pantalonovna, as some of her customers call her—is not merely a lace-peddler; lace-peddling is a cover for her essential business. She is a procuress, or, putting it more kindly, a matchmaker, an arranger of "marriages," sometimes permanent, but more often temporary. She is thus a purveyor to the secret sexual needs of the capital; and in this capacity she obtains a unique under-view of the real life of Petersburg.

"The Battle-axe" may be said to continue the "physiological" tradition in Russian literature, a tradition going back to two collections of essays and stories brought out by Nekrasov and Belinsky in the 1840s, the *Petersburg Miscellany* and the *Physiology of Petersburg*, themselves modeled on similar "physiologies" of Paris and London. Seeking to capture for literature the increasingly prestigious scientific method, the literary "physiologists," aggressively repudiating the romanticism of their fathers, undertook to view life as objectively as the biologist views the worm he dissects. And the wormier the better: they delighted in exhibiting maximally grubby slices of slum and underworld life to titillate their middle-class audiences. The "physiological" tradition had been revived in the 1860s in such works as *The Slums of Petersburg*, published anonymously by Leskov's friend Vsevolod Krestovsky. Having assisted his friend in some of his "research" on the low life of Petersburg, Leskov was by no means averse to making use of such material himself.[6]

The first half of Domna Platonovna's "physiological" narrative forms an essential unity. In an eighteenth-century novel it might have borne a title like "The History of Lekanida Domukhovskaya; or, How High-class Prostitutes Are Made." Lekanida is a young woman of Polish origin, but Orthodox religion, who has left her husband, a doctor, and come to Petersburg to escape him, with no clear idea how she is going to maintain herself. She takes a large apartment, planning to rent rooms; one of the rooms is taken by a man who is "refined, educated, and kind"; and soon she is having an affair with him. Before long his refinement and kindness turn to extortion and beatings; but Lekanida is unable to extricate herself from her predicament. She drifts on until she is abandoned by her lover and evicted for nonpayment of rent.

The two foreground characters, Lekanida and the narrator, Domna Platonovna, offer a perfect contrast. Lekanida is a delicate flower, a romantic, accustomed to being treated with gentleness, unused to dealing in hard realities. She uses romantic fig-leaves to cover her moral nakedness: true, she had an affair, but that was a romantic infatuation legitimized by genuine sentiment; neither cold sensuality nor calculation played any part in it. The earthy Domna Platonovna, on the other hand, specializes in base realities. She takes the world as she sees it, and she simply cannot understand all Lekanida's tergiversations, wailings, and spiritual refinements. When Lekanida is nearly destitute, Domna Platonovna takes her in and offers what seems to Domna the perfect solution: a rich general Domna Platonovna knows is looking for a new mistress; he likes refined types like Lekanida; Domna Platonovna will "fix them up."

But Lekanida can only wring her hands and lament her lost innocence and her beautiful childhood, spent with her darling mother, now an angel in heaven. Lament or no, there is no other way out; as Domna Platonovna says, nobody gives rubles for tears. Lekanida does not have the money to go back to her husband, who does not answer her letters. To earn the train fare, she consents, just for once; but when the general comes—Domna Platonovna tactfully absents herself—Lekanida cannot bring herself to open the door. Domna Platonovna is furious. Lekanida has not only spoiled a good business deal, arranged in Lekanida's own interest; she may have jeopardized Domna's standing with the general and his family (Domna supplies both him and his son with mistresses and also procures well-muscled student boarders for the general's wife). Her anger is so great that she berates Lekanida violently and beats her.

Destitution and pressure at last force Lekanida to succumb and become the mistress of the general, who is persuaded to pay another visit, and she eventually gives up all thought of returning to her husband. Later, she develops a romantic interest in the general's son as well and even a sentimental friendship with the son's wife. Seemingly secure in her position, she allows herself the satisfaction of calling Domna Platonovna a "vile woman" and a "scoundrel" (*merzavka*)—which Domna considers the height of ingratitude. In revenge Domna denounces her to the general's daughter-in-law, and the result is such a row that the general decides to get a new mistress.

The confrontation and contrast of the two disparate types, Domna Platonovna and Lekanida, is effective in itself. But Leskov has a difficult technical problem, for the narrator of the contrast is Domna Platonovna herself. Since she tells the story, to all appearances the author has surrendered control over it. How, then, can he right the moral balance, communicate his own judgment, or even make us feel that we know the whole truth? He cannot let Domna Platonovna's morality have the last word: in nineteenth-century Russia, where attitudes toward such matters tended to be both puritanical and sentimental (stories of noble-hearted young men "rescuing" prostitutes, often by marrying them, are legion in this period), a cynically French, Balzacian attitude toward Lekanida's predicament would not have been tolerated. Nor did Leskov, at least on the surface, have any intention of taking issue with conventional morality. He must therefore somehow show that he deplores Domna's cynicism, despises her claims to charity, and sympathizes with Lekanida as a pathetic fallen angel.

Leskov accomplishes this task in a variety of ways. First, the reader's repudiation of Domna Platonovna's morality is inherent in the situation: approval would have been unthinkable. If we are told how a sensitive young woman refuses to prostitute herself and for this is abused and beaten by a middle-aged procuress, we naturally side with the victim, no matter who tells the story. Second, besides conveying her own feelings, Domna reports objective facts and, to a degree, the attitudes of others. Thus when she tells us, in a shocked tone, how Lekanida called her a "vile woman" and a "scoundrel," we are made aware that Domna's response to the events is not the only possible one.

Finally, the frame narrator never wholly abandons the stage to Domna Platonovna's tale, occasionally injecting his own reactions into the transcription. To avoid spoiling the skaz, Leskov holds the frame narrator's interventions to a minimum. He remains a shadowy figure and a passive one, hardly more than a receptacle for Domna's outpourings (he even lies sick in bed during part of her narrative). Apparently he is too virtuous to have any business dealings with the procuress; she treats him as a confidant on the basis of their common origin in Oryol. But despite his passivity, the frame narrator does from time to time interpose comments and questions, and on rare occasions he ventures a moral reaction.

On one of these occasions Domna Platonovna has just expressed her uncomprehending amazement at Lekanida's unwillingness to finance her trip home to her husband by a single act of prostitution ("how long did she play around with that pock-marked boarder of hers without getting anything for it; and now, for the sake of her own advantage and peace, to restore herself to an honest life, she can't take one step"). At this point the frame narrator feels obliged, even if very cautiously, to speak out (though only to the reader) in the name of decency: "I looked again at Domna Platonovna. In her there was nothing of what is usually so clearly imprinted in those women who specialize in creating victims of our social illness. The woman sitting in front of me was quite ingenuous. She uttered her abominations in the unshakable conviction of her own kindness and the impenetrable folly of Mme Lekanida" (1:167). The word "abominations" (*merzosti*), which the frame narrator uses to detach himself morally from Domna Platonovna, is etymologically the same as the curse (*merzavka*) Lekanida has finally hurled at the procuress. Officially, the "author" thus takes his stand alongside Lekanida and the prevalent sentimental-romantic morality of the nineteenth century.

But one of the most interesting things about this story is that this judgment does not entirely stick; the ultimate moral conclusion to be drawn from "The Battle-axe" remains ambiguous. To be sure, neither Leskov nor we can condone Domna Platonovna's trafficking in human desperation, however she may try to disguise her operations as charity; we inevitably find her unsavory and ludicrous. Nevertheless, at times we cannot help siding with her. In her judgments of Lekanida she is often right. Hers is the voice of reality, of truth; and we feel a certain satisfaction when the truth cuts through a protective tissue of self-justifying myths. The truth may not be romantic, but it is good to know it.

Moreover, Domna Platonovna is good-hearted, according to her lights; the story would have lost much of its subtlety if Leskov had made her into a villainous white-slaver. In many of her operations, including Lekanida's case, she is less concerned with her own profit than with the "artistic" gratification of successfully completing a complex arrangement and advancing the welfare of everyone concerned. When Lekanida first tearfully announces her decision to return to her husband, throw herself at his feet, confess all, and if necessary remain with him as his servant, Domna Platonovna thinks it over and decides it is not a bad idea, in Lekanida's own interests. Her argument is a refreshingly realistic antidote to Lekanida's fantasy of a beautiful, tear-washed scene of contrition and absolution: "I thought it over and approved of that idea of Lekanida's being her husband's servant. She's a good-looking girl, I thought, and even if he stays mad for a while at the beginning, when she is right there in front of his eyes, I'll bet the spirit that cometh in the darkness will tangle them up again; and maybe it will all blow over. The night-time cuckoo always out-cuckoes the day-time cuckoo, you know" (1:162).

The frame narrator may claim to feel shocked at the abominations so unblushingly uttered by Domna Platonovna; but aloud he never protests or criticizes (the word "abominations" is said only to the reader). One feels there is something symbolic about this acquiescent silence. The "author" is a passive voyeur, who, whatever his conscious moral attitude, is unwilling to cut off the flow of Domna Platonovna's titillating tales; and perhaps secretly he too likes Domna Platonovna, abominations and all, is refreshed by her realism, and exasperated by Lekanida's sentimental evasions.

The account of Lekanida's downfall constitutes only the first part of "The Battle-axe." So far, the story is flawless, and from the point of view of thematic unity and structural symmetry it would have been better to end it there. But Leskov did not do so. For one thing, he wanted to round out the character of his heroine and give her a dimension in time. In the first part, Domna Platonovna stands essentially outside of time, the stationary point from which we view the degeneration of Lekanida; she is the ageless and indestructible busybody, leading, as she calls it, the most "unceasable" life (*samaja prekratitel'naja žizn'*). Too bad to deprive her of such enviable immortality! But Leskov gives her a "before" and an "after," the "after" containing an ironic retribution for her sins. In the second part of "The Battle-axe," through a series of flashbacks, we get the story of Domna Platonovna's beginnings in Mtsensk, her marriage (she earned the title "Battle-axe" from her titanic warfare with her husband), and her initiation into the world of Petersburg "lace-peddlers. Unfortunately, Leskov does not succeed here in giving greater psychological depth to his characterization; the retrospective episodes are only a series of anecdotes lacking the emotional intensity and unity of the Lekanida sequence.

The "after," the account of Domna Platonovna's come-uppance is even more questionable. It may be ironically satisfying, but psychologically it is not convincing; we are not prepared to accept such a complete change in the leading character. After many years of catering to the passions of others, while herself remaining aloof and unmoved, Domna Platonovna succumbs to the power of eros. At well past forty, she falls desperately in love with a youth of twenty. He is a rogue and exploits her thoroughly. For him she sacrifices everything, her money, her connections, and even her profession. When he falls afoul of the law and is taken off to prison, Domna Platonovna has nothing to live for, and she dies. With her last breath she asks that her pitiful effects, a little trunk, a pillow, and a jar of jam, be delivered to the "author" for him to give to the "person he knows about," that is, her imprisoned lover.

It is a neat and affecting finale; but it seems dictated more by the laws of conventional morality than by those of psychology or art.

Perhaps the nadir of Leskov's entire career as a writer is the short novel *The Islanders*, a work that exhibits all his vices in concentrated form and none of his strengths. The causes hitherto singled out for Leskov's failures do not apply to *The Islanders*.[7] This is not a polemical tract against the nihilists; neither political passion nor personal vindictiveness is present to distort artistic judgment. Its only ideological content is a brief discussion of art theory and the policies of the official Petersburg Academy of Arts; and in this argument, although he ridicules the "annihilation of art" advocated by the nihilist critics Pisarev and Zaitsev, Leskov supports strongly the more moderate "progressive" position that art should serve moral and social ends, not isolate itself in the ivory tower of the academy.[8] Nor is *The Islanders* a long novel, a mass of material too bulky for Leskov to organize artistically: it is less than two-hundred pages long. Likewise, it contains no undigested autobiographical material, no wishful punishments inflicted on erring friends and relatives. There is no alter ego character to be gratified and vindicated; and for once Olga Vasilievna is left in peace. Most important, the main characters of *The Islanders*, with one exception, do not belong to Russian educated society. Thus the lack of distance or aesthetic perspective, the principal cause of Leskov's failure in his other novels, seems to have been avoided. To all appearances, Leskov has applied here his basic defense against novelistic error: his principal characters are distanced from himself by social status and nationality.

The island in question is Vasilevsky Ostrov, a district of Petersburg on an island in the Neva. The inhabitants are semi-Russified Germans, lower-middle-class tradespeople who, although they have lived in Petersburg for two generations or more, have retained their German identity and Lutheran religion. They are bilingual in German and Russian (as far as one can tell: it is sometimes impossible to determine whether a given Russian dialogue is being presented in the original or in the author's translation). They display a host of "German" virtues considered notably un-Russian, such as cleanliness, thrift, and sturdy self-reliance. Such a picturesque island of Russian life would seem the ideal background for one of Leskov's genre stories.

What then went wrong with *The Islanders*? The crux of the matter seems to lie in the author's familiarity with the milieu and character types he describes. In his successful genre stories, Leskov dealt with social milieus and personality types he knew well. He had lived among the peasants of the Gostomlya and the merchants and petty tradespeople of provincial towns like Mtsensk since his childhood, and he understood them by instinct.

But the Germans of Vasilevsky Ostrov were another matter. Leskov did not speak German; he had never lived in Germany; his ideas about Germans were mostly secondhand stereotypes. Even with Petersburg Germans his acquaintance must have been very superficial; his biography shows no trace of any close connections. Lacking knowledge of the society he had chosen to describe, Leskov was forced to invent. And, as he later admitted, invention was the aspect of artistic creativity he found most difficult. "I have powers of observation and perhaps a certain capacity for analyzing feelings and motives," Leskov wrote in 1884. "But I have *little imagination*. To invent is difficult and painful for me, and therefore I have always needed living models."[9]

The trouble with *The Islanders* is that its "living models" were not living. The characters were derived not from experience or knowledge, but from literary stereotypes, popular myths. The Petersburg German coloration given these familiar puppets is only the thinnest of facades; underneath, there are well-worn international *Schablonen*. Among them are the irresistible, irresponsible Bohemian artist; the fragile ingenue who falls desperately in love with him; the heroine's industrious, long-suffering mother; a saintly spinster sister; and so on. From this cast of characters the action is all too predictable. After a long campaign, the innocent maiden will be "ruined" by the otherwise lazy, but sexually very enterprising artist, bringing disgrace and sorrow upon her family; both he and she will be appropriately punished for their sin; and after many tribulations they will find, not happiness —that is forever denied them—but contrition and spiritual peace.

Many of the episodes in this hackneyed plot can only be read as comedy, though this was far from Leskov's intention. There is the affecting scene when, at the news of her granddaughter's downfall, the heroine's aged grandmother, who has spent years in a wheelchair, suddenly rises up, walks, pronounces a curse upon her sinning descendant, and keels over dead. In another scene (in fact borrowed from Gogol's comedy *The Marriage*, although Leskov presents it seriously), the hero, returning after an absence of several months, is maneuvered into visiting his pregnant sweetheart. He suspects a shotgun conspiracy and spectacularly leaps out of the window, like Podkolyosin, into freedom. Finally, there is the laughable scene when the heroine, now respectably married to a real German German, complete with a castle in a good German forest, has an accidental encounter with her erstwhile lover, now wandering around Germany, nearly blind, known as the "Russian Ivan" who "makes shapes" out of clay with his fingers. As a neighboring *Hausfrau* relates the story: " 'Ivan' took off his eyeshade; she cried out 'Ach!'; he cried out 'Ach!'; he began to shake and tremble; she fell down senseless; and this beast, this accursed Herrnguter [her husband] took her in his arms, ran with her into the yard, and rode off" (3:154). As Vsevolod Setchkarev has appropriately observed,[10] you would think you were reading a parody if it were not clear that the author is in dead earnest.

The Islanders must be written off as Leskov's offering on the altar of the Victorian *Zeitgeist*. Gross sentimentality, particularly about women and children, nowadays seems one of the most unbearable, and incomprehensible, features of that highly creative period, marring the work of some of its greatest masters. The writer whose faults most immediately suggest those of *The Islanders* is Dickens, the mawkish, lachrymose Dickens of Little Nell and Agnes Wakefield, the Dickens who wrote the story which most closely parallels that of Manya Nork in *The Islanders*—the account of the heartless seduction of Peggoty's niece by the rich, handsome, and cruelly irresponsible Steerforth. It is not necessary to claim direct influence here, although this is not impossible—Leskov was an admiring reader of Dickens.[11] The point is that in their weaker moments both writers, instead of dealing honestly with certain subjects, especially sex, took the easier course of pandering to their sentimental public and to that aspect of their own nature which yearned to evade the truth. Fortunately, neither of them allowed this trap to hold him for long.[12]

10

A Theatrical Spendthrift

In the early phases of his career Leskov gives the impression of explosive energy bursting in all directions at once. Some writers go through a period of slow, methodical growth, of gradual acquisition of technical mastery and critical judgment. Leskov, however, seems to lunge wildly now here, now there, from subject to subject, style to style, genre to genre, sometimes rising to real greatness, sometimes collapsing in ignominious failure. He did not always know where he had succeeded and where he had failed. It was difficult for him, as for most artists, to take an outsider's view of his own creations, and he was also constantly blinded by extra-literary passions. He always believed that his works were valiant blows struck in the best of causes: to defend Russia from the demonic forces of nihilism and to destroy his own enemies, public and private, demonstrating to the world his perfect innocence and righteousness.

The critics and the public were likewise of little help in enabling Leskov to gain a clearer view of his own strengths and weaknesses. The weak novel *No Way Out*, though denounced as the act of a scoundrel in the pay of the police, had a considerable *succès de scandale*, which the author could interpret as a vote of public confidence, running through two editions in two years. Yet Leskov's best works of the period, stories like "The Mocker," "The Musk-ox," "Lady Macbeth," and "The Life of a Peasant Martyress" (which have since been recognized as classics) passed almost unnoticed at the time they appeared. As Leskov never tired of pointing out in later years, Russian criticism failed him terribly. After *No Way Out*, the critics, most of them radicals, could see no virtue in Leskov no matter what he did; their judgment was subordinated to their partisanship. Even the distinguished writer Saltykov-Shchedrin, who should have been capable of more independent judgment, in a lengthy review written in 1869 of a two-volume collection of Leskov's stories, several of them masterpieces, could only emit vicious innuendoes concerning *No Way Out*, the police, and "Russian Society in Paris." Not a word of encouragement or even artistic criticism: everything is tarred with the same ideological brush.[1]

Embittered and furious as he was, Leskov nevertheless kept plunging ahead. Despite his failures, which he only dimly recognized anyway, he felt within himself the powerful force of his talent and an overwhelming will to conquer. At times he displays an almost megalomaniac confidence in his powers. He would master every field, every form: he was an economist, a political journalist, an ethnographer; an expert on vodka-distilling, peasant colonization, women's rights, the Old Believers, and Russian society in Paris; he was the author of long novels, short novels, long stories, short stories, sketches, and memoirs—all this in the six years since he had arrived in Petersburg. And in 1867 he set out to conquer another piece of literary territory, the drama.

Leskov had a long-standing interest in the theater. In his days as an official in Kiev, his friend Gromeka had drawn him into the amateur theatricals presided over by Princess Vasilchikova, the governor-general's wife, in which he had shown a natural histrionic talent. Later, while working for Scott, he made frequent trips to Petersburg and Moscow and probably took advantage of the opportunity to attend the theater: there is an authentic autobiographical ring to the narrator's account, in "The Musk-ox," of how he almost nightly escorted his provincial friends to the Petersburg theaters. And after he had settled permanently in the capital, Leskov's stage fever showed no signs of abating.

In 1866 he managed to persuade his friend and mentor Stepan Dudyshkin, the editor of *Notes of the Fatherland*, to assign him a regular position as theater critic, and during that and the following year he produced four substantial reviews of current plays and productions.[2] The death of Dudyshkin in 1866 and the subsequent transfer of the magazine to the radical editors Nekrasov and Shchedrin brought to an end Leskov's long association with *Notes of the Fatherland*, but he continued the series with two more articles in the short-lived *Literary Library*.[3] In the midst of this theater-going and reviewing, Leskov decided to write a play himself.

In "Lady Macbeth of the Mtsensk District" Leskov had shown that he could, although with some strain, handle a dramatic structure, with a logically developed sequential plot, vivid, somewhat exaggerated characters, and a development accomplished primarily through scenes and direct confrontation of characters rather than through analysis and exposition by the author. ("Lady Macbeth" was indeed successfully adapted as a play and, in 1934, as a remarkable opera by Dmitry Shostakovich, which was denounced with vehemence and long suppressed because Stalin was irritated by its cacophony).[4]

For his play *The Spendthrift,*[5] dated May 26, 1867, Leskov returned to the milieu of "Lady Macbeth," the provincial merchantry. By this choice he was in effect invading the territory of the man considered the greatest Russian dramatist then living, Aleksandr Ostrovsky, for Ostrovsky had made his reputation, beginning in the 1840s, with a series of remarkable genre plays about the Moscow merchant class, on which he seemed almost to have a patent. Ostrovsky, however, as Leskov pointed out with acerbity in a critical article, had given up writing those rich, salty, and vigorous merchant plays which he handled so well and had been turning out dreary poetic dramas on Russian history like *Minin Sukhoruk* and *Tushino.*[6] With his *Spendthrift*, Leskov would seized the torch from the faltering hand of the master and carry it to new heights.

Leskov felt that he could improve on the technique of Ostrovsky's best genre plays. Ostrovsky, writing in a period of reaction against romantic bombast, had tried to base his merchant plays on the drama inherent in the ordinary lives of commonplace people, avoiding conventionally dramatic scenes and violent events. His are dramas of restraint and implication, of pent-up feeling and off-stage climaxes. Even "Lady Macbeth" may have been conceived as a riposte to Ostrovsky's *Thunderstorm:* Katerina Izmailova is a bigger, bolder, and more "Russian" heroine than the pathetically weak Katerina of Ostrovsky's play; and the story is crammed with the explosive action and melodrama Ostrovsky avoided.[7]

Leskov decided to write an Ostrovskian genre play, but one brought up to date and with the bright colors and dramatic action he felt were the rightful properties of the theater. The result, unfortunately, was a bad play, though in many ways an interesting one, both for its manifest content and for its revelation of the author's feelings.

The central character, though not the hero in either the technical or the moral sense, is that endlessly potent figure in Leskov's emotional constellation, the bad father, ultimately based on Mikhail Strakhov. In *The Spendthrift* Strakhov is reincarnated as an old merchant named Firs Knyazev ("Prince"). The invented name is a clue to the power he wields and to Knyazev's position as an aristocrat in disguise: he is the "first man" in a Russian town from which the gentry are strangely absent. Knyazev is the embodiment of power as Leskov seems to have fundamentally felt about it: malignant, unscrupulous, ruthlessly dedicated to the maintenance of its supremacy and the gratification of its desires. Knyazev is the classic capitalist exploiter, the merchant-shark who sticks at no swindle, cruelty, or crime in order to turn a profit; he is also a sexual "devourer," an aged satyr who treats the female population of the town as if they belonged to his harem, just as the classic Russian landlord-despot treated his women serfs. At sixty Knyazev spends much time plotting his sexual conquests, using all his resources to bully young women into submission.

Knyazev's lust dominates his avarice. For him, money is but a means to pleasure; he is a dissipater, not an accumulator, of capital. He is avaricious about pleasure. "The worst thing I can imagine," he says, "is that after my death wine, money, and beautiful women will be left on the earth." His sexuality has a sadistic tinge. His most volup-tuous fantasy is to "kiss" a young woman who is weeping because she has no recourse but to submit to him: "Sometimes I love women when they are crying. [*Passionately!*] Just then, when they are crying, their lips are so hot and they are all a-tremble, like a butterfly on a pin. It's a long time since I've kissed one like that." (1:392)

All action in the play emanates from Knyazev. The other characters are either marionettes he manipulates, or, in the case of the good ones, helpless victims of his machinations, futilely struggling to resist his will. As a fantasy image, a mythical deity of evil power, "Satan in all his glory," as one of his minions calls him, the figure of Knyazev is an effective artistic creation. Perhaps he is not a possible human being in a real world, but he represents an archetypal image. Such personified absolutes have a valid place in art.

But the problem of including a colossal fantasy figure in a realistic play about nineteenth-century Russia proved beyond Leskov's artistic powers. Satan, to be believable, must appear, as Milton showed him, in an environment proportionate to his size, on a cosmic stage far above the everyday realities of our world; or, if he does come down to the ordinary earth, he must himself be debased, as Dostoevsky under-stood, made to share human pettiness and triviality. To incarnate a heroic Satan as a Russian merchant in a nineteenth-century Russian town is like confining a shark to a goldfish pond.

Knyazev's antagonist, and the real hero of the play, is a well-to-do young industrialist, educated and Westernized, who contrasts with the medieval, bearded merchants of Ostrovsky's world. His name, Ivan Molchanov ("silent"), symbolizes his basic moral quality, both a virtue and a fault: his silence is gentleness, nonaggression, willingness to listen to others; but it is also passivity, inability to "speak," to assert his will, to challenge effectively the power of Knyazev. In Leskov's syllogism, if power is by definition evil, it follows that its antipode, the good character, must be a passive and helpless martyr, a victim of the evil despot.

Molchanov's passivity is his dominant trait. As a child he had been extraordinarily submissive, even unmasculine. His sweetheart remembers him: "A wonderful child he was! But I was growing up as vicious as a wasp. Shameless girl that I was, I used to take him somewhere far off into a ditch or a garden and beat him up. (*Wipes away her tears.*) If he had something, I would take it away, and he would put up with it [. . .] Once my late mother saw how I pushed him down in a flower-bed and for that wouldn't give me anything to eat; and so he wouldn't eat either [. . .] How do you like that! (*Weeps*)" (1:453).

Molchanov's basic goodness, like Knyazev's evil, is presented as innate, a natural submissiveness in the face of aggression. Such a figure might have been workable if magnified to the titanic dimensions of Knyazev, represented as an archetypal figure of humility and suffering. The drama would then have become a reenactment of the conflict between absolutes of good and evil, Christ and Satan. But Molchanov is no Christ. Although his goodness is inherent, Molchanov is otherwise psychologized, treated as a formed human being whose life history has made him what he is. The human Molchanov is no valid antagonist for the demonic Knyazev; in fact, the Molchanov we see simply could not be the product of the experiences he is supposed to have had.

Molchanov is the son of a rich (but unbelievably stupid and credulous) manufacturer who had been murdered by Knyazev after making a will appointing Knyazev his son's guardian. The orphan Molchanov was brought up under Knyazev's tutelage, and the monster made a systematic—and initially successful—effort to corrupt him, teaching him "at eight to drink sweet vodka, at ten bitter, at fifteen rum and champagne, while he himself in his apartment placed French girls and dancers on my knees [. . .] He clad my soul in rags" (1:409). By a senseless provision of his father's will (dictated by Knyazev) Molchanov is forced to marry a certain girl or lose half his inheritance; and the girl turns out to be another Olga Vasilievna, vulgar, mean, shrewish, and disloyal, who browbeats her passive husband. Somehow, Molchanov's innately virtuous nature survives, or revives. At the beginning of the action he has returned from three years' study in Germany a modern industrialist, thoughtful and humane, a new Robert Owen, resolved to raise his workers to a higher level of existence, sober and circumspect in his private life. It is not a believable transformation. The implausibility of Molchanov's psychological development is a major weakness of the play.

Still worse is the utter implausibility of the action. Molchanov initially tries to outmaneuver Knyazev by donating to some orphanages in Petersburg 200,000 rubles he has coming to him from the settlement of Knyazev's guardianship. Because Petersburg is involved, the settlement would be adjudicated by an outside court which Knyazev would be unable to control or bribe; this was the time (1867) when the great judicial reform of Alexander II had just been carried out. Knyazev easily thwarts this design by having the local court, which he does control, declare Molchanov an incompetent, a spendthrift dissipating the rightful inheritance of his children (Molchanov's wife is a party to Knyazev's plot). Thus the donation of a spendthrift is legally void. Despite his alleged intelligence and German training, it never occurs to Molchanov that his obvious defense is to appeal the local court's decision, if necessary to the Senate, which Knyazev could not buy or intimidate. Molchanov's sweetheart Marina (perhaps an incarnation of Katerina Bubnova) does suggest this course; but for no clear reason it is never carried out. Instead, Molchanov stays meekly in the town, his only resistance being a futile burst of rage when he sees Knyazev before him. As punishment for this outburst, Knyazev has him declared a madman and locked up.

The action moves on to a Shakespearean catastrophe. Three months later, Molchanov, now genuinely mad, breaks out of the asylum and sets fire to the whole town, himself perishing in the process; Marina takes poison rather than fall into the clutches of Knyazev. Until the last moments of the play it looks as if satanic evil has triumphed: the good characters have destroyed themselves, and the villain is victorious. Leskov then resorts to a deus ex machina to right the moral balance. *The Spendthrift* ends, something like Gogol's *Revizor*, with the sudden announcement that Knyazev and all his cohorts are to be brought to trial the very next day in one of the *new* courts in the provincial capital.

Besides the general implausibility of this melodramatic plot, Leskov's stagecraft is weak. He does not come to grips with the technical differences between the drama and narrative fiction. In the drama, the author can never comment; everything communicated to the audience must be said or done by the characters. If the audience must be informed about antecedent action, for example, it must be reported on the stage by one character to another. Dramatists must exert considerable ingenuity to make this "informing of the audience" believable. Leskov's solutions to the problem are crude. Characters tell things their interlocutors have known for years, as when Molchanov regales Knyazev's own factotum with a long narrative of the villain's crimes. Elsewhere Leskov arbitrarily introduces a "stranger," so that some workmen can fill him in on what has been going on in the town, and he can ask the appropriate questions. Leskov even puts the soliloquy to use for this purpose. We may accept the soliloquy as a stage convention enabling the author to communicate a character's private thoughts and feelings; but when a solitary character, in an otherwise realistic play, turns to the audience and tells what has happened offstage, the audience is likely to draw unfortunate conclusions about the author's stagecraft. Toward the end of *The Spendthrift* Marina escorts her blind mother out of the shed where Marina has been hiding from Knyazev, and into which the mother has "accidentally" wandered. On her return Marina turns to the audience and says—to herself: "Oh! Oh! They saw me! Now all is lost [. . .] I couldn't restrain myself. I led her to the porch and wanted to turn back. But there in the entryway she slipped in the darkness [darkness is apparently also a problem for the blind] . . . I thought she had hurt herself. . . . jumped out after her. . . . and they opened the door and brought lights" (1:479).

As in *The Islanders*, the melodramatic scenes in *The Spendthrift* verge on parody. At the end of act 4, for instance, Knyazev appears on stage with a crowd of henchmen and catches Molchanov drinking with Marina. He declares that Molchanov has stolen money from him, orders him seized, and confiscates his wallet. Molchanov escapes into the woods, leaving Knyazev to turn his amorous attentions to Marina. To trick the villain, she agrees to go off into the woods with him; as they are walking, she pushes him against a hollow tree that happens to be the hiding place of Barefoot Alyosha. (Barefoot Alyosha is a former merchant who has been mad ever since Knyazev almost drowned him at the time he killed Molchanov's father; a kind of Shakespearean fool, Alyosha symbolizes Knyazev's bad conscience.) As Knyazev falls against the tree, Alyosha seizes him, calling, "I drown! I drown!" Momentarily overcome by superstitious horror, Knyazev cries out, "Maksim! Maksim! [Molchanov's father] Let me go! I will repent!" He raises his arms in fear, giving Marina an opportunity to recapture Molchanov's wallet; "laughing hysterically," she runs off with it.

Besides the fool, Leskov resurrects a number of other antique pieces of Shakespearean stage equipment. "Vulgar," lower-class characters form a chorus to comment on the action in appropriately folksy language. The dénouement is foreshadowed by portents and prodigies; and the catastrophe itself takes place during a tremendous storm, with thunder, lightning, and violent wind serving to fan the fires set by Molchanov and to provide suitable orchestration for his and Marina's tragic demise. But the Renaissance stage machinery creaks noisily in this nineteenth-century play.

The Spendthrift was produced at the Aleksandrinsky Theater in Petersburg on November 1, 1867, and repeated there six times during the season—a moderate success. (Then, as now, Russian theaters were operated on the repertory system.) It was given at the Maly Theater in Moscow the following year and subsequently widely performed in the provinces. Although never a mainstay of the Russian theater, it was occasionally revived during the nineteenth and early twentieth century and is sometimes performed today: its melodramatic vigor and vivid characters may provide relief from the drabness of Soviet morality plays.

Leskov retained a certain affection—defensive, as usual—for this unique dramatic child. Only a few weeks before his death he told an interviewer who had asked him whether he customarily drew up plans for his works: "Even the play *The Spendthrift* I wrote without a plan. You are so young that you surely don't remember it. It was denounced, like everything I wrote, but people say that it is not wholly bad; and when it was first performed, Gedeonov [the director of the Imperial theaters] assured me that it would last for ten years; and now a quarter of a century has gone by, and it is still on the boards."[8]

Somewhat earlier Leskov had been more forthright about the play's faults. "Twenty years ago I wrote my single, very weak theatrical play *The Spendthrift*. In its day [it] was unanimously attacked by all the critics, and only P. Shchebalsky, one of the more tolerant reviewers, noted that I had caught the new mores and currents in the merchant milieu. But since my play was bad, my sketches of the new characters and tendencies in the milieu remained unnoticed."[9]

The critics' unanimity against *The Spendthrift*, as usual in the 1860s, had little to do with the play itself. Partly encouraged by a silly preface attached to the play by the editor of *Literary Library*, the radicals interpreted Leskov's play as an attack on judicial reform. Since the new court is the deus ex machina that resolves the action, Leskov felt indignant about this misinterpretation: "In *The Spendthrift* I showed how unjust was the justice of the prereform courts, and meanwhile *everyone*, headed by Suvorin and Burenin in Korsh's *Petersburg News*, wrote that I was 'vilifying the *new courts'*—although the concluding words of the play are as follows: 'So this is how the *new courts have caught us.'* "[10]

Leskov also had difficulty persuading people that he had his legal facts straight, that it was possible to have a sane person legally declared a spendthrift and deprived of control over his property. The censors objected on these grounds, and Leskov was obliged to cite three actual cases in order to convince them that he was not unfairly besmirching Russia's legal dignity. Since similar skepticism was prevalent among the public, Leskov took the peculiar step of publishing, in an anonymous article written by himself, a defense of the legal accuracy of the play:

> The appearance of the drama *The Spendthrift*, with its somewhat original, but by no means supernatural plot, caused an uproar, not only in the Theatrico-Literary Committee [the censorship] but even in the press, the organs of which [. . .] beat the drums, some asserting that it was only an anecdote on which it was impossible to construct a play, and others, still more reasonably, that it was simply made up by the author and a slander of Russian life, whereas [. . .] in Petersburg five individuals are known who to this day bear on themselves all the weight of that arbitrary abuse of power on which Mr. Stebnitsky's drama is based.

Leskov gives their names: Mr. Ya——v in Petersburg, Sergei Ku——n from Moscow, Or——v from Kashino, and so on, as if they were witnesses for the defense.[11]

According to his son, Leskov was so disheartened by the hostile and unfair criticism showered upon *The Spendthrift* that he lost confidence in his powers and abandoned the theater.[12] A few later lists of characters and sketches of plots for plays were never worked up.[13] But judging by *The Spendthrift* we may suspect that Leskov's aesthetic instinct contributed to his decision. He was beginning to discover that he was not a universal genius. A genius he was; but his gifts lay in another area.

ぴ11ひ

A Chronicle of Old Town

Early in 1866 Leskov began one of the most original, and ultimately most successful, artistic enterprises of his career. Seeking respite from his war with the nihilists, he undertook to search deeply, both in his own heart and in the heart of his country, for something more meaningful and lasting than the word-battles of Petersburg. There was more to Russia, he knew, than journalistic tempests and more in himself than the vindictive anger he had poured into *No Way Out*. The true Russia was not the Petersburg of ink-pot vendettas. The real life of the country lay in the depths of those vast spaces, where a peaceful population lived its age-old life of toil and repose, joy and suffering, thinking thoughts altogether different from those that agitated the deracinated literati. Leskov had never felt comfortable with intellectuals, that "rootless and characterless herd of Petersburg scribblers";[1] and his attempts to portray them in fiction had proved disastrous. Despite his intense reading, he still felt insecure in the world of European culture. But he was proud of his Russianness: his roots in his country were deep and his experience wide. He determined to take a long view, to try to see what Russia had been, what it was, and what it was to be. So he began the "chronicle" that eventually became *Cathedral Folk*. This work, in its final form, came to be regarded as the apotheosis in Russian literature of the Orthodox clergy and thus of Leskov's ancestors, the long line of priests from the village of Leski that had been broken by his father's secularization. Revile it as the intellectuals might, the Orthodox church was still the most authentic cultural voice of the Russian people, the repository of its ideals and its art. If you wanted to comprehend the soul of Russia, you had first to understand its religious life.

Originally, Leskov did not intend to limit himself to the priests or a priestly view of Russia. He planned to represent the inner life of all the classes, from gentry to peasantry, especially those who had remained genuinely Russian, not become would-be Europeans. In his Stary

173

Gorod ("Old Town," later contracted to Stargorod) he would show a microcosm of the true Russia in a single town, with its organic life, its ancient traditions and loyalties. The life of this town was by no means stagnant or motionless. Its inhabitants aspired to social justice, truth, and progress, but its fundamental spirit was alien to the hot-house notions cultivated by the Petersburg intellectuals.

In Leskov's conception, the Russian people were, as in the Gospel story, waiting for the angel to stir the water and give it the power to heal their afflictions. Hence the original title of Leskov's "chronicle": "Waiting for the Moving of the Water" (*Čajuščie dviženija vody*), a quotation from John 5:3-4: "In these [the five porches of Bethesda] lay a great multitude of impotent folk, of blind, halt, withered, waiting for the moving of the water. For an angel went down at a certain season into the pool, and troubled the water: whosoever then first stepped in was made whole of whatsoever disease he had."

Leskov was determined to avoid the novel proper, which for him was indissolubly associated with Petersburg and with the angry, recent, "literary" side of his career. His Old Town would know nothing of that imported and artificial form, by very definition an invention, a fiction, which furthermore seemed to require the writer to take up the hackneyed subject of "romance." Leskov undertook instead to write the *history* of Stary Gorod. However, the use of the term "history" to denote an account of fictional events in a fictional place is an illusionistic device and cannot be taken at face value. As Thomas Eekman has observed, *Cathedral Folk* remains a novel in spite of Leskov's denials, if that term is defined broadly enough to encompasss any substantial work of fiction.[2] Moreover, Leskov himself often slipped and referred to *Cathedral Folk* as a novel.[3] Nevertheless, especially at the time he was writing it, Leskov insisted that his work belonged to a different genre. He sometimes called it "history" or a "history of bygone years,"[4] but his final designation was *khronika*, "chronicle." The Greek word seemed more flexible than the Russian equivalent *letopis'*, which perhaps evoked too exclusively the Russian medieval annals. Morever, *khronika* was already current as a literary term, having been used, for instance, in Sergei Aksakov's masterpiece, *A Family Chronicle* (1856). Initially, Leskov even put forward a compromise term, "novelistic chronicle" (*romaničeskaja xronika*), as he describes the work in a letter to his first publisher: "I urgently request that in the advertisement in the next issue [of *Notes of the Fatherland*] you print not 'a large work of fiction,' but simply announce it [. . .] as a '*novelistic chronicle*'—'Waiting for the Moving of the Water,' for it will be a chronicle, and not a novel. So it was conceived, and so it grows by God's grace. It is not a usual thing with us, but we can learn."⁵ Early in 1866 the overall plan and theme for this nonnovel had been discussed in detail and agreed upon with Semyon Dudyshkin, the editor of *Notes of the Fatherland*, who accepted it in advance and gave Leskov encouragement. Part one was delivered to Dudyshkin in July 1866 (10:362). Dudyshkin was the only editor, perhaps the only Petersburg intellectual, whom Leskov trusted and, indeed, loved; his sudden death, on September 18, 1866, was a tremendous blow to Leskov and to the progress of his chronicle. For a brief period after Dudyshkin's death the magazine was edited by its hard-bitten old publisher, Andrei Kraevsky, a man with whom Leskov's relations were far from cordial. "Waiting for the Moving of the Water" thus began a six-year career of tribulations with its publishers, until it finally emerged as *Cathedral Folk* in Katkov's *Russian Messenger*.

Three installments of "Waiting for the Moving of the Water" appeared in *Notes of the Fatherland* in the spring of 1867. Before the third installment came out, Leskov was engaged in an acrimonious dispute with Kraevsky over what he considered arbitrary editorial changes made to anticipate the objections of the censors. At that time *Notes of the Fatherland* was not subject to preliminary censorship, but could be punished by fines and suspension of it published something objectionable. To protect himself, Kraevsky privately hired government censors to blue-pencil his magazine in advance. According to Leskov, when he saw the first installments of his novel full of gaps and distortions, he begged Kraevsky not to publish any further parts without his prior agreement to any changes; to allow him to confront the censors and defend his text; and if that failed, to let him fill in some of the gaps left by their reckless scissors. When the third installment appeared, substantially changed without the author's knowledge, Leskov angrily withdrew the book altogether.⁶

Leskov was embittered by this experience and nursed a grudge over it for years: his resentment became more acute when he discovered how difficult it was to sell a half-published work to any other magazine. No doubt he had good reason to be indignant about Kraevsky's high-handedness. But the cessation of the book's publication in *Notes of the Fatherland* did force Leskov to reconsider his whole conception of it; and the enforced slowdown in its production ultimately worked to its advantage. Leskov had been rescued from his own excessive ambitions.

For in his original design of "Waiting for the Moving of the Water," Leskov had started something he would never have been able to finish or shape into a unified whole. As he later acknowledged, "When I am conceiving a plan, I overreach myself and try to take in whole worlds and harm myself in this way."[7] His chronicle grew like a huge, branching plant. Individual episodes were lopped off and became independent stories or novels; others withered and died without reaching maturity. *Cathedral Folk* is only one part of a vast, amorphous complex including several independent and separately published units, only some of which overlap with the final text of *Cathedral Folk*.

This body of interlocking material potentially resembles Zola's *Rougon Macquart* or Faulkner's Yoknapatawpha County series, providing a complete sociology of its locality, class by class, and its history as well. But Leskov seemed to lack the artistic stamina to carry through such a grandiose scheme; and the results, except for *Cathedral Folk*, remain fragmentary.

The parts of this Old Town complex are listed below in chronological order, for identification purposes.

1. "Waiting for the Moving of the Water." Three installments of a large-scale "chronicle."[8]

2. "Kotin the He-Cow and Platonida." A short story, originally constituting chapters 4-9 of "Waiting for the Moving of the Water"; revised and published as a separate work in 1867.[9]

3. "Dwellers in God's House" (*Božedomy*). Described as "episodes from the unfinished novel 'Waiting for the Moving of the Water,' " it was published in the first two numbers of *Literary Library* for 1868.[10] This is the section of the original chronicle that dealt with the clergy; it corresponds roughly to part one of *Cathedral Folk*. *Literary Library* ceased publication after the second number for 1868; and so the "Dwellers in God's House" were once again left up in the air.

In the summer of 1868 Leskov managed to sell "Dwellers in God's House" to V. V. Kashpirev's new magazine *Dawn* (*Zarja*) and received a substantial advance. Publication was to start early in 1869. Kashpirev intended to continue in *Dawn* the moderate liberal line adhered to in Dudyshkin's time by *Notes of the Fatherland*, which had just been captured by the radicals. Leskov, along with Dostoevsky's friend Nikolai Strakhov and the antiradical novelist Viktor Klyushnikov, was to be a member of the editorial board.[11] But before the end of the year, these hopes had been dashed.

When he received the manuscript of "Dwellers in God's House," Kashpirev claimed that it was twice as long as had been agreed upon;

furthermore, he alleged that Leskov had violated their contract by simultaneously selling "The Dwarfs of Plodomasovo," which he insisted was an integral part of "Dwellers in God's House," to Katkov's *Russian Messenger*. Kashpirev therefore canceled the contract and in the summer of 1869 brought suit against Leskov for the money he had advanced. Leskov brought a countersuit, claiming damages for Kashpirev's violation of the contract. At the trial, held on August 12, 1869, both parties were denied damages. Leskov, however, was required to repay, in installments, the advance he had received from Kashpirev.[12]

In 1870-71 Leskov attempted to sell "Dwellers in God's House" to S. A. Yuriev's new Slavophile magazine, *Colloquy* (*Beseda*). But Yuriev balked at reprinting so much material that had been published before, even though the author offered to let him have it free. Leskov finally sold his novel to Katkov for *Russian Messenger*, where it was published as *Cathedral Folk*.

4. "Old Times in the Village of Plodomasovo." In the meantime, Leskov had separated from his original chronicle the section dealing with the gentry, on which he now planned to write a separate novel or even a trilogy.[13] This novel was never completed, but three parts of it were published independently in 1869, two of them, "Boyarin Nikita Yurievich" and "Boyarinya Marfa Andreyevna," under the general title "Old Times in the Village of Plodomasovo."[14] All three parts were also included in the volume of Leskov's short stories published the same year.[15]

5. "The Dwarfs of Plodomasovo." This is the third part of "Old Times in the Village of Plodomasovo." It was published separately in *Russian Messenger*, being Leskov's first contribution to that magazine.[16] With a slightly different text, it was included in its entirety in *Cathedral Folk*. It was also reprinted separately in Leskov's collected works.[17]

6. *Cathedral Folk*. This is essentially the same work as "Dwellers in God's House," but carried through to completion. It first appeared in *Russian Messenger* in 1872.[18]

"Waiting for the Moving of the Water" is indeed a history. Leskov begins his narrative in the seventeenth century, when Old Town's inhabitants, true to the antiquity of their city (though not an important historical site, it is twice mentioned in the primary Russian chronicle, which deals with events up to the beginning of the twelfth century) repudiated the "Nikonian" innovations of the official Orthodox church and clung to the "ancient piety" of their fathers. The action, however, commences at the end of the eighteenth century, with a fully drawn portrait of the leader of the Old Town Old Believers, the merchant Mina Silych Kochetov, an ideal patriarch, revered by his followers as an "ark gilded by the spirit [. . .] carried above the waters of the sea of life, saving us [. . .] from the flood of sin and eternal death." Under Catherine II and Paul, Kochetov had been persecuted and imprisoned for his faith, but was released on the accession of Alexander I. The national crisis of 1812 aroused his patriotic spirit; and after he had attended the famous "estates general" in Moscow (described in *War and Peace*), when the Russian classes offered themselves up to their young tsar for his crusade against the invader, Kochetov was moved to reconcile himself with the state church. His moral authority was such that half the population of Old Town followed him into Orthodoxy, the other half remaining Old Believers.[19] The portrait of Kochetov, presented in archaized language, is striking, despite the idealization; but his conversion to Orthodoxy seems inadequately motivated, perhaps dictated by ideological rather than artistic considerations—a charge also brought against the similar conversion of Old Believers at the end of "The Sealed Angel." The return of the Old Believers to the church, however desirable from the official and even the human point of view, appeared improbable to Leskov's contemporaries. Especially in the eyes of his nihilist enemies, he seemed to be serving up official wish fulfillments in an effort to curry favor with his imperial masters.

After the defection of Kochetov, the remaining Old Believers in Old Town elected a new elder, Semyon Deyev, a grimmer figure, "vengeful and inclined toward anger." His gloomy, prisonlike house on the edge of town is a symbol of his character and of the austere, unyielding spirit of the Old Believers and their merchant leaders. Leskov originally intended to recount in detail the experiences of these hard-core schismatics in the face of the persecutions and pressures of the nineteenth century, but he never carried out this plan. In the final version of *Cathedral Folk*, the Old Believers are relegated to a subsidiary position, a foil for the generosity of Father Tuberozov and a manifestation of the incompatibility of his humanity with bureaucracies, both ecclesiastical and secular. And even in "Waiting for the Moving of the Water" as originally published, the story concerning the Old Believers is no representative sampling of their experiences. It rather consists of the very atypical series of episodes that formed the plot of the short story "Kotin the He-Cow and Platonida." After "Waiting for the Moving of the Water" was abandoned, Leskov evidently felt that the narrative material of this section was sufficiently integrated to stand as an independent unit. He was only partly right: this story still shows the ragged edges left when it was torn from the parent novel. Despite its faults, "Kotin the He-Cow and Platonida" remains a revealing work.

One night a girl of eighteen was ejected from Deyev's schismatic fortress for illicit pregnancy—a crime doubly heinous for an Old Believer, since her child's father was the Orthodox sexton. A year later this sexton's accidental death left the mother and her infant son destitute. She survived only by disguising her son as a girl and entering a convent with "her." This son, Konstantin Pizonsky, is the first hero of the story, and one of the first in Leskov's long series of righteous men.

Brought up in the convent until the age of twelve, Konstantin believed himself a girl. When his puberty forced his mother to take him out and restore him to the male sex, he never could break the habit of using feminine grammatical forms, which made him the object of savage ridicule from his schoolmates. Although not stupid, he is so terrified by the school that despite repeated floggings he cannot even learn to write his name properly; he either hypnotically stretches it out to an infinitely long *Konstantintintintintintin*, or chops it off at a mere *Kotin*. This anecdote, perhaps implausible but picturesque and effective, is told with a flourish: it is one of those glittering narrative beads strung together in many of Leskov's stories. The anecdote itself and the character of Konstantin—much altered but recognizable—are drawn from an acquaintance of Leskov's Kiev days, a semiliterate sexton also known as Kotin. He appears under this name in "Pechersk Eccentrics," with the surname "Lomonosov" ("Broken-Nose"), not from any kinship with the eighteenth-century scientist and poet, but because of the actual state of his nose—a feature also shared by the he-cow Kotin.

The sexual confusion of Pizonsky will no doubt cause Freudian eyebrows to be raised. Although Leskov does not delve into the psychological ramifications, it transpires that the femininity of the hero has a particular meaning for the author. After some time Pizonsky is expelled from the seminary and sent as a recruit into the army. Years later he is discharged and returns to Old Town to find himself destitute and alone: his mother is dead, and his Deyev relatives will have nothing to do with him. He tracks down a cousin in a neighboring village only to find that she too, along with her husband, is dead, leaving two infant daughters, who are being cared for—very badly—by a blind old beggar woman. Pizonsky abducts these two children and carries them back to Old Town in a sack.

Leskov then describes in detail how, little by little, starting from nothing, Pizonsky establishes a household for himself and the little girls. Pizonsky initially obtains some material assistance from his relative (by marriage), Platonida Deyeva, the young wife of the middle-aged scion of the Deyev dynasty. (This assistance is, until the very end, the only manifest connection between the "Kotin" and "Platonida" parts of the story. There is an implied parallelism and contrast between these two main characters and their fates, which provides an abstract unity for these otherwise disparate halves of the story.) By ingenuity and persistence Pizonsky establishes a reputation as a handyman, making himself indispensable all over town. Eventually the city fathers let him occupy a vacant island in the middle of the river, where he builds a cozy house and garden for his family. Always self-effacing, physically unprepossessing with his bald head and crooked nose, Pizonsky personifies that selfless love combined with practical competence, self-reliance, and perseverance which for Leskov are the essential qualities of righteousness.

Leskov calls Pizonsky a *doílets*, a nonexistent masculine form coined from the feminine *doílitsa*, an affectionate term used of a good cow, a "feeder," a "nourisher." This concocted masculine variant of a feminine noun symbolizes the ambiguity of Pizonsky's sexuality. He is essentially a mother, a breast-feeder, a he-cow. The adoption of the girls enables him to fulfill himself as a woman, to play a maternal role at home while functioning as a male in his economic life. He never shows a trace of masculine sexual interests, or of overt sexuality of any kind. It seems, then, as was suggested in the case of Artur Benni, that in Leskov's moral system desexualization is often the price of male sainthood. Positive masculinity seems to imply an aggressiveness and self-assertion incompatible with the meekness and humility of the saint. Moreover, Leskov, like St. Paul, tends to regard sexuality itself as intrinsically sinful. A surprising number of Leskov's male saints are, in effect, *castrati*. Furthermore, practically all Leskov's fictional representations of active, youthful sexuality are illicit, adulterous, or even incestuous, and associated with crimes and punishments. Leskov's endemic antisexualism has much in common with the position later expounded in extreme form by Tolstoy in "The Kreutzer Sonata"; and it is therefore not surprising that the elder Leskov found these views so congenial.

In the early 1880s, after the break-up of his marriage with Katerina Bubnova, Leskov tried to act out his own literary scenario, with himself in the role of Pizonsky. In 1883 he acquired a new cook, an Estonian woman with a four-year-old daughter named Varya. The mother he discharged two years later, but Varya stayed with Leskov, without her mother, from the time she was six until his death, when she was sixteen. She was not his illegitimate daughter, as he affirmed on numerous occasions, but an "orphan" to whom he had "given shelter," following the commandments of his heart and his Savior. A large literature and correspondence developed on the subject of orphan-love, with Leskov subtly but gratifyingly exhibiting himself as a shining example of Christian charity. He responded with fury if anyone suggested that the bachelor flat of an old man was not a suitable place for a little girl to grow up, or that he had wrongfully bullied Varya's mother into signing away her natural claim to her daughter. Although he never formally adopted Varya nor treated her as a full social equal, Leskov in 1892 made a will granting her a share of his estate equal to that of his daughter Vera and his son Andrei, a share which she duly inherited on his death, much to their resentment. Soon after that she married and lost all contact with her Leskov "relatives." Unfortunately, she left no memoirs.[20]

The orphan is from the beginning an important figure in Leskov's emotional constellation. The love of orphans, besides enabling a man to be a mother, proves to be one of the most gratifying of all loves. Since the orphan has no unquestioned rights, no enforceable moral claim, the nurturer can bask in the glow of his virtue, while retaining complete power to set whatever limit he likes, both to the nurture and to the love. Sons or daughters may take their nurture for granted, knowing instinctively that it is their natural right; but the sheltered orphan must carry an everlasting debt of gratitude, reinforced by the threat, whether stated or implied, of renewed abandonment if the bills are not regularly paid. And the shelterer himself can freely engage in that endlessly satisfying pastime, moral self-congratulation, perhaps with the bonus of social approbation.

The reverse side of Kotin's antisexual virtue is displayed in the second, "Platonida" part of the story. Here Leskov repeats the essential elements of the plot of "Lady Macbeth," except that the sex and violence are rendered as attempts or wishes rather than deeds. Nevertheless, the consequences are almost as dire.

Like Katerina Izmailova, Platonida Deyeva is a lush, big-breasted young beauty married to a man twice her age who duplicates the dourness, grimness, and despotism of his old father. Like Katerina, she is childless: the inability of these middle-aged tyrants to fertilize their young wives seems to symbolize their emotional and social sterility as well. A virile young lover is available: her husband's younger brother, Avenir, who resembles the Sergei of "Lady Macbeth" in Sergei's earlier appearances. Platonida, however, remains virtuous, despite the ardent attentions of Avenir and her affection for him. The climax comes when her husband unexpectedly dies—a natural death this time. On the night after the funeral, not Avenir but her old father-in-law, his lust aroused by vodka, climbs in her bedroom window. Platonida struggles with him, calling for Avenir's help, and in her desperation strikes at the old man with an ax. He falls senseless to the floor, and Platonida, thinking she has killed him, rushes from the house and disappears forever. Actually the ax had struck old Deyev only a glancing blow on the shoulder, just at the moment when, unseen by Platonida, Avenir had seized his father from behind and forced him to the floor.

This scene of the attempted rape is powerfully told, only slightly spoiled by the implausibility of the finale: it is hard to believe that Platonida would not have seen Avenir, or that he would have let her rush away without speaking to her. But Leskov cannot allow Avenir and Platonida to come together: they must be punished for their incestuous and murderous wishes as if they were deeds. Platonida hides out with Pizonsky—thus establishing a second link between the two halves of the story. The next day the old man, showing his wound, publicly accuses his son and daughter-in-law of trying to kill him. Avenir is arrested, and a fruitless search is made for Platonida. Pizonsky is arrested on suspicion of complicity, but he will reveal nothing of Platonida's whereabouts.

In the 1867 book version, Leskov broke off "Kotin the He-Cow and Platonida" there, adding only a postscript: "When the novel was printed in the magazine, this chapter ended with the words, 'We will see how valid were the suppositions concerning Konstantin Ionych's involvement in the affair of the lost widow.' Now we must change this conclusion and say that we will never see this, for the novel 'Waiting for the Moving of the Water,' for many reasons not dependent on the author, cannot be continued."[21]

More than two decades later, on the urging of Suvorin, who planned to issue "Kotin the He-Cow and Platonida" as a separate volume in his "Cheap Library," Leskov undertook to finish the story. Apparently he wrote the ending on the proof sheets of the book, since in a letter he irritably asks Suvorin not to press him for it until the proofs are ready, since he has not yet "thought it out."[22] The result shows how difficult it is for an artist to return successfully to a long-abandoned work. The new, final chapter, though only half a page long, is a disaster.

Platonida, it turns out, had hidden herself among some eremitic nuns, eventually becoming their elder. She had "wept out her eyes" and is blind. Avenir had been sent as a soldier to the Caucasus and for heroism in action commissioned an officer and had married a general's daughter. Years later he returns to Old Town and pays a visit to Platonida's hermitage. This visit, adapted from one of Turgenev's most affected and unsatisfactory scenes, Lavretsky's glimpse of Liza as a nun at the end of *A Nest of Gentlefolk*,[23] brings the story to an unbearably false, pseudo-romantic close: "The blind old woman, feeling his head, asked, 'Is this head repentent or is it still unrepentent?' Avenir replied, 'It is repentent.' 'Good,' said the elder Ioil [i.e., Platonida]. 'Feed [sic] with reason thy path toward the good and peaceful haven,' and then added, 'And now farewell, with God, forever' " (1:262).

Leskov used the same ghastly image, the contrite nun with wept-out eyes and even with little icons inserted in the eye-sockets, again in "Pavlin" (1874). In both these cases, and in that of Katerina Izmailova as well, it seems that the sexually radiant woman must be punished, by blindness, life imprisonment, or death, for having, like Eve, acted the part of temptress of the "innocent" male.

After the disappearance of Platonida, the original "Waiting for the Moving of the Water" went on to describe the fates of the two girls adopted by Pizonsky. The older one, Glafira, grows up to be an irritable, hysterical woman, who marries the stupid heir of a rich merchant family so that she can rule him. A good deal of attention is given to her and her unhappy marriage before Leskov drops this thread to introduce Father Tuberozov and his diary, one of the most successful parts of *Cathedral Folk*. After the end of the diary, we learn that in old age Pizonsky had adopted another orphan, a boy this time, the offspring of the town half-wit, who had been seduced by a soldier and had committed suicide after giving birth to this child. At this point "Waiting for the Moving of the Water" breaks off.

Pizonsky himself reappears in the final version of *Cathedral Folk*, but with details inconsistent with those in "Kotin the He-Cow" and "Waiting for the Moving of the Water." Leskov eliminated the two girls and their life histories, but he wanted to retain Pizonsky as an illustration of orphan-loving saintliness. Leskov therefore transfers the episode of the adoption of the bastard *boy* to Tuberozov's diary. There, under the year 1837, it is related how a year earlier, Pizonsky, already elderly and living alone on his island, had given shelter to this abandoned infant. Later, in an entry under the year 1861—one of the many strangely careless chronological slips in this diary—Pizonsky is still caring for the same "little boy," who by that time would have been twenty-five. Clearly, Pizonsky was an eternal image of benevolent tenderness, and his orphan charge could not be allowed to grow up.

In Tuberozov's 1837 entry Leskov's panegyric to orphan-love is sung in its purest and most affecting form. Seeing from his window Pizonsky's joy in caring for this unwanted baby, Tuberozov is moved to tears and to making a famous entry in his diary concerning Russian charity, which ends with the oft-quoted apostrophe, "O my soft-hearted Russia, how splendid thou art!"[24] Later, the priest pronounces a sermon on the same subject, alluding, though not by name, to the saintly example of the humble Pizonsky: "I talked of how sweet it is to warm the defenseless bodies of children and to implant seeds of good in their souls. When I said this, I felt that my eyelids were moist, and I saw that many of my listeners had begun to wipe their eyes and to look about the church for the one to whom my heart alluded, Kotin the beggar, Kotin the feeder of the orphaned" (4:36-37).

Tuberozov's parishioners, Leskov's readers, and obviously Leskov himself found this scene immensely moving. Victorian eyes were always ready to mist at such spectacles of sinless love and saintly virtue in humble circumstances. Twentieth-century readers, however, their innocence lost to Freud, may be aware of the self-indulgences disguised in the fantasy. Pizonsky's sexual confusion makes his motherhood hard to accept as pure Christian charity, and Tuberozov's admiration of such "lesser brethren" may seem too patronizing to be genuine.

Although his paternal ancestry and religious concerns gave him a feeling of deep involvement with the Orthodox clergy, Leskov's basic sense of identity was by no means that of a priest or a priest's son. His father had effectively broken the family's ecclesiastical connections, and Leskov was born a gentleman, a *barchuk* (lordling), as he liked to say. Through Mikhail Strakhov, he got, early in his life, an intimate view of the life of a high-born nobleman. Thus Leskov claimed identity with the ruling class of Russia, which possessed wealth and power and, since the eighteenth century, had replaced the clergy as the country's chief bearers of culture. In an all-embracing survey of Russian life as epitomized in Old Town, the top of the social pyramid would obviously demand much attention. For many reasons this class was an attractive subject for literary treatment. With his advantages of education, travel, and service in the capitals, the gentleman's range of experience was more varied than that of the stuck-at-home local, and his mental life richer and more accessible to literary expression.

In the literary complex centered around Old Town, Leskov planned to give the gentry their due in a big novel dealing with the Plodomasovs, the leading aristocratic family of the region, whose manor house and estates lay a few hours' drive from the town. This family was to be viewed in a long historical perspective, its fortunes traced back to the reign of Peter the Great. Leskov abandoned this ambitious project long before it was completed. Three related short stories or "sketches," as the author called them, remain: the two-part "Old Times in the Village of Plodomasovo" and "The Dwarfs of Plodomasovo."

"Old Times in the Village of Plodomasovo" displays Leskov's gift for pure narrative—the vivid presentation of events. These tales are simply good stories, beautifully written, with plenty of action and appropriate well-drawn, but not deeply perceived characters. By moving to the eighteenth century, Leskov seemingly liberated himself from the ideological and moral concerns that for him were inescapably bound up with mid-nineteenth-century themes; his narrative gift appears in its purest form.

In the first of the sketches, "Boyarin Nikita Yurievich," Leskov again draws on the figure of Mikhail Strakhov. Here the Strakhov image is projected back into the middle of the eighteenth century, the heyday of the Russian gentry, when their power and prestige were at their height, when each landlord ruled as an independent monarch on his own demesne and could do what he liked to anyone beneath him in rank, wealth, or influence. Equality before the law was not even a

185

legal fiction: one's civil rights varied in direct proportion to social standing and wealth.

In the main action of "Boyarin Nikita Yurievich," we see the hero, Nikita Plodomasov, in 1748, at the age of fifty-one. After a brief, enforced career in the service under Peter, he returned to his estates with the aim of devoting the rest of his life to enjoyment. With his army of retainers, he held vast hunting parties, trampling down his peasants' and his neighbors' fields; exacted exorbitant tolls from the merchants obliged to cross his lands; and established a large harem of serf girls. In late middle age he suddenly decides to marry the fifteen-year-old daughter of an impoverished neighbor. But the neighbor (unlike Leskov's grandfather) unexpectedly and daringly refuses Plodomasov's proposal, although the marriage would bring him advantages: he cannot bear to surrender his beloved daughter to the old reprobate.

The furious Plodomasov kidnaps the girl, Marfa Andreyevna Baitsurova, and forcibly marries her, although the authorities attempt to intervene. There is lots of stirring action: the wild ride of Plodomasov's army back to his estate bearing the captive girl; the presentation to Plodomasov of official orders, one of them signed by the Empress Elizabeth, to curb his wild ways and surrender his prey; finally the siege of the Plodomasov estate by the governor of the province with three companies of dragoons. The climax comes when the governor, victorious in his siege, is about to carry Plodomasov off to prison. Though married with a gag in her mouth, his young wife is still undefiled because of her threat to hurl herself from the second-story window if her husband attempted to touch her. A formal statement from her is required attesting that she had been married against her will. In this moment of truth she turns the plot upside down by announcing that her marriage had been voluntary and that she has no complaint to make against her husband. The charges against Plodomasov are dropped, and a new, married life begins for them both. From that time onward Plodomasov is a changed man. His violence and his lawlessness have departed from him. Humbly grateful and subservient to his strong-willed girl-wife, he spends his last years in anguished repentance for his sins. The psychology may not be convincing, either the unexpected decision of Marfa Andreyevna to rescue the dissolute old man and become his real wife, or his subsequent reform. But within the artistic framework of this story it does not matter. Such sudden psychological transformations seem suited to the precipitous action, and in adventure stories like this our standards of verisimilitude are in any case likely to be less severe.

In the sequel, "Boyarinya Marfa Andreyevna," we see the heroine as a beautiful young widow with an infant son. Unwilling to give up her independence and power, she rejects all suitors, electing to spend the rest of her life as the solitary monarch of the Plodomasov estates. She is a good monarch and a courageous one. In the climax of this story, a gang of thieves invade her mansion, and she endures horrible tortures rather than deliver to them the key of a strongbox. The box contains nothing of value, but it symbolizes her refusal to submit to violence. Her authority in her domain is absolute. In the other principal episode of the story, her twenty-year-old son, by this time a guards officer, meekly submits when his mother orders him whipped by the priest for getting a serf girl pregnant; she listens outside the bathhouse while the flogging is being carried out.

Although he admires her intellectually and tries to show her in the best possible light, Leskov's—and therefore the reader's—overall attitude toward Marfa Andreyevna remains ambivalent. There is clearly a high degree of idealization: Marfa Andreyevna is conceived as a *pravednitsa*, a pillar of undeviating virtue in the midst of a violent and corrupt society. Yet she is a despot who uses her power to humiliate her son; and having become a grandee, she treats those beneath her with condescension or contempt. On the whole, Leskov accents her positive qualities. In revising the story for his collected works (for the second volume 6, issued in 1890 to replace the one forbidden by the censors), Leskov eliminated a chapter in which he had described, as a counterweight to Marfa Andreyevna's puritanical indignation at her son's fornication, her amused and voyeuristic interest in her house serfs' sexual shenanigans.[25] In 1890 Leskov felt that his image of the ideal female autocrat was besmirched by this vicarious prurience.

Like many of Leskov's works of this period, "Old Times in the Village of Plodomasovo" reflects an obsessive concern with illicit sexuality. We can guess the reasons for this fascination: on one level Leskov's guilt over his abandonment of his lawful wife and daughter and his own illicit union with Katerina Bubnova; and on another, the Oedipal conflicts of his childhood. Associating it with violence and crime, Leskov represents sexuality as morally repugnant, though still charged with excitement. Until after his marriage, the sexual power of Nikita Yurievich is an aspect of his power as a slaveholder. His serf mistresses exist for him as female bodies to be penetrated, not as women. Only by desperate courage does Marfa Andreyevna avoid being raped by him. When she does submit to him, it is on her condition, as it were, that he transfer to her his masculine power: this was apparently her object in accepting the marriage.

Sexuality in the father is thus again identified with the cruelty and aggression of Strakhov. The good, strong mother resists it, then symbolically emasculates the father, and after his death renounces sexuality altogether (as Leskov's mother had done), retaining a monopoly of power. The son's attempt to emulate his father's erstwhile sexual authority over serf girls is met by the (perhaps jealous) mother with a childish and degrading (and thus also emasculating) punishment. After her son's departure, she "atones for" this behavior by an extraordinary display of tenderness toward his serf mistress and their bastard child. Finally, the mother is shown "investigating" the amorous carryings-on of her house serfs; but this scene is later expunged as unworthy of her.

The virulent antisexualism of Leskov's later years, his contemptuous repudiation of the "cult of penis and vagina"[26] was, we observe again, deeply rooted in his personality and amply anticipated in his early work.

The third of Leskov's "sketches" differs from the other two. Here there is no stirring action or derring-do, no gripping and cinematic scenes. The basis of this story is what Formalist critics have called realization of a metaphor. In relation to aristocratic despots like Marfa Andreyevna most people "feel small"; to symbolize this feeling, Leskov therefore creates characters who are literally small: two dwarf serfs bought by Marfa Andreyevna to amuse her bastard grandson (and herself). We are then made to see the world from their nanoid point of view. They are permanent children in the power of an almighty mother, with no chance of growing up and escaping her power. The smallness of the dwarfs gives Leskov and his readers an opportunity to indulge their Victorian fondness for quaintness, and Leskov a chance to display his command of the extraordinary wealth of hypocoristic forms in the Russian language.

The story gives the life history of the dwarfs, told as skaz by the male, Nikolai Afanasevich. At the time he relates his narrative he is an old man, looking back on a lifetime spent in the service of Marfa Andreyevna and her son. As a symbol of humble virtue, he is the perfect counterpart to Marfa Andreyevna's imperious righteousness. Nikolai Afanasevich is the ideal slave: docile, submissive, grateful for his mistress's kindnesses, tolerant of her foibles. He has not a drop of rebelliousness, nor of male sexuality. He is Marfa Andreyevna's faithful dog, whose only will is her wish.

Once again, this sequence of stories illustrates Leskov's grimly pessimistic attitude toward the battle of the sexes. He seems unable to imagine a relatively equal, give-and-take relationship; or perhaps such a relationship has no excitement for him. There is no middle ground between despotism and slavery. Moreover, there is an agonizing moral conflict, especially for the man, because male sexuality seems to lead inexorably to criminality. The sexually active male is at best an irresponsible fornicator and at worst an abductor and rapist; and both these crimes are ultimately punished by symbolic castration, administered by the woman. If a man (or boy) wants to be good, it would appear that he must renounce his sexuality altogether, voluntarily accept the castration, and meekly prostrate himself, like the dwarf, at the feet of the omnipotent Mother. With the fantasy of such a catastrophic dilemma lurking in his unconscious, it is not hard to understand why Leskov had such difficulty with the love theme, both in literature and in his life.

Although he himself once (correctly) described "The Dwarfs of Plodomasovo" as "a little anecdote having no connection whatever with the novel,"[27] Leskov nevertheless included the entire text in the final version of *Cathedral Folk*. These dwarfs appealed both to him and to his readers. In a note published while *Cathedral Folk* was appearing serially in *Russian Messenger*, Leskov claimed to have received numerous oral inquiries and letters from readers asking about the fate of the dwarfs and imploring him not to exclude them from the novel. He reassured them that the beloved dwarfs would be resurrected in part two.[28] Leskov evidently felt that the looseness of the chronicle form permitted such digressive material—background narratives on subsidiary characters—even when they had no connection with the main plot.

Marfa Andreyevna Plodomasova also appears as a character in *Cathedral Folk*, in the retrospective narrative of Nikolai Afanasevich and in the early parts of Father Tuberozov's diary. By including her and her dwarfs in his clerical novel Leskov created impossible chronological anomalies. To fulfill his original purpose, he would have had to compose additional stories or whole novels treating the two subsequent generations of Plodomasovs, Marfa Andreyevna's son and grandson, in order to bring the family down to the 1860s and provide a character to participate in the main action of *Cathedral*

Folk. Without this intervening material, Leskov had to stretch out his characters' lives to impossible lengths to reach from the kidnapping of Marfa Andreyevna in 1748 to the "present" (1867) of *Cathedral Folk.* If we calculate with Leskov's dates, Marfa Andreyevna lives to be 117; Nikolai Afanasevich is at least 97 when he tells his story in *Cathedral Folk,* and there are other instances of extraordinary longevity.[29]

The big, three-generation novel on the Russian gentry remained on Leskov's long-range agenda. He attempted it again in 1874 with *A Decrepit Clan* and again gave it up before he reached his goal. The task of representing historical successivity within a series of generations seemed to tax Leskov's powers beyond their capacity.

12

In God's Holy House

While he was writing *Cathedral Folk* and its various antecedents, Leskov was intermittently aware that he had undertaken something far more lasting and significant than his antinihilist novels. At bottom, Leskov knew that *No Way Out, The Bypassed,* and *At Daggers Drawn* were not major works of art. They were, as he said, "hasty, journalistic jobs." Yet he too, like his contemporaries, was influenced by two characteristic mid-nineteenth-century notions—or prejudices. These were, first, the ideology prejudice, still rampant in the Soviet Union, according to which the most important thing about a work of literature is not its artistic quality but its political or philosophical line; and second, the size prejudice, according to which sheer bulk is regarded as a measure of artistic importance and seriousness. A writer is to be judged by his major efforts, his longest and most substantial works. In Leskov's case this meant his big novels, which were second-rate. Therefore Leskov was pigeon-holed by critics as a second-rate, minor writer, "very close to Melnikov and on a level with Avdeyev," as one critic put it as late as 1891—an absurd misestimate typical of the period.[1] Leskov might be credited with a few pretty good short stories, but no one could buy his way to top artistic rank with such small change.

Yet one work of Leskov's was bulky enough to qualify as a heavy-weight and also shared the artistic quality of "Lady Macbeth" or "The Battle-axe." That work, of course, was *Cathedral Folk. Cathedral Folk* is the only one of Leskov's long works that on its own merits can be ranked as an indisputable classic. For that reason, it has perhaps been rated even higher by Leskov's defenders than it deserves. Especially in an age dominated by giant novels, it was comforting to have one large success to point to, one universally acknowledged monument with which its author's name could be linked as an appellative: Leskov, the author of *Cathedral Folk,* that "magnificent book," as Maxim Gorky called it.[2] But now, with the perspective of a century of time and the fact of several reputations, such as Maupassant's or Chekhov's, resting on short stories rather than novels, we find ourselves able to do our author full honors without pinning them all on *Cathedral Folk*. We may even concede that this novel does not quite rank among Leskov's very best works.

Cathedral Folk is indisputably a big book, and a good, if not a great, one. The author had ample reason to regard it with special fondness. "I love my *Dwellers in God's House* so much that I am ready to fuss over them again and again," he wrote in 1871, not discouraged by the many trials he had undergone in attempting to get the book published. "For the sake of your love of art and the idea of art, bestow your love on my *Dwellers* and take care of them. I place my greatest hopes in them."[3] Much later, when translations of *Cathedral Folk* began to appear in Western languages, Leskov felt his special affection for this work confirmed: "Akhilla is opening for me the doors into European literature," he wrote in 1886.[4] Leskov continued to take pride in the artistic quality of *Cathedral Folk* long after he had repudiated its ideology.

The strength of *Cathedral Folk* lies principally in its characterizations, especially that contrasting, but wonderfully integrated trio of dwellers in the Old Town cathedral: Father Savely Tuberozov, the thoughtful, courageous, though sometimes bull-headed archpriest; Zakhariya Benefaktov, Tuberozov's subordinate, the essence of gentleness and self-abnegation; and most picturesque, Deacon Akhilla Desnitsyn, a living oxymoron, a Cossack in a cassock, a man of giant physique, born to ride the steppes like a warrior of old, doing battle with his tsar's enemies, who finds himself incongruously clad in a clerical gown and living in the prosaic, small-spirited, overcivilized nineteenth century.

The technical means Leskov uses to realize these three characters are as diverse as their personalities. The middle figure, Father Zakhariya, is defined mostly by reflection of light from the other two: he is the valley between their peaks. In comparison with Akhilla he is small, weak, and gentle; in contrast with Savely, he is fecund in body,[5] but feeble in intellect and passive in spirit. He is a praying, not a thinking, Christian. Since Leskov seems to have little insight into this kind of spirituality, our view of Zakhariya is external, and a little patronizing. It is presented mostly in the form of direct analytical comparisons from the author.

In the case of Akhilla, the representation is also external and more than a little patronizing. The controlling attitude toward him, which the reader is made to share, is one of benevolent amusement. He is an eternal child, a child sometimes obstreperous, but good-hearted, loyal, and utterly guileless. Leskov's chief means for portraying him is a series of illustrative anecdotes that reveal his character and stand as semi-independent narrative gems as well. Akhilla provides the comic relief to the solemn Tuberozov, and the novel contains many hilarious episodes of which this comic Achilles is the hero, interposed with the serious and the tragic events in Tuberozov's life.

The comedy begins in Akhilla's seminary days. He had a magnificent bass voice—one of the essential attributes of a Russian deacon—and while in the seminary was called upon to perform a solo during an important church festival. He sang the solo superlatively, but was so carried away by his excitement that he could not stop singing, and kept on bellowing the words "And by griefs He was pierced" (*I skorb'mi ujazvlen, ujazvlen, ujazvlen*), until he had to be forcibly carried from the church.[6] Similarly, Akhilla's famous "duel" over a human skeleton (whose nonburial he considers sacrilegious) with the nihilist schoolteacher Varnava Prepotensky (who wants to use it for "atheistic" anatomical demonstrations to his pupils) is also essentially another comic anecdote: a tug-of-war over some bones between an oversized but underbrained deacon and an overaged adolescent prankster, eager to demonstrate his emancipation from convention and tradition. Spun out through several chapters, this puerile struggle constitutes the main action of the first part of the novel.

Throughout most of *Cathedral Folk*, Akhilla is an unchanging character. Perhaps recognizing his difficulty in representing psychological development, Leskov at the outset renounces any attempt to investigate the formation of his characters' personalities: "The years of early youth of these people [the clerical trio] do not concern us, nor the time of their childhood" (4:5). At the end of the book, however, the last comic anecdote involving Akhilla leads to a kind of transfiguration. Akhilla, the warrior for Christ, at last confronts the ultimate antagonist, the devil. This devil is in reality a local scamp who has terrorized the superstitious populace by dressing up with horns and claws and attacking people at night. Yet Akhilla's physical triumph over him—locked in lethal embrace, they fall together into an icy canal and nearly freeze to death—is symbolically elevated into a spiritual triumph over the real devil, the devil of his own childishness. Though he ultimately perishes from the exposure, Akhilla dies possessed of a wisdom and maturity he had lacked all his life.

The real protagonist of *Cathedral Folk* is Savely Tuberozov. Toward this character condescension is impossible: the reader must view him as an equal; and for a nineteenth-century Russian reader— that is, a member of the cultural elite—to view an Orthodox priest as an equal demanded a spiritual revolution. Two conventional attitudes toward the clergy were possible: patronizing benevolence if you were a believer, contemptuous hostility if you were not. Educated Russians who took their religion seriously and revered their priests as instruments of God still found it hard to respect them as men. It was only too true that the average Russian village or town priest was ignorant, poor, obsequious toward the gentry, grasping toward his peasant parishioners, unkempt, and frequently addicted to drink.

As the protagonist of his long novel designed to show the living spirit of Christianity burning bright in Russian Orthodoxy, Leskov was therefore obliged to create an idealized priest: intelligent, well read, warm-hearted, and courageous. Such is Savely Tuberozov. The danger in any such idealization is that the resulting character may turn out to be neither believable nor attractive—virtuous characters in literature often turn into unbearable prigs. But Leskov's Tuberozov manages to be both believable and likable.

For one thing, Father Tuberozov is a healthily flawed and human saint. He is conscious of his superiority to most of his clerical brethren. When a parishioner gives a carved walking-stick to each of the three cathedral-dwellers, Tuberozov is incensed that Zakhariya and Akhilla are treated as his equals. He immediately takes steps to make the canes suitably hierarchal, confiscating Akhilla's altogether and having his own and Zakhariya's inscribed with appropriately different Biblical quotations. Savely also inclines toward self-indulgence, through which he occasionally comes close to hypocrisy. He takes up pipe-smoking, but reprimands Akhilla for smoking cigarettes in public. Smoking remains a symbol of spiritual deterioration throughout the middle period of Tuberozov's life. His rise to moral grandeur, at the end of his life, is accompanied by a renunciation of tobacco.

Finally, despite the social revolution carried out by Leskov in obliging his readers to regard Tuberozov as their equal, the fact is that he does permit us after all to retain a certain measure of condescension in our attitude toward his priestly hero. Although Savely is intelligent, thoughtful, and surprisingly well read, he remains intellectually both a provincial and a priest. He reads history, the church fathers, and

two notable Englishmen, neither of them at all in literary fashion—
John Bunyan and Laurence Sterne (both favorites of Leskov). In
general, there is something quaint, old-fashioned and otherworldly
about Tuberozov. We feel toward him as toward a kindly old uncle—
charming, admirable, and lovable, but not a part of the sophisticated
modern world.

In order to present us with an interior view of this character, Leskov
resorts to a familiar device, the diary, a written analogue of the skaz.
More than half of part one of *Cathedral Folk* is taken up with Father
Tuberozov's "Demicoton Book"—the title symbolizing the quaintness
and old-fashionedness of its author. Demicoton was a heavy cotton
fabric widely used in Russia in the early nineteenth century, but by
1872 as picturesquely obsolete as Napoleonic uniforms. Father
Tuberozov's demicoton book is actually a calendar bound in this
fabric, on whose blank pages he has inscribed over many years his
occasional comments and reflections about his life.

The artistic success of the Demicoton Book depends partly on its
contents, a judicious mixture of public matters (Tuberozov's aspirations and difficulties as a priest) and private themes (his warm relationship with his wife, their grief over their childlessness). But the
content would not affect us so much if the style were not perfectly
appropriate to it. Leskov conveys the priest's thoughts in a language
precisely Tuberozov's own: a little bookish and antiquated, yet
vigorous and strong, seasoned with priestly Church Slavonicisms,
quotations from Scripture or the liturgy, plus some less exalted
specimens of "in-group" ecclesiastical jargon.

It is difficult to transpose these stylistic effects into another
language, and the translations of *Cathedral Folk* inevitably lose some
of its flavor.[7] The following parenthetically commented passage from
the Demicoton Book may suggest some of Leskov's verbal wizardry:

> The sexton Yevtikheich [the use of the patronymic alone is both
> colloquial and somewhat condescending—sextons were far
> beneath priests in status; moreover, the name itself is unusual
> (Greek Eutyches), rather uneuphoneous in Russian, and therefore
> slightly ridiculous] returned from the provincial capital [literally,
> "from the province," a common old colloquialism] and reported
> [using another archaic colloquialism] that between the Bishop
> [using not the precise technical term *episkop*, nor the common
> neutral term *arkhierei*, but *vladyka*, literally "master," a more in-
> group and emotion-laden term, also used as a mode of deferential

address] and the governor there took place a certain contention [the words for "certain" and "contention" are bookish] over a reciprocal official call.

2nd October. The rumors about the official-call contention [this adjectival form, and especially its combination with a substantive denoting an emotional event, sounds odd in both languages. We might accept "official-call etiquette," but hardly "official-call anger"] are confirmed. The governor, on his appearances in the cathedral on the tsar's name-day and birthday [the governor only attends church on official state occasions when his presence is required] has the custom at such time of conversing rather loudly. The Bishop resolved [an archaism, put in the deferential third-person plural] to put an end to this proceeding [bookish] and sent his staff-bearer [an acolyte specially assigned to carry the Bishop's staff] to ask His Excellency to conduct himself more decorously. The governor received the reprimand most choleric-ally [literally, "ambitiously": this Latinism is the most marked word in the whole passage, especially redolent of the seminary] and within a brief time renewed his loud colloquies with the gendarme colonel [in the original, "his loud with the gendarme colonel colloquies": this word order is more acceptable in Russian than in English, but very stilted]; but on this occasion the Bishop himself stopped and said loudly: "Then I, Your Excellency, shall be silent and shall begin when you have finished."

Of this act of the bishop's I heartily approve.[8]

Considering the pride Leskov took in Tuberozov's diary and the number of times he reworked the text,[9] it seems surprising that he allowed many gross chronological inconsistencies to remain. For example, the years 1837 and 1863 are repeated three times, with three different sets of events. In 1863 the events of January 13, 18, and 19 follow an event of February 2. The nihilistic official's wife Bizyukina appears as a married woman in an entry of 1849, but in the main part of the book, which takes place in 1867, she is still described as a "young matron." If Leskov noticed the mistakes, he considered them too insignificant to correct.[10] (Leskov's editors, both magazine and book, allowed these mistakes to survive many editions. There is no evidence in Leskov's published correspondence that any editor called them to his attention.)

Many contemporaries considered Tuberozov's diary the apex of Leskov's literary achievement, a moving view of the inner world of a Russian provincial priest in the austere Nicolaitan age. Leskov de-fended it against the cutting recommended by a critic friend with the assertion that it was "tenderly loved by the public and much honored."[11] If we venture to qualify this assessment, it would be on two grounds.

First, in the diary we occasionally catch a whiff of nineteenth-century sentimentality. The recurrent orphan theme is invoked again, linked with Savely's and his wife's grief over their childlessness. Tuberozov claims to be greatly touched when his wife, after many disappointments with hoped-for pregnancies, asks him if in his youth he had not sired any bastard children whom they might now adopt. His negative reply puts an end to the thought of adoption as the solution to their loneliness, even though the noble example of Pizonsky the he-cow is not only before their eyes, but enshrined in their hearts. One feels, therefore, that the genuineness of the couple's grief is called into question by their unwillingness to take steps to alleviate it. Such behavior is a perfect example of sentimentality: treasuring for their own sake emotions at least partly spurious. The couple's refusal to adopt—especially for a priest whose greatest homiletic moment is a sermon on orphan-love—seems to indicate that the original grief has become pleasurable in itself and that they are unwilling to relinquish this pleasure. Leskov must also be charged with the sentimentality, since he plays up Tuberozov's "sweet sorrow" as if it were the genuine article.

An additional disappointment in Tuberozov's diary is the limited view it gives us of the priest's inner life. We never see Father Tuberozov, either as man or as priest, in direct relations with his God. We see his church as a moral institution of this world, not as a means of contact with the next. The characters undergo no religious, as distinct from ethical, experiences. We learn a great deal about Father Tuberozov's view of the church and his program for its reform—his ecclesiastical sociology, so to speak—but we find out nothing about his theology. We never see him in his sacerdotal roles—not at the supreme moment in the Eucharist when the apostolic power he wields transforms humble bread and wine into the body and blood of Christ, nor, for that matter, at any other moment in the liturgy. Nor do we ever see him in the confessional, exercising the awesome power vested in him to absolve men of their sins.

Instead, our most powerful impression of Savely in the church is his performance as a preacher, delivering sermons that burn the hearts of men, until the hierarchy seals his lips. To treat the sermon as the pastor's central religious act is a Protestant, not an Orthodox position, the more so since Tuberozov's sermons are focused on moral issues facing his parishioners in this world, not on their relations with God. Such sermons cannot be regarded, from an Orthodox point of view, as a fulfillment of a priest's most basic function. For in Orthodoxy, as in Roman Catholicism, the most vital mission of the church and of its priests is not to seek the amelioration of this sinful world, but to save souls. God has granted his church certain means to promote that salvation, among which are the sacraments. And there is scarcely a mention of sacraments in *Cathedral Folk*.

In view of this latent Protestantism, it is not surprising that only three years later Leskov repudiated *Cathedral Folk* and the church it idealized. Leskov's allegiance to Orthodoxy had always been qualified. A letter of 1871, written in connection with *Cathedral Folk*, appears forthrightly to declare his Orthodox allegiance: "I am not an enemy of the church, but her friend, or rather I am her humble and devoted son and a convinced Orthodox—I do not wish to vilify her; I wish her honorable progress out of the stagnation into which she has fallen, crushed by her involvement with the State."[12] Yet the negative cast of this statement stands out. It begins not with an assertion of devotion, but with a denial of enmity, and the tone throughout is critical and condescending. This son of the church may be devoted, but he is neither humble nor blind to her faults.[13]

The view of the Orthodox church Leskov presents in *Cathedral Folk* is that of a sympathetic Protestant outsider. Largely ignoring the question of the church as intermediary between man and God, Leskov concentrates on its worldly situation, its strengths and weaknesses, its enemies and friends in the Russian reality of his time. He paints a stark and gloomy picture. He shows us a church so beset by external enemies and undermined by internal flaws that its chances of survival, let alone revival, appear dark. It thus seems strange that *Cathedral Folk* was received with such enthusiasm by the Russian clergy and the Orthodox faithful.[14] In fact, *Cathedral Folk* reads more like the Doomsday Book of Orthodoxy.

As shown in the novel, two principal enemies confronted the church in the mid-nineteenth century. The first was the enemy "from below," the Old Belief, to which millions of simple Russians remained fanatically devoted. The second was the enemy "from above": the secularism and atheism widespread among the educated classes, an atheism that in its most radical form totally rejected the church as an outmoded, repressive institution.

Leskov originally planned to demonstrate both these assaults on the church in his novel, integrating them as fundamental conflicts in his plot. But they proved too diverse to bring together. The theme of the Old Belief is gradually crowded into the background by the more current, and to intellectual readers much more meaningful, subject of atheism. In the novel the schism is relegated to the past, to the early portions of Tuberozov's diary, while the confrontation with atheism is acted out in the present, the 1860s.

Although the Old Belief is no longer a major theme, Leskov demonstrates what he considers the essential moral dilemma of the official church in relation to the schismatics and his own strong opposition to official policy. As he points out in the letter quoted above, the central moral fault of the Orthodox church was its unholy alliance with the autocratic state. According to the church, the Old Believers were heretics, their salvation jeopardized by their separation from the apostolic church; according to the state, they were seditionists, a source of political danger against whom defensive measures were required. This defense, as usual, meant persecution. Since the church was a state institution, it became the agent of, or a collaborator in, the persecution.

Leskov was a vehement opponent of religious persecution in any form; and in the early parts of Tuberozov's diary he effectively demonstrates the disastrous effects of this official policy. As a promising young priest, Tuberozov had been sent to Old Town, known as a hotbed of the Old Belief, in order to carry on the struggle with the schism. But experience soon teaches Savely that no struggle, at least on terms morally acceptable to him, is possible. The authorities want him to keep up a steady stream to headquarters of *donosy*, that is, he is to "finger" active Old Believers with damaging details so that they can be prosecuted. Tuberozov wants to engage in missionary work, to endeavor to reconvert the schismatics by the force of reason and moral example. He knows that the moment he collaborates in police persecutions, he will lose all potential moral influence among the Old Believers. He refuses to be an informer. The result is a head-on collision between him and his superiors, ecclesiastical and secular; and in the end the power of their authority proves stronger than the will of one man.

Tuberozov is forbidden to engage in his most cherished missionary project, a series of public discussion meetings with leading Old Believers. He then tries to resist the time-honored, but to him morally repugnant, custom of collecting Easter donations from schismatic households—donations that in effect bought the givers immunity from persecution. The gifts formed an important part of the Orthodox clergy's annual income; and it was no wonder that the deacon—Akhilla's predecessor—was so incensed by Tuberozov's prohibition of the practice that he denounced Savely for secretly abetting the Old Belief, though Tuberozov had paid him the expected tribute out of his own meager funds.

The climax of the government's campaign against the schismatics was the demolition of their chapel. As the building was being pulled down by soldiers, an iron cross from the cupola came loose and hung on a chain; then, "being enragedly urged by the hooks of the destroyers toward falling," it broke away and fell on the head of a soldier, killing him (4:33). The fact that the soldier proved to be a Jew, and that the Christian Russian government was revealed as sending Jewish soldiers to pull down schismatic Christian crosses, incenses Tuberozov more than the fate of the unfortunate victim.[15] The persecution arouses indignant sympathy among the Orthodox population for their schismatic brethren; and the Old Believers' dedication to their faith is intensified by their sufferings. They march through the streets of Old Town singing "Pharaoh the tormentor."

Immobilized in his missionary efforts, Tuberozov gives up struggling with the Old Belief. Gradually he learns to live with it according to the traditional patterns, under which persecution is mitigated only by the inefficiency and corruption of the system. At last Tuberozov sinks low enough to participate in the annual collection of Easter tribute. As he rationalizes his surrender, it is no use kicking against the goads. With Tuberozov's moral collapse, the whole subject of the Old Belief slides out of the novel.[16]

The confrontation between the church and secular rationalism was a more potent subject than the Old Belief. Under the aspect of eternity, the conflict between official Orthodoxy and the Old Belief was a local, transient, and somewhat technical issue, of little interest outside its social and historical context. In the conflict of the church with secularism and atheism, however, the future of Christianity itself was in question. The crisis of Christianity (and other religions) in modern times has resulted not from sectarianism or schism, but from the defection of a large part of the cultural elite. The Russians were among the first to perceive and articulate this threat: because of its peculiar intellectual and social weaknesses the Orthodox church had few defenders among Russian intellectuals, and the crisis of faith is nowhere more powerfully expressed than in the novels of Dostoevsky and Tolstoy.

Unfortunately, Leskov does not match either their cosmic sweep or their emotional intensity. He shows us no Konstantin Lyovin or Ivan Karamazov wrestling agonizingly with the "accursed questions" of the existence of God and the moral order of the universe. Instead the whole theme is externalized and trivialized. First, Leskov makes a childish, propagandistic equation of faith and morality: the good believers, the clergy and the faithful, are lined up on one side and the wicked atheists arrayed on the other. The battles that take place across this moral barricade are on the level of humorous anecdote. Leskov never sees, as Dostoevsky did, that the most significant battle is not the external struggle between atheists and Christians, but the internal conflict between faith and unfaith in the hearts of individuals. Apart from Akhilla's short-lived and ludicrous doubts, acquired during a trip to Petersburg, there is no inner struggle for faith in *Cathedral Folk*.

Even as an external confrontation of forces, the conflict between atheism and faith in *Cathedral Folk* is trivialized. Akhilla's war with Varnava Prepotensky over the human skeleton is no more than the puerile mischief of two naughty adolescents. Yet in its symbolic implications this is the war of the century—the battle between science and religion, here reduced to a provincial anecdote. Equally trivial are the "devastating questions" put to poor Father Zakhariya Benefaktov by a prankish schoolboy, at Prepotensky's prompting: Since whales are known to have small gullets, how could Jonah have been swallowed by one? Unable to deal with the question intellectually, this saintly old priest denounces the boy to his father for insubordination, and the father duly whips his son. However time-honored it may be, particularly in Russia, the whip as the answer to an intellectual argument cannot be said to resolve the conflict in favor of Christianity.

A more formidable enemy of the church than Prepotensky is the Petersburg atheist and exrevolutionary Termosyosov, the chief villain of the novel. This moral monster, who lacks convictions of any kind, determines to turn to his own advantage Father Tuberozov's conflicts with the authorities. Although he himself has a revolutionary past, he denounces Tuberozov to the authorities as a seditionist, hoping thereby to gain himself a lucrative position in the secret police. He succeeds in this, but his greed proves his undoing: he is caught counterfeiting banknotes. (This motif of the police counterfeiter was picked up much later in Chekhov's "In the Ravine.") He undertakes the seduction of the naive nihilist matron Bizyukhina in order to use her in his machinations; and he controls his colleague, Prince Bornovolokov, by means of blackmail and intimidation. As these details indicate, Termosyosov is ridiculously overdrawn, one of Leskov's superblack devils. Like some of the characters in *At Daggers Drawn*, he is supposed to illustrate Leskov's theory that by the end of the sixties the erstwhile nihilists had cast aside their ideological fig-leaves and become out-and-out criminals, a theory partly inspired by the Nechaev affair and its most important literary repercussion, Dostoevsky's *Devils*. But Termosyosov is a comic-strip villain who nearly wrecks the novel by his presence. The Termosyosov sections of *Cathedral Folk* are as bad as anything in *At Daggers Drawn*, and they belie the view that *Cathedral Folk* is a tranquil, art-focused, apolitical book, free from the ax-grinding of the antinihilist novels.[17]

A more serious threat to the church than the avowed atheism of the radicals was the widespread religious indifference of the upper classes, who staffed the administrative apparatus of the government, and therefore the de facto indifference to the church among the civil authorities, whatever the official rhetoric in Petersburg. Tuberozov (and Leskov) externalizes this problem as well. He attributes the officials' coolness toward the church to the fact that many of them were of Polish or Baltic German origin and hence hostile to Orthodoxy as Catholics or Lutherans. Thus the crucial nineteenth-century problem of intellectuals' loss of faith is evaded by Leskov, and a paranoid, xenophobic myth is substituted. In Leskov's novel, for the purpose of substantiating this myth, the administrative apparatus of this ultra-Russian province is represented as nightmarishly un-Russian, filled with sneering Poles and haughty Germans contemptuous of Russia, her church and her people. It was more comfortable to blame the troubles of Orthodoxy on the non-Orthodox minorities than to confront the fact that most educated Russians had ceased to have any but casual contacts with the church.

Thus Tuberozov's denunciations of atheists are met with indifference on the part of the authorities. "They are all like that," Tuberozov is told when he complains against the schoolteacher Prepotensky. (Tuberozov has no compunctions about using the secret denunciation, or *donos*, against atheists.) "If we discharge him, the next will be still worse." The "foreign" state bureaucracy is thus shown to be an unreliable defender of the state church. Likewise, except for the antique Marfa Andreyevna Plodomasova, who dies in 1850, the local gentry, though unimpeachably Russian in blood, have little interest in church affairs, let alone willingness to fight the bureaucracy on its behalf.

Even at the top of the social pyramid there was little support for the church. Much to Father Tuberozov's discouragement, a church-supported temperance campaign is halted by the minister of finance, who needs the vodka revenues to balance his budget. Rubles weigh heavier than souls. Since the minister of finance would need the assent of the emperor to overrule the Holy Synod, Leskov thus implies that the Orthodox tsar himself did not care much about Orthodoxy.

The situation inside the church, as Leskov and Father Tuberozov saw it, was even more disheartening. The church's structure showed weaknesses at every point. The village pope, supposed to be a source of moral and spiritual enlightenment for his peasant flock, was badly educated and so poor that he was constantly tempted to squeeze his parishioners to the utmost on occasions such as baptisms, weddings, and funerals when they could not dispense with his services. In the peasants' eyes, he became another exploiter, and his moral influence was lost. He was surrounded by indifferent officials and gentry and subjected to a harsh ecclesiastical bureaucracy, in which corruption was rife. Finally, between this village priest and his bishop there was an enormous social gulf. The bishops ruled their domains like mitred autocrats, with little spirit of Christian humility or even humanity. This theme of the bishops' tyranny and pomposity is only touched on in *Cathedral Folk*, left smouldering to flare up seven years later in *The Little Things in a Bishop's Life*.

Father Tuberozov's main struggle, and his ultimate feat of saintly courage and martyrdom, are directed against this internal rottenness of the church, the stagnant spirit of timidity, time-serving, and subservience to authority. Tuberozov's reforming zeal comes in two bursts. The first occurs at the beginning of his ministry, when as an idealistic young priest he feels strong and brave enough to challenge the system. The system proves stronger than Tuberozov's idealism, and his efforts to halt the persecutions of Old Believers trail off in defeat. Similarly, his most substantial intellectual undertaking, a long memorandum entitled "On the Condition of the Orthodox Clergy and on Means of Improving the Same for the Good of the Church and the State," which he submits after months of toil to his ecclesiastical superiors, has no reverberation whatever. There is neither reproof nor commendation—nothing. The treatise is buried in some bureaucratic file and forgotten.

Tuberozov in his old age again rises to do battle as a Christian soldier. After a lifetime of accommodations to the system, he has undergone a transfiguration. Once, while traveling, he took shelter in the woods during a violent rainstorm and is only a few yards from a giant oak tree when it is struck by lightning and felled. The storm scene is described by Leskov with power and beauty. Tuberozov is not hurt, but the lightning seems to have struck his soul. As he puts it, his life (*žizn'*) is over and his martyrdom (*žitie*) begins.

On the next day, which is a solemn state festival—probably the tsar's birthday—Tuberozov summons all the officials of the town, on pain of denunciation, to appear in church. Before them he delivers a blistering sermon, incredibly bold for a Russian priest, on the text "Give the king thy judgments, O God, and thy righteousness unto the king's son" (Psalm 72). The word "king" appears as "tsar" in both Slavonic and Russian Bibles, and the direct application to Russian conditions is immediately apparent. The gist of the sermon is the prayer that God hold the tsar's heart in his hands and protect it, since the monarch is surrounded by corrupt and un-Christian servants, money changers who should be driven from the temple; it ends with the plea that God not let his holy Russia become a laughingstock among nations because of the wickedness of her false servants.

For a Russian priest to pass such harsh moral judgments on the secular authorities seemed the utmost in subversion. As Termosyosov exclaims with delight, it is rebellion, *bunt*. By implication Tuberozov's sermon conjures up a cataclysmic prospect: the church, far from being a prop to the state and the throne, might become the most powerful revolutionary organization imaginable. Its network covered the nation, and its mythology lived in the hearts of the people as no political ideology ever did. Tuberozov is arrested three days later and led off to ecclesiastical confinement. He and his wife live in sequestration for months. His friends pull every wire they can, but the authorities are adamant. Finally it is arranged that if Tuberozov will go to the governor and apologize, he will suffer no further consequences of his seditious act, and he will be released. But Savely will not do this: he exhibits the same stubbornness once displayed by Leskov's father in a somewhat similar situation.

The poor *protopopitsa*, Savely's wife, dies, and it looks as if Savely will do the same. But his friends devise a legalistically satisfying, if morally dubious, formula. If Tuberozov is *ordered* to acknowledge his guilt, he will do so, since he will bear no moral responsibility for what he does under orders. Savely pens the required apology and is released, allowed to go home to die.

Most of Leskov's contemporaries, especially those of the conservative, pro-Orthodox camp, were seduced by Tuberozov and his colleagues. They acclaimed *Cathedral Folk* as the artistic embodiment of the preeminent virtues of Orthodoxy, disregarding the bleak pessimism of Leskov's picture of the church. As one of Leskov's archiepiscopal correspondents put it, with characteristic xenophobia, "The two priestly types, Father Savely and Father Zakhariya, and also the *protopopitsa*, are so fine and so morally elevated that with them our clergy can take its stand before any enlightened public [. . .] Compared with the Catholic clergy, even Akhilla is a righteous man and a moral personality."[18]

But one of Leskov's correspondents was more discerning. He complained to Leskov that all three good clerics are dead at the end of the novel. There are no successors, no new generation of courageous young priests to show Orthodoxy the way out of its difficulties. Nor is there a glimpse into a brighter future. Leskov's reply, quoted in part above ("I am not an enemy of the church, but her friend"), is a fascinating document, both as an expression of his forlorn hopes for the future of Orthodoxy and as a statement of his principles of "realism," that is, of faithfulness to the reality he knew:

As for the lack of good people to replace Tuberozov, Zakhariya, Akhilla, and Nikolai Afanasevich, there is nothing to be done about it; and no matter how much I would like to gratify your respected love for good people, I cannot find them in the clergy of the Russian church at the present turning point. The types I have depicted are conservative types; but what the present church will produce in its progress, that I do not know and am afraid of making mistakes. A chronicle like "Dwellers in God's House" must be strictly faithful to the truth of the day; and I am indignant at you my most noble mentor. I wish to leave matters with the statement that the "hour of general renewal has struck for the priest's house of Old Town." [This is a slightly altered, memory version of the last sentence of *Cathedral Folk*.] But what sort of renewal of the church this will be with Dmitry Tolstoy tied to the cross around its neck, that my artistic instinct does not venture to predict to me, and by making such a demand of me, you, I think, are committing the sin of constricting the freedom of artistic feeling.[19]

In the in-fighting of the late 1860s, Leskov himself had sometimes committed the same sin, constricting the freedom of his artistic sensibility and wandering far from the "truth of the day," in order, as he thought, to promote the good cause and destroy his enemies. But on the subject of religion Leskov refused to be swayed by the propagandistic needs of his party. In *Cathedral Folk* Leskov still struck some final blows on his old political anvil, clanging away at the diabolical nihilist rascals. But on the subject of religion and the church, he told the truth as he saw it; and artistic truth remains clean and alive when the party truths of all ages have settled into the dust of the past.

13

The End of Nihilism

The years when he was writing *Cathedral Folk* were the most agitated of Leskov's life. No doubt the peacefulness of the Old Town cathedral and the radiant simplicity of its "dwellers" were created partly as an antidote to the turmoil of the author's existence. Although much of this turmoil was associated with Leskov's protracted war with the nihilists, his rage spewed onto enemies of all political hues. Indeed, it is hard to believe that public affairs alone could account for the fury that gripped Leskov during those years. The frustrations of his private life must have kept reinforcing it.

Of the nature of these private tensions we can make some plausible guesses. First, there were serious economic difficulties, especially in the period before 1869. Through his union with Katerina Bubnova Leskov had acquired many new responsibilities when his literary income was particularly unstable. He no longer had any regular position as a journalist, his old base of operations, the *Northern Bee*, having passed out of existence—without paying Leskov the money it owed him. The "thick" magazines where he had published his serious work were also evaporating. Boborykin's *Library for Reading* had gone bankrupt, leaving Leskov's large honorarium for *No Way Out* still unpaid. Dostoevsky's *Epoch* had been suppressed by the censorship; left saddled with its debts—the honorarium for "Lady Macbeth" being one of them—the editor had to escape abroad to avoid prison. Harassed by editorial duties and alarmed by the dwindling list of subscribers, the wily Kraevsky had seized the opportunity to recoup the fortunes of *Notes of the Fatherland* by turning it over to the radicals Nekrasov and Shchedrin, left temporarily stranded by the suppression of the *Contemporary*. The insignificant *Literary Library*, where "Dwellers in God's House" had made a second attempt to emerge into public view, had gone bankrupt after the second number for 1868. Katkov's *Russian Messenger* was far away in Moscow, and as yet Leskov had no contacts there. He was desperate for money. Pisarev's excommunication seemed to have caused a general slamming of editorial doors in Leskov's face. As he wrote in 1868 to Dostoevsky's friend Nikolai Strakhov, "There is nowhere for me to work [. . .] No way out for him who wrote *No Way Out*."[1] Strakhov had a position with the government-subsidized *Journal of the Ministry of Education*, which published only dry scholarly articles on history, philology, and pedagogy; but Leskov begged Strakhov, in vain, to try to find him a position there. There was the struggle to publish *Cathedral Folk* and the lawsuit with Kashpirev; there was the refusal of a loan by the Literary Fund. The shortage of rubles was acute and constant, relieved only by the fortuitous death of Mikhail Bubnov in 1868. And by the time Bubnov's estate was settled, Leskov had again established a regular position with a newspaper, the *Stock-Exchange News*, for which he wrote a large number of signed and unsigned articles during 1869 and 1870, including a regular weekly column entitled "Notes on Russian Society."[2]

Leskov had also assumed a heavy load of moral responsibilities in his second marriage. He had induced a married woman to forgo her respectability and assume the ambiguous position of his "civil" wife, a position which must often have been humiliating for her; and Katerina's insecurity undoubtedly contributed to the tension at home. Moreover, there were four of Katerina's children and one more of theirs together for whom he had to serve as father—protector, teacher, and example. Finally, Leskov's conscience still had to contend with the guilty fact of his abandonment of Olga Vasilievna and his daughter Vera, especially the latter, whom he had irresponsibly surrendered to the vagaries of her demented mother.

Only such an accumulation of private stresses could account for the violence of Leskov's literary fury during this period, as shown, for instance, in the following episode. In 1866 M. A. Khan, known as a writer of scientific textbooks and popularizations, was preparing to publish a new literary magazine, *Universal Labor*. Its political orientation was to be conservative, and many of Leskov's antiradical friends gravitated to it, men like Pisemsky, Vsevolod Krestovsky, Vasily Kelsiev, and Aleksandr Milyukov. Leskov, too, was invited to collaborate. Hearing of his difficulties with Kraevsky over "Waiting for the Moving of the Water," Khan twice made Leskov advantageous proposals for transferring the novel to *Universal Labor*. Leskov turned them down because at that time he still felt committed to *Notes of the Fatherland*.[3]

Yet a few months later, writing anonymously in *Literary Library*,

Leskov asserted that "Dr. Khan's magazine has hitherto evoked only the malicious laughter of the literary hangers-on and the amazement of serious friends of literature, who merely shrug their sholders at the rubbish printed in it."[4] This judgment was grossly unfair: *Universal Labor* had made a notably good start that year, publishing among other works a new play by Ostrovsky and a novel by Pisemsky. Whence all this malice? It is hard to say. Leskov had probably known Khan since his Kiev days: at the beginning of the sixties Khan had collaborated with Aleksandr Valter in publishing *Contemporary Medicine*, in which some of Leskov's first journalistic pieces had appeared. Perhaps Leskov still nursed some old grudge against Khan dating back to that time; perhaps something happened between them in the summer of 1867.

Further, one of the envoys Khan had sent to Leskov was a young man named Nikolai Solovyov, who had been engaged as the chief literary critic for the new magazine. Solovyov, like Khan, was a medical doctor turned littérateur. The fact that Solovyov was chosen to negotiate with Leskov suggests that they were already acquainted. Solovyov had also written for *Notes of the Fatherland* in the Kraevsky-Dudyshkin days; and the relationship may have been older than that. Solovyov had studied medicine at Kiev University in the early 1850s, when Leskov's uncle would have been one of his teachers, and they might have met. They were exactly the same age. Yet in the *Literary Library* article just cited Leskov writes venomously of the

> utterly stupifying articles of Mr. Solovyov, in which it is stated in all seriousness that in the literature of the English there has been almost no cynicism, whereas in that literature there are Swift and Sterne, or that in our literature there was no romanticism, *because we are of the Orthodox persuasion* [. . .] To deny romanticism in our literature is to talk stupid nonsense, which reveals in the members of the editorial board [of *Universal Labor*] an unforgivable ignorance, a complete and all-inclusive nonacquaintance with those literatures about which Mr. Solovyov writes his interminable articles, which are linked only by the unity of uninterrupted nonsense. (10:53)

Later the same year Solovyov published a substantial article on Leskov and Vsevolod Krestovsky. It was the first extended piece of criticism devoted to Leskov's work, and the only one almost to the end of his life that made any attempt to assay his work from an artistic or philosophical rather than an ideological point of view. Unfortunately,

Solovyov was not a first-rate critic, and his formulations run to meaningless antitheses, such as "The novelist needs observation of life, while the dramatist requires knowledge of the human heart." But the tone of the article is friendly, though it came after Leskov's vicious attack on its author.[5]

There must have been some nonliterary reason for Leskov's anger against the Kiev doctors. Solovyov died in 1874. Some twenty years later, on the eve of his own death, Leskov wrote an amusing story called "The Lady and the Wench," the gist of which is the contrast between the hero's shrill and shrewish wife and his comfortable, tolerant, lower-class mistress.[6] The story is subtitled "From My Literary Reminiscences" and purports to deal with a "writer" (*literator*) whom Leskov had met in 1865 on the staff of *Notes of the Fatherland*. According to Andrei Leskov, the real person this hero resembles is Nikolai Solovyov—except that Andrei can recall nothing about a "wench" associated with him. The lower-class mistress, Andrei Leskov maintains, is a reincarnation of Pasha, an equally comfortable housekeeper and mistress Leskov himself had kept in the late seventies and early eighties.[7] But in "The Lady and the Wench," the mistress, with her name changed only from Pasha to Prasha, and a wife who again closely resembles Olga Vasilievna, are both bestowed upon a resurrected literary image of Nikolai Solovyov. Why? It is a mystery, but the fact surely suggests some connection in Leskov's unconscious mind between Solovyov and himself.

Besides his critical thrusts at Khan and Solovyov, Leskov slashed about in other directions. He wrote an extraordinarily acerbic critique of a fellow writer of "reactionary" novels, Vasily Avenarius (later better known as a writer for children), pronouncing an annihilating judgment of Avenarius's entire literary work and voicing personal insults as well (10:41-54). This article was the first in a projected series entitled "A Chronicle of Literary Oddities and Horrors." The second (and last) was an equally vitriolic polemic over the legitimacy of literary pseudonyms and whether it was proper for critics to reveal the names behind them.[8] It is crammed with innuendos: against Leskov's old friend Suvorin, who wrote under a pseudonym, but made a practice of revealing the pseudonyms of others; against the radical poets Vasily Kurochkin and Nekrasov, who despite their professed radicalism had for tactical purposes written patriotic verses; against nihilists in general, who were too cowardly to fight duels; and once again against Solovyov, who eschewed a pseudonym, but whose articles were so stupid that it would be better if he had not signed them.

Although Leskov's anger was undiscriminating, its most frequent targets were the radicals. Of all his many demons, they were the most consistently hated. Toward the end of the sixties, Leskov's fury at the radicals even increased in intensity and his own originally gradualist ideology began to gravitate toward the right. Ironically, the label "conservative," which had wrongly been pinned on Leskov by his enemies in 1863, had by 1870 become a reasonably valid description of his position. At the time Pisarev wrote that no self-respecting Russian publisher except Katkov would ever again print anything signed by "Stebnitsky," Leskov had not yet published a single line in any of Katkov's organs; but by 1870 Leskov had become—temporarily, to be sure—a loyal worker for Katkov's conservative-nationalist propaganda machine.

Leskov's rightward ideological evolution in the latter half of the 1860s ran parallel to general tendencies among the ruling circles in Petersburg. The liberalism that had been fashionable in the late fifties and early sixties had spent itself in the Emancipation and its aftermath. The pressure for a new era of reform did not build up again until late in the seventies. His feelings hurt by the ingratitude of the peasants and the effrontery of the Poles, the emperor turned to heavy-handed, no-nonsense generals who promised to maintain order. The most egregious effrontery was the shot fired at the tsar on April 4, 1866, by Dmitry Karakozov. The aftermath of the Karakozov affair was inevitably a time for responsible citizens to rally ostentatiously around the throne, expressing their abhorrence for such acts of violence, and a time for the government to put aside thoughts of reform until it had reestablished its grip on the country.

Leskov moved with the tide. On April 14, 1866, twelve days after Karakozov's shot, he was inspired to write the only poem he ever penned (or published). Entitled "A Humble Petition," it addressed the happily surviving tsar in the sugary accents of pseudo-"folk" verse:

A shudder gave Orthodox Rus
When she learned of Thy mischance:
From out Thine own sovereign land
Came murderers seeking Thy life!

The Russian people, the poem goes on, are grateful for the reforms, for the Emancipation, for the increased freedom of the press, and for the renovation of the law courts. They do not venture any wish with regard to the captured miscreant: let justice be done.

We have only one favor to beg of Thee, O Father,
For our dear people, for our very selves:
With one voice we all pray to Thee,
With one plea we bow to the earth before Thee:
Doubt not that Rus is with Thee.[9]

We can only be grateful that Leskov's career, both as poet and as royal sycophant, ended as abruptly as it had begun, with this maudlin petition.

Many years later Leskov reported, in a self-justifying letter to Suvorin, that once the devil had appeared to him "in the shape of M. N. Muravyov. I could have had an estate near Vilna, and all around me there was nothing but the 'stones of the wilderness' and malicious slander. It is enough that for those who know me I remained a 'well-ordered and honorable man,' and for the public an 'entertaining and clever writer.' I am satisfied with that."[10]

Mikhail Muravyov was one of the no-nonsense generals to whom Alexander had turned after the Polish revolt. He was assigned the task of "pacifying," by executions and deportations, the territory of Lithuania. His vigor at this task won from Alexander the hereditary title of count and from the populace the sobriquet "Muravyov the Hanger." After the Karakozov attempt, he was chosen to head the investigating commission, which not only swiftly dispatched Karakozov to the gallows but used his crime as the pretext for a series of repressive measures. At this time or earlier, just after the Polish revolt (it could not be later, because Muravyov died late in 1866), Muravyov apparently approached Leskov with the proposal that he become a propaganda writer for the government, offering him a confiscated Polish estate as a reward. If this is true, it is, as Leskov says, to his credit that he resisted the temptation, despite his straitened financial circumstances.

Leskov's rejection of temptation entitled him, he felt, to celebrate a moral triumph over the radical potentate Nekrasov, whose major political sin was his attempt, in 1866, to save the *Contemporary* from suppression by reciting at a public reception, in Muravyov's presence, a poem celebrating "the hanger" as the savior of the fatherland. Nekrasov's sycophancy failed: Muravyov nevertheless had the *Contemporary* suppressed. Leskov, bubbling over with malice, triumphantly and repeatedly exhibited to the public this stain on the radical banner.[11] Yet Leskov later professed many times to respect Nekrasov both as a poet and as a man; and Nekrasov was one of the few radicals who recognized Leskov's talent and expressed regret for the treatment he had received in the left-wing press.[12]

Leskov's effort to vex or injure people he considered his enemies was continued in two long articles published in 1867 entitled "Specialists on the Distaff Side." He begins his discussion of the problem of women's rights and feminine emancipation by denying its existence: there was no problem at all; it had been invented by radical publicists. This nonexistent problem was nevertheless sufficient pretext for fifty pages of vituperation, in which Leskov attempts to draw blood from almost every Petersburg journalist then alive. The avowed female emancipationists receive the heaviest fire, among them Leskov's old enemies Vasily Sleptsov, Varfolomei Zaitsev, Dmitry Pisarev, and the "nihilizing" official, Yury Zhukovsky. Nikolai Solovyov gets another going-over, rougher than one in "A Chronicle of Literary Oddities and Horrors." And there are many other victims.

The problem of the status of women is given short shrift. Unhappy marriages are not the result of a "woman problem," but of a human problem. The country needs good wives and mothers much more than it needs women doctors or women officials. Nihilistic agitation about women's rights demoralizes women and lures them away from their primary roles. After a brief experiment with their admission, the government has again closed the doors of Russian medical schools to women; but the responsibility for that exclusion lies wholly on the women themselves, since they did not conduct themselves with modesty, but acquired a reputation for sexual laxity. Nadezhda Suslova (the sister of Dostoevsky's famous mistress), who was the first Russian woman to complete a medical education (in Switzerland), will do a great service by showing people that a woman doctor can be a positive asset to the country. But most feminist agitation is designed only to justify sexual misbehavior and cannot be too vehemently condemned.

On December 27, 1867, Artur Benni died of gangrene in St. Agatha's Hospital in Rome. Expelled from Russia for his revolutionary activities, he had taken a position as correspondent for the London *Spectator* covering Garibaldi's campaigns and had been wounded at the battle of Mentana. News of his death appeared in the Petersburg press on February 7, 1868. Even the obituaries contained allusions to the rumor that Benni had been an agent of the Russian secret police, and Turgenev made a public protest against the besmirching of the dead man's memory.[13]

213

The revived charges against Benni and the intervention by Turgenev stirred Leskov and gave him, as it were, authorization to rake over the Benni story—ostensibly as a means of clearing his friend's name. Leskov's motives were in fact more personal and less chivalrous than that. It was not only Benni who had been accused of collusion with the police and suffered the abuse of the nihilists. In riding forth in defense of Benni's innocence Leskov could vindicate himself and slash away at people who had humiliated him in the past.

Leskov therefore determined to write the life history of Artur Benni so as to prove his own and Benni's virtue, demonstrate his superior political wisdom, and convict his enemies of libel. He set about writing immediately, and the work was finished that same spring, by the beginning of May 1868.[14] With its antiradical bias, Leskov evidently considered his vindication of Benni.ideal grist for the Katkovian propaganda mill, an appropriate entrée into the Katkov empire. This plan received an unexpected rebuff: Leskov's work, despite its ideological correctness, was rejected by *Russian Messenger*.

On May 25, 1868, we find Leskov pleading with one of Katkov's assistants:

From the spirit of Pyotr Karlovich's letter [i.e., P. K. Shchebalsky, a critic and close friend of Leskov's, through whom he had submitted the manuscript to Katkov] I gather that this piece will hardly be deemed worthy of *Russian Messenger* (which, of course, will be extremely painful for me, since I consider it an honest and far from uninteresting work, and furthermore have nowhere else to place it if you refuse it). Before you pronounce your final sentence, permit me to call your attention to the following: (1) the contents of the manuscript consist entirely of facts, the truth of which I guarantee; (2) Benni lived with me and confided in me more than in anyone else; (3) of all the promoters of that comic revolution *he is the most honorable* and the most popular [. . .] I am very eager to strike a blow against [revolutionary] "enterprises" and to restore the good name of a libelled man.[15]

Leskov's pleas were in vain. He was unable to publish "An Enigmatic Man" until 1870, when it appeared serially in the *Stock-Exchange News*, to which he was then a regular contributor.[16]

The following year Leskov brought out a separate, revised and expanded, edition of "An Enigmatic Man," despite the fact that Benni's brother Herman had requested him not to do so.[17] Herman Benni then carried out his threat to make a public protest, repudiating Leskov's "defense" of his late brother and in the process stripping away the fig leaf of Leskov's honorable intentions: "Let this announcement serve as the vocal protest of all our family against the shameless author of 'An Enigmatic Man.' Not only did he concoct utter falsehoods and slanders against a man whose life and way of thinking were absolutely unknown to him or else were deliberately represented by him in a false light; but he does not even know the simple rules of decency."[18] But Leskov did not change his course. He kept flailing away at his phantom enemies with this flimsy and "enigmatic" weapon.

"An Enigmatic Man" belongs to a borderline genre between the historical sketch and the fictional story. The author would like us to think that it lies closer to history, but he also wants to make our impression more complete and lifelike than written history can legitimately produce. Therefore he resorts to such techniques of fiction as transcriptions of conversations at which he was not present. He gives the work the subtitle *istinnoe sobytie*—a "veritable event" or more colloquially a "true story"—and he assures us frequently that his narrative is grounded in fact. Indeed, he insists on this so relentlessly that at last we begin to question it.

In order to defend Benni's innocence and at the same time attack his own radical enemies, Leskov had to arrange his material so as to produce a moral segregation: Benni, who was good, had to be separated from his ideas, his actions, and his associates, which were bad. Leskov had begun to learn that ridicule is a more effective technique of denigration than invective; and so he presents the revolutionary period of the early 1860s as a "comic time," a vaudeville of absurdities staged by scoundrels and clowns. If a person who participated actively in such a movement is to be given a moral plus sign, he must be a fool, a holy innocent who knew not what he did. This is what happens to Benni in "An Enigmatic Man."

The aim of ridiculing the revolutionary movement dictates the selection of materials in Leskov's "true story." The major concentration of the work is on two absurd episodes in Benni's career, both distorted to make them appear as senseless as possible.

The first of these is the story (which may or may not be true—we have no evidence other than Leskov's account) of how Benni, while still in London, became involved with a Siberian gold-miner named Tomashevsky. During a trip abroad, Tomashevsky posed as a red-hot revolutionary in order to make an impression in Herzen's circle. Benni took him at his word and accompanied him back to Russia, intending to assist the gold-miner in his impressive plans for underground work. These plans turned out to be nothing but ad hoc fantasies, concocted in London for effect; and even before they reached the Russian border, the "revolutionary" Siberian was energetically dissociating himself from the young enthusiast. Thus in Leskov's presentation Benni arrives in Petersburg looking like a credulous fool.

Leskov assiduously maintains this impression in the second episode, which concerns the journey undertaken by Benni with the ill-starred Andrei Nichiporenko to collect signatures on a petition for a constitution.[19] In Leskov's account, the primary purpose of the tour, the collection of signatures, is mentioned only once, and with extreme vagueness. It is referred to as "a certain proposal" which Benni vainly urged Katkov to sign. Instead of being a quest for public support of constitutionalism—an aim Leskov could not have represented as ludicrously extremist—the enterprise is reduced to abortive agitation in taverns and ineffective attempts to distribute copies of Herzen's *Bell.* Even these are never given out: one night in a provincial hotel Nichiporenko has a bad dream and makes a disturbance. The hotel clerk and a policeman come to investigate the noise. They find nothing, but when they have gone, Nichiporenko, still shaking with terror, burns all the copies of the *Bell* in the stove.

Such acts of poltroonery are typical of Nichiporenko as Leskov presents him. All the resources of caricature are brought into play to make him as repulsive as possible: dirty and ill-mannered, he is fond of mouthing blood-curdling revolutionary phrases, but in action he shows himself a coward, a liar, and an informer. Many details are carried over from *No Way Out,* where Nichiporenko appears as Parkhomenko. But here Leskov's taste is more questionable. In "An Enigmatic Man" he caricatures, under his own name, a man who had died in the fortress before his case had come to trial, and with whom he himself had once been on terms of intimate friendship. As a reviewer pointed out, Leskov had not always found Nichiporenko's habits so disgusting: a photograph existed of Leskov and Nichiporenko embracing each other.[20]

Leskov then sketches Benni's return to Petersburg, his journalistic and philanthropic activities there, and his trial, imprisonment, and banishment. His political innocence is rubbed away by friction with reality, and his belief in the imminence of a socialist revolution in Russia is abandoned as a chimera. Benni's arrest and banishment, Leskov maintains, were due to the gratuitous denunciation by Nichiporenko; and his death was an ironic blow of fate, coming just when he was about to emerge from childish innocence and become a responsible adult.

Leskov's ostensible purpose in writing "An Enigmatic Man" had been accomplished: people ceased to believe that Benni had been a spy. But in his general aim of making the revolutionary movement appear corrupt and ridiculous, he overshot the mark. The traces of personal venom are too obvious, and the literary means employed are inappropriate to the ideological end. People who had lived through the heroic days of the early sixties did not regard them as a comic time, nor, in fact, did Leskov: in *No Way Out* this very period had been described as an "epoch of rebirth," "one of the great poetic epochs of our history."

The last major campaign in Leskov's war with the nihilists was the novel *At Daggers Drawn,* written in 1870-71 and published serially in Katkov's *Russian Messenger* the same year, hot from the author's pen.[21] This novel is certainly the longest (over 800 pages) and one of the worst of Leskov's works. In later years, the author occasionally acknowledged it as such. A few weeks before his death, an interviewing journalist asked him if he had ever dictated his works to a stenographer. "I don't find it convenient," Leskov replied. "Only once I tried to dictate, and the results were terrible. I was ill and dictated the novel *At Daggers Drawn.* And that, in my opinion, is the sloppiest of all my inferior works."[22] Twenty years earlier, we have a report that Leskov agreed with Ivan Goncharov that *At Daggers Drawn* was the worst of his works and "The Sealed Angel" the best.[23] Andrei Leskov recalls that throughout his later life Leskov was ready to spring to the defense of *No Way Out,* but of *At Daggers Drawn* he seldom spoke.[24] Leskov's published correspondence, although studded with allusions to *No Way Out,* contains almost no references to *At Daggers Drawn* after its publication in *Russian Messenger* had been completed. Nevertheless, Leskov did include *At Daggers Drawn* in his collected works, published in 1889-90: perhaps he felt it was too bulky to sweep under the rug.

Even at the time he was writing it, Leskov seemed to sense that all was not well with *At Daggers Drawn.* Characteristically, he tried to shift the blame from himself to his editors, denouncing in his letters the monsters in Katkov's editorial rooms. "Against the editors of *Russian Messenger* it is hard not to complain [. . .] In a word, I am finishing the novel with vexation, malice, and irritation, sticking everything together anyhow, just to meet the schedule."[25] Though Katkov's editors were notorious for their arbitrary tampering with author's texts, Leskov's irritation was doubtless mostly a reflection of his own sense of artistic failure.

In view of its low artistic quality and its lack of psychological and autobiographical immediacy, a few general observations about *At Daggers Drawn* will suffice. The historical message of the novel may be summed up: the generation of radicals that had flourished at the beginning of the sixties had been succeeded, toward the end of that decade, by a generation of vipers. As Leskov puts it, with paronomastic playfulness, the old nihilists, the *nigilisty*, have been replaced by *negilisty*, people who have cast aside all the old *gil*, or rubbish, about ideals, loyalties, decency, and self-sacrifice for the cause. In place of this *gil*, they have hit upon new, all-encompassing ethical principles, distilled from the pages of Darwin: "Gobble up others lest they gobble up you." "All is permitted."

The discovery that all is permitted, which so much affected Raskolnikov and other Dostoevskian characters, is carried by the *negilisty* to its logical conclusion. For them there are no moral barriers of any kind, no positive emotional bonds between individuals; friendship and love do not exist. The weaker, backward *negilisty* cover their amorality with the rationalization that the end justifies the means: their crimes will make possible a better society. According to this theory, in order to lead man out of the jungle, the revolutionaries must fight according to the laws of the jungle. "We do not despise power; we concern ourselves with money; and when we shall have in our hands both money and power, then we shall accomplish our common cause."

But the true, more advanced *negilisty*, like Termosyosov in *Cathedral Folk*, no longer bother with rationalizations. The old "end," the better society in whose name their crimes were committed, for them becomes a means, and a means of deception at that: it is a myth with which they can seduce the remaining idealists in the movement. For them there is no cause, no human solidarity, no goal, no society even, only a jungle in which every individual seeks to devour the next. In the life of the backward *negilist*, there inevitably comes the moment of disillusionment when he discovers the truth about the movement: the box is empty; there is nothing inside, nothing at all. "It's all nonsense, it's all deception, nothing more; and in reality it's every man for himself."

There may have been some historical truth in this picture. Human societies, like human individuals, tire of excessive demands for altruism. The revolutionary excitement prevalent in the late fifties and early sixties had dissipated, giving way to weariness and cynicism. The Chernyshevsky-Dobrolyubov-Pisarev generation had receded into the past, their doctrines propounded and their blood shed seemingly for nothing. The movement itself began to seem tarnished. The Nechaev trial, held in the summer of 1871, revealed terrifying scenes of revolutionary duplicity and crime. Among revolutionaries, professed idealistic motives seemed to have degenerated into lust for power.

But this perception of Leskov's did not inspire a first-class novel. Dostoevsky's *Devils*, which immediately followed *At Daggers Drawn* in *Russian Messenger*, showed that a great novel could be written incorporating the same historical vision. The trouble was not in Leskov's sociology so much as in his psychology. Leskov did not understand, as Dosteovsky did, that the depiction of abnormal or criminal characters does not mean abrogation of the laws of psychology. The need for accurate observation and adequate representation remains as stringent for extraordinary as for ordinary types. Leskov never grasped that there is a basic difference between human beings and demons. The demon, a creature of absolute evil and destruction, is not a possible human type. It is an artificial construction, an ideal. The human criminal, even the basest, is not a demon. His heart is an all-too-human congeries of conflicting passions and self-justifying rationalizations. No matter how monstrous his crimes, the human criminal is never totally alone: he always has, at least in potential, some "we" for whose benefit, or by whose permission, the crimes are committed. But the position Leskov ascribed to his advanced *negilisty*, total emotional isolation and a totally exploitative attitude toward every other human being, is not human at all. Leskov's *negilisty* are in fact demons, far more diabolical than Dostoevsky's devils.

If we cannot believe in the existence of Leskov's demons, we cannot take their actions seriously. And if we disbelieve them, the book is destroyed. The whole long, immensely complicated plot crumbles to nothing: it is somebody else's nightmare. The intrigues, disguises, and trap-door disappearances, the forgeries, blackmail, and extortion, the adulterous and nonadulterous promiscuity, the fake marriages in Moldavia and the true marriages never consummated, the duels, poisonings, knifings, and suicides—all lose meaning and relevance. Even if the Jewish usurer and blackmailer Kishensky is drawn from a real model, as Leskov asserts in an otherwise disingenuous letter to Suvorin,[26] we cannot consider him other than preposterous. Despite occasional flashes of unconscious humor (the sexy villainess in black tights who carries a stiletto concealed in a riding whip), these annals of senseless crime are unbearably tedious. *At Daggers Drawn* is a bore.

There are a few redeeming features. Leskov's positive characters are more convincing, particularly those who stand apart from the main action, such as the inimitable Vanskok. Vanskok's real name is Anna Skokova, but in her hurried pronunciation it comes out as "Vanskok," and so she has come to be known. Vanskok is a reincarnation of Bertoldi, one of the good nihilists in *No Way Out*—the short-haired, sexually unattractive female revolutionary, not very bright, often ridiculous in her revolutionary fetishes, forever working at something but accomplishing nothing, yet thoroughly good-hearted, unselfish, and devoted. Even Dostoevsky, who was by no means friendly to Leskov, was impressed by Vanskok. As he wrote to his friend Maikov,

> Are you reading Leskov's novel in *Russian Messenger?* There is a lot of fibbing, a lot of the devil knows what, as if it were happening on the moon. The nihilists are distorted to the point of scoundrelism, but on the other hand, certain types! What about Vanskok! Even Gogol never did anything more typical or truer. I have seen this Vanskok, I have heard her myself, it's as if I had felt her. An amazing character! If the nihilism of the sixties dies out, this figure will remain for eternal remembrance. It's a work of genius! [. . .] Strange is the fate of this Stebnitsky in our literature. Such a phenomenon as Stebnitsky should be analyzed critically, and in a more serious way.[27]

Likewise Maxim Gorky—for once—agreed completely with Dostoevsky about Vanskok: "This girl is a type masterfully extracted from life by the hand of a Russian artist, depicted with amazing art, utterly alive—such Vanskoks the Russian revolutionary movement created by the dozen."[28]

Unfortunately, however, it would require more than a few successful minor characters to redeem this confused and unconvincing novel. If it were not for the author's reputation, *At Daggers Drawn* would long since have faded into oblivion.

ᏣᏲ 14 ᏲᎲ

Laughter and Grief

At Daggers Drawn marks the end of a major phase of Leskov's career. He was now finished with the nihilists as subjects for his art. These daggers were never drawn again. But by 1871 Leskov's antinihilist war had pushed him a good deal farther to the right than he belonged by temperament or conviction. In his yearning for allies and for a reliable magazine outlet, he had identified himself with the chauvinistic and conservative *Russian Messenger*, and to some extent, during the next five years, he accommodated his writings to the Katkov party line. Nevertheless, despite this political displacement, Leskov's "Katkovian" years, between about 1870 and 1875, were among the most fruitful of his life. One after the other there emerged, mostly in the pages of *Russian Messenger*, the major works on which his reputation chiefly rests: *Cathedral Folk*, "The Sealed Angel," "The Enchanted Pilgrim," *A Decrepit Clan*, "At the Edge of the World."

This sequence of successes is not, of course, the result of Leskov's association with the conservatives or the beneficent influence of Katkov, although it was doubtless reassuring to be accepted and well paid for one's efforts; and the emotional security provided by membership in the Katkovian family may have contributed to the artistic serenity that pervades Leskov's works of this period. But the price of ideological conformity was high, and the masterpieces of the early seventies might have been even better if it had not been for Katkov: Leskov certainly thought so in later years.[1] It was rather the termination of the debilitating antinihilist war that made possible Leskov's burst of creativity. All the energy and talent he had dissipated on his puerile pursuit of vengeance were now liberated. With the confusions and irritations of the war eliminated, he could draw for artistic inspiration on his deeper self. Symbolically, just at this time he abandons his pseudonym. M. Stebnitsky, the scourge of the nihilists, was dead; but N. Leskov was very much alive.

The first work in the post-1870 series is *Laughter and Grief*, a satire partly on contemporary (but not antinihilist) themes. It was written sometime during 1870 and at once dispatched for approval to Katkovian headquarters in Moscow.[2] Partly because of financial pressures and partly because of the topicality of the latter part of the work, Leskov was anxious to have *Laughter and Grief* published as soon as possible.[3] Katkov, however, refused to have two long works by Leskov appearing in *Russian Messenger* at the same time. Since *At Daggers Drawn* was running there from October 1870 through October 1871, it might look, Katkov felt, as if Leskov had taken over the magazine, or as if he were short of contributors. Leskov tried to persuade him to let *Laughter and Grief* appear in *Russian Messenger* under a new pseudonym, Merkul Praotsev, while *At Daggers Drawn* was appearing there under his real name; but in the end Leskov had to agree to allow *Laughter and Grief* to be serialized in the less prestigious *Contemporary Chronicle*, a weekly supplement to Katkov's daily newspaper.[4]

In this new work Leskov turned away from the conventional narrative forms of the time, the novel and the short story, toward a genre both more original and more congenial to his talent. Perhaps the most serviceable designation for this genre is the one provided, partly facetiously, by Leskov himself, when in early editions he gave it the subtitle "A variegated potpourri from the motley memories of a faded man."[5] It is indeed a motley collection—of anecdotes, jokes, gossip, philosophical arguments, social and historical disputes, and satirical portraits of various figures from contemporary life. An anonymous reviewer in *Russian Messenger*, perhaps Leskov's friend Shchebalsky (to whom the separate edition of 1871 was dedicated), strained to produce two more metaphors to define the genre of *Laughter and Grief*. He called it "not a picture, but a bas-relief, a ribbon with figures depicted on it."[6] The ribbon image is suggestive. *Laughter and Grief* unrolls like a figured ribbon, displaying an extraordinary variety of scenes. It does not possess the structural unity we expect in a single picture or story, being bound together only by the character of its central protagonist and by the idea which his various adventures illustrate.

Laughter and Grief is also a frame narrative, but it is not strictly speaking a skaz, since the narrator, an educated man, speaks standard Russian, and the impression of oral delivery is not maintained. The "author" or frame-narrator and his uncle, Orest Markovich Vatazhkov, are taking part in a discussion of the old custom, then apparently dying out, of giving "surprise" presents to children on Palm Sunday, gifts hung from their beds with ribbons and decorated with palms and winged cherubim or amoretti. The "author's" uncle, "an extraordinarily reserved and well-mannered man," expresses disapproval of this custom, saying that "all surprises are harmful and should have no place in education, and especially in Russia." This unexpected remark arouses curiosity, and Vatazhkov is prevailed upon to tell his story, his "potpourri of surprises," which will refute the nonsensical idea that life in Russia is monotonous. On the contrary, he asserts, he has to go abroad for long periods to rest from the kaleidoscopic variety of Russian life.

The inner narrative is thus introduced apropos of a discussion, to illustrate a point. Here it provides a demonstration of a melancholy proposition, which Leskov spelled out in a letter several years later: "Regarding our earthly life as a 'transition,' I would observe that this transition is especially difficult in Russia, where nothing can be accomplished by honest labor, and where there is no consistency in anything except in persecuting a man, if not by sharp torments, then by dull harassment."[7]

Any attempt to produce an impression of oral delivery in Orest Vatazhkov's speech is abandoned after the first few chapters. His tale proceeds without interruption, with scarcely any indication of the presence of an audience, for nearly 200 pages. Its termination is never clearly indicated. At the end of chapter 86 the "author" breaks in: "At this point, my honored reader, I think we might close; but one last narrative we must have, and my chronicle is finished" (the last clause is an adaptation of a line from Pushkin's *Boris Godunov*). He reports that the prolonged "conversation"—his uncle's monologue—had been interrupted by the arrival of the uncle's servant, bringing the alarming news that two officers of the secret police had just appeared at his apartment. With heavy heart, Vatazhkov repairs to investigate this apparition, and the "one last narrative" is provided by the "author."

Vatazhkov's potpourri may be divided into two unequal parts. The first contains the narrator's memories of his childhood and youth, up to the death of Nicholas I and the accession of Alexander II; the second consists of his observations and experiences a decade later, in 1867, when he returns to Russia after a long sojourn abroad. The first of these parts is the more satisfactory from a literary point of view. It presents a string of anecdotal reminiscences illustrative of the constant "surprises" of life in Russia, invariably unpleasant. These "surprises" are graphically associated with the original subject of the Palm Sunday presents. Vatazhkov recounts how *his* eccentric uncle, in order to

223

prepare the boy psychologically for the unpleasantnesses awaiting every Russian, one Palm Sunday substituted a bundle of birch rods for the expected present hung from his bed, and in the morning burst in upon his nephew and gave him a severe flogging—for no reason. The rhymed inscription his uncle attached to the rods reads: "He who expects to get joys for nought will receive the sorrow his folly hath brought."[8]

In these anecdotes Leskov displays unparalleled powers as a literary raconteur. One after the other they roll off his pen, varied, delightful, perfectly told. He manages to avoid the repetitiousness of a catalogue of funny stories. He knows how to vary the pace. Some of his anecdotes are related *lento*, developed at length, extending over many pages an incident that might have been exhausted in a few words. One of these slow episodes is the opening story of the general's wife at a wayside inn, forced to pay seventeen rubles for a roast turkey—an exorbitant price. This trivial incident is built up into a wonderful genre scene, full of the atmosphere of Russian travel in prerailroad days, with several vivid characterizations—the worldly-wise servant of the narrator and his mother, the extortionist innkeeper, and the poor *generalsha*, so pompously self-important at the beginning of her stay and reduced to impotent fury and tears at the end. Elsewhere, material that might have been expanded is tossed off *allegro*, in a few words, for instance, the tale of how the narrator's uncle, a misanthrope who wanted no visitors interrupting his bucolic solitude, drove away a female relative who insisted on seeing him by coming out stark naked to greet her; or the story of how the same eccentric anticlerical uncle constructed a literal golden calf to which he obliged the local priest to make obeisance: a turn of a crank then caused the calf to emit a coin, which was given to the Baal-worshipping priest.

The most substantial part of the first section centers on the character of the "light-blue Cupid," Captain Postelnikov, an officer in the secret police, through whose agency occur several of Vatazhkov's most unpleasant surprises. (Light blue was the color of a gendarme's uniform, and Postelnikov is a cupid in his babyish appearance; he is thus another reincarnation of a Palm Sunday cupid, complete with birch-rod "surprises," hanging from Vatazhkov's bed. His name, furthermore, is derived from *postel'*, "bed.") Admitting himself "completely unfit for the service he is in," Postelnikov, at a moment of crisis in his career, resorts to denouncing his "friend" Vatazhkov for possessing a forbidden book which Postelnikov had planted in his room. Though duly arrested, Vatazhkov is disarmed by the following confession: " 'Dear boy, I offer you five million apologies, but there was nothing else to be done [. . .] I might have lost my job, and yesterday this is how bad things were for me,' and Postelnikov expressively drew his hand across his throat. Then he rushed over to kiss me."

For his "crime" Vatazhkov is expelled from the university and rusticated to his uncle's estate. Later, through another denunciation of the same Postelnikov, he is forced to take a commission in the hussars. The crime he is charged with this time reaches the ultimate in absurdity. The nickname "Filimon" (Philemon) had been bestowed on him by one of Postelnikov's friends. It transpires that Saint Philemon's day falls on December 14, the day of the 1825 uprising. From this association Vatazhkov automatically becomes a suspicious character, unfit to study at the university (which he had managed to reenter after some wire-pulling by his uncle).[9]

Such is the absurdity of life under the despotism of Nicholas I. At any moment the unexpected may happen. One's desires and plans are of no account, and there is no rationality anywhere. Everything happens as if in jest. And yet that happening may be painful or tragic. For instance, an order goes out from Petersburg to the effect that it is disrespectful for schoolboys to "answer in the imperative mood." In consequence, all over Russia hundreds of floggings are administered for such rude responses as "Divide the quotient and multiply the divisor," even though this is the form in which the answers appear in the textbooks.[10]

Vatazhkov's most tragic surprise is his uncle's final "joke." After he is expelled from Moscow University, Vatazhkov is met by this uncle in the provincial capital. Before leaving for their estate, they spend the night in an inn. While Vatazhkov is sleeping, he hears a terrible cry. It turns out that Vatazhkov's mother had made her way to the town independently; to punish her for her "sentimentality," the uncle had loudly sung a funeral hymn when his sister approached the room where her son was sleeping. Believing her son dead, she uttered the terrible cry Vatazhkov had heard and then fell dead of heart failure. Thus, as Vatazhkov summarizes his experiences, "Expelled from Moscow *in jest*, I arrived in my native town only to be a witness of how *in jest* a man killed the mother I loved so passionately."

Leskov has frequently been criticized for the "toothlessness" of his satire as compared, for example, with the corrosive ironies of Shchedrin.[11] The oppressive reign of Nicholas I, these critics insist, was no comedy of errors. In Leskov's recreation of it, they maintain, one feels not the Gogolian "laughter through tears," but simply laughter, or laughter *at* tears—the last a reprehensible manifestation of callousness. The grief Leskov advertises in his title is not felt in the text.

There is a modicum of truth in this criticism. Laughter and grief are not present in the story in the same proportions, and not on the same level of consciousness. Laughter is one's immediate response to Leskov's ribbon of absurdities, whereas the method of narration prevents us from feeling grief, which must be intellectually deduced. But the grief is there all the same. We may laugh at the idea of punishing boys for answering in the imperative mood, but we know that the floggings hurt. Leskov's technique of distancing, dissociating the reader from the sensations of the characters is a valid literary procedure: it gives us perspective, allows us to keep our wits about us and pass rational judgment on the events described. It is a device Leskov may have learned from Gogol, whose "tears" must also be deduced.[12] Leskov insisted in a dedicatory letter prefaced to the first separate edition that the public had simply overlooked the grief he had embodied in his text: "In *Laughter and Grief* the public noticed and deemed worthy of its attention only the laughter and did not perceive any grief at all" (10:550). But the public did what anyone would do in response to Leskov's technique: first laugh, and then deduce the inherent sorrow of the situations. The public and many critics mistakenly assumed that since the grief was not felt in the text, the author *could* not feel it. Leskov was fully aware of the horrors of Nicholas's reign and could depict them palpably enough when he chose, as in "The Sentry," "Vale of Tears" or "The Toupee Artist."

The comedy of *Laughter and Grief* is partly a literary mode, partly an emotional defense, and partly a philosophical idea. The idea Leskov wants to demonstrate might be called an existential one. The trouble with human life is not that we are victimized by deliberate human wickedness: real villainy is rare. Most of our misfortunes stem from the fact that we cannot control our destinies. Our will is powerless before the play of fate, folly, and human cross-purposes. As we have learned from some modern dramatists, the "absurd" is only a way of looking at life in general, and such absurd societies as Leskov's pre-reform Russia are only extreme cases of our common predicament.[13]

The second part of *Laughter and Grief* is weaker than the first. After a ten-year absence abroad, Orest Vatazhkov returns to discover a new and reformed Russia, the Russia of Alexander II. But the Russia he finds in 1867 proves to be almost as absurd as the one he had left a decade earlier. Vatazhkov is eager to examine and acclaim the many changes and improvements; but as he makes his pilgrim's progress, he finds new absurdities to go with them. Beneath the talk of reform and renovation, too often there is nothing but the same old sham and mockery. The clergy, for example, terrified by the recent decree reducing the number of parishes by half, are now frantically denouncing each other to the authorities. One priest looked through the shutters of his colleague's house and duly reported him to the bishop for "galloping and dancing and indecently striking his under-cassock with his heels." It turns out that these lewd capers were actually undertaken to soothe a crying baby which the "galloper" had in his arms. Nor is the propensity for violence diminished. A strong-arm general, a hero of the Polish campaigns of 1863, boasts that if given his way he would swiftly solve all the problems of Russian foreign policy: he would march through Europe with a Russian horde armed with birch rods and administer a sound thrashing to the entire European population.

Worst of all are the civil servants, the agents of reform. Vatazhkov is given an assignment, which he accepts enthusiastically: he is asked to draw up a project recommending reforms in the medical and sanitary services available to the peasants in a certain province. He consults with doctors and officials, discusses alternatives, collects material, and meditates at length. But eventually he gives up the project in disgust. Once again, it turns out to be a joke. Medical services for the peasants cannot be reformed because they do not exist, and the peasants do not want them. A doctor tells Vatazhkov how he was once paid by peasants to go away and let an old man (whom he could easily have cured) die in peace. The man had settled his affairs, made his farewells, and was ready to depart; neither he nor his family had any wish to prolong his life. As the same cynical doctor says, the peasants need to be cured of three great maladies—hunger, cold, and stupidity; and medicine cannot help with any of them. Many years later, the hero of Chekhov's "House with a Balcony" was to feel the same way: the poverty and backwardness of the Russian countryside are so appalling that it is ridiculous to talk of such refinements as hospitals and schools, which only increase the peasants' burdens, since in the end they must pay for them.

Vatazhkov concludes that the "renovation" of Russian life exists mostly on paper or in conversations. Liberalism has become a game, to be played by the frivolous, self-important governor, his monocle-wearing, "emancipated" wife ("God is oxygen"), and the sycophantic officials who seek their favor.[14] All persons, plans, and projects, including Vatazhkov and his medical investigation, become pawns to be manipulated in the game of bureaucratic intrigue. In the self-contained structure of provincial administration, nothing real has reality. Vatazhkov at last throws up his hands and flees.

Russia plays one last joke on him. While waiting in Odessa to take ship for Europe, he is accidentally present during the pogrom of April 1871, when anti-Semitic riots broke out, perhaps tacitly instigated by the government. (Pogroms were so instigated later, under Alexander III and Nicholas II; but the charge may not be true for 1871.) In putting down the riots, the Russian troops resorted to indiscriminate flogging of people seized on the street. Although he is a completely innocent bystander, the luckless Vatazhkov is one of the victims—flogged for nothing, *in jest,* as he had been in his childhood. For poor Orest Markovich it was the last straw, and he gives up the ghost, lying on his stomach in his hotel room, with his steamship ticket on the table beside him. Before he dies he writes ironically to his nephew: "Being in this situation on account of Jews and Greeks whom I did not have the honor to know before this pleasant event, I am consoled by the fact that I am dying with the satisfaction that I was at least flogged by my own compatriots."[15]

Looking back long afterward on the period when he had written *Laughter and Grief,* Leskov remarked: "I began to think responsibly when I wrote *Laughter and Grief,* and since that time I have remained in the same mood—critical, yet insofar as I was able, unmalicious and benevolent."[16] The observation is correct: Leskov had reached a new phase of maturity. He could now allow himself to be critical without anger and benevolent without sentimentality.

15

"The Sealed Angel"

Laughter and Grief was intended to force upon the Russian consciousness a painful truth, the author's conviction that life in Russia, even under the reformed regime of Alexander II, was precarious and irrational, a parody of life in the more advanced countries in the West. In the intensity of the anger brought on by the comparison, Leskov failed to articulate explicitly the universal implication of that story—which might have proved comforting—that the "Russian condition" in the last analysis only epitomized the fragility and irrationality of the human condition itself. But in any case, life in Russia was harder. As Leskov put it, Russia is a country where the "transition" from this earthly life to eternity is "especially difficult, where there is no consistency in anything" except persecution.[1] If such a statement had been made by a foreigner, it would have been taken as a national insult. Yet it was made by a fullblooded Russian, a man intensely involved with his country, even in love with her, who treasured every detail of her physical geography "from the Black Sea to the White and from Brody to Krasny Yar."[2] How could such love and hate coexist in the same heart?

It was hard to be an educated Russian in the nineteenth century. "I love my fatherland, but with a strange love," Lermontov wrote in 1841; yet a few months earlier he had gleefully shaken from his heels the dust of "unwashed Russia," the "land of masters" and their obedient slaves. Almost every great Russian writer has left statements about his national identity as ambivalent as these.

How was the cultivated and Europeanized Russian to relate to the vast and appallingly laggard country in which he lived? Was the nation's "inferiority"—its poverty, the ignorance of its peasant population, the ineptitude of its government—to be interpreted as a mark of his personal inferiority? Clearly not; yet throughout the nineteenth century intellectual Russians reacted as if just this inference had been drawn. It was they who were accused; they who felt responsible.

229

Through their identity as Russians they seemed to feel obliged to assume a burden of responsibility, or guilt, for their country's faults. The burden was heavy and painful to bear. Realistically, the only means of relief was work: you could add your strength to the forces trying to propel Russia forward into the modern world. But the problems were huge, the forces attacking them puny, and the resistances great; and it was hard not to fall into despair. Was there not some easier way?

Perhaps the problem could be shown to be a calumny or at least a mistaken calculation. If so, there was no inferiority at all. Much nineteenth-century historical philosophizing in Russia was an effort to establish this point. Perhaps the "backwardness" was not a defect but a virtue—a state of pastoral purity irrevocably lost in the grimy, petty, soulless, money-grubbing industrial societies of the "rotten" West. If this were true, then there was no need to "catch up"—quite the reverse; the problem was rather to preserve Russia's innocence, to protect her from infection. So thought Nicholas I, Leontiev, Pobedonostsev, Dostoevsky, and many other nationalist conservatives. And, paradoxically, many socialists adopted the same position, or a variant of it. They did not hold up nineteenth- (or seventeenth-) century Russian society as the paradise lost by the industrial West. But they, too, made a virtue out of Russian backwardness. "Russia is 'young,' " they said. "She is unspoiled, uncorrupted by the sickness of capitalism and industrialism; and therefore she can 'leap' right over the advanced civilizations of the West into a glorious future." So believed Herzen, Lavrov, and, essentially, Lenin. How comforting such views were to the despairing Russian heart, whether conservative or radical! A wave of a verbal wand, and presto! that painful inferiority not only vanishes, but a gratifying superiority appears on the very spot.

Leskov did not adopt either of the two magic solutions outlined above. He had too acute a sense of the human misery caused by Russia's backwardness to claim it as an advantage. He knew that Russia had to "catch up." And he knew that the problems were more than material. One of the chief obstacles was the obstinate conservatism of the Russian peasants themselves, their refusal to accept changes from which only they would benefit. This obtuse clinging to the past, and the exasperation and despair it caused the proponents of progress, are among the favorite themes of Leskov's later years, most explicitly in "The Cattle Pen" (1893). "If the ideas of Rakhmetov [the socialist hero of Chernyshevsky's *What Is to Be Done?*] were to triumph," Leskov said prophetically not long before he died, "the Russian people, on the very next day, would choose themselves the most savage police chief they could find."[3] Rather than dream of Utopias, Russians would do better to set about solving their innumerable concrete problems.

Leskov was unwilling to accept sleight-of-hand solutions to the problem of Russian backwardness. He had to acknowlege the truth: Russia was poor, her resources undeveloped, her institutions outmoded, her veneer of civilization thin. Yet Leskov loved that dark Russia even as she was, with all her faults, her backwardness, and her sloth, and he loved without excusing or denying those faults.

Such a clash of opposites in a man of Leskov's passionate temperament produced a violent oscillation of the emotional pendulum between love and exasperation or despair. *Laughter and Grief* had marked one extreme in the pendulum's swing. Leskov seizes his countrymen by the collar, shakes them, and cries, "Look what a senseless and ridiculous country this is!" With his vexation temporarily appeased, Leskov's pendulum then begins to swing back toward national eulogy. But it is eulogy of a peculiar, Leskovian sort. Despite his conservative opinions and his association with Katkov, Leskov never boosts the Russian government or social system. Nor does he find much to admire in the Russian intelligentsia or among the upper classes. He looks for manifestations of virtue, intelligence, and creative talent among ordinary Russian people. Finding them, he can then call attention to areas of real beauty, moral as well as aesthetic, in Russian life, thus helping to lift the national ego out of its despair.

A particularly successful product of one of these pro-Russian swings of Leskov's pendulum is the story "The Sealed Angel" (1873),[4] a work cherished by generations of Russians both because of its high artistic quality and its gratifying celebration of their national virtues. In this story Leskov exploited two areas of his special expertise: his longstanding interest in the Old Believers and his more recent fascination with icon-painting. The two were not hard to combine, since the Old Believers had a special reverence for icons, especially pre-Nikonian ones; and insofar as icon-painting still existed as an art, it flourished mainly among them.

Such a combination involved a readjustment in Leskov's attitude toward the Old Believers. He still basically considered the schismatics to be as he had described them in "The Musk-ox," *No Way Out*, and "Waiting for the Moving of the Water"—stubborn, nit-picking, bigoted people. But they were Russians; and they were colorful and different. Leskov had in the meantime discovered the beauties of Russian icon-painting; and he knew that the Old Believers cultivated and cher-

231

ished this national art. Within the crucible of his story, when Old Believers and icon-painting are mixed together, the artistic beauty of icons is transmuted into the moral beauty of the Old Believers who cherished them.

Leskov became fascinated by Russian icon-painting in the late 1860s. He had always been fond of the visual arts: he was an indefatigable museum- and exhibition-goer. In a characteristically bitter, self-pitying statement, Leskov claimed that this interest had arisen because of the exile imposed upon him by his radical enemies: "During the rather lengthy period when I had been cast out of literature, boredom and inactivity led me to become interested in and even excited about church history and the church as such, and incidentally I devoted byself to the subject of church archaeology in general, and icon-painting in particular, which I liked."[5] Since Leskov had never stopped writing for a moment, despite the efforts of some radicals to "cast him out" of literature, this statement cannot be taken at face value. But the interests he enumerates were real.

Nowadays the exceptional beauty of Russian icons, especially those of the fifteenth century and earlier, has been generally recognized in Russia and elsewhere. Albums of colored reproductions are sold widely in the West, although in Soviet Russia the icons have had to contend, not always successfully, with official atheism. But in singing the praises of icons in the 1860s and 1870s, even in Russia Leskov was a pioneer. To be sure, there had been several earlier treatises on the subject, most notably the "General Concepts of Russian Icon-Painting" (1866) by the noted Slavist and folklorist Fyodor Buslaev.[6] All these earlier studies, however, had treated icons exclusively as manifestations of Russian religiosity, as a miraculous survival into modern times of the spirit of medieval Christianity, rather than as works of art.[7]

Leskov must have read Buslaev's article soon after it appeared, and about the same time he had the good fortune to make the acquaintance of an icon-painter then living in Petersburg, Nikita Savostianovich Racheiskov. Racheiskov earned his living by painting original icons and by restoring old ones, and Leskov probably first sought him out to restore an icon he had bought. Even in his less affluent days Leskov was an insatiable frequenter of antique shops and art dealers, and by the early seventies he had accumulated a small collection of paintings and objets d'art in which he took great delight. Leskov's son Andrei recalls being frequently taken to Racheiskov's workshop in a slum quarter of Petersburg inhabited mostly by Old Believers, and he has left us a fine portrait of the painter: "Nikita Savostianovich himself had style from his head to his heels. Absolute Stroganov school. Tall, with a rather lean figure, in a black peasant tunic reaching almost to the floor, buttoned up to the top, creaky Russian boots. What a picture! At work, a chintz shirt, silver spectacles, holding in his hand a tiny little brush with only a few bristles, all attention and piously absorbed in the creation of Holy Trinities, Saviors, angels, heavenly battles, and a vast variety of saints."[8] After Racheiskov's death in 1886, Leskov wrote a warm appreciation of his personality and talents, mentioning that "The Sealed Angel" had been "composed entirely in Nikita's hot and stuffy workroom" and adding with legitimate author's pride that after the publication of the story Nikita had had a sudden rush of orders for icons of angels.[9]

Although the statement that "The Sealed Angel" was "entirely" composed in Racheiskov's workroom is probably an exaggeration, Leskov did spend long hours there, studying, watching, talking, learning the technical terms and distinctions of what was then essentially a folk art, and trying to grasp the mentality of the master, who was a painter-craftsman in the medieval sense, eons removed in spirit from the nineteenth-century academic or Bohemian "painter." Leskov was exceedingly good at this. He knew how to talk to people of the lower class without either patronizing them or pretending that they were his equals. His interest in them was deep and genuine, and they recognized it; but he never tried to push through to an intimacy that might embarrass them. His rule was friendliness and frankness combined with full recognition of the other's dignity and privacy.

So Leskov had a splendid stock of materials for his story: his long-established familiarity with the picturesque Old Believers; his newly acquired knowledge of icon-painting, including what he could find in written literature about its history and meaning, and the results of his own researches into its technique and psychology; and an excellent unifying personality for a model, a man who was both an Old Believer and one of the best icon-painters of his time. Whether in Racheiskov's workshop or his own, Leskov set about applying his masterful technique to the task of transforming these materials into a story.

For all his love of visual shape and color, Leskov's feel for a milieu and a period and his most effective means for conveying that feel were derived from language. "Man lives by words," he once said,[10] and stories are made of words; by making his story a skaz and the narrator an Old Believer who is an art connoisseur, Leskov plunged his reader into two new word-worlds at once.

This skaz is built with particular adroitness. The opening chapter establishing the frame is less perfunctory than usual: it creates a vivid scene at a lonely wayside inn, isolated in the midst of a blizzard and crammed with travelers who have taken refuge. The room is so full than there is not even space for people to lie down. Sleep is impossible; a conversation ensues, in the course of which the topic of guardian angels comes up; one man seems to speak with authority on this subject; this authority, it turns out, is based on actual experience; and the man is therefore begged to relate the story of his experiences.

The setting for the narrative is concrete, almost palpable, and the narrator's voice sounds real in our ears. This narrator, as he describes himself, is "no more than a peasant," uneducated, a stonemason by trade, and "born in the ancient Russian faith." But his modesty is excessive. A man of piety, whose life is shaped by religion, he is literate, well read, and even erudite. His learning, however, belongs to a culture quite alien to the nineteenth century, a culture that shows no impact of science, industry, the West, or anything that has happened in Russia since Peter the Great. He is a walking survival of the Middle Ages, steeped in Scripture, saints' lives, and sermons.

The narrator's language is a product of this pre-Petrine culture, filled with ecclesiasticisms, archaisms, Church Slavonicisms—phrases, words, and even grammatical forms—many of them echoes of Scriptural quotations, prayers, or liturgical formulas. It is a bookish language, but not the language of the books written by or for the contemporary Westernized intelligentsia. It is colloquial, both because the narrator is speaking, and because to his ear the distinctions between literary and spoken Russian are not those made in the "standard language," the language of the educated classes. Most of all, the narrator (and the author) loves the shape and feel of these old words: they breathe the spirit of the "ancient piety" he adores.

The narrator soon introduces the subject of icons, on which he reveals himself an expert, and his narrative draws on another stock of highly marked vocabulary, the technical terms of the art—a vocabulary that in places would have been hard for the average educated Russian to comprehend. The effect is inescapable: the words are arresting in themselves, and we cannot help recognizing that their remarkable scope and precision demonstrate exceptional mental capacities on the part of the narrator, including an impressive command of this recondite subject.

The following passage, containing the original description of the angelic icon around which the story centers, will give some idea of the extraordinary range of this language. Since this is descriptive "appreciation," the language is less technical (and thus a little easier to translate) than it becomes later, when he deals with the actual process of painting: "This angel was verily something indescribable. His countenance, as I see it now, is most luminously divine and, so to say, swift to succor; his gaze is tender; his little ears are with thongs, in sign of his ability to hear in all directions and places; his raiment gleams, closely studded with golden ornaments; his armor is feathered; his shoulders begirded; on his breast he bears an image of the infant Emmanuel; in his right hand is a cross and in his left a flaming sword. Wondrous! Wondrous!"[11]

Leskov is not merely showing off his verbal wizardry here. The archaic, bookish vocabulary and forms make this voice from a cultural past come alive. It is as if the icon itself began to speak. The effect is incantatory, almost hypnotic. It is, to be sure, idealized language, like the person who uses it and the story itself; no nineteenth-century Old Believer would have spoken so perfectly in character. But this idealization was the essence of Leskov's method, and Dostoevsky was surely wrong to attack him for it. Dostoevsky argued that such language was unrealistic—too perfect, too quintessential; but Leskov, in endowing his narrator with a linguistic talent of this kind, was no more trying to represent the average Old Believer than Dostoevsky was trying to represent the average radical in Pyotr Verkhovensky.[12]

The discussion of religion and icon-painting, on which the narrator lavishes so much detail, has still another use within the framework of the story, that of narrative retardation. "The Sealed Angel" is an exciting story, full of tension and suspense; the tension is created partly by means of cleverly enforced delays in the action. Among the delays are landscape descriptions, subsidiary episodes involving characters tangentially connected with the main action, technical discussions of icon-painting, and disquisitions on the religious mentality of the Russian people. Leskov applies these brakes with remarkable skill. The pictures we see and the sounds we hear as the plot slows down are so interesting that we are scarcely aware of the author's delaying artifice; it seems simply as if the story were moving at the pace of life itself.

Thus, the story of the seizure and sealing by Russian officials of a beautiful icon especially cherished by a group of schismatic workmen and of their desperate efforts to recover it builds up slowly to a climax. In the finale, Luka Kirillov, the leader of the Old Believers, carrying the icon, must cross the Dnepr on a stormy night, balancing himself on a high chain suspended between the piles of the new bridge then being built, with the wind tearing at the chain and masses of ice crashing into the piles below. It is a magnificent cinematic scene, and we cannot help agonizing over Luka's every step until at last his foot touches solid ground on the other side of the river.

Although it appeared in *Russian Messenger,* "The Sealed Angel" is far from being a Katkovian party-line parable. Its tone of ancient piety conceals a subversive modern message. The story pits the good, hardworking, devout Old Believers, who belong to the lower class, against the powers that be, the upper class and officials of a large Russian town on the Dnepr, presumably Kiev. The chief villains are the officials. The Old Believers have learned to expect nothing but evil and persecution from Russian officials; they regard the administrative apparatus of the government—and in fact the upper classes generally— with intense suspicion and hostility, and their suspicions are confirmed by the events of the story. All evil in the story emanates from above: from a flighty, silly, superstitious lady, who plays the game of using the Old Believers' prayers magically to gain her private ends; and especially from her corrupt husband, a high official in the civil service. The heroes' only allies in the world of educated society are not Russians at all, but an English engineer and his wife, who perceive the moral goodness of the Old Believers and the aesthetic beauty of their icons and undertake to fight the system on their behalf.

The primary emotions inspired by the story are indignation against the Russian authorities for their senseless cruelties and sympathy for their persecuted victims. This was not Katkovian propaganda. Nevertheless, many liberally inclined readers and critics, though otherwise admiring the story, have objected to the ending, in which the group of Old Believers is suddenly and dramatically reconciled to the Orthodox church. In the aftermath of their leader's exploit of crossing the river, a "miracle" occurs (for which Leskov carefully supplies a naturalistic explanation): the sealed angel on the icon is suddenly unsealed, and the face of the angel, over which melted sealing wax had been poured, is revealed radiant and pure. Encouraged by the Orthodox bishop, the Old Believers interpret this unsealing as a miracle wrought by the official church and decide in a body to seek readmittance to the fold of the faithful.

This ultimate reconciliation with official Orthodoxy seems to clash with the anti-official spirit of the rest of the story; and since it appeared in *Russian Messenger,* some critics have attributed the ending of "The Sealed Angel" to Leskov's desire to conform to Katkovian doctrine. Some even assert that Leskov tacked on this ending at the insistence of Katkov.[13] There is some external evidence that appears to support this view. Many years later Leskov told one Yelizaveta Akhmatova, an old friend of his, that if he were writing "The Sealed Angel" then (about 1884), he would have ended it differently.[14] Similarly, Ilya Shlyapkin reports that in 1877 he discussed "The Sealed Angel" with the rector of the Petersburg Roman Catholic seminary. The rector said he considered the ending an artificial appendage. Shlyapkin says he reported this statement to Leskov and that Leskov agreed with it. Shlyapkin further records Leskov as saying in 1892: "For a long time I was under the influence of Katkov—in the ending of 'The Sealed Angel' and in *The Spendthrift*."[15]

But these statements do not prove that Leskov changed the ending of "The Sealed Angel" to suit Katkov. Leskov admitted to Akhmatova and agreed with the Catholic rector only that there was something wrong with the ending; if he had written the story later in his career, he would have done it differently. By the middle 1870s Leskov had passed through a religious crisis, as a result of which he severed his allegiance to the Orthodox church and repudiated the idealizations of that church in earlier works like *Cathedral Folk* and "The Sealed Angel." In his post-1875 mood, he would not have wanted to lead his idealized Old Believers into the arms of the church—or idealize them at all. But there is still a difference between the supposition that after 1875 Leskov would have produced a very different "Sealed Angel" and the assertion that in 1873 he appended the conversion of the Old Believers, against his own convictions, in order to maintain the favor of Katkov.

What about the explicit statement Shlyapkin attributes to Leskov in 1892, that he was "under the influence of Katkov" in shaping the ending of "The Sealed Angel" and in *The Spendthrift?* This assertion must also be regarded with suspicion, especially the link between "The Sealed Angel" and *The Spendthrift.* Katkov had nothing to do with *The Spendthrift:* he did not publish it, and Leskov at that time had no contacts with him. How, then, can we account for the statement? One explanation is that Shlyapkin misreported what Leskov said. In general, although the author was a trained literary scholar, a specialist on Old Russian literature, Shlyapkin's article on Leskov is surprisingly careless. The second possibility is that Leskov did make such a statement in 1892, erroneous as it was. As other autobiographical utterances show, Leskov's memories of the events and personalities of his earlier years were often blurred. He knew that *The Spendthrift* was poorly written, and he now also disliked the ending of "The Sealed

Angel." He also disliked the memory of his own association with the Katkov empire. Therefore, why not blame Katkov for some of his own artistic mistakes? Such a procedure, perhaps unconscious, was very much in keeping with Leskov's defensive character.

The evidence so far cited fails to prove that in 1872-73 Leskov deliberately altered the ending of "The Sealed Angel" to suit Katkov. There seems to exist no other external evidence that could decide the question. Leskov's letters to his friend P. K. Shchebalsky, the most revealing personal documents for this epoch, are missing for the period between May 6, 1872, and January 4, 1874—precisely the period when "The Sealed Angel" was written and published. Nor are there any other extant letters to Katkov or his assistants concerning the story. The first mention of the story in Leskov's correspondence is in 1874, when Leskov complains that he cannot afford to spend six months working on a story the length of "The Sealed Angel," for which he had received only 500 rubles.[16]

In the absence of external evidence, therefore, we must turn to the story itself. First, the broader question, the conversion of the Old Believers to Orthodoxy: was this a deus ex machina tacked on to the end of an otherwise superlative story? Even a cursory reading shows that it was not: the conversion is carefully prepared for almost from the beginning. The narrator, although he thoroughly infects us with his feeling of antagonism against the persecuting officials and the feather-brained lady, carefully avoids attributing any of this persecution to the impetus of the "reigning church." For the ending to surprise us, as it is intended to do, the narrator must conceal the fact that at the time he relates his narrative he is no longer an Old Believer; he simply avoids making any statement about his present religious allegiance. But the absence of the schismatics' usual hostility in the narrator's statements about the official church might lead a shrewd reader to guess the ending. More important, the central portion of the story is an account of the narrator's journey with a young companion in search of an icon-painter skillful enough to duplicate their sealed angel. In the course of these wanderings, the narrator's own faith in the Old Belief is deeply shaken, first, negatively, by his experiences in the schismatic community in Moscow, in which he finds no light of inner spirituality, only "obstinacy"; and second, positively, through his encounter with a holy Orthodox hermit named Pamva. The impression of Pamva's sanctity is so strong that the narrator's companion, who is mortally ill, on his deathbed induces Pamva to baptize him into the church.

This episode is included in order to motivate and anticipate the later conversion of the Old Believers.

Secondly, the conversion of the Old Believers—in fact, the entire story—correctly illustrates not Katkov's, but Leskov's own convictions of 1872-73. Although he continued to see much evil in the Russian bureaucracy and officialdom, this was the period when Leskov regarded the Orthodox church as a potential force of moral progress and enlightenment. Thus, to convert the Old Believers to Orthodoxy at the end of "The Sealed Angel" was, at least in theory, to point the way of intellectual and spiritual growth for such ideal, if retarded, Russians as the narrator and his comrades. This was the way out of the mire of the Old Belief, the road to a future spiritual reunion of the whole Russian people in the embrace of the one holy church, a reunion Leskov passionately desired. Therefore, there can be no question that by converting his Old Believers to Orthodoxy Leskov was violating convictions of his own. The dislike of many critics for this ending may not be an artistic judgment at all, but a reaction against any triumph of the official church, especially when proclaimed from the patriotic pages of *Russian Messenger*.

The question remains whether the ending is faulty from an artistic point of view. First, there is nothing wrong with the conversion as such: it serves as a valid climax to the religious quest of the narrator and his companion, and it is adequately motivated as the culmination of their spiritual and intellectual growth. If we try to imagine alternative endings, they seem flat by comparison. For instance, the Old Believers might fail to recapture their angel, but nevertheless remain true to their original faith; perhaps their leader, Luka, should fall from the chain to his death in the icy river. Such an ending, by intensifying the tragic desperation of the Old Believers, would correspondingly strengthen the indictment of the system that caused the tragedy. But the movement of the story would be essentially circular; the Old Believers would be left as before, mental inhabitants of the Middle Ages. Leskov's ending represents a fulfillment of the Old Believers' experience *in the story*; conversion is an appropriate psychological consequence of what life has taught them.

The ending of "The Sealed Angel" might be validly criticized, however, for the sudden and "miraculous" manner in which the conversion take place. That Leskov's heroes are so affected by the apparently magic freeing of the angelic face from wax that they are ready immediately to be baptized into the church—this is hardly a manifestation of spiritual growth. Nor does the bishop's willingness to exploit their credulity do him any credit. Such a conversion has nothing in common with Pamva's spirituality: it is a conjuror's trick.

In his later years, Leskov himself often expressed distaste for the idealizations he had created in *Cathedral Folk* and "The Sealed Angel." During one of the deflationary swings in his artistic pendulum he ostentatiously undertook to puncture the balloon from which "The Sealed Angel" is suspended. In the last chapter of "Pechersk Eccentrics" (1883), a collection of anecdotes on life in Kiev in the "old days," during the reign of Nicholas I, Leskov discusses the supposition, frequently expressed in print, that the unspecified locale of "The Sealed Angel" was Kiev, and that the story of the Old Believer who crossed the Dnepr on a chain was based on a real occurrence. To these hypotheses Leskov replies:

> The first is quite true, but the second is not. The locale in "The Sealed Angel," as in many of my other stories, does actually resemble Kiev—which is explained by my habitual associations with Kievan scenery; but *such an event* as is reported in the story *never took place in Kiev*, that is, no Old Believer ever stole an icon and carried it across the Dnepr on chains. In reality there was only the following: once, when the chains had already been tightened, a certain stonemason from Kaluga, on commission from his comrades, during the Easter midnight service crossed from the Kiev to the Chernigov bank *on the chains*, but not for an icon, but *for vodka*, which at that time was sold much cheaper on the other side of the Dnepr. Having poured himself a pail of vodka, the intrepid tightrope walker hung it around his neck, and with a staff in his hand which served as a balance, returned safely to the Kiev shore with his contraband burden, which was then consumed to the greater glory of Holy Easter.[17]

This wonderful tale of the debonair Russian daredevil risking his life for a pail of cheap vodka is not a possible alternative ending for "The Sealed Angel." It is an ironic finale to a very different story, a story written in a different tone and from a different point in the swing of Leskov's pendulum. As the pendulum swings away, Leskov reaches back, as it were, to kick over an icon he had reverently set up ten years earlier.

16

The Russian Superman

In the summer of 1872 Leskov undertook an excursion by steamer on Lake Ladoga, an inland sea close to Petersburg but rarely visited by its residents. The land of woods and lakes immediately north of the capital was an area Leskov had not yet explored, an area exceptionally rich in Russianness. Originally settled by pioneering citizens of Great Novgorod, the northern region, even after it came under Muscovite power, had never been parceled out as the property of private landlords. The land was difficult to farm, and the climate did not make it attractive as a setting for gentlemen's residences. Its peasant inhabitants thus had no private masters. They were never enserfed, remaining "peasants of the state," subject only to the taxes and impositions levied by the tsar's officials. Relatively isolated from the rest of the country, and with no gentry to serve as the medium for the penetration of Western ideas and fashions, the northern peasants and fishermen preserved into the nineteenth century an archaic mode of life and a highly developed folk culture, among the manifestations of which were the oral epics, the *byliny*, long since lost by the more civilized people further south.

The north was also noted as a locale of monasteries, outgrowths of hermitages originally established by men who wished to find in the silence of the northern forests escape from the vanity of the world and a place to devote themselves to contemplation of the deity. Some of these hermitages eventually grew into large and substantial monasteries, of which the most celebrated is Solovki, on the Solovetsk Islands in the White Sea, later unhappily famed as a Soviet concentration camp. The islands of Konevets and Valaam on Lake Ladoga were also the sites of well-known monasteries, the latter then particularly prosperous under the administration of Abbot Damaskin (1795-1881).

Leskov wrote up his Ladoga experiences as a straightforward travel essay, published the following year under the title "Monastic Islands on Lake Ladoga."[1] This travelogue is chaotic and disorganized. It records the traveler's experiences, miscellaneous and confusing as they were, without giving them focus or coherence: the way the steamer tickets were sold, the layout of the ship, the food, the appearance of the water and of the various passengers, together with the author's random associations with these impressions. Leskov in later years expressed dislike for this work. "Some people like it," he wrote to a friend; "but I can't stand it and always tear it out [of the separate volume it shared with "The Sealed Angel"] and throw it away. I haven't got a copy of it just because I don't like it."[2] The literal reproduction of experiences could not satisfy. Encumbered with trivial facts, it did not reach through to essences, to deeper truths about human life. The artistic imagination was a far more penetrating tool.

There was, however, a product of the Ladoga journey more significant than "Monastic Islands." The enforced idleness on board the steamer, the detachment from the cares and anxieties of Petersburg, the surrounding landscape, "oppressive and dreary," the visit to the ancient Russian town of Korela, "than which it would be hard to conceive anything more melancholy," and especially the sight of the monks who were fellow passengers aboard the ship, with faces that seemed almost like maps of their life histories—all this set Leskov's imagination to working. In his mind he tried to reconstruct the monks' biographies. What experiences had led them to renounce the world in this way? What sins were they expiating, what sorrow had they left behind? Leskov probably talked with some of these monks. In any case, he came away from this journey with the setting and the theme for a new story, one of his best known and most successful, "The Enchanted Pilgrim," the imaginary life history of a Ladoga monk. Following his familiar narrative strategy, Leskov establishes a frame situation, a conversation aboard ship among travelers of disparate social backgrounds, recounted ostensibly as fact by the "author" speaking in the first person. This primary narrator transcribes for us the autobiographical saga of the second, inner narrator, the enchanted pilgrim himself.

Very likely the actual conversations with the monks aboard the steamer—if we can judge from those recorded in "Monastic Islands"—were not especially interesting. Yet Leskov received from them a powerful stimulus. If Orthodox monasticism was the end of the road for these typical Russians, what had been the beginning and the middle of this road? Was monasticism the apotheosis of the Russian spirit? If so, one of these monks could be made to represent the epitome of the Russian national experience, personifying the national character of the

242

Russian people. It was an opportunity for a far-reaching generalization.

The monastic pilgrim was therefore to be a Russian of the Russians, a folk hero, a single person embodying in concentrated form the basic features of the Russian character. A folk hero is far from a "typical" everyman possessing precisely average amounts of average qualities. Rather, he intensifies, exalts features found in the average man, magnifies them so that they appear in sharp outline. He is larger than life, freed from ordinary life's contingencies and contradictions. "The Enchanted Pilgrim" is not a *bylina* or even a literary imitation of a *bylina;* but it comes from the land where the *byliny* still lived, and its hero, as the author observes, resembles the *bylina* hero Ilya Muromets, a Russian Hercules, a giant-hero of fantastic physical strength and courage. In "The Enchanted Pilgrim" the clerical garb covers a man of huge physique, like "Achilles" Desnitsyn in *Cathedral Folk,* a *bogatyr,* a mighty man of war; and as his story unfolds, we find that his life, too, is epic in events and proportions.

The pilgrim's name—Ivan Severyanovich Flyagin—is full of generalizing implications. "Ivan" is *the* name for the Russian male; and among neighboring peoples, including the Tatars invoked in the course of the narrative, it is used as an appellative for "Russian." "Severyanovich" is derived from *sever,* "north": Russia is a land of the north, and the north of the north, where the author encountered the hero, is the most Russian part of Russia.[3] Finally, the surname "Flyagin" comes from *flyaga,* "flask"—thus symbolizing that passion for drink which ever since the time of Saint Vladimir has been the favorite national vice. The hero's name might therefore be translated "Ivan Northson Flaskman."

Born a serf on the huge estate of "Count K." in Oryol Province,[4] Ivan was shaped by the serf's lot. The institution of serfdom and its psychological repercussions—which continued, like those of slavery in America, long after the institution itself was abolished—were evidently the determining factors in the formation of the Russian national character as it appeared in the nineteenth century. One of the most striking features of the serf mentality, and the underlying philosophy of Ivan Flyagin's life, is its fatalism. As Leskov had shown so graphically in *Laughter and Grief,* life in Russia was precarious for everybody, even for gentlemen; but for a serf this insecurity was augmented many times. A serf had little power to control his destiny, little chance to build his future. The agricultural peasants were so encumbered with assessments and obligations and so oppressed by landlords, bailiffs, and their own collective council, to say nothing of the eternal uncertainties of weather and pestilence, that they had little hope of improving the conditions of their life. They just hung on, hoping to survive from one year to the next. The house serfs, though somewhat better off materially, were more vulnerable to the caprices of their owners. The closer a serf was to his master, the less power he had over his fate. Defenseless and without rights, he was subject body and soul to the whim of a despot who might either shower him with favors or order him flogged to death. In an environment like this such bourgeois virtues as thrift, diligence, and persevering pursuit of some distant goal have little meaning. Helpless in the grip of forces more powerful than himself, the individual only tries to roll with each blow of man or fate. One must not stake too much on the permanence of anything; only disappointment can result. One travels light, grabbing what gratifications one can as the opportunities arise.

Under such conditions survival and sanity depend on endurance, the Russian endurance that is still proverbial—under both physical hardship and man-inflicted misery. No one is born with such endurance; it must be learned. Ivan Flyagin's education included a typical course. His father was a coachman, and as a boy of eleven Ivan was trained to be a postilion: he rode astride one of the front horses in the team pulling the count's carriage, shouting for all to make way for His Excellency, who was fond of fast driving and not accustomed to move aside or slow down for anyone. On long trips Ivan had to be tied to the saddle so that he would not fall off from weariness; and at the end of such journeys he was sometimes lifted off the horse unconscious from exhaustion and given horseradish to smell to make him come to his senses. "But then I got used to it," he says, "and all that was as nothing to me." "I got used to it": hardship was not something exceptional, to be survived with groans and remembered with moans; it was man's lot.

The capacity to endure physical pain and exhaustion is often combined with a willingness to inflict pain on others. If one's own person is not sacred, then neither is anyone else's, especially not those of members of one's own class, since among serfs property cannot serve as a substitute for the human body. If no one has anything, one cannot attack or punish a man by taking something from him; one can only hurt him physically. The gentry applied this principle in the corporal punishment they inflicted on their serfs so constantly, regardless of age or sex; and the serfs adopted it with equal avidity. Flyagin's career is one long sequence of episodes of physical violence—most of them endured, but some inflicted by him.

The first of these episodes is an act of manslaughter Flyagin committed as a young boy, the event which led to his "enchantment." While serving as the count's postilion, he galloped up to a hay wagon that had made no move to clear the way for the count's carriage. On top of the hay a man lay asleep, letting the horse go home of its own accord. Exulting in his power and enjoying the élan and dash of the ride, the boy rose up in his stirrups and fetched the man a tremendous blow across the back with his whip. The man turned out to be a monk from a nearby monastery, old and decrepit, and the blow killed him. Such acts epitomize that senseless, almost impersonal violence that made existence in Russia so uncertain. As Leskov had observed in *Laughter and Grief*, in Russia one was always liable to be beaten "by mistake."

By means of bribes Ivan's master managed to forestall any legal consequences of this crime; and of course he ordered the boy to be severely flogged. That night Ivan has a vision of the murdered monk, who makes a prophecy concerning Ivan's life—a fatalistic prophecy epitomizing the destiny of every Russian. Because of its play on the Slavic verbal aspects, this prophecy is hard to translate epigrammatically into English, but the following is an attempt: "Many times wilt thou be in peril, but not once wilt thou perish, until thy real perdition is upon thee; and then thou wilt [. . .] take the tonsure."[5] A conviction, then, that the conditions of life are fundamentally precarious and that survival depends on our ability to endure arbitrary acts of violence: this is the first key to the Russian character as Leskov sees it.

Russian fatalism and violence both seem Asiatic to the Western bourgeois (*Grattez le russe et vous trouverez le tartare*), but Leskov shows these very Tatars in an exhibition of the "Russian" qualities of endurance and cruelty which go to extremes that leave even Russians aghast. The Tatars also share another fundamental Russian trait—a willingness to throw everything to the winds for the sake of some immediate gratification. No wonder Flyagin in spite of his show of contempt for heathen orientals recognizes the Tatars as kindred spirits. This kinship is brought out and sealed in blood in a series of gruesome initiation procedures through which Flyagin becomes, for a substantial period of his life, an adoptive Tatar.

The first of these procedures is a flogging duel, a spectacle which might have been treated as a particularly revolting display of bloodthirsty brutality, but is distanced by Leskov (since we see it through the eyes of Ivan Severyanovich) into an exciting description of a tribal custom.[6] Two Tatars, both well-to-do, are first seen bidding against each other for a beautiful horse. The price is pushed up to astronomical heights, with money, land, horses, and even daughters thrown into the balance. To prevent the winner from being ruined by his victory, public opinion at last demands that the matter be settled by a flogging duel. The two men sit on the ground facing each other, stripped to the waist, left hands clasped, and with each bracing his feet against the other's. Then with their right hands they flog each other across the back with a whip, until one of them admits defeat, faints, or dies. After witnessing one of these duels and learning the technique of winning them, Flyagin volunteers to participate in one of them. Being a man of superhuman strength, he wins the duel; but unfortunately his opponent, too stubborn to give up in time, falls over dead. To avoid unpleasant consequences with the police Flyagin has to flee into the steppe with a group of Tatars, who bear him no grudge for beating one of them in a fair fight.

Like Ilya Muromets, Ivan Flyagin spends many years among the Tatars, kept a prisoner so that he may serve them as a doctor "for horses and women." He is prevented from running away by another gruesome display of Tatar cruelty: they strip the skin from the soles of his feet and insert bristles in the flesh, afterwards sewing the skin back on again. After the wounds have healed, the man cannot stand on his feet without excruciating pain. He must learn to hobble around on the sides of his feet.

Eventually Flyagin does escape from the Tatars and on returning to European Russia begins a new phase of his life, this one focused on yet another basic ingredient of the Russian character, the *flyaga* strain, or alcoholism. Alcoholism is an external symptom of an underlying emotional pattern which, in the case of the lower-class Russian, again seems related to serfdom. As Flyagin uses alcohol, he is not an addict, that is, he does not require a regular dose each day in order to make life endurable. On the contrary, he remains sober for long periods of time. Then suddenly he feels the impulse to go on a spree, and these sprees sometimes last for several days. He consumes enough vodka to make himself lose consciousness—and since he is a *bogatyr* and a practiced drinker, the amount required is prodigious—and then begins drinking again as soon as he comes to himself. This goes on until his spirit is sated, or the "zeal" (*userdie*), as he puts it, passes by.

During this alcoholic period Flyagin serves as assistant to a cavalry officer assigned to buy horses for the army. In this capacity Flyagin often has custody of considerable sums of government money. He is absolutely scrupulous and would not dream of embezzling. When he feels a spree coming on him, he dutifully reports the fact to his officer, turns over to him all the government's money, and disappears from sight for several days. The spree, or *vykhod*, "going out," as he oddly calls it, is represented as something like a spell of stormy weather, inevitable, uncontrollable, completely external to the will of the individual. The only thing to do is to batten down the hatches and ride it out as best you can.

This externalization of desire is a recurrent feature in the mythology of Russian alcoholism, and Ivan Severyanovich perfectly fits the national pattern. This giant, so powerful in other respects, has no power over himself. The passion for alcohol is rationalized as something independent of the self, a demon that cannot be denied. Everything must make way before it. This mythology is readily accepted by other Russians. No matter how much he is inconvenienced by Ivan's sprees, the officer tolerates them without demur. The two of them, in fact, work out a system of mutual dependence. When Ivan is on a spree, the officer must guard the money and do Ivan's work for him. In return, the officer has his own aristocratic passion, gambling. He too is recurrently tempted to play with the Treasury's money. When in the grips of this "devil," he begs, pleads, and even threatens Ivan, trying to extract the money from him. But Ivan is always adamant, and the officer afterward thanks him for his firmness. If your demon, your passion, is outside yourself, the counterforce must also come from outside. Like a child, the Russian must depend on others, temporarily cast in the role of parent or master, to protect him from himself.

One can see how serfdom might create such a pattern of dependence. The serf is dependent by definition, subject to all sorts of external controls. In a sense he is never permitted to grow up. He is still punished physically, like a little child. If he develops any internal controls, they are likely to be only those adaptive ones that enable him to present an acceptable façade of compliance. But in a system where authority is both despotic and capricious, and from which there is no emancipation, the serf is unlikely to develop rational self-control. "No," the serf says in effect, "if they are going to force me to behave in a certain way, then let them do the forcing, and the restraining; my behavior is their responsibility, not mine. And every now and then I will show them that their power over me is limited after all: I will get royally drunk." Drunkenness is a pleasure that can occasionally be extorted from a largely hostile environment, and at the same time it is a safe mode of rebellion. A serf insensate from alcohol is no good to anyone; he has escaped. There is no satisfaction even in beating him, since he cannot feel it.

If Flyagin's Russian alcoholism can be interpreted in this way, as the self-obliterating rebellion of a slave, what about the behavior of the officer? Though a man of wealth and a prince, he too is dependent; he relies on a servant to prevent him from committing theft. Is he too a spiritual serf? Not exactly, but the Russian gentleman's situation does have a good deal in common with the serf's. It is a much more comfortable and privileged position; nevertheless, a dependent mentality is deeply ingrained in him, and his dependence, too, is a product of serfdom. The keystone of the middle-class ethos, that a man by work must provide for himself and his family, is essentially as alien to the master as to the serf. The serf does not provide, in a psychological sense, for himself and his family. He is made to work; but the master, or God, provides; and if they do not, there is nothing he can do. As for the master, he need not provide for himself: his estate (that is, his serfs) will do that; there will always be an income. Money is a naturally available resource, like air. Any suggestion that it is finite brings on the floundering of a man being suffocated. Russian nineteenth-century history and literature record countless instances of Russian gentlemen recklessly squandering their estates, with utter disregard for their own future, let alone that of their descendants. "How dare they limit my pleasures?" they seem to say. "My desires are law. I'll show them."

The gentleman may choose to serve, to do a stint in the army or civil administration. But even if he does, the stint is generally not long, nor does he live on his salary. Furthermore, while he is in the service, he in turn is in effect a serf of the tsar, protected and cared for, but obliged to do or die according to the whim of his imperial master. Thus all through the system there is mutual dependence, reliance on external restraints and self-destructive rebellion against them, and a total absence of that sturdy self-reliance idealized by the middle-class societies in the West.

In the epic of Ivan Flyagin, the mutual protection system eventually breaks down. One day the prince is out of town when the spree zeal descends upon Ivan. For a time Ivan tries to fight off his demon by himself. Then, while he is drinking tea in a tavern, of all places, he falls into conversation with a miserable wretch of a drunkard, a man in the last stages of degradation and despair. Though he cannot use it himself (he has so many sins on his conscience that he considers his degradation a just punishment), this drunkard offers Ivan an infallible cure for alcoholism. He will "magnetize" Ivan and drive away his demon forever. The first stage in this magnetization, as might be expected, is one last spree, a spree to end all sprees. But the magnetic cure turns out to be something more than this inevitable rationalization. Its secret, it transpires, is to drive out the demon of drink with the demon of lust. Ivan, dead drunk and loaded with five thousand rubles of government money, is taken to hear the singing of a beautiful gypsy girl. Before the night is over he has thrown all the money, in the form of "white swans"—hundred-ruble notes—at her feet.

The prince, of course, is legally responsible for this money. When his master returns, Ivan therefore presents himself, confesses, and assumes the position for a beating, expecting to work out the five thousand rubles over many years of service. But the prince unexpectedly absolves him. It turns out that in this respect too they are kindred spirits, true Russians. For the love of the same gypsy girl, the prince has mortgaged all his lands and paid a fantastic sum—fifty thousand rubles—to buy her from her *tabor* or camp. Furthermore, the prince at once recognizes their community of spirit. They are both "artists," he says, and of course he himself is the greater artist, since he sacrificed more and got the girl into the bargain. But the nature of this artistry is not only what the prince and Ivan represent it to be—simply a heightened capacity for aesthetic appreciation, a total response to the beauty of the girl and her singing. This capacity for uninhibited, total response, whether aesthetic or emotional, constitutes one of the most cherished ingredients of the Russian soul as idealized by its apologists. Many writers, including Herzen, Dostoevsky, and others, paid homage to this spiritual "breadth," contrasting it favorably to the niggling, constricted spirit of the shopkeeping West. But in their admiration for the broad sweep of the Russian spirit, the apologists often overlooked the reverse of this shiny coin, its self-destructive and depressive aspects. There is something narcissistic and also suicidal in the wild abandon described by the writers. The artist, whether Ivan Flyagin or his master (or Dmitry Karamazov), is more excited by the spectacle of his own destruction, of the sensation he is creating by throwing away all that money, than he is by the gypsy girl. His real message is not so much "I want her" as "Look at me." And further, "Since you won't restrain me, I'll destroy myself, and then you'll have to pick up the pieces."

In the prince's case, the basic narcissism of his act is demonstrated by succeeding events. Having won the girl, he soon loses interest in her. Before long he moves her from his house, in the last stages of pregnancy, to make room for an aristocratic wife whom he must marry to recoup his depleted fortunes.

An underlying motif of self-destruction and suicide is also a basic ingredient of the complex of Russian dependency. An alcoholic stupor, after all, is a simulation of death. The close connection between alcoholism and suicide is worked into the structure of "The Enchanted Pilgrim." Flyagin's life history is preceded by an apropos anecdote on the subject of whether those who commit suicide are irrevocably damned. It is true, Flyagin admits, that Orthodox Christians are normally not permitted to pray for the souls of self-murderers. But he knows of one exception to this rule, a wretched little priest who was specifically authorized by the metropolitan to continue praying for "those who lay hands on themselves." This priest had been condemned to be unfrocked for habitual drunkenness. Contemplating suicide himself, he began to pray for the souls of other suicides. When he heard the priest's story, the metropolitan, after some prodding from Saint Sergius (who appeared to him in a vision), decided both to leave the priest in his parish and to authorize him to continue praying as before.

Suicide and self-destruction run through the tale of the enchanted pilgrim. Early in his life, despairing from a cruel and unending punishment imposed by Countess K., Flyagin attempts to hang himself, but he is rescued by a gypsy, with whom he runs away on two of his master's horses. The flogging duel, the sprees, the throwing away of the five thousand rubles—what are they but mitigated suicides? Likewise, the gypsy girl, Grusha, the stimulus for Ivan's and the prince's "artistry," resolves on suicide after being abandoned by the prince. Dependent as any full-blooded Russian, she cannot bring herself to perform the act of self-destruction with her own hands. Instead, she first binds Ivan by terrible oaths and then requires him to murder her. In an agony of love, he hurls her from a precipice, thus taking another murder on his already burdened conscience. To expiate this crime, he volunteers to take another man's place as a recruit in the army and then offers himself for the most dangerous service in the Caucasus, where war was incessant. But because of his enchantment, the curse laid upon him by his first victim, he cannot manage to get himself killed, or even arrested for the girl's murder, which he confesses to a superior officer. As in the monk's prophecy, his "perishing" must remain in the imperfective aspect, incomplete and continuing.

Finally, Flyagin's entry into a monastery is a substitutive suicide, a renunciation of life. And for Flyagin, unlike the hero of the seventeenth-century Russian *Tale of Woe-Misfortune*, even monasticism is not the end of his long road of perishing. While in the monastery he begins to prophesy war, citing the words of Saint Paul: "When they shall say, Peace and safety, then sudden destruction cometh upon them, as travail upon a woman with child, and they shall not escape."[7] At the age of fifty-three, though wearing a monk's habit, Flyagin longs to take up arms again: "I have a great longing to die for my people," he proclaims. It is at this point we leave him, his enchantment still upon him.

Thus to transmute "The Enchanted Pilgrim" into a disquisition on the Russian national character may be going beyond the bounds of legitimate literary analysis. Yet the story contains an inner striving toward universality, and the universals explicitly transmuted above are implicit in the story. Perhaps Leskov did not understand them intellectually to the extent of being able to formulate them as abstract statements, but his artistic intuition perceived them and epitomized them perfectly in concrete images.

To write at this level of generalization is difficult and artistically dangerous. It is hard to embody an abstract generalization in a concrete image that will retain its individuality and its credibility as a real instance taken from life. Therefore, throughout "The Enchanted Pilgrim," Leskov goes to great lengths to anchor his story in reality, to provide his universals with concrete ballast.

By making the hero talk and tell his own story, Leskov convinces us of his reality; we feel the concrete shapes and sounds of his words. Flyagin's is the vigorous, open-air speech of a man of intelligence but little education; a man who has learned a great deal about life from varied experiences but has read few, if any, books. (He is not illiterate, as we learn from the mixture of newspapers, the Gospels and writings of Saint Tikhon of Zadonsk that inspire his latter-day prophecies; but we are never told how he learned to read.) Throughout Flyagin's narrative, the intonation and syntax of oral speech are consistently maintained, and the impression of oral delivery is reinforced by occasional questions and comments from his audience.

Another kind of concretizing ballast is supplied by horses. By birth, profession, and natural inclination Ivan Severyanovich is what he calls a *connoisseur*—an untranslatable Leskovian pun, since the French word transliterated as *konesèr* is interpreted by Flyagin as a derivative of the Russian *kon'*, "horse." Flyagin is a connoisseur of horseflesh. He has an almost miraculous understanding of the animals; he sees to the depth of their souls. Among other things, this connoisseurship gives Ivan Severyanovich the opportunity to regale us with horse stories and with elaborate descriptions of the bodies and personalities of horses, using extraordinary technical language, some of which must have been obscure to the ordinary Russian reader even in those pre-automobile times. These technical words help to convince us of the concrete individuality of the enchanted pilgrim, despite his universal Russianness.[8]

In terms of its structure, "The Enchanted Pilgrim" must be understood as part of Leskov's long-continued polemic against the structural unity of the mid-nineteenth-century novel. Life, Leskov seems to say, is not so neat or symmetrical. Life is more like a journey. We move constantly onward, leaving behind places, people, and problems, and encountering new ones to take their place. Leskov imitates this journey with his "string of beads" structure. The populist critic Mikhailovsky (as frequently with nineteenth-century Russian critics, he was a political and social thinker masquerading as a literary critic) correctly perceived and defined this structure, perhaps originating the metaphor that describes it. "In 'The Enchanted Pilgrim,' " Mikhailovsky writes, "one is especially struck by the absence of any center; so that strictly speaking there is no plot, but rather a whole series of plots, threaded on a string like beads; and each bead is quite separate and may very easily be removed, replaced with another; and you could thread as many more beads as you like on the same string."[9] Mikhailovsky considered this lack of center a grievous fault: a proper story has a proper plot with a well-determined center. In fact, however, Leskov was working in a different architectural form, an elongated one without a center. This form has no precise name, although Leskov at one point in Flyagin's narrative (in an author's commentary) introduces the odd term "dramocomedy" to describe it. It is a hybrid form made up of elements of other genres, including the folk epic and its nineteenth-century imitations (for example, the ballad on Ilya Muromets by A. K. Tolstoy actually cited in the text); the old picaresque novel; the didactic court novel of eighteenth-century France; and the largely English eighteenth-century novel of travel and adventure.

In the original newspaper version Leskov's story bore a characteristic eighteenth-century subtitle: "The Enchanted Pilgrim: His Life, Experiences, Opinions, and Adventures"—an echo of the "lives and adventures" of many eighteenth-century heroes, such as Tom Jones, Peregrine Pickle, or Gil Blas. The "opinions," however, are clearly those of Tristram Shandy, a favorite of Leskov's. All these novels consist of "bead strings" of adventures, unified only by the personality of their hero. In an early, unpublished version, "The Enchanted Pilgrim" was entitled "A Black-Earth Telemachus"—thus echoing the *Odyssey*, Fénelon's didactic novel, and the real epic into which this novel had been transformed by the eighteenth-century Russian poet Trediakovsky.[10] Leskov himself pointed further to a structural connection between both *Laughter and Grief* and "The Enchanted Pilgrim" and Gogol's *Dead Souls*, itself a remote descendant of the picaresque novel.[11] One of Leskov's friends had criticized "The Enchanted Pilgrim" on the grounds that Leskov had kept his hero too much in the foreground, failing to exploit all the artistic possibilities of the different milieus described. Leskov vehemently rejected this contention, and in so doing provided further confirmation of his work's literary ancestry: "Why should the personality of the hero necessarily fade into the background? What sort of a requirement is that? What about Don Quixote, Telemachus, Chichikov? Why shouldn't the hero and the milieu move along together?"[12]

Besides these structural models, "The Enchanted Pilgrim," as the Soviet scholar I. Z. Serman has pointed out (4:552-553), also reverberates with other echoes from Russian literature, including two stories published a year earlier. Leskov must have had in mind Turgenev's story "The End of Chertopkhanov," later attached to *A Sportsman's Sketches*, but first published in 1872, when "The Enchanted Pilgrim" was being written. Turgenev's story is in turn an ironic echo of Lermontov's "Bela." In all three stories a central theme is the rise and decline of a romance between a Russian gentleman and an exotic, non-Russian girl—Circassian in the case of Bela, gypsy in "Chertopkhanov" and "The Enchanted Pilgrim"—as well as a competition between women and horses for the first place in a man's heart. Turgenev had exploded Lermontov, so to speak, by reversing the sexual roles and having his gypsy girl abandon her aging Russian lover not because of a rival passion, but simply from boredom. Leskov in turn has rescued the male honor (and paid a last tribute to romanticism) by having his Grusha insist on death when she loses the prince's love. But Leskov's position is far from romantic. He may give his prince the satisfaction of driving a girl to suicide from unrequited love for him, but that prince is no Pechorin. In later scenes he is thoroughly deflated and made to appear not only irresponsible and callous (these qualities might still be romantic), but childish and foolish.

Serman also calls attention to the parallel between "The Enchanted Pilgrim" and another great Russian story published in 1872, Tolstoy's

"Prisoner of the Caucasus"—like "The End of Chertopkhanov," an ironic echo of Russian romanticism. Tolstoy had taken the theme of Pushkin's poem and punctured it by having the highly romantic plot narrated in a down-to-earth style by a peasant soldier. Leskov too has taken up the prisoner theme and deromanticized it, even more than Tolstoy had done, in the story of Flyagin's captivity with the Tatars. His prisoner-hero is no handsome young officer, but an earthy serf, and Leskov's Tatars are not dashing Caucasian mountaineers. Their flogging duels and their "bristling up" of a man's feet are savage and brutal; and their life at home seems sordid and unpoetic in the extreme.

Furthermore, Ivan has anything but a romantic, poetic image of his own captivity. He adapts himself to his captors' way of life, among other things accepting their unromantic attitude toward women. In one tribe he is given two wives as an anodyne for the ills inflicted on him, and he accepts them and begets children by them. Then he is traded to another tribe and acquires new wives and new children. Toward neither set of wives and children does he form any emotional attachment. As a Russian, he considers himself superior to these Asiatics (among whom he includes his own children), and he abandons them without a qualm when his chance comes to escape. He uses religion to rationalize his indifference: since they are not baptized, these wives and offspring do not count. The romantic hero's passion for the Circassian girl may fade, as Pechorin's did, but at least it was there to begin with. Flyagin, on the other hand, like any good Tatar, considers his wives merely servants with whom he has sexual relations.

For all its vitality and originality, "The Enchanted Pilgrim" was far from winning immediate recognition as a masterpiece. Leskov apparently first submitted it to V. P. Meshchersky, editor of the conservative weekly *The Citizen*, with which Dostoevsky had a close connection.[13] The story was not accepted. If Viktor Vinogradov is right in his suppositions, this rejection was instigated by Dostoevsky himself.[14] Leskov then sent the story to his new haven, Katkov's *Russian Messenger*, and on May 10, 1873, received a rather ungracious reply from Katkov's factotum, N. A. Lyubimov:

Mikhail Nikiforovich [Katkov] has read "A Black-Earth Telemachus" and after some hesitations has come to the conclusion that it will not be convenient to publish this piece. Not to mention certain episodes, for instance about Philaret and Saint Sergius [which Katkov considered disrespectful to Philaret Drozdov, the late metropolitan of Moscow], the whole piece seemed to him raw material for the creation of figures which are now quite murky rather than a finished description of something actually possible and occurring. I am not reporting to you, of course, what Mikhail Nikiforovich said in his exact words, but only in the most general terms. He advises you to wait before you publish this piece, the theme of which itself, in his opinion, might be developed into something worthwhile.[15]

On this letter, probably at some later date, Leskov wrote: "Received 10 May, 1873. Appraisal of *Telemachus* by the editors of the *Russian Messenger*, a month after they had finished publishing *Baal*." *Baal* was a sensational satirical melodrama, absurdly overdone, by Pisemsky; apart from its weakness as a work of art, Leskov undoubtedly considered this play the last word in moral cynicism (among other things, in the course of the action a husband urges his hitherto virtuous wife to "use her charms" on a government official who is threatening him with financial ruin, and she complies). In any case, Leskov felt that the acceptance of such a work over his "Enchanted Pilgrim" was a good measure of the false values that prevailed in the editorial offices of the *Russian Messenger*. His anger was justified and has been vindicated by posterity. *Baal* is forgotten, but "The Enchanted Pilgrim" lives on, one of the great imaginative products of the Russian spirit.

17

The Decrepit Nobility

Leskov now turned his attention to the antithesis of the "people" in Russian society, the gentry. In the metaphor employed by one of his gentleman characters, the peasants were the "stomach" of Russian society—admittedly a vital organ, but an inarticulate and partly insensate one. The "head" of that society, its eyes, ears, and brain, was the gentry—smaller in numbers, but incomparably more important as the country's political, cultural, and economic nerve-center. What sort of head was it?

Leskov had given much thought to the state of the gentry, that class to which he precariously belonged. Like Chekhov, Leskov was a natural sociologist, with an instinct for social dynamics. Like a good engineer, he had a keen eye for the weak spots in class relationships, signs of friction or decay that might cause the structure to sag. His observations were generally couched in moral rather than in scientific terms, but his awareness of the practical realities of class relationships was so acute that his judgments of Russian society still seem right and even prophetic. They do not have the dated, incomplete, self-deluding air of the social statements made by many of his contemporaries. As a critic of Russian society, Leskov has stood up remarkably well—much better than his later master Tolstoy, whose extreme anti-urbanism and anti-intellectualism now seem dated and crankish.

For the gentry, the nineteenth century was a period of crisis. The Emancipation of 1861 had been a belated recognition on the part of the government that the old feudal system of serfdom for the peasants and civil service (often evaded or curtailed) for the nobles was no longer viable. The country was being drawn inexorably forward along the road of capitalism. Would the gentry adapt to capitalist conditions of agriculture? Would there be a place for them in industrial society? Leskov's cold answer to these questions, in 1873, was no. The Russian gentry, he concluded, is doomed. Whatever its contributions in the past, it will not succeed in adjusting to present realities; it is riding toward its own destruction. He was right.

Leskov's view was not that of a detached modern historian. He stood very close to the deteriorating gentry, bound to it by many personal ties. Tenuous as his membership was, he always listed the gentry as *his* class. But that tenuousness gave him a perspective that a fullfledged gentleman would not have possessed. His ancestral gentry roots were shallow, going back on his father's side only to 1825; he had long ago given up government service, the traditional pursuit of a gentleman, and launched upon a bourgeois, capitalistic career, first as Scott's employee, later as a journalist and free-lance writer. Having thus made the jump to capitalism, he could now turn back to look at the other "lordlings" still huddled on the other shore. Would they make it or not?

Leskov decided to resurrect the gentry section of the three-part chronicle he had projected in 1866. The clergy section had eventually become *Cathedral Folk*, but only fragments of the gentry chronicle had been completed, published under the title "Old Times in the Village of Plodomasovo." "Old Times" contains two images of eighteenth-century Russian aristocratism: tyrannical power (male); and well-ordered despotism (female). In both cases the nobility is seen in its heyday, not in the later decline Leskov saw so inexorably menacing the gentry of his own day. Moreover, both those images were too exceptional to be sociologically representative.

In 1873 Leskov felt that he had more to say on the gentry question, especially in its contemporary aspects. Instead of returning to the abandoned Plodomasovs he decided to write a new gentry chronicle, ostentatiously entitled *A Decrepit Clan* (*Zakhudaly rod*)—the deterioration of one family would represent the declining fortunes of the entire class. (The metaphorical associations of the Russian *zakhudaly* are biological: derived from *khudoi*, "thin," it implies "wasted," "emaciated.") This new gentry clan, the Protozanovs, bear a name resembling that of their predecessors, the Plodomasovs. And there are other similarities, as well.

Leskov worked on this new chronicle during most of 1873 and probably well into 1874.[1] Though still uncompleted, *A Decrepit Clan* was accepted for serial publication in *Russian Messenger,* and the first installment appeared in July 1874. There were further installments in the August and October numbers. Then the explosion occurred.

In the past, Leskov had repeatedly been angered by the editorial high-handedness of Katkov and his assistants. The assistants, without consulting their authors, made substantial changes in the texts of the works they published, sometimes on ideological, sometimes on aesthetic grounds. When he saw the mutilations of his novel in the October number of *Russian Messenger*, Leskov blew up. Large chunks of important matter had been excised; pages had been rewritten, their tone and emphasis changed, their philosophical message blurred. Even the names of characters had been arbitrarily altered.[2] Infuriated, Leskov decided to break with Katkov altogether and to withdraw his novel from *Russian Messenger*.

Katkov and his henchmen had grossly transgressed the legitimate boundaries of their editorial function, and Leskov's wrath was justified. Nevertheless, in view of the fact that the same thing had happened to Leskov before, not with Katkov, but with Kraevsky, we might question the emotional use Leskov made of Katkov's misbehavior, especially Leskov's conclusion that *because* of Katkov's tampering with his text, he could not finish the novel. Leskov decided to issue immediately, in book form, the first two parts of *A Decrepit Clan* in their original, non-Katkovian text. He thus put a seal of finality, as it were, on the uncompleted work, making it more difficult to return to it later.

"I've sold *A Decrepit Clan* to Bazunov, as much as has appeared," Leskov wrote to Ivan Aksakov. "I will publish the second part with all the cuts restored; but I am quite unable to finish writing the novel now, after all this turmoil, and I am postponing it to a more peaceful time."[3] And a few days later, to the same correspondent: "It's impossible to finish *A Decrepit Clan* now, even despite the fact that it is almost entirely completed in rough form. My heart is no longer in it, and it is a hundred times easier and pleasanter for me to think about a new work than to return to this aching wound. It is beyond my strength! Perhaps after some time has passed, I'll manage to add something, but now— too much black blood has collected in my heart from this. First of all I have to forget about it."[4]

One can understand Leskov's exasperation. Yet one would have thought that instead of hysterically throwing up his hands and refusing to touch the novel again, he would have been all the more determined to complete it, to vindicate himself by exhibiting it whole to the world. It looks as if Leskov did not want to finish this novel and seized upon Katkov as a convenient excuse. Several months later, in a rare moment of frankness, Leskov came close to admitting this: "the novel began to get mixed up in my head, and I had to drop it."[5]

Curiously, in after years the author professed especial fondness for this abandoned and unfinished work. In the late 1880s, A. S. Suvorin issued a series of cheap reprints of popular fiction, designed to be sold in such places as railway stations. A number of Leskov's stories were published in this series, and he was much gratified by their success. The financial rewards were substantial, and he was pleased to think that he would now reach a new species of reader, the kind of person who would never enter a bookstore or a library or read a literary review, but might pick up a story to amuse himself on the train. In 1888 Leskov wrote to Suvorin, strongly urging him to issue *A Decrepit Clan* in this series:

> I am sending you, Aleksei Sergeyevich, a copy of *A Decrepit Clan*. I want you to like it and to publish it. *I love this piece* more than *Cathedral Folk* or *The Sealed Angel*. It is more mature than they and painstakingly written. Katkov valued it and praised it [How time, self-interest, and the needs of rhetoric blur the memory!], but it was not noticed by the critics and is little read by the public. If you have leisure, glance through it. It will just make a small book worth 50 copecks, and that will be convenient for you, the public, and me. I will be impatient to receive your answer, because *this is my favorite piece.*[6]

Suvorin seems to have been unimpressed, and a year later Leskov renewed his plea in stronger terms:

> Among this material is a piece *I especially love, love most of all* and know that it is good—this is *The Decrepit Clan of the Princes Protozanov*. It was admired by Katkov and Aksakov and Cherkassky and Pirogov. It is dearer to me than anything else I have written, and I would ardently wish to see it distributed as widely as possible [. . .] You have published incomparably weaker works of mine; please do not refuse me this great literary favor— publish "The Protozanov Princes" in the *Cheap Library*! Really, they deserve it! I am asking you, you understand, not for any petty reason, but my spirit hungers and thirsts for it. It is an urge, a demand of my soul.[7]

Perhaps irritated by what he considered illegitimate emotional pressuring, Suvorin remained adamant, and *A Decrepit Clan* never appeared in the "Cheap Library." It was reissued in 1889-90 in Leskov's collected works, and the nature of the revisions carried out for that edition will be considered later. But whence this love? Does *A Decrepit Clan* merit such praise from its creator?

Leskov provided *A Decrepit Clan* with a double subtitle: *The Family Chronicle of the Princes Protozanov* (*From the Notes of Princess V. D. P.*). [8] More than Leskov's earlier chronicle of the clergy, this aristocratic subtitle calls attention to his indebtedness to Sergei Aksakov's *Family Chronicle*. Aksakov's work was the classic evocation in Russian literature of the pre-Emancipation gentry and their life in the country—idyllic in relation to nature if sometimes inhuman in relation to their serfs. To challenge such a classic on its own ground was a bold act. Perhaps Leskov's anticipation of the inevitable comparisons partly accounts for the pains he took with the book and for his inability to finish it.

Aksakov's chronicle presents under a thin fictional disguise the author's actual memories of his forebears and his childhood. Lacking aristocratic memories of his own, Leskov presents instead the fictitious memories of an imaginary character, a contemporary descendant of an aristocratic family. His narrator, Princess V. D. P. (Vera Dmitrievna Protozanova), by no means limits herself to her own memories, however; they play a small part in the completed sections of the novel. Rather, as the self-appointed historian of her clan, she undertakes to reconstruct a more distant past, mostly by questioning persons whose memories antedate hers by a generation. Although this mode of narration has advantages—in particular, the controlled point of view of a character directly associated with the action seems less fictitious than a presentation by an omniscient author—it involved Leskov in technical difficulties, since the narrator here (or memoirist) neither participates in nor observes much of the action. We are thus twice removed from many of the episodes recounted: a fictitious princess tells what she has learned from survivors about events that happened before she was born; and if these survivors (mostly old exserfs) were not themselves present at some important event, they in turn must have heard about it from someone else or have witnessed it as eavesdroppers. The chain of relayed reportages becomes too long for convenience and for credibility. Ivan Aksakov, son of Sergei Aksakov, had similar misgivings about the intricacies of this structure and advised Leskov to revert to a more conventional, omniscient-author point of view. As Leskov reported the matter to a friend, "Ivan Sergeyevich Aksakov [. . .] praised me for *A Decrepit Clan*, but said that it was too bad I had not chosen an overall novelistic structure, but had written it as a memoir, as if coming from a fictional character. Ivan Sergeyevich even pointed out to me certain passages where my own face could be clearly discerned from behind the fictional character presenting the memoir."⁹ This inherent confusion may have been another reason for Leskov's abandonment of the novel.

Like "Old Times in the Village of Plodomasovo," the chronicle of the Protozanovs begins with a brief glimpse of the family's remote past, before the founding of the Muscovite principality; it is a long lineage, and a distinguished one, though one of its representatives earned the distinction of having his head chopped off by Peter the Great—for peculation. Four generations of his successors, however, were men of upright life and unimpeachable virtue. Except for their beheaded forebear, therefore, the Protozanovs thus fit the Leskovian moral pattern familiar from *No Way Out*: nuggets of gleaming goodness set against a background of evil.

This historical excursus is handled with dispatch, as if Leskov were afraid of again being carried away with eighteenth-century ancestors and failing to reach the nineteenth-century generations on whose decrepitude he had planned to focus. He needed the procession of righteous Protozanov prototypes in order to establish the moral foundation for the novel: the doctrine of *noblesse oblige*, which a hundred years earlier the poet Sumarokov had tried to inculcate in the Russian gentry. Nobility of class calls for nobility of character.

The culminating figure in the parade of Protozanov *pravedniki* is not the ultimate male descendant of the peculator executed by Peter, but a person who married into the family, the wife of a Protozanov killed in 1812. Just as in "Old Times in the Village of Plodomasovo," the shining exemplar of aristocratic virtue, the person who lives according to the principle of noblesse oblige, is a woman, Princess Varvara Nikanorovna Protozanova née Chestunova—her maiden name echoing the honesty and honor (*chest'*) of her character. On the appearance of Princess Varvara, the swift-moving parade of *pravedniki* ends, and the action of the novel properly begins.

With this character Leskov found himself trapped in almost the same snare that had prevented him from working out the fortunes of the Plodomasov clan. He got stuck, fascinated by this radiant image of what the old nobility *should* have been. Enchanted, he was unable to proceed to the decrepitude promised in the title. The published portions of *A Decrepit Clan* have nothing decrepit about them at all; they are almost wholly concerned with this splendid and impressive figure, Princess Varvara Nikanorovna. In her, as in Marfa Andreyevna Plodomasova, nobility of birth and nobility of character are joined.

There are many similarities between these two women. Each was born to a poor family and married into a rich one; each was widowed at an early age and left sole possessor of the lands and wealth passed down to her husband from his ancestors; each proved an excellent custodian of that wealth and a benevolent ruler of her estate; each refused to marry again and remained a queen regnant to the end of her days. Both characters were modeled on the same real person, or perhaps the same two real persons, important figures from Leskov's childhood.

The first of these models is identified in Leskov's own testimony:

> In the Kromy district of Oryol province, in the village of Zinovievo, there lived a landowner named Nastasia Sergeyevna, née Princess Masalskaya. In her youth she had received a brilliant education in Paris, and she enjoyed general respect for her intelligence and for her noble, independent character. Her fortune was modest (500 souls), but her well-situated house was open to all guests, invited and uninvited. She was much revered, and people came to see her from far away, not for the sake of pomp or hospitality, but "to pay their respects"—out of veneration. There was hospitality in the Zinoviev house, but it was simple, comfortable, and often quite merry. Moreover, the Zinoviev house was also to a considerable extent a source of enlightenment for the whole region. Most of the neighbors borrowed books from the library, which the owner had inherited from Masalsky [her uncle, a minor writer of the early nineteenth century], and this helped to maintain quite a high standard of literacy in the surrounding society.
>
> When I was taken as a boy to Zinovievo, Nastasia Sergeyevna was already an old lady, but I remember her very well, and I have sketched some of her traits in my portraits of "Boyarinya Plodomasova" (in *Cathedral Folk*) and "Princess Protozanova" (in *A Decrepit Clan*).[10]

Obviously this grand lady made a powerful impression on the young Leskov. First, there were the wealth and the nobility themselves. Five hundred souls may have been "modest," but it was still a great deal compared with the Leskovs' fifty. And the proprietress of these five hundred souls was a *knyaginya*, a "princess"—a fairly common, but still prestigious aristocratic title indicating blood a good deal bluer than the average gentlewoman's. From Leskov's childish point of

view, the Zinoviev household must have seemed a luxurious and dazzling one indeed.

Second, Nastasia Sergeyevna was a widow. Widowhood placed the
woman in a partly masculine social position: in the case of a Russian
aristocrat, she assumed full responsibility for her estate. Thus Nastasia
Sergeyevna, as a relatively rich landowner managing her own estate,
was a figure of economic power in Leskov's neighborhood. Perhaps
this female power was attractive and exciting to Leskov. In the hands
of a woman, power seemed to him more benevolent, less harsh and
arbitrary, than when wielded by a man like his uncle Strakhov. On
the other hand, the widow assumed only half the social role theoreti-
cally assigned to her male counterpart. The other half, service to the
state, was not expected of her (or open to her at all). Thus, by the nature of things, a Nastasia Sergeyevna was more detached in relation to
the government, more independent in her attitude toward official
pieties, than a male exofficial turned squire would usually have been.
Wealthy, powerful, and a woman, Nastasia Sergeyevna was a uniquely free moral agent.

Finally, Nastasia Sergeyevna was distinguished by her culture, her
brilliant education in Paris, and her outstanding library. And she
evidently had a personality suitable to her social attributes: a combination of warmth, dignity, and moral uprightness that aroused affection and admiration in others. According to Leskov, people did not
care to take advantage of her generosity; they revered her.

In migrating through Leskov's imagination to fictional reincarnation
in Marfa Andreyevna Plodomasova and Varvara Nikanorovna Protozanova, Nastasia Sergeyevna underwent significant modifications.
Both fictional heroines have far more wealth; they are the richest proprietors for miles around. His heroines are said to be excellent admin-
istrators, and in the case of Varvara Nikanorovna, Leskov goes into
considerable detail concerning the economics of her estate—her financial relations with her peasants and her commercial transactions with
the outside world. In this picture the superior moral qualities of Varvara Nikanorovna are exemplified in her everyday economic behavior.

On the other hand, the element of cultural superiority that distinguished Nastasia Sergeyevna is virtually eliminated from her two fictional reflections. Neither heroine "received a brilliant education in
Paris." About Marfa Andreyevna's intellectual interests little is said:
we know only that she took her religion seriously and, though devoutly Orthodox, had a generally low opinion of the Orthodox clergy.
Varvara Nikanorovna, though more thoughtful than Marfa Andrey-

evna, is not cultivated in the usual sense. Her intellectual life has little to do with books, especially contemporary ones. She speaks French correctly, but considers it pretentious to do so with people who can speak Russian. She is a natural philosopher: she meditates about her life, her responsibilities as a mother, as a landowner, as a human being, and as a Christian, trying to think out a consistent ethical position and to apply her ethics in her life.

The elimination of cultural superiority as a quality of these mother-heroines may provide us with a clue for identifying another model for the righteous widows in Leskov's fiction: the author's mother. Marya Petrovna Leskova claimed no brilliant education, nor an impressive library, nor wealth; but she did have some of the moral qualities Leskov admired in Nastasia Sergeyevna. Even before her husband's death in 1848 she had assumed the reins of power on the little Panino estate and made it yield enough to support her sizable family. Moreover, there is evidence that Marya Petrovna won the respect and admiration of her neighbors, if not for her mildness and benevolence, at least for her administrative ability and practical intelligence.[11] In merging his mother's image with that of Nastasia Sergeyevna Zinovieva, Leskov eliminated both his mother's poverty and her roughness and harshness, for which he could never forgive her.

The core of Varvara Nikanorovna's characterization is her striving for a consistently humane, Christian ethic. To expatiate too long on such matters, however, would have turned the novel into a moral treatise. Varvara Nikanorovna therefore rarely expounds her ideas in words; she reveals them through her actions and her relations with others. These others have lives of their own, each one providing a pretext for introducing anecdotal material of independent narrative value. Thus, time and again the main action must be halted while these tangential stories are told.

There are many such subsidiary characters, at first mostly persons dependent on Varvara Nikanorovna, beneath her in class status. Among them are Olga Fedotovna (the source of much of the information gleaned by the memoirist, Princess V. D. P.), born a house serf on the Protozanov estate and eventually promoted to be Varvara Nikanorovna's closest retainer and one of her oldest friends, and the deaconess Marya Nikolayevna, who exemplifies Leskov's ideal of selfless humility by sacrificing herself for her family in a ridiculous marriage to a man much younger than herself.[12] Though never denying her superior status, Varvara Nikanorovna recognizes and respects the worth of these characters as human beings. She is a spiritual, though not a social, democrat.

Farther up the social scale are the impoverished gentry, the class from which Varvara Nikanorovna originally sprang. The outstanding figure from this group, and one of the most picturesque characters in Leskov's fiction, is Dorimedont Rogozhin, the Russian Don Quixote, a poor but noble-hearted and eccentric gentleman who bears innumerable scars from wounds received in quixotic battles for justice and human dignity. Rogozhin is a fighter for the ideal he shares with Varvara Nikanorovna: noblesse oblige. Since his noblesse does not provide him with the wherewithal to display ethical nobility in his economic behavior, he evinces it in physical action. He is an anachronistic knight in armor, wandering around the nineteenth-century Russian countryside in an absurdly decrepit carriage drawn by caricatures of horses, tilting with indomitable courage against the injustice and cruelty he encounters at every step. He and Varvara Nikanorovna recognize their spiritual kinship and become devoted friends, despite the enormous difference in their fortunes.[13]

As free, nonserving gentry, Rogozhin and Varvara Nikanorovna feel strongly antipathetic toward that "other nobility" that dominated the Russian provinces in the nineteenth century, the officialdom, the representatives of Germanic "Sankt-Peterburg" and its parasitic bureaucracy. As the "true" Russian gentry, they acknowledge the tsar as their rightful sovereign lord; but they feel that they are his rightful representatives on the land. What need for this arrogant army of plundering "German" officials?

Associated with the Germanic bureaucracy is the villainous figure of Count Funkendorf, a Baltic baron and Petersburg grandee who has bought land in this ultra-Russian neighborhood and is introduced to Varvara Nikanorovna by the governor of the province. Varvara Nikanorovna is not impressed: as a bearer of the ancient Russian title *knyaginya*, she has no inclination to humble herself before a mere *graf*, a Germanic rank introduced into Russia by Peter the Great. The main action of the novel as we have it—much retarded by anecdotal material connected with secondary characters and by philosophical matter—concerns the plot of Count Funkendorf to capture the princess's wealth, first by marrying her, then, when that scheme fails, by wedding her sixteen-year-old daughter. Though the count is past fifty (Mikhail Strakhov again), the second plot succeeds: the young princess is a mindless ingenue recently released from an exclusive Petersburg institute for high-born maidens: and her only thought is to escape from her mother's irksome tutelage into the arms of the first man who seeks her hand, provided that he is acceptable in the eyes of that Society whose values she shares.

In *A Decrepit Clan*, as in Tolstoy's moral squiredom, the locus of evil is Petersburg, the teeming center of both officialdom and high society, which seems to radiate corruption into the country it is supposed to govern. Several times in her life Varvara Nikanorovna is sucked into its orbit, and each time something dear to her is lost or spoiled. Her most important encounters with Funkendorf take place there; and there she must confront Funkendorf's ally and her distant relative, the bigot and hypocrite Countess Khotetova, an immensely rich spinster who displays her ultra-Orthodox religiosity by buying silver and jewel-studded icon-cases and making large donations to monasteries with money obtained by grinding the faces of the poor peasants on her estates.[14] Countess Khotetova and Count Funkendorf conspire to "rescue" the young Princess Protozanova from the clutches of a mother they consider eccentric and dangerous; and the young princess is only too ready to be rescued. To Varvara Nikanorovna, the seduction of her daughter into an inappropriate marriage and the corruption of her daughter's spirit that made the seduction possible are both characteristic products of Petersburg.

Her daughter's dowry confronts Varvara Nikanorovna with a formidable moral-economic problem, one that illustrates the precariousness of the serf's lot, even under the best of masters. Among the serfs included in the dowry are several who had become prosperous and had with their own money bought land to add to their farms. Since serfs could not legally own land, the title to the land they bought lay with their owner. When the serfs were passed on in the daughter's dowry, "their" land went with them; and when Count Funkendorf saw fit thereafter to take it away from them—its rightful, but not legal, owners—there was nothing the serfs could do. Feeling she has betrayed their trust, and unable to prevail upon her son-in-law to reverse his decision, Varvara Nikanorovna then turns over to those peasants other lands remaining in her possession, for their free use and profit. In Russian serfowning society, this was the act of an ethical fanatic.

With her first-born child lost to the forces of evil, Varvara Nikanorovna takes all the more seriously the education of her two younger children, both boys. How is it possible to bring up aristocratic children to be noble? How can she instill in their hearts the ideals by which she herself lives and armor them against the false gods of Petersburg? The princess resolves to find an ideal teacher, a man whose integrity is even greater than his intellectual attainments; and then to teach them at home. Varvara Nikanorovna's search for a tutor is thus also a search for truth and righteousness. It brings her into contact with some real, nonfictional people, from a nonservile, nonaristocratic class: Mikhail Speransky, then in disgrace, the exseminarian who rose to the pinnacles of power under Alexander I; and one of the important "righteous men" of Leskov's own youth in Kiev, Dmitry Zhuravsky, the "first abolitionist," the economist and estate administrator who spent his own meager earnings buying peasants their freedom. Through the good offices of these two real people, Princess Protozanova meets the fictional character Mefody Chervyov—from an ideological, if not an artistic, point of view one of the most important characters in *A Decrepit Clan*.

Mefody Chervyov embodies an even more alienated vision of Russian society than Varvara Nikanorovna's. Her dealings with him thus test her system of ethics from the left, so to speak—Chervyov stands much further outside the Russian class system than she does. He is a social outcast. Originally a professor in an ecclesiastical seminary, he had been dismissed for unorthodox views. He then served as a teacher in a provincial private school. The unexpected deaths of his wife and son left him alone in the world, free from all "baser" human ties. With no one to support, he decides to abandon his burdensome position in the school and to simplify his way of life still further. He is willing, however, to assume the responsibility for educating the two Protozanov princelings. Their future wealth and power, he believes, will make the virtue he can instill in their hearts all the more effective in the world.

Though deeply impressed by Chervyov's character, Varvara Nikanorovna is taken aback by the extremism of his views. How could two princes live with such ideas as Chervyov's? Attracted and repelled at the same time, the princess hesitates. Fate decides the question for her. Even if she had agreed to accept Chervyov, Russia, it turns out, would not have permitted it. The day after her interview with Chervyov, she receives the news that he has been arrested. Accused of propagating seditious ideas, he is banished to a monastery in the White Sea, to live out his life as a laborer under monastic supervision. At the same time the princess receives an order from Petersburg (Countess Khotetova and Count Funkendorf have been busy intriguing against her), advising her that as a noblewoman she must "educate her sons in conformity with their high station." In other words, they too must be sent to a Petersburg institute. This blow shatters the princess's life and marks the beginning of the decline of the Protozanov clan.

In the version of *A Decrepit Clan* published in 1875, the chronicle ends at this point, with Chervyov in exile and the princess broken in spirit. In revising the text for his collected works, Leskov rounded off the ending and made some essential changes, especially concerning the ideology of Chervyov. Unfortunately, these alterations, like the chapter appended to the end of "Kotin the He-cow and Platonida," prove again how difficult it is for a novelist to return to a work laid aside years before. If the characters no longer live in his imagination, they cannot be resurrected on paper.

In 1889, at the time he carried out this revision of *A Decrepit Clan*, Leskov was an ardent Tolstoyan. Stifling his artistic instincts, he undertook to transform this unfinished novel of fifteen years earlier into a vehicle of Tolstoyan propaganda. He did not bother to rewrite the entire work. Instead, he hastily tacked onto the end of the novel a large placard covered with Tolstoyan maxims. The idealistic teacher Chervyov was the obvious candidate for carrying this poster. In 1889 Chervyov was transformed into a full-fledged, letter-perfect Tolstoyan—a Tolstoyan considerably *avant la lettre*, since the main action of the novel takes place about 1820.

The anachronism is palpable, but that is not the worst of it. In the version of 1889, the Tolstoyan Chervyov almost ruins an otherwise powerful piece of fiction. Until his appearance on the scene, the moral center of the novel is Princess Varvara Nikanorovna. At the very end, in marches Chervyov. He has one extended conversation with the princess, and her moral edifice collapses. All her ideas, her standards, her philosophy of personal ethics and social responsibility—everything is shattered. Orthodoxy? Her scrupulous, though never fanatical adherence to the religion of her ancestors and her people is senseless, since God "dwelleth not in man-made temples." Patriotism? Her allegiance to the tsar and her wish to see her country justly and efficiently governed—this too is a delusion: all governments are intrinsically evil, and the only good government is one that strives to abolish itself and place in its stead the government of God. Before this onslaught of Christian anarchism all the princess's beliefs fall in ruins, the convictions of her entire life demolished in a hour's dialogue. For the ideals of an ideal character to be so suddenly annihilated and replaced by another, even more austere set of ideals is psychologically unconvincing and leaves the novel disastrously unbalanced in structure.

This destruction was wrought in 1889. But a more basic confusion of design had prevented Leskov from finishing the novel back in 1874. What was the cause of the confusion? We can formulate a hypothetical answer to this question. Several fragments of the continuation of *A Decrepit Clan*, apparently dating from 1873-74, have survived in manuscript and have now been published (5:518-551). These are first drafts, written only "lengthwise," as Leskov liked to say, not yet revised "crosswise." They deal with the figure of Prince Yakov Lvovich Protozanov, the elder son of Varvara Nikanorovna and the uncle of the putative memoirist, Princess V. D. P. With him the chronicle of the Protozanovs thus moves down another generation, into the reign of Nicholas I. Known improbably as Prince "Kiss-Me-Quick" (in English) from the rose-bud shape of his mouth, Prince Yakov Lvovich, despite his Petersburg education, has grown up to be another *pravednik*, known throughout the province for his generosity and fairness. Most of the fragments consist of anecdotes illustrating his nobility of character, especially his moral authority as a judge, a marshal of nobility, and a guardian and trustee for orphans. He is another of Leskov's selfless saints, his character made more believable by his folly in marrying a narcissistic, high-society nitwit very much like his sister.

In itself the characterization of Prince Yakov Lvovich is interesting and well done; it is good Leskov. But in a novel dealing with the fortunes of a decrepit clan, this characterization was a blind alley. Essentially Prince Kiss-Me-Quick is only a masculine copy of his mother. While such similarity between son and mother may be plausible in psychological terms, it blocks the progress of the novel. The much-anticipated degeneration of the Protozanov clan cannot proceed. Although there is some deterioration of their economic situation when the estate is divided after Varvara Nikanorovna's death, none of her children squanders borrowed money, which was the historical cause of decrepitude for most gentry families in Russia. Vera Dmitrievna, the memoirist, keeps telling us that her family has become "emaciated," but we never learn how this happened. And except for the Countess Funkendorf, Yakov Lvovich's sister, there is no moral emaciation of the Protozanovs either.

The confusion in *A Decrepit Clan* thus seems to come down to a difficulty in moving from the exceptional to the typical. Leskov begins by portraying a character of exceptional moral beauty. From this beginning the only plausible development was degeneration. The exile of Chervyov and the forcible placing of the young Protozanov princes in a Petersburg institute were clearly the signals for moral decrepitude to set in. The young princes could have been demoralized and "Petersburgized," have lived beyond their means, mortgaged their estates and died leaving nothing a pile of promissory notes. But Leskov was unable to shift into this new key. Apparently he could not bear to see the beauty of Varvara Nikanorovna's righteousness fade. He was proud of having created such a vital model of moral excellence, and to destroy it before the action of the novel had reached the present time seemed too disheartening. He therefore caused Varvara Nikanorovna's virtue to reappear intact in the next generation, as a sign that goodness was just as possible in the middle of the nineteenth century as it had been at its beginning. But this static moral truth was at cross purposes with the historical decline of the Russian gentry and with the internal dynamics of his novel about that decline. There now seemed no way to introduce the decrepitude, and the novel had to be abandoned.

Thirty years earlier, the continuation of *Dead Souls* had foundered on Gogol's inability to transform a comically conceived and static "bad" hero, the personification of petty corruption, into a full-grown human being struggling toward morality and truth. *A Decrepit Clan*, on the contrary, broke down because of the author's unwillingness to permit corruption to touch his saints, to allow the typical folly of the world to be victorious over his ideal models of virtue.

Part III

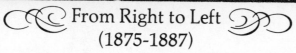

From Right to Left
(1875-1887)

❧ 18 ❧

A Virtuous Peacock

From the time of *A Decrepit Clan* onward, the search for literary righteousness became almost obsessive with Leskov—*eine Art Manie,* as Vsevolod Setchkarev calls it[1]—as he portrays one eccentric, exceptional, noble character after another. Some of these portraits of virtue were brought together in 1880 and provided with a programmatic introduction.[2] The series was expanded to fill the second volume of the collected works of 1889-90. Leskov took pride in this collection of "good" characters, rightly considering his ability to portray them one of the outstanding features of his talent.

> People still describe me as the castigator of the progressive movement in Russian life [Leskov said in the 1890s]. But I myself think that the denunciatory side of my works is the weakest of all. My Prepotenskys, Bizyukinas, Termosyosovs, Bornovolokovs [all atheistic intellectuals from *Cathedral Folk*] and other nihilists are pathetic pieces of patchwork; but the real strength of my talent lies in positive Russian types. It is I who have given the reader positive types of Russians. The whole second volume [of the 1889-90 edition] under the title "The Righteous" [*Pravedniki*] consists of these heart-warming products of Russian life [. . .] This volume of my works I consider the most significant of all. It clearly shows whether I was blind to the bright sides of Russian life. Show me another writer who has such an abundance of positive Russian types.[3]

Leskov was indeed more successful with his positive characters than most writers of his time. But a fundamental confusion between ethics and aesthetics underlies his characteristically defensive-aggressive statement. "Good" people do not necessarily make good stories—the history of literature seems to prove the reverse. Leskov knew this; but he almost succeeded in convincing himself that they do. The number of "positive Russian types" in his pages becomes a measure of his stature as an artist. As he grew older, Leskov became more insistent on the didactic function of his art: he wrote to teach, to make men better. As the medieval hagiographers understood, one way of making men better is to give them better models to imitate. Leskov did have a talent for producing convincing portraits of virtuous people; all the same, the virtue of the character is no guarantee of the success of the portrait. By no means all of Leskov's "righteous" stories rank among his best work.

The major problem in creating virtuous characters is to provide convincing motivation, to make their virtue consistent with the dynamics of the human personality. Vice is easier to manage. Vice is passion, and everyone understands the dynamism of passion. Vice is desire and the will to gratify desire, regardless of the consequences to others. The reality of a fictional miser, bully, robber, or rake is not hard for us to accept, because we recognize in ourselves the potentiality of his passion. Only when villainy becomes demonic, as in *At Daggers Drawn*, when it displays an unlimited willingness to do gratuitous injury to others without guilt or even rationalization, do we question its reality.

Virtue is another matter. Some forms of virtue may also be grounded in passion, especially in love—a genuine (not self-sacrificing) love that sees the welfare of loved ones as a means of its own gratification. Likewise, ambition—or sublimated love—may be expressed through creative endeavor, which may enrich and improve the world. In addition to such "passionate virtue," there also exists what might be called dispassionate virtue, virtue of rational origin, stemming from an intellectual recognition that the virtuous act is the only way to solve a given problem. But it seems that much of what we call virtuous conduct, especially when it is ostentatious, is neither passionate nor rational, but an effort to please the imaginary parent we bear within us. And this parent is notably corrupt: all too often having appeased it with an act of demonstrative public virtue, we feel free to indulge our private meannesses.

We are likely to accept virtuous characters in literature only if the dynamics of their virtue is plausibly accounted for. We believe the righteousness of Varvara Nikanorovna in *A Decrepit Clan* partly because we understand that a rich and powerful woman derives gratification from the exercise of her power, even if she does so benevolently. She enjoys having others dependent on her, subordinate to her will. Within the confines of her estate she is an omnipotent goddess, and her virtue lies in the fact that she chooses to exercise this omnipotence by being kind to people, rather than flogging them.

Pure virtue for the sake of virtue is no more believably human than demonism. Yet the myth of free and unrewarded virtue has always had appeal, especially for people like Leskov who congratulate themselves for their generous acts in order to mitigate the guilt they feel for their ungenerous ones. Such people delight in the basically sentimental, prettified image of the self-abnegating saint. This basic sentimentality vitiates many of Leskov's *pravednik* stories; the remarkable thing is that it did not spoil them all.

The next example in the *pravednik* series is the short story "Pavlin." Probably written immediately after *A Decrepit Clan,* "Pavlin" was published in 1874 in the mass-circulation magazine *Ploughland* and reprinted in 1876 in a separate volume with the novel *Childhood Years.*[4] For unknown reasons neither story was included in the collected works of 1889-90. If the omission was an oversight, that in itself is evidence of the author's lack of favor. The exclusion seems unaccountable, in any case. Though it is by no means a perfect work of art, "Pavlin" has merit and is far better than many pieces Leskov did include in the collected works.

The hero of the story, the "righteous man," is a doorman in a large apartment house in Petersburg. His alliterative and somewhat ridiculous-sounding name is Pavlin Petrovich Pevunov. The first name, Pavlin, also means "peacock," and the surname suggests something like "songbird," a person who loves to sing. Although Pavlin does somewhat resemble a peacock when dressed up in his doorman's uniform, no one could be less of a songbird. To all appearances he is the dourest, grimmest, glummest man alive.

In his stories of *pravedniki,* Leskov is fond of this paradoxical effect of providing his righteous hero with a forbidding and repellent exterior: then the story gradually reveals the human warmth behind the façade. Often these heroes are given inhumane jobs to perform. In "The Pygmy," for example, the virtuous hero is a supervisor of the corporal punishments administered in police stations under court orders. From an artistic point of view, the rigorous conscientiousness with which such heroes perform their grim functions serves in part as an antidote against sentimentalization.

Pavlin too is a fanatically conscientious executor of cruel duties. The owner of his building, a society lady, is a heartless skinflint, and she relies on Pavlin to serve as her collection agent. All rents in the building must be paid accurately a month in advance. If they are not, after one day's grace the windows in the apartment are removed; on the second day, the tenant is evicted. Pavlin carries out these procedures with implacable severity, making his rounds followed by two janitors armed with a hatchet and tongs to remove the windows—a potent measure in a Petersburg winter. All the poor tenants regard Pavlin as a bloodthirsty monster; but pleas have no effect on him. He carries out his orders; his own feelings are irrelevant; and he knows that his mistress is inexorable.

This initial "paysage and genre," to use a designation Leskov applied to several later stories, is a vivid evocation of the practical realities of Petersburg life. It is presented from the point of view of a young boy, relating much later his memories of this period in his youth. The boy is a nephew of the landlady, which provides him with information about her and also gives him a class status higher than Pavlin's. Pavlin is thus one of the *pravedniki* on whom we can look *down* the social ladder—a perspective of superiority that perhaps makes it easier for us to accept his virtue.

As long as the picture remains static, the story is on Leskov's highest literary level. But a plot is required to demonstrate Pavlin's humanity and for this Leskov resorts to a series of sentimental clichés.

Into one of the apartments in the building move a family of three women—grandmother, mother, and little daughter. They are destitute and cannot pay the rent. Although it is bitter cold outside, along come Pavlin and his henchmen to take out their windows. The narrator's family comes to their aid, first inviting them into their apartment and then paying their rent. It transpires that the lady's husband, the little girl's father, a military doctor, has been killed in action in Hungary (the time is 1848-49), and they are left destitute. To avoid burdening her daughter, the old lady commits suicide. A month later the daughter succumbs to a "cruel malady." The little girl is thus left an orphan—that figure of infinite appeal for Leskov.

The implacable Pavlin now displays his hidden generosity. He is a man of fifty and a bachelor, who has refrained from marrying so that he might play the benefactor to his relatives, whom he bought out of serfdom. These have recently all died of cholera, and he thus needs a new object for his self-sacrifice. So Pavlin adopts the orphan Lyuba, evoking again the image so strangely appealing to Leskov, the male mother, the unmarried man who nurtures a child without the help of a woman.

Pavlin's righteousness emerges when Lyuba has grown into a beautiful girl of sixteen. Shallow and ungrateful, she looks down on her adoptive father, whom she calls a "lackey," and she attaches herself to the miserly landlady, who has a dashing officer son. The landlady, with ulterior motives of her own (she hopes to save money by providing her son with a cheaper mistress than the French belles of the Petersburg demi-monde), urges Lyuba to marry Pavlin: Pavlin is devoted to her and will not deny her anything. It would be better than the slavery of a milliner's shop. Pavlin, long in love with his ward, is dazzled by the idea of marriage and astounded when Lyuba agrees to it.

So they are married, and before long Lyuba becomes the mistress of Dodichka, the landlady's son. For some time she lives the wild life of the demi-monde, and her self-abnegating husband knows nothing about it. After the lurid description of glittering and illicit pleasure, the inevitable moral whip is cracked. Dodichka tires of Lyuba and drops her, and then they are both arrested for a theft Dodichka has committed.

Lyuba is cleared of the charge; and Dodichka, to "save the honor" of his uniform, is transferred to a distant station, presumably in Siberia. Pavlin now performs the ultimate act of self-sacrifice. Although he knows that Dodichka is a good-for-nothing, he also knows that Lyuba still loves him and is carrying his child. Pavlin therefore decides to enable, even force them to marry by arranging a fictitious death for himself. Substituting a dead man's passport for his own and distributing a few bribes, he assumes the dead man's identity, accompanies the widow, his former wife, to Siberia, and there compels Dodichka to marry her. After that Pavlin keeps in touch with the newlyweds by letter. Dodichka is later killed, and Lyuba, now penitent, returns with her former husband to European Russia, where they both retire to monasteries. Ultimately we learn that before she died in the convent, the fallen woman, the former Lyuba, had "wept out her eyes," and that little mother-of-pearl icons had been inserted in the sockets. This is the same preposterous and sentimental image that Leskov later used for the new finale of "Kotin the He-cow and Platonida"—which may account for the exclusion of "Pavlin" from the collected works. Certainly one set of wept-out eyes is more than sufficient for any writer's corpus.

Thus the story that began so effectively with the genre picture of Pavlin's administration of his apartment house founders on the attempt to develop him from a rigid executioner into a self-sacrificing saint. Leskov does not want to explore the emotional underpinnings of Pavlin's virtue. Surely in the real "economy" of such a personality the self-sacrifice on behalf of distant relatives would serve as a kind of payment for the sadistic pleasure derived from the relentless exercise of power over the tenants. But Leskov cannot afford to reveal the nature of these transactions, or perhaps to perceive them himself.

Leskov likewise advertises Pavlin's self-sacrifice on behalf of Lyuba as far more genuine than that of the hero of Chernyshevsky's *What Is to Be Done?*. Chernyshevsky's hero, in the name of feminine emancipation and freedom of individual choice, obligingly steps aside to enable his wife to fulfill her love for another man. (Afterward, the three of them cozily have tea together, an image Leskov considered cynical and immoral.) Chernyshevsky does not examine the emotional roots of this behavior, which would nowadays probably be interpreted as masochistic and homosexual. But the motivations for Pavlin's generosity are just as assiduously veiled and idealized.

Leskov does not explore the implied sexual ambivalence in Pavlin's assuming the role of mother to Lyuba, even though this ambivalence is confirmed by his later behavior as her husband. It is not clear whether Pavlin and Lyuba ever have sexual relations. It seems unlikely. She is always out with Dodichka, while supposedly Pavlin naively believes that she is sleeping at the landlady's. This blindness on Pavlin's part requires psychological explanation, but Leskov does not provide it. We might speculate, for instance, that Pavlin has an unconscious wish to encourage Lyuba's downfall in order to punish her for not loving him, or even for being a woman, and then to triumph over her with his virtue—a pattern Dostoevsky demonstrated penetratingly in the tortured relationship between Dmitry Karamazov and Katerina Ivanovna. But Leskov cannot push his understanding to this level. He is determined to hold up Pavlin as an icon of pure-hearted selflessness.

Besides its psychological weaknesses, "Pavlin" also shows some signs of hasty composition and carelessness. The narrator reports many events at which he was not present, without accounting for his knowledge, and the point of view shifts disconcertingly from the narrator's "I" to the omniscient author. But the most striking indication of Leskov's carelessness is the fate of Lyuba's baby: after sending her to Siberia pregnant with Dodichka's child, Leskov forgot to bring the poor infant into the world.

19

The Case for Spontaneity

During 1874 Leskov returned to his stubborn battle with the novel. Inveigh as he might against the restrictiveness and artificiality of the genre, he could not escape the implicit scale of values of the nineteenth-century public: a big reputation in literature could rest only on big books. He had tried to displace the novel with a looser, more congenial form, the chronicle; but this substitute brought new problems of its own. The chronicle was too open-ended, lacking logical limits. Its scrolls kept unwinding endlessly—several were finished only by abruptly breaking them off and publishing them as admittedly incomplete fragments.

Thus in 1874, with the loose ends of *A Decrepit Clan* dangling before him, Leskov began to look for another narrative form that would demand neither the unlifelike neatness nor the love story he considered obligatory in the novel. The form he hit upon was the fictional autobiography. The fictional autobiography is, in effect, a quantitative extension of the memoir Leskov had already exploited successfully in shorter pieces like "The Mocker" and "The Musk-ox." It is a memoir increased in bulk so as to qualify as a major work, and with the focus shifted from the outer world of observation to the inner world of subjective experience. The result of this effort was serialized the following year in the mass-circulation family magazine *Ploughland* under the title "Will-o'-the wisps (The Autobiography of Praottsev)." In 1876 it was reprinted in book form, together with "Pavlin," under a new title, *Years of Childhood (From the Reminiscences of Merkul Praottsev).*[1]

Judging by an incomplete manuscript fragment (5:605-608), Leskov's original intention in *Years of Childhood* had been to present his hero's reminiscences as a skaz. This fragment is a preface, excluded from the final text, which establishes a typical frame setting. A group of Petersburg acquaintances, among them the "author," are spending the summer together in the country. They become friendly with a

monk in a nearby monastery, Father Gordy. Father Gordy proves to
be a man of exceptional cultivation, and a talented artist and musician
as well. The "author" and his friends wonder what could have induced him—well educated, good-looking, and still in his early forties
—to immure himself in a monastery. The answer to this question will
obviously be a story, as in "The Enchanted Pilgrim," the monk's narrative of his life. In both published versions, however, the "author"
and his friends have been eliminated, and the monk addresses the
reader directly, in written form, without providing any external explanation for the existence of his text.[2]

This nonnovel (which may very well be called a novel, depending
on one's definition) begins with a polemic with the novel form, one of
Leskov's fullest statements on the subject:

> It seems [Father Gordy writes] that I shall inevitably have to write
> down my story, or I should rather say my confession. I think so
> not because I have found my life exceptionally interesting and
> instructive. Not at all: parts of stories like mine can be found in a
> great many contemporary novels; and as far as sheer novelty
> goes, I shall perhaps relate nothing so new that the reader has
> never known or even seen its like before. But I will not tell it in
> the way such stories are told in novels,—and that, I think, may
> create a certain interest and even, perhaps, novelty, and even
> prove instructive.
>
> I will not pare down the significance of certain events and mag-
> nify that of others: I am not obliged to do that by the artificial
> and unnatural form of the novel, which requires a rounding off of
> plot line and a concentration of everything around one main cen-
> ter. In life it is not like that. A man's life moves like a parchment
> unwinding from a scroll, and in the notes presented here I will un-
> wind my life like a ribbon, just in that way. (5:279)

There were acknowledged novels in world literature—*David Copper-
field*, for example—that followed precisely the same autobiographical
procedure. But Leskov, smarting from the failure of his own self-de-
fined novels, tried to retaliate against the genre by adopting a narrow
definition of it and then rebelling against the limits imposed by his
own definition.

What Leskov found most uncongenial about the novel as he defined
it was the "rounding off" of the plot line and the concentration of the
action around a single center—in other words, an integrated and symmetrical organization of the material, focusing on crucial events in the

life experience of one or two central characters and with a basic conflict in the hero's life rising to a climax and resolved in a dénouement. Another important aspect of this roundness—a more specific product of the nineteenth century, with its scientific bias—is the insistence on causality, on making one event follow another as the logical (causal) consequence of the characters' actions and interactions. Both these requirements, symmetry and causality, Leskov found difficult to satisfy. He therefore discovered that neither symmetry nor logical causality is typical of real people's lives. Most human beings stagger chaotically and unsymmetrically through a series of accidents fortuitously connected with one another. Their lives do not form a tight structure created by their personalities, but consist of a loose series of last-minute, improvised attempts to cope with unpredictable events in their environment. Leskov's characters live in a world of unexpected "surprises"; it is not a world that fits the structural unities of the conventional novel. Hence the additive, linear organization of most of Leskov's narratives is consonant with his philosophical conviction about human life.

So *Years of Childhood* begins with a disclaimer: it is to be an autobiography, not a novel. For the first third of the book the disclaimer holds true: the work is a characteristically Leskovian chain of incidents, each a unit in itself.

The first episode epitomizes Leskov's negation of psychological causality, translating into narrative terms the principle on which his repudiation of novelistic structure had been based. Beginning *ab ovo*, as he says, the narrator recounts his earliest memory. As a tiny child, left alone with servants, he had climbed out on the sill of a fifth-story window. Happening to return home at that moment, his parents saw him precariously hanging by his hands, in imminent danger of falling to his death. His father dashed upstairs and rescued him in the nick of time.

A conventional novelist would have used such a scene of intense emotion for psychological exposition, to lay bare a whole matrix of feelings within the family constellation, and perhaps also to serve as the cause of changes in these relationships. Leskov, however, uses it for the very opposite effect—to illustrate his conviction that human psychology is genetically determined, independent of experience and environmental influence, and that causal sequences are of little importance in our chaotic, improvised lives. His hero, Merkul Praottsev, had climbed out on the window sill because he had been *born* with a dreamy, impractical nature; the incident only reveals an existing fact.

Moreover, by way of explaining the cause of his son's imprudent behavior, Merkul's father relates a story from his infancy. In the hour of his birth, before the world could have had any effect on him, instead of crying vigorously like a proper newborn baby, Merkul had silently contemplated first the midwife's face and then the colored patterns on the window cornice. Then and there his father had concluded that he was a *verkholyot*, a dreamer and fantast, "of which we have quite enough already." The adventure on the window sill confirmed this diagnosis: Merkul was a born visionary, mentally suspended between heaven and earth, incapable of preserving himself in the real world. Since the hero's deepest traits are already established at birth, his life can only constitute the fulfillment of an ordained destiny, not the evolution of a personality interacting with the world.

After this symbolic episode, *Years of Childhood* continues with a string of loosely connected anecdotes. There is a visit by the narrator, as a small boy, and his mother to his Baltic German grandmother, a benevolent despot with a passion for washing people, which she gratifies on her helpless grandson, among others. Despite his frenzied resistance, he is stripped naked and energetically washed in the bathhouse by his grandmother, assisted by a bevy of husky Lettish girls. There is an anecdotally severe inspection of the regiment of Merkul's father (he is an army colonel) by a choleric high dignitary, followed by his father's disgrace and death from a heart attack, after which Merkul is separated from his mother and placed in a military boarding school.

Except for these incidents, Merkul's "years of childhood" are in fact passed over entirely. In Leskov's instinctive view of narrative art, only "interesting" events are worth telling; the trivia of everyday life, especially a child's life, have no place. We also learn little about Merkul's years in boarding school; instead, the action jumps forward to his expulsion from the school, at the age of sixteen, for participating in a cadet revolt against the floggings to which they were constantly subjected.[3]

Following his expulsion from the military academy, Praottsev, along with several schoolmates, is shipped home to his mother. She is living in Kiev; the year is approximately 1850; and Leskov therefore has the opportunity to describe another of those prerailway journeys through Russia, of which he had taken so many in his younger days and from which he drew so much of his literary material. This Leskovian journey is almost a literary form in itself, a spatial analogue of the chronicle. The simple fact of progression through space constantly confronts the hero with new situations, new personalities, new adventures to be described and enjoyed for their own sake. Usually these travel experiences have little plot connection with one another, except that they happen to the same person.

The adventures of Merkul Praotsev are in the best Leskovian tradition. One of the most effective is the story of how the boys' coachman, a sly muzhik with an insatiable love for vodka, managed to induce the tradespeople of a small Ukrainian town to load his coach with "donations." One of the excadets, a Pole with a taste for exotic clothing, had bought himself a brightly colored peasant blouse, a pair of baggy Ukrainian trousers, and a Turkish fez, in which bizarre costume he loved to strut through provincial marketplaces. The coachman, Kirilla, spread the word that this oddly attired young man was a *kat*, a special executioner being sent to Kiev to administer a flogging to a Polish countess who had mistreated her peasants. The Ukrainians had a custom, something like warding off the evil eye, of offering presents to an executioner "so that he would beat more mercifully." Thus the magic word *kat* enabled Kirilla to collect an enormous tribute, with which he and his charges happily drove off toward Kiev. But he soon paid dearly for his gains. At some distance from the town a carriage overtook them bearing a police official and a soldier. The official ordered their coach to halt and examined the boys' papers. Then, turning to Kirilla and flinging him to the ground, he had the accompanying soldier, right there on the road, give him a hundred lashes with a leather whip. Such was Russian roadside justice in the halcyon days of Nicholas I.

For all its color, this particular episode, like many others, has no structural function in Praottsev's autobiography. It simply stands by itself as a scene, a picturesque piece of narrative prose. There are, however, a few incidents in the journey that Leskov makes a half-hearted attempt to "novelize," that is, to connect them as part of a causal chain in Praottsev's life. For instance, the boys stop over in Tver, where the family of one of them lives. There Merkul falls desperately in love with his friend's older sister, glimpsed briefly at a ball. The sister turns out to be nearly thirty (to his sixteen). Nevertheless, later in the journey he writes her a long and passionate love letter—a scandalous breach of etiquette. After Praottsev's arrival in Kiev, Leskov for some time tries to keep alive this affair of the improper letter, with several suspenseful references to its supposedly disastrous consequences. But when the consequences are revealed, they prove anything but disastrous. The girl's brother writes Praottsev a rude and insulting letter; despite Praottsev's wish to hide the matter from her, the letter falls into his mother's hands; but instead of censuring him, she absolves him of wrongdoing. He had acted on the basis of genuine feeling, and his breach of propriety had been committed inadvertently, out of ignorance of social custom. The suspense created by the letter thus dissolves into nothing. The tolerant reaction of Merkul's mother does, however, demonstrate her character and her system of values; and the revelation of her ethical system is the philosophical core of the narrative.

In another novelized episode from the journey, Merkul, downcast and guilt-ridden because of the ill-starred love letter and because of the loss of his virginity with a wayside prostitute (an event mentioned, but not described), decides to enter a monastery. He stops at the first monastery they pass, planning to confess his sin to the abbot and ask admission as a novice. But his act of contrition has an unexpected outcome. There follows a hilariously incongruous scene, in which the troubled and penitent boy is obliged to have tea with the abbot and a lady visitor. The abbot, a fat and jovial Greek, is much more interested in his spread of delicacies than he is in Praottsev's sins. Poor Merkul never gets a chance to confess; instead, he is forced to listen while the abbot regales his visitors with lurid tales of his own adventures in the world, before he had taken the tonsure.

From a structural point of view, this episode might perhaps have been intended to anticipate the hero's later entry into a monastery. Although in the published versions Father Gordy has disappeared, the narrator, whom we know only by his secular name, still describes his confession as an answer to the reader's anticipated question, "How did you come to be a monk?" Whatever Leskov's original intentions, the action is never carried to that point. Furthermore, such an ironic and satirical scene could not serve as a suitable anticipation of a genuine religious experience to come later. Thus once again an incident with latent novelistic possibilities remains unnovelized. It is one of Leskov's brightly colored narrative beads, alluring and glittering, but lacking any integral connection with what follows.

After Merkul's arrival in Kiev, the nature of his autobiography changes. From this point onward Leskov abandons his string of anecdotes and transposes his novel into a new, philosophical key. It is to be a problem novel, a *Bildungsroman* in a literal sense, a work designed to illustrate the faults and virtues of a particular theory of education. In this respect it has an eighteenth-century flavor, reminding us of *Émile*, for example.

Unfortunately, the ideas presented in this fictional guise are not distinguished for profundity or originality; nor is the attempt to make them live through the lives of the characters successful. The literary quality of *Years of Childhood* falls off considerably. The work becomes a tedious, abstract demonstration of a psychological and educational truth. Leskov warns us that it is dangerous to overplan one's life or the lives of one's children. Room must be left for the play of chance and for the individual's own spontaneity—the unpredictable sparks of inspiration, talent, or passion that make life worth living. The intellect is a powerful and useful instrument, but it is only a tool for dealing with the world. Our real "liveness" comes from our feelings, our hearts; and our hearts must be left free to respond with spontaneity to what life offers.

This doctrine of the primacy of feeling is linked with a popular national stereotype, a self-congratulating myth Russians used to mark themselves off from Germans (or Englishmen). Germans, so the myth runs, are an overrational, overorganized people, their lives dessicated and their natures deformed by rules and schedules. With their "broad" natures, Russians, though seemingly chaotic and unsystematic, possess a freedom of emotional expression more in harmony with man's true self. This spontaneity exploits man's creative potential and ultimately provides deeper satisfactions in life.

Elsewhere—in "The Mocker," for instance, or later in "Iron Will"— Leskov presents with more hostility this contrast between the anal Germanic peoples and the oral Russians, to use the Freudian terminology. But in *Years of Childhood* Leskov is gentler and more balanced; the Germanic rationality, though ultimately discredited, is allowed to state its case. Praottsev's mother, the representative of rationality, is a symbolic ethnic compromise. By birth a Baltic—semi-Russian—German, she had married a Russian and in her later years was converted, at least pro forma, to Orthodoxy. She is presented throughout the novel, with a wearisome piling on of superlatives, as a paragon: intelligent, thoughtful, gentle, kind, virtuous. Yet she has retained the fatal Germanic flaw: overrating the intellect, she leaves no room, in her life or her son's, for the free play of emotion; and the action of the novel is designed to show her up.

When Merkul arrives in Kiev, his mother has already drawn up a blueprint for his life. He is to have an undemanding post in the civil service, which will take little of his time, but will enable him to build up seniority. In his free hours he will study, partly under his mother's guidance (during her widowhood she has acquired an erudition most unusual for a Russian woman of that time) and partly under that of a local professor with whom she is friendly, a formidable list of subjects: Greek, Latin, French, English, history, and mathematics, plus Bible readings in German (which he has known from childhood) and "recreation periods" devoted to music and to Russian literature. Merkul proves to be a natural student, and he applies himself with enormous diligence to this strenuous program. Too much diligence, it turns out. His spirit is willing, but his body, speaking with the voice of his "true nature" (and articulating the author's case against Merkul's mother) rebels. He has a series of illnesses that serve as warnings of an inherent disharmony in his life.

Eventually the disharmony comes to the surface. Sent away from Kiev on a brief official journey, Merkul makes the acquaintance of a painter engaged in frescoing a provincial church. Merkul is immediately fascinated with this process. Quickly assimilating the technique, he is permitted to paint a little. He proves to have real talent and with it, a passion for art, for plastic creativity. This was precisely the area for which no allowance had been made in his mother's scheme. And yet fate, nature, or God had decreed that art would be the spiritual center of Merkul's life. Such is the first "Germanic" error: even the life of the intellect, one's education in the narrow sense, should not be overplanned. We do not always know where our greatest talents lie.

Parallel to Merkul's experience runs the account of another life in which the inadequacy of Mme Praottseva's benevolent rationality is again displayed. Khristya Altanskaya, the professor's daughter, allows Merkul's mother to manage the life of her heart as she supervises that of Merkul's mind. Khristya loves a young man named Serge, whose social situation is superior to her own and whose mother is counting on him to restore the family's deteriorated finances by marrying an heiress. Serge presses Khristya to marry him despite his mother's disapproval, but she hesitates. She recognizes that Serge is a weak and dependent personality, incapable of facing the world on his own; if deprived of his inheritance and excluded from his customary society, he would soon feel miserable and come to hate her as the instrument of his degradation. Merkul's mother agrees with these considerations. Whatever the urging of passion, reason dictates that Khristya resolutely refuse Serge's proposal and sever all contact with him.

Khristya carries out this painful prescription, and subsequent events seem to fulfill Khristya's and Mme Praottseva's predictions. Much to his mother's satisfaction, Serge marries a girl with an adequate fortune, and it seems as if he and Khristya are parted forever. But the heart is not so easily gainsaid. Serge's wife proves to be a shrew almost the equal of Olga Vasilievna, and she makes Serge's existence miserable. After some time he renews his contacts with Khristya. Her dormant love is reawakened, reinforced by jealousy of his wife and rationalized as pity for his misfortunes. Khristya becomes Serge's mistress.

In terms of nineteenth-century official moralities this means ruin and ostracism; Khristya virtually cuts herself off from all human contacts. She is astonished to discover that the noble Mme Praottseva will still receive her in her house. The illicit love affair, however, as Khristya knows, is doomed. Before long Serge's wife and mother-in-law manage to get him transferred in the service, first to Petersburg and then abroad. Swearing eternal fealty to Khristya, Serge submits to "fate" and departs, since the alternative would be financial ruin for himself and his mother. Khristya had expected nothing else. She knew that such a love could not survive long. She wants only to die, since she now feels that at least she has really lived: she has loved and been loved. Fate is obliging. Shortly thereafter she dies giving birth to Serge's child, which also succumbs.

This tragic outcome seems to give the lie to the reasoned righteousness of Mme Praottseva. Mme Praottseva had prevailed upon Khristya not to marry Serge, when marriage was a possibility, on what seemed well-considered grounds. But experience had shown that in Khristya's case, not marrying proved worse than the worst possible marriage. Khristya's life had come to a tragic end; and it gradually dawns on Mme Praottseva that some of the responsibility lies with her.

Khristya's fate, for Mme Praottseva, is an object lesson, demonstrating the inadequacies of her system of rational morality. But the lesson could not be learned in time to salvage two other lives whose creative spark had been dampened by her excessive rationality—her own and her son's. Mme Praottseva's experience, we eventually learn, had been analogous to Khristya's, although she had never stepped off the straight and narrow of sexual virtue. A baroness by birth, she had been wooed by an indigent artist named Kolberg, a suit her parents had rejected out of hand as socially impossible. She had dutifully acquiesced, and eventually she married the hero's father. Years later, after she had become a widow, Kolberg, ever faithful, had renewed his suit and was again rejected, this time by the lady herself, on the grounds that duty now required her to devote her full attention to her son. In consolation, she offered Kolberg her friendship—an epistolary one. They carried on a lengthy correspondence in which the events of her life and his were analyzed and moralized about in extenso.

Mme Praottseva had thus voluntarily renounced personal happiness in the name of her maternal obligations. All the more terrible, therefore, is her gradual realization that she has sacrificed for a chimera. Her son is chafing at her tutelage, both intellectual and moral. His love for her is lukewarm. The feeling she inspires in him, as in everyone else, is respect, admiration, gratitude—anything you like, but not love. Moreover, even her *Bildungsentwurf* has proved a failure. Her son does not want the kind of life she had so painstakingly mapped out for him. Her curriculum had no place for the plastic arts, and yet his talents lay precisely in that area. In short, she had overcalculated her life and the lives of others; her morality lay like a heavy yoke on the shoulders of her loved ones. Confronted with the "rational" wreckage of three lives, Mme Praottseva's final act of "rationality" is to poison herself.

This ending, though potentially moving, is dry and abstract as Leskov presents it: his demonstration of the insufficiency of a cerebral life is itself essentially cerebral, and also hasty and perfunctory.

Years of Childhood must be regarded as a largely unsuccessful experiment with a more intellectually conceived, philosophical mode of fiction than was usual for Leskov. His artistic imagination does not seem to function easily when moving from an abstract truth to its concrete demonstration. His talent seems to require the very spontaneity, he prescribes in the story as necessary for life. When, as in the first part of Merkul's autobiography, Leskov is operating as a free artist, a master raconteur, his narrative is vivid and alive. But when his abstract conception forces him to concoct characters and events to prove a predetermined principle, the narrative becomes, as Merkul says of his life before he caught the excitement of artistic creativity, "gloomy and dull." The moralist and the artist in Leskov were not always effective collaborators.

◁℃ 20 ℈▷

Renounce and Denounce

Self-pity, self-justification, and moral indictments of others are persistent themes in Leskov's life. "How hard I tried, and how unfairly I was treated!"—how often this lachrymose refrain recurs in his biography! In the middle seventies, however, it was played at an absolute maximum of frequency and volume. This was Leskov's heyday of renouncing and denouncing, a time of crisis in every aspect of his life—his literary career, his family, and his religious beliefs.

There was, to be sure, no question of renouncing literature, giving up the writer's profession. Despite his complaints about lack of recognition, and despite some feints, à la Turgenev, at proclaiming that he had had enough, Leskov's commitment to literary art was deep and indestructible. Though literature was immune to attack, the literary arena always provided many targets for renunciation and fury—critics, fellow writers, literary schools, editors, magazines.

The most recent and most fateful renunciation had been that of Mikhail Katkov. That monarch of Moscow conservatism had served five years as Leskov's literary father. He had been a haven of refuge and support after the furious battles with the nihilists. He had been financially generous,[1] and the Katkov years were relatively free from the pressures of penury that otherwise beset Leskov until late in his life. Katkov had on occasion been unusually indulgent—for instance, in agreeing to reprint, as part of the serialized *Cathedral Folk*, the section called "The Dwarfs of Plodomasovo," which had appeared as a short story in the same magazine only three years before. But Katkov had also insisted on a monarch's privileges: he might choose to be indulgent, but his will was law. Fundamentally Katkov (like Russia's present-day monarchs) regarded literature not as an art form, but as a means for propagating a political line—in his case, nationalist, conservative, imperialist. Katkov regarded his writers as employees, to be treated generously, but in the last analysis expected to do his bidding. Least of all did he consider himself *their* subordinate, an acolyte whose duty was to elevate their sacred Words to the altar of print. Conflict with Katkov was an inevitable part of any writer's relations with *Russian Messenger*, as the bitter experience of Turgenev, Dostoevsky, Tolstoy, and others had shown.[2]

Leskov had long been accumulating resentments: the rejection of "The Enchanted Pilgrim," the ideological pressuring, and, most of all, the high-handedness of Katkov's editors. For a time these resentments were held in reserve. The moment to release them had come in 1874, when Leskov felt unable to continue *A Decrepit Clan*. To assume full responsibility for a failure of this kind was difficult for Leskov, and in such situations he always sought to blame someone else. In this case the candidate was obvious: Katkov. Katkov's editors *had* been outrageously arbitrary in their treatment of his chronicle. There had also been a genuine ideological conflict between Leskov and *Russian Messenger*. *A Decrepit Clan* was designed to illustrate Leskov's conviction of the inevitable decline and fall of the Russian nobility, a point of view decidedly heretical in the eyes of Katkov, who still regarded the gentry as the natural "head" of Russian society.

So Leskov's "renounce and denounce" machine was put into operation with Katkov as its target, and it kept grinding away, off and on, for years. Samples of its output follow.

I value many of Katkov's accomplishments and am grateful to him for many things, but on me personally *as a writer* his influence was not always beneficial and was sometimes simply terrible, so terrible that I inwardly came to consider him a man harmful to our literature. His very indifference to it, which was never concealed, but on the contrary expressed in almost contemptuous forms, oppressed me and reduced me to despair. The despair was warranted, because I could work *only with that man* and with no one else.[3]

I am as fond as ever of Mikhail Nikiforovich [Katkov], but primarily when he is so coarsely and stupidly reviled— then I am for him; but when I am sitting alone, I cannot help feeling toward him what a literary man must feel toward the murderer of his national literature. He discourages every initiative and knocks the life out of every thought with his hateful arrogance.[4]

How long, how long I believed in Katkov as a man of letters. I felt that I myself, personally, needed nothing but a place to publish where the beliefs were similar to mine, and I did not perceive that in that very place purely literary interests were belittled, disregarded, or adapted to the service of interests which have nothing whatever in common with any kind of literature [. . .] I think that no one in all Russia holds literature in such contempt as he.[5]

And the most famous of Leskov's pronouncements on Katkov, made in 1891, perhaps with some rewriting of history:

Katkov had a great influence on me, but during the printing of *A Decrepit Clan* he was the first to say, to Voskoboinikov: "We are mistaken: that man is *not ours!*" We parted company (over our view of the nobility), and I did not attempt to complete the novel. [Ideological differences still seemed a much more acceptable reason for not finishing that work than the artistic muddle Leskov had admitted to Aksakov in 1874.] We parted politely, but firmly and forever, and then he said again, "It's nothing to be sorry about: that man is *not ours!*" He was right, but I did not know whose I was. "The Gospel, well read" clarified that for me, and I straightway returned to the free feelings and allegiances of my childhood.[6]

And there are many more.[7]

Leskov's rupture with Katkov was a complex act. First, there had always been potential ideological discord. For all his anger at the radicals, Leskov had never become a nationalist conservative of the Katkovian stamp. Leskov's mentality was fundamentally progressive, in the literal sense: he wanted visible progress, real, practical improvements in the country's economic and political life. He hoped for parliamentary institutions of some kind; he advocated equality of classes and national minorities before the law; he opposed religious persecution; he had little interest in Russia's military glory or the expansion of her borders. In that sense, Katkov was right: Leskov was "not ours."

On the literary plane, Katkov and his henchmen had shown little respect for Leskov's texts, and Leskov may have been right in ascribing to Katkov a contempt for literature as art. On a deeper emotional level, Katkov had more and more come to play, in Leskov's inner drama, the role of "bad father." He was a new Strakhov, to be hated and rebelled against (and secretly envied and admired). The precipitating cause of the break was Leskov's impasse with *A Decrepit Clan.* And so Leskov's links with the Moscow empire of *Russian Messenger* were broken off "firmly and forever" in 1874.[8]

Leskov perhaps did not fully realize how drastic the effect of his rupture with Katkov would be. Bridges are easier to burn than to build. A Russian writer in those days depended on magazines for his income; royalties from most book editions, except in extraordinary cases, were small.[9] In the eyes of the Left, even the very moderate Left, Leskov was still labeled an arch-Katkovian reactionary and even a police agent. The doors of radical organs like *Notes of the Fatherland* and *The Cause* and even the moderate liberal *Messenger of Europe*, Turgenev's long-term literary home, were closed to Leskov. The curse of Pisarev was still potent. "Lots of magazines [Leskov wrote bitterly to Shchebalsky] would be *glad* to take my work (as I said to Goncharov), but—'You know, he's got such a reputation, and all that business with Katkov, and besides, they say he's close to the Third Section.' What a joke that is, when that same Katkov has just about knocked out of me the strength to screw my lips up into a smile."[10]

There was nowhere for Leskov to go, no respectable literary magazine in which he could publish. The prestigious "fat reviews," the focus of Russian cultural life during the nineteenth century, were to remain entirely barred to Leskov for more than a decade. Only in 1886 was he able to publish a story in *Russian Thought*,[11] then at the beginning of its rise to prominence; it was not until 1891 that Vladimir Solovyov persuaded the self-righteously liberal editor of *Messenger of Europe*, M. M. Stasyulevich, to publish Leskov's "Night Owls."[12] In the meantime, Leskov had to scrounge for outlets, and his bibliography for those years reveals his desperation: the *Orthodox Review*, *The Church and Social Herald*, *The Pilgrim*—party organs of Orthodoxy, subsidized, not very generously, by the government; children's magazines; daily newspapers; lowbrow magazines aimed at lower-class and provincial readers, like *A. Gattsuk's Gazette*; and semiacademic historical magazines, such as *Kiev Antiquities* and *Historical Messenger*—the latter remained one of Leskov's major outlets for years. The only remotely literary magazine to which Leskov had access at this time was the ultraconservative *Citizen*, edited by Prince V. P. Meshchersky (on a secret subsidy from the privy purse).[13] *The Citizen* was distasteful: Meshchersky was an unsavory literary lightweight, a writer of high-society potboilers and a man without intellectual or moral standards, who spent his life cashing in on his court connections. *The Citizen's* line was even more stridently chauvinistic than *Russian Messenger's*. Apart from Meshchersky, it was dominated by the personalities of Dostoevsky, with whom Leskov was hardly on speaking terms, and the poet and critic Apollon Maikov, whom Leskov could not forgive for treating him with aristocratic hauteur.[14]

Worst of all, *The Citizen* had a wretchedly small circulation and did not pay well. "There is no work for me in *The Citizen* [Leskov wrote to Shchebalsky]. There the editor himself is lazy, and the magazine itself is too small to provide a man even with bread, let alone support. Besides, my (and your) friend Apollon Maikov (no longer a Slavophile) is there, with his 'this lofty . . . this Christian' ability not to love another human being."[15] Nevertheless, Leskov had to go knocking at *The Citizen's* doors. There he published several of his major works of the later seventies: "At the Edge of the World," "The Pygmy," "The Unbaptized Priest."

In the immediate aftermath of his break with Katkov, the satisfactions of "renounce and denounce" were doubtless great. But as time passed, the reality closed in: no magazines, no publications, no money. And at home there was a collection of mouths to feed. The tone of Leskov's letters became more desperate, even hinting at suicide:

My state of mind is the most agonizing possible [. . .] I have *nowhere* to publish. I see nothing on the literary horizon except party, or better, party-line lies, which I understand all too well and cannot serve. That is all! What is ahead? Can it be that this is already *the end?*[16]

There is literally nothing for me to live on and nothing to lay hold of; nowhere to work and nowhere to get the strength to work; and I cannot exist with a family on 1,000 rubles a year [his salary from a part-time official post]. I have no expectations, and I'll probably go to my brother's village to serve as his clerk, in order not to die of starvation or be put in debtors' prison. My situation is without a *glimmer of hope, and my spirit has fallen into despair,* which prevents me from either thinking or hoping. If something happens to me, my papers will be sent to you.[17]

There was much exaggeration in this: Andrei Leskov points out that his mother had an income of about 3,000 rubles a year from her property in Kiev;[18] so the family was not nearly so close to destitution as Leskov claims. All the same, Leskov's situation was critical.

Before the break with Katkov, Leskov had begun casting about for some nonliterary solution to his economic problems. He longed for a position that would provide a steady income, free him from the caprices of editors and the literary market, and yet not consume too much of his time and energy. He wanted a sinecure or a subsidy. Yet a year earlier he had waved aside an opportunity to enjoy the favors of the court. A highly placed general, S. E. Kushelev, had appeared on Leskov's doorstep with the news that "The Sealed Angel" had been read aloud to the royal family by Boleslav Markevich, and the Empress Maria Aleksandrovna had expressed a desire to hear the same story read by the author himself. Leskov apparently did not care for the role of court entertainer, despite the substantial rewards it promised, and did not respond to the imperial wish.[19]

Nevertheless, the sign of royal favor was put to use. The tsar's messenger, General Kushelev, became a family friend of the Leskovs. Later he was mobilized, along with Boleslav Markevich and other well-connected friends, to wangle an official position for Leskov with a regular salary and duties not too onerous. The best these efforts could produce was a post in the Ministry of Education—a seat on the "Learned Committee" that passed judgment on the suitability of books distributed among the peasantry. The salary was a mere thousand rubles a year, but even that helped. Leskov accepted, and the appointment became official on January 1, 1874. Thus after fourteen years of "retirement," Leskov once again became a civil servant, with the rank of provincial secretary, third from the bottom in the Table of Ranks established by Peter the Great.

This appointment solved none of Leskov's problems and in the end added to them. The meager salary did not fill the deep hollows in the family exchequer, and the pressure to publish or perish remained undiminished. Furthermore, Leskov had to spend much time reading the tedious manuscripts submitted to the committee. Most of them were patronizing moralities designed to spiritualize the uncouth masses (and at the same time turn a profit, since the committee's endorsement automatically brought mass orders for school and public libraries). Leskov worked up some of his government reports as salable articles.[20] But he developed an aversion to his immediate superior, Aleksandr I. Georgievsky; and his antagonism toward Count Dmitry Tolstoy, the minister of education, was already sharp at the time of his appointment. It was a position in which the rewards were few and the opportunities for frustration and conflict abundant. Nevertheless, Leskov worked at the job conscientiously for nearly a decade, until his notorious dismissal "without request" in 1883. Doubtless even a thousand rubles a year was a financial prop he could not afford to forgo, and he may have hoped that in time the ministry would recognize the value of his services and see fit to increase his emolument. It never did. Only two years after his appointment he was begging

Shchebalsky to help him get a more lucrative post as school inspector in the Caucasus, but equally without result. He concludes the letter, "I am a pillar on which both people and dogs urinate" (10:444).

Not long after obtaining this civil service position, Leskov began casting about for some additional nonliterary means of support. As his new sponsor or "good father," he turned to Ivan Aksakov, son of the distinguished chronicler of Russian gentry life and himself the leading spokesman of latter-day Slavophilism. For several years, during the mid-1870s, Aksakov received intensely revealing letters from Leskov, full of complaints, bitterness, self-pity, and—literary gossip. Leskov hoped to use Aksakov's influence to obtain a position in the personal secretariat of the well-known millionaire, V. A. Kokorev, who, after amassing one fortune in the vodka monopoly, was proceeding to make several more in oil, banking, and railroads. Aksakov did his best, and Leskov had several apparently congenial interviews with Kokorev, writing a review for him of a project for the oil industry drawn up by one of the financier's subordinates; but in the end nothing came of the connection (except the material for the story "At the Edge of the World"). Kokorev wanted a more pliable and less stiff-necked literary factotum who would write public relations pieces to order. Leskov, however, immediately began to express strong opinions of his own—for instance, about the route of a new railroad then being projected. Moreover, he refused to write anything for such magazines as *Notes of the Fatherland* on the grounds of his own literary quarrels with their editors.[21] It appeared that for Leskov commercial employment was as constricting, and therefore unworkable, a solution to his economic difficulties as the service of the crown.

Undoubtedly the frustrations of Leskov's public life were translated into tension at home, where there was enough already. The romance between Leskov and Katerina Bubnova had faded, and the fact that their union was not a legal marriage made it even more fragile. "A man's enemies are the men of his own house" (Micah 7:6) became one of Leskov's favorite quotations, and he meant it literally. The "men of his house" (in Russian *domašnie*, "domestics") were his own family and principally his wife. They were fair-weather friends like all the rest, ready to share in his triumphs, caring nothing for his adversities. "What do they care about my convictions?" Leskov asked bitterly in a letter to Shchebalsky. "They are 'friends of the moment, worshippers of success.'"[22] There also seems to have been jealousy over the children between Leskov and his wife. Nikolai Bubnov tells a depressing story of being obliged to destroy, in the presence of his mother and Leskov, a potted palm tree Leskov had given him—this in order to "prove" that his love for Leskov was genuine and not bought by such bribes.[23] Leskov and his wife were not ready for a permanent rupture, but they apparently agreed on a temporary separation. In the spring of 1875 Leskov decided to flee from his troubles and make a second trip to Europe, alone.

He set off early in May, stopping first in Moscow to pay a visit to his new father-confessor, Ivan Aksakov.

About May 15th I plan to go abroad [Leskov wrote to Aksakov before his departure]. I want at least for a while not to see all the things that have deprived me of my strength and vitality. I am thinking of joining a party of French pilgrims and walking with them to Lourdes. Perhaps the religious awakening of people whom I know mostly for their lack of religiosity will arouse my interest, and I won't have to think about those things about which my thoughts are so painful and so fruitless. More than that, I don't know why I am going; I only feel an irresistible need to go away, and for as long a time as possible.[24]

At the beginning of June, by the Gregorian calendar, Leskov arrived in Paris. He evidently though of the trip as a flight in time as well as space, a reenactment of his first Parisian adventure in 1862, when he had likewise fled from political warfare and domestic squabbles. He again took a room in the Latin Quarter. But the years had taken their toll. He was now forty-four. The charms of bohemia had faded, and the rive gauche was unbearably noisy. Before long Leskov made a move, symbolic of the change in his age and status, to a quiet pension near the Champs Élysées. Among the inhabitants there was the distinguished Moscow philologist, Fyodor Buslaev.[25]

The pilgrimage to Lourdes did not take place. The Garonne had flooded the town, as Leskov reported in a letter to his son and stepchildren[26] (his estrangement from his wife was symbolized by his addressing all his letters from abroad to the children, not to her). As he indicated in another letter, it was too expensive and "I see and understand quite clearly what these pilgrimages are."[27]

Nevertheless, the subject of religion absorbed Leskov during this sojourn abroad. The relative isolation from the stimulations and stresses of Petersburg made it possible for him to think hard about religious questions that could not be readily explored in Russia; and he set about a thoroughgoing reconsideration of his own Weltanschauung. It proved to be one of the most significant intellectual enterprises of his life.

Aksakov had asked Leskov while in Paris to look up Father (formerly Prince) Ivan Gagarin, a Russian exile who had lived in France since 1843 and had become a Jesuit priest. Gagarin had written a book on the Russian Orthodox clergy,[28] which was of great interest to Leskov and Aksakov. Aksakov wondered if Leskov could obtain from Gagarin information concerning the rumor that Gagarin had been the author of the anonymous letter that precipitated Pushkin's fatal duel. (He was not, as Leskov subsequently demonstrated in a special article.)[29] Leskov liked Gagarin and was touched by his cordiality and that of other Russian Jesuits. They took him on a tour of their schools, which impressed him, and in his letters home the Jesuits are favorably contrasted with the "nihilists," many of whom were also congregated in Parisian exile.

> Gagarin is a sweet old gentleman [*milyj barin*], who still exudes the atmosphere of the Pushkin circle. What a difference from all that Russian scum [*svoloč'*] who have formed the present-day Russian reading room in Paris! O, if you could only see what scum they are![30]

> Judging by the attitude toward him of the other Jesuits (I was introduced to many of them, including the rector himself) they evidently consider Martynov [Ivan Martynov, a Russian Jesuit writer and archaeologist] a valuable man, and he is always either writing something for them or going off somewhere. He keeps going away and coming back; but Gagarin they good-naturedly pat on the tummy and sometimes make fun of him a bit [. . .] I have also been in the nihilist rookery established by Iv. S. Turgenev; but that is simply repulsive. In general, I didn't like Paris this time.[31]

Cordial as his relations with the Parisian Jesuits were, Roman Catholicism never appealed to Leskov. It shared the same "magic," sacramentalist conception of Christianity and the church that he deplored in Orthodoxy, and it had some disturbing features of its own which he could attack from what looked like an Orthodox point of view. His letters to Gagarin, recently discovered and published by William B. Edgerton,[32] contain polemics on several points at issue between Catholicism and Orthodoxy: the Immaculate Conception of the Virgin, proclaimed as a Catholic dogma in 1854; the worship of the "sacred heart" of Jesus (construction of the famous church of the Sacré Coeur on Montmartre was then about to begin); and most of all, the Catholic tone of assurance in speaking about matters that to Leskov seemed beyond human knowing. In Gagarin's book on the Russian clergy, Leskov noted with approval the view that most agreed with his own, that the chief fault of the Russian clergy was its subservience to the state.[33] He argued, however, that Gagarin had not done justice to Russian monasticism, citing a long list of holy men who had borne witness to the spirituality latent in Orthodoxy.

Although in his relations with the Jesuits Leskov tended to defend Orthodoxy, the most significant result of his religious experiences in 1875 was a decided move in the direction of Protestantism. He met Louis Naville, son of the Swiss Protestant theologian Ernest Naville. "I had a meeting with the young Naville," Leskov later wrote to Shchebalsky, "and [. . .] was shaken in my views."[34] Leskov read several books by Ernest Naville and by other Protestant theologians, including Frederick William Farrar, Philip Schaaf, and Roger Hollard. He also read the text, forbidden in Russia, of the catechism of the Russian "spiritual Christians," known colloquially as the Molokans or "Milkers," from their willingness to drink milk during Lent.[35]

The end product of these readings and meditations was increasing alienation from the Orthodox church.

I am taking the cure, feeling depressed, and not working at all because of my insuperable depression [Leskov wrote to Shchebalsky from Marienbad, where he had gone from Paris in July to to take the waters], but I have read a great, great deal [. . .] In general, I have become a "turncoat" and no longer burn incense to many of my old gods. Most of all, I am out of sympathy with ecclesiasticism, on questions concerning which I have read my fill of works not admissable into Russia [. . .] More than ever I believe in the great significance of the church, but nowhere do I see that spirit which would be in keeping with a society bearing the name of Christ [. . .] I will say only one thing, that if I had read everything I have now read on this subject and if I had heard what I have now heard, I would not have written *Cathedral Folk* in the way I did, for that would have been disagreeable to me. Instead, I have a craving to write the story of a Russian heretic—a clever, well-read, and free-thinking *spiritual Christian* [note this term], who has experienced every hesitation in the course of his search for the truth of Christ and has found it only in his own soul. I would call such a story "Fornosov the Heretic," and would publish it—Where would I publish it? Ugh, these "tendencies"![36]

Leskov's break with the Orthodox church did not become complete for several years; but by the end of 1875 he was already well on the road to what eventually came to be called "Tolstoyanism"—farther along than Tolstoy himself. It was the greatest renunciation of Leskov's life.

However questionable the medicinal value of the mud baths and mineral waters of Marienbad, Leskov believed in them. Whether because of his belief, or the waters, or the enforced exercise and rest, Leskov began to recuperate in Marienbad from his physical and psychic ills. He claims that he literally "sweated bile"—much as the Jewish hero of "Episcopal Justice" was to "sweat blood"—and after that began to "regain color and health."[37] Refreshed in body and renovated in spirit, he was ready, by the end of August, to return to the moil and turmoil of Petersburg.

❦ 21 ❧

Bishops and Baptisms

For several more years after his personal religious crisis Leskov continued to regard the Orthodox church as at least potentially a force for spiritual enlightenment of the Russian population. After all, the vast majority of Russians were, at least nominally, Orthodox Christians. If Christianity were really to affect their lives, therefore, the church was at least the most efficient and possibly the only channel through which its message could be brought to them. In his own religious life, however, Leskov in 1875 had basically severed connections with the church. He was no longer, as he claimed to be in 1871, a "convinced Orthodox."

Unlike so many of his contemporaries, however, Leskov did not escalate his break with the church into a break with Christianity itself. Apart from his philosophical ideas on the subject, he preserved unshaken to the end of his life a firm, nonrational faith in a personal God and in personal immortality.

> My religion is with me [he wrote to Shchebalsky, who had expressed concern about the suicide hints contained in some of Leskov's letters to him], and Christ, with His suffering and endurance, is my strength, which both supports and shames me. I recognize the saving power of undeserved sufferings as an edifying school for the spirit, the immortality of which I do not doubt for an instant. I acknowledge a personal, not an elemental immortality, and I am not troubled by the fact that I cannot understand it. I am troubled not by the fear of reasoning about it, but because it is not my business and in general not a human business: to understand it would mean to understand God, and it is given to us only to feel Him, not to provide Him with commentaries, either from a Protestant or from an Orthodox-priestly [popovskij] point of view. *Scio quod Redemptor meus vivit.*[1]

Nevertheless, the "Protestant point of view" was by now much closer to Leskov's truth than the "priestly-Orthodox" one.

Back in Petersburg and ready to take up his pen, Leskov found himself in a difficult situation. Never an advocate of "art for art's sake," he wanted to use his literary talent to propagate the truth as he now saw it: to show Russians how far their national church had strayed from the ideals of true Christianity. The great theme that now beckoned to him was "Fornosov the Heretic," an unwritten novel that was to affirm genuine Christian ethics. The quest for "spiritual Christianity" in an un-Christian society was to lead the intrepid seeker-hero (as it had the author) beyond Orthodoxy into a new realm of freedom and truth. But as Leskov put it in his letter to Shchebalsky, where was he to publish the account of such a quest? The official censorship was obstacle enough; and the only publishing outlets available to Leskov in the later seventies were either the party organs of Orthodoxy itself or the archconservative *Citizen.*

The course Leskov chose and pursued with adroitness for the next five years was to contrive to present his new, subversive message in a form so disguised that the censors (never distinguished for their perspicacity) and even his editors and publishers would be fooled by it. The trouble with such a successful disguise was that the common reader might also be deceived. Leskov hoped, however, that the effect of his spiritual subversion would be felt through the disguise. The common reader might not be able to pinpoint the author's heresy; but from Leskov's stories he would *feel* the difference between official Orthodox truth and Christian truth.

The first of these camouflaged anticlerical time bombs was the story "At the Edge of the World," probably written in the autumn of 1875, soon after Leskov's return from Marienbad, and then planted on the unsuspecting pages of *The Citizen.*[2] Leskov employed a sly technique in this piece of literary secret weaponry. Using the skaz form, he brought forward as the oral narrator of his anti-Orthodox parable an Orthodox bishop. At first glance this looks like another application of the "negation of the negation" principle Leskov had employed in "The Battle-axe" (and was to use again in "Night Owls"): to place a skaz narrative in the mouth of a morally repugnant character, thus ensuring the reader's repudiation of the narrator's values. The bishop-narrator of "At the Edge of the World," however, is represented as a most attractive person, responsive, self-critical, intelligent. Yet he is unimpeachably Orthodox, devoted to his church. Where was the catch?

The "camouflage" function of the bishop's attractiveness is obvious. Such a sympathetic portrait would disarm the censors and win friends for the story among the partisans of the church. The pro-Orthodox party would react, Leskov hoped, as they had in 1872, when they had gratefully hailed Father Tuberozov as a radiant example of Orthodox virtue, conveniently forgetting his catastrophic moral isolation within his church. Now they would think that the bishop-narrator of "At the Edge of the World" was simply a new Tuberozov, promoted to a higher rank. By and large the trick worked.

Furthermore, the bishop Leskov chose for his narrator was a real person. As he often did, Leskov took pains to propel his fiction over the border separating literature and life. In the story the bishop-narrator is never named, although he presents his narrative as authentic reminiscence. But in "Episcopal Justice," published the following year with the ostentatious subtitle, "A *pendant* to the story 'At the Edge of the World,' " Leskov undertook to underscore the reality of his fiction. The narrator of "At the Edge of the World," he now announced, was a real person, Bishop Nilus (Russian form Nil, secular name Nikolai F. Isakovich), who had died in 1874 as Bishop of Yaroslavl. Nilus, who had previously had a long period of service in Siberia, had "*himself* related this event, which *had happened to him*, to a most respected person, V. A. K——v, who is still alive and thriving here in Petersburg," (Leskov's italics). This "V. A. K——v" (in whom, with some assistance from Andrei Leskov,[3] it is not hard to identify Vasily Aleksandrovich Kokorev, the millionaire banker-industrialist whose secretariat Leskov had vainly tried to join) had in turn passed the story on to Leskov, who in his turn had "developed" it very little, "only in certain details and that from a prepared canvas" (6:89). Thus Leskov's attack on Orthodox sacramentalism was made to emanate from a respected real bishop, recently deceased, the author of a treatise on Buddhism in Siberia and of a book of Siberian travel memoirs.[4]

An early draft of "At the Edge of the World," under the title "Man of Darkness," has been preserved and published.[5] A comparison between the draft and the finished story reveals a great deal about Leskov's artistic mastery. We can reduce the draft story to two basic structural skeletons, the one narrative, the other ideological. The narrative core is the autobiographical adventure story Kokorev probably heard from Bishop Nilus and passed on to Leskov. Once while engaged in missionary work among shamanist tribes in Siberia (he was then bishop of Irkutsk), Nilus had been lost in a blizzard and would have perished if it had not been for the resourcefulness, self-sacrifice, and devotion of his driver, who was a heathen. The basic prescription for transforming the anecdote into literature is clear: amplification, concretization, vividness of detail.

The theme is archetypal: man against nature, with nature at her cruelest, and man, the naked ape, the creature of the tropics, struggling through ingenuity and determination to survive in an environment for which he is totally unsuited by physical endowments. Leskov's task was to capture the "feel" of the experience, the external sense impressions, the sights and sounds of that grim and inhospitable world (beautiful in its way), and the emotions of the hero, alternating between despair and hope. A corollary theme is the classic reversal of roles, the abasement of the mighty and the exaltation of the humble. The bishop hero, the representative of civilization and human authority, is alien and helpless in that world of forest, snow, and wolves, and thus wholly dependent on his "savage" guide. Leskov accomplished the task of realization brilliantly: "At the Edge of the World" must be ranked among the great blizzard stories of Russian literature, alongside Pushkin's and Tolstoy's "Snowstorm" and Tolstoy's "Master and Man." ("Master and Man," written twenty years later, may well have been influenced by Leskov's work; it combines in a similar way the excitement of sheer peril with the moral transfiguration experienced by characters *in extremis*).[6]

"At the Edge of the World" (and "Man of Darkness" before it) also has an ideological core, the subversive message Leskov wished to implant in his readers' hearts. This message comes in several layers of accessibility and generalization. There is a manifest sermon, itself disturbing enough, and there are implied conclusions that go much further. Leskov's stated moral is that the efforts of the Orthodox church to baptize the heathen and introduce Christianity among primitive tribes in Siberia are not only worthless, but harmful. Since civilization is mainly represented by the Russian civil and military bureaucracies, both of them staffed with hard-drinking, rapacious, bribe-taking officials, its penetration into northern Asia, with Christianity in its baggage train, had brought about a deterioration in the moral and ethical standards of the local populations. The baptism of shamanists, often accomplished by intimidation and bribery, is not a sacrament, but an impious fraud. Such conversions exist only in lifeless government statistics; in human terms they are meaningless. When the magic rite of baptism is performed wholesale on hordes of primitive people, often without religious instruction, at the most a new set of vaguely understood gods is added to their pantheon. Moreover the new gods may not be placed in the first rank: the meek and

303

suffering Khristosik strikes these heathens as a weakling, inspiring pity and sympathy, but not awe. In their minds the concrete rewards they receive for undergoing the ceremony—often vodka—or their fear of the consequences of refusal outweigh the religious content of the conversion.

Leskov's message was in part a Russian version of the general crisis of doubt over the value of missionary work. The old sureness had been shaken. The bland assumption of religious superiority was weakening and a sense of cultural relativism developing. People were coming to realize that the "benefits" of civilization brought by the missionaries included alcohol, syphilis, and economic exploitation, as well as the destruction of much that was admirable in the cultures assumed to be in need of Western enlightenment.

Further, by implication, Leskov was questioning baptism itself, if regarded as an automatic ticket to the Kingdom of God. (The "ticket" image, later brilliantly developed by Ivan Karamazov, is employed in Leskov's text.) True baptism was only of the spirit, manifested in its effect on life on earth. Still further, an attack on the sacrament of baptism implied an attack on ecclesiasticism as such—the granting of absolution by priests is also questioned in the course of the story—and thus on the Orthodox church. How could a devout Orthodox bishop be made the vehicle for carrying such a message?

Leskov's literary strategy is simple. The story is constructed as a *Bildungsroman*, depicting the education through experience of a young and energetic bishop, recently arrived in his Siberian diocese, full of zeal to bring salvation to the heathen. Little by little the truth forces itself upon this bishop's consciousness. The activities and the moral example of the Russian bureaucracy are not civilizing, but oppressing and corrupting the primitive peoples on whom they have imposed their rule. His church lacks the human and spiritual resources to accomplish any genuine Christian enlightenment. His monks and priests are lazy and ignorant, unwilling to learn the local language[7] and themselves no shining examples of the Christian life.

The experience in the snowstorm is the culmination of the bishop's education. He is forced to recognize that there may be more natural Christianity, that is, human solidarity, responsibility, and love for one's neighbor, in his heathen guide than in all the Orthodox Christian Russian officials put together. On the basis of this hard-won wisdom the bishop concludes that, discouraging as the fact may be, the missionary efforts of Orthodoxy are a harmful delusion. The best thing he can do, as a Christian leader, is to administer his diocese as humanely and efficiently as possible, try to set and inspire a better moral example on the part of the Christian community, and leave the baptism of the heathen to the initiative of God and a better day to come.

To place such ideas in the mind of an Orthodox bishop was risky, to say the least. The bishop was beginning to sound a good deal like Fornosov the heretic. Leskov took pains to modify the risk. First, he counterbalanced the bishop's implicit heresy with an explicit affirmation of his Orthodoxy. In the final version of the story, Leskov introduced a long chapter, missing from "Man of Darkness," in which the bishop is given an opportunity to underscore his loyalty to the church. In the introductory, frame section of the final version, before the bishop begins his narrative, there is a discussion between the aged bishop and his guests concerning the relative effectiveness of Orthodox and Protestant missions. A naval captain attacks Orthodoxy as incapable of preaching the Gospel. The bishop unexpectedly agrees with this part of the captain's argument; but when the captain goes on to assert that the Orthodox clergy "hardly understand Christ," the bishop objects. He opens an album in which he has collected great representations of Jesus in European art: Rembrandt, Rubens, Titian, Guercino, and Metsu are alluded to, as well as some nineteenth-century artists forgotten today, such as Robert Cauer (a German sculptor) and Alexandre Lafond (a French painter of biblical subjects).[8] The bishop turns the pages of the album and comments briefly on each picture. However admirable aesthetically, all these products of Western art are found wanting in their grasp of the divine personality. They do not succeed in representing pictorially the perfect union in Jesus of God and man. The audience is then asked to turn to the corner of the room, where they see an ancient Russian icon of the Savior, the true Jesus. "Our simple-hearted painter," the bishop concludes triumphantly, "*understood* better than any of them Him whom he had to paint." "And so," the bishop goes on, "to the extent that our national art has, in my opinion, grasped the external features of Christ's representation more simply and successfully than any other, so, perhaps, our national spirit has come closer to the truth of the internal features of His character." On this basis the bishop can assert with confidence that "in Russia Our Lord is understood no less than in Tübingen, London, or Geneva," let alone the centers of Roman Catholicism, of whose cult of the sacred heart the bishop speaks with especial disdain.

Thus the bishop vigorously asserts his Orthodoxy, meshed with an emotional force perhaps even more powerful, Russian nationalism. Like Dostoevsky and Tyutchev, whose lines on the "Russian Christ"

Leskov cited as the epigraph to the edition of 1876,[9] Leskov's bishop seems to be subjecting Jesus to a program of Russification. And in another part of the story the list of "Christianities" to which Russian Orthodoxy is deemed superior is increased by yet another—the Or-thodoxy of the Greeks, whose "sumptuous Byzantinism," the bishop insists, is poles apart from the humble Russian Christ, who "walks everywhere in simplicity, without incense" (5:465).

Thus the bishop's combination of patriotism with Orthodoxy has been ostentatiously exhibited before he begins his narrative. There is, however, an implicit weakness in the conclusion the bishop draws from his exercise in art appreciation, perhaps a trap Leskov has placed beneath his feet. The great art of Russian icon-painting, as the bishop explicitly states, belongs entirely to the past: the secret of the ancient masters "died with them and their rejected art." Might not one there-fore conclude that the superior understanding of the deity by "our national spirit" had also perished along with the medieval culture to which the "rejected art" belonged? If so, there was not much comfort for nineteenth-century Orthodoxy in the ancient icons.

A second significant change Leskov carried out between the early and late versions of "At the Edge of the World," more interesting from a technical than from an ideological point of view, is a kind of fission that takes place in the character of the bishop. In "Man of Darkness" the bishop must accomplish his education alone. He must learn entirely through his own bitter experiences that with the meager spiritual resources at his command, he can do almost nothing to advance the cause of Christianity in Siberia. The course of wisdom, one often hard for the young and energetic to accept, is essentially to attempt nothing. The time is not ripe; one can only "watch and pray."

After completing his first draft, Leskov apparently decided that such wisdom was too hard to acquire by oneself. Perhaps to make the bishop's *Bildung* psychologically more convincing, perhaps to dilute the impression of heresy by dividing it among two people, Leskov determined to supply his bishop with a teacher. A new character therefore appears in "At the Edge of the World," Father Kiriak, an old, frail, and saintly Orthodox monk. Father Kiriak has already been through the experiences the bishop must undergo and learned the lessons the bishop must master. Father Kiriak understands all too well the futility and immorality of missions, which are hopelessly con-taminated by their association with what he calls *vrazhki*, the "little enemies," the Russian officials. Kiriak thus becomes an image of the bishop's future: patient, beyond worldly ambitions, content to proselytize only by his own example of quiet kindness.

Father Kiriak in "At the Edge of the World" is assigned what in "Man of Darkness" had been the bishop's own past. He now relates to the bishop (a skaz within a skaz) as stories fr⌣m *his* childhood several experiences which in the original version had happened to the bishop himself, in particular the "miracles" with which he had been favored as a child. Once he had been miraculously rescued (after prayer) from a school flogging by the appearance of a visiting school inspector; once, likewise after prayer, he was miraculously absolved from taking a dreaded examination by having his arm broken in a game of leapfrog. Transferring these "miracle" anecdotes from the bishop's memories to Father Kiriak's preserves the bishop's dignity and gives him an appearance of greater sophistication as he listens with scepticism to Kiriak's tales; at the same time it gives Kiriak a winning air of naiveté and sweetness.

With the presence in the story of two genuine (though Orthodox) Christians, Leskov is able to introduce a symbolic—and deeply ironic —addition to the plot. In "Man of Darkness" the bishop is accompanied on his dog-sled expedition by a Father Peter, a young priest eager to advance his career by chalking up "statistical" baptisms. He senses an enemy in a bishop whose intelligence and devotion to Christian principles would inevitably thwart his, Peter's, ambitions. In the new version the only character resembling Father Peter is a nameless missionary priest from the next diocese. But in "At the Edge of the World" the bishop's companion on the journey into the taiga is not this un-Christian priest, but Father Kiriak.[10] One of their two drivers is a heathen and the other a baptized Christian; and Father Kiriak, with his spiritual insight, assigns the *heathen* driver to the bishop as the more dependable of the two, taking the unreliable Christian for himself. His self-sacrificing wisdom is borne out by the event. The bishop is heroically saved by his pagan driver, while the Christian abandons Kiriak to his fate. The old monk is ultimately rescued, but with limbs so badly frozen that he dies of gangrene in the bishop's arms. The Christian driver's desertion is proof that baptism without spiritual content may sever a man's moral roots and leave him a worse human being than he was before.

A third difference between "At the Edge of the World" and "Man of Darkness" is the addition of a large quantity of diverse associative material. "Man of Darkness" lacks the ramifications through digres-

sion that give the final version its fullness. In some of Leskov's works, for example in the second part of *Laughter and Grief*, an overabundance of topical digressions blurs the artistic focus of the story and weakens its impact. But in "At the Edge of the World" the additions sharpen our impression. The associative material is kept strictly relevant to the basic problem and appropriate to the characters who introduce it.

The cultural associations of the bishop and Father Kiriak take us again into that "archaic" bookish world of Christian religiosity, so distant from the bibles of the Petersburg intellectuals: from Tertullian, St. Augustine, and St. Cyril of Jerusalem through Massillon, Bourdaloue, and Karl Eckhartshausen, to Kirik of Novgorod (a Russian writer of the twelfth century), Cyril of Turov (a great preacher of the same period), and Stefan Yavorsky (one of the greatest Russo-Ukrainian homilists of the seventeenth century). Also invoked are the ominous examples of Paul (Konyushkevich), an eighteenth-century metropolitan of Tobolsk whose missionary zeal was rewarded by his dismissal from his post and confinement to a monastery,[11] and Arsenius (Matseyevich), once Metropolitan of Rostov, who in 1763 denounced Catherine's seizure of monastic lands and ended his life confined to a prison in Reval under the name of Andrew the Liar, with a lock on his mouth. Leskov skillfully studs his ecclesiastical heroes' speech with nuggets from the Slavonic Bible. Father Tuberozov's priestly diary is surpassed in the speech of Father Kiriak and his episcopal pupil. Never forced, these scriptural quotations appear as a natural verbal resource of persons whose minds reverberated continually with biblical phrases, as Leskov's evidently did.

As an essay in camouflage, "At the Edge of the World" was a brilliant success. Prince Meshchersky accepted it without demur, and it appeared on schedule in his *Citizen*, apparently without encountering any trouble with the censors; the book edition sold out rapidly; and a copy was presented, with a warm recommendation, by the archreactionary ideologue K. P. Pobedonostsev to his pupil, the future Alexander III. One could hardly hope to plant a spiritual bomb any higher than that. As Leskov put it, his "little story" had had "a certain success."[12]

Some of the more perceptive pillars of Orthodoxy, however, deduced the hidden implications of Leskov's subversive sermon, and they rose up in indignation. Had their advocate become a turncoat? How dare anyone depict a bishop "who countenanced unbelief and was even indifferent to the salvation of souls through Holy Baptism" (6:88)? Leskov was eager to continue the war. Delighted with the pretext provided by his ecclesiastical critics, he returned to the attack with another "apropos" story dealing with the misguided missionary efforts of Orthodoxy. It was called "Episcopal Justice." Leskov managed to place it in a Church-sponsored magazine, *The Pilgrim*.[13]

Following up the original subtitle, "A *Pendant* to the Story 'At the Edge of the World' " (dropped in later editions), Leskov begins by registering the published praises of that story and also the disapproval of "certain highly respected and quite well known personages in the clergy," which had reached him privately. These private criticisms he now made public—partly to make sure no one would miss the hidden message of "At the Edge of the World," partly to provide himself with a starting point for his new story. It was certainly wrong, he claimed, to charge him with "indifference to the salvation of souls through Holy Baptism." He had only insisted that baptism be a spiritual, not a purely formal event. And he happens to have another "bishop" story to make his point clear.

This new story is purported to come from the author's reminiscences: Leskov is recalling his experiences as an army recruiting agent in Kiev in the early 1850s. One presumes that the story has a foundation of fact. It is stuffed with real names, people, and places; and the author did hold such a post.

Ideologically, the point in "Episcopal Justice" is the same as in "At the Edge of the World." The ceremony of baptism by itself has no religious value and under certain circumstances may be immoral. These circumstances obtained in the early 1850s, when the Russian government was striving for its own "final solution" to the "Jewish problem" by inducting twelve-year-old Jewish boys into the army and forcibly subjecting them to Orthodox Christian baptism. By Leskov's implication, a church that perpetrated these cruelties could not call itself Christian.

This savage attack required an elaborate camouflage. Leskov's overall strategy might be called *atypicality*, the reverse of the *tipichnost'* ("typicality") which is urged upon Soviet writers, enjoining them from dealing with unpleasant facts of Soviet life on the ground that they are not "typical" and are therefore unworthy of artistic representation. The story Leskov chooses is no representative sample of his experiences as a legal persecutor of Jewish children. It is a unique case in which a "good" Russian official, Prince Illarion Vasilchikov, the governor-general of Kiev, and a "good" Russian prelate, Metropolitan

Philaret Amfiteatrov, intervened on behalf of one child and kept him out of the army.

No doubt one function of this "exceptionality" was to assuage Leskov's guilt for having presided without protest over so much man-made agony. On another level, the anodyne for Leskov's conscience worked as a soporific for the censors. In such an atypical case, both church and state are made to appear much better than they were in fact. As in "At the Edge of the World," we are shown a very humane and attractive bishop—wise, kind, a little abrupt, but with a saving sense of humor.[14] There is an attractive high official, Prince Vasil-chikov, whose basic good-heartedness in this case wins out over the obstacles set in its way by legalism, bureaucracy, and the misguided enthusiasms of his wife, whom he is too weak to oppose. Leskov never pretends that the intervention of the governor-general and the metro-politan was anything but exceptional; nevertheless, it leaves us with a glow of satisfaction. Even in the Russia of Nicholas I there was an occasional victory for humanity. We know that the rescue of one child in no way rights the moral balance for the hundreds of other victims. But the emotional satisfaction from this atypical case helps to make more tolerable, for us and for the censors, the horrifying statistical truth of the typical cases.

Another means of slipping the story past editorial and censorship boards was the distance in time. The Russia of 1877 was very different from the Russia of 1850—"unbelievably different," Leskov says. The atrocious policy described in the story had been abrogated by Alex-ander II. To attack a policy abandoned decades before could not be seen as subversion.

As the final touch to his camouflage, Leskov appeared to proclaim publicly the personal Orthodoxy he had privately renounced: "I grew up in the gentry family I was born in, in the town of Oryol, with a father who was a very clever man, very well read, and a connoisseur of theology [no doubt the result of this "gentleman's" having attended a seminary, which is not mentioned] and a mother who was very God-fearing and pious; I learned religion from the best and in his time very well-known teacher, Father Euphemius Ostromyslensky, for whose good lessons I shall always be grateful to him" (6:125). Leskov adds that he learned to think "in an Orthodox way" both from his father and from this priest, that his Orthodoxy was still intact at the time of his narrative, the early fifties, and that "as an Orthodox Chris-tian" he considered absolute the theological authority of Metropolitan Philaret (Amfiteatrov). This sounds like a pledge of Orthodox allegiance. But the statement about his father's "Orthodoxy" is a fabrication. Moreover, in the pledge Leskov never places his own Orthodoxy securely in the present tense. It is unobtrusively "distanced" to the time of the action. In its context, the statement gives the impression of "well-intentioned" loyalty. Thus the Orthodox facade of "Episcopal Justice" seems impeccable.

The story at face value relates an exceptional instance in which a bumbling, benevolent governor and a saintly bishop rescue a Jewish child from a pernicious official policy—a policy long since abandoned. Furthermore, the full horror of the government's policy is never represented. We do not witness the separation scene, when the child is wrenched from his parents' arms, nor the miseries of the child soldiers later. Leskov concentrates on the sufferings of the father, who is an absurd and contemptible figure.

Nevertheless, the implied message is explosive. The sacrament of baptism is even more degraded than it was in "At the Edge of the World." If a sacrament can be so misused, can it have any sacred content? Can such a church be Christian? Do the laws of a government that perpetrates such crimes have any validity? Might not disobedience to the law be the only possible moral position for a believing Christian and for a truly Christian church? The implied answers were not likely to strengthen the reader's allegiance to the altar or the throne.

In general, "Episcopal Justice" is not as successful a work of art as "At the Edge of the World." The moral ambiguities of the author have taken an artistic toll. Most of all, the scurrilous caricature of the Jewish father is simply odious; it reflects a tendency toward thinking (and feeling) in terms of ethnic stereotypes. Leskov lays great stress on the father's ridiculous, offensive, and even despicable qualities. The wretched Jew squeals, grovels, cringes, sleeps on the floor like a dog, jabbers incoherently, and—worst crime of all for a language-lover like Leskov—writes an absurd mixture of Russian, Ukrainian, and Yiddish, though he claims to be a learned man. He lacks any personal dignity and is ready for any self-abasement in order to gain his end. Symbolically, even the blood he supposedly "sweats" in his anguish has a disgusting odor. If we pity such a figure, we despise him even more.

Second, Leskov tries to shift the moral responsibility for this suffering from the Russian government, which in fact caused it, to the Jewish community. The sufferings of the Jews, he claims, were greatly aggravated by "the boundless cruelty of Jewish deceit and chicanery,

311

practiced in all possible forms" (6:90). Thus Leskov's retrospective stance is one of respectful dissent from an official policy already abolished; but the vehemence of his moral indignation is seemingly directed against the one element from which he himself was completely dissociated, the Jewish community.

"Episcopal Justice" also suffers from some serious technical flaws. The "memoir" form here seems partly incompatible with the narrative core. The true hero of the story is the Jewish father, the bookbinder, whose desperate efforts to save his son provide the energy that in turn propels the action and sets in motion the other characters. The rest of the story is padding. But in the memoir form as Leskov employs it here, the hero cannot be given his due. The memoirist, identified with the author himself, is excessively distanced from his protagonist, partly by prejudice and partly by ignorance. The narrator perceives the bookbinder's anguish and feels some far-off compassion for him, but these sentiments do not lead to empathy. Our vision of the tragedy is thus blurred.

The process of lateralization in "Episcopal Justice," the typically Leskovian branching out into associative connections, starts from the wrong point. Leskov's associations amplify our image of the persecutors, not the persecuted. We get a vivid picture of the life of provincial Russian officials in the last years of Nicholas's reign and striking portraits of historical personalities, such as Princess Vasilchikova; but they are largely irrelevant to the plot.

In effect, therefore, "Episcopal Justice" is two separate, superimposed works sharing a narrow piece of common ground. One is the story of the Jewish bookbinder who almost lost his only son into the clutches of the baptizing army, but who by self-sacrifice and tremendous perseverance, plus a bit of luck, managed to save him. The other is a genre picture, taken from the author's memories of his youth, of the world of provincial Russian officialdom in 1850. The two stories are not satisfactorily fused into one.

The impact of "Episcopal Justice" is further weakened by the epilogue or, as Leskov labels it, the "Chapter in Lieu of an Epilogue." The Jewish bookbinder is seen some years later. His son is dead; his wife is also dead; and the bookbinder has become a convert to Orthodox Christianity. Such a surrender to the culture and religion that caused him so much misery, though perhaps humanly possible, seems in the context just another slur on the hero's integrity.

Leskov almost redeems himself with a final, post-Epilogue chapter in which he employs to perfection his archly ironical, tongue-in-cheek manner. The newspapers recently (February 1877) had been full of the story of a "Jerusalem baron" who sought a contract as a supplier for the Russian army. Denied it because of his religion, he converted to Orthodox Christianity, with the benevolent assistance of some "all-powerful patronesses." Therefore, Leskov wryly concludes, his story "At the Edge of the World" has wrought no changes in the views or the activities of these "high-society baptizers," and so his episcopal critics might be persuaded to forgive him. They and their patronesses can, one infers, continue to their hearts' content to dishonor the sacrament of Holy Baptism; neither Leskov nor literature can stop them.

The climax to Leskov's battle with baptism came in the same year, 1877, in a story again planted in the archconservative, ultra-Orthodox *Citizen*, where Dostoevsky, in his *Diary of a Writer*, was rallying the Orthodox with the vision of victorious Russian armies restoring the cross on the Hagia Sophia in Constantinople. Leskov's message could hardly be more contrary to this call to an Orthodox jihad. In his new story the antibaptismal motif appears in the title: "The Unbaptized Priest."[15] The priest-hero is not only unbaptized, but unorthodox and essentially un-Orthodox. He is a Protestant minister in Orthodox sacerdotal robes, preaching Leskov's Protestant sermon within the walls of the Orthodox sanctuary.

Leskov's cagey camouflage is here laid on in several strata. First, there is a powerful distancing effect in his choice of geography and social class. This is a Ukrainian peasant story, full of local color and speech. Although earlier he had written stories with Ukrainian settings, such as "The Sealed Angel" and *Years of Childhood*, this is the first story in which Leskov fully exploited his superb knowledge of the Ukrainian milieu and the Ukrainian language. The tone of "The Unbaptized Priest" is reminiscent of some of the gayer stories in Gogol's *Evenings on a Farm Near Dikanka*; but Leskov is more audacious than Gogol had been in his use of Ukrainian in a Russian story, including whole sentences and paragraphs. This use of Ukrainian, besides imparting a ring of geographical authenticity to the characters' voices, has a distancing value of its own. It sounds funny. To the Russian ear, there is something a little ludicrous about the Ukrainian shape of the familiar Slavic words; and an unbaptized *pip* ("priest") is more of an absurdity than an unchristened *pop* would have been. Thus the characters are firmly anchored "out there," in an ethnographic, linguistic distance from which Leskov's cultivated Russian readers felt safely separated; and so disarmed, Leskov hoped, those readers would be receptive to his didactic message.

Second, despite their linguistic artistry, the characters of "The Unbaptized Priest" are markedly "dumb" peasants. Just as Gogol's readers had, as it were, been authorized to condescend to Rudy Panko and his friends, so Leskov's readers are entitled to look down on the unbaptized priest and his flock. The attitude toward the characters programmed for us is one of hearty, backslapping amusement. These are ignorant, wayward children whose antics entertain us, but whose ideas are not to be taken seriously.

Third, the jocularity of tone is part of Leskov's technique of literary subterfuge. All this rollicking Ukrainian laughter functions as a means of facilitating the story's passage not only through *The Citizen*'s editorial rooms and the censor's scissors, but into the readers' hearts.

This multilayered camouflage is wound around a narrative nucleus that in itself seems innocent. Two godparents taking an infant to be baptized in a neighboring parish are caught in a blizzard and cannot reach their destination They are rescued unharmed, but are so terrified of the child's father that they falsely report their mission accomplished and the child duly baptized. Eventually the child grows up to become a priest. Many years later, on her deathbed, the godmother confesses her crime: the priest was never baptized! The consequence is great alarm in the church: if the priest is unbaptized, does this not invalidate all the sacraments he has performed? Are not all the village children therefore likewise unbaptized, all the marriages unions in sin, and worst of all, all the departed souls doomed to eternal torments in hell since they died without absolution?

Leskov provides an approved Orthodox (and common-sense) solution to this problem, dispensed by the bishop. The bishop applies the argument of St. Paul (in I Corinthians 10:1-4) to the case of Savva, the unbaptized priest, concluding that he was baptized after all. His would-be godparents had passed through a "cloud of moisture" (the blizzard) in their quest for baptism, and they had made the sign of the cross on the infant's forehead with melted snow in the name of the Holy Trinity. What more could God possible require? This was as surely a baptism as that of the Israelites in the Red Sea.

Again, a subversive conclusion lurks beneath the surface of this narrative. The ceremony of baptism in itself is clearly of no great importance; what matters is its spiritual content. Infant baptism symbolizes a dedication of the child to God; in no sense is it a magic rite with special power to influence the child's fate.

Other equally un-Orthodox conclusions can be drawn from the story. If the ceremony of baptism can be dispensed with, what about other church ceremonies? Perhaps the priest should not be regarded as a dispenser of magic tickets to salvation; perhaps his only valid function is that of a spiritual teacher, a moral force in his community. Leskov shows Father Savva in precisely this role. Savva is the realization of what the musk-ox should have become, embodying Leskov's positive ideal for the church, including its Protestant coloration.

Dedicated from birth by his mother to God, Savva Dukachov grows up under the tutelage of Okhrim Pidnebesny, a representative of a "new and very interesting Little Russian type which began to take shape and form in the trans-Dnepr settlements as early as the first quarter of the current century" (6:189). This new type, which "perhaps" traced its origin to German colonists in the Ukraine, was essentially Protestant, "Puritan." Its representatives placed fundamental stress on the Scriptures, especially the Gospel, and believed that in the "human traditions" followed by the Orthodox clergy "everything had been corrupted and distorted" (6:190). Men like Pidnebesny did not shun society or labor, "but were even models of industry and domesticity." Pidnebesny operated a free school for children, and in the evenings entertained young adults with nuts and honey while he talked to them about Christ. "His interpretations were of the simplest, quite devoid of any dogmatism and theological formulations, but almost exclusively aimed at the moral education of man according to the ideas of Jesus" (6:192). Those young people who fell in love at these gatherings invariably formed happy marriages, "since their coming together took place in a peaceful atmosphere of spirituality, and not in a burst of unbridled passion, when choice is governed by desire of the blood, and not the sensitive inclinations of the heart" (6:191). Pidnebesny himself, however, was a virgin, like Artur Benni and many of Leskov's other saints.

Thus Pidnebesny constitutes a source of Protestant virtue and enlightenment, radiating the light of Gospel truth and moral purity into the surrounding Orthodox darkness. And his pupil, Savva Dukachov, becomes the agent for introducing this light directly into the Orthodox church itself.

Despite his un-Orthodox early education, Savva dutifully goes through the Orthodox seminary. There his record is so good that he is

315

invited to continue his studies at the Academy, with the prospect of being made a bishop. Savva refuses this offer and elects to become a parish priest. (This decision obliges him to marry and thus lose his saintly virginity. But Leskov quickly dispatches his wife as if she hardly existed. As a widower Savva follows Pidnebesny's example of sexual abstinence.) Becoming a priest, Savva systematically introduces Protestant content into Orthodox forms. For penances he assigns practical good works, such as making clothes for orphans, instead of recitation of prayers or pilgrimages to Kiev; he makes no dietary prescriptions at all; contributions or penitential offerings he spends on orphans "and not for incense and candles"; a handsome bequest is used to build a school rather than to buy a church bell. In short, Father Savva, though remaining nominally Orthodox, represents that active, practical Christianity of good works that Leskov had long admired in the "shtundists," an evangelical sect then becoming widespread in the Ukraine.[16]

"The Unbaptized Priest" is not entirely satisfactory as a work of literature. Despite the camouflage, the didacticism seems too obvious, the narrative too flimsy a vehicle to carry the heavy truths loaded on it. The characterizations of the two Protestant saints, Pidnebesny and Father Savva, suffer from faults Leskov generally avoided with his virtuous characters: they remain essentially abstractions, not believable human beings. For both of them life is too easy; there seem to be no obstacles to the triumphant march of their faith. Savva has no psychological conflicts of any kind, and his innovations in ecclesiastical practice are accepted by his parishioners without the slightest resistance. His moral precepts are instantly effective: for instance, a harsh stepmother is immediately transformed by Savva's admonition into a loving mother. Furthermore, Leskov gets trapped in an impossible contradiction in his description of Savva's sacerdotal mission. On the one hand, Leskov shows Savva as a teacher and reformer of superhuman powers; on the other hand, Leskov's need for social distancing and humor requires Savva's peasant parisioners to remain as unenlightened and superstitious at the end as they were at the beginning. They know, for instance, that it is the duty of every "real Orthodox Christian," if he happens to meet a witch, to deal her a tremendous blow with any weapon that comes to hand; they believe that Savva's baptismal troubles are due to the fact that his patron saint, Savva (or Sabbas) is weaker than the "Muscovite" St. Nicholas, who has been intriguing against him in celestial realms; and they think that they can "beef up" (*podsilivat'*) St. Savva for his fight with St.

Nicholas by burning countless candles before his image; finally, they threaten to "depart to the Turkish faith" if the bishop deprives them of their beloved Savva. Are these the fruits of Savva's enlightenment?

Whatever its faults, "The Unbaptized Priest" remains a powerful statement of Leskov's ideals. Most of all, it is convincing evidence that as early as 1877, Leskov's religious position was already close to that which he and Tolstoy were later to share—long before Tolstoy arrived at this position himself.

◈ 22 ◈

The Germans

Leskov found time, during his trip to the West in 1875, to play the tourist's game of comparing cultures. This game arouses conflicting feelings in most people: some of "their" ways strike us as better than "ours," yet to acknowledge this superiority seems almost an act of self-treason. An emotional tug-of-war ensues, in which "we" normally emerge victorious. All the same, some residue of cultural relativism usually survives the war—an awareness that one's own national system of beliefs and social practices is only one of many possible adjustments to the human condition.

For an educated Russian in the nineteenth century, this game was hard to win. It was all too clear that in France, Germany, and England most people were better fed, better clothed, and better housed than they were in Russia; public services were more efficient; political institutions more responsive to popular will; levels of education and literacy higher; industrialization much further advanced. On the Russian side there was little to put in the balance. There were the extraordinary creative achievements of the Russian cultural elite during the preceding century, especially in literature; but the totality of these achievements hardly matched the cultural wealth accumulated in the West since the Renaissance. The Russian could only resort to intangibles: national character, the nation's "youth" (whatever that might mean), its pristine vigor. "Our" people, as people, were clearly better —nicer and more human. And of course God loved them most (and, as Bishop Nilus had demonstrated, they understood Him best).

Leskov had been an aficionado of the game of culture-matching from childhood. His aunt Aleksandra's marriage to an Englishman, semi-Russified though he was, had exposed Leskov to a juxtaposition of two ways of life. If an admired uncle were one of "them," "our" ways could not seem, even to a child, so divinely ordained.

This theme of the foreigner in Russia—the counterpart of the Russian abroad—fascinated Leskov all his life. The confrontation of two

318

cultures provided dramatic energy and a means of casting new light on Russian society and the Russian national character. Several times he resorted to direct literary incarnations of his uncle, Alexander Scott, who makes full-scale appearances at the beginning ("The Mocker," 1863), middle (*The Little Things in a Bishop's Life,* 1878), and end ("The Cattle-pen," 1893) of Leskov's literary career; and he is referred to tangentially in many other works. Very likely Leskov's own experience in 1875 as the Russian abroad reactivated the corresponding theme, the foreigner in Russia.

After completing "At the Edge of the World," Leskov took up this theme again. He focused this time not on Scott, but on a former employee of his, a German engineer named Krüger. As an archetypal specimen of his nation, Krüger was given a treatment even more mocking than that administered to Scott in "The Mocker."[1]

Like most Russians, Leskov had ambivalent feelings about Germans. The nineteenth-century educated Russian found much in the Germans to admire and envy. German philosophers provided the foundation for most of the "Russian" ideologies of the nineteenth century, from Romantic idealism (Schelling, Fichte, Hegel) through mid-century materialism (Feuerbach, Moleschott, Büchner) to "scientific" socialism (Marx, Engels) and "decadence" (Nietzsche). German music was supreme, German literature outstanding, and German science and scholarship preeminent. German manufacturing rivaled England's. And under the sagacious rule of the "Iron Chancellor," the Prussian crown had subjected to its rule all the petty German principalities, and had inflicted humiliating defeats on Austria and France. Germany, which had entered the century politically divided and economically backward, had now "caught up with and overtaken" France and England as Russia still only aspired to do. Thus for many Russians Germany was the model for their future.

Admiration, however, was inevitably accompanied by jealousy, aggravated by various current sources of friction. Russia's major antagonist for the time being was Germanic Austria, her rival for the spoils of the disintegrating Ottoman Empire. Russian imperialist ambitions in the Balkans were intensified and Russian emotions heightened against both Austria and Turkey by uplifting notions of pan-Slavic solidarity with Balkan Slavs and pan-Orthodox solidarity with Balkan non-Slavs. As long as Bismarck ruled, however, Germany remained neutral in this conflict and tried through the *Dreikaiserbund* to keep its imperial partners on negotiating terms. But outside the government there was already alarming talk in Germany about *Lebensraum* and the *Drang nach Osten,* which augured ill for the future.

The Russians' attitude toward Germans in Germany remained favorable during the latter 1870s, as feelings aroused by the Franco-Prussian War subsided. Toward Germans in Russia, on the other hand, antagonism was increasing. Here the chief villains were the Baltic (Livonian) barons. These relics of the ancient glories of the Teutonic Order and the Knights of the Cross had managed to retain their lands and their dominance over the indigenous Lettish and Estonian populations through several changes of national flag. After the area's incorporation into Russia in the eighteenth century these German nobles came to play an increasingly important role at the Petersburg court and in the Russian administration generally. Some of them eventually became Russified in language and culture, with only their names serving as emblems of their Germanic origin; but those who retained their connection with their ancestral Baltic lands generally preserved their German speech and Lutheran religion.

These Baltic provinces, moreover, had never been fully incorporated into the Russian administrative and judicial systems, but were allowed to retain their local law and customs; the German language there had equal status with Russian in the courts. This anomaly of an enclave of German territory within the Russian Empire, with German officials presiding over its destinies, began to trouble race-conscious Russian patriots as the nineteenth-century tide of ethnocentric nationalism began to engulf the older, "feudal" notion of multinational monarchical suzerainty. If political allegiance were based on ethnic and cultural identity, how could these Germans be trusted to serve the tsar rather than the kaiser? How could you be a Russian and a German at the same time?

The noted Slavophile Yury Samarin had for years been conducting a campaign of journalistic indignation against German rule in the Baltic provinces, calling for the government to institute in that area something like the policy that was later adopted, in the reigns of Alexander III and Nicholas II, bearing the ill-fated name "Russification." For the time being, however, Samarin's articles had to be published outside of Russia, and his patriotic propaganda evoked punitive action against him from the Russian government.[2]

Leskov visited the Baltic area many times, beginning with his subsidized excursion in 1863 to Riga to investigate the secret schools of the Old Believers. At that time the Baltic barons had received a favorable assessment from Leskov. As Protestants and non-Russians, they could not understand, or sympathize with, the Russian government's persecution of the Old Believers, which was then Leskov's chief concern; thus he could use their German tolerance as a means of shaming the Russian intolerance he deplored. The Baltic German officials, he reported, carried out "with disgust" the repressive orders of the Russian government.[3]

Leskov's sentimental idealization of the Petersburg Germans in *The Islanders* (1866) seems to mark the height of his early pro-German sentiments. In the later 1860s, he began spending the summers at Baltic resorts, and his feelings about Russian Germans took a turn for the worse. First, there was the holy water and cigar affair. Although he claimed he was not, as the Germans charged, the first to publicize this incident in the Russian press, Leskov energetically broadcast it later. In 1866, in the Estonian town of Wesenberg (now Rakvere), the resident Russian officials and clergy held a public service of thanksgiving for the emperor's survival of Karakozov's assassination attempt. This Orthodox ceremony, held in the public square, involved the consecration of holy water. The local German burghers considered themselves spectators rather than participants in the ceremony, whatever their feelings about the emperor's survival; and they stood by their shops or in the square to watch the arcane Orthodox antics of their Russian compatriots—without, apparently, deeming it necessary to remove their hats or extinguish their cigars. During the ceremony some behatted and cigar-smoking German crowded up indecently close to the priest performing the service. A Russian major promptly had the German arrested for his insolence. This act aroused other Germans to come to his defense, and a melee ensued, in the course of which some Germans supposedly lit their cigars from the candles burning on the Orthodox altar. In the aftermath, the German officials of the Baltic region took no action against the arrested German and instead managed to get the major and the priest transferred out of their territory. This was a story designed to arouse righteous anti-German indignation in Russian breasts, and Leskov made the most of it.[4]

Even closer to home was Leskov's own "wie Rauch" affair, which took place in 1869 or 1870. One evening in Reval Leskov and a Russian friend named Dobrov got into a tavern argument with three young Germans. Quoting Turgenev's novel with malicious satisfaction, one of the Germans proclaimed that *Smoke* offered the most basic of all insights into the destiny of Russia: Russia was a country where every undertaking "would dissolve like smoke" (*wie Rauch*). The good Dobrov rose to his country's defense, breaking a cane over the Germans' heads. According to his own account, Leskov remained aloof from the physical combat, but he was nevertheless made a defendant in a suit for assault brought by his German antagonists. The suit dragged on for years in the courts, with Leskov patriotically refusing to respond to German legal papers served on him in Petersburg, insisting that they be translated into Russian. The case went all the way to the Senate, where Leskov was apparently let off with a small fine—having made much journalistic capital out of the affair.[5] Leskov's dislike of Baltic Germans, however, had become a permanent emotional resource, to be drawn on for xenophobic caricatures like Count Funkendorf in *A Decrepit Clan.*

In 1875 Leskov seems to have returned from abroad with a renewed animus against Germans. He vented these feelings in the story "Iron Will," utilizing anecdotal material dating back to his days in Scott's employ.

Like "The Mocker," "Iron Will" was based on the confrontation of two national archetypes, the "oral" Russian and the "anal" European. In a Russian story on this theme we would expect the national oriflamme (or favorite orifice) to be thoroughly vindicated. Leskov, however, as in "The Mocker," *Laughter and Grief,* "The Cattle-pen," and other works in which he deals with the theme of national character, avoids the superficial satisfactions of chauvinism. His technique is to spread his irony over Russian and foreigner alike. If the foreigner comes to grief in Russia, it is because his character is not suited to Russian conditions. These conditions are in no way presented as better than those in the West; they are simply a reality to which the Westerner must adapt or perish.

"Iron Will" begins as a discussion, in the course of which the main narrative is brought in by way of illustration. The author's spokesman, Fyodor Afanasievich Vochnyov, reminds us of Bishop Nilus and a little of Orest Vatazhkov: the wise oldster, reflective and rich in experience, benevolent and tolerant, acutely aware of the imperfections of human nature and the frequent ironies of human fate.

Like Nilus, Vochnyov is a patriotic Russian; and he narrates a story that at first seems like the ultimate Russian put-down of the Germans. Vochnyov-Leskov, however, puts the Germans to shame without making the expected corollary claim of Russian superiority; he even makes the German's ignominy a source of ironies directed against his own country. Vochnyov is fond of "ironic boasts," if this oxymoronic genre can be said to exist. The Russians are assured a great future, he announces, because a people that could produce such a scoundrel as

Chichikov is invincible![6] With their thousand years of recorded history, he insists, the Russian claim to national youth is an absurdity. And the antidote to German rationality, he suggests, is simply Russian stupidity! As he quotes a Russian general, "What do we care if they [the Germans] make clever calculations? We'll do something so stupid to them that they won't even be able to open their mouths."[7] Likewise, the counterforce to Bismarck's iron is Russian "dough": "All right, so they're made of iron . . . and we are simply dough, soft, raw, unbaked dough. But you should remember that a mass of dough can't be cut with an axe, and you may even lose your axe in it." Or, to use the Russian proverb that appears as the epigraph to the story: Rust eats iron.

The narrative material of "Iron Will" consists of a series of anecdotes, connected, on the narrative plane, by the personality of the hero, and on the plane of abstraction, by the idea the whole story is supposed to demonstrate, namely, the futility and even danger of iron will as a basic human stance, especially in an environment of dough-like Russians. Leskov deftly avoids giving the impression that the illustrations have been concocted to justify the conclusion. Exaggerated as they are, they have the ring of human authenticity.

The central character in "Iron Will" is a German engineer named Hugo Pectoralis (Krüger), imported into Russia by the narrator's English employers to service their milling machinery. This Pectoralis is the anal character incarnate, magnified to the point of caricature against the background of Russian orality. He is competent—a good engineer, conscientious, responsible, and technically resourceful; however deficient he may be in human relations, he deals most effectively with objects. He is dependable, knows his job, and gets his work done on time. All these virtues contrast with the characteristic vices of the Russian oral character—slapdash performance, unreliability about time and obligations, achievement in word rather than deed. Similarly, Pectoralis is a fanatic practitioner of postponement of gratification, showing a stupendous capacity for stifling the urgings of his id. For Pectoralis life in the present is almost totally denied in the name of the power and glories he aspires to in the future. He lives in anticipation of the day when he will proclaim his independence of his employers, establish his own business, marry, and commence the production of a new generation of solid, dutiful, responsible German accumulators.

Pectoralis is in the end reduced to ignominy and his dream swallowed up in the sticky dough of Russian life. The virtue he most values in himself, his iron will, his capacity for self-control, proves his undoing. Pectoralis's iron will is bound up with two fatal flaws of character: a rigidity so extreme that it cannot adjust to important realities in the world, and an overwhelming vanity that renders him unable to distinguish between self-interest and fatuous face-saving.

Vochnyov relates with gusto a series of episodes in the Russian experience of Hugo Pectoralis. The German is stoicism carried to absurdity, enduring countless wasp stings without a murmur and drinking glass after glass of tea so strong it is almost pure tannic acid. These and many other self-injurious acts are performed in order to avoid the impossible alternative of admitting his own fallibility. The great Pectoralis cannot make a mistake or require human aid.

Pectoralis's dream of glory is carefully measured out with money. When his savings reach 3,000 thaler (a goal he has set himself before leaving for Russia), he sends for his German fiancée, and they are legally married. To the amazement of Pectoralis's weak-willed Russian associates, it later transpires that the German had set himself another, unspoken test of his gigantic will power: he will not consummate his marriage until his savings reach 10,000 thaler! Such pointless abstinence proves too much for his wife, who first consoles herself with another German, a laborer, and finally departs in search of a husband with more blood and less iron.

Pectoralis, in short, is an inhuman and thoroughly unpleasant character, his meanness redeemed only by his absurdity. But the two Russians who serve as his chief antagonists exhibit only the vices and not the virtues of the Russian character. (It should be admitted, however, that these vices as Leskov represents them seem less vicious, more human, than Pectoralis's.) The first is a horse trader named Dmitry Yerofeich—a notorious swindler, but a swindler who cheats people not in a dry, prosaic, "German" manner, purely for gain, but exhibitionistically, for the fun of it, "as an artist," "for glory." Without too much difficulty this Dmitry Yerofeich manages to con Pectoralis into buying a blind horse, the animal's physical blindness appropriately symbolizing its new owner's spiritual anopsy. When Mr. Iron Will discovers the fraud, he says nothing, preferring to accept the loss rather than make a public admission of his folly. This stoic silence so unnerves the rascally Russian, used to soul-satisfying scenes with his swindled victims screaming at him, that he lives in terror of the dire plot he assumes the German must be hatching against him. To forestall it, he is eventually reduced to sending Pectoralis a good horse! But even now the German cannot admit his original mistake. He contemptuously rejects the new horse, remarking scornfully to Dmitry Yerofeich: "I'm ashamed of you. You haven't got any will power at all."

Dmitry Yerofeich is a man of considerable intelligence and verve, however knavish the purposes to which they are put. These qualities are lacking in Pectoralis's chief Russian antagonist, Safronych. Safronych is the epitome of "Russian" weaknesses. As the German's rival in the foundry business, Safronych is hopelessly inferior—sloppy, incompetent, unreliable, and without the slightest ambition to improve. Where Pectoralis's life is a mountain of "cares," Safronych by contrast is "careless," that is, carefree, *bespechnyi*—a Russian word hard to translate fully, with all its overtones of lighthearted irresponsibility, frivolousness, and oral dependency. This archetypal Russian failure is addicted to the national oral vice, alcoholism.

In a fair fight between these two specimens of ethnic identity, we would naturally expect the hard-working, self-denying, persevering German to emerge victorious, however appealing the Russian might be. But the German's rigidity proves more self-destructive than the Russian's irresponsibility. Pectoralis is ordered by a court either to reopen the passage, which he had barred off, between Safronych's house and the street (Safronych's house and workshop can be reached only by a right-of-way across Pectoralis's land) or to compensate Safronych for his lost business at the rate of 15 rubles per day. Confronted with the choice between backing down or saving face by making payments greater than he can possibly afford, Pectoralis stubbornly chooses the latter course. As he boasts in court, "I have an iron will, and everybody knows that what I have once decided must remain as I have decided and cannot be changed. I will not open the gate." Grimly announcing that he will "eat pancakes at Safronych's funeral," Pectoralis squeezes out the daily contribution required of him. Financial ruin is preferable to compromise.

The ensuing situation ironically illustrates the fatal flaws of both character types. For the oral Russian, Pectoralis's daily subsidy, unexpected and unearned, represents the realization of his most cherished infantile dreams. He can now revert to a state of total dependency, with no labor or productive output required of him, comfortably lie back and suck his bottle, as it were, in blissful idleness. Safronych thus ingests a prodigious quantity of alcohol, more than his body can long tolerate. At last Pectoralis, though financially ruined, fulfills his vow to eat pancakes at Safronych's funeral. German rigidity would thus seem to have gained a symbolic triumph.

But the victor is soon vanquished, financially and physically, swallowed up in the maw of Russian orality. At Safronych's funeral feast Pectoralis foolishly engages in a pancake-eating contest with a monumentally obese, gouty old priest, "who loves anything made from dough." Doggedly determined as ever, Hugo goes on desperately cramming down pancake after pancake until at last he slides under the table, dead. "And Father Flavian crossed himself, sighed, and whispering 'God with us,' reached for a new pile of hot pancakes."

As a story, "Iron Will" shows Leskov near the top of his form. The anecdotal material is amusing in itself, and it accomplishes its argumentative purpose. The various episodes are skillfully dovetailed into one another; and the major event, the contest between Pectoralis and Safronych, is beautifully delayed by various means, including an anecdote within an anecdote that shows how credulous lower-class Russians could be (the drunken Safronych, sleeping off a binge in the attic of his house, is taken for a ghost, and an elaborate campaign of exorcism is undertaken against him). The general irony, the characteristically Leskovian wryness of tone, neutralizes the chauvinistic spirit of the material. In the moral balance the Russians fare little better than the German. The only valid criticisms of "Iron Will" are, first, that Leskov belabors his point excessively, harping endlessly on the phrase "iron will" and its absurd consequences; and second, that the limits of our credulity are pressed a little too hard by the exaggerations of caricature. The demise of poor Pectoralis from a belly overstuffed with doughy Russian *bliny* may strike us as more obedient to the laws of poetic justice and artistic timing than those of human physiology.

"Iron Will" clearly ranks among Leskov's better stories. Yet the author unaccountably excluded it from his collected works. We do not know whether he forgot about it or had turned against it for some reason.[8]

The subject of Germans and Russians occupied Leskov in later years, and ironic needling of Russian chauvinism remained one of his favorite gambits. His "celebration" of the Russian talent for peculation in the story "The Cynic" (1877) has already been examined in connection with Leskov's own experiences during the Crimean War. This was not the clarion call to patriots one would expect from a "well-intentioned" writer just when Russia was beating the drums for a new war with Turkey. A similar irony pervades "A Flaming Patriot" (1881), which treats the "Germanic" theme in an Austrian variant.[9] Despite its title, "A Flaming Patriot" is not at all of the hurrah-patriotic sort. It is rather the reverse: a sobering lesson in the need for caution in making both claims to national virtue and charges of national sin against others.

In the main anecdote the narrator, during a stay in Vienna, is taken in a carriage by a Russian princess to the Prater park, where they have the luck to behold the reigning emperor, Franz Josef, graciously drink a glass with the simple folk in a Biergarten. To view the scene more closely, the princess has her carriage advanced past the point her Viennese coachman—and the public—consider seemly; afterwards she expresses scornful disapproval of the kaiser's undignified currying of public favor. All this arouses the indignation of her simple Russian maid, Anna Fetisovna, who had been impressed by the emperor's unceremoniousness and ashamed of her mistress's display of arrogance and tactlessness. Anna Fetisovna's displeasure is so great that she abruptly leaves the princess's service and returns to Russia alone.

The flame of this flaming patriot is thus a very modest one. Russians abroad, Anna Fetisovna senses instinctively, should preserve a dignified awareness of their own worth, avoiding both self-flattery and self-abasement; at the same time they should be sensitive to the feelings of their hosts and ready to appreciate their virtues. It is a good lesson, but unfortunately not a particularly good story; the didactic kernel never really sprouts into narrative art.[10]

Leskov turned to the Baltic Germans with two substantial articles of the early eighties, "Herod's Work" and "Russian Statesmen in the Ostsee Region."[11] In these articles Leskov's strategy is similar to that in "The Cynic" and many other stories: through irony and ostensibly naive commentary to force the material to lead to conclusions different from the expected ones.

"Herod's Work" is an ironic deflation of the career as Livonian governor-general of the recently deceased Prince Aleksandr Suvorov (1804-1882). A thoroughbred Russian, grandson of the great general, this Suvorov, according to Leskov, consistently favored the interests of the German aristocracy over the Estonians and Letts; he was contemptuous of the Russian Orthodox clergy in Livonia and harshly oppressive toward the Russian Old Believers. "Herod's Work" is a vigorously acid piece of writing, an effective antidote to the saccharine obituaries that had filled the Russian press with eulogies of Suvorov. In a letter to his editor Leskov accurately advertised it as "a lively article, half-historical, half-polemical, with the admixture of several amusing and characteristic anecdotes."[12]

One of the balance wheels in Leskov's psychic mechanism, preventing him from veering off too violently in the direction of anti-German nationalism, was his spiritual affinity with German Protestantism. Whatever their faults, the Germans, in Leskov's view, had come closer than the Russians to making Christianity a meaningful moral force in their daily lives, which for Leskov was the chief value of religion.

"Russian Statesmen in the Ostsee Region" continues from where "Herod's Work" left off. Leskov uses an old letter by Samarin to blacken further the name of Suvorov and to polemicize with Samarin himself and the policy of Russification he advocated. Leskov poses as an ordinary Greek Orthodox Russian; but in his exposition he continually makes unfavorable comparisons between the ritualism and superstition of the Orthodox, including the Old Believers, and the sobriety and enlightenment of the Germans. In one of his anecdotes a simple and friendly old German, an amateur Gospel preacher, expatiates in bad but eloquent Russian to some Old Believers about the universal brotherhood of men in Jesus Christ. The Old Believers tell him that the Scriptures are all right in their place, but that he should read other, presumably more interesting, holy books too. In the *Ray of the Spirit*, "it is written how a young widow used the abomination of women [menstrual blood?] to save herself from the demon of concupiscence." In such a comparison it is clear where Leskov's (and his readers') preference lies.

The Russo-German theme and the same slyness of manner were combined for more strictly literary ends in "Kolyvan Husband" (1888).[13] The confrontation of Russian and German archetypes is here represented as an aspect of the battle of the sexes, which perhaps confuses the national issue. Kolyvan is the medieval Russian name for the town called by Estonians (and present-day Russians) Tallinn, by Germans and other Europeans Reval, and by nineteenth-century Russians Revel. The hero of the story, the ill-fated husband, is a Russian of the Russians, Ivan Nikitich Sipachov, born deep in the heart of Kaluga province to parents of impeccable Russian ancestry. He has a Slavophile Moscow uncle who is an authority on Slavic archaeology and a friend of the Kireevskys and the Aksakovs. As a Russian naval officer in Reval, however, Sipachov marries into the local German gentry. His wife is a woman of unimpeachable character and great beauty, and her mother and other female relations are also paragons of Protestant virtue; but each time a child is born to the Sipachovs, these wily German females manage in the father's absence to have it baptized a Lutheran. Thus, instead of the long-awaited Nikita Ivanovich, heir to the Sipachov dynasty, there is a succession of anomalous Teutonic non-sons: Gottfried, Oswald, and Günther. Each time Sipachov rages and storms, threatening violence and murder and suicide; but after a while his oral outburst subsides, followed by an aftermath of remorse and efforts to make amends. Meanwhile, the quietly persistent women make no concessions. "Yes, we are stubborn Germans," one of them says, "and we have the bad habit of pursuing a matter through to the end."

Fifteen years later, on a visit to Dresden, the narrator learns of the final ironies in the ultra-Russian career of Ivan Nikitich Sipachov. His wife Lina had died, on her deathbed bequeathing him to the tender mercies of her equally Germanic and even stronger-willed cousin, Aurora, whom he dutifully married. The marriage was illegal in Russia, however, and so at Aurora's insistence Sipachov had retired from the Navy (as a rear admiral) and moved to Dresden. There he had died, after begetting three daughters to match the three sons he had by Lina. He was buried in a German Protestant cemetery; and his six sons and daughters, despite their Slavic surname and their blood bonds with Kaluga, have lost all traces of Russianness and become devoted citizens of the Reich.

"Kolyvan Husband" is much inferior to "Iron Will" both as a work of art and as a representation of national types. Its ambiguities are neutralizing rather than energizing, and the role of the narrator is unsatisfactory, both ideologically and technically. The narrator is purely a spectator, and his lack of motivated connection with the action causes difficulties in the narration, requiring much implausible eavesdropping and confusion in characterization.

Ostensibly repudiating Sipachov's strident nationalism (of word, not deed), the narrator repeatedly tells us how charming and beautiful and virtuous the German girls are and how noble their mother and their grandmother. But there is a glaring discrepancy between these assertions and the women's behavior. In action these lovely Teutonic maidens and matrons are shown as quite insufferable—self-righteous, arrogant, unforgiving, and deceitful. Thus the narrator's professed feelings seem out of keeping with his narrative material, and this disharmony is not explained or utilized in any way.

Officially and doctrinally, Leskov opposed national exclusiveness and advocated tolerance toward all nations and toward national minorities in particular; but on the emotional plane, Leskov disliked Germans. As a result, feelings and doctrine work at cross purposes in the story. In the characterizations of the German women, the attractiveness so insistently asserted by the narrator is never made believable, because the author does not believe in it himself. Nor is it made comprehensible why Sipachov, passive as he is, should twice allow himself to be maneuvered into marriage to a castrating prig. The element of ironic amusement in our attitude toward Sipachov has nothing to match it in our response to the women. There is nothing amusing about them, and no poetic justice in their grim conquest of their Russian male victim. Finally, our ideological response is confused. What was apparently intended as a plea for tolerance and a camouflaged attack on the policy of Russification of the Baltic area has the opposite effect: we feel sympathy for the basically warmhearted, if ineffectual Sipachov and anger at the unyielding will to power of the German females. The story has been read by some Soviet commentators as an anti-German, nationalist tract, which would surely have shocked Leskov.[14]

&23&

Russia's Spiritual Janitor

Despite the increasingly Protestant coloration of his religious views, Leskov was not ready, in the later seventies, to make a public break with Orthodoxy. He still hoped he could use his artistic talent to awaken the church from within, exposing to view its many problems and faults; then the moral pressure of public opinion would become irresistible and reform inevitable. The censorship seemed an insurmountable obstacle to this program, but the threat of the censor's blue pencil seemed only to stimulate Leskov's ingenuity and enhance his artistic powers. And so he appointed himself Russia's spiritual janitor, assigned, as he later put it in a letter to Tolstoy, to "sweep the rubbish from the temple."[1] The result was a series of satirical articles and stories culminating in the underappreciated masterpiece entitled *The Little Things in a Bishop's Life*.

An earlier, and the most substantial, nonfictional item in this series is the treatise entitled *A High-Society Schism*, first published serially in the *Orthodox Review* and then as a separate book.[2] Hitherto this work has been considered chiefly in terms of its manifest content: to all appearances it is a pro-Orthodox attack on a Protestant heresy, and it appeared in a respectably official, Orthodox magazine with an Orthodox imprimatur. Its subject—one that indeed fascinated Leskov —is presumably conveyed by the subtitle, *Lord Radstock, His Doctrine and Sermon*. It is a detailed examination of the life, personality, and religious ideas of the heterodox British lord who stirred Petersburg society in the mid-seventies with his evangelical preaching. Nevertheless, it is now clear that the "high-society schism" is as much a disguise as a subject. The patent censure of the schism conceals a criticism of Orthodoxy.

In the winter of 1874, Granville Augustus William Waldegrave, the third Baron Radstock (1833-1913), appeared in Petersburg and began preaching his version of the Gospel in high-society salons. This version was not aristocratic, nor was it theologically sophisticated. Its inspiration was plebeian: on a visit to the United States in 1859, Radstock had been impressed by the standard techniques of American advertising—the endless repetition of a few simple formulas, addressed not to the mind but to the unconscious. Like many American revivalist preachers, he sought to apply this method to Christian propagandizing, and with considerable success. The British blueblood, a former army officer with no seminary training, became the Billy Graham of his day, a box-office star in many countries with his simple Christian advocacy. He preached a strong emphasis on faith over works; the notion that one could earn salvation was a satanically prideful claim. The core of his message was the Redemption: God so loved the world that he gave his only begotten Son to redeem it; provided we believe, that love and that sacrifice have assured our salvation. Christians should put aside their accumulated ecclesiastical differences, abandon vain efforts to reason too much about religion, and in their love for one another try to emulate God's love for them.[3]

Lord Radstock came to Russia several times between 1874 and 1878. He became a major attraction in Petersburg society and made a number of conversions among aristocratic ladies. Several prominent Russian noblemen also became his disciples, including a former minister, Count Aleksei Bobrinskoy, and Count Modest Korf, son of a distinguished member of the Council of State. One of Radstock's most enthusiastic converts was Vasily Pashkov, a wealthy retired Guards officer, who proceeded to devote great energy and considerable means to the propagation of Radstock's teachings among the peasants on his estates. As a result of these efforts "Pashkovism" (the name "Radstock" did not survive the "sinking" of this *Kulturgut* into the lower classes) eventually became an authentic folk religion, one of the many heretical sects that flourished among the Russian masses, though persecuted by the government. By the twentieth century the *pashkovtsy* had merged with the Baptists.[4]

As a phenomenon of upper-class Russian intellectual life in the seventies, Radstockism had noteworthy literary repercussions. Dostoevsky went to hear Radstock preach and wrote two articles about him in his *Diary of a Writer.*[5] He was unimpressed: "I did not find anything special in him: he spoke neither especially cleverly nor especially dully." Dostoevsky attributed Radstock's successes to the deracination of the Russian upper classes, their separation from the sacred "soil" in which lay the deep Orthodox roots of the Russian people. To separate Christianity from the church, Dostoevsky felt, was like trying to carry a precious liquid without a vessel: it is soon spilled on the ground and lost.[6] Likewise Lev Tolstoy, despite his isolation at Yasnaya Polyana, did not remain unaffected by Radstockism. Then in the early stages of the religious crisis he externalized as that of Konstantin Lyovin in *Anna Karenina*, Tolstoy heard about Radstock from acquaintances. Among these were Count Bobrinskoy, who visited him in February 1876, full of his new faith. Though Tolstoy was impressed by the faith itself, as a psychological phenomenon and a source of obvious happiness to Bobrinskoy, he could not share it, either intellectually or emotionally. Even earlier, Tolstoy had learned through a mutual friend that his old love Maria Peiker was undertaking to bring Radstock's message to the Russian peasant masses in a magazine called *The Russian Workman*. As Leskov was to do publicly,[7] Tolstoy wrote privately a substantial critique of Mme Peiker's magazine, though not her religion.[8] But he basically disliked her religion too: it smelled of Petersburg drawing rooms, and he satirized it harshly in *Anna Karenina*.[9]

But the most substantial Russian literary response to Radstock was Leskov's. Like Dostoevsky, Leskov was acquainted with one of Radstock's devoted Russian followers, Yulia Denisovna Zasetskaya, a daughter of Denis Davydov, the poet and guerilla hero of the war of 1812. In 1876, on the verge of his final separation from Katerina Bubnova, Leskov took his son Andrei and, much to Andrei's displeasure, spent the summer alone with him at a country house in Finland owned by Mme Zasetskaya. She was not there, but through correspondence Leskov craftily exploited her as a source of information about Radstock (whom she had known earlier in England) and his teachings. The result of these researches was *A High-Society Schism*.[10]

One might have expected Leskov to welcome, at least covertly, the advent in Petersburg of a Protestant Lord Apostle, but this Protestantism had little appeal for him. The crudity, the low intellectual level of Radstock's preaching, his American technique of the gut appeal repelled Leskov. As an amateur of church history and a connoisseur of the Bible, Leskov set high intellectual standards for those who presumed to interpret God's word, especially to an educated audience. He found Radstock intellectually wanting on every count: uninformed about church history, ignorant of contemporary religious thought, shaky in his knowledge of Scripture, uninterested in the biblical scholarship that was making such enormous strides in the nineteenth century. In short, he was a publicity man, not a thinker.

As a literary artist, Leskov found fault with Radstock on aesthetic grounds. "All kinds of literature are good except the dull kind" was one of Leskov's favorite sayings. Radstock, he felt, was dull. Life in Petersburg was not very exciting in 1876, "but all the same this lord, with his colorless language, his use of a fair barker's tricks, his huge boots with which he stamps like a horse with its hoofs, is really not the best of entertainments."[11] There were better Protestant preachers in circulation, some resident in Petersburg: Hermann Dalton, pastor of the German Reformed Church and a prolific author on religious subjects, and Adolf Masing, pastor of another German evangelical church, who preached in Russian.[12] There were good Orthodox preachers too, among whom Leskov particularly praises Archpriest Ivan Polisadov, the religious instructor at the *gymnasium* of the Imperial Philanthropic Society. He also mentions the "brilliant Father Hyacinthe," whom he may have heard preach in Paris.[13] Leskov claims that even the Old Believer peasant preacher Ivan Ivanovich Androsov had more style than Radstock. In short, according to Leskov, the Lord Apostle was born to the manor but not the manner. He had no talent.

Leskov credits Radstock with good intentions and admires his Christian spirit. As William Edgerton has suggested (perhaps overstating the case a little), by the end of *A High-Society Schism* Radstock's portrait is almost ready to be hung in Leskov's gallery of the quixotic righteous—at one point he is explicitly compared to the visionary knight.[14] Leskov concedes that Radstock's moral influence was good; he managed to arouse religious feelings in people who had never experienced them before. Leskov thought he had played fair with Radstock in *A High-Society Schism,* giving him every credit he deserved. The anger with which many Radstockites, including Mme Zasetskaya, reacted to his book was therefore, he insisted, quite undeserved. It is a familiar note in Leskov's career.

The real issue, however, was not Leskov's portrait of Radstock; his basic target lay elsewhere. Radstockism was a Petersburg fad; in the long run, the chief vehicle of Russian spirituality was still the Orthodox church. The fact that Radstock could create a stir was a sign that something was lacking in that church. Leskov's investigation and critique of Radstockism was thus by implication an investigation and critique of Orthodoxy.

How was it, he asked, that such a fine woman as Yulia Zasetskaya, with a deeply religious nature, could desert the church of her fathers and follow Radstock? The answer was that, although nominally Orthodox, she had imbibed in her childhood the universal upper-class contempt for the clergy. She had seen her impatient father disdainfully bribe a priest to speed up a long-winded service in their house. How could an educated person seek spiritual guidance from a mindless and grubby purveyor of superstition like the average Russian *pop*, clad in a grease-spotted cassock and smelling of vodka?

By thus appearing to analyze the motives for defection from Orthodoxy, Leskov was able to make the *Orthodox Review* print harsh judgments about the national church, which he then affected to refute. The Russian church was "ritualistic and lifeless," the incipient Radstockities had concluded. It had been unable to resist the tide of atheism engulfing the educated classes. Not only did it lack intellectual resources, but it was constantly tempted to resort to the secular arm, defending itself by force rather than idea or spirit, and in the process corrupting itself and alienating its friends. Hinting at the hated Ober-Procurator of the Holy Synod, Count Dmitry Tolstoy—and probably at most of the leading bishops as well—Leskov describes the church as led by men "who stand only for the external side of religion and have no scruples about employing threats and punishments" (p. 98). Few were the priests who could converse on equal terms with educated people, though there were some noble exceptions to this rule, a few of whom Leskov carefully mentions.[15]

Further, the Russian church was shamefully neglectful of its responsibility to provide the faithful with moral instruction. Sermons of any kind were rare, and good ones rarer. Even its prayers had little meaning for most Russians, including well-educated people, since they were recited in an archaic foreign language (Church Slavonic). In an appendix to *A High Society Schism*, as a substitute for these unintelligible Slavonic prayers, Leskov slyly offered his translations into Russian of the prayers of Eugène Bersier, a French *Protestant* minister.

Finally, the Russian Orthodox Church, in Leskov's opinion, had been a disgracefully poor agency for eleemosynary activities. He disapproved of the extravagant "charity" balls of high society: "Can mankind really have sunk so low that it can do good deeds only with the lure of pleasures?" (p. 98). Furthermore, the Russian church, like the English, had been infected by the Mrs. Jellyby-syndrome: with desperate needs at home, charitable donations were being shipped far off to support fashionable causes, such as that of the oppressed Orthodox in the Balkans.

Nevertheless, in his conclusion Leskov appears to hold out hope for the church—on the condition that it undertake far-reaching reforms. Most of all, it must emerge from its bureaucratic cocoon. It must take advantage of the human resources available to it, engaging the active participation of the lay faithful, particularly from the educated classes.

"Those of our educated people who have the rare good fortune not to lose, as a result of their acquisition of knowledge, their faith in the saving power of the Christian religion, for the time being only want the opportunity to receive vital instruction in the churches and to participate directly in parish activities" (p. 106). "The insufficiency of close and vital communion [in Orthodoxy] between the clergy and the laity," Leskov maintains, "is neither necessary nor eternal; it is the artificial product," he hints darkly, "of conditions alien to the Church," (p. 106). In the reformed Orthodoxy Leskov envisions "the preaching of the Gospel during church services will be revived and strengthened, and Christian charity will be practiced within the church community, i.e., in one's own parish" (p. 107).

Leskov's image of a renovated Orthodoxy, however skillfully camouflaged, is thoroughly Protestantized. Not a word about sacraments; not a word about the church as man's intercessor with God; not a word about the apostolic succession of the clergy. Leskov's ideal church is an evangelical, teaching, preaching, praying, alms-giving community of the faithful, at last freed, he implies, from its long enslavement to the state. And if such a transformation of Orthodoxy is not carried out, Leskov warns, there will be not a high-society schism, but a real schism; and the responsibility will not lie on such as Lord Radstock and his Russian followers, but on "those who postpone reforms in the Church"—by implication, the hierarchy, the Synod, the ober-procurator, and the government, including the emperor.

Thus for a few more years Leskov intermittently warmed to the hope that renovation of the Orthodox church was possible. He knew there were thoughtful, vigorous, and reform-minded men among the clergy; an alliance between the progressive clergy and the progressive laity might rescue the church from stagnation. And one man, whom Leskov had always admired, had the power to make reforms real, including reform of the church. This was the tsar, Alexander II, then moving into the second "reform" period of his reign. Perhaps the heart of the Orthodox tsar could be moved to action by the cry of literature.

If these were Leskov's hopes (he could not express them openly in print), they were soon dashed. In 1880 Alexander at last relieved Dmitry Tolstoy of his position as ober-procurator of the Holy Synod, only to replace him by a man whose views were even more conservative. This new ober-procurator, Konstantin Pobedonostsev, to use Aleksandr Blok's image, was to cast the "dark shadow of his gigantic wings" over Russia and her long-suffering church for twenty-five years, until 1905, a whole decade after Leskov's death. As long as

"Lampadonostsev" (as Leskov invariably called him)[16] ruled, there was no hope for church reform, and Leskov's was a voice crying in the wilderness. The final blow was struck when, in 1881, the tsar liberator was forcibly removed from the scene, to be replaced by his stolid, frightened, much less intelligent son. As the reactionary tenor of the new reign became palpable, Leskov cast aside his last, lingering hopes for Russian Orthodoxy.

But before all these catastrophes, in the last years of Alexander II's reign, Leskov determined to have one more go at the church with his spiritual broom.

The camouflaged critique of Orthodoxy in *A High-Society Schism* was tangential to the main subject of the book. Less perceptive readers may not have recognized Leskov's true target. Furthermore, *A High-Society Schism*, as a nonfictional treatise on a contemporary religious movement, had limited appeal, being of interest mainly to the few Russian intellectuals who concerned themselves with religious matters. Although it was more successful than Leskov probably anticipated—it went through two book editions in a single year—it left Leskov with a feeling of incompleteness. The social philosopher in him had more to say about Orthodoxy, and to render the message accessible to a larger public was the task of Leskov the artist. He had accumulated a rich store of vivid church material crying out for exploitation, from which he produced his brilliant satire, *The Little Things in a Bishop's Life.*

The journalistic dimension of *Little Things* is underscored by its mode of publication. With the prestigious literary reviews closed to him, Leskov turned to the daily newspapers. Newspapers were the first mass media, read by far more people than literary reviews; and for a writer who seriously believed in the power of literature to change men and society, they presented a great opportunity. Unfortunately, the pay was bad for a writer who worked slowly and took pains with his style. But Leskov had little choice. *The Little Things in a Bishop's Life: Pictures from Nature* was first serialized in the newspaper *News and Stock-Exchange Gazette* in thirteen scattered numbers in the latter part of 1878.[17] It was Leskov's last great literary confrontation with Orthodoxy.

Leskov's strategy in *Little Things* is to take off from a current topic of journalistic debate, thus firmly basing his art in the real world. Assuming an ostensibly nonpolemical air of benign reasonableness, in these semifictional "arguments" Leskov professes to offer a broader, more balanced view of his subject than the short-memoried newspaper writer could do. His topic was church administration, a subject widely discussed in the press during 1878 in connection with proposed reforms. The papers, relatively bold in this period of relaxed censorship, had carried a number of revealing stories about Orthodox bishops that tended to show those exalted personages (they were officially addressed as *vaše preosvjaščenstvo*, "your most consecratedness") as anything but paragons of Christian virtue. They were comic in their self-indulgent, pompous eccentricities, and frequently petty despots in their ecclesiastical domains, haughtily unresponsive to public opinion.

These newspaper stories provided Leskov with his opening gambit. Were the bishops really as bad as they were portrayed? In his preface, Leskov slyly professes to be writing *in defense* (his italics) of the bishops, though not in the manner of those "narrow and one-sided people who consider any discussion of bishops an offense to their dignity," that is, the right-wing, pro-Orthodox publicists. If the bishops have faults, Leskov insists, the blame lies on society itself, for the situation in which it has placed them.

Valid as this point may have been, in large part Leskov's ostensible defense is a ruse. His covert intent was to attack the very principle of ecclesiastical hierarchy—a system in conflict, Leskov believed (as did most radical Protestants), with the basic egalitarianism of Christian doctrine. If all men are equal in the eyes of God, what need have God's earthly representatives for the trappings of majesty? Indeed, has Christianity any real need for such things as bishops? These questions, of course, are more implied than spelled out; but it is hard to see how their implications could be missed.

Leskov's artistic problem, as always, was concretization—the specific illustrations that give credibility to his abstract idea. Here the concrete "little things" in bishops' lives have a satirical function as well, that of belittling, showing that beneath their regalia the bishops are ordinary human beings like the rest of us. Leskov spelled out his intentions in a letter to Mme Peiker: "The book must be understood *correctly*. Its aim is to cut through the pomp and show that they [the bishops] are the most ordinary mortals, who sneeze and get constipated and need 'instrumental treatment.' "[18]

Leskov's concrete material consists of a string of anecdotes, bishop stories accumulated during his long career as a clergy-watcher. In his use of seemingly trivial anecdotal material, Leskov tries to let his readers in on the secret. The accent on "little" things is partly a camouflage for deceiving censors; it is also a means for discovering and thinking concretely about big things:

> those little things of life in which a man most of all is revealed as a living man and not a stand-in for a registry cipher. (6:535)

> Most [bishops] are known only from their dry, official side, while a man, as we all know, is *best revealed in little things* (6:502; Leskov's italics).

In *The Little Things in a Bishop's Life* Leskov's skill as an anecdotist —he uses the word himself (6:524)—is unsurpassed. He tells these little stories with exactly the right mixture of descriptive and narrative detail, of foreshadowing, authorial commentary, and condensation alternating with retardation. Leskov's contemporaries could not help feeling the force of his talent. But accustomed as they were to big chords and dazzling cadenzas, they found it hard to imagine that an art of little things could be a major art. "From the author of *Cathedral Folk* [. . .] we have the right to expect [. . .] that he should not fritter himself away on 'little things,' but should give us a series of major scenes and types," wrote one reviewer.[19] He had missed the point: "littleness" was the essence of the matter.

Although arithmetically the good and bad bishops in *Little Things* are quite evenly balanced, the manner and order of their presentation assures a negative overall response. Long before we catch a glimpse of a good bishop, we are full of vivid impressions of bad ones. The first bishop we encounter is the first one Leskov learned about in real life, Bishop Nicodemus of Oryol, who had delivered up Leskov's cousin, the son of his father's sister Pelageya, to a twenty-five-year term of military service. Enraged by this act, Leskov's father, then still the fearless detective, had "in his [Nicodemus's] own episcopal residence had it out with him very sternly" (6:399). Whether this "having it out" amounted to anything more than a volley of abuse is not clear, nor the fate of the recruit cousin—one never hears of him again in this or any other of Leskov's "memoirs." But the impression of the bishop's cruelty and tyranny is underscored at the outset of *Little Things*—and symbolized by the black color of the black clergy to which he belonged: "In our [Leskov's parents'] house the black clergy in general were not liked, and the bishops in particular. I was simply afraid of them, probably because I long remembered my father's fearful anger at Nicodemus and the frightening assertion of my nurse that the bishops crucified Christ. Christ I had been taught to love from childhood" (6:399-400). Thus before launching into his first major anecdote, Leskov has already generalized a negative response to the black clergy as a whole, and suggested, by quoting a misinformed popular superstition, a basic opposition between the Orthodox bishops and Christ. The nurse's belief may turn out to be symbolically true.

This emotional foundation is reinforced by the first of Leskov's full-length bishop portraits, again a sharply negative one, Smaragdus of Oryol. If Nicodemus was the first bishop Leskov heard of in his Oryol childhood, Smaragdus was the first he actually saw.[20] Smaragdus is our first developed image of episcopal pomposity and tyranny. These qualities are demonstrated in three types of relationships—with the civil authorities, with the educated lay public, and with the lower clergy

Smaragdus' counterpart in the civil hierarchy is the governor of Oryol Province, Prince Pyotr Trubetskoy, another of Leskov's favorite bugbears.[21] Trubetskoy was an even more capricious despot than his ecclesiastical colleague, although his character is not so fully illustrated in *Little Things* as in his other appearances in Leskov's corpus. As Leskov presents them, Trubetskoy and Smaragdus were a match for each other. For years they carried on petty warfare, greatly amusing the Oryol public with their antics. Trubetskoy, according to Leskov, fought like a rooster, ruffling up his feathers and pecking away furiously at anything in sight; Smaragdus fought in capric style, restraining his anger and cunningly waiting for an opening in his enemy's defenses.

This practice of associating human characters with animals is a well-established technique of satire, one Leskov might have learned from Gogol. In this zoomorphic tradition, the skirmishes in the Trubetskoy-Smaragdus war were reported to the Oryol public, Leskov tells us, by means of a permanent puppet display (which he calls "the first glimmer of a free press" in Oryol; 6:407): a goat and a rooster were shown in various stages of mortal combat, their positions ingeniously reflecting the blows and counterblows the bishop and the governor dealt one another.

Besides its function of debasing the two combative potentates, this anecdote, in its "little" way, adumbrates the big question of church-state relations. Although the two antagonists appear as equals, it is significant that the bishop is the more circumspect of the two warriors. In a church-state showdown in Russia, the state almost always proves stronger; and even a bishop must watch his step. Leskov vehemently denies (but reports) the tale, ascribed to Smaradgus' career variously in Oryol, Saratov, and Ryazan, that the bishop "had gone on foot to the police station in procession with banners and to the ringing of church bells to visit a priest who had been arrested by the night patrol [for violation of curfew] on orders from Prince Trubetskoy, while that priest was taking the sacrament to a sick person" (6:400-401). This fantasy of a Russian Orthodox bishop dramatically defying the Russian state in defense of liberty and justice was an electrifying one: what power for good the church could exert if it only would! But it was only a fantasy. Smaragdus, Leskov assures us, never did any such thing. In his conflict with Trubetskoy nothing more was at stake than petty vanities and jealousies.[22]

In the Smaragdus story the representative of the educated lay public, a symbolic stand-in for the author, is Major Aleksandr Schultz, a retired officer living in Oryol. Schultz—whose middle name is Khristianovich—is the "publisher" of Oryol's first uncensored newspaper; he is the puppeteer behind the rooster-goat display. Though apparently Orthodox himself, despite his German name, and a friend of the Slavophile Kireevsky family, Schultz is described as a better Christian than all "Orthodox Oryol Christendom." Above all, he practiced what was for Leskov the essential Christian virtue—practical charity, giving money (he was the only man in Orthodox Oryol Christendom who gave more than pennies) and using his influence for such purposes as getting state scholarships for orphans.

The contrast between Schultz's secular Christianness and Smaragdus' Orthodox un-Christianness is made explicit. Schultz's link to the author is his role as a "journalist," a journalist of a Leskovian stamp —sly, adroit, tongue-in-cheek. Leskov's characterization of Schultz's manner of mocking the "many vulgarities and savage displays of tyrannical self-indulgence of those 'good old days' " is an excellent description of his own technique for needling despotism and pomposity in high places: "Schultz's subtle and mocking humor was directed mostly at local luminaries, but directed with such adroitness and apparent naiveté that no one dared think of retaliating" (6:403).

The concluding anecdote on Smaragdus shows him at his tyrannical worst, in his relations with the lower clergy. To set the stage for this encounter Leskov employs a device he was to use on several other bad bishops: he strips "his most consecratedness" of his sacerdotal robes, revealing that the naked body underneath is distinguished from those of other middle-aged human males only by its bloated proportions,

341

the product of too much eating and too little exercise. Like Gogol, Leskov directs attention to the less respectable areas of the episcopal anatomy, particularly the lower reaches of the digestive tract. These anal associations are elaborately developed later in the case of Porphyrius, suffragan bishop of Kiev, who summoned Leskov's brother Aleksei, a gynecologist, and asked Aleksei to use his obstetrical instruments to relieve him of his constipation and gas pains; his agony alleviated, the grateful bishop pleaded that a medical dissertation should be written on "episcopal constipation." Smaragdus too suffers from "severe attacks apparently of a hemorrhoidal nature" (6:414).

These and other allusions to the anal region raised the Victorian hackles of some of Leskov's contemporaries, notably Ivan Aksakov, who rebuked the author for "vulgarity," "mauvais goût," and "mauvais genre," urging him to take his pen out of the gutter and follow Schiller up into "die schöne Regionen."[23] A sophisticated modern critic, Leonid Grossman, has expressed similar disapproval of Leskov's alleged bad taste.[24] But as Chekhov pointed out in answering a similar criticism, manure plays a basic functional role in an agricultural landscape.[25] Leskov's alleged coprophilia in Little Things performs a valid artistic function, showing symbolically that bishops are as much bound as any of us by the mundane requirements of our animal nature. In no sense does he relish coarseness for its own sake.

Besides his hemorrhoids, Smaragdus also suffers from "pressure between the wings." Concerning this curious anatomical designation Leskov comments ironically, "the episcopal interalium [mežudukrylie] is located on the back, in the area where ordinary mortals have shoulder blades" (6:414)—thus also ridiculing the age-old monastic claim to angelic rank. Smaragdus' doctor prescribes exercise as the remedy for his "interalic" pains, thus providing the basis for Leskov's next anecdote.

Orthodox bishops had absolute authority in disciplinary cases concerning the lower clergy. Erring priests, deacons, and subdeacons had to appear before their mitred judges and humbly accept the penances and punishments meted out to them. Smaragdus' practice was to hold such persons under arrest without bail, as it were, waiting around his consistory for months and even years until he deigned to consider their cases. No provision was made for their maintenance during this period, and the already poor village clergy were soon reduced to destitution. Leskov's specimen is a village subdeacon (d'jačok) named Lukyan, who was hauled before the bishop's court after an unfortunate amorous escapade. Wretchedly poor, Lukyan, during his long months

of waiting for episcopal justice, had nothing to eat but wild horseradish, a diet, Leskov comments, that would have done in "not only the
most muscular German, but even the hardiest of the mighty ancient
Russian heroes." Lukyan, however, survived.

Smaragdus had chosen wood-sawing as his mode of therapeutic
exertion. His practice was to man one end of a two-man saw, the other
being held by one of the many clerical underlings clustered around his
office, including persons whose cases were *sub judice*. To become the
bishop's sawing partner was a recognized means of advancing one's
case through the costive channels of episcopal justice: it meant that
one might at last be noticed. But Lukyan had an even more subtle
plan. First, he managed to wangle an appointment as the bishop's co-
sawyer. Then he selected the thickest, knottiest logs he could find and
placed them on the sawhorse. The effort of cutting such monsters was
more than Smaragdus had bargained for, but his pride would not allow him to lay down his saw until the job was finished. His anger,
however, mounted in proportion to his fatigue, especially since he
correctly perceived an element of mockery in the selection of the logs.
After the second such episode the good prelate's ire boiled over, and
he cracked the deacon's head with his crutch.

This blow was exactly what Lukyan wanted. As he had been told,
following one of these outbursts of violence the bishop's temper was
briefly softened, and he was sometimes moved to show mercy toward
his victim. The scheme worked. The next day Smaragdus called for
Lukyan's case and then dismissed him, with no other punishment than
the blow he had already received from the bishop's consecrated hands.
(This ironic variant on the traditional episcopal prerogative of "laying
on of hands" is carried further in *Little Things*, when the learned Innocent, bishop of Crimea, punishes an erring lay brother by "laying on"
not only his hands, but his feet as well.) Does this incident not teach
us, Leskov ironically concludes, that "we must never despair of the
clemency of Russian bishops"? "Although some of them may be wont
to show wrath, even this wrathfulness is at times subject to mitigation" (6:418).

Smaragdus' Oryol is a microcosm of Leskov's archetypal "Nicolaitan" world (Smaragdus reigned in Oryol from 1844 to 1858)—a world
of *proizvol*: tyranny, physical violence, absence of legal rights or
means for the redress of grievances, despotism mitigated only by an
underling's skill at manipulating the quirks in his master's character.
In all this the church faithfully reflected the spirit of the age.

The reverse image of these despotic prelates would be Leskov's ideal of a good bishop. The antithesis of tyranny and pomposity is gentleness, kindliness, and simplicity—qualities sometimes possessed by Russian bishops, as Leskov shows. But in his presentation the good bishops are good in spite of their rank; their goodness is part of their basic personalities, which have resisted the corruption of power.

Leskov again invokes the figure of Metropolitan Philaret (Amfiteatrov) of Kiev, characterized at length in "Episcopal Justice": a lovable old soul, genially tolerant of human foibles, incapable of harshness to anyone. Yet Philaret's lovability does admit and perhaps require condescension on our part. The old man is childish, sublimely naive. In one of Leskov's anecdotes he is associated directly with children (he secretly helps some schoolboys steal fruit from his own garden), and he is compared with them in another (trying to frighten a drunken and roistering deacon, the metropolitan banged his hand on his desk, hurting his finger, which he then "blew on like a child").

In presenting his positive episcopal ideal, Leskov executes two clever maneuvers. First, he draws a contrast (suggested earlier in "At the Edge of the World") between the simplicity and humility of true Russian Orthodoxy and the pompous "Byzantinism" of the Greeks, the latter foolishly idealized by some misguided Russians. Thus the powerful force of national pride is identified with the cause of ecclesiastical democracy, and a wedge is driven into the episcopacy: "Casting aside Byzantine formalism, which was forcibly imposed on them and never suited them, they [the good bishops] of their own accord seek to *simplify themselves in the Russian way* [*oprostit'sja po-russki*] and become men of the people, with whom it will at least be pleasanter to await some *real* measures designed to slake our spiritual thirst and restore the life-giving spirit to the worn-out faith of the Russians" (6:439; Leskov's italics). If the bishops stepped down from their thrones, gave up their four-horse carriages, and *walked* among men, they would not only get over their chronic constipation, as Bishop Porphyrius wistfully points out, but "perhaps might teach people something good and restrain them and advise them. Otherwise, what's the use of us?" (6:445). Merely to dispense "blessings," Leskov and some of his good bishops argue, is useless, especially if the act of benediction is superstitiously believed to possess magic power ("grace"). The church's proper job is to *teach*, not to traffic in efforts to manipulate the divine will.

Leskov's second sly maneuver, in presenting his positive ideal, is employed in his stories about Bishop Neophytus of Perm.[26] The trick here is sleight-of-hand reversal: the evils of "Byzantinism" are associated with a *layman*, a wealthy landowner enamored of Orthodox ceremonials, while the antiritualist, the simplifying "protestant," is the Orthodox bishop himself. The effect is to underscore the point that Byzantinism is alien to the Russian spirit, an artificial imposition repudiated by the better elements in the Russian higher clergy. This landowner, in Leskov's language, is a *pravoslavist*, an "Orthodoxist"—in other words, not a Christian. He maintains a sumptuously decorated village church where punctilious services are conducted by disciplined priests, services sometimes attended *"by no one at all"* (Leskov's italics). Such soulless services even the clergy call inhuman.

Expecting a visit to his estate from Archbishop Neophytus, the pious gentleman has planned a series of welcoming solemnities. Neophytus brushes aside all the folderol, specifically requests and takes delight in some purely secular music performed by his host's children, and for his bedtime reading chooses *Notes of the Fatherland*, with a story by Shchedrin, rather than *The Pilgrim* or *The Orthodox Colloquist*. In general, this bishop is an attractive human being, responsive, intelligent, endowed with a keen sense of humor and, best of all, a sense of natural human values.

Most of the other good bishops in Leskov's roster are shown from a more restricted point of view than Neophytus and Philaret, usually as they respond to a particular problem. As the touchstone of their humanity (as opposed to their Orthodoxy) Leskov focuses several times on an issue close to his heart, the church's function as the regulator of sexual relations. This question was very much in the air in the late 1870s, as *Anna Karenina* shows. The possibility of amending the harsh laws on marriage and divorce had been raised in the Synod by the ober-procurator, Dmitry Tolstoy; but the majority of its episcopal members opposed any changes, and eventually the matter was dropped—a "fiasco," Leskov calls it. The rigidity of the bishops, Leskov asserts, helped alienate many otherwise naturally religious people from the church. At the same time Leskov shows some understanding of the bishops' position: they felt they had neither right nor power to alter age-old canon laws sanctioned by tradition and, they believed, by divine authority.

As the state's agent in the sphere of marital relations, the church was empowered to legislate and to enforce its laws, at least on all the legally Orthodox inhabitants of the empire (and anyone with an Orthodox parent was legally Orthodox). These laws included several relics of medieval rigor no longer supported by public opinion: the severe limitations on divorce, the injunction forbidding remarriage of widowed priests, the rule prohibiting the marriage of first cousins or of a widow or widower to his or her late spouse's sister or brother.

Leskov offers illustrations of the last two situations, his manner of presentation clearly indicating his strong disapproval of the church's rules. In both cases the solution of the problem is offered by a good bishop, who, though discreetly and unofficially, advises evasion of the law. It augured ill for the church, Leskov implies, that as an institution it could not bend to meet legitimate human needs, thus forcing otherwise moral Christians either to leave its fold or to resort to illegal subterfuges. Certain bishops could and did seek ways to meet those needs, but they could do so only by acting counter to their official responsibilities.

In themselves such cases may seem "little things." But there is grave danger to the moral order of a community when official morality diverges too widely from public belief and practice. The inevitable results are, first, a black market in the forbidden goods or services and, second, corruption and cynicism among the enforcers. What can be said of the moral condition of a church when one of its *good* bishops says, " 'I don't know where, but I've heard more than once that there are priests who for 500 rubles will marry you not only to your sister-in-law, but even to your mother!' " (6:512) and then *recommends* that his suppliant resort precisely to such a priest?

If such a bishop, however humane, appears dangerously cynical in his attitude toward the law, in "Russian Cryptomatrimony," published as a supplement in the 1880 edition of *Little Things,* cynicism and corruption in the church are carried to greater extremes. Here the "author" (specifically identified as "the author of 'Deacon Akhilka' ") is regaled by a member of the white clergy, an archpriest rich in "underground" experiences, with a long series of tales of the ecclesiastical black market in illegal marriages. The ultimate in symbolic cynicism seems to be reached when a petitioner is told that the most convenient time and place for negotiating a covert deal with a priest is *within the sanctuary* after the liturgy: " 'If there is anything a bit dubious, they always discuss it inside the sanctuary, because that's their kingdom' " (6:606). In a world where vital human needs are thwarted by lifeless laws, a black market becomes not a necessary evil, but a positive good: "These days even the most reckless 'marrying padres' are also in their way necessary and useful [the archpriest argues]. I mean it: useful. In a big enterprise there's a use for everything. And although in principle I don't approve of their method of sewing without stitches, I know that even in that way they did good to many people" (6:612).

The Orthodox church, as Leskov represents it, was thus almost up-side-down morally: its good bishops recommend violations of canon law, its good priests condone all sorts of chicanery, and its "useful" priests traffic in fake marriages within Orthodox sanctuaries. This picture of moral chaos is unambiguously revealed in another supplement to *Little Things,* "Diocesan Justice," an appalling compilation, assembled by Leskov over several years from the legal columns of the *Novgorod Diocesan News,* of the offenses with which clergymen had been charged before the bishop's court. The enormity of the offenses—endless cases of drunkenness, drunken misbehavior in church, embezzlement of church funds, and even an ironic instance of "iconoclasm" (an icon was apparently broken over a wife's head during a marital brawl) —is matched only by the legal irregularities and arbitrariness of the diocesan judicial system.

The Orthodox church, Leskov says in his conclusion, is "in a state resembling decay or, to put it more accurately, *crisis,* a crisis, to be sure, affecting all ecclesiastical Christianity" (6:538; Leskov's italics). The devout Christian would seem to have little recourse but to flee from "this shameful sight" into the peace of the *shtunda* (6:463), to abandon Orthodoxy for Protestantism. Though he never identified himself with the shtundists or any other Protestant sect (unless one counts Tolstoyanism), that is what Leskov had done: he had abandoned Orthodoxy for Protestantism.

Leskov's contemporaries, and posterity as well, have mostly judged *The Little Things in a Bishop's Life* as a treatise, an ideological document. Right-wing and pro-Orthodox spokesman were indignant. The bishops rose to their own defense, publishing several attacks on Leskov, mostly on grounds of general disrespectfulness of tone or of factual inaccuracies.[27] They did not debate with him publicly about the larger questions he had raised. Leskov deftly counterattacked, needling Bishop Nicanorus for his "amazingly bad style."[28] A Perm archpriest named Yevgeny Popov wrote that Leskov's disrespect for bishops was a manifestation of the generally deplorable state of morals in the modern age, with its predilection for "robbing and shooting."[29] At this Leskov exclaimed mordantly, "Yes, yes, that is actually what is written there: you cannot say that bishops may have fits of caprice or even suffer from catarrh of the stomach without sharing in the general immorality of our times, with its 'robbing and shooting.' "[30]

Privately, Leskov's friend Ivan Aksakov expressed similar, more sophisticated dismay, criticizing Leskov for the "littleness" of his technique: "To objurgate seriously, to denounce baseness and vileness does not have that corrupting effect on the spirit that such techniques have as snickering and the like, in situations where one should preserve respect for the office along with the capacity for indignation at an individual displaying unworthiness for his office. [. . .] When necessary, [bishops] should be beaten with a cudgel, not treated with fillips."[31]

Aksakov had hit on the main point at issue. Aksakov advocated respect for the bishop's office combined, if necessary, with reprobation of unworthy individuals holding it; Leskov basically, if covertly, repudiated the office, yet freely acknowledged the goodness of certain individuals serving in it. It was a fundamental difference, and Leskov's friendship with Aksakov did not long survive its appearance.[32]

In his reply, Leskov avoided this fundamental issue, limiting himself to defending his accuracy and the effectiveness of his "snickering," his ridicule of "little things": "I have never ridiculed the clergy as such, but have depicted its members truly and realistically, and I see no fault in that [. . .] My only sin in *The Little Things in a Bishop's Life* (out of ignorance) was to represent the prelates, as one intelligent bishop wrote me, as 'better than they are in fact.' You say, 'Beat them with a cudgel.' But they are not afraid of your cudgel, whereas my pinpricks make them scowl."[33] Left-wing critics, though suspicious of Leskov for his anti-radical past, grudgingly acknowledged that he had written with talent in a good cause.[34] In this connection Leskov's later bibliographer Pyotr Bykov reports an encounter in a cafe. Someone said to Leskov, "For your *Little Things in a Bishop's Life* much can be forgiven you, but not the novels *No Way Out* and *Mirage*."[35] But the author of *Mirage*, another antinihilist novel of the 1860s, was Viktor Klyushnikov, and Leskov's accuser later admitted never having read *No Way Out*.

Despite the mixed critical reception, *The Little Things in a Bishop's Life* was a commercial success. The book edition of 1879 sold out rapidly and a second, revised and expanded edition appeared in 1880. The subsequent fate of the work might serve as a tolerance indicator, a thermometer measuring the heat of censoring zeal in successive periods of Russian history. Permitted and fully published in the last years of Alexander II's reign, *Little Things* fell into official disfavor soon after the accession of Alexander III. In 1883 it helped bring about the author's dismissal from his post in the Ministry of Education (11:275). In 1884, by imperial decree, it was withdrawn from circulation in libraries, a prohibition that lasted until 1905 (11:823, 6:669). And in 1889 it was the principal reason for the suppression of volume 6 of Leskov's Collected Works (6:667-669). The censors deemed the book "an impudent attack both on church administration in Russia and on the degeneration of the morals of our clergy" (6:667). The volume was sequestered and eventually burnt.

In 1897 Rostislav Sementkovsky, the editor of the second and third (posthumous) editions of Leskov's works, managed to get a mutilated text of *Little Things* through the censorship by judicious omissions and rearrangement of the text, putting the good bishops first and generally blunting the edge of Leskov's satire. Sementkovsky's version was reprinted unchanged in the mass edition of 1902. Thus two generations of Russians knew *Little Things* chiefly in this corrupt, "sweetened" version, unless they took the trouble to dig out, if they could, the original editions.

Ironically, in Soviet times the durable coin of censorship has merely been reversed. In editions of Leskov's selected works published in 1937 and 1952 the chapters on bad bishops were resurrected in their original form, while the good ones were omitted entirely (ostensibly for reasons of space).[36] Only in the "thaw" edition of 1957 has the full original text of *The Little Things in a Bishop's Life* at last been reprinted, for the first time since 1880.

A century later, read in its unadulterated form, *The Little Things in a Bishop's Life* still encounters formidable obstacles to full recognition as a literary classic. From the artistic point of view, the nineteenth-century prejudice against "littleness" of form, though weakened, is still potent. Readers are awed by bulk, which they sometimes equate with depth, and by solemnity of tone. They find it hard to assign top rating to a string of seemingly inconsequential, "snickering" anecdotes, some "in questionable taste." And if we set aside the issue of taste and grant that littleness may outweigh bigness on a more sophisticated scale, still we must admit that *Little Things* has artistic faults. It suffers from Leskov's besetting sin of excessive structural looseness. As noted, the second (1880) edition was published with three "appendices"—originally separate bishop articles—which Leskov never bothered to integrate into the main text. The main text itself consisted of originally disparate stories and articles. In particular, the final, six-

Nikolai Leskov

teenth chapter, on the literary predilections of Metropolitan Isidor, belongs to a different genre (as does "Diocesan Justice"), largely expository or descriptive, nonanecdotal.

On the ideological side, too, *Little Things* encounters prejudice. From the official Soviet point of view Leskov in general and this book in particular have proved hard to use for purposes of "engineering human souls" according to Communist specifications. Some attempts were made to isolate the bad bishop stories and use them for anticlerical propaganda; the full text, as published in 1957, is supplied with a commentary stressing its "denunciatory" features (6:663-664). But, though *Little Things* is indeed a denunciation of Orthodoxy, the present regime hardly wants its subjects led to Leskov's destination, a spiritualized, vital, and self-reliant Protestantism. However you turn him, Leskov does not fit the slot of the militant atheist.

Furthermore, Leskov's denunciation has seemed too weak and timid to some Soviet critics. If you are going to denounce the bishops, they say, why not do a good, Vyshinsky-like job of it? Leonid Grossman complains that "rereading these sketches in our times, one is struck by the paltriness of their subject matter and the innocuousness of their invective. Was this the kind of anticlerical satire unfurled by Rabelais, Boccaccio, Voltaire, or Swift?"[37]

Those who do not share official Soviet values may also find it hard to respond favorably to Leskov's satire. For many the question of the moral condition of the Orthodox church in tsarist Russia is too distant to be of interest. And others, especially Russians, mindful of the subsequent fate of that church, the cruel persecution it has undergone since 1917, may feel reluctant to recall the church's faults in a past that now seems impossibly remote.

Yet some readers will recognize that the values expressed are universal, though art requires concrete labels of time and place. We can read *The Little Things in a Bishop's Life* as an attack not on bishops or Orthodoxy, but on any species of pomposity, tyranny, and cruelty; and an advocacy not of Protestantism, but of individual moral responsibility, tolerance, and the spiritual equality of all men.

24

A Roster of the Righteous

In his retrospective old age, Leskov perceived two basic moral impulses propelling his literary talent, two magnetic poles that made it
vibrate. The negative pole, manifested in *The Little Things in a
Bishop's Life*, he associated with what he called his "police chief's
nose."[1] By this he meant his capacity, which he considered exceptional, to sniff out the fishy odors in human motive and behavior, to
detect what was rotten, false, callous, or cruel, however artfully hidden. This ability had been demonstrated in a formidable array of
satires, extending from *No Way Out* to "A Winter's Day," written at
the end of his life against the corruption he then discerned among his
fellow Tolstoyans. Yet the "police chief's nose" reacted to fragrance as
well as to malodor; and looking back on his career, Leskov took
greater pride in his ability to capture moral fragrance for literature
than in his fetid accomplishments as a spiritual janitor. "In every party
there are attractive and noble people."[2] "Outsize characters have
always been dear to me . . . I have depicted martyrs for an idea and
sufferers for the sake of others."[3] "The strength of my talent is in positive types."[4] These are pronouncements of Leskov's later years.

In an article written in 1882, Leskov referred in similar terms to
Russian medieval saints' lives: "The characters of the persons about
whom these hagiographic narratives were composed constitute the
'spiritual beauty' of our people. And art must and is even obligated to
preserve insofar as possible all the features of this national 'beauty.' "[5]
First unconsciously, later with deliberate intent, he set about transposing this hagiographic tradition into modern literature. Late in the
seventies he began formally to conceptualize this process. In 1879 he
published a short story entitled "The Monognome" (*Odnodum*—the
title refers both to the single-minded "saint" himself and to his anthology of Biblical quotations, and no existing English word seems
adequate to it). This story, judging by its full original title, was intended as the first of a larger cycle: "Russian Eccentrics (From Tales of

the Three Righteous Men). The Monognome."⁶ It begins with a preface (relegated to the footnotes in the Soviet edition; 6:641-643) in
which the author, in his anecdotal style, presents the conceptual basis
for his modern revival of the hagiographic genre.

Referring anonymously, though transparently, to his friend and fellow novelist Pisemsky (a "major writer" and dramatist, not a Peters-
burger, who has a taste for pungent language and for self-dramatization), Leskov contrasts his older colleague's somber view of human
nature with his own benign one. Pisemsky, as Leskov quotes him, saw
nothing but "nastiness" in the Russia around him and nothing but
"vileness" in his own soul or in Leskov's. This misanthropic outburst
—Pisemsky, Leskov says, was "in the process of dying for the forty-
eighth time," which contributed to his pessimism—enabled Leskov to
set up an introductory straw man. Taken aback by Pisemsky's misan-
thropy, Leskov tells us, he began to ask himself (and, slyly, his readers): "Can it be that there is nothing but filth either in my soul or in
that of any other Russian? Can it be that all the kindness and goodness
discerned by the artistic eye of other writers is nothing but fantasy and
nonsense? This is not only sad, it is terrible. If, according to the folk
belief, no city can stand without three righteous men, then how can a
whole country stand with nothing but the filth that lies in my soul and
yours, my dear reader?" (6:642). So, Leskov continues, he thereupon
set out in search of those "three righteous men" without whom the
Russian city would fall. Happily, the results were favorable: he found
not only the Monognome and the requisite two others, but the whole
population of worthy Russians who inhabit the second volume of the
original (1889) edition of Leskov's collected works. Russian righteousness, thank Heaven, was still alive. Leskov's quest for the virtuous
had begun long before the (probably apocryphal) exchange with
Pisemsky. His earlier portraits of Rainer-Benni, Pizonsky, Tuberozov,
Flyagin, Father Kiriak, the Peacock, and perhaps even the Musk-ox,
might easily qualify for his later gallery of authorially certified saints.
And in 1876, three years before the Pisemsky preface was written, the
association of sainthood with the magic number three had been made:
a story called "The Pygmy," later included in the formal hagiographic
cycle, originally bore the title "Three Good Deeds."⁷ The folk motif of
the three righteous men had been on Leskov's mind perhaps since
childhood. It crops up in *The Little Things in a Bishop's Life,* where
Leskov refers in passing to the family of one of his *gymnasium* classmates "which in childhood seemed to me the family of those three

righteous men for the sake of whom the Lord suffered on the earth the 'crackpots' of Oryol" (6:409).

"The Monognome," with its conceptualizing preface, was followed the next year by "The Cadet Monastery" and "A Russian Democrat in Poland."[8] Joined by "The Pygmy," this virtuous threesome appeared together in book form early in 1880, along with an apparent stowaway, a story about a presumed nonsaint called "Sheramur."[9] The volume bore the enigmatic—and inaccurate—title *Three Righteous Men and One Sheramur.*[10] (Actually, the number of righteous men in this collection is not three, but seven or possibly eight, depending on one's definition.)

Leskov's hagiographic gallery kept on growing throughout the eighties. The assortment in the 1889 volume 2 included "Deathless Golovan" (1880), "The Unmercenary Engineers" (1887), "The Left-hander" (1881), "The Sentry" (1887), "The Enchanted Pilgrim" (1873), and even "Sheramur," who thus seemed to have been promoted to the elect.[11] Besides these officially certified righteous ones, several others, both early and late, might be counted. "Figura" (1889), for instance, though not placed in the righteous volume 2, had originally been given the subtitle "From My Recollections of Righteous Men."[12] For our present analysis, we shall limit ourselves to those whom their creator formally designated as *pravedniki,* "righteous ones," particularly the stories in *Three Righteous Men and One Sheramur.*

I count sixteen major *pravedniki* in volume 2. All are male. Elsewhere, Leskov had created images of female virtue—Princess Protozanova in *A Decrepit Clan* or Klavdia in "Night Owls." But no females appear as major saints in volume 2. Even the entourage of these male saints is overwhelmingly male. Only one secondary character, Pavla from "Deathless Golovan," could be said to equal her male counterpart in virtue (though not in narrative importance). The reason for this apparent exhibition of male chauvinism is not so much misogyny as antisexuality: one of Leskov's criteria for canonization is renunciation of sexual activity; and some of his saints prefer to repudiate not only sexual activity, but all feminine society.

Leskov's saints vary considerably in age, as does the extent of their lives during which we view them. They are all seen at least into maturity. Leskov's tests for righteousness generally require long-term demonstration; he looks for staying power, wisdom, and persistent fortitude—qualities seldom exhibited in youth. The flashes of spectacular courage of which young people are capable seem to impress him less.

Leskov's saints also display considerable variation in class status, though they avoid the social extremes. After *A Decrepit Clan* Leskov seemed to have written off the landed gentry; none of his later *pravedniki* is drawn from this favored class. On the other hand, unlike his late master Tolstoy, Leskov apparently found little evidence of sainthood among the agricultural peasants, who made up the vast majority of the population. From "The Cattle-pen" (1893) and many other utterances we know that Leskov took a pessimistic view of the "dark masses" of the peasantry; he saw there far more savagery than sanctity. The lowliest saints on his roster are thoroughly emancipated peasants, detached from their original milieu, such as Ivan Flyagin, the runaway serf turned soldier, horsetrader, Tatar, and monk; or Deathless Golovan, a liberated serf turned dairyman. Golovan, though he lives by husbandry, is essentially an Oryol townsman.

The middle ranges of society were closer to Leskov's identity and experience, and they provided him with a richer source of prototypes. Furthermore, he had a moral reason for concentrating on them. It was harder, he felt, to be virtuous in dependent situations where you had to accommodate yourself to the authority and whims of your superiors. Thus in the middle classes, especially in the bureaucracy, virtue was even more to your credit than among freer agents. As the narrator puts it in "The Cadet Monastery": "Righteous men have not become extinct among us, nor will they. People just don't notice them, but if you look closely, they exist. I now recollect a whole habitation of righteous men [. . .] And note that none of them is from the common people or from the aristocracy, but rather from serving officials, dependent people for whom it is harder to preserve virtue" (6:315). The official class predominates among Leskov's *pravedniki*: of the sixteen major figures, seven are army officers and four are civil servants. One is a clergyman; one is an artisan; two are expeasants. The sixteenth is the ambiguous Sheramur, whose class status is confused: he is the illegitimate son of a gentleman and a serf girl, later adopted by a petty official to whom his mother's marriage was arranged by his father. His experience led him to become for many years a vagabond, a total drop-out from the social system. We last see him married to the proprietress of a Parisian hash-house.

As a final point of social statistics, it should be noted that all the *pravedniki* of volume 2 are Great Russians. Evidently no members of national minorities or foreigners, though many virtuous examples appear in other works, could be used to shore up the Russian city.

There are three basic areas in which Leskov's saints exhibit their righteousness: let us call them the political, the economic, and the sexual. Usually they must distinguish themselves in at least two of these areas to qualify.

The composite image of Leskov's idea of *political* virtue is an interesting one, especially in psychological terms. (The term "political" is used here in a very broad sense, to include all relationships and activities within the governmental or administrative system.) First of all, one is struck by the aura of authority and power. Nineteenth-century Russian society was indeed highly stratified, with an enormous distance between its top and its bottom. It placed few restraints—especially in the first half of the century—on the power of superiors over their subordinates; the model of autocracy was endlessly repeated, on a diminishing scale, throughout the social system. Yet Leskov exaggerates these features, marked as they were in reality. Most of these stories are dated in the "classic" era of Nicholas I, a despotic time when every petty official with a modicum of authority played the little tsar within his little domain, and when the threat of physical violence hung over everyone except the most privileged.

In such a situation, the "normal" response is to present to one's superior an acceptable façade of servility and vent one's anger on those below (or on wives or children). In these terms, "righteousness" would be the opposite behavior: heroic uprightness, refusal to be cowed by a tyrant. Leskov's saints act out this archetypal pattern to a large extent (perhaps its most primitive form is the young boy first taking a moral stand against an authoritarian father).

The authorities confronted by Leskov's saints are dazzlingly exalted, and the social gulf they must cross makes the saints' deeds all the more heroic. The Pygmy, for example—a minor Russian prison official—is moved by compassion to extend himself far, far beyond his normal administrative purview, to the brink of treason. In 1853, when Russia is on the verge of war with France and England, he ventures to appeal directly to the French ambassador, asking him to appeal in turn to the emperor that the latter remit at the last minute a sentence of flogging and branding imposed unjustly on a Frenchman probably too frail to survive it. It is an unprecedented feat of bureaucratic daring, the opposite of the "normal" administrator's philosophy of play-it-safe, keep-your-nose-clean, pass-the-buck, and don't-stick-your-neck-out.

The Monognome, Alexander Ryzhov, a minor provincial police official, performs a more spectacular, if less generously motivated, exploit of nonservility. Scandalized by the presumptuous behavior in church of his ultimate superior, the governor of the province, Sergei Lanskoy (a real person, later count and minister of the interior), Ryzhov goes up to the governor in the church and, with the words "Servant of God, Sergius! Enter into the house of God not proudly, but humbly, displaying thyself as the greatest of sinners, thus!" physically forces the governor's back into a suitably respectful position before the solium.

Perhaps the ultimate is represented by Mikhail Persky, "abbot" of the "cadet monastery" (a military boarding school), who, without violating a single canon of official etiquette, talks back to his august majesty, Nicholas I. Persky exonerates his youthful charges of seditious intent in feeding some of the mutinous soldiers wounded in the Senate Square on December 14, 1825. To the tsar's angry accusation, "They fed the mutineers!" Persky calmly replies, "They have been taught, your Majesty, to fight the enemy, but after victory to care for their wounded enemies as if they were their own." Though his wrath is not appeased, the tsar can think of no counter to this perfect riposte and departs speechless.

These are glorious moments, exhibitions of great courage. There are, however, two peculiarities in Leskov's treatment of such confrontations. First, within the confines of Leskov's art such acts of moral defiance are almost always successful and almost always go unpunished. In each instance the exalted authority figure is humbled and chastened with impunity; on occasion he even expresses gratitude for the lesson administered by his presumptuous subordinate. Lanskoy, for instance, is moved not to wrath, but to curiosity by the Monognome's extraordinary action—in effect a public physical assault—and he eventually gets Ryzhov a medal for his exemplary conduct in office. Nicholas sends a gift of 1,500 rubles to the Pygmy with a holographic note, "I thank you." Though Persky gets no thanks from the tsar, at least he wins his point and suffers no evil consequences.

Such instances of courageous defiance evoking a magnanimous response in the high and mighty are mythic in character, and the presentation of myth is one of the central features of hagiography. Like the stories of Daniel before Nebuchadnezzar or Belshazzar, these stories represent a species of human wish-fulfillment: the moral triumph of an underdog. Comforting as these happy endings are, the fate of Private Postnikov in "The Sentry"—a "mild" flogging of two hundred strokes

356

with birch rods—seems, alas, the more likely outcome of such confrontations. Perhaps a Pisemsky would say that the most realistic archetype would be the fate of the great Chinese historian Ssu-ma Ch'ien, whom the Emperor Wu ordered castrated for his insistent—and quite disinterested—defense of a disgraced general.

Besides the attribution to his authority figures of unrealistic magnanimity, many of Leskov's "righteous" stories display another peculiarly Leskovian "political" paradox. Leskov locates several of his saints on rungs in the social ladder where one would least expect to find them: the army and the police. Leskov seems to take perverse delight in presenting cases that confute "liberal" prejudices. The Pygmy, a prison official and a supervisor of corporal punishments, would be an object of automatic moral revulsion to most liberal or radical intellectuals. Yet this person risks his career and perhaps his life to save an innocent man from his knout. Likewise the Monognome, Ryzhov, is first a town policeman (*kvartal'nyj*) and is later promoted to police chief (*gorodničij*)—positions treated with marked disfavor in Russian life and literature, beginning with Gogol's immortal archetypes of brutality and corruption, Derzhimorda and Skvoznik-Dmukhanovsky. Yet this Ryzhov takes no bribes (more an economic than a political virtue), and he performs a heroic feat of insubordination in calling a governor to order.

By casting his saints in unholy roles, Leskov makes two anticonventional points. For one thing, he is saying that moral reality is more complex than ready-made ideological formulas admit, and that each case should be judged on its own merits. For another, he is asserting the very opposite of that social determinism professed by "progressive" intellectuals of that day and this. "The individual is a predictable product of his socioeconomic environment," say the social determinists. "Not at all," Leskov replies. "The individual human being is uniquely himself." Saints, like criminals, may crop up anywhere, on the most unpromising social soil. Their sainthood, as Leskov sees it, is not determined by social origin, occupation, or even cumulative experience: it is rather a manifestation of pure individuality, a triumph within the individual soul of the psychic forces of good.

This conviction of the ultimate moral independence and responsibility of each individual was firm in Leskov. It later drew him to Tolstoy, who came to hold similar views, and it made him skeptical of the social panaceas of the revolutionaries. From the literary point of view, however, his conviction was associated with a system of psychological portrayal different from Tolstoy's—more "medieval," static, and ab-

solute. Even a late Tolstoyan "saint" like Father Sergius must grow
and develop, winning sainthood—if he does win it—only after severe
moral struggles and catastrophic failures. Leskov's saints are "given,"
like phenomena of nature; their goodness is in their blood; it is revealed, not achieved. Such undeveloping figures live much more comfortably in the short story—or the medieval *vita*—than in the modern
novel.

In the area of *economics*, Leskov's righteous men display their virtue in more conventional ways. They are all *bessrebrenniki*, "silverless," like the engineers of Leskov's title, which is here inadequately
translated "The Unmercenary Engineers." The quality celebrated is
not poverty, but a basic moral indifference to money—the most common feature of Leskov's saints. Money may talk, but they won't listen.
They will not focus their lives on material things. The Monognome
performs the feat, unheard of for a policeman in the early nineteenth
century, of living on his minuscule salary. The Russian democrat in
Poland—a high official—turns down a latifundium offered him by the
Russian government from Polish lands confiscated after the 1831 uprising; he then resigns from the service as a sign of his disapproval of
the policy of granting huge Polish estates to Russian magnates.[13]

Though his saints refuse to care about money, Leskov by no means
regards poverty as a self-evident badge or a necessary accompaniment
of righteousness. The Protestant ethic in its economic aspects, such as
self-reliance, thrift, and enterprise, is vividly manifested by many of
these righteous, nominally Orthodox Russians. Poverty, furthermore,
often leads to dependency, a condition which may have psychological
consequences incompatible with righteousness. Moral sturdiness, Leskov feels, goes hand in hand (or hand in pocket) with economic self-
sufficiency. The Monognome could subsist and even support a family
on his ludicrous policeman's salary of 10 paper rubles a month (equivalent to 2.87 silver rubles); but even he could not have lived on nothing. Righteousness requires subsistence, however minimal.

Though poverty had been celebrated as a virtue and a means of spiritual therapy, in a medieval tradition still strong in Russia (Tolstoy's
Father Sergius is again an example), Leskov became increasingly suspicious of the very idea of the holy mendicant. Even his enchanted pilgrim had been self-supporting, until he entered the monastery; and in
Leskov's late fiction Orthodox "pilgrims," as in "Deathless Golovan"
or "Night Owls," are treated with harsh satire. In Russia's "holy peo-

ple" who wandered from shrine to shrine and monastery to monastery Leskov saw more superstition, sloth, and chicanery than sanctity.

Economic self-sufficiency, furthermore, makes possible another manifestation of righteousness, charity. Money is not in itself an evil; it can be used for other than selfish ends. Several of Leskov's saints are ardent practitioners of that commandment on which he laid so much stress in his own life: *prelomi i dažd'*, "break [bread] and give [it]."[14] It is remarkable to what extent Leskov's saints display their charity in the most primitive "biological" form: bread-breaking, feeding. Man may not live by bread alone, but bread he must have; and one of the most basic manifestations of human solidarity, therefore, is to feed the hungry. Feeding as the fundamental act of charity loomed especially large in a country where famines were not infrequent. Leskov's works are full of feeders, beginning with Kotin the He-Cow, and many of them were later numbered among the certified saints. Deathless Golovan, for instance, by profession a dairy farmer, "would break bread from his loaf with any man without distinction who asked for it [. . .] Even to the Jew Yushka from the garrison he gave milk for the children" (6:373).

Feeding is an obsession with two of Leskov's *pravedniki*, Andrei Bobrov from "The Cadet Monastery" and Sheramur. Bobrov is the quartermaster in the First Saint Petersburg Cadet Corps, in charge of its supplies and physical maintenance; but he cares most about feeding his boys. "Dinner and all other food we invariably received in his [Bobrov's] presence," the narrator reports. "He loved to 'feed,' and he fed us very well and very satisfyingly" (6:331). Bobrov gave away his entire salary in the form of graduation presents for the poor among his "scoundrels," as he called them: two silver soup spoons, four teaspoons, and three changes of underwear ("If a comrade drops in, you'll have something to give him to eat his cabbage soup with, and for tea two or three of them may drop in" 6:333). It was in character for a "silverless one" to give away silver.

As for Sheramur, at first he seems an unlikely candidate for sainthood, economic or otherwise. As a "child of Cain"[15] he is a "fugitive and a vagabond in the earth." Poverty, misfortune, and what we would call mental illness have so crushed him that the act of eating is the only meaningful event in his life. He deprives even this event of its human dimensions by habitually using the word *zhrat'* for "eat," equivalent to German *fressen*: what animals, not people, do to food.

Yet Sheramur has a deep-seated philanthropic impulse, the basis of his sainthood, if he possesses it. Though he cares only about stomachs, he is as much concerned to fill others' as his own. As Leskov succinctly puts it, "Sheramur is a *hero of the belly;* his motto is *zhrat';* and his ideal is to *feed others*" (6:244). At the end of the story he is at last able to fulfill this nutritive ideal. The money he has saved during service in the Serbian war (1875-1877) he invests in the low-class Parisian bean-ery managed by the bosomy, superannuated "Tante Grillade," whom he marries. Thus he can realize his dream: "feed two men [gratis] twice a week or, still better, three every Sunday. And besides that, once a year give a special banquet attended by nobody but homeless *voyous*" (6:297).

Apart from his eleemosynary exploits and his poverty and vaga-bondage, Sheramur is still an exponent of the Protestant ethic. He is mostly self-supporting, faithful in carrying out the clerical jobs he takes on, and punctilious about money. When he asks to borrow two francs and is given five, he brings the change the next day. Despite the author's Sternean disclaimer (he says he put Sheramur into the same volume with the "three righteous" only so that the book might have the requisite number of pages), Sheramur meets the qualifications for Leskovian sanctity, though perhaps only in the special category which the Russians call *yurodivy:* the "touched" saint, the fool-in-Christ. Ac-cording to Leskov's facetious subtitle, Sheramur is a *chreva-radi yuro-divy,* which we might translate as "touched" not in the head, but in the belly.

Sheramur's decidedly unromantic and stomach-centered marriage is only an eccentric variety of the sexual behavior of most of Leskov's saints. Not only his marriage, but his very name is a parody of sexual-ity. Because of his immense beard and small stature he had been called "Chernomor," after the dwarf magician in Pushkin's *Ruslan and Lyud-mila;* this nickname was in turn twisted into *Cher amour* by a buxom Englishwoman who tried unsuccessfully to seduce him.[16] Like the Musk-ox before him, Sheramur is a sexual puritan.

Leskov's image of sanctity thus incorporates the puritan antisexual-ity typical of most official Christian ethics. Although he made no at-tempt until conveniently late in his life to practice asceticism him-self, Leskov, as many of his stories show, carried a heavy load of guilt about his sexuality. Sexual activity in his works is repeatedly as-sociated with ghastly crimes and condign punishments. He admires persons able to follow the preferred course of St. Paul, absolute celi-bacy. The Russian word for "male virgin," *devstvennik,* occurs more than once in Leskov, usually italicized and followed by an exclamation point. The four saints of the "cadet monastery," the director, quartermaster, doctor, and chaplain, are all celibate, though only the archimandrite chaplain is bound by religious vows. Except for the archimandrite, they rarely venture beyond the walls of their "abbey," preferring the society of adolescent boys to any other, especially female. (The pre-Freudian Leskov apparently has no inkling of the probable homosexual impulses behind such behavior.)

The most remarkable case of righteous asexuality, however, is Deathless Golovan. As Leskov presents Golovan's *vita*, sexual abstinence is given the highest, climactic position among his exploits of virtue. From a literary point of view this apical position is paradoxical. Other aspects of Golovan's life appear to offer more promising literary possibilities—his courage in caring for the sick during an epidemic or his final act: during the great Oryol fire of 1848 he fell into a seething privy pit "while saving somebody's life or somebody's property" (6:352). Yet Leskov passes quickly over these dramatic events, saving his primary attention for his hero's mysterious sexual behavior.

The resolution of this mystery is skillfully withheld until the last. Golovan, we are told early in the story, inhabits a remodeled barn, together with five women. Of these one is his mother and three his spinster sisters. The fifth is called Pavla or, by the townspeople, "Golovan's sin." This Pavla is a tall, pale woman with "amazingly black and regular eyebrows" that make her look like "a Persian maiden resting on the knees of an aged Turk." The general assumption is that Pavla is Golovan's mistress, since they are known to love each other and she lives in his house. We know better, however, because Leskov's manner of referring to "Golovan's sin" has subtly led us to doubt its authenticity. Furthermore, we have been informed in passing of the concrete fact that "summer and winter" Golovan sleeps in a cattle-stall alongside not Pavla, but his beloved red Tyrolian bull, Vaska.

We have thus assumed from the start that Golovan is innocent of "Golovan's sin," though we cannot yet fathom the reason for his enigmatic continence. Consequently we are hardly startled by the exclamation encountered in the final chapter: "Golovan was a *virgin!*" (Leskov's italics; 6:395). This astounding fact is reported by the "author's" grandmother, who had heard it from the priest to whom the now dead Golovan had confessed: so we can take it as authentic. The reason for Golovan's virginity, it transpires, was as follows. Pavla was already married, to a scoundrel who had deserted her. After she had taken refuge in Golovan's house, the husband reappeared, incog-

361

nito, and took advantage of the opportunity to blackmail the "lovers." Since Pavla and Golovan knew that her husband was alive, they could not in good conscience resort to the Russian law that permitted remarriage after a spouse had not been heard from for five years. And since they also would not live in sin, there was "no way out": Golovan was obliged to remain a *virgin!* "Then because of him [the husband] they deprived themselves of all happiness!" the "author" exclaims to his grandmother. "It depends on what you call happiness," she replies. "There is righteous happiness and there is sinful happiness. Righteous happiness will not step over anyone, while the sinful kind will step over anything." "Why, they were amazing people!" the "author" again exclaims. "Righteous people," his grandmother corrects him (6:397).

To us, however, Golovan's and Pavla's genital inactivity may seem pointless, and we may also criticize Leskov for refusing to look beneath this chaste surface at its probable unconscious components—masochism, narcissism, and veiled hostility. Such terms, to be sure, smack of our age rather than his, but the phenomena are as old as mankind itself, and Leskov should have been able to perceive them.

Taken together, Leskov's righteous ones do not share a uniform system of religious, as opposed to ethical, ideas. Many of them, such as the Pygmy or the Russian democrat in Poland, appear to be motivated either by a secular humanistic philosophy or by feelings of human compassion, unencumbered by ideology. In several of his "righteous" stories, however, Leskov expresses his own developing religious convictions. Righteousness, one concludes from the *pravedniki* cycle, is virtually incompatible with orthodox Orthodoxy.

The Monognome, for example, though he never formally breaks his connection with the church, makes his confessions regularly and takes the sacrament, is nevertheless a very deviant churchman. Most of all, he reads the Bible and has actually read it through, "as far as Christ"; and in Russia all Orthodox Christians, according to Leskov, know that from anyone who has read the Bible and "got as far as Christ" no further sensible behavior can be expected (6:222). The demonstrative rebuke Ryzhov administered to Governor Lanskoy for his impiety was an affirmation of religious propriety rather than a defense of Orthodoxy. No doubt, however, it helped to make the story acceptable to the censors and perhaps more insidiously effective in the hearts of Orthodox readers. In any case, once again a line was drawn between Christian and Orthodox.

In "The Cadet Monastery" Leskov similarly plants some half-concealed barbs directed at Orthodox piety. Leskov's narrator[17] recalls with bitterness General Nikolai Demidov, ordered by Nicholas to "tighten up" discipline in the cadet corps. Demidov is described oxymoronically as "a man extremely devout and absolutely pitiless" (6:324)—his superstitious bigotry offering no obstacle to his cruel treatment of the cadets.

Leskov's technique of planting among his righteous partly hidden anti-Orthodox scoffs is carried furthest in "Deathless Golovan." Like the Monognome, Golovan technically maintains his membership in the Orthodox church; but like Ryzhov's, his Orthodoxy is in doubt. To his fellow townsmen his faith "seemed strange," and they punningly called him a *molokan*, a "milker"—perhaps, Leskov observes slyly, "simply because he dealt in milk," but perhaps because they suspected him of religious heterodoxy. When asked to what parish he belongs, Golovan replies, "I am of the parish of the Creator Almighty." "And there was no such parish in all Oryol," the narrator adds with ostensible naiveté.

Leskov's most potent anti-Orthodox sally in "Deathless Golovan," however, is contained in a long flashback used to introduce the nefarious character of Pavla's husband. In this excursus Leskov gives a satirical picture of the scenes accompanying the canonization of a new Orthodox saint. It is a most unedifying picture: the crush and frenzy of the crowds, the ubiquitous thieves, imposters, and touts, the fraud and fakery, the superstitious expectation of miracles. Like any Protestant, Leskov finds abhorrent the idea that some magic power called "grace" inheres in the mortal remains of a saint, and he satirizes it mercilessly. In "Deathless Golovan" a well-to-do merchant seeking a miraculous cure for his daughter goes to great lengths to be near the saint's coffin at the moment of opening, when the out-flow of concentrated "grace" is presumably greatest—something like the alcoholic exhalations from a freshly uncorked bottle of spirits.[18]

ᑕᖇ25ᘓ

Two Ties Are Unbound

The late seventies and early eighties were a period of upheaval for Leskov, one which wrought profound changes in his private mode of existence and in his public image. Leskov of the middle years—a solid family man and citizen, regarded as a deep conservative, a Katkovian stalwart, and the most faithful advocate of Orthodoxy among Russian writers—is transformed into the late Leskov, a cantankerous old celibate, crustily at odds with all "establishments" of church and state.

The religious and philosophical aspects of this transformation were far advanced by the second half of the seventies. Inwardly, Leskov after 1875 was already a radical Protestant, espousing many ideas that would later be proclaimed and systematized by Tolstoy. But around this new and well-formed religious core a good many other pieces had to be fitted.

First, a painful reordering of his private life had to be carried out. By 1875 it was clear that the second of Leskov's attempts at "family happiness," like the first, was anything but happy. Leskov began to realize that temperamentally he was not suited for family life—something that few creative artists have managed successfully. As his relationship with Katerina Bubnova passed the point of rupture, Leskov's defensive structures began to give a little. Though he still mechanically went through the motions of "renounce and denounce," trying to pin the blame on her, in the late seventies one can detect some new notes.[1] Along with the usual self-pity and self-justification there are hints of acknowledgment that the blame was not all on one side; and as time passed a deeper recognition emerged that the problem, for Leskov, was not the woman, but marriage itself: a relationship with a woman socially his equal with whom authority in the household had to be shared. In 1879, two years after their separation, he wrote to his former wife, perhaps in response to a suggestion of reconciliation, "I am sincerely glad to entertain guests, but I don't like equal masters in one lair; and I am by now so old that it is difficult and useless for me to try to adjust to anyone else's character."[2]

Unlike the explosive sundering of his first marriage, the termination of his second was accomplished quietly. By 1877 both parties had come to recognize that they had drifted so far apart that their common life had become an affliction. Mme Bubnova made a business trip to Kiev in the spring of that year. When she returned in August, the decision was final: separation, "untying" (*razvjazka*), to use Leskov's word,[3] which in Russian has the secondary, literary sense of "denouement."

Mme Bubnova with her four Bubnov children moved to another apartment in the same building; Leskov and their son Andrei, with the maid Dunyasha, took a flat in another part of Petersburg. For some years[4] Leskov and Andrei took Sunday dinners *en famille* in the Bubnov ménage, as of old. But as time passed and the children grew up, the contacts dwindled away. Ultimately, after her children had completed their education, Mme Bubnova moved back to her native Kiev, where she eventually died. Though the picture is not entirely clear from Andrei Leskov's biography—virtually our only source on the subject—it seems likely that Leskov hardly ever saw his former wife after the mid-eighties.[5]

This quiet separation was harder for Leskov to endure than a stormy severance. Separations evoke guilt feelings; and for Leskov guilt feelings were intolerable. He always strove desperately to throw them back at the other party ("It's all your fault"). A tranquil separation left Leskov nowhere to unload his guilt. In the meantime he was confronted with the multiple pain of remorse, loneliness, isolation, rejection. The normally assertive, domineering Leskov, usually businesslike and proud of his sense of practical realities, sure of what was right and wrong, suddenly evinced the opposite qualities. In his depression he became passive, hesitant, and docile, dependent for practical decisions on his eleven-year-old son. The boy became for a time the center of household authority, keeping the accounts, choosing the menus, managing the laundry, supervising the maid. The roles had been reversed: the son had become the father (or perhaps the mother), and the father a child who had lost its mother. The depression did not last, and before long the old authoritarian tendencies reasserted themselves, to the discomfiture of the eleven-year-old housekeeper who was taking pride in his new responsibilities. When given a bad mark for inattentiveness in class, the boy, normally an excellent student, was ignominiously birched by the father toward whom he had been feeling so protective and paternal. "Resentment flooded my soul," Andrei Leskov wrote many decades later of this episode.[6] It is clear from his book that the accumulated resentments, from this and many other spiritual blows received from his father, never left him, even in his old age.

From a selfish point of view we might be grateful for Andrei Leskov's unfortunate fate: both the fact that he was left with his father, to bear witness to his private life, and that he amassed so much rancor against him, for it is mostly the negative side of his ambivalence that fires the engine of his superb biography. No doubt Andrei took pride in being the son of a great writer; but one feels that the more potent force behind his book is the wish to show the world the human reality behind the façade of "righteousness" and Christian benevolence his father had artfully constructed. His "kin according to the flesh" knew another Leskov: temperamental, self-righteous, unreasonable, sometimes cruel, and always difficult.

Andrei Leskov never knew how he had been assigned to live with his father, away from his mother's household. The subject was so painful that even as an adult he never dared raise it, either with his father or his mother. More than a decade after his father's death he learned from his uncle Aleksei that as early as 1874 he, Aleksei Leskov, and his wife had been so concerned about Andrei's situation in the stormy Leskov-Bubnov ménage that they had considered removing him permanently from it by adopting him. This proposal had evidently been rebuffed with such acerbity that the memory of the episode was still rankling in Aleksei thirty-odd years later.[7]

Andrei Leskov spent his adolescent years sharing the bachelor lair of his literary father, until maturity and a commission in the army made possible his escape. Subsequently his relationship with his father suffered the fate of Leskov's relationships with so many others: accusations, recriminations, periods of "disgrace" and estrangement. A blood tie, however, cannot be severed like a friendship, and there were also periods of reconciliation and mutual affection. His experience with his father was not pleasant for Andrei Leskov to endure or remember. Perhaps the bitterest sentence in his book is the one that concludes the most personal chapter, "Pro domo": "Using two of his late titles, one may say with assurance that his [Leskov's] entire personal life was 'vexation of spirit,' and that life with him was a 'vale of tears.' "[8]

Life with Leskov was difficult for many reasons, but the most basic was his commitment as an artist: his art came first. All other values were sacrificed on its altar. Everything that interfered with the exercise of artistic talent was ruthlessly pushed aside. When confronted with a choice, he chose art over love. Andrei Leskov writes with indignation, for instance,[9] of his father's continued intense literary activity in Petersburg when Andrei lay at death's door in Kiev, suffering from malignant typhus. Using the rationalization that Andrei was being well cared for by his uncle and aunt and that there was nothing for him to do there, Leskov did not come to Kiev to join the watchers. His son never forgave him. No doubt such behavior is inhuman. From our selfish point of view, however, we can be grateful for Leskov's callousness, for it made possible his art.

Many of Leskov's stories reveal his deep ambivalence about sexuality. He was ultimately to realize his ideal of celibacy, but only after age and illness had blunted physical desire. By the late seventies he had learned that marriage was for him no solution to the problem of sexuality, since it brought with it even worse problems: two masters in the same lair, too many emotional demands, too little freedom for artistic work. The ideal compromise seemed to lie between celibacy and marriage. The best of all worlds would be a lower-class mistress who would have no rights or pretensions, could make no claims, and would play no part in the writer's social or literary life. She would be a woman who knew her place, and her place was the bed and the kitchen, not the living room or study.

In the early 1880s Leskov realized such a relationship, achieving what his son calls, citing one of his father's letters, peace with "female equilibrium."[10] The woman was a housemaid called Pasha (Ignatyeva), hired early in 1880. She devotedly nursed Leskov through a severe case of pneumonia and in the concomitant intimacy became his mistress. Pasha was an excellent housekeeper, quietly arranging all the external details of the writer's existence exactly according to his wishes, often sensed rather than expressed. She never presumed beyond her station, and she seemed content to subordinate her life to his. Unfortunately, it turned out that even Pasha aspired beyond the lot of the perfect slave, and that her aspirations did not involve Leskov. In 1882 she abruptly left him to get married.

Leskov's puzzling literary incarnation of Pasha in the good-humored late story "The Lady and the Wench" (1894) has already been mentioned:[11] under the transparent name of Prasha she is there mysteriously linked with Leskov's long-deceased friend-turned-enemy, Nikolai Solovyov. It is clear from the story that Pasha's image had remained with Leskov as an archetype, the model of the artist's (or male chauvinist's) perfect woman.

Leskov never found a successor to Pasha. Whether any of the women who in later years presided over his kitchen also penetrated to his bedroom is not clear. By the late 1880s Leskov had apparently settled, reasonably comfortably, into the life of celibacy he idealized.

The departure of Katerina Bubnova created a financial crisis. Reluctant as he had been to admit the fact, her substantial private income had been the mainstay of the family during the difficult years of literary isolation, when Leskov had had to peddle heavily camouflaged stories and articles, poorly remunerated, to the *Orthodox Review* and the *Church-Social Herald*, and to supplement his literary earnings by taking a part-time position in the Ministry of Education. Leskov had been a capable worker in this post, yet year after year had gone by without his receiving any advance in rank or a single ruble's increase in salary. None too eager about him in the first place, his superiors had found him annoyingly independent and stiff-necked, and they evidently hoped to freeze him out. Furthermore, in the course of these years Leskov accumulated other slights and affronts which he deeply resented.[12] That a man as opinionated and intractable as Leskov would not fit easily into a bureaucratic machine is not surprising; the only puzzle is why he stuck it out so long. Apparently those thousand rubles a year represented a psychological refuge, a last-ditch insurance against destitution, for which he was willing to pay a high price in frustration and humiliation.

Soon after his separation from Mme Bubnova, Leskov obtained, through the good offices of his most highly connected friend, General S. E. Kushelev, a second part-time government post, also with a salary of 1,000 rubles a year. He was named an official on special assignment on the staff of Count P. A. Valuev, the minister of state property. Unlike the position in the Ministry of Education, this one was apparently a sinecure, involving few duties, if any.[13] With his two government posts, Leskov could count on a steady income of 2,000 rubles a year, with literary earnings in addition. It was enough to maintain his motherless ménage in modest comfort. For some reason, however, the position in Valuev's office was not of long duration. On December 23, 1880, Leskov was dropped from the rolls of the Ministry of State Property "at his own request" (11:818). The existing sources do not reveal the reasons for Leskov's resignation. Most likely there was a budgetary squeeze to which this sinecure had to be sacrificed, and

resignation was the graceful way of withdrawing. Leskov's temperament being what it was, one feels that if there had been some intrigue
against him in the Ministry of State Property, the resulting fireworks
would surely have left some mark in his correspondence, as his dismissal from the Ministry of Education was soon to do.

By 1880 Leskov's literary income must have taken a leap forward;
so the loss of the government post was not a disaster. Though he was
still excluded from all the big literary reviews, he was now publishing
extensively in three daily newspapers (*News, New Times,* and *Petersburg Gazette*) and also in Suvorin's newly founded *Historical Messenger.* Nevertheless, Leskov clung to his position in the Ministry of Education until the bitter end.

The "event of March 1" (1881), as it was always euphemistically
called, the assassination of Alexander II, marked the beginning of a
disastrously reactionary period in Russian political history. At a time
when industrialization was causing rapid social and economic
changes, the government of Alexander III resisted making any political changes whatever. Its central resolve was preservation of the autocracy, an institution already outmoded and lacking wide support in
the country. Furthermore, the government continued to alienate even
its potential allies among the more privileged segments of society. Intellectuals were regarded with suspicion and their literary representatives plagued with a censorship more captious and capricious than it
had been since Nicholas I. Toward the radicals the government pursued a vindictive policy of arrests, exiles, and executions.

As the government moved to the right, Leskov moved left, "against
the currents," to use the title of one of his biographies—not to the
"official" left of the secular radicals, whether populist or Marxist, but
left nevertheless. Yet he was still a member of the Learned Committee
of the Ministry of Education, dutifully writing reports and attending
the Tuesday meetings of the committee. At the same time he was publishing stories and articles that were anything but well-intentioned.

Like a smoldering volcano in the aftermath of a major eruption, Leskov continued to emit addenda, codicils to *The Little Things in a
Bishop's Life,* in which, usually under the guise of historical analogy,
he contrived to lay bare the weaknesses of the Orthodox clergy and to
make unfavorable comparisons between Orthodox and Protestant
Christianity. In "Priestly Leap-frog and Parish Caprice," for example,
citing historical documents in *Historical Messenger,* Leskov gleefully
recounts how in 1727 a certain drunken priest named Kirill "within the
holy sanctuary and in his sacerdotal garments had mounted the back

of the deacon and ridden him around the altar."[14] In "A Celestial Serpent" Leskov enumerates the crimes of an Orthodox bishop in the sixteenth-century Ukraine, inquiring why with such bishops the people had not turned to Protestantism, "where Christian morality of course stood much higher and closer to the evangelical ideal."[15]

From behind these historical masks, Leskov sometimes directed his barbs not at Orthodoxy in general, but at certain of its pillars then living. In "A Celestial Serpent" he cites a speech given in Kiev by Konstantin Pobedonostsev, the ober-procurator of the Holy Synod, in which that potentate had admitted that the great weakness of Orthodoxy was the poor quality of its clergy. And who, Leskov inquires cuttingly, has the power to do something about that if not the ober-procurator?[16] In another article, supposedly referring to personalities of the early nineteenth century, Leskov wonders whether the development of Orthodoxy in Russia might have been hampered by the "lack of faith of certain ober-procurators and the harsh despotism of others."[17] It was not hard for his contemporaries to recognize an allusion in the first case to Dmitry Tolstoy, known to be an indifferentist in his own religious beliefs, and to Pobedonostsev in the second. And in an earlier article Leskov had referred to Tolstoy by name, in a tone hardly appropriate for a bureaucratic underling speaking of a minister. In his other positions, Leskov wrote, Tolstoy "had managed to win himself the general disfavor of the entire country." But as ober-procurator of the Synod, presumably because he was not afraid to deal roughly with the bishops, "among his many mistakes he may well have done a good deal of good."[18] These powerful men retaliated, using their bureaucratic weapons. They were joined in the conspiracy to punish Leskov by another of his former friends, Terty Filippov, then assistant comptroller of state, who aspired to the post of either ober-procurator or minister of education.[19] Pressure was brought to bear on the new minister of education, Count Ivan Delyanov, to put a gag on his insubordinate literary subordinate or get rid of him altogether. Delyanov complied.

The confrontation between the two men took place on February 8, 1883, perhaps the most heroic day of Leskov's life. Here is his own account of the affair, given in a letter to his Kiev friend, the historian Filipp Ternovsky, who was soon to be a victim of Pobedonostsev's tyranny (later that year Ternovsky was dismissed from his post in the Kiev Theological Seminary for an article criticizing the late metropolitan of Moscow Philaret [Drozdov]):[20]

There is not much to tell. The affair took place on February 9th [actually February 8th, since Leskov went to the ministry on Tuesdays]—face to face with Del[yano]v, who kept begging me "not to get angry" [and saying] that "he himself had nothing to do with it," that "it was all pressures from outside." The satellites of that lackey [. . .] spread it around town that the "pressure" came from the Emperor himself, but that of course is a bald lie. The pressurers proved to be Lampadonostsev and Terty. I did not request permission to resign, and when he asked me to allow him to "refer to [such] a request," *I did not agree.* I said: "I can't allow that, and I will protest." I *wanted* to force them out into the open, and I succeeded. I am not in the least aggrieved, but I was very angry, and I spoke bluntly and told him many home truths. To the question "Why do you want such a dismissal?" I replied "For my obituary" and left.[21]

From his memories of Leskov's oral rendition of this scene, Andrei Leskov gives a variant finale. During the conversation Leskov in his nervousness had sat down on a windowsill while Delyanov remained standing—a marked breach of etiquette. Still hoping to elicit a "voluntary" resignation, the minister took no notice of Leskov's bad manners. "But why, Nikolai Semyonovich, do you insist on being dismissed rather than resigning?" At this point Leskov came down from the windowsill and flung at the astonished minister, "I need it! If nothing else, for the obituaries, mine—and yours!"[22]

The "Armenian enlightener of Russia," as Leskov was to call him later,[23] achieved an unenviable immortality in Russian history, though not as the perpetrator of this affront. By the time Delyanov's obituaries were written, in 1897, he had been minister of education for fifteen years and had committed so many more outrages that the memory of this one had faded.[24]

In time and in accordance with his wish Leskov was listed as dismissed "without request" (and without explanation) from the Ministry of Education. The writer did not allow the incident to rest there; he meant to exhibit the dirty work to the public eye. So he arranged for an anonymous article to be planted in the *News,* saying that the dismissal "without request" of the "well-known writer N. S. Leskov" had created a "sensation." Moreover, the lack of an explanation had "aroused perplexity in many people."[25] In order to relieve this perplexity, Leskov felt obliged to explain the circumstances of his dismissal, in a "Letter to the Editor" of the same newspaper:

I was dismissed from the Ministry "without request" for reasons lying entirely outside my official work, which for ten years was recognized as useful and had never evoked a single reproach or reprimand from three ministers [. . .] No fault of mine was adduced as the reason for my dismissal from the service; I was only told that my literary activities were "incompatible" with service. Nothing more.

In the fact that I was dismissed not at my own request, but "without request" there is also nothing damaging or offensive to me. I was given full opportunity to resign according to the procedure that is usually considered more comfortable, but I myself preferred the one which in my view more accurately reflected the true state of affairs.[26]

For the last eleven years of his life Leskov's only "service" was to literature.

ᏨᎬ 26 ᏕᎲᎧ

The Christmas Story

During the late seventies and early eighties Leskov's literary work became decentralized. The small forms, particularly the short story, came to prevail over the larger genres. Leskov had begun his career in belles lettres as a writer of short stories. But if we arbitrarily define the short story as any work of prose fiction less than thirty-five pages in length, then Leskov had produced no short stories between "The Mocker" (1863) and "The Pygmy" (1876), whereas in the following decade, up to 1886, he turned out more than twenty-five of them. In a parallel development, after 1878 the process of diversification affects the subject matter and aim of Leskov's art: it becomes more independent of didactic purpose.

Apart from psychological speculations, two practical reasons for this development may be suggested. First, the short story was a convenient size for insertion in newspapers, where many of Leskov's works now made their first appearance. Second, the theme of the Orthodox church and its frailties becomes less obsessive after *The Little Things in a Bishop's Life.* Leskov did not abandon it, but now his energy and talent went in other directions as well.

In pretelevision days newspapers were called upon to provide more in the way of features or entertainments, than they do now; among the standard offerings were Christmas stories—fictional pieces tailored for a traditionally expanded Christmas number of the paper. Leskov produced a considerable number of such short stories. It is difficult to make an exact count, since stories slide easily in and out of the Christmas category. By 1886 enough Christmas stories had accumulated for Leskov to bring out a volume of them, entitled *Stories of the Christmas Season.*[1] The Christmas story had become a standard item in Leskov's repertory, a subgenre in itself.

In the lead-off story in that volume, "Pearl Necklace" (1885), Leskov executes a Sternean literary maneuver (in a Leskovian variant), turning his art in on itself.[2] Stressing the artificiality of literary form,

373

he "lays bare" some of the technical problems of the Christmas genre. "Pearl Necklace" is a skaz, but its frame is of novel design. Instead of the familiar group discussion of some problem into which the narrator inserts his story, we have a frame made up of writers' shop talk.

The frame narrator is a writer and thus presumably identified with the author; he passes on some professional scholia heard from his illustrious confrere, the late Aleksei Pisemsky, this time identified by name. Anticipating the unorthodox literary fraternity of the 1920s called the Serapion Brothers, the discussants had been deploring the impoverishment of plot and inventiveness in Russian fiction of the late nineteenth century. At this point the "author" injects a comment, which he attributes to Pisemsky and transmits in Pisemsky's style of jaundiced cynicism.

The reason for the pallor of Russian plots, Pisemsky is quoted as saying, is—railroads! Travel by rail is too fast and too easy; it leaves no impressions. In the bumpy days of coach journeys, you might have a scoundrel of a driver, insolent fellow passengers, and have to stop over at an inn where the proprietor was a swindler and the cook a botcher; and you would be left with a marvelous stock of pungent impressions to be transmuted into literature. But when you travel by train, "the only impression you'll get is that you'll be shortchanged by a flunkey and you won't even have time to enjoy cursing him out" (7:432-433).

One of the guests objects that in England everyone travels by fast train, yet Dickens "saw and observed a great deal, and the plots of his stories do not suffer from poverty of content" (7:433). The only exceptions are his Christmas stories. "They too, of course, are splendid, but they are a bit monotonous." But that is not Dickens's fault, since monotony is the nature of the genre:

[The Christmas story] is a species of literature in which the writer feels himself a prisoner of too constricted and precisely organized a form. The immutable requirements of the Christmas story are that it should be linked to the events of some evening between Christmas and Epiphany, that it should be somewhat supernatural, that it should carry some sort of moral, if only the invalidation of some harmful prejudice, and finally, that it absolutely must have a happy ending. In life there are few such events, and therefore the author forces himself to invent and to contrive a plot to fit this scheme. And therefore in Christmas stories you find great artificiality and monotony. (7:433)

374

Still another discussant, the future skaz narrator, objects to this somber view and insists that the Christmas story can fulfill all the stated requirements and yet "present a remarkable variety while reflecting both the times and the ways of men" (7:433).

Since he has the last word, the final speaker's position may plausibly be taken as Leskov's own. Leskov evidently regarded the Christmas story as something like a prose sonnet, its limitations a stimulating challenge to a writer's ingenuity. Within its scanty plot of ground, fenced in by many tight requirements, he had to devise narrative designs that give the impression of infinite variety, of unlimited spaciousness and freedom. On balance, Leskov met this challenge with notable success. Though his Christmas stories are not all masterpieces, some of them may be placed alongside the Dickensian model, even the matchless, if now unbearably hackneyed, *Christmas Carol*.

Narrow as the specifications for the Christmas story are proclaimed to be in "Pearl Necklace," in practice the holiday costume in most cases could be slipped on and off rather easily. Of the twelve stories in *Stories of the Christmas Season*, only four were from the outset designed as Christmas stories and made their debuts in the Christmas numbers of magazines or newspapers. The rest were given a superficial cosmetic revision to make them acceptable for the 1886 Christmas volume. Likewise, Christmas details were sometimes removed later. The first true Christmas short story Leskov wrote was originally entitled "Christmas Eve with a Hypochondriac"; it appeared in the Christmas number of *New Times* for 1879.[3] This original version contained two frame chapters of discussion on the subject of belief and unbelief. The skaz narrator, Ivan Ivanovich, then recounted the transcendent experience whereby he claimed to have recovered his Christian faith, which had earlier "dissolved." That experience was to witness his uncle, a rich Moscow merchant,[4] engage in a saturnalia of drunkenness and debauchery, followed by an orgy of penitential prayer before a celebrated icon of the Virgin.

In this original version, cutting against the grain of his Protestant convictions, Leskov had forced himself to treat this display of alcoholic idolatry as a serious religious experience, padding his frame with pious commentary about the natural religiosity of the Russian people. His publisher, Suvorin, had evidently been dissatisfied with an earlier draft and demanded changes. Leskov complied; but the defensive irritation he expressed in the accompanying letter probably stemmed from his sense of guilt at having violated his own beliefs: "Of course it is *greased* [*smazano*, Leskov's italics]. What else can you do? I wrote it in haste while *sick in bed*. I just didn't want to refuse you and did *the best I could*. Now I've redone it *the way you wanted*. The main thing is the picture of the Khludov debauch, which took place *last year* and which Kokorev attended. It will make lively reading. I've now told it more intelligibly, but you can do with it what you like; I have no empty vanity and value matter more than nonsense" (6:654).

On Christmas Day, 1879, with the issue of *New Times* in his hands, Leskov wrote Suvorin again. After praising three Christmas poems it contained, he continued *pro domo sua:*

> My piece, I think, is no worse than theirs, although there is "grease"; but (I forgot to say) that really a Christmas story can rarely do without some such grease. It sometimes shows through like white threads [sic] even in Dickens. It doesn't matter: the main thing is that some vivid image should remain. Now I see what should have been done—I should have tossed out the editorializing introduction, which necessitates the generalizations at the end, and simply made a story of a *day's round*—what a Russian can rampage through in a day.[5]

When two years later Leskov did revise this story for his *Russian Miscellany* collection,[6] he wiped off the Christmas "grease" he had smeared on at Suvorin's insistence. With a new, ironic title, "Exorcism," the story was stood on its ideological head. It was no longer a Christmas story, but a brilliant satire of the superstitions and pseudo-religiosity of the Moscow merchantry. In twelve pages it offers a perfect, mocking rebuttal of the dubious Dostoevskian notion, "sin your way to Jesus." The ultimate symbol of "Orthodox" hypocrisy in Leskov is the reprobate old moneybags in the church, lying prostrate and sobbing, in an attitude of overwhelming contrition, while his feet continue to tap out the *trepak*, the stamping folk dance he had capered through during the previous evening's carousal.

If we discount the decommissioned "Exorcism," the first stable Christmas story Leskov wrote was "White Eagle," published in the Christmas number of *New Times* for the following year, 1880.[7] Like "Exorcism," "White Eagle" was written under the pressure of the Christmas deadline. As late as December 17 it was still unfinished: Leskov wrote Aksakov that he was "scrambling with all possible haste to put together a Christmas story for Suvorin."[8]

Except for its Christmas dating, "White Eagle" is essentially a ghost story, of a kind in vogue in the 1870s and 1880.[9] People were beginning to tire of the flatness of high realism and to look back with nostalgia at the glamors of romanticism—its freedom, its naked egoism, its mysteries. These ghost stories are perhaps the first straws in the wind that was to blow symbolism into power a generation later. The late nineteenth-century reader, however, with all his scientific indoctrination, remained proudly skeptical of the supernatural, and the road back to the romantic mysteries seemed blocked. The writer's problem was to titillate him with a realistically plausible ghost story. The typical solution was artificial ambiguity—a plot so contrived that the sober reader could interpret the spooky apparitions naturalistically, yet still enjoy toying with the notion that there might be "more things in heaven and earth" than naturalism could account for.

"White Eagle" is Leskov's first work in this ambiguous tradition. It is a very professional story, cleverly put together—perhaps too cleverly to carry full conviction. The title is neatly integrated into the plot. The skaz narrator, Galaktion Ilyich, is a government inspector sent out from Petersburg to investigate the malfeasance of a provincial governor.[10] He has been promised the award of a white eagle medal if he successfully carries out his mission. In the provincial capital Galaktion Ilyich is assigned the services of an attractive young official whose name, by an extraordinary coincidence, is Akvilyabov (from *aquila alba*), and who is known as the "white eagle" for his handsomeness and winning personality.

The story's game is to play upon the mysterious correspondence between man and medal. The much beloved Akvilyabov inexplicably dies, and Galaktion Ilyich, a man whose physical appearance is terrifyingly ugly, is accused of putting the evil eye on him. Afterward the ghost of the "white eagle" appears to pursue the hideous inspector and by a series of tricks prevent him for three years from receiving the promised "white eagle." After that interval the ghost's need for vengeance is apparently satisfied, and Galaktion Ilyich receives his long-awaited award.

The ghost's appearances can be read as the hallucinations (the word is used in the text) of its victim, who is said to have suffered all his life from ill health. But to link Galaktion Ilyich with the "mad officials" of Gogol and Dostoevsky, as Leonid Grossman does,[11] goes too far. Referring vaguely to "the classic images of Dostoevsky and Gogol," Grossman further connects "White Eagle" with Leskov's other tales of insanity, the early "A Short History of a Case of Private Derangement" (1863) and the late masterpiece "The Rabbit Warren" (written 1891-1894). These analogies seem too loose to be significant, especially since Galaktion Ilyich, except for his hallucinations (if such they are), is not described as "mad."

Maria Goryachkina[12] tries to make a more specific case for a connection between "White Eagle" and Gogol's "Nose." Leskov was indebted to Gogol in many ways; but here Goryachkina shows only that both stories make use of the oxymoronic effect of introducing fantastic apparitions into the humdrum world of bureaucracy, and that the phantoms of neither author observe the usual rules of ghostly decorum. Gogol's story seems the weirder and more original of the two, since it dispenses entirely both with the convention that phantoms are the spirits of dead people and with any naturalistic explanation for their appearances. Leskov's is a more conventional dead man's ghost, though the posthumous Akvilyabov does unghostly things like slamming doors, singing jaunty songs, and speaking bad Russo-French.

Vsevolod Setchkarev offers an ultranaturalistic explanation for Akvilyabov's sudden death, namely that he might have been poisoned by the governor, who feared exposure of his crimes.[13] The suggestion is appealing, but one wonders whether Leskov thought of it. Setchkarev does not make clear why Akvilyabov should have been poisoned rather than Galaktion Ilyich, nor, more importantly, explain why Leskov did not plant in the text some allusion to this possibility.

Though its connection with the Christmas season is tenuous—only the fact that medals and commendations were traditionally given out on New Year's Day—"White Eagle" complies with most of the other Christmas story requirements outlined in "Pearl Necklace." It could be said to have a happy ending, if a ghoulish one: the conflict over the medal is ultimately resolved to the narrator's satisfaction and apparently the ghost's as well; and the potentially tragic death that produced the ghost in the first place has been distanced so as to minimize its pathos. Certainly the story is a good deal more than somewhat supernatural. But it is difficult to say what harmful prejudices "White Eagle" eradicates: perhaps the prejudice that ghosts have no sense of humor.

Ghostly impishness is also the leitmotif of Leskov's next Christmas story. In this case, the contrived mystery and ambiguity have been eliminated, with advantageous results. Though he was not immune to belief in spirits, Leskov was at his literary best in unadulterated satire of the spiritualist fad. His story "The Spirit of Mme Genlis" (1881) deftly scoffs at spiritualist credulity and at Victorian prudery.[14]

The protagonist is a high-society princess who relies on the advice of the ghost of Stéphanie-Félicité de Genlis (1746-1830) in making crucial decisions. The opinions of that once-famous writer were obtained by opening volumes of her works at random and reading whatever struck the eye.[15] The princess favors Mme Genlis because of her high moral tone, which she contrasts with the shocking immorality of later (Victorian) literature, especially its Russian branch, from whose filth she guards her virginal daughter. (The princess is scandalized, for example, by Oblomov's sybaritic contemplation of the "elbows" of Agafya Pshenitsyna.)

Leskov appears as narrator *in propria persona*, as the author of "The Sealed Angel," a victim of literary persecution, and an acquaintance of the Parisian Jesuit Prince Gagarin. In the story, "literature," in the person of Mme Genlis's irreverent ghost, administers a bitter lesson to the prudish princess. First, as narrator, Leskov vigorously argues with her, defending the freedom of literature against her puritanism; in the process of arguing, he anticipates the climactic scene by relating the anecdote about the prudish French lady who could not bring herself to say the word *culotte*. When circumstances obliged her to utter it in the presence of the queen, she made matters infinitely worse by stumbling to a halt after the frightful first syllable.

In the climax the princess's daughter is called upon to read aloud a passage from Genlis, picked at random for prophetic purposes. She naively comes forth with an unseemly, hilarious anecdote. The blind Mme Dudeffand, who customarily felt the faces of new acquaintances with her hands, mistook the noble visage of the monumentally obese Edward Gibbon for his . . . *cu*. The princess may not have been cured of her prudery by this catastrophe, but she lost her faith in the spirit of Mme Genlis.

"The Spirit of Mme Genlis" was not originally a Christmas story, but it was not hard to make it into one. It dealt authentically, if a bit disrespectfully, with the world of spirits; it aimed to invalidate harmful prejudices; and it had what may qualify as a happy ending—for us, if not for the princess. Thus all it needed to become a certified Christmas story was some connection with the Christmas calendar. This Leskov easily arranged in preparing the story for the book edition: he staged the climactic scene on New Year's Eve.

In 1882 Leskov produced four stories that were eventually included in the 1886 Christmas volume. The first of these chronologically is "The Darner," published in March under the title "The Moscow Ace."[16] The story deals with the fury of the "Moscow ace"—a rich parvenu—

at the discovery that a mere darner (a clothes-repair tailor) has the same surname as his. In the original version of the story this unhappy secret was given away in the initial frame, which led off with a discussion of the problem of the coincidence of literary names with those of real people. There were allusions to Gogol (doubtless the opening paragraphs of "The Overcoat") and to Zola (his unsuccessful defense in the lawsuit brought against him in 1882 by a barrister who had the same name as one of the characters in *Pot-Bouille*). In altering the story for the Christmas genre, Leskov cut away the discursive frame and substituted a single holiday sentence: "What a stupid practice it is to wish everyone some new happiness in the new year, but sometimes something like that really does come" (7:793).

The frame narrator, presumed to be the author, recounts how he met the skaz narrator. The latter is the darner, a Russian of the Russians, from the most Russian part, the "Zamoskvoreche," of the truly Russian capital, Moscow (not Petersburg). Yet his shop sign advertises the services of one "Maitr taileur Lepoutant" [sic]. The "author" persuades him to explain how he came to bear his un-Russian appellation.

"Maitr Lepoutant" recounts in excellent, if not strictly literary, Russian a series of adventures he had undergone, all dated Christmas, New Year's Eve, or Epiphany. The last of these had been a typically Russian (or Leskovian) "laughter and grief" display of fate's inconstancy. First, he had his ears boxed by the parvenu "ace"; then the same man presented him with a 35,000 ruble house in free gift, on the sole condition that he transform himself into the outlandish Lepoutant. In this final version, only much later does he—and we—learn the reason for the fury and the generosity, namely that parvenu and tailor both bear the surname Laputin, an ordinary, plebeian name that has repeatedly interfered with the parvenu's aristocratic ambitions. As Boris Bukhshtab has pointed out (7:516-517), the Christmas adaptations greatly improved "The Darner." It now acquired an element of suspense lacking in "Moscow Ace."

In its final version "The Darner" is an amusing and gratifying Christmas anecdote. For all its gaiety, however, it reiterates one of Leskov's bitter criticisms of Russian society, the helpless vulnerability of its lower orders to the caprice of their betters. One suspects, alas, that boxes on the ears were a much more realistic epiphany of this social reality than gifts of houses from parvenu Santa Clauses.

The second of Leskov's 1882 Christmas stories, "Yid Somersault,"[17] is the most offensive and morally tainted product to come from Leskov's pen. That it could be included in a Christmas volume and accepted there without demur by reviewers and apparently by most readers indicates the extent to which anti-Semitic prejudice had become endemic in the Russian consciousness (see Chapter 33).

In "An Apparition in the Engineers' Castle," the third of his 1882 Christmas stories,[18] Leskov attempts a new solution to the problem of the nineteenth-century ghost story with great success. Here he resorts neither to contrived ambiguity nor to satirical mockery. In outward appearance this is one of his most straightforward narratives, for once not a skaz. But beneath the straightforwardness Leskov has hidden a piece of narrative wizardry.

The main stratagems in "An Apparition in the Engineers' Castle" are two. First. a dual angle of vision is established. One belongs to the young denizens of the Engineers' Castle, an eighteenth-century palace in Petersburg, once the residence of Paul I, but now used as a school for future army engineers. These children, especially the younger ones, believe in the reality of ghostly apparitions and are terrified by them. Such dread seems appropriate in that dismal place, the scene of the grisly assassination, in 1801, of the mad emperor.[19] The second angle of vision is ours and the author's, which is distanced from that of the youthful engineers and systematically discounts their naive terrors. Thus there is no ambiguity about the reality of the castle's ghosts: we know that they are nothing but figments of the boys' imaginations. To underscore this point, Leskov relates in detail how several of the terrifying apparitions had been prankishly staged by the older boys. (One of these boys, however, was rumored to have been flogged to death for this escapade, thus creating a new specter to haunt the castle.)

We thus begin with the naturalistic world: the Engineers' Castle, as a microcosm, has enough real horrors; it needs no reinforcements from fairyland. On this "scientific" foundation, Leskov constructs a frightening ghost story, complete with a corpse, a nocturnal vigil by its side, mysterious noises, and finally an apparition in white that terrifies the young corpse-watchers and us as well. Ultimately it turns out that the apparition has an acceptable, and even touching, natural explanation.

Leskov displays the utmost in narrative skill, first in forcing us to identify with the boys and thus share their feelings, even though we repudiate the superstitions on which those feelings are based; and second, in postponing the resolution as long as possible. Tension is built up during a long series of preliminary episodes, associations, and digressions, in the course of which a clue to the ultimate solution is carefully but unobtrusively dropped. "An Apparition in the Engineers' Castle" is a tour de force of narrative art.[20]

Curiously, the only one of Leskov's 1882 Christmas stories published on Christmas Day—its original title was "Christmas Night in a Railway Carriage"[21]—is in many ways the least Christmas-like (except for the infamous "Yid Somersault"). "A Journey with a Nihilist," as it was rebaptized for the 1886 volume, is a pure anecdote. It is based on a story Leskov had heard in 1879 from a friend of his daughter's, a Mme Sarandinaki. Since Andrei Leskov provides us with his recollection of the original version of the tale as he heard it from that "uninhibited and widely experienced lady,"[22] we have an unusual opportunity to compare this oral raw material with the finished product.

On a Christmas rail trip to a provincial town, a fellow passenger of Mme Sarandinaki's had refused to remove a suitcase from the seat of the compartment he was sharing with several others, replying to every request that he do so with a curt "I don't care to." Enraged by his arrogant incivility, the other passengers planned to denounce him to the railway authorities on reaching their destination. On their arrival, however, the antisocial gentleman was greeted with a great show of respect by the local officials: apparently he was a bigwig of some kind. It also turned out that the offending suitcase was not his.

To transform the nuclear anecdote, Leskov first injected an ingredient of political satire. In Leskov the churlish official is taken by his fellow travelers for a "nihilist," a revolutionary terrorist (this was the year after Alexander II's assassination), because of his unconventional attire and hairdo. His obstinate refusal to move the odious luggage, here transformed into a laundry basket, is thus doubly suspicious. The final irony is that he is revealed to be a public prosecutor, among whose official obligations is the defense of society against nihilists.

As he had shown in *Laughter and Grief*, Leskov was fond of poking sly fun at the many absurdities of nineteenth-century Russian political "policemanship." He satirizes particularly the tendency of the average philistine, in periods when police paranoia is rife, to take vicarious pleasure in contemplating the authorities' relentless pursuit of "subversives," sometimes trying to join in the chase themselves. Here, as in the late and more substantial story "The Rabbit Warren," the ridiculous confusion between pursuer and pursued symbolizes how misguided, unfair, and dangerous such efforts are.

Leskov's representative philistine, in "A Journey with a Nihilist," is a provincial deacon, who leads the passengers' campaign against the putative terrorist and, while doing so, emits a steady stream of Leskovian verbal girandoles, including favorites from other works.[23] The difficulty of translating these verbal displays has kept this vital dimension of "A Journey with a Nihilist" locked within Leskov's Russian.

The story may be adjudged a successful display, in small compass, of Leskov's narrative art, though it is marred by a basic implausibility. Would anyone, no matter how surly, *six times* repeat "I don't care to" when asked by a railway conductor to move a basket, without once adding the phrase that would instantaneously have solved the problem (and destroyed the anecdote), "It's not mine!"?[24]

Leskov was later granted an opportunity to claim that life was being true to his fiction. In January 1885, a Russian newspaper carried an account of an incident that had just occurred in Italy. The president of the Ravenna district court at the railway station in Forlí picked up an anarchist paper he found lying on a table and was thereupon arrested as an anarchist. In "Ancient Psychopaths," published shortly thereafter, Leskov wove this story, together with a recapitulation of "A Journey with a Nihilist," into a discussion of the often perverse relations between literature and life. Perhaps, he suggests facetiously, it is not literary invention that is becoming impoverished, but life itself, which has been reduced to "playing on its keys the imperfect products of our composition." For although there had been "certain changes in characters and setting corresponding to the conditions of the locale, the whole plot is the same" (7:450).

The year 1883 produced four more stories for the Christmas volume, including some of the most famous. The first of these is a gem called "A Little Mistake,"[25] published, like "The Spirit of Mme Genlis," in *Fragments*, the low-brow weekly humor magazine of which the young Chekhov was just becoming a mainstay. Like the revised "Exorcism," "A Little Mistake" is pure satire, again directed at the superstitious pseudoreligiosity of the Moscow merchantry.

The target here is the misguided reverence bestowed by uneducated and credulous Muscovites on Ivan Koreisha (1780-1861), a half-wit confined to an insane asylum, whose mutterings were considered oracular and his prayers infallibly efficacious. Leskov tells an ironic anecdote about a little mistake in the use of Koreisha's magic powers. When Koreisha is asked to beseech God to bestow the gift of children on the infertile eldest daughter of a Moscow tea and sugar merchant, a mix-up over names occurs. As a result, his second, unmarried daughter is rendered pregnant by the half-wit's prayers. Leskov fills out this skeleton anecdote skillfully, producing a particularly charming characterization of the jovial, childless son-in-law, who, although his faith —especially in the moronic thaumaturge—is shaky, extracts the family unscathed from its predicament.

"A Little Mistake" required minimal changes for the Christmas collection: the discussion about belief and unbelief into which the anecdote was inserted as skaz was simply dated "in the Christmas season" (*na svjatkax*).

Shortly after "A Little Mistake," Leskov published a longer tale originally called "The Featherbrains."[26] Later, under the title "Deception," it was changed in the same superficial way by dating the preskaz discussion "just before Christmas." Like "The Melamed from Österreich" and "Yid Somersault," this skaz emanates from the military milieu; and like them, it exudes the offensive odor of anti-Semitism. It is also full of a more unusual prejudice, anti-Rumanianism. The Rumanians, according to the narrator, an exofficer turned policeman, although they are "of the same Orthodox faith as we," are nevertheless "such scoundrels the like of which the world has not yet seen."[27] His narrative demonstrates this unexpected opinion.

The narrator's displeasure with the Rumanians has been aroused by differences between Balkan economic and sexual mores and those of northern Europe. Leskov's account of these ethnographic varieties, though accurate, lacks interest; the old soldier is dull and repellent; and his tales of sexual frustrations in Moldavia are so interminably drawn out that they become tedious. "Deception" is not one of Leskov's artistic successes.

Nor is the story morally satisfactory. In the frame finale the narrator reiterates his substitution of anti-Rumanianism for anti-Semitism, proposing a toast "to the Yids and to the confusion of those evil swindlers, the Rumanians." Such a toast may sound intrinsically absurd and therefore ironic, intended to mock the very prejudices it expresses. That is the generous interpretation given to the story by its skillful English translator, William Edgerton;[28] and he is probably right with regard to Leskov's conscious intent. To set aside one's anti-Semitism in favor of anti-Rumanianism would seem ridiculous, even to inveterate neighbor-haters. The moral conclusion is that we should set aside not only anti-Semitism, but all ethnic prejudice. Leskov draws this conclusion in the closing lines, when a member of the narrator's audience proposes a Christmas toast: "Let us wish all men good and no one evil."[29]

Yet one wonders whether Leskov's readers would have derived this message from "Deception." It would seem easy for ordinary Russians to discount these pieties and simply add the Rumanians to their list of despised peoples.[30] In the context of pogrom-wracked Russia of the early 1880s, a playful treatment—"gentle scoffing," as Edgerton calls it[31]—of the subject of ethnic prejudice seems inappropriate artistically and morally. Murder and mayhem call for stronger responses than gentle scoffing. In view of Leskov's ambiguous record on this question, it seems that the timid ironies of "Deception" may stem from the author's lingering ambivalence about Jews.[32]

Leskov wrote two stories explicitly for the Christmas of 1883. The first is a parable for children called "The Magic Ruble"[33]—the ruble that remains intact no matter how many times you spend it, provided you do so wisely and unselfishly. This sentimental fable is of no literary interest.[34]

The other story Leskov published for Christmas 1883 is perhaps his most successful in that genre—"The Wild Beast," one of Leskov's most popular.[35]

"The Wild Beast" (together with "Pearl Necklace") reproduces the basic theme of Dickens's *Christmas Carol,* the moral transformation, under psychological pressures associated with Christmas, of a bad man into a good one. For his Scrooge, Leskov, at the age of fifty-two, resurrected for the last time that archetypal figure from his childhood, the "bad father," "Mr. Fear," Mikhail Strakhov. His name is withheld —perhaps to avoid offending family sensibilities, more likely to enhance his universality. It is as if Leskov were finally able to exorcize this demon by having him, in a literary reincarnation, undergo the classic metamorphosis of Scrooge.

There are many clues that such quasi-autobiographical stories as "The Wild Beast" or "Vale of Tears" had psychological significance for Leskov. He hides nuggets of autobiographical fact in his fiction, yet they have no literary significance, since they could not have been perceived by his contemporary readers (except for a few members of his own family). His reason, therefore, cannot be to enhance versimilitude by claiming that the events "really happened." In "The Wild Beast," for example, why does he leave his cruel uncle nameless, yet use the real name of the German tutor, Kolberg, in his uncle's household (11:13)? Why does the narrator's detective father go to the very place, Yelets, where the elder Leskov had gone on one of his investigative missions (11:10)? Like the appearance in "Vale of Tears" of a wholly fictional character bearing the name of Leskov's aunt, these bumps of private fact embedded in public fiction seem to indicate that some inner reality of the author's is being expressed.

Whatever its psychological significance, "The Wild Beast" is a superb exhibition of the storyteller's art, one which through symbol radiates generalizing energy, yet retains distinct features of individuality. The narrative line gracefully and unobtrusively oscillates between the polarities of the general and the particular, now sketching in the background with its habitual or repeated occurrences, now singling out the unique narrative events that make the story a story.

The narrative is told directly as reminiscence by an "I" whom the naive reader will identify with the author. This narrator was only five years old at the time of the main action, which takes us back to the "archetypal" period of Nicholas I. Though some use is made of the child's reactions—especially the natural sympathy between children and animals—no attempt is made literally to reproduce the child's point of view. The episodes of the plot are partly recalled directly, but partly reconstructed and newly comprehended by the narrator as a reasoning adult.

The plot utilizes two archetypal conflicts, appearing in unusual and confusing variants, superimposed upon one another. The first is the hunt: the primitive confrontation of man and beast, with man as predator asserting his supremacy in the animal kingdom. Through manipulation of the child's point of view and through the negative characterization of the chief hunter, this archetype is up-ended: the reader identifies more with the hunted animal than the hunting man. The second archetype is "master and man," a relationship involving the power of one human being over another, power bestowed by society, not nature.

The archetypes are intertwined. One of the principal antagonists, the main representative of man the hunter, is also an authority figure, the bad father. Being a rich Russian landowner in the days of serfdom, this bad father is a human god, if a terrible one, endowed with power of life and death within his domain. The other principal antagonist is a bear, captured by men as a cub, selected for its unusual intelligence and gentle character, brought up tame, and allowed to run free on the master's estate. During five years in a human environment this bear, named Sganarelle, had led a blameless life, from the point of view of

386

human ethics. But at last its feral nature had asserted itself, and it had begun to molest domestic animals and people. For these crimes the master sentenced it to die, and its elaborately staged execution was to provide an entertainment for his guests on Christmas Day.

As intermediary between these two antagonists stands the third major character, Ferapont or Khraposhka, a young serf huntsman whose duties include supervision of tame bears.[36] Ferapont enjoys a natural rapport with animals, and he and Sganarelle love one another: "they were, in fact, friends," the narrator says (7:265). The slaughter of Sganarelle promises to be an excruciating experience for Ferapont. Sensing this, the sadistic master requires him to serve as one of his friend's executioners. It is a test of the master's power over the man; it is well understood that any hint of resistance will be ruthlessly punished. The climactic scene, the staged hunt of Sganarelle, is described with verve and excitement; and the reader heaves a huge sigh of relief when, through an almost miraculous series of accidents, Sganarelle escapes the destiny decreed for him by the Man. In our emotions this bear has become a symbol of the tragic destiny of an individual trapped in a tyrannical social system. We rejoice in his liberation.

To enable him to play such an exalted role, the bear must be individualized and partly humanized. Though Russian bears are invariably called "Mishka" ("Mike"—originally a human nickname, but through constant use transformed into an appellative and often written with a small letter), this one is given an elegant Italian name, perhaps taken from Molière's *Précieuses ridicules*. In his moments of agony, Sganarelle is compared with King Lear; and, most poignant detail of all, as he emerges from the pit to face his executioners, he absurdly dons a peasant hat given him earlier by Ferapont. During the ensuing battle the bear exhibits moral qualities usually admired by human beings. He fights back against seemingly hopeless odds with courage and even cleverness; and after being treacherously betrayed by his erstwhile human companions, he remains loyal to his friend Ferapont, refusing to extend his anger to the entire human species. Sganarelle is indeed a noble figure.

The most questionable part of "The Wild Beast," as of *A Christmas Carol*, is the aftermath, the redemption of the Man. Impressed by Ferapont's display of love for the bear and deeply moved by an impromptu sermon delivered by the local priest on the text of the Slavonic hymn "Christ is born," the hitherto pitiless old master unexpectedly *"weeps"* (Leskov's italics). Ferapont is forgiven his part in permitting the bear to escape and offered his freedom. Like other manumitted serfs in Leskov (for instance, Patrikei Semyonych in *A Decrepit Clan*), Ferapont refuses to leave his master. Together they spend the old man's last years performing deeds of charity in the slums of Moscow. Eventually the master dies and is buried in the Vagankov Cemetery (the site of Mikhail Strakhov's grave; 11:13); and Ferapont is eventually buried there too, at his master's feet, like a faithful dog.

This moral metamorphosis is psychologically unconvincing and sentimental in conception, like the extraordinary forbearance and generosity of some of Leskov's other threatened authority figures, such as Governor Lanskoy in "The Monognome" or Nicholas I in "The Pygmy." But we can accept the change in Leskov's hero not as realistic representation but as myth, and in this case an imaginative and gratifying reenactment of the Christian myth itself.

It is tempting, in this Christmas story, to perceive analogies, albeit heretically formulated, between its main conflicts and fundamental points of Christian theology. (The validity of these analogies does not depend on Leskov's being consciously aware of them.) Viewed this way, the humanized bear paradoxically represents man, with a small letter, the original sinner, caught with blood on his hands, yet worthy of redemption, of loving and being loved. The tyrannical uncle stands for the "bad god"—perhaps Jehovah in his most primitive, capricious, and implacable aspects. Ferapont, finally, would represent Jesus, as intercessor between God and man, who through love and voluntary sacrifice gains the gift of life for the beast (i.e., man). Ferapont's example has the effect of "taming the beast" (this phrase in thus used metaphorically in the finale) within his lord, not only reconciling him to the actual beast (the bear), but transforming him into an agent of mercy rather than of doom. Christians may consider the formulation blasphemous, but it would appear that in their basic myth the hitherto vengeful Jehovah is similarly reformed through the sacrifice of his son, Jesus the Redeemer. His anger against his creature, man, somehow appeased by his son's unjust execution, he now consents to grant man the possibility of eternal felicity, a possibility previously denied even to the most virtuous.

Leskov's next Christmas story, "Choice Grain," began to appear early in January 1884, still in the Christmas season.[37] It does not seem to have been written as a Christmas story, since it had to be given a superficial revision for the 1886 Christmas volume (another frame discussion in a railway compartment dated to New Year's Eve).[38]

In an illuminating study, William Edgerton has called "Choice

Grain" "Leskov's parody on Gogol."[39] The word "parody" is too strong. Though the story is full of Gogolian echoes and allusions, especially to *Dead Souls,* Leskov in "Choice Grain" is not mocking or imitating Gogol's great "poem." What he does, as Edgerton effectively shows, is to employ certain Gogolian images to make an un-Gogolian point.

This point is an ironic, Leskovian one, by now familiar from "Iron Will," "The Cynic," and many other "national character" stories. Prince Bismarck may have said that the Russians "had begun to make excessive use of their stupidity" and that there was nothing left for Russia to do but "perish."[40] But Russians have no intention of perishing. They will show themselves such artists at knavery that no one could doubt their capacity not only to survive, but to prosper at the expense of others, especially the Germans.

The story is called a "trilogy," designed to demonstrate the universality of the Russian talent for roguery. In its three sections a landowner, a merchant, and a village of peasants perpetrate a series of clever swindles, culminating in a glorious and unpunished swindle of a German insurance company.[41] It is hardly a celebration of the glories Gogol had prophesied at the end of *Dead Souls* for Russia's *troika;* nor is it a Christmas sentiment. "Choice Grain" illustrates, as Edgerton shows with quotations from Leskov's letters written the previous summer, the writer's deep pessimism about Russia's future in the civilized world.

Shortly after "Choice Grain" Leskov brought out another satirical story later superficially revised for Christmas, "The Old Genius."[42] The theme here is the scandalous social irresponsibility of certain persons with high court connections and their immunity to legal judgments brought against them. The story reaches its happy ending when the hero, the old genius, following a favorite Leskovian pattern, exhibits his mental powers in the form of practical know-how. Despite the seeming untouchability of the villain, a high-society shark, the old genius finds a way to force him to repay a poor widow the money she had naively loaned him. "The Old Genius" is entertaining to read; but the characters are little more than clichés, and the genius's genial solution to the widow's dilemma is implausible.

The last of the stories in the 1886 Christmas volume to be written was the programmatic "Pearl Necklace."[43] Because of its suitability as a critical introduction to a collection of Christmas stories, it was moved to first place in that book and also in the corresponding volume of the collected works. Apart from the literary discussion with which it opens, "Pearl Necklace" is less effective than Leskov's best Christmas stories, especially "The Wild Beast," whose theme it shares. Nevertheless, it is not without its charm.

Written before Leskov had officially joined the Tolstoyan "church," "Pearl Necklace" points to an orthodox Tolstoyan moral: when good is returned for evil, the moral effect on the aggressor is transforming. The chain of aggressive action and aggressive reaction is broken; the aggressor is forced to reorder his pattern of thinking, feeling, and acting. Chekhov, too, in his brief Tolstoyan period, was to make this point with such stories as "An Encounter" (1887).

In "Pearl Necklace" a bearish old skinflint has cheated two of his daughters out of their dowries; in consequence they and their husbands have bitterly broken off relations with him. The third daughter is fortunate enough to find a man who marries her only for love—or perhaps mutual esteem would be a better term for it, since the element of sexual passion is absent. The bridegroom is comfortably off and does not concern himself about his bride's dowry. The chain of malignancy is thus broken. The new husband refuses to be drawn into a quarrel with his miserly father-in-law, demanding nothing from him and insisting that he and his wife continue to love and respect her parent both for his sake and for theirs. Her father is so nonplussed by this display of benevolence and lack of greed that he presents them on the spot with 150,000 rubles. They insist, of course, on sharing the money (conveniently divisible into three) with the two disgraced sisters. Like the uncle in "The Wild Beast," the hitherto malevolent old man actually weeps when his heart is at last opened to love and the joy of giving.

Again, this edifying metamorphosis is not psychologically plausible, despite the narrator's assertion that it "really happened." But perhaps we can accept it, outside the usual criteria of realism, as a myth, another instance of moral wish-fulfillment. By Leskov's own testimony, the story of Mary Magdalene may not be psychologically plausible either, as the etymology of our word "maudlin" suggests.[44]

After the publication of *Stories of the Christmas Season* in 1886 (it was placed on the market in time for the Christmas trade of 1885; 11:824), Leskov wrote few narratives identified with Christmas. As he moved back, in the late eighties, to the literary reviews, he evidently felt less pressure to work in this form. He vaguely classified two Oryol "memoir" pieces, "The Bugbear" (1885) and "A Robbery" (1887), as Christmas stories, but in neither case does the Christmas connection have a bearing on the form or content of the story.[45]

In his last years Leskov dutifully turned out several Tolstoyan moral fables, two of which, "Offended before Christmas" and "The Pustoplyasians," he called Christmas stories.[46] These fables have more in common with other didactic tales of the Tolstoyan period than with the earlier Christmas stories (except for "Christ Visits a Muzhik"). They will therefore be considered in their chronological place.

Left, Left, Left

In 1881, at the age of fifty, Leskov wrote his best-known short story, the work Russians associate with his name as we connect *Tom Sawyer* with Mark Twain's: "The Tale of the Crosseyed Lefthander from Tula and the Steel Flea (A Workshop Legend)," as it was originally called.[1] In the collected works (1889), the nameless hero's appellation, *Levshá*, "The Lefthander," was established as the main title, the long one becoming a parenthetical subheading.[2] The story will be referred to here as "The Lefthander."[3]

During the spring of that year Leskov's friend Yelizaveta Akhmatova, a translator and writer for children, had begun importuning him to contribute to a volume of miscellanea she was planning to issue as a bonus for purchasers of a set of her collected works. Leskov was not eager to do so: it was an obscure place to bury one of his stories, and Akhmatova could not pay well. She was persistent, however, and eventually he succumbed: "I am pursued by fate [Leskov wrote to Ivan Aksakov] in the person of Mme Akhmatova, who has dreamed up some sort of jubilee almanac and has been tormenting me with demands for an article. I agreed to let her use my name, but did not promise any work, since I want to write the story I long since promised to *Russian Speech*. However, Akhmatova got the best of me, and I'll have to write something for her."[4]

But the little piece Leskov had intended to knock off quickly for Akhmatova outgrew the modest dimensions he had assigned it and consumed much time and energy. As the story gained in quality and quantity, Leskov begrudged giving it to Akhmatova. As he wrote to Aksakov:

> I began to write for her a little piece of about thirty pages, in which I decided to be free of all constraint. But suddenly I fell in love with it and decided to steal it from her and give it to you and to write her something more in the petticoat style [. . .] I've

written three little sketches (some 30 pages altogether) under the general title "Historical Characters in Fabulous Folktales of Recent Composition," and they've turned out very lively and humorous. These are pictures in folk style concerning three emperors: Nicholas I, Alexander II, and Alexander III ("the economical"). They are all very lively, very funny, and full of movement. In short, everyone I've read them to has liked them, and I think I'm not likely to write anything better, especially since I haven't got time. And you will be able to squeeze it through the censorship, for it's not disrespectful, but affectionate, although not without some home truths. In brief, they are passable and inoffensive. (7:500)

Like many letters of writers to their publishers, not all is "home truth" in this missive, in particular the stated ratio between work planned and work accomplished. In May 1881 Leskov had not in fact completed three "little sketches," but was working on two of them. The one portraying Alexander III, finished later that summer, was to become "Leon the Butler's Son"; this was the story "more in petticoat style" that Leskov exchanged for "The Lefthander."[5] The story with Alexander II as its hero apparently never got written (though "Leon the Butler's Son," nominally about Alexander III, deals mainly with his father's reign). The story about Nicholas I was the one Leskov fell in love with. Pushed back to include Alexander I as well, it grew to the size originally planned for all three little sketches together. It became "The Lefthander."

The original title of this work had included in parentheses a semiserious genre designation: "a workshop legend." In the original magazine version Leskov had appended a footnote to this subtitle; in the separate edition of 1882 he raised the footnote to the status of "Preface." In the collected works, for reasons discussed below, he eliminated it.

In this excluded note Leskov had explicitly claimed folk origin for the tale, assigning himself the role of transcriber:

I cannot say exactly where the tale of the steel flea was first wound up, that is, whether it was in Tula, on the Izhma, or in Sestroretsk; but evidently it came from one of those places. In any case the tale of the steel flea is specifically an armory legend, and it expresses the pride of Russian masters of the gunsmith's trade. In it is depicted a contest between our masters and English ones, out of which ours emerged victorious, and the English were put to shame and humiliated. Here too is elucidated a certain secret reason for our military misfortunes in the Crimea. I transcribed this legend in Sestroretsk from the oral recitation of an old gunsmith who lived there, a native of Tula, who had moved to the Sestra River back in the reign of Alexander I. The narrator two years ago was still in good health and of sound memory; he liked to recall old times, greatly revered the Emperor Nicholas I, lived "according to the Old Belief," read pious books, and kept canaries. People treated him with respect. (7:499)

In this quasi-genetic footnote Leskov was following a familiar procedure. First, appearing as "author" in an initial frame (the note functions as a frame), he makes the acquaintance of a colorful character, who then tells the core story as oral narrative or skaz, with the "author" ostensibly playing the role of stenographer. The "author" then reappears in the closing frame to point the moral or comment on the story's wider implications.

In "The Lefthander," this narrative machinery collided with the naiveté and prejudice of contemporary readers and critics, and it broke down. The trick succeeded too well. Indeed, the reception of "The Lefthander" illustrates an important, if seldom noticed, fact about literature: there is a crucial difference between belief and suspension of disbelief. It is a little like the game of hide-and-seek, the object of which is to be found (though not too soon). The realist may use all his tricks to create the illusion that the people he describes are real and that the events happened. But to appreciate his art we must retain a subliminal awareness that it is, after all, an illusion. For if art is life, what becomes of the artist?

In "The Lefthander," much to Leskov's chagrin, people took him at his word and accepted the story as an actual transcription of a "gunsmith's legend," crediting the author at best with being a good secretary. "Mr. Leskov's authorial participation [. . .] in the narrative," wrote one reviewer, "is limited to simple stenography. And one should do Mr. Leskov justice: he is a superb stenographer."[6] Other reviewers suggested with some disapproval that Leskov might have made up part of the story or distorted its original oral form.[7] But almost to a man they took literally Leskov's disingenuous statement: "I transcribed this legend."

Leskov's literary vanity was piqued. His letter to Aksakov shows that in writing "The Lefthander" he had felt himself at the peak of his powers. He had put enormous effort into the stylization. As he wrote later of "Pamphalon the Mountebank," "I worked very, very hard on it. This language, like the language of 'The Steel Flea,' does not come easily, but with great difficulty, and only love for his task can induce a man to undertake such mosaic work."[8] Yet even professional critics had perceived his laborious mosaic art as mere stenography.

In self-defense Leskov then made a public confession. In the form of a letter to the editor of *New Times* he published a note entitled "On the Russian Lefthander (A Literary Explanation)." One of the problems touched on in this note was the story's ideological ambiguity. But the question of originality bothered Leskov even more:

> With one voice [the critics] assert that the tale of the lefthander is an "old and well known legend." This requires correction, and I ask permission to make it. All there is of pure *folk* origin in the "tale of the lefthander from Tula and the steel flea" consists of the following joke or witticism [*pribautka*]: 'The English made a flea out of steel, and our Tula men put shoes on it and sent it back to them.' There is nothing more about the "flea"; and about the "lefthander" as the hero of the whole story and as the representative of the Russian people there are no folk tales, and I consider it impossible that anyone could have "long ago heard" about it, because—I must confess—I *made up* the entire story in May of last year, and the *lefthander* is a character *invented by me*. As for the shoeing by the Tula men of an English flea, it is not a legend at all, but a short joke or witticism, like the "German monkey" which "a German invented," but it could not sit down (it kept jumping) until a Moscow furrier "took and *sewed a tail* on it— then it sat down." (11:219-220)

Unfortunately, the damage had been done; probably few of Leskov's readers saw this disillusioning note. He kept trying. In "Ancient Psychopaths" (1885), in an excursus on the paradoxes of the literature and life relationship, he again asserted, in italics, that "The Lefthander" had been *made up* by him (7:449). And in 1889, in a brief article defending the authenticity of his "The Felon of Ashkelon," Leskov affirmed yet again that "there [was] no legend about a 'lefthander from Tula,' and that plot *I myself invented*."[9]

Finally, in that same year, 1889, when preparing "The Lefthander" for his collected works, Leskov in exasperation excised entirely the note about the author's "transcribing" the narrator's legend. Like the early "Life of a Peasant Martyress," "The Lefthander" in its final text begins frameless, with only the folksy language signaling that someone other than the author is speaking ("When the Emperor Aleksandr Pavlovich [Alexander I] had finished up the Council of Vienna, he felt like doing a bit of traveling and taking a look at the wonders in various countries").

One might have thought that now Leskov's readers would have grasped that "The Lefthander" was the product of a literary artist contriving to sound like a folk narrator. But as late as 1905 the first piece of scholarly research devoted to the story again treated it as a transcription of folklore (and a bad one at that: the author, an artillery colonel working in the Tula arms factory, noted with indignation that no Tula gunsmith would speak in the florid language of Leskov's narrator).[10]

In any case, the question of the sources of "The Lefthander" was not settled by Leskov's disclaimers. Perhaps the author had made up the figure of the lefthander; perhaps there had been no legend, no transcription, and no pious old gunsmith with canaries. But the "witticisms" cited by Leskov remained—the one about the Russian shoes on an English steel flea and the analogous one about the German monkey. Furthermore, Leskov had spent the summer of 1878 in Sestroretsk, a town on the Gulf of Finland, where there was an arms factory. While there he had lived in the house of a master gunsmith and had become friendly with the assistant director of the factory.[11] Any literary biographer knowing these facts would feel himself on solid ground in surmising a connection between the Sestroretsk summer of 1878 and the Sestroretsk gunsmith's legend of 1881. Yet Andrei Leskov, who was there, claims that no such connection existed. According to him, before coming to Sestroretsk his father already had in mind the germ of a story, the "joke" or "witticism" about the steel flea recounted in Leskov's note, and during that summer he tried to "find its roots" by questioning the gunsmiths. These efforts were in vain. "Everyone smiled and admitted that they had heard something of the sort, but [added] that it was all foolishness." "And so," Andrei Leskov concludes, " 'The Lefthander' remained in no way indebted to the summer spent in the armorers' village in the gunsmith's cottage. Nor was there any 'old migrant from Tula' there."[12]

One might question whether a twelve-year-old could have such complete information about his father's activities and social contacts. But in view of Leskov's explicit disclaimers and his frequent practice of ascribing his tales to imaginary folk narrators, it seems advisable to accept Andrei Leskov's denials. The question, therefore, still remains: if Leskov's Sestroretsk inquiries were fruitless, where did he get the idea for "The Lefthander" and has it any connection with Russian folklore?

This question has been investigated by two reputable Soviet scholars, E. S. Litvin and Boris Bukhshtab.[13] They first reassayed a nugget of historical reality first unearthed by the artillery colonel. A pair of genuine Tula gunsmiths had been sent to England in 1785. One of them became a drunkard and never returned, but the other came back to Tula, presumably full of impressive tales of English gadgetry which presumably passed into an oral tradition presumably recorded in Sestroretsk by Leskov, who fused the two prototypes into one character—drunken, but repatriated. However, in view of the lack of evidence that any such oral tradition existed and the considerable differences between these facts and Leskov's legend, a genetic connection between those peripatetic gunsmiths and the lefthander seems doubtful.[14]

Next, a demonstrably real prototype to be investigated was the Don Cossack ataman, Count Matvei Platov (1751-1818), who appears in the story as the lefthander's sponsor. Platov did become the hero of Cossack folk songs dealing with the Napoleonic wars, and Leskov's picture of him as the rough, hearty, homespun Russian, unmoved by European baubles and blandishments, the antipode to Alexander's effete cosmopolitanism, is close to the one presented in the songs. However, Bukhshtab correctly stresses the fact that in Leskov's treatment of this figure there are two distinct images: the narrator's positive Platov, corresponding to the Platov of folklore, and the author's partly negative one. Though the negation is never explicitly spelled out, the author and his readers are presumed to share a system of values that does not condone such acts of Platov's as repeated physical assaults on his social inferiors, including the lefthander, or his proposal to have the guiltless lefthander thrown into prison and held there "until such time as he might be needed." The naive narrator accepts such behavior as the natural order of things, part of the fabric of Russian society; but it is clear that the author does not.[15]

Finally, in addition to folklore sources, Litvin discovered many close parallels between Leskov's account of the lefthander's experiences in England and another historical source, a transcribed oral report presented to the real General Platov by one of his Cossacks. This report had been published in a magazine in 1814[16] and not subsequently reprinted; Litvin has no explanation of how Leskov happened to come across it. Nevertheless, he might have done so—he loved rummaging through old books and magazines—and an analogous case cited by Bukhshtab lends credence to the possibility. Bukhshtab reports the discovery by the noted Soviet literary scholar Ilya

Serman, in a magazine dated 1808, of an anecdote reproduced almost verbatim in "The Lefthander" (a pistol greatly admired in England by Alexander I turns out on close examination to have been made in Tula).[17]

Finally, there are the "witticisms" cited by Leskov as the only bona fide folklore analogues of "The Lefthander." As Bukhshtab convincingly argues, the first of these, at least in the form Leskov presents it, is nothing but a synopsis of the plot of "The Lefthander," and that Leskov admitted having "invented." The only attested folk saying resembling it is a locale joke: "The Tula-ites have shod a [live] flea" (a clever but useless thing to do). An adage analogous to the second "witticism" is also attested: "The Germans invented the [live] monkey"—a humorous expression of the Russian peasants' amazement at the wonders of German technology. These together may be the folk seed from which "The Lefthander" sprang.

In conclusion, Bukhshtab reports the discovery of another obscure printed source for "The Lefthander," a little article in the newspaper *Northern Bee* for April 6, 1834. The parallels are striking. There appeared in Petersburg a peasant craftsman who made tiny locks "almost no bigger than a flea," with keys so minute that you had to "examine them through a magnifying glass." Only the huge but deft fingers of their maker could fit one of these microscopic keys into its lock. The craftsman boasted of his locks to a gentleman. The latter thought him mad and ordered him arrested. When he was searched at the police station, some of the locks were found on his person. Vindicated, he was "released with honor." "Of course," the author concludes, "it is a useless thing, but a rare one, for which the English are willing to pay huge sums." The article was signed only "V. B."[18]

Bukhshtab shows how Leskov might have hit on this obscure newspaper piece almost fifty years old. Investigation revealed "V. B." to be Vladimir Burnashov, a hack writer whom Leskov knew personally and whose obituary he wrote.[19] Burnashov's memoirs had been published in *Russian Messenger* at the time Leskov's *Cathedral Folk* was being serialized there. Though the story of the locksmith is not in these memoirs, it seems possible that Burnashov, who met Leskov around this time, told Leskov about it or referred him to the issue of the *Northern Bee*.

To these specific sources for "The Lefthander" one more might be mentioned: Hoffmann's *Meister Floh* (1822). Though the stories otherwise have little in common, Leskov might well have derived from Hoffman the general theme of microscopic vision and in particular the image of a flea in boots. It should be noted, however, that Hoffmann's flea is very much alive![20]

"The Lefthander" was far from achieving instant recognition as a classic. Contemporary critics, blind to Leskov's structural subtleties, charged it, quite unjustly, with moral ambiguity. One of the reasons for critics' persistent misunderstanding is the double angle of moral vision in the story. Two sets of judgments are implanted in the text, one immediate and explicit, the other derived and implicit. The first belongs to the narrator, the naive, semieducated, culture-bound gunsmith. The second is that of the "author," who speaks with his own voice only in the concluding chapter, but whose moral presence can be felt. By implication he—and we—condemn behavior the narrator considers normal, such as Platov's pulling out by the roots great gobs of the lefthander's hair.[21] Readers who thought the story a pure transcription of folklore could not acknowledge the double perspective, though they still inconsistently ascribed to Leskov views expressed in the story of which they disapproved. Thus the problem of the story's origin became integrally bound up with the question of moral interpretation.

One moral issue raised by "The Lefthander" is our response to the narrator's chauvinism. Although they are somewhat neutralized by the humorous style in which he expresses them, the narrator's ethnic aggressiveness and boastfulness were and are offensive to many readers, including Russians; and some of them, quite wrongly, have imputed these attitudes to the author. Yet anyone even superficially acquainted with Leskov's many stories dealing with confrontations of national types would know that he is anything but a jingoist. Within "The Lefthander" it is clear from the linguistic bizarreries alone that the narrator and the author are not to be equated. And apart from style, the outcome of the plot—the tragic fate of the talented Russian artisan in his own country, especially compared with the much more favorable experience of his English friends—hardly sounds like blind insistence on Russian superiority.

Yet there were critics who took Leskov to task for what "The Lefthander" does not say. Blinded by their prejudices against the author of *No Way Out* and hostile to anything that had first appeared in Aksakov's Slavophile *Rus*, left-wing ideologues decided that "The Lefthander" was just another bought-and-paid-for product of a well-known servant of "patriotic" reaction. "You can't help thinking," *Notes of the Fatherland* wrote with heavy irony, "that if uneducated

Russian masters are like this, what would come of them if you taught them from arithmetic the four rules of addition,[22] and you can't help soaring way up high over Europe, singing the praises of Russian talents and patriotic loyalty and chanting 'Ai lyuli, se tre zhuli.' "[23]

In Soviet times, blatant sounding of the national horn no longer evokes the opprobrium it did a century ago. In her analysis of "The Lefthander," Maria Goryachkina praises Leskov (and with just as little justification) for the very chauvinism and xenophobia for which her nineteenth-century predecessors had reprobated him. "The liberal cosmopolites," she writes, "were especially indignant at Leskov's patriotism, his defense of the national individuality of the Russian people, his celebration of their natural giftedness."[24] Writing in 1963 (and showing some lack of political foresight), Goryachkina triumphantly marshaled in support of her "truly Soviet" appreciation of Leskov's patriotism that distinguished literary critic Nikita Khrushchev, who had once given a pep talk in Tula in which he reminded the "happy descendants of Leskov's lefthander" of the "pride in our people" evoked by the story.[25]

It seems the height of irony to associate Leskov with Khrushchev's shoe-pounding chauvinism. Goryachkina goes further, attributing to Leskov as well an Anglophobia of which he could not have been less guilty. The "profoundly mediocre" English, as Goryachkina calls them,[26] may represent "smugly secure, uninspired practicality and self-satisfaction."[27] But in Leskov's story it is the English who most admire the lefthander's workmanship, so undervalued in his own country, and they offer him not only money, but an English bride as well and urge him to settle there permanently. Moreover, the lefthander's only defender during his later misfortunes at home is an Englishman, the hard-drinking, Russian-speaking "half-skipper"[28] of the ship that returns the lefthander to his native land.

Left-wing critics in the nineteenth century also disregarded the strong elements of social criticism in "The Lefthander," whereas party-minded Soviet ones reinterpret them to fit their own stereotypes. Conflicting interpretations of the nuclear plot illustrate this point. The dextrous lefthander and his colleagues do show extraordinary skill in putting shoes on the English steel flea. Skillful as it was, however, this feat is not only useless but harmful. The weight of the shoes prevents the flea from doing its dance. The ingenious mechanism is spoiled. When the English point this out to him, attributing the oversight to his insufficient education, the lefthander ruefully acknowledges the justice of their remarks: "There's no argument that we didn't get very far in our studies, but all the same we're truly devoted to our country" (7:50).

However admirable the lefthander's patriotism, the fact of Russian technological backwardness and social injustice thus remains. Leskov symbolically stresses it, though he rightly adds that the backwardness in no way results from the Russians' lack of talent. It is a product of social conditions. Russians as natively gifted as the lefthander are not offered the opportunity to acquire even a rudimentary education; they are therefore not equipped to assimilate, let alone match, the technical achievements of their Western counterparts.

Even worse, Russian society and its rulers show scandalous lack of appreciation for the accomplishments of their talented countryman. Instead of a triumphal return from England the poor lefthander gets a very "Russian" reception, pointedly juxtaposed with the treatment, afforded the English "half-skipper" in the British Embassy. The two friends, Russian and Englishman, reach Petersburg in a state of acute alcoholic poisoning. The Englishman is examined in his embassy by a doctor, given a hot bath and a "gutta-percha pill," laid on a feather-bed, covered with a sheepskin coat, and left to sweat out the poison; orders are given that no one in the embassy is allowed to sneeze until he wakes up. By the next morning he is himself again. Even the humorous exaggerations in this account indicate the awareness of Leskov's narrator that among the English, ordinary citizens are treated by their civil "servants" with consideration.

By contrast, the semiconscious lefthander is taken to a Petersburg police station, where he is robbed of his clothes, his watch, and his money, and then sent off in the bitter cold, without blankets, in an unpaid sledge, to any hospital that will take him. However, since General Platov had rushed him off from Tula to Petersburg without giving him time to collect his "tugaments"[29] (identification papers), hospital after hospital refuses to accept him. Finally the lefthander is brought to a hospital where "all those of unknown estate are admitted to die" and dumped on the floor. The next day his English friend finds him in a moribund condition.

The loyal "half-skipper" now rushes from one high Russian official to another, trying to rescue the lefthander, but he is repeatedly rebuffed. He is ushered unceremoniously out of the office of Count Kleinmichel for reminding that dignitary that the lefthander has a human soul.[30] At last a doctor is dispatched to examine the now dying lefthander, and to him the folk hero imparts his testamentary message: Tell the tsar that the army should stop cleaning gun bores with brick dust. This was an English technological advance he wished his country to assimilate, fearing dire military consequences if it failed to do so. The message encounters bureaucratic resistance and never reaches the emperor. The result is the Russian defeat in the Crimean War.

In its picture of the treatment the returning folk hero receives in his beloved fatherland, Leskov's story is the opposite of a rightist panegyric to Russian national superiority. Indeed, "The Lefthander" powerfully expresses the leftward leanings of the author's later years. Especially after the assassination of Alexander II, Leskov felt anguish and despair about Russian society—especially the lack of inviolable individual rights and the indifference of its rulers to the fate of their plebeian countrymen. For that reason the second, bitter half of "The Lefthander" pleased Leskov particularly. " 'The Flea' has been much noticed here [in Petersburg], even by the *literati*," he wrote to Aksakov soon after the issue of *Rus* containing the story had come out, "but all the same I think the best part is the ending,—the left-hander in England and his tragic demise."[31]

From the opposite camp conservative nineteenth-century critics rebuked Leskov for the excessive pessimism of his image of Russian society,[32] and some Soviet scholars have used the lefthander's fate as a pretext for venting their righteous wrath at the "venal and greedy pack of rulers of autocratic-serf-owning Russia,"[33] who deliberately "destroyed [. . .] talented Russian patriots."[34] (Such writers of course say nothing about how many "talented Russian patriots" have been destroyed by the Soviet regime.) But the most succinct and penetrating appraisal of the ideological significance of "The Lefthander" was offered by one of the "liberal cosmopolites" Goryachkina so hotly despises. Alone among his impercipient colleagues, the anonymous reviewer for *Messenger of Europe* understood what Leskov was doing. "The entire tale," he wrote, "appears to be designed to support Mr. Aksakov's theory about the supernatural capacities of our people, who have no need of Western civilization; but at the same time it contains within it a very sharp and malicious satire of that very theory."[35]

From the artistic point of view, the most outstanding feature of "The Lefthander" is the "mosaic" of its language, which, as Leskov himself pointed out in letters to a German translator,[36] is impossible to render intact into another tongue. Attempts have been made, of which the best in English is William Edgerton's; but it cannot be said that many of them recapture the sparkle of the original.

Pure linguistic fun is surely one of the artistic aims of this language, perhaps the primary one.[37] Some of Leskov's most successful malapropisms and folk etymologies have become Russian "household words."[38] Despite the resplendence of these verbal fireworks, most nineteenth-century critics and even fellow writers, indoctrinated with the sober canons of realism, expressed disapproval of them, calling them excessive, unnatural, overdone.[39] Perhaps with our modern eclectic capacity to appreciate the most varied styles, including the Baroque, we may be more willing than our great-grandfathers were to enjoy these stunts for their own sake.

But Leskov's verbal tricks actually serve serious and integrating artistic functions. First, they characterize the speaker who uses them and the social milieu from which he sprang. In a programmatic introduction to "Leon the Butler's Son," Leskov laid bare some of these ulterior stylistic motives. The uneducated or semieducated man, when he tries to describe events and personalities drawn from a social world higher than his own, strains to employ language he thinks appropriate to that world. The results are often laughable:

> His language is studded with bizarre deposits of wrongly used words from the most varied milieus. The latter is the result, of course, of too great effort on the part of the originators [of such stories] to reproduce the conversational tone of that social stratum from which they derive the personages represented. Unable to assimilate the true style of such people's colloquial discourse, they think to attain the greatest vividness in transmitting it if they have these persons utter words as quaint and colorful as possible, so as not to resemble ordinary speech. This constitutes a typical feature of *oral popular literature* when it represents persons with a way of life removed from the peasant milieu. (7:61)

Leskov had made good use of this technique in "The Battle-Axe" and was to do so again in "Night Owls"—in both cases with even more structural effect than in "The Lefthander," since in those stories the narrator is a central figure in her own tale and thus partly characterized through her own speech. In "The Lefthander," the folk narrator, the old Sestroretsk gunsmith—even in the 1881-82 version with the initial frame intact—plays no part in his own story. He therefore need not be depicted as an active participant in events. Yet even as a disembodied voice the folk narrator plays an important structural role in the story. Through his mode of narration—choice of words, selection and arrangement of detail, ordering of events, commentary, evaluation—the narrator projects his "point of view" in both senses of the term—the angle of vision from which he sees the events and his attitude toward them. Since the author distances himself from the narrator's attitude, he creates dynamic tension between the narrator's judgments and his own (which we presumably share).

Furthermore, of the two viewpoints, the author's or final one may contain elements unacceptable to certain readers and especially to censors; they must therefore be insinuated by hint and implication. Bizarre language is thus part of the camouflage beneath which Leskov hoped to slip his subversive message through censorships, official and private, and into his readers' hearts. Unfortunately, the continuing critical confusion indicates that in this aim he failed: readers may have enjoyed the story, but too many of them have misunderstood its moral import.

The camouflage function of linguistic bizarreries is more apparent in the case of "Leon the Butler's Son." The subject of this story was also politically sensitive: the corruption that had flourished in high places during the last years of Alexander II's reign. In dealing with this taboo topic the folk narrator distracts attention with his linguistic eccentricities, and his inexperience and incomprehension can be used to motivate intentional confusion of the plot. Leskov described this procedure in the same letter to Aksakov quoted above:

> In a few days Akhmatova will publish a similar [to "The Left-hander"] legend about the present sovereign [Alexander III], under the title "Leon the Butler's Son; A Dinner-Table Predator." It is not as good as "The Flea," but people praise it too. Only it was written in haste and is therefore not so well finished off. Here there is the mania for "predacity" with allusions to certain people, but naturally everything is confused so you can't be sure who this "Leon" is—whether a flunky or someone a bit higher up. There is a Hapfrau [a contamination of *Hauptfrau* with Russian *xapat'*, "to grab, steal, take bribes"] and a Leibmeister [contamination of court titles, Leibmedick and Zeremonienmeister] and his Ober-excellency [. . .] I'm sorry that I left a lot unsaid in my fear of the feminine foolishness of the editor [. . .] The tsar in the story is

very simple, very warmhearted, and (in my opinion) very attractive. The story is funny, jolly, and in the same unsophisticated tone as "The Flea."[40]

The "affectionate" treatment of Alexander III was part of the camouflage. In life Leskov had little affection for this autocrat and regarded even the outset of his reign with deep pessimism. Alexander's reaction to the murder of his father, Leskov well understood, would be a series of vengeful and repressive measures, beginning with the gruesome execution of the assassins.[41] Furthermore, since he had become the heir apparent only on the death of his older brother Nicholas, when he was nearly full grown, Alexander had not received the more comprehensive education given a future tsar. He was ignorant, bigoted, and profoundly influenced by his former tutor, the archreactionary Pobedonostsev, the "Russian Torquemada," as Leskov called him,[42] who now wielded immense power and influence. When on April 29, 1881 (just before "Leon the Butler's Son" was written), the new tsar published a manifesto, written by Pobedonostsev, affirming his "faith in the strength and truth" of the autocracy and his determination to preserve it unchanged, Leskov went out and bought a portrait of Loris-Melikov, the liberal minister of Alexander II's last years whose constitutional project was now summarily abrogated. The portrait stood on Leskov's desk to the end of his days.[43]

Nevertheless, in "Leon the Butler's Son" Leskov used a sentimental image of Alexander III to sugar a bitter pill. He sought to contrast the "sweetness" and incorruptibility of the new Alexander with a satirical picture of the peculation and speculation that had pervaded the royal court in the old Alexander's later years. For in one respect, Leskov may have sympathized with the new tsar, Alexander "the economical": a devoted family man, modest in his personal expenditures, he did try to set a moral tone in financial and sexual matters that contrasted with his father's laxness.

In "Leon the Butler's Son," as in "The Battle-axe," Leskov through his confused folk narrator presents a deliberately confusing worm's-eye view of these high-society piracies. This narrator is "a trading peasant who frequently visited Petersburg and knew here many people who, in his strange words, 'had broad acquaintances in the public and could know at court various absolute circumstances' " (7:62). He is not characterized further, and the contrast between the sentimental frame and the satirical core makes it difficult to believe that they could both be the product of one narrator.

In any case, the author's frame (in which he meets the narrator) is followed by a sugary introduction showing the future Alexander III as a boy, concerned to discover the truth about the life of ordinary people despite the obstacles placed in his path by scheming courtiers. This introduction is followed by the narrator's account, highly confused, of the efforts of Leon the Butler's son—a household official at Alexander II's court—to make the financial most of his position. We are shown a phantasmagoria of bribes, inflated bills, triple bookkeeping, and enforced payoffs of other venal courtiers, including the wily "Hap-frau," who rakes in hush money, plays the stock market, and stashes her gains in a foreign bank.[44]

The picture of these financial machinations is intermixed with that of the complicated sexual capers engaged in by Leon, his wife, and his associates. A deus ex machina resolution is provided by the virtuous Alexander III, who has now ascended the throne. The new tsar uncovers Leon's peculations, dismisses him, and issues a decree that "wherever a predator is discovered, all shall be judged equally by the same law" (7:78). The country rejoices at this wise command, because "the whole land was sickened by predators even worse than by its worst enemies."

As Leskov admitted, "Leon" is no match for "The Lefthander." Though it contains some of his most ingenious and effective folk etymologies,[45] the saccharine image of Alexander III is almost more sickening than the crookedness of the courtiers. Moreover, the mixture of false sentiment with satire does not yield an artistic unity. It may be for this reason—and perhaps because by 1889 his dislike of Alexander III had become much stronger—that Leskov excluded "Leon the Butler's Son" from his collected works. Or he may simply have forgotten about it.

28

Southern Memories

Leskov spent the summers of 1880 and 1881 in Kiev, renewing ties with relatives and friends and revisiting the haunts of his youth. Though much had been changed—"Europeanized," as Leskov puts it —these were the same streets, the same houses, the same churches, squares, and hills he had first gazed on with rapture in 1849, when he had escaped there from the provincial dullness of Oryol. Kiev had been a revelation: the big city, the bright lights, culture, the stimulating company of the young professors in his uncle's house, mind-stretching philosophical conversations in the upper garden, and "first loves"—both the agreeable experiences with the good-natured prostitutes of Kresty and Yamki, and the blind passion that brought about his first marriage. (The equally ardent romance that led to his second marriage also had its setting in Kiev, though fifteen years later.) Thus, Kiev was a city charged with Leskov's memories.

The Leskov of 1880, however, was a different person from the starry-eyed eighteen-year-old of 1849 or the intense, battle-scarred young journalist who in 1864 had fallen in love with the beautiful Mme Bubnova. By 1880 he had behind him two disastrous failures at family life. Though he never acknowledged his full share of responsibility for these failures, he had come to the sad but firm conclusion that "family happiness" was not for him. He also had behind him a literary career not without its successes, even brilliant ones, but marred by enmities, battles, and wounds remembered more vividly than the triumphs. The world had been grudging about granting even his successes the recognition they deserved. It was a bruised and bitter Leskov who in 1880 came to the ancient Ukrainian city in search of time past.

The first visit went well. Provided with every comfort in his brother's well-managed household, Leskov enjoyed reviving memories and acquaintances, even with the poignant realization that they were irrecoverable. His hospitable relatives persuaded him to come again the following year. But the repetition proved vain. The Kiev of

407

1881 seemed alien and repellent. The well of poetic nostalgia had run dry. Leskov no longer saw the romantic Kiev of his youth, but the Kiev of the present, a city absorbed in crass commercialism. To the Petersburg man of letters this middle-sized commercial town seemed the very opposite of what it had been in 1849: it was now small, dull, backward, money-grubbing, uncultured, and above all provincial. It was a backwater, and he was bored with it. Much to the disappointment of his son Andrei, who reveled in the warm family life he so much missed in Petersburg, Leskov cut short this second visit and departed for home on July 21, 1881. He never set foot in Kiev again.

Two years later, he put his ambivalence to brilliant artistic use, in a work in which his youthful memories were nostalgically, and humorously, resurrected and set against the repulsive "banking tendency" (7:203) of latter-day Kiev. One of the old Kiev friends whose acquaintance he had renewed there, Feofan Lebedintsev, retired in 1882 from his position as supervisor of local ecclesiastical schools and founded a magazine, *Kiev Antiquities*, devoted to the history of the region. In this effort Lebedintsev was encouraged and partly assisted by another, much admired friend of Leskov's, Filipp Ternovsky, professor of history at the Kiev Theological Seminary, who was soon to lose his position for incurring the displeasure of Pobedonostsev. The tsarist censorship required that such a magazine be published in Russian, not the "Little Russian dialect"; but in essence *Kiev Antiquities*, in a limited way, was an organ of Ukrainian cultural self-assertion. Without making political demands or claims (which it would not have been allowed to do), it stressed as much as it could what was different, particular, and independent about the Ukrainian past.

Soon after the magazine had been launched, Lebedintsev wrote Leskov asking for a contribution.[1] The writer responded warmly: "I'll write you and send you without fail a little sketch (about fifteen pages long), but well planned and integrated—gay, and with historical relevance to Kiev. It will be called 'No Prayer for the Tsar'; or, if 'that pious old fool, our censorship so cruel' doesn't like that, then put 'The Ancient Malafei and His Youthful Servant.' It is a type, and a genre picture, and something that perhaps people will read and smile at; and that's enough for a storyteller like me."[2]

Once again, the creative impulse got out of hand. Like "The Lefthander," this "little sketch" of fifteen pages refused to conform to its author's blueprint. A month later Leskov wrote to Lebedintsev: "I am doing a little work for you and will soon finish it. It will be something on the order of my recollections of Kievan eccentrics of the 1850s. It will be called 'Pechersk Workers of Wonders.' If the words 'workers of wonders' (not 'wonder-workers')[3] do not sound well in the censors' ears, than you may put 'eccentrics.' Here there will appear the celebrated improviser (or simply liar) Kesar Berlinsky, the Old Believer sage Malafei Pimych and his young servant Giezy. These are all lively people with characteristic traits and very funny."[4] This letter shows that a new section, devoted to the great "improviser" Kesar Berlinsky, had been added during the month that had passed since the previous letter, rendering the old title obsolete. Yet the new one, "Pechersk Eccentrics," was an invitation to further expansion: it seemed that Leskov's memory or imagination could always conjure up one more unforgettable character.

Another month passed, and "Pechersk Eccentrics" was still being described in the future tense: "I am trying to make for you an article not without interest. Naturally, this will not be history, but facetiae [*pobasënki*], perhaps insignificant in worth, but lively; and 'without them (as Gogol used to say) the reader begins to nod and may go to sleep altogether.' "[5]

Watching this offspring grow uncontrollably, Leskov was beginning to feel trapped by his own generosity. Not surprisingly, *Kiev Antiquities* was more worthy than popular; it had few subscribers and a shoestring budget. Leskov had therefore not expected to receive his usual honorarium, and for a "little sketch" of fifteen pages the difference did not matter much. Lebedintsev was a friend, and the cause was a good one. But "Pechersk Eccentrics" was becoming a major work, and the author began to fret over the financial loss incurred by letting it go so cheap. "Naturally I can't give it away," he wrote the same day to Ternovsky, "nor exchange it for a baked apple." It had been hard labor: "Funny stuff is fun to read, but it's much harder to turn out than the most boring things (which, of course, are supposed to be called 'serious')."[6]

The work continued to grow. Still another major "eccentric" was added in the succeeding month, the priest Yefim Botvinovsky, and after him several minor ones (the Kiev "strongmen").[7] The final text runs to nearly ninety pages. It was finished on December 20, 1882: Leskov so dated it in the published text, as if to emphasize the long historical perspective from which these "memories" are viewed.

Leskov took pains to dissociate "Pechersk Eccentrics" from the historical articles surrounding it in *Kiev Antiquities*. In an introductory note in the magazine version, later expunged, he claimed that he was "in general not a connoisseur of history. I highly value and love that science, but I can only serve it from one side, the one which was somewhere characterized by the late Sergei Mikhailovich Solovyov [the great historian] as the lightest and most superficial side, the side where are represented unimportant people—people, however, who in their very lives to a certain degree express the history of their time."[8]

"Pechersk Eccentrics" might qualify as social rather than political history, or as a spiritual typology of a place and an era; but neither category would do justice to its artistic dimensions. An earlier letter of Leskov's had described it as "a type and a genre picture and something that may make people smile"; the published work was subtitled "Fragments from My Youthful Reminiscences"; and the text contains several references to "legends" and "fairy tales." Perhaps the best genre classification would be the facetious one Leskov had invented for his *Laughter and Grief*: "a multifarious potpourri."

Either because of its genuine flaws—the beginning and middle are much better than the end—or because of its unserious, ironic, and informal tone, the work has not to this day received the recognition it deserves. Flaws and all, it is a work of great art, bearing Leskov's stamp on every page.

One of Leskov's trademarks is the playful manipulation of the categories "truth" and "fiction." In the first chapters of "Pechersk Eccentrics" the author appears in something like his *propria persona* and announces that he is going to relate his memories of his youthful years in Kiev: "In literature I am considered an Oryol man, but I was only born and spent my childhood years in Oryol and then in 1849 moved to Kiev" (7:134). These statements are true; and except for the date (also accurate), they were probably known to Leskov's contemporary readers. Such readers would therefore conclude, and were meant to do so, that the "I" here is the real author, Nikolai Leskov, telling about his own experiences. Then the author adds (7:136) that on his arrival in Kiev he had been "completely alone and left to [his] own devices." The contemporary reader had no way of knowing that this statement—not important in itself—was an "improvisation," pure fiction. Leskov's omission of the uncle with whom he lived in Kiev may have been motivated by an old grudge Leskov bore, of which there is other evidence,[9] but it may have an artistic purpose as well. In this work the author is exclusively an observer, not an actor; and his observations come from outside his social sphere. Therefore Leskov may have sought to avoid cluttering the text, as he had that of "Episcopal Justice," with "irrelevant" personal details, such as the identity of this uncle, less colorful and "eccentric" than the Pechersk originals on whom he planned to concentrate. Perhaps the author's loneliness was also needed to provide a motive for his attraction to the run-down Pechersk quarter of Kiev and his acquaintance there with three of his principal "eccentrics," Kesar Berlinsky, Giezy (or Gehazi), the young Old Believer, and the ancient prophet Malafei (or Malachi). Whatever the motivation, this omission of Uncle Sergei is significant mainly as testimony that in his "memoir" pieces Leskov did not feel bound to reproduce exactly the version of the "truth" served up by his conscious memory.

Reordering of autobiographical truth had been one of Leskov's standard procedures since his first short story, "A Case That Was Dropped," in 1862. In "Pechersk Eccentrics," as in Leskov's other "memoirs," we thus find ourselves in an epistemological no-man's land. Except for the author, the characters here, as he put it, were "unimportant people," historically speaking. In the case of Kesar Berlinsky and Father Yevfim Botvinovsky, we know that individuals existed bearing these names.[10] But Malachi and Gehazi might well be fictional characters, created according to the canons of nineteenth-century realism: they are described so vividly that we willingly suspend our disbelief in their real existence.

Further along in "Pechersk Eccentrics," Leskov performs a more unusual juggling feat with "truth" and "fiction." In a work written for a historical magazine, a work that claimed to portray characters who "to a certain degree express the history of their time," Leskov temporarily repudiates not only "history" but also the very principles of realistic fiction. He demonstratively eschews all illusionistic claims and aggressively asserts the total fictionality of his fiction. What he offers us in this section, he says, is not "truth" (real history) nor fiction pretending to be truth (realism), but fiction denying any connection with truth.

The part in question is the hilarious tale of the toothache of "Bibikov's mother-in-law" (Dmitry Bibikov was governor-general of Kiev Province, and thus a real person; but this "mother-in-law," apparently, was imaginary) and of the miraculous medicine invented by Kesar Berlinsky's nephew, "Nikolavra." In telling this story Leskov takes repeated pains to *deny* its truth. It is one of the innumerable boastful yarns spun by Berlinsky, the renowned "improvizer" (or, as Leskov put it in his letter, liar). The text of this "improvization," as transmitted by the author, mostly in indirect discourse, is peppered with the Russian conjunction *budto* or *budto by*, which signals that the speaker has grave doubts about the veracity of the discourse he is reporting. (Our spoken language can create the same effect by a special "doubting" intonation, but written English has no exact equivalent of this *budto*; we must resort to such locutions as "supposedly," "claimed that," and the like.) Further, Leskov begins the tale of "Bibikov's mother-in-law" in heavily marked fairy-tale style; and he even places the poor lady in ironic quotation marks, raising doubt about her very existence: "Once upon a time, supposedly [*budto*], there was 'Bibikov's mother-in law,' a lady 'very stout and most enormous,' and she arrived, supposedly, to spend the summer in the country, somewhere not far from Kiev" (7:150).

Coming down with a terrible toothache (she insists on cracking a hard nut with her teeth), Bibikov's mother-in-law sends her bailiff to town to fetch Berlinsky's nephew, a doctor celebrated for his infallible toothache medicine (though it only works on lower teeth, and it is one of her upper teeth that hurts). The bailiff arrives in Kiev in the night and bangs so hard on the doctor's shutters that the servants warn him he may make the windows fall out of their frames, "and now it is the dead of winter, and we might freeze with our little children." Here Leskov reassuringly comments, "The story was told just like this; during these negotiations mention was made of 'winter' and 'cold,' and the reader should not be troubled at the fact that these events took place during the summer visit of Bibikov's mother-in-law to her estate. Soon we will again see gay and sultry summer instead of dull, dead winter" (7:151-152). In other words, the movement of the seasons may be whimsically speeded up or slowed down *ad libitum*, to meet the expressive exigencies of the story. Could anything be more at variance with the realistic code than this?

Yet as pure narrative the toothache story loses nothing by this "disillusioning," though one may question whether it "expresses the history of [its] time." Rather, it is unadulterated art, freed, as D. S. Mirsky said of Pushkin's fairy tale *Tsar Saltan*, from "all the irrelevancies of emotion and symbol, 'a thing of beauty' and 'a joy for ever.' "[11] It is a perfect narrative, beautifully told, with skillful retardations, rising to a magnificently absurd climax—a perfect peripeteia—and tapering off in an equally absurd anticlimax. It would be invidious to say more here about these "supposed" events, for that would be to give away the secret of how upper teeth can be transformed into lower ones, and why afterwards there was such an epidemic of toothache among the ladies of Kiev.

Good as it is, however, the tale of Bibikov's mother-in-law is only an appetizer. The pièce de résistance in "Pechersk Eccentrics," the nucleus from which it grew, is its central section, the story of the Old Believer prophet Malachi and his servant Gehazi. This section, besides its value as narrative, is of great importance as an ideological proclamation of a significant change in the author's views of the Old Belief. In the final paragraphs of "Pechersk Eccentrics," Leskov roguishly cuts the ground from under his earlier idealization of the Old Belief in "The Sealed Angel" when he reveals that the prototype of the heroic Luka crossed the Dnepr on a chain not for an icon, but for a pail of cheap vodka. This was indeed a hard chunk of "realism" to throw at an earlier "romance."

The shattering effect of "Pechersk Eccentrics" on "The Sealed Angel" is greater than the explicit ironies of the last chapter. As the late Boris Drugov suggested, the story of Malachi and Gehazi may be regarded as a parody of the tale of the noble votaries of the sealed angel.[12] Instead of the exemplary sweetness, talent, and intelligence (however misguided) exhibited by those simple Russians in the earlier story, the devotees of the "ancient piety" in "Pechersk Eccentrics" display the very opposite qualities. They are characterized by Berlinsky as "splendid people and fools," and the old "prophet" himself labeled a "fool eternally blessed." In short, the image of the Old Believers in "Pechersk Eccentrics" is sharply negative. It indicates a reversion on Leskov's part to his earlier view of the Old Belief (as expressed by the Musk-ox): in their abysmal ignorance, gross superstition, and fanatical obsession with trivial details of ritual or diet, the Old Believers are even further than the Orthodox from the true spirit of Jesus Christ.

The Old Believer mentality is graphically illustrated in the characters of Gehazi and Malachi. First of all, their relationship is anything but a loving discipleship like that of Levonty and Pamva in "The Sealed Angel." It is more like a case history from Krafft-Ebing. The old slavedriver repeatedly flogs his young disciple with a rope, usually wetted to make it hurt more. Gehazi masochistically submits to this discipline and on one occasion even requests it, *ad majorem Dei gloriam*. On another occasion the prophet bestows on his servant such a blow in the face that the poor youth's lips "were instantaneously bespattered with blood." This buffet too is accepted; when bystanders attempt to defend him, the youth pushes them aside. "It's all in the family," he says.

The impression of ugliness and squalor produced by this sick relationship is reinforced by Leskov's description of its physical setting— the horrid hovel where the Old Believers are obliged to hide from the police. It is a dilapidated shed hidden in a back courtyard, the latter filled with a huge—and symbolic—pile of manure. "The hut had three windows, and all of them in a row gave on the above-mentioned manure pile or rather manure hill" (7:168). This manure hill provided the view for another set of windows, belonging to a hut occupied by a rival group of Old Believers, the *tropari*. The two sects differed over the question of whether the tsar could be included in their prayers, despite his use of the heretical three-fingered cross or "salt-pinch," as the Old Believers scornfully called it; and these differences were frequently carried to the point of physical combat, with stone-throwing and window-smashing. Though it is made to seem ludicrous in Leskov's description, the picture of these combative bigots is in fact another melancholy illustration of the inexhaustible human propensity for discord over trivia, and the limitless ability of self-styled Christians to distort or deny the most basic teachings of their Founder.

The central episode in the tale of Malachi and Gehazi is the most pointed anti-idealization of the fanatical pair, and especially of the "prophet" himself. Malachi proves a bad prophet. His vengeful and deluded mind had imagined a triumphal scene. During the ceremony (held in 1850) dedicating the new bridge across the Dnepr, the tsar, Nicholas I, would walk to the middle of the structure and there ostentatiously sign himself with the true, two-fingered cross. It would be as momentous an event as the adoption of Orthodox Christianity almost nine hundred years earlier by his ancestor St. Vladimir Svyatoslavovich, when the idol of the pagan god Perun had been cast into that same Dnepr. It would signal that the tsar and the Russian government had at last come to their senses and changed sides. The hated "Nikonians" (the official Orthodox church) would be cast into outer darkness, and the formerly outcast Old Believers could joyfully commence to persecute the Nikonians as they themselves had been persecuted, including the administration of such blows on the face as Malachi had just dealt his faithful Gehazi.

Of course Nicholas did nothing of the kind, and instead of the Nikonians, the prophet himself is put to shame. By means of exaggerated retardations and digressions as well as an immensely detailed, heroicized description of the setting and the major actors, Leskov builds the scene up to a tremendous climax. The air is positively electric with "expectension," to coin an English analogue to one of Leskov's favorite folk etymologies (*ažidacija*), as the august monarch strides onto the bridge. The collapse of Malachi's ill-founded hopes is therefore all the more devastating—a poignant blend of the tragic with the ludicrous.

The ludicrous aspect of the scene is reinforced by a skillfully dovetailed subsidiary episode. At the climactic moment, when he reaches the center of the bridge, the tsar is observed to walk over to the edge and there physically touch and apparently converse with two Kiev gentlemen, who had managed to ensconce themselves there, in a position to get a superb view of all the proceedings. The more distant spectators, and especially the ecstatic Malachi, attribute great significance to the momentous words His Majesty had been observed to utter; they must be laden with symbolic and even prophetic meaning. There prove to have been just two of these words, as the author subsequently learns from the gentlemen themselves: "Get out!" (*Pošli proč'!*). So much for the vaticinations of the "fool eternally blessed."

Leskov concludes the Malachi-Gehazi section with an account of an accidental meeting with Gehazi many years later, at the railway station in Kursk. (The scene is reminiscent of the author's similar "post scriptum" encounter with the Jewish bookbinder in "Episcopal Justice.") Gehazi, long liberated from his slavery to Malachi, shows no moral improvement: when the author discovers him, he is engaged in a ghastly procedure—one after the other beheading tiny quail with a twist of his fingers and letting them fly headless until they drop.[13] He has, however, gone over to the state church, like the Old Believers in "The Sealed Angel." Unlike theirs, however, his "conversion" was not the product of religious experience. Gehazi claims that from the terrible fasts enforced on him by his old master he had contracted cancer of the stomach. "And with a stomach like mine what kind of faith can you have?" "In the church faith you can live easier." And so, Leskov observes ironically, "without reading the Encyclopedists and other accursed writers, [Gehazi] had with his own intellect arrived at the theory of Diderot and placed religion in dependence on physiology" (7:202).[14] "Pechersk Eccentrics" was Leskov's last artistic encounter with the Old Believers, and a devastating one it had surely been.[15]

After Malachi and Gehazi have been disposed of, "Pechersk Eccentrics" does not sustain such a high level of artistic quality. The section on Father Yefim Botvinovsky is less impressive, though it illustrates Leskov's contrary broadmindedness. He includes this Orthodox priest among the ranks of his "righteous ones," pointedly commenting,

"When people talk to me about the notorious 'greediness of priests,' I always remember that the most unselfish person I ever saw—to the point of irrationality—*was a priest*" (7:209).

But the characterization of this priest fails to come alive, perhaps because Leskov is so anxious to stress Botvinovsky's goodness rather than his colorful eccentricities—his worldliness, his fondness for dancing, hunting, and billiards. These unpriestly activities, which might have helped to fill out the abstraction, are only mentioned in passing, never realized. On the other hand, Botvinovsky's greatest moral exploit—financially ruining his own family in order to rescue a man he hardly knows from impending disaster—may strike us as immoral. As Vsevolod Setchkarev observes, it smacks more of mental derangement than of Christian love.[16]

After Botvinovsky "Pechersk Eccentrics," like *The Little Things in a Bishop's Life*, trails off in a hurried jumble of anecdotes, as if Leskov had simply emptied out his remaining literary scraps concerned with Kiev. Nevertheless, the final chapter, on "The Sealed Angel," remains a powerful specimen of authorial self-irony: reaching beyond the limits of the work itself, Leskov demonstratively topples one of his most admired earlier creations. It was like a penitential act, a pledge of new allegiance. The post-1875 Leskov could no longer tolerate the idealizations of his Katkovian past.

Two years later Leskov paid a return literary visit to the Ukraine with "Ancient Psychopaths"[17]—as the similar title suggests, an apparent effort to replay "Pechersk Eccentrics" with some new material concerning more Ukrainian "characters." The results were much less successful.

The "psychopaths" in question—they are not especially "ancient," since they date from the time of Nicholas I—are a rich Ukrainian landowner named Ivan Vishnevsky and his Russian wife. Vishnevsky's type is familiar in Leskov and many other Russian writers describing the age of serfdom—the "little tsar," absolute master of his petty kingdom, who exacts subservience to every whim. Vishnevsky "psychopathically" abuses his powers in two major areas, official and sexual. The local bureaucracy walks in terror of him. He dislikes all government officials, as well as all Protestants, Catholics, and Jews; and in the course of the narrative he contrives—with impunity—to have a considerable number of free persons belonging to these categories taken to his stable and flogged. Legal redress was out of the question.

In his domestic arrangements Vishnevsky takes maximum advantage, as many Russian landowners did, of his *droit de seigneur,* begetting innumerable children (whom he does not acknowledge as his own) on an endless succession of his female slaves. Like Humbert Humbert, he has a predilection for pubescent girls, and his estates provide a constant supply of them. In selecting, training, and outfitting his sexual partners Vishnevsky is aided by his wife, who thus expresses her own brand of psychopathy. (It is explained that after the birth of her second child she had somehow been rendered unfit for any further sexual activity.)

The sexual material in "Ancient Psychopaths" caused difficulty with the censors,[18] though from the modern point of view it seems mild. More important is the fact that it is not sufficiently analyzed to be interesting. Leskov does little but point; he does not penetrate. Moreover, he does not seem to know what attitude to adopt toward Vishnevsky's antics. Are they to be regarded, like the "improvizations" of Kesar Berlinsky, as the amusing eccentricities of a vanished era, or are they moral outrages? Leskov vacillates between these two alternatives, and as a result the image of his "psychopaths" is blurred.[19]

CHAPTER 29

Abraham the Hebrew

The decade of the eighties brought the culmination of Leskov's long and tortuous involvement with the so-called "Jewish question."[1] As "Episcopal Justice" demonstrated, the moral problem posed by the Jews was an intensely personal and emotional one for Leskov, with roots reaching back to his experiences as a young man in the recruiting agency in Kiev, when he had been witness to—and collaborated in producing—so much misery and horror, the worst of which had been the conscription of Jewish boys with the aim of forcibly "converting" them to Christianity. Though in later years Leskov publicly expressed disapproval of this impious procedure, "Episcopal Justice," in its contemptuous caricature of the Jewish hero-victim, had revealed a deep, unresolved ambivalence in the author's attitude toward Jews. Leskov, like most educated Russians of his time, had imbibed the ideals of fairness, tolerance, and universal human equality that were part of the moral heritage of liberalism, whether or not associated with the ethical doctrines of Christianity. He publicly deplored the government's discrimination against Jews and advocated equality of all Russian citizens before the law. Public profession, however, was not always in harmony with inner self, that unregenerate, self-aggrandizing part of us only too ready to assimilate ethnic prejudice as a means of elevating itself at the expense of others.

Confined by law to a "Pale of Settlement" along the western border of the empire, the Jews of nineteenth-century Russia were a typical pariah people. They clung to an alien culture, an alien language and an alien religion. That religion stood in an ambiguous relationship to Christianity, at once its parent and its negator. There were thus quasi-religious rationalizations for disliking and persecuting them. Outnumbered and intimidated, they offered no effective resistance; and the authorities understood that their constituency wanted them to enforce the unwritten laws of prejudice rather than the written laws of justice. Moreover, in their struggle to survive in a hostile environment the

418

Jews had developed behavior patterns toward which the Russians felt moral distaste. The Jewish façade of cringing obsequiousness and compliance seemed to hide a clannish conspiracy to exploit the *goyim* by extortion, corruption, and commercial deceit.

It would have been hard for any Russian official in the Pale, however liberal his convictions, not to feel aversion for these grubby Jewish outcasts and to take pleasure in his own secure membership in the ruling elite, with all its cleanliness, comforts, and culture. And in Leskov's case there was the added factor of the guilt he still felt for his complicity in the oppression of Jews. The end product of all these divergent pressures, in Leskov, was permanent confusion and conflict—liberal or Christian ethics struggling with underlying anti-Semitic impulses.

This conflict had already found expression in "Episcopal Justice." Whatever its faults, that story had expressed disapproval of the old oppressions and showed compassion for the Jews who had suffered them. Having made this gesture, Leskov seemed to feel freed to vent his underlying anti-Semitic feelings. For his reputation as an anti-Semite chiefly rests on the two "Jewish" stories which follow: "The Melamed of Österreich" (1878) and "Yid Somersault" (1882).[2]

"The Melamed of Österreich," like "Episcopal Justice," was in part a response to the renewed anti-Semitic agitation in Russia that accompanied the Russo-Turkish War of 1877-78 and its aftermath, the Congress of Berlin. Leskov published this story in Katkov's *Russian Messenger*, his last appearance in that ultranationalist organ, with which he had severed connections four years before. According to the formula broadcast by the yellow press, the fruits of victory bought in that war by Russian arms and Russian blood had been stolen away by the machinations of international finance capital—chiefly Jewish— led by the epitome of Jewish guile, Disraeli. Right-wing Russian journalists engaged in verbal fist-shaking at this lord of international Jewry. Lord Beaconsfield lay beyond their physical reach; but his Russian fellow Jews did not, and there can be no doubt that these anti-Semitic journalistic campaigns helped prepare the ground for the terrible outbreak of pogroms in the early 1880s. To this campaign Leskov contributed his ambiguous bit, "The Melamed of Österreich."

No doubt one should be cautious about the ideological conclusions one draws from a work of fiction. It is dangerous to assume without corroborative evidence that in any work of the creative imagination the author is expressing personal convictions. He may be simply "performing," taking experimental stances, observing, exhibiting, trying to understand—not speaking in his own name. In "The Melamed of Österreich" this basic ambiguity of art is twice reinforced. The author, through the structure of the story, removes himself from responsibility for the contents of the narrative. Subtitled "A Tale on Bivouac," "The Melamed of Österreich" is transmitted to us by two military narrators, a young *junker* who in turn acts as tape recorder for the main (oral) narrative of his superior officer, an old-line major. Can we blame the author for their anti-Semitism?

Ambiguity also appears in the argumentative purpose for which the major's narrative is introduced. In the course of the war, the *junker* tells us, there had been much talk among the newspaper-reading junior officers about the diplomatic jockeying among the powers, "the cunning of Beaconsfield, the wrigglings of Andrassy," through which Russia was being deprived of her rightful spoils. At the root of the trouble, the officers conclude, lie the wily intrigues of the Jews, against which simplehearted Russians are helpless.

These are no longer the days when in all matters you can rely on your own strength and courage; nowadays you need brains and calculation and capital. . . . the side that has the capacity for far-sighted thinking, subtle calculation and capital—that's the side that will come out on top. And we have neither the one nor the other. It's the Yids who are the winners: a Yid in London, Yids in Vienna, masses of Yids everywhere, and even here in Russia they're getting to the top. We're being fed by a concessionaire married to Beaconsfield's niece, and even the Slavs we're fighting for are in the hands of Viennese Yids. It's a gloomy outlook. The Yid is scary: he'll plot it all out, get everything in his paws, and then tie everybody up.[3]

The old-fashioned, true-blue major, a descendant of Lermontov's Maksim Maksimych, customarily deplores political arguments among his officers and refuses to participate in them; he belongs to the "theirs not to reason why" school. But when he hears this frightening description of Europe ensnared in the net of the "scary" Yid, the major is moved to speech. "Come now," he snorts. "What are you going to think up next? Tell me another! The Yid scary, indeed!" The major then tells his tale to exorcize the officers' phantom.

The major's story is a long, heavily embellished, and not very effective anecdote, which Leskov said he had learned from the "customs-office priest in Olkusz,"[4] a tale full of the atmosphere of "Jewish" frontier chicanery which Leskov had experienced in Radziwiłłów-Brody, on the Russo-Austrian border, back in 1862. The major is no Judophile: in his narrative he recounts with gusto the comeuppance received at the hands of a simple Russian Cossack by the wiliest and most knavish of Galician Jews. But in the context of the officers' argument, this outsmarting of a Jew by a Russian, and a rank-and-file Cossack at that, is designed to show that there is no need for Russians to be frightened by Jews. The ultrapious and ultradeceitful *melamed* from Österreich (the major says that among Jews these two qualities always come together) is made a laughing-stock, all his power and prestige demolished.

Though the anecdote need not be retold here, one further point might be made. The major's attitude toward Jewish religiosity is disdainful, the tone of his descriptions mocking and ironic:

> When [Skharia, the *melamed*] prayed, he always straightened out his legs in the first position, rocking and shaking without sparing his knees so that the angels would see how greatly fear made him tremble before the Omnipresent One. He first shouted out his prayers in Hebrew and then dispatched special prayers in Syrian and Chaldean so that the angels, who do not understand these languages, would not be envious of his requests from the coming Messiah. Even more subtle care was required against the devil, lest that intriguer should get wind of Skharia's requests and do him an injury. But that was taken care of: the devil could never find out what Skharia was asking for because the devil also does not know Syrian or Chaldean and can never learn these languages because his "swinish" pride does not allow him to study from human beings. If Skharia chanced to spit during his prayers, he performed this impolite act not otherwise than to the left, so as not to bespatter the crowd of angels admiring him from the right.[5]

Yet, despite his contempt for Skharia's Jewish piety, Major Pleskunov shows a thorough acquaintance with the forms of this "piety," indicating, one surmises, a good deal of research on his creator's part. Such detailed knowledge indicates serious interest, a knowledge of Jewish ceremonies Leskov was to demonstrate later in a series of newspaper articles.[6]

One might adduce from "The Melamed of Österreich" one final ambiguity in Leskov's favor: the fact that Skharia's Cossack antagonist is represented as in no way morally superior to the Jew. He is a bully, a thief, and an extortionist, showing that the Jews have no monopoly of iniquity. Skharia's servant, the Ukrainian peasant woman Oksana, drives the point home: "What's the good in you being baptized if you steal and my masters beat me for it afterwards?"[7] Nevertheless, although the Jew and the Cossack are objectively in moral equilibrium, the emotional scale is weighted in the Russian's favor. The Cossack's victory over Skharia and his general bullying of Jews are presented as good-humored and "funny," without a trace of indignation or sympathy for his victims; while Skharia's mixture of superstition and rapacity is presented with scornful disapproval.

The redeeming ambiguities of "The Melamed of Österreich" are almost entirely lacking in "Yid Somersault," published four years later in the low-brow provincial magazine *A. Gattsuk's Gazette*. Ominously, the date of publication was 1882, the year after the first Odessa pogrom, with which it is thematically connected. "Yid Somersault" is the most vicious thing Leskov ever wrote, far worse than the polemical novels for which he was ostracized by the Russian Left.

The tone of the first paragraph is indicative. Beginning with a direct reference to the pogroms, Leskov expresses no indignation, but rather irritation with the victims, as if to say, "How offensive of the Jews to incite Russian mobs to beat and rob them!" To be sure, the language of the passage, the element of hyperbole, and particularly the manner of making outrageous statements in a calm, matter-of-fact tone—all this indicates some authorial distance from the attitudes expressed. This is *erlebte Rede*, not the author's own voice. Nevertheless, the tonal distance does not seem great enough to force the reader, as in "The Battle-axe," to negate the moral attitudes of his narrator.

"Yid Somersault" begins as follows: "It was Christmas time after the big Jewish pogroms. These events had served everywhere as the subject of lively and sometimes very strange discussions on one and the same theme: what are we to do with the Jews? Where shall we escort them to, on whom shall we bestow them, or shall we reshape them for our own use? Some people wanted to give them away, escort them out, but the most practical among the discussants found inconvenience in both these solutions and were more inclined to think that it would be better to make use of the Jews for our domestic purposes, primarily enfeebling ones, which would cause their race to decline."[8] War is proposed as a solution. "Instead of shedding Russian blood on the field of battle," a practical disputant argued, "wouldn't it be much better to water the earth with Jewish blood?" This seemed to be a clever means of furthering Russia's foreign policy at the expense of her disruptive Jewish subjects; but there is a serious objection: the Jews are wretched fighters. "They are cowards and quite devoid of bravery and courage."[9] One of the discussants, however, an experienced military man, says that he knows a way to "pour bravery and courage into Jewish hearts." He tells a story to illustrate the technique.

This inner story takes us back to Kiev in the 1840s and to the theme of Jewish conscription under Nicholas I. The author again operates at double narrative remove: the "experienced military man" in 1882 only passes on stories he had heard long ago in Kiev from yet another experienced military man, a Colonel Stadnikov. Colonel Stadnikov was relating in the 1840s events that had happened to him long before that. So there is great narrative and temporal distance from the author of 1882.

The theme of Jewish conscription is introduced with a subanecdote, which, Leskov explicitly indicates, is of questionable authenticity. Early in the reign of Nicholas I, Colonel Stadnikov asserts, high government circles were discussing the possibility of exempting all Jews from military service on the grounds that they were unfit to fight and would be a pernicious influence in the army. The Jews of Petersburg attempt with barrels of gold to bribe the tsar's ministers into adopting such a policy, but there is one they cannot bribe: Nikolai Semyonovich Mordvinov.[10] At last, even Mordvinov is tricked into accepting a Jewish bribe; but it buys only his silence, not his support for the exemption. However, when all the ministers argue in favor and Mordvinov remains silent, the wise tsar understands that all have been bought. He decrees that the Jews must be subject to military service "equally with others."[11]

Colonel Stadnikov never explains how this "equality" involves the special conscription of Jewish children, who are mentioned only in passing: "Both adult and underaged Jews were conscripted into the army; the latter were supposed to be more than twelve years old. . . . The little ones were put into battalions of military cantonists, where our spiritual fathers, at the behest of our father-officers, in the twinkling of an eye brought these youngsters to knowledge of truths of the Orthodox Christian faith and baptized them to the glory of Lord Jesus's name."[12] The statement is ironic; and the irony is easy for us perceive in the context of Leskov's other ironic treatments of Orthodox baptisms. But one wonders whether the readers of *A. Gattsuk's Gazette* saw it.

The iniquitous Jews, the Colonel goes on, were so strangely reluctant to give their lives for the tsar or to see their children taken from them and baptized that they resorted to maiming and disfiguring:

> Such nasty things as they did to themselves I don't think our Sarmatian land had ever seen before. Some covered themselves up to the neck with the most malignant scrofulous mange, such as had not been seen until then on a single Russian dog; others gave themselves epilepsy; still others deprived themselves of a leg, an eye, or a hand [. . .] In Berdichev there were rumors that a doctor had let it be known that for a hundred rubles a "rescription" he would "make your guts come out while your soul stayed in" your body [. . .] [The Jews] preferred the most terrible mutilations to the captivity of the service. They simply did not want to die, so as not thereby to diminish the Israelite race.[13]

Colonel Stadnikov's main subject, however, is the technique for "pouring" courage into adult Jewish hearts. His anecdote describing this is apparently supposed to be funny, in rollicksome, hearty, military style.

The adult Jews conscripted into the army by Nicholas's decree proved to be a problem. Jews are not cut out to be warriors. Furthermore, the Jewish soldiers conspire to appear more cowardly than they are in the hope of convincing the Russian authorities to grant them general exemption. In accordance with this conspiracy, the three Jewish soldiers in Stadnikov's company (he was then only a lieutenant) refuse to fire their rifles, even in practice; every time they are ordered to do so, they simply flop down on the ground as if in terror. For this insubordination their goodhearted Russian officer orders them flogged, so severely that they now have to do their sewing lying on their stomachs. (Business-minded like all Jews, they engage in tailoring on the side.) But the flogging does no good. "God did not create the Jew," the Jews themselves say, "to shoot from a rifle."[14] At a loss, the Russian officer consults with a Polish corporal, as one more experienced in dealing with Jews. The "Polish" solution, it transpires, is to flog the Jews again, but from the front rather than the rear. After this operation they must do their sewing in a standing position; but they still stubbornly do their "Yid somersault" when ordered to fire a gun. Next a Baltic German lieutenant is called. The "German" solution is to beat the Jews so viciously about the face that they look as if they were covered with bee stings; "even their Jewish noses were out of shape." But they still persist.

As in "The Melamed of Österreich," it takes a simple Russian

private to outsmart the Jews and make them abandon their somersault. His trick is to order them to fire their rifles while standing on a
plank extended over a river. They dare not flop down lest they fall in
and drown: *moze, tu gliboko* (It might be deep here), as they put it in
their garbled Judeo-Ukrainian.[15] The Jews now gallantly accept defeat. The conspiracy has failed; the word swiftly gets around through
the Jewish grapevine, and the somersault is abandoned throughout
the army.

It is a stupid anecdote. The tone of swaggering "humor" and of
malicious satisfaction in the Jews' painful punishments and humiliating defeat is hard to forgive Leskov. His elaborate literary packaging,
the side trips, the funny subsidiary characters, the verbal tricks—none
of them can hide the malevolent core of this story.

We do not know whether Leskov felt ashamed of the prejudices
manifested in "The Melamed of Österreich" and "Yid Somersault."
There is no record of contrition in his writings or published correspondence. Apparently he did not, since he felt no compunction about
republishing these stories.[16] Nevertheless, in 1883, soon after issuing
"Yid Somersault," Leskov undertook a reassessment of the "Jewish
question." At the end of this process, despite some backsliding, he
emerged transformed—from a literary trafficker in anti-Semitic
anecdotes into an outspoken defender of the Jews and a proponent of
equality and fraternity between Jews and Russians.

The immediate impetus for this moral reordering was a commission
Leskov received from representatives of the Jewish community in
Petersburg. They asked—or engaged—him to write a treatise in
defense of the Jews to be presented to the governmental body charged
with investigation of the Jewish problem. How or why Leskov was
chosen for this task we do not know. It seems odd that the Petersburg
Jews would appeal for assistance to the man who had just published
"Yid Somersault." They may not have known about it, however: few
of them would have read *A. Gattsuk's Gazette,* and the story was not
reprinted in a book collection until 1886. Probably Leskov's series of
inoffensive newspaper articles on Jewish ceremonies had caught their
attention. There is evidence also that Leskov had acquaintances
among Jewish intellectuals in Petersburg;[17] perhaps these people knew
that his attitudes toward Jews were more complex and fair-minded
than those articulated in "Yid Somersault." Among Russian writers he
was considered the leading expert on religious matters, and apparently
the Jews felt he could be trusted to do an effective job for them.[18]

Andrei Leskov's account of the episode—perhaps somewhat white-washed—follows:

At the beginning of 1883 there appeared in Leskov's study a little figure almost caricatural in aspect: a very short, flamboyantly dressed brunet, with a shaved upper lip, a black goatee, and close-cropped, coarse hair. He announced himself as the representative of Baron [Abraham] Zak, Baron H[orace] O. Günzburg and other leading figures of the Jewish community in the capital. He gave his name as P[yotr] L[vovich] Rozenberg, Candidate in Law from Kazan University. In the name of those who sent him he transmitted a request that Leskov compose a treatise on the position of the Jews in Russia, designed to be presented subsequently to the so-called "Pahlen Commission," which had been created to discuss measures for preventing in the future such Jewish pogroms as had broken out in the South in 1881-1882.

For Leskov, who since his childhood years had meditated on the fate of the Russian Jews and at the very beginning of his literary career had hotly disputed with I. S. Aksakov on the question of granting certain rights to the "descendants of Moses living under the shelter of the laws of the Russian Empire," the proposal was appealing, both to the mind and to the heart. He sat down to work.

On December 21, 1883, censorship authorization was obtained, and in January of the following year there appeared, in an edition of fifty copies, a book entitled *"The Jew in Russia; Some Notes on the Jewish Question.* (Not placed on sale.) St. Petersburg, 1884." The author of the treatise was not indicated.

On one of the two copies of this edition which I had preserved there was a handwritten inscription by Leskov: "This book, printed with the permission of the Minister of In[ternal] Af[fairs] C[ount] Dm[itry] Andreevich Tolstoy, was written by me, Nikolai Leskov, and delivered to the press by a certain Pyotr Lvovich Rozenberg, who is recorded as its nominal author. N. Leskov." [19]

We have no record of payment for this work, but we know Leskov could not have afforded to produce it for nothing. Leskov's was one of several documents commissioned by Jewish leaders, especially Baron de Günzburg, for presentation to the Pahlen Commission;[20] these documents were too important to be entrusted to volunteers. Ambiguity therefore remains in interpreting *The Jew in Russia* as a document in Leskov's spiritual biography. Does it embody its author's convictions, or is it the brief of a literary lawyer?

In any event, *The Jew in Russia* is a remarkable piece of writing, heavily stamped with Leskov's literary personality. Its key is pitched low, its ostensible attitude one of calm reasonableness; but it has Leskov's familiar undertone of tongue-in-cheek slyness. In form it refutes, one after the other, the principal arguments used for rationalizing anti-Semitic prejudice.[21]

Is the faith of Orthodox Christians threatened by the presence of Jews? Hardly, since Judaism is the least proselytizing of the great religions, and conversions of Christians to Judaism are rare. There is greater danger of Orthodox Christians' being converted to Protestantism, Roman Catholicism, or even Islam than to Judaism; yet votaries of these religions do not suffer the disabilities under Russian law imposed on the Jews.

Leskov puts his finger on the absurdity of the policy of the Pale of Settlement: if the Jews are so dangerous, why are the good Orthodox Ukrainians and Belorussians singled out for maximal exposure to their noxious influence? Would it not be better to dilute the poison throughout the empire? Moreover, the Ukrainians feel less hostility toward the Jews than toward the Great Russians. And even among the Great Russians, Leskov adds, the Jew stands low in the hierarchy of Mediterranean deceitfulness and trickery. According to the proverb Leskov cites, "The [Russian] peasant can be cheated by a Gypsy; the Gypsy by a Jew; the Jew by an Armenian; the Armenian by a Greek; and the [Orthodox!] Greek can be cheated solely by the devil himself, and then only if God permits it."[22]

Leskov cites evidence that the level of public morality was higher among the Ukrainians and Belorussians living in the Pale than among the Great Russians. The Jews were accused of debauching and impoverishing the Orthodox peasantry in the Pale by operating taverns. But drunkenness is worse in the Great Russian area; moreover, drunkenness has been a Russian problem since the time of Saint Vladimir. The Jews are not responsible for it.

The efforts of Nicholas I to assimilate the Jews forcibly had proved a failure; likewise the thirty-ruble bonus paid by the government to Jewish converts to Christianity—a sum reminiscent, Leskov notes, of the thirty pieces of silver paid to Judas for the betrayal of Jesus. Leskov welcomes the abolition of these practices by Alexander II, as well as further measures of liberalization, especially in the sphere of education. The failure of Nicholas's attempts to create Jewish farmers was caused, Leskov correctly maintains, by the faults of the government's program, particularly its refusal to supply the Jewish colonists with capital loans.

The moral standards of the Jews are higher then those of the surrounding Christians. Leskov goes through the Ten Commandments one by one, demonstrating that the Jews come out better or equal on every count. Finally, the charge of ethnic arrogance imputed to Jews is widespread among peoples, including Russians. Conversely, the virtue of charity is particularly developed among Jews, a charity often bestowed on Gentiles as well as fellow Jews.

The wish to impose restrictions on the Jews comes from those who fear their competition. This fear cannot be shared by the Russian government, which is thus free to resolve the "Jewish question" from the point of view of justice. Justice demands that the Pale of Settlement should be abolished, the Jews permitted to live where they like and engage in any occupation they choose; all other legal inequalities should be eliminated, and taxes and civic responsibilities imposed on the Jews equally with other citizens. "Only such a solution of the Jewish question," Leskov concludes "will be correct and in consonance with the true interests of that great state which is in the process of equalizing Russian subjects of the Jewish faith with all other subjects of the Russian nation without regard to their tribal origin or creed."[23]

The rulers of that "great state" chose to disregard this sensible advice. The Pahlen Commission eventually recommended the gradual abolition of the legal disabilities imposed on Jews in Russia; but to this recommendation the loutish tsar, Alexander III, perhaps at the behest of the fanatic Pobedonostsev, responded by abolishing the commission and imposing new restrictions on the Jews.[24] The human losses, not only to the Jews, but to all Russian citizens, resulting from this idiotic policy are incalculable.

Although *The Jew in Russia* marked the beginning of Leskov's gradual emancipation from anti-Semitic prejudice, the process was still far from complete, as several works from this period demonstrate. We have already considered the dubious ironies of "Deception," written that same year, with the "sly" suggestion that the Rumanians are even more despicable than the Jews. Two years later, in a story called "Fish Soup without Fish," Leskov again made literary use of an anti-Semitic anecdote, resurrecting the time-worn stereotype of Jewish avarice, trickery, and clannishness. In the story Palashka, a poor Christian girl with an illegitimate baby, is begging for a ruble to have her child baptized. A well-off Jew named Solomon has just won five rubles at cards. He gives Palashka the five-ruble note, on the condition that she return him four rubles in change and work out the remainder by doing his laundry. Solomon's friend criticizes him for giving good money to a goy beggar, especially for baptism. Solomon retorts that, first, Palashka will do two rubles' worth of work for the one he has given her; and, second, the money was counterfeit, and he did not want to pass it to a fellow Jew. When Palashka dutifully brings the four rubles of good change, Solomon's friend acknowledges his wisdom. This was one of those rare and happy instances, Leskov concludes, where there were no losers: the Christians regarded Solomon as a generous man; Palashka considered him her benefactor and worked the whole winter for the single ruble; the other Jews honored him as a sage; and Solomon himself got the four good rubles and regular clean clothes. The further adventures of the counterfeit note are not reported.[25]

This minor specimen of anti-Semitic recidivism, however, was followed the same year by Leskov's most forthright pronouncement—this one uncommissioned—in favor of tolerance and equality between Jews and Christians, a didactic Tolstoyan fable, analogous in conception to Tolstoy's parables, "What Men Live By" or "How Much Land Does a Man Need?" It was entitled "The Tale of Theodore the Christian and His Friend Abraham the Hebrew."[26]

Like many of Leskov's (and Tolstoy's) didactic tales of this period, the nucleus of the plot, somewhat altered, is derived from the Old Russian *Prolog* (*Synaxarion*, a collection of brief saints' lives and moral fables designed to be read aloud in churches). Set in fourth-century Byzantium, the story tells of the childhood friendship of two boys, Theodore and Abraham, Christian and Jew, whose families live in harmony side by side. The boys grow up inseparable. They attend a secular school run by a pagan philosopher named Panphilus: "Among all the people here [Panphilus says] there are many different faiths, and there is no evil in that; the evil is that every person thinks his own faith the best and the truest and without good reason contemns others. But since I do not know all the faiths, I cannot judge their truth in all its fullness, and therefore I do not set any faith lower than another, nor exalt any either."[27] Such ecumenism is unacceptable to the officials of the empire; since they now possess the "truth," they wish to assert it by force. The indifferentist school is closed, and Theodore and Abraham are forcibly separated, Theodore sent to a Christian school and Abraham to a (suspiciously anachronistic) *heder*. They are forbidden to associate with one another and taught that the other's religion is to be despised. This lesson is eventually learned. The boys begin to quarrel, calling each other *zhid* and *goy*. The quarrel becomes a fight, in which first the mothers join, then the fathers, and finally the neighbors. It becomes a brawl. Soldiers come and put a stop to it, arresting the instigators (apparently the two fathers). The governor, however, behaves like the Russian police during a pogrom: he orders the Christian released and the Jew beaten and fined. After this the enmity of the two families is total; Theodore's and Abraham's houses are separated by a high stone wall.

Years pass; Abraham and Theodore grow up and succeed to their fathers' professions. Theodore is a merchant engaged in shipping and foreign trade; Abraham is a gold- and silversmith. One day Abraham is beaten and robbed by Christian ruffians who claim they are justly punishing him both for working on a Chrisian holiday and for not removing his hat in front of a Christian icon. Seeing his erstwhile friend being assaulted, Theodore is moved to come to his defense. He argues, very cogently, with Abraham's assailants that "work is never a sin" and that for a Jew to keep his hat on is actually a sign of respect. For this sermon the pogromists beat up Theodore as well.

After this affair the friendship of Theodore and Abraham is revived, despite the strong disapproval of Theodore's coreligionists. Theodore points out to them that Christ commanded us to love all men and hate no one; to this they reply, "Except the Jews." A seller of myrrh—a symbol of Orthodox ritualism—claims to have had a vision foretelling disaster for Theodore, God's punishment for his consorting with a Jew.

This prophecy seems to be fulfilled. A series of calamities strikes Theodore: the destruction of his house by lightning, the deaths of his wife and children, and two shipwrecks in which all his goods are lost. Despite these signs of divine wrath, three times Abraham rescues his friend from destitution by lending him, without security, a thousand litrae of gold. After the second shipwreck, Theodore has an immensely successful voyage, becomes rich, and repays all his debts to Abraham with interest. Abraham refuses to accept the interest; and Christian and Jew together endow a "home where children of all faiths without distinction may receive food and shelter, so that they will become accustomed to one another from childhood and not be divided."[28]

"This tale," Leskov concludes, coming out from behind the rather flimsy scenes, "is not a fable invented by a writer at leisure. It is a true story, which really occurred in ancient times and in those ancient times was written down by the hand of a contemporary respecter of God and a lover of men. Now it has been taken from the old writings and presented in a new exposition for the possible pleasure of the friends of peace and humanity, who are offended by the intolerable spirit of fraternal hatred and abuse."[29]

This statement is not wholly ingenuous. There is no evidence of the historical authenticity of this *Prolog* tale, and the "new exposition" involved substantial changes in the original plot. It would have been impossible for an early Christian writer to assert the equality of Jew and Christian, for to do so would imply the equality of the two religions and thus negate the Christian claim to a unique possession of truth. It was therefore necessary for Leskov to edit out two crucial episodes from the original story (contained in the *Prolog* for October 31). In the *Prolog* the final payment of Theodore's debt is brought to Abraham not by Theodore in person, but miraculously, in a casket cast by the Christian into the sea and conjured, in the name of Jesus Christ, to deliver the money to his Hebrew friend and creditor. The Jew is so impressed by this magic display that he decides to be baptized, "with his entire household." The *Prolog*'s moral, therefore, was a clear demonstration of Christianity's superiority, not tolerance of an alien faith; and the latitudinarian features of the plot—the "pamphilic" secular school and the interfaith orphans' home—were Leskov's invention.

The tale is not an artistic success, as Leskov was well aware. The characterizations are undifferentiated, abstract, and sentimental, the setting colorless and unrealized, the plot excessively linear and predictable. Leskov seems to have recognized these shortcomings. Though he published the story originally in *Russian Thought*, a relatively high-brow magazine, he defended himself against criticisms by asserting that it was "good only for the savage and dark mass of the people."[30] It was designed to "exact from the muzhik a moment of reflection on the Jew."[31]

Leskov did plan to publish "Theodore and Abraham" in a cheap edition for mass distribution, preferably with the "Posrednik" firm managed by Tolstoy's disciple Vladimir Chertkov. In this way he hoped to reach the "muzhik" with his message of tolerance. Chertkov, however, did not like the story. He apparently disapproved of its mercantile spirit and of the shower of wealth bestowed on Theodore at the end. He wrote Tolstoy,

> I am sending you another story of Leskov's, written for us. In spite of the repulsive Leskovian style, I think the first part of the story is full of content in a good sense and that if the censorship permits, it would be a valuable and useful addition to the publications of "Posrednik." Religious intolerance is terribly developed among our peasants and seems to be increasing among the masses in proportion as individuals become filled with the true spirit of Christ's teaching. The ending of the story, about the borrowing of money and the misfortunes of the Christian merchant [. . .] seems to me utterly unnecessary, tiresome, and overdone. If it was necessary to say that the Jew helped the Christian, it would have been enough to say it in a few words. Leskov does not want to eliminate the ending, but he will agree to do so if we won't accept it otherwise. But everything will work out better and to our common satisfaction if you will write me that you agree with my impression.[32]

Tolstoy resisted, however. "Leskov's article [sic]," he replied to Chertkov, "is excellent, except for the language, in which one feels artificiality. In my opinion there is no need to change anything in it, but we should make every effort to have it printed as it is. It is a spendid thing."[33] Tolstoy even rebuked Chertkov for his pedantic judgments of works of art.

Chertkov affected to accept this reproof with Christian humility: "Your remark about my pedantry with respect to artistic works I will remember," he replied, "and I shall try to be as attentive as possible in this respect." On rereading it he still found the ending of Leskov's story objectionable, and he confessed naively to his lack of aesthetic sensitivity: "In general it is hard for me to make a distinction between what is represented in artistic form and what we should try to carry out practically in our actions."[34]

In the same letter Chertkov says that Leskov had agreed to cut the ending. Leskov's letters to Chertkov do not bear this out: "Let them [Theodore and Abraham] engage in business. There's no harm in that. Remember what L[ev] N[ikolaevich] says about the 'pail of slops' in which there is a precious stone [. . .] Furthermore, this is, after all, from the Prolog; so to a certain extent it is a historical legend! And the Jew respected the Christian's love of and faith in the 'man of Galilee.' What more do you want? Otherwise you can dessicate and dissect everything, line everybody up like tin soldiers, and you will have tedious works and with them the loss of the readers' interest."[35]

Tolstoy relented and offered to let Chertkov have his way. "I approve of and understand your letter to Leskov," he wrote. "It would be better the way you write him [with the ending cut], but it is good as it is."[36] However, Leskov refused to change the ending of "Theodore and Abraham." He gave the publishing rights gratis for two years to the firm of A. A. Levenson in Moscow, which brought out a separate edition in 1887.[37] That autumn, when Chertkov expressed renewed interest in the story, Leskov replied that it had already been published in a large number of copies and was selling well; there was now no need for a "Posrednik" edition. "Moreover," he added, "unfavorable attention has been paid to 'The Jew' at the behest of the Ministry of Education, which has perceived something harmful in the story. Consequently, a new edition, especially by your firm, would hardly be permitted now."[38]

A more powerful and sinister figure, Konstantin Pobedonostsev, had also been roused to anger by "Theodore and Abraham." Learning of the separate Moscow edition, Pobedonostsev wrote to Yevgeny Feoktistov, the chief censor—an old enemy of Leskov's—that "it should not be permitted to be published again."[39] Pobedonostsev arranged for the Holy Synod to proclaim the story "extremely harmful."[40] And he also bestirred himself to prevent the publication of a volume of Leskov's *Prolog* stories, including "Theodore and Abraham." "I am afraid," he wrote Feoktistov, "lest there might be some irregularities with regard to a book which has ecclesiastical significance. Please give orders—don't you think it is necessary?—in the right quarters that the matter should be looked into."[41] To this Feoktistov sent a reassuring reply: "With regard to Leskov's book you may be at ease. Measures have been taken."[42]

Though it was included in several prerevolutionary editions of Leskov's collected works, "The Tale of Theodore the Christian and His Friend Abraham the Hebrew" was not reprinted in another mass edition for more than thirty years. In 1919, the same year *The Jew in Russia* was for the first time made available to the general public, the Publishing House of the Petrograd Soviet of Workers' and Red Army Deputies brought out a new edition of "Theodore and Abraham" as part of a campaign against anti-Semitism. Since that date the tale has not once been reprinted in the U.S.S.R., not even in the eleven-volume "thaw" edition of Leskov's collected works (1956-58), which included many items hitherto forbidden, such as *No Way Out* and *Cathedral Folk*.

"Theodore and Abraham" proved to be Leskov's last public pronouncement on the "Jewish question." As a spokesman for the Russian literary conscience and for Tolstoyan Christianity Leskov had finally wrestled down his prejudices and come out, strongly and unambiguously, in favor of tolerance and fraternity. It was a sign of genuine spiritual growth, for which he deserves more credit than he has received.

In private, residual prejudice remained, though the ideal of human unity was genuine. In a letter to his German translator, whose wife had apparently expressed reservations about the possibility of a Jew being as generous and attractive as Abraham, Leskov wrote this reply:

> In practice, "for today" your wife may be on firmer ground than we in her judgment of Abraham, but with respect to the "length of days," the truth will prove to be on our side, even though I would prefer to order work from a Russian or a German than from a Jew. The point is that the story of Theodore and Abraham is given thus in the Prolog (7th century), from where I derived the plot. Further: "True is not that which is and was, but that which might be according to the capacity of the human soul" (Lev Tolstoy), and finally: "Use every man after his desert, and who should escape whipping?" (Shakespeare, *Hamlet*) [. . .] In my life I have known two or three Jews who are men of high caliber, but I agree with your wife that the percentage of bad people among Jews is extraordinarily high. Unfortunately, exact comparisons are impossible here. I do not like Russian, and expecially Muscovite, morality, and I detest Prussian militarism and Baltic baronialism; but we must avoid tribal disharmony. "The unity of the human race," whatever you may say, is not a utopia; a man is first of all worthy of sympathy because he is a man. I understand his condition, to whatever nationality he may belong. "Kinship according to the spirit is greater than kinship according to the flesh." The priests have made nonsense out of that, but the real meaning is that a man close to me in thought is more akin than one of the same tribe with me but with ideas quite different from mine. That is what is meant by "kinship according to the spirit" and "kinship according to the flesh" [. . .] Kinship according to to the spirit is to come together with one another in thought, and then "There is neither Jew nor Greek. . . . for ye are all one in

Christ Jesus" [Galatians 3:28]; for "thought," that is, the proclivi-
ties which govern us, are in Him, and He is the "carpenter's son
from Nazareth, and we know it" [cf. Matthew 13:55]. And He
knew them very well and they tormented Him to death, and He
prayed for them, and they transmitted Him to us much better
than the Greeks did. In my name ask your wife's indulgence for
those for whom Our Lord wept and prayed.[43]

ᴄᴋᴇ 30 ᴄ꙰

The People in Retrospect

Since the beginning of his career as a writer of fiction, Leskov had often used his putative memories as a means of defictionalizing that fiction, giving his readers the illusion of having been led from literature into life. "A Case That Was Dropped" (1862) was the first in a series of apparent nonfictions in which the "author," using the first person singular, presented what purported to be recollections of real experiences. In the age of realism, however, the word "real" must be regarded with suspicion, and this rule applies to Leskov as much as any other writer of that era. But suspicion should not lead to wholesale denial of Leskov's "real" claims. Perhaps the most unusual, and most characteristic, feature of his memoirs is ambiguity. His formula for combining remembered fact with invented fiction was unique.

To enhance the illusion of fictional reality was not the only function of the memoir form for Leskov. It was convenient as a motivation for the story, providing a plausible explanation for the author's knowledge of the events he relates. In addition, by relating memories the author can claim deeper understanding: the years presumably have given him perspective and, with it, wisdom.

Leskov loved historiography. Though he never considered himself qualified to write history, he collaborated in historical magazines, especially Suvorin's *Historical Messenger*, supplying it with raw material—documents, scenes, anecdotal narratives, sketches of personalities—for the professional historians to assimilate and interpret. Awareness of the past, Leskov felt, was a hallmark of civilized man, giving every generation and every individual a sense of distinct identity, a feeling that life was more than endless turns of the biological wheel. As he grew older, Leskov fought to counteract the pervasive human tendency to forget the past, and especially the predilection of youth to regard its problems and discoveries as unprecedented in human history. In this fight Leskov's chief tactic was the adduction of historical

436

precedents—finding analogues from the past to juxtapose with the issues of the present.

The past could also be used as a political weapon and a ruse. During the 1880s, as Russian society drifted to the right, Leskov moved decisively to the left in religion and politics. His break with Orthodoxy widened; his Protestantism became more recusant; and his antagonism toward the reactionary regime of Alexander III grew. Impelled by these emotions, he found another use for the memoir form: camouflaged criticism of the present. By dwelling on analogous troubles of the past he could express apprehension about the problems of "Lampadonostsev's" Russia. For Alexander III, in diluting the reforms of his father, seemed to be reverting to the reign of his formidable grandfather, Nicholas I. Therefore memoirs from Nicholas's era—Leskov's favorite source of materials—could serve a dual function: provide historical perspective on the present, and at the same time evade some of the censors' taboos against public discussion of present problems. Thus reminiscences of the authoritarian Russia of Nicholas I offered a mirror image—though a caricaturing one—of the authoritarian Russia of Alexander III.

Finally, there is yet another "Dichtung und Wahrheit" paradox inherent in Leskov's literary uses of history. Through the magic of art, specific, concrete images may lead to universal, timeless truths about man's nature and fate. In this way Leskov's carefully "dated" memories of the Russia of Nicholas I may become not only camouflaged critiques of a later Russia, but specimen cases of universal human nature, illustrating man's innate propensities for good or evil. Using a group of retrospective stories written by Leskov in the eighties and nineties, we can construct a sociology of Nicolaitan Russia, a Russia which serves some of the functions of caricature, both of the Russia of Leskov's present and beyond that, *mutatis mutandis*, of some endemic imperfections of all human societies and of the human nature that created them.

We begin our sociology at the bottom of the pyramid, with the peasant class. Of all the social evils in the Russia of Nicholas I, the most egregious was the institution of serfdom. In Russia, as in America, until past the middle of the nineteenth century, human beings were bought and sold like cattle; and the moral as well as social weight of this fact lay heavy on the consciences of both countries, not to mention their economies.

This weight lay heavy on Leskov. In many of his earlier stories, for instance "The Life of a Peasant Martyress" and "The Enchanted Pilgrim," he had given graphic illustrations of the corrupting effect of slavery on both owner and slave. For Leskov the Emancipation Act of 1861 had been the central event of the nineteenth century, and all his life he revered the Tsar Liberator who had issued it.

Leskov did not believe that Alexander III would attempt to reestablish serfdom. But by stressing the inhumanity of the slavery from which the second Alexander had delivered his country, Leskov could indirectly call attention to the difference in spirit of the two reigns: an Alexander who acknowledged social evils and compassionately endeavored to relieve them, and an Alexander who regarded all social change as a potential threat to his throne. Therefore, to what is perhaps the most harrowing of all his pictures of the serf society, "The Toupee Artist: A Graveyard Story" (1883), Leskov attached a demonstrative dedication: "To the sacred memory of that blessed day, February 19, 1861."[1]

As in "The Wild Beast," the situation of master and man is shown in "The Toupee Artist" in its extreme and personal form, the relationship of a lord with his house serfs. What happens to human beings when one of them has absolute power over the lives and bodies of others who share his home?

For the lord in this story, Leskov scanned the landscape of his Oryol childhood for despots and chose an even more flagitious example of the "bad father" than Mikhail Strakhov: the repulsive figures of the Counts Kamensky, already celebrated in literature in Herzen's story "The Magpie-Thief."[2] Herzen had portrayed Count Kamensky under the transparent pseudonym of Prince Skalinsky,[3] but Leskov leaves the real name intact. Using the pretext of the blurriness of his childhood memories, however, he fuses two generations of that infamous family, thus concentrating in a single image the worst features of both generations.[4]

The Kamenskys had been famous both for their cruelties to their human chattels—in 1809 Field Marshal Mikhail Kamensky had been murdered by his desperate serfs—and for the private theater in which those same human chattels were trained to perform. Leskov chose his representative Russian slaves from the company of this theater.

Serf actors constituted a paradoxical social case. The theater belonged to the world of high culture, with which peasant serfs ordinarily had no contact. By calling his serf hero an "artist" and making his serf heroine a talented actress, Leskov makes the point, as Turgenev had done in such stories as "The Singers," that Russian peasants are just as capable as their gentry owners of displaying artistic talent and responding to aesthetic stimuli.

But Leskov has a different point as well. Unlike Turgenev's singers, his serf actors are not "natural" peasants performing products of their own folk culture. They are expeasants artificially turned into vehicles of European high culture. A cultured, "European" serf is uncomfortably close to upper-class identity. The gentleman could regard the sweaty muzhik as a beast of burden with sensibilities as refined as an ox's; but could he feel that way about a serf "artist"?

Leskov refrains from pushing this possibility to its limit, exploiting the obvious theme of the brilliant slave whose ascent of Parnassus is blocked by his servile status. Instead, he makes his hero, Arkady, a "toupee artist," a hairdresser in the serf theater. The hairdresser's back-stage position symbolizes the ambiguous, half-way status of the cultured serf. Arkady is a hanger-on, a semiparticipant in the gentry culture. Though his services are indispensable, he is not a part of it.

Leskov underscores this point with the verbal symbolism of the title —as bizarre a phrase in Russian as it is in English—a borrowed French word given a Russian adjectival form. Leskov amplifies the symbolism by an introductory discussion of artistry among jewelers, tailors, and even undertakers.[5] A toupee artist may be an artist, but he is at best a subordinate and rather undignified one.

"The Toupee Artist" dramatizes the confrontation not only of master and man, but also of master and woman, thus adding a sexual dimension to the theme of class antagonism. Unlike Mikhail Strakhov, Count Kamensky is not a "bad father": indeed, he has not advanced on the evolutionary scale to the point of assuming any paternal responsibility. He is simply a bull, an impregnator of heifers. But under the conditions of slavery even this primitive role has been corrupted. Kamensky is also a sadist. He takes delight in deflowering the carefully guarded virginity of his female chattels, staging an elaborate scene of defilement, with his victims costumed as Saint Cecilia, virgin and martyr.

This motif of sexual tyranny is combined with the explosive theme of sexual rivalry between master and man. The pressure reaches the detonation point when the toupee artist receives orders to make up as Saint Cecilia, for his lord's delectation that evening, the girl he loves and who loves him in return. Under this intolerable stress the serf's emotions, and the story's plot, explode. Arkady's desperate efforts to rescue his sweetheart propel the swift-moving action of the concluding chapters of the story. A series of stirring episodes—the abduction, the chase, the betrayal, the capture, the terrible punishments—is followed by the hero's triumphant return and tragic death.

In resolving his plot almost fortuitously, Leskov takes artistic risks. After being tortured by the count and sent as a soldier, Arkady rises to become a commissioned officer. Now a free man and the count's legal equal, he returns with the intention and the money to buy his sweetheart into freedom. But the night before he is to negotiate this transaction, the innkeeper cuts his throat for the girl's ransom. To dispose of his hero so arbitrarily could appear to be motivated more by a need to give the story a tragic ending than by causal forces operating within it. A happy ending would have been jarring in this somber tale, told in a graveyard. The hero and heroine cannot emerge victorious from a system so prejudicially arranged to exploit them. But Leskov needs his semifortuitous resolution of the plot, and he seems to get away with it. By having his hero die at the hands of an outsider he makes the additional point that serfs are subject like any of us to the ironies of fate and the malice of their fellow men. Here the irony is double, since the hairdresser perishes by his own instrument, the razor, an outcome foreshadowed earlier. Once while shaving the count's brother, in a moment of desperate defiance, when the brother threatened to shoot him if he so much as nicked his face, Arkady had replied that if the nobleman made any move to reach for his pistols, he, Arkady, would slit his throat.

Besides the skillfully integrated, if risky, development of its plot, "The Toupee Artist" displays technical mastery and literary daredeviltry of a high order. Leskov contrives an ingenious modification of his patented skaz form. At the outset he seems to be following his familiar formula. The narrator or "author" (again Leskov introduces real names like "my grandmother Alferieva," so that we are encouraged to identify the narrator with the real author) is passing on a story he says was told him in his boyhood by his brother's nurse, Lyubov Onisimovna, who is the former serf actress and the heroine of the plot. But Leskov does not let the old nurse tell the whole story. Her skaz is not consistently maintained. Often without quotation marks or explanatory verbs of speaking, the role of narrator slides imperceptibly back and forth between Lyubov Onisimovna and her auditor-turned-author. The latter sometimes unobtrusively acquires an authorial omniscience out of keeping with his role as boy auditor, such as knowledge of private conversations between the count and his brother. Elsewhere the narrator makes deft use of reported speech (*erlebte Rede*), relaying the nurse's narrative not precisely in her own words, but retaining enough of her diction to give the style some of her personality.

Among the sources of that flavor are typically Leskovian puns, malapropisms, and folk etymologies. In this case, however, these verbal oddities are not humorous in their effect, nor intended to be. One of the most poignant verbal symbols in Leskov is the word *plakón*, a contamination of the Western loan-word *flakón*, "flask, phial," with the Russian verb *plákat'*, "to weep." *Plakón* is the old nurse's name for the vodka bottle which has been her inseparable companion ever since the tragic demise of her beloved; and after reading the story we may well feel like reaching for a *plakón* ourselves.

The basic strategy of "The Toupee Artist" is to represent a maximal contrast of the moral hierarchy with the social one. The highest positions in Russian provincial society are occupied by "noblemen" whose behavior is the opposite of noble. The Counts Kamensky are vicious psychopaths. Yet it did not occur to prereform Russian society to protect a serf against his master. Lyubov Onisimovna comments bitterly that "the [provincial] authorities dared not think of intervening" on behalf of the serf victims of Kamensky's ghastly tortures.[6]

The only authority recognized by the Kamenskys was that of the tsar; and the former toupee artist avails himself of that authority (though only with the count's permission) in escaping from his servile status through service in the tsar's army. But Leskov explicitly symbolizes the complicity of the tsars in the crimes of the Kamenskys. The climax of the plot is reached in connection with a special performance in the Kamenskys' serf theater attended by the tsar—Leskov's narrator "can't say" whether it was Alexander I or Nicholas I, thus generalizing the indictment beyond personality. The imperial presence in the serf theater symbolizes the tsars' responsibility for the slave system. With their private theater, and their tyrannies as well, the Kamenskys were imitating the royal example as best they could.

Leskov knew that his image of a moral order directly opposed to the social order was not historically true. It was a simplification, a propagandistic schema. The wicked Kamenskys were real, but they were not typical; and the noble, brave, and steadfast serfs were not typical, either. As if to right the balance, in his next peasant story, "The Bugbear,"[7] Leskov presented benevolent specimens of the Russian gentry and a less idealized picture of the serfs.

In "The Bugbear" Leskov shows the isolation of even benevolent gentry from the culture of their own people. The mass of the Russian populace still lived within the forms of a primeval folk culture which the gentry had long since repudiated and of which they had little understanding. Leskov's point, however, is not the upper classes' lack of appreciation for the beauties of Russian folklore, but the enormity of the cultural gulf between them and the peasants. For as he represents it, the folk culture, for all its richness and color, may be a source of moral evil. The peasants' ignorant superstitions may lead to cruelties almost as dreadful as the Kamenskys' sadism.

Leskov once again makes effective use of a semioutsider's point of view, an intermediary between the two worlds. The narrative vision is a complex, double one. The essential experiences related are those of the "author" as a child, a *barchuk* or gentleman's son, whose contacts and emotional bonds with the serf servants were closer than with his parents. These experiences are told as adult recollections from the distant past. The memoir form enables Leskov to veer back and forth in time, as if he were manipulating the zoom lens of a movie camera. Through the child's eyes he presents the events with freshness and immediacy, infused with the child's emotions; then he withdraws to an adult perspective and passes appropriate judgments.

Leskov establishes this dual point of view at the outset. He invokes what purport to be (and probably were) his own memories.[8] Although all the action takes place in the country, the narrator begins his tale in Oryol. Stressing his social elevation as the son of "noble parents," with a father "known by everyone in town," the narrator in the opening chapter reports his strong desire as a child to descend from that elevation. He envies the peasant boys who are allowed to frolic naked in the shallow waters of the Oka, and he sympathetically identifies with the soldiers whom he sees being beaten every day as they are drilled on a field near his house. The narrator's move from Oryol to a country estate—corresponding to the Leskovs' move from Oryol to Panino in 1839—enables him to close the cultural gap that separates him from the peasants.

In the country the lordling-narrator undertakes a course of study in the folk culture. His first teacher is an old miller named Ilya, who instructs him in the habits and habitats of the many local goblins and sprites. In recapitulating these lessons, Leskov does not reproduce the child's wide-eyed credulity, but imposes his adult point of view, using ironic vocabulary: "By virtue of his duties as miller Grandfather Ilya had rather close connections with the water sprite who *was in charge of* our two ponds, the upper and lower one, and of the two swamps.

This demon had his *principal staff headquarters* underneath an in-operative outlet of our mill."[9]

The folk culture assimilated by the boy is not merely a collection of quaint fairy tales. The peasants' misperceptions of moral reality lead them to commit acts of gross injustice. These misperceptions center on the figure of Selivan, the principal hero of the story. The plot consists of the gradual refutation of the peasants' false image of Selivan: he is a good man wrongly believed to be a bad one. The narrator "unlearns" the false image of Selivan he has absorbed from his peasant teachers and replaces it with the true one, forced on him by experience.

Selivan is technically not a peasant serf, but a free artisan who operates a poor, almost unfrequented inn in the neighborhood. The peasants are prejudiced against him because he has an ugly red birth-mark on his face (thought to be a sign of moral taint and divine dis-favor) and because he had befriended and later secretly married the crippled daughter of a retired executioner, abhorred by all for her father's bloody past. The truth is that Selivan is a *pravednik*, a man of righteousness; and the peasants' ascription to him of satanic powers, tricks, and crimes is as unfair as Count Kamensky's treatment of Arkady.

Despite his sympathies, the narrator is forced to acknowledge this fact: "[We] landlord's children harbored the tenderest feelings toward our serf servants and faithfully kept their secrets [from our parents . . .] My childhood friendship with our former serfs to this day is one of my pleasantest and warmest memories. From them we got to know all the needs and cares in the poor lives of their relatives and friends in the village, and we learned to *pity the peasants*. But these good peas-ants, unfortunately, were not always just" (8:34; Leskov's italics).

The truth about Selivan's goodness, already sensed by the narrator, is brought to the surface and forced upon the popular consciousness by the hero's heroic behavior in a series of adventures involving the narrator—dramatic rescues and displays of integrity, all related with verve. As Vsevolod Setchkarev has pointed out,[10] the plot is resolved with a Dickensian happy ending perhaps more in keeping with the emotional demands of the story's original readers (it was first pub-lished in a children's magazine) than with the probabilities of real life. Selivan is not only vindicated, but amply rewarded for his virtue.

The narrator, having outgrown his early prejudices, articulates his moral growth in terms of the principles of true Christianity. These are enunciated, for once, by an Orthodox priest, a "real" figure, the

Father Yefim (or Yefimy) Ostromyslensky (or Ostromysleny) whom Leskov mentions in other contexts as a beneficial influence on his childhood.[11] Father Yefim points the moral: "The bugbear was not Selivan, but you yourselves—your suspicion of him, which prevented you from seeing his good conscience. His face seemed dark because your eyes were dark" (8:52).

Leskov was proud of "The Bugbear." In 1887 he wrote to Suvorin, recommending the story for the latter's "Cheap Library": "I have a half children's, half peasant story called 'The Bugbear' which was published three years ago in Volf's children's magazine as a Christmas story. It depicts a good, honest peasant, an innkeeper, who was considered a thief and a robber for no other reason than the fact that he was scary looking and unsociable and also concealed his wife, who was the daughter of a retired executioner. It was a real incident in Kromy. The peasant returns a large sum of money to a traveler who forgot it in his house. The story was read with pleasure by both grown-ups and children."[12] They can do so still.

In the 1890s, after his declaration of allegiance to the religion of Tolstoy, Leskov extracted several more stories from his "peasant memories." The first of these, "Vale of Tears,"[13] has already been discussed as a late variation on the theme of Leskov's first short story, "A Case That was Dropped." In the thirty years between those stories, Leskov's view of the Orthodox clergy had changed drastically: in his Tolstoyan old age he no longer regarded the church as even a potential agency of moral enlightenment among the peasants.

But Leskov's view of the peasants themselves had undergone little change. This view had several facets. Leskov always insisted on placing foremost the principle that no matter how degraded, socially and morally, the peasant must be acknowledged as a fellow human being. As the narrator of "The Bugbear" learned, this truth had to be assimilated emotionally as well as intellectually. Their abysmal poverty made the peasants objects of compassion, but to be meaningful that compassion had to be *practical*, expressed in effective measures of relief. In "Vale of Tears" the author's ideal of charity is exemplified by two of his most attractive "righteous ones," the narrator's Aunt Polly and her devoted friend, the English Quaker Hildegarde. Fearless of infection, these ladies set up a lazaret where they nurse the sick and dying peasants.

Compassion must not blind us to the truth about its objects, however. In the case of the starving Russian peasants of 1840, part of that truth consisted of atrocities committed by the starvelings. The ghastly murder they perpetrate in the effort magically to bring rain symbolizes the dense spiritual darkness still engulfing the Russian peasantry in the enlightened nineteenth century. As Aunt Polly says, in their vale of tears they suffer not only from hunger of the body, but from "hunger of the mind, hunger of the heart, and hunger of the soul." On a larger scale, the murder and the mumbo-jumbo accompanying it represent the universal tendency of men to resort to magic, in thought or deed, when confronted with forces beyond their power to control.

Leskov's aim in "Vale of Tears" was to give his readers historical perspective on the famine of 1891, through which they had just passed, by conjuring up pictures of the even more terrible famine he had seen in his youth.[14] In his introductory chapter he calls attention to what he considers the most important differences between the two famines. In 1891 the miseries of the starving had been mitigated by organized relief measures. Volunteers, including some foreigners, had been roused to action by journalism. In 1840, on the other hand, Nicholas I had forbidden mention of the famine in the press, on the grounds that it would damage the country's prestige and be taken as a sign of military weakness. At that time the only private charities permitted had been those undertaken on the spot by people of good will like Leskov's righteous heroines; no public fund-raising campaigns were allowed.[15]

The social response to misfortune had been better in 1891 than in 1840, and Leskov wanted to call attention to social progress: relative freedom of public discussion had led to relief of human suffering. To establish the fact of this progress in the public mind was important. Even in 1891, as Leskov's readers knew, the Russian government had continued to censor published accounts of the famine and had regarded private relief undertakings with suspicion. As an instrument of social activism, "Vale of Tears" was designed to demonstrate the progress made by Russian society during the preceding half-century, mainly during the reign of Alexander II. At the same time it was intended to exert covert pressure on the government of Alexander III by subtly praising it for policies it had adopted reluctantly.

"Vale of Tears" was thus a work of literature bound up with life, seeking to act upon it. It was no more a precise record of historical or biographical fact than Leskov's other quasi memoirs had been. As Leskov wrote in a letter to an old friend from Oryol:

445

On "Vale of Tears" I wrote you that it was all true, but sewed together like a patchwork quilt by one of our Oryol tradeswomen from behind the Ilyinka. The times are depicted accurately, therefore, and the artistic aim is achieved. I have characters there from both Kursk and Tambov. For my purposes (to provide a picture of mores) it doesn't matter. In that whole region the mores are the same; and what happened in Oryol, Kursk, and Tambov can all be splendidly mixed together and laid out on one palette. I had to call it memoirs to show that it was not invented. I did not invent it: I brought together in one story events of the same time and nature.[16]

Some readers questioned one historical fact in "Vale of Tears:" the presence of Quakeresses in Russia of 1840. People knew that in 1891 the Quakers had brought famine relief from abroad to the "breadbasket of Europe"; but were there Quakers in Russia in those far-off times? Leskov claimed to have received a flood of queries, and he made use of his readers' putative doubts in order to attach a postscript to "Vale of Tears," a quasi-historical article entitled "On Quakeresses."[17]

The core of this article is a historical document that Leskov says he obtained from Veniamin Astashev, a major general and former gold miner in Siberia; it proved that there had been Quakeresses in Russia—apparently Russian, not English ones—as early as 1744, when twenty-two of them had been exiled for their heresy to an Orthodox convent in Tomsk. This document, which also contains several discreditable instances of perfidy on the part of the Orthodox clergy and of inhuman callousness on the part of the Russian bureaucracy, is "framed" with more of Leskov's nonconformist Protestant associations, mainly some further recollections of his Scott relatives.[18]

Leskov's statement in this article about the Protestant influences of his childhood is confirmed by other sources and can be read as authentic autobiography: "With Protestants in our family circle we maintained particularly close connections, since one of my aunts was married to an Englishman and all of us (who were then young) grew up with respect for the beliefs and piety of our English relations, whom our elders frequently held up to us young people as examples of an active Christian life" (9:314).

Containing autobiographical data and a historical document as well, "On Quakeresses" presumably lies outside the realm of fiction. Yet even here that "historian" performs a trick. In this straightforward historical context, he boldly asserts the historicity of what his son has described as the "semiapocryphal Aunt Polly" and the "even less authentic Englishwoman Hildegarde."[19]

Associations with the Scotts were revived in Leskov's next opus in the "memories of peasants" genre, "A Product of Nature" (1893).[20] Although this story was written from a compassionate impulse as a contribution to a volume published to raise funds for the relief of peasants being resettled in Siberia from the overpopulated regions of European Russia, the work seems designed to demonstrate the limitations of compassion and the need for the hardest kind of realism when dealing with the "dark" people. Again Leskov takes us back to the days of serfdom, recounting what purport to be his own experiences with analogous resettlements of peasants thirty-five years before.

When managing the estates of the Naryshkins and Perovskys, Leskov's uncle, Alexander Scott, had been instructed to buy up serfs in central Russia for resettlement on virgin lands acquired by his employer in the steppe regions of the southeast. Scott assigned Leskov to accompany one of these expeditions. As Leskov elusively describes the arrangement, he was not then a regular employee of his uncle's firm, but at Scott's suggestion was using this experience to test his preferences and capacity for this kind of work: would he prefer private business to government service? This description of his situation may well have been correct—in 1857 Leskov had worked "on trial" for Scott while on leave from his government post; but whether biographically true or not, there were sound literary reasons for establishing greater distance between the narrator and his uncle's business. To be penetrating, the narrative point of view must be that of a relative moral outsider—someone whose commitment to the system is not final, who has not acquired the moral calluses of habit and is still capable of being troubled by what he sees.

Through inclination and on his uncle's assignment, the narrator plays a compassionate role toward the peasants being resettled. He is given clemency powers, authorized to grant exceptions to the harsh regime imposed on the migrants. Though he is nominally in charge, the real head of the expedition is a hard-bitten, tough-minded peasant whom Scott calls his "Pizarro": "The peasant [Scott explains] will sit on the neck of a softhearted person and start kicking him with his bast shoes. You need Pizarros, and I have just the Pizarro I need" (9:342). This Pizarro, alias Pyotr Semyonov, has a physique to match his character: "[He] was a dark, curly-haired peasant of about forty-eight or fifty, muscular, strong, and lively, with fiery black eyes, black eyebrows grown together over the nose, a turned-up nose, and a short, thick black beard. The expression on his face was strong, bold, decisive, and rather cruel" (9:343). The action of the story amounts to a test case, an experimental comparison of the narrator's soft line toward their charges with "Pizarro's" hard one.

As the hard line goes, once one accepts the basic premise that peasants are to be involuntarily uprooted and transported en masse over great distances, the conclusion becomes inescapable that compassion is a liability. There is as little room for it as there was in the Spanish conquest of Peru. The peasants have to endure; and as military leaders know, harsh discipline makes it easier for men to endure harsh realities. They develop automatic reflexes of obedience, and they need not feel any responsibility for their sufferings.

In this instance the harshest of the peasants' realities is lice. In Leskov's "A Product of Nature" these loathsome insects make as vivid an appearance in Russian literature as Gogol's cockroaches or Dostoevsky's spiders. Lice were not a usual subject even for realistic literature, as Leskov himself observes: "Filth is disgusting, and you don't sing songs about it while sitting at the piano, and you don't compose ballads on the subject; but we must set aside our squeamishness and speak insistently about filth in order to eradicate it" (9:355). "A Product of Nature," therefore, might be called Leskov's ballad on lice.

Under the crowded conditions on the barges the lice become a torture. The traditional methods for controlling them, the steam bath and the bonfire (for roasting them out of clothing), cannot be employed on the barges, and the peasants refuse to bathe in the cold waters of the river. The lice, they assert, multiply in cold water; and the rules of modesty could not be maintained. So there is nothing for it but to endure; yet the agony is unendurable.

For the narrator, apparently free from physical contamination in his private cabin, the situation becomes psychologically unendurable. At length he authorizes a party of male peasants to go ashore to visit a bathhouse they claim to see in the distance. Once on land, the crazed desperadoes set off for home on foot, abandoning their families on the barges. When the news leaks out, there is danger of a general rebellion; and it is feared that the runaways may stir up trouble in the villages they pass through. The narrator with his compassion is disgraced and discredited, and the triumphant Pizarro has him ousted from the expedition.

In the aftermath the runaways are caught, flogged, and forcibly returned to the barges by a police clerk. The clerk, though he has only three decrepit Cossacks at his disposal, intimidates the peasants with his peremptory manner and his dashing cape, from the inside of which gleams a large buckle, made to appear like a medal. This clerk is a variant of the Pizarro type, a more articulate and philosophical one, filled with contempt for the docile human cattle whose rebellion he has easily suppressed:

My boss is away, and I myself am a nobody and have no powers. I'm simply a clerk, a secretary, nothing more. But I know these people. So I took three cripples, put on a cape with a big buckle pinned to it, caught the runaways and ordered them, "Back, you scum!" And I brought them all back and flogged the whole lot. My buckle has an amazing effect: I chase them back like Pharaoh, bring them here and whip them all; and don't forget that I whip them with their own magnanimous and benevolent assistance. They hold one another by the legs and arms and sit on each other's heads; and then I send them back to their barges and it's all over. They sail off, and I stand on the bank and think, "Oh, you Slavic rubbish! Oh, you native-born trash!" Let anyone with three helpers try to play such a trick on forty Frenchmen. Fat chance! But here everything goes splendidly. And that, don't forget, is with my mere buckle. But if I had a real medal! Oh, if only I had a medal! With a real medal I could flog the whole of Russia by myself!" (9:354)

In her humorless, orthodox-Soviet manner, Maria Goryachkina takes this speech as a "sarcastic direct exposé, by his own self-description, of a character" who is "the personification of the machinery of autocracy not only of prereform, but also of postreform times."[21] She has missed the point of Leskov's irony. The police clerk may be a cog in the "machinery of autocracy," but he is not a typical cog or a "personification"; nor is Leskov's attitude toward him as hostile as Goryachkina seems to assume. Like his creator, he is a social realist and a humorist; he is capable of viewing himself and his role with ironic detachment; and he understands that any system of tyranny requires massive collaboration by the oppressed in their oppression.

Leskov shared the clerk's scorn, so heretical from the official Soviet point of view, for the submissive "Slavic rubbish" who cooperated in flogging one another. "If a police scribe by himself could flog a whole crowd of peasant runaways from my barges, and with their own collaboration, where can you go with such a people? *Nowhere!*"[22] And on another occasion Leskov said of "A Product of Nature": "I was humane and had various ideas on this subject, but life demanded Cossacks and birch rods. And my peasant "transferees," under my own authority, were caught by Cossacks and flogged. There are your clever ideas for you! But that's what happened."[23]

"A Product of Nature" epitomizes two problems connected with the compassionate impulse and the compassionate act. The first of these might be called the "working within the system" problem, or "reform versus revolution." It would be generally agreed that anything that relieves human suffering is a positive good. Still, it is sometimes the case that no effective measures for the relief of suffering are possible within a given system. One must then confront the moral necessity of repudiating the system itself and seeking to change it. Is it possible, for example, to be a moral (or a Christian) slaveholder? The "practical Christian" Alexander Scott evades the moral implications of this problem. He would argue that he cannot change or alleviate the miseries of the serfs he manages, at least while they are in transit. (A larger question is whether Scott's job itself is morally acceptable.) A realist, he resorts to "Pizarros," distancing himself from the horror by staying at home and by making jokes and inventing verbal ironies, one of which is the title of his nephew's story.[24] The peasants, Scott says, like the lice that infest them, are only "a product of nature." If their bellies are filled, they can knock off a thousand versts "like dancing a cotillion." The ironic image of a cotillion being danced by these miserable, vermin-ridden people is repeated several times.

The second of the "compassion problems" is that of physical and moral squeamishness. Poverty is often repulsive. Leskov's picture of the louse-covered bare breast of a nursing mother brings vividly home the overwhelming reversal of feeling produced by squalor. "Stopping alongside a young woman nursing a baby at the breast, with shameless insolence ['Pizarro'] cast the light of his lantern on her exposed breast. There was something gray on the breast like tulle, and that tulle was moving, mixing by the nipple with drops of blue milk from which the child had drawn back. Pizarro's lips curled into a contemptuous smile, and he pulled away the lantern and said, 'Isn't it nice that my son can respond to such charms?' "[25]

The poor may also evoke moral squeamishness. The Russian peasants, as Leskov realistically viewed them, were ignorant and superstitious, untrustworthy, and capable of brutal cruelty, especially to one another. Harking back to the muck-raking social realists of the early sixties, the "people" in Leskov's "Vale of Tears" and "A Product of Nature" anticipate Chekhov's shockingly brutalized "Muzhiks" (1897) and the repugnant denizens of Bunin's *Village* (1909). Leskov's point is that true compassion must recognize the degraded physical and moral state of its object and be able to survive the knowledge.

In a letter written later that year Leskov claimed that "A Product of Nature" had been turned out too hastily. There were several details he wished he could add: the louse-races with which the peasants on the barges had tried to amuse themselves, and a Penza whipping post in the form of a cross or T, with a police captain who before a flogging would intone in liturgical Slavonic, "Let us inscribe him who was crucified for us."[26]

Life gave Leskov no time to make further revisions in "A Product of Nature," but it did allow him to turn out one more story on the peasant theme.

Leskov's final pronouncement on the peasant question is "The Cattle-pen."[27] It is a work difficult to classify by genre. Leskov himself called it a "survey":[28] it combines current journalistic commentary with historical reminiscences and with satire of contemporary life.

Leskov's immediate stimulus for writing "The Cattle-pen," according to his own assertion,[29] was an "excellent article" by his friend and correspondent, the literary critic and journalist Mikhail Menshikov, then a sympathizer with Tolstoyanism. Menshikov's article, Leskov said, was entitled "On the Chinese Wall."[30] By this metaphor—the more recent term is "iron curtain"—he meant the means by which Russia has periodically attempted to isolate herself from the rest of the world, especially Western Europe.[31] For Leskov the "Chinese Wall" was an explosive subject, and he had plenty of dynamite ready— thirty to forty pages of "illustrations," as he called them.[32]

He begins "The Cattle-pen" by citing with indignation a Russian adaptation (1857) of an old German work in theoretical economics, *Der isolierte Staat* (1826) by Johann-Heinrich Thünen, as one among many meretricious attempts to idealize and justify the ugly fact of Russia's backwardness.[33] Backwardness, Leskov insisted, like any problem, had to be acknowledged before it could be solved, and many educated Russians refused to do that. They claimed that backwardness was an illusion, that in higher senses Russia was more advanced than her Western neighbors. To Leskov such claims were vicious nonsense, undermining people's will to work; and in "The Cattle-pen" he provides a string of "illustrations" of their wrongness.

The metaphor of the cattle-pen, he says, is derived from a printed picture circulated as an illustration to the Thünen book. It showed "a dark cattle-pen, surrounded by a wall broken here and there by little cracks through which weak rays of light reached us in our unbroken darkness" (9:357). The most benighted occupants of this dark cattle-pen are the peasants; and to illustrate this fact Leskov brings forward more autobiographical reminiscences, including some from his "Scott" period.

Though presumably real, this material is presented with the vividness of fiction, a fact noted by Tolstoy. After delivering the manuscript of "The Cattle-pen" to his editors, Leskov had written Tolstoy asking for an assessment:

> I have written a piece for *The Week*, and it's already set in type, but somehow everyone is scared of it, and therefore I don't know whether it will come out or not. It's called "The Cattle-pen." In essence it is a *survey*. Everything is copied from nature. If it does come out, please read it and tell me whether it is harmless or harmful. I don't need praise, but I need to test myself by the judgment of someone I trust. The point is not whether it is well written or not, but whether it meets the needs of this day. People also talk this way and that to me; and I am alone, and my mind is shaky [. . .] Please have a look at it.[34]

Tolstoy had long been troubled by the moral ambiguities of fiction. The essence of realistic fiction, he knew only too well, was legerdemain, making readers believe in the reality of the unreal. Writing fiction was therefore a form of deceit; and the world's greatest writer of fiction, which Tolstoy might validly have claimed to be, was therefore the world's biggest liar! Earlier that year Tolstoy had written Leskov: "I was about to begin further work on a certain piece of fiction, but believe me, it hurts my conscience to write about people who never existed and who never did anything of the kind. Something is wrong. Is it that the form of fiction has outlived itself, or that stories are outworn or that I am outworn? Do you experience anything like this?"[35]

Leskov's patchwork truth, with its apparently solid facade of "real" facts, struck Tolstoy as an excellent solution to the lying problem. Leskov, it seemed, had no need to lie: he wrote with the techniques of fiction about real people and real events! When Tolstoy read "The Cattle-pen," he wrote to Leskov: "I liked it and especially the fact that it is all truth and not invention. It is possible to make the truth just as interesting as invention or even more so, and you know how to do this superbly. What did people tell you you shouldn't say? Maybe that you don't sing the praises of the old days? But they are wrong. The old days were fine, but freedom is still better."[36]

Overjoyed by the master's praise, Leskov replied with an interesting restatement of his epistemological principles in writing such stories: "I thank you humbly for your lines about my 'Cattle-pen.' I am very fond of this form of story about what "was," introduced "by the way" (apropos), and I don't think it is harmful or supposedly improper, since it touches on people who are still alive. For I am not moved by either enmity or friendship; I note those phenomena from which you can see the times and the movement of the vital currents of the mass."[37]

In the memoir portions of "The Cattle-pen" Leskov presents graphic "illustrations" of Russia's backwardness. He displays vividly the peasants' primitive agricultural implements and inefficient practices; their resistance to the efforts of "enlightened" landlords, like Scott, to introduce improved techniques; their refusal to live in fine new stone houses built for them by a benevolent owner. (They use the stone houses as privies, while living in chimneyless wooden "smoke huts" they construct alongside.)[38]

The peasants' obstinacy, Leskov implies, is not a moral fault; it is the product of ignorance and ingrained suspicion of their masters. The majority of landlords, however, disapprove of efforts to improve the peasants' lot and rejoice at the peasants' rejection of such attempts. Such people, in Leskov's books, are not ignorant: they are wicked. Out of narrowly conceived self-interest, they knowingly side with darkness and evil.

Worse still, he believes, are "intellectuals" who articulate this position publicly, trying to idealize Russia's backwardness as a positive good. Leskov's examples of these pernicious efforts include a pamphlet by his one-time acquaintance Vladimir Burnashov proclaiming the alleged miraculous medicinal properties of the shiny soot scraped from the walls of peasant smoke huts. There was no reason, Burnashov implied, to try to provide peasants with better houses than the *kurnye izby* or smoke huts. Misguided liberals might regard the smoke huts as hovels where the peasants spent long winters being smoke-cured like hams, in an atmosphere thick with sweat and soot, to the enormous detriment of their eyes and lungs. In reality, Burnashov maintained, the smoke huts were an asset: they were warm and cozy, and they produced a wonderful medicinal soot for which Europe would soon come begging.

Nikolai Leskov

In his presentation of Burnashov's outrageous argument something new happens to Leskov's literary manner. The familiar dry, ironic mode is abandoned, and the author's indignant fury breaks through. First we hear the old Leskov:

In the brochure on soot [. . .] it was said positively that by its means, with God's blessing, you could cure almost all human diseases, and especially "diseases of the female sex." You only had to have the knack of how to collect the soot, that is, whether to scrape it from above downward or from below upward. This affected its medicinal properties. If garnered in one direction, it lifted that which was fallen, whereas if taken the other way it lowered that which needed moving downward. And you could get it only in Russian smoke huts and nowhere else [. . .] The West has no such asset, and the West will come to our cattle-pen for our soot.

Then his anger is revealed:

The cattle-pen was content. Depraved people who had lost their shame and their sense undertook to prescribe how to treat yourself with soot. The "glistening soot" was to be dissolved in vodka and water and taken internally by people of all ages, especially children and women. Who can say how many people paid for this with their lives?[39]

Scott's bitter words about the Russian character as quoted in "The Cattle-pen" sum up the author's final judgment as well. The peasants were "savage and dark." But worse than that, as Scott said, they were being lied to and told that the bad was good and the good bad. "Mark my words," Scott had warned. "The reckoning for this will come when it is least expected" (9:368-369).

These words correspond closely to pronouncements made by Leskov himself in his last years:

Our peasants drink from morning till night. No noble principles can be instilled in such people. L. N. Tolstoy's Karataev [in *War and Peace*] is an exception; the real peasants are in *The Power of Darkness*.[40]

To this day the peasants cultivate the earth with the implements of Gostomysl [a ninth-century ruler of Novgorod], treat themselves with soot from the stove, and on holidays like not to read the newspaper, but to hunt for lice in each other's hair, or in a

454

drunken stupor to bloody each other's mugs with their fists or their sticks. But who knows, maybe such people are more capable than writers of voting fine laws, war and peace, credit and so forth.[41]

From the point of view of artistic unity—never Leskov's strong point—it might have been better to end "The Cattle-pen" with Scott's dire forecast. But in the mood of indignant wrath that possessed him during those years Leskov wanted desperately to make people see that the evils of Russian society could not be relegated to the "old days," as Tolstoy put it. Though their shape had changed, they were still alive. He therefore continues his "illustrations" with a series of contemporary scenes, drawn from his experiences in the Estonian resorts where he had been spending the summers in recent years.

The central figure in this section is an unsavory rascal named Yefim Volkov, ludicrously called "Mifim" by the Estonian populace. The apex of Mifim's myth-filled career was to pass himself off as an Orthodox priest, in disgrace for having performed an illegal marriage.[42] The *generalshi* (the wives of generals or high officials) who frequent the resort believe this tale and seek to avail themselves of Mifim's magic in winning suitors for their unmarried daughters. And sometimes, it appears, they avail themselves of a different kind of "magic" that Mifim has to offer, one "the memory of which brings roses to the cheeks." In short, the intellectual and spiritual level of the *generalshi* is no higher than that of the benighted and brutalized peasant serfs of forty years earlier. It is morally lower, since the ladies have access to the light and consciously reject it.

The picture Leskov drew of the shallow, corrupt world of Russian upper-class society was intensified in "A Winter's Day." Filled with moral indignation, the old Leskov looked around him at the Russia of his day and saw only a generation of vipers living in a dark cattle-pen. At times it seemed to him that there had been no progress since the days of *No Way Out:* "Everything stands in the same place in the same *cattle-pen.* Once again we begin to daydream about Europe, about science, about medical schools for women, about freedom of the press, and again from the beginning and again. . . . It will be a long time yet. And all this I prophesied in *No Way Out.*"[43]

Feeling his life nearing its end, Leskov had renewed the dire prophecy, and he was proud of it: "This ['The Cattle-pen"] is my posthumous work. I am glad that even in my declining days I succeeded in capturing the spirit of the times and the characters of men."[44]

ᘓᕟ 31 ᕯᘗ

Other People in Retrospect

Leskov's backward gaze was not riveted solely on the peasants. In view of the developments in his spiritual life since 1875, it would not have been hard to predict what Leskov's retrospective view of the Orthodox clergy would reveal in 1884. Long before he formally allied himself with Tolstoy, Leskov had concluded that the Orthodox church had no connection with the true message of Jesus Christ. Its moral state was doubly corrupt, since it actively strove to conceal or distort the teachings of Jesus, keeping the light of Christianity from penetrating the dark "cattle-pen."

To convey in censored print this view of the church was a formidable undertaking, even for an experienced camouflage artist like Leskov. Nevertheless, in 1884 he attempted this impossible task; and for once he failed, at least partially. The censors penetrated his disguises and forced him into silence before his tirade was complete.

The work in question is "Notes in an Unknown Hand," published serially in *A. Gattsuk's Gazette*.[1] Leskov resurrects the eighteenth-century device of representing the text as a real manuscript that has somehow fallen into the author's hands and which he only edits. This trick was also supposed to disarm the censors, since an editor should presumably not be held responsible for heretical ideas expressed by the original author. And if the notes are in an unknown hand and in a markedly archaic style, then the supposed author is obviously not only obscure, but dead and buried, safely beyond the reach of censors and police. Moreover, as heretical ideas recede in time, they lose their virulence, becoming mere curiosities. Finally, in this case even the place where the manuscript was acquired is symbolically "distanced": the author says he bought it from an antique bookseller on his "last visit to Moscow."

The author's introduction describes the text as "an artless representation of events that at one time interested a certain social circle, evidently very respectable, original, and seriously inclined" (7:322).

456

This "certain social circle" proves to be the clergy; but the censor might not guess it even from the lead-off story in the series of anecdotes which constitute the "notes." The first story is the only one that does not mention the clergy at all, but deals with the familiar theme of bureaucratic corruption. Perhaps Leskov hoped that censors would not read past this point.

A further camouflage function is served by the titles of the individual anecdotes, such as "Speed Is Required in Catching Fleas, but in Business Circumspection Is Required." They label each chapter as if it were an old-fashioned fable, devoid of specific social relevance. Further, some of these titles are of questionable relevance to the stories they head; they seem to be deliberate false leads.

The most important and sustained camouflage device in "Notes in an Unknown Hand" is the style, which comes close to being an artistic liability. The "notes" are written in heavily stylized, archaized prose, ostentatiously dry and void of emotion. It is a church style, full of Slavonicisms and ecclesiasticisms, but different, for instance, from Father Tuberozov's diary. It is deliberately stripped of grace, charm, and sentiment. Such prose makes neither easy nor pleasant reading.

Apart from its camouflage functions, Leskov employs this style to unmask covertly a discreditable narrator. The narrator (the supposed author of the "notes") expresses moral judgments which the true author wants his readers to repudiate; he is therefore given a symbolically ugly style to match. The danger in this procedure is that the reader, irritated by the creaky, stiff, graceless sentences, will repudiate not only the narrator, but the work itself. Finally, some of the "humorous" anecdotes in "Notes in an Unknown Hand" are simply bad jokes: the pseudo-author's taste in humor is as corrupt as his moral principles.

For these reasons "Notes in an Unknown Hand" falls short of being an artistic success; it is often tedious and dry. Its most vivid narratives were the two connected chapters, "On Petukh and His Children" and "A Simple Means," which had just been readied for publication when the censor struck; they remained in manuscript until 1917.[2] These two chapters, in contrast to the others, form an effective short story in themselves. The plot is a variation on that of "Old Times in the Village of Plodomasovo": a young gentleman in love with a serf girl and his efforts to marry her despite the disapproval of society and the opposition of his mother. In this quasi novella Leskov's natural gift for narrative seems to have overcome his conscious efforts to stifle it and simulate the "artlessness" of an old-fashioned ecclesiastical moralist.

"Notes in an Unknown Hand" has also been criticized for lack of satirical vehemence, but unjustly.[3] The cumulative picture these anecdotes present of the moral state of the Russian clergy in the pre-reform era seems altogether too vehement. The clergy as Leskov represents them are contemptible: ignorant, drunken, and squalid, associated with belching, spitting, lice, and bedbugs; cowardly and rapacious; servile toward the gentry and toward their ecclesiastical superiors, arrogant and prone to acts of physical violence against those beneath them. These alleged servants of God lack redeeming features of any kind. The picture is too bleak to be wholly credible.

In their relations with peasant serfs the clergy of "Notes" show themselves to be callous and exploitative. They see nothing wrong with the slave system, only regretting that they do not enjoy the gentry's privilege of owning serfs. They are always eager to side with the gentry against the peasants in the hope of receiving some crumbs from the lord's table. As in "The Life of a Peasant Martyress," the priests have no scruples, for instance, about defiling the sacrament of matrimony by obediently marrying a serf girl against her will, but at her mistress's command, to a degenerate moron twice her age. The clergy never show any sense of responsibility to provide religious instruction. For them religion is a business, and they are only interested in ceremonies that pay.

Among themselves, Leskov's clergy are full of backbiting, intrigue, tale-bearing, petty rivalries, disloyalty, and pompous displays of rank. The priests are obsequious toward the gentry, who regard them with contempt: as coarse, cloddish creatures who, for instance, use a bread knife to remove calluses from their feet; and as servile subordinates whose "religious" services are always for sale, and cheap.

Worst of all is the relation of the clergy to the state power. Twice Leskov slips in direct allusions to the priests' most shameful betrayal: reporting confessional secrets to the police. This practice seems to be accepted by the nominal author and his colleagues as natural. "That which is revealed to us in secret," one of his priests says, "must forever remain secret from all, except the political authorities alone" (7:332).

Other than its police function, the main purpose of confession, in the priests' view, is income. They prefer the pro forma confession of an atheistic political exile who leaves a ten-ruble note in their pocket to the lady who confesses three times a year in great detail and leaves only a wretched coin. Penance seems perfunctory, lacking moral force. Leskov manages slyly (and unfavorably) to contrast Orthodox confessional procedures with Roman Catholic practice (which insists on exploring the psychological background and motivation of the sins) and with Protestants, who urge the individual to confess his sins directly to God. A bishop's defense of the Orthodox penance sounds like an admission of moral collapse: "As Orthodox we must not despise our own [confessional practice], but hold to it, particularly since with us the confession in any case has a special use for the civil administration, which it is better for us not to touch. And therefore don't try to destroy it, but let us lead a quiet life in all piety" (7:335).

The same bishop is about to reprimand a priest for having attended a discussion with a visiting foreign preacher (*predikant*—a typical seminarian Latinism in the "author's" style), a Protestant, something like a precursor of Lord Radstock. The bishop's wrath dissolves, however, when he hears that the governor of the province had attended the same meeting: for him the governor's presence is a seal of divine approval.

Leskov smuggles his positive religious ideals into this depressing context and contrasts them with the debased practices of the Orthodox. Only under pressure from foreign Bible societies, for example, does the Holy Synod at last print and distribute copies of the New Testament in Russian, rather than Slavonic; but the clergy continue to feel uncomfortable about having God's word so readily and comprehensibly accessible to the laity.

As Leskov sees it, Orthodoxy and Christian piety are incompatible. A learned archimandrite proclaims his intention of "stripping off his angelic rank" and living in the world as an ordinary man. He is unmoved by arguments that he might soon become a bishop. The archimandrite's explanation by implication calls into question the whole system of monasticism and ecclesiastical ranks: "No, I have come to know myself, and there is nothing angelic in me. I am only an ordinary man with all a man's weaknesses. I feel tenderness of heart for ordinary people, my equals, and I seek to share an equal fate with them, both in this life and in another, about which we know not" (7:375).

It was suspected that this exmonk's secret plan was to marry a rich widow, and several women came forward with proposals. But the ex-archimandrite rejects them. His only wish is to lead a "simple, healthy life," earning his bread "in the sweat of his brow." He becomes a teacher; but as an unfrocked monk he encounters difficulties. At last he dies gruesomely of scurvy; and this unseemly death is taken by the Orthodox, including the "author," as divine punishment for his apostasy.

Positive values may be derived from secular sources as well. In a chapter entitled "On the Harm Which Many Experience from Reading Secular Books" the purveyor of these values is Charles Dickens, called "the Anglic writer Dickents" [*aglickij pisatel' Dikenc*] in the quaint style of the manuscript. In her readings of Dickens a young seamstress (who anticipates the noble Klavdia of "Night Owls") loves to contemplate "the emulation of nobility of character and principles in those modest individuals who are portrayed by that author in the most ordinary circumstances of life and find their strength in the gentle loftiness of the Christian spirit" (7:347). The seamstress's ideal of female virtue is Little Dorrit.

Overwhelming pressure is brought to bear on this girl's sweetheart, a seminarian, not to renounce the priesthood in order to marry her. He ultimately succumbs and marries instead the priest's daughter designated for him. The seamstress dies in poverty, and he commits suicide. In short, the tale is of a sentimental intensity worthy of "Dickents." In this instance the lachrymose narrative is improved by the dry style in which it is told and by the "author's" attitude toward these events—not only unsentimental, but full of disapproval of these young people's efforts to place the integrity of their feelings above social convention.

The social element closest to the clergy in prereform Russia, in status and in culture, was the merchantry; and in his story called "A Robbery" (1887) Leskov lights up this colorful class with his retrospective searchlight and symbolically conveys that social closeness.[4] Leskov knew provincial merchants only externally, from his years as a court clerk in Oryol; yet his story succeeds in conveying a vivid picture of their life as seen from the inside—except for the brief, though pungent "Exorcism" (1879), something he had not attempted since the sixties.

"Robbery" is structured as a skaz. Leskov leads off with a flimsy frame setting, a group discussion in 1887 of a recent bank robbery or embezzlement in Oryol, which gives the narrator, an "old Oryol merchant," his pretext for launching into a reminiscence of another Oryol robbery of fifty years before. The stylization of this old merchant's speech, as Vsevolod Setchkarev has noted,[5] is one of Leskov's most brilliant tours de force. Though less spectacular than some of his other

displays of verbal ingenuity, such as "The Lefthander," it is more successfully integrated with narrative purpose, more strictly functional.
The narrator, his style, and his story are all of a piece: they work harmoniously toward the same end. The narrator's language is picturesque and colorful, but it does not leap out of the story and become an
independent value in itself.

The atmosphere of "Robbery" is very different from Leskov's earlier
merchant tales. His perennial anger at the Orthodox clergy has been
sublimated into humor, and the darkness of the merchant world similarly relieved. This story stands as a major exception to Andrei Leskov's rule that in his father's fiction the Great Russian stories, mostly
with their locus in Oryol, are gloomy and depressing, in contrast with
the sunny Ukrainian stories, brimming with jollity and laughter.[6]
"Robbery" is one of Leskov's funniest tales, and in Andrei Leskov's
own phrase it is "permeated through and through with the flavor of
life in old Oryol."[7]

The humor of "Robbery" is cinematic. It could be made into a Marx
Brothers type of film: a quick-moving sequence of absurdities, drunkenness, obtuseness, silly, superstitious women, mistaken identities,
and mutual deceptions. It exudes a narrative spirit Leskov called "gay
confusion," one which he distilled successfully in "Night Owls" and
"The Rabbit Warren." Leskov describes the story in an "advertising"
letter to a magazine editor: "At this moment (8 A.M., November 24,
1887) I have a story on my desk: ready, recopied, and once again thoroughly scribbled over. It remains only to submit and print it. It is
about thirty pages long; it is called 'A Favor from a Kinsman.' In genre
it is a story of everyday life; in plot it is gay confusion; the setting is
Oryol and partly Yelets. In the narrative fact is mixed with fancy, and
in general it is funny reading and a true picture of life in that thievish
town of sixty years ago, in the time of Trubetskoy and Kurilenko."[8]

"Robbery" is by no means devoid of social and moral import. In
old Oryol, among the merchants, one encounters not religion, but "lerigion" (*leregija*, a symbolic folk corruption also used by Leskov elsewhere). "Lerigion" consists on the one hand of superstitious formalism, of both the Orthodox and the Old Believer variety (between
which Leskov now sees little to choose); and on the other of aesthetics
and showmanship. What the merchants look for in their clergy is the
quality of an ecclesiastic's singing voice: going to church is a form of
entertainment, and their fervor is aroused not by a sermon or prayer,
but by a deacon who can make the rafters vibrate with a low D.

The climactic scene in the story is an "audition," conducted by two merchants, of the vocal powers of two deacons who are competing for a lucrative position in Yelets. The description shows that for all his moral contempt for Orthodoxy, Leskov was still a connoisseur of church singing: "They fortified themselves [with a tumbler full of "pure Jamaica rum"], and the deacon began from the bottom 'in blessed death eternal peace' and started going up the scale and then in a thick sub-bellow 'to all the departed bishops of Oryol and Sevsk, Apollos and Dositheus and Jonah and Gabriel and Nicodemus and Innocent,' and when he got to 'gra-a-a-ant them,' even his whole Adam's apple stuck out from his throat like a ball, and he let out such a roar that awe descended upon us, and Uncle began to cross himself and to thrust his feet under the bed" (8:131). It turns out that there are "spies" hiding under that bed; so the awestruck feet set off a further chain of events.

The merchants' world is depicted as narrow, dull, and bigoted—an archaic world untouched by liberalizing emanations from the West. As prescribed in the *Domostroy*, the sixteenth-century Russian handbook of household management, children, even when virtually grown, are expected to be subservient to their parents; and marriages are arranged by parents without consulting the children. The antiquity of this way of life is symbolized by several allusions to the beautiful seventeenth-century *Tale of Woe-Misfortune*, a Russian merchant-class variation on the prodigal son theme.

The author's heaviest thunderbolts in "Robbery" are hurled at the civil administration. Like the archetypal setting of Gogol's *Inspector-General*, Leskov's old Oryol is a model of administrative corruption: a "thievish town" where the chief robbers are the police. Though Leskov does not express his indignation so vehemently in "Robbery," the savage description he was to give to old Penza in "The Cattle-pen" would fit the Oryol of the earlier story:

The streets were kept in the condition of swamps, and the sidewalks were built in such a way that *no one* dared walk on them. These sidewalks were of boards, and under the boards were ditches full of water. The nails with which the boards were held down had come out, and the boards lowered the pedestrian into a cloaca where he met his death. Police officials robbed people in the public square; dogs belonging to the Marshal of Nobility bit people in Lekarskaya Street in the direct view of the general on one side and police chief Frolov on the other; the governor with his own hands beat people on the street with a whip; the most terrible and yet plausible rumors circulated about rapes of women lured by invitations to parties into the houses of persons of the most blue-blooded class. In a word, it was not a town, but some sort of robbers' den. (9:369)

In 1888 Leskov set up again as his target for a final fusillade his favorite archetypal tyrant, Prince Pyotr Trubetskoy, governor of Oryol in the days of Leskov's youthful service in the criminal court. The topic of Trubetskoy's most picturesque performance, his "war" with Bishop Smaragdus, had already been exploited to the limit in *The Little Things in a Bishop's Life*; but Leskov dredged up some new material, tales he had heard from Afanasy Markovich, who served on Trubetskoy's staff. These newly unearthed memories were incorporated in a brief, but effective reminiscential sketch called "The Dead Estate."[9]

"The Dead Estate" has a tripartite structure: three main sections embodying three basic anecdotes. In the first two of these the infamous prince exhibits his nefarious qualities; in the third he receives a long-deserved comeuppance. The retribution is symbolic, rather than punitive; and it does not come from the imperial government, which first appointed him, but through a fortuitous encounter with a "good" governor, the beloved Ivan Funduklei, governor of Kiev from 1839 to 1852.

The mysterious title is explicated in the first anecdote, which illustrates both the prince's imbecility and the political paranoia that infected Russia in those days. Someone had anonymously denounced a *gymnasium* history teacher for subverting his pupils' minds with interpretations of the "rights of the third estate" in eighteenth-century France. The governor loved dressings-down and reprimands. He therefore ordered his staff to compose a stinging rebuke for the historian and his superiors as well. When asked what the French lower classes should be called if the term "third estate" was forbidden, Trubetskoy decreed that they should be called the "dead estate," since he was told that all the people in question were no longer living.

The title thus functions as a double symbol. On one level it illustrates the governor's ignorance and inane refusal to listen to reason. Figuratively, the "dead estate" suggests, from the vantage point of 1888, the remoteness of the tyrannical era of Nicholas I and of such provincial simulacra of the tyrant as Trubetskoy. As Leskov concludes the story, "Now all these persons themselves already constitute a 'dead estate'; but when you happen to recollect their time, you can hardly believe that all this really happened, and moreover comparatively recently" (8:462).

But this distancing disclaimer should not be taken literally. Leskov has planted an antidote to it in his opening paragraph: "People who love to recall not too remote old times and to juxtapose them with the present may find this story not devoid of interest" (8:450). The message of the seemingly innocent conclusion, therefore, is that although Trubetskoy's Nicolaitan style may have faded into the past, its spirit and substance are alive in the Russia of 1888 and, beyond that, in the timeless recesses of the unregenerate human heart.

To complete his "survey" of Nicholas's Russia, Leskov had to include the highest circles of society, of which he had no personal experience. For accounts of these spheres he was obliged to rely on the memories of others. His method of working from these memories, however, was different from a historian's.

In 1887 he published in *Russian Thought* a long piece entitled "Everyday Apocryphas (From Oral Traditions about Fathers and Brothers). The Unmercenary Engineers (From Stories of the Three Righteous Men)."[10] The magazine version contained a preface, later expunged,[11] in which Leskov deals in straightforward critical language with the theoretical problems involved in a "retrospective" art. He takes up again the question of the literal truth of the historian versus the synthetic truth of the artist (what he later, in connection with "Vale of Tears," called "patchwork" truth).

In this preface Leskov also draws a distinction of genre and method between his species of retrospective art and that of historical novelist. The latter, he says, "invents," creating purely fictional characters and placing them in real settings; he, on the other hand, never invents, but only collects, selects, and synthesizes. However, his method differs from that of the uninventing historian. When working from other people's memories, he feels justified in perpetuating the inaccuracies and even inventions found in his sources, on the grounds that these are themselves revelatory of the spirit of the time and its actors.

Historicity in a larger sense was important to Leskov. He refers in the same preface to some of his earlier retrospective pieces—his "documentaries," not his personal reminiscences—some of them based on written evidence, such as the notes of Filipp Ismailov, the former secretary of the Holy Synod,[12] others derived from transcriptions of (real) oral narratives, such as "The Cadet Monastery." Leskov takes pride in the fact that the data presented in these works had not been publicly challenged—"refuted" or "rejected." Such pieces presumably qualify in his eyes as history, factually accurate and dependable.

Leskov has in his possession other historical materials which he considers factually less reliable, yet in their way equally interesting and illuminating, and on these he proposes to create an intermediate genre, neither historical fact nor historical fiction:

> [These materials] reveal events to us not in that dry, though exact form in which monographs and documents present them; we see them rather as they seemed to contemporaries who formed their conceptions of them from their own vivid impressions and amplified them with their own ideas, conjectures, and guesses. Such presentations may not be wholly dependable, but they are curious and present their pictures no less juicily than a historical novel or story in which the very plot and details are the invention of the author. In any case, I myself invent nothing here; I only transmit how things appeared to people who lived then and interpreted in their own way whatever they saw and heard [. . .] From what they *invented* about people under the influence of their own inclinations and conceptions one can derive a rather clear understanding of the tastes and mentality of the inventors themselves; and that undoubtedly characterizes the spirit of the times. (8:588-589; Leskov's italics)

"The Unmercenary Engineers," the work supposed to illustrate this theory, thus stands in an ambiguous relation to "truth." For despite the disarming disclaimers of the introduction, to the effect that factual accuracy may occasionally have been sacrificed in the name of faithfulness to flavorful contemporary sources, Leskov nevertheless writes in the style of an "objective" monograph, without ever identifying the "juicy," but unreliable sources of his "oral traditions."[13] At the same time he undermines that objectivity by periodically inserting footnotes in which he casts doubt on the validity of statements made in the main text. The effect is an almost whimsical "now you see it, now you don't"; yet the tone of the narrative is serious. It cannot be said, therefore, that this intermediate form achieves the object the author claimed for it.

As the original subtitle indicated, Leskov intended to include "The Unmercenary Engineers" in his "righteous men" series. Its heroes were three young aristocrats, Dmitry Bryanchaninov, Mikhail Chikhachov, and Nikolai Fermor, living in what Leskov described as "the terrible time of the base and hypocritical period of muteness" (of the press and public discussion).[14] They attended a school for military engineers enjoying the special patronage of the emperor (a relationship begun when Nicholas was still grand duke). But their spirit contrasts with the time-serving careerism and cynical hedonism prevalent in those days. They take religion seriously as a pervasive influence on everyday life.

These "unmercenary" and devout engineers seem to fit Leskov's pattern for *pravedniki*—isolated exemplars of virtue in an environment of sin. They did not fit into Leskov's artistic machinery, however, and the result is a work that gives a confused ethical as well as factual impression and fails to carry conviction.

First of all, the men were historical persons, too prominent to be freely reshaped according to Leskov's specifications—one of them had had a book written about him.[15] Thus, to a considerable extent the author's artistic hands were tied by history. These "righteous ones" stubbornly strove for their own ideals, not Leskov's.

The first two, Bryanchaninov and Chikhachov, were ultra-Orthodox in their convictions, adherents of the Orthodox revivalist movement inspired by the personality and writings of the late metropolitan of Petersburg, Michael (Desnitsky, died 1821). They both resigned from the army to become Orthodox monks; and Bryanchaninov rose to become a bishop. Although he tries to pay them their due, these adepts of official Orthodox piety did not appeal to Leskov. His model of courageous religiosity was the *rasstriga*, the self-unfrocked monk of "Notes in an Unknown Hand." Neither Bryanchaninov nor Chikhachov did anything like this. Except for a few anecdotes, Leskov therefore limits himself to their earlier life, when they were still in the army.

Still another difficulty arose with the third engineer, Nikolai Fermor. In Fermor's case what Leskov tries to represent as inflexible rectitude was actually a developing psychosis. His is a tragic story—psychologically interesting, but hardly inspiring morally—of deteriorating mental health and eventual suicide. In his saner years Fermor had resisted the outrageous peculation being committed by the Russian army engineers in Poland after the suppression of the 1831 uprising; but his incorruptibility eventually degenerated into a sanctimonious priggishness and ended in psychotic despair, a feeling of total isolation and helplessness in an absolutely wicked world.

A final source of confusion in "The Unmercenary Engineers" is the image of Tsar Nicholas I. In depicting a monarch, even a dead one, Leskov faced problems not only of historicity, but of censorship. A harshly satirical portrait like the savage one in Tolstoy's "Hadji Mu-

rad" would not have been permitted in 1887. (Tolstoy's "Nikolai Pal-
kin," though written then, was not published until 1891, and in Geneva.) Furthermore, Leskov seems to have had ambivalent feelings
about this tsar, the supreme father symbol of his childhood years. Although he repeatedly expressed intense dislike for Nicholas's reign, he
continued to harbor feelings of admiration and awe for the monarch
himself, "the most powerful sovereign in the world, who possessed
intelligence, spiritual strength, and nobility."[16]
In "The Unmercenary Engineers" Nicholas is first shown slightly
satirically, as taking pride in his ability to judge character from first
impressions. Later we see the implacable tyrant in an unexpected
guise. Toward the demented Nikolai Fermor, Tsar Nicholas displays
not so much majestic benevolence as paternal *tendresse* and even
plants an imperial kiss on the madman's brow. Whatever the historicity of this episode, it does not meet Leskov's criteria of revealing the
"spirit of the age."

That spirit appears in a much more convincing incarnation in the
short story "The Sentry (1839)," published earlier the same year.[17] The
narrative strategy in this magnificent story is in many respects similar
to that of "The Unmercenary Engineers." Again Leskov works from
the memoirs, evidently transmitted to him orally, of a long-lived and
high-ranking acquaintance, Lieutenant General Nikolai Miller (died
1889).[18]
Concealing their source, Leskov transposes Miller's memories into
an omniscient author narrative. Like the engineers, the characters in
the tale are presumed to be real, and most are attested historical personalities. The events related, Leskov asserts, are likewise real, though
they are not of the kind that would find their way into an ordinary
history book: "This is an anecdote, partly from the court, partly from
history, which gives a good picture of the customs and tendencies of a
very curious, but meagerly recorded era, the fourth decade of the
nineteenth century, which is now drawing to its close. In the narrative
to be related there is no invention whatever" (8:151).
General Miller's tale, unlike Pavel Fermor's, was in full harmony
with Leskov's moral views and fitted well an artistic mold Leskov had
employed successfully many times before. According to this pattern,
an obscure but morally sound personality, an incipient *pravednik*,[19]
finds himself at moral odds with the social system in which he lives;
when put to the test he remains true to his basic ethical sense, regardless of the consequences to himself.

The heroic personality is a private soldier named Postnikov, assigned to nocturnal guard duty at the Winter Palace. One January night, after a tremendous inner struggle, he leaves his post to rescue a man drowning among the ice floes in the Neva. Desertion of a sentry's station was the most heinous of military crimes. The expected punish- ment in that "forceful time," as Leskov puts it, would have been in effect capital: running the gauntlet enough times to cause death. The magnanimous sentry has thus risked his life doubly, defying first nature and then society.

The aftermath is a display of the adroit maneuvers by which people with "knack" and "tact" succeed in manipulating the bureaucratic system so that "the wolves are sated and the sheep still whole" (almost). The case is never fully reported to the tsar; no military court is convened; an unscrupulous officer receives a medal for a rescue he did not perform; and the true rescuer, Postnikov, receives a mere two hundred blows with birch rods—enough to put him in the hospital, but far less than he feared.

Postnikov's heroism is a case like the Pygmy's, when natural human solidarity breaks through the terrifying structure of official rules and official inhumanity. As Leonid Grossman has wittily observed, the "man on duty," to translate the Russian title literally, showed that he could be a man *even* on duty.[20] Yet in the iron-fisted Russia of Nicholas I even the rescue of a drowning man has become an illegal act subject to Draconian penalties and requiring extraordinary courage to attempt. As Postnikov quaintly puts it, he is "guilty without mercy before God and the sovereign."

Nicholas's Russia is a world where power invariably takes precedence over people. Though the chief drill sergeant never appears, his spirit pervades the scene. All tremble in terror that, if he learns that a sentry has deserted his post, his wrath will descend not only on the hapless soldier himself but on all his superior officers, moving up the hierarchy of responsibility.

Nicholas's stand-in is the Petersburg police chief, General Sergei Kokoshkin, a man "very severe and very frightening [who] aroused in everyone great fear of himself" (8:163). But Kokoshkin has a weak spot for prankish officers in trouble; and like the "old genius," he is a past master at the art of manipulating the system. So he accepts a report he knows is false and awards a medal to a man he knows does not deserve it; these questionable acts are preferable to the alternative— an outburst of imperial anger, two permanently blighted careers, and a soldier flogged to death.

Leskov loves to confront his readers with the realities of "lesser evil" choices. Theory-loving intellectuals with a taste for absolutes, he believed, find it hard to accept the necessity for such moral compromises. Leskov takes pleasure in the effort to force them to live in the realm of the possible, facing the real alternatives of the real world. Within the limits of the system Kokoshkin's lesser evil may be adjudged a positive good. But what can we say of a system which offers only such alternatives? With all the mighty Kokoshkin's tact and skill, and a bit of luck besides, the *best* solution it allows is that a hero who has saved another man's life "gets off" with a mere 200-stroke flogging.

To cap the moral climax, Leskov introduces, as representative of the Nicolaitan state's official spirituality, Philaret (Drozdov), metropolitan of Moscow from 1821 to 1867, who was then visiting in Petersburg. When he learns the truth about the Postnikov episode, Philaret gives the "lesser evil" solution his unqualified moral approval, condoning both the deception of the tsar ("half truths are not lies") and the punishment of Postnikov. Concerning the flogging of Postnikov, Philaret sanctimoniously intones, fingering his rosary: "Punishment on the body is not harmful to a plebeian and does not conflict either with the custom of nations or the spirit of Scripture. It is much easier for a man to endure the rod on his coarse body than subtle suffering of the spirit" (8:173).

In contrast to God's self-proclaimed representative, in his brief concluding chapter Leskov makes bold to "venture the supposition that God Himself was satisfied with the modest soul of Postnikov, which He had created." For the sentry was one of "those mortals who love the good simply for the sake of the good itself and expected no rewards for it in any place whatever."

In his concluding words Leskov describes the tale as "accurate and artless." "Artlessness" may be taken to signify a deliberate unsophistication—an intentional naiveté perhaps designed to harmonize with the "simplicity" of the hero. In his opening paragraph, for example, Leskov announces, like an excited child, that the tale he is about to relate is "touching and terrible in what it meant to the chief hero."

The chief suspense-building device in "The Sentry" is by no means so artless in its operation. This is Leskov's extraordinary success in creating a sense of time pressure. The unusually short chapters have something to do with it, some only a paragraph long—terse log entries, as it were, recording hour by hour the events of that fateful night. Many of them contain or end with actual clock readings:

"about two A.M.," "it was almost three o'clock," "it was already the beginning of the fifth hour of the morning." The hours extend from the time the "crime" is reported to Captain Miller to the inexorable moment when General Kokoshkin must make his morning report to the tsar. The relentless movement of the clock seems to symbolize the relentless spirit presiding over the fate of the "man on hours" or "man on the clock," to give two even more literal translations of the title.

The only artistic flaw in "The Sentry" is the final scene with Metropolitan Philaret, which seems somewhat artificially tacked on. But the scene as such is so good and its moral implication so important to Leskov that one may pass over the weakness of the links by which it is joined to this masterful story.

32

The Pen Apropos

In 1883 Mavriky Volf, a well-known Russian publisher of Polish origin, died—according to Leskov, on the day he had planned to sign a contract to publish an edition of Leskov's collected works.[1] His son and heir Aleksandr did not see fit to carry through his father's intention, preferring, Leskov added bitterly, to publish Boborykin (an immensely prolific writer, mostly of topical novels). "And he did well to do so, because he [Boborykin] at least has some sort of support."[2] It was six years before an edition of Leskov's complete works appeared.

The "new Volf," however, had a use for Leskov. In 1884 he launched a "family" magazine called *Virgin Soil* (*Nov'*). (The title was identical with Turgenev's ill-starred last novel and similar to the magazine's chief competitor and also model, A. F. Marks's immensely successful *Plowland* [*Niva*], founded in 1870.) The family magazine was a middle-class, middle-brow affair, less relentlessly serious than the literary reviews, softened with illustrations, women's and children's departments—testimony to the increasing diversity of Russian society and the growth of a literate public. Leskov was pressed to contribute to *Virgin Soil*, and he agreed: even at this late date he was excluded from the high-brow reviews.

The first two issues of the magazine each contained two works by Leskov: two installments of a full-fledged novel called *A Faint Trace* and two parts of a series entitled "Stories Apropos." The novel was abandoned after these two installments; but the series of short stories and articles, "Stories Apropos," proved sturdier. It lasted through thirteen installments in *Virgin Soil* during 1884-1886, and in 1887 Volf brought out a collection of the stories in book form.[3]

The practice of writing artistic prose "apropos" of some current issue was a favorite of Leskov's. Many of his "memory" stories were apropos in character and were so designated in private letters ("The Cattle-pen," "A Product of Nature"). Making his works relevant to contemporary life was a fundamental tenet of Leskov's commitment as an artist and was his most beloved literary strategy. In a letter to Tolstoy written in connection with "The Cattle-pen," Leskov says: "I am very fond of this form of story about what 'was,' introduced 'by the way' (apropos)."[4]

Leskov still bore the marks of his origin as a journalist. Of the great Russian writers, not excepting Dostoevsky, he is the most "journalistic." But the pejorative connotation that word sometimes carries seems inappropriate to Leskov. In his case journalism was rarely a pretext for dealing in ephemeral topics, nor was it an excuse for hasty and slipshod writing. For him the interaction between art and current life proved stimulating and fruitful.

Taking off from a current "question," Leskov propelled himself by analogy into his favorite literary territory, a partly fictional, partly real time past. Leskov admittedly found "invention" difficult; and besides, he shared some of Tolstoy's doubts about whether invention, in literature, might not just be a euphemism for lying. The apropos story seemed a perfect solution: without any inventing, the writer moved easily from the real present to the real past, altered here and there in the name of synthesis, to present a truth of essences rather than accidents.

The group of apropos stories included in the *Virgin Soil* series is uneven in quality and contains only a few of Leskov's best specimens of this genre. Some are not stories at all, but topical articles; many—including one story of high quality—were later excluded from the collected works.

The series led off unpromisingly with a topical essay called "New Testament Jews"[5]—an account of four Jews Leskov knew who had been converted to Christianity: a medical student, a middle-aged artisan, a sick and destitute old man, and a dynamic young exrabbi who eventually emigrated to England and became a missionary in the colonies. Leskov again makes an unfavorable comparison between Russia and England. In England there is a special religious society ministering to the needs of ex-Jewish Christians, while in Russia they find themselves isolated—despised by the Jewish community and regarded with anti-Semitic prejudice by their new co-religionists.

"Two Swineherds,"[6] the second in the series, is more a set of illustrations for a philosophical abstraction than a story. Though it contains some apparently authentic memoir material, it is interesting chiefly as a statement of Leskov's religious convictions in this period.

472

The two case histories illustrate what to Leskov was the enormous distance that separated the "sentimental piety" of the Radstockites, with their (to him) frivolous attitude toward sin and expiation and their simplistic view of the Redemption as a "free" key to salvation, from the down-to-earth Shtundists, who insist that Christianity is meaningful only if it leads the sinner to real amendment of life here on earth.[7]

The third of Leskov's stories apropos in *Virgin Soil* was the first to be included in the collected works: "An Enigmatic Incident in an Insane Asylum."[8] The material for this work, like that for "On Quakeresses," was derived from a historical document, in this case some papers Leskov bought from an antiquarian book dealer.[9]

Leskov begins with a discussion about whether the old judicial system in existence before the reform of Alexander II (1864) had not been swifter and more just than the new jury trials conducted in public. Loyal to the Great Reforms, especially the court reform, Leskov takes the opposite view, which he demonstrates with two examples. They show conclusively that the old court system was anything but swift; nor is there any reason to believe that the closed bureaucratic system of Nicholas I produced any more justice than the reformed courts of Alexander II.

One of Leskov's cases is taken from his own memories (and possibly his father's practice): an Oryol forester of the 1840s named Krasovsky who was accused of embezzling lumber from crown forests. Krasovsky's case became the Jarndyce & Jarndyce of old Oryol, on which generations of law clerks cut their teeth, and in the end it was left unresolved. After spending twelve years in prison while his case was under investigation, Krasovsky—who, people said, would have been a perfect model for Little Dorrit's father—is released with no charges proved against him.

Leskov's second case is drawn from the papers he had acquired, the archives of Yevgeny Pelikan, at one time chairman of a medical council in Voronezh.[10] It concerns the mysterious death in 1853 of five inmates of the women's ward of an insane asylum in Voronezh. All of them died peacefully, in one night, without any signs of violence. Though their bodies did show some symptoms of poisoning, other inmates who had eaten the same food and breathed the same air were in perfect physical health. No motive for the murder could be imagined. The authorities conducted an investigation; but twenty-five years later Pelikan noted that the cause of death was still undetermined.

This case of the Voronezh madwomen seems anything but "apropos," having little to do with the old justice or the new. No jury trial was involved, and there is no reason to believe that the case would have been any easier to solve after than it was before the reform. The main value of "An Enigmatic Incident" lies in the interest of its bizarre details and the rare glimpse it affords of a provincial insane asylum for women in prereform days (a great deal more humane and "modern" than one might have expected).

Beyond this, Leskov seems to be playing a literary, Sternean game with his array of inconclusive "life" materials. People expect a story to have an end, a resolution, yet here the author has left his readers up in the air. Who killed the women, and why? We never learn. "The writer of these lines fully acknowledges the legitimacy of such displeasure," Leskov slyly concludes, "and indeed experienced it himself when he read the case he has just related."

Leskov's next story apropos, "The Co-functionaries: A Bucolic Tale on a Historical Canvas,"[11] is unquestionably a piece of narrative art, though in a form unusual for Leskov. It is a genuine story, and the apropos element is weak. It is supposed to illustrate the evils of "co-functionism" (*sovmestitel'stvo*), the practice of allowing officials to retain one position (and apparently continue to collect its salary) while being farmed out on commission to other offices. The story turns the title into a pun. The real trouble with "co-functionism," it transpires, arises when two or even three functionaries are trying to "function" with the same woman.

Leskov tells it as an overextended anecdote, a bedroom comedy smacking more of the eighteenth than the prudish nineteenth century. The central figure is a real person, Count Yegor Kankrin (1774-1846), at the time of the action minister of finance, an office he held from 1823 until 1844. Leskov claims in the opening paragraph that he heard the story in oral form from a "high-born and truthful man" and is simply transmitting it "almost in the same words I heard it." Nevertheless, the story is not a skaz, since no attempt is made to give the narrative any oral flavor.

The narrative piquancy of "The Co-functionaries" is derived from a new twist given to the traditional triangle, or, in this case, quadrilateral. The old minister (Kankrin), who keeps a mistress more as a status symbol than from sexual interest, has grown sick of his young lady's incessant caprices and demands. He determines to get rid of her and subtly recruits for the purpose a young officer. However, when Kankrin and the officer drop in on her, they accidentally discover that Kankrin's design has been anticipated by a gallant, curly-haired young official who is found hiding under a dressing table in the lady's boudoir. Unruffled, the count simply grasps the opportunity to substitute one "co-functionary" for the other. He is thus able to end his burdensome affair, after a genial conversation *à quatre*, over cocoa, with his exlady and his two "rivals."

The lady and her enterprising young lover soon learn to capitalize on the count's good humor. First timidly, then more and more brazenly he and the lady (they are soon married, with the count serving at the ceremony as her surrogate father) exploit her ex-lover's favor to the limit.

Young Ivan Pavlovich rises meteorically in the service (somewhat misinterpreting the count's initial signs of favor, subordinate officials outdo themselves in propelling him up the bureaucratic ladder); his impeccably faithful wife maintains a salon, where she parades quotations from Belinsky and Khomyakov and acquires a reputation for intellectuality. Eventually she becomes a provincial grande dame, all the while taking "the most desperate bribes, even with reference to departments in which her husband had no direct influence."

The lady's (and her husband's) is a worldly success story; and Leskov's an amusing variant on the satirical career-and-society story of the Pushkin era. Such lighthearted cynicism was not in style in the 1880s. The story was not in Leskov's best style, either, for his feet tread heavily amidst the boudoir lace.

Leskov's next *Virgin Soil* story apropos was "Pearl Necklace," displaced out of the apropos collection to round off Leskov's 1886 volume of Christmas stories (see chapter 26 above).

"Pearl Necklace" was followed by another jewel story, "The Alexandrite: A Natural Fact in a Mystical Light."[12] In the summer of 1884 Leskov made the third and last of his trips to Western Europe, this one a modest health-seeking pilgrimage to Marienbad. On the way home he stopped off in Prague, where he was robbed of his wallet. Nothing daunted, he made Prague the setting of his new jeweler story; the wallet incident, modified, was displaced to "Interesting Men."[13] "In the summer of 1884," Leskov accurately reports, "I happened to be in Bohemia. Having the restless tendency of becoming enamored of various forms of art, I there became quite interested in the local jewelers' and gem-polishers' work."[14]

Nikolai Leskov

On his return to Petersburg Leskov wrote to his friend Mikhail Pylyaev, who had recently published a book on precious stones,[15] asking for technical assistance:

> I have an irresistible desire to write a superstitiously fantastic story, based on the passion for precious stones and, combined with this passion, belief in their mysterious influence. I have begun it and have entitled it "The Fiery Garnet," and for an epigraph have taken five lines from your book, and the qualities of one of the characters I have borrowed from traits I saw and observed during the summer in Prague among the families of the traders in garnets. But I feel that I am not well enough acquainted with ancient superstitious ideas about gems, and I would like to know some stories from the gem trade.

After flattering his correspondent, Leskov asks for bibliography on jewels, especially pyropes: "I gazed at pyropes to my heart's content and learned to understand their beauty, which I assimilated and came to love, so that I want to write [about them], but I don't want to talk nonsense."[16]

The story was finished by the autumn of 1884. Leskov evidently did not at that time intend to include it in the apropos series. He first tried to place it in the *Rus* of Ivan Aksakov, with whom his relations were still cool. Because a jewel story from Prague would be ideally suited for Aksakov's pan-Slavic organ, Leskov offered it in bequiling language:

> The last time you wrote me, when you sent the honorarium for "The Left-hander" [three years earlier], you asked me, "If you have some *special* piece, very refined and polished," to send it to you for *Rus*. Since then I haven't had anything like that:
>
> > They've no use for the zither's tones,
> > Serve them up marketplace goods.
>
> Those of us who are condemned to struggle in order to "boire, manger, et sortir" manage only to serve up what is in urgent demand. But sometimes you cook up a piece that you fall in love with and do it differently for your own pleasure. That is what has happened now. I started putting together for Christmas a fantastic little story and got caught up in it and began to polish it, and then, when I had polished it, I felt sorry about tossing it where I had thought to [. . .] It's a tiny little story (eight pages), fantastic, touches on the Emperor Alexander II and "his stone." As spokes-

476

man I portray an old gem-polisher, a Czech from the "dry hills of Merenica." Of course everything is respectful and (I think) entirely *original*. It is a poetic caprice, an *objet d'art*, a *Kunststück*, in which invention is fused with reality and exudes both mountain superstition and horrible reality. Shall I send it? [. . . A postscript:] The story I am writing is called "An Underground Sooth sayer." It would be best to find a place for it around Christmas time, since it is *fantastic*, although not happy—rather, sad.[17]

Aksakov responded favorably, but made several avuncular, but aculeate remarks about Leskov's "tarnishing his muse" and "besmirching" his God-given talent, especially by gossiping about the higher clergy.[18] Very likely Aksakov's reply made Leskov so angry that he broke off negotiations—and relations. He and Aksakov exchanged no further letters before Aksakov's death in 1886. And the new story, now entitled "The Alexandrite," was published in *Virgin Soil* after all.

Others rate this work less highly than Leskov did. It is a poorly integrated amalgam of gem lore, travel impressions, an effortfully quaint character, and reverence for Alexander II—the whole steeped in an artificial solution of "fantastic" mystery.

The title is the name of a precious stone, the first specimen of which was found in the Urals in 1834 and named in honor of the future Alexander II, then crown prince, who had just come of age. The gem, a variety of chrysoberyl, has the unusual property of dichromism, appearing green in daylight, but red under artificial light. After Alexander's tragic death, Leskov tells us, some of his admirers acquired alexandrite rings to wear in his honor. One of these admirers was Leskov, who, his son reports,[19] until the end of his days wore an alexandrite ring with two small diamonds, just as he described it in his story, the alexandrite representing the tsar liberator, and the diamonds "the two most glittering deeds of the last reign—the emancipation of the peasants and the establishment of a better judicial system in place of the old 'black injustice.' "[20]

On his trip to Prague, the author informs us, he was commissioned by a friend to buy a fine Czech pyrope, not available in Russia. This mission led him into intensive contacts—implausibly prolonged— with a picturesque Czech jeweler named Vencel, saturated with gem lore and looking like a seedy version of King Lear. There is a lot of talking and even dreaming, mostly by Vencel, about jewels and their mystic properties, and a tirade, again by Vencel, against the "Swabians" and their crass inability to appreciate the Slavic soul of the pyrope;[21] but there is no plot other than the long-delayed acquisition by the author of this deeply Slavic gem.

The real point of the story is reached on the last page, at the narrator's final encounter with old Vencel. It has nothing to do with the pyrope. Unaccountably, the sharp-eyed old man has hitherto not noticed the author's alexandrite ring. But at this final meeting he does so with a vengeance, crying out in rapture over this "prophetic Russian stone" and offering an interpretation of its prophecy. The alexandrite is green with hope in the morning and stained with blood in the evening—the fate of its royal namesake. This neatly symbolic linkage has appeal as a *jeu d'esprit*, but it cannot make the story.

"The Alexandrite" was followed in the *Virgin Soil* series by "Ancient Psychopaths," discussed above in chapter 28. After that came the longest and most literary story in the collection, "Interesting Men."[22] "Interesting Men" is a full-fledged story, with genuine characters and a plot, not a *feuilleton* with illustrations. Its "apropos" relevance is literary, involving the names of two of Leskov's most illustrious living colleagues, Tolstoy and Gleb Uspensky.

A group of friends, the narrator tells us, had gathered together expecting to read aloud the new story by Tolstoy promised for the February (1885) number of *Russian Thought*. The long-awaited issue contained instead a pink slip stating that the Tolstoy story could not be published. No reason was given, and that fact made the reason obvious to every Russian: censorship. Disappointed, the friends read instead a sketch by Uspensky, whom Leskov characterizes as "one of the few members of our literary fraternity who does not sever his connections with vital truth, who does not lie and does not cater to the so-called 'tendencies.' "[23]

In Uspensky's story, called "What Has Happened to a Certain Good Russian Type?", a middle-aged lady complains that men are not as "interesting" as they used to be in the days of her youth. After the reading is finished, this remark leads to one of Leskov's familiar group discussions on the subject of how "interesting" men used to be in the old days; one of the company offers to illustrate the point with a story about someone he knew, not as dashing or dazzling as a Lermontov hero, but interesting nonetheless.

This story in turn has literary ramifications. Although its plot and characters are ultimately taken from real life, Leskov derived them from a book written a decade earlier by Vsevolod Krestovsky, his sometime friend and fellow antinihilist, now turned army officer and military historian: *A History of the Fourteenth Uhlan Yamburg Regiment* (1873).[24]

Krestovsky's history related the bare facts concerning a sad episode that had occurred in 1860. A group of officers, including a young cornet named Nikolai Desyatov, were occupying a hotel room in Tver next to that of a foreigner. The foreigner found that he had been robbed of 250 rubles. Suspicion fell on the officers, who were thereupon searched—with their own consent, but without result. The cornet, however, felt the whole episode such a stain on the regiment's honor and his own that he shot himself. Later the thief was discovered: a servant in the hotel.

The historical Cornet Desyatov was clearly deranged, an unbalanced young man whose ego structure collapsed at one breath of suspicion. This asthenic and paranoid melancholic would not qualify as "interesting," especially to a middle-aged lady. Leskov therefore first had to restore him to some degree of mental health or at least give him a more poetic motive for committing suicide. The solution was obvious: love. Leskov at last could make use of his number two novel plot, "He fell in love and shot himself." The middle-aged commander of the regiment has proposed to, married, and is expecting a baby from a girl named Anya, with whom the cornet (called "Sasha" in the story) had fancied himself in love. The birth of the colonel's child is thus a living symbol of Anya's betrayal—both her unromantic choice of a middle-aged bridegroom and her carnal relations with him.

This imminent birth provides a plausible explanation for Sasha's mental distress on the fateful night. And—though the point is not explored by Leskov—it offers another, implicit motivation for his suicide: to punish someone else. Its message to Anya was not only "See how noble I am!" (to sacrifice myself for your sake), but "How could you do *this* to me and *that* with him?"

Leskov gives the foreigner of Krestovsky's account concrete definition as a Pole, Avgust Matveich, as he is called in Russia, where he is employed as an estate manager. Avgust Matveich is not a bad sort, but a bit self-important and—à la polonaise—excessively punctilious in his manners. Besides these national qualities, the Pole is endowed with a gift of spiritual insight bordering on the supernatural, learned during travels in "Scotland and Hindustan." This capability not only helps to make him "interesting," though not in the way the lady meant, but greatly assists the author in his task of dramatic foreshadowing.

The sum stolen from the clairvoyant Avgust Matveich is augmented from 250 to a much more "interesting" 12,000 rubles in large bank-notes. The Pole is too tactful to express openly any suspicions of the officers. He accuses no one. As he and all the officers have been playing cards in one room, it seems clear that no one else could have the money. As a matter of honor, therefore, the officers strip naked and have their clothing searched.

During this process the colonel arrives with the news that his wife has been delivered of a daughter, and—almost simultaneously—Sasha refuses to strip. He insists that his refusal is itself a matter of honor—a higher order of honor than the one impelling him to comply. He rushes into another room and shoots himself. It is later revealed that next to his skin he was wearing an inscribed aquarelle portrait of Anya —"the token," the narrator adds, "not so much of passionate love as of pure childhood friendship and chaste vows." Thus to die "preserving the honor" of the girl he wanted to punish for rejecting him was a doubly rewarding path to glory, and much more "interesting" than the dreary suicide of the real Cornet Desyatov.

By his characterization of the thief, the hotel servant, Leskov contrives to thrust more barbs into Orthodox false religiosity. To atone for his theft, the pious servant, Marko, had ordered a new bell cast for his church, paying for it with one of the stolen notes (it is through this note that he is caught); the rest of the money is found hidden in his room beneath his icon-stand. This behavior symbolizes Leskov's view of Orthodox morality: while making no serious demand on the sinner for amendment of life, it offers him a system for bribing God to wink at the unrepented sin.

Leskov has spun Krestovsky's story out with scenes, characters, and anecdotes which do not add to its structural strength or integrity, as the expansive narrator admits. When enumerating the distinguished ladies present at Sasha's funeral, he stops the clock in order to characterize the most interesting of them, known as the "snake," and to relate an anecdote about her.[25] At this point the narrator comments, "Against all the rules of architectonics and economy in constructing a story, right at the end I have introduced this new character, and so I must tell you about this lady" (8:100). Leskov delighted in demonstrating that he could throw together all sorts of jerry-built narrative structures, violating all the "rules of architectonics," and still get away with it. "Interesting Men" surely proves his point.

Leskov was fond of it. Two years later Aleksei Suvorin read it in the book edition of *Stories Apropos* and wrote Leskov how much he liked it. Much gratified, the writer replied: "The Pole and Sasha are just as you find them. The nicest character is Sasha, after him the captain with the armpits, and after him the regimental chaplain. In the Pole there is a predominance of reserve and good breeding, through which his contempt for Russians nevertheless shows."[26]

As A. I. Batyuto has pointed out (8:569), there is another literary question connected with "Interesting Men." In 1897 Aleksandr Kuprin published a story called "The Bréguet Watch," which rehearses the same plot as "Interesting Men," with all Leskov's motivational adaptations of the Krestovsky raw material, but "straight," without the anecdotal accretions and without the apropos discussion about interesting men. The two stories might be compared, not only as a problem in literary "influence" (not to say plagiarism), but also as an aesthetic test for the reader: do you like your stories straight or curved, rules intact or rules broken?

Leskov had dealt with the military milieu earlier, in a short story called "The Voice of Nature," later included with the apropos stories.[27] In that story he mentions two historical personages who also appear in "Interesting Men," Field Marshal Aleksandr Baryatinsky (1814-1879), the unfortunate husband of the "snake," and General Rostislav Fadeyev (1824-1883), who, despite his portliness, made himself interesting to women.

"The Voice of Nature" is an inconsequential anecdote about how Baryatinsky recognized an old bugler, who had served under him years before, only when the bugler put his instrument to his lips, "puffed out his cheeks, and emitted one crackling tantara." Leskov creates out of this unpromising material an amusing genre picture of small-town provincial life galvanized by the presence of a big shot from the capital, a picture subtly enhanced by partly hidden ironies.

The story's suspense seems contrived: the bugler makes the puzzled marshal wait interminably until the "voice of nature" will reveal his identity. But the artificiality is redeemed by the irony inherent in the defeat of our expectation that the title phrase, repeated *ad nauseam*, refers to something sexual. A more fundamental and bitter irony lies in the fact that the old bugler, singled out long ago and rewarded by the field marshal for his "honesty"—and now toasted again for the same quality—has done very well for himself during his postmilitary years by dishonest means. He serves as an inspector in a military supply depot, and there "together with the rats" he gnaws "bread crusts and leather soles" belonging to the government. Over the years, the author tells us, he has managed to "gnaw himself a pretty little wooden house with a balcony," where he now entertains his former commander. The authentic voice of nature, it appears, is human greed.

Mention may be made here, by virtue of its probable date of composition (1883-84), of another story presumably destined for the apropos series, but never printed in Leskov's lifetime. Two variants of it survived among his manuscripts, both published in the Soviet period. Though they bear different titles—"A Wild Fantasy" and "A Just Man"—and have totally different texts, their plot and moral conclusion are identical.[28]

"A Just Man," apparently the later of the two, is almost a parody on Leskov's theme of the three righteous men without whom no nation can stand. The narrative is related "apropos" of an alleged general belief, supposedly expressed in recent newspaper articles, to the effect that not a single just man could be found in the whole of Holy Russia. The narrator refutes this calumny. He knows of one impeccably just Russian, and he relates the experience of his acquaintance with this paragon.

Our expectations of meeting another Leskovian *pravednik*, radiating lonely virtue through the darkness of provincial Russia, are upended. The "just man," it turns out, is nothing but an obnoxious and vulgar bourgeois (though "educated" and fond of quoting Gogol), whose stalwart defense of justice consists only of raising a drunken row in the town park because the band keeps playing a march dedicated to the late General Mikhail Skobelev, hero of the Russo-Turkish War of 1887-88, thus neglecting the much greater military paladin, Field Marshal Aleksandr Suvorov, who died in 1800.

The two variants of this anecdote reveal Leskov's methods of work and the exacting standards he set himself. Neither is a revision of the other. "A Wild Fantasy" seems to have been written first. Apparently finding it too wordy, Leskov did not attempt to cut it, but simply started again, rewriting the story from scratch. This second, shorter version, "A Just Man," was then severely pruned. Despite this effort, Leskov apparently remained dissatisfied and put both versions to rest in a drawer of his desk, presumably to await further revision. Possibly he feared difficulties with the censorship, but there is no evidence that either version was ever submitted to a magazine, let alone to the censors. Leskov seems to have lost interest in the story and never returned to it.

If artistic dissatisfaction was the reason for Leskov's suppression of "A Just Man," it seems sufficiently justified. Though not without merit, the story does not rank among his masterpieces. It could hardly have been redeemed by pruning, since prolixity was not its problem. Both versions are skillfully told, the first perhaps better than the second. The picture of the shabby provincial park, with its philistine populace, mindless music, and joyless "gaiety," is effectively drawn, with a wealth of concrete detail; and the climactic scene is vivid, when the "just man," who has climbed up on a table to proclaim the pre-eminence of Suvorov over Skobelev, is pulled down by the police in a chaos of flying footwear, spilled wine, and smashed crockery. But the basic anecdote is too weak to support the superstructure; and on the plane of abstraction, the link between this anecdote and the ironic conclusion to be drawn from it—the vulgarity, triviality, and moral decay of Russian society in the late nineteenth century—is tenuous. In its scornful vision of a society, "A Just Man" can be seen as a harbinger of the much more powerful satires of the 1890s, such as "Night Owls" and "A Winter's Day."

The next story in Leskov's apropos series, "Mysterious Omens,"[29] follows a familiar structural pattern: a nuclear anecdote, greatly retarded, is made the vehicle for a series of satirical "pictures" and commentaries having little to do with the original subject.

Here the lead-off topic concerns omens of war. (There was a war scare in the spring of 1885 over Anglo-Russian rivalry in Afghanistan.) This theme recalls other omens and other war scares, in particular a portent that presaged the outbreak of the Crimean War in 1853. This omen had to do with a visit by the then metropolitan of Petersburg, Nicanorus, to the Valaam Monastery on Lake Ladoga. But before this visit can be described, the story jumps by analogy further into the past, to other visits to Valaam by other metropolitans and one by the Emperor Alexander I in 1819.

These bits of prehistory were derived by Leskov from the unpublished memoirs of Andrei Vagner.[30] Vagner had in the early 1850s been part of the entourage of Andrei Muravyov (1806-1874), an ultra-Orthodox writer and poet, whose pretentiousness and bigotry Leskov had ridiculed in *The Little Things in a Bishop's Life*. The great longing of Muravyov's life was to be appointed ober-procurator of the Synod. His hopes were never fulfilled, partly, Leskov claims, through his own maladroit bureaucratic maneuver. The post went instead to Count

Nikolai Protasov, who held it for nineteen bitter years (1836-1855).[31]

The Vagner memoirs contained an account of the mysterious incident on Valaam which constitutes the only real plot of "Mysterious Omens," and a great deal of gossipy material about Muravyov as well —his circle, his activities, his relations with various members of the higher clergy, his finances, and even his clothes. This material, decidedly off-center from the narrative point of view (Muravyov does not even make the expedition to Valaam), forms the core of the work in position, bulk, and extraliterary significance as well.

The portrait of Muravyov is devastating: renowned in his time as its most learned and devout Orthodox layman, he is shown "in reality" to be a petty, domineering, self-important man, not only far from learned, but scarcely even literate. He kept a small army of lay spies who were sent to various churches throughout Petersburg to detect any irregularities in the celebration of the liturgy, and he would then report any offending clergyman to the latter's bishop. Muravyov, in short, personified everything Leskov hated about false piety (which he tended to identify with Orthodoxy).

By contrast, as in the Neophyte episodes in *The Little Things in a Bishop's Life*, the clergy, including Metropolitan Nicanorus, come off rather well. The metropolitan is kind and sensible; in his suite there are clerics of high caliber, such as Ignatius (Bryanchaninov), later depicted fully in "The Unmercenary Engineers," and Muravyov's sworn enemy, Archimandrite Avvakum, a noted Chinese scholar. There is a poetic description of an open-air liturgy celebrated by the metropolitan and his assistants on the deck of the ship on the way to Valaam. Nor does Leskov belittle monasticism.

The final "omen" anecdote, however, has a generalized anti-Orthodox air about it. The readiness of educated men like Muravyov[32] to believe that some hay on Valaam had been raked and gathered by spirits symbolizes for Leskov the Orthodox preference for "miracle, mystery, and authority," to use Dostoevsky's phrase, over righteousness and truth.

This intervention of the supernatural (for which Leskov has a natural explantion) is taken as an omen of war (perhaps the "mowing of warriors" image, familiar in medieval literature). But Leskov—or fate—plays an ironic trick. The fact that the hay was gathered not by spirits but by human agents should presumably have deprived the incident of divinatory value. Yet it actually turned out to be an omen: the Crimean War broke out a year later.

The next three "stories apropos" in the *Virgin Soil* series are not stories. The first, "The Debauchers,"[33] is an article on peasant girls who come to the city and end as prostitutes. Their real "debauchers," Leskov maintains, are their avaricious parents, who make exorbitant financial demands on their daughters, money they can obtain in no other way.

The article has no literary value, but it contains an explicit statement by Leskov of his objections to the idealization of the peasantry by the populists, anticipating the grim pictures of peasant savagery Leskov was to draw in "Vale of Tears" and "The Cattle-pen": "The Russian plebeian family only in very rare, exceptional cases exhibits those simple virtues, worthy of respect, with which it is adorned by the tendentiously inclined imagination of the unlimited admirers of the village. The Russian plebeian family is morally as sick in the country as it is in the city [. . .] The cause of the moral sickness in all probability lies in the fact that in the imperfect nature of man there is an [innate] tendency to evil."[34]

The next piece in the series, "Unlimited Goodness,"[35] demonstrates that isolated individuals—*pravedniki*—conquer the universal tendency to evil. Leskov's case is the recently deceased Yevgeny Karnovich (1823-1885), a journalist and historian with a talent for practical generosity. Though Leskov's admiration for Karnovich was genuine, his treatment of the man here is peripheral and perfunctory.

"Sleepy Memories at the Trial of Sarah Becker"[36] recounts two overextended anecdotes, attributed to Pisemsky, directed against an unnamed writer who was distinguished for his vanity and pomposity. The target is possibly Boleslav Markevich, but Leskov had much better stories about him than these.[37]

The final work in the *Virgin Soil* series was "Fish Soup without Fish," which has already been discussed in Chapter 29. Leskov contributed nothing more to *Virgin Soil* after this story. He retained, however, his fondness for the cover title, "Stories Apropos,"—and for the literary strategy it represented. The title was used, as noted, on the book collection brought out by Volf in 1887, and Leskov twice defended in print his rights to it against an anonymous collection published in Moscow under the same title.[38]

Leskov used the phrase "story apropos" in the title or subtitle of a number of later works. And the editors of the two pre-Soviet posthumous editions of Leskov's works included under this rubric a number of works not specifically so labeled by Leskov. Some of the latter are late, nonliterary historical articles, similar to many Leskov published in the 1880s in *Historical Messenger*, but did not include in his collected works. They are of interest as indicators of the writer's ideological preoccupations.

"Siberian Scenes of the Eighteenth Century"[39] extracts from the same Astashev papers Leskov used for "On Quakeresses" some depressing evidence of the enormous harm that results when the police power of the state is applied in religious matters. Peter the Great in 1716 had decreed that all Russian citizens were to make their confession to an Orthodox priest at least once a year; those who did not were to be fined. Applying as it did both to Old Believers and shamanist tribesmen—and also to people who lived at great distances from any church or priest—the decree proved unenforceable, at least in Siberia. Naturally it led to a miserable cesspool of bribes, lies, and extortion, which Leskov describes with gusto.

In "Inspired Vagabonds,"[40] Leskov displays characteristic literary guile in relating two historical cases, one of the seventeenth and one of the eighteenth century, in which Russian adventurers had sought favors from the state after returning from long periods of captivity abroad, mostly in Turkey. Then, by analogy with these safely remote examples, he slyly introduces a much hotter, contemporary affair, the case of Nikolai Ashinov, which Leskov regarded as symptomatic of the moral decay of Russian society in his time. Ashinov, by origin an artisan from Penza, had transformed himself into a "free Cossack" and with a band of equally dubious mercenaries and adventurers had attempted in the 1880s to raise the banner of Russian imperialism in East Africa. Though Ashinov had the open support of Katkov and secret encouragement from Pobedonostsev,[41] the Russian government was not prepared to undertake any major commitment in Africa, especially at the risk of war, and Ashinov's venture foundered because of strong French and British reluctance to admit Russia to the club of Africa-carvers.

A third article is "Descent into Hell,"[42] written to explain that a pre-seventeenth-century Russian icon depicting, on three planes, Christ's descent into hell and liberation of the patriarchs, his resurrection, and his ascent into heaven, was not a product of the "artist's imagination," as some ill-informed French journalists had written, but based on a well-known New Testament apocrypha of great antiquity, the Gospel of Nicodemus, which Leskov cites *in extenso*. (The journalists were as ignorant of Western as of Eastern art, since this iconography is familiar in Western medieval art, for instance in the panels on the opposite side of Duccio's great *Maestá*. The scene is known in English tradition as the "harrowing of hell.")

Leskov's final work in the à propos genre—in the magazine version it carried the additional subtitle "Stories Apropos"—was "The Lady and the Wench: From My Literary Reminiscences."[43] This was the last work by Leskov to be published in his lifetime. Though there is evidence that an early draft goes back to the late 1880s,[44] Leskov worked hard on it during the last year of his life, revising it again and again. A brief account of these revisions will give some idea of the exacting standards Leskov set himself, even as a sick old man.

On June 4, 1894, Leskov wrote his editor that the story was "quite ready."[45] Three weeks later, however, it had been "finished and recopied and again scribbled over."[46] Two months later the manuscript was again being recopied.[47] By October the story was in the editors' hands, but it was returned to Leskov when he asked for an opportunity to make further revisions in the proofs. (Though printing was much less costly in those days, editors still preferred that authors finish their revisions before delivering a manuscript—a preference frequently honored in the breach.) On November 16 Leskov returned the newly revised manuscript to *Russian Thought* with a comment describing his attitude toward all these revisions:

> I am returning the manuscript of the "The Wenches" [sic] to you today. It has again been drastically corrected, but nevertheless it is in sufficiently presentable condition so that it will be quite easy for the printers to work from. I am very glad that it paid me another visit and that I was free to rework it. It is very important for an author to get away from a work he has completed and then read it as a reader. Then you see a lot of things you never notice when you are writing. The main thing is to weed out the *longueurs* and mannerisms and attain the simplicity that comes so hard. Now I am satisfied and at peace. It would be better to send me proofs for just one day; but if you are in a hurry, don't bother.[48]

Leskov's peace, however, did not last long. Three days later he regretted his offer to forego proofreading and withdrew it:

> Three days ago I sent you the manuscript of "The Wenches" in condition to go to the printers, and I wrote Viktor Aleksandrovich [Goltsev] that he needn't send me any proofs. But now I

want to take back my words. I am so finical and such an incorrigible scribbler that I can't help correcting myself, and I ask you immediately to give orders that the proofs of "The Wenches" also be sent to me without fail. I beg this of you most urgently; I can't live without it! I promise you that I won't keep the proofs more than one day. You can count on me. In the meantime, I am enclosing a sheet on which I have written something to be inserted. Please send it to the printers [. . .].[49]

After the story had appeared in print in *Russian Thought*, Leskov in the last weeks of his life gave it another revision for inclusion in the twelfth volume of collected works, which did not appear until after his death.[50]

Throughout this correspondence Leskov assured his nervous editors that his new story was "peaceful," unlike "A Winter's Day," which they had somehow managed to squeeze through the censorship in the fall of 1894. That caustic satire had evidently given them many anxious moments, and they were not eager to repeat the experience. Leskov wrote them soothingly, "The story ['The Lady and the Wench"] has content, but is quite peaceful."[51] "It's utterly innocent, like a toothless child."[52] However, these assurances were misleading.

Though the story bore the subtitle "From My Literary Reminiscences," this phrase, to quote Andrei Leskov, "proved far from descriptive of the real content of this work, which is partly polemical, partly fictional, and least of all reminiscential."[53] The "reminiscential" ingredients, such as they are, have already been discussed—the story's evocation of Leskov's love affair in the early 1880s with his housemaid Pasha, the source of his short-lived "feminine equilibrium" (See Chapter 25).

From a literary point of view, representing a fictional story as a "memoir" and introducing into it several real people under their real names (the editors Dudyshkin and Kraevsky, the children's writer Aleksandra Toliverova-Yakobi, and others) enhance the illusion of substantiality and justify the reader's limited knowledge of events. The narrator represents himself as a friend of the "lady's" husband and a benefactor of the "wench"; thus as an actor in his own story, he cannot be omniscient about the characters' lives.

The reminiscing narrator is equated with the real author by concrete, factual references. At one point, for example, the narrator is comparing the poverty writers had endured in the 1860s with the relative affluence of the eighties and nineties. To illustrate, he says that in the sixties, after his nameless hero's death, with all his efforts he had been able to collect only 200 rubles for the writer's mistress and illegitimate child. This he contrasts with the 2,000 rubles he raised in the eighties with comparative ease to support the child of "A. I. Palm" (9:472). This was a lump of real fact. Aleksandr Palm was a writer who died in 1885, leaving destitute an (apparently) illegitimate daughter, since his legal heirs received all his assets. On her behalf Leskov had conducted a fund-raising campaign from the pages of *New Times*, raising more than 4,000 rubles, according to Andrei Leskov,[54] although none of Leskov's articles mentions a sum this large. Very likely there is more of Palm than of Nikolai Solovyov in the hero of "The Lady and the Wench."

Reducing the fictional content of "The Lady and the Wench" to an abstract schema, one could describe the story as a contrast of three female types, placed along a scale according to their responses to the male sex. At one end of the scale is the "lady," a fanatical, castrating man-hater, who married the unfortunate critic in order "in his person to take vengeance on all men for their oppression of women" (9:462). He had married her out of pity—a poor motive for marriage, Leskov comments; and for several years she made his life as hellish as Leskov's own had been with Olga Vasilievna. Like Olga Vasilievna and her literary incarnations, the "lady" "possessed that happiest of female talents, not to be afraid of any sort of scene" (9:458). She makes scenes in public and in private, even tearing up one of her husband's manuscripts, and badgers his editors and his superiors in the civil service with complaints about him.

In the sexual area, however, the relationship of the critic and the lady differs from the passionate attraction believed to have marked the early stages of Leskov's marriage to Olga Vasilievna. Neither the critic's pity nor the lady's vengefulness had much sexuality in it. Although somehow they have produced a child, their sexual relations are extremely infrequent. The lady announces to the narrator that "her husband is ridiculous and good for nothing, especially *vis-à-vis d'une femme*." She claims to prefer it that way, since "a woman should be higher than nature, because 'nature is a pig' " (9:463-464). The critic, for his part, "most naively" confesses to the narrator, " 'You know, where we got him [their child] from I truly can't even imagine' " (9:462). (The possibility of its being another man's child seems precluded by the lady's general unattractiveness, ill-nature, and hostility to men; it is never raised by the narrator.)

At the opposite end of the androphile-androphobe scale is one of Leskov's "wenches" (in his letters to his editors he regularly referred to the story as "The Wenches," since there are two of them, not one). This "androphile" wench is not Prasha, the critic's comfortable refuge from his shrewish spouse, but her youthful aunt—equally plebeian in origin, but with the aristocratic name of Zinaida Pavlovna Potyomkina. Zinaida is the incarnation of female lust—a subject on which Leskov was in general much franker than most writers of his time, both in Russia and elsewhere; he refused to pay homage to the common Victorian myth that sexual desire was an exclusively male phenomenon.

The illegitimate daughter of a soldier's wife and an itinerant Pole, Zinaida is a great beauty. At fifteen she is sold by her mother to a merchant and later married to a shoemaker so jealous that on his deathbed he made her vow before an icon of the Virgin Intercessor of Kursk never to marry again. This vow does not prevent Zinaida from having a long series of lovers—and children. There is a brief period of continence during her partnership with Prasha; but when Prasha marries, Zinaida's concupiscence gets the better of her.

Eventually Zinaida breaks her vow and remarries; is again widowed; and at last enters a convent. But even there she finds "many various holy things, but also many temptations." She "prays in the daytime, but at night she sometimes sews herself a pilgrim's bag and yearns to run away; but as soon as they ring the bell for matins, the devil flies away from her" (9:499).

The antithesis to both Zinaida's nymphomania and the lady's frigidity is Prasha. Prasha is the male chauvinist's (insecure male's) ideal of the perfect woman: affectionate, devoted, modest, unassertive, undemanding, but at the same time competent, practical, and self-reliant.

Prasha nurses (mothers) her literary lover through a serious illness (as Pasha had nursed Leskov), and after his death she uses the 200 rubles the narrator collects for her to set herself up in the laundry business. Prasha eventually remarries, a middle-aged clerk of Polish origin, who reads aloud to her Fénelon's *Télémaque;* has more children by him; and is eventually widowed. When her children are grown, she retires to a cottage in Finland, where a local sadhu (Protestant) helps her to find inner peace. Death, which he taught her not to fear, soon overtakes her there.

Prasha was "an ordinary Russian woman," Leskov concludes, "who perfected herself in this earthly life" without much help either from her literary lover, "whom she loved, or her husband, who loved her." She was a good woman for both of them because to each she gave "the treasure of her kind heart" (9:500).

The polemic or didactic aspect of "The Lady and the Wench" is apparent. The story is a plea for a broader, more tolerant view of sexual relations than was characteristic of many Christian moralists, including Tolstoy. Denial of "nature," sexual abstinence, is no virtue in itself, Leskov seems to be saying. It is often practiced by mean and spiteful people like the "lady"—and is perhaps one of the causes of their meanness, although Leskov does not explore this possibility. On the other hand, promiscuity is no better: it is self-centered and restless and leads to inner emptiness, a life devoid of lasting human ties (Zinaida has little feeling for her lovers or even for her children). What counts between a man and a woman, Leskov maintains, is not ceremonies or vows—he cares little for the legalities of church or state— but love and devotion.

These views conflict with the extreme antisexual position Tolstoy articulates in "The Kreutzer Sonata" and its famous "Afterword." Leskov commented specifically—though ambiguously—on Tolstoy's doctrines in his posthumously published story "Concerning 'The Kreutzer Sonata.'" There, however, he had to announce himself publicly, for or against Tolstoy. But in "The Lady and the Wench," Leskov quietly worked out a decidedly anti-Tolstoyan position on the sexual question, a Leskovian position, less shrill and doctrinaire than Tolstoy's, but didactic and moralistic nevertheless. He was far from Chekhov's "descriptive" or "scientific" neutrality in these matters.

A more specific polemical intent in "The Lady and the Wench" is to strike one last blow on Leskov's ever-ready anti-Orthodox anvil. The "Orthodox" career of Zinaida, with its silly vows to an icon and its "sacraments" of marriage to men she did not love, ends in an Orthodox convent, full of "temptations," where—of all things—the shrewish "lady" has become the "directress" (*načal'nica*—Leskov avoids using the correct term, *igumen'ja*, "abbess"). Prasha's life ends ideally in the simple peace taught by a Finnish Protestant who can scarcely speak Russian.

⟪33⟫

The Form That Failed

During his life as a writer Leskov completed three novels, that is, three works of narrative prose of substantial length not specified by the author as belonging to some other genre. The three finished novels are early: *No Way Out* (1864), *The Bypassed* (1865), and *At Daggers Drawn* (1871). *No Way Out*, Leskov claimed, had been an act of "witnessing" on his part, a truthful reflection of its time; and it had required great moral courage to write. For his defiance of the intellectuals' accepted orthodoxy he had been, he believed, severely and unjustly punished. Looking back on the book in his old age, he reveled in the image he saw there of his youthful valor.[1] An admission occasionally leaked from Leskov that the novel was not of high artistic quality, though even that was the fault of others: the pressure of serial publication, censorship, the carelessness of the publisher who lost or hid the revised proofs for the second book edition.[2] Whatever its artistic faults, *No Way Out* remained for the old Leskov a symbol of his virtue, his ticket of admission to the ranks of martyred literary *pravedniki*. *The Bypassed* and *At Daggers Drawn* were another matter. The latter was "the most unprepossessing of my inferior works" (partly as a result of having been dictated).[3]

At Daggers Drawn, however, contained an interesting critical excursus on the novel form. Pre-Reform Russian fiction, Leskov reports, had been described by a French reviewer as superb in execution but poor in content (an odd judgment: one could argue just the reverse). Leskov accepts the dictum, but ascribes the poverty of content to censorship. Prevented from dealing with public issues, Russian fiction, he says, developed into an art of the miniature. It concentrated on descriptions of private affairs and inner experiences in the most subtle detail, like Gerard David painting in the pupil of a man's eye the reflection of a window and in the window a passer-by. But the relative liberalism of the age of the Great Reforms had changed the situation. Beginning with *On the Eve*, Russian fiction had acquired a broader

492

scope and dealt in larger public questions, although the public did not always recognize the truth of the artist's vision.[4]

Truth and objectivity were scarce in *At Daggers Drawn*. Although the novel contained fine distillations of sociopsychological types, as Dostoevsky and, later, Gorky recognized, its documentary value had been vitiated by the author's vindictive rage and obtrusive *parti pris*. *At Daggers Drawn* also foundered on the author's inability to impose order on chaos. Leskov simply got lost in the vastness of the novel form.

Nevertheless, he kept trying: once more in the seventies, three times in the eighties and nineties. He would start a novel, commence serial publication in a magazine, and then abandon it unfinished. This process began with *A Decrepit Clan*, left hanging at the end of 1874 after three installments in *Russian Messenger*. The true explanation for the abandonment of that novel was the author's inability to cope with the problem of structure. As Leskov in a moment of frankness had confessed to Aksakov, "The novel began to get mixed up in my head, and it had to be abandoned"[5]

Yet the novel still beckoned. Apart from authorial pride and prestige, magazine editors liked novels, for so did the public; and serialized novels lured subscribers. Furthermore, the novel seemed to Leskov, as it did to many writers of the period, the most appropriate medium for saying something big about the big questions.

After *A Decrepit Clan*, Leskov almost immediately began work on a new novel, already entitled *Falcon Flight*.[6] He seems to have done little work on it until 1881. Early in 1882 he sent a "notebook" containing the opening chapters to his friend Aleksei Gattsuk, editor and publisher of *A. Gattsuk's Gazette*. Gattsuk was favorably impressed; but, wise in the ways of writers with serialized novels, he thought it advisable not to begin publication until he had more of the manuscript in hand.[7] Gattsuk then hoped to start publishing in May 1882; but almost a year later, on January 10, 1883, he wrote Leskov that he was expecting more of *Falcon Flight* and was afraid to begin publication until he had received it. Either he went ahead against his better judgment, or Leskov delivered additional text; for the first installment of *Falcon Flight* appeared in *A. Gattsuk's Gazette* on February 19, 1883.[8] Two more installments were published in February and early March. Then together with the fourth installment there appeared a letter to the editor from Leskov announcing that there would be no more of them:

To my own regret and to the evident vexation of the editors and perhaps of certain readers, I must refuse to continue publication of the novel *Falcon Flight*, which was begun in your magazine. I recognize all the awkwardness of this refusal, but I cannot do otherwise. The writing of this novel was begun a long time ago— more than two years back, under circumstances which for the press were very different from the present ones. [Alexander II was on the throne and censorship less severe.] [. . .] I know well that [*Falcon Flight*] would not have been in harmony with current views about literature; and come what may, I *call a halt*. I call a halt simply because—correctly or not—I consider the present time completely unsuitable for a social novel written truthfully, as I at least try to write, without submitting to party or any other pressures.[9]

According to the author, *Falcon Flight* was conceived as another act of political "witnessing," something like a replay of *At Daggers Drawn*. It was to be a sequel to *No Way Out* that would show how a decade or two later the erstwhile fire-breathing revolutionaries had become renegades: "In the novel I wanted to depict the 'flight' from ideas I described twenty years ago in the novel *No Way Out* to ideas of modern times. In the novel *Falcon Flight* many characters were to appear known to the public from *No Way Out*, which in one of the critical articles of Mr. P. Shch[ebalsky] was called 'prophetic.' "[10]

More specifically, though he did not so specify in the sign-off letter, Leskov had intended in *Falcon Flight* to take up the "Polish question," always a keen touchstone for testing the sincerity of Russian radicals. Those who had supported the Polish rebellion of 1863 would be shown in the seventies and eighties "transformed into devoted servants of the tsarist government, actively carrying out the government's policy of Russifying the kingdom of Poland and the Western Provinces."[11] The topic would have been risky even in the tolerant days of Alexander II. But to begin serializing such a novel in 1883, as Leskov did, when the Pobedonostsev reaction was already in full sway, seems almost a deliberate challenge to the censorship. Leskov must have known that he would never be permitted to say what he wanted to say on this subject. He could therefore make a big show of helpless frustration, abandon his novel scarcely begun, and thus call the public's attention to the increasing restrictions on the Russian press.

Whether the cessation of *Falcon Flight* was deliberate or not, Leskov never got far with the novel.[12] The first installment was marked

"Part One; Book One; Chapter 1," seeming to presage great future growth. But only four brief installments appeared, extending up through chapter 13 (still within part 1, book 1).[13]

The action begins "in the autumn of 1863, during the beginning of our reaction and our upheavals, which were still in their infancy." The scene is a prison in the Western provinces, somewhere near the Austrian frontier. The prison is a liberal one, under the influence of its enlightened warden, Pavel Petrovich Kolybelnikov, a veteran of Sevastopol. Kolybelnikov believes that a humane regime is just as effective in keeping his prisoners imprisoned and obedient as the traditional whips and chains, and much more effective in rehabilitating the criminals. In his program of rehabilitation he has been successful, aided by his fifteen-year-old daughter, Susanna (he is a widower), whom he allows to associate freely with the convicts. They adore her. Corporal punishment has been virtually abolished; shackles are taken off on holidays; sick prisoners are sent to a prison farm; unguarded prisoners are sent into town on errands; and there have been no escapes. It is a model of penal progressivism.

An inspector has come from Petersburg, however, with the warning that reports of laxness in the prison administration have aroused disapproval in official quarters. His big news is that the prison is to become a political one (presumably for Poles arrested in the aftermath of 1863, although this is not stated). The final, thirteenth chapter ends with the shocking assertion by Susanna, made to amplify the definition of "political criminal," that "Jesus Christ was accused of a political crime." This unseemly remark augurs a plot based on crossed loyalties and crossed moralities: probably the warden's daughter torn between her father and one of the political prisoners he is obliged to incarcerate, with whom she falls in love.

The announcement of the "politicization" of the prison is as far as the action of *Falcon Flight* proceeds. The characterization of neither Kolybelnikov nor his daughter is developed beyond sentimental stereotype: the kindly widower who worships, and cannot control, his precocious, charming, and self-willed daughter. In the opening scene, for example, Susanna is observed riding a billy-goat down a fire escape attached to one of the prison windows—perhaps, as Leonid Grossman suggests, foreshadowing an escape attempt to come.[14] Leskov has put more effort into the characterization of Fromon, the inspector from Petersburg—a satirized figure who resembles Leskov's late exfriend, Stepan Gromeka, the former liberal businessman and journalist who ended as vice-governor of Siedlce in Poland, persecuting the Uniate church.[15] In novelistic (not short story) fashion, Fromon's character, in the existing chapters, is mostly displayed not in his actions or words, but in analytical statements, usually ironical in tone, by the author. These are of greater interest as documents in Russian social and intellectual history—and in Leskov's intellectual biography—than as realized elements of an artistic creation.

Fromon belongs to the "humanitarian," progressive party among up-and-coming Petersburg officials, one patronized by Prince Vladimir Odoevsky.[16] Like Leskov and Gromeka, Fromon had been an amateur student of philosophy and of political economy, "then being made fashionable by Vernadsky, Bezobrazov, Babst, and Molinari."[17] Fromon himself had only published two or three articles; after he moved up the bureaucratic ladder, he stopped writing altogether, "since to do so is still considered improper in our country," that is, for an official. Fromon's bureaucratic ascent has apparently taken him into the upper reaches of the secret police. He has been assigned a confidential mission involving political prisons, and he is "responsible only to one person in the world"—presumably either the head of the Third Section or the tsar himself.

Fromon, in short, is a chameleon-like bureaucratic careerist, a man who avoids definite commitments, yet takes on the glow of fashionable ideas. He is neither a Westernizer nor a Slavophile; he admires old Russian forms, but not those that have outlived their usefulness; he reveres the law, but understands that laws are not always flexible enough to fit life's needs.

In chapter 10 of *Falcon Flight* a new character is mentioned: Adam Lvovich Bezbedovich, Susanna's tutor. The son of a Uniate priest, he is a university graduate in mathematics. His name is ominously marked with two minus signs in Fromon's little book. Though Susanna denies it, her father believes Bezbedovich to be the source of the outré remark about Jesus Christ as a political criminal. That is all we learn about Bezbedovich in *Falcon Flight*. But he—or at least his name—appears in Leskov's next unfinished novel, *A Faint Trace*.[18]

Despite Leskov's assertion, none of the characters in the existing chapters of *Falcon Flight* is a straightforward revival of any character from *No Way Out*. Characters similar in type or derived from the same prototype are possible. This is true of Bezbedovich. If, as Andrei Leskov plausibly suggests, in Bezbedovich "in many ways there is a suspicion of something from A[rtur] Benni,"[19] then to bear out Leskov's claim he should have the same name as Benni's embodiment in *No Way Out*, Wilhelm Reiner. But he does not; and his curriculum vitae is different from Reiner's (Reiner is half Swiss, half Russian, somehow fluent in Polish, while Bezbedovich is a borderline Polono-Ukraino-Russian). But there are basic elements of similarity among Reiner, Bezbedovich, and Benni: higher education in a nonliberal discipline (mathematics or engineering); association with non-Orthodox Christianity; involvement with Russian and Polish revolutionaries (only implied in the case of Bezbedovich). But unless Reiner was to appear later *in propria persona* (which seems unlikely, since he and Bezbedovich are too much alike), we must conclude that Leskov's statement about *No Way Out* characters in *Falcon Flight* cannot be taken so literally as he implies.

Leskov concludes his sign-off letter to the editor: "Instead of this novel I will write for you and submit for publication this year a novel devoted to purely private, everyday life, on a motif drawn from one of those situations always convenient for novelistic development: 'He fell in love and got married' or 'He fell in love and shot himself' " (11: 223). Whether this promise was serious or not is unclear. In commenting on Leskov's letter, Gattsuk made no reference to the offer of a new, "private life" novel, but held out the hope for a continuation of *Falcon Flight* itself: "And so, in accordance with the author's wish we are ceasing the printing of his novel *Falcon Flight*, in the hope of continuing it when the time shall have passed when it is so difficult to express in print honest and truthful thoughts."[20]

Leskov published neither a continuation of *Falcon Flight* nor any other novel in *A. Gattsuk's Gazette*, unless "Notes in an Unknown Hand" is, by stretching the term, considered a novel. He immediately began work on another genuine (again unfinished) novel, but he did not destine it for *A. Gattsuk's Gazette*. Nor did he, insofar as we can judge, intend to make it a purely "private" or "everyday" novel hung on one of his two standard plots. Rather it was to be another attempt, in the teeth of the censors, at a "social novel" on the still-elusive theme of Poland.

Some seventeen chapters of *A Faint Trace* appeared in the two inaugural issues of *Virgin Soil* in November 1884.[21] They are again from a section labeled "Part One," which bears the overall title "Domestic Roof." After those two installments, publication was broken off and never resumed. From an artistic point of view this fragment of a novel is more interesting than what we have of *Falcon Flight*. It is a fictionalized reflection of certain scenes from Leskov's father's biography.

The novel is presented as an *Ich-Erzählung,* a retrospective memoir or "family history," as the subtitle puts it. The narrator is the younger son, Ivan, of the Bezbedovich family.[22] Although they have moved to the "Great Russian provincial capital of O———" (we read Oryol), the narrator's family, like their homonymous counterpart in *Falcon Flight,* have strong Polish associations. Their forefathers, in the style of the celebrated Prince Kurbsky, had fled from Russia to Lithuania in the time of Ivan the Terrible; and there they had gone over to the Uniate church. The narrator's father, like Leskov's, had studied for the priesthood, in his case the Uniate, but eventually pursued a secular career. Furthermore, though he remained nominally Uniate, "his beliefs were somewhat different," just as Semyon Leskov's were "somewhat different" from strict Orthodoxy. Again like Leskov's father, Lev Bezbedovich had acquired a better education than the average seminarian, although the range of subjects is amplified: "He knew the theological and philosophical sciences, ancient and modern languages, a little medicine, and music very thoroughly."

Though he regarded Polish as his mother tongue and was well acquainted with Polish literature, Bezbedovich *père* spoke Russian perfectly and considered himself a Russian. He "did not like either Polish culture or the Polish character." In "Lithuania," where he lived (modern Belorussia is probably meant), Lev Bezbedovich identified with the oppressed local peasantry, and he hoped to serve them as a priest. This ambition was thwarted when, at the instance of a member of the local nobility, he was banished to O——— as a political subversive (perhaps an echo of the fate of Leskov's beloved mentor, Afanasy Markovich).

In O——— Bezbedovich is thus something of an alien body. In Poland he had been a Russian, but in Russia he is considered a Pole. As an alien he can make comparisons and pass judgments from an outsider's point of view. This visual alienation and dual nationality are given a—too obvious—physical symbol: he has one brown and one blue eye. The elder Bezbedovich has served as estate manager for an apparently wealthy nobleman named Brasov; and while in Brasov's service he learned an important, if melancholy, truth. In Polish territory he had attributed the cruelty of the Polish gentry toward the Belorussian or Lithuanian peasantry to their ethnic and religious differences; but in O——— he makes the Marxian discovery that Russian gentlemen are just as ruthless in exploiting their fellow Russians.

The Brasovs, the gentry family Bezbedovich serves, are in a state of open moral and hidden financial decay; they are far more decrepit a clan than the Protozanovs. The youngest daughter has escaped the moral rot. She falls in love with Bezbedovich and eventually elopes with him (her family considered him socially far beneath them, as the Alferievs considered Semyon Leskov). For her disobedience she was cursed by her father, and all relations between Brasovs and Bezbedoviches were severed.

Although the marriage of Leskov's parents had been a prosaic affair (since the Alferievs could afford no dowry, they had to settle for the ex-seminarian), it took place in 1830, precisely the year of Bezbedovich's elopement. And 1831, the year of Leskov's birth, is the year when Adam Lvovich Bezbedovich was born. Apparently Adam Bezbedovich was to become the main hero of *A Faint Trace*, but in the existing text his father is the central figure. Lev Bezbedovich, again like Semyon Leskov, had become an investigator or detective attached to the governor's office, where he acquires a Leskovian reputation for intelligence, industry, and stiff-necked integrity. He refuses to make the little moral compromises expected of a person in a subordinate situation; and his obduracy eventually proves his undoing, as it had Leskov's father's.

The first turning point in Lev Bezbedovich's life comes with the death of his father-in-law. Lying on his deathbed, old Brasov seeks to be reconciled with his youngest daughter. Since it is—perhaps symbolically—the season of thawing rivers and breaking ice, she must undertake a dangerous journey to reach the parental estate from town. The trip is described by Leskov with a vividness almost worthy of the blizzard scenes in "At the Edge of the World." (Her husband happened to be away on an investigative mission, just as Leskov's father was away when "Deathless Golovan" saved Leskov from a mad dog.)

The dying Brasov knows that his financial affairs are "in disarray," as the conventional euphemism had it: his expenditures had for many years exceeded his income. He urges his daughter to prevail upon her husband to take charge of what is left of the Brasov estate. Through a complicated arrangement Bezbedovich receives in his own name title to a small property, plus a large debt.

The creditor is a villainous extortionist named Nemchinov, married to an even more villainous "regimental widow." They are implacable misers and tyrants. Mme Nemchinova in turn has as her lover a still more villainous character, the serf coachman Sadok, an absolute brute of a man who habitually extorts both financial and sexual favors from the Nemchinovs' serfs and debtors alike; he also serves with pleasure as their chief flogger.

While dressing for a fancy ball (Leskov surveys the competitive *haute couture* in the Russian provinces), Mme Nemchinova in a fit of rage strikes her maid with a pitcher; by bad luck the blow proves fatal. Ordinarily such acts of manslaughter or even murder of serfs by their owners, including the not-too-uncommon deaths under the rods, were easy to cover up, and the Nemchinovs had successfully done so several times before. Morally supine as always in Leskov, the local priest, under instructions from Sadok, "peacefully and quietly" buries the murdered girl without thought of protest to the authorities.

But in this unique case the victim's mother and fiancé, driven to desperation, decide on a reckless effort to obtain justice. They dream of appealing to the tsar himself. On their way to town they pass through the Bezbedovich estate and are found there half-frozen. Bezbedovich is therefore faced with a crucial moral choice. Will he report the runaways to their owners, or will he assist them in their quixotic quest? Not only gentry class solidarity, but the desirability of keeping on good terms with his hard-fisted creditor would incline him to the former solution; but he opts for the latter. Like Semyon Leskov, who once refused a huge bribe designed to induce him to cover up an atrocious crime, Bezbedovich is a *pravednik*.

He shelters the runaways and gives them warm clothing and a little money (which they foolishly use to buy forged passports). Ordinarily, Leskov says, their case would have been hopeless: the provincial administration was run by and for the provincial gentry. But it just happened that a senatorial investigation of the provincial administration was in progress. The police therefore "did not dare not to report to the governor that a charge of murder had been brought; and the governor did not dare to quash the matter." To save his own skin Sadok testifies against his mistress, and on his instructions several skeletons are dug up from the Nemchinovs' yard, the remains of peasants officially listed as unapprehended runaways.

For the murder of the maid Mme Nemchinova is banished to Siberia. Nemchinov escapes punishment. Leskov never makes clear what legal action, if any, was taken in the matter of the skeletons, and he needs to keep Nemchinov on hand for the purposes of the plot. The villain demands immediate full payment of the debts, both Bezbedovich's own and that of his mother-in-law. There are no resources to meet this demand. Most of the property therefore has to be sold, and the Bezbedovich family is reduced to destitution. They are left with a tiny remnant of their former property, a mini-farm rather like the Panino "estate" where Semyon Leskov wasted his last years. Helpless against the poverty, Lev Bezbedovich loses interest in the farm and devotes himself instead to the education of his older son, Adam (something Semyon Leskov failed to do with his eldest son).

When the time comes to send Adam to a *gymnasium*, there is no money for it. Requests for a Treasury scholarship are denied. Even the senator who once pushed the case of the Nemchinov serfs now has the police formally notify Bezbedovich that he must not "burden responsible officials with irrelevant petitions in a most insolent tone." Despairing of being able to raise his sons above the status of cobblers, Lev Bezbedovich suddenly dies, as Semyon Leskov had, of cholera.

Bezbedovich *mère*, however, is no replica of Marya Leskova. She is a loving, but weak-willed and totally passive woman; and the sudden death of her husband leaves her utterly prostrate. Fortunately, the family is befriended by the picturesque and faithful Deacon Flavian, more a tradesman than a clergyman in spirit, who becomes their pillar of strength.

Here part 1 of *A Faint Trace* ends, and with it the entire novel. Obviously Lev Bezbedovich's day is over, and the fictional future belongs to the young Adam, of whom his dying father says, with a somewhat cryptic explanation of the title, "He has an excellent heart. Above it the dove flew early, and beneath it the serpent crawled; and they both left a faint trace. If God preserves him, he will not live in vain."

Despite signs of carelessness or haste, which could easily have been ironed out in later revisions, *A Faint Trace* shows great promise, and it is a pity Leskov abandoned it. The figure of Lev Bezbedovich, the virtuous Russian and almost-Pole, has cast a deep moral shadow for his sons to grow up in, and there are several other promising characterizations: Father Flavian; his orphan-loving wife; the narrator's eccentric aunt, Mme Brasova née Poslova; her Russian companion, Marya Morevna, who, though hopelessly in love with Bezbedovich, had helped arrange his elopement with Darya Brasova; her English companion Belle. Leskov seems to have in mind a *Bildungsroman*, with Adam Bezbedovich as the poor boy from the provinces, further alienated by his semi-Polish background, gradually learning the truths of the Russian world and groping his way through its moral pitfalls.

The biggest of these pitfalls was the theme of Russia vs. Poland, which in the nineteenth century meant Russian oppression of Poland.

It was a theme that needed confronting by some courageous Russian writer, able to face up to the moral dilemma. Pushkin had failed: his poem "To the Slanderers of Russia," written in the aftermath of the Polish rebellion of 1831, is a childish burst of chauvinistic bombast, for which Mickiewicz called him bitterly to order. The hate-filled "Christian" Dostoevsky had peopled his novels with contemptible Poles who obviously deserved to be oppressed. Tolstoy's Polish record was better;[23] but for him, as for Turgenev, the problem was too removed from direct experience.

In many ways Leskov was better equipped to face this moral dilemma and make literature out of it than any other major Russian writer. Ever since his youth in Kiev the "Polish question" had been on his mind. It was revived and focused through his friendship with Artur Benni and dramatized for him by the Paris confrontations of 1863. Surely these personal experiences, feelings, and images, especially with the perspective of years, could have been transmuted into artistic symbols epitomizing the national moral dilemma. Leskov yearned to do it, as both *Falcon Flight* and *A Faint Trace* testify. But each time he shied away—perhaps from fear of censorship, perhaps from misgivings about his ability to create a work of the dimensions the theme required, perhaps because of his emotional ambivalence.

Like most Russians, Leskov generally disliked Poles, but felt guilty about oppressing them. And guilt about oppression led to more dislike. The dislike was predictably confirmed by the Poles' defensive contempt for alleged Russian "barbarism" and by their pompous, self-serving celebration of their supposed "martyrdom." ("We are the Christ among nations.")

In order for a Russian writer to make great literature out of the Polish theme, the emotional tangle would have to be sorted out and the vicious circle broken. Whether Leskov had the intellectual and spiritual strength to accomplish this feat is open to question; but it is a great pity that he did not give it more of a trial. Eventually the theme was taken up by Aleksandr Blok for what he, too, hoped would be his most substantial work, the lyrico-epic *Retribution*; but Blok was, as it were, defeated by the Poles also, and *Retribution* was left unfinished. The theme of Poland still awaits adequate Russian exploitation.

After giving up on *A Faint Trace*, Leskov seems for some time to have toyed with the idea of tackling the Polish theme again, perhaps through another rebirth of Bezbedovich. The two published installments of *A Faint Trace* had appeared in November 1884, but it was not until September 1885 that Leskov announced publicly that he was abandoning the novel; and even then he apparently made the announcement only under pressure from the editor of *Virgin Soil*. His reasons are vague: "Various unfavorable circumstances about which it would be inappropriate to speak here have prevented me from fulfilling the obligation I took upon myself."[24] Such allusions were generally taken to refer to censorship, and they have been so interpreted by some scholars.[25] But since no sensitive matters had yet been touched upon in *A Faint Trace*, it seems wiser to concur with the cautious assessment of I. Aizenshtok: "The reference to 'unfavorable circumstances' preventing the continuation and completion of the novel as begun cannot be clarified with full assurance. Most probably, Leskov had simply lost his enthusiasm for his conception of a 'family novel.' "[26]

Nevertheless, the figure of Adam Bezbedovich still haunted Leskov, a spirit longing for a literary body. He appears, for instance, on a list of characters, date uncertain, for an unwritten play: "Adam Lvovich Bezbedovich, a music teacher just under 50, an unmarried ladies' man, a friend of old Treplyov."[27] ("Old Treplyov," incidentally, is a colonel and "inspector of a correctional institution," rather like the Kolybelnikov of *Falcon Flight*.) Bezbedovich flashes by again in a letter of 1889 to Tolstoy's disciple and future biographer, Pavel Biryukov. Arguing for a more moderate application of Tolstoy's social and economic principles, one that would allow for continuing small landholdings rather than insisting on pure Tolstoyan communes, Leskov says: "A mass of small landowners, landowners with a good Christian orientation, remains for me the surest step for the present time as I see it. I want to write such a novel, a little one, and call it by the name of its hero 'Adam Bezbedovich' (from the Polish evangelicals). The Poles are spendidly capable of settling down in the country."[28]

This work remained unrealized, however, and two years later Leskov wrote to Tolstoy, "I want to write 'Bezbedovich'—a little novel with a hero of simple understanding, and I would like to talk to you about this character and sketch out the 'artistic spots of the picture.' "[29] This "little novel" likewise remained unwritten.

The most substantial unfinished novel of Leskov's late years is *The Devil's Puppets*, published in the January 1890 issue of *Russian Thought*.[30] It was reprinted the same year in the tenth volume of the collected works. Since the tenth was the final volume of the series (two supplemental ones were issued subsequently by a different publisher), and since *The Devil's Puppets* was the last work in that volume, its position of finality gave it a special significance.[31] It is a summing up, through the medium of fiction, of Leskov's most cherished ideas about his art—its meaning in relation to life, its power as a moral force, the artist's dependence on and responsibility to the society in which he lives.

In terms of genre, *The Devil's Puppets* might be classified as an extended parable or as a "problem novel" with a thesis. Fiction is used as a means of exploring age-old problems in the ethics and socioeconomics of art: its relationship to money, patronage, politics, and power—and to sexuality. As Leskov described his plan in a letter to his editor: "I have in production on my desk something you might call a novel or maybe a chronicle, but probably closer to a novel, about 250-300 pages long. Its plot is taken from papers and traditions about the thirties and touches on the exalted of our land—mostly or even exclusively from the aspect of their amatory capers and amatory heartlessness."[32]

Leskov had a collection of "papers and traditions" to work from: the career of the noted Russian painter Karl Bryullov (1799-1852), who may also have inspired some of the features of Istomin in "The Islanders."[33] Leskov saw Bryullov as an artist of enormous gifts and technical skill whose career had failed—from moral weakness, not from insufficiency of talent or energy. For Leskov, Bryullov's life demonstrated that ability without integrity leads to disaster.

On summons from Nicholas I, in 1836 Bryullov had returned from Rome, where he had been studying and painting for years, to assume a professorship at the Petersburg Academy of Arts. In Russia he had been showered with money and favors by the tsar, but had also been favored with royal "suggestions" about subjects for his pictures. Nicholas liked heroic historical scenes, and Bryullov spent his last years struggling with a gigantic canvas depicting the siege of Pskov in 1581-82, which was still unfinished at his death. Isolated from the vital currents of European art, immune from criticism (at least in Russia), Bryullov's painting, according to Leskov, sank into sterile academicism. He had sold his artistic soul for a mess of Nicholas's pottage.

In illustrating the pernicious effects of subordinating art to political power, Leskov also alluded to the potent and sacrosanct figure of Pushkin. Like Bryullov, Pushkin had entered into an ambiguous dependent relationship with Nicholas I. Like Bryullov, Pushkin had received royal "favors"—less than generous ones—for which he ultimately paid dearly (though not with loss of his artistic integrity).

Pushkin too had received imperial "suggestions" about the topics and even form of his works. And in his last years Pushkin, like Bryullov, had been sucked into court life and court intrigues, involving the rumor of a love affair between his wife and the tsar.[34]

Leskov sought to reexamine these cases in fictional form, using Bryullov for his basic model, but infusing ingredients from the life of Pushkin. This synthetic image in turn became the vehicle for a philosophical study of the moral and economic basis of art. Does he who pays the piper always call the tune? What does "freedom" mean for an artist? What are his moral responsibilities, and to whom?

The Bryullov-Pushkin cases in their political and sexual aspects could not be treated openly in the censor-ridden Russian press. Even the usual disguises—changes of names, details, situations—would not hide the inevitable *lèse-majesté*. As Leskov put it to his editor:

> *Au naturel* it would be impossible, and therefore it is written in the form of events which happen no one knows when or where— in the form of a "discovered manuscript." The names are all non-Russian and sound intentionally made-up, like nicknames. It is a device like Hoffmann's. In general, it is an interesting story to read; and in particular, well-informed people will understand that it is not just a story. Its chief element is *seraglio* vice and the mores of *seraglio* magnates. Not the "struggle with flesh and blood," but simply vice of the will combined with emptiness of heart and external hypocrisy. I call this novel in accordance with the character of the characterless personages who appear in it *Devil's Puppets*.[35]

Thus Leskov de-nationalized his subject, transported it out of Russia, partly to a colorless Rome (where Leskov had never been), partly to an unnamed, never-never land (though one scene resembles the Pushkin-Lermontov Caucasus), presided over by a nameless "Duke" (Herzog), who represents "you know whom," as Leskov put it in his letter—Nicholas I.

The de-nationalization was conventional. On one level, as Leskov notes in his letter, readers in the know (nowadays those supplied with a scholar's commentary) could treat *The Devil's Puppets* as a roman à clef and read Bryullov and Pushkin back into it. On a higher level, the abstraction through de-nationalization symbolizes the universal relevance of the theme. For Bryullov and Pushkin are instances of a problem that arises *mutatis mutandis* in any culture where there are professional artists. Into the abstractions provided by the novel, the reader

—Russian or otherwise—can reintroduce concrete images of his own, applying its lesson to his own society or time.

As a technique of censorship evasion, de-nationalization succeeded, for the work (part 1) passed the censors unscathed. But the artistic cost was enormous. For Leskov, writing an abstract, de-nationalized novel was like working blindfolded, ears stuffed with cotton, and a bad cold in the head. His art depended on the concrete textures of the real world. Yet here he had had to banish himself from that world. Even the speech of the stateless characters had to be "translated" into colorless literary Russian.

Despite its un-Leskovian abstractness, *The Devil's Puppets* remains a powerful sermon on the subject of art and freedom. To study the problem, Leskov created two additional artist characters to set off the central one. In the center is Bryullov-Pushkin, alias "Febufis" (an infelicitous corruption of *fils de Phèbe,* "son of Apollo," given the hero for his physical beauty as well as his artistic talent). On one side of Febufis is his satellite Pik, who views him with unqualified admiration and is corrupted by his example. On the other side stands the upright Mak, the author's spokesman and alter ego, who believes in the moral commitment of art and will not sell his brush to any "duke."

When we meet them, the three young painters are on the same level (though Febufis is the most talented): ex-students now free-lance artists living the *vie de Bohème* in Rome. Their paths soon diverge, when Febufis forms his "friendship" with the traveling Duke and departs with him. After that Pik and Mak at first function as commentators on the stages of Febufis's career. Later Pik joins his idol and acts out a caricatured mirror image of Febufis's degeneration.

Though Febufis is the central character, he does not represent a basic philosophical position. He is a passive body being pulled toward the more powerful of two poles. If Pik is his satellite, he in turn becomes a satellite of the Duke. The Duke and Mak represent the two extremes of principle: the serving artist vs. the free artist.

The philosophical issues at stake had been much debated in the 1830s, the presumed period of the novel's action. Should the artist pursue "art for art's sake," as the Romantics believed, disdainful of "contemptible utility" (Pushkin's phrase), and denying, as Pik claims to do in the novel, "all exterior aims save only pure beauty" (8:488)? Or should he put his God-given talent to the service of his society? And if the latter, who is to define society's need—its rulers? By the 1850s, when Leskov cut his philosophical teeth, the utilitarians, mostly radical, had prevailed. Art should serve—not the tsarist state, of course, but the "people."

In *The Devil's Puppets* the utilitarian position is Mak's, and it was also Leskov's, as attested by numerous extraliterary utterances and by his practice as an artist in his late years. Though they disagreed strongly on political tactics, on this issue Leskov was at one with Chernyshevsky: "[Mak] was concerned with social problems: he grieved over the miseries of mankind and thought deeply about the service aims of art" (8:488).

On the Italian scene, though he is not Italian, Mak's hero is Garibaldi; but he does not pose the question of how his art might serve Garibaldi's cause, nor what the situation of art would be if Garibaldi were to attain political power. In that conveniently uncomplicated world all political power is in the hands of reactionary dukes (or popes), who are opposed by noble (but powerless) revolutionaries. The definition of "freedom of art," therefore, is simply independence of political authority, a principle which Mak upholds with vigor.

Even before Febufis's meeting with the Duke, Mak had inspired him to paint an illustration of the text "Cast thyself down." This Satanic command is interpreted (by Febufis, but citing Mak) as "moving from God's truth to the truth of dukes and kings, entering into an alliance with them." "And you know," Febufis goes on, "Christ didn't do it!" Later, when Pik offers to share with Mak some of the Duke's money— so that Mak will have the leisure to paint his "big canvas"—Mak's reply is "Get thee behind me, Satan!" We are reminded of Leskov's own reply (at least as he tells the story) when offered an estate in Lithuania by "Muravyov the Hanger." But Febufis himself makes the opposite decision. Succumbing to Satan's lures, he "enters into an alliance" with the Duke.

At each stage of Febufis's increasing entanglement with the Duke, Mak makes a gloomy and sardonic comment. Mak's position is uncompromising: for the artist, at least in modern times, the "king's" touch is invariably morbific. When Pik argues that with the Duke's support he and Febufis will be able to "serve art and high ideas in general," Mak replies: "I do not believe in the possibility of serving high ideas when in the service of dukes" (8:526).

Like Leskov (as he rationalized his failure with the "big forms"), Mak cannot afford the time to paint a "big canvas." He must support himself day by day with "little genres." But he consoles himself that these are "doing a job which is better than the biggest picture, for they 'stir some people's consciences.'" Just as Leskov published in low-brow media like the *Petersburg Gazette* in order, as he hoped, to exert a moral influence on the "300,000 lackeys, janitors, cooks, soldiers, shopkeepers, spies, and streetwalkers,"[36] so Mak rejoiced that his "little genres" were being hung in taverns.

The polar opposite of Mak in *The Devil's Puppets* is the Duke (Nicholas I). The Duke is well advanced on the road to a "totalitarian" view of art: the artist must serve the state, or else. As Mak puts it: "Believe me, the man to whom you have entrusted the 'talent' you mention is not afraid of any shame. I think he would think it shameful to know that there is such a thing as fear of shame; and as for your 'talent,' they'll settle its score quickly. There's nothing to stop him from leaving that talent without canvas and without paints and even without God's world" (8:533). Though the possibility of terror thus exists, within the first part of the novel the Duke prefers to rely mainly on blandishments.

The Duke's commanding voice is muffled by an "ideological" orchestration, an ostensible espousal of "art for art's sake." The official line at the Duke's court is that "pure art perishes from the corrupting pressure of social tendencies." Febufis has understood this principle, and therefore "to preserve the sacred vessel intact, he has brought it and laid it at the feet of the Duke. The Duke did not spurn it, as he spurns nothing he can save" (8:536). While thus serving "pure art," on the Duke's payroll, Febufis receives a "command" (the word is used) to paint a huge canvas depicting a subject more splendid and bold than that of Kaulbach's "Battle of the Huns and the Romans."[37]

Besides such uplifting heroics, the Duke allows, as subjects for artists to work on, "the pastoral, religion, the family, and peaceful bucolics." He is adamant, however, against any "sticking of noses into social questions" (8:538). "Art must be national, like everything else" is another of the Duke's dicta (8:544). "The historical too is possible, I do not deny the historical, but only from our correct point of view, and not from theirs [the artists' own]. Social questions do not concern art. The artist must stand above that. That's the kind we need! Find me people who can in this way be useful to art and bring them here. To meet their financial needs is my business. We can even give them ranks and uniforms [. . .] Our calling is to bring about a renewal of art" (8:538).

The words are window dressing, "unrealizable nonsense," as even Febufis "understood." What concerns the Duke is "possessing" the artist, controlling and using him. "You are mine!" he twice exclaims triumphantly to Febufis, reminding us of Katkov's immortal words about Leskov: "That man is *not ours!*"[38]

A great deal of the ideological screen for the Duke's policy of controlling and manipulating artists is supplied by the artists themselves, Febufis and Pik. They must justify the Duke's policies in order to rationalize their own surrender to him. To save their necks, or face, or mere creature comforts, they collaborate in their own enslavement.

Early in his career in the Duke's service Febufis dreams of reversing the lines of force, using his art to "direct [*napravljat'*] the Duke and through him to develop taste in his subjects and be their benefactor: 'to embellish their sky' " (8:525). It soon becomes clear that all the "directing" will be done by the Duke, and Febufis's hopeful bubble bursts. Though disillusioned, he cannot summon the courage to extricate himself from his cage.

Later, when attacked in the European press for the sterility of his paintings, Febufis writes a defensive article, sophistically asserting that in fact he is freer than his critics, enslaved as they are to ideas alien to art; and that he refuses to yoke his muse and make her walk a treadmill "under the supervision of despotic critics" (8:539). The Duke approves this treatise, but decides it would be more dignified not to publish it. Febufis's manuscript is not returned to him. Instead, he is graciously allowed (by a courtier) to view the royal words written on it: "I approve and quite agree." In lieu of publication Febufis receives the reward of "an estate in a picturesque corner of the dukedom."

Besides his wish to control art and use it to glorify the nation's destiny and his own, the Duke has another use for art: pornography. His original encounter with Febufis in Rome came about through his desire to view a "naughty" picture painted by Febufis. The picture showed a diplomat's wife (she had jilted Febufis for a cardinal) represented as Pandora, being obscenely embraced by the cardinal in the guise of Epimetheus, with Febufis himself shown at the bottom of the picture as a satyr being led away by an old woman with a candle. The Duke is amused. As Mak later puts it, an artist at the Duke's court has two tasks: to paint battle scenes and to paint "naked women on the mirrors in the Duke's apartments" (8:527).

The ironic equation of "pure art" with pornography was a favorite idea of Leskov's. In the last year of his life, in an interview with a newspaper reporter, he made the following sententious pronouncement (though the style is garbled, the ideas are Leskov's): "I love literature as a means which enables me to express what I think is true and good; if I cannot do that, I do not value literature. To look on it as an art is not my point of view. I absolutely do not understand the principle of 'art for art's sake.' No, art must be useful—only then does it have definite meaning. The art of drawing naked women I do not acknowledge. It is the same with literature. If by its means you cannot serve truth and goodness, there's no reason to write; you should give up the occupation."[39]

One of the most interesting features of *The Devil's Puppets* is the way Leskov blends this theme of "naked women" (or "seraglio vice," as he put it in his letter) with that of the philosophy of art. Indeed, it would appear from Leskov's correspondence that the vice was the original nucleus and the philosophical element a later accretion:

> I repeat that the novel is primarily an *erotic* one, and all about Moscow and Petersburg high-society "devil's puppets" (whores) of refined delicacy with names like Pomon, Neud, Delli, etc., who genuflect before the Duke, who is modeled on you know whom and has no other name but the "Duke." Along with him are served up Bryullov and *tutti frutti*. It all sounds like a fable or bit of ancient history, but then suddenly you catch yourself up and feel that there's something familiar about it all. It's all written like Hoffmann's "Serapion Brothers." There are no deep or accursed questions at all. "Much for their sake have I suffered."[40]

But the "deep" questions did creep in, perhaps deeper than Leskov realized. For in some sense the theme of ducal dominance of art is an analogue of an archetypal fantasy of paternal sexual dominance. The Duke "possesses" artists as the sultan possesses his seraglio. Thus the subject of pornography in art forms an integrating link between the fully conscious, philosophical theme of the relation of art to political authority, and a partly unconscious one of sexual tyranny. The link is manufactured out of the Duke's hypocrisy. Though posing as a model spouse and enforcing puritanical rules on others (Pik undergoes a brief "paternal" arrest, a bit like a spanking, for allowing his girl pupils to sketch male torsos), the Duke allows himself the secret titillation of obscene pictures (and more direct gratifications as well).

Another link in the novel between the philosophical and sexual themes is the use of women as prizes. The Duke serves as matchmaker for his two artistic minions, Pik and Febufis. For each a lovely and well-connected bride is found; and in each case the powerful hand of the Duke moves aside difficulties presented by the girl or her parents. Even after the marriages the Duke supervises the adjustment of the spouses and is well-informed even about private, bedroom matters. ("He knows everything except the needs of his people!" Pik bitterly exclaims.) It transpires that it is not only the Duke's eye that is ubiquitous. The female "puppets" he uses to ensnare the artists are not quite brand new. Pik's bride is revealed to have been a mistress of the Duke's and there is suspicion that Febufis's Gelia has also been—or will be in the immediate future (in the final scene the Duke carries her into his castle—ostensibly to protect her from her enraged husband). It seems that the royal penis, like the royal eye, has been everywhere.[41]

By thus farming out his cast-off mistresses, the Duke both provides for them and further tightens the bonds around his artists. But the example of royal hypocrisy and sexual predacity proves infectious. The Pik marriage takes place first. Before his own, which is never consummated, Febufis contrives to have an affair with his friend's wife. The affair is discovered by Pik, and the solidarity of the two artists thus destroyed. They are now totally isolated in their relations with the Duke. It seems that sexual integrity is as necessary to art, and as impossible under a ducal regime, as intellectual integrity.

By the beginning of December 1889, Leskov had almost ready a fair copy of part 1 of the novel and perhaps the remainder in rough draft. He wrote *Russian Thought* that he would prefer to keep the manuscript a year or so longer, until he had finished it; but that if they wished, he would agree to have them publish the first part immediately. They would have to trust him to produce the remaining parts, as Boborykin had trusted him with *No Way Out* and Katkov with *At Daggers Drawn*. Once again he asserted, "The plot is purely erotic; and the further it goes, the more interesting it gets; but it is *touchy* and rather unusual, although it's all taken from real people and events."[42]

Soon thereafter Leskov advised *Russian Thought* that *Russian Survey* and *Motherland* were also interested in *The Devil's Puppets*. *Russian Thought* evidently responded suitably to this competitive prodding and agreed to publish forthwith. On December 15 we find Leskov asking for only one more day before delivering the final manuscript.[43] In the same letter, he claims an odd assortment of new literary ancestors for his *Devil's Puppets:* Aristophanes's *Clouds;* an anonymous eighteenth-century lampoon on Potyomkin called *Pansalvin, the Prince of Darkness;* and another eighteenth-century Russian satire, Khemnitser's *Bloody Rod.*

Tired after his intense work on the first installment, Leskov asked his editors for a respite. He would not try to deliver the second installment in time for the February issue, but would surely have it ready for the March one.[44] But when March came, there was no installment; and after that the continuation of *The Devil's Puppets* receded into a remote future.

Leskov's inspiration seemed to come in single spurts. Having delivered a batch of manuscript to a publisher, he felt finished with it, wrote it off in his mind, and turned to something new. The spring of 1890 was full of other events: a visit to Tolstoy at Yasnaya Polyana, the appearance of the final two volumes of the collected works. In the last of these volumes Leskov inserted the published first part of *The Devil's Puppets*, giving it the subtitle *Chapters from an Unfinished Novel*, which must have increased the impression, both his own and his readers', that the novel had been abandoned. Yet he still kept alive the hope, at least of his editors, that he intended to go on with it. When they pressed him, he first pleaded his state of despair over the "arrest" by the censors of the sixth volume of the collected works (although that had occurred many months earlier). In compensation, he dangled the prospect of a new story, "Concerning 'The Kreutzer Sonata' "; but about the novel he was vague: "I will write you some new considerations concerning *Devil's Puppets*, which everyone here likes very much and finds interesting. I think it may be possible to go on with it."[45]

Five months later Leskov was offering *Russian Thought* still another new story and the rather unrewarding prospect of further "talk about *Puppets*."[46] Nine months later still, in May 1891, Leskov was advising his patient editors: "By autumn I want to finish up and send you the third part of *Devil's Puppets*. The second is untenable [*neudobna*, meaning either politically too risky or sexually too risqué], but the third is tenable and interesting."[47]

Whether any of these tenable or untenable parts was actually written remains unclear. Of the surviving manuscripts of *The Devil's Puppets* all are variants of the earlier work with that title. The fate of any manuscript containing further parts of the 1890 novel, as Andrei Leskov notes, "is unknown."[48]

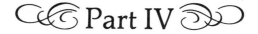

Part IV

Together with Tolstoy
(1887-1895)

ℭ₰ 34 ₰℘

The Rushlight and the Torch

On April 20, 1887, Leskov had his first meeting with Lev Tolstoy, the man who for the rest of his days was to be his beacon, his guide, the fountainhead of his most cherished ideas. Before the meeting took place, Leskov had been "cleared"—and encouraged—by two of Tolstoy's disciples, whom he had already known for several years: Pavel Biryukov and the disciple-in-chief, Vladimir Chertkov. They saw Leskov as a valuable recruit for the Tolstoyan cause; and the final solemnity of his initiation was to be a visit with the master. Informed that Tolstoy planned to be in Moscow the following week, Leskov wrote him requesting an interview—the first letter in a long and fascinating, though sadly one-sided and incomplete, correspondence that has come down to us.[1] On April 19 he took the train to Moscow; and apparently finding a favorable response from Tolstoy awaiting him at his hotel, the next day he was at the door of the Tolstoy townhouse at 15 Dolgokhamovnichesky Lane.

The encounter seems to have been a pleasant one for both participants. Back in Yasnaya Polyana, on April 25, Tolstoy wrote Chertkov, "Leskov came. What an intelligent and original man!"[2] Andrei Leskov heard from his father many vivid stories of the meeting; but by the time he wrote his biography, several decades later, his memory of them had faded. He could no longer distinguish them from accounts of Leskov's second (and last) face-to-face encounter with Tolstoy, in January 1890, when with Chertkov as his Palinurus he made the pilgrimage to Yasnaya Polyana. One symbolic episode Andrei Leskov did recall; it happened in either 1887 or 1890. During the conversation one of Tolstoy's daughters accidentally blew out a candle by puffingly pronouncing before it the explosive word *pop*, meaning "Orthodox priest."[3]

The emotional impression left on Leskov by his first meeting with Tolstoy was overwhelming. A long unsatisfied need to give love, admiration, and devotion had found a worthy object. Since child-

515

hood, Leskov had borne within him a deep craving for something his father had never given, or had given insufficiently: not only love and attention, but instruction, guidance, and the image of what a good man should be. Except for his distant glories as the incorruptible detective, Leskov's real father had failed him on these counts. Withdrawn and depressed, he had presented an image of defeat and despair; and then he had died, just when his family needed him most. But his son's emotional yearning lived on and sought substitutes. There had been a long series of father-surrogates (or older brothers); yet one after the other they had failed Leskov as his father failed him, the relationship ending in disillusionment or death or both.

The first father-substitute was Uncle Alexander Scott. Scott provided Leskov with a potent image of male uprightness: rigor, self-discipline, sturdy insistence on his own rights and dignity, and, in his dealings with peasants, a delicacy and humanity that contrasted with the common practice of Russian serf-owners. It was also an image of religious differentness: no priests or icons or incense, but simple private devotions, hymns, Bible readings, and an effort to make religion part of everyday life. There had later been some friction with Scott in the days of Leskov's employment in Scott's firm and a good deal of resentment about its termination. But after Scott's death his spirit remained alive in Leskov, undergoing frequent literary reincarnations. He was the primary exemplar of practical, Protestant virtue.

Then came Opanas Markovich, the gentle and cultivated Ukrainian-in-Oryol, who had fed Leskov's hungry mind as neither family nor school had fed it. But contact with Markovich had been lost after Leskov's move to Kiev in 1849. In the Kiev days the role was filled mainly by Stepan Gromeka, the fellow official who helped promote Leskov's emancipation from the civil service and his initiation as a writer. But Gromeka had ultimately betrayed the ideals he preached to Leskov. From the independent businessman and liberal free-lance journalist, he was metamorphosed into a zealous policeman and religious persecutor. Thus he came to represent for Leskov the frailty of human idealism.

After Gromeka had come the "enigmatic" Artur Benni, chronologically younger than Leskov, yet a radiant image of culture and idealism. But the idealism had been frustrated by impracticality and bad luck, and Benni's untimely death at Mentana had symbolized the fruitlessness of his disjointed life. Then Leskov's favorite editor, Semyon Dudyshkin, the man who had perceived his talent when others denied it, who had counseled and encouraged and inspired him, died suddenly and prematurely, in 1866. No later editor ever took his place in Leskov's heart.

After Dudyshkin came Pyotr Shchebalsky, the closest intellectual friend of the Katkov period (Katkov was too overbearing to be a satisfactory father-substitute). But in later years Shchebalsky, like Gromeka, had gravitated to the right as Leskov moved left. He had worked his way far up the bureaucratic ladder, even serving at one time as police chief of Moscow—a curious post for a literary critic. He and Leskov drifted apart, and they had lost contact long before Shchebalsky's death in 1886. For a brief period the mantle fell on Ivan Aksakov. But Aksakov tended to patronize Leskov, and he and Leskov were in disagreement on many fundamental questions, especially the Orthodox church. Contact between them had ceased three years before Aksakov died.

The closest spiritual ally of the post-1875 period was Filipp Ternovsky, fellow lover of church history and fellow victim of Pobedonostsev. But Ternovsky too had died prematurely, in 1884, though with his integrity intact. After Ternovsky's death Leskov's need for a father-surrogate was left unfilled until the meeting with Tolstoy.

In Tolstoy, Leskov had found the most satisfactory of all his substitute fathers or mentors by correspondence (after the 1860s every one of Leskov's kindred spirits lived somewhere else; none was a daily presence in Petersburg). Tolstoy was satisfactory, that is, as an image of power and virtue: true emotional closeness he did not offer. Certainly Tolstoy was an imposing model, a veritable giant—as an artist, as a thinker, as a moralist. He seemed to be power itself, a bottomless reservoir of creativity and courage.

He challenged everything and everybody. History, government, philosophy, law, medicine, pedagogy, Biblical exegesis, every Christian thinker before himself, including Saint Paul—all were weighed in Tolstoy's balance and contemptuously swept aside so that he, unhampered and alone, could confront the ultimate questions: what does it all mean, why am I here, what should we do? Confront them he did, and along with them the psychological realities of his own nature in a manner that Leskov could with justice call "sincere to the point of sanctity."[4] Here was a man of godlike dimensions. As a living icon for Leskov to worship from afar, Tolstoy was perfect.

Leskov's "conversion" was immediate and total. Only a few months after the meeting he wrote to Chertkov a pledge of allegiance: "About L[ev] N[ikolaevich] everything is dear to me and everything is ineffably interesting. I am always in agreement with him, and there is no one on earth who could be dearer to me than he. I am never bothered by what I cannot share with him; dear to me is the overall, so to speak, the governing formation of his soul and the fearful penetration of his mind. Where he has weaknesses—there I see his human imperfection, and I am amazed how rarely he is mistaken, and then not in the main thing, but in practical applications, which are always transitory and dependent on contingencies."[5]

Leskov's admiration for Tolstoy did not arise from nothing in a Moscow living room in 1887. For decades he had regarded with awe the gargantuan artist who had given the nineteenth-century novel a depth and grandeur matched only by the great epics. In the 1860s, when Leskov was a struggling journalist, Tolstoy must have seemed to loom impossibly far above him. A count who dwelt on a lofty Olympus, removed from the squabbles of literary Petersburg, he had dispensed to the world one of the most magnificent works of literary art it possesses, *War and Peace*. Leskov had recognized at once the stature of this book and of the man who wrote it, at a time when many Russians, including most of his literary colleagues, were trying to cut the giant down to their own petty size or to enlist him in their political factions. Leskov wrote in 1869, after the appearance of the fifth volume of the first, six-volume edition of *War and Peace*, "Before I. S. Turgenev, as before all of us during the past year there has grown and risen to a height we have hitherto not known the author of 'Childhood and Boyhood,' and in his most recent work, which has brought him glory, in *War and Peace*, he has shown us not only a gigantic talent, mind, and spirit, but also (which in our enlightened age is much rarer) a big character, worthy of admiration."[6] And in another, largely expository, article Leskov gives *War and Peace* almost unstinted praise. Expressing regret only about some clumsiness of style, he extols the vividness of its characters and scenes, its subtlety and psychological rightness. Because of the depth and power of his vision, Leskov maintains, Tolstoy should be called not a "realist" —the word for Leskov evidently had some of the dunghill connotations "naturalism" bore later—but a "spiritualist."[7] For all its concreteness, Leskov insisted, *War and Peace* is a deeply spiritual book.

Leskov wrote little that could be called literary criticism after 1870, but he followed Tolstoy's output with undiminished admiration. He was so delighted by *Anna Karenina* that he poured out his enthusiasm to Dostoevsky, of all people, with whom he had been at swords' points ever since their squabble over "The Sealed Angel" in 1873.

Impressed by Dostoevsky's article on *Anna Karenina* (included in his *Diary of a Writer*[8]), Leskov admiringly wrote its author: "What you said about the 'scoundrel Stiva' and the 'pure in heart Lyovin' is so fine—so pure, noble, intelligent, and perspicacious that I cannot resist conveying to you my warm thanks and heartfelt greetings. Your spirit is splendid—otherwise it could not have understood things *so* well. It is the analysis of an intelligent soul, and not of the head."[9]

The unforgiving Dostoevsky did not deign to reply to this eulogy,[10] but Leskov's letter shows that his response to *Anna Karenina*, as it had been to *War and Peace*, was more than aesthetic pleasure. It was a spiritual experience of the deepest kind.

By 1887 Leskov perceived Tolstoy not merely as a literary artist far greater than he could ever be, but as a transcendent religious thinker, a teacher whose lessons fit Leskov's soul exactly. Tolstoy's celebrated "crisis" of 1878-1880 and the outpouring of treatises and tracts that followed it showed that he had leaped to a philosophical position close to that which Leskov had occupied ever since his much less dramatic, and less well-advertised, "crisis" of 1875. But on Tolstoy's map the positions were drawn with a surer hand and on a scale Leskov never attempted. (For one thing, Leskov was obliged by economic necessity to publish in the censored press, while Tolstoy could afford to write for unremunerated clandestine distribution.)

Tolstoy repudiated the Orthodox church and with it all churches claiming that their "sacraments" were an indispensable means of "salvation"; so did Leskov. Tolstoy sought a Christianity freed of rituals and magic, a religion that would induce people to lead better lives here on earth; so did Leskov. Tolstoy regarded with scorn and ridicule the churches' claims to exact knowledge of such things as the structure of the Godhead, the geography of heaven and hell, and the nature of the afterlife; so did Leskov. In short, as Leskov liked to put it, he had "coincided" with Tolstoy, not been overpowered by him. "I said the same thing *before* he did, but not eloquently, not with assurance, but timidly and haltingly."[11]

In an interview held some years after Leskov's death, Tolstoy was generous enough to acknowledge that Leskov had anticipated many of his ideas, even crediting him with one "Tolstoyan" attitude he had never really shared, a totally negative view of economic progress and political change: "He [Leskov] in the sixties was the first idealist of a Christian type and the first writer who in his *No Way Out* showed the insufficiency of material progress and the danger for freedom and ideals from depraved people. Even then he had turned away from materialistic doctrines concerning the benefits of political progress if people remain wicked and vicious [. . .] Leskov was my follower, but not out of imitation. He had long been going in the direction I am now moving. We met, and I am touched by his agreement with all my views."[12]

The route by which Leskov came to this agreement was different from Tolstoy's. Though he ended in an attitude of "protest" against the "apostolic" Christian churches, Tolstoy was never much interested in Protestantism. It would never have occurred to Tolstoy to eulogize Luther as Leskov did: "a bold fighter for freedom of conscience against the yoke of papal tyranny."[13] Through Tolstoy's glass the Protestant churches looked almost as bad as the Orthodox or Catholic: their ministers crowned kings, blessed wars, administered oaths, accompanied criminals to the scaffold—in short, shared in and sanctioned the official violence and crime of their societies. When he later found that there were some Protestants, such as the Quakers, who did not do these things, Tolstoy applauded them, but he was not seriously influenced by them.

Furthermore, Tolstoy could never be a follower of anyone. He soon decided that the amassed heritage of Christian thought was rubbish, to be swept away. Not even the New Testament could be accepted as it stood. Saint Paul in particular had blunted the edge of Jesus's teaching, especially by his "divine right" sanction of governmental authority. And the Gospels had been mistranslated and even miswritten, since they contained nonsense about the divinity of Jesus and the thaumaturgic tricks he allegedly performed. Tolstoy was therefore obliged to provide a corrected version. That done, he proceeded stone by stone to construct the edifice of his new and rationalized Christianity: its theology (*A Critique of Dogmatic Theology* and *What I Believe*), sociology (*What Then Must We Do?*), political science (*Christianity and Patriotism*), ethics (*The Kingdom of God Is within You*), aesthetics (*What Is Art?*). It was all done with enormous self-assurance, the doubts and contradictions hidden as deep inside as he could bury them.

Leskov's modus operandi was different. Where Tolstoy loved to deal in abstractions and absolutes, Leskov's mind clung to the specific and concrete. His religious judgments were essentially of people, or social units, not theologies; he felt for the spirit, the tone of human relationships. His earliest Protestant impressions came from the "real presence" of his Scott relatives: there in the heart of Orthodox Russia were beloved people who possessed no icons, burned no candles, and sprinkled no holy water, but who tried to make Christianity manifest in their daily lives. In institutions and even in books Leskov looked for the specific, the practical, the real; he had a horror of abstract schemata. He always wanted to know not how the machine looked in the diagram, but how it actually worked.

Tolstoy attacked the Orthodox church from the standpoint of moral absolutes arrived at not by observation of its actual operations—he did very little of that—but by rational deductions from what he considered unassailable premises. He, Tolstoy, knew what Jesus meant (or perhaps what he should have meant); the church had flagitiously distorted that message; Tolstoy therefore had no further use for it. He never paid much attention to the social personality of the church in Russia, the priests and deacons and bishops and ober-procurators. He was no connoisseur of icon-painting or church music. It was precisely in his sensitivity to these things that Leskov excelled. For Tolstoy church history was as meaningless as history *tout court*: another sorry record of man's folly and crime. Once that fact was established, why catalogue the details? Tolstoy seemed to have none of the hoarder's instinct, the loving accumulation of things or facts; on the contrary, he was a great rejector, a thrower-away.

Leskov's mind was relativistic and pragmatic. Where Tolstoy insisted on all or nothing, Leskov generally preferred to settle for *something*. If existing institutions could be put to good ends, use them. For a long time he applied this doctrine to the Orthodox church itself, hoping that it could become a moral force for good. Similarly, as long as Alexander II reigned, Leskov continued to regard the Russian state as a potential force for social improvements. It was only after he felt the inexorably conservative hand of Pobedonostsev gripping both church and state that he finally renounced them both. The mood of growing social and moral anger affecting Leskov after the accession of Alexander III made it possible for him to accept the sweeping negativism of Tolstoy. In that era of stagnation and repression Tolstoy's was the loudest solo "No!" being uttered, at least from a religious standpoint; and Leskov was glad to join the chorus.

Leskov's enrollment in this chorus was accomplished gradually, between 1883 and 1887. First, he had to discover what Tolstoyanism was: Tolstoy's religious writings could be published in Russia only in heavily bowdlerized versions. The full texts circulated in underground editions, hand-copied or hectographed. These were expensive and not easy to obtain. Leskov refers to the problem in a sly "advertisement" of these illegal editions which he published in 1884. Handwritten copies of Tolstoy's *Confession* and *Gospel*, he reports, were then selling for 25 rubles in Petersburg.[14] It therefore took some time before Leskov first accumulated the basic Tolstoyan "scriptures" and then studied them and assimilated their ideas.

Leskov's first public response to Tolstoyanism as a religious system was ambiguous: a "negation of a negation," and not wholly his own. Nevertheless, it was strongly pro-Tolstoy. In 1883, with the author's permission, he rewrote a long article by his friend Filipp Ternovsky of Kiev and then published it under his own name as two separate newspaper articles.[15] The original article was an attack by Ternovsky, from what he considered a Christian point of view, on a nominally Orthodox, but in Ternovsky's opinion very un-Christian, book by Konstantin Leontiev called *Our New Christians*. Leontiev's book in turn was an attack on the Christian teachings of both Dostoevsky and Tolstoy. In attacking Leontiev, Ternovsky was perforce defending the two great novelists; and since he rewrote the article and signed it, these opinions must be regarded as equally Leskov's.

Leontiev had first criticized Dostoevsky for holding out, in his celebrated "Pushkin speech," the hope of an ultimate union of nations, inspired by Russian "pan-humanism," in a spirit of Christian love and harmony. For Leontiev this was sentimental nonsense, a misguided effort to evade hard truths about the basic sinfulness of the world, the necessity of suffering, and the grim inexorability of the Last Judgment. Christ, Leontiev asserted, never promised a universal brotherhood to be realized in this world. Leskov and Ternovsky agree that *Russia* will not succeed (as Dostoevsky had dreamed) in showing Europe the way out of its spiritual anguish; but they argue that Dostoevsky's ideal of universal love is more authentically Christian than Leontiev's "gnashing of teeth."

Though he made an effort to pay him his due, Leskov had far too much "residue in his liver" from his personal contacts to regard Dostoevsky as a spiritual beacon. He therefore turns with pleasure to the other "heresiarch," who, in his view, is better informed than Dostoevsky about religious questions. This, of course, is Tolstoy. But before leaving Dostoevsky, Leskov could not resist inserting the following footnote, obviously his and not Ternovsky's, in which he contrives to batter one of his "clients" with the other:

The writer of these lines knew F. M. Dostoevsky personally and many times had occasion to conclude that that very gifted man, who passionately loved to dwell on questions of religion, to a considerable extent lacked adequate knowledge of religious literature, with which he began his acquaintance only rather late in life; and because of the passionate intensity of his sympathies he could not find in himself the tranquillity to study it attentively and soberly. Quite different in this respect is the devoutly inclined and philosophically free mind of Count L. N. Tolstoy, in whose works, both those published and still more those that have not been published but are known only in manuscript, one can see both extensive and thorough reading and deep thoughtfulness.[16]

Ternovsky and Leskov rise to the defense of Tolstoy's story "What Men Live By," which Leontiev had attacked for favoring the lower classes at the expense of the upper and for stressing divine love rather than punishment. Christianity, Leskov and Ternovsky insist, is preeminently a "religion of love." The real "heresiarch," therefore, is neither Dostoevsky nor Tolstoy, but Leontiev himself, the proponent of a "religion of fear" he mistakenly identifies with Christianity.[17]

As early as 1883, then, Leskov had regarded Tolstoy as a serious, well-informed, and responsible religious thinker, deserving of great respect, though not yet of the extravagant veneration lavished on him after 1887. Leskov still had doubts and hesitations.

Not long after this joint public defense of Tolstoy against Leontiev, Leskov commented privately on Tolstoy's well-publicized refusal of jury service in September 1883. These remarks, though strongly anti-Orthodox, show that Leskov was not yet a full-fledged Tolstoyan. Without any firsthand knowledge of Tolstoy's motives, Leskov argued that his refusal could not have been based on the grounds that Christians are forbidden to "judge" (since they are not). Tolstoy refused because Christians are forbidden to "swear by God." Tolstoy had refused to "swallow" the frightful words of the required oath, as some "non-juring" Russians did.[18] Actually Tolstoy could have refused for either of these reasons, since he abhorred both swearing and judging; or more profoundly, because he considered all law courts evil, as ultimately based on violence. Leskov had evidently not yet assimilated this central tenet of Tolstoy's teaching.

But Leskov looked not only for Tolstoy's manifest reasons for refusing jury service; he also sought the unconscious motives. With shrewd intuition he discerned in Tolstoy a craving for martyrdom, a "thirst to suffer," which he identified as a typical feature of the Russian peasant mentality. "Do you know what Tolstoy really wants!

He's gone wholly peasant and 'thirsts to suffer.' Believe me, it's true!"[19] Leskov's correspondent apparently raised some objections to this interpretation, and Leskov's reply shows that while he may have had a few reservations about Tolstoy's "eccentricities," he basically considered him a close Christian consociate:

> About Lev N. Tolstoy I am precisely of the same opinion as you, but that does not exclude the validity of my hypothesis concerning his "wish" to suffer. He will be glad if they try him for heresy; but as you correctly think, it won't happen. His desire to suffer is directly expressed at the end of the preface to his Gospel. Undoubtedly he walks unsteadily [*vixljaetsja*], but he sees a true point: Christianity is a *vital* teaching, and not an abstraction, and it has been spoiled by being made an abstraction. "All faiths are right till the priests them do blight." We have Byzantinism, not Christianity; and Tolstoy is fighting that with dignity, seeking to point out in the Gospel not so much the "road to heaven" as the "meaning of life" [. . .] The old Christianity evidently has simply outlived itself and can no longer do anything for the "meaning of life." There is no use fuming against ecclesiasticism, but also no use bothering about it. Its time has passed and will never return, while the aims of Christianity are *eternal*. Tolstoy's actions are "eccentric," but in the peasant spirit.[20]

During the next two years, 1884 and 1885, Leskov's interest in Tolstoy remained intense, though its literary echoes were temporarily less frequent. In 1884 he apparently wrote a substantial defense of Tolstoy against some "very stupid book," but the piece was rejected by Suvorin—presumably as too demonstratively partisan—and has been lost. In his accompanying letter to Suvorin, Leskov says of Tolstoy: "I love and respect that writer and follow his work passionately."[21]

In the same year Leskov's article on Pashkov and the Shtundists[22] evoked a protest by Chertkov, which in turn led to the beginning of Leskov's stormy relationship with that stiff-necked apostle.[23] Chertkov helped Leskov obtain authentic texts of Tolstoy's unpublished writings and may also have offered his own interpretations of these illicit scriptures. Leskov was doubtless flattered when Chertkov, as head of the Tolstoyan publishing house "The Intermediary," asked permission to bring out a mass edition of his fable "Christ Visits a Muzhik." He readily gave his assent and asked no remuneration.[24] He and Chertkov subsequently quarreled, however; among other things Leskov could not stand Chertkov's "doctrinaire mind and professorial tone."[25] Eventually Leskov would find it necessary to "renounce and denounce" the whole array of Tolstoyan saints; only the master himself survived.

The year 1885 passed with only three brief, unsigned newspaper articles dealing with Tolstoyan questions,[26] but 1886 marks the high point of Leskov's confrontation with Tolstoyanism, in the sense of debate and independent criticism on major points of doctrine. After 1887 his attitude shifted to allegiance and discipleship; criticism thereafter becomes muffled and minor, or is turned against fellow disciples only.

Early in March 1886, Leskov received from Moscow some new unpublished works by Tolstoy and sat up until five A.M. reading them. It was then that the exclamation burst from him about Tolstoy's sincerity "to the point of sanctity." To the same letter he added a postscript crediting Tolstoy with bringing about a moral vivification of Russian literature: "Have you noticed that Lev Tolstoy even in his present mood is *enlivening* literature? He stirs the conscience, awakens thought, transforms attitudes towards persons and reputations."[27]

In April Leskov again took up arms in defense of Tolstoy's folk-style fables. He gleefully pointed out that the plots of many of them, charged by Orthodox-minded critics with heresy, had been derived from an ecclesiastical source, the Byzantine "Prolog."[28] By way of illustrating what a "Prolog" story is, Leskov relates three of them.

The first, like Tolstoy's "Three Hermits," makes the subversive point that ecclesiastical rank on earth may not be a measure of a man's standing in the eyes of God: the prayers of a poor old woodcutter, the "best supplicator," prove more efficacious in bringing rain than those of a bishop and all his retinue. The second story argues that splendid choral displays in churches and exact performances of rituals have less spiritual value than the silent prayers of a hermit, especially one who lives by his own toil. And the third story underscores this point, reiterating Leskov's case against religious parasitism. Even two self-supporting eremites hear a voice informing them that a certain poor shepherd is spiritually more advanced than they. Whereas they maintain only themselves, he gives a third of his income to the poor, a third to wayfarers, and keeps only a third for his own and his wife's expenses. In short, Leskov takes satisfaction in citing ancient *Orthodox* authorities in support of his favorite argument that practical good works are morally worth more than monastic asceticism and ecclesiastical abracadabra.[29]

From the point of view of his religious thought, Leskov's most important works of 1886 are three other articles: "On the Kitchen Muzhik, Etc.," published in June; and two published in November, the first written the previous spring, "A Ghostly Witness for Women" and "About Goads: An Appeal to the Sons of Resistance."[30]

In the vividly written "Kitchen Muzhik" Leskov uses the live Tolstoy ("the greatest contemporary literary talent in the whole world"; 11:138) to batter the dead Dostoevsky. According to Leskov, in his late, successful years Dostoevsky liked to strike an exalted pose as the nation's chief prophet and guide, a stance Leskov regarded with marked skepticism. Filled with his faith in the messianic mission of the Russian people, Dostoevsky advised some cosmopolite Petersburg ladies to "study" at the feet of their "kitchen muzhik" (a domestic servant of peasant origin). The ladies laughingly wondered what subjects such an instructor could teach: history? geography? To this Dostoevsky sullenly replied, "Everything."[31]

For ten years thereafter the phrase "kitchen muzhik" was bandied about Petersburg salons; but light on the problem was cast only by Tolstoy's great story "The Death of Ivan Ilyich." In that story the peasant Gerasim has a valid and important lesson for his educated master (how to face death with dignity) and another one for his master's relations (how to bring aid and comfort to a dying man). Both these things, Leskov concurs, the Russian peasants do well and the educated classes badly; the latter would therefore be well advised to "study" with such as Gerasim. But it is doubtful whether this is precisely what Dostoevsky meant by "everything."

In any case, Leskov continues, Russians have three great teachers to choose from. They are Dostoevsky, who offers Russian nationalism and Orthodoxy; Turgenev, representing secular humanism; and Tolstoy, "the moralist and practical Christian." Leskov's vote is not hard to guess. His literary admiration for Tolstoy already knew no bounds, and it was now infused with a veneration bordering on idolatry.

In the second of these 1886 articles, "A Ghostly Witness for Women," and in a letter concerning it, Leskov is still "unconverted" enough to voice some highly critical sentiments. The article deals mostly with a specific question, higher education for women; but it also touches upon the cornerstone of Tolstoyan ethics, the so-called "nonresistance to evil." As Leskov wrote to his editor:

The article consists of a long, thirty-page letter from Nikolai Pirogov with a foreword and afterword by me [. . .] The article is in the highest degree interesting in both a historical and philosophical sense, since it has a vital relation to the questions of women and of resistance to evil, which are being so foolishly mishandled [*jurodstvenno koverkaet*] by Tolstoy. Pirogov's views, of course, are the opposite of Tolstoy's; and they annihilate the latter by both the intelligence and the seriousness of Pirogov [. . .] The article will pass the censors, and I set great store by it. It is inspiring, serious and intelligent, and it is now apropos.[32]

The issue of higher education and responsible work for women is interesting, because it forced Leskov to confront the nihilistic and absolutist side of Tolstoy. The "pedagogic ravings" of Tolstoy,[33] who thought a simple religious education sufficient for women, affronted Leskov, and he triumphantly counters such nonsense with the unimpeachable authority of Pirogov. He insists that if women want to study and work, they should be encouraged to do so, and society will be the richer for their efforts.

Leskov did not then realize that the extremes of Tolstoy's views went beyond the conventional conservatism Leskov attributed to him—confining women to *Kinder* and *Küche*, if not *Kirche*. Tolstoy did not favor higher education even for men. What could education do but corrupt them morally, deracinate them from the soil, and transform them into committed servants—government officials, doctors, lawyers—of that civilization he viewed as God viewed Sodom and Gomorrah. Why contaminate women with the same poison? But Leskov had not yet perceived the extent of his master's maximalism, and he therefore treats the subject only as a feminist issue.

To "nonresistance" Leskov devoted a special article, "About Goads."[34] There he first makes the essential point, not to this day understood by many superficial commentators on Tolstoy, that the unfortunate phrase "nonresistance to evil" does not mean that a moral person should condone evil, accept it, or submit to it inertly. Evil *should* be resisted; the whole question is how, by what means. Where, then, does this misleading phrase come from? Leskov intimates that he is "not free" to discuss this question in print—an obvious hint at censorship difficulties. People as steeped in Scripture as Leskov knew that the phrase is derived from the Sermon on the Mount (Matthew 5:39), a passage better known for the image of turning the other cheek than for the absolute formula extracted by Tolstoy. In any case, Leskov understands that Tolstoy does advocate resisting evil, but by nonviolent means. (Tolstoy argued that the Greek word ἀντιστῆναι means specifically "resist by violence," not "resist in general.")

Psychologically speaking, Leskov continues, the only force capable of overcoming evil is love, that "perfect love" of which Saint Paul said that it "seeketh nothing for itself." Therefore the practitioner of non-violent resistance must be sure that he is acting in the spirit of love: he must cleanse himself before he seeks to cleanse others.

Leskov thus seems ready to accept the validity of Tolstoy's doctrine of nonviolent resistance, at least as an ideal strategy in the relations between individuals. He has, however, many reservations about its universal applicability. The objections are familiar, but interesting as illustrating Leskov's relativistic cast of mind. Wars are evil, but some wars have good results: for instance, the American Civil War led to the emancipation of the slaves. Tolstoy believes that if one of two warring armies refuses to fight, the other will be morally over-whelmed, and men can then settle their differences in a spirit of frater-nal love instead of hatred and murder. But Leskov knows too many examples of soldiers beating and killing nonresisting women and chil-dren. Why were these soldiers not morally transformed by their vic-tims' nonviolence? What is a man to do if his sister, wife, or mother is being raped before his eyes? Some years earlier two little girls had been raped in the Kiev Botanical Garden by convicts assigned to work there. Leskov argues that if a bystander had struck one of these rapists on the head with an iron bar, he would have committed no crime.

It was not in Leskov's antitheoretical style even to try to raise such examples to a higher level of generalization, to formulate principles that would make the necessary allowances for "acceptable" violence. In Isaiah Berlin's unforgettable image, Leskov is the perfect "fox," who "knows many things," while Tolstoy (qua prophet and moralist) is the "hedgehog," who "knows one big thing." Of course, as Berlin bril-liantly demonstrates, Tolstoy's hedgehog was really a mask worn by an imperfectly suppressed fox.

Leskov's allegiance to Tolstoyanism found many different forms of expression, artistic and otherwise. As an artist, he tried to harness his muse to the Tolstoyan plow. The results of these efforts will be chron-icled in subsequent chapters. Here it remains only to sketch the intel-lectual and emotional consequences of the conversion.

As was noted earlier, once Leskov joined the Tolstoyan "church," he to a certain extent lost his freedom of action. He was no longer an outsider, even a sympathetic one, who could judge and compare freely, accept what he liked and reject what he didn't. Even though there was no formal membership, Leskov nevertheless acquired a certain insider's feeling of responsible belonging. In consequence, the Tolstoyan period is intellectually, though not artistically, the most unproductive in Leskov's life. He no longer tries to pursue the "big questions" himself, but is content to incorporate the ready-made answers supplied from headquarters at Yasnaya Polyana. His nonfictional articles in defense of Tolstoy are mostly trivial, dealing with questions like the thickness of the cream in Tolstoy's coffee.[35] The humility is stultifying, though touchingly expressed in repeated variants of the "torch" and "rushlight" image:

> I have said and say that I long sought what he seeks, but did not find it, because my light is weak. Then when I saw that he had found something that satisfied me, I felt that I no longer needed my insignificant light, and I am following him and I seek nothing of my own but see everything in the light of his enormous torch.[36]

> About Lev Nikolaevich Tolstoy we should use language different from that we have hitherto used about him. We don't want to call him by his real name, but he may be boldly called a sage [*mudrec*]. Place him side by side with Epictetus and Socrates. That's where his place is. But we compose verses about him à la Velichko and write feature articles. What a petty society! After him it will be a desert. Then everyone will feel it. People say that I imitate him. Not in the least! When Tolstoy was writing *Anna Karenina*, I was already close to what I am saying now. I was already digging in that pile where Lev Nikolaevich later began to dig. But his light is brighter, and I followed him with my rushlight. He has an enormous torch, and I a flickering little rushlight. I am hurrying after him! Hurrying![37]

And to Tolstoy himself the self-abasement would be almost sickening if it were not so obviously sincere:

> What value can my opinions have before your intellect? Only the value of an understanding reader. If that is so, then the truth is that I do have a capacity for understanding, and I love the same thing you love and I believe what you believe; and it so happened by itself and so it continues. But I always take my fire from you to light my splinter-lamp.[38]

> Since my early years of life I have had a penchant for questions of faith and began writing about religious people when it was considered indecent and impossible (*Cathedral Folk, The Sealed*

Angel, "The Monognome," *The Little Things in a Bishop's Life*, etc.), but I kept getting confused and was content to "rake away the rubbish from the sanctuary," but I did not know how to enter the sanctuary [. . .] Although there were glimmerings in my mind of the same things I discovered in you, in me it was all chaos, murky and unclear, and I had no confidence; but when I heard your interpretations, logical and powerful, I grasped everything as if I had remembered it, and I no longer needed anything of my own, and I began to live in the light I saw in you and which I liked better because it was incomparably stronger and brighter than that in which I had been digging on my own. Since then you have had a significance for me that cannot fade, for I hope to pass with it into another existence, and therefore there is no one who could be as dear and memorable to me as you.[39]

Though the tone of these utterances may jar the ear, Leskov's image is basically apt. The light of Tolstoy's "great torch" did clarify and confirm Leskov's ideas, most of which he had already worked out for himself many years before.

In theology proper Tolstoy was more radical than Leskov, but it is hard to set down Leskov's credo—he could not spell it out in legal print, and he did not write underground treatises. Leskov seems to have retained a residual belief in the divinity of Jesus and in personal immortality not shared by Tolstoy. In a scolding letter to Suvorin written early in 1887 Leskov asserts, for instance, that "the resurrection was necessary" and adds (inaccurately) "and Tolstoy does not deny it."[40] Much later he wrote to Mme Chertkova: "In my thoughts about the human soul and about God I have been strengthened in the direction I believed before, and Lev Nikolaevich Tolstoy has become still closer to me as a co-believer. I think and believe that 'I shall not all die' [a quotation from Pushkin's version of *Exegi monumentum*], but a certain spiritual essence will leave the body and will continue an 'everlasting life'; but in what form this will be—about this one cannot form a conception here [on earth], and later God knows when it will be clarified."[41]

In general, however, Leskov avoided theological questions, on the grounds that these were things man cannot know in this life and about which it is better not to speculate. Man can only sense that the Kingdom of God is within him. Leskov cites with approval Tolstoy's dictum that the dogmatic theology of the church is what Jesus meant by "blasphemy against the Holy Spirit."[42] Nevertheless, he begged Tolstoy to complete a "Catechism" that would capsulize the Tolstoyan doctrines (not theology) in an easily accessible form.[43]

Leskov eventually went along with most of the lesser points in Tolstoy's teachings, including vegetarianism and abstention from alcohol and tobacco. Like Tolstoy, he found it hardest to give up smoking, but had done so successfully even before his "conversion," more for reasons of health than religion. (If Leskov's dating can be credited, he stopped smoking in 1878, at the age of forty-seven, before Tolstoyanism existed.)[44] As for alcohol, he seems to have continued, like Saint Paul, to take a little wine for his stomach's sake, once asking Tolstoy's blessing for this practice.[45]

After he began having angina attacks, his doctor recommended a vegetarian diet, and Leskov began energetically preaching the spiritual benefits to be derived from meatless and bloodless Tolstoyan living. But he himself seems to have cheated a good deal on the recommended boycott of the butchers. In 1892 he confessed to the same doctor that he was eating meat once a week,[46] and after his death the secret leaked out from his household that to the end he had remained "especially fond of partridge."[47]

There were a number of issues on which Leskov differed not only from the practice of the Tolstoyans, but from the doctrines of Tolstoy. Out of loyalty he preferred not to air them publicly: "There is no reason to trot his [Tolstoy's] faults out into the street and trouble his old age. That is only 'making a noise,' not seeking the truth."[48] But in his letters and in recorded oral statements Leskov voiced objections and reservations concerning Tolstoy's ideas.

Leskov found it difficult to condone the moral compromises in Tolstoy's way of life at Yasnaya Polyana. Here was the austere prophet who repudiated private property, deplored the unnecessary consumption of the propertied classes, and had demonstratively renounced the copyright of his own writings, at least those written since his conversion. Yet he continued to live comfortably on his ancestral estate and even (indirectly) to enjoy the income collected by his wife from his earlier works. "Lev Nikolaevich [Leskov wrote to Chertkov], besides his great talent, may be credited with nobility of spirit and with a brilliant interpretation of Christianity. He has given mankind everlasting aid. But in his actual life there is an enormous mistake which forces itself on one's attention and *harms the cause*."[49]

Leskov had some inkling of how hard it was for Tolstoy to reconcile his new teachings with his old responsibilities to a recalcitrant wife and children. He proposed a compromise (though he hadn't the nerve to propose it directly to Tolstoy): Tolstoy should legally withdraw his own share from the estate and give *that* to the peasants, leaving the rest to his family to dispose of as they liked. When he spoke of this proposal to Lidia Veselitskaya, she unkindly asked him why he didn't set an example for Tolstoy by distributing some of *his* property. "But I haven't got anything," Leskov exclaimed. "Well now," she countered. "Everybody can find *something*. Remember the widow's mite." Leskov's explosively defensive reaction might have been predicted; he did not take her advice.[50]

Leskov never accepted all the extremes of Tolstoy's *Kulturnihilismus*, as Brigitte Macher aptly calls it. He had none of Tolstoy's antagonism to medicine, and he objected vehemently to Tolstoy's repudiation of science and learning. "Why does he attack learning? Do we have such a lot of it, and is it hindering anybody? Let them study! Why deny that?"[51]

And the fetishisms of "simplification," as practiced by the Tolstoyans, simply irritated Leskov: "Soap and combs and bathtubs and all that. You can't do without them, but he thinks they're unnecessary. He's a joker, that Lev Nikolaevich! Why on earth shouldn't a woman concern herself with her beauty and elegance? Why come visit me without galoshes and tramp mud all over my clean floor?"[52]

Leskov severely scolded Chertkov for insisting that his wife, though ill, breast-feed their child—a Tolstoyan fetish that long antedated Tolstoyanism: "I am sorry about her illnesses and infirmities and can in no way justify your insistence that she feed the child with her feeble breast. You write about 'harmony.' Can one woman not help another in the other's weakness? I do not understand you and do not approve of what you are doing with your wife and child."[53]

Leskov had deep reservations about the extremism of Tolstoy's sexual doctrines. "Though in all things I subordinate myself to the greatness of Lev Nikolaevich's mind [Leskov wrote to Veselitskaya], I cannot accept his view of the relations between the sexes. It is inconsistent with the demands of nature and the task of mankind—to perfect itself in a whole chain of generations obliged to appear according to the command 'Be fruitful and multiply.' "[54] On this sexual issue Leskov began what would have been his only public (though ambiguous) literary disagreement with a Tolstoyan doctrine. His story "Concerning 'The Kreutzer Sonata,' " however, remained unfinished—perhaps because he could not bring himself to oppose Tolstoy publicly. The completed portion of the story was published only after Leskov's death.[55]

Even on this question, however, Leskov avoided theorizing and tried to see the positive side of Tolstoy's extremism. "In 'The Kreutzer Sonata,' " he said, "the important thing is not at all the call for an ideal abstinence by people from carnal love, but how Tolstoy turns us away from the area where we debauch ourselves and women."[56]

The most revealing account of Leskov's "anti-Kreutzerism" is recorded by Lyubov Gurevich, his only woman editor—a glimpse past all the moralizing into the erotic depths of the Leskovian unconscious. She quotes the following oral tirade by Leskov:

> He [Tolstoy] wants what is higher than human nature, what is impossible, impossible because that is how we are made. I know it myself. All my life I have been a demon [*aggel*]. I have done things that no one knows about. And now I am old and sick, but still there are things seething in me such that I myself cannot say how and what. I have such dreams, terrible dreams which cannot be described in words. And who knows what that is and why and wherefore and whence? Should it be called sensuality? But what is sensuality? Who can say? And why do I have it? I need nothing, with my reason I want nothing, I seek peace for my soul; but something keeps tormenting me.[57]

For all his antagonism to the government of Alexander III, Leskov never followed Tolstoy to the limits of his Christian anarchism. He hated militarism and snorted as scornfully as Tolstoy at the jingoistic drum-beating that accompanied the Franco-Russian alliance of 1893.[58] But he continued to look back with nostalgia on the reformist regime of Alexander II as a time when the Russian state had seriously tried to use its power for good ends, something Tolstoy considered impossible by definition. Leskov just did not believe that all government is intrinsically evil.

Against the Tolstoyans, Leskov felt freer to vent his negative emotions. Valid as many of these criticisms were, it sometimes seems that Leskov was using the Tolstoyans as scapegoats, discharging on them some of the frustration and constriction he felt within Tolstoyan doctrine. His irritation gave him a prophetic understanding of how little would be left of the Tolstoyan "church" when the founder was gone. The self-important posturing of the Tolstoyans reminded Leskov of the antics of the nihilists he had ridiculed long before in *No Way Out*; and the Tolstoyan "communes" seemed to him like rural replicas of Sleptsov's ill-starred "Domus Concordiae." Such doings were nothing but games, intellectuals playing "peasant," and they would end in ignominious failure. "What you write about the 'Tolstoyans' is very interesting," Leskov wrote to Veselitskaya in 1894. "I too do not let them out of my sight, and I think that it's time to take them up seriously; but one must be sure to distinguish them absolutely from the man who gave them their name or their label [. . .] I don't believe in Biryukov's ability to plow. If he plows, I pity his poor horse."[59] The principal result of Leskov's observations of the Tolstoyans was "A Winter's Day," and it did not endear him to their hearts.

Beneath the ideas lay Leskov's emotional need, the old yearning for a strong and righteous father who would give him the answers and on whom he could lay his burdens. This need became more intense in the last years. Leskov was more and more lonely—"very much alone," as he wrote to Tolstoy.[60] His son Andrei had grown up and married. His daughter Vera, with whom he had never been close, lived far away in the Ukraine, also married. He was estranged from most of his other relatives. Friends one after the other had been cast aside; many had died. For all his advertisements of orphan-love, his stepdaughter Varya cannot have been a rewarding companion.

And then in 1889, supposedly at the news of the "arrest" of the sixth volume of his collected works, received while he was standing on the steps of Suvorin's publishing house, came illness, angina pectoris or "chest toad," in the vivid Russian phrase. For the rest of his life Leskov suffered frequent, acutely painful seizures; and he knew that any one of them might mean the end. Death became a constant presence. Feeling weak and alone, he turned for aid to Tolstoy: "Many people do it [die] with dignity," he wrote Tolstoy in 1893, "but fear can disfigure and spoil it [. . .] If you can, say something to me about it, more than it [death] has 'gentle eyes.' Your words help me. I am ashamed to importune you, but I am weak, and I seek the support of a man stronger than I."[61]

Support, approval, recognition, love: the need is powerful, and the cry for it touching: "Today [the Tolstoyans] Vanya Gorbunov and Sytin visited me and said that you [Tolstoy] knew about my illness and even wanted to come [to Petersburg] to see me. This agitated and touched me terribly, and I sweetly and joyfully wept. I do not want to speak to you about my feelings toward you. You are a penetrating person, and there is no need to utter to you what loses its essence in verbal articulation and takes on something extraneous. You know what good you have done me."[62] In his moral strength Tolstoy was a model. He too had confessed to a stormy and sinful past; but he had grappled with his unregenerate self and wrought a metamorphosis:

> To remake oneself altogether may be impossible, but undoubtedly intentions engender decisions, decisions efforts, and efforts habits, and there is formed what is called "behavior." Just remember what L[ev] N[ikolaevich] was like and compare what he is now. It was all done by efforts to control himself and not without backslidings and "returns to his vomit" [. . .] But if he hadn't tried to "correct" himself, what would he be like with that passionate and wrathful face? But he remade himself, and of course he became dearer to everyone and pleasanter to himself.[63]

In her perception of Leskov's need for a moral model, a person with passions like his who had mastered them by persistent effort of mind and spirit, once again the most illuminating memoirist is Lyubov Gurevich:

> Sometimes—and perhaps more often towards his old age—he [Leskov] was *frightened* by himself. He felt like seizing hold of someone who in many things, though not in such frightening ones, had surmounted himself or was at least on the way to doing so, was striving to do so with hope of success and faith in its possibility. That is the reason for his attraction to Tolstoy, which was also not complete, but uneven, like everything in him, interrupted both by criticism of "Tolstoyanism" and by an organic disinclination for any form of asceticism, except perhaps a fanatic and frenzied one, a frenzy in which he could find an outlet for his insupportable passions.[64]

For the sake of perspective it may be interesting to view the Tolstoy-Leskov relationship through the eyes of the other partner. Leskov never meant to Tolstoy anything like what Tolstoy meant to Leskov. On the literary level, Tolstoy probably read some Leskov in the years before their spiritual alliance; but if he did, it left no trace in his letters or diaries. The first mention of Leskov in Tolstoy's papers occurs in the 1880s, in connection with the Leskov fables being reprinted by the "Intermediary" firm. After their meeting in 1887, and especially after the publication in 1889-90 of Leskov's collected works, which were sent to Tolstoy, Tolstoy read a great deal of Leskov. Some of his judgments of individual works have been or will be considered in connection with the particular text. In general, however, Tolstoy's literary assessments of Leskov, though very erratic, boil down to two basic points. First, the closer a work adheres to Tolstoy's moral doctrines, the better marks he gives it. Second, even if a story passed the moral test, Tolstoy was frequently put off by what he considered Leskov's florid mannerisms, his verbal trickery and stylistic *embarras de richesses*. For Tolstoy "simplicity" was an absolute standard of aesthetic excellence, and Leskov seldom measured up to it.

On the personal level, Tolstoy's feelings about Leskov were as ambivalent as his literary judgments. After the charm and flattery of the original meeting had worn off, he sometimes found Leskov's adulation a bit sticky: "Received letters, an unpleasantly ingratiating one from Leskov, and from Ge," Tolstoy wrote in his diary on November 12, 1890.[65] Perhaps he also found the emotional dependence tiring.

Again the most perceptive observations were made by Lyubov Gurevich. She visited Tolstoy in the summer of 1892 and spoke of Leskov: "I have one recollection which it is hard to convey in words, because the essence of it lay in what was left unsaid and in Tolstoy's intonation. I was talking with him about various people as we walked through the apple orchard, and when we touched on N[ikolai] S[emyonovich], Tolstoy said, 'Yes, he sometimes writes to me. Only sometimes there's such a tone . . . It's too . . . Sometimes unpleasant. Well, of course you probably understand yourself.' "[66]

Nevertheless, not all was saccharinity in Leskov's behavior toward Tolstoy. In 1892 he resolutely stood up to Tolstoy on behalf of his friend, the British journalist E. J. Dillon, who, he felt, had been unjustly treated by Tolstoy. In Dillon's cause Leskov pursued Tolstoy relentlessly, smoking him out of his evasions and even his efforts to avoid controversy with his wife. Eventually Leskov extracted from Tolstoy an apology to Dillon. This time there were tears on both sides. Gurevich testifies that Tolstoy wept at Leskov's exposure of his moral tergiversation.[67] And when Tolstoy wrote Leskov that he had been convinced by the latter's arguments and had actually written an apology to Dillon, Leskov's floodgates were opened: "I was frightfully struck how powerfully he struggled with himself and nevertheless found the strength to say to me that I alone was 'right' and that he had been 'wrong' and that I had 'conquered' him. I sobbed like a child reading these lines."[68]

Thus the real Tolstoy and the idol Leskov worshipped may not have been quite identical; nor did the idol adequately reciprocate, or even respond to, its votary's veneration. But in the life of Leskov the important thing is the veneration itself: the extraordinary adoration bestowed by one restless and willful seeker on another greater than he.

35

He Spake in Parables

In a letter written in 1879 Leskov had pronounced a judgment concerning the nature of his talent and at the same time uttered a prophecy and also a prayer concerning the direction he hoped it would take in the future. Speaking of *The Little Things in a Bishop's Life*, he wrote, "It is not a sermon, of which I am incapable, and which I hope, by the grace of God, never to undertake."[1] Leskov assigned himself only the satirist's job of "clearing away the manure piled up by the doors of the temple"; and in subsequent years he made frequent and effective use of the literary pitchfork. But the impulse to preach, positively as well as negatively, already apparent in "The Unbaptized Priest" and inherently present much earlier, began to assert itself. Especially after his "conversion" to Tolstoyanism, the urge to don the preacher's robes was irresistible.

In contrast to muckraking, the task of broadcasting the Tolstoyan message in positive literary form confronted Leskov with new problems. Foremost among these was a dilemma keenly felt by Tolstoy as well, stemming from the wish to escape from the "prison of the intelligentsia." If you felt inspired to burn men's hearts with God's truth, it followed that you wanted the number of scorched hearts to be as large as possible. Yet most "literature," as Tolstoy was only too bitterly aware, was consumed only by the educated elite; and of all human hearts, Tolstoy believed, theirs were the least receptive, corrupted as they were by their elitism and jaded by the surfeit of ideas and impressions to which they were constantly exposed. Amidst the ever-increasing journalistic clamor, it was hard to get a hearing, let alone exert a moral influence on the educated public. But surely the "people" were different, as yet unspoiled by newspapers and clashing ideologies. Tolstoy thought so; and Leskov, though more skeptical than his master about the innate virtues of the folk, was impressed by their numbers and the consequent importance of trying to convert them.

If one wished to reach a mass audience in those days, one had to write sermons that the folk would read. Always on bearish terms with the urban intelligentsia, Tolstoy had been occupied with this problem off and on since the early 1860s. At that time one of the by-products of his pedagogical experiments with peasant children on his own estate had been the aggressively provocative article "Who Should Teach Whom to Write, We the Peasant Boys or the Peasant Boys Us?"—in which the world's greatest novelist had proclaimed that his rustic pupils innately possessed not only virtue, but superlative "natural" artistic abilities, including literary talent equal or even superior to his own. (Never one to fear inconsistencies, Tolstoy proceeded directly from the "Who Whom?" article to commence writing *War and Peace*.) In the 1870s renewed pedagogical interests had involved Tolstoy in the production of primers and readers. At first these had consisted mostly of nondidactic stories, borrowed by Tolstoy from the storehouse of world legend and then stylistically and structurally pruned to the bare-bones form he regarded as alone suitable for child or folk consumption. But the opportunity to inculcate ideals of virtue in children's (or peasants') hearts was too alluring to let slip; and even before his dramatic conversion, Tolstoy had begun to make use of his school books for homiletic purposes.

Leskov was a specialist on the subject of didactic folk and children's literature: from 1874 to 1883 he had sat on the Learned Committee of the Ministry of Education whose job it was to screen material proposed for school distribution. A series of reports he composed for that committee had been published in 1876 as independent articles in the *Orthodox Review*. They contain vigorous prescriptions about how one should, and especially how one should not, write for the "people." In "Sentimental Piety" he severely criticized *The Russian Workman*, a Radstockist organ published as a philanthropy by a Petersburg lady named Maria Peiker (who, despite the criticism, later became his friend). The magazine's effectiveness, Leskov maintained, was vitiated by its editor's ignorance of the mentality and way of life of the Russian peasants to whom it was addressed. Consisting of material adapted from English Protestant sources, it was full of undigested, un-Russian lumps of English life.[2] Similarly, in "Energetic Tactlessness" Leskov had had even harsher words for *The People's Sheet*, a clumsy attempt to stuff peasants' heads with crude right-wing propaganda as the antidote to populist agitation.[3] (The *Sheet* encouraged peasants to lynch suspected revolutionaries.) Finally, in "A Pedagogical Monstrosity" Leskov had castigated a children's magazine called *Kindergarten*, which had been approved for use in schools sponsored by the Ministry of War (not the Ministry of Education). *Kindergarten* was full of left-wing, especially feminist propaganda (though generally liberal on the issue of women's rights, Leskov counters the demand for equal educa-tion of girls with the "common sense" statement that after all, girls cannot be allowed to climb trees and "wave their legs about").[4]

Amidst this scathing censure of the purveyors of such "people's" and children's literature, there is one name that even in 1876 elicits from Leskov only praise: Count L. N. Tolstoy. In this instance it is not Tolstoy the artist Leskov venerates, but Tolstoy the pedagogical theo-rist and pioneer. Though it dates from the 1860s, long before his ser-vice in the Ministry of Education, Leskov shows himself thoroughly familiar with the theoretical positions enunciated in Tolstoy's short-lived pedagogical magazine, *Yasnaya Polyana*.[5] But more important than theories was the concrete example Tolstoy set. For Leskov, Tol-stoy was in 1876 already the model both of what to say to children and how to say it. He had shown that it was possible to write for both peasants and children without the simpering and patronizing of *The Russian Workman* and to use a simplified, "folk" style without sinking to the vulgarity of *The People's Sheet*.[6]

One of Tolstoy's most successful early (pre-Tolstoyan) sermon-stor-ies was the now well-known fable "God Sees the Truth but Waits," first published in 1872 and later included by the author in his *Third Russian Reader*. This fable is an expanded version of a sermon preached by Platon Karataev in the closing pages of *War and Peace*.[7] It is a parable of Christian forgiveness, the story of a convict, Aksyo-nov, who after twenty-six years of penal servitude in Siberia by chance is brought face to face with the man who committed the crime for which he has unjustly suffered. Aksyonov ultimately forgives his enemy, though not—in the later version—without a moral struggle. His forgiveness works such psychological wonders in the guilty man that the latter insists on confessing the original crime. The final irony is that by the time this confession works its way through the bureau-cracy to effect Aksyonov's release, death has already claimed him. Thus the strongest impression left by the story is not so much of the power of forgiveness as the nihilistic Tolstoyan belief in the irrele-vance and futility of seeking justice on earth, especially from the cor-rupt human institutions called ministries of justice.

Leskov knew Tolstoy's fable in the *War and Peace* version, perhaps in the reader as well. Though he may have forgotten its source, the basic plot lay dormant in his literary storehouse. He used it in 1880 as the theme for a Christmas story he had promised his friend Tatyana Passek, the editor of a children's magazine called *Toy*. Under the title "Christ Visits a Muzhik," it appeared there in the January number for 1881.[8] By comparing Leskov's and Tolstoy's treatment of the same plot, we can clearly perceive their philosophical and stylistic differences.[9]

Leskov presents a more conventional, Christian face than Tolstoy. Leskov, apparently, could not tolerate the bleakness of the Tolstoyan finale. With the final shock of Aksyonov's unliberated death, Tolstoy's story appears to leave a disturbing imbalance in the moral reckoning. "By rights" the hero should get some earthly reward for his virtue and suffering; he should be released, vindicated, restored to his family, allowed to enjoy at least a few years of terrestrial happiness. But the force of Tolstoy's plot lies precisely in the frustration of this expectation. The moral pendulum never completes its swing; it forces us to confront what (in earthly terms) seems to be the basic disequilibrium of human fate. Aksyonov and the reader must take what satisfaction they can in the forgiveness itself, as an absolute good. Aksyonov's final revelation, as his enemy weeps on his knees before him, is that man cannot attempt to measure right and wrong. The moral order of the universe lies beyond our comprehension. (Tolstoy does not doubt that there is one.) "Perhaps I am a hundred times worse than you," Aksyonov says, weeping; and this acknowledgment, like Ivan Ilyich's final vision of light, releases him from attachment to the things of this world, including hopes for human justice. "And he ceased to pine for home, never wished to leave the prison, and thought only about his last hour."

Leskov's moral vision is much less bleak. His world is the human world, men in their relations with one another. At his hands the rough edges of the Tolstoyan plot are smoothed and softened all around. The Tolstoyan crime had been the robbery and murder of one man by another, a stranger; for this deed the innocent Aksyonov was flogged, branded, and imprisoned for the rest of his life. In Leskov's version the crime is the embezzlement by an uncle of his nephew's inheritance; the victimized nephew, whose name is Timofei, is banished to Siberia for having assaulted his uncle with a deadly weapon, which he did. Further, an Oedipal dimension, reminiscent of Leskov's play *The Spendthrift* and of the act of his uncle Strakhov, is added to the sexless Tolstoyan plot. Timofei's elderly, but evilly vigorous uncle has not only "mortally aggrieved the hero's father and driven his mother to an early grave," but manages to compel the parents of Timofei's own tender-aged fiancée to marry the girl to him. Being a merchant of the first guild, Leskov's Timofei is not knouted and branded for his assault, nor even incarcerated. He is simply compelled to resettle in Siberia. Finally, although his uncle has stolen nine-tenths of his property, even the remainder is sufficient so that he can set himself up in business in his new abode. And the business prospers: unlike Tolstoy, with his idealization of poverty and his strong sense of the moral taint involved in property-owning, Leskov exhibits a characteristically practical, Protestant feeling that God approves of thrift and enterprise and does not always "wait" until the next life to reward them. Material prosperity thus assuages Timofei's psychological wounds; and to make the healing process faster, the exile finds himself a nice Siberian girl, marries, and settles down to a happy family life. With all these mollifying experiences, Leskov's hero certainly has less reason than Tolstoy's to nurse an undying grudge against his enemy; and thus the basic conflict between the Christian impulse of forgiveness and the "natural" craving for vengeance is less satisfactorily motivated in Leskov's plot.

On the other hand, Leskov avoids two serious technical weaknesses in Tolstoy's version of the story. To make his hero seem still more isolated in his lonely prison cell, Tolstoy rather implausibly has Aksyonov lose all contact with his former life. Though his marriage had been a happy one, his wife readily believes that he committed the murder; and she apparently severs relations with him. During his entire exile he gets no letters from home. Aksyonov in prison is thus totally alone with his God, a state Tolstoy needs as symbolic of man's ultimate existential condition; but it conflicts with the picture painted earlier of his family life. Secondly, Tolstoy needs to give Aksyonov the power to take vengeance on his old enemy, Makar Semyonov, if he should so choose, for it is his refusal to do so that effects Semyonov's moral transformation. Yet for Aksyonov to denounce Semyonov to the authorities for the murder committed long ago, the very crime for which he, Aksyonov, had been punished, will obviously not carry much conviction: he has no new evidence, and who would believe him if Semyonov refused to confess? Therefore, Tolstoy must have Semyonov commit a new crime. He digs a tunnel out of the prison, secretly disposing of the dirt outdoors during the daily exercise period. But here Tolstoy slips badly. A guard catches Semyonov disposing of the dirt in this way and goes on to discover the tunnel; yet inexplicably Semyonov is not singled out as the suspected digger. All the prisoners are questioned, and all, including Aksyonov, refuse to give the culprit away. What Tolstoy needed was the "confrontation" scene, when Aksyonov is interrogated by the commandant of the prison in Semyonov's presence. In this moment of truth the hero tells the lie that represents a higher truth: passing up his opportunity for revenge, he denies any knowledge of who dug the tunnel. This episode seems a clumsy, un-Tolstoyan gaffe, surprising in a story so frequently revised: it would seem so easy to have the guards discover the dirt and the tunnel, but not the man.

Even more striking than these differences of motivation and philosophy are those of style and structure. For Tolstoy a requirement in stories for peasants or children is extreme simplicity of language and form. Sentences are generally short, simple in syntax; coordinate are preferred to subordinate clauses. Expressive means, especially adjectives, are held to the minimum. Diction is colloquial, avoiding words of marked literary origin, but without ostentatious folksiness. Plots are linear and straightforward, with events related in chronological order and following reasonably plausible patterns of causality.[10]

Much as he admired Tolstoy's simplicity, Leskov found it impossible to write this way. Later, in his committed Tolstoyan period and under direct pressure from the master, he did make an effort to do so. But in 1880 he followed his own literary devices. In "Christ Visits a Muzhik" he presents the events as a memoir, a retrospective narrative related by a character only peripherally involved in the action. This narrator, however, cannot claim the usual Leskovian identification with the "author," even in quotation marks: the milieu of Siberian merchants is too remote. As narrator Leskov must create a new character, a Siberian merchant like Timofei himself. Such a narrator allows him to stylize the language in a literate, but folk idiom rather like that employed in "The Sealed Angel."

Leskov's narrator offers additional advantages. He has ample opportunity to observe Timofei's spiritual development over the years, since the two men have strong religious interests and confide in one another. Leskov develops an effective contrast between the narrator and the hero as spiritual types. Timofei is the cleverer, the more literate of the two, more adept at manipulation of scriptural texts; but his cleverness becomes a source of pride and therefore leads to error. The less intelligent narrator feels humble on account of his intellectual inferiority, but his humility helps him achieve a spiritual wisdom deeper than Timofei's.

The most notable difference between the two plots is indicated by Leskov's title: the visit of Christ. As the instrument of Timofei's spiritual growth Leskov injects a supernatural element into Tolstoy's plot.

Appalled during a Gospel reading by the behavior to Our Lord of the inhospitable Pharisee (Luke 7:36-50), Timofei begs Jesus to pay him a visit so that he can make amends. There is an audible reply: "I shall come." Thereafter a place of honor is always set at Timofei's table; but despite the promise, for weeks all expectations are disappointed. On Christmas Day, however, the revered guest does at last appear, escorted by an "indescribable pink light" and guided by a "hand white as snow." However, the guest turns out to be not Jesus, but the very uncle who had once done Timofei wrong. The old miscreant has somehow lost his wealth (no details are given) and his family and has been in search of Timofei to beg his forgiveness. Under such circumstances and with such obvious evidence of divine sponsorship, the plea could not be refused. Timofei's heart melts; the penitent old man is placed in the Lord's seat of honor; and he remains with Timofei until his death.

With its sticky sentimentality, Leskov's story is less satisfactory as a work of literature, more dated than Tolstoy's "God Sees the Truth but Waits."[11] Doubtless aware of its defects—the story had been written in great haste—Leskov must nevertheless have been much gratified to learn that "Christ Visits a Muzhik" had found high favor with Tolstoy's disciples Chertkov and Biryukov. As we saw earlier, this story was the pretext for their making Leskov's acquaintance, and it was through them that Leskov arranged his first meeting with Tolstoy. But the honor brought by the story was even greater than this passport to the master.

In 1884 Chertkov conceived the idea of founding a publishing house for the production of Tolstoyan literature in cheap editions for mass distribution. For this purpose he made the surprisingly shrewd move of allying himself with an existing publisher, I. D. Sytin, who was already in the business of producing and distributing "pulp" fiction. Sytin had the know-how and the distribution network the Tolstoyans lacked; and he was flattered to be employed in the Tolstoyan cause and to become the publisher of prestigious writers whose names he had never dreamed would adorn his lists: Tolstoy, Leskov, Korolenko, Garshin, "and others."[12] Thus was born the Tolstoyan publishing firm *Posrednik* ("The Intermediary"), which was to survive until the Revolution. Its first four booklets appeared on April 1, 1885, in the gaudy style Sytin's humble customers found enticing: pink and blue covers with red borders and drawings by A. D. Kivshenko. They sold for one and one-half kopecks each. The titles of the first four in this illustrious series were: *A Prisoner of the Caucasus, What Men Live By,* and *God Sees the Truth but Waits,* all by Tolstoy; and *Christ*

Visits a Muzhik by Leskov. Twelve thousand four hundred copies of Leskov's story were printed, and they sold out within a year. New editions were brought out in 1886, 1891, 1893, and 1894.[13] It was a triumph indeed.

Despite the immense success of "Christ Visits a Muzhik," Leskov did not return for several years to the didactic fable. In 1886 he embodied his belatedly professed principles of tolerance toward Jews in a long narrative based on a plot taken from the so-called *Prolog;* and "Theodore and Abraham" proved to be the first in a series of such stories in which early Christian settings are used not only to demonstrate the moral principles of Tolstoyanism, but to show how far the official Christian churches of the nineteenth century had strayed from their founder's path. Not until 1888 did Leskov again take up the short, didactic fable. During the Christmas holidays of that year, apparently in two days' time, he produced a folk-style parable entitled "Malanya Muttonhead."[14]

From manuscript materials it appears that the immediate source of "Malanya Muttonhead" was a Flemish folktale.[15] The theme, however, is an international migratory one: a personified Death is immobilized by some human agency (necessarily with the aid of supernatural powers); the resultant immortality proves unendurable for erstwhile mortals, and Death is ultimately released and allowed to proceed with its grim but necessary work. At Leskov's hands the tale undergoes far-reaching changes, including a change of genre. The original story is essentially an attempt through imagination to answer the wishful question, "What if there were no death?" Leskov shows only perfunctory interest in this question. Instead, he makes use of the old plot nucleus to present a parable of Christian love.

In the Flemish original the trapper of Death is an old woman allegorically named Want. Leskov substitutes for this allegoricism another personified abstraction, but withholds her identity until the end. He also eliminates a satirically portrayed secondary character in the original tale, Death's assistant Dr. Medicus. In place of Want, Leskov installs as his central character one of his own "righteous ones," a poor peasant woman nicknamed Muttonhead by her fellow villagers for the stupidly selfless generosity she displays. Among her good deeds is the archetypal Leskovian act of charity, the adoption of two orphans; and in her case the credit is compounded, since both orphans are cripples. Though she leads a hand-to-mouth existence, Malanya shares what she has, living according to Christ's prescription, "Take no thought for the morrow." Thus at the outset the story's moral force appears to be derived from the familiar Leskovian contrast between the generosity and goodness of the isolated individual and the self-centered worldliness of the surrounding society, reminding us of "The Monognome" and "Deathless Golovan."

The motif of the arrest of Death appears to have no logical place in this moral context, and its appearance causes the story to veer off into abstraction and allegory. When some of Malanya's tactless neighbors remark that Death might mercifully deliver her from her deformed charges, the heroine cries out in anguish, "I won't let her [the Russian 'death' is in the feminine gender] cross my doorstep!" Subsequently, by showing hospitality to a poor old wanderer (named Living Soul), she gains the power to carry out this threat. Thus, when Death comes for the orphans, Malanya imprisons her and dries her up.

As Leskov tells it, the chief problem caused by the absence of death is the power given the cruel to oppress the weak. There is no longer any fear—either of capital punishment or of the torments of hell—capable of intimidating the wicked; and the human world becomes a hell of exploitation and terror. At last, after a hundred years of universal immortality, Malanya is persuaded to release Death, who at once sets to work at the long backlog on her list. Malanya herself, however, is exempt from Death's attentions: her immortality is now permanent. Her old name has been forgotten, but a new one has fallen from heaven, carved on a heart-shaped stone: Love.

Leskov's story is related with great skill, so much so that Leonid Grossman considers it a "little *chef d'oeuvre.*"[16] It seems, however, that the celebration of a model of charity and righteousness has little to do with the folk motif of the arrest of death. It is a bad fit. The two disparate themes are held together only by the abstraction, stated allegorically but undemonstrated, that "love conquers death."

The author may well have sensed the structural frailty of "Malanya Muttonhead." He apparently chose not to publish the story.

Leskov's alliance with the Tolstoyans, cemented by his meeting with the master in 1887, stimulated his production of fables or parables designed for the edification of semiliterate, unsophisticated readers. Several of these were later issued in mass editions by the Tolstoyan publishing firm, The Intermediary. From both a literary and a psychological point of view, these works are particularly interesting as the products of direct interaction between the two writer-preachers, with Leskov, a veteran with thirty years' literary experience, incongruously placing himself in the role of a humble pupil of the great sage of Yasnaya Polyana.

Our first well-documented case of a work produced from this novel apprenticeship is "Figura" (1889).[17] Its literary quality is not high: the preacher overpowers the artist. Yet in "Figura" Leskov applied techniques that had served him well in the past. It is a memoir story, like "Pechersk Eccentrics." A narrator, apparently to be identified with the real author, again reminisces about an "eccentric" he had known in old Kiev, in the reign of Nicholas I. Accompanied, he says, by a well-known real person, the much-admired "first abolitionist" Dmitry Zhuravsky, the author-narrator frequented the society of the story's hero, a Ukrainian "character" named Vigura, punningly known as "Figura" for the striking figure he cut. After the original meeting and characterization of the hero by the frame narrator or author, "Figura" tells his story. It contains what should have been an effective satirical portrait of another real person, the famous general Count Dmitry Osten-Saken (1790-1881), a hero of the Napoleonic campaigns who was still alive and active in the Crimean War, when Tolstoy had served under him.[18] The narrative kernel of "Figura" is thus a confrontation between a *pravednik* (touched up to meet Tolstoyan specifications) and Osten-Saken, exemplifying a negative type Leskov had effectively scored off many times before—the Pobedonostsev-style Orthodox bureaucrat-bigot, like the infamous Nikolai Demidov in "Cadet Monastery." One would have expected the clash of these two familiar figures, so well established in Leskov's repertory, to produce fireworks. Instead, there is a fizzle.

In the case of "Figura," the problem is excessive idealization. Vigura may have been a real man: in a letter to Tolstoy Leskov said that his hero was the "founder of the Ukrainian Shtunda" and that almost everything in the story was true.[19] Yet on paper "Figura" seems all too unreal. Like Chervyov, the dissident tutor belatedly grafted onto *A Decrepit Clan*, Figura is a letter-perfect Tolstoyan. He is a lifelong vegetarian, un-Orthodoxly eschewing not only meat, but even fish ("anything that has consciousness of life"); he is a "simplified" small landowner who works the soil with his own hands like a peasant; he is a sexless ascetic who lives, like Deathless Golovan, in chastity with a woman he has rescued from sin, and with her illegitimate child, who is not his (the "orphan" again); he is a Bible-reading, moral Christian, nominally Orthodox, but indifferent to the manifestations of Orthodox religiosity—icons, rituals, monasticism, pilgrimages. Figura is too perfect, and he thus becomes abstract, inhuman, as lacking in personality as the Dick and Jane of a child's primer. Leskov attempts to remedy his hero's colorlessness with daubs of Ukrainian paint, using Ukrainian speech to create an atmosphere of hearty joviality. But the jollity does not cover up the hero's priggishness.

The core of Figura's narrative is the story of his confrontation with Osten-Saken. As a young army officer, before his "simplification," he had refused to discipline a soldier who had drunkenly assaulted him. The nonviolent response has a miraculous psychological effect. The now-sober soldier is overcome with remorse, and he confesses his sin to the chaplain. The chaplain, like other Orthodox priests in Leskov's stories, betrays to the authorities the secret heard in the confessional. Ultimately Figura is summoned before the commanding general, Count Osten-Saken, and his resignation from the army demanded for his breach of discipline.

Osten-Saken was the incarnation of fanatical Orthodox piety. The confrontation between the two men, representing "true" and "false" Christianity, therefore should have given Leskov an opportunity to make his didactic point with a vivid and effective scene. But the verbal dialogue between the two is a failure: too long, too predictable, and not interesting. The count's bigotry proves as lifeless as Figura's virtue.

Leskov understood that his lesson-story lacked the vitality of artistic detail, and he turned to his master for aid. On April 30, 1889, he wrote Tolstoy:

> Yesterday I sent you by registered mail my new little story "Figura." It is the same story concerning the founder of the Ukrainian Shtunda about which I once wrote you, asking your advice about making a short novel out of it. Receiving no answer, I threw it all together in the form of a short story, done very hastily. There is very little invention in it, it's almost all real, but the vexing thing is that I have forgotten something important from that reality and can't recall it. Besides that, I never saw Saken and have no information about his habits. For that reason, probably, his image came out pale and without character. May I ask you to salt this lump with your hand and from your salt-cellar? Won't you indicate on the proofs where and what I should insert to give flavor and clarity about Saken, whom, I think, you knew and remember? (11:427)

Tolstoy apparently obliged, if perfunctorily. His reply is lost, but from Leskov's counterreply we can get an idea of the master's unfavorable judgment and also of the psychological effect of that judgment on Leskov. Leskov's second letter is a veritable battlefield on which his old-style wounded pride and defensive self-justification contend with his newly acquired reverence and submissiveness toward Tolstoy.

> Everything you write is true. The story is thrown together and "cold"; but I kept seeing before me the repulsive bugbear of the censorship, and I was afraid to develop the warmth. That, I think, is why it turned out cold, but after all, the story did get by in a censored publication [Tolstoy published most of his religious material in illegal or foreign editions, and therefore had no worries about the "bugbear."] Shadows on Figura's face are needed, and I will try to introduce them when I revise the story for the fifth volume of my collected works; but under the censorship let the story circulate as it is. [I'm in no great hurry to carry out your suggestions.] The story may have a good effect even in this form. I thank you for what you noted about Saken; I knew nothing about him except what I wrote. [Note that my problem was lack of information, not lack of skill.] I won't send you an offprint of "Figura" a second time [you don't deserve it] so as not to bother you. What you said is enough for me. [Turned around: the way I wrote it is good enough for you. But now the emotion of reverence surges back, and the letter concludes on a note of official humility.] I cherish my love and gratitude toward you with great joy of the spirit, for through you I received much light and strength and consolation.[20]

Leskov reworked the story later that year for his collected works, making use of some of Tolstoy's criticisms. The changes have been ably analyzed by A. I. Batyuto (8:622-624). To the portrait of Saken Leskov added a detail presumably communicated by Tolstoy, that the bigoted Saken could not distinguish real piety from the fake variety assumed by his self-seeking subordinates. Further, Leskov placed some "shadows" on Figura's face and figure, making him a little coarser and more decisive. But it was not enough to make the character come alive, and in the meantime Leskov had moved on to other projects.

The relative failure of "Figura" apparently convinced Leskov that his private brand of realistic reminiscential story was difficult to use as a vehicle for Tolstoyan didacticism, especially in addressing a mass audience. He therefore turned to the master for fresh instruction. Tolstoy evidently advised him to try using the folktale model he himself had employed in such works as "The Tale of Ivan the Fool and His Two Brothers" (1886); and he offered Leskov a specific theme. The assignment was to take a folk-style tripartite riddle, "didacticized" in the Tolstoyan spirit, and build a story around it. The riddle Tolstoy supplied went as follows: What time is the most important of all, what person the most needed, and what action the most valuable? The replies epitomize the Tolstoyan ideal of "disengagement"—renunciation of long-term commitments and calculations, even personal relationships, in favor of an impersonal, here-and-now benevolence. The most important time is the present, the most important person the one you are dealing with right now, and the most valuable action the good you can do that person. The corresponding literary riddle Tolstoy set Leskov was how to incarnate these questions and answers as the nucleus of a work of narrative art. And though he labored over the task with great industry, Leskov again failed, at least in his teacher's opinion.

Leskov's work is called "The Hour of God's Will."[21] In Russian folk riddle-tales, the riddles are usually set by a king or tsar—presumably the only person able to offer an adequate reward for solving them or punishment for failing to do so.[22] Thus, Leskov automatically introduces a king figure into his plot. The problem was how to connect Tolstoy's riddle, which contains a private moral addressed to ordinary men in their personal lives, with the symbol of political power. The presence of a king in the story presented the temptation of politicizing the fable and thus overcomplicating it.

In conceiving a plot framework for Tolstoy's riddle, apparently the first association Leskov evoked was his memory of a fairy tale by E. T. A. Hoffmann, one which he had mentioned in passing in an article on church history published several years before.[23] As Leskov remembered it, it was the story of a king who wanted everyone to be happy, but somehow could not bring it off. This Hoffman model, even as modified in Leskov's memory, proved an unfortunate choice. There was no logical connection between the well-wishing king and Tolstoy's riddle, although the Hoffmannesque theme by itself might have provided the basis for an effective story demonstrating the Tolstoyan truth that no ruler, however good-willed, can promote the well-being of his subjects, since all governments, being based on violence, are intrinsically evil.

Apparently the specific government Leskov had in mind was that of the young Kaiser Wilhelm II. On ascending the throne in June 1888, the new emperor of Germany had made several pronouncements and issued rescripts concerning his intention to carry out large-scale social reforms. Leskov had reacted to the Kaiser's proclamations with a mixture of admiration and skepticism. As he wrote to the editor of the magazine where "The Hour of God's Will" first appeared: "I am interested in the efforts of the German emperor, with which I deeply sympathize, despite the fact that I do not expect any great result from them in the immediate future; but nevertheless these are efforts of great significance, and his 'beginning is worth more than money' [a Russian proverb]. However, in any case he won't accomplish anything now, and I think it can be seen exactly why he won't."[24] The reason, as articulated in the story, approximates the celebrated Actonian dictum: Absolute power corrupts absolutely. The German model had to be hyperbolized to prove this point. Despite his original Germanic inspiration, Leskov's King Goodwill, with his apparatus of torturers and executioners and his practice of holding hostages to enforce the return of travelers abroad, bears more resemblance to Ivan the Terrible (or to Lenin-Stalin) than to either the Kaiser or Alexander III.

The inevitable corruption of power, however, has nothing to do with the "hour of God's will." Throughout the latter part of the story one senses an almost frantic effort on the author's part to fill the unbridgeable gap. Detail after detail is added, character after character; the story is as stuffed with tidbits as a fruit cake.

King Goodwill at last obtains from a wise maiden the correct answers to the three questions; but instead of acting upon them, he orders the story written down and placed "on the bottom of a golden box hidden away in the cellar of the king's private quarters behind seven locks and sealed with seven seals" (9:31). The political moral may be clear, but the private one is obscured. The relevance of Tolstoy's riddle for ordinary people in their everyday lives gets buried in the story's cellar among the ironies of royal politics.

Leskov put immense effort into "The Hour of God's Will." Among his papers are preserved two manuscripts containing three basic variants of this story. The first text was composed by the author and written down by him, then covered with corrections. A new copy incorporating these corrections was then made by a scribe. This fair copy was then again completely covered with authorial emendations and in that form sent to the printers. The process of revision was continued on the printers' proofs.[25] Several samples of these variant texts have been published.[26] They show that, once established, the characterizations and plot sequences of the story remained fixed. All the effort of revision went into language, stylization. In "The Hour of God's Will" Leskov was trying to achieve the incantatory effect of "poetic" and rhythmicized folk language. It has many distinct features of vocabulary, including a massive use of hypocoristic forms, many idiosyncrasies of syntax and even morphology. The effects in themselves are striking,[27] but one feels they are merely window dressing.

Leskov's friend-enemy Suvorin (in an inextant letter) evidently needled him about the excesses of stylization in "The Hour of God's Will" and about the story's subversive message. In defending himself against these charges, the author virtually denied his didactic purpose. The moralist, he said, had been swallowed up by the artist:

> It is tiresome to write folk tales in contemporary language. I began in jest to ape the language of the seventeenth century, and then, as Tolstoy says, became "intoxicated with success," and sustained the entire tale in that unified tone. [Leskov then needles Suvorin for professing incomprehension of certain archaisms in the story.] Your ignorance is a pretense. The tale is simply a "little piece" which is artistic and amusing, but without ulterior aim [*zamysel*], and it evokes a smile and a little reflection. But experienced writers like you and Tolstoy probably felt: "What a lot of work went into this!" I simply wanted to give the public a pretty piece. The state doesn't concern me at all.[28]

Much more meaningful to Leskov was Tolstoy's reaction. The master was not favorably impressed with Leskov's story, though he tried to express his displeasure as tactfully as he could: "I began to read, and I especially liked the tone and the extraordinary command of language, but . . . then there intruded your especial defect, which it would seem so easy to correct and which in itself is a [good] quality and not a defect—*exubérance* of images, colors, and characteristic expressions which intoxicate you, and you are carried away. There is much that is superfluous and disproportionate, but the *verve* and the tone are amazing. The tale is very good all the same, but it's too bad that if it weren't for a superfluity of talent, it would be even better."[29]

Tolstoy's true opinion, unmitigated by diplomacy, was recorded in his diary several years later: "Leskov made use of my theme, and badly. My marvelous thought was three questions: what time is the most important of all, what person and what action? The time is now, this very minute, the person is he with whom you are dealing, and the action is to save your soul, i.e., to do the work of love."[30] Several years later still, in 1903, Tolstoy undertook to do the job himself. He resurrected his "marvelous thought" as the theme for one of three tales he had promised Sholom Aleichem for a Yiddish anthology being published to aid victims of the Kishinyov pogrom.[31] Besides the Yiddish translation, Tolstoy's story was published in the original Russian in 1903 by his own Intermediary firm, under the title "Three Questions."[32]

It cannot be said that Tolstoy had any greater success than Leskov. He fell into the same royal trap that had caught Leskov. "Riddle" evokes "king," and yet the notion of king confuses this riddle. Tolstoy's solution is to depoliticize the king. His monarch goes for solitary walks in the country, spends hours digging in an old hermit's garden, and with his own hands performs first aid on a man's bleeding wound. The implausibility of these acts and situations is matched by the artificiality with which the events are contrived to fit the riddle. The "marvelous thought" did not inspire a marvelous story, either at Leskov's hands or at Tolstoy's own.

In 1890, Leskov had no premonition of the posthumous competition he would encounter. Receiving Tolstoy's much tempered criticism, he humbly kissed the (well padded) rod and begged for a new assignment: "For the opinion you expressed I thank you heartily. You correctly notice a certain 'curliwurliness' [*kučerjavost'*] and in general 'mannered' style—this is my defect. I feel it and try to refrain from it, but I don't succeed in doing so. Give me another theme for a nice little folktale. I'll try to write it without curlicues. It's easy and pleasant for me to write on your themes."[33]

The hours of toil Leskov spent over "The Hour of God's Will" did not redeem its artistic flaws. By ironic contrast, a little newspaper story he dashed off for the Christmas of 1890 without any prior consultation with his instructor set the bells ringing at Yasnaya Polyana. The unexpected success was "Offended before Christmas," published in the holiday number of the *Petersburg Gazette*.[34] In didactic intent it is a Tolstoyan fable, but not a mannered folktale stylization like "The Hour of God's Will." Leskov reverts here to the "realistic" problem story, his typical first-person narrative form with a setting in the nineteenth century present. The frame narrator or "author" relates an incident in the life of a friend;[35] in the course of the discussion, two other analogous events are recounted. One of these involves a new set of characters; the other is taken from the frame narrator's experience. The two latter stories are illustrations designed to help the friend solve a moral problem. This structure might have proved overintricate. But the narratives neatly interlock and reinforce each other, effectively pointing up the same moral lesson. The story is simple, short, clear, and impeccably Tolstoyan: no wonder the master was pleased.

Furthermore, the Tolstoyan principle preached in "Offended before Christmas" is the cherished "resist not evil." In the first "analogy" story a merchant by chance apprehends a child who is being used by a gang of thieves to burglarize his storehouse. Instead of using the boy as a hostage to pursue the robbers (one of whom is the child's father), the merchant adopts him, brings him up, and eventually marries him to his own daughter. Much later, after the adoptive father's death, the adopted son and exthief, now himself a prosperous merchant, refuses to serve on a jury. Not having himself been judged, he cannot bring himself to judge.

The second antilegal tale, the "author's" story, shows the reverse side of this moral coin. The "author's" doorkeeper, against his will, takes legal action against a poor tailor who had absconded with an expensive fur coat belonging to the "author." The only consequence of this legal quest for justice is all-around misery. The tailor is caught and thrown into prison, leaving his wife and children destitute. Though compelled by conscience and compassion to support his victim's family, the "author" derives no satisfaction from his benevolence. The family members are not grateful, since they blame him for depriving them of their breadwinner; and he feels guilty for all the suffering the law has caused on his behalf.

The ecstatic response of Tolstoy to this fable is well documented. His initial rapturous letter to Leskov has not come down to us, but from other materials its tone can be surmised. Tolstoy sent a copy of Leskov's story to Chertkov with the comment, "What a delight! It is the best of all his stories. And how fine it would be if we would publish it" [in the Intermediary series]. At the same time a second copy was sent to another of Tolstoy's favorite disciples, Marya Schmidt, with the comment, "Rarely has anything moved me so."[36] And Leskov's reply to Tolstoy glows with pleasure. "I didn't expect *such* praise from you," he purred. He hoped Tolstoy would approve his having published the story in such a despised medium as the *Petersburg Gazette*, from which, he said, it had been "read off adroitly or laboriously spelled out in janitors' quarters, taverns, and filthy places, and perhaps some bits of good have stuck in some people's minds."[37]

The subversive message of "Offended before Christmas," that one should not prosecute thieves, was bound to arouse alarm in the propertied establishment. On January 7, an article attacking the story appeared in Suvorin's *New Times*, entitled "Life and Phantasmagoria."[38] It offered the predictable arguments: that punishments are necessary for the maintenance of social order; that the well-to-do can afford to forgive thieves, but the poor cannot; that Christ's admonition "Render unto Caesar" implies an acceptance of legal systems. Leskov replied with an article entitled "Possessed Salt."[39] He argued that he had been illustrating a "fully reasonable and noble" ideal, that of forgiveness, a higher human impulse than punitive vindictiveness, and one suitable in a Christmas story, "in which it is customary to present a plot that softens hearts and to treat that plot in the spirit of the Gospel and not that of political economy or the Codex on the prevention or forestalling of crime."[40]

The implication here that the moral principles expounded in "Offended before Christmas" might be only an attribute of a literary genre seems to weaken the argument. Nevertheless, Tolstoy was almost as pleased with "Possessed Salt" as he had been with the story. When Leskov, who was afraid the master might disapprove of his replying,[41] sent him a copy, Tolstoy replied: "Your defense is a delight. May God help you to teach people thus. What clarity, simplicity, strength, and gentleness. Thanks be to them who evoked this article. Please send me as many copies as you can."[42]

Leskov was again delighted by the praise, but he tried to reply circumspectly: "You, Lev Nikolaevich, are spoiling me with your kindness, but I receive it with moderation and will try not to become puffed up with the praises of such a writer as you."[43] Nevertheless, he obtained a hundred copies of the article for Tolstoy and in a letter written several months later to his stepson was still proudly advertising the master's praise.[44]

Though for unknown reasons it was omitted from all the editions of Leskov's collected works, "Offended before Christmas" had a distinguished Tolstoyan career. Its first story, the tale of the merchant and the boy-thief, was published under the title "A Thief's Son" in 1892 in a Tolstoyan miscellany called *To Russian Mothers*.[45] This same fragment was reprinted in 1894 in another charitable miscellany called *Poor Children*.[46] The same year the whole text was reprinted in yet another miscellany, *The Good Cause*.[47] Then in 1905 Tolstoy abridged it for inclusion in the first edition of his meditation handbook, *A Circle of Reading*. Since he did not approve of the ecclesiastical associations of the word "Christmas," he changed the title to "Offended before the Holiday." His abridgement was not substantial: two apostrophes to the reader and a digression on Leskov's archetypal merchant,

Ivan Ivanovich Androsov,[48] were eliminated, but the story retained its essential flavor. In this form it appeared in the *Circle for Reading* and was reprinted many times.[49]

In its second incarnation, however, "Offended before Christmas" was more profoundly transformed. In February 1908, the octogenarian master improvised from memory a new version of Leskov's story. This improvisation was recorded on a phonographic cylinder for use in the Yasnaya Polyana school. The oral text was then transcribed by a secretary, corrected by Tolstoy, and under the old title "A Thief's Son"[50] published in a revised edition of the *Circle of Reading*.

In this new story the "problem" structure, the author-narrator, the "apropos" recollection, all this Leskovian stock-in-trade is discarded, although Tolstoy inserts a Leskovian touch lacking in the original—a skaz. The aged merchant who refuses jury service explains his reasons in his own words. In Tolstoy's version of the old merchant's narrative, the character of the father, the original thief, is much more vividly realized than in Leskov (he is a good man when not stupefied by drink). Likewise his mother (who never appears in Leskov's version): the traditional Russian mother, benevolent but weak, the fellow victim with her children of her husband's brutality. The boy's feelings in the aftermath of the burglary are also more fully articulated. Thus Tolstoy out-Leskoved Leskov—though one might argue that the sacrifice of the tailor and fur coat story, less dramatic but psychologically more convincing, was too high a price to pay.

In his next Tolstoyan parable, "Vexation of Spirit," Leskov reverted to the pseudo-memoir form, as indicated by the subtitle, "From My Adolescent Memories."[51] In this case the literary sleight-of-hand was even trickier than usual. Leskov extracted, and caused to reappear as the German teacher in his own "classic" childhood environment at the Strakhovs', the Swiss tutor from Alexander Herzen's novel *Who Is to Blame?* (1845).[52] (The character is similar, though the plots have nothing in common.) Leskov's tale begins effectively with a vivid scene not found in Herzen. A poor gardener's son is whipped for picking a prize plum in his master's orchard. The crime was actually committed by a visitor, the son of the provincial governor, a dreadful *enfant gâté*, who is perfectly content to keep silent while the other boy suffers for his misdeed. The narrator and his brother, who know the truth, though greatly troubled, also keep silent: they have taken an oath not to reveal the secret. Their "honorable" silence thus involves dishonorable moral complicity in the injustice—a fact that gives the German tutor the opportunity to preach a Tolstoyan sermon against oath-taking.

This tutor, despite his possible origin in Herzen's pages, had become a Leskovian *pravednik*. Unencumbered by family responsibilities or by social or economic ambitions, he cannot be intimidated by "establishment" threats. He speaks unwanted truths before the high and mighty, a practice which has made most of his positions of short duration. In this case he denounced the true plum-thief before the latter's outraged mother and her scandalized hosts. For his pains he is summarily dismissed, which enhances his moral triumph. It is an excellent scene: the lonely man of virtue courageously challenging and indicting a corrupt and complacent power structure, regardless of the consequences to himself. After the tutor's moment of glory, however, the story trails off badly into a long and sentimental farewell sermon implausibly preached by the tutor to the narrator and his brother while they all stand on the road.

Despite its perfect Tolstoyan orthodoxy, "Vexation of Spirit" seems to have evoked little response in Tolstoyan circles. It was never circulated by The Intermediary.

"The Little Fool" (1891)[53] similarly fails satisfactorily to realize the Tolstoyan message in a convincing fictional context. The genre here is again the memoir.[54] As usual, the narrator, presumed to be the author, reminisces about his childhood, identifying himself as a gentleman's son in the days of serfdom. The hero, Panka, is the underdog incarnate—both a serf and an orphan, known even among serfs as a "little fool" for his selfless generosity. Panka is totally defenseless, does not resist the aggressions of others, willingly does others' work for them, and even volunteers to receive a flogging in place of another boy. Later, during the Crimean War, he offers himself for the army (to spare someone else), and he gladly serves out the war as a latrine-digger. (The censor apparently forbade Leskov to state openly that he refused to bear arms.)[55] His final exploit, performed while serving as herdsman for a Tatar horse magnate, is to risk his life by releasing a prisoner his master had planned to torture.

As a realistic hero, Panka might have had psychological possibilities: he could be a perfect specimen of the masochistic type who strives to win love by allowing others to abuse and exploit him, eventually internalizing a confusion of pleasure with pain. But Leskov, perhaps blinded by his "nonresistant" dogma or perhaps because he invested too little effort in this children's story, fails to penetrate below the official Tolstoyan surface of this character. To delve deeply into Panka's unconscious might have forced his creator to confront some disturbing questions about the general psychological health of the Tolstoyan ideal of self-abnegation.

In Leskov's treatment, Panka remains an icon. He undergoes no development and experiences no conflicts. Like an automaton he mechanically gives the correct Tolstoyan response to a series of stimuli. But the "average" reader, endowed with a normal quotient of self-assertiveness and aggression, will write him off, as do his fellow serfs, as a "little fool."

Tolstoy seems to have reacted in this way. He was not impressed with the story and did not recommend it for The Intermediary. It lacked "sincerity," he wrote to Chertkov—the very quality he had found in such abundance in "Offended before Christmas."[56] "Sincerity" was not the right word: both Panka and Leskov are sincere. It is the illusion of life that is missing; also questionable is the viability of a masochistic type as a universal ideal. But Tolstoy could no more acknowledge that problem than Leskov could. For to dislodge that shaky stone might cause the edifice of super-Christian ethics to collapse, and with it Tolstoyanism itself: a religion that sets man at odds with his instinctual nature.

In "The Pustoplyasians" (1893) Leskov experimented with yet another form for conveying his Tolstoyan sermon: the concealed allegory.[57] At first glance this bit of disguised didacticism appears to follow the Leskovian "apropos," skaz formula; but the nature of the inner narrative has changed.

The narrator, a Russian peasant, is recollecting events from his distant youth, fifty years before. The action of his tale takes us back to the reign of Nicholas I. But before long we realize that these memories are illusory. The action has nothing to do with historical time or place, but occurs in the land of allegory, where the characters are personified virtues, vices, and follies. And then we find that the detour by way of allegory had landed us not in the Russia of Nicholas I, but back at the point of origin, the Russia of 1893.

Our first clue is the title. The word "Pustoplyasians" ostensibly designates the inhabitants of a Russian village with the odd name of Pustoplyasovo. But this toponym has an etymological meaning: "a place of idle dancing," which proves descriptively significant. During a year of disastrous drought, the fields of Pustoplyasovo unaccountably produce a bountiful harvest. The inhabitants are thus faced with a moral dilemma: how to enjoy their prosperity in the face of their starving and begging neighbors. Their solution is the casuistry of moral indifferentism. God must have intended to reward them and punish their neighbors; who are they to thwart his purposes? They therefore freely proceed with their drinking, meat-eating, and "idle dancing," until at last a calamitous fire reduces them to destitution even worse than their neighbors'.

The abstract moral is obvious; and contemporary readers could easily follow the trail from the abstraction to their own time. The nation had just passed through the famine of 1891-1892; the "idle dancers" during that year had been the members of Russia's elite classes (including virtually all of Leskov's readers), who had been able to justify enjoying their comforts amidst their starving fellow-countrymen. The fire at Pustoplyasovo might be taken as a prophecy of the revolution that was to drive the Russian Pustoplyasians from their fields of privilege. The central character, the old peasant moralist Fedos, who vainly urges the Pustoplyasians to show charity toward their neighbors, comes to sound like that old "peasant" Lev Tolstoy. Not only is his basic message the same; but Fedos confesses à la Tolstoy to a youth of sin and selfishness. In his old age Fedos harbors his greatest enemy within his own house: the most energetic and vicious resistance to his wisdom comes from his granddaughter (read: wife); and it is she who ultimately causes the fire that brings about the "dancers' " downfall.

The author provided an unambiguous key to the allegory in his letter to Tolstoy of January 10, 1893:

The story itself came into my head all at once (for lack of a plot) after an argument about you with [Sergei] Tatishchev [a conservative historian]. "What would the peasants say and what would he say to the peasants?" I hastily put together such a dialogue in a peasant milieu on subjects which come up in talks about you. The day before yesterday Lyub[ov] Yak[ovlevna Gurevich] came to see me and said that the censor had told her that he had "understood everything," and what he understood was that he had been "tricked," because the Pustoplyasians are the gentry and the man lying on the stove and talking is Tolstoy. Sytin has reportedly been forbidden to publish it. That's what they busy themselves with![58]

Leskov understood that "The Pustoplyasians" was not a successful work of literature. In the letter quoted above, he prefaces his explanations with excuses for the story's defects. He had been sick, he says, when he wrote it, with a fever of "39° [C.] in the blood," and under "repulsive conditions of censorship, according to which you can't make changes in the proofs" (11:521-522). But the basic trouble lay in the constraints imposed on Leskov's talent by the requirements of Tolstoyan didacticism.

"The Pustoplyasians" was the last fable Leskov published in his lifetime. Among his papers another was discovered, of uncertain date, but unquestionably from the Tolstoyan period. Entitled "Brahmadatta and Radovan," it first appeared in 1903 in the third edition of the collected works.[59]

Apart from its literary interest, "Brahmadatta and Radovan" illustrates an important tendency of latter-day Tolstoyanism (and Leskovianism): the effort to see beyond the "parochial" confines not only of institutional Christianity, but of Christianity itself, into the universal moral truths lying at the root of all the great religions. For as the name of its first title character suggests, "Brahmadatta and Radovan" is non-Christian in origin, a refugee from ancient India drafted into the service of Tolstoyan Christianity. It is a Buddhist legend, the prototype of which is found in the Pāli *Vinayapiṭaka* or "Book of Obedience," part of the basic canon of Buddhist scriptures.[60]

In its original incarnation, the story is a parable related by the Lord Buddha to illustrate a sermon. Some of his bhikkhus, or monastic followers, had lapsed into dissension, and it fell to their master to reaffirm in their hearts his fundamental ethic of peace, of goodwill toward men. His parable tells of a king who learns through experience to put aside his sword and rule according to higher principles of justice and mercy; the lesson for the Buddha's disciples is that "if such is the forbearance and mildness of kings who wield the scepter and bear the sword, so much more, O Bhikkhus, must you so let your light so shine before the world."[61]

In the climactic episode of the tale, a young prince named Dhigavu (Long-life) is granted a perfect opportunity to avenge the deaths of his father and mother, who had been executed in the aftermath of a war of conquest by a neighboring king, Brahmadatta. With Brahmadatta asleep before him, three times Dhigavu draws his sword to slit his enemy's throat and three times restores it to its sheath, remembering his noble father's last words: "Not by hatred is hatred appeased; by not-hatred is hatred appeased." He spares the king's life; and in return the awakened king, morally overwhelmed, not only spares Dhigavu's life, but "gave him back his father's troops and vehicles, his realm, his treasuries and storehouses, and he gave him his daughter."[62]

This parable fits the ethical core of Tolstoyan Christianity, as Leskov quickly recognized. From the ethical point of view only slight changes were required to suit it to other Tolstoyan fables. One episode from the original had to be screened out. In the original version the prince's mother, while pregnant with him, experiences the "longing of pregnant women [. . .] to see an army, with its four hosts set in array, clad in armor, standing on auspicious ground, and to drink the water in which the swords were washed."[63] The aim of this "longing," which the mother gratifies, is to ensure that her offspring will be a boy, a hero, and ultimately a king. Neither the means nor the ambition was acceptable in Tolstoyan terms. Likewise, the fairy-tale reward for Dhigavu's virtue, the restoration of his kingdom and the hand of Brahmadatta's daughter, was too materialistic for a Tolstoyan hero. Leskov therefore says nothing about his hero's marriage or restoration.

Other changes illustrate the differences between the "poetics" of an authentic parable-folktale as found in the *Vinayapiṭaka* and a nineteenth-century simulation. The bareness of the original seems intolerable to the nineteenth-century writer: the "empty," abstract characters, the absence of props, the lack of plausibly motivated sequences. In the original version, after lamenting his parents' death, Dhigavu goes to Brahmadatta's elephant stables and apprentices himself as a trainer. His nocturnal singing and lute-playing there attract the king's attention, and the story moves on as he is invited to join the king's inner circle. Leskov cannot leave it at that. He first manufactures an unemployment crisis to force Dhigavu into his undignified work of elephant-tending. Then, to explain the vacancy among the king's elephant keepers, Leskov proceeds to characterize a particular elephant as so savage and bloodthirsty that several trainers have been trampled to death or seized in its trunk and beaten against its stall. The regular trainers refuse to go near it, even on pain of execution. The scene is thus set for the hero to tame the beast with his courage as well as his musical talents, and thus gain access to the king. Through these episodes a whole little world, the royal elephant stables, comes vividly alive at Leskov's hands, complete with distinct personalities, including an elephant's; the interactions of the personalities fill out a narrative sequence.

The contrast between these two versions provides a revealing measure of the two distinct poetic systems, both endeavoring to inculcate in men's hearts the same ideal: "not by hatred is hatred appeased; by not hatred is hatred appeased."

36

The *Prolog*

Alongside the "fables," the didactic impulse of Leskov's late years found its major outlet in a series of stories identifiable more by source than by precise genre characteristics: his *Prolog* tales. As noted earlier, the *Prolog* is the Slavonic title (preserving an ancient confusion) of the Greek *Synaxarion*, a collection of short lessons, or *exempla*, mostly narratives from saints' lives, arranged according to the church calendar. Various versions of the *Prolog* had been circulating in Russia since the early Middle Ages.[1] A printed edition was brought out as early as 1640, and others were issued periodically during the eighteenth and nineteenth centuries under the auspices of the Holy Synod, mainly to be read aloud in churches. The Synod's editions were not acceptable to the Old Believers, who kept the *Prolog* alive in manuscript and in printed editions of their own. An avid collector of antiquarian books, especially on religious subjects, Leskov owned several copies of the *Prolog*, including an Old Believer edition he considered richer in piquant material than the official one.[2]

Unlike the much fuller and more elaborated saints' lives included in the *Chet'i-Minei* or Menologia, the *Prolog* stories are related in naked, naive, artless form—"simple and stupid," as Leskov once bluntly described their style[3]—without elaboration of the characters or realization of the background. They are narration at its most primitive, strings of "and then and then and then," their order prescribed only by chronology, and their main interest, at least for their original audience, lying in the unusual or spectacular nature of the events recounted.

In the early Christian context evoked in the *Prolog* stories, the unusual ingredient mostly consists in displays of the supernatural powers acquired or invoked by saints: practical demonstrations of the new religion's efficacy, graphic manifestations of its God's potency. The educated nineteenth-century reader, even a devout one, might well have regarded many of these stories with skepticism or dismay, for the display of credulity is obvious.

In making use of these old legends as vehicles for Tolstoyan lessons, therefore, Leskov risked resistance on the part of his educated readers. He also knew that because of their church associations his *Prolog* tales would automatically be submitted to the ecclesiastical censorship. The latter might disapprove of his amendments of several *Prolog* plots and might suspect a satirical aim in the very resurrection of these relics of ancient fantasy. Leskov therefore took pains to minimize doctrinal significance in the *Prolog* itself. In a programmatic introduction to "The Legend of Conscience-stricken Daniel," for example, he maintained that the *Prolog* heroes were not saints. "Their stories were presented in olden times simply as entertaining and edifying reading 'with the aim of spiritual instruction' [. . .] The reader must not forget that such legends do not in our day carry any church authority whatever. On the contrary, they have even been subjected to ridicule by such theologians as Feofan Prokopovich, who in his *Spiritual Reglament* openly calls them 'idle and laughable tales.' "[4] Similarly, in a letter to Suvorin, who was also worried about the ecclesiastical censorship, Leskov reiterated that the *Prolog* was "not a holy and not even a church book, but a repudiated (*otrečennaja*), so to speak, 'retired' (*otstavnaja*) one."[5]

The statement is inaccurate, perhaps deliberately so. Though its editions may have become less frequent or been edited, the Orthodox church never repudiated or "retired" the *Prolog*: the Synod published a new edition of it the year after Leskov's death.[6] Nevertheless, the stories in it epitomize a difficulty besetting Christianity in modern times: how to tone down miraculous legends in order to suit the skeptical spirit of a scientific age and at the same time avoid alienating the millions of "unenlightened" believers who still take the magic at face value.

To a nineteenth-century professional writer the *Prolog* must have seemed like an immense store of undeveloped plots: narrative seeds needing the literary soil and water needed to make their picturesque episodes come to life. "The *Prolog* is rubbish [*xlam*]," Leskov wrote to Suvorin, "but in that rubbish there are such pictures as you couldn't dream up."[7] With his interest in church history and church literature and his fondness for relics of the medieval past, Leskov had good reason to turn to the *Prolog* for literary inspiration. It represented part of the stream of Russian national culture, reaching deep into the Middle

Ages and, via Byzantium, back to antiquity. Though neither anti-Western nor a "kvas patriot," Leskov was conscious of the cultural roots of his Russianness. The *Prolog* for him was a Christian cultural resource, thoroughly Russified and assimilated, "suiting the taste," as he maintained, of the "plebeian readers" he most hoped to influence.[8]

By the time he began using the *Prolog* for literary raw material, Leskov had widely diverged from official Orthodoxy. There was therefore an insidious motive in his turning to that source, a characteristic slyness. Fighting his ecclesiastical enemies with their own ammunition, he undertook to extract from the *Prolog* stories a very different ideal of Christianity from that propagated by the church. Keeping an eye on the censorship and assuming a pose of scholarly straightforwardness, Leskov contrived to present his counterideal as if it were the "natural" content of the *Prolog* stories, saying nothing about any changes he might have made in their meanings or their plots. He was, he pretended, simply retelling in modern language stories the church regarded as edifying, at least for uneducated believers.

Leskov had another, more literary motive directing him to the *Prolog*. With their settings in the ancient Near East, Egypt, Palestine, and Byzantium, the *Prolog* stories brought him to the locus of a current European literary fashion. Whereas the classic eighteenth-century literary tourist (Sterne, Mme de Stael, Fonvizin, Karamzin) had seldom strayed from civilized Europe, the Romantics had developed a taste for more exotic climes, from Chateaubriand's America to Byron's Albania. The realists and neoromantics of the late nineteenth century energetically traveled to the remotest parts of the globe in search of literary material (Gautier, Melville, Conrad, Kipling, Goncharov, Chekhov, and a host of others). The fascination with displacement in space was paralleled by a love for imaginary movement through time. Scott's novels had provided the model for numberless literary junkets to distant times and places. Finally, in such works as *Salambô* the two trends seemed to merge: the author's dutiful tramping about the ruins of Carthage matching the compulsive conscientiousness of his library researches.

In addition to the temporal and spatial voyages of its professional writers, the nineteenth century also produced an efflorescence of straightforward scholarly research into the pasts of many nations, especially the great Mediterranean civilizations of antiquity. Much of this research was then popularized for a wider public, sometimes by the scholars themselves. Among these were the great Egyptologists Leskov specifically mentions among his sources: Georg Ebers (1837-

1898) and Gaston Maspero (1846-1916). Ebers, a professor of Egyptology at Leipzig, had an immensely successful secondary career as a historical novelist, though his fiction does not seem to have survived time's ravages as well as his famous papyrus.[9]

Leskov's involvement with this tradition is peripheral. He never visited the sites of his "Oriental" stories, not even Constantinople. He was far less a scholar than Flaubert. He knew no ancient languages (apart from a smattering of Latin). Except for his medieval Slavonic texts, he relied on modern popularizations for his historical material. Furthermore, his *Prolog* tales represent only a small, and relatively minor, part of his total *oeuvre*. Nevertheless, for a period of about five years, from 1886 to 1891, Leskov devoted himself intensively to fictional recreations of the ancient world, hoping to make of them an efficient vehicle for conveying the Tolstoyan message into simple Russian hearts.

The precise chronology of the composition of Leskov's *Prolog* tales is not easy to determine. Many of them encountered difficulties with censorship and were not published until many years after they were written. It seems reasonably clear, however, that the lead-off piece in the *Prolog* cycle was "The Tale of the God-favored Woodcutter," incorporated into the pro-Tolstoyan article entitled "The Best Suppliant."[10] This article was a follow-up of Leskov's earlier defense, with Filipp Ternovsky, of Tolstoy's story "What Men Live By."[11] Though he had not recognized the ultimate *Prolog* roots of Tolstoy's story (which he simply identified as a folktale), Leskov says he subsequently began to "sense ancient prologues" behind several of Tolstoy's later folk-style stories; and he triumphantly reports that a visitor at Yasnaya Polyana had seen a copy of the *Prolog* in Tolstoy's study.[12] Thus, as early as 1886 Leskov saw Tolstoy's "torch" as lighting the way not only to the larger truths of a purified Christianity, but to the *Prolog* as a compendium of early Christian stories that could be used to illustrate these truths.

"The Tale of the God-favored Woodcutter" set the fundamental pattern for Leskov's selection of *Prolog* material. The unadulterated original (September 8) points one of Leskov's favorite morals: the prayers of a poor woodcutter prove dearer to God than those of a bishop. That God's preferences are demonstrated through a drought-ending rainstorm contributes to the naive charm of this early Christian stylization; the scientifically minded nineteenth-century reader, if he liked, could take the rain as an accident of timing which symbolizes the moral irrelevance of the church hierarchy. The only traces of authorial irony in the accounts of supernatural manifestations are punctuational: the ellipsis (. . .) following the words "beneficent rain" and the quotation marks enclosing the "voice from heaven" that informs the bishop which person's prayers are to be solicited in order to relieve the drought. And the fact that the bishop, both in the original story and in Leskov's version, is presented as a good and kind Christian (after the prayer episode he supports the woodcutter for the rest of his life) further helps to camouflage the subversive Leskovian intent. But the implication is clear that if God prefers the prayers of a poor woodcutter to those of a good bishop, who is a specialist in prayers, perhaps the need for a professional clergy should be reconsidered.

Leskov's next *Prolog* adaptation to be published was "The Tale of Theodore the Christian and His Friend Abraham the Hebrew," already discussed in chapter 29. The artistic shortcomings of this story perhaps made Leskov more aware of the difficulties of utilizing early Christian plots in a nineteenth-century literary environment. One remedy was, like Flaubert, to play the literary archaeologist and load one's pages with authentic physical detail. Another, which appealed to Leskov, was to combine lavish physical detail with lushness of language, including ostentatious rhythmicization of the prose. It was as if the profusion of shapes, physical and verbal, would compensate for inherent weaknesses of characterization and plot. Leskov sought to apply both "Flaubertian" remedies in his next *Prolog* tale, "Pamphalon the Mountebank,"[13] Both these solutions were far removed from the austere simplicity prescribed by Tolstoy.

The subversively anti-Orthodox moral of "Pamphalon" is much like that of "The Tale of the God-favored Woodcutter" (even its original title, "The Tale of a God-pleasing Mountebank,"[14] was similar): Christian virtue (love) is manifested not in feats of ascetic self-mortification—a useless, egocentric, parasitic procedure—but in active good works among men. This moral is perhaps in some sense inherent in the original story (*Prolog* for December 3), but it is never explicitly drawn there. In that version a high Byzantine official, the exarch Theodulus, disgusted with the vanities of the world, withdraws from earthly concerns and spends thirty years as a stylite. A message from heaven informs him that a certain Cornelius, a public entertainer in Damascus, is a man "of great virtue and worthy of the kingdom of heaven." Theodulus comes down from his perch, seeks out Cornelius, and extracts from him the story of his life, which consists mainly of extraordinarily self-abnegating acts of charity. Cornelius's *vita* is a graphic illustration of a Christian ideal the opposite of Theodulus's self-centered asceticism: active love for others. Apparently satisfied, but having learned nothing, Theodulus in the original story returns to his pillar; and the pious author, missing the implications of his own material, regards both his "saints" with equal veneration. There is no conclusion.

Leskov cannot let his self-centered stylite get away with such imperviousness to heaven's lessons. His Theodulus, renamed Hermius to appease the censors,[15] must be forced to admit that the good works of a lowly mountebank have more value in God's eyes than all his own self-inflicted suffering, and that his, Hermius's, withdrawal from his responsibilities as a Byzantine official had been a selfish and cowardly act, a cop-out. God, according to Leskov, wants us to stay in there fighting: "man must serve man," as he puts it (8:230). At the end of his career, like Tolstoy's Father Sergius (a story Leskov could not have known at this time), Hermius expiates his previous selfishness by a life of *useful* humility, serving peasants as a goatherd and teaching their children.[16]

Thus, in Leskov's reshaping of the legend Hermius's character shows moral growth and acquires psychological interest.[17] The same, however, cannot be said of his moral instructor, the mountebank Cornelius, renamed Pamphalon. Unlike Hermius, Pamphalon remains on the plane of medieval "absolute" characters, unchangingly good. Although Leskov tries to render his goodness humble and not priggish, Pamphalon's character does not develop, and he experiences no internal conflicts. He simply "illustrates" his natural goodness. Although such combinations of absolute and complex characters in the same work are not unknown in nineteenth-century fiction (for example, in Dickens), it is open to question whether the mix in "Pamphalon the Mountebank" is a successful one.

Leskov tries to avoid psychological monotony within Pamphalon's life story by introducing another "growth" character, Magna, the object of Pamphalon's most spectacular charity. Magna is a sympathetic, morally sensitive girl, insulated in her early years by affluence and prudery from the realities of life. To outgrow her naive self-righteousness she must go through the school of hard knocks, eventually to be rescued from total degradation by the ever-generous Pamphalon.

Like several of Leskov's other supermoral voyages into antiquity, the edifying story of Magna's corporal fall and spiritual elevation also provides the author with a convenient pretext for describing the world of ancient vice—the opulent abodes of elegant hetaerae. As Chekhov put it later in relation to "Legendary Characters," Leskov confronts us all at once with a curious "mixture of virtue, piety, and fornication"—

567

highly original and entertaining, but in the last analysis perhaps a case of the author's irrepressible id interfering with his conscious moral purposes.[18]

The artistic center of gravity in the story thus shifts to its superficies, to its physical and verbal "texture." Leskov took pains in "Pamphalon the Mountebank" to weave a decorative fabric full of ancient color and to create verbal rhythms of which the following translation can only be a pale reflection: " 'Stop!' I [Pamphalon] cried. 'I recognize thee. Thou art indeed the noble Magna, daughter of Ptolemy, in whose gardens with thy father's permission I often amused thee in thy childhood with my games and received from thy loving hands coins and wheaten bread, raisins, and pomegranates! Tell me quickly what has happened to thee, where is thy spouse, the rich and luxurious Byzantine Rufinus, whom thou lovedst so dearly? Can he have been swallowed up by the waves of the sea, or has his young life been cut short by the sword of some barbarian Scyth who has sailed across the Pontus? Where are thy family, the children?' "[19]

This brief specimen of antique stylization brings out another technical problem besetting Leskov's *Prolog* stories: the neutralization of the skaz narrator. Following the Leskovian formula, Pamphalon tells Hermius his story in his own words. But how can the words of an early Christian Greek speaking nineteenth-century Russian be made to sound individual and personal? Such authentically picturesque, socially marked language as Father Tuberozov's is impossible. The need for linguistic color forced the author to look elsewhere. As this passage shows, his only recourse was to an incongruous ultra-literariness: the lowly mountebank is made to speak bookish and conventionally poetic literary Russian.

Aleksei Suvorin, who had also been undertaking some literary excursions into antiquity,[20] apparently criticized Leskov's story for its linguistic artificiality. Stung, Leskov replied that his correspondent had himself "antiquicized" in a similar way the language of his play *Medea*, just as Flaubert had done in *The Temptation* [Leskov says *Vision*] *of St. Anthony*. Such simple prose as that of Tolstoy's "Prisoner of the Caucasus," Leskov insisted, "would have been inappropriate" for "Pamphalon the Mountebank." To describe Leskov's style Suvorin had evidently used the vivid, but pejorative Russian word *zalizannyj*, literally "licked," slick, overpolished. In his defensive tirade Leskov tried to turn even *zalizannyj* into a positive quantity, evidence of how exacting his artistic standards were by comparison with others. " 'Polish' [*zalizannost'*] there is [in "Pamphalon the Mountebank"], i.e., great and excessively painstaking execution; but I think it can be tolerated, since it is met with so rarely nowadays."[21]

Suvorin's jibe continued to rankle, however. When a favorable review of the story appeared in *Russian Thought*, singling out the language for especial praise, Leskov triumphantly wrote not to Suvorin himself, but to his factotum Shubinsky, the editor of *Historical Messenger*, where the story had first appeared:

> The magazine [. . .] sings the praise of Pamphalon, valuing especially the story's language—"original and reminiscent of ancient tales,"—and also its "clarity, simplicity, and irresistibility." This must be pleasant for you, since you were the first and for a long time the only one who appreciated this story, which cost me particular labor in simulating the language and studying the way of life of a world we have not seen and about which the Josephite *Prolog*, in the life of St. Theodulus, gives only a weak and very brief hint. This praise and the fact that "The Mountebank" is *universally* liked and beloved give me little personal satisfaction, but I am very glad for you—because of the sadnesses and vexations you endured and because of the stupid cavils of those who should have thanked you for your discrimination in acquiring a genuinely "artistic work," as it is now described. "The Mountebank" will long outlive much that owes its reputation to publicity and advertisement. I worked over it a great, great deal. This language, like that of "The Steel Flea," does not come easily, but with great difficulty, and only love for the task can induce a man to undertake such mosaic work. But I was reproached for this very "original language"; and so they [Suvorin] made me spoil it somewhat, deprive it of color. May God forgive these unjust judges! They must have forgotten that there are people who do not merely turn out products for the market, without corrections, straight to the printers, "let the shit freeze just the way it comes out." But the public has fallen in love with "The Mountebank," Lev Tolstoy gives it his blessing, and the critics praise it [. . .] So you have been vindicated manyfold, and I rejoice for you, my good friend: we have given the public a real literary work in these days of total decadence and hucksterism.[22]

This outburst of thinly disguised self-congratulation perhaps hid a lack of confidence in the artistic merits of this "universally beloved" story. To Suvorin, who neither loved nor praised it, Leskov had written wistfully, in the letter eliciting the criticisms that angered him, "Is 'The Mountebank' really altogether bad? Out of cowardice I spoiled it terribly."[23] And in later years, when his defensive enthusiasm had cooled, Leskov's doubts revived. In 1888 he expressed surprise that the story had been selected for translation into German, proclaiming that, of his early Christian cycle, "The Beauteous Aza" was notably better.[24] Later he rated "The Mountain" higher than both "Aza" and "The Mountebank."[25]

Still excited by its literary potential, Leskov in 1887 undertook to make a comprehensive survey of The *Prolog*, ostensibly to provide other writers with a guide to its riches. Though he was planning to polish the choicest nuggets himself, Leskov first wrote his "survey" as a straightforward article.

In order to approach the subject in this journalistic manner, he required some angle of attack, some "àpropos" theme that would give direction and unity to the disparate material. He chose a theme not only topically relevant, but also piquant. He mined the *Prolog* for comparative material concerning the "woman question"; and he extracted from that anthology for ascetics not only the expected moralizing about sexuality, but a surprising amount of what today's lawyers call "prurient interest."

Leskov structured his survey, ultimately entitled "Legendary Characters," as a refutation of an allegedly prevalent misconception, that in the medieval saints' lives, "which our forefathers believed in," women were invariably presented in a bad light, as temptresses whose aim was to "lure men away from the lofty tasks of life and immerse them in a life of irrationality and sensuality." Leskov maintains vehemently that this charge is false. To prove his point he trots out, one after the other, a series of female characters appearing in the *Prolog*. Are they wanton temptresses or not?

According to Leskov's statistics, the *Prolog* contains exactly one hundred plots "more or less suitable for representation in narrative or plastic art." Women characters figure in only thirty-five of these. Since the *Prolog* was presumably compiled by and designed for the edification of male monks, this paucity of women characters is not surprising. What is surprising is the honesty of these monastic homilists in dealing with the problem of human sexuality.

Some of the monks were tempted by real women, some by female creatures of their imaginations; but in either case the *Prolog* legends, as Leskov recounts them, do *not* adhere to the expected formula, blaming women for the lust men feel for them. On the contrary, the stories make clear that in most cases, sexual desire arises spontaneously in the men's psyches. In most of the stories the women are passive figures; when they are active, it is to resist male tempters.

According to Leskov's statistics, in seventeen of the thirty-five *Prolog* stories dealing with erotic temptations, the women make no effort to seduce the men, but "on the contrary, the men themselves are carried away in that direction with extraordinary ease and lack of discrimination."[26] In only four cases do active temptresses appear, and in all but one of these their seductive efforts come to nothing; the men resist their enticements. Of those three, one is a prostitute and another a former one; a third is a young girl who is mentally disturbed. In nine cases the women are models of virtue, helping their male counterparts to overcome *their* sensual inclinations. And of the remaining five *Prolog* women, Leskov considers only two clearly evil: one who murders her children in the hope of pleasing her lover, who has reproached her for them; and one who commits abortion (at least in intent). The remaining three are either morally neutral or clearly pardonable, such as the girl forced into prostitution to support her widowed mother. (She has a brother, but he has "died unto the world" in a monastery and will do nothing for his relatives.) The case of the irresponsible brother—one of many instances Leskov cites of callous self-centeredness on the part of otherworldly "saints"—illustrates one of Leskov's covert purposes. These ingenuous case histories provide ample illustrations of some of his favorite truths, especially the many "temptations" inherent in the structure of institutional Christianity.

For the most part Leskov makes little attempt in "Legendary Characters" to develop these case histories into full-fledged narrative art. There are too many of them for that. Two of the plots, however, were so appealing that they were given more extended development in "Legendary Characters" and later appeared as independent works: "The Mountain" and "The Beauteous Aza" (the latter virtually unchanged from "Legendary Characters"). Most of the other plots are given summary treatment. Yet the procession of artless summaries, in which piquant material is embedded, as if naively, in pious commentary, makes a quaint, striking impression, as Chekhov noted ("virtue, piety, and fornication").

The manifest displays of "fornication" in "Legendary Characters," combined with suspicions of the author's anti-Orthodox intentions, proved too much for the censors and for friendly editors as well. Leskov had completed the work by the end of 1887, as his letter to Suvorin of December 26 shows (11:362). He hoped to publish it in *Historical Messenger*, which Suvorin owned, but ran into an unexpected obstacle. The editor, Shubinsky, considered the article shockingly immoral and rejected it with indignation.[27] Other attempts to publish it proved equally fruitless. Parts of the survey were read aloud by Leskov in the pious environs of The Intermediary (Tolstoyan) bookstore on May 1, 1888, and again in the studio of the painter Ilya Repin on February 23, 1889;[28] but it was not until 1892 that the survey finally appeared in print.[29] As Leskov wrote to Stasyulevich on February 8, 1895, only a fortnight before his death, his "Survey of the *Prolog*" had "slept" in his desk for five years (11:607). In the meantime several of the stories summarized there had already been published in fully "Leskovized" form.[30]

Leskov's next "prolog"[31] to be completed was not taken from this "pornographic" series. It focused on violence. With his "Legend of Conscience-stricken Daniel" Leskov moved from the titillating Seventh Commandment to the lurid Sixth.[32]

The original story, found in the *Prolog* for June 7, tells of a hermit on Mount Sinai who was three times kidnapped by "barbarians." The first time he was ransomed and the second he managed to escape. The third time, driven to fury by torments, he picked up a stone, killed his captor with it, and fled. Afterwards he deeply repented this bloody deed and in search of absolution went to Alexandria and confessed his crime to the patriarch. That dignitary brushed aside the sin as less then venial: to kill such a "beast" was no sin. Dissatisfied, Daniel undertook an "ecumenical" tour of all the high prelates of Christendom, including the pope of Rome and the patriarchs of Constantinople, Ephesus, Jerusalem, and Antioch, querying each about his point of conscience. All are in agreement: to kill a barbarian kidnapper is no sin. The secular authorities prove equally unwilling to inflict the desired punishment. Daniel's "prince" tells him, "Would that thou hadst killed seven more of those barbarians!" So Daniel assigns his own penance: to attach himself to a crippled and disfigured leper and care for him until death.

The reason for this story's appeal to the Tolstoyan in Leskov is obvious: even in the original version the conscience-stricken Daniel sets higher standards of Christian morality than the church hierarchy. In particular, he insists on a universal application of the Sixth Commandment. In the original, no conclusions are drawn from the ecclesiastical casuistry. Daniel seems to be offered as an illustration of moral maximalism, pleasing to God, but not appropriate for responsible church officials or for Christians generally.

Leskov exults at the opportunity to expose once again the moral weaseling of the hierarchs. He stresses particularly the ironic point, not mentioned in the *Prolog* at all, that the prelates were much more concerned with the minute doctrinal differences they detected in one another than with larger moral issues. But on the central question they were all in un-Christian agreement: extremism in the cause of Christ is no crime; it is all right to kill pagan barbarians. To underscore his irony, Leskov adds a gleeful footnote, derived, he says, from the "church history of Gasse," to the effect that the patriarch Timothy of Alexandria mentioned in the text was Timotheus Αἴλοδρος [Leskov's spelling], which he translates as "Timothy the Tergiversator," a "monophysite," who "according to circumstances accommodated himself wherever it was most advantageous."[33] With regard to secular hierarchs, Leskov also sharpens the *Prolog's* satirical edge. Where the original had Daniel spend a mere thirty days in the "prince's" dungeon waiting for trial, Leskov keeps him there "not one day, not two, and not a month, but many years," since the prince is too busy hunting, fighting, feasting, and horse-racing to attend to his judicial duties.

Otherwise, Leskov fleshes out the legend with detail, bringing to life some of the personalities and adding a few of his own creation, such as the wife of the man Daniel killed. Particularly effective is the personification of Daniel's bad conscience, his Ethiopian victim, whose image haunts him mercilessly, much as Boris Godunov was tormented by the "bloody boys" in his eyes. Leskov's gruesome description of the leper doubtless owes a good deal to the conclusion of "St. Julien l'hospitalier," though there is horror enough in the *Prolog* original, which Leskov tones down (he evidently could not stand the *Prolog* account of how Daniel takes food from the leper's mouth and eats it when the leper is unable to swallow).

In "Conscience-striken Daniel" Leskov was striving for Tolstoyan simplicity; in a preface to the original newspaper publication, he described its style as "in the spirit of the folktales of L. N. Tolstoy."[34] And the master was at first duly appreciative. Both "Conscience-stricken Daniel" and "The Beauteous Aza" are "splendid," Tolstoy wrote to his disciple Pavel Biryukov. "Aza," however, was too "curly," while "Daniel" was "simple and charming."[35] A year later, however, the story was apparently read aloud at Yasnaya Polyana, and this time Tolstoy's reaction was the opposite. "[We] read 'Conscience-stricken Daniel,' " he wrote in his diary. "Not good [*nexorošo*]."[36] He gives no indication of the basis for this drastically revised judgment. In the meantime his disciples had already taken steps to give "Conscience-stricken Daniel" mass distribution.[37]

The companion piece Leskov incongruously assigned to "Conscience-stricken Daniel" was "Beauteous Aza," a work in which Leskov tried again to show off the austere principles of Tolstoyanism against a lush background of Oriental sensuality.[38]

The nuclear plot for "The Beauteous Aza," taken from the *Prolog* for April 8, tells of a young pagan woman, an orphan left by her parents with a substantial fortune, who discovers a man about to hang himself in her vineyard. She persuades him to postpone his act of desperation; and when she learns its cause, hopeless indebtedness, she undertakes to pay the debts herself, even though it will cost her entire fortune. Her generosity leaves her destitute, and she is reduced to prostitution. Subsequently, she seeks to become a Christian. The puritanical Christians spurn her as a harlot: no baptismal sponsors can be found. The impasse is resolved by angels, who, assuming the shape of some local clergymen, present themselves as her sponsors, and the baptism is accomplished. An investigation by the bishop then reveals both the miracle and its explanation, the woman's previous feat of charity. After this she happily dies in the Lord.

Leskov's development of this tale moves in two opposing directions. The filling out of the skeletal plot, though serving to provide a more concrete image of characters and scenes, vividly realizes details of a torrid, pagan world charged with sexuality—the opposite of the chilly northern landscape of Tolstoyanism. None of these details are found in the *Prolog*. For instance, in Leskov's version, the heroine, when she discovers the would-be suicide in her vineyard, is just returning from a bath in the Nile. Her "enchanting, virginal body" is therefore only barely concealed by a "light coverture." She then invites the unhappy man indoors for a more extended interview. "She ordered a maid to serve fruits and cooling beverages, and seating her guest among soft pillows on a luxurious rug, went out to change her bathing dress for another. When Aza returned, she sat down there beside her guest, and behind them stood two black maidservants and by a light movement of silken tassels began to set in motion a huge fan made of large variegated feathers, steeped in perfume, which was suspended from the ceiling" (8:293). It is hardly an ascetic setting. Nothing improper occurs between Aza and her guest; but neither the reader's nor the writer's thoughts can be said to be wholly concentrated on the suicide's troubles.

The borrowed plot of "Aza" gives Leskov an opportunity to treat his favorite subject, "bishops and baptisms." The implied conclusion, even of the *Prolog* version, is not "Orthodox." First, the heroine while still a pagan displays more charity than could be expected of a devout Christian. Secondly, the Christians, despite Jesus' example, are as bigoted and self-righteous toward the selfless harlot Aza as the Pharisees. What, one asks, has been the moral force of baptism?

Leskov cannot pursue too far the notion that people's responsiveness to others, their basic "goodness" or "badness," has little to do with religious indoctrination. For if that were true, what would be the use of writing Tolstoyan fables? But he stresses how irrelevant to larger moral truths is the obsession of the Christian clergy with religious technicalities. To bring this point home, Leskov changes the shape of the final miracle. In his version the rescuing angels no longer eliminate the obstacles to Aza's earthly baptism. The two "radiant persons" simply dress her body in baptismal robes and carry her soul off with them to the "habitation of the living." No baptismal ceremony is performed. Admission to paradise, Leskov implies, can be gained by the virtuous without a baptismal ticket. The clergy, faced with this demonstration of divine indifference to their "sacrament," at once find a new technicality to worry about: what sort of burial can be given to the body of this officially unbaptized harlot?[39]

In this story of an unbaptized, pagan paragon there seems to be no room for human representation of "true" (Tolstoyan) Christianity. The angels have preempted the role. Nevertheless, Leskov the preacher, perhaps fearing that his readers might miss the symbolic message of the silent angels, introduces a Tolstoyan *raisonneur* into the story. Like the Tolstoyan tutor Chervyov inserted in the late version of *A Decrepit Clan*, Leskov sends a saintly Syrian philosopher to comfort Aza when she is at her lowest ebb of despair. This "stranger" gives her some Tolstoyan lessons, which she hardly needs ("We are all sent here by God to show love to one another and to help one another in sorrow"), and to tell her that her sins have been forgiven. But since the lessons are unneeded and the divine forgiveness is authoritatively demonstrated by the angels, the "Tolstoyan" teacher is artistically superfluous.

Leskov is also unable to repair the chief weakness of the original plot, the lack of contact, after her original benefaction, between Aza and the man she has rescued and his family. A "Hellene," he might have returned to Greece after paying his debts. But would he and his family, which included a girl Aza's age, have gone off without any thought of their benefactress? If so, his characterization is inconsistent, for he is represented as a devoted family man ready to kill himself to save his daughter from the lascivious clutches of his creditor. Why did Aza not apply for aid to this family?

Neither the *Prolog* nor Leskov provides answers. To point the moral the heroine must voluntarily reduce herself from affluence to destitution. The destitution is symbolically important, a measure of the scope of her generosity. Since *Prolog* stories seldom concern themselves with psychological loose ends or even verisimilitude, in that context we may perhaps accept this motivational lacuna as an attribute of the genre; but in a nineteenth-century version it is less tolerable.

The original story shows covert awareness of the problem. To investigate the reasons for her melancholy state, Aza's first angelic visitor appears to her in the shape of the man she had rescued. Only later does the angel recruit quasi-clerical assistants to serve as her baptismal sponsors. Leskov, however, eliminates this detail. He apparently felt that to pick up the figure of the rescued Greek again, even in the form of an angelic impersonator, would create more problems than it solved. Better to ignore him altogether after his purpose, obliterating Aza's fortune, has been served.

Leskov was aware that "The Beauteous Aza" might raise problems with the censorship. In the original newspaper version he therefore included a "diversionary" preface, hoping to throw the censors off the scent. There he vehemently inveighed against those, including his former friend Vsevolod Krestovsky, who misinterpreted Jesus' famous words concerning the woman who washed his feet with her tears, popularly identified with Mary Magdalene ("Her sins, which are many, are forgiven, for she loved much"; Luke 7:47). For vulgarians like Krestovsky "loving much" simply meant "loving" many different men. Leskov ostensibly offers the story as an antidote to this gutter view of Christian love.[40]

Leskov had high hopes for the didactic effect of Aza, and he took pleasure in contemplating how "ideas of mercy" would reach the uncouth hearts of the folk (11:369). He also delighted in contemplating the skill he himself had repeatedly shown in maneuvering these stories aroud the censors' roadblocks. His self-congratulation had a certain defensiveness, however. Impeccable as were the Tolstoyan principles in the story, some of Leskov's fellow Tolstoyans were not unaffected by its sensuality. What if the "exuberance" of Leskov's style, as Lyubov Gurevich discerned, were an expression of the author's passionate sensuality, imperfectly papered over with Tolstoyan morality?

When charged with literary voluptuousness, Leskov leapt to his own defense, invoking his all-purpose excuse: censorship. The lushness that disturbed his Tolstoyan brethren was a decoy for the censors. It was the "colored paper" in which a Tolstoyan fable had to be wrapped in Russia if it was to circulate legally. "Accept my work as I can do it," he half begged, half admonished the implacable Chertkov. "I am used to polishing my works and cannot work more simply." "To write as simply as Lev Nikolaevich is something I cannot do. It is not among my talents" (11:369).

Though, in his letter to Biryukov, Tolstoy had expressed disapproval of "Aza's" "curliness," Leskov vociferously claimed that Tolstoy had "approved and praised ['Aza'] from head to toe" and had advised him to "write another like it."[41] As Andrei Leskov has pointed out, immediately after citing this praise Leskov adds, "But I am very tired and exhausted and enough of that genre."

Almost simultaneously with "The Beauteous Aza" Leskov published in the children's magazine *Toy* his Tolstoyan version of the story of Saint Jerome and the lion.[42] The original legend is found in many versions within the Christian tradition, and the basic theme— the miraculous taming of a savage beast—is doubtless as old as mankind itself. Leskov's primary source was the *Prolog* (entry for March 4), but he almost certainly knew others, such as the *Golden Legend* and the *Spiritual Meadow* of John Moschus.

The medieval versions differ among themselves in various details, but Leskov's retelling stands radically apart from all its predecessors. Some of his changes are ideological in motivation—Tolstoyan twists to the old plot. First of all, to avoid entanglement with the ecclesiastical censors, he is at pains not to claim any connection between his hero and the historical Saint Jerome. Though the name is retained (Russian form Gerásim), the term "elder" (*starec*) is carefully substituted for "saint,"[43] and there is no reference to Saint Jerome's scholarship or other activities.

Other changes reflect a fundamental difference between the early Christian and the nineteenth-century mind. In the original versions, as in most Christian legends, including many parts of the Gospels, the basic strategy is to evoke wonder, to astound the reader with accounts of supernatural happenings; the miraculous provided clear evidence of divine power. Most nineteenth-century readers believed that all events without exception have natural causes, though we may not know them.

If the nineteenth-century writer is retelling a medieval legend, this upending of etiologies confronts him with contradictions. He may decide, as Leskov did in the case of Aza's angels, to leave some of the supernatural manifestations intact, as "accessories," quaint survivals of his medieval source. By tone and style, however, he makes clear that he is not taking responsibility for them; and the modern reader is free to regard them either as symbols or simply as picturesque fantasies. His other alternative is to offer naturalistic explanations for events his source presents as supernaturally caused.

Leskov uses both these methods in his "The Elder Jerome's Lion." That an adult lion is suddenly gentled and offers itself as a beast of burden—this event even in Leskov's presentation remains essentially miraculous. But it is enmeshed in a characteristic nineteenth-century pattern of psychological interaction that almost accounts for it causally. The cause of the lion's supposed gratitude is not just removal of the thorn (in Leskov's version a sharp stake), but the cumulative effect on the animal of Jerome's spiritual qualities, his combination of kindness and total fearlessness. Least of all is it due to magic powers acquired by the saint through ascetic practices.

More specifically Tolstoyan is Leskov's refusal to contaminate his leonine psychology with quasi-Orthodox ritualism. In the *Prolog* version, the lion is ultimately released from servitude to Saint Jerome and allowed to return to the wild. Nevertheless, it voluntarily comes back from its mountain every Sunday to make obeisance to its former master. Leskov has expunged this quaint detail, perhaps sensing that even in a nineteenth-century child it might evoke a skeptical smile rather than awe at God's wondrous ways.

Leskov also eliminates the *Prolog's* "sentimental" conclusion to the story, the lion's overwhelming display of grief at the saint's death. Discovering that its beloved master is no more, the *Prolog* lion bellows mightily and then expires atop Jerome's coffin. Even Moschus feels obliged to explicate this detail with a theological commentary. The lion's anthropic behavior does not show, he tells us, that the beast possesses human reason or a human soul. It is rather a sign from God "who seeks to glorify those who glorify Him, not only during their lives, but after their deaths"; and it also reminds us of the important fact that before he committed the original sin, all the beasts had been subject to the rule of Adam.[44]

Neither of these theological points, however, is acceptable to the Tolstoyan Leskov. He therefore stops his story short of the death of either main character, man or beast. Instead, he introduces a good Tolstoyan demonstration of the overpowering moral effect of Jerome's "nonresistance" on the robbers who stole his donkey. Their dread chieftain, Amru, is so overwhelmed that he offers to donate a tent so that Jerome can live closer to his water supply. The elder rejects this offer: the luxurious tent would only be a temptation and a pretext for further disputes over property, and it was to escape such discord that he had originally withdrawn from the world.

Leskov's next two *Prolog* tales, "The Felon of Ashkelon" and "The Mountain," are both expanded versions of "women" stories already selected and written up for "Legendary Characters." That anthology had not yet found a publisher. Leskov therefore undertook to out-maneuver timid editors and captious censors by doling out his legendary characters piecemeal. The maneuver was ultimately successful, though by no means easy, particularly in the case of "The Mountain," which was finally published, after great difficulties, only in 1890. "The Felon of Ashkelon" came out a little earlier.[45] Though written later than the original version of "The Mountain," it is treated here first.

The legend on which "The Felon" is based is found in the *Prolog* for June 14. It tells of a well-to-do merchant who loses his entire fortune in a shipwreck and is cast into prison by his creditors. His virtuous and beautiful wife, who regularly visits him in prison and brings him food, is offered the means to set him free: if she will spend a single night with a Byzantine magnate whose fancy she has caught, the latter will pay all her husband's debts. It is a poignant moral dilemma, a classic problem of ends and means: is the husband's liberty worth the price of the wife's virtue? Would the generous motive for the sacrifice of that virtue cancel out the sin? What would be the consequences?

The *Prolog* cannot permit any serious doubts on this score. Moral compromises and ambiguities can never be condoned, especially in the sexual sphere; and the Lord must be trusted to find a better way out. Christians should consider the problem not only from the perspective of this life, but of the next: there the balance will be righted. In this case, happily, Providence acts with dispatch. The wife insists on consulting her husband concerning the magnate's proposal, and the husband nobly spurns the very idea. At this point the much-needed deus ex machina appears. A frightful brigand, a co-prisoner of the husband's, who overhears this conjugal discussion, is touched by its display of purity and mutual loyalty. Knowing himself doomed, he reveals to the meritorious pair the location of his cache of ill-gotten gold. The amount proves more than sufficient to pay all the husband's debts; the magnanimous felon is duly beheaded; and the reunited couple, their bed undefiled, presumably live happily ever after.

This skeletal plot, despite its implausibilities, seemed a promising prospect for modern adaptation. First of all, the skeleton story needed flesh. The most obvious source had been shown by Flaubert in "Hérodias"—"archaeology." Leskov's "Felon" is loaded with period artifacts, the clothing, jewelry, food, and utensils of ancient Palestine.[46] Digging up these relics, even from readily accessible archaeological handbooks,[47] Leskov found a disconcertingly laborious task, much harder than working with the Russian settings he knew by instinct: repeatedly he complained—or boasted—about the immense labor his Oriental tales cost him. "Here every word requires reading and research," he wrote Suvorin.[48]

The archaeological artifacts, however, proved easier than resurrecting the human characters. The piquant *Prolog* plot potentially had great psychological interest. The possibilities are almost limitless, especially if the wife were permitted to accede to the proposal. With his own tangle of conflicting literary purposes, however, Leskov was unable to take full advantage of them. Again there proved to be an unbridgeable distance between a Christian parable and a modern short story.

First, presumably to make the heroine's experience more poignant, Leskov greatly intensifies the pressures on her to succumb. With her husband, Faldei, in prison, Tenia is the sole support of her two children and of her aged mother-in-law (all unknown in the *Prolog*). For a time she succeeds in providing this support by performing self-composed songs to her own harp accompaniment. But this source of income dries up when some imported Nubian belles appear with a strip-tease act ("There's a wasp buzzing somewhere inside my gown") that has greater box-office appeal. The mother-in-law begs her to sacrifice her virtue ("O Tenia, save us with thy beauty!"). And at last Faldei wavers: the conditions of his life in prison are appalling, and he faces the prospect of starvation if his wife ceases to bring him food.

Nevertheless, Tenia refuses to defile herself. Her resolute virtue in the face of these overwhelming pressures is perhaps conceivable psychologically, though surely its underpinnings would need more convincing demonstration than Leskov gives. But from a novelistic point of view, it certainly would have been more satisfactory if Tenia had given way. The aftermath of sin would have been more interesting than the magic reward of virtue. Could the transgression have been limited to "just this once"? What would have been the psychological repercussions, the effect on the husband, their marriage, the children, the mother-in-law, and on Tenia's idea of herself?

Fascinating as these questions were, Leskov felt precluded from pursuing them. Though he often made significant changes in the *Prolog* plots, in this case he professed himself bound by considerations of genre. The didactic fable, he believed, required exemplars of virtue, not vice. "It would have been better to end the story in 'sin,' " he wrote to Suvorin. "That would have been more probable [*statočnee*]. But I held to the genre and therefore wrote something closer to the outcome given in the *Prolog*."[49] Only in the essentially non-Christian "Insulted Neteta" was he able to explore the erotic possibilities of the alternative plot.

Holding to the genre, however, did not prevent Leskov from making a most insidious, ideologically motivated change in the *Prolog* plot, including the version of it he himself retold in "Legendary Characters": in "The Felon of Ashkelon" the *Prolog's* exemplary and virtuous *Christian* heroine, Tenia, is a pagan! This transformation enables Leskov to revive the strategy of "At the Edge of the World" (and also "The Beauteous Aza"), where the Siberian shamanist is endowed with more "natural" Christianity than most Orthodox Christians, including a priest. Though she has never been converted, Leskov's Tenia cites Jesus against the casuistry of her Mammon-serving Christian husband (in his preprison days): "Your Teacher bade you do good and not accumulate wealth," she insists, while he argues that after he has enriched himself his power to do good will be much augmented. (But even then he plans to bestow his charities only on those of his own faith.) And Tenia's pagan virtue proves impervious to the seductions and intimidations of the *Christian* viceroy, who to gratify his lust for her is prepared to spend money entrusted to him for the charities of the Empress Theodora. By this sly alteration in the original plot, Leskov once again calls attention to the gulf he perceived separating the Christianity of Jesus from the Christianity of the official Byzantine (read: Russian) establishment.

Suvorin, who had used the same *Prolog* source, expressed surprise at Leskov's undercover substitution of a pagan for a Christian. In his defense Leskov argued that Tenia's paganism made her moral conflict more meaningful. It would be "illogical," he insisted, for a Christian woman "at her husband's wish to go to another man's bed"; for her there could be no moral issue and therefore no conflict. But a pagan woman faced a dilemma about which she could "reason."[50] In fact, however, the heroine's rigid virtue seems just as impervious to reason under the pagan label as it had under a Christian one. Despite the pressures on her, Tenia never seems likely to give way. She has internalized an absolute taboo and can no more violate it than a music box can change its tune. As a result, for all its lavish color and despite the rhythmic prose of which Leskov was so proud, "The Felon of Ashkelon" cannot be said to have made the leap from the medieval to the modern with complete success. It remains a two-dimensional icon incompletely redrawn in three-dimensional perspective.

The most elaborate, and possibly the best, of all Leskov's adaptations of *Prolog* stories is "The Mountain," finally published, after many vicissitudes with the censorship, in 1890.[51] This short novel—it runs to nearly a hundred pages—illustrates, in extended form, the same features observed in earlier *Prolog*-based works: liberties taken with the plot of the original to render suitably Tolstoyan the Christian moral being preached; lavish detail, evoking an image of Oriental lushness; and signs of a fierce conflict over sexuality between the author's puritan principles and his voluptuous imaginings.

The plot of the original story, the *Prolog* lesson for October 7, is itself more complex than usual, involving two connected, but relatively independent episodes. A Christian goldsmith in Alexandria is tempted to fornication by one of his female customers. In resisting the temptation, he stabs himself in the eye, following literally the famous "castration" precept of Jesus (Matthew 5:29): "And if thy right eye offend thee, pluck it out." The woman flees in horror. At that time the Saracen ruler of Alexandria had also apparently been reading the Gospel according to Saint Matthew. Seizing upon the opportunity to extort another huge "contribution" from the Christian community, he summons the bishop and orders him to put into practice Jesus' exhortation (Matthew 17:20): "If ye have faith as a grain of mustard seed, ye shall say unto this mountain, Remove hence to yonder place; and it shall remove." The Christians are commanded to take Mount Adar and by the power of their faith cast it into the Nile; otherwise all their property will be confiscated.

The outcome of such a predicament, in a medieval Christian legend, is not hard to predict. All the Christians are summoned by the bishop to a night of prayer on the mountain; the woman who had attempted to seduce the goldsmith tells the bishop of his feat of self-mutilation; the goldsmith is summoned to join the prayers; and when he does, the mountain moves. Now the terrified populace have to beg the Christians to stop it before it buries their city. By the bishop's own prayers the mountain's movement is successfully braked; and—not surprisingly—"many barbarians believed in the Holy Trinity and were baptized."

Leskov had already given this tale fairly extended treatment in "Legendary Characters," where it is represented as one of the rare appearances in the *Prolog* of true seductresses. There he had followed the original plot, only transposing the action from Saracen back to Roman times, thus making Alexandria pagan rather than Moslem. Islam was a living religion; and with his commitment to tolerance, Leskov did not want, in a country with a large Moslem minority, to appear to be inciting the Christian majority against them. Furthermore, the antique props Leskov had collected in his literary researches would have been of little use in a description of Saracen Alexandria. Finally, the "Cleopatra" image would not have been in character in a Moslem city. Otherwise, the *Prolog* plot is left intact in "Legendary Characters," though the possibility is left open that the miracle may have a naturalistic explanation: an earthquake and landslide, by coincidence, may have occurred just when the Christians needed them.

Though these general outlines remain the same in "The Mountain," changes have occurred. The anti-Orthodox theme had to be worked into the story. Besides the bishop, now represented as a bumbling old man (his mountain-braking final prayer is eliminated, and the landslide stops by itself), Leskov introduces a wily patriarch. That mitred Macchiavelli decamps for parts unknown just before the ruler's decree about mountain-moving is published, leaving the bishop and the faithful to fend for themselves. Only after everything is over does he return to share the credit and extort what advantages he can from the badly shaken ruler.

In both the *Prolog* and in "Legendary Characters" the reason Zeno the goldsmith's prayers are not at once invoked by the Christians is, first of all, because the bishop does not know of his ascetic deed and has no reason to believe that his prayers would be efficacious. Secondly, he considers Zeno's occupation (like that of Pamphalon the mountebank) sinful—adorning with jewelry the depraved bodies of pagan women. But in "The Mountain" a new motive for the bishop's avoidance of Zeno is introduced: heresy. Zeno, it appears, may never have been properly baptized. He had been converted to Christianity by a "Syrian immigrant" and "did not think about everything exactly the way the other Christians in Alexandria were expected to do, without reasoning" (8:303). Though he does not criticize anyone publicly, Zeno holds himself aloof from the Christian community and attends no services. He communes with God directly, through prayer, not rituals. For him Christ is always the Teacher, a source of moral truth, not a deity endowed with supernatural powers. Though it appears to have moved a mountain, Zeno admits at the end that his faith is "weak" and variable. "Sometimes it barely flickers, like the glimmering of dawn; sometimes it burns bright and then illuminates everything for me" (8:389).

Even on their way to the mountain, where everything will depend on the strength of their faith, the other Christians are still arguing with the Old Believers: whether one should pray with the arms extended in the form of a cross; whether both palms should be turned upward or only the right one; or only the left one. Zeno comments only that he himself prefers to pray inwardly, "in devout silence," but condemns no one else's practice. All that is needed is that the "hands of the suppliants be free of cupidity and the spirit free of all evil" (8:378). The final irony is that when the landslide has started and the ruler seeks out the Christians to beg them to stop it, he finds them still arguing about how to pray. Encamped on the side of the mountain, they did not realize that it had already "moved," before they had gotten around to praying for it.

The censors first disallowed "The Mountain" on the grounds that in the figure of the patriarch Leskov had meant to satirize his old abomination, Metropolitan Philaret Drozdov. The charge was false, Leskov insisted.[52] There is no particular resemblance, except the general qualities of an adroit ecclesiastical politician; and it seems odd that the censors would resort to such a far-fetched identification if they wanted to suppress this genuinely subversive, anti-Orthodox story. If they insisted on making *à clef* identifications, they might have found a closer parallel between the evil old pagan priest Peochus, who reads holy scrolls by the light of a *lampada* (in Russian, "icon-lamp"), and the man Leskov always called "Lampadonostsev" (Pobedonostsev). "Contemporary Egyptians from the rabble considered Peochus a great zealot of the faith and went to him for advice as a man endowed with a sharp, penetrating mind, acuminated by implacable hatred of everything not in accord with antiquity. Peochus with equal implacability hated all faiths not in accord with the faith of the ancient Egyptians and was ready to do injury to every heterodox person" (8:329). *Mutatis mutandis*, it would have fitted Pobedonostsev pretty well. Further, Peochus incited the Egyptian rabble to *pogroms*—this word is used—against the Christians, just as the virulent anti-Semite Pobedonostsev was believed (although apparently falsely) to have condoned, if not incited, pogroms against Jews in Russia.[53] And apart from Pobedonostsev himself, the motivation for the Egyptian government's incitement, or at least toleration, of pogroms against the Christians was precisely that of the Russian government in relation to the Jews: pogroms were a safety valve, deflecting popular anger away from the mistakes, ineptitudes, and crimes of the government itself. "Poor and infuriated ignoramuses, instead of feeling indignant at the callousness of the government, vented their anger on the Christians and thus appeased their discontent" (8:330).

"The Mountain" encounters the same artistic difficulties as afflicted Leskov's other *Prolog* stories. The chief weakness is psychology: how to develop an iconographic figure and make it a believable human being. It cannot be said that Leskov accomplishes this with either of his principal characters. The goldsmith Zeno is the weaker of the two: too perfect, too static, too lacking in conflict to resemble a live man. His act of self-injury is supposed to be a last resort, a desperate effort to master overwhelming passion. But in the context, there is no passion to master. The seduction scene does not show Zeno convincingly tempted. If we feel any passion, it is hers, Nephora's, not his. What a contrast with the finger-chopping scene in Tolstoy's "Father Sergius," or the scene from the autobiography of the seventeenth-century archpriest Avvakum, forced to burn his hand with a candle-flame when the too graphic confession of a female parishioner aroused his lust. Leskov makes much of Zeno's artistic nature; and as in "The Alexandrite," one senses the author's spirit in the loving description of the jeweler's painstaking art. But Zeno's moral nature remains an abstract ideal, not a human reality.

Nephora is more interesting, though her character is not wholly convincing either. Her early representation as a "Cleopatra" or "Venus in Furs" figure, ordering her slaves whipped when they bring disappointing news from Zeno, has vitality, although perhaps she belongs more to the masturbation fantasy of a male masochist than to real life. In "The Mountain," however (as distinct from the *Prolog* and "Legendary Characters," where she is immediately chastened and guilt-stricken after Zeno's deed), her rage at Zeno's rejection ("hell hath no fury . . . ") is effectively used to motivate the later development of the action. Nephora extends her wrath against the whole Christian community, plotting against it with the evil witch Bubasta (*borodataja baba Bubasta*, "bearded granny Bubasta," an obvious alliterative steal from Baba Babarikha in Pushkin's "Tsar Saltan") and even agreeing to marry the ruler's half-witted son Dunaz in order to influence his father against the Christians. Later, by posing as a Christian and applying directly to the bishop, Nephora makes sure that Zeno will be included among the Christians mobilized to pray Mount Adar into the Nile and therefore, as she expects, dooms him to disgrace. That all this vengefulness is only an inverted form of Nephora's passion for Zeno seems plausible, as is her sudden break from the sadist's to the masochist's role ("I will be thy slave," she declares to him on the mountain).

Less convincing is Nephora's transformation, under Zeno's benevolent tutelage, into a humble and serene Christian Baucis. When she has voluntarily divested herself of her wealth through benevolences, the one-eyed Zeno decides that she meets his moral and sexual specifications, and they are married. In this state "they lived a long time and were useful to men and useful to God" (8:389). Maybe so, but one suspects that it would take more then Zeno to transform Cleopatra into Florence Nightingale.

As in other *Prolog* stories, Leskov attempts to compensate for psychological deficiencies by avoiding close-ups, limiting descriptions to large groups of people. "The Mountain" contains several mass scenes that would made a splendid film. The climactic episode on the mountain is narrated with superlative skill, tension building as Leskov describes the social groups and classes journeying from Alexandria to Mount Adar.

Like other *Prolog* stories, "The Mountain" is lavishly ornamented, visually and orally. Leskov lays on layer after layer of "archaeological" details, culled from the pages of "Ebers, Maspero, and other Egyptologists."[54] He also orchestrates the language to the point of musicality, which greatly impressed one of the story's first reviewers. "The simple, supple, pictorial and at the same time musical language," he wrote, "harmonizes amazingly well with the nobility and depth of content."[55]

Leskov was immensely pleased by this review and hurried off a triumphant letter to Shubinsky:

Trubachev is very kind to me, but he did not flatter me and did not distort the truth: "The Mountain" required extraordinarily hard work. It is something you can do only "out of love for art" and with the assurance that you are doing something of use to people, trying to subdue in them their coarse instincts and fortify their spirits to endure trials and undeserved offenses. "The Mountain" was recopied so many times that I have lost count of the number, and therefore it is true that in places the style attains "music." I knew that and it is true and it does Trubachev honor that he noticed this "musicality of language." There is no flattery here: I worked for this "musicality," which suits the plot like a recitative.[56]

Leskov did work long and hard on "The Mountain," but to the modern reader he seems to have overworked it, to have forced a theme he could not handle through instinct and intuition. "The Mountain" seems like a cake that is nothing but frosting.

Leskov's enthusiasm for "The Mountain" waned quickly. As early as 1889 he wrote the artist Repin that it was "not especially good, but *hard.*"[57] To Lavrov he wrote that others found "The Felon of Ashkelon" better than "The Mountain."[58] And to Goltsev later that year he voiced that opinion as his own.[59] "The Mountain" had quickly fallen from the author's favor.

The last of Leskov's *Prolog* adaptations to be published was "Innocent Prudentius"—yet another effort to fuse together the discordant themes of Tolstoyan morality and antique sexuality. The offspring of this misalliance was designed to articulate a "philosophy of love" that would be "Leskovian" rather than pure Tolstoyan—a compromise position, less grimly celibate than the bleak prescriptions of the "Afterword to the Kreutzer Sonata."[60] Though not printed until 1891, "Innocent Prudentius" was probably written, or at least drafted, several years earlier, as recently published correspondence proves. The story is of interest because it shows Leskov in literary interaction not only with Tolstoy and his ideas, but with another of the great Russian luminaries of the nineteenth century, Ivan Goncharov.[61]

One of the "sex" stories Leskov had culled from the *Prolog* (in the lesson for August 14) and retold in "Legendary Characters" ran as follows. A merchant seeks to marry the beautiful and virtuous widow of a friend. Though she likes him, she has decided to devote her life to religion. But she agrees to put her insistent suitor to a test: if he will faithfully follow her instructions, she will accede to his desire. He must remain without food in his room until further notice. After three days of starvation he is summoned to her abode, scarcely able to walk from hunger, and offered a choice: the marriage bed or dinner. He chooses the dinner. Thus made to realize, apparently, that life cannot be grounded in the transitory yearnings of the flesh, the merchant gives all his wealth to the poor and enters a monastery. His beloved becomes a nun.

In "Legendary Characters" Leskov had treated this story straight-forwardly, eliminating only the monastic ending. Like the model Tol-stoyan Klavdia and her ascetic fiancé in "Night Owls," the woman and her would-be husband must express their celibate religious com-mitment in the world. But even this purified ending apparently left Leskov dissatisfied. After all, the widow's lesson demonstrates not so much the superiority of spirit over flesh as simply of the stomach over the nether parts; and it was hard to see Tolstoyan virtue in that.

Puzzling over this problem, Leskov seized the occasion of their re-newed relationship to apply for advice to Goncharov. Goncharov's interesting reply has recently come to light:

> After your visit I kept thinking about the denouement of that legend and could not come to any logical conclusion. The salt, that is, the meaning of the denouement, still escapes me. If the widow simply wanted to get rid of an excessively insistent adorer, she could have thought up a more subtle, feminine, and moreover natural stratagem. As I understood from your narrative, she agrees to gratify his passion if he will endure the trial she pro-poses, i.e., a struggle with his passion. And the merchant readily accepts the proposal, prepared to endure ten [sic] days of starva-tion. She could have proposed an even simpler test: for instance, not to breathe for ten minutes, it's the same thing. Her stratagem is not clever and not natural. She mixed and confused physiolog-ical processes—and one can only regret that the merchant did not know physiology and psychology: he would have shown her that he *had not lost* at all. "She did not want to kill him," but in the meantime she was ready to turn him into a corpse, and even so, she would not have deflected him from his passion if he had re-mained alive. You asked my opinion; this is what came into my head. When you have written up this legend, I will of course be very curious to learn how you have cut this Gordian knot.[62]

Leskov replied, gratefully, if noncommittally, the same day: "I thank you heartily for your attention to my legend. They are all very naive, and they always have to be 'shaped up' [*prisnorovljat'*]. I feel the jus-tice of your observations and greatly value your attention."[63]

Goncharov did not live to see how Leskov cut Prudentius's Gordian knot,[64] and one is left wondering what his judgment would have been. Perhaps he would have felt that Leskov's solution, though it shows ingenuity, did not suceed in resolving the story's artistic and psychological confusions, not only in the ending, but in its whole design. The main problem, as Goncharov's remarks indicate, is one of characterization: how to endow these didactic stick-figures with the flesh and blood of realistic literary life.

In the effort to give the characters psychological depth, Leskov vastly expanded the *Prolog's* anecdote, among other things extending its time span. We first meet the widow, Melita, as a beautiful, virtuous young woman married to the dour Alceus. Though he is twice her age, Melita is "happy"—serenely faithful to her stern spouse and without an adulterous thought. The "friend" of the original story has been changed to the youthfully innocent Prudentius, son of Alceus's former partner. Further, an aura of criminality has been added. The widow's husband and his colleague are pirates, and early in the action Alceus apparently murders his partner, Prudentius's father. When Alceus in turn is brought back a corpse from one of his piratical expeditions, suspicion of a vengeance murder falls on the seventeen-year-old Prudentius, who had replaced his father in the partnership with Alceus; but the boy proves his innocence—thus living up to his sobriquet, "Innocent Prudentius." He had earned this epithet earlier, by his refusal to accede to the sexual temptations placed in his way by Alceus, who, like Knyazev in Leskov's play *The Spendthrift*, had hoped to corrupt the youth's soul, appropriate his property, and eventually get rid of him. The reason for Prudentius's imperviousness to seduction is not natural virtue or religion, but the fact that he is desperately in love with Melita.

This intrigue was apparently invented by Leskov, both to give a firmer psychological foundation to the *Prolog* starvation anecdote and to provide a quasi-allegorical illustration of the Leskovian erotic philosophy. From the psychological point of view, the prehistory was necessary in order to give Prudentius an opportunity to fall in love with his exquisite neighbor, Melita, four years his senior, who had chastely—her sexual feelings are apparently never stirred—served as his tutor, athletic instructor, and playmate.

Leskov's representation of Prudentius's developing "passion" is disastrously unconvincing, culminating in a transcription of delirious sleep-talk that surely belongs in the department of "raves I doubt ever got raved": "O, go not away, go not away, Melita! Show mercy unto me. Step with thy foot on this leaf which grows by the path. Touch it with thy foot, so that poor Prudentius may afterwards kiss it. Do this so that I may have relief in my grave torments! I shall take this leaf and cover it with my kisses. I shall wipe it with my tears which I shed for thee day and night, hiding from everyone that for which I really weep, and then I shall place this leaf on my heart, so that it should cease to beat, should cease to live, because life without thee is for me filled with torment, and on earth there is no one who would mean anything to me. I am going, I am fading, O Melita!" (9:84). (All this is said while asleep, though conveniently overheard by his mother and Melita's beautiful slave, Marema.)

For his allegorical purposes, Leskov needed the early non-*Prolog* section of the story in order to establish a moral spectrum, along which Prudentius (and later Marema) represent the center, the average human being, suspended between the two extremes, the saintly Melita on one side and the wicked and murderous pirates on the other. Prudentius may be innocent of murder and of promiscuity, but he is guilty of the "original sin" of all mankind, sexual desire. Leskov allows this passion to appear in its purest and most poetic form, the unrequited first love of an innocent young man for a lovely and virtuous woman. The old Tolstoy had taken a hard look at this much-celebrated facet of human experience, glorified by poets and novelists, including Lev Tolstoy, and it had withered beneath his gaze. All sex, he concluded, is selfish, bestial, and degrading. It has no "acceptable" forms, not even the conjugal bed; and the true Christian will strive to renounce it in thought and deed. In Leskov's story this "correct" Tolstoyan position is articulated and lived up to by Melita after her widowhood (her original marriage had occurred before her conversion, when she was too young to know better). Once freed, she has no intention of binding herself in another marriage, but plans to devote the rest of her life to good works, as her Christian friend Erminia had done (though not as a nun). Leskov here seems intellectually to accept this celibate ideal, but he is more willing than his master to allow ordinary human beings an acceptable way out of their sexual dilemma. Though starved out of his passion for Melita, Prudentius is offered— by Melita, standing in for Leskov—a consolation prize, her dark and lovely exslave, Marema (a reincarnation of Zarema, from Pushkin's "Fountain of Bakhchisarai").

The scene of the starvation test is transferred to a picturesque island, where the late pirates had established a well-supplied hideout. There two caves are conveniently arranged in such a way that Melita and Marema (who refuses to take advantage of her manumission, since she is necessary to the plot) can live in the lower one while the starving and love-lorn Prudentius suffers up above. He does not starve alone, since one of Leskov's Gordian knot modifications is to have Melita observe the same fast. She endures it with much more fortitude than either he or Marema (who downs a raw gull egg on the sly).

In the finale, after being carried by Marema to his "wedding feast," Prudentius pays no attention to Melita, but laps a potful of gravy and gnaws at some unfilled pastry-shells. While he is thus engaged, the ethereal Melita fades away—leaving the island and joining her saintly friend Erminia. Prudentius is left alone with Marema. After a year has passed, Melita and Prudentius's mother come to visit and take the couple back to the mainland, and they find a pair of healthy twin boys. The story ends with the grandmother's squeal of delight over these babies.

Leskov thus offers in "Innocent Prudentius" a significant modification of the guilt-ridden Tolstoyan sexual doctrines. The austere precepts of "The Kreutzer Sonata" can be followed, Leskov maintains, only by the elect, people like Melita and Erminia. Ordinary creatures like Prudentius and Marema will always need to gratify "that by which nature ordinarily binds a man and a woman."

After its appearance as a separate book in 1892, "Innocent Prudentius" was severely criticized by one Grigory Georgievsky (not the "red-nosed" Aleksandr Georgievsky, Leskov explained, his former colleague and enemy in the Ministry of Education) for its departures from the *Prolog* original. That source, Georgievsky wrote, Leskov had "transmitted inaccurately, giving the story his own tendency and discarding from it everything that reminds the reader of the Church and her age-old precepts and procedures." Thus the *Prolog* tale has been transformed "from a pious and strictly ecclesiastical 'lesson' into a tendentious agglomeration of the empty phrases of coarse materialism."[65]

Leskov was moved to defend his offspring (and himself) against the charge of falsification. There is nothing wrong with altering a *Prolog* plot, Leskov wrote to Suvorin.

It is not obligatory that a *Prolog* theme be exactly reproduced. A theme is a theme; I can make of it what I find possible. Otherwise there would be no point in adaptation. You should simply take it and reprint it. And it would come out as simple and stupid as the *Prolog* itself. And a university professor doesn't understand that! As for "Prudentius," I thought a long time about it and sought the advice of Goncharov, and I am enclosing a genuine letter of that great artist, from which you will see that Goncharov also thought over my Prudentius theme and found it impossible in the form it has in the *Prolog*.[66]

However, though moved to defend "Prudentius" against an Orthodox-minded critic, Leskov had no great affection for it. In a letter to the critic M. O. Menshikov written the next year concerning the eleventh, supplementary volume of his collected works, Leskov wrote, "That volume contains the repulsive [*gadostnyj*] 'Prudentius,' put there because another, somewhat better one reflects on the clergy, and I am tired of being confiscated."[67]

At last putting the *Prolog* aside—"I am terribly sick of legends and disgusted with them" he wrote to Tolstoy[68]—Leskov determined to have one more go at the theme of ancient sexuality. But this time he took as his source a plot derived from a non-Christian historical text, the *Jewish Antiquities* of Josephus Flavius. It proved a most revealing change.

Unlike the legendary *Prolog*, a historical source is a record of the real doings of real people. If these doings illustrate a moral, it must be deduced from the material. Possibly because it derives from a nonhagiographic source, "Insulted Neteta," the last of Leskov's antique revivals, escapes the faults of so many of his *Prolog* stories; it is the most successful of the lot.[69]

The nucleus of the plot is found in book 18, chapter 3 of the *Jewish Antiquities*, in a section following the famous "Christian" passage in that work. A beautiful, happily married Roman matron named Paulina—in Leskov's version her name is Neteta—was pursued relentlessly by a wealthy patrician named Decius Mundus. He showered her with presents and offered bribes, escalating the price as high as 200,000 Attic drachmae for a single night. When money proved useless, Mundus tried the "Prudentius" discipline: starving himself in the hope of arousing the lady's compassion. Though Paulina remained impervious, a woman servant of his named Ide was more sympathetic; and she devised an ingenious plan to enable her master to gain his end. The priests of the temple of Isis, where Paulina frequently worshipped, were bribed to tell her that the god Anubis had fallen in love with her. The devout Paulina was much affected by this annun-

592

ciation; and with her husband's approval she agreed to spend a night in the temple in the arms of the god. The god was in fact Decius Mundus, whom Paulina did not recognize in the darkness. The triumphant lover, however, not content with a single night of passion, could not resist three days later boasting to his victim of his conquest, and in such terms that she could be in no doubt that he was privy to the most intimate secrets of her communion with Anubis. Ashamed and incensed, she reported the deception to her husband, who in turn reported it to Tiberius. The emperor's response was drastic. The temple of Isis was to be demolished and its priests crucified, along with Ide. Toward Mundus himself, however, Tiberius showed a touch of "romantic" compassion, "because he supposed that what crime he had committed was done out of the passion of love."[70] The adulterer was only banished.

Many years earlier Leskov had discovered this "vivid, colorful, passionate, and tender" story, as he described it in a letter to Lavrov,[71] and he had energetically recommended it to his literary colleagues as a "marvelous plot for a dramatic work."[72] Though he saw "a whole opera or a ballet" in the Josephus story,[73] Leskov decided to write it up not as a play—that form he had abandoned forever after *The Spendthrift*—but as a "light sketch."[74]

As the letter to Lavrov shows, the Paulina story stood high on Leskov's literary agenda as early as December 1889. Though it was "still all only in [his] head" at that time, he hoped to finish it by the following February. *Russian Thought* apparently did not jump at the bait, and Leskov therefore promised the story to Prince Dmitry Tsertelev for his *Russian Survey*. In a letter to Tsertelev of September 1890, he reaffirmed his promise, but admitted that the story was not ready. "It is a very complicated and difficult thing, for which you have to read a great deal and piece it together like a mosaic."[75] He was too tired and sick to do it, however, especially since he was then involved in another project, the story that became "The Hour of God's Will." A month later he wrote Tsertelev again, now reporting that Adolf Marks had expressed interest in the unfinished story for his mass-circulation magazine *Ploughland* (*Niva*). Leskov felt bound by his promise, he said, but wouldn't Tsertelev accept "Night Owls" instead?[76] Curiously, a few weeks earlier Leskov had written Marks, asking *him* to accept, as a substitute for the Josephus story, a work even further from completion, or even commencement, called "Fragments from My Literary Reminiscences of Thirty Years."[77] Neither Marks nor Tsertelev was willing to accept the substitute. As late as

December 1891, he was still offering Tsertelev a choice between the long unpublished "Legendary Characters" and the risky "Rabbit Warren." Eventually Tsertelev had to settle for "Legendary Characters."[78]

In the meantime, Leskov had concluded a tentative agreement with Marks to publish "Insulted Neteta" in *Ploughland*, with pictures by the well-known illustrator Elisaveta Bem. This arrangement put Leskov in the novel situation of direct interaction, during the process of composition, with the illustrator of one of his stories. (Earlier illustrations of his works, for instance those by Repin, had all been done after the fact.) Leskov's correspondence with Mme Bem, though only partly published, provides a fascinating record of a developing creative relationship. Perhaps helped by the difference in sex, the writer and the artist got along famously. Leskov was not only delighted with Bem's sketches, one of which stood on his desk to the end of his days,[79] but found that her pictures of his characters actually helped him to understand them better.

Both Leskov and Bem seem to have worked hard on their collective venture during 1891 and 1892, but in the end it was not completed. The reason is not documented, but the conjecture of Aleksandr Izmailov, the editor of "Insulted Neteta," is probably correct: when Marks found out what Leskov's story was about, and looked at Bem's sketches, he was aghast. It was too lurid for *Ploughland*, a "family" magazine; and he vetoed the project. Without pressure from a publisher and deprived of the collaboration of the illustrator (Bem was on contract to Marks and could not take her work elsewhere), Leskov lacked the impetus to finish the work. "Insulted Neteta" might have proved the masterpiece in his series of ancient stories.[80]

In "Insulted Neteta" Leskov made substantial changes in the plot he found in Josephus. The changes are almost entirely psychological in motivation, not doctrinal. Christianity is only a distant echo in "Insulted Neteta," strange rumors brought to Rome by Palestinian vagabonds about people who "take no pride in their ancestors and have no desire to avenge themselves, but on the contrary do not consider it a dishonor to endure an insult and even hasten to do good to those who do them evil" (p. 171). But this lesson in nonresistance, though topically relevant to the plot, has no influence on its outcome. Though in his version Neteta abandons her quest for vengeance, her motives are not Christian.

Leskov has taken Josephus's flat, linear tale of sexual cozenage and revenge, intended to illustrate the general depravity of the Romans, and transformed it into a passionate demonstration of the redeeming power of eros. His story is more a hymn to Venus than to Isis, let alone to the God of "The Kreutzer Sonata." His Neteta and even her cynical seducer are transfigured—purified—by their night together. Though at first outraged by her discovery of the trick, Neteta comes deeply to repent having revealed it to her husband Saturninus, a dull and coarse man much older than she, and having thus set in motion the grim machinery of imperial justice. For in the "god's" arms, Neteta had experienced sensations never before aroused in her, and in retrospect the memory of them has blossomed into love.

But it is too late. In Leskov's version, Tiberius allows the injured husband to select the adulterer's punishment. Saturninus condemns Decius Mundus to be burnt at the stake. Thus a tremendous spectacle is to be staged for the titillation of the jaded Romans: the razing of the temple of Isis, the crucifixion of its priests, and the auto-da-fé of Mundus. Tiberius would not dare call it off, and in any case Neteta cannot gain admission to the imperial presence to plead for mercy. Tormented by love and remorse, she wanders dazedly about the streets until her friend Polivia arranges a final meeting with her lover, the night before his execution.

Decius Mundus too has been touched by the wand of Venus. The cold seducer has fallen deeply in love with his victim, so much so that he even regards his execution as a punishment well deserved for his cruel deception of her. He plans to die shouting "I love thee, Neteta!" As a nobleman and man of honor, Mundus is allowed the freedom of his jailer's house and garden, and there he and Neteta pass a second, final night of love together. The next day, like the most virtuous of Hindu wives, Neteta throws herself into the flames consuming her lover.

Leskov was right: "Insulted Neteta" would make a marvelous opera. Such hyperbolic tales of romantic passion are out of style in literature nowadays. Yet they answer a genuine need for larger-than-life images that express the powerful emotions we sometimes feel, by comparison with which our "real," external lives seem petty and drab. The story shows that there remained in Leskov levels of feeling and imagination deeper and more potent than any touched by the pious proprieties of the *Prolog*.

37

John of Kronstadt

The high point of Leskov's involvement with *Prolog*, as a source of texts for Tolstoyan sermons, had been reached by 1888. Though his ancient stories extend into the nineties, in most cases he was only publishing works written several years before, but held up by censorship. By 1891 he proclaimed himself "terribly sick of legends and disgusted with them."[1] He attributed the same feelings to his readers. Trying to sell Prince Tsertelev, editor of *Russian Survey*, on accepting the contemporary satire "Night Owls" in place of the unfinished "Insulted Neteta," Leskov wrote, "The 'day's evil' will always evoke more response in the hearts of readers, who are incensed by incense and the censer."[2] The ponderous preacher's robes began to weigh on him, and he looked with renewed favor on his old satirist's pitchfork. In the last five years of his life Leskov's prowess as a satirist reached its apogee, producing works that rank among his most durable contributions to Russian literature.

The first target he chose was Pobedonostsev's Orthodox church, whose degeneration became epitomized for Leskov during this period by Father John of Kronstadt, a secular (married) priest who, at the turn of the century, became a major spiritual leader of Russian Orthodoxy. For Leskov, there was only one spiritual leader, Lev Tolstoy, and only one form of true Christianity. Father John was a fraud and an impostor, a focus of the corruption in Russian society. As Leskov saw it, Russian spiritual life in the 1890s was suspended between two poles: a pole of good, located at Yasnaya Polyana, and a pole of evil, entrenched at Kronstadt. Between them Russians had to make an existential choice. "You cannot love both Lev Tolstoy and John of Kronstadt," he said to his friend Lidia Veselitskaya a few months before he died.[3]

John of Kronstadt (Ivan Ilyich Sergiev) was born in 1829, the year after Tolstoy, in the village of Sula in the province of Archangel, the son of the local sexton. He attended an ecclesiastical school and was graduated from Petersburg Theological Seminary in 1855. Only the last accomplishment was unusual: most secular priests received far less education. He was at once ordained a priest, married, and, by arrangement with his father-in-law, was assigned to the Cathedral of Saint Andrew in the fortress town of Kronstadt.

No one would have predicted for him anything but a life of obscurity, since it was impossible for the married clergy to rise in the church hierarchy. Yet he had a spectacular career. By some mysterious process of social psychology, he gradually acquired the reputation of a wonder-worker and living saint. People began flocking to Kronstadt from all over Russia to ask his blessing, beg him to remember them in his prayers, and perhaps to seek practical assistance, as large sums of money were presented to him to distribute as he saw fit. His influence extended upward in society as well as outward geographically, and in 1894 he was summoned to the Crimea to administer the sacrament to the dying Alexander III. The veneration of John of Kronstadt even spilled over into religious heterodoxy: during the 1890s a sect arose, which regarded him as an incarnation of Christ. Sergiev repudiated the sect, but it grew and spread nonetheless.[4]

During the latter 1890s the conflict between John of Kronstadt and Tolstoy became as acute in reality as it had been in Leskov's mind. While Tolstoy, for reasons of principle, abstained from attacking the "great thaumaturge" personally, Sergiev had no such scruples; his public utterances bristled with denunciations of Tolstoy and his teachings, and he published a pamphlet against him entitled *An Exposé of the False Doctrine of Count Lev Tolstoy.*[5]

After the turn of the century the figure of Father John took on new dimensions as spiritual chaplain to the extreme Right in Russian politics. He "consecrated the first banner" of the anti-Semitic Union of the Russian People,[6] and during the Revolution of 1905 stood firm by the scepter of absolutism; in the radical press he was caricatured training a cannon on the insurgent masses.[7] Just before his death in 1908 he was appointed a member of the Holy Synod, the first secular priest to attain that office.

This apogee of Sergiev's career occurred long after Leskov's angry glare had ceased to follow him, but at the beginning of the 1890s Leskov kept malicious track of his every movement. Leskov's letters to Tolstoy are filled with ironic comments about "Ivan Ilyich" (Leskov delighted in the identity of his name with that of the antihero of Tolstoy's story);

I observe how "Ivan Ilyich" comes to our hospital to perform cures and always mumbles only over one of the patients and for some reason doesn't pray for all of them at once. I posed this question to the "sisters of mercy," and they were embarrassed. His sphere of action keeps on expanding "by God's mercy"—on the day of his jubilee, when (according to the gossip columnists' accounts) he consumed three dinners in a row and "got up from the table with astonishing jauntiness"—Archpriest Mikhailovsky, the chairman of the Temperance Society and celebrated Petersburg religious teacher, erred in measuring the wine he had consumed and, having taken into his insides more than was fitting for a Leader of the Sober, did not get up at all, but was carried out in the arms of his spiritual children, and Ivan Ilyich did not cure him of that, but has himself been appointed to his position, since he drinks no wine but madeira from the Zmeev Brothers' factory in Kashino.[8]

Ivan Ilyich alone performs miracles. A few days ago he came to cure an acquaintance of mine, a young lady named Zhukova, and a priest who lives above me. Both of them died, and he did not bury them. Recently some sailors invited him to open a reading room for them; at his instigation your works are excluded from it. What do messieurs the sailors need with him?[9]

In the literary work of Leskov's later years the sharpest expression of the Sergiev-Tolstoy polarity occurs in the short novel "Night Owls," which first appeared in the liberal organ *Messenger of Europe* in November-December 1891.[10] Even the place of publication was significant of the ideological revolution through which Leskov had passed: M. M. Stasyulevich, the editor of *Messenger of Europe*, was an upright Westernizer-liberal of the most orthodox sort, whose ears still rang with the anathema pronounced against Leskov by Pisarev in 1865; in the late 1880s he could still say to A. F. Koni, when the latter suggested his publishing something by Leskov, "What are you saying! *Leskov is someone I will never publish in Messenger of Europe.*"[11] Only vigorous persuasion by Koni, Vladimir Solovyov, and others induced him to change his mind.[12]

Though not published until the end of 1891, "Night Owls" had actually been written the previous year. The first mention of it in Leskov's correspondence occurs in the letter to Prince Tsertelev dated October 23, 1890: "I have a piece ready which is also not devoid of artistic bouquet, but contemporary and somewhat 'tendentious' (anti-pharisaical) [. . .] My story is *ready* and is called 'Night Owls' "

(11:466). The main composition of the story can be approximately dated in the summer and early autumn of 1890.

Leskov often wove his stories around anecdotes picked up in conversations with his friends, in their letters, or even in the newspapers, and it seems clear that the initial impulse that inspired the writing of "Night Owls" was a letter written to Tolstoy by one of his followers, a copy of which was sent to Leskov, describing a comic encounter with John of Kronstadt. This Tolstoyan disciple was Prince D. A. Khilkov, a former officer in the Hussars and veteran of the Russo-Turkish War, who had arrived independently at a Tolstoyan philosophy of life, resigned from the army, distributed his lands among the peasants, and lived by cultivating a small plot on his erstwhile estate. Like Leskov, he first met Tolstoy in 1887.[13] Khilkov's mother was strongly opposed to his new convictions—her opposition was to assume a more violent form later on—and she decided to enlist the aid of Father John in the hope of turning her son back from the path of error. In the summer of 1890 Sergiev visited the estate of the Kalugins, a family of landowners who lived near Khilkov's farm, and Khilkov was induced by his mother to put in an appearance. Here is Khilkov's description of the scene:

> [After the church service, which I refused to attend, was over] I went to the place where Father John was supposed to be having tea. A good many noblemen, acquaintances of the Kalugins, were waiting for him. When he arrived, my mother said something to him, and he started walking in my direction. He was wearing a white under-cassock (for some reason the whole day long this under-cassock looked to me like a dish of junket) and a straw hat; he was quick in his movements and kept putting his hands on his hips. His first words were, "Well, good afternoon, my son." [*Zdravstvuj,* in the second person singular.] His tone was contemptuous, haughtily ironic. I didn't like it, but I thought, "It is because his faith is so strong; he is scandalized because I didn't go into the church." Then he patted me on the head and gave me his hand. I shook it. At that his cheekbones took on just a tinge of red. He asked me whether I had any children, how old was my son, and whether he had been baptized. (He knew all the answers beforehand and had told my mother to have me come; otherwise I would not have gone, or would have gone independently.) I said, "No." "Why not?" he said. Seeing that he was getting angry, and had put his right hand on his hip, I said I thought it would be better not to talk about it, that his tea was waiting for him, and that my reasons could hardly interest him. He was mollified and

showed me a Gospel saying, "Do you believe in this?" I replied, "I do." "And do you believe in the Church?" "No," I said, "I do not." He reddened, and there was a look of malice in his eyes. "That is pride," he said, "obscurantism," etc. I realized it would be better to say nothing and again reminded him of the tea and of all the people who were waiting for him. He insisted, "Baptize them. John baptized." "How could John baptize when Jesus had not yet been crucified and the word did not yet exist?" [This argument rests on the etymology of the Russian word for "baptize," *krestit'* from *krest*, "cross."] "Well, he cleansed them. Jesus baptized everyone." "How?" I asked. "With water," he replied. "What water?" I asked. "There are various kinds of water. There is the water found in rivers and wells, and there is the water Jesus promised to give to the Samaritan woman; which did he baptize with?" He poured out a whole flood of words, denouncing my ignorance, pride, and obscurantism, and concluded thus: "It is impossible to talk to you; I put an end to this discussion." He went up to a chair, turned it around noisily, and sat down.[14]

Whether or not Leskov had begun writing "Night Owls" before receiving his copy of Khilkov's letter, he took advantage of the anecdotal material it contained to point up his characterization of John of Kronstadt, adapting it to suit his purposes. As the incident is presented in the story, Khilkov's part is given to the Tolstoyan heroine, Klavdia Stepeneva, while John of Kronstadt appears in his own person, though referred to only by the pronoun "he." As was the case with Khilkov, "he" is brought to this encounter by Klavdia's mother in a vain effort to dissuade her daughter from following the precepts of Tolstoyanism.

[As soon as *he* had gone into Klavdia's room], he at once laid his hand on her head and said, as priests do, "Good afternoon [*zdravstvuj*], my daughter." She took his hand in hers and, removing it very gently from her head, simply shook it and answered, "How do you do?" [*zdravstvujte*]. (9:190)

He elevated his shoulders and said, "It is terrible how inconsistent you are."
   She replied that to save a person's life one could even be inconsistent. "It's simply obscurantism!" (9:192)

The discussion about water and baptism is considerably altered, and one can guess the reasons: it might have given the regular censors the notion of turning the story over to the ecclesiastical censorship board, which was notoriously severe; moreover, it is not effective as a Tolstoyan argument. Leskov changes the water to salt and brings off a typical joke. The priest in this scene is not "he," but the local parish curate.

> Again he [the priest] said to her [Klavdia], "You are oversalting it! You are oversalting terribly!" [Meaning that she was raising too many critical questions.] She joked with him. "That's better, but if the salt shall lose its savor—that's worse. Then wherewith shall it be salted?"
> But the priest caught her up nicely on that one. "It is not enough, Miss," he said, "to know texts. You must know more. The salt that loses its savor is not the salt that everyone uses now-adays, but a weak Palestinian salt. . . . We have our own proverb about salt: 'Undersalted—on the table; oversalted—on the back. . . . You can add salt to something undersalted, but for oversalting you are whipped." (9:151-152)

Otherwise, the concrete factual material on John of Kronstadt seems to have been drawn from the press[15] and from private conversations no longer traceable; there is no evidence that Leskov had any direct experience with him. Most of the details are verifiable: Sergiev's commerce with wealthy merchant families,[16] his practice of riding around paying visits and performing "cures" for various corporeal and psychological ills,[17] the intense competition for his favors among his wealthy patrons, and the scramble for alms among the poor, the crowds that gathered wherever he went, even his fondness for expensive silk robes—all this is well attested in contemporary sources. The portrait, though hostile, is not so vicious as one might expect from reading Leskov's letters; the priest is presented as pompous and pretentious, but not irretrievably wicked. It remains an open question to what extent this "softening" of the caricature was due to Leskov's fears of the censorship and how much to an official Tolstoyan attitude of humility and forgiveness (an attitude as remote from Leskov's character as it was from Tolstoy's).

Fears of the censorship were much in Leskov's mind while the story was being written. It required considerable audacity to attack John of Kronstadt in print; and despite the artistic camouflage, Leskov was afraid that the censors would forbid the story. Despite the "advertisement" letter quoted above, Leskov apparently never submitted the story to Tsertelev. "I'm afraid it wouldn't suit your quadrille," he wrote Tsertelev later.[18] (*Russian Survey* was a conservative magazine, enjoying a personal subsidy from the tsar.[19]) Leskov hesitated for a long time before offering it elsewhere. "I still have my story with me," he wrote to Tolstoy on January 4, 1891, "and I am in no hurry—I am afraid. Shouldn't I call it *An Overture*? To what? An opera called *A Frightened Crow*?"[20] And in another letter, "I'm going to keep my story in my desk. Surely no one will print it under present conditions."[21] And still later, "However, in my opinion *that* story is hardly printable anywhere *right now*."[22]

"Night Owls" was at last carried off to Stasyulevich by Vladimir Solovyov, and Stasyulevich squeezed it through the censorship in the last two numbers of his magazine for 1891. He had originally planned to publish it in April,[23] and it may be that delay was caused by difficulties with the censors. Leskov wrote Tolstoy in February that Stasyulevich considered the story entirely passable.[24]

The process of composition was not completed with the delivery of the manuscript. Leskov was a fanatical reviser of his own texts, and his emendations were not confined to matters of style. Even in February 1891 he wrote Tolstoy, "During the time the manuscript has been away from home, I have accumulated a great number of very characteristic additions."[25] Unfortunately, the manuscript and proofs of "Night Owls" are apparently lost, and it is impossible to identify the changes made in the story during 1891. But its appearance in *Messenger of Europe* did not put an end to alterations. It was reprinted in volume 11 of Leskov's collected works, published by A. F. Marks in 1893,[26] and the second version exhibits striking differences from the first.

Leskov was evidently emboldened by the relative ease with which the story had passed the censorship in the magazine version. But there was a more important reason for revision: the camouflage had worked too well; the artistic disguise attracted far more interest and admiration than the message hidden beneath. "In 'Night Owls' it is evidently the comic side that wins people over," Leskov wrote to Tolstoy, "but there are other sides to it, and they are what made me afraid [of the censors], since they are primarily in our spirit."[27] Now that his apprehensions were somewhat allayed, Leskov set about intensifying the "other sides"; as a result, the second version is a far more forthright piece of Tolstoyan propaganda than the first. The following examples will illustrate the ideological motives behind the new redaction.[28]

In the second version Leskov corrects a few slips from orthodox Tolstoyanism. For instance, it was one of Tolstoy's fundamental notions that the Gospel is a universally applicable guide to life, simple, direct, and comprehensible to everyone. This point is now brought out in the new text. Marya Martynovna, the narrator of the main part of the story, is describing Klavdia's religious behavior, which to her appears strange and unintelligible. The earlier version reads:

> Right off she would reach for the Gospel and pick out some text the likes of which I never heard in my life; but she just couldn't understand it properly—she would draw out of it something completely extraordinary.[29]

And the new version is:

> Right off she would reach for the Gospel and pick out some text the likes of which I never heard in my life; but she just couldn't understand it properly—she would draw out of it something completely simple and ordinary, so that it wasn't even interesting. (9:149)

New anticlerical details are added. John of Kronstadt, who has been summoned by Klavdia's mother to "cure" her daughter of Tolstoyanism, now recommends that the mother use prayer to bring about Klavdia's return to a mundane life, one like that of everyone else, in which the guiding principle is the calculation of one's worldly advantage. That is, from the Tolstoyan point of view, he recommends the use of prayer for an essentially immoral purpose. The earlier version is:

> He [John of Kronstadt] comforted her [Margarita Mikhailovna, Klavdia's mother] like an angel and said, "Grieve not, grieve not! Many things happen in one's youth, but afterwards they pass. If she [Klavdia] does not want to come out and see us, can't I drop in on her?"[30]

The later version of this passage:

> [He] comforted her like an angel and said, "Grieve not, grieve not! Many ill-advised things happen in one's youth, but afterwards people perceive their advantage and abandon them."
> "May God grant it" [. . .] Margarita said again.
> "And God will grant it! It shall be unto you according to your

faith.[31] And now, if she doesn't want to come out and see us, can't I drop in on her?" (Chapter 10)

A third example. The second version includes a Tolstoyan creed absent from the first, as well as a new "inquisitional" statement by the priest. Klavdia is speaking with John of Kronstadt:

"Can you be so deceived [he says] that you think you have a better understanding of God than anyone else?"
    She couldn't answer that one and admitted, "I have a very poor understanding of God and believe only in what I need to believe."
    "And what do you need to believe?"
    "That God exists, that is is His will that we should do good and not think our real life is here, but should prepare ourselves for eternity. And so, when I keep my mind only on that, I know what God requires of me each moment and what I must do: but when I begin to consider what it is proper for different people to believe, where God is, and what He is like—then I get all mixed up. Allow me not to go on with this conversation; you and I will never agree."
    "No, we will never agree," he said, "and I will tell you that you are fortunate to be living in this feeble age of ours, or else you might be obliged to smolder on a stake."
    "And perhaps you would lead me there?" she replied. [9:195]

One might compare Klavdia's credo with the following brief statement by Tolstoy in his "Reply to the Synod's Edict of Excommunication" (1901):

I believe in this: I believe in God, whom I understand as spirit, as love, as the source of all [. . .] I believe that man's true welfare lies in fulfilling God's will, and this will is that men should love one another and should consequently do to others as they wish others to do to them [. . .] I believe therefore that the meaning of life of every individual man is to be found only in increasing the love that is in him; that this increase of love leads the individual man, even in this life, to ever greater and greater good, and after death gives him the greater good the more love he has in him.[32]

In the second version Leskov stresses the fact that the priest, in spite of his reputation for supernatural perspicacity, fails to see through the tricks and deceptions practised by his entourage. The motif of Tolstoyan pity and forgiveness is also reemphasized. Both these two themes appear in the following passage, which is also missing from the first version:

[The mother is speaking.] "What sort of a seer is he when you can use trickery and trick him into someone else's carriage?" [The priest had made appointments to visit various houses during the day, but this schedule was not kept at all. The names on the list leaked out, and by representing themselves falsely under those names people succeeding in luring him into their carriages and making off with him.]

[Klavdia] "Oh, let's not argue about that, Mama."

"I intended to send him five hundred rubles, but now I'll send him a thousand on account of the unpleasantness."

"Send more, Mama. I am sorry for him."

"What is there to be sorry for?"

"How can you ask, Mama? What a responsibility to take on oneself! What a part to play! People see him and lose their senses, run around and crush one another like wild beasts and beg for '*money, money!!*' Isn't it dreadful?" (9:202)

And one last example. One of the most effective details in the story, symbolic of its moral lesson, was introduced after the original publication. It occurs twice:

He [the priest] looked at the chair and sat down and did not notice that he had accidentally knocked her little Gospel off the table with his sleeve. (9:191)

And with that she deigned to stretch out her little hand toward the spot where her little Gospel always lay, but it wasn't there, because he had accidentally knocked it off. (9:193)

This is by no means an exhaustive list of the instances of ideological sharpening that distinguish the second edition from the first, but it indicates Leskov's direction. In spite of his efforts to point up the moral and intensify the satirical mood in "Night Owls," even the second version seems attenuated from our vantage point. The tone is genuinely gay: the comic side won out after all. For the modern reader the most remarkable thing about "Night Owls" is not the ironical portrait of a pharisaical priest and not the gentle heroism of a Tolstoyan girl, but the brightly colored, fantastical cascade of words that streams from the mouth of Marya Martynovna.

Marya Martynovna is the narrator of the skaz that forms the core of "Night Owls," and hers is one of Leskov's most dazzling exhibitions in this genre, a consummate display of verbal acrobatics.[33] In an age whose critics valued literature solely for its sobering revelations of social evils, such stunts seemed irrelevant and even wicked. To a man, the critics reproved Leskov for his "unbelievably bizarre, distorted language, [which] disgusts the reader."[34] But actual readers refused to be intimidated by these stern prescriptions, and to this day they continue to take delight in the literary acrobatics of "Night Owls."

To set the stage for Marya Martynovna's performance Leskov first appears himself. His introductory remarks constitute the frame section of the skaz, providing the motivation for the inner narrative. The author then shifts his role to that of audience. The lights are thrown on the narrator, and hers is the star performance. After the skaz is over, the author reappears briefly to point the moral and ring down the curtain.

In "Night Owls" this duality of structure is underscored in the subtitle, "Paysage and Genre"—the "paysage" roughly corresponding to the frame and the "genre" to the skaz, although the analogy with painting is not entirely satisfactory, since even the introductory descriptive section bears a much closer resemblance to genre painting than to landscape. In the two introductory chapters ("paysage") the author tells of an excursion he made to an unnamed town (Kronstadt). This town had become a center of pilgrimage because of the residence there of a certain celebrated ecclesiastic (Father John), a wonderworker and potential saint. The author stops in a hostelry frequented by the pilgrims, which is to be the setting for the skaz. This curious institution is then described in the minutest detail: it is as if the author feels a need to gorge himself on visual impressions while he still can, since during all the rest of the story his only organ of perception will be his ears. For two chapters his eye takes in the *Azhidatsia*, as this odd inn is oddly named,[35] from the top to bottom. The human beings who inhabit and run it figure here only as parts of the "landscape."

The next step is the motivation of the skaz itself. Through the thin partitions of his room the author overhears two separate conversations going on in the rooms on either side. On one side a drunken old man and his wife are discussing various underhanded projects for winning the favor of the powers that be in the town and for covering up their previous rascally behavior. This cynical dialogue is an overture which sets the tone and states the main themes to be developed later. The conversation going on between the author's two female neighbors in the other room, which has vaguely lesbian overtones, is quickly transformed into skaz. One of its participants consciously takes on the role of storyteller, and the stage is hers from then on. The other, as visible audience, is limited to occasional interjections, queries, and marginal comments, while the author himself, as eavesdropper, is a hidden recording machine. By ordinary criteria of verisimilitude this motivation of the skaz by eavesdropping seems flimsy, but it has a symbolic significance. The author, as it were, deliberately blinds himself in order to give a virtuoso performance of the skaz in its purest form. From behind the partitions he must play by ear, and his only instrument is the human voice.

The owner of this voice, Marya Martynovna, is a variation on a female type Leskov had created twenty-five years before with Domna Platonovna in "The Battle-axe"—the half-educated, colorful, flamboyant, middle-aged *meshchanka* or *petite bourgeoise*. Marya Martynovna too has had a checkered career, though not quite so meretricious as Domna Platonovna's. Left penniless after two disastrously unsuccessful marriages (there are hints at sexual difficulties, perhaps stemming from Marya Martynovna's lesbianism and symbolized by the needle she supposedly has wandering around in her body), she supports herself by serving as "companion" to widows of the merchant class. One of these is the audience for her tale, Aichka, a young woman who seeks the assistance of John of Kronstadt in conjuring the man she loves to abandon his silly Tolstoyan notions and marry her. Aichka's predecessor was the widow Margarita Stepeneva, whose daughter Klavdia is to be the Tolstoyan heroine of the story and the chief antagonist of John of Kronstadt; and the main subject of Marya Martynovna's disjointed narrative is a retrospective account of her experiences in the Stepenev household.

Mary Martynovna's language, like Domna Platonovna's, is a hodgepodge symbolic of her social (and moral) confusion, suspended between the folk speech of her origin and the "educated" language of the class she admires. It is full of distortions, absurdities, and incongruities—spoonerisms, malapropisms, and folk etymologies—perhaps more concentrated than in any other work by Leskov. They are enough to drive any translator to despair.[36] Brief examples of these verbal fireworks will be cited here.

Perhaps the most famous of the *slovechki* or trick words in "Night Owls" is a triple pun. As mentioned above, the name of the inn where the "author" stays and where he hears Marya Martynovna's story is *Azhidatsia*. This is not only a contamination of the Russian *ozhidanie* ("expectation"; phonemically /ažidan'ija/) with the Western *azhitatsia* ("agitation"), but it is also used in the sense of *audientsia* ("audience").[37]

Occasionally these verbal stunts are combined into interlocking systems, of which the "grammatic" theme in "Night Owls" is one of the subtlest and most ingenious. At the beginning of her narrative Marya Martynovna announces that she will tell her capricious auditor a "grammatic story of her life." One takes "grammatic" as another of the Western pun distortions and lets it go at that. But Leskov is not finished: the story turns out to be "grammatic" after all. Throughout Marya Martynovna's monologue there is recurrent punning on grammatical terms, such as *roditel'nyj* ("genitive"), *neopredelennoe naklonenie* ("infinitive mood"), *mezhdometie* ("interjection"), and *mnozhestvennyj* ("plural"). Unfortunately, few of these puns can be readily carried over into English, but such approximations as "put an item on the gender" and "I agree to all your prepositions" may suggest something of the flavor.

Though it may have helped distract the censors' attention from the story's subversive content, the use of such a skaz narrator as Marya Martynovna has risks. The verbal fireworks can be too diverting: enthralled readers may not notice the Tolstoyan moral. The moral itself must be deduced by the reader, reconstructed; it is not handed to him. After all, Marya Martynovna is a most unlikely lecturer on Tolstoyan morality. This is a serious technical difficulty of the skaz: if the narrator's attitude toward the events recounted is different from the author's own, a correctional factor must be provided so that the reader can draw the right conclusions without explicit statement. Since Marya Martynovna is the moral opposite of Klavdia, we must learn to place an ideological minus sign before Marya Martynovna's judgments and attitudes.

This Leskov carefully prepares us to do. The seemingly balanced, objective description of the "Azhidatsia" is interspersed with occasional ironic remarks, unobtrusive in themselves, which rouse our suspicions about the inn. Then the overture conversation between the drunken old man and his wife discloses unexpected depths of duplicity and criminality in this Orthodox Mecca. Finally, when Marya Martynovna makes her appearance, she is first presented as a sycophant, a potential thief, and a lesbian. Later on she reveals herself as a spy and a hypocrite, and at the end she proposes murder as a solution for Aichka's amatory problems. After that, if she offers us the negation of Tolstoyanism as her positive moral ideal, we are well prepared to negate the negation. Thus linguistic technique and ideological purpose are blended in an artistic unity. Marya Martynovna's linguistic distortions of literary Russian are symbolic of her moral deformations of true Christianity; and just as her unconscious verbal innovations often ricochet off into areas of meaning she does not suspect, so her moral values are deflected and turned against her.

38

Sodom and Gomorrah

The midnight immolation of Father John of Kronstadt was the last engagement in Leskov's war with the Orthodox church. In the seventies, Leskov had still hoped that the church might loosen the shackles that bound it to the state and become a positive moral force in Russian society. Instead, his worst fears had been realized. In the fifteen years since *The Little Things in a Bishop's Life*, the moral level of the church had noticeably sunk, as Father John's publicity-seeking fakery demonstrated.

And what about the rest of society? As he looked around him in his old age, Leskov saw a moral jungle, a dark "cattle-pen" of depravity, whose vast expanse was only faintly illuminated by the solitary beacon shining at Yasnaya Polyana. The moral rot had spread through every class: the long "decrepit" nobility; the ever corrupt bureaucracy; the "new" merchantry, awakening to the wheeling and dealing of European-style stock-exchange capitalism; and finally the "people," still as benighted and savage as they had been under serfdom, when Leskov had accompanied his louse-ridden "product of nature" down the Volga.

In the early 1870s *At Daggers Drawn* had expressed a similarly bleak view of Russian society, and especially of its left-wing intellectuals. Then, however, the darkness of Leskov's view had seemed partly an expression of unabated rage against the "nihilists" who had drawn their daggers on him. But in the 1890s no such ad hominem explication could apply. Most of the old wounds were healed; recognition had come, if grudgingly; and relations with the literary establishment were more amicable than ever before. Yet Leskov's view of Russian society at large—and of mankind as a whole—now descended to its nadir of pessimism. Leskov saw the shadow of doom on his country.

The Tolstoyan preaching of the late 1880s had been a desperate effort to shore up Russia's moral bulwarks, to inject into her veins

610

some antidote against the spreading poison. But even while sermon-izing, Leskov sometimes puts aside the gleaming specimens of *Prolog* virtue and in their place holds up grim pictures of the moral chaos in which his contemporary "parishioners" lived.

In 1888, at the height of his career as a *Prolog* preacher, one of these breaks occurred in Leskov's literary work—the metamorphosis of an antique prologue into a contemporary satire. In the summer of that year, which he spent at a resort in Estonia, away from libraries, Le-skov had written to his new friend and co-believer Tolstoy asking him to look up in the *Prolog* the story of the "forty martyrs of Sebastia." Leskov did not plan to apply to this *Prolog* tale his usual formula for modernization and Tolstoyification. Rather, it was to be introduced as an illustration in a story of contemporary life, where it would serve as a moral lever, a catalyst—much as Leskov hoped his own "ser-mons" would do.

My plan is as follows. A boy from an Old Believer family which has gone over to the reigning church lives with his grandfather, a kind old fellow, but a backwoods [*dremučij*] nit-picker, in a wretched earthen hovel, and reads to him about the martyrs in Sebastia and at the age of twelve discovers in the book what his grandfather "read, read, and saw not." Learned men come, and the twelve-year-old boy will argue with them about the *spirit*, and "his word will be harsh unto them," and "lest he destroy their traditions," they will have him sent up as a soldier, like "bad grass—from the field away!" And there he will "run the gauntlet" [undergo flogging] and will be a latrine-digger[1] in fulfillment of orders. His kindness, honesty, mockery of him, that he is a *proxvost* [blackguard]. A pious judge advocate will teach him to be the "transport executioner" [*oboznyj palač*]. He is ordered to strangle a Pole and a Jew. The "latrine-digger" refuses and be-comes a martyr in the Sebastia style. That is my plan or my con-coction, but I don't know what is written about the Sebastians.[2]

Tolstoy obligingly set his daughters to work on the *Prolog*; but if they unearthed anything on the martyrs of Sebastia, Leskov never used it. Eventually the hagiographic nucleus of the latrine-digger theme as outlined here would form the basis of the short fable "The Little Fool" (1891).[3] But in that work one can hardly recognize the plot outlined in the letter to Tolstoy. The climax is drastically changed: instead of the ordered execution of a Pole and a Jew followed by the hero's refusal and martyrdom, we have the hero's release, apparently with impunity, of the man his Tatar employer had planned to torture. But the motif of the Judeo-Polish execution was not forgotten. It was transferred to another work, one outside the fable genre, the story enigmatically entitled "Antukà."[4]

The enigma can be solved by ear. *Antukà* is an attempt to render the Russian pronunciation of the French phrase *en tout cas*. An epigraph provided by Leskov further explains that in Russian the word *antukà* was also used (as indeed was *en tout cas* in French) as the name for an all-purpose umbrella, good for both rain and hot weather. No such umbrella is unfurled in the story, but the word stands as a symbol of the moral shiftlessness of the modern world, its lack of solid convictions, principles, or even style. Nowadays, Leskov seems to be saying, everyone comes equipped with plastic umbrella convictions *en tout cas*, principles that can be adjusted to any weather.

The story illustrating this conviction had to be heavily camouflaged and distanced—in this case across the Russian border. Like "Yid Somersault," "Antukà" is a skaz encased in a double frame. On a train between Vienna and Prague the "author" meets a "Slav" who in turn partly relates his own thoughts and impressions, but mostly passes on a long story he had heard from someone else. In an "apropos" discussion with the "author" about the moral state of contemporary mankind, the first narrator illustrates what he perceives as a general decline in morals by contrasting the two successive proprietors of a provincial Polish inn. The former owner had been a gentleman of the old school, steady in his principles, sure of himself and his worth, deep in meditation about the fate of his country—a veritable personification of *stara Polska*. The new one is a typically modern *en tout cas*—nervous, ingratiating, full of words but not of substance, uncertain even of his national identity. With a German name (Moritz), he answers readily either to Herr Moritz or Pan Moric, and is equally at home in Polish or German, though he considers his bad French more chic than either. His kitchen serves tasteless food, about which he pronounces the most fulsome oral advertisements.

In this inn the first narrator hears the tale of the second, an Austrian gendarme. The gendarme, it appears, had once participated in a Slavic revolt against a foreign oppressor—probably the Polish revolt against Russia in 1863, though this is never made clear, doubtless for reasons of censorship.[5] He had been ordered by his chief, a Catholic priest, to hang two deserters, and had done so, first treacherously breaking a promise to them. Years later, feeling remorse, he sought absolution from a holy man living in a forest. This sylvan "saint" turned out to be

Father Flavian, the very priest who had ordered the execution. After this encounter the executioner's convictions underwent a cynical metamorphosis, and he happily entered the service of the Austrian police—an ironic peripeteia typifying the moral instability of the contemporary world.

"Antukà" is structurally overcomplicated for its size; furthermore, the execution scene, on which the indictment of the *en tout cas* gendarme largely depends, is so distanced as to seem hardly real. But the linguistic execution, as Leonid Grossman points out,[6] is superb: in a story written in Russian Leskov miraculously gives the flavor of a "Slavic" narrator who in turn reproduces the distinctive speech of various characters speaking Poznan Polish, Galician Polish, Judeo-Polish, and bad French!

The famine of 1891 inspired Leskov to evoke in "Vale of Tears" his vivid memories of the famine of 1840. From that comparison he derived consolation, especially from the fact that in 1891 the government allowed the plight of the populace to be broadcast at home and abroad and private relief measures undertaken, whereas in 1840 the subject had been regarded as a military secret. Thus one could point to increased enlightenment at the top of the social pyramid. But the bottom remained shrouded in primeval darkness. Despite the Emancipation, the spiritual condition of the starving peasants seemed no better in 1891 than it had been half a century before. Their hunger was still not only of the body, but of the mind, the heart, and the soul.

For Leskov the most bitter and ironic symbol of this spiritual starvation was the fact that in the following year, 1892, when an epidemic of cholera broke out, some doctors administering public health and quarantine measures in country districts (an activity, incidentally, in which Anton Chekhov was energetically engaged) had been murdered by the peasants they were trying to help. The muzhiks suspected the doctors of deliberately infecting them with the disease.

Leskov took a variant of this misunderstanding and made a story out of it, "The Improvisers."[7] In his version the rumor circulates among the *Lumpenproletariat* in Estonia (where the author is again spending the summer) that in Petersburg doctors kidnap people and inject them with poison, of which they die, or at least reach a state close to death, in a matter of hours. The doctors' motives for committing these murders are not explained; apparently it is pure satanism. In the core anecdote a retired general miraculously rescues his butler from the doctors' evil clutches. He then proceeds to shoot two of them and beat up a third, challenging the last, when the beating is over, "Go ahead, go complain!" The folk "improvisers" of this tale take especial delight in this brutal retribution and refuse to listen to the author's skeptical remonstrances. With equal glee they report another rumor, to the effect that in that very Estonian resort area a doctor, apparently testing the sea water for contamination, had been suspected of deliberately infecting it, beaten, and barely escaped with his life.

Yes, the "people" are indeed "dark." But the educated classes are little better. To make this point, Leskov begins his tale by reporting that in Petersburg someone had arranged a window exhibit showing a comma-shaped cholera bacillus. It was supposedly the real thing: first enlarged under a microscope, then taken out in its enlarged state and permanently mounted. It was actually a Japanese beetle; but its authenticity was widely credited—and feared—by numerous persons of "notable position." If the enlightened classes of society are so ignorant and credulous, Leskov implies, can we blame the masses for *their* savagery? And what hope can there be for society?

Leskov's most searing indictment of that society is embodied in the novella "A Winter's Day," written in the last year of his life. Getting this jeremiad published was a miracle. Leskov first offered it to *Messenger of Europe*, but the editor, Mikhail Stasyulevich, who had long regarded the reactionary Leskov with liberal aversion, thought it much too risky. "You have concentrated everything there to such a degree that it bowls one over," he wrote Leskov. "It is a fragment from Sodom and Gomorrah, and I dare not appear before God's world with such a fragment."[8] Leskov next tried *Russian Thought*. That journal too had in the past been far from audacious in challenging the censorship on Leskov's behalf. But this time, perhaps nettled by the writer's jibes about their timidity,[9] its editors Goltsev and Lavrov decided to take the plunge; and they and the story survived unscathed. With the "fragment from Sodom and Gomorrah" *Russian Thought* appeared before God's world in September 1894.[10]

Partly because of the smokescreen with which Leskov surrounded it to distract the censors, "A Winter's Day" may be difficult for latter-day readers to perceive in all its contemporary virulence. As in both "Night Owls" and "The Rabbit Warren," Leskov's primary stratagem is deliberate confusion. The waters are muddied so that we cannot see clearly what lies beneath. Leskov's befuddled narrative sequences remind one strikingly of techniques devised much later in cinema and television, often with the aim of creating an atmosphere of anxiety or bewilderment. Disparate images rapidly succeed one another on the screen, none of them remaining long enough so that the viewer feels sure he has identified it, let alone understood all its implications. Explanations and background information are lacking, or must be pieced together as the action proceeds. It is a form that demands considerable participatory effort on the part of the reader or viewer.

As William Edgerton has pointed out,[11] the structure of "A Winter's Day" is essentially dramatic rather than novelistic. There is no narrator, no skaz, no "apropos" discussion; and the omniscient author by and large refrains from moralizing or offering interpretations of his own. He does, especially at first, program our negative response to his characters by dropping a few evaluative remarks masquerading as description; for instance, "The hostess is old, and her appearance might be called respectable if her face did not bear the imprint of too much attentiveness and obsequiousness" (9:397). But for the most part the reader must assemble his own understanding of the events and pass his own judgments.

As he did in "Night Owls," Leskov gives "A Winter's Day" the subtitle "Paysage and Genre," calling attention to its pictorial and descriptive qualities. The "landscape" here is an *intérieur*, though it has wider implications. The action is confined to a single house and virtually to a single room, a "living room of the second rank," apparently in Petersburg, belonging to an elderly widow, a gentlewoman a bit down at the heels, with two grown sons. In fact, a good deal of the "action" is not action, but discussion of events, past, present, and future, taking place elsewhere. The discussants naturally are much better informed than the reader about the causes and significance of these events, many of which, furthermore, are the kind one speaks about only in hints and whispers, and it therefore takes some time for us to figure out exactly what is going on. But gradually the picture comes into focus. And an ugly picture it is—a "paysage" of unlimited egotism, treachery, betrayal, extortion, and sexual depravity.

The cast of characters, some of whom never appear on the stage, is as follows. The widow and mistress of the house (whose name we never learn) has two brothers and one sister. One of the brothers, Luka, is very rich, but estranged from the rest of the family, except for one niece; it later comes out that his disgruntled and greedy relatives are hatching plots for forging his will in their favor. They also contemplate denouncing the favored niece to the authorities as a political subversive. The second brother, Zakhar, a general, is a spendthrift and a philanderer. Long ago he had had a love affair with the widow's guest and interlocutor during most of the "action," a woman of unsavory character, evidently an agent of the secret police, who uses her position for purposes of extortion. This guest is also unnamed, except for the sobriquet "Kamchatka" given her as the place of exile to which the victims of her denunciations are sent. Employing her sick old husband to deliver blackmail letters to her exlover, during this winter's day she collects 1,000 rubles from Zakhar—one of a series of such payments—as the price for suppressing some information contained in a notebook he had inadvertently let fall into her hands. After Zakhar has paid his bill and departed, the money is at once appropriated by the hostess's younger son, Valerian, apparently his fee for serving Kamchatka as a gigolo.

Thus it is gradually revealed to us that all these characters are caught up in a complex network of spying, blackmail, and intrigue, each struggling to survive and then to exploit someone else. All positive human bonds have rotted away; sexuality has become a commodity and a means of exploitation. The gigolo Valerian, we learn, has other, more personal sexual interests besides his contracted services. A Chinese maid in his mother's house is pregnant by him. She in turn tries to use her condition to extort money from him; at the same time she arranges to sell herself to Uncle Zakhar. Valerian's older brother, Arkady, is a homosexual; and for that reason, though people are said to be more tolerant than they used to be of this form of deviance, his career in the diplomatic service may be jeopardized by threats of blackmail, which his mother must ward off. Zakhar's daughter Nina, a woman in her twenties, has married for money a man past seventy; she is now pregnant, not by him, but by her cadet nephew.[12] Finally, as if not to be outdone by the carryings-on of her employers, even the widow's cook, a large woman of forty-five with a "two-story chin," is enthusiastically engaged in teaching the secrets of love to the grocer's thirteen-year-old delivery boy. Such, we must conclude, is the reality behind the official Victorian facade of nineteenth-century life. As Leskov puts it in his concluding sentence, "They [his sex-obsessed characters] seem to recognize as genuine 'acts' only those acts of nature that multiply life, without caring for its meaning or significance" (9:455). As Vsevolod Setchkarev has convincingly shown, this sentence is almost a direct quotation from Schopenhauer (who is mentioned in the text earlier); and the whole "Winter's Day" could be taken as a graphic illustration of the pessimistic philosophy of Schopenhauer, of whom Leskov, like Tolstoy, was a great admirer.[13]

Some Lot figure was needed to provide relief in this pageant of depravity. Leskov supplies two of them, one on each social level. Among the servants there is the young maid Theodora (whom her mistress for some reason insists on calling Katya). Theodora is a Tolstoyan; and she shows that even a servant can be a moral catalyst in a corrupt household, or at least a signpost marking its deviation from standards of truth and righteousness. Though a good worker and very cheap, Theodora arouses her mistress's wrath for refusing to lie, even to the extent of telling unwanted callers that her mistress is not at home. The widow advises her to consult "any priest" concerning the distinction between permissible and forbidden lies, but Theodora has passed beyond the reach of priestly casuistry. She has abandoned personal happiness, and all her earnings go to help support a sister and the sister's illegitimate children.

On the upper-class level, Leskov implants another Klavdia-like heroine, the mistress's niece Lidia, also a Tolstoyan, though an independent one. Lidia is going to college (or "higher women's courses," as they had to be called in Russia in those days) and at the same time working as a medical assistant. This is deviant behavior for an upper-class girl; but to make matters worse, she is much more interested in her work and her intellectual life than in pursuing the conventional goals of marriage and children. Like Theodora, she is the perfect liberated woman à la Tolstoy, one who has transcended the pursuit of egotistic love based on sexuality in favor of a generalized charity toward mankind as a whole.

Unfortunately, despite (or perhaps because of) her array of virtues, Lidia, like her colleague Klavdia, never really comes alive as a character. In Andrei Leskov's vivid phrase, both Lidia and Klavdia are "mannequins who speak bookishly and artificially from phonograph discs recorded by the author."[14] At times one even feels some sympathy with the criticisms of her voiced by the gossipy and meretricious old ladies: she is "pure, but cold"; she seems to be governed "not by the heart, but by mathematics" (9:422). The relative lifelessness of his ideal heroine, when compared with her malignantly vital relatives, was pointed out to Leskov after the story had appeared in print. Characteristically, he blamed the failure on the immaturity of his models, not on himself. "What do you expect?" he exclaimed. "Don't forget that these are women of the future who are still young and haven't yet had time to make their mark. Are A. A. and Mlle L. fully developed types? No, but they exhibit the beginnings of a certain [social and moral] tendency, and that is what I sought to depict."[15]

Much has been made of the criticisms of Tolstoy and the Tolstoyans articulated by Lidia, which Leonid Grossman interprets as evidence that in his last years, partly under the influence of Vladimir Solovyov, Leskov was moving away from Tolstoyanism altogether.[16] Regardless of one's interpretation of "A Winter's Day," there is abundant biographical evidence that this view is mistaken, that Leskov's reverence for Tolstoy and his fundamental allegiance to Tolstoyanism remained unshaken till his death. As for Solovyov, Leskov had long admired that philosopher's independence and moral vigor; his was one of the few first-rate intellects in Leskov's Russia seriously concerned with religious questions. They became personal friends in the latter 1880s and for a time saw a good deal of one another. But Solovyov's mystical, Neoplatonic cast of mind was fundamentally alien to the practical Protestant Leskov, and they seem to have drifted apart during the last two or three years of the writer's life. The most explicit statement of Leskov's feelings about Solovyov vs. Tolstoy is found in a letter he wrote late in 1893, in which he forcefully asserted his own discipleship and his "coming together" with Tolstoy, at the same time proclaiming (quite correctly) that "Solovyov is not a co-believer with L[ev] N[iko-laevich] and cannot be his defender."[17]

In "A Winter's Day" Lidia does indeed speak quite harshly, *No Way Out* style, about the Tolstoyan "nonresisters" [*neprotivlënyši*]—their fetishism of dirtiness, their endless talk and little action, their general incompetence in practical matters; she also refuses to subscribe to the party line against science and learning set forth by Tolstoy himself. In all these points she speaks for the author. But Leskov never wavered in his allegiance to the sage of Yasnaya Polyana. In his last surviving letter to Tolstoy, written four months before his death, Leskov writes with eager anticipation of the "catechism" of Tolstoyan beliefs on which the master was then working, and in the same letter speaks pathetically of his plan—never realized—to travel to Moscow during the Christmas season of 1894 in order to "take two weeks of rest to-gether with people who share my beliefs," in other words, the very Tolstoyans, including Tolstoy, he was supposed to have repudiated in "A Winter's Day."[18]

After Leskov had finished writing "A Winter's Day," he again found that life was contriving to imitate his art. While his "fragment from Sodom and Gomorrah" was still in the patronizing hands of Stasyulevich, the newspapers were full of news about a scandalous trial. The *Kammerjunker* Count A. V. Sollogub, son of a well-known writer of the Gogol era, was implicated in a plot to forge the will of the millionaire V. I. Gribanov. Stasyulevich noted how faithfully the Gribanov trial bore out Leskov's view of the state of Russian society: "Of course, dear Nikolai Semyonovich, the trial of Count Sollogub lends a great deal of credence to what is said and done in your 'Winter's Day,' but [. . .]"[19] And in the letter accompanying the manuscript which he offered the next day to *Russian Thought*, Leskov took pleasure in the evidence of his prophetic powers which the newspapers were providing: "The contents [of "A Winter's Day"] are lively and for the most part copied from nature. Just as I sensed *No Way Out*, so I seemed to have had a premonition of the Sollogub socialites."[20]

In a letter written later that summer Leskov names some of his prototypes, most of them high-society connections of his from long before, some of whom were already dead. Among them were General Veniamin Astashev, the Siberian gold-mine operator who had provided Leskov with materials for his "Siberian Scenes of the Eighteenth Century"; Major General Prince Aleksandr Shcherbatov, a close friend of Leskov's in the seventies; and Adjutant General Sergei Kushelev, the courtier to whom "The Enchanted Pilgrim" was dedicated and who had brought Leskov the news of the pleasure of the emperor and empress at hearing "The Sealed Angel" read aloud. Also mentioned in the letter, presumably as the prototype of Cousin Olimpia of "A Winter's Day" (a bustling woman with high connections who loves to meddle in politics and lives mostly abroad), is Mme Olga Novikova, known as the "M. P. for Russia," a long-term resident of London and author of several books in English written in defense of Russian foreign policy.

Leskov also names two prototypes for his composite Tolstoyan heroine, Lidia: "the daughter of Maksheyev and Lörberg; both are medical assistants [. . .] It's amazing that in the women's college somehow they've already found out about it and shouted yesterday, 'Lörberg, you're described in *Russian Thought!*' "[21] Perhaps not surprisingly, these young Tolstoyennes seem to have left fewer marks on history's pages than their less savory elders, and they have not been identified further.[22]

Leskov knew very well that in many quarters "A Winter's Day" would raise hackles. "There are lots of places in 'A Winter's Day' that will make people bellow," he wrote to Goltsev. "It's inevitable: 'There's no use blaming the mirror if your mug is awry.' "[23] The Tolstoyans were offended. Though he knew Leskov was mortally ill, Chertkov still avoided coming to see him, settling the score for "A Winter's Day," as Andrei Leskov puts it.[24] "I was supposed to protect them [the Tolstoyans] and not tell the truth," Leskov wrote bitterly to Veselitskaya, just a few days before his death.[25]

There is no record of Tolstoy's reaction, but his wife transcribed her own characteristic response: "After dinner the boys were doing their lessons," she wrote her husband, "and I read aloud to Lyova [Lev junior] Leskov's story "A Winter's Day"—dreadful vileness [*užasnaja gadost'*] in all respects. I had not liked Leskov even before, but now he became still more repulsive to me, since his filthy soul shows through his supposed humor, but we didn't laugh but were simply disgusted."[26] Had he known of this contumelious judgment, Leskov might not have been distressed. To some extent he reciprocated the Countess's hostile feelings—he thought she was a bad influence on her husband—and he had hoped his story would hurt: "My latest works about Russian society are very cruel [he said to Faresov]. 'The Cattle-pen,' 'A Winter's Day,' 'The Lady and the Wench.' The public isn't pleased with these pieces because of their cynicism and directness. But I don't care to please the public. Let it even choke on my stories as long as it reads them. I know how to please, but I don't want to please any more. I want to scourge and torment the public. The novel becomes an indictment of life."[27] "I myself like 'A Winter's Day,' " Leskov said on another occasion. "It's downright insolent to write like that. 'Sodom,' people say about it. They are right. As society is, so is 'A Winter's Day.' "[28]

39

The Rabbit Warren

Onopry Peregud, the mad protagonist of Leskov's last story, "The Rabbit Warren," perceives the utter madness of the "sane" human world—its self-serving delusions, its needless cruelties, its self-destructiveness. Filled like his creator with the afflatus of the prophet, he yearns to save men's souls by searing their hearts with God's truth. But he perceives with equal clarity that his message of salvation cannot be delivered through the medium of "Gutenberg's invention," for, as he puts it, "printing cannot fight against prohibitions." Madman that he is, Onopry therefore is endeavoring to invent a means to emblazon his message on the sky, beyond the reach of any human censors.

This megalomaniac fantasy obviously expresses the feelings, if not the hopes, of Onopry's creator. Leskov had experienced not only the frustration of all prophets at the unresponsiveness of men, but, more specifically, the obstacles placed in the path of nineteenth-century Russian prophets by the tsarist censorship. Viewed retrospectively, Leskov's literary career from beginning to end sometimes seems like a prolonged cat-and-mouse game played with the censors, with Leskov in the role of the mouse-daredevil of the cartoons, the one who delights his audience by sauntering up to the dozing cat, setting it some painful trap, then pulling its whiskers and dashing to safety, there to relish the spectacle of his enemy's frustration and humiliation. Of all the great nineteenth-century Russian writers, Leskov, perhaps together with Saltykov-Shchedrin, should be awarded the grand prize for acrobatic censor-baiting.

For a censor-defying literary daredevil in a police-ridden country like nineteenth-century Russia, the most dangerous topic—except the character and private life of the reigning monarch—was the police, especially the secret or political police. From the time Catherine II packed the noble Radishchev off to Siberia until the long-dreaded revolution cast them from their throne, the tsars spent an enormous amount of money and human energy (though nothing to match the

outlays of their Communist successors) on what is now called "state
security"—the pursuit of "subversives," "rockers of foundations," and
"shakers of thrones," as Leskov's madman calls them. The Third Section of His Majesty's Own Chancellery was an all too palpable presence in the lives of many Russians, especially the members of the educated classes. Yet the gendarmes were a subject rarely alluded to, let
alone explored, by most writers of the period. (Dostoevsky, Tolstoy,
and Chekhov did deal with the related subject of prison and exile,
though mostly from the perspective of common rather than political
criminals.) Leskov, however, in *Laughter and Grief* and "A Journey
with a Nihilist," had deftly touched on the forbidden topic of the "sky-
blue [gendarme] uniforms," as Lermontov called them, and treated it
with a light, mocking irony more deflating than the most ardent
philippic.

In the angry mood of his last years, Leskov decided to take up the
police theme again, and on this high-risk subject turned out two of his
most brilliant stories, "Administrative Grace" and "The Rabbit Warren." But times had changed. Although in both these stories Leskov
employed his best disguises and literary sleight-of-hand, he did not
succeed in getting either one published. The last round in the cat-and-
mouse game appeared to have been won by the cat. The censors' victory was by default, however, since neither story was submitted to
them. No magazine editor could be found bold enough to do even
that. "The Rabbit Warren," completed in 1894, had to wait until 1917
to be published; "Administrative Grace," written in 1893, did not see
the light of day until 1934.[1]

"Administrative Grace" is less than ten pages long, but it embodies
what Shaw might have called the quintessence of Leskovism. It exhibits in concentrated form the devious, upside-down slyness and
wryness that are the hallmarks of Leskov's literary personality; and
though on the surface it gives the appearance of callous cynicism,
underneath it glows with the fire of his moral indignation.

In structure "Administrative Grace" is typically Leskovian. An
illustrative anecdote, safely relegated to the past to mask its subversive intent, is recollected and related apropos by a participant in a
contemporary discussion. The discussion is on a risky subject: the
measures the state should, or should not, employ in defending itself
against internal enemies such as disruptive students and liberal professors. The "author" or frame-narrator remains a passive auditor, but
he relays with sarcasm the absurdities uttered on both sides: the anti-

Katkov effusions of a "liberal" general's wife, upset by recent police reprisals against the *jolis garçons* (radical students), the sight of whose muscular shoulders stirs her fading passions; and the Russia-first, Europe-be-damned fulminations of a school principal, himself "maybe a Czech and maybe a Croat," who insists that "the root of evil must be extirpated."

The frame narrator refers specifically to the notorious expulsion from Moscow University, in the 1880s, of the liberal professors S. A. Muromtsev and M. M. Kovalevsky by the "mighty hand" of Leskov's old abomination, the "Armenian enlightener of Russia," Count Ivan Delyanov. The apropos anecdote is then introduced ostensibly to illustrate how much more skillfully such matters had been handled earlier, under the Machiavellian regime as minister of "enlightenment" of Delyanov's predecessor, Count Dmitry Tolstoy (equally an abomination of Leskov's, though in this story his aversion must be deduced by the reader). The basis for this anecdote, though the victim is never identified by name in the story, was the "quiet" removal of a professor from the university, in 1879, during Tolstoy's ministry.[2] This act of deft repression is held up by the narrator as a perfect specimen of "administrative grace."

The narrator of this retrospective illustration at first glance appears to be another of Leskov's typical "wise oldsters," a man rich in practical know-how and experienced in the workings of bureaucracies, more concerned with concrete results than with scoring verbal points or taking public stances. Such people know that it is often expedient to attain one's end by other than prescribed routes. This narrator seems to be cut from the same cloth as the "old genius" or the Petersburg police chief in "The Sentry." But those earlier manipulators had clearly been working for good ends (though in the second case, "good" with qualification). The narrator of "Administrative Grace" is another matter. Like Marya Martynovna in "Night Owls," he proves to be one of Leskov's "negated narrators." As William Edgerton puts it, the story is related "in approving terms by a character who turns out to be himself a target of Leskov's attack."[3] The episode this character relates as a perfect example of "graceful" administrative practice, Talleyrand-style (Talleyrand's pet phrase, *pas de zèle*, is cited in the text), must be read by us as a particularly repulsive case of administrative cynicism.

As the top official in a southern university town, the narrator had felt obliged to take action against both students and liberal professors: his predecessor had been assassinated.[4] One professor in particular, called only Lasalle in the story, seems to be a center of agitation, and he is therefore marked for removal. Unlike Delyanov, however, the narrator seeks to avoid open confrontations. As he puts it—in a phrase perhaps too aggressively repeated in the story's subtitle—he prefers *zahme Dressur*, the gentle method of lion-taming, to the more spectacular *wilde Dressur*, with its noisy display of guns and whips. So, after a consultation with the local bishop, a *donos* (secret denunciation) of the subversive professor is routed to Petersburg, not through the insecure channels of the Ministry of Education, but through the clergy, since the arch-conservative Dmitry Tolstoy was at that time (presumably 1879) head of both the Ministry of Education and the Holy Synod. Thus Leskov again strikes at a favorite target, the collaboration of the Orthodox clergy in police repression.

As a result of this *donos*, an adroit bit of *zahme Dressur*, apparently at Tolstoy's behest, is performed by the local chief gendarme. A lawyer named Parasolka, a Pole and Lasalle's chief rival for leadership of the local radicals, receives a summons to appear before the gendarme colonel. Soon after his arrival, the colonel excuses himself, pleading urgent business, leaving Parasolka alone in his office. There Parasolka discovers a (carefully planted) unfinished letter addressed by the colonel to Petersburg and reporting information supposedly brought to the police by none other than Lasalle himself. After (dishonorably) reading this letter, the liberal lawyer experiences "the greatest joy accessible to a progressive intellectual, the discovery of something nasty about his neighbor."

Of course Parasolka loses no time in spreading this scandalous news among his radical constituency, and Lasalle is soon reduced to ashes—first disgraced and spat upon by his former adulators (who make no attempt to verify Parasolka's story), and then killed, either murdered or a suicide. Only later is it discovered, by means of large bribes distributed among gendarme clerks, that no such report had ever been sent to Petersburg. This revelation in turn discredits Parasolka, who is suspected of making up the story of Lasalle's treachery, and Parasolka is obliged to depart in disgrace "for the banks of the Vistula." Such, concludes the dignitary, is the very essence of administrative grace: without public action by the government, two subversive leaders were removed from the scene, and some gendarme clerks were not only enriched, but have established a credibility and a secret contact with the radicals which can be exploited in the future. Perfect!

The reader is not expected to share the narrator's delight over these "graceful" maneuvers. A problem posed by the story, as by others with "negated" narrators, is how Leskov maneuvers us into the negative judgment. Leonid Grossman felt he did not succeed. "Frequently Leskov's reader is genuinely perplexed," he maintains, speaking of "Administrative Grace," "as to whose side the satirist is on, whom he is condemning and for whom fighting."[5] In the case of such stories as "Yid Somersault" and "Deception" I too have registered a similar complaint, feeling that the negation of the narrators was inadequately programmed, at least for the average Russian reader, and even imputing some of the inadequacy to the author's own ambivalence about Jews. But regarding "Administrative Grace" Grossman's strictures seem undeserved. Few readers could fail to perform the necessary upending of that story's narrator.

First of all, the frame discussion has been reported with heavy irony; all the participants in it have been scored off before the inner narrative begins. And the skaz narrator, though little is said to deflate him directly, speaks in a pompous and self-satisfied manner, a style befitting the appellation *sanovnik* with which he is several times designated—a Russian word for "high official" or "dignitary," here used with ironic overtones. Secondly, the narrator's cynicism is too extreme, his values too deviant from ethical norms common to civilized mankind. Leskov evidently relies on his reader's application of an "average" standard of compassion and ethics. The cool glee with which both the narrator and his bishop consultant greet the news of Lasalle's death would signal, even to the most case-hardened reader, that the values of such people are to be repudiated. Neat as it is, the whole "graceful" procedure for eliminating both the professor and the lawyer, in which the narrator takes such pride, will not be acceptable to any reader who feels that administration should strive not only for "grace," but for justice and humanity.

Grossman notwithstanding, there is little ambiguity about Leskov's position in "Administrative Grace." And despite the efforts of some Soviet commentators to assert otherwise, the thrust of his satire is directed not only against police cynicism, but against the heartless credulity and shallow faddism of the radicals. As the narrator expresses it, the dirt of his repressive action is left not on the government, but on society itself, which obligingly does the police's dirty work for it. Historically, Leskov's vision of this dirt proved prophetic, though doubtless even he did not imagine the extremes to which both police cynicism and public complicity in police crimes would go in the twentieth century.

A more substantial evocation of the policemanship theme is found in Leskov's last story, "The Rabbit Warren." This final work is both a trenchant satire and artistically one of Leskov's most brilliant performances—a fitting swan song indeed.

Though its final text unquestionably dates from the last months of Leskov's life, the full history of this story's composition is far from clear. As early as 1873 the newspaper *Russian World* had advertised a forthcoming story by Leskov, "The Devil in Peregudy," described as "fantastic scenes from Ukrainian peasant life"—a description which bears some resemblance to the contents of "The Rabbit Warren."[6] No such story appeared in print, and there seems to be no trace of it in Leskov's surviving manuscripts. Again in 1881 the magazine *Historical Messenger* advertised a forthcoming story by Leskov entitled "The Idle Dancer from Peregudy."[7] This story too never appeared in print. These titles, however, may represent early versions, or unwritten plans, for "The Rabbit Warren." (The "Idle Dancers," though not from Peregudy, made their debut later in the Tolstoyan parable with that title.) And the village of Peregudy—a rather absurd name, pronounced in Ukrainian *perehúdi* and suggesting something like "outroar"—was also mentioned in "The Unbaptized Priest" (1877); it was evidently part of Leskov's permanent stock-in-trade of "funny Ukrainian" materials.

After the advertisement of 1881 nothing is heard of Peregudy for another decade. Then, in Leskov's correspondence for 1891, we find evidence of an intensive effort on his part to peddle a story—obviously completed, since the manuscript was submitted—one of whose proposed titles was "The Rabbit Warren." This story was first offered to *Russian Thought*, but it aroused acute censor-panic and the skittish editors, Lavrov and Goltsev, dropped it.[8] It was then submitted to Prince Tsertelev for *Russian Survey*. To him Leskov reassuringly represented his story as "very funny and not without pin-pricks, but nothing to bother the censors."[9] A few days later he wrote Tsertelev a more detailed account of the story's origin and shifting titles:

> I have entitled the manuscript differently from what it was. It used to be called "An Invasion of Barbarians," but now it will be called "The Rabbit Warren." The new title is less aggressive and *less comprehensible*, and at the same time it is sonorous and enticing, which is good for a magazine cover. And the title had to be changed, because the persons who had the story with its old title [the editors of *Russian Thought*] have the habit of "consulting"

with people whom they should decidedly not consult [the official censors]. Very likely, the title, has already been noticed there, and it is awkward to brandish it before their eyes again.[10]

Tsertelev proved no more willing than Lavrov and Goltsev to confront the censors with Leskov's "Rabbit Warren," and the work returned to the author's desk.[11]

Whether this "Rabbit Warren" of 1891 is the same work as the one published under that title in 1917 is open to question. From the letter just quoted it is clear that the story first submitted to *Russian Thought* and later provisionally titled "The Rabbit Warren" was the one originally called "An Invasion of Barbarians." And from the descriptions of that work given in letters to Goltsev written earlier in 1891, it seems equally clear that this was a different story from the "Rabbit Warren" published in 1917. The 1891 work was a *conte à clef*, characterized as "memoirs" "built according to the tales of Zhomini and representing Ashinov, M——v's daughter, the Bulgarians, and our patriots and the diplomats' conflict with them. It is a gay and funny episode."[12] A few days later Leskov wrote Goltsev a more detailed key to the story's prototypes; among the personalities identified there is the same Olga Novikova who figures in "A Winter's Day."[13] But none of this material is to be found in the later "Rabbit Warren," and it is therefore possible that the work referred to in the 1891 correspondence is an entirely different one.[14] On the other hand, in a letter to Vladimir Solovyov of May 20, 1892, Leskov speaks of the necessity of "redoing" a story called "The Rabbit Warren," apparently to render it publishable;[15] and a later letter to A. F. Marks refers to "The Rabbit Warren" as "a piece that has been lying [unpublished] for a long time 'out of fear.' "[16] Thus the final "Rabbit Warren" may be a revision, if a very drastic one, of the original "Invasion of Barbarians."[17]

In any event, nothing more is heard of rabbit warren or barbarians until 1894. Late in that year Leskov again offered to *Russian Thought* a story now unquestionably the one we know as "The Rabbit Warren," though temporarily bearing another title, with two variants, "A Game with a Dummy" or "With a Dummy." Again Leskov tries to reassure the editors that although the story contains "delicate matter," "everything ticklish is very painstakingly disguised and intentionally confused. The coloration is Ukrainian and insane."[18] This new satire, he asserts, is much milder than "A Winter's Day," which had just made its way into print unscathed in that same *Russian Thought*. But Goltsev and Lavrov apparently had no inclination to experience again their nervousness over "A Winter's Day"; and so this new "Rabbit Warren," like its predecessor, was hastily rejected. "V[iktor] A[leksandrovich Goltsev] and I read your manuscript," Lavrov wrote Leskov, "and we decided that at the present time it is absolutely impossible to print it. Precisely with respect to those questions you touch on in it [the secret police] the censorship will turn savagely both on us and on you. It's very sad, but we hope you won't hold against us what should be entirely attributed to the current state of affairs. Though with heavy hearts, we are returning your manuscript."[19]

Leskov had time for one last try. In January 1895 he sent his manuscript to *Messenger of Europe* with another accompanying description both enticing and reassuring:

> The manuscript was ready, but I still cannot settle on a title, which sometimes seems to me too sharp, sometimes too obscure. However, let's try out the one I have given it now, that is, "The Rabbit Warren," in other words, the absurd places settled in by the "rabbits whose refuge was a rock."[20] The piece is written in a whimsical manner, on the order of the narratives of Hoffmann and Sterne, with digressions and ricochets. The setting is transferred to the Ukraine because there was a particular lot of nonsense there about "catching subversives, meaning those who rock thrones," and with Ukrainian humor the subject seems to go more smoothly and appear more innocuous. Perhaps it would be better to call it by the name of the hero or "dummy," i.e., "Onopry Peregud of Peregudy; His Life, Experiences, and Adventures." If you like the piece, we'll agree on a title.[21]

But Stasyulevich was just as frightened by Leskov's rabbits as Lavrov and Goltsev had been. His rejection was coolly gracious: "Again with no little pleasure I read your 'Rabbit Warren,' but I cannot dream of taking the risk of sharing the pleasure with others."[22] With an attempt to echo Leskov's wit, Stasyulevich added that he was afraid of suffering the fate of the "angered eelpout" in Leskov's story and landing in the bishop's soup.

In his reply, apparently the last literary letter he wrote in his life, Leskov accepted the rejection with resigned equanimity: "There is a proverb, 'Drunk or not, if people say drunk, better go to bed.' I'll follow that precept. I don't consider my 'jolly story' so terribly dangerous, but I will put it to bed. It's become a habit with me. *Cathedral Folk* slept in my desk three years. The 'Survey of the *Prolog*' ["Legen-

dary Characters"]—five years. Let this one sleep too. I believe you
that there is reason to be afraid, and of course I don't blame you in the
least, and I appreciate very much your effort to 'sugar the pill.' Let's
wait. Perhaps the weather will improve."[23]

The painted masks and colorful costumes of "The Rabbit Warren"
are so eye-catching that it is difficult to decide which is the more important part of the story—they or the satirical core they are supposed
to conceal. For at Leskov's hands the "Ukrainian and insane coloration" has acquired artistic value in itself. But there can be no doubt of
the author's judgment: the camouflage, however ingenious, was only
a devious means to a moral end.

Even lacking the author's celebrated "police chief's nose," the censors might have sniffed out some of the "delicate matter" Leskov had
hidden beneath the "mad" disguises. The basic satirical aim in "The
Rabbit Warren" is to reduce to absurdity the antisubversive police
paranoia chronic in Russian (and other) governments, and to show its
contagious effect on Russian society at large. The trick, in visually
belittling or shrinking an apparently formidable object, is to change
the proportions; if the scale is sufficiently reduced, the object is literally trivialized. Questions of state that seem portentous and deadly
serious in the councils of star-studded Petersburg generals become
ludicrous when perceived against the background of a sleepy Ukrainian village with the absurd name of Peregudy. An American parallel
(not so remotely impossible) would be to imagine the mayor of Ot-
tumwa, Iowa, ordering his police chief to investigate Communist in-
filtration of the town's first-grade teachers.

Onopry Peregud, the narrator-hero of Leskov's tale, by a fortuitous
series of circumstances is appointed police chief (*stanovoj*) in the village of Peregudy, a post for which he is totally unqualified and un-
trained. All goes well as long as he devotes himself to the village policeman's time-honored task of catching horse thieves. His methods
are unorthodox—he browbeats suspects into confessing by reading
them terrifying accounts, in Church Slavonic, of the punishments
awaiting them in the next world. It is only after he is infected by the
modern police contagion of rooting out the "sicialists" who "rock
thrones" that Onopry comes to grief. After that, like the "coney"
behind the rock, he can only take refuge in private madness from the
public insanity he had temporarily shared.

The details of Peregud's anti-"sicialist" manhunt are made maximally absurd. In the climactic anecdote, the overzealous police chief

first arrests as a suspected revolutionary a genuine secret police agent engaged in undercover pursuit of genuine revolutionaries. Then he discovers, too late to do anything about it, that the true revolutionary had been his own coachman, who has just successfully and insolently vanished. And beneath the seat of his own carriage the would-be detective hero discovers a large cache of revolutionary leaflets.[24]

Besides thoroughly shrinking his dummy of a policeman, Leskov also implicates the Orthodox clergy in the succession of police idiocies and contrasts its sacramentalist formalism with the true Christian piety of Tolstoyanism and Shtundism. What inspires Leskov's "dreamy maniac" to join the ridiculous hunt for subversives is partly the competitive example of the local priest, Father Nazary, who has received a medal for some secret political denunciation. Still worse, the information the perfidious priest has reported to the authorities was apparently extracted from his parishioners during their confessions.

By contrast with this representative of police Christianity, one of the suspicious-looking "women with cropped hair and spectacles," Yulia Semyonovna, turns out to be one of Leskov's ideal Tolstoyan heroines, a vegetarian, celibate, and performer of good works for the poor, among them the knitting of stockings, the last being the activity that later occupies Peregud in his madness. In an episode full of multiple ironies, Peregud, thinking to trick this saintly girl into giving evidence against herself, persuades her to write down for him those subversive sentences about rich and poor he has just heard her utter. The two pronouncements she obligingly transcribes, which Onopry then triumphantly incorporates in his *donos*, are later shown to be New Testament quotations (Matthew 13:22; James 2:6). The case is especially ironic, in Leskov's best anti-Orthodox spirit, in that it took a Lutheran, Baltic German clerk in the district police headquarters to identify the quotations, whereas Peregud, who had excelled in the special schooling given the Orthodox bishop's choir boys, has no inkling of their source. What Peregud did learn to perfection in that school were such Orthodox "essentials" as the "thirty-nine times an acolyte must bow before the bishop during the liturgy, including when to bow once and when three times in succession."

The anticlerical bias of "The Rabbit Warren" was intensified in a last-minute revision[25] involving the introduction of a new character, Yevgraf Ovechkin, alias Vekovechkin, an expriest unfrocked for suspicion of having murdered his wife.[26] Vekovechkin is the instructor of the bishop's choir boys; and in what Leskov considered typical Orthodox style, if hyperbolized, he obliges them to commit to memory an array of vital Orthodox statistics concerning how many saints are honored each month ("in September there are 1,100 saints, in October 2,543, in November 6,500, and in December even more, 14,400"). Similarly, the boys must learn the important fact that "the Holy Virgin was born in the summer of the year 5486, and the Annunciation occurred in the year 5500, on Sunday, at ten o'clock in the morning, in the twelfth year and seventh month of her age."[27] There are many more anticlerical and antipolice darts stuffed into the quiver of this story. The apprehension of the editors of *Russian Thought* and *Messenger of Europe* does not seem surprising: these are deadly weapons.

The poisoned arrows were expertly camouflaged, however, and on that camouflage Leskov lavished so much talent that the cover, consisting of manipulations of structure, characterization, and style may have come to outweigh the core. Leskov pointed out the main feature of his structural camouflage: a proliferation of "digressions and ricochets" causing "deliberate confusion." Never one to be overscrupulous about structural symmetry, in "The Rabbit Warren" Leskov had the perfect "rationalization" for his censor-deluding disorder: his narrator is crazy! From the serenity of his madhouse Peregud recollects the series of catastrophes that had brought him there; and realistically, one could hardly expect a madman to tell his story in logical sequences.

Along with this confusion, one of Leskov's devices of structural camouflage is to cover his satirical core with irrelevant matter. Since Onopry tells his story as autobiography, he naturally does not come to the final, police period of his "sane" life until his tale is far advanced. Thus, if the story is classified as a satire on policemanship, then its whole first half must be viewed as a digression. This digression, dealing with Onopry's early life, consists of a series of disconnected and seemingly harmless anecdotes, such as the one about the "angry eelpout" earmarked for the bishop's soup (gourmets know that the eelpout's liver swells when it is provoked, and its flesh is thus rendered more delicious).[28]

Dimly aware of the fortuitousness of these sequences, the narrator lays bare their absurdity by such enigmatic remarks as, "You have to know a little about the lay of the land in our village of Peregudy, because otherwise you'll never understand what's coming about my father, about the eelpout fish, and about my benefactor, the bishop" (9:510). On the level of pure narrative development, none of this background geography proves essential to the reader's understanding.

However, as anecdote follows absurd anecdote, it dawns on us that an architect other than Peregud has secretly imposed his own organizing principles on the madman's chaotic narrative. Besides the angry eel-pout, the author has his own satirical fish to fry.

Thus before we get to the police, we begin to realize, though the narrator does not, that a second satirical target, the Orthodox clergy, has already been effectively riddled by these seemingly random pot-shots. One after the other, Onopry's early anecdotes add up to a devastating picture of a priesthood concerned only with its own material well-being and physical satisfaction, or with obsessive minutiae of ritual. It seems uninterested in, and unaware of, the moral basis of Christianity. The typical figure is fat-bellied Pop [Priest] Prokop of Peregudy, who celebrates the liturgy wearing red boots, teaches his parishioners that "their faith is better than all other faiths in the world," and with the help of the landowner, whom he has assisted in reducing free Cossacks to serfdom, drives all Catholics and Jews out of his village, after which he himself becomes the village usurer.

Not only the clergy are scored off. One of Onopry's most innocently devastating anecdotes is based on a weird, but authentic article, "On Capital Punishment," written by the poet Vasily Zhukovsky in 1849.[29] There Zhukovsky seriously proposed that in Russia executions be treated like a religious rite, conducted decorously behind high walls, with church bells ringing and people kneeling outside while the hangman did his grim work within. As Leskov ironically paraphrases this scheme, Zhukovsky offers a procedure for "executing Orthodox Christians in such a way that it should prove not coarse, but instructive for all and for [the victims] themselves easy and spiritually beneficial" (9:532).

Furthermore, it turns out that apart from their content, the series of structural nonsequiturs that makes up the first part of "The Rabbit Warren" conceals another philosophical irony. In relating episodes from the basic phases in his life, each of them unconnected in any rational way with the one before, Onopry is unconsciously making the same point Leskov had made twenty years earlier in *Laughter and Grief:* that human lives, especially in Russia, are existentially absurd. They are chains of fortuitous events, often ludicrously incongruous, with links established only by the play of chance.

Onopry's early biography is thus in effect a parody of the *Bildungs-roman:* since whatever the hero learns in one period of his life is of no use in the next, no experiential *Bildung* can take place. In a world governed wholly by chance, one enters each phase of life unprepared to deal with its new problems. The end product of such an education could only be lunacy. Onopry's situation is rather like that of the pig in the famous experiment, driven to madness because it cannot decide whether to undertake the enormous effort required to open a door when the existence of the reward on the other side has been deliberately made uncertain.

The character of this mad dummy of a narrator is also a part of Leskov's camouflage, and a particularly delightful one. Peregud's personality is disarming. Even the most captious censor could not have been alarmed by the queer ramblings of this lovable old lunatic. For Onopry is not only mad, but a good soul. The favorite of the asylum, he sits eternally knitting stockings to cover the "cold blue feet" of his fellow inmates. When he recounts the story of his ludicrous life so genially and so delightfully, in such a bizarre mixture of Russian and Ukrainian, who could be so churlish as to see subversion in his tale?

Finally, that ear-catching linguistic mixture, as in so many of Leskov's stories, has become not only a means for distracting censors, but a tour de force of extraordinary ingenuity. The texture of the verbal crazy quilt is impossible to reproduce in any translation, since the original is made up of verbal material taken from two languages, closely related and mutually comprehensible, but nevertheless distinct.

Leskov's use of Ukrainian is much more subtle than the obvious formula of skaz plus frame—Peregud's Ukrainian skaz surrounded by a frame in the "author's" literary Russian. Apart from the fact that a skaz in pure Ukrainian would have been hard for some Russian readers to comprehend, such a structure would have suited neither the character of the narrator nor the author's stylistic designs. First, the "author" allows his own diction to be contaminated by that of the narrator, whose speech he first paraphrases rather than reports directly. Then, when we hear Peregud's own words, they are anything but pure Ukrainian. As a more or less educated man and an administrative official, Onopry knows Russian well and is accustomed to using it a great deal; and to make matters more complicated, his ecclesiastical education has left him with a residue of Church Slavonic associations. The style of "The Rabbit Warren," therefore, constantly drifts, incongruously and comically, from Russian to Ukrainian and back again, with occasional "quotations" in Church Slavonic, sometimes all three of these absurdly coexisting in the same sentence. The linguistic mishmash aptly symbolizes the mental and cultural confusion of Onopry Peregud.

In general, the consensus of critics competent in Ukrainian seems to be that Leskov is one of the very few Great Russian writers at home in that language, able to exploit juxtapositions and interlardings of the two linguistic cousins for the most varied artistic effects.[30] But a translator cannot duplicate these stunts. He has trouble enough with the usual array of puns, malapropisms, and folk etymologies.[31]

Literary scholars have concerned themselves with detecting the influences of other writers on this comic masterpiece. Leskov has indicated the principal ones, either in his correspondence or in the story: Hoffmann and Sterne, the latter for the "life and adventures" subtitle, for disjointed structure, and for "toying with the form"; Gogol, for Ukrainian comedy generally and for some specific satirical tidbits, for instance the parallel between policeman Peregud's ambitious dreams of medals and promotions and the fantasies of Petersburg glory indulged in by Gogol's immortal police chief, Skvoznik-Dmukhanovsky. The Ukrainian writer Grigory Kvitko-Osnovyanenko (1778-1843) is mentioned in the text as a model for description of the Ukrainian landscape; and the Ukrainian philosopher Hryhory Skovoroda (1722-1794) is cited several times as a source of various bits of quaint wisdom, including the epigraph, from which Leskov extracts not only a double pun on *bolvan*, "blockhead" (used by Skovoroda in the older sense of "idol, image," and in Leskov's earlier title in the additional sense of the "dummy" in a card game), but a picturesque formulation of the Platonic notion that the concrete Appearances (which are the essence of realistic art) are only mirror reflections of the true or spiritual Idea of Man.[32]

Along with these well-attested sources, Leonid Grossman has adduced two new and surprising ones, which, if valid, are instances of the younger generation influencing the older: Vsevolod Garshin and Anton Chekhov.[33] Garshin's "Red Flower" and Chekhov's "Ward No. 6," particularly the latter, may have had something to do with Leskov's use of the mad *raisonneur* who, from the vantage point of the lunatic asylum, lays bare the madness of the outside world—though, to be sure, Leskov's literary interest in insanity goes back to the very beginning of his career ("A Short History of a Case of Private Madness," 1863). Grossman also points out that Chekhov's early story "Oversalted" (1885) has a plot somewhat similar to the core anecdote of Peregud and his revolutionary coachman.[34] Whatever its derivation, however, as a finished work of art "The Rabbit Warren" sprang unmistakably from the pen of one of the most "self-natured" (to use Tolstoy's phrase) literary talents of the nineteenth century, Nikolai Leskov. It could have been written by no one else.

40

A Winter's Night

Mystical premonitions of impending death had come over Leskov several times in his later years, and they acquired a powerful physical reinforcement after he suffered a heart attack in August 1889, standing on the steps of Suvorin's publishing house, when he heard the news that the sixth volume of his collected works had been "arrested." From that time on, for the few years of invalided life remaining to him, the recurrent, excruciating attacks of angina were a potent *memento mori*. It was time to pack his spiritual bags.

In some ways this packing process was easier for Leskov than it was for Tolstoy. Despite his fervent allegiance to Tolstoyan principles, Leskov retained to the end a comfortably firm belief in personal, conscious immortality; thus he did not have to face the prospect of the extinction of personality. Where Tolstoy saw immortality as a rather bleak, Nirvana-like merging of the individual soul into the ultimate One, Leskov had a cozier view of the next world as a place much like this, where the individual soul retained its identity and apparently its earthly memories. He was not being entirely facetious when he said after his melodramatic reconciliation with his lifelong enemy Terty Filippov, "At least we will bow to each other in the next world."[1] And although eruptions of generalized guilt and contrition occasionally burst from him, Leskov seemed confident that the balance sheet of his life was solidly in the black. In his youth he may sometimes have been an *aggel*, a demon, but he was sure that the combination of his literary work (regarded as a moral force for good) and the Tolstoyan reforms of his old age would qualify him for the company of angels. Therefore, at least in theory, for Leskov death had no sting. It was an "interesting day," as he had called it in *Laughter and Grief* (3:488), a "great step,"[2] a moment of ultimate truth, more revealing than any other in all experience, an "awakening from the sleep of life."[3]

All the same, death was frightening—frightening not because it threatened the extinction of consciousness (since it did not, in theory), nor out of excessive attachment to the things of this world (by now the flesh was a source of more pain than pleasure, though the life of literature excited Leskov to the very end). Nevertheless, the "step" of departure was not only "great"; it was "fearful."[4] Whatever the consolations of philosophy, the organism clings instinctively to life. A letter to Suvorin, written in response to an invitation to a New Year's Eve party, reveals Leskov's struggle to accept the reality of death:

> It [the thought of death] is very stern, but as you learn to live with it, it seems to become more merciful. For in it lies concealed the most powerful force for consoling and for humbling yourself. Except for death, at a certain age everything becomes very petty and no longer even stirs you deeply. I have read in the works of ascetics, heard from thoughtful old men, and L[ev] N[ikolaevich] has told me that the *most essential* thing is to make your peace (i.e., get on good terms) with the idea of the inevitability of death. For a long time I have been going to bed and getting up with it; and since I have learned to live with it, I have seen the light: everything has become easier for me, and a sort of boldness has entered my spirit which was not there before. L[ev] N[ikolaevich] says that afterward "an imperturbable peace should come," but I have felt that only once, and for a short time; but on the other hand it was an amazing condition of such happiness that I even took fright and began forcibly to remind myself that people suffer the loss of loved ones, humiliations and torments. The Orientals say that they love "talks about death," and perhaps for that reason they are more tranquil than we are, but among the English too it is not considered improper to speak of death, and some people think the English die no worse, but rather better than our common folk. But our "in-between people" are terribly scared of death, which therefore catches them like chickens and tears off their heads, also like chickens. This is a very pathetic condition, and so-called "piety" can do absolutely nothing to help a person with it. Remember how Aleksei Tolstoy puts it.: "Like a thief it laid me low." Then everything flies to the winds—all your dreams and hopes. But to get used to expecting this guest helps a great deal.[5]

Some of Leskov's fear was not of death, but of the process of dying; how to die with dignity, unlike Ivan Ilyich, without wails of *ne khochu . . u . . u* ("I don't want to . . oo . . oo"). A vividly positive model had been Leskov's friend and fellow antisacramentalist, Herzen's cousin Tatyana Passek. As Leskov described her death, "In the night she summoned Gattsuk and said, 'All right, I am floating away. Strike some chords on your guitar.' He began to strike chords, and she 'floated away.' She was a woman of intellect, and she 'floated away' in the full light of reason, without tears, without squeals, and without the muttering of priests."[6]

This was the way Leskov wanted to die, but he was afraid he would bungle it: "Thoughts of death never leave me [he wrote Tolstoy in 1894], and they come instantaneously, even at the very first moment I wake up in the night. I consider this a blessing, since in this way all the same you come to accept the inevitability of the fearful step. Of writers on death I prefer to read chapters from your book *On Life* and Seneca's letters to Lucilius. But no matter how much you study the theory, in practice all the same it will be happening for the first time, and you'll have to get through it somehow or other, since it will be a 'new thing.' "[7]

Whether from good fortune or strength of spirit, Leskov's "fearful step" proved more like Tatyana Passek's than Ivan Ilyich's. Though he remained an invalid and was increasingly troubled by shortness of breath, in the last year of his life the angina attacks were mitigated. Leskov seemed, as he said, to have been granted a reprieve. No one, least of all Leskov, expected the end to come when it did.

On February 13, 1895, he went out to attend the opening of the twenty-third exhibition of the "Itinerants" in the Academy of Arts. Among the pictures publicly displayed there for the first time was the now well-known portrait of Leskov by Valentin Serov. As Andrei Leskov remarks, it is a pity that this is the most accomplished portrait of Leskov we have, since it shows him already "sick and doomed," though it succeeds in conveying that "penetrating gaze, full of life and thought."[8] Leskov had liked the portrait earlier. But for the exhibition it had been given a heavy, almost black frame. It looked like an obituary portrait, and Leskov returned from the exhibition full of gloomy premonitions.

The following day he began to run a fever. On February 18, sick of being cooped up in his stuffy apartment and finding it hard to breathe, Leskov got up and, contrary to doctor's orders, went outdoors. As he had so often done in the past, he hired a sleigh and took a drive around the Tauride Garden, gratefully sucking the fresh, cold air into his sick lungs. It was an act that his horrified son and doctor considered suicidal.

Although the next day he seemed no worse, the favorable signs were illusory. On the night of February 20, the lungs again began to fill with fluid. No attempt was made to drain them artificially, and Leskov was never hospitalized. An oxygen tent was brought, and digitalis administered. Though earlier the shortness of breath had bothered him, at one A.M. Leskov went peacefully to sleep. And about two A.M., February 21, 1895, his son Andrei, who was keeping vigil in his father's study, went in and found Leskov dead. His wish for an end "peaceful and free from shame" and been fulfilled. He had "floated away" in his sleep, "without tears, without squeals, and without the muttering of priests."

The next day Leskov's "Last Request," written several years before, was read and subsequently published widely, provoking considerable comment. It is a quirky, Leskovian document.

A rather querulous opening paragraph asks that an autopsy be performed "so that the causes may be found of the heart disease from which I have long suffered, despite the assurances of doctors that there were no pathological changes in my heart whatever." This antimedical sally provoked Dr. Chekhov to remark, in a letter to Suvorin, "He needn't have written in his will that the doctors didn't know what was happening to his heart. The doctors knew very well, but they concealed it from him."[9] The autopsy was performed and revealed such fatty degeneration of the heart that it seemed miraculous that Leskov had lived as long as he did.

Four paragraphs of the "Last Request" are devoted to funeral and burial arrangements. The tone is discordant—a mixture of manifest humility, muffled self-congratulation, suppressed self-pity, and pleas for love and recognition masquerading as proud unconcern: "At my burial I ask that no speeches be made. I know that in me there was much that was bad and that I merit no praise or regrets. He who wishes to speak ill of me should know that I contemned myself [. . .] I select no place of burial for myself, since in my eyes that is a matter of no importance, but I ask that no one place on my grave any monument other than an ordinary, simple wooden cross. If this cross deteriorates and someone is found who wishes to replace it with a new one, let him do so and accept my appreciation for the remembrance. If there should prove to be no such well-wisher, it means that the time to remember my grave has passed."[10]

Sandwiched in between two of the funeral paragraphs was paragraph five, which provided for the disposition of property. All of Leskov's assets were bequeathed in equal shares to his daughter, his son, and his "orphan" ward, Varya Dolina. This is the only mention of Vera and Andrei in the will, but on Varya he expatiates for five more paragraphs. Those who wish to show love for Leskov are asked to transfer it to "poor Varya, whom I loved" and help her with life's financial and other problems. He explicitly denies the rumor that Varya is his bastard daughter: "I don't know why I should conceal it, but it is not true." Then he launches into his familiar "orphan" sermon, reiterating that "a man can love his own and another's child equally."

True as this formula may be, it can be, and certainly was, read in a much less benign spirit by the real son and daughter. Even if they recognized that one of its purposes was to stroke their father's ego ("Was I not a noble and generous spirit to adopt an orphan?"), they also perceived in it a message much less friendly to them. To them it said, "You thought you could bind me by ties of blood, but I had the last laugh: I loved her more than you." Andrei never forgave him.

Even in the transcendental final paragraph of the will the note of self-pity for undeserved injury seems to sound louder than the official humility: "Then I ask forgiveness of all those whom I have insulted, grieved, or to whom I was unpleasant, and with all my heart I forgive all people everything unpleasant that was done to me, either out of insufficiency of love or in the conviction that by doing me harm they were rendering service to God, in whom I believe and whom I have tried to serve in spirit and in truth, suppressing in myself my fear of people and strengthening myself in love according to the word of my Lord Jesus Christ."

The funeral was held on February 23. Leskov's instructions could not be carried out to the letter: the Orthodox clergy won a posthumous victory over their old enemy. Andrei Leskov purchased for his father a plot in the "Writers' Bridges" section of the Volkovo Cemetery in Petersburg, incongruously near the graves of such radical luminaries as Belinsky, Dobrolyubov, Pisarev, and Shelgunov. According to law, burial in that cemetery was not allowed without the "muttering of priests," that is, an Orthodox funeral service. The priests, therefore, were permitted to "mutter" over Leskov's corpse. Contrary to custom, however, and at his specific request, the coffin was kept closed. No speeches were made, either in the church or at the graveside.

And so, as one of those present in both places, Leskov's friend Lidia Veselitskaya wrote: "Nikolai Semyonovich departed with his coffin into that cold, slimy hole, away from the severe illness which had exhausted him, from the vengeance of his enemies and the slander of his friends, from all injuries and sorrows, from readers and admirers, from his literary brethren, and from his heirs, already quarreling among themselves. But the incorporeal and ageless monument he erected to himself stands firm and secure."[11]

Leskov's study in the 1890s.

Notes

References to Leskov's works cited by volume and page number only are to the following edition: N. S. Leskov, *Sobranie sočinenij*, ed. V. G. Bazanov et al. (Moscow, 1956-1958), 11 vols. Some works not included in that edition are cited from the last pre-Revolutionary edition: N. S. Leskov, *Polnoe sobranie sočinenij* (St. Petersburg, 1902-1903), 36 vols., abbreviated in the notes as "*P.s.s.*" The abbreviation "ANL" refers to the standard biography of Leskov by his son: Andrej Leskov, *Žizn' Nikolaja Leskova po ego ličnym, semejnym i nesemejnym zapisjam i pamjatjam* (Moscow, 1954). The abbreviation "SPb." is used throughout for St. Petersburg.

1. Class, Family, and Mr. Fear

1. Leskov to M. A. Protopopov, Dec. 23, 1891 (11:508). See also 11:16.

2. In a letter to P. K. Shchebalsky dated May 7, 1871, referring to *Laughter and Grief*, Leskov uses the first person singular for the presumably fictitious narrator. He mentions a letter identified in the story as a document received by the narrator from his uncle, and alludes to it as "his [Vatazhkov's] final letter to *me* about *my* quarrel with the Germans" (10:318; italics mine). In 1870 Leskov had a row with some Germans in Reval, about which he later wrote an amusing article, "Zakonnye vredy," *Russkij mir*, nos. 313, 320 (Nov. 30, Dec. 11, 1872).

3. Leskov to P. K. Shchebalsky, April 16, 1871 (10:310).

4. The most reliable source concerning the elder Leskov's career is his "service record" (*formuljarnyj spisok*), which is cited at length in ANL, pp. 19ff.

5. One of these children, according to Leskov's autobiographical sketch (11:8), was his mother, Marya Petrovna Alferieva, then living with her family in the household of Mikhail Andreevich Strakhov; but see below, note 15.

6. In his autobiographial sketch Leskov stresses how deviant such incorruptibility was: "According to his own account, this post [in the Caucasus] was such a 'fat' one [*doxodnoe*] that you could have 'taken in as much as you wanted' [. . .] But my father took in nothing from the Caucasian 'vodka operations' but the 5,000 paper rubles he received as a bonus when he left the post in 1830" (11:9). Leskov's true feelings about his father's exemplary con-

duct may have been ambivalent: his father had his honor and his spotless conscience, but it is money that gives power and prestige in this world, besides the benefits it confers on one's relatives. Naturally Leskov could not acknowledge such feelings, even to himself.

7. The letter is quoted in ANL, pp. 22-24.

8. A. N. Leskov, "N. S. Leskov," *Literaturnyj sovremennik*, no. 3 (March 1937), p. 160.

9. As Andrei Leskov observes, "Semyon Dmitrievich's closeness to Ryleev and Bestuzhev remains without confirmation from any known materials, testimonials from outside the family, or from family traditions. The conditions and motives for [S. D. Leskov's] move to Stavropol are unmistakably set forth in his formulary"—that is, he wanted to go to an outlying area where promotions would come faster (ANL, p. 22).

10. ANL, p. 22.

11. "Russkie demonomany," in N. S. Leskov, *Russkaja rozn'; očerki i rasskazy* (SPb., 1881), p. 228.

12. In the same passage in which he sends a "low bow" of gratitude to Ostromyslensky, then alive and well, Leskov claims that he "learned to think in an Orthodox way" from his father. The explanation for this falsehood is that in that story Leskov needs to represent himself as wholly Orthodox in background so that he will not be suspected of anticlerical motives in denouncing, as he does in this work, the forcible conversion to Christianity of young Jewish boys conscripted into the army for this purpose.

13. Leskov to P. K. Shchebalsky, June 8, 1871 (10:329).

14. Leskov to L. I. Veselitskaya, June 27, 1893 (11:529).

15. The chronology of this tutorship is not clear. As Leskov represents it in his autobiography, it occurred during the period after his father left the seminary and before he entered the government service: "With his forty kopecks father came to Oryol and was taken 'for his keep' into the house of a local landowner named Khlopov, whose children he taught, and apparently successfully, since he was 'lured' away from Khlopov by the landowner Mikhail Andreevich Strakhov, who was then serving as marshal of the nobility in Oryol District. Then father taught the children in the family of the Alferievs, who had fled Moscow from the French, and by this time received some sort of pay, probably very little. But it is noteworthy that among his little pupils was the girl who was later to become his wife and my mother. While he was tutor in the Strakhovs' house, father attracted attention with his excellent mind and his honesty, which was the outstanding feature of his whole long-suffering life. From being a teacher he was persuaded to enter the service" (11:8).

However, Semyon Leskov left home in 1808 or 1809 and entered the government service in 1811 (see ANL, p. 20)—*before* the Alferievs came to Oryol from Moscow and two years before Leskov's mother was born. The only explanation for this discrepancy is that Semyon Leskov must have continued to give lessons in his spare time long after he had become a civil servant.

The passage quoted above is an excellent illustration of the psychological ambiguity in Leskov's attitude toward his good and bad fathers. Though his own father is credited with long-suffering honesty, Leskov seems especially eager to emphasize his poverty, insignificance, and dependence on such a mighty figure as Mikhail Andreevich Strakhov, the local marshal of the nobility. The spelling out of all three of Strakhov's names and the high-sounding title are evidence of the unacknowledged reverence Leskov felt for this man.

16. "Dvorjanskij bunt v Dobrynskom prixode," *Istoričeskij vestnik*, no. 2 (Feb. 1881), p. 371.

17. Marya Petrovna Leskova to Leskov, Aug. 23, 1883. Originally in the Prague Archive, this letter was copied into a notebook by Pierre Kovalevsky, who made it available to me. On this notebook and its contents see William B. Edgerton, "Missing Letters to Leskov: An Unsolved Puzzle," *Slavic Review*, no. 1 (March 1966), pp. 120-132. Edgerton's article apparently stimulated the "discovery" of most of these letters in Moscow, where they were transferred from Prague in 1945. This letter is now in the Central State Archive of Literature in Moscow. See V. G. Zimina, "Iz arxiva N. S. Leskova," *Zapiski otdela rukopisej Gosudarstvennoj Ordena Lenina Biblioteki SSSR imeni V. I. Lenina*, issue 30 (Moscow, 1968), p. 208.

18. ANL, p. 31.

19. Leskov to Aleksei Leskov, Aug. 22, 1879 (ANL, p. 36).

20. Leskov to Marya Petrovna Leskova (ANL, p. 35). The Sergei Petrovich whom Leskov sideswipes in this letter is his uncle, Marya Petrovna's brother. Leskov lived in his house for several years after moving from Oryol to Kiev. As this passage and others show, Leskov harbored a long-standing grudge against this uncle. About the alleged expulsion from his house of Sergei Petrovich's mother, Leskov's grandmother Alferieva, I have no further information.

21. ANL, p. 43.

22. "Iz odnogo dorožnogo dnevnika; okončanie," *Severnaja pčela*, no. 351 (Dec. 29, 1862). According to Andrei Leskov, Natalia Petrovna had seven children by Strakhov and eight by her second husband, L. I. Konstantinov. Aleksandra Petrovna Scott had at least two sons (ANL, pp. 121-122), but apparently no daughters. Marya Petrovna had four sons and three daughters. This adds up to twenty-four grandchildren. Sergei Petrovich might account for the other three, but apparently he was childless.

23. Leskov to S. N. Shubinsky, Feb. 1, 1883 (11:273-274).

2. The Ineducable Autodidact

1. ANL, p. 74.

2. Leskov's lengthy series of articles entitled "Russian Society in Paris" contains an elaborate account of the cultural and political activities of the Russians, Poles, Czechs, and Serbs in Paris in 1862-1863, as well as a detailed

sociological description, evidently based on personal experience, of Parisian grisettes and the way they looked after their Slavic lovers. See "Russkoe obščestvo v Pariže," originally in *Biblioteka dlja čten'ja*, no. 6 (June 1863); reprinted, in a much expanded version, in *Očerki i rasskazy M. Stebnickogo*, 1 (SPb., 1867); and in *Sbornik melkix belletristiceskix proizvedenij N. S. Leskova-Stebnickogo* (SPb., 1873). The grisettes are also dealt with, in passing, in "Kak otravljajutsja ugol'nym čadom v Pariže" ("How people are poisoned by coal fumes in Paris"), *Severnaja pčela*, no. 70 (March 14, 1863), which, despite its ominous title, ends "Oh, how fine it is to live in Paris!"

3. Leskov from Paris to his son, stepson, and stepdaughter (10:405). In that publication the letter is dated June 12/24, 1875, but Edgerton has given cogent arguments for dating it June 30/ July 12. See William B. Edgerton, "Leskov's Trip Abroad in 1875," *Indiana Slavic Studies*, 4 (The Hague, 1967): 89n.

4. Leskov to P. K. Shchebalsky, July 29/ Aug. 10, 1875, from Marienbad (10:411). The editors of volume 10, A. M. Bikhter and N. I. Sokolov, make no attempt in their annotations to identify the "young Naville" referred to in this letter, but William B. Edgerton has offered convincing arguments that he was Louis Naville, the son of the noted theologian Jules-Ernest Naville, with whose books Leskov was well acquainted ("Nikolai Leskov: The Intellectual Development of a Literary Nonconformist" [Ph.D. dissertation, Columbia University, 1954], pp. 358-359). It is known that Louis Naville read Russian; but if Leskov had been able to speak Russian with a Swiss theologian, he would probably have thought it worthy of comment in this letter.

5. Leskov lived in a pension where several other Russians were staying, among them the noted Slavist F. I. Buslaev (see 10:402, 412, 452). The Jesuits were I. S. Gagarin (1814-1882) and I. M. Martynov (died 1894); see Leskov to I. S. Aksakov, July 29/ Aug. 10, 1875, from Marienbad (10:415). Leskov wrote a whole article dealing with Gagarin's alleged complicity in Pushkin's fatal duel: "Iezuit Gagarin v dele Puškina," *Istoričeskij vestnik*, no. 8 (Aug. 1886).

6. See Leskov to I. S. Gagarin, June 11 (n.s.), 1875, in which he comments in detail on Gagarin's *Le clergé russe* (Brussels, 1871). This letter has been published by Edgerton, "Leskov's Trip Abroad," pp. 90-92. Edgerton, incidentally, shows that Leskov's date is incorrect and that the letter was actually written on June 1/13, 1875. In a letter to S. N. Shubinsky dated Aug. 17, 1883 (11:283), Leskov, in a spirit of exasperation at the censorship and the torpidity of Russian literary life, exclaims, "I can't forgive myself that I never mastered the French language sufficiently to work in it. I wouldn't stay in Russia for an hour forever after."

7. Leskov to A. P. Milyukov, July 12/24, 1875 (10:410-411).

8. In the late 1880s Leskov was reading in Russian a collection of the maxims and "wisdom" of Goethe, *Izrečenija v proze Gete* (SPb., 1885); see also ANL, pp. 596, 647. But he reviewed a volume entitled *Die vierte Saecul-*

arfeier der Geburt Doctor Martin Luthers by C. F. V. Walther in *Novosti i birževaja gazeta*, no. 89 (March 30, 1884), p. 4.

9. The breadth of Leskov's acquaintance with English poetry and prose is demonstrated in his correspondence with his stepson, B. M. Bubnov, in *Šestidesjatye gody; materialy po istorii literatury i obščestvennomu dviženiju*, ed. N. K. Piksanov and O. V. Cexnovicer (Moscow and Leningrad, 1940), pp. 359-376. Unfortunately, many of these letters were not included in the collected works published in 1956-1958.

10. On Leskov's pan-Slavic interests, see William B. Edgerton, "Leskov and Russia's Slavic Brethren," *American Contributions to the Fourth International Congress of Slavicists* (The Hague, 1958), pp. 51-76.

11. For an anecdote about fellow pupils, see 11:71-72. The story about privies is in "Zametka o zdanijax," *Sovremennaja medicina*, no. 29 (July 28, 1860), pp. 517-518. The projected autobiography, begun in 1885, was never completed. A copy of part of it was made by the literary critic A. A. Izmailov for his manuscript on Leskov (never published; the only copy extant is now in the Pushkin House, Leningrad). The original was in the archives of the publisher A. F. Marks and was probably destroyed during the Revolution (see ANL, pp. 7-8). The description of Leskov's landlady is in "Kak ja učilsja prazdnovat' "; quoted in full in ANL, pp. 70-71.

12. Leskov's school record is given in ANL, pp. 73-74.

13. "Smert' strogogo čeloveka," *Peterburgskaja gazeta*, no. 38 (Feb. 8, 1892); quoted in ANL, p. 73.

14. It was written in 1890 for V. G. Shvetsov, the editor of the magazine *Zhivopisnoe obozrenie*. See also ANL, p. 15.

15. The date of S. D. Leskov to D. N. Klushin, March 17, 1848 (ANL, pp. 25-26), seems to settle the question as to whether he might have died in 1847 (Edgerton, "Nikolai Leskov," p. 67n).

16. Quoted in ANL, p. 26.

17. Chekhov has an amusing remark about this: "Writers are as jealous as pigeons. Leikin doesn't like it when somebody writes about merchant life, and it's unpleasant for Leskov to read stories of clerical life not written by himself" (A. P. Chekhov to I. L. Leontiev, Feb. 4, 1888, in *Polnoe sobranie sočinenij i pisem*, 14 [Moscow, 1949]: 30).

18. A. I. Faresov, *Protiv tečenij; N. S. Leskov; ego žizn', sočinenija, polemika i vospominanija o nem* (SPb., 1904), p. 69.

19. "I. Èm," "Kak rabotajut naši pisateli: N. S. Leskov," *Novosti i birževaja gazeta*, no. 49 (Feb. 19/ March 3, 1895), p. 2.

20. A. I. Faresov, "Umstvennye perelomy v dejatel'nosti N. S. Leskova," *Istoričeskij vestnik*, 143 (March 1916): 805, 808. Two letters from Leskov to Srebnitsky, both written in 1891, are preserved in the Pushkin House, Leningrad, but neither has been published.

21. ANL, pp. 82-83.

22. V[iktor V.] P[rotopopov], "U N. S. Leskova," *Peterburgskaja gazeta*,

no. 326 (Nov. 27, 1894), p. 2. The references to Mme Zinovieva's·library, though numerous in Leskov's writings, are inconsistent. Sometimes the library is located in Oryol, sometimes on a country estate; the lady is variously called Anna N. Zinovieva, Nastasia Sergeevna Zinovieva, and Nastasia Sergeevna Ivanova. It seems clear that the library must have been in Oryol in Leskov's student days there, or he would hardly have been able to peruse it as thoroughly as he claims to have done. See Leskov to I. S. Aksakov, March 23, 1875 (10:388); "Dvorjanskij bunt v Dobrynskom prixode," *Istoričeskij vestnik*, no. 2 (February 1881), p. 358; 11:182; ANL, p. 75. Leskov's acquaintance with Gromeka dates from his Kiev period (after 1849) and is discussed in Chapter 3.

23. From an unsigned and untitled note in *Novosti i birževaja gazeta*, no. 104 (July 16, 1883); quoted in 11:683-684.

24. Leskov to S. N. Shubinsky, July 23, 1883 (11:282). On Markovich, see L. I. Levandovskij, "N. S. Leskov o Marko Vovchok i A. V. Markoviče," *Voprosy russkoj literatury*, 1 (Lvov, 1966): 49-54.

3. My Universities

1. ANL, p. 89.
2. Ibid., p. 113.
3. The subject of recruiting Jewish boys had been touched on much earlier in "Neskol'ko slov o vračax rekrutskix prisutstvij," *Sovremennaja medicina*, no. 36 (Sept. 15, 1860). It is also alluded to in "Ovcebyk."
4. Leskov uses this quotation (Jeremiah 31:15; Matthew 2:18) repeatedly.
5. The story originally appeared under the title of "A Naval Captain from the Dry Nedna": "Morskoj kapitan s suxoj Nedny; rasskaz *entre chien et loup* (Iz besedy v kajut-kampanii)," *Sbornik morskix statej i rasskazov* (monthly supplement to the naval newspaper *Jaxta*), nos. 2-3 (Feb.-March 1877). The revised version under the title of "Besstydnik" appeared in N. S. Leskov, *Sobranie sočinenij*, 6 (SPb., 1890): 324-338.
6. Leonid Grossman asserts that the development of the story "clearly breaks off in this anecdotal finale, which is unworthy of its great and tragic theme" (*N. S. Leskov: zizn', tvorcestvo, poètika* [Moscow, 1945], p. 241). Apparently Grossman believed that the "great and tragic theme" of wartime corruption called for a philippic against the wicked and unpatriotic embezzlers.
7. Pilyankevich, Yakubovsky, and Vigura are mentioned in 11:24. Bogorodsky, along with Yakubovsky and Zhuravsky, is referred to in an unfinished autobiographical note (11:17).
8. Zhuravsky crops up many times in Leskov's writings, and is always referred to in the most glowing terms: "the most sincere of abolitionists, who had devoted to the peasant question his entire life and *all his means*" (5:162), "a character of the first magnitude" (3:558). In 1870 Leskov prepared a whole article on Zhuravsky, consisting mostly of the latter's correspondence with his

employer, L. A. Naryshkin. Leskov was unable to publish it, and it remains in manuscript to this day: "Iz gluxoj pory; perepiska Dmitrija Petroviča Žuravskogo i dva pis'ma L'va Aleksandroviča Naryškina (kasajuščiesja ličnosti Žuravskogo) 1843-47 goda," preserved in the Central State Literary Archive, Moscow. See 10:544; ANL, p. 620.

9. Leskov to I. S. Aksakov, Dec. 2, 1874 (10:371).

10. There is an extended discussion of Feuerbach in *At Daggers Drawn* (P.s.s., 23:117). In the same novel there is a discussion of the "Tübingen theologians" and their great successor, Renan (24:73).

11. Louis Reybaud, *Études sur les réformateurs, ou socialistes modernes* (Paris, 1842-1843).

12. "Vladyčnyj sud" (6:116-117). In this typical memoir many of the characters—such as Prince and Princess Vasilchikov and Metropolitan Philaret (Amfiteatrov)—appear under their real names. Gromeka, however, is called Andrei Ivanovich Drukart, the name under which he appears in "Pechersk Eccentrics." This has led B. Ya. Bukhshtab, editor of the seventh volume of the recent Soviet edition of Leskov, to annotate Drukart as a real person (7:531). S. A. Reiser, editor of the sixth volume, in which "Episcopal Justice" appears, also fails to make the identification with Gromeka. The identity of the two had been pointed out by William B. Edgerton ("Nikolai Leskov: The Intellectual Development of a Literary Nonconformist," [Ph.D. dissertation, Columbia University, 1954], p. 90) and is obvious from the statement made in "Episcopal Justice" itself: "[Drukart] very recently died in the post of vice-governor of Siedlce, in which he took part in the final destruction of the Uniate church" (6:115). The vice-governor of Siedlce who died in 1877 was S. S. Gromeka, and Leskov cites the same details about his career as a religious persecutor, but using Gromeka's real name, in 11:97n.

13. "Rossijskie govoril'ni," *Biblioteka dlja čten'ja*, no. 11 (Nov. 1863), p. 70; 10:22.

14. M. L. Slonim, *Tri ljubvi Dostoevskogo* (New York, 1953); I. M. Grevs, *Istorija odnoj ljubvi: I. S. Turgenev i Polina Viardo* (Moscow, 1927).

15. L. I. Veselitskaja, "Pis'ma N. S. Leskova," *Literaturnaja mysl'*, 3 (Leningrad, 1925): 265; reprinted in *Vstreči s pisateljami* (Leningrad, 1929).

16. ANL, p. 100

17. N. D. Baxareva, pseud. (N. D. Poljuškina, née Noha), "Nikolaj Semenovič Leskov (Memuary vnučki N. S. Leskova pisatel'nicy Natalii Dmitrievny Baxarevoj)" (deposited in Archive of Russian and East European History, Columbia University), p. 4.

18. Ibid.

19. "Iz odnogo dorožnogo dnevnika," *Severnaja pčela*, no. 337 (Dec. 13, 1862).

20. This is the date given by Andrei Leskov (ANL, p. 106) and, probably on the strength of his testimony, by K. P. Bogaevskaya, who compiled the "Chronological Outline of N. S. Leskov's Life and Works" appended to the

collected works (11:801). The same date is given in the much more detailed, but still unpublished, outline of Leskov's life and works compiled by Mme Bogaevskaya's late husband, S. P. Shesterikov, notes on which were kindly made available to me by William B. Edgerton. However, Vera Leskova's daughter, Natalia Bakhareva, says that her mother was born in 1858. In Leskov's own writings the only direct evidence is the figure of Varya Rozanova in *No Way Out*, who is closely modeled on Leskov's daughter, Vera. Varya was five years old in 1861; she would thus have been born in 1856 (2:169). There are many mistakes and inaccuracies in Mme Bakhareva's memoirs, but it does seem surprising that she should err in the date of her mother's birth.

21. L. Levandovsky has discovered archival materials in Kiev showing that Leskov resigned from the service in 1860 because he refused to take part in a cover-up of a police robbery. See "N. S. Leskov v Kieve (novye materialy)," *Russkaja literatura*, no. 3 (1963), 104-109.

22. The hypothesis of a visit to Petersburg by Olga Vasilievna is largely based on the account in *No Way Out*, which shows Dr. Rozanov's wife creating a new series of miseries for her husband among a new set of friends in Petersburg. She even becomes involved in a love affair with Beloyartsev, the leader and organizer of the notoriously libidinous "commune," who is modeled on Leskov's archenemy, Vasily Sleptsov. If based, even partially, on fact, these events would have taken place in 1861-1862. Bakhareva, however, reports that her grandmother visited Petersburg only after Leskov established a permanent menage with Katerina Bubnova—which did not happen until 1865. Andrei Leskov mentions no such visit, but P. D. Boborykin recalls seeing Olga Vasilievna in Petersburg in 1863 or 1864 (P. D. Boborykin, *Vospominanija,* 1 [Moscow, 1965] 358).

23. Leskov to A. S. Suvorin, March 3, 1887 (11:332).

24. ANL, p. 109.

25. Bakhareva, "Memuary," p. 9.

26. ANL, p. 111.

27. Leskov to A. S. Suvorin, Oct. 17, 1888 (11:393).

28. ANL, p. 61. The word Leskov used was *aggel*, a good example of the checkered etymological lives of some words. In Byzantine Greek the word *angel* had automatically become *aggel*, since all /-ng-/ groups were assimilated into /-gg-/. The medieval Russians, however, refused to submit to this law of Greek phonology and saw the hand of Satan trying to sully a sacred word. They preserved *angel* in its original sense and assigned to *aggel* the opposite meaning of "devil."

29. Leskov to P. K. Shchebalsky, April 16, 1871 (10:311).

30. "I. Em," "Kak rabotajut naši pisateli; N. S. Leskov," *Novosti i birževaja gazeta,* no. 49 (1st ed., Feb. 19, 1895), p. 2. In this interview Leskov exaggerated the length of time by a factor of two, claiming he had worked for Scott for "six to seven" years.

31. Leskov to I. S. Aksakov, Nov. 27, 1874 (10:365).

32. 9:315. See the English translation by William B. Edgerton, "Leskov on Quakers in Russia," *Bulletin of Friends Historical Association*, vol. 40, no. 1 (1951), pp. 3-15.

33. The milling is referred to in 6:419; the vodka distilling, in several articles written in the early 1860s, especially "Očerki vinokurennoj promyšlennosti (Penzenskaja gubernija)," *Otečestvennye zapiski*, no. 4 (April 1861), pp. 419-444.

4. Journalist, "Revolutionary," and Pariah

1. "Pis'mo k redaktoru," *Ukazatel' èkonomičeskij*, no. 195 (June 18, 1860), pp. 677-679; "Kiev; korrespondencija," *Sankt-Peterburgskie vedomosti*, no. 135 (June 21, 1860), pp. 699-700.

2. "Zametka o zdanijax," *Sovremennaja medicina*, no. 29 (July 28, 1860), pp. 513-523.

3. "O rabočem klasse," *Sovremennaja medicina*, no. 32 (Aug. 18, 1860), pp. 561-569.

4. England is "a country of well-ordered, model governmental institutions and a rational economy, where there is no delay in applying the findings of science to the *practical* forms of life," Leskov proclaims in "A Note on Buildings," pp: 522-523. Robert Owen is mentioned in a number of articles written in 1861-1863, always in the most favorable terms. He exemplifies Leskov's ideal of practical virtue and charity. See especially "Russkie ljudi, stojaščie 'ne u del'," *Russkaja reč'*, no. 52 (1861), p. 787; 10:21.

5. "Neskol'ko slov o vračax rekrutskix prisutstvij," *Sovremennaja medicina*, no. 36 (Sept. 15, 1860), pp. 633-645; "Neskol'ko slov o policejskix vračax v Rossii," ibid., no. 39 (Oct. 6, 1860), pp. 689-699; "Policejskie vrači v Rossii," ibid., no. 48 (Dec. 8, 1860), pp. 842-849. Leskov noted the bribe-taking rife among police doctors. The Ministry of the Interior subsequently demanded that he reveal the names of individual bribe-takers, but he refused. See L. Levandovskij, "N. S. Leskov v Kieve (novye materialy)," *Russkaja literatura*, no. 3 (1863), p. 107.

6. "Očerki vinokurennoj promyšlennosti (Penzenskaja gubernija)," *Otečestvennye zapiski*, no. 4 (April 1861), pp. 419-444. Leskov preserved in his archives an offprint of this article inscribed in his own hand, "Leskov. First trial of the pen. With this commenced [my] literary work. 1860" (ANL, p. 128). In the magazine the article is dated "Odessa, April 28, 1860" (p. 444).

7. The only direct evidence of Gromeka's role is Leskov's vague statement that he was "finally enslaved to literature" by Gromeka in 1860 (11:19). Gromeka was in Petersburg in 1860-1861 and active in the world of journalism; it is highly probable that he was instrumental in luring Leskov not only into literature but to Petersburg.

8. "Pis'mo iz Peterburga," *Russkaja reč'*, no. 25 (1861), p. 396.

9. Ibid., nos. 22, 25, 30 (1861); and later, "O russkom rasselenii i o polit-

iko-èkonomičeskom komitete," *Vremja*, no. 12 (Dec. 1861), section 4, pp. 72-86.

10. "Russkie ljudi, stojaščie 'ne u del'," *Russkaja reč'*, no. 52 (1861), pp. 786-788; "Praktičeskaja zametka; ob iščuščix kommerčeskix mest v Rossii," *Otečestvennye zapiski*, no. 3 (March 1861), section 6, pp. 1-6.

11. "Pis'mo iz Peterburga," *Russkaja reč'*, no. 31 (1861), pp. 489-490.

12. "O naemnoj zavisimosti," *Russkaja reč'*, no. 37 (1861), pp. 542-543; "Torgovaja kabala," *Ukazatel' èkonomičeskij*, no. 221 (Feb. 12, 1861), pp. 145-148.

13. "Russkie ženščiny i èmancipacija," *Russkaja reč'*, nos. 44, 46 (1861), pp. 655-658, 688-690.

14. "Kak otnosjatsja vzgljady nekotoryx prosvetitelej k narodnomu prosveščeniju," *Russkaja reč'*, no. 48 (1861), pp. 719-722.

15. "Poslednjaja vstreča i poslednjaja razluka s Ševčenko," *Russkaja reč'*, no. 19-20 (March 9, 1861); reprinted in 10:7-12.

16. "O rabočem klasse," ibid., p. 569.

17. M. A. Antonovič, "Asmodej našego vremeni," *Sovremennik*, no. 3 (March 1862); reprinted in *Izbrannye stat'i*, ed. V. Evgen'ev-Maksimov (Leningrad, 1938); and in *Literaturno-kritičeskie stat'i*, ed. G. E. Tamarčenko (Leningrad, 1961).

18. "O zamečatel'nom, no ne blagotvornom napravlenii nekotoryx sovremennyx pisatelej," *Russkaja reč'*, no. 60 (1861), pp. 126-128; signed "V. Peresvetov."

19. The phrase is quoted from the memoirs of E. P. Vodovozova, *Na zare žizni i drugie vospominanija*, ed. B. P. Koz'min, 2 (Moscow and Leningrad, 1934): 49. Its spice stems from the incongruity of Yakushkin's wearing peasant attire, and at the same time eyeglasses, which few Russian peasants could afford.

20. For evidence see Aleksandr Herzen (Gercen), *Polnoe sobranie sočinenij i pisem*, ed. M. K. Lemke, 16 (Petrograd, 1919-1925): 74; S. M. Levin, *Obščestvennoe dviženie v Rossii v 60-70-ye gody XIX veka* (Moscow, 1958), pp. 196-234.

21. *Severnaja pčela*, no. 38 (Feb. 8, 1862); reprinted in ANL, p. 142.

22. "Kak otnosjatsja," *Russkaja reč'*, p. 722; M. K. Lemke, *Očerki osvoboditel'nogo dviženija "šestidesjatyx godov"* (SPb., 1908), pp. 9-13.

23. "Pis'mo iz Peterburga," *Russkaja reč'*, no. 31 (1861), pp. 489-490.

24. Lemke, *Očerki*, pp. 39-65, 143-154, 183-223; N. A. Serno-Solov'evič, *Publicistika; pis'ma*, ed. I. B. Volodarskij and G. A. Kajkova (Moscow, 1963).

25. B. P. Koz'min, "Artel'nyj žurnal 'Vek'," *Russkaja žurnalistika'*, 1 (Moscow and Leningrad, 1930); reprinted in B. P. Koz'min, *Iz istorii revoljucionnoj mysli v Rossii; izbrannye trudy* (Moscow, 1961), pp. 68-98.

26. Lemke, *Ocerki*, pp. 110-112, 140-141, 183.

27. Ibid., p. 110.

28. [A. S. Suvorin?], "Nezagadočnyj pisatel'," *Vestnik Evropy*, no. 8 (Aug. 1871), p. 900.

29. This petition had been drawn up the previous year in collaboration with Ivan Turgenev. For evidence see my article "Leskov and His Enigmatic Man," *Harvard Slavic Studies*, 4 (1957): 208-209.

30. Vasily Kelsiev was a specialist in the Old Believers, who were regarded by radicals as a potentially seditious element. In the spring of 1862 Kelsiev made a secret trip to Russia, using a forged Turkish passport, with the aim of promoting rebellion among the religious dissidents. In 1867, convinced of the futility of these efforts, he spectacularly repented of being a revolutionist and threw himself on the mercy of the tsar. He was forgiven and permitted to return to Russia unmolested. His memoirs, *Lived Through and Thought Through* (*Perežitoe i peredumannoe*, SPb., 1868) made a sensation. The fuller version or "Confession" remained in the police archives until 1941, when it was published in *Literaturnoe nasledstvo*, 41-42 (Moscow, 1941).

31. On Ivan Kelsiev, see *Političeskie processy 60-x gg.*, ed. V. P. Alekseev and B. P. Koz'min (Moscow and Petrograd, 1923), pp. 120-135; "I. I. Kel'siev—Gercenu i Ogarevu," ed. P. G. Ryndzjunskij, *Literaturnoe nasledstvo*, 62 (1955): 219-258; "K biografii I. I. Kel'sieva," ed. I. Zverev. ibid., 41-42 (1941): 105-110. On Zaichnevsky and Argiropulo, see Koz'min, *Iz istorii*, pp. 127-345. On the student disturbances in Moscow in 1861 see V. I. Orlov, *Studenčeskoe dviženie Moskovskogo Universiteta v XIX stoletii* (Moscow, 1934); P. D. Šestakov, "Studenčeskie volnenija v Moskve v 1861 g.," *Russkaja starina*, 55 (Sept. 1887): 641-662; ibid., 60 (Oct.-Nov. 1888): 203, 353-370.

32. Leskov helped Benni place an article on the Mormons in *Russian Speech*, first polishing up Benni's unidiomatic Russian (3:335). The article, presumably, was "Neskol'ko slov o mormonax," *Russkaja reč'*, no. 61(1861), pp. 241-243. Benni also published an article on the Mormons in Dostoevsky's *Vremja*: "Mormonizm i Soedinennye Štaty," *Vremja*, no. 10 (Oct. 1861), pp. 320-355.

33. See esp. 11:34-44. There Leskov maintains that his position had always been identical with Melnikov's. Earlier, however, he had tried to take a stand midway between Shchapov and Melnikov: see *S ljud'mi drevlego blagočestija* (SPb., 1863), p. 3 (originally in *Biblioteka dlja čtenija*, no. 11 [Nov. 1863], pp. 1-64.

34. The evidence for this identification is presented in my Ph.D. dissertation, "Studies in the Life and Art of Leskov" (Harvard University, 1956), pp. 66-70.

35. After escaping from prison in Russia, Ivan Kelsiev met his death (from typhus) while proselytizing among émigré Old Believers in Rumania. The sectarians were thus something of a family specialty, and it seems more than probable that Kelsiev was already displaying a political interest in them in Moscow at the time Leskov knew him there in 1861.

36. *Literaturnoe nasledstvo*, 41-42: 105-110.

37. M. K. Lemke, *Političeskie processy v Rossii 1860-x gg. (po arxivnym dokumentam)*, 2nd. ed. (Moscow and Petrograd, 1923), pp. 1-54; Koz'min *Iz istorii*, pp. 127-290.

38. See William B. Edgerton, "Leskov and Russia's Slavic Brethren," in *American Contributions to the Fourth International Congress of Slavicists* (The Hague, 1958), p. 61.

39. See ANL, p. 79.

40. K. P. Bogaevskaya (11:804) assigns Olga Vasilievna's arrival in Moscow to August or September 1861—which is probably an attempt to make somewhat more definite Andrei Leskov's vague phrase "toward autumn" (ANL, p. 140). Both Bogaevskaya and Andrei Leskov imply that the scandals and the rupture with Countess Salias occurred almost immediately thereafter. Andrei Leskov suggests that only contractual obligations required both Leskov and the countess to prolong his collaboration on *Russian Speech* until November. But if the interpretation presented above of Dr. Rozanov's activities during the student affair of October 1861 is correct, it shows that even at that late date Leskov not only still frequented the countess's house socially, but in a time of crisis repaired there first of all.

41. Her capital exhausted, the countess had departed in November for western Europe, leaving *Russian Speech* in the hands of Yevgeny Feoktistov (another of Leskov's friends turned life-long enemy); and it ceased publication altogether early in 1862.

42. Nebolsin is mentioned in "Pis'mo iz Peterburga," *Russkaja reč'*, no. 36 (1861), p. 532; Perozio is not mentioned in Leskov's reports of 1861, but in an article written in 1863 he is referred to as an habitué of the meetings. See "Učenye obščestva," *Biblioteka dlja čtenija*, no. 5 (May 1863), p. 76.

43. Lemke, *Očerki*; Benni to V. I. Kelsiev, Feb. 7/19, 1862; quoted in *Literaturnoe nasledstvo*, 62 (Moscow, 1955): 27.

44. See N. Aristov, "Žizn' Afanasija Prokof'eviča Ščapova," *Istoričeskij vestnik*, no. 10 (Oct. 1882).

45. *Sovremennik*, no. 4 (April 1862), p. 305; quoted in ANL, pp. 144-145. The attribution to Yeliseyev is corroborated by A. M. Bikhter and N. I. Sokolov in 10:530. There is no evidence for the ascription of the article to Chernyshevsky, as is done in J. G. K. Russell, "Leskov and His Quarrel with the Men of the Sixties," *Canadian Slavonic Papers*, vol. 12, no. 2 (1970), p. 109. (Russell's article is filled with numerous other errors.) It is possible that the editorial may actually refer to Nichiporenko rather than Leskov, and Nichiporenko did go to London shortly thereafter. However, lacking further evidence, I follow Andrei Leskov in identifying Leskov as the addressee—which is at least equally likely.

46. *Severnaja pčela*, no. 142 (May 29, 1862); quoted in ANL, pp. 144-145. Leskov did go abroad that year, but his antagonism toward the radicals had become so great that he decided not to make the pilgrimage to Herzen. In an

article written considerably later, dealing with his European experiences, he felt obliged to offer a long explanation of this omission and of his conclusion that he had nothing to learn from Herzen. See "Russkoe obščestvo v Pariže" (revised version), in N. S. Leskov, *Povesti, očerki i rasskazy*, 1 (SPb., 1867); reprinted in *Sbornik melkix belletrističeskix proizvedenij N. S. Leskova-Stebnickogo* (SPb., 1873).

Another indication of Leskov's continued friendly association with radicals in the spring of 1862 was his presence at a meeting held in Benni's apartment at which Dostoevsky's *Notes from the House of the Dead* were read aloud. Among those present were Vasily Sleptsov, and Varfolomei Zaitsev, an exuberantly ruthless critic from the radical magazine *Russkoe slovo*. Leskov later regarded both of them with implacable hostility. See "Russkie dejateli v Ostzejskom krae," *Istoričeskij vestnik*, no. 12 (Dec. 1883), pp. 508-510.

47. No convincing evidence of arson was ever produced, but the charge is still bandied about in the historical literature, latter-day "revolutionary" historians preferring to accuse the reactionaries or even the government itself of starting the fires in order to provide an excuse for cracking down on the radicals. But there is as little evidence for this as for the opposite charge. See Solomon Rejser, "Peterburgskie požary 1862 g.," *Katorga i ssylka*, no. 10 (1932), pp. 79-109.

48. The text of Leskov's editorial in *Severnaja pčela*, no. 143 (May 30, 1862) has been reprinted in A. I. Faresov, *Protiv tečenij* (SPb., 1904), pp. 30-32.

49. *Severnaja pčela*, no. 144 (May 31, 1862).

50. Ibid., no. 151 (June 7, 1862).

51. Ibid., no. 157 (June 13, 1862).

52. "Russkoe obščestvo v Pariže," in Leskov, *Povesti*, 1: 512; 3:347. The texts are identical except that in the first the phrase "and we ask it to do this" is added at the end.

53. Faresov, *Protiv tečenij*, p. 34, reporting a conversation that presumably took place in the early 1890s.

54. "Russkoe obščestvo v Pariže" (revised version), in Leskov, *Povesti*, 1: 513.

55. On Leskov's Slavic connections, see Edgerton, "Leskov and Russia's Slavic Brethren."

56. "Iz odnogo dorožnogo dnevnika," *Severnaja pčela*, no. 351 (Dec. 29, 1862).

57. Ibid., no. 335 (Dec. 11, 1862). Józef Korzeniowski (1797-1863) and Józef Ignacy Kraszewski (1812-1887) were leading Polish novelists of the mid-nineteenth century; ignorance of them meant ignorance of contemporary Polish literature in general. Edward-Antoni Odyniec (1804-1885) was a dramatist and translator, now chiefly remembered for his close association with Mickiewicz. Władysław Syrokomla (pseudonym of Ludwik Kondratowicz, 1823-1863) was a minor poet, now little remembered.

58. "Russkoe obščestvo v Pariže," *Biblioteka dlja čten'ja*, no. 9 (Sept. 1863), p. 4.

59. Leskov, *Povesti*, 1:454. In this article, written in Leskov's most anti-Polish period (1867), the "soft, birdlike" Czech is used as a means of belittling Polish, now described as a "hissing and jangling language." Still later Leskov wrote, doubtless facetiously, that he wanted his works translated into all languages except Czech, since he disliked that language particularly. See Leskov to P. K. Shchebalsky, April 3, 1878 (10:455).

60. "Ot tebja ne bol'no," *Severnaja pčela*, no. 95 (April 12, 1863), translation dated Paris, Dec. 25, 1862. On Leskov and Nemcova, see T. S. Karskaja, "Tvorčestvo Boženy Nemcovoj v ocenke N. S. Leskova," *Izvestija Akademii Nauk SSSR*, literature and language series, vol. 27, issue 3 (1968), pp. 259-264; and T. S. Karskaja, "Leskov—avtor očerka o Božene Nemcovoj," *Russkaja literatura*, no. 2 (1969), pp. 157-163.

61. See "Kak otravljajutsja ugol'nym čadom v Pariže," *Severnaja pčela*, no. 70 (March 14, 1863); 7:135.

62. Leskov, *Povesti*, 1:416. It should be noted that this description is missing from the version Leskov published in 1863. It was added only in 1867, when he was eager to advertise his Russian patriotism by comparing Napoleon unfavorably with Alexander II; he also took advantage of the opportunity to deride the Poles' hopes that Napoleon would provide support for their cause.

63. Leskov deserves credit, however, for recognizing the artistic merit of Russian icon painting, which most cultured Russians of the nineteenth century scorned as crude and primitive. On Leskov and the graphic arts, see Leonid Grossman, *N. S. Leskov: žizn', tvorčestvo, poètika* (Moscow, 1945), pp. 204-224.

64. V. P[rotopopov], "U N. S. Leskova," *Peterburgskaja gazeta*, no. 256 (Sept. 18, 1894).

65. As suggested by Edgerton, "Leskov and Russia's Slavic Brethren," p. 67.

66. Leskov, *Povesti*, 1:407.

67. Ibid., p. 443.

68. Ibid., p. 385.

69. Ibid., p. 407.

70. Ibid., p. 410. It should be pointed out that Leskov also performed some rather tricky verbal footwork in this connection. In 1863, when writing of his experiences in Lvov, Leskov consistently referred to the Ukrainians either as *rusiny* or *malorossy*, distinct terms applied to them alone. In 1867, however, these very same Ukrainians, the nationalists in Austrian Lvov, are referred to simply as *russkie*, "Russians." By this means Leskov not only by implication denies the separate identity of the Ukrainians, but what in 1863 had been Polish hostility to *Ukrainian* cultural and political ambitions now becomes Polish contempt for *Russian* culture. Similarly, in 1867 Leskov views the liberation of the Ukrainians in Austria as a "Russian" cause, claiming that

there were only a few extremists who could "rave of detaching Malorossia from Great Russia." See "Russkoe obščestvo v Pariže," *Biblioteka dlja čten'ja*, no. 9 (Sept. 1863), p. 4; and the same in Leskov, *Povesti*, 1:407, 425.

71. On Leskov's later attitudes toward Poland, see Edgerton, "Leskov and Russia's Slavic Brethren."

72. See "Iskanie škol staroobrjadcami," *Birževye vedomosti*, no. 44 (Feb. 14, 1869), where Leskov speaks respectfully of Subbotin. Later he attacked Subbotin, who had become a henchman of Katkov and generally a supporter of religious persecution. See "O suščnosti i značenii raskola," *Istoričeskij vestnik*, no. 12 (Dec. 1881), pp. 840-842; "Kto napisal? Vopros iz Moskvy," *Novoe vremja*, no. 2118 (Jan. 20, 1882), p. 2; "Irodova rabota," *Istoričeskij vestnik*, no. 4 (April 1882), pp. 198, 199.

73. *O raskol'nikax goroda Rigi, preimuščestvenno v ostnošenii k školam* (SPb., 1863). A copy of this exceedingly rare book is in the library of Columbia University.

74. "S ljud'mi drevlego blagočestija," *Biblioteka dlja čtenija*, no. 11 (Nov. 1863), pp. 1-64; no. 9 (Sept. 1864), pp. 1-45. Both parts were issued separately as pamphlets (SPb., 1863, 1865).

75. "Iskanie škol staroobrjadcami," *Birževye vedomosti*, nos. 28, 30, 37, 43, 44, 48, 65, 71, 89, 102, 134 (1869); "Propavšaja kniga o školax," *Russkij mir*, no. 56 (1874); Leskov to S. N. Shubinsky, April 23, 1883 (11:278). The work was reprinted posthumously, in A. E. Burcev, *Slovar' redkix knig i gravirovannyx portretov*, vol. 5, no. 1932 (SPb., 1905), pp. 45-98.

5. The Leap into Fiction

1. See Chapter 2, note 22.

2. V. P[rotopopov], "U N. S. Leskova," *Peterburgskaja gazeta*, no. 326 (Nov. 27, 1894), p. 2.

3. Ibid. The letters have been lost, but they must have contained accounts of Leskov's adventures, descriptions of out-of-the-way places, and portraits of remarkable characters—much like his later travelogues.

4. The neighbor's name was Selivanov, as attested in two autobiographical notes (11:17, 18). The first name is not given. The individual has been commonly identified as Ivan Vasilievich Selivanov, a writer, but he lived some distance away, while Scott's nearest neighbor was a landowner named Fyodor Ivanovich Selivanov. See Leonid Grossman, *N. S. Leskov* (Moscow, 1945), p. 45n, citing the Penza scholar, A. Khrabrovitsky.

5. Though his article contains numerous errors and misunderstandings, Benjamin must be credited with this fundamental insight. Entitled "Der Erzähler," his essay originally appeared in *Orient and Okzident* (1936); reprinted in Benjamin, *Schriften*, 2 (Frankfurt-am-Main, 1955): 229-258; and in an English translation by Harry Zohn in Benjamin, *Illuminations*, ed. Hannah Arendt (New York, 1968).

6. "Pogassee delo (Iz zapisok moego deda)," *Vek,* no. 12 (March 25, 1862), pp. 139-143. Although twice reprinted in subsequent years under a new title, "Drought," this story was not included in the collected works of 1889-1896, nor in any subsequent edition, and is therefore virtually unknown to present-day readers. See "Zasuxa," in N. S. Leskov (M. Stebnickij). *Rasskazy,* 2 (SPb., 1869); and in N. S. Leskov, *Sbornik melkix belletrističeskix proizvedenij* (SPb., 1873). In these editions it is joined with "The Mocker" under the general heading of "For What People Here Used to Go to Penal Servitude" (*Za čto u nas xaživali v katorgu*).

7. Andrei Leskov (ANL, p. 85) offers this hypothesis.

8. "Za aksiosy da ob stol mordoju." In his first story Leskov displays his fondness for oddities of clerical speech. During the ordination ceremony the Greek word *axios* ("worthy") was loudly intoned by a deacon when the tonsure was given; the word came to mean the hair itself.

9. Leskov, *Sbornik,* p. 116.

10. Ibid., p. 122.

11. "Judol'," originally in *Knižki Nedeli,* no. 6 (June 1892); reprinted in 9:218-312. For an extended analysis of the background and ideology of the story see L. G. Čudnova, "Krest'janstvo v tvorčestve N. S. Leskova 1890-x godov (povest' 'Judol')," *Iz istorii russkoj literatury = Učenye zapiski Leningradskogo Gosudarstvennogo Pedagogičeskogo Instituta imeni A.I. Gercena,* 245 (Leningrad, 1963): 313-334. Like many Soviet apologists for Leskov, Chudnova tries to accommodate him to Soviet ideology, emphasizing his socially critical and progressive features and playing down his pessimism about the peasantry.

12. "Razbojnik," originally in *Severnaja pčela,* no. 108 (April 23, 1862); reprinted in 1:1-10.

13. It is difficult to convey in translation the full oral impression of the original: "Strax menja obujal smertnyj, nekogda, vižu, dumat'-to, podnjal dubinu-to da kak svistnu ego vdol' po xripu, so vsego, znaeš', s razmaxu. Tak on i povalilsja, i ruki v storony rastoporšil" (1:8). The four main verbs are in parallel, the first three without conjunctions (asyndeton), alternating the perfective past with the historical present. For the last verb, which is introduced by the colloquial conjunction *da kak,* the speaker employs the perfective "future" in its colloquial usage as a past tense, focusing more vividly on the act itself. Other such features are the repetition of the preposition (*so vsego . . . s razmaxu*); the use of the singular *znaeš',* even though several people are listening; the enclitic *-to;* the use of *xrip* in the sense of "backbone" (*xrebet* in literary Russian); and the mouth-stretching *rastoporšil,* probably a misprint for *rastoporščil,* a free coinage with the intensifying prefix *ras-,* substituting for the more usual *vstoporščil,* "spread out wide." Finally, *obujal* would now be apprehended as a bookish archaism, but in this context it might be regarded as an oral expression.

14. "My posmotreli na atletičeskoe složenie xozjaina i peregljanulis' " (1:9).

Note that the use of the literary loanword *atletičeskoe* places the frame narrator linguistically among the intelligentsia, marking his social distance from the peasant storyteller.

15. "V tarantase," *Severnaja pčela*, no. 119 (May 4, 1862); reprinted in Leskov, *Tri rasskaza M. Stebnickogo* (SPb., 1863), but not subsequently. The editors of the most recent Soviet edition of Leskov's collected works were taken to task for not including it: see A. Narkevič, "Leskov i ego kommentatory," *Voprosy literatury*, no. 12 (Dec. 1959), p. 195.

16. For an interesting analysis of "The Robber" and "In a Coach" with interpretations differing from mine in many respects, see Thomas L. Aman, "Leskov's First Series of Sketches," *Slavic and East European Journal*, no. 4 (Winter 1968), pp. 424-434.

17. "Ovcebyk," *Otečestvennye zapiski*, 147, no. 4 (April 1863), pp. 558-625; in Leskov's lifetime reprinted in 1867, 1873, 1890. The date and place of composition appear in all these editions. The validity of the date is questioned by Andrei Leskov, ANL, p. 167; however, he presents no arguments and offers no alternative. Among other things, he was doubtless puzzled by the fact that "From You It Doesn't Hurt" is dated "Prague, December 3, 1862," since Leskov went to Paris after Prague. This discrepancy could be explained by Leskov's having used the Julian calendar in one case and the Gregorian in the other. Perhaps Andrei Leskov also suspected that his father would not have been able to complete the story so soon after arriving in Paris from his long trip through Slavic Europe.

18. See V. Bazanov, *Pavel Ivanovič Jakuškin* (Oryol, 1950). Leskov's memoir on Yakushkin, written in 1883, is reprinted in 11:71-89.

19. In later years Yakushkin made a solid contribution to Russian ethnography with his publications of folklore texts, and he also acquired a reputation as a writer of ethnographic sketches and stories in the Sleptsov-Levitov tradition.

20. Leskov relates a similar anecdote about Dostoevsky in "On the Kitchen Peasant and Other Matters" (*O kufel'nom mužike i proč.* [1886], 11:149-154).

21. Upon graduating from the seminary (colloquially known as *bursa*), the Russian had two options. He could marry and take orders as a parish priest, or he could continue his studies in an "academy," hoping eventually to rise to high position in the hierarchy. In the latter case he had to take vows of celibacy. The celibate clergy were known as "black"; the married priests, "white."

22. As I too have done, both with regard to Akilina Alferieva and the narrator-author's remarks about the intellectual preoccupations of his "university" days. But it is a dangerous practice unless there is confirming evidence from some clearly nonfictional source. Barring this, we can only take our stand on the slippery ground of the general plausibility of such quasi-autobiographical material, especially in relation to more firmly established facts.

23. He may have been on a temporary assignment at Zvenigorod (ANL, p.

113), but that does not get him to Kursk. It is conceivable that before his move to Kiev in 1849, while he was serving in the Oryol criminal court, he may have carried messages to Kursk, but that was much earlier. In general, "business" like this would have been more appropriate for Leskov's father than for Leskov.

24. "Jazvitel'nyj," *Jakor'*, nos. 12, 13, 14 (1863). R. Norman has translated it into English under the title of "The Stinger," but I consider "The Mocker" somewhat closer to the definition of *jazvitel'nyj* given in the standard Russian dictionary by D. N. Ushakov: "striving to vex, unpleasantly nagging someone, maliciously derisive." (Here the adjective is used substantively.) The Norman translation is found in *The Tales of N. S. Leskov*, 1 (all published; London, 1944). The publication of this story in *Anchor* is one of the few bits of evidence connecting Leskov with Grigoriev. Others are Leskov's report of Grigoriev's reaction to his *No Way Out* (10:169) and his statement in an autobiographical note written in 1890: "Apollon Grigoriev perceived and supported or encouraged my belletristic talents" (11:19). Grigoriev died in 1864; his influence on Leskov's artistic development could have been only brief.

25. In the original version of this story (inadvertently reprinted posthumously in the twelfth volume of Leskov's collected works), the narrator's mother, like the grandmother in "The Musk-ox," is referred to by her "real" Christian name and patronymic, Marya Petrovna; in the 1869 version, however, she remains nameless. See *P.s.s.*, 22 (1903): 127, which reprints the magazine version, and 1:23, the revised version.

26. Leskov's father had a good friend among the Oryol merchants, Ivan Ivanovich Androsov, who was probably the model for this character. He is invoked in two other works written in 1863, "Um svoe i čort svoe," *Severnaja pčela*, no. 17 (Jan. 18, 1863); and "S ljud'mi drevlego blagočestija," *Biblioteka dlja čten'ja*, no. 11 (Nov. 1863), p. 31. He appears again in 6:364, 393, and in 7:223, 540.

27. Leskov later allowed his positive judgment of Scott to prevail. In an article written a few years after "The Mocker," his characterization of his English uncle seems flatly to contradict the image of Dane: "In the Lower Volga provinces, on the estates of Counts Perovsky and Naryshkin, until rather recently the manager was one Aleksandr Yakovlevich Scott—an Englishman by birth, but a man completely Russified, *remarkably well acquainted with the Russian people and skillful at winning the confidence of the peasants he supervised* [emphasis added]. He is now dead, but people still know and remember him in Simbirsk and in Penza and in Samara" ("Naša provincial'-naja žizn'," *Birževye vedomosti*, no. 238 [Sept. 3, 1869]; quoted from ANL, p. 121).

28. "Žitie odnoj baby," *Biblioteka dlja čten'ja*, nos. 7, 8 (1863). Finding no satisfactory English equivalent for *žitie* ("vita," "saint's life"), I have tried to convey the same effect through the word *martyress*.

29. According to the preface to the first volume of Leskov's collected short stories, *Povesti, očerki i rasskazy* (SPb., 1867), a work entitled "Amour in Bast Shoes" was to be included in the second volume. When that volume appeared two years later, however, it did not contain any such item, nor did any subsequent pre-Revolutionary edition of Leskov's collected works. The manuscript of *Amour in Bast Shoes* was eventually given, about 1889, to Leskov's friend, the bibliographer P. V. Bykov. After the Revolution Bykov brought out a separate edition of this text: *Amur v lapotočkax; krest'janskij roman* (Leningrad, 1924). In his preface Bykov writes that "at the end of the 1880s" he attended a gathering where Leskov read aloud the original version of the story (presumably "The Life of a Peasant Martyress" from *Library for Reading*) and then announced his intention of revising it. This he did, but according to Bykov he was unable to publish the revised version because of censorship. Boris Eikhenbaum (1:502) has questioned the plausibility of this account and especially the dating of the new version on the grounds that (1) "The Peasant Martyress" is much too long to be read aloud at one sitting; (2) it is odd for a writer to read aloud a work published twenty-five years before and then announce his intention of revising it; (3) the reference to *Amour in Bast Shoes* in the preface of 1867 is sufficient evidence that at that time the revision had already been carried out. William B. Edgerton, "The Intellectual Development of a Literary Nonconformist" (Ph.D. dissertation, Columbia University, 1954), p. 214n, argues in favor of a revision in the 1880s on the grounds that the nonappearance of the work in 1869 probably meant that the promised revision had not actually been completed; and that since Bykov and Leskov were not on good terms in the late 1860s, Bykov could not have been present at any reading given then. Leskov would almost certainly have chosen to read aloud only a work with which he was actively involved; and therefore he must have made the revision in the 1880s. Although Edgerton's arguments have merit, I am inclined to agree with Eikhenbaum, on the further ground that if Leskov had revised "The Peasant Martyress" in the 1880s and attempted to publish the revision then, the effort would almost certainly have left some trace in his correspondence. Most of Leskov's letters to the editors of the magazines where he customarily published in the 1880s have been preserved and published, and there is not a trace in them of *Amour in Bast Shoes*. My surmise is that by 1924, when Bykov wrote the preface, his memory had formed a connection between two disparate phenomena: he had indeed been present at a reading by Leskov in the 1880s, but the work read was not "The Life of a Peasant Martyress," but something shorter and more current. During the same period, perhaps even on the same occasion, Leskov presented Bykov with the manuscript copy of *Amour in Bast Shoes*, a youthful work he no longer cared to publish.

30. "Russkoe obščestvo v Pariže," *Biblioteka dlja čten'ja*, vol. 178, no. 5 (May 1863), p. 18. The "guardian and benefactor" was presumably Strakhov. One wonders, however, whether a five-year-old—Strakhov died when

Leskov was five—would have been able to play the role of benevolent intercessor so effectively. In the 1867 version of the article Leskov eliminated the reference to his "guardian and benefactor," leaving the intercession general. See Leskov, *Povesti*, 1: 320.

31. Leskov, *Povesti* 1:320.

32. Malen'kij mužičonko byl rjuminskij Kostik, a zljuščij byl takoj, čto upasi Gospodi.

33. Po čulanam da po pun'kam libo po podkletjam. The Ushakov dictionary lists *punja* as a regionalism.

34. Leskov's brother, Mikhail, was born in 1841 and therefore can hardly be identified with the boy who was fourteen "last summer" (1862?), when the narrator revisited his home territory. But the name and the school are right.

35. For a brief but judicious comparison of the two versions see N. S. Pleščunov, "Zametki o stile povesti Leskova," in *Literaturnyj seminarij*, ed. A. V. Bagrij, no. 6 (Baku, 1928). *Amur v lapotočkax* was not included in the edition of 1956-1958, but may be found in *Izbrannye proizvedenija*, ed. S. M. Petrov (Moscow, 1949).

36. The real case histories on which the story is based are outlined briefly in "Slučai iz russkoj demonomanii," *Novoe vremja*, nos. 1529, 1533, 1536, 1542 1552 (1880); under the title of "Russkie demonomany" also included in *Russkaja rozn'* (SPb., 1881), pp. 228-293. Leskov discusses several instances from his childhood of insanity among women, a subject he knew from his experiences with his wife.

37. "Um svoe i čort svoe," *Severnaja pčela*, no. 17 (Jan. 18, 1863); "Kratkaja istorija odnogo častnogo umopomešatel'stva," ibid., no. 159 (June 17, 1863); "Kochanko moja! Na co nam rozmowa," ibid., no. 180 (July 3, 1863).

38. P. V. Bykov, *Siluèty dalekogo prošlogo* (Moscow-Leningrad, 1930), p. 164. Boris Eikhenbaum quotes some passages from this unpublished revised version, showing its florid language much toned down. See B. Ejxenbaum, *Literatura, teorija, kritika, polemika* (Leningrad, 1927), p. 219.

39. "Kratkaja istorija odnogo častnogo umopomešatel'stva" was reprinted first under the title "Istorija odnogo umopomešatel'stva" in Leskov, *Tri rasskaza*. In 1869 and 1873 it appeared under still another title, "Otčego ljudi sxodili s uma; Kuverkov; Soveršenno neverojatnoe sobytie," in Leskov, *Rasskazy*; and Leskov, *Sbornik*. I have not been able to consult the text in *Tri rasskaza*. The comparison here is therefore between the newspaper version and the one in the volumes of 1869 and 1873 (which are identical).

6. No Way Out

1. Leskov to Kraevsky, May 23, 1863 (10:251-252).

2. P. D. Boborykin, *Za polveka; moi vospominanija*, ed. B. P. Koz'min (Moscow-Leningrad, 1929), p. 274.

3. "Perly i adamanty russkoj žurnalistiki," *Russkoe slovo*, no. 6 (1864); reprinted in V. A. Zajcev, *Izbrannye sočinenija v dvux tomax*, ed. B. P. Koz'min, 1 (Moscow, 1934): 224-225.

4. Most of these identifications have long been established. See, among others, Leonid Grossman, *N. S. Leskov; žizn', tvorčestvo, poètika* (Moscow, 1945), p. 133; ANL, p. 175n. The identification between Persiantsev and Ivan Kelsiev was first suggested in my doctoral thesis, "Studies in the Life and Art of Leskov" (Harvard University, 1956).

5. "Nikolaj Gavrilovič Černyševskij v ego romane 'Čto delat'?," *Severnaja pčela*, no. 142 (May 31, 1863); reprinted in 10;:13-22.

6. V. Sleptsov had appeared in Countess Salias's circle in Moscow as early as 1860. See Kornej Čukovskij, *Ljudi i knigi šestidesjatyx godov* (Leningrad, 1934), pp. 168-169. Both he and Leskov were present at a reading of Dostoevsky's *Notes from the House of the Dead* in Petersburg early in 1862. See "Russkie dejateli v Ostzejskom krae," *Istoričeskij vestnik*, no. 12 (Dec. 1883), pp. 508, 510.

7. See Čukovskij, *Ljudi i knigi šestidesjatyx godov*, pp. 221-252; V. G. Bazanov, *Iz literaturnoj polemiki 60-x godov* (Petrozavodsk, 1941), pp. 118-128. William Craft Brumfield in his doctoral dissertation, "Vasilij Slepcov" (University of California, Berkeley, 1973), pp. 42-43, has justifiably taken me to task for an earlier, more pro-Leskovian version of this episode included in my dissertation.

8. The commune lasted from September 1863 until May 1864. See "Xronologičeskaja kanva žizni i raboty Slepcova," in V. A. Slepcov, *Sočinenija*, ed. K. I. Čukovskij, 1 (Leningrad, 1932): 587.

9. A. I. Faresov, *Protiv tečenij* (SPb., 1904), p. 60.

10. Ibid., pp. 59-60. It is hard to see how Pomada, a holy innocent of a Pole, sweet, naive, and utterly ineffective, can be called either a "nihilist" or a "Russian revolutionary."

11. Leskov's inscription on a copy of *No Way Out* presented to his friend, P. K. Shchebalsky, dated April 18, 1871 (10:169). I. V. Stolyarova discovered the article by Shelgunov on which the statement by Leskov is based in *Delo*, no. 12 (Dec. 1869). See her "Roman-xronika Leskova," in *Istorija russkogo romana*, ed. A. S. Bušmin, et al., 2 (Moscow-Leningrad, 1964): 416-438. Benni may have served as the model not only for the hero of "An Enigmatic Man" and Wilhelm Reiner in *No Way Out*, but also for Adam Lvovich Bezbedovich, who appears briefly in the unfinished novel *Falcon Flight* (1883). A Benni sort of figure was destined to play a major part in the also unfinished novel *A Faint Trace* (1884). See *Pis'ma Tolstogo i k Tolstomu; jubilejnyj sbornik* (Moscow-Leningrad, 1928), p. 102, note by S. P. Shesterikov, citing Andrei Leskov.

13. 2:629. Krasin is another rude radical, perhaps based on Vasily Kurochkin.

14. "Ob'jasnenie," *Biblioteka dlja čtenija*, no. 12 (Dec. 1864), p. 1.

15. Leskov to M. A. Protopopov, Dec. 23, 1891 (11:509).

16. 2:642-643. It is a curiosity of twentieth-century academia that the structure of this chaotic novel has been given a full-dress, formalistic analysis in Bodo Zelinsky, *Roman und Romanchronik* (Cologne and Vienna, 1970), pp. 9-74.

17. 2:429. Bertoldi is modeled on Princess Yekaterina Aleksandrovna Makulova, one of the inmates of the Znamensky Commune. See Ekaterina Žukovskaja, *Zapiski,* ed. Kornej Čukovskij (Leningrad, 1930), p. 167.

18. Quoted in *Russkie pisateli o literature,* ed. S. Baluxatyj, 2 (Leningrad, 1939): 303. Oral statement of the 1890s, transcription in the archive of Andrei Leskov.

19. "Propuščennye glavy iz romana 'Nekuda'," *Sankt-Peterburgskie vedomosti,* no. 200 (Sept. 11, 1864); quoted in V. G. Bazanov, *Iz literaturnoj polemiki šestidesjatyx godov* (Petrozavodsk, 1941), p. 164. Bazanov ascribes this anonymous article to V. Burenin, another radical who was later a reactionary publicist. Suvorin's authorship seems to me more probable, however, since Suvorin knew Leskov better, and was more able to reveal, as he threatened to do in future articles, the "real truth" behind the slanders in *No Way Out.* The attribution to Suvorin is made by B. P. Koz'min in Zajcev, *Izbrannye sočinenija,* p. 505; and by Andrei Leskov, ANL, p. 176.

20. That this sentence was to be read as a statement about Leskov's treatment of his wife is clear from the pseudodenial in "Pis'mo v redakciju," *Sankt-Peterburgskie vedomosti,* no. 218 (Oct. 1, 1864), signed Znakomyj g. Stebnickogo.

21. "Ob'jasnenie," p. 2.

22. D. I. Pisarev, *Polnoe sobranie sočinenij v šesti tomax,* 4 (SPb., 1897); 328-331.

23. "Russkoe obščestvo v Pariže," in Leskov, *Povesti, očerki i rasskazy,* 1 (SPb., 1867): 389. See also the unpublished article "O šepotnikax i pečatnikax" (1882); quoted in ANL, p. 179.

24. Quoted in Faresov, *Protiv tečenij,* p. 60.

25. Leskov to A. S. Suvorin, April 12, 1888 (11:384).

26. S. F. Librovič, *Na knižnom postu* (Petrograd-Moscow, 1916), pp. 212-213.

27. Leskov repented of his satirical portrait of the Novosiltsev sisters, who remained benefactresses of his daughter, Vera, despite his attack on them. See Leskov to A. S. Suvorin, Feb. 3, 1881 (11:250); and to I. S. Aksakov, Dec. 9, 1881 (11:256). Leskov also once admitted that Feoktistov might have valid reasons for hating him: see Leskov to P. K. Shchebalsky, Jan. 15, 1876 (10:441). But elsewhere he reduces the insult to Feoktistov to "two lines" in *No Way Out*—again, a minimization considerably less than the truth: see Leskov to A. S. Suvorin, Nov. 24, 1888 (11:399-400).

28. Leskov to A. S. Suvorin, March 11, 1887 (11:339). For a discussion of *No Way Out* in connection with the typology of antiradical Russian novels,

see Charles A. Moser, *Antinihilism in the Russian Novel of the 1860's* (The Hague, 1964). N. S. Pleshchunov, in his *Romany Leskova "Nekuda" i "Sobor-jane"* (*Baku, 1963*), attempts to rehabilitate Leskov in terms of Soviet ideology by stressing the "progressive" and "realistic" aspects of his antiradical novels. This is also the strategy of Stolyarova in her "Roman-xronika Leskova."

7. Katerina Bubnova

1. "Russkij dramatičeskij teatr v Peterburge," *Otečestvennye zapiski,* 169 (1866): 275.

2. "Neulovimyj mnogoženec (Iz istorii bračnyx zatrudnenij)," *Novoe vremja,* no. 1710 (Nov. 30, 1880), p. 3n. This article is sufficient to refute the assertion of Leskov's granddaughter, Natalia Bakhareva, that he could easily have obtained a divorce but did not because he felt remorse over causing his wife's madness. See N. D. Baxareva, "Nikolaj Semenovič Leskov," manuscript deposited in the Archive of Russian and East European History, Columbia University, pp. 6-7.

3. This article, "Brakorazvodnoe zabven'e: pričiny razvodov bračnyx po zakonam greko-rossijskoj cerkvi," was printed in the Dec. 1885 issue of *Historical Messenger* but at the last minute cut out of the issue and burned. The text is apparently lost. See ANL, p. 530; 11:691.

4. Leskov to A. S. Suvorin, Nov. 30, 1888 (11:401).

5. These details are mostly derived from the "Vospominanija" of Leskov's stepson, Nikolai Bubnov, a manuscript deposited in the library of the Slovenian Academy of Sciences, Ljubljana, Yugoslavia, as quoted by William B. Edgerton, "The Intellectual Development of a Literary Nonconformist" (Ph.D. dissertation, Columbia University, 1954), pp. 266ff.

6. It is possible that Katerina Stepanovna's husband agreed to pay for Nikolai's tuition in the German boarding school, but Bakhareva's report that he supplied his wife with 15,000 rubles on her departure for Petersburg to live with Leskov seems highly questionable if only in view of Leskov's clearly attested financial difficulties during this period. In general Bakhareva is unreliable, and she seems to have a predilection for piquant inventions concerning Katerina Bubnova. Bakhareva's greatest feat of imagination is the tale that after breaking up with Leskov in the late 1870s Katerina Stepanovna returned to her husband. He supposedly received her kindly and said, "I'm glad, Katya, that you've come back." See Bakhareva, "Nikolaj Semenovič Leskov," pp. 7-8. In fact, Bubnov had died ten years earlier.

7. The identification of Katerina Bubnova with Polinka Kalistratova was first suggested by Edgerton, "The Intellectual Development," p. 266. It is also asserted, without argumentation or confirming evidence, by N. I. Totubalin in his notes to *No Way Out* (2:718). There are, however, some serious chronological difficulties about this identification. During 1864 *No Way Out* was appearing in installments. Polinka Kalistratova makes her appearance in

chapter 22 of book 2, which was printed in the August number of *Library for Reading*. Yet Leskov is supposed to have met Bubnova only in July, according to K. P. Bogaevskaya in her chronological table of Leskov's life (11:807). Although the August number did not actually appear until October, judging by the date of the censor's approval, and although Leskov may have met Bubnova somewhat earlier in 1864 than July, it is hard to believe that a writer could in so short a time create for a novel already in progress a new, major character based on so recent an acquaintance.

8. ANL, p. 218.

9. "Memoirs of E. I. Zarina-Novikova," a manuscript cited in ANL, p. 226.

8. Lady Macbeth

1. "Obojdennye," *Otečestvennye zapiski*, nos. 18-24 (Sept. 15-Dec. 15, 1865). In a letter dated December 7, 1864, to N. N. Strakhov, who collaborated with the Dostoevsky brothers in editing the magazine *Epoch*, Leskov wrote that he was then "finishing" this "big work" (10:253). On March 6, 1865, writing again to Strakhov, Leskov describes it as a "novella, almost a novel" and offers it to *Epoch*. Although allegedly finished, it did not yet have its final title, but was called "Vsjak svoemu nravu rabotaet" (10:256). Probably the final version was not completed until the summer of 1865.

2. See esp. "Russkie ženščiny i èmancipacija," *Russkaja reč'*, nos. 44, 46 (1861); "Specialisty po ženskoj casti," *Literaturnaja biblioteka*, nos. 18, 24 (Sept. 15, Dec. 15, 1867).

3. As "Ledi Makbet našego uezda," it appeared in Èpoxa, no. 1 (Jan. 1865); under the new title in N. S. Leskov, *Povesti, očerki i rasskazy*, I (SPb., 1867). In the latter edition the story is dated "November 26, 1864; Kiev."

4. Leskov to N. N. Strakhov, Dec. 7, 1864 (10:253).

5. "Kak ja učilsja prazdnovat';" quoted in ANL, p. 71.

6. It is noteworthy that, in the adaptation of Leskov's story for the opera by Dmitry Shostakovich, this third murder was the one eliminated. Shostakovich's motives were ideological, as he himself has explicitly stated: he sought to treat Katerina Izmailova as an intrinsically good "folk" character whose nature had been warped by the corrupt social system. Her murders for love could be condoned, but not a murder for avarice. Shostakovich's remarks, written for the Moscow production of 1934, are quoted in Victor Ilyich Seroff, *Dmitry Shostakovich: The Life and Background of a Soviet Composer* (New York, 1943). This attempts to "rehabilitate" and to make heroic a merchant murderess was one of the ideological sins charged against Shostakovich during the attacks on "Lady Macbeth" in 1936. See Chapter 10, note 4.

7. Note by Andrei Leskov in N. S. Leskov, *Izbrannye sočinenija* (Moscow-Leningrad, 1945), p. 453. This information is given more fully in another article by Andrei Leskov that I was unable to consult: "Kak N. S. Leskov pisal

'Ledi Makbet Mcenskogo uezda'," in *Sbornik statej k postanovke opery "Ledi Makbet Mcenskogo uezda" Leningradskim gosudarstvennym akademičeskim malym teatrom* (Leningrad, 1934).

8. I. K. Markuze, "Vospominanija o V. V. Krestovskom," *Istoričeskij vestnik*, no. 3 (March 1900), p. 989.

9. "The Battle-axe" and The Islanders

1. Leskov to P. K. Shchebalsky, April 19, 1871 (10:312).

2. "Voitel'nica," originally in *Otečestvennye zapiski*, no. 7 (April 1, 1866). It has been translated into English by David Magarshack under the title of "The Amazon."

3. A. I. Faresov, *Protiv tečenij* (SPb., 1904), pp. 274-275.

4. Boris Ejxenbaum, "K 100-letiju roždenija N. Leskova," in N. S. Leskov, *Izbrannye proizvedenija* (Moscow-Leningrad, 1931), pp. xlviii ff.

5. A more detailed discussion of the language of "Voitel'nica" is to be found in Valentina Gebel', *N. S. Leskov; v tvorčeskoj laboratorii* (Moscow, 1945), pp. 201-206. On the skaz generally, see Irwin Titunik, "The Problem of *Skaz* in Russian Literature" (Ph.D. dissertation, University of California, Berkeley, 1963).

6. ANL, pp. 662-663, quoting an oral statement by Leskov, and a letter published by another "physiological" friend, the artist Mikhail Mikeshin, in *Petersburgskaja gazeta* in 1895. On the "physiological" sketch, see A. G. Cejtlin, *Stanovlenie russkogo realizma (Russkij fiziologičeskij očerk)* (Moscow, 1965).

7. "Ostrovitjane," originally in *Otečestvennye zapiski*, nos. 21-24 (Nov. 1-Dec. 15, 1866).

8. On this question see I. Z. Serman's commentary in 3:584-587.

9. "Avtorskoe priznanie; otkrytoe pis'mo k P. K. Ščebal'skomu," dated Dec. 10, 1884 (10:229).

10. Vsevolod Setschkareff, *Nikolai Leskov; sein Leben und sein Werk* (Wiesbaden, 1969), p. 60.

11. See Leskov to Pisemsky, May 17, 1871 (10:320-321).

12. There exists an elaborate study of prose rhythms in this story by M. P. Štokmar: "Ritmičeskaja proza v 'Ostrovitjanax' Leskova," *Ars poetica*, ed. M. A. Petrovskij and B. I. Jarxo, 2 (Moscow, 1928): 183-211.

10. A Theatrical Spendthrift

1. N. Ščedrin (M. E. Saltykov), *Polnoe sobranie sočinenij*, ed. V. Ja. Kirpotin et al., 7 (Moscow, 1937): 365-372.

2. They all bear the title "Russkij dramatičeskij teatr v Peterburge": *Otečestvennye zapiski*, Sept. 1, Nov. 1, Dec. 15, 1866, March 1, 1867. Only one of them, the fourth, has been reprinted, 10:23-40.

3. *Literaturnaja biblioteka,* Oct. 1, Dec. 1, 1867.

4. Stalin's inspiration of the massive journalistic attack on Shostakovich is now acknowledged in Soviet sources. See L. Danilevič, *Naš sovremennik: tvorčestvo Šostakoviča* (Moscow, 1965), p. 38. Danilevich's comment illustrates some of the agonizing ambivalences of contemporary Soviet intellectual life: "formalistic, abstractionist pseudo-art" is still very much to be condemned, but the application of this category to Shostakovich's opera was Stalin's mistake. The opera was "rehabilitated," slightly revised by the composer, and produced again in 1963.

5. "Rastočitel'," originally published in *Literaturnaja biblioteka* (July 1, 15, 1867).

6. "Russkij dramatičeskij teatr v Peterburge," 10:23-40.

7. This suggestion was made by B. M. Drugov, *N. S. Leskov: očerk tvorčestva* (Moscow, 1957), pp. 30-36. Drugov, however, interprets this "polemic" more in political than in artistic terms.

8. "I. Em," "Kak rabotajut naši pisateli," *Novosti i birževaja gazeta,* no. 49 (Feb. 19, 1895), p. 2.

9. Cited in Leonid Grossman, *N. S. Leskov: žizn', tvorčestvo, poètika* (Moscow, 1945), p. 148.

10. Leskov to P. K. Shchebalsky, Oct. 16, 1884 (11:294). For effect, Leskov fibs a bit here: the quotation he identifies as the concluding words of the play actually comes a little earlier.

11. "Specialisty po ženskoj časti," *Literaturnaja biblioteka,* no. 24 (Dec. 15, 1867), p. 270.

12. ANL, p. 193.

13. They are cited in Grossman, *Leskov,* pp. 150-152.

11. A Chronicle of Old Town

1. "Bespočvennaja i beznaturnaja staja peterburgskix literaturščikov," Leskov to I. S. Aksakov, Nov. 16, 1874 (10:362).

2. Thomas A. Eekman, "The Genesis of Leskov's *Soborjane,*" *California Slavic Studies,* 2 (Berkeley and Los Angeles, 1963): 124.

3. For instance, in Leskov to I. S. Aksakov, Dec. 9, 1881 (11:256).

4. A variation on the title of the primary medieval Russian chronicle, *Povest' vremennyx let.* See Leskov to S. Yuriev, December 5, 18, 1870 (10:279, 281).

5. Leskov to A. A. Kraevsky, undated, ascribed to Sept. or Oct. 1866 (10:260).

6. All this is recounted in great detail in Leskov to E. P. Kovalevsky, secretary of the literary fund, May 20, 1867, in which he asks for a loan in view of the difficult financial circumstances brought on by the withdrawal of his novel (10:262-265).

7. Leskov to P.K. Shchebalsky, June 8, 1871 (10:329).

8. "Čajuščie dviženija vody," *Otečestvennye zapiski,* nos. 6, 7, 8 (March 15-April 15, 1867).

9. In N. S. Leskov, *Povesti, očerki i rasskazy,* 1 (SPb., 1867). The title there is a long one: "Stargorodcy (Otryvki iz neokončennogo romana 'Čajuščije dviženija vody') I. Kotin doilec i Platonida." There was, however, no continuation beyond number "I."

10. "Božedomy," *Literaturnaja biblioteka,* nos. 1, 2 (Jan.-Feb. 1868). The manuscript of the continuation of "Božedomy" survives, now preserved in the Central State Literary Archive in Moscow (f. 275, ed. xr. 3, list 137). It is extensively quoted in Valentina Gebel' *N. S. Leskov* (Moscow, 1945); and N. S. Pleščunov, *Romany N. S. Leskova "Nekuda" i "Soborjane"* (Baku, 1963). See also A. Baboreko, "Rukopis' 'Soborjan' N. S. Leskova," *Voprosy literatury,* no. 9 (Sept. 1959), pp. 254-256.

11. See Leskov to the poet A. A. Fet, Aug. 16, 1868 (10:270-271).

12. The details of this legal battle are outlined in 10:537-538.

13. See the inscription in the copy of the second (1869) volume of stories presented to P. K. Shchebalsky; cited in Gebel', *Leskov,* p. 130n.

14. "Starye gody v sele Plodomasove," *Syn otečestva,* nos. 6-9 (1869).

15. *Rasskazy M. Stebnickogo,* 2 (SPb., 1869).

16. "Plodomasovskie karliki," *Russkij vestnik,* no. 2 (Feb. 1869).

17. The differences between the two texts are analyzed in Eekman, "Genesis," pp. 133-134.

18. "Soborjane: Stargorodskaja xronika," *Russkij vestnik,* nos. 4-7 (April-July 1872).

19. Leskov was fond of these saintly schismatic patriarchs, who also appear in *No Way Out,* "The Sealed Angel," and "Pechersk Eccentrics." They are probably based on people he met during his researches on the schismatics, such as Vasily Khmelinsky, the leader of the Old Believer community in Pskov, or Zakhar Belyayev, who held a similar position in Riga. See *O raskol'nikax goroda Rigi,* pp. 15, 50.

20. On Varya "Dolina"—a Russian surname Leskov gave her to replace her Estonian one, Kukk—see ANL, pp. 488-497; the footnotes provide a bibliography of Leskov's many articles and letters touching on the "orphan question." Andrei Leskov is naturally very hostile toward this intruder, whom his father seemed to prefer to his own children.

21. Leskov, *Povesti,* 1: 292. Leskov goes on to make a series of jibes at Kraevsky's supposedly "uncensored" magazine.

22. Leskov to A. S. Suvorin, May 16, 1888 (11:389).

23. As suggested by Vsevolod Setschkareff, *Nikolai Leskov: sein Leben und sein Werk* (Wiesbaden, 1959), p. 70.

24. 4:36. In "Božedomy" the same scene is included in Tuberozov's diary, but there the orphans are the two girls instead of the boy. If this arrangement had been retained, it would have straightened out some of the chronological troubles in *Cathedral Folk,* since the boy could have been adopted much later.

But Leskov evidently did not want to devote so much space and attention to these now episodic figures, and so the two adoptions were telescoped into one.

25. The excised chapter is given as an appendix in 3:571-580. The editor of this volume, I. Z. Serman, believes (p. 599) that the excision was motivated by Leskov's fear of the censorship. However, there are many pages more lurid than these in the collected works that passed unscathed through the censor's hands.

26. Leskov to B. M. Bubnov, May 4, 1891 (*Šestidesjatye gody* [Moscow, 1940], p. 361).

27. Leskov to A. S. Suvorin, Dec. 5, 1870 (10:276).

28. "Čitateljam 'Soborjan' ot avtora," *Russkij mir*, no. 119 (May 7, 1872); cited in full in 3:598-599. These well-timed "inquiries" and the author's obliging response may have been a diversionary operation carried out by Leskov in order to justify to his readers and perhaps to Katkov the fact he was planning to reprint, as part of the text of *Cathedral Folk* being serialized in *Russian Messenger*, a short story that had appeared in the same magazine only three years before.

29. These discrepancies are discussed in detail in Eekman, "Genesis," pp. 136-137.

12. In God's Holy House

1. M. A. Protopopov, "Bol'noj talant," *Russkaja mysl'*, no. 12 (Dec. 1891), p. 265. Pavel Melnikov (1819-1883), Leskov's "tutor" in matters regarding the Old Believers, was the author of bulky ethnographic novels (written under the pseudonym of Andrei Pechersky) that try to get the maximum artistic mileage out of Russian couleur locale. The best known are *In the Woods* (*V lesax*, 1871-1875) and *On the Mountains* (*Na gorax*, 1875-1881). Although still remembered, reprinted, and read, Melnikov is a minor figure among the Russian literary luminaries of the nineteenth century. Mikhail Avdeyev (1821-1876), a novelist and critic now almost totally forgotten, made an ephemeral splash in 1860 with a novel called *Underwater Stone* (*Podvodnyj kamen'*) that dealt daringly with the titillating topic of free love.

2. In his introduction to Leskov's *Izbrannye proizvedenija*, 1 (only volume published; Berlin, 1923): 9. Gorky's admiration for Leskov has been the subject of numerous Soviet scholarly efforts; and Gorky's endorsement has frequently been used—not always successfully—as a lever to push the dubiously reactionary and religious Leskov through the Soviet censorship. See, among others, B. M. Drugov, "A. M. Gor'kij o Leskove," *Literaturnaja učeba*, no. 6 (June 1941), pp. 21-43; Leonid Grossman, *N. S. Leskov* (Moscow, 1945) pp. 294-311; K. D. Muratova, "Gor'kij i Leskov," *Voprosy izučenija russkoj literatury XI-XX vekov* (Moscow-Leningrad, 1958), pp. 253-259; N. S. Pleščunov, *Romany Leskova "Nekuda" i "Soborjane"* (Baku, 1963); F.

M. Ioffe, "Zametki M. Gor'kogo o tvorčestve N. S. Leskova," *Russkaja litera-tura*, no. 2 (1968), pp. 22-35.

3. Leskov to P. K. Shchebalsky, June 8, Oct. 7, 1871 (10:329, 335).

4. Leskov to S. N. Shubinsky, June 17, 1886 (11:320).

5. As Thomas Eekman has pointed out, these children of Father Zakhariya are one of the curious chronological inconsistencies of the novel. Zakhariya is said to be "a little older than Father Tuberozov, who has lived beyond the sixth decade of his life." Yet Zakhariya has a vast number of little children. This would be impossible for a Russian priest, who was obliged to marry at the time of his ordination and was not permitted to remarry even if widowed. See Thomas A. Eekman, "The Genesis of Leskov's *Soborjane*," *California Slavic Studies*, 2 (Berkeley and Los Angeles, 1963): 136.

6. The critic Protopopov disapproved particularly of such "improbable and vulgar anecdotes" as unworthy of a serious artist—a good illustration of the basic clash between Leskov's artistic method and prevailing nineteenth-century aesthetic value systems. See "Bol'noj talant," p. 263.

7. Unfortunately, the only English translation to date of *Cathedral Folk* (New York, 1924) was made by one of the most tone-deaf of the late-Victorian amateur translators, Isabel F. Hapgood. The fact that no better translation exists is another illustration of the state of Russian-to-English translating gen-erally.

8. In the Russian text cited here, lexical items that are stylistically "marked," whether commented on in the translation or not, are italicized.

15-e avgusta. Vernulsja *iz gubernii* ponomar' *Evtixeič* i *skazyval*, čto meždu *vladykoj* i gubernatorom proizošla nekaja *rasprja* iz-za vzaimnogo *vizita*.

2-e oktjabrja. Sluxi o *vizitnoj raspre podtverždajutsja*. Gubernator, *byvaja* v carskie dni v sobore, *imeet obyčaj* v *sie* vremja dovol'no gromko razgovarivat'. *Vladyka* položili prekratit' *sie obyknovenie* i poslali svoego kostyl'nika prosit' ego prevosxoditel'stvo vesti sebja *blagopristojnee*. Gub-ernator prinjal zamečanie ves'ma *ambicionno* i črez *maloe* vremja snova vozobnovil svoi gromkie s žandarmskim polkovnikom *sobesedovanija*; no na sej raz vladyka uže sami ostanovilis' i gromko skazali: "Nu, ja, vaše pre-vosxoditel'stvo, zamolču i načnu, kogda vy končite."

Očen' èto so storony vladyki odobrjaju (4:55-56).

9. In addition to manuscript variants, there are four different printed ver-sions of the diary: in "Waiting for the Moving of the Water" (1867); in "Dwell-ers in God's House" (1868); in the 1872 version of *Cathedral Folk*; and the re-vision of *Cathedral Folk* for the collected works (vol. 1, 1889).

10. On this see Eekman, "Genesis," and Boris Tomaševskij, *Pisatel' i kniga* (Leningrad, 1929), pp. 126-127, or 2nd ed. (Moscow, 1959), pp. 140-141.

11. Leskov to P. K. Shchebalsky, June 8, 1871 (10:328).

12. Ibid., (10:329).

13. On Leskov's relation to the church see Brigitte Macher, "Nikolai Leskovs Verhältnis zur Orthodoxie" (dissertation, Marburg, 1952).

14. See the long anonymous article, "Naše duxovenstvo po belletrističe-skim proizvedenijam," *Pravoslavnoe obozrenie*, no. 1 (Jan. 1872), pp. 73-105, 304-333. It is devoted entirely to an enthusiastic review of *Cathedral Folk*.

15. The idea of making this soldier a Jew was an afterthought on Leskov's part, added to the 1872 version, perhaps with the aim of pleasing his anti-Semitic publisher, Katkov. There is no mention of the soldier's religion either in the "Waiting for the Moving of the Water" or the "Dwellers in God's House" version of the diary.

16. In the early drafts of "Dwellers in God's House" Leskov invoked directly the figure of Avvakum, the great seventeeth-century leader of the Old Believers and himself a writer with a "Leskovian" feel for the Russian language. With his intransigence and courage in the face of persecution, Avvakum was to be a moral model for Tuberozov, even appearing to him in a vision during Tuberozov's "transfiguration" scene. In the published versions of *Cathedral Folk* all direct references to Avvakum have been eliminated—possibly because the paradox seemed too extreme of an Old Believer providing moral guidance to an Orthodox campaigner against the Old Belief. See I. Z. Serman, "Protopop Avvakum v tvorčestve N. S. Leskova," *Trudy Otdela drevnerusskoj literatury Akademii nauk SSSR*, 14 (Moscow-Leningrad, 1958): 404-407.

17. Thomas Eekman, "Genesis," is eloquent on this point.

18. Paul, Bishop of Kishinyov (Petr Lebedev), to Leskov, Sept. 25, 1872; quoted from notes made by Pierre Kovalevsky in the early 1930s and later made available to me. The letter is now in the Central State Literary Archive in Moscow. See V. G. Zimina, "Iz arxiva N. S. Leskova," *Zapiski otdela rukopisej Gosudarstvennoj Ordena Lenina Biblioteki SSSR imeni V. I. Lenina*, issue 30 (Moscow, 1968), p. 209; William B. Edgerton, "Missing Letters to Leskov: An Unsolved Puzzle," *Slavic Review*, no. 1 (March 1966), p. 128.

19. Leskov to P. K. Shchebalsky, June 8, 1871 (10:328-329). Count Dmitry Tolstoy, with whom Leskov later crossed swords many times, in 1871 simultaneously occupied the posts of minister of education and ober-procurator of the Holy Synod. He was regarded as an extreme reactionary.

13. The End of Nihilism

1. April 4, 1868 (10:268).

2. "Russkie obščestvennye zametki," *Birževye vedomosti*, Aug. 3, 1869, et seq. Two (out of more than twenty-five) of these articles have been reprinted in 10:72-96. On Leskov's journalism of this period see I. V. Stoljarova, "N. S. Leskov v *Birževyx vedomostjax* i *Večernej gazete* (1869-1871 gg)," *Učenye zapiski Leningradskogo godudarstvennogo universiteta*, philological sciences series, no. 295, issue 58 (1960), pp. 87-119; "Obščestvennaja i literaturnaja

pozicija N. S. Leskova v konce 1860-x—načale 1870-x godov," *Vestnik Leningradskogo universiteta*, history, language and literature series, no. 2, issue 2 (1961), pp. 112-122. Stolyarova has painstakingly established the attribution to Leskov of numerous articles not listed in the Bykov and Shesterikov bibliographies. She also tries valiantly, but in my opinion not wholly convincingly, to rescue Leskov's democratic reputation by placing his position further to the left than is customary in the scholarly literature on him.

3. See Leskov to E. P. Kovalevsky, May 20, 1867 (10:262-263).

4. "Literator-krasavec," 10:54; originally in *Literaturnaja biblioteka*, no. 8 (Sept. 1867).

5. Nikolaj Solov'ev, "Dva romanista: kritika *Peterburgskix truščob* V. V. Krestovskogo—*Nekuda, Obojdennyx, Voitel'nicy, Čajuščix dviženija vody* i *Rastočitelja* M. Stebnickogo," *Vsemirnyj trud*, no. 12 (Dec. 1867), pp. 35-66.

6. "Dama i fefela," originally in *Russkaja mysl'*, no. 12 (Dec. 1894).

7. ANL, p. 422.

8. "Letopis' literaturnyx strannostej i bezobrazij," *Literaturnaja biblioteka*, no. 20 (Oct. 15, 1867), pp. 215-225.

9. "Čelobitnaja; stix," *Otečestvennye zapiski*, no. 8 (April 15, 1866).

10. Leskov to A. S. Suvorin, April 22, 1888 (11:385).

11. He alludes to it in "Specialists on the Distaff Side," *Literaturnaja biblioteka*, no. 18 (Sept. 15, 1867), pp. 196, 200; and again in "An Enigmatic Man" (3:364).

12. See Leskov to I. S. Aksakov, April 23, 1875 (10:397) and Dec. 9, 1881 (11:256); and an article by Suvorin of 1889, quoted in 11:741.

13. The relevant texts are quoted in 3:604.

14. The date of composition given by I. Z. Serman in the apparatus to 3:604 ("the latter half of 1868") is incorrect, as shown by Leskov to N. A. Lyubimov, May 25, 1868 (10:269). This error was pointed out by K. P. Bogaevskaya in her review of Leskov's collected works in *Russkaja literatura*, no. 3 (March 1959).

15. Leskov to N. A. Lyubimov, May 25, 1868 (10: 269-270).

16. *Birževye vedomosti*, nos. 51, 54, 56, 58, 60, 64, 66, 68, 76, 78 (1870). As early as Jan. 4, 1869, Leskov had written to his friend A. P. Milyukov to ask the latter's help in placing it in a Petersburg newspaper (10:272).

17. N. S. Leskov, *Zagadočnyj čelovek* (SPb., 1871).

18. German Benni, "Pis'mo k redaktoru *S.-Peterburgskix vedomostej*," *Sankt-Peterburgskie vedomosti*, no. 256 (Sept. 17, 1871).

19. The evidence for this assertion, as well as a detailed comparison of the facts of Benni's career and Leskov's treatment of them in "An Enigmatic Man," is to be found in my article, "Leskov and His Enigmatic Man," *Harvard Slavic Studies*, 4 (1957): 203-224.

20. "Nezagadočnyj pisatel'," *Vestnik Evropy*, no. 8 (Aug. 1871), p. 900. Probably by A. S. Suvorin; see Leonid Grossman, *N. S. Leskov* (Moscow, 1945), p. 97.

21. "Na nožax," *Russkij vestnik*, nos. 10-12 (1870) and 1-8 (1871). The

novel appeared in a separate edition in 1871 and was reprinted in 1875, 1885, and in the first three editions of Leskov's collected works, but not in the Soviet edition.

22. "I. Èm," "Kak rabotajut naši pisateli: N. S. Leskov," *Novosti i birže-vaja gazeta*, no. 49 (Feb. 19, 1895), p. 2.

23. This statement was entered in the diary of I. A. Shlyapkin under "January 1875." Shlyapkin, who later became a well-known professor of Russian literature, was at that time a university student and a friend of Leskov's stepson, Nikolai Bubnov. See I. A. Šljapkin, "K biografii N. S. Leskova," *Russkaja starina*, 84 (Dec. 1895): 213.

24. ANL, p. 182.

25. Leskov to P. K. Shchebalsky, April 16, 1871 (10:307).

26. May 20, 1871 (10:297). The individual to whom Leskov alludes remains unidentified.

27. F. M. Dostoevskij, *Pis'ma*, 2 (Leningrad, 1930): 320-321. When Leskov read this letter in a collection of Dostoevsky materials published after Dostoevsky's death, he wrote bitterly to his friend Shchebalsky, "In the published volume of the letters of F. Dostoevsky he speaks even about some sort of 'genius' of mine and mentions my 'strange position in Russian literature,' but in print he played the sly dog and tried to put me in the shadow" (Oct. 16, 1884 [11: 295]). On Leskov's relations with Dostoevsky see V. V. Vinogradov, *Problema avtorstva i teorija stilej* (Moscow, 1961), pp. 487-555.

28. M. Gor'kij, "Predislovie," in N. S. Leskov, *Izbrannye proizvedenija*, 1 (Berlin, 1923): 7.

14. Laughter and Grief

1. Leskov to I. S. Aksakov, April 23, 1875 (10:396).

2. I. Z. Serman (3:615) and K. P. Bogaevskaya (11:810) believe that the manuscript of "Laughter and Grief" was sent to Moscow as early as March or April 1870. Their evidence is Leskov to P. K. Shchebalsky, April 16, 1871 (incorrectly cited by Serman as May 7), in which Leskov complains that the editor of *Russian Messenger* (probably N. A. Lyubimov is meant) had kept the manuscript "under his desk *for a year*, aiming to kick it away with his feet" (10:308; italics mine). But it seems to be unwarranted to attribute so much definiteness to this probably hyperbolical "year." The only sure evidence for the date of composition is Leskov to P. K. Shchebalsky, Dec. 19, 1870 (10: 284), which indicates that the manuscript was then in Moscow and had been there at least long enough to be read and tentatively accepted—and probably a good bit longer, if it was to serve a term as Lyubimov's football. I would estimate that Leskov finished *Laughter and Grief* in the summer of 1870.

3. See Leskov to P. K. Shchebalsky, Dec. 19, 1870 (10:284).

4. "Smex i gore," *Sovremennaia letopis'*, nos. 1-2, 8-16 (1871).

5. *Raznoxarakternoe* potpourri *iz pestryx vospominanij polinjavšego*

čeloveka. In addition to the original publication in *Contemporary Chronicle*, this subtitle was repeated in the separate editions of 1871, 1886, and 1887, but was eliminated from the collected works (vol. 5, 1889). The term "potpourri" remains in the text of chapter 1.

6. *Russkij vestnik,* no. 12 (Dec., 1871), p. 632; quoted in 3:616.

7. Leskov to P. K. Shchebalsky, Jan. 15, 1876 (10:440).

8. *Kto ždet sebe ni za čto ni pro čto radostej, tot doždetsja za to vsjakix gadostej.*

9. Leskov based the "Philemon" episode on an actual occurrence. Prince S. G. Golitsyn, known among his friends as "Firs," was summoned for questioning during the investigation of the Decembrist uprising because the feast of St. Firs (Thyrsis) was also celebrated on December 14 (3:620).

10. *Razdeli častnoe i umnoži delitelja.* The "disrespectful" aspect is perhaps somewhat greater in Russian, since the imperative customarily used in such expressions is the singular, "thou" form.

11. Some contemporary reviews are quoted in 3:616-617. Leonid Grossman shares this opinion (*N. S. Leskov* [Moscow, 1945], p. 237). It is energetically disputed by M. S. Gorjačkina, *Satira Leskova* (Moscow, 1963), pp. 51-53.

12. Much later, in a letter to A. S. Suvorin of April 22, 1888, Leskov himself pointed to the connection between *Laughter and Grief* and Gogol: "A tour of landowners like Chichikov's has always attracted me, and I made some small attempts at it in *Laughter and Grief* and in 'The Enchanted Pilgrim' " (11:385).

13. Leonid Grossman's argument for downgrading *Laughter and Grief* shows that he missed the point of Leskov's "laughter." Grossman's reasoning goes: *Laughter and Grief* is a satire; a good satire is a strong indictment of social evil; *Laughter and Grief* is not this; therefore, *Laughter and Grief* is a failure. An analogous argument would be: an apple is good; an apple is red; this fruit is not red; therefore this fruit is not good—stated while holding a ripe pear in one's hand.

14. Andrei Leskov (p. 123) suggests that the governor and his wife in *Laughter and Grief* are portraits of the Vasilchikovs, the governor-general of Kiev under whom Leskov had served in the late 1850s and the wife in whose amateur theatricals he had performed. V. Setchkarev (*Nikolai Leskov* [Wiesbaden, 1959], p. 142n) believes that Leskov may have drawn on the figures of von Lembke and his wife from Dostoevsky's *Devils.* The similarity exists, but the date of composition makes any influence (of Dostoevsky on Leskov) highly improbable. *Laughter and Grief* was completed well before the end of 1870, and *The Devils* did not appear until 1871.

15. This episode, since it dealt with events of 1871, was necessarily a last-minute addition to the separate edition published in that year (see Leskov to P. K. Shchebalsky, May 7, 1871 [10:317]). In the magazine version, Vatazhkov is stabbed by mistake by "some sort of Spanish republican," who took

him for Marfori, traveling in Odessa incognito. Marfori was the notorious steward and lover of the recently deposed Isabella II.

16. Leskov to A. S. Suvorin, Nov. 30, 1888 (11:401-402).

15. "The Sealed Angel"

1. Leskov to P. K. Shchebalsky, Jan. 15, 1876 (10:440).

2. Ibid., April 16, 1871 (10:311). Brody is a town to the northeast of Lvov, at that time on the Austrian side of the border. Leskov had been there in 1862: see "Iz odnogo dorožnogo dnevnika," *Severnaja pčela*, no. 350 (Dec. 28, 1862). Krasny Yar is a town on the Caspian in the Volga estuary near Astrakhan. Leskov probably went there during his travels as a commercial agent in the employ of his uncle, Alexander Scott, in 1857-1860.

3. A. I. Faresov, *Protiv tečenij: N. S. Leskov: ego žizn', sočinenija, polemika i vospominanija o nem* (SPb., 1904), pp. 43-44.

4. "Zapečatlennyj angel," *Russkij vestnik*, no. 1 (Jan. 1873), pp. 229-292.

5. "Blagorazumnyj razbojnik (ikonopisnaja fantazija)," *Xudožestvennyj žurnal*, no. 3 (1883); quoted in ANL, p. 288.

6. F. I. Buslaev, "Obščie ponjatija o russkoj ikonopisi," originally in *Sbornik na 1866 god, izdannyj obščestvom drevne-russkogo iskusstva pri Moskovskom publičnom muzee* (Moscow, 1866); reprinted in F. I. Buslaev, *Sočinenija*, 1 (SPb., 1908): 1-193.

7. On this subject see I. Z. Serman's notes in 4:541-544, which list the essential bibliography.

8. ANL, pp. 288-289.

9. "O xudožnom muže Nikite i o sovospitannyx emu," *Novoe vremja*, no. 3889 (Dec. 25, 1886).

10. Faresov, *Protiv tečenij*, p. 274.

11. In the Russian text below, stylistically "marked" items are italicized and their "markings" are indicated in parentheses after the marked word according to the categories in the *Tolkovyj slovar' russkogo jazyka*, ed. D. N. Ušakov et al. (Moscow, 1935-1940), as follows: A = archaic (*ustareloe*); B = bookish (*knižnoe*); C = colloquial (*razgovornoe*); D = diminutive, generally colloquial in effect; E = ecclesiastical (*cerkovnoe*); R = regional (*oblastnoe*); SC = substandard colloquial (*prostorečie*); and X = words not listed in Ushakov's dictionary.

Sej (AB) angel *voistinu* (B) byl *čto-to neopisuemoe* (B). *Lik* (E) u nego, kak sejčas vižu, samyj *svetlobožestvennyj* (X) i *ètakij* (C) *skoropomoščnyj* (X) [both these composita were perhaps coined by the narrator]; *vzor* (B) umilen; *uški* (D) s *torocami* (X) [a quasi-Slavonic plural form, derived from *toroka*, a word of Mongolian origin meaning "saddle-ties"; in icon-painting the word was used to indicate the symbolic stream of light emanating from the ears of an angel or divine figure] v znak povsemestnogo otovsjudu *slyšanija* (X) [this construction with verbal substantive and the word order are also bookish]; *odejan'e* (AB) gorit, *rjasny* (X) [an echo, in Church Slavonic, of Psalm 44 (45):13] *zlatymi* (ABE) *preispeščreno* (X); *dospex* (AB) pernat, *ramena* (ABE) *prepojasany* (AB); na *persjax* (BE) *mladenčeskij* (B) *lik* (E) *Emanuilev* (E); v pravoj ruke krest, v levoj *ognepalaščij* (X) *meč* (B). *Divno! divno!* (AB)

12. See "Rjaženyj," in Dostoevskij, "Dnevnik pisatelja," *Sobranie sočinenij*, 11 (Leningrad, 1929): 90. For a general discussion of this judgment and its implications, as well as the context of the argument, see V. V. Vinogradov, "Dostoevskij i Leskov," *Problema avtorstva i teorija stilej* (Moscow, 1961).

13. See Leonid Grossman, *N. S. Leskov* (Moscow, 1945), p. 169; ANL, pp. 293-294; Vinogradov, *Problema avtorstva*, pp. 526-527.

14. An unpublished memoir on Leskov by Akhmatova is preserved in the Pushkin House in Leningrad. See ANL, p. 294.

15. I. A. Šljapkin, "K biografii N. S. Leskova," *Russkaja starina*, vol. 84, no. 12 (Dec. 1895), p. 214.

16. Leskov to P. K. Shchebalsky, Jan. 4, 1874 (10:360).

17. "Pečerskie antiki" (1833), 7:219.

16. The Russian Superman

1. "Monašeskie ostrova na Ladožskom ozere," *Russkij mir*, nos. 206-208, 219, 220, 224, 226, 227, 232, 233, 236 (1873); reprinted the following year in a separate volume with "The Sealed Angel": *Zapečatlennyj angel; Monašeskie ostrova na Ladožskom ozere* (SPb., 1874). It is not included in any of the editions of Leskov's collected works.

2. Leskov to A. S. Suvorin, March 25, 1888 (11:371).

3. Andrei Leskov also points out that this patronymic is a variant of that of Nikita Savostyanovich Racheiskov, the model for the icon-painter in "The Sealed Angel," from whose tales some of the material for Ivan Flyagin's biography was also derived (ANL, p. 288). But it is surely no accident that of all the variants of Racheiskov's patronymic Leskov selected the form *Severyano*-vich.

4. Probably Count Sergei Mikhailovich Kamensky (1771-1835) or his father Mikhail Fedotovich (1738-1809), whose images Leskov invoked many times as typifying the despotic landowner of pre-Reform days—most notably, and under their full names, in "The Toupee Artist" (1883).

5. *Budeš' ty mnogo raz pogibat' i ni razu ne pogibneš' poka pridet tvoja nastojaščaja pogibel' i togda [. . .] pojdeš' v cernecy.*

6. One of the means of distancing this scene is the punning name Flyagin gives it. The Tatars, he says, engage in duels *naperepor*, from *porot'*, "to flog," punning with *naperekor*, a common adverb meaning "in spite of, contrary to."

7. I Thessalonians 5:3.

8. On the sources of this horse material see M. P. Čerednikova, "Ob

odnom fol'klornom motive v povesti N. S. Leskova 'Očarovannyj strannik'," *Russkaja literatura*, no. 3 (1973), pp. 139-144. On the Tatars, see A. A. Gorelov, "'Talarskie' èpizody 'Očarovannogo strannika' N.S. Leskova i 'Istorija Rossijskaja' V. N. Tatiščeva," *Russkaja literatura XIX-XX vekov* = *Učenye zapiski Leningradskogo universiteta*, philological sciences series, no. 355, issue 76 (Leningrad, 1971), pp. 193-195.

9. N. K. Mixajlovskij, "Literatura i žizn'," *Russkoe bogatstvo*, no. 6 (June 1897), p. 105. On the structure of the story see M. P. Čerednikova, "O sjužetnyx motivirovkax v povesti N. S. Leskova 'Očarovannyj strannik'," *Russkaja literatura*, no. 3 (1971), pp. 113-127.

10. Leonid Grossman, though superficial, I think, in his basic interpretation of this story, has some interesting observations on its relation to Fénelon's *Aventures de Télémaque*. See *N. S. Leskov* (Moscow, 1945), pp. 164-165.

11. Leskov to A. S. Suvorin, April 22, 1888 (11:385).

12. Leskov to P. K. Shchebalsky, Jan. 4, 1874 (10:360).

13. See Leskov to Meshchersky, March 18, 1873 (10:357-358).

14. V. V. Vinogradov, *Problema avtorstva i teorija stilej* (Moscow, 1961), p. 494. Angered by this rejection, Leskov then initiated a petty squabble with Dostoevsky in print.

15. Quoted in ANL, p. 296.

17. The Decrepit Nobility

1. Leskov to P. K. Shchebalsky, Jan. 4, 1874 (10:360), shows that a substantial portion, probably the first two parts as we possess them, were then complete and were being sent to Shchebalsky for comment.

2. For details see Leskov to I. S. Aksakov, March 23, 1875 (10:388).

3. Ibid., Dec. 5, 1874 (10:368).

4. Ibid., Dec. 23, 1874 (10:370-371).

5. Ibid., April 23, 1875 (10:396).

6. Leskov to A. S. Suvorin, Feb. 11, 1888 (11:366; italics mine).

7. Ibid., March 2, 1889 (11:418; italics mine). Vladimir Cherkassky (1824-1878) was a leading Slavophile, a friend of Ivan Aksakov's. Nikolai Pirogov (1810-1881) was a prominent surgeon and educational theorist.

8. "Zaxudalyj rod; semejnaja xronika knjazej Protozanovyx (Iz zapisok Knjažny V. D. P.)," originally in *Russkij vestnik*, nos. 7, 8, 10 (1874); reprinted as a separate volume, with "restored" text (SPb., 1875). A new version appeared in volume 6 of Leskov's collected works, issued in 1889, but was immediately suppressed, seized by the censors, and burned (a dozen or so copies of this volume survive). The suppression had nothing to do with *A Decrepit Clan*, but was provoked by other works included in that volume. The new *Decrepit Clan* therefore successfully appeared in the "second" volume 6, issued in 1890 to replace the suppressed one.

9. Leskov to F. I. Buslaev, June 1, 1887 (10:451).

10. "Presyščenie znatnost'ju" (1888), 11:182. Leskov elsewhere gives conflicting testimony about the location of this lady's library and even her name. But her personality and the fact of the library's existence remain constant.

11. See "Dvorjanskij bunt v Dobrynskom prixode," *Istoričeskij vestnik,* no. 2 (Feb. 1881), pp. 371-372.

12. She too had a real-life model, apparently named Marya Nikolayevna (we never learn her surname), the same woman who inspired the portrait of Tuberozov's wife in *Cathedral Folk.* See "Karikaturnyj ideal" (1877), 10:225; and "Presyščenie znatnost'ju" (1888), 11:183: "the deaconess Marya Nikolayevna (actually a deacon's daughter) was a timid, middle-aged spinster, especially respected by Nastasia Sergeyevna 'for her virtue and modesty.' "

13. Dorimedont Rogozhin also had a real-life model, an Oryol gentleman named Ilya Ivanovich Kozyulkin (or Kazyulkin). Refuting the charge that Rogozhin was overdone or exaggerated, Leskov claimed that in his youth Oryol had "teemed" with types suggestive of a Kozyulkin. See Leskov to I. S. Aksakov, March 23, 1875 (10:388); and "Presyščenie znatnost'ju" (11:183). I. V. Stolyarova has discovered some other interesting examples of real Don Quixote or Robin Hood types among the Russian nineteenth-century gentry. See her "Roman-xronika Leskova," in A. S. Bušmin et al., eds., *Istorija russkogo romana,* 2 (Moscow-Leningrad, 1964): 435-436, and "Russkie donkixoty v tvorčestve N. S. Leskova," *Učenye zapiski Leningradskogo gos. universiteta imeni A. A. Ždanova,* philological sciences series, no. 355, issue 76 (1971), 77-95.

14. The model for this character is Countess Anna Alekseyevna Orlova-Chesmenskaya (1785-1848), daughter of one of the assassins of Paul I and one of the richest women in Russia, known for her bigoted and intolerant Orthodoxy.

18. A Virtuous Peacock

1. Vsevolod Setschkareff, *Nikolai Leskov: Sein Leben und sein Werk* (Wiesbaden, 1959), p. 80.

2. In *Tri pravednika i odin Šeramur* (SPb., 1880). It is reprinted in 6:641-643.

3. A. I. Faresov, *Protiv tečenij* (SPb., 1904), p. 381.

4. *Pavlin (rasskaz); Detskie gody (Iz vospominanij Merkula Praotceva)* (SPb., 1876).

19. The Case for Spontaneity

1. "Bluždajuščie ogon'ki (Avtobiografija Praotceva)," *Niva,* nos. 1, 3-18 (1875); *Pavlin (rasskaz); Detskie gody (Iz vospominanij Merkula Praotceva)* (SPb., 1876). Leskov did not include this work in the collected works of 1889-1890. In the edition of 1902-1903, published as a supplement to the same

Ploughland, the magazine rather than the (later) book version was used, apparently inadvertently. The recent Soviet edition (5:279-450) correctly reprints the book version of 1876 as the last printed text to pass through the author's hands.

2. L. B. Domanovsky, the editor of the fifth volume of Leskov's works, believes (5:608) that the elimination of this preface was carried out at the demand of the censors, on the ground that Father Gordy was too worldly a figure for a proper monk, since he painted and played the cello instead of chanting and praying. This hypothesis seems to me unconvincing. Surely Ivan Flyagin is a much more worldly figure than Gordy, and yet the censors had not troubled him. I think that the decision to eliminate the skaz was partly an artistic one. The speech of Father Gordy, as an educated man, could not be satisfactorily individualized. Another reason may have been that after dragging out several installments of an increasingly abstract and tedious Bildungsroman, Leskov grew so tired of Merkul Praottsev and all his works that he decided to terminate the autobiography before his hero even reached the monastery for which he was destined. The change in title to *Years of Childhood* supports this hypothesis.

3. This "revolt" episode was not included in the magazine version of the story, undoubtedly for reasons for censorship.

20. Renounce and Denounce

1. "Katkov was a noble man in relation to his collaborators," Leskov wrote to A. S. Suvorin many years later. "Why did he pay me 150 rubles [per signature] when, like Kashpirev, he could have given 50, and when for me there was no other 'way out.' And he *gave* me the [book] edition of *Cathedral Folk*" (April 22, 1888 [11:384]).

2. Katkov had made extensive, ideologically motivated changes in *Fathers and Sons* and *Smoke*, in which Turgenev acquiesced, though under protest. By the end of the 1860s, Turgenev had withdrawn from *Russian Messenger* and made his home in *Messenger of Europe*. In the 1870s, Katkov's most famous acts of editorial tyranny were his suppression of the celebrated "At Tikhon's" chapter in Dostoevsky's *Devils* (on grounds of indecency) and his refusal to print the final installment of *Anna Karenina* (on the ground that Tolstoy's attitude was too derisive toward the Russians who volunteered to fight for Serbia).

3. Leskov to I. S. Aksakov, April 23, 1875 (10:396).
4. Leskov to P. K. Shchebalsky, July 29/ Aug. 10, 1875 (10:412).
5. Leskov to I. S. Aksakov, Dec. 16, 1875 (10:433).
6. Leskov to M. A. Protopopov, Dec. 23, 1891 (11:509).
7. For further details on Leskov's relations with M. Katkov, see Andrei Leskov's afterword and annotations to Leskov's remarkable obituary article, "Na smert' Katkova," *Zven'ja*, 3-4 (Moscow-Leningrad, 1934): 894-901. Le-

skov's article was written for Suvorin's *New Times* immediately after Katkov's death in July 1887 and actually set up in type. It was suppressed before
publication on the personal order of Suvorin, who scribbled on the galley
proof "Take this crazy thing out!" The article is a bold and sly attack on Katkov's career, especially on the three major policies insistently advocated by
his propaganda machine: the compulsory study of classical languages in the
gymnasia, the Russification of Poland, and the Franco-Russian alliance. In all
of them Leskov saw the seeds of future disaster for Russia. The article is reprinted in 11:159-163, but without Andrei Leskov's valuable commentary. An
earlier unpublished article on Katkov by Leskov, also full of sly innuendoes,
has recently been discovered and published. See N. Sokolov, "Neizvestnaja
stat'ja N. Leskova o M. Katkove," *Russkaja literatura*, no. 3 (1960), pp. 161-
165.

8. Leskov published one more short story in *Russian Messenger* four years
later, "Rakušanskij melamed" (1878). M. Katkov's publishing house also
brought out the separate editions of *Sentimental'noe blagočestie* (Moscow,
1876); and *Velikosvetskij raskol* (Moscow, 1877). These belated echoes did
not signify a reentry into the Katkovian camp.

9. The only way to make money out of books, Leskov wrote bitterly in a
letter to I. S. Aksakov, is to write potboilers like Meshchersky's, preferably
spiced up with a bit of pornography (Dec. 16, 1875 [10:435]).

10. Leskov to P. K. Shchebalsky, Nov. 10, 1875 (10:430).

11. "Skazanie o Fedore-xristianine i o druge ego Abrame-židovine," *Russkaja mysl'*, no. 12 (Dec. 1886), pp. 1-23.

12. On Leskov's reconciliation with Stasyulevich, see my article, "Leskov
and Ioann of Kronstadt: On the Origins of *Polunoščniki*," *American Slavic
and East European Review*, vol. 12, no. 1 (Feb. 1953), 97-98n.

13. The subsidy in 1892-1895 was 80,000 rubles a year, according to Sergei
Witte, and had been paid for some time before that, probably at least since the
beginning of Alexander III's reign. See the appendix, "Knjaz' Meščerskij," in
S. Ju. Vitte, *Vospominanija*, 2 (Berlin, 1922): 510-518. It is possible, however,
that no subsidy was paid in the 1870s, when Alexander II was still on the
throne. (Meshchersky had been chosen as a childhood playmate for Grand
Duke Nikolai Aleksandrovich, the heir apparent who died in 1865, and for the
rest of his life he exploited to the utmost his intimacy with the royal family.)

14. Andrei Leskov wrote of his father's relations with Maikov: "Father's attitude was respectfully chilly. He valued his [Maikov's] poetic form, but he
could not forgive him either his general's rank [in the civil service: Maikov
eventually became chairman of the censorship committee for foreign books]
or his dry manner of a literary general" (*Vestnik literatury*, no. 7 [1920], p. 6;
cited from 11:753). In the late 1860s, Maikov had helped Leskov with some
letters of introduction. Such a letter of Maikov to Terty I. Filippov (later one
of Leskov's bitterest enemies) is cited in A. I. Faresov, "Umstvennye perelomy
v dejatel'nosti N. S. Leskova," *Istoričeskij vestnik*, no. 3 (March 1916), p. 787.

15. Nov. 10, 1875 (10:431).
16. Leskov to I. S. Aksakov, April 23, 1875 (10:397).
17. Leskov to P. K. Shchebalsky, Oct. 5, 1875 (10:426-427).
18. ANL, p. 345.
19. Ibid., p. 295. On the other hand, Leskov's granddaughter, Natalia Bakhareva, maintains that her mother inherited from Leskov a diamond-studded gold watch and a gold tobacco box presented to him by the empress for reading "The Sealed Angel" at court (from her letter to William B. Edgerton, Aug. 5, 1953). Without further evidence, it is hard to ascertain the truth in this matter. On the one hand, Andrei Leskov, in his efforts to maneuver his father's image (and his own book) around various Soviet taboos, had reasons for denying any court connections his father might have had, regardless of the truth. Nevertheless, in view of the scrupulousness of Andrei Leskov's biography in general, and the sloppiness and inaccuracy of Bakhareva's "memoirs" (actually she did not know her grandfather at all and passes on mostly second-hand gossip), I am inclined to believe Andrei Leskov.
20. For instance, "Pedagogičeskoe jurodstvo (Pedagogičeskij žurnal 'Detskij sad')," *Pravoslavnoe obozrenie*, no. 7 (July 1876), pp. 519-526; "Sentimental'noe blagočestie (Ežemesjačnoe izdanie 'Russkij rabočij' M. G. Pejker)," ibid., No. 3 (March 1876), pp. 526-551; "Ènergičnaja bestaktnost' ('Narodnyj listok,' prostonarodnaja gazeta M. M. Dmitrieva)," ibid., no. 5 (May 1876), pp. 128-149.
21. Leskov to I. S. Aksakov, March 1, 1875 (10:382).
22. Leskov to P. K. Shchebalsky, Nov. 10, 1875 (10:431).
23. Quoted in Edgerton, "The Intellectual Development," p. 352n.
24. April 23, 1875 (10:397).
25. Leskov to Andrei Leskov, June 11/ 23, 1875 (10:402-403). Leskov and Buslaev became friendly. The story "The Unbaptized Priest," published in *The Citizen* in 1877 and as a separate book in 1878, was dedicated to him.
26. June 30/July 12, 1875 (10:404). As William B. Edgerton has shown, the letter is incorrectly dated in that volume. See "Leskov's Trip Abroad in 1875," *Indiana Slavic Studies*, 4 (The Hague, 1967): 89n.
27. Leskov to A. P. Milyukov, June 12/ 24, 1875 (10:406). On this question see also Edgerton, "Leskov's Trip Abroad," p. 89n.
28. I. S. Gagarin, *Le clergé russe* (Brussels, 1871).
29. "Iezuit Gagarin v dele Puškina," *Istoričeskij vestnik*, no. 8 (Aug. 1886), pp. 269-273.
30. Leskov to A. P. Milyukov, June 12/ 24, 1875 (10:407).
31. Leskov to I. S. Aksakov, July 29/Aug. 10, 1875 (10:419).
32. See Edgerton, "Leskov's Trip Abroad."
33. Leskov to I. S. Gagarin, June 13 (n.s.), 1875, in Edgerton, "Leskov's Trip Abroad," p. 90.
34. July 29/ Aug. 10, 1875 (10:411). Concerning the identity of the "young Naville," see above, Chapter 2, note 4.

35. *Veroispovedanie duxovnyx xristian, obyknovenno nazyvaemyx molo-kanami* (Geneva, 1865). In an article published in the *Orthodox Review*, Leskov managed to cite from this forbidden text. See "Ėnergičnaja bestaktnost'," *Pravoslavnoe obozrenie*, no. 5 (May 1876), p. 134. On the general question of Leskov's Protestant readings in 1875 and later, see Edgerton, "Leskov's Trip Abroad," p. 97.

36. July 29/ Aug. 10, 1875 (10:411-412).

37. Leskov to A. P. Milyukov, Aug. 3/ 15, 1875 (10:413).

21. Bishops and Baptisms

1. Nov. 10, 1875 (10:431-432). Without consulting the manuscript, I have taken the liberty of correcting the Latin of the quotation (Job 19:25), although in both Soviet publications of the letter the word *meus* has been misread as *mens* and a corresponding translation concocted, at some violence to the rules of Latin grammar. See 10:432n; *Šestidesjatye gody: materialy po istorii literatury i obščestvennomu dviženiju* (Moscow-Leningrad, 1940), p. 335.

2. "Na kraju sveta (Iz vospominanij arxiereja)," *Graždanin*, no. 52 (Dec. 28, 1875); ibid., nos. 1-4, 6 (Jan. 5, 12, 18, 25, Feb. 8, 1876). It was issued immediately thereafter as a separate book (SPb., 1876); again in 1880, together with "Episcopal Justice," under the combined title *Russkie bogonoscy: religiozno-bytovye kartiny* (SPb., 1880); again in the collected works of 1889-1890. There is little evidence with which to date the composition of the story. In "Episcopal Justice" Leskov explicitly states that he "wrote it" in 1876 (6:88), which is clearly impossible, since publication began in 1875. Oddly, the story does not figure at all in Leskov's extant correspondence for 1875 and 1876, perhaps because his letters to Prince V. P. Meshchersky for this period have not survived (see 10:561).

3. ANL, p. 306.

4. *Buddizm, rassmatrivaemyj v otnošenii k posledovateljam ego, obita-juščim v Sibiri* (SPb., 1858); *Putevye zametki* (Yaroslavl, 1874).

5. "Temnjak," 5:552-573. The manuscript was given by Leskov to Ivan Shlyapkin on February 18, 1876, according to a note in Shlyapkin's handwriting (5:634). The manuscript shows several crossed out alternative titles, characteristic of Leskov's always intense efforts to "baptize" his "children" appropriately: (1) *Two Preachers (told by His Eminence N.); a true story* [the portion in parentheses was then altered to read "told by His late, lamented Eminence Nilus: a tale"]; (2) *God in the Wilderness; a Tale;* (3) *The Savage;* (4) *Three Miracles.*

6. The only recorded pronouncement by Tolstoy on "At the Edge of the World" comes from some ten years after "Master and Man": " 'At the Edge of the World' is very good. The Tungus is shown to have a simple, sincere faith, and his acts are appropriate to it, while the bishop's faith is artificial." (Oral statement recorded on February 22, 1905, by D. P. Makovitsky; see *L. N.*

Tolstoj v vospominanijax sovremennikov, 2 [Moscow, 1955]: 188). Characteristically, Tolstoy's harsh judgment of the bishop's faith has more to do with Tolstoy's feelings about Orthodox bishops than with the content of "At the Edge of the World."

7. In "Man of Darkness" the language is mistakenly identified as Samoyed, a Uralic language spoken by Finno-Asian peoples in the extreme north of European Russia, east of the White Sea, but much further west than the locale of the story. In "At the Edge of the World" the mistake has been corrected, and the language is now Yakut, a Turkic language spoken in the Lena region of northeastern Siberia.

8. For the attribution of pictures not identified by Leskov, I am indebted to the notes by L. B. Domanovsky in 5:619-620. He adds that Leskov's "Metsu" is probably a mistake for Quentin Metsys, since Metsu did not paint religious subjects.

9. Udručennyj nošej krestnoj,
  Vsju tebja, zemlja rodnaja,
  V rabskom vide car' nebesnyj
  Isxodil, blagoslovljaja.

    (From "Èti bednye selenija," 1855)

10. Ivan Shlyapkin records Leskov as saying in 1892 that he "still liked" "At the Edge of the World"—testimony to the fact that the ideology of this pseudo-Orthodox story was compatible with the ardent Tolstoyanism of Leskov's late years. Leskov added that he would have provided a different motive for the bishop's journey into the wilderness. Unfortunately, Shlyapkin did not question Leskov any further on this statement, and we do not know what the new motive would have been. In "Man of Darkness" the bishop and Father Peter plan to engage in actual missionary work, with Peter baptizing and the bishop instructing the natives in Christianity. In "At the Edge of the World," the bishop and Father Kiriak are simply making an inspection tour of remote parts of the diocese seldom visited by its bishop. See I. A. Šljapkin, "K biografii N. S. Leskova," *Russkaja starina*, no. 12 (Dec. 1895), pp. 214-215.

11. At least so it was widely believed in Leskov's time. Ironically, later research revealed that Paul's disgrace came about partly because of his cruelty to his subordinates, and partly because he engaged in precisely the missionary practices Nilus refused to permit, the combined use of intimidation and vodka. See V. Ikonnikov, "P. Konjuškevič, mitropolit tobol'skij," ibid., no. 3 (March 1892).

12. 6:88. Pobedonostsev's letter of presentation is published in *Pis'ma Pobedonosceva k Aleksandru III*, 1 (Moscow, 1925): 44. I am indebted for the reference to William B. Edgerton, "The Intellectual Development," p. 379n. Edgerton, however, has confused the two Alexanders, II and III.

13. "Vladyčnyj sud; byl' (Iz nedavnix vospominanij)," *Strannik*, nos. 1, 2 (Jan., Feb. 1877), pp. 38-72, 226-258. A separate edition of the story appeared

in the same year (SPb., 1877); again in the following one (SPb., 1878); it is also included in *Russkie bogonoscy* (SPb., 1880); and in the collected works. See chapter 3.

14. Along with other anecdotes about Philaret, Leskov introduces an allusion to the metropolitan's dislike for Petersburg and his quarrels with the Holy Synod.

15. "Nekreščenyj pop," *Graždanin*, nos. 2)-29 (Oct. 13-31, 1877); reprinted in a book edition the following year (SPb., 1878); and in the collected works.

16. On Leskov and the shtundists, see William B. Edgerton, "Leskov, Paškov, the Štundists, and a Newly Discovered Letter," *Orbis Scriptus; Dmitrij Tschiźewskij zum 70. Geburtstag*, ed. Dietrich Gerhardt et al. (Munich, 1966), pp. 187-200.

22. The Germans

1. Krüger's name is found in an address book of Leskov's dating from the 1850s. See Andrei Leskov's note in N. S. Leskov, *Izbrannye sočinenija* (Moscow, 1945), p. 454.

2. Samarin's "Letters from Riga" (1849) urged the Russian government to base its authority in Livonia on the Lettish and Estonian peasantry, not on the German barons. For this work Samarin was arrested and administratively banished to Simbirsk. Later he continued the campaign with *The Borderlands of Russia* (Berlin, 1868-1876), which again led to legal action against him, terminated only by his death in 1876. Samarin cannot, of course, be blamed for the repressions perpetrated in the name of Russification under Alexander III and Nicholas II, but, nevertheless, his advocacy pointed in that direction.

3. "Iskanie škol staroobrjadcami," *Birževye vedomosti*, no. 37 (Feb. 7, 1869); "Irodova rabota," *Istoričeskij vestnik*, no. 4 (April 1882), p. 196.

4. Leskov tells the story in "Zakonnye vredy," *Russkij mir*, nos. 313, 320 (Nov. 30, Dec. 11, 1872); in "Russkie dejateli v Ostzejskom krae," *Istoričeskij vestnik*, no. 12 (Dec. 1883), pp. 493-494; and again in "Podmen vinovnyx," ibid., no. 2 (Feb. 1885), pp. 327-340.

5. The details of the case (from Leskov's point of view) are set forth in "Zakonnye vredy." Writing in 1872, Leskov says there that the incident had taken place three years before (1869). Andrei Leskov, however, dates the affair in 1870, attributing the Germans' arrogance to their pleasure at their compatriots' victories in the Franco-Prussian War (ANL, pp. 235-236). The truth could probably be ascertained from court records, but no one has dug them out. Leskov also refers elusively to the case in *Laughter and Grief*.

6. A similar Gogolian insight is attributed to Artur Benni in "An Enigmatic Man": "No noble principles can take hold among these Chichikovs and Nozdryovs" (3:368).

7. The general referred to is the Crimean War hero Stepan Aleksandrovich Khrulev (1807-1870), a "character" noted for his unconventional style,

and from whom Leskov perhaps heard the remark directly. Leskov was fond of it. He had used it before in *Laughter and Grief* (3:544); and cited it again in "Kartiny prošlogo," *Novosti i birževaja gazeta* (May 12, 1883). See ANL, p. 115.

8. "Železnaja volja" first appeared in *Krugozor,* nos. 38-44 (1876). It was not reprinted in any of Leskov's collected works, including the commodious Marks edition of 1902-1903. With assistance from Andrei Leskov, it was rescued from undeserved oblivion in 1942, when it was reprinted in the Soviet magazine *Zvezda* (no. 3-4), obviously considered appropriate grist for the Russian war propaganda mill. It has subsequently been reprinted many times. The only explanation I have seen for Leskov's exclusion of "Iron Will" from the collected works is that given by B. M. Drugov in his afterword to the separate edition of 1946, "lack of space." But this is absurd: the story is only eighty pages long, and the edition was in twelve large volumes. See B. M. Drugov, "Posleslovie," in N. S. Leskov, *Železnaja volja* (Moscow-Leningrad, 1946), p. 198.

9. The story first appeared under the title "Imperator Franc-Iosif bez ètiketa," in *Istoričeskij vestnik,* no. 1 (Jan. 1881), pp. 139-146. It was reprinted in Leskov's *Russkaja rozn'* (SPb., 1881), pp. 203-214, under the title of "Imperator Franc-Iosif i Anna Fetisovna." It acquired the title of "Plamennaja patriotka" only in the collected works.

10. Leskov did not rate "A Flaming Patriot" very high. In a letter to Ivan Aksakov, who had evidently read it in manuscript, Leskov calls it "an insignificant little story [*rasskazec ničtožnyj*] but very uncontentious." Aksakov had apparently taken Franz Josef's beer drinking as an implied criticism of the Russian emperor, who had no such "democratic" tendencies. Leskov reassured him that he had no such intention: "In the scene with the Austrian emperor you saw a great deal more than is there. [. . .] Actually, I've sewed a tail on it to shift its weight in another direction" (Dec. 17, 1880 [10:475]). The "tail" is probably the final encounter in Russia between the "author" and the maid, when the latter stresses more her disapproval of her exmistress's bad manners than her rapture at the Kaiser's "simplicity."

11. "Irodova rabota," *Istoričeskij vestnik,* no. 4 (April 1882), pp. 185-207; "Russkie dejateli v Ostzejskom krae," ibid., nos. 11, 12 (Nov., Dec. 1883), pp. 235-263, 492-519.

12. Leskov to S. N. Shubinsky, Oct. 8, 1882 (11:262).

13. "Kolyvanskij muž (Iz Ostzejskix nabljudenij)," *Knižki nedeli,* no. 12 (Dec. 1888), pp. 1-77.

14. This is the interpretation of Leonid Grossman, *N. S. Leskov* (Moscow, 1945), p. 187; and of ANL, pp. 238-239. Both of these books, however, were written either during or immediately after World War II. Andrei Leskov is perfectly aware—and the fact is emphasized in the excellent commentary to the story by A. I. Batyuto in 8:610-613—that the story is also a satire on lat-

ter-day pan-Russianism and on Leskov's erstwhile mentor, Ivan Aksakov, who had died two years earlier.

23. Russia's Spiritual Janitor

1. Jan. 4, 1893 (11:519). Earlier, Leskov had put it even more pungently. Writing of *The Little Things in a Bishop's Life*, he described it as "not a sermon, of which I am incapable and which with God's grace I hope never to undertake; it is rather the cleansing of the manure piled up by the doors of the temple. This I can do and consider my calling" (undated [1879?] letter to M. G. Peiker [10:456]).

2. "Velikosvetskij raskol; Grenvil' Val'digrev lord Redstok, ego žizn', učenie i propoved'," *Pravoslavnoe obozrenie*, nos. 9, 10 (Sept., Oct. 1876), pp. 138-178, 300-326; ibid., no. 2 (Feb. 1877), pp. 294-334; *Velikosvetskij raskol* (Lord Redstok, ego učenie i propoved'); očerk sovremennogo religioznogo dviženija v peterburgskom obščestve (Moscow, 1877; 2nd ed., SPb., 1877). The two editions in one year were evidence of the book's popularity. Some of the Orthodox hierarchs, however, saw through its camouflage. "A most crafty book," it was called by the tsar's confessor, protopresbyter V. B. Bazhanov. Ivan Šljapkin, "K biografii N. S. Leskova," *Russkaja starina*, no. 12 (Dec. 1895), p. 213.

3. On Radstock's life and teachings see Mrs. Edward Trotter, *Lord Radstock: An Interpretation and a Record* (London: Hodder & Stoughton, n.d.).

4. A. I. Klibanov, *Istorija religioznogo sektantstva v Rossi (60-ye gody XIX v.—1917 g.)* (Moscow, 1965), pp. 200-203.

5. F. M. Dostoevskij, "Lord Redstok" and "Miraži; štunda i redstokisty," originally published in *Graždanin*, March 1876, Jan. 1877. Dostoevsky's colleague and editor, Prince Meshchersky, quickly knocked off a whole novel on Radstock, *Lord Apostol* (1875). In this roman à clef, he attributed to Radstock all sorts of reprehensible acts, including charlatanism and financial chicanery.

6. F. M. Dostoevskij, *Dnevnik pisatelja za 1877 god* (Paris: YMCA Press, n.d.), p. 13.

7. "Sentimental'noe blagočestie," *Pravoslavnoe obozrenie*, no. 3 (March 1876), pp. 526-551.

8. Tolstoy to Baroness E. I. Mengden, Feb. 1875 (L. N. Tolstoj, *Polnoe sobranie sočinenij*, 62 [1953]: 143-144).

9. *Anna Karenina*, part 7, chapter 21. The self-righteous bigot, Countess Lidia Ivanovna, tortures Stiva Oblonsky by making him listen while she reads aloud in English such uplifting tracts as "Safe and Happy" and "Under the Wing" (the titles are in Radstock's spirit) and then after consulting a phony medium (spiritualism was also a fad in Petersburg at the time) persuades Karenin not to grant Anna a divorce.

10. ANL, pp. 338-343.

11. N. S. Leskov, *Velikosvetskij raskol* (Moscow, 1877), p. 38. Leskov later may have somewhat revised his opinion of Radstock, crediting him with intelligence, linguistic talent, and a "rather remarkable" knowledge of scripture. See "Čudesa i znamenija, nabljudenija, opyty, i zametki," *Cerkovno-obščestvennyj vestnik*, no. 40 (April 2, 1879); quoted ANL, p. 342. But see below, Chapter 32, note 7.

12. "Sentimental'noe blagočestie," *Pravoslavnoe*, p. 532.

13. Charles Loyson (1827-1912), an apostate French Catholic priest married to an American widow, author of many books, and later pastor of the "Gallican Catholic" church in Paris.

14. Leskov, *Velikosvetskij raskol*, p. 90; William B. Edgerton, "Leskov, Paškov, the Štundists and a Newly Discovered Letter," in Dietrich Gerhardt et al., eds., *Orbis Scriptus: Dmitrij Tschiževskij zum 70. Geburtstag* (Munich, 1966), pp. 192-193.

15. Bishop Philaret (Gumilevsky, 1805-1866), a distinguished church historian, and Leskov's friend and correspondent Father Ivan Bellyustin (1820-1890), author of a much discussed book, *A Description of the Village Clergy* (*Opisanie sel'skogo duxovenstva* [Leipzig, 1858]).

16. *Pobedonostsev* means "victory-bearer"; *lampadonostsev*, "bearer of icon-lamps."

17. "Meloči arxierejskoj žizni," *Novosti i birževaja gazeta*, nos. 236, 239, 240, 244, 248, 253, 259, 265, 272, 278, 285, 292, 298 (Sept. 14, 18, 19, 23, 28, Oct. 4, 11, 17, 25, 31, Nov. 7, 14, 20, 1878). Chapters 14, 15, 16, under the titles "Vladyčij vzgljad na voennoe krasnorečie," "Slučaj s generalom u mitropolita Filareta," and "Mitropolit Isidor v ego literaturnyx interesax," appeared in *Istoričeskij vestnik*, no. 6 (June 1880), pp. 255-267, 326-332. The appendices originally appeared as follows: "Arxierejskie ob'ezdy" under the title of "Arxierejskie vstreči" in *Novosti i birževaja gazeta*, nos. 145, 152, 159, 170 (June 9, 16, 23, July 5, 1879); "Eparxial'nyj sud" under the title of "Duxovnyj sud," ibid., nos. 153, 154, 159 (June 12, 13, 18, 1880); "Russkoe tajnobračie," ibid., no. 322 (Dec. 16, 1878), nos. 4, 7, 13, 28 (Jan. 5, 9, 15, 28, 1879). The book editions were *Meloči arxierejskoi žizni* (SPb., 1879, without the appendices); and 2nd ed., revised and enlarged (SPb., 1880). Some further revisions were made for the suppressed sixth volume of Leskov's collected works in 1889; this final version is reprinted in 6:398-623.

18. Leskov to M. G. Peiker (undated; first half of 1879?), 10:456.

19. "N. K.," *Novoe vremja*, no. 1108 (March 30, 1879), p. 3; quoted 6:665.

20. Secular name Aleksandr Krizhanovsky, died 1863; bishop of Oryol, 1844-1858.

21. 1798-1871, governor of Oryol, 1841-1849. He is mentioned many times by Leskov, notably in *Laughter and Grief*, 1871 (3:538); "A Robbery," 1887 (8:112); and "The Dead Estate," 1888 (8:451).

22. In "Pribavlenie k rasskazu o Kadetskom monastyre" (1885), Leskov

shows the consequences of a more serious challenge to the state by a bishop. Bishop Ireneus (Nesterovich, died 1864) was declared officially insane by A. S. Lavinsky, governor-general of eastern Siberia, whom he had defied, and confined to a monastery in Vologda (6:350, 657). This concept of "official insanity," first employed by Nicholas I against Pyotr Chaadaev, has been revived by the Soviet authorities for use against intellectual dissidents.

23. A. I. Faresov, "Umstvennye perelomy v dejatel'nosti N. S. Leskova," *Istoričeskij vestnik*, no. 3 (March 1916), p. 789. I. S. Aksakov to Leskov, Nov. 15, 1884.

24. Leonid Grossman, *N. S. Leskov* (Moscow, 1945), p. 240.

25. A. P. Chekhov to Maria Kiseleva, Jan. 14, 1887 (*Sobranie sočinenij v dvenadcati tomax*, 11 [Moscow, 1963]: 107).

26. In the original text identified only as N—— of P——. One of Leskov's ecclesiastical critics, Archpriest Yevgeny Popov, removed this figleaf of anonymity, spelling out the names in full, as Leskov noted caustically in a footnote to the second edition (6:465n.). Popov's book was entitled *Velikopermskaja i permskaja eparxija* (Perm, 1879). Leskov attacked Popov again in "Iz meločej arxierejskoj žizni," *Novoe vremja*, no. 1325 (Nov. 5, 1879); reprinted in 10:244-246; and "Poslednee slovo o 'Meločax' (Pis'mo v redakciju)," *Novoe vremja*, no. 1330 (Nov. 10, 1879); reprinted in 10:521.

27. The critical response is summarized, with some quotations, by S. A. Reiser in 6:664-666.

28. "Poslednee slovo o 'Meločax,' " 10:521.

29. Quoted by Leskov in "Iz meločej arxierejskoj žizni," 10:244.

30. Ibid.

31. Faresov, "Umstvennye perelomy," p. 788. I. S. Aksakov to Leskov, Jan. 4, 1881.

32. They carried on an active correspondence, only part of which has survived, between 1874 and 1881. In 1881, I. S. Aksakov apparently took umbrage at Leskov's constant efforts to besmirch the memory of Metropolitan Philaret (Drozdov) of Moscow; he may also have been offended by Leskov's angry reply, dated Jan. 7, 1881, to his criticisms of *Little Things*, though Aksakov's response was conciliatory (he still wanted Leskov to contribute to his newspaper, *Rus'*). Aksakov's letter accompanying the honorarium for "The Left-hander," published at the end of 1881, was the last for several years. In 1884 Leskov wrote Aksakov again (11:297-298), hoping to publish "The Alexandrite" in Aksakov's newspaper, but Aksakov did not take the bait. Aksakov died in 1886.

33. Leskov to I. S. Aksakov, Jan. 7, 1881; quoted 6:664 and 11:667-668.

34. Samples are quoted in 6:665.

35. P. V. Bykov, *Siluèty dalekogo prošlogo*, ed. B. P. Koz'min (Moscow-Leningrad, 1930), pp. 162-163.

36. *Izbrannye sočinenija*, ed. B. M. Drugov (Moscow-Leningrad, 1937),

pp. 237-264; *Izbrannye proizvedenija,* ed. S. M. Petrov, 2 (Petrozavodsk, 1952): 328-359.

37. Grossman, *Leskov,* p. 240.

24. A Roster of the Righteous

1. A. I. Faresov, *Protiv tečenij* (SPb., 1904), p. 51.

2. Ibid., pp. 59-60.

3. Ibid., p. 61.

4. Ibid., p. 381.

5. "Žitija kak literaturnyj istočnik," *Novoe vremja,* no. 2328 (Aug. 17, 1882), p. 2.

6. "Russkie antiki; iz rasskazov o trex pravednikax," *Eženedel'noe novoe vremja,* no. 37-38 (Sept. 20, 1879); no. 39 (Sept. 27, 1879).

7. "Tri dobrye dela; iz bylogo," *Grazdanin,* no. 14 (1876), pp. 372-376. Not included in the Soviet edition—one wonders why. It is an interesting exercise in historical comparison to try to imagine a contemporary version of the plot of "The Pygmy"—an officer in the Lubyanka prison in Moscow in 1938 asking a foreign ambassador to appeal to Stalin to save some foreign national from Yezhov's tortures.

8. "Kadetskij monastyr'," *Istoričeskij vestnik,* no. 1 (Jan. 1880), pp. 112-138; "Russkij demokrat v Pol'še; iz rasskazov o trex pravednikax," ibid., no. 3 (March 1880), pp. 533-546.

9. Judging by its original title, "Children of Cain," "Sheramur" was intended to lead off a different series: "Deti Kaina, tipičeskie raznovidnosti; očerk pervyj; Šeramur; èpizodičeskie otryvki fatal'noj istorii," *Novoe vremja,* nos. 1352, 1359, 1361, 1362, 1366 (Dec. 2, 9, 11, 12, 16, 1879).

10. *Tri pravednika i odin Šeramur* (SPb., 1880); reissued (SPb., 1886) with new title page. See 6:639n.

11. The question of Sheramur's "righteousness" is discussed, a bit naively, but with citation of further materials, in 6:645.

12. "Figura; iz vospominanij o pravednikax," *Trud,* no. 13, book 1 (July 1889), pp. 1-26.

13. The "Russian democrat" is no Polonophile. His plan is for Russia to abandon ethnic Poland entirely, but to assimilate the formerly Polish-held territories of Lithuania, Belorussia, and the Ukraine by "conquering them with the samovar," colonizing them with retired Russian officers who would settle there permanently. This story, too, was excluded from the 1956-1958 edition: the topic of Russo-Polish relations is apparently too sensitive, even today.

14. The phrase, in Church Slavonic, is apparently a transposition to the imperative of words occurring several times in the New Testament in the past tense in connection with the Last Supper and the feeding miracles of Jesus, such as Matthew 14:19: "He blessed, and *brake,* and *gave* the loaves." Leskov cites his imperative version, for instance, in his letter to Tolstoy of June 12,

1891 (11:494). Andrei Leskov has a chapter with this title (pp. 208-214), detailing some of Leskov's remarkable acts of generosity.

15. "Children of Cain" was the original title of the story. See above, note 9.

16. Besides *cher amour—černomor*, Leskov cannot resist still another pun on this name, *černomordyj*, "black-mugged," referring to the hero's copious black beard.

17. The narrator of "A Cadet Monastery" was a real person, Grigory Pokhitonov (1810-1882), whose stenographic memoirs Leskov reworked at the author's request. Leskov treated the story as if it were his own, unlike his procedure with "Spiridony-povoroty" (*Russkaja mysl'*, no. 8 [Aug. 1889], pp. 1-38), his reworking of the memoirs of the book dealer Nikolai Sveshnikov (1839-1899), which he never claimed as his. The Pokhitonov text has been preserved, but no systematic comparison with Leskov's version has been made. Apparently the changes were not very substantial. See 6:656.

18. Leskov's account may be based on reports of scenes accompanying the opening of the relics of St. Tikhon of Zadonsk in 1861, at which some 220,000 people assembled. See E. E. Golubinskij, *Istorija kanonizacii svjatyx v russkoj cerkvi* (2nd ed., Moscow, 1903); reprinted (Westmead, Farnborough, 1969), p. 182. Leskov had several other sallies on the issue of holy relics. There is one in the last chapter of *The Little Things in a Bishop's Life* (6:533-534), where Leskov speaks of relics waiting in line to be opened and even, as it were, jockeying for position. In 1894, he wrote an article entitled "Where Fake Relics Are Obtained." Because of censorship, the article had to be shortened and the title made less provocative. It appeared as "Zametka" in *Russkaja žizn'*, no. 83 (March 23, 1894); reprinted in *Izbrannye sočinenija*, ed. B. M. Èjxenbaum (Moscow-Leningrad, 1931), pp. 737-739, but not in the 1956-1958 edition. The full text, "Gde dobyvajut poddel'nye mošči," was published in *Krasnaja niva*, no. 17 (1930), p. 19.

25. Two Ties Are Unbound

1. Especially in the unfinished continuation of the autobiographical story "Javlenie duxa" (*A Ghostly Apparition*) published in ANL, pp. 353-360. The first part of the story, based on the death of Leskov's son Dmitry and his quarrels with his first wife, had appeared in *Krugozor*, no. 1 (Jan. 3, 1878). It is reprinted in ANL, pp. 101-105.

2. Leskov to Katerina Bubnova, Sept. 14, 1879; cited ANL, p. 369.

3. Ibid., May 1877; cited ANL, p. 352.

4. ANL, p. 363.

5. Andrei Leskov has little to say about his mother's whereabouts after the separation, perhaps because he considered the subject irrelevant in a biography of his father, perhaps because of his own ambivalence toward her (he alludes [pp. 363, 523] to a coolness between them) and his embarrassment about his illegitimacy. He does make clear that she continued to live in Peters-

burg for "several years" (p. 363) after the rupture; in 1885 she returned to live there again for the sake of her daughter's education (pp. 523, 526); she was still living there in 1886 (p. 385) and 1887 (p. 536). Thus Natalia Bakhareva's tale of her alleged return to her first husband, Bubnov, immediately after the separation from Leskov is evidently pure fiction. See Natal'ja Baxareva, pseud. (Natal'ja Dmitrievna Poljuškina, née Noha), "Nikolaj Semenovič Leskov (Memuary vnučki N. S. Leskova pisatel'nicy Natal'i Dmitrievny Baxarevoj)," manuscript deposited in the archives of Columbia University.

6. ANL, p. 366.
7. Aleksei Leskov to Andrei Leskov, Jan. 25, 1908; cited ANL, p. 361.
8. ANL, p. 543.
9. Ibid., p. 528.
10. Leskov to his stepdaughter, Vera Bubnova, Jan. 2, 1883; cited ANL, p. 422.
11. See above, chapter 13.
12. Leskov enumerates them in a letter to Ivan Aksakov dated Nov. 25, 1881 (11:254-255).
13. ANL, p. 366.
14. "Popovskaja čexarda i prixodskaja prixot'," *Istoričeskij vestnik*, no. 2 (Feb. 1883), p. 268.
15. "Rajskij zmej; iz meločej arxierejskoj žizni," *Novoe vremja*, no. 2131 (Feb. 2, 1882), pp. 2-3.
16. Ibid.
17. "Sinodal'nye persony; period bor'by za preobladanie, 1820-1840," *Istoričeskij vestnik*, no. 11 (Nov. 1882), p. 409.
18. "Dvorjanskij bunt v Dobrynskom prixode," *Istoričeskij vestnik*, no. 2 (Feb. 1881), p. 388.
19. 11:676. Leskov had met Filippov through Apollon Maikov in 1868, but they quarreled in the mid-1870s and remained bitter enemies until a few weeks before Leskov's death, when Filippov unexpectedly appeared in Leskov's apartment, fell on his knees, and begged Leskov's forgiveness for all the evil he had done him. Not wishing to raise him up "in royal fashion," Leskov knelt down beside him, and both men burst into tears. Though genuinely moved by the scene, Leskov at least in retrospect was aware of some inherent ironies. After the dramatic moment had passed, it was hard to find a safe topic of conversation; neither man had changed his beliefs or allegiances one iota. See A.I. Faresov, *Protiv tečenij* (SPb., 1904), pp. 137-140; ANL, pp. 660-661.
20. F. A. Ternovsky's article, "Mitropolit Filaret: ego naučnoe i obščestvennoe značenie," *Novoe vremja*, nos. 2466, 2467 (Jan. 9, 10, 1883), was commissioned by A. S. Suvorin at Leskov's instance. The furious reactions of Filippov and Pobedonostsev are described in Leskov to F. G. Lebedintsev, Jan. 22, 1883 (*Istoričeskij vestnik*, no. 10 [Oct. 1908], pp. 168-169; quoted 11:677-678).
21. Leskov to F. A. Ternovsky, March 12, 1883 (11:275).

22. ANL, p. 436; see also Faresov, *Protiv tečenij*, p. 96.

23. "Administrative Grace," written in 1893 (9:388). First published in 1934.

24. Delyanov was responsible for the dismissal from Moscow University of two liberal professors, S. A. Muromtsev in 1884 and M. M. Kovalevsky in 1887 (Leskov alludes to these episodes in "Administrative Grace," 9:388). Perhaps the most notorious outrage of this "minister of enlightenment" was his circular issued in 1887: it proclaimed that the government should endeavor to *prevent* "the children of coachmen, laundresses, petty shopkeepers and the like" from obtaining a secondary education. This circular passed into Russian folklore as the "decree about cooks' sons." Leskov responded to it with a caustic article, "Temnejuščij bereg" (*Darkening Shore*). Apparently destined for *Novoe vremja*, it was not published there and remained in manuscript until 1958, when it was printed in 11:164-170. Leskov also alludes to Delyanov's circular in "Ob odnoj pračke," *Novoe vremja*, no. 5215 (Sept. 5, 1890), p. 2.

25. *Novosti*, no. 63 (March 8, 1883); quoted 11:655.

26. "Pis'mo v redakciju (ob otčislenii N. S. Leskova 'bez prošenija' ot služby v učenom komitete Ministerstva narodnogo prosveščenija)," *Novosti*, no. 65 (March 10, 1883); reprinted 11:221-222. The letter was reprinted in two of Leskov's other outlets, *Novoe vremja*, no. 2526 (March 11, 1883), and *Gazeta A. Gatcuka*, no. 10 (March 12, 1883). See ANL, p. 437.

26. The Christmas Story

1. *Svjatočnye rasskazy* (SPb., 1886). The word *svjatočnyj* refers to the whole holiday season, *svjatki*, the "twelve days" from Christmas to Epiphany, as contrasted with *roždestvenskij*, the specific adjective for Christmas proper. Twelve stories were included in that book.

2. Sterne had long been a favorite of Leskov's. He was rereading him in this period and refers to him in a letter written on Christmas Day, 1879 (10:469).

3. "Roždestvenskij večer u ipoxondrika," *Novoe vremja*, no. 1375 (Dec. 25, 1879). Leskov's original title was "Dissolution" (*tajanie*—"thaw" would be a more usual translation, but the title refers metaphorically to the "dissolution" of religious faith). The Christmas substitute was supplied by his publisher, A. S. Suvorin, with Leskov's permission. See Leskov to Suvorin (undated; presumed Dec. 1879; quoted 6:654).

The first piece of fiction by Leskov to be specified as a "Christmas story" was "The Sealed Angel," published in the January number of *Russian Messenger* for 1873. However, though he gave it the subtitle of *roždestvenskij rasskaz*, in terms of length it qualifies as a *povest'* or "novella"; thus it is not a true "Christmas [short] story," according to the definition used here. The same remarks apply to "At the Edge of the World," which in its original magazine publication also bore the subtitle of *roždestvenskij rasskaz*, eliminated in subsequent editions.

4. Modeled on some member of the wealthy Khludov family. See Leskov's undated letter to A. S. Suvorin and S. A. Reiser's note in 6:654.

5. Dec. 25, 1879 (10:468).

6. "Čertogon," *Russkaja rozn'; očerki i rasskazy (1880-1881)* (SPb., 1881), pp. 187-202.

7. "Belyj orel; svjatočnyj rasskaz," *Novoe vremja,* no. 1735 (Dec. 25, 1880).

8. Dec. 17, 1880 (10:475).

9. For instance, Turgenev's "Song of Triumphant Love" and "Klara Milich." Andrei Leskov recalls his father's reading aloud in 1878 two of Turgenev's other ghost stories, "The Dog" and "Knock, Knock, Knock" (ANL, p. 372).

10. The governor in question is given the name P——v (7:8), from which Andrei Leskov concludes that the story is based on "something that in part perhaps really happened in Penza, during the career there of the infamous governor [Aleksandr] Panchulidzev [1789-1867]" (ANL, p. 396), who was forced into retirement after a senate investigation (7:495). This may be true, but perhaps another source is the equally infamous career in Oryol of Prince Pyotr Trubetskoy. In "A Surfeit of Gentility" (1888) Leskov describes an investigation of Trubetskoy's activities carried out by a Petersburg official named Telepnyov, which resembles the situation described in "White Eagle." As another instance of life imitating literature, Telepnyov was accompanied by two subordinate officials named Ivan Ivanovich and Ivan Nikiforovich ("Presyščenie znatnost'ju," 11:182-183).

11. Leonid Grossman. *N. S. Leskov* (Moscow, 1945), pp. 192, 249.

12. Marija Gorjačkina, *Satira Leskova* (Moscow, 1963), pp. 106-107.

13. Vsevolod Setschkareff, *Nikolai Leskov: sein Leben und sein Werk* (Wiesbaden, 1959); p. 110.

14. "Dux gospoži Žanlis; xarakternyj slučaj (Iz literaturnyx vospominanij)," *Oskolki,* nos. 49-50 (Dec. 5-19, 1881), pp. 387-390, 399-402. Leskov's unfinished story "A Ghostly Apparition" (*Javlenie duxa,* 1878) was based on his belief that there was some mystic connection between his dead son Dmitry and his live son Andrei (ANL, pp. 353-356). Andrei Leskov also recounts (pp. 350-351) an anecdote illustrating his father's willingness to believe that Andrei had seen an angel in the courtyard of their apartment house.

15. Though the princess reads Genlis in the original, in the tiny volumes of "an edition superbly printed in Paris" (7:80), Boris Bukhshtab has conclusively demonstrated (7:513) that Leskov used a Russian translation of her memoirs, an 1809 edition that must have been a rarity in Leskov's day. (Leskov reproduces from that edition misprints of several French proper names.)

16. "Moskovskij kozyr' (Malen'kij žanr)," *Gazeta A. Gatcuka,* nos. 10, 11 (March 6, 13, 1882). In 1886 the title was changed to "Štopal'ščik."

17. "Židovskaja kuvyrkalegija," *Gazeta A. Gatcuka,* nos. 33-36 (1882), pp. 579-582, 595-598, 610-614, 626-630.

18. Third in order of publication. It was originally published under the title of "Poslednee prividenie Inženernogo zamka; rasskaz," in *Novosti i birževaja gazeta,* nos. 294-295 (Nov. 5, 6, 1882). In *Svjatočnye rasskazy* the title was changed to "Prividenie v Inženernom zamke." There is evidence that the story had been written the previous year for *A. Gattsuk's Gazette,* but ran into trouble with the censorship. See note 19, below.

19. Because of the censorship, references to this event, as to the recent assassination of Alexander II, had to be made very circumspectly. Here it is called the "sudden end" of Paul I (7:110, 111). The story seems originally to have been written for *A. Gattsuk's Gazette,* for on November 15, 1881, Gattsuk wrote to Leskov that the censors were worried lest a story submitted by Leskov refer too explicitly to the "demise" of Paul I. He added that for this reason the story had been submitted to the censor, P. P. Vyazemsky. The letter is unpublished. It is preserved in the Central State Archive of Literature and Art in Moscow. I cite the "Kovalevsky notebook." See William B. Edgerton, "Missing Letters to Leskov: An Unsolved Puzzle," *Slavic Review,* no. 1 (March 1966), pp. 120-132; V. G. Zimina, "Iz arxiva N. S. Leskova," Gosudarstvennaja ordena Lenina biblioteka SSSR imeni V. I. Lenina, *Zapiski otdela rukopisej,* issue 30 (Moscow, 1968), p. 208.

20. Even the frequently hypercritical Setchkarev rates this story "ein kleines chef d'oeuvre" (Setschkareff, *Nikolai Leskov,* p. 111).

21. "Roždestvenskaja noč' v vagone (Putešestvie s nigilistom)," *Novoe vremja* no. 2453 (Dec. 25, 1882).

22. ANL, p. 382.

23. *Poverxnostnaja kommissija* (for *Verxovnaja*), *prosit' proščady,* and *rojal'noe vospitanie* (for *real'noe*), also found in "Polunoščniki." Others are *naxalkikanec iz-za Taškentu, buteršaft,* and *binamid* (for *dinamit*).

24. In Leskov's version the owner of the basket is a Jew who had been hiding under the seat to avoid paying his fare. Conceivably, therefore, the boorish "I don't care to," rather than "It's not mine," might have been designed to avoid exposing this man. But surely a more polite disclaimer would have served the purpose better. And would a Russian prosecutor be likely to help a Jew cheat the railroad?

25. "Malen'kaja ošibka," *Oskolki,* no. 43 (Oct. 22, 1883).

26. "Kartiny prošlogo: Vetrenniki," *Rossija,* nos. 10-15 (1883). In *Svjatočnye rasskazy* the title was changed to "Obman."

27. *P.s.s.,* 18:95.

28. *Satirical Stories of Nikolai Leskov* (New York, 1969), pp. 105-106

29. *P.s.s.,* 18:123.

30. Boris Eikhenbaum told William B. Edgerton in 1955 that "Deception" would be excluded (as it was) from the multivolume Soviet edition of Leskov's works "lest the Rumanians should be offended" (*Satirical Stories,* p. 106).

However, I suspect that the subject of anti-Semitism constituted a more potent taboo. Except for "Episcopal Justice," every one of Leskov's "Jewish" stories was excluded from that edition.

31. Ibid., p. 203.

32. See below, Chapter 29.

33. Literally, "The Unexchangeable Ruble." "Nerazmennyj rubl'; roždestvenskaja istorija," *Zaduševnoe slovo,* no. 8 (Dec. 24, 1883), pp. 140-147.

34. Nineteenth-century taste favored such didactic syrup. Of all Leskov's Christmas stories, this one was chosen for translation into German and featured in the Christmas number of the Berlin *Echo* for 1890, a fact of which Leskov boasted in a letter to his brother, Aleksei, Dec. 12, 1890; quoted in ANL, p. 626. An English translation by Olga Vitali (née Izvolskaya) was published in *Our World* (Dec. 1924), pp. 81-84.

35. "Zver'; roždestvenskij rasskaz," *Gazeta A. Gatcuka,* Christmas supplement (Dec. 25, 1883), pp. 1-7.

36. The name, of Greek origin, means "attendant," from *therapōn, theraps,* but Leskov doubtless punningly linked it with *thēr,* "wild beast."

37. "Otbornoe zerno; natural'naja trilogija," *Živopisnoe obozrenie,* nos. 1-3 (1884), pp. 2-4, 22-23, 33-35. In the second two installments the subtitle was changed to "original'naja trilogija."

38. Setchkarev perceives here the influence of Bret Harte's story "A Sleeping-Car Experience," referred to by name in "The Toupee Artist," written the same year. Setschkareff, *Nikolai Leskov,* p. 122n.

39. William B. Edgerton, "Leskov's Parody on Gogol': *Otbornoe zerno,*" *Lingua viget* (*Commentationes Slavicae in honorem V. Kiparsky* (Helsinki, 1965), pp. 38-43.

40. 7:280, 304. Soviet scholars have been unable to find the source of Bismarck's alleged statement. See 7:545.

41. It is amusing to observe Maria Goryachkina (*Satira Leskova* [Moscow, 1963], pp. 114-115) wax indignant at the "rapacity and rascality" of the landowner and merchant, while exculpating the peasants entirely. "The participation of the peasant," she writes, "in the dirty swindle of the merchant does not evoke the animadversion either of the author or the reader: the peasant offends nobody. He simply appropriates a part of what had been stolen by the merchant and the landowner."

42. "Staryj genij," *Oskolki,* nos. 4, 5 (1884).

43. "Žemčužnoe ožerel'e; svjatočnyj rasskaz (Posvjaščaetsja besprimernomu masteru rasskazyvat' Ivanu Fedoroviču Gorbunovu)," *Nov',* no. 5 (Jan. 1, 1885), pp. 117-125. Ivan Gorbunov (1831-1895) was a well-known actor, an acquaintance of Leskov's from the 1860s. For some reason the dedication to him was eliminated from the book version.

44. "Unizitel'nyj torg," *Istoričeskij vestnik* (1885). The article deals with the "Magdalene refuge" for repentant prostitutes established in Kiev under the patronage of Princess Vasilchikova. The reforms were a sham. The "dogs"

invariably "returned to their vomit," in Leskov's application of the biblical phrase (Proverbs 26:11), meaning that the prostitutes, often with the connivance of their new soldier husbands, returned to their time-honored profession.

45. "The Bugbear" was identified as a Christmas story only retrospectively, and perhaps incorrectly, through a lapse of memory, in Leskov to A. S. Suvorin, Nov. 9, 1887 (11:357); the text itself bears no trace of any such classification. "Robbery," in its magazine publication, *Knižki Nedeli*, no. 12 (Dec. 1887), p. 1, bore the subtitle "Svjatočnyj rasskaz," but this designation was eliminated in the collected works.

46. "Pod Roždestvo obideli," *Peterburgskaja gazeta*, no. 354 (Dec. 25, 1890); "Pustopljasy," *Severnyj vestnik*, no. 1 (Jan. 1893).

27. Left, Left, Left

1. "Skaz o tul'skom kosom Levše i o stal'noj bloxe (Cexovaja legenda)," *Rus'*, nos. 49, 50, 51 (Oct. 17, 24, 31, 1881), pp. 20-23, 19-21. A separate edition was published the following year under the title of *Skaz o tul'skom Levše i o stal'noj bloxe (Cexovaja legenda)* (SPb., 1882).

2. "Levša (Skaz o tul'skom kosom Levše i o stal'noj bloxe)." The question of the final or canonical title of this work, as of its canonical text, is confused by the fact that in 1894, the last year of Leskov's life, the publisher M. M. Stasyulevich brought out a new book edition of the story under yet another title: *Stal'naja bloxa: skaz o tul'skom Levše i o stal'noj bloxe (Cexovaja legenda)* (SPb., 1894). According to accepted principles of textology, this title and text would be considered canonical, since they were the last to appear in the author's lifetime. Except for its title, however, this 1894 edition reproduced exactly the separate edition of 1882, ignoring the changes Leskov had made for the collected works. Since many of those changes had been substantial, incorporating Leskov's efforts to defend himself against critics, it seems inconceivable that in 1894 he would have chosen to ignore these emendations and revert to the 1882 text. The presumption is, therefore, that the use of the 1882 edition was a mistake of Stasyulevich's, that Leskov himself did not supervise the 1894 edition, and that therefore the 1889 text from the collected works should be regarded as the final one. The point is well argued by Boris Bukhshtab in 7:499.

3. Translators have also been capricious with this title. Variations include: "The Steel Flea" (Hapgood; Deutsch-Yarmolinsky; Edgerton); "The Left-handed Artificer" (Magarshack); "Lefty; Being the Tale of the Cross-eyed Lefty of Tula and the Steel Flea" (Hanna). Apart from the title, the best translation is Edgerton's; Magarshack's and Hapgood's are the least satisfactory.

4. May 12, 1881; quoted 7:499-500.

5. It was literally buried there. Omitted from the collected works, it was not reprinted until 1958.

6. *Delo*, no. 6 (June 1882), p. 102.

7. The critical response is summarized in B. Buxštab, "Ob istočnikax 'Levši' N. S. Leskova," *Russkaja literatura*, no. 1 (1964), p. 50.

8. Leskov to S. N. Shubinsky, Sept. 19, 1887 (11:348).

9. "Ob Irodovoj temnice (Pis'mo v redakciju)," *Novoe vremja*, no. 4962 (Dec. 20, 1889); reprinted 11:242-243.

10. S. A. Zybin, "Proisxoždenie oružejnič'ej legendy o tul'skom kosom Levše i o stal'noj bloxe," *Oružejnyj sbornik*, no. 1 (1905), section 2, pp. 1-58. As B. Bukhshtab has shown ("Ob istočnikax," p. 51), Zybin must have used either the book edition of 1882 or its 1894 reprint, for he took no account of the changes Leskov made in 1889, nor of any of his previous disclaimers. Zybin continues to take literally Leskov's "I transcribed" statement.

11. ANL, p. 372.

12. Ibid., p. 373.

13. È. S. Litvin, "Fol'klornye istočniki 'Skaza o tul'skom kosom Levše i o stal'noj bloxe' N. S. Leskova," *Russkij fol'klor: materialy i issledovanija*, 1 (Moscow-Leningrad, 1956): 125-134; Buxštab, "Ob istočnikax."

14. In 1947 Zybin's hypotheses were reiterated, without any new evidence, by Viktor Šklovskij, "Ob odnoj cexovoj legende," *Ogonek*, no. 19 (1947), p. 16.

15. Buxštab, "Ob istocnikax," pp. 58-59.

16. *Russkij vestnik*, book 1 (1814), p. 66; cited in Litvin, "Fo'klornye," p. 133. The report was later reprinted in *Russkaja starina*, no. 3 (March 1905), p. 712, under the title "Rasskaz kazaka Aleksandra Zemlenuxina grafu M. I. Platovu, zapisannyj dežurnym podpolkovnikom Krasnokutskim."

17. [S. N. Glinka], "Ot izdatelja," *Russkij vestnik*, part 2, no. 4 (1808), pp. 117-118; quoted in Buxštab, "Ob istocnikax," p. 53.

18. "V. B." [Vladimir Burnašov], "Il'ja Junicyn," *Severnaja pčela*, no. 78 (April 6, 1834); quoted in Buxštab, "Ob istočnikax," pp. 60-61.

19. "Pervenec bogemy v Rossii," *Istoričeskij vestnik*, no. 6 (June 1888), pp. 534-564. V. Burnashov is also mentioned in "The Cattle-pen" (9:365). Incidentally, Burnashov was guilty of the crime of which Leskov was falsely accused, writing on assignment from the secret police.

20. I am indebted to Alexis Emerson for calling this parallel to my attention. Like most Russians of his generation and the one before, Leskov was well acquainted with Hoffmann's work. He mentions Hoffman specifically in letters in connection with details of technique in "The Devil's Puppets" (11:431) and "The Rabbit Warren" (11:606).

21. In the original, magazine version Platov only "grabbed the lefthander by the hair and began to yank him about." In the 1882 text Leskov changed this to "began to yank him this way and that so that tufts went flying." See 7:44, 498.

22. This is a quotation from the story, an example of the narrator's linguistic oddities. The Russians conventionally referred to the four basic arith-

metical processes as *pravila*, "rules." But to speak of the "four rules of *addition*" is nonsense.

23. *Otečestvennye zapiski*, no. 6 (June 1882), section 2, p. 257; quoted 7:502. The last phrase (7:48) is the ditty sung by the lefthander as he careens drunkenly through Europe, nourished only by vodka. It combines a nonsense, tra-la-la refrain from Russian folk songs with his distortion of *c'est très joli*. The last word is also perhaps contaminated with Russian *žulik*, "crook."

24. M. S. Gorjačkina, *Satira Leskova* (Moscow, 1963), p. 76.

25. *Pravda* (Feb. 17, 1959); cited in Gorjačkina, *Satira*, p. 77.

26. Gorjačkina, *Satira*, p. 75.

27. Ibid., p. 72.

28. *Polškiper*, a malapropism for *podškiper*, literally "subskipper," in other words, "first mate." William B. Edgerton's equivalent: "thirst mate."

29. A folk etymology for *dokumenty*, "documents," contaminated with *tugoj*, "tight, stiff, tough," and perhaps also *pergament*, "parchment."

30. The original has a quaint rhyming formula: *xot' i šuba ovečkina, tak duša čelovečkina* (7:57), which we might paraphrase, "Though calloused his hands, yet his soul is a man's."

31. Oct. 26, 1881 (11:252).

32. For example, "Leskov o russkom narode," *Novoe vremja*, no. 2224 (May 30, 1882); partly quoted 7:502-503.

33. Gorjačkina, *Satira*, p. 74.

34. Valentina Gebel', *N. S. Leskov; v tvorčeskoj laboratorii* (Moscow, 1945), p. 36.

35. *Vestnik Evropy*, no. 7 (July 1882), wrapper; cited 7:503.

36. " 'The Flea' is too Russian and hardly translatable (because of its language)"; Leskov to K. A. Grehwe, Oct. 26, 1888 (11:395). "If you translate 'The Lefthander,' you'll be the 'foremost magician' "; Leskov to Grehwe, Nov. 29, 1888 (11:400). "It will be hard for you to cope with 'The Lefthander and the Flea.' Here knowledge of colloquial German is not enough. What will you do with the sound effects and the plays on words: 'kleveton' instead of feuilleton [the loanword *fel'eton* contaminated with *kleveta*, "slander"], 'spiral' instead of *spertyj vozdux* ["stuffy air," a folk etymology from *spirat'*, "to crush," confused with *spiral* (coil) and also perhaps with some echo of Latin *spirare*. It is not clear whether this was a genuine folk formation or was invented by Leskov], 'dosaditel'naja ukušetka' [in the story the form is *dosadnaja ukušetka*, the "couch of vexation" on which Platov lies; *couchette* is contaminated with *ukusit'*, "to bite"], etc.? Of course something will come of it, but the general tone of such a piece cannot be conveyed in another language" (Leskov to Grehwe, Dec. 5, 1888 [11:405]).

37. Some Soviet commentators, for instance, Gebel (*Leskov*, p. 197), disapprove of such fun for fun's sake.

38. For example, *melkoskop* for *mikroskop*, "microscope," combining

melkij "small"; *dolbica* (for *tablica*) *umnoženija*, "multiplication table," combining *dolbit'* "to drill, to learn by rote"; *buremetr* for *barometr*, "barometer," combining *burja*, "storm."

39. Many of these criticisms are cited or summarized in Gebel' pp. 194-197. Leskov's critics included Dostoevsky and Tolstoy.

40. Oct. 26, 1881 (11:251-252).

41. The rope from which the heavy Timofei Mikhailov was to be hanged broke twice under his weight, and he crashed down, hurting himself, and then had to mount the scaffold again. When he heard this story, Leskov reminded some visitors that a similar mishap had occurred in 1826, at the executions of the five Decembrists, and of Muravyov's bitter remark, "Even this we manage not to do properly." See ANL, p. 401.

42. Ibid.

43. Ibid.; also A. I. Faresov, *Protiv tečenij* (SPb., 1904), p. 312.

44. So far no one has attempted to uncover the real personalities alluded to in this conte à clef. I have not done so systematically either, but I suspect that the "Hapfrau" may refer to Princess Yekaterina Dolgorukaya, later Yurievskaya, the mistress and subsequently the morganatic wife of Alexander II. Several memoirists assert that her influence with the emperor was used to obtain lucrative railway concessions for her confederates. See E. M. Feoktistov, *Vospominanija; za kulisami politiki i literatury*, ed. Ju. G. Oksman (Leningrad, 1929), pp. 307-309; "Rasskazy o Romanovyx v zapisi P. I. Barteneva," *Golos minuvšego*, nos. 7-9 (July-Sept. 1918), pp. 228-229.

45. *Propuganda*, combining "propaganda" with *pugat'*, "to frighten"; *kvazimorda*, Hugo's Quasimodo plus Russian *morda*, "ugly face"; *bezbel'e*, *déshabille* interpreted as *bez*, "without," plus *bel'ë*, "underwear."

28. Southern Memories

1. Lebedintsev's letters to Leskov are preserved in the Central State Archive of Literature and Art in Moscow, but have not been published. See William B. Edgerton, "Missing Letters to Leskov: An Unsolved Puzzle," *Slavic Review*, no. 1 (March 1966), p. 124; V. G. Zimina, "Iz arxiva N. S. Leskova," Gosudarstvennaja ordena Lenina biblioteka SSSR imeni V. I. Lenina, *Zapiski otdela rukopisej*, issue 30 (Moscow, 1968), p. 208.

2. Sept. 7, 1882, in V. V. Danilov, "K biografii N. S. Leskova," *Istoričeskij vestnik*, no. 10 (Oct. 1908), p. 163. The rhymed phrase in the original runs, "esli 'bogomol'noj našej dure, sliškom čopornoj cenzure' èto ne ponravitsja." It is a slightly garbled quotation from Pushkin's mildly obscene poem, "Car' Nikita žil kogda-to" (1822).

3. The distinction here is hard to reproduce in English. To avoid the official ecclesiastical term *cudotvorec*, "wonder-worker," translating Greek *thaumatourgos*, a category of sainthood, Leskov uses an unsuffixed form, *čudotvor*, which he apparently coined.

4. Oct. 14, 1882 (Danilov, "K biografii," p. 165). In Lebedintsev's reply to this letter, dated Oct. 20, 1882, he expressed a preference for *čudotvory* over *antiki*, but added, "as the censorship will dictate." (I cite the "Kovalevsky notebook.") In subsequent correspondence, however, written before the work had been submitted to the censors, Leskov refers to the work as "antiki." (See, for example, Leskov to Lebedintsev, Nov. 12, 1882 [Danilov, "K biografii," p. 167].) The title, therefore, has remained "Pečerskie antiki," apparently by the author's choice, not the censors'. Soviet editors are doubtless correct in leaving the title thus, despite their usual textological principle of undoing changes clearly made solely to appease the tsarist censorship.

5. Leskov to Lebedintsev, Nov. 12, 1882 (Danilov, "K biografii," p. 166).

6. Leskov to Ternovsky, Nov. 12, 1882 (11:267).

7. See Boris Bukhshtab's commentary in 7:523.

8. "Pečerskie antiki," *Kievskaja starina*, nos. 2, 3, 4 (Feb., March, April 1883), pp. 235-268, 493-527, 691-708. The omitted introduction is quoted in 7:522.

9. See above, chapter 3.

10. Leskov's correspondence with Lebedintsev, for instance, contains references to both Berlinsky and Botvinovsky as real people whom Lebedintsev had also known. Andrei Leskov also unearthed a corroborative reference to Berlinsky in the memoirs of L. G. Dejč, *Počemu ja stal revoljucionerom* (Petrograd, 1921), pp. 12-13. See N. S. Leskov, *Izbrannye sočinenija* (Moscow, 1946), pp. 457-458.

11. D. S. Mirsky, *A History of Russian Literature*, ed. Francis J. Whitfield (New York, 1949), p. 93.

12. Boris Drugov, *N. S. Leskov; očerk tvorčestva* (Moscow 1957), p. 87.

13. This scene was based on a personal experience of Leskov's, recounted orally to a group of friends. See F. G. de la Bart, "Literaturnyj kružok 90-x godov," *Izvestija obščestva slavjanskoj kul'tury*, vol. 2, book 1 (Moscow, 1912), p. 18.

14. As B. Bukhshtab points out in his commentary (7:533), in *A Decrepit Clan* (5:83) Leskov had attributed the same idea to Voltaire.

15. Confusing art with journalism, Leskov included in the text of "Pechersk Eccentrics" (7:196-197) his personal Old Believer refrain, already repeated many times and filled with accusations, self-justification, and self-pity. He had been unfairly reviled for rejecting the views of the late Afanasy Shchapov, the populist historian who had regarded the Old Believers as potential revolutionaries. Yet he, Leskov, and his mentor in these matters, Pavel Melnikov (Pechersky), had been proved right, while a radical such as Shchapov had done the Old Believers great harm by inciting the government to persecute them. In life Leskov may have been correct, but in art he was surely mistaken to insert this alien lump into a beautiful story.

16. Vsevolod Setschkareff, *N. S. Leskov: Sein Leben und sein Werk* (Wiesbaden, 1959), p. 124.

17. "Starinnye psixopaty," *Nov'*, nos. 8, 9 (Feb. 15, March 1, 1885), pp. 626-633, 96-110. The story belongs to the series *Rasskazy kstati*, but has been treated here for purposes of juxtaposition with "Pechersk Eccentrics."

18. See letter to Leskov from the publisher of *Nov'*, Mavriky Volf, dated Feb. 1, 1885, and obviously referring to this story: "In 'Stories à propos' by demand of the censorship the frankness must be reduced." (I cite the "Kovalevsky notebook.") B. Bukhshtab points out (7:565) that in preparing the text for the collected works Leskov evidently restored many of these "frank" passages, which had been "reduced" to suit the censors.

19. As B. Bukhshtab has shown (7:565), there is something wrong with the text of "Ancient Psychopaths," even in the collected works. What promises to be a major episode in the plot, the "tragic story" (Leskov's phrase) of Vishnevsky's fifteen-year-old concubine, Hapka Petrunenko, is never told, though it is explicitly promised at the end of chapter 6. Bukhshtab assumes that the censorship would not allow Leskov to tell Hapka's story (as he suggests, she probably committed suicide); but it seems equally possible that the omission was simply carelessness on Leskov's part. In revising the text for the 1889 edition, he may have forgotten to restore the cut made by the 1885 censors.

29. Abraham the Hebrew

1. The bulk of this chapter is a condensed version of my article "Theodore the Christian Looks at Abraham the Hebrew: Leskov and the Jews," *California Slavic Studies*, 7 (Berkeley and Los Angeles, 1973): 65-98.

2. "Rakušanskij melamed; rasskaz na bivuake," originally in *Russkij vestnik*, no. 3 (March 1878), pp. 291-325; cited here from *P.s.s.*, 14:130-165. I have tried to approximate Leskov's use of the Czech word for "Austrian," *rakušanský*, incomprehensible to most Russians, by giving the country its German name in translating the title into English. "Židovskaja kuvyrkalegija, povest'; ob odnom kromčanine i o trex židovinax," *Gazeta A. Gatcuka*, nos. 33-36 (1882), pp. 579-582, 595-598, 610-614, 626-630; cited here from *P.s.s.*, 18:140-168.

3. *P.s.s.*, 14:134. I have not been able to discover the identity of "Lord Beaconsfield's niece." Lord Beaconsfield had no niece, in the strict sense of the word (his sole nephew, Coningsby Disraeli, was only a child and did not marry until much later); the reference must be to a more distant relation.

4. Leskov to N. A. Lyubimov, March 8, 1878 (10:453-454).

5. *P.s.s.*, 14:138.

6. "Religioznye obrjady evreev," *Peterburgskaja gazeta*, nos. 244, 245, 252, 254, 255 (1880), nos. 1, 8, 14, 20, 26, 38 (1881); "Obrjady i sueverija evreev," ibid., no. 68 (1881); "U evreev," ibid., no. 251 (1884); "Evrejskaja gracija," ibid., no. 265 (1884); "Radostnyj den' u evreev," ibid., no. 268 (1884) "Religioznaja illjuminacija u evreev," ibid., no. 348 (1884). Unfortunately, all these articles were inaccessible to me. Their tone is described as one of "abso-

lutely conscientious impartiality" by V. Vodovozov in *Evrejskaja ènciklo-pedija*, vol. 10 (SPb., n.d.), cols. 415-418. Curiously, Leskov originally offered them to the rabidly anti-Semitic *New Times*. See Leskov to A. S. Suvorin, Dec. 25, 1879; and to S. N. Khudekov, Nov. 26, 1880 (10:468-469, 473-474). There Leskov advertises the articles as "gay and unmalicious" (p. 473).

    7. *P.s.s.*, 14:164.

    8. Ibid., 18:140.

    9. Ibid.

    10. A prominent Russian naval officer and statesman (1754-1845).

    11. *P.s.s.*, 14:145.

    12. Ibid., p. 148.

    13. Ibid., p. 147. Many years before, in an article in *Contemporary Medicine* in which he had taken up the theme of Jewish conscription, Leskov had reported that young *Russians* hoping to be medically disqualified for military service would appear at the physical examination with bloody ram's intestines protruding from their anuses. See "Neskol'ko slov o vračax rekrutskix prisutstvij," *Sovremennaja medicina*, no. 36 (Sept. 15, 1860), pp. 633-645.

    14. *P.s.s.*, 14:157.

    15. Ibid., p. 167.

    16. "The Melamed of Österreich" was included in *Russkaja rozn'* (1881) and in the collected works; "Yid Somersault," in *Svjatočnye rasskazy* (1886) and in the collected works.

    17. "Pervenec bogemy v Rossii," *Istoričeskij vestnik*, no. 6 (June 1888), p. 559.

    18. Another possibility is that Leskov was recommended by his immediate superior in the Ministry of Education, Aleksandr I. Georgievsky, who was a member of the Pahlen Commission and an advocate of equal rights for Jews (Louis Greenberg, *The Jews in Russia* [New Haven, 1944]: 1:36, 2:103). However, Leskov and Georgievsky were on far from cordial terms (ANL, pp. 425-428), and Leskov was abruptly dismissed from his post in the ministry that same year.

    19. ANL, pp. 465-466.

    20. Greenberg, *The Jews in Russia*, 2:130.

    21. The edition I used was N. S. Leskov, *Evrei v Rossii; neskol'ko zamečanij po evrejskomu voprosu* (Petrograd, 1919), with an introduction by the noted Russo-Jewish historian, Yuly I. Gessen (Hessen). This edition has recently been reproduced photographically (New York, 1969). The title of the original edition, however, was in the singular: *Evrej v Rossii*.

    22. *Evrei v Rossii*, p. 29.

    23. Ibid., p. 96.

    24. The official title of the Pahlen Commission was "High Commission for the Reexamination of Laws Currently in Force concerning the Jews in the Empire" (*Vysšaja kommissija dlja peresmotra dejstvujuščix o evrejax v Imperii*

zakonov). It was formed by imperial decree in 1883 and dissolved in 1888. Its unofficial name is taken from its chairman during most of this period, Count and Senator K. I. Pahlen (Palen). See *Evrejskaja ènciklopedija*, vol. 5, cols. 862-863.

25. "Uxa bez ryby," *Nov'*, no. 7 (Feb. 1, 1886), pp. 352-358. Not included in any collected works. In the preface to his excellent translation of this story (*Satirical Stories*, pp. 203-204), William B. Edgerton interprets Solomon's act, more benevolently than I would, as "a maneuver that brilliantly combines philanthropy and economic self-defense with poetic justice."

26. "Skazanie o Fedore-xristianine i o druge ego Abrame-židovine," *Russkaja mysl'*, no. 12 (Dec. 1886), pp. 1-23.

27. *P.s.s.*, 30:92.

28. Ibid., p. 111.

29. Ibid.

30. Leskov to K. A. Grehwe, Oct. 26, 1888 (11:395).

31. Leskov to V. G. Chertkov, Jan. 28, 1887 (11:329).

32. Jan. 15, 1887 (L. N. Tolstoj, *Polnoe sobranie šocinenij*, 86 (1937): 12-13n).

33. Jan. 23, 1887 (ibid., p. 18).

34. V. G. Chertkov to Tolstoy, Feb. 9, 1887 (ibid., p. 26n).

35. Leskov to V. G. Chertkov, Jan. 28, 1887 (11:329).

36. Feb. 13, 1887 (Tolstoj, *Polnoe*, p. 28).

37. *Skazanie o Fedore-xristianine i o druge ego Abrame-židovine* (Moscow: A. A. Levenson, 1887).

38. Leskov to V. G. Chertkov, Nov. 4, 1887 (11:355).

39. June 12, 1888 (*Literaturnoe nasledstvo*, books 22-24 [1935], p. 537; cited from 11:712).

40. Cited from 11:729.

41. May 28, 1888 (*Literaturnoe nasledstvo*, books 22-24, p. 534; cited from 11:729).

42. *K. P. Pobedonoscev i ego korrespondenty*, vol. 1, book 2 (Moscow, 1923), p. 851; cited from 11:729.

43. Leskov to K. A. Grehwe, Dec. 5, 1888 (11:404-405). I must register here my disagreement with what seems to me an excessively favorable account of Leskov's various treatments of Jewish themes in William B. Edgerton, "Nikolai Leskov," *Encyclopaedia Judaica*, vol. 11 (Jerusalem, 1971), col. 46.

30. The "People" in Retrospect

1. "Tupejnyj xudožnik; rasskaz na mogile," originally in an issue of *Xudožestvennyj žurnal* (no. 2, Feb. 1883) dedicated to the twenty-second anniversary of the Emancipation. The magazine version had a slightly altered inscription: "St. Petersburg. February 19, 1883. The day of the liberation of the serfs and the Saturday for remembering the departed" (cited 7:538).

2. The connection of these two stories was noted by Leonid Grossman (*N.*

S. Leskov [Moscow, 1945], p. 190) and is explored by B. M. Drugov (*N. S. Leskov* [Moscow, 1957], pp. 76-77).

3. The name Kamensky comes from *kamen'*, "rock"; Skalinsky from *skala*, "crag."

4. Field Marshal Count Mikhail Fedotovich Kamensky (1738-1809) and his sons, Counts Sergei Mikhailovich (1771-1835) and Nikolai Mikhailovich (1779-1811). The historical inconsistencies are analyzed by Boris Bukhshtab in 7:538-539.

5. In these examples Leskov inaccurately invokes literary references from Heine and Bret Harte. See B. Bukhshtab's notes in 7:538-539 and also his interesting comments on Leskov's apparently unconscious distortion of the plot of Harte's story "A Sleeping-Car Experience" in "Ob istočnikax 'Levši' N. S. Leskova," *Russkaja literatura*, no. 1 (Jan. 1964), p. 56.

6. 7:231. Leskov added this phrase in 1890 in revising the story for the collected works. See 7:538.

7. "Pugalo; rasskaz dlja junošestva," *Zaduševnoe slovo*, nos. 10, 11 (1885). The subtitle was dropped in the collected works.

8. Andrei Leskov (ANL, pp. 52-54) points out some minor distortions of historical fact.

9. 8:7; italics mine. The phrases "in charge of" and "principal staff headquarters" as applied to a demon imply adult derision of childish superstition.

10. Vsevolod Setschkareff, *N. S. Leskov* (Wiesbaden, 1959), p. 105.

11. "Vladyčnyj sud" (6:125); "Russkie demonomany," *Russkaja rozn'* (SPb., 1881), p. 292. A letter from Ostromyslensky to Leskov is cited in the "Kovalevsky notebook."

12. Nov. 9, 1887 (11:357-358). Although it contains Christmas references, "The Bugbear" was not "published as a Christmas story," but ran serially between March and July. A. S. Suvorin apparently agreed to publish "The Bugbear" in the "cheap library," but for unknown reasons the edition never appeared (11:713).

13. "Judol'; iz istoričeskix vospominanij," *Sbornik "Nivy"*, 2 (June 1892): 553-634.

14. In the original magazine version the story bore the subtitle "From [my] historical reminiscences," changed in the collected works to "A Rhapsody."

15. Arcadius Kahan, "Natural Calamities and Their Effect upon the Food Supply in Russia," *Jahrbücher für Geschichte Osteuropas*, no. 3 (Sept. 1968), pp. 353-377.

16. Leskov to Vasily L. Ivanov, Aug. 7, 1892, in A. I. Faresov, "Umstvennye perelomy v dejatel'nosti N. S. Leskova," *Istoričeskij vestnik*, no. 3 (March 1916), p. 812.

17. "O 'kvakerejax'; Post-scriptum k 'Judoli'," *Sbornik "Nivy"*, no. 10 (Oct. 1892), pp. 21-29. For translation and commentary see William B. Edgerton, "Leskov on Quakers in Russia," *Bulletin of the Friends' Historical Association*, vol. 40, no. 1 (Spring 1951).

18. See William B. Edgerton, "The Intellectual Development of a Literary

Nonconformist" (Ph.D. dissertation, Columbia University, 1954), pp. 32-36, for further details on the Scotts. Astashev's documents were also used for "Sibirskie kartinki XVIII veka," *Vestnik Evropy,* no. 3 (March 1893).

19. ANL, pp. 33, 342.

20. "Produkt prirody," *Put'-doroga; naučno-literaturnyj sbornik v pol'zu Obščestva dlja vspomeščestvovanija nuždajuščimsja pereselencam* (SPb., 1893).

21. M. S. Gorjačkina, *Satira Leskova* (Moscow, 1963), p. 111.

22. A. I. Faresov, *Protiv tečenij* (SPb., 1904), p. 65; in the original the last word in this statement is *nekuda,* the title of the Leskov novel that I have translated as *No Way Out.*

23. Ibid., p. 21.

24. Besides Scott's use of the phrase in the text, the title is derived from the Russian translation of Carlyle's *French Revolution,* quoted as an epigraph. In the English original the phrase is "outburst of Nature" (referring to a "mob"), which does not work well in Leskov's context.

25. 9:351. The younger Semyonov, a replica of his father, had been amusing himself with that woman.

26. Leskov to M. O. Menshikov, Aug. 3, 1893 (11:556).

27. "Zagon," *Knižki Nedeli,* no. 11 (Nov. 1893).

28. Leskov to L. N. Tolstoy, Nov. 1, 1893.

29. Ibid., Oct. 8, 1893 (L. N. Tolstoj, *Perepiska s russkimi pisateljami* [Moscow, 1962], p. 573).

30. In his notes to the first publication of this letter, in *Pis'ma Tolstogo i k Tolstomu* (Moscow, 1928), p. 148, S. P. Shesterikov explained this title as a reference to Menshikov's signed article, "Dve pravdy," *Knižki Nedeli,* nos. 4-5 (April-May 1893), which contained a contrasting analysis of conservatism and liberalism. More plausible is the more recent identification of the title, by S. Rozanova in her notes to Tolstoy's correspondence (*Perepiska* p. 574), as referring to an anonymous article, "Kitajskaja stena," from the weekly newspaper *Nedelja,* no. 37 (Sept. 12, 1893). It seems odd, however, that in a letter to Menshikov dated Oct. 18, 1893 (11:560), Leskov refers, as his inspiration for "The Cattle-pen," to "articles"—in the plural—from *Nedelja* "on the Chinese wall" and does not mention that he knew at least one of these "articles" to be by his addressee.

31. In the text Leskov attributes the phrase "Chinese wall" not to Menshikov but to a speech given in September 1893 at a session of the Society for the Promotion of Russian Industry and Trade: "Russia must stand apart, forget the existence of other western European states, and *separate herself from them by a Chinese wall*" (9:356; Leskov's italics).

32. Leskov to L. N. Tolstoy, Oct. 8, 1893 (*Pis'ma Tolstogo,* p. 146).

33. It is a curious fact that Thünen's book was published in a new, full Russian translation in 1926: apparently its arguments were felt to be useful as supports for Stalin's theory of "socialism in one country."

34. Nov. 1, 1893 (11:567-568).
35. July 10, 1893 (L. N. Tolstoj, *Polnoe sobranie sočinenij*, 66 [1953]: 366).
36. Dec. 10, 1893 (ibid., p. 445).
37. Dec. 14, 1893 (11:569).
38. Leskov had discussed this subject a decade earlier in two newspaper articles: "O krest'janskix vkusax," *Novosti i birževaja gazeta*, no. 58 (Feb. 28, 1884); and "V saže i v kopoti (À propos des bottes)," ibid., no. 107 (April 19, 1884). The latter article contains anecdotal material used in the first part of "The Cattle-pen," though less effectively presented.
39. 9:366-367. Judging by the material adduced by A. I. and S. I. Gruzdev in 9:623, Leskov's source may not have been the (perhaps mythical?) pamphlet by Burnashov, but an old medical handbook by Osip Kameneckij, *Kratkoe nastavlenie o lečenii boleznej prostymi sredstvami* (9th ed., SPb., 1864), containing a section, "On the use of shiny soot," that indeed specified an important medicinal distinction between soot scraped upward and soot scraped downward.
40. Faresov, *Protiv tečenij*, p. 253.
41. Ibid., p. 265.
42. Actually Yefim had already spent two years in Leskov's storehouse, awaiting literary exploitation. As early as 1891 Leskov had written to Tolstoy with a description of this ex-soldier, "hypocritical, insolent, and vile," as a typical agent of "Russification" in the Baltic area (July 12, 1891 [11:494-495]). At that time, however, Yefim had apparently not yet begun his "religious" career. The satirical section on Yefim was apparently the first part of "The Cattle-pen" to be written. On Sept. 3, 1893, Leskov wrote to Menshikov that he would soon send *The Week* a "Mereküla study" (Mereküla was the resort Leskov frequented), to be called "At the Pig Trough" (11:558).
43. Faresov, *Protiv tečenij*, p. 66.
44. Ibid., p. 288.

31. Other People in Retrospect

1. "Zametki neizvestnogo," *Gazeta A. Gatcuka*, nos. 2, 5, 9, 10, 11, 12, 13, 14 (1884). The magazine received a "first warning" from the censorship for the sections in numbers 9, 10, 11, and a "second warning" for number 14, in which Gattsuk had not only continued to publish the offending series, but had inserted an editorial note objecting to the censor's report that his magazine was displaying an "indubitably harmful attitude." A third warning meant suspension of the magazine, and so "Notes in an Unknown Hand" came to a sudden end, with the "to be continued" in number 14. Three additional chapters, ready in manuscript at the time of the second warning, were not published until after the Revolution. See below, note 3. For a more detailed account of the censorship history see Andrei Leskov's afterword to the reprint of seven of the "Notes" in *Zvezda*, no. 7 (July 1935), pp. 224-226.

2. "O Petuxe i ego detjax" and "Prostoe sredstvo," *Niva*, nos. 51-52 (1917). An additional chapter, "Preusilennoe stesnenie v temnoe vremja protivnoe proizvodit," correctly placed before "O Petuxe i ego detjax" in volume 7(195), was first published in ibid., no. 1 (1918).

3. Leonid Grossman, for instance (*N. S. Leskov* [Moscow, 1945], p. 241), says that "the satirical element, as usual with Leskov, is evasive and not definite." He further quotes N. S. Pleshchunov ("Zametki o stile povestej Leskova," in A. V. Bagrij, ed., *Literaturnyj seminarij*, 6 [Baku, 1928]: 52): "There is a sort of ambiguity, unclarity in the work. [The author] plays tricks and while trying to be serious is essentially smirking." I should mention that Grossman was taken severely to task for his gross misestimate of Leskov's satires by Maria Goryachkina (*Satira Leskova* [Moscow, 1963], p. 6). Goryachkina (pp. 88-92) correctly credits the anticlerical virulence of "Zametki neizvestnogo," though she reduces his message to the standard Soviet clichés.

4. "Grabež; svjatočnyj rasskaz," *Knižki "Nedeli"*, no. 12 (Dec. 1887), pp. 1-52. The subtitle "A Christmas Story" was dropped in the collected works.

5. Vsevolod Setschkareff, *N. S. Leskov* (Wiesbaden, 1959), pp. 122-123.

6. ANL, pp. 89-90.

7. N. S. Leskov, *Izbrannye proizvedenija* (Moscow, 1945), p. 460.

8. Leskov to V. M. Lavrov, Nov. 24, 1887 (11:358-359). Trubetskoy is Prince Pyotr Ivanovich Trubetskoy (1798-1871), governor of Oryol from 1841 to 1849, who appears in several of Leskov's other reminiscential works, including *The Little Things in a Bishop's Life* and "The Dead Estate," as a living symbol of capricious tyranny and brutality. The editor of volume 11 (I. Ya. Aizenshtok) fails to identify Kurilenko. From the context one would guess that he was police chief in Oryol at that time, the prototype of Tsyganok in the story. Earlier, on October 30, 1887, Leskov had written Lavrov that the plot was based on the "story of Kastovsky (1837)" (11:355), a reference also left by Aizenshtok without any explanation. This was probably an actual criminal case in Oryol, possibly one in which Leskov's father was involved. For some reason the story was not accepted by Lavrov for *Russian Thought*, and Leskov gave it instead to Pavel Gaideburov for the monthly supplement to *The Week* (*Knižki "Nedeli"*). Gaideburov seems to have disliked the title "A Favor from a Kinsman" (*Rodstvennaja usluga*) and rechristened the story "Robbery," apparently with Leskov's approval (Gaideburov to Leskov, Nov. 24, 1887; cited from the "Kovalevsky notebook").

9. "Umeršee soslovie (Iz junošeskix vospominanij)," *Knižki "Nedeli"*, no. 5 (May 1888), pp. 1-16. The title of "The Dead Estate," like that of "Robbery," was suggested by Gaideburov, according to a letter from Gaideburov to Leskov cited without date in the "Kovalevsky notebook."

10. "Bytovye apokrify (po ustnym predanijam ob otcax i bratijax); Inženery bessrebreniki (Iz istorij o trex pravednikax)," *Russkaja mysl'*, no. 11 (Nov. 1887), pp. 119-175. The first part of the title was intended as an overall label for a series of "apocryphas," of which "The Unmercenary Engineers"

was to be the first. The project was not carried out, and in the collected works the series title was dropped along with the preface.

11. This preface was written on the proofs of the story, as if Leskov suddenly felt the need to guard his flank "in case something turns out to be historically not quite accurate." See Leskov to V. M. Lavrov, Oct. 30, 1887 (11:354).

12. In 1882 Leskov had obtained from his friend Filipp Ternovsky the diary of Ismailov (1794-1861) and extracted from it a whole series of articles: "Sinodal'nye persony; period bor'by za preobladanie (1820-1840)," *Istoričeskij vestnik*, no. 11 (Nov. 1882), pp. 373-409; "Kartiny prošlogo: Bračnye istorii tridcatyx godov; po zapiskam sinodal'nogo sekretarja. I. Vysečennaja polkovnica. II. Očarovatel'naja smoljanka. III. Sinodal'nyj Iosif," *Novoe vremja*, nos. 2461, 2469, 2475, 2483 (Jan. 4, 12, 18, 26, 1883); "Kartiny prošlogo: Patriaršee jurodstvo i Seničkin jad v tridcatyx godax XIX veka (Po zapiskam magistra F. F. Ismajlova)," *Novosti i birževaja gazeta*, nos. 19, 25, 38, 40 (1st ed.) (April 21, 27, May 10, 12, 1883). Some of this material was included in a revised form in the suppressed volume 6 of the collected works, but otherwise has not been reprinted.

13. The source of at least part of Leskov's material is known: the memoirs of Lieutenant General Pavel Fyodorovich Fermor (1810-1888) concerning his brother Nikolai. A "conspectus" of Pavel Fermor's memoirs survived among Leskov's papers: see Valentina Gebel', *N. S. Leskov* (Moscow, 1945), p. 75. Since Pavel Fermor was still alive when the story was first published, Leskov may have wished to avoid openly questioning the reliability of his source's memories. He therefore takes the responsibility for them himself, referring only vaguely to their origin. Concerning Leskov's sources on the other two "unmercenary engineers" I have no information except what he himself provides.

14. Leskov to V. M. Lavrov, Oct. 5, 1887 (11:353).

15. Leskov cites as his source (8:233n.) a book entitled *Žizneopisanie episkopa Ignatija (Brjančaninova)*, but I have not been able to verify it or identify it more fully.

16. "Sinodal'nye persony" *Istoričeskij vestnik*, no. 11 (Nov. 1882), p. 384.

17. The original title was "Spasenie pogibavšego (1839)," *Russkaja mysl'*, no. 4 (April 1887), pp. 117-135. It was changed in the collected works to "Čelovek na časax (1839)."

18. Andrei Leskov (in Leskov, *Izbrannye proizvedenija*, p. 460) reports that Miller's daughter and her husband, Baron A. E. Shtromberg, lived next door to Leskov in 1880-1885; through them Leskov became friendly with her father.

19. In a letter to S. N. Shubinsky dated April 29, 1887, Leskov wrote that Postnikov was "also numbered among the righteous" (11:345), and in the arrangement of the collected works Leskov placed him in their midst.

20. Grossman, *Leskov*, p. 194.

32. The Pen Apropos

1. Leskov to A. S. Suvorin, March 14, 1887 (11:342). The account of this dramatic coincidence is not consistent with Leskov's report of the same events in a letter to Suvorin written a year later, April 22, 1888 (11:383).

2. 11:342. On Leskov's relations with the Volf firm, see Sigismund F. Librovič, *Na knižnom postu: vospominanija, zapiski, dokumenty* (Petrograd, 1916), passim.

3. *Rasskazy kstati* (SPb., 1887). In a note he published in 1885 Leskov said that several other stories written in 1884 for the *Virgin Soil* series had been forbidden by the censorship. Except for "Substitution of the Guilty," later published in *Istoričeskij vestnik* (Feb. 1885), he does not identify them. See "Ob"jasnenie po trem punktam," *Novosti i birževaja gazeta*, no. 40 (Feb. 10, 1885); reprinted 11:234.

4. Dec. 14, 1893 (11:569).

5. "Rasskazy kstati. Novozavetnye evrei," *Nov'*, vol. 1, no. 1 (Nov. 1, 1884), pp. 71-84. It is doubtless more symptomatic of Soviet paranoia concerning the "Jewish question" than of the actual contents of Leskov's innocuous article that in the year 1973 the authorities of the Lenin Library in Moscow refused to make a xerographic copy of this article. I am grateful to Irina Corten for making a synopsis of it for my use.

6. "Rasskazy kstati. Dva svinopasa," *Nov'*. vol. 1, no. 2 (Nov. 15, 1884), pp. 302-309.

7. Andrei Leskov (ANL, p. 342) maintains that his father repented the severity of his criticism of Radstockism in *A High Society Schism* and in later years came to regard the schism more favorably. In particular, according to Andrei Leskov, Leskov regretted his harsh treatment of the Radstockites Yulia Zasetskaya and Maria Peiker and tried to make it up to them, even apologizing in print. This assertion is doubtless true on the level of personal relations. But Andrei Leskov adds, "On the 'new faith' itself Leskov left a sufficient number of no less respectful [*uvažitel'nye*] testimonials than about the two female votaries of that doctrine." He cites in evidence seven articles written by Leskov between 1883 and 1886 (ANL, p. 342n), *not* including "Two Swineherds." I was able to check five of these, and in my opinion they do not confirm Andrei Leskov's point. Their assessment of Radstockism seems to me anything but "respectful." The most explicit is "Knjaž'i navety," *Novosti i birževaja gazeta*, no. 253 (Sept. 13, 1884), which deals with precisely the same topic as "Dva svinopasa," the comparison of Radstockism with Shtundism. Leskov again asserts that the two are diametrically opposed, and his own position is obviously at the Shtundists' end of that diameter. The Radstockites, he again asserts, place all their stress on pure faith, are ignorant of Scripture, and acknowledge Christ the Savior, not Christ the Teacher. Their success is due mainly to the adherence of Pashkov himself, who is not only a sincerely religious man, but rich to boot. After Pashkov's death, Russian Rad-

stockism will either disappear or be transformed, but not into Shtundism. The Shtundists, on the contrary, are interested mainly in the didactic parts of the Gospel and make their religion a guide to leading a better life, emphasizing chastity, industry, and sobriety. Salvation, they feel, is God's business and better left to Him. The only thing the Shtundists and the Radstockites have in common is their rejection of the Orthodox clergy and the sacraments; but this is true of all priestless sects. This article evoked a letter of protest from Pashkov, dated Sept. 22, 1884, and published in A. I. Faresov, "Umstvennye perelomy v dejatel'nosti N. S. Leskova," *Istoričeskij vestnik,* no. 3 (March 1916), pp. 794-799. This letter in turn evoked a lengthy reply from Leskov, published in William B. Edgerton, "Leskov, Paškov, the Štundists, and a Newly Discovered Letter," *Orbis Scriptus* (Munich, 1966), pp. 187-200, where the subject is reviewed discerningly.

8. "Rasskazy kstati. Zagadočnoe proisšestvie v sumasšedšem dome (Izvlečeno iz bumag E. V. Pelikana)," *Nov',* vol. 1, no. 3 (Dec. 1, 1884), pp. 414-421. It was not included in the Soviet edition of 1956-1958 and is cited here from vol. 20 of the A. F. Marks edition (1903), pp. 105-118.

9. As testified by that dealer. See N. I. Svešnikov, *Vospominanija pro-pašČego Čeloveka,* ed. L. B. Modzalevskij and S. P. Šesterikov (Moscow-Leningrad, 1930), p. 308n.

10. Leskov also used Pelikan's papers for an article on the white slave trade in Riga, "Unizitel'nyj torg," *Istoričeskij vestnik,* no. 5 (May 1885), pp. 281-298; and a short, unsigned article, "O nekotoryx bumagax Pelikana," *Peter-burgskaja gazeta,* no. 286 (1884)—the latter inaccessible to me.

11. "Rasskazy kstati. Sovmestiteli; bukoličeskaja povest' na istoričeskoj kanve," *Nov',* vol. 1, no. 4 (Dec. 15, 1884), pp. 611-628.

12. "Rasskazy kstati. Aleksandrit; natural'nyj fakt v mističeskom osve-ščenii," *Nov',* vol. 2, no. 6 (Jan. 15, 1885), pp. 290-297.

13. As noted in ANL, p. 508.

14. *P.s.s.,* 20 (1903): 94.

15. *Dragocennye kamni; ix svojstva, mestonaxoždenija i upotreblenija* (SPb., 1877).

16. Aug. 9, 1884 (11:291). The epigraph from Pylyaev, like the title "The Fiery Garnet," did not survive later revisions. Pylyaev's book is quoted in the text.

17. Nov. 10, 1884 (11:297-298). The lines quoted are from A. K. Tolstoy's poem, "Pantelei the Curer" (1866). Leskov writes the words *boire, manger, sortir* in Cyrillic characters, as semi-Russified loanwords. The word *sortir* has acquired in Russia a euphemistic sense unknown in its homeland.

18. I. S. Aksakov to Leskov, Nov. 15, 1884, in A. I. Faresov, "Umstvennye perelomy v dejatel'nosti N. S. Leskova," *Istoričeskij vestnik,* no. 3 (March 1916), pp. 789-790.

19. ANL, p. 467.

20. *P.s.s.,* 20:94.

21. Vsevolod Setchkarev (*N. S. Leskov* [Wiesbaden, 1959], p. 117) takes strong exception to this passage, accusing Leskov of pandering to public prejudice with "Hurrapatriotismus," even contrary to his own convictions. This charge seems unfair, for the following reasons. First, the anti-"Swabian" diatribe is not the author's, but Vencel's, and is a plausible part of Vencel's characterization. Vencel is by no means a wholly positive character; on the contrary, he is more than half mad, and his words might well be discounted by the reader. Second, the admiration for Alexander II expressed in the story was sincere on Leskov's part.

22. "Rasskazy kstati. Interesnye mužčiny," *Nov'*, vol. 3, nos. 10, 11 (March 15, April 1, 1885), pp. 215-228, 441-458.

23. Actually, Tolstoy's piece was not a "story," but part of the treatise *What Then Must We Do?* It was censored in January 1885 from the February number of *Russkaja mysl'*. On Leskov and Uspensky see I. V. Stoljarova, "N. S. Leskov i G. I. Uspenskij," *Russkaja literatura*, no. 3 (1974), pp. 76-93.

24. *Istorija 14-go Ulanskogo Jamburgskogo polka, sostavlennaja poručikom V. Krestovskim 1-m* (SPb., 1873). See Valentina Gebel', *N. S. Leskov* (Moscow, 1945), pp. 72-74. Gebel derived her information from an unpublished article by the distinguished Leskovist S. P. Šesterikov, "Smert' korneta Desjatova," in which the historical facts are analyzed in connection not only with Leskov's story, but also with a manuscript by Chernyshevsky, one not published until 1936. Andrei Leskov (ANL, p. 508n) says cryptically that the juxtaposition of Leskov's story and Desyatov's suicide "is hardly in all respects justifiable," but he does not elaborate.

25. Andrei Leskov, in his notes to the story in N. S. Leskov, *Izbrannye proizvedenija* (Moscow, 1945), p. 459, says that the "snake" is modeled on the wife of Field Marshal Aleksandr I. Baryatinsky.

26. March 15, 1887 (11:343). During the search the captain's hairy armpits looked like two rats. The regimental chaplain is a genial, but mindless, priest who answers "yes, yes, yes" to all questions and lacks any moral influence.

27. "Golos prirody," *Oskolki*, no. 12 (March 19, 1883).

28. "Dikaja fantazija; polunoščnoe videnie," *Literaturnyj sovremennik*, no. 12 (Dec. 1934), pp. 98-103, with an afterword and notes by Andrei Leskov. "Spravedlivyj čelovek; polunoščnoe videnie," 7:305-312. The arguments for the dating and relative chronology of the two variants are succinctly presented by Boris Bukhshtab in 7:547-548.

29. "Rasskazy kstati. Tainstvennye predvestija," *Nov'*, vol. 3, no. 12 (April 15, 1885), pp. 613-628.

30. The manuscript of Vagner's memoirs was preserved among Leskov's papers. See Gebel' *Leskov*, p. 75.

31. Leskov describes this intrigue in "Sinodal'nye persony," *Istoričeskij vestnik*, no. 10 (Oct. 1882), pp. 373-409.

32. In "Aleutskij duxovidec," *Èpoxa*, no. 2 (Feb. 1886), pp. 97-106, Leskov extracts from Muravyov's papers yet another example of the latter's superstitious credulity. It is an account recorded by Muravyov from the lips of Metro-

politan Innocent (Veniaminov), who had served as a missionary in Siberia. The report concerned an Aleut Christian who had performed various healing and prophesying miracles and was regularly assisted by two spirits, who gave him instruction in biblical history, Christian morality, and Orthodox dietary rules. All this is reported by Muravyov in a tone of "sentimental piety," to use Leskov's phrase.

33. "Rasskazy kstati. Pagubniki," *Nov'*, vol. 7, no. 1 (Nov. 1, 1885), pp. 124-143.

34. Ibid., p. 136. This assertion of the tenacity of the old Adam, even in the country, runs counter to the Rousseauistic opinions of the peasantophile Tolstoy.

35. "Rasskazy kstati. I. Bezgraničnaja dobrota; anekdotičeskie vospominanija o Karnoviče," *Nov'*, vol. 7, no. 2 (Nov. 15, 1885), pp. 228-292.

36. "Rasskazy kstati. [. . .] II. Dremotnye vospominanija na dele Sarry Bekker," *Nov'*, vol. 7, no. 2 (Nov. 15, 1885), pp. 292-295.

37. See, for example, Leskov to A. S. Suvorin, Sept. 30, 1887 (11:349-350); ANL, pp. 299-300.

38. "Čužoe zaglavie (pis'mo v redakciju)," *Novoe vremja*, no. 4206 (Nov. 13, 1887); reprinted 11:236. The offending publishers, Mikhail and Yevgeny Verner, replied in "Otvet g. Leskovu," *Novoe vremja*, no. 4211 (Nov. 18, 1887), saying they had never heard of Leskov's book and the title was too general to be legally his. To this Leskov wrote a mordant reply, published in the same issue (untitled; reprinted 11:237), saying the Moscow editors evidently considered as decent and proper anything that was not actually punishable by law.

39. "Sibirskie kartinki XVIII veka," *Vestnik Evropy*, no. 3 (March 1893).

40. "Vdoxnovennye brodjagi," *Severnyj vestnik*, no. 10 (Oct. 1894).

41. Leskov also dealt with the Ashinov case in a series of articles in *Peterburgskaja gazeta*: "Gde vojuet vol'nyj kazak," no. 314 (1887); "Vol'nyj kazak v Pariže," no. 326 (1887); "Vol'nyj kazak v literature," no. 28 (1888); and "O vol'nom kazake," no. 33 (1888). He also appears in "Na smert' Katkova," written 1887, published in *Zven'ju* 3-4 (Moscow-Leningrad, 1934); and in "The Cattle-pen."

42. "Sošestvie vo ad (Apokrifičeskoe skazanie)," *Peterburgskaja gazeta*, no. 104 (April 16, 1894). This article was written in 1887 (ANL, p. 470). Leskov had tried unsuccessfully to peddle it to *Russian Thought, New Times,* and *The Week*; but the editors of all three, evidently afraid of the ecclesiastical censorship, demurred. See Leskov to V. M. Lavrov, Feb. 11, 1888 (11:365-366); to A. S. Suvorin, March 26, 1888 (11:375) and April 15, 1888 (11:379); to V. A. Goltsev, May 10, 1894 (11:582).

43. "Dama i fefela. Rasskazy kstati; iz literaturnyx vospominanij," *Russkaja mysl'*, no. 12 (Dec. 1894).

44. The "Kovalevsky notebook" records the existence of a letter from P. A. Gaideburov, the editor of *The Week*, asking Leskov to submit "The Lady and the Wench" for the November issue" of *Books of The Week*. The reference is

undated, but it is associated with letters dated 1888 and 1889. Gaideburov died in 1893.

45. Leskov to V. A. Goltsev, June 4, 1894 (11:585).
46. Leskov to V. M. Lavrov, June 28, 1894 (11:586).
47. Ibid., Aug. 20, 1894 (11:587).
48. Leskov to V. A. Goltsev, Nov. 16, 1894 (11:599).
49. Leskov to V. M. Lavrov, Nov. 20, 1894 (11:600).
50. See the note by A. I. and S. I. Gruzdev in 9:638. The Gruzdevs correctly decided to use this, the last revised text, even though the usual textological rule required them to use the magazine version, as the last text actually *published* in the author's lifetime.
51. Leskov to V. M. Lavrov, June 28, 1894 (11:586).
52. Leskov to V. A. Goltsev, Oct. 14, 1894 (11:598).
53. ANL, p. 422.
54. ANL, p. 210. Andrei Leskov lists the various appeals for Palm's daughter that Leskov published in *Novoe vremja.*

33. The Form That Failed

1. Leskov made many statements to this effect, orally and in letters. A vivid one is quoted by Faresov, *Protiv tečenij* (SPb., 1904), pp. 59-63.
2. See Leskov to M. A. Protopopov, Dec. 23, 1891 (11:509).
3. I. Èm, "Kak rabotajut naši pisateli; N.S. Leskov," *Novosti i birževaja gazeta*, no. 49 (Feb. 19, 1895), p. 2.
4. *P.s.s.*, 26:122-124.
5. Leskov to I. S. Aksakov, April 23, 1875 (10:396).
6. This title first occurs in a letter from Leskov to his son, Andrei, and his stepdaughter, Vera Bubnova, written from Paris on July, 1-13, 1875: "In Marienbad I hope to finish writing a story [*povest'*] that I have begun and that will be called 'Falcon Flight' " (10:409). The relationship of this "story" to the later "novel" is not clear.
7. See A. Gattsuk to Leskov, Feb. 28, 1882. I cite the "Kovalevsky notebook."
8. "Sokolij perelet. Roman. Čast' I. Kniga 1," *Gazeta A. Gatcuka*, nos. 7-10 (Feb. 19, 26, March 5, 12, 1883), pp. 139-144, 162-164, 178-179, 194-198; never reprinted. Since the texts of *Falcon Flight* and *A Faint Trace* are so difficult of access, their contents are described here in greater detail.
9. "Pis'mo v redakciju," *Gazeta A. Gatcuka*, no. 10 (March 12, 1883), p. 206; reprinted 11:222.
10. Ibid. Shchebalsky's reference to *No Way Out* is found in his article, "Naš umstvennyj proletariat," *Russkij vestnik*, no. 8 (Aug. 1871), p. 641.
11. This is the formulation of I. Ya Aizenshtok in his note to the "Letter to the Editor" (11:656). Aizenshtok refers to some early drafts of the novel preserved in manuscript.

12. I have not examined them, but all the surviving drafts appear to be variants of the beginning. See 11:656, Valentina Gebel', *N. S. Leskov* (Moscow, 1945), p. 122.

13. The chapter numbering in the magazine is confused and incomplete. The chapters are numbered as follows: 5, 8, 7, 10, 11, 13. It is not clear whether these are misprints or marks of the censor's scissors. The sequences seem uninterrupted.

14. Leonid Grossman, *N. S. Leskov* (Moscow, 1945), p. 246.

15. See "Otkuda pošla glagolemaja 'erunda' ili 'xirunda'," *Novosti i bir-ževaja gazeta*, no. 243 (Sept. 3, 1884); reprinted 11:90-99. See esp. p. 97.

16. Prince Odoevsky (1803-1869) was a man of great distinction in many fields—literature, music, science, scholarship, education, charity. At the time of his death he was director of the Rumyantsev Museum in Moscow.

17. Ivan Vernadsky (1821-1884) was an old acquaintance of Leskov's, once professor of political economy at Kiev University, later an official in Petersburg and editor of the *Economic Index*, where Leskov published some early articles. Vladimir P. Bezobrazov (1828-1889) was a noted economist and statistician. Ivan K. Babst (1824-1881) was professor of political economy at Moscow University. Gustave Molinari (1819-1912) was a Belgian economist with extensive Russian interests and connections, whose textbook of political economy was translated into Russian.

18. The name Bezbedovich also occurs in early drafts for a novel bearing the title "Devil's Puppets" (*Čortovy kukly*), used later for an entirely different work. See Gebel',' *N. S. Leskov*, pp. 122-127.

19. As quoted by S. P. Shesterikov in the notes to *Pis'ma Tolstogo i k Tolstomu* (Moscow, 1928), p. 102.

20. "Ot redakcii," *Gazeta A. Gatcuka*, no. 10 (March 12, 1883), p. 206.

21. "Nezametnyj sled; roman (Iz istorii odnogo semejstva). Čast' pervaja. Domašnij krov," *Nov'*, nos. 1, 2 (Nov. 1, 15, 1884), pp. 116-134, 220-232; never reprinted.

22. As pointed out above, note 18, the early drafts entitled "Devil's Puppets" have more in common with *A Faint Trace* than with the work later published under that title. Not only the name Bezbedovich, but also the name Brasov—also prominent in *A Faint Trace*—occurs in these drafts. See Gebel', *Leskov*, pp. 122-128.

23. See Wacław Lednicki, *Tolstoy between War and Peace* (The Hague, 1965). It should be noted that the pro-Polish sentiments belong to the old Tolstoy. In real life, in 1863, ex-Lieutenant Tolstoy had been ready to leap on his horse and ride off to do battle against the rebels. See Tolstoy to A. A. Fet, May 1-3, 1863 (L. N. Tolstoj, *Perepiska s russkimi pisateljami*, [Moscow, 1962], p. 253).

24. Untitled letter to the editor, published in *Nov'*, no. 23 (Oct. 1, 1885); reprinted 11:235.

25. By S. Shesterikov in his note to Leskov to L. N. Tolstoy, Feb. 26, 1891

(*Pis'ma Tolstogo*, p. 102.)

26. 11:661.

27. Gebel', p. 109.

28. Leskov to Biryukov, Jan. 7, 1889 (11:412).

29. Feb. 26, 1891 (Tolstoj, *Perepiska*, p. 538).

30. "Čortovy kukly," *Russkaja mysl'*, no. 1 (Jan. 1890), pp. 97-167. As mentioned above, note 18, this title occurs much earlier in Leskov's letters, but refers to a different work. On June 5, 1871, for example, Leskov wrote to Shchebalsky about a novel to be called "Devil's Puppets" that would be "all about women" (10:327). On December 20, 1871, he received a letter from Katkov's factotum Voskoboynikov reporting that the editors of *Russian Messenger* considered the title "Devil's Puppets" "too sharp" (I cited the "Kovalevsky notebook"). Four years later Leskov wrote to A. P. Milyukov that he was working on a satirical piece resembling *Laughter and Grief* and had named it "Devil's Puppets" (Aug. 3-15, 1875 [10:415]).

31. In his notes to the text in 8:627-631, A. I. Batyuto presents an interesting short essay on the novel, including a cogent refutation of some wild conjectures put forward by N. S. Pleshchunov in "K voprosu o zamysle romana N. S. Leskova 'Čertovy kukly'," *Trudy Azerbajdžanskogo gosudarstvennogo universiteta imeni S. M. Kirova*, philological series, issue 2 (Baku, 1947). (The pagination given by Batyuto [8:627] of the position of *The Devil's Puppets* in volume 10 of the original collected works is incorrect. It should read 420-510).

32. Leskov to V. M. Lavrov, June 14, 1889 (11:431).

33. The subject of the genesis of *The Devil's Puppets* and the prototypes of its characters has been explored in an excellent article by S. Eleonskij, "Nikolaj I i Karl Brjullov v 'Čortovyx kuklax' N. S. Leskova," *Pečat' i revoljucija*, no. 8 (Dec. 1928), pp. 37-57. Some early drafts are analyzed in I. V. Stoljarova and A. A. Šelaeva, "K tvorčeskoj istorii romana N. S. Leskova 'Čertovy kukly'," *Russkaja literatura*, no. 3 (1971), pp. 102-112.

34. It seems that Bryullov's wife, née Timm, may also have been a mistress of Nicholas I (Eleonskij, "Nikolaj I i Karl Brjullov," p. 56); the marriage broke up two weeks after the wedding, perhaps because Bryullov discovered the truth.

35. Leskov to V. M. Lavrov, June 14, 1889 (11:431).

36. Leskov to L. N. Tolstoy, Jan. 4, 1891 (11:472).

37. This picture by Wilhelm Kaulbach (1805-1874), painted in 1834-1837, was greatly admired in its time,—by Leskov among others.

38. Leskov to M. A. Protopopov, Dec. 23, 1891 (11:509).

39. V. P[rotopopov], "U N. S. Leskova," *Peterburgskaja gazeta*, no. 326 (Nov. 27, 1894), p. 2.

40. Leskov to V. M. Lavrov, June 14, 1889 (11:431). The female names do not occur in the existing text, but are similar in type to Pelegrina, Pik's wife, and Gelia, Febufis's.

41. The theme of the amours of Nicholas I was evoked by Tolstoy at

almost the same time, in both "Father Sergius" (published 1911, written 1889-1898) and "Hadji Murad" (published 1912, written 1896-1905). It is hard to say whether there was any mutual influence, and, if so, in which direction. I have no evidence that Leskov knew either of these stories by Tolstoy, which he would have had to read in manuscript; but the possibility is not excluded. I also find no direct reference in Tolstoy's papers to *The Devil's Puppets*. Leskov visited Yasnaya Polyana in January 1890, just after the novel appeared in *Russian Thought*, and it seems possible that Tolstoy read it and that they discussed it. Tolstoy's diary contains only a note from more than a month later: "I am still reading Leskov. Bad, because untruthful" (L. N. Tolstoj, *Polnoe sobranie sočinenij*, 51 [1952]: 25). Unfortunately, Tolstoy did not specify which work he was reading, and the possiblities are almost infinite, since he had just acquired the first nine volumes of Leskov's collected works.

42. Leskov to V. M. Lavrov, Dec. 7, 1889 (11:445).

43. "The night of December 14-15, 1889": Leskov not infrequently used such nocturnal dating to create an atmosphere of urgency or of his own weary toil. The letter is to V. M. Lavrov (11:449).

44. Ibid.: "A break in February is essential. Otherwise I won't manage it in time."

45. Ibid., March 13, 1890 (11:455).

46. Ibid., Aug. 9, 1890 (11:461).

47. Leskov to V. A. Goltsev, May 10, 1891 (11:487).

48. ANL, p. 459.

34. The Rushlight and the Torch

1. Of Leskov's letters to Tolstoy, fifty-one survive. Of these, forty-nine were published, with excellent annotations by S. P. Shesterikov, in *Pis'ma Tolstogo i k Tolstomu; jubilejnyj sbornik. Trudy Publičnoj biblioteki SSSR imeni V. I. Lenina* (Moscow-Leningrad, 1928). Twenty-nine of these are reprinted in full in volume 11; others are quoted in the apparatus. There were once more of these letters: there are two big gaps, in 1889-1891 and 1891-1892. Of Tolstoy's letters to Leskov only ten survive, published in volumes 65-67 of the Jubilee Edition. The others perished as a result of the misfortunes that beset Leskov's archives during the Revolution, on which see William B. Edgerton, "Missing Letters to Leskov: An Unsolved Puzzle," *Slavic Review*, no. 1 (March 1966), pp. 120-123. Nevertheless, it is clear that Leskov wrote Tolstoy a great deal more often than Tolstoy wrote him. Leskov's first letter is dated April 18, 1887 (11:344-345). The entire correspondence, including two more hitherto unpublished letters from Leskov to Tolstoy, has been reprinted, with commentaries by S. Rozanova, in L. N. Tolstoj, *Perepiska s russkimi pisateljami* (Moscow, 1962), pp. 511-608.

2. April 24-25, 1887 (L. N. Tolstoj, *Polnoe sobranie sočinenij*, 86 [1937]: 49.

3. ANL, p. 601.

4. Leskov to A. S. Suvorin, March 3, 1886 (11:310).

5. Leskov to V. G. Chertkov, Nov. 4, 1887 (11:356). Chertkov forwarded this letter to Tolstoy, who commented, "Leskov's letter was such a joy to me" (Tolstoy to Chertkov, Nov. 22, 1887 [Tolstoj, *Polnoe*, 86:101).

6. "Russkie obščestvennye zametki," *Birževye vedomosti*, no. 340 (Dec. 14, 1869)) reprinted 10:90.

7. "Geroi otečestvennoj vojny po gr. L. N. Tolstomu," *Birževye vedomosti*, nos. 66, 68, 70, 75, 98, 99, 109 (March 9, 11, 13, 18, April 11, 12, 25, 1869); cited from 10:146.

8. F. M. Dostoevskij, *Dnevnik pisatelja za 1877 god, Sobranie sočinenij*, ed. B. Tomaševskij and K. Xalabaev, 12 (Moscow-Leningrad, 1929): 201-233.

9. Letter dated "The night of March 6-7, 1877" (10:449).

10. See ANL, p. 292; F. M. Dostoevskij, *Pis'ma*, ed. A. S. Dolinin, 2 (1930): 466.

11. Leskov to M. O. Menshikov, Nov. 12, 1893; cited ANL, p. 605.

12. A. I. Faresov, *Protiv tečenij* (SPb., 1904), pp. 69-70.

13. Review of C. F. von Walther, *Die vierte Saecularfeier der Geburt Doctor Martin Luthers*, *Novosti i birževaja gazeta*, no. 89 (March 30, 1884), p. 4.

14. "Kak dorožat pisanijami grafa L'va Tolstogo," *Novosti i birževaja gazeta*, no. 36 (Feb. 5, 1884), pp. 3-4. This article suggests that the "new notebooks" of Tolstoy referred to in Leskov to A. S. Suvorin, March 3, 1886 (11:310), could not be *A Confession* and *What I Believe* as stated by I. Ya. Aizenshtok (11:695). Leskov had read *A Confession* long before 1886.

15. "Graf L. N. Tolstoj i F. M. Dostoevskij kak eresiarxi (Religija straxa i religija ljubvi)," *Novosti i birževaja gazeta*, nos. 1, 3 (April 1, 3, 1883); "Zolotoj vek; utopija obščestvennogo pereustrojstva. Kartiny žizni po programme K. Leont'eva," ibid., no. 87 (June 29, 1883). As evidence of Ternovsky's authorship see Leskov's letters to him dated Feb. 19 (11:270), March 12 (11:275-276), April 6, 1883 (11:276-277). Leskov shared the honorarium fifty-fifty, but did not mention Ternovsky's name in the published text. The original Ternovsky article had first been rejected by *New Times*. Leskov was angered by this affront to his friend, but still considered Ternovsky's style too academic for a popular medium.

16. "Graf L. N. Tolstoj," *Novosti*, p, 2.

17. A decade later, taking sole credit for this article, Leskov proclaimed it the "warmest and most difficult word" he had uttered in defense of Tolstoy. He further asserted that it had brought about his dismissal from the Ministry of Education. See his letter to M. O. Menshikov dated Nov. 11, 1893; quoted ANL, p. 605. In fact he was dismissed before this article appeared.

18. See Leskov to A. S. Suvorin, Oct. 8, 1883 (11:286), which in turn refers to Leskov's article "Snedaemoe slovo (O kljatve Bogom)," *Rus'*, no. 46 (1882), pp. 11-12. In the letter Leskov reports that, at the request of General Rostislav Khreshchatintky, he rewrote the Russian soldier's oath "briefly, with style, in a Christian spirit, without threats or overconfidence" (11:286).

19. Leskov to A. S. Suvorin, Oct. 8, 1883 (11:287).

20. Ibid., Oct. 9, 1883 (11:287).

21. This undated letter (11:301-302) is assigned to the "end of 1884" by Andrei Leskov (ANL, p. 596) and by I. Ya. Aizenshtok. Neither presents any arguments for the date or identifies the "stupid book."

22. "Knjaž'i navety (Po povodu stat'i 'Graždanina' o Paškove)," *Novosti i birževaja gazeta*, no. 253 (Sept. 13, 1884), pp. 2-3; see above, Chapter 32, note 7.

23. See Leskov to V. G. Chertkov, Oct. 15, 1884 (11:292).

24. See ibid., March 8, 1887 (11:336). On the story and "The Intermediary" edition see below, Chapter 35.

25. Leskov to V. G. Chertkov dated "The night of April 8-9, 1889" (11:425).

26. "Tri pervoklassnyx pisatelja," *Peterburgskaja gazeta*, no. 45; "Torgovaja igra na imja gr. L. N. Tolstogo," ibid., no. 262; "Novye brošjury, pripisyvaemye peru gr. L. N. Tolstogo," ibid., no. 265 (1885), all inaccessible to me. The first apparently ridicules Leskov's old enemy, the critic A. M. Skabichevsky, for speaking of Gleb Uspensky and especially N. Zlatovratsky in the same breath with Tolstoy as "three first-class Russian writers." See N. K. Gudzij, "Tolstoj i Leskov," *Iskusstvo*, books 1-2 (1928), p. 97.

27. Leskov to A. S. Suvorin, March 3, 1886 (11:310).

28. "Lučšij bogomolec," *Novosti i birževaja gazeta*, no. 109 (April 22, 1886); reprinted 11:102. On the *Prolog*, see below, Chapter 36, note 2.

29. The story ends on the "Kreutzerian" note that the shepherd and his wife "keep their bed undefiled" (11:112)—written before "The Kreutzer Sonata." It is not completely clear whether this means they refrained from intercourse or simply from adultery.

30. "O kufel'nom mužike i proč.," *Novosti i birževaja gazeta*, no. 151 (June 4, 1886) and 161 (June 14, 1886); reprinted 11:134-156; "Zagrobnyj svidetel' za ženščin; nabljudenija, opyty i zametki N. I. Pirogova, izložennye v pis'me k baronesse È. O. Raden," *Istoričeskij vestnik*, no. 11 (Nov. 4, 1886). "O rožne; uvet synam protivlenija," *Novoe vremja*, no. 3838 (Nov. 4, 1886). "O kufel'nom mužike" was published in *Novosti* because Suvorin in *Novoe vremja* would not let Leskov "tell the whole truth about Dostoevsky." See Leskov to A. S. Suvorin, April 24, 1887 (11:327).

31. This story is suspiciously similar to one Leskov told on Pavel Yakushkin, who allegedly advised Leskov and his brother Aleksei to "study" at the feet of their former serf, Matvei Zaitsev. See 11:81.

32. Leskov to S. N. Shubinsky, June 14, 1886 (11:317-318). Pirogov (1810-1881) was a distinguished surgeon and educational theorist.

33. Ibid., June 17, 1886 (11:319).

34. "About Goads" was evidently completed by early October, 1886, since the main points are outlined in Leskov's letter to Suvorin dated Oct. 8, 1886 (11:323). On October 29 Leskov wrote to S. N. Shubinsky (11:324) complaining that A. S. Suvorin, out of "nervousness," had held up the article for a month. The proofs had long since been corrected and returned, but the article

had not appeared. Leskov asked Shubinsky to return it so that he could publish it somewhere else. Apparently the threat was sufficient; Suvorin ran the piece in *New Times* on November 4. On this article and its significance see esp. William B. Edgerton, "Leskov and Tolstoy: Two Literary Heretics," *American Slavic and East European Review,* 12 (Dec. 1953): 524-534.

35. This subject is discussed in "Kurskaja trel' o Tolstom (Pis'mo v redakciju)," *Peterburgskaja gazeta,* no. 23 (Jan. 24, 1891), reprinted 11:245-246. Others of this caliber are "O xoždenii Štandelja po Jasnoj Poljane," *Novoe vremja,* no. 4550 (Oct. 28, 1888); "Devočka ili mal'čik?," ibid., no. 4559 (Nov. 6, 1888), reprinted respectively 11:195-199, 200-202. A possible exception is "Obujannaja sol'," *Peterburgskaja gazeta,* no. 12 (Jan. 13, 1891), a defense by Leskov both of Tolstoy and of his own story, "Offended before Christmas."

36. Leskov to Lidia Veselitskaya (V. Mikulich), June 1, 1893 (11:534).

37. Faresov, *Protiv tečenij,* pp. 307-308. V. L. Velichko (1860-1903) was a poet and literary critic who wrote for A. S. Suvorin's *New Times.*

38. Leskov to L. N. Tolstoy, Aug. 28, 1894 (11:591).

39. Ibid., Jan. 4, 1893 (11:519-520).

40. Leskov to A. S. Suvorin, March 11, 1887 (11:340).

41. Leskov to A. G. Chertkova, March 2, 1894 (11:577).

42. Leskov to A. S. Suvorin, March 11, 1887 (11:340).

43. Leskov to L. N. Tolstoy, Aug. 21, 1894 (11:589).

44. Leskov to V. V. Protopopov, Sept. 10, 1892; quoted ANL, pp. 614-615. See also Leskov to A. S. Suvorin, Oct. 12, 1892 (11:516-517).

45. Leskov to L. N. Tolstoy, July 12, 1891 (11:494).

46. Leskov to Lev B. Bertenson, Feb. 20, 1892 (Bertenson, "K vospominanijam o Nikolae Semenoviče Leskove," *Russkaja mysl',* no. 10 [Oct. 1915], pp. 89-95).

47. ANL, pp. 618-619.

48. Faresov, *Protiv tečenij,* p. 214.

49. Leskov to V. G. Chertkov, Dec. 29, 1888; quoted ANL, p. 602.

50. V. Mikulič, "Pis'ma N. S. Leskova," *Literaturnaja mysl',* 3 (Leningrad, 1925): 290. Andrei Leskov (ANL, p. 606) cites a self-justifying letter from Leskov to Menshikov in response to Veselitskaya's barb.

51. Faresov, *Protiv tečenij,* p. 314; also ANL, p. 609.

52. Faresov, *Protiv tečenij,* p. 315. In the transcription of the same statement as published by Andrei Leskov (ANL, pp. 609-610), probably Faresov's original version, the muddy-footed Tolstoyans are identified by name: Ivan Gorbunov-Posadov and Pavel Biryukov.

53. Leskov to V. G. Chertkov, March 5, 1888 (11:369).

54. Leskov to Lidia Veselitskaya, June 9, 1893 (11:540).

55. "Po povodu 'Krejcerovoj sonaty'," *Niva,* no. 30 (1899); reprinted 9:32-49. As noted earlier, "The Lady and the Wench," because less explicitly identified with Tolstoy's doctrines, perhaps conveys Leskov's criticisms more fully and authentically.

56. Apparently a transcription by Faresov. See ANL, p. 610.
57. Ljubov' Gurevič, *Literatura i èstetika; Kritičeskie opyty i ètjudy* (Moscow, 1912), p. 301. On Lesko·/ and Gurevich, see P. V. Kuprianovskij, "L. N. Tolstoj i N. S. Leskov v žurnale 'Severnyj vestnik'," *Lev Tolstoj i ego sovremenniki=Učenye zapiski Ivanovskogo gos. pedagogičeskogo instituta imeni D. A. Furmanova*, 29 (Ivanovo, 1962).
58. Leskov reacted with rapture to Tolstoy's article "Christianity and Patriotism": see his letter dated "Night of October 15-16, 1893" (11:562). He wisely advised Tolstoy to publish it first in England, not in Germany—which Tolstoy did (it first appeared in the *Daily Chronicle* in 1894).
59. Leskov to Lidia Veselitskaya, April 6, 1894 (V. Mikulič, "Pis'ma N. S. Leskova," *Literaturnaja mysl'*, 3 [Leningrad, 1925]: 294).
60. Leskov to L. N. Tolstoy, Sept. 14, 1891 (*Pis'ma Tolstogo*, p. 118).
61. Ibid., Jan. 10, 1893 (11:521).
62. Ibid., Jan. 4, 1893 (11:519).
63. Leskov to A. S. Suvorin, Dec. 31, 1889 (11:452).
64. From L. Gurevich to Andrei Leskov, April 9, 1937 (ANL, p. 607).
65. L. N. Tolstoj, 51:104.
66. L. Gurevich to Andrei Leskov, April 9, 1937 (ANL, p. 606).
67. Gurevič, *Literatura i èstetika*, pp. 278-279.
68. Leskov to E. J. Dillon, Aug. 12/24, 1892 (*Russkij literaturnyj arxiv*, ed. M. M. Karpovich and D. I. Čiževskij [New York, 1956], p. 151).

35. He Spake in Parables

1. Leskov to Maria Peiker, undated; assigned to the first half of 1879 (10:456).
2. "Sentimental'noe blagočestie," *Pravoslavnoe obozrenie*, no. 3 (March 1876), pp. 526-551.
3. "Ènergičnaja bestaktnost'," *Pravoslavnoe obozrenie*, no. 5 (May 1876), pp. 128-149.
4. "Pedagogičeskoe jurodstvo," *Pravoslavnoe obozrenie*, no. 7 (July 1876), pp. 510-526.
5. Cited by Leskov as demonstrating the inappropriateness for Russian schools of the ideas of Friedrich Fröbel, the originator of "kindergartens," "Pedagogičeskoe jurodstvo," p. 514.
6. "Ènergičnaja bestaktnost'," *Pravoslavnoe*, p. 131.
7. "Bog pravdu vidit, da ne skoro skažet," originally in *Beseda* (1872), included in *Tret'ja russkaja kniga dlja čtenija* (1875). Karataev tells the story in book 14 of *War and Peace*. Much later, in *What is Art* (1898), Tolstoy specifically exempted only this story, along with *A Prisoner of the Caucasus*, from those of his own works he assigned to the category of "bad art" (chapter 16, note).
8. "Xristos v gostjax u mužika," *Igrušečka*, no. 1 (Jan. 1881), pp. 1-12.

Because of his friendship for Mme Passek, Leskov accepted a small honorarium for this story, according to Passek to Leskov (1880; otherwise undated); cited in the "Kovalevsky notebook."

9. Ivan Shlyapkin (*Russkaja starina*, no. 12 [Dec. 1895], p. 211), without mentioning the affinity with Tolstoy's story, asserts that the plot of "Christ Visits a Muzhik" was taken from Afanasiev's *Legendy russkogo naroda*. Shlyapkin gives no details, and I suspect that this may be another of the many inaccuracies in his article.

10. The style and structure of Tolstoy's didactic tales are intelligently analyzed in L. Myškovskaja, *Masterstvo L. N. Tolstogo* (Moscow, 1958), pp. 369-389; and more conventionally by Z. S. Melkix, "Tolstoj i fol'klor (Narodnye rasskazy 70-80x godov)," *Voprosy literatury* (Minsk, 1960), pp. 3-20.

11. Misdating "Christ Visits a Muzhik" in 1885, Vsevolod Setchkarev (*Nikolaj Leskov* [Wiesbaden, 1959], p. 136) compares it, most unfavorably, not with "God Sees the Truth but Waits," but with "Where Love Is, There God Is," a story Tolstoy wrote in 1885, adapting the plot from a Russian translation of a French story by Ruben Saillens. (The translation was published in *The Russian Workman*, the very magazine Leskov had criticized so severely). Actually, "Christ Visits a Muzhik" shares with "Where Love Is" only the motif of a symbolic "visit" by Christ turning out to be an opportunity for charity—a common theme in Christian literature. In view of the dates, the only possible genetic connection between the two stories would be a borrowing by Tolstoy from Leskov, which seems unlikely because of the known French source for Tolstoy's plot.

12. I. D. Sytin, "Iz perežitogo," *Polveka dlja knigi* (Moscow, 1916), pp. 21-28, cited from L. N. Tolstoj, *Polnoe sobranie sočinenij*, 85 (1935): 122. On the history of "The Intermediary" firm, see Thais S. Lindstrom, "From Chapbooks to Classics: The Story of *The Intermediary*," *American Slavic and East European Review*, 16 (1957): 190-201.

13. S. P. Šesterikov, "K bibliografii sočinenij N. S. Leskova," *Izvestija otdelenija russkogo jazyka i slovesnosti Akademii Nauk SSSR*, 30 (1925): 268-310. On January 8, 1891, Leskov wrote to Tolstoy, apparently without foundation, that the edition of that year had been forbidden by the censorship (11:474).

14. I follow the dating of K. P. Bogaevskaya in 11:828; the basis for it is not stated. "Malan'ja—golova baran'ja" was not published in Leskov's lifetime. It first appeared (as far as I know) in *P.s.s.*, 33 (1903): 196-201.

15. The manuscripts are extensively cited in Gebel', *N. S. Leskov* (Moscow, 1945), pp. 82-83. Several further folktale analogues (but not the Flemish original) are discussed in J. G. K. Russell, "Leskov and Folklore" (Ph.D. dissertation, Princeton University, 1971), pp. 262-272.

16. Leonid Grossman, *N. S. Leskov* (Moscow, 1945), p. 234.

17. "Figura," *Trud*, no. 13 (July 1, 1889), pp. 1-26. The magazine edition bears the subtitle of "Iz vospominanij o pravednikax." The story was reprinted in a separate edition (Moscow, 1889).

18. During the campaign Tolstoy either wrote or transcribed a soldiers' ditty satirizing General Saken's ostentatious piety: "A tam Saken-general/ Vse Akafisty čital/ Bogorodice" (*And then General Saken kept reciting hymns to the Virgin*); cited from *Pis'ma Tolstogo i k Tolstomu* (Moscow-Leningrad, 1928), p. 74. The song is echoed in Leskov's story.

19. April 30, 1889 (11:427-428). There seems to be no trace of this Vigura in the historical literature on the Shtunda. The only authenticated personality is Ivan Martynovich Vigura (1819-1856), professor of law at Kiev University, who is vaguely alluded to in the story as a distant relative of the hero's. Leskov probably met Vigura through Leskov's uncle Alferiev and might then have met the hero, if he existed at all, through his relation.

20. May 18, 1889 (11:428-429). Though there is no doubt that Tolstoy disliked the story, I am inclined to question the conjecture of the editors of the Jubilee Edition of Tolstoy's works (50:338) to the effect that an entry in Tolstoy's diary dated Nov. 18, 1889, refers specifically to "Figura." The entry reads: "Read Leskov. Artificial. Bad" (50:184). The editor's hypothesis that Tolstoy was referring to "Figura" is based solely on the fact that the story had just appeared in "The Intermediary" edition. But Tolstoy had read "Figura" months before. In the meantime he had received the first volumes of Leskov's collected works and was reading them; his strictures could therefore have been directed at almost anything.

21. "Čas voli Božiej; skazka," *Russkoe obozrenie*, no. 11 (Nov. 1890). The story was first offered to *Russian Thought*, but rejected, presumably out of fear of the censorship. See Leskov to V. M. Lavrov, Aug. 9, 1890 (11:461); to D. N. Tsertelev, Dec. 14, 1891 (11:506). In Leskov to A. K. Sheller, Sept. 26, 1890; and to D. N. Tsertelev, Oct. 12, 23, 1890 (11:463-465), Leskov speaks of "toning down" the story to ease its passage through the censorship.

22. Some analogous folk riddle-tales are adduced in J. G. K. Russell, "Leskov and Folklore," pp. 272-274.

23. "Cerkovnye intrigany; istoričeskie kartiny," *Istoričeskij vestnik*, no. 5 (May 1882), p. 379. The actual source in Hoffmann is not clear. Leskov was perhaps recalling "Klein Zaches genannt Zinnober" (1819), which evokes an Arcadian paradise presided over by a do-nothing prince named Demetrius. Demetrius's successor, Prince Paphnutius, is an "activist" ruler and ruins everything by trying to make his realm conform to the rationalist principles of the *Aufklärung*.

24. Leskov to D. N. Tsertelev, Sept. 20, 1890 (11:462).

25. In ibid., Oct. 23, 1890 (11:465), Leskov apologizes for (but at the same time justifies) the immense number of textual changes made in the proofs: "I can't refrain from corrections and revisions as long as there is any possibility of making them, and a printer's proof for some reason always has the property of revealing defects in a work that you don't notice in a manuscript, even one recopied many times."

26. Gebel', *Leskov*, pp. 143-150.

27. For instance the following rhythmic sentence added in proofs: "Zdrav-

stvuj, krasnaja devica, do drugix do vsex laskovaja, do sebja bezzabotnaja, ja prišel k tebe iz dalekix stran i prines poklon ot korolja našego batjuški, on menja poslal k tebe za bol'šim delom, kotoroe dlja vsego carstva nadobno" (ibid., p. 151).

28. Leskov to A. S. Suvorin, Dec. 14, 1890 (11:470-471).

29. Tolstoy to Leskov Dec. 31, 1890 (L. N. Tolstoj, *Perepiska s russkimi pisateljami* [Moscow, 1962], pp. 519-520).

30. Entry of June 12, 1898 (Tolstoj, *Polnoe*, 53 [1953]: 198).

31. Tolstoy felt obliged to assure Aleichem that he was not plagiarizing from Leskov, since the idea had originally been his. See his letter dated Aug. 25, 1903; quoted in ibid., 34 (1952): 556.

32. See B. M. Eikhenbaum's notes in ibid., pp. 554-560.

33. Leskov to Tolstoy, Dec. 6, 1890 (Tolstoj, *Perepiska*, p. 520).

34. "Pod Roždestvo obideli" *Peterburgskaja gazeta*, no. 354 (Dec. 25, 1890).

35. In a letter to Tolstoy Leskov identified the friend as Mikhail Pylyayev, the popular historian whose gem lore he had exploited for "The Alexandrite." He added that everything in the story was "real": "From beginning to end nothing was invented" (Jan. 4, 1891 [11:472]).

36. Jan. 15, 1891 (Tolstoj, *Polnoe*, 87 [1937]:68); Feb. 1, 1891 (ibid., 65 [1953]: 235).

37. Leskov to L. N. Tolstoy, 4, 1891 (11:472).

38. "Žizn' i fantazmagorija," *Novoe vremja*, no. 5337 (Jan. 7, 1891), pp. 2-3. The article was signed "A——t," the pseudonym of V. K. Petersen.

39. "Obujannaja sol'," *Peterburgskaja gazeta*, no. 12 (Jan. 13, 1891).

40. Inaccessible to me; cited from Tolstoj, *Perepiska* pp. 532-533.

41. Leskov to L. N. Tolstoy, Jan. 20, 1891 (11:479).

42. Tolstoy to Leskov, Jan. 20-21, 1891 (Tolstoj, *Perepiska*, p. 533).

43. Leskov to Tolstoy, Jan. 23, 1891 (Ibid., p. 533).

44. Leskov to B. M. Bubnov, May 14, 1891 (11:490).

45. "Vorovskoj syn," in *Russkim materjam*, ed. I. I. Gorbunov-Posadov (Moscow, 1892).

46. *Bednye deti* (Moscow, 1894); reprinted 1901.

47. *Dobroe delo* (Moscow, 1894).

48. An acquaintance of Leskov's father's, mentioned in "The Musk-ox," "The Mocker," and several other works.

49. "Pod prazdnik obideli," *Krug čtenija. Izbrannye, sobrannye i raspoloẑennye na kaẑdyj den' L'vom Tolstym mysli mnogix pisatelej ob istine, žizni i povedenii*, 3 (New York, 1921:78-90). There is an account by N. N. Gusev of Tolstoy's editing work in the apparatus to Tolstoj, *Polnoe*, 42 (1957): 590-591; Tolstoy was reminded of the story and assisted in the editing by F. A. Strakhov. The text of this version, however, was not reprinted in the Jubilee Edition.

50. "Vorov syn"; reprinted in Tolstoj, *Polnoe*, 41 (1957): 22-25.

51. "Tomlenie duxa; iz otročeskix vospominanij," N. S. Leskov, *Sobranie*

sočinenij, 6 (SPb., 1890): 510-519. It was originally published under the title "Koza" (Nanny-goat) in *Jubilejnyj sbornik žurnala "Igrušecka"* (SPb., 1890) and reprinted with a new title in the "replacement" volume 6, issued later the same year.

52. As pointed out by Grossman, *Leskov*, p. 200.

53. "Duračok," *Igrušečka*, no. 1 (Jan. 1891).

54. Grossman (*Leskov*, p. 234) classifies "Duračok" as a "fairy tale" (*skazka*), perhaps because the title suggests the traditional folktale figure, used, for instance, in Tolstoy's "Tale of Ivan the Fool," of the (ultimately vindicated) underdog, the "third brother." But Leskov's hero, Panka, bears little resemblance to this figure, and otherwise the story has nothing in common with the fairy tale form.

55. See Leskov to L. N. Tolstoy, July 28, 1893 (11:553); to M. O. Menshikov, Aug. 3, 1893 (11:556). In these letters Leskov says that in "The Little Fool" he made use of a story he had heard from his friend General Rostislav Fadeyev (also the source for "The Voice of Nature") concerning some Dukhobors who had similarly volunteered to serve out the Crimean War as latrine diggers. Leskov originally planned to call the story "Proxvost," a word whose rich etymological history, insofar as he knew it, must have delighted him. The word begins as Late Latin *praepositus*, "one set in authority," from *praeponere*, "to place before." In Old French the word becomes *provost*, but with the same meaning, and in this form it crossed the Channel to England. In Germany, first changing its shape to *Profoss*, it acquired in addition to its original meaning a new, specialized one: "naval rating in charge of punishing sailors who have violated ship's regulations." In the seventeenth century the Russians borrowed *Profoss* in this special sense. The phoneme /f/ does not occur in native Slavic words, and *profos* was therefore popularly rendered as *proxvos*. Then, by an obvious folk etymology restoring the final "t," this version led in turn to *proxvost* through contamination with *xvost*, "tail." It was passed on by the navy to the army, and in the land service, in addition to the parallel meaning, "military policeman who administers corporal punishments to arrested soldiers," it acquired (through association with "tail"?) a new meaning, "soldier in charge of digging or cleaning latrines." Neither role led to popular acclaim, and in the course of time *proxvost* acquired its meaning in modern Russian, which is simply, "dishonorable man, scoundrel, blackguard." Leskov of course, intended a play on the current meaning, but with the older "latrine" associations present as well. The effect survives in the text itself, but the censors evidently considered the word unsuitable for a children's magazine.

56. Tolstoy to V. N. Chertkov, Jan. 15, 1891 (Tolstoj, *Polnoe*, 87 [1937]: 68). Tolstoy must have made some similar remark in a lost letter to Leskov. At any rate, in Leskov to Tolstoy, Jan. 20, 1891 (11:478), Leskov makes the admission, "I know 'The Little Fool' is bad."

57. "Pustopljasy; svjatočnyj rasskaz," *Severnyj vestnik*, no. 1 (Jan. 1893), pp. 220-230.

58. 11:552. According to a note by S. Rozanova in Tolstoj, *Perepiska*, p. 561, "The Pustopliasians" was actually published by "The Intermediary," but without any publisher's imprint. I have no record of this edition. Lyubov Gurevich was the editor of *The Northern Messenger*; Sytin, publisher of "The Intermediary."

59. "Bramadata i Radovan," *P.s.s.*, 30 (1903): 179-92. The editor of that edition, R. I. Sementkovsky, provides only the following cryptic footnote: "This Indian tale, beautiful in form and profound in its basic thought, was prepared for the press in final form by the late writer and did not appear in his lifetime because of fortuitous circumstances" (p. 179n). Sementkovsky gives no further information concerning the manuscript or the "fortuitous circumstances." The story was not included in any Soviet edition of Leskov's works, and to my knowledge no Soviet scholar with access to Leskov's papers has adduced any information that would make possible any more precise dating. "Brahmadatta and Radovan" is not mentioned in K. P. Bogaevskaya's chronology of Leskov's life (11:825) and is not referred to in any of Leskov's published correspondence.

60. For identification of the source of this story I am greatly indebted to my Berkeley colleague, Barend A. van Nooten, who instantly spotted the outlines of the Pāli original, even through the dark glass of my summary of Leskov's version. An English translation of the Pāli story is to be found in *Vinaya Texts*, trans. T. W. Rhys Davids and Hermann Oldenberg, part 2 = *Sacred Books of the East*, ed. F. Max Müller, 17 (Delhi-Varanasi-Patna, 1965 [a reprint of the original edition published at Oxford in 1882]): 293-306. I have not been able to determine just where and in what form Leskov encountered the story.

61. Ibid., p. 305.

62. Ibid.

63. Ibid., p. 295.

36. The Prolog

1. N. I. Petrov, *O proisxoždenii i sostave slavjano-russkogo "Prologa"* (Kiev, 1875).

2. "There are new, significantly abridged Prologs," Leskov wrote in 1886, "and these are used in the offical church; and there are old, fuller Prologs, and these are to this day printed in Moscow, on the printing-press of the 'one-creed' monastery there for the one-creeders. [The "one-creed" church (*edinoverie*) was a government sponsored compromise between official Orthodoxy and the less radical Old Believer sects.] The one-creed Prologs [. . .] are sold openly everywhere, cost 36 rubles, and in content are in no way different from the old, patriarchal Prologs" ("Lučšij bogomolec," *Novosti i birževaja gazeta*, no. 109 [April 22, 1886]; reprinted 11:102). In another article written the same year Leskov cites a presumably Old Believer *Prolog* printed in

Grodno ("Prolog grodnenskoj pečati") that he may also have owned. See "O rožne," *Novoe vremja*, no. 3838 (Nov. 4, 1886), p. 3. Despite these assertions, it would appear from a comparison of Leskov's versions with a Synodal *Prolog* of 1896 that the nuclei of Leskov's plots might just as well have been derived from the official text. This conclusion is supported by the research of Stephen Lottridge, "Nikolaj Leskov and the Russian *Prolog* as a Literary Source," *Russian Literature*, no. 3 (The Hague, 1972), pp. 16-39. See also Lottridge, "Nikolaj Leskov's Moral Vision in the *Prolog* Tales," *Slavic and East European Journal*, no. 3 (1974), 252-258; V. J. Troickij, "Nekotorye sjužety i obrazy drevnej russkoj literatury u N. Leskova," *Russkaja literatura na rubeže dvux èpox (XVII-načalo XVIII v.)*, ed. A. N. Robinson (Moscow, 1971), pp. 338-396. It seems possible that Leskov's talk about discrepancies among various versions of the *Prolog* was an effort to deflect attention from the many changes he introduced in those stories.

3. Leskov to A. S. Suvorin, Nov. 9, 1892 (11:517).

4. "Dve legendy po starinnomu Prologu: 'Sovestnyj Danila' i 'Prekrasnaja Aza'," *Novoe vremja*, no. 4286 (Feb. 3, 1888); cited 11:714. Feofan Prokopovich (1681-1736) was Archbishop of Novgorod and the chief supporter within the church hierarchy of Peter the Great's reforms.

5. Dec. 25, 1889 (11:451).

6. *Prolog* (SPb., 1895-1896), 2 vols.

7. Dec. 26, 1887 (11:362).

8. "Lučšij bogomolec" (11:108).

9. A Russian translation of his novel *Uarda* (1877) was reissued as late as 1963: *Uarda; roman iz žizni drevnego Egipta* (Moscow, 1963).

10. "Povest' o Bogougodnom drovokole," incorporated in "Lučšij bogomolec." Under the title "Bogougodnyj drovokol; legenda," the story was included in the collected works without the surrounding discursive article. I am puzzled by the statement in K. P. Bogaevskaya's chronology of Leskov's life (11:825) that the "Tale of the God-favored Woodcutter" was forbidden by the censors on April 30, 1886, since the story had just appeared in print (April 22) as part of "The Best Suppliant." Perhaps the prohibition applied to a proposed separate publication of the tale.

11. See above, Chapter 34.

12. 11:102. Leskov ascribed the source of "What Men Live By" to the Afanasiev collection of Russian folk legends. Actually Tolstoy based the works on a tale he had heard narrated by the famous *bylina* singer, V. P. Shchegolyonok, in 1879. The latter was indeed ultimately derived from the *Prolog*. See L. N. Tolstoj, *Polnoe sobranie sočinenij*, 48:207.

13. "Skomorox Pamfalon; vostočnaja legenda," *Istoričeskij vestnik*, no. 3 (March 1887), pp. 481-526.

14. This is the title on the proof sheets preserved in the Pushkin House in Leningrad. See 8:579.

15. The change of names was insisted on by the ecclesiastical censor, who

decreed that since the name Theodulus was found in the calendar of saints, it should not be used in a secular story. (What, one might ask, about "Ivan"?) See Leskov to V. G. Chertkov, Feb. 1, 1887 (11:330). A report, dated Feb. 3, 1887, by the censor Archimandrite Tikhon is quoted in 11:702-703. Correctly identifying the *Prolog* source, Tikhon regarded the phrase "God-pleasing mountebank" as improper, and he further insisted on the blunting of the satirical edge of Leskov's presentation of Theodulus's asceticism. Finally, he ruled that the name Theodulus could not be used because it attributed to the saint acts not attested in his offical vita.

16. The reform of Hermius was an afterthought, introduced by Leskov in the proofs. See 8:580.

17. The extent of the changes made in the *Prolog* plot seem to me the reason why Leskov decided to omit the preface originally written for this story and published by A. I. Batyuto in his apparatus (8:580-583). In that canceled introduction Leskov had openly acknowledged the *Prolog* derivation of his tale, which he was adducing apropos of refuting the charge that Russia's Byzantine literary heritage was "monotonous, coarse, and boorish" by comparison with its western counterpart. The latter was (unfairly) illustrated by Leigh Hunt's "Legend of Florence" (1840), a Russian translation of which had just been published and supposedly had given rise to this anti-Byzantine judgment. Leskov summarizes Hunt's preposterous plot, with its uninspired exemplars of male nobility toward women, and offers in their stead a "more genuine, simple, and powerful" Byzantine legend, one that presents a more edifying model of virtue.

But after he had found it necessary to make substantial changes in this "genuine, simple, and powerful" Byzantine plot in order to prove his moral point, Leskov's argumentation was weakened. He evidently decided that it would be prudent to cover his Byzantine tracks: few of his readers (other than Archimandrite Tikhon) would notice his changes. This explanation for the omission of the preface (put forward by A. I. Batyuto) seems to me much more convincing than a second one, also suggested by Batyuto and enthusiastically seconded by Stephen Lottridge, to the effect that Leskov canceled the preface because it appeared to claim that his treatment of medieval material was superior not only to Hunt's, but also to Tolstoy's. This hypothesis rests on what seem to me strained interpretations of certain passages in the preface referring to Tolstoy, references that I consider the opposite of disparaging. Leskov simply says that his own aims and principles of selection from the *Prolog* are different from Tolstoy's, not that they are superior; and he describes Tolstoy's exploitation of *Prolog* material as exhibiting "matchless mastery" (8:582).

18. Chekhov to A. S. Suvorin, March 11, 1892 (A. P. Čexov, *Polnoe sobranie sočinenij i pisem*, 15 [Moscow, 1944-1952]: 341).

19. 8:211. It might be argued that the use in the translation of the archaic English second person singular has a distorting effect, deviating further from normal speech patterns than the original does. However, even in Russian Le-

skov's use of this grammatical category differs markedly from nineteenth-century social customs and therefore constitutes an element of stylization. In the nineteenth century a "low-class" entertainer addressing an aristocratic lady would certainly employ the polite plural. Pamfalon's failure to do so is not a sign of boorishness, but a linguistic symbol of alien time and place.

20. For instance, his play "Medea" (1883), written jointly with V. P. Burenin.

21. Leskov to A. S. Suvorin, March 14, 1887 (11:342).

22. Leskov to S. N. Shubinsky, Sept. 19, 1887 (11:348-349).

23. March 11, 1887 (11:338). A. I. Batyuto (8: 579-580) cites passages from the corrected proofs of this story showing that Leskov made quite drastic cuts in the course of his revision, creating a minor inconsistency in the plot, which he failed to correct in any subsequent editions.

24. Leskov to K. A. Grehwe, Oct. 31, 1888 (11:397).

25. Leskov to V. A. Goltsev, Nov. 14, 1888 (11:398).

26. *P.s.s.*, 33:141.

27. See Leskov's bitter protest in his letter to A. S. Suvorin, May 17, 1888 (*Pis'ma russkix pisatelej k A. S. Suvorinu*, ed. D. I. Abramovič [Leningrad, 1928], p. 83); also the more circumspect public statement in "O dobrom grešnike," *Novosti i birževaja gazeta*, no. 133 (May 15, 1888).

28. Leonid Grossman, *N. S. Leskov* (Moscow, 1945), p. 225; also "O dobrom grešnike."

29. "Legendarnye xaraktery," *Russkoe obozrenie*, no. 8 (1892).

30. Leskov's recent editors have not correctly identified the work referred to in his correspondence of the late 1880s as the "Legendary Characters" published in 1892. Referring to the "survey of the *Prolog* 'as a narrative source' " mentioned in Leskov to A. S. Suvorin, Dec. 26, 1887, I. Ja. Aizenshtok, for example, states categorically that "the manuscript [of this work] was not published in Leskov's lifetime and has not been preserved" (11:714). Similarly, for the work that "slept" in Leskov's desk for five years, Aizenshtok provides no explanation whatever. In 1891 the work was brought out and offered to D. N. Tsertelev for *Russian Survey* (where it ultimately appeared). Leskov first refers to it (11:505) by the title "Female Types according to the *Prolog*," previously used for the newspaper publication of "The Beauteous Aza," but here alluding to a survey article as yet unpublished. Leskov says it has long been ready for print, but has been held up *straxa radi*, "out of fear" (of the censorship). He asserts that "There is nothing bad in it," but the censors will forbid it anyway "out of malice and stupidity" (11:505). The same failure to identify "Legendary Characters" occurs in A. I. Batyuto's notes to "The Beauteous Aza" (8:598) and in K. P. Bogaevskaya's chronology of Leskov's life (11:825). The error was noted by A. Narkevich in his review of the edition (*Voprosy literatury*, no. 12 [Dec. 1959], p. 200), but he does not indicate all the instances where it occurs.

31. Characteristically, Leskov makes use of a Slavic folk etymology for the

Greek word πρόλογος. With a change of prefix, it becomes alternatively *pri-log*, interpreted as a synonym of the archaic *priklad*, "example," used, for instance, in the seventeenth-century translation from Polish of the medieval *Speculum magnum exemplorum*. See O. A. Deržavina, *"Velikoe zercalo" i ego sud'ba na russkoj počve* (Moscow, 1965). As Derzhavina shows (pp. 146-153), Leskov was familiar with this work, which contains several of the same stories as the Byzantine *Synaxarion*, and he drew on it for certain details in both "Pamphalon the Mountebank" and "The Mountain."

32. "Dve legendy po starinnomu Prologu. I. Sovestnyj Danila," *Novoe vremja*, no. 4286 (Feb. 3, 1888). It was published the following year together with "The Beauteous Aza" under the title *Sovestnyj Danila i prekrasnaja Aza; dve legendy po starinnomu Prologu* (Moscow, 1889). In the collected works it was given the title "Legenda o sovestnom Danile", cited here from *P.s.s.*, 30: 3-20.

33. There are several mistakes here, though it is not clear whose they are— Leskov's, his German authority's, or his printer's. In the first place, the church historian referred to must be not "Gasse," but Wilhelm Gass (1813-1889), who published a *Neuere Kirchgeschichte* in three volumes between 1874 and 1880. Though a Protestant, Gass was noted in Russia for his favorable attitude toward, and interest in, eastern Orthodoxy. The monophysite patriarch of Alexandria was Timotheus Aelurus, Αἴλουρος, "the cat," died 477, so-called for his stealthy movements, who was excommunicated by Pope Leo I. There is no Greek word * αἱλοδρος as cited by Leskov (*P.s.s.*, 30:12n.); possibly he has confused αἴλουρος with αἰόλος, "nimble, changing."

34. Quoted 11:714.

35. Letter to P. I. Biryukov, April 14, 1888 (Tolstoj, *Polnoe*, 64[1953]:161). Because of the odd way Tolstoy phrased his comment, there has been some confusion about which story he dubbed ''simple'' and which ''curly.'' I. Ya. Aizenshtok has them reversed in his note in 11:723, even though the identification is given correctly in the Tolstoy edition he quotes and even more clearly stated in Biryukov's biography of Tolstoy, where it was first published (P. I. Birjukov, *Biografija L'va Nikolaeviča Tolstogo*, 3 [Moscow, 1922]: 87). In fact, anyone who has read the two stories could have no doubts about which was "simple" and which "curly."

36. Tolstoj, *Polnoe*, 50 (1952): 90.

37. See Leskov to V. G. Chertkov, March 5, 1888 (11:368). Chertkov postponed publishing "Conscience-stricken Daniel" and "The Beauteous Aza" together in one book, for which he had the censor's permission, hoping to be allowed also to issue them separately. The delay greatly annoyed Leskov (see his letter dated March 28, 1889 [11:424]), since he was afraid the censors might reconsider the original permission. Nevertheless, all went well: the combined edition with "Aza" came out in 1889 (see above, note 32); and a new, more expensive one with illustrations by Repin appeared the following

year (Moscow, 1890). Leskov greatly disliked the Repin illustrations; see Leskov to V. G. Chertkov, May 15, 1889; cited in ANL, p. 462.

38. "Ženskie tipy po Prologu; prekrasnaja Aza," *Novoe vremja*, no. 4347 (April 5, 1888); reprinted with "Conscience-stricken Daniel" in 1889 (see above, note 32) and 1890; there was also a separate edition of "Aza" alone (Moscow, 1889), with Repin illustrations. The text of "The Beauteous Aza" was lifted with slight changes (mainly calling the heroine "Aza" instead of "the Egyptian girl") from the latter part of "Legendary Characters" (not yet published). Apparently Leskov had despaired of publishing the larger work and decided to make what capital he could out of pieces carved from it. Later both "Legendary Characters" and "The Beauteous Aza" were included intact in the collected works.

39. In view of these substantial changes in the ending of "The Beauteous Aza," Leskov's claim, in his letter to A. S. Suvorin dated April 12, 1888, that it was "written *exactly according to the Prolog*" (Leskov's italics) can only be regarded with astonishment. "I may compose variations," he goes on, perhaps aware that his letter is a considerable "variation" on the truth; "but I cannot depart from the original. [. . .] How could I give a different ending! I could only poeticize the scene—which I did" (*Pis'ma russkix pisatelej k A. S. Suvorinu* [Leningrad, 1928] , p. 69).

40. The preface is reprinted in 8:597-598. Privately, Leskov admitted that the dedication (to the poet Yakov Polonsky) and the preface had been explicitly designed to "mask its [the story's] spirit and tendency with accessories of a literary-polemical sort" (Leskov to V. G. Chertkov, March 5, 1888 [11:368-369]). But "any intelligent man," he added, "will understand why [it] is served with such a garnish and not au naturel. Au naturel it would have sat still and not been carried in 30,000 copies to all the ends of Russia. Later we can throw out the garnish and serve 'Aza' in her pure form." For once Leskov was as good as his word. In the later editions of "Aza" the preface was eliminated.

41. Leskov to A. S. Suvorin, April 19, 1888 (11:380). Tolstoy's letter to Leskov is not extant.

42. "Lev starca Gerasima; vostočnaja legenda," *Igrušečka*, no. 4 (April 1888), pp. 149-158; reprinted (Moscow, 1890) in an "Intermediary" edition together with the "Tale of the God-favored Woodcutter"; and in volume 10 of the collected works. The story had been written, at least in a preliminary draft, the previous December. In Leskov's letter to the editor of *Toy*, Aleksandra Peshkova-Toliverova, dated December 17, 1887, he reports that he has just read the *Prolog* version of the St. Jerome story and promises to work up an adaptation for her magazine. "But the story," he continues, "as usual with saint's-life descriptions, is dull and requires elaboration and reworking, and that in turn requires resurrecting in one's mind and memory the circumstances of eremitic life in the first centuries of Christianity, when St. Jerome flourished in Arabia" (11:361). A later letter (11:363) shows that he had finished a first

draft by December 26. The work was completed and read aloud to Repin, who did an illustration for it, on February 11, 1888 (11:365).

43. Leskov stresses the tactical importance of this verbal avoidance in his letter to Peshkova-Toliverova dated Dec. 26, 1887 (11:363).

44. Cited from a Church Slavonic version published under the title *Sinajskij paterik*, as the work was generally called in Russia, ed. V. S. Golyšenko and V. F. Dubrovina (Moscow, 1967) p. 187; checked with *Le pré spirituel*, ed. M.-J, Rouët de Journel, S. J. (Paris, 1946), p. 157.

45. "Askalonskij zlodej; iz sirijskix predanij," *Russkaja mysl'*, no. 11 (Nov. 1889), pp. 18-69.

46. When attacked by his persistent enemy, the populist critic A. M. Skabichevsky, for allegedly "inventing" the features of Herod's prison as depicted in the story, Leskov wrote a mordant reply, "Ob Irodovoj temnice," *Novoe vremja*, no. 4962 (Dec. 20, 1889); reprinted 11:242-243. He insists that he invented nothing, but copied everything from "Prologs and Menologia." He refrains from citing the chapter and verse of his sources.

47. For instance, the "albums" of Hottenroth and Maspero mentioned in Leskov to Z. P. Akhochinskaya, March 15-20, 1889 (11:422). Friedrich Hottenroth wrote a popular book on ancient artifacts, a book that Leskov owned.

48. Dec. 9, 1889 (11:447). Almost simultaneously with Leskov's story, A. S. Suvorin published one of his own based on the same *Prolog* plot: "Askalonskaja vernost'," *Novoe vremja*, no. 4967 (Dec. 25, 1889). In a prefatory note Suvorin graciously commended Leskov for the "erudition, labor, and talent" he had expended on *his* story, especially in presenting an accurate picture of everyday life, a task which he, Suvorin, had not attempted. The note is quoted in 11:746. Leskov was greatly moved by this praise, especially coming from the usually critical Suvorin. See Leskov to Suvorin, Dec. 25, 1889 (11:450).

49. Letter dated "The night of Dec. 9-10, 1889" (11:448). In an earlier letter to A. S. Suvorin, dated Dec. 9, 1889 (11:447), Leskov had also conceded that a different ending would have been closer to "true life." But after making this admission he at once defensively invoked the historian Klyuchevsky, who, he claimed, "strongly approves of my conception and considers that it was done in the spirit of that time."

50. Leskov to A. S. Suvorin, Dec. 25, 1889 (11:451).

51. "Gora," *Živopisnoe obozrenie*, nos. 1-12 (1890); reprinted the same year in a separate edition (SPb., 1890); and also in volume 10 of the collected works. The story was first submitted to *Russian Thought* in the fall of 1888, set up in type, but withdrawn at the last minute by the editors out of fear of the censorship. It was subsequently offered to P. A. Gaideburov for *The Week*; but when Gaideburov asked Leskov to "sacrifice the [ideological] thrust" of the story, the author indignantly refused. The editor of *Živopisnoe obozrenie* ("Pictorial Review"), the novelist A. K. Sheller (Mikhailov), managed, much to Leskov's amazement and delight, to squeeze the story through

the censorship under its new title (it had formerly been called "Zeno the Gold-smith") and with the names of the principal characters changed. In the collected works the original character names, Zeno and Nefora, were restored, but the new title, "The Mountain," was retained. See A. I. Faresov, *A. K. Šeller* (SPb., 1901), pp. 135-136; Leskov to V. A. Goltsev, Oct. 5, 1889 (11:439). This material is also cited in 8:600-603.

52. See Leskov to Tolstoy, Oct. 1, 1888 (L. N. Tolstoj, *Perepiska s russkimi pisateljami* [Moscow, 1962], p. 518. In that edition and in the earlier publication of the letter, in *Pis'ma Tolstogo i k Tolstomu* [Moscow, 1928], p. 72, the letter is misdated 1889, though indexed correctly in the 1962 volume). In the letter Leskov asked Tolstoy to help him place a letter to the editor of the Moscow newspaper *Russian News* in which he explained, insofar as possible in a censored publication, the reason why the story had not appeared in *Russian Thought* in the Fall of 1888. Tolstoy apparently obliged; at any rate Leskov's letter, under the title "Concerning the story 'Zeno the Goldsmith'," was duly published: "O povesti 'Zenon zlatokuznec'; pis'mo v redakciju," *Russkie vedomosti*, no. 12 (Jan. 12, 1889); reprinted 11:240-241; also 8:601-602. Leskov denied as "absolutely false" the rumor that there was any connection between any character in the story and "a certain recently deceased person of Russian origin who lived and operated in Moscow." He also denied that he and the editors of *Russian Thought* had had any falling out. The latter claim is demonstrably false, as several angry letters from Leskov to V. A. Goltsev show. Though their magazine was not subject to preliminary censorship, Goltsev and V. M. Lavrov had *voluntarily* submitted Leskov's story to the ecclesiastical censors; and that seemd to Leskov an act of gratuitous cowardice, which, furthermore, the two tried to conceal from him. See Leskov to Goltsev, Nov. 14 (11:398), Nov. 20, Nov. 29, 1888 (11:731); to Lavrov, Dec. 30, 1888 (ibid.); to P. I. Biryukov, Dec. 30, 1888 (11:497-408). On Jan. 1, 1889, Tolstoy went with Biryukov to the editorial offices of *Russian Thought* to investigate the fate of "Zeno the Goldsmith." He was told that after receiving the unfavorable report of the ecclesiastical censors in Moscow, Lavrov had gone to Petersburg to appeal their decision. The appeal, however, was to the chief censor, Leskov's long-standing enemy, Yevgeny Feoktistov, and no help was likely to be obtained from him. Feoktistov simply referred the case to the main Moscow censorship board, which got the hint and prohibited the story. See Biryukov to Leskov, Jan. 3, 1889, in V. G. Zimina, ed., "Iz arxiva N. S. Leskova," Gosudarstvennaja biblioteka imeni V. I. Lenina, *Zapiski otdela rukopisej*, issue 30 (Moscow, 1968), pp. 228-231.

53. On Pobedonostsev's anti-Semitism, see Robert F. Byrnes, *Pobedonostsev: His Life and Thought* (Bloomington and London, 1968), pp. 202-209. The identification of Peokh with Pobedonostsev is hinted at (though denied) in Leskov to P. I. Biryukov, Jan. 7, 1889 (11:411). Without reference to this letter, the possibility of an implied connection between the anti-Christian pogroms in "The Mountain" and anti-Jewish pogroms in Russia was raised in an article

by Ivan Rozanov, "Ešče o Leskoviane," *Knižnye novosti*, no. 23-24 (1937), p. 108. Though Rozanov makes a number of obvious factual errors, I would not dismiss the connection with as much assurance as does A. I. Batyuto in 8:604.

54. "O povesti 'Zenon-zlatokuznec' " (11:241). A. I. Batyuto (8:692n) lists Herodotus and Strabo among the "Egyptologists" consulted by Leskov! He adduces convincing evidence (8:608-610) of Leskov's use of current Russian translations of Herodotus, Strabo, and Theocritus, and also of Ebers's immensely popular novel *Aegyptische Königstochter*.

55. S. T[ruba]čev, *Istoričeskij vestnik*, no. 6 (June 1890), pp. 679-681.

56. Leskov to S. N. Shubinsky, June 2, 1890 (11:459-460).

57. Leskov to I. E. Repin, Feb. 18, 1889 (11:414).

58. Leskov to V. M. Lavrov, July 20, 1889 (11:435).

59. Leskov to V. A. Goltsev, Oct. 5, 1889 (11:438).

60. "Nevinnyj Prudentij; legenda," *Rodina*, nos. 1-6 (1891); reprinted in a separate edition (Moscow, 1892); and in the supplementary volume 11 (1893) of the collected works.

61. Leskov and I. A. Goncharov had been acquainted for many years, at least since the early 1870s (ANL, pp. 376-377), but the relationship remained formal and distant, though marked by mutual respect. In the late 1880s, besides the consultation over "Innocent Prudentius," there was a flurry of correspondence between them in connection with an article about Goncharov by Viktor Rusakov (Librovich) ("Slučajnye vstreči s I. A. Goncarovym," *Nov'*, no. 7 [1888], pp. 137-144), against which Leskov wrote an anonymous defense of Goncharov ("Literaturnyj grex," *Peterburgskaja gazeta*, no. 38 [February 8, 1888]). Leskov, however, did not acknowledge his authorship of this article to Goncharov, who hated publicity of any kind. See Zimina, "Iz arxiva," pp. 222-228.

62. Feb. 11, 1888 (Zimina, "Iz arxiva," pp. 223-224).

63. Feb. 11, 1888 (11:365). The "legend" referred to is wrongly identified in 11:716 as "Conscience-stricken Daniel." This exchange of letters shows that the conception of "Innocent Prudentius" goes back to a time several years before its publication date. In Leskov's published correspondence there is no further evidence of when the story was written.

64. I. A. Goncharov was alive when the story appeared in the newspaper *Native Land*, but ill and living in total seclusion. He died later the same year (September 15, 1891). There is no evidence that Leskov sent him the final text of "Innocent Prudentius."

65. G. Georgievskij, "Apokrifičeskoe skazanie ili literaturnaja fal'sifikacija," *Russkoe obozrenie*, no. 10 (Sept. 1892), pp. 946-959; quoted 9:602-603; also 8:584.

66. Leskov to A. S. Suvorin, Nov. 9, 1892 (11:517).

67. June 27, 1893; quoted ANL, p. 470; also 9:602.

68. Jan. 23, 1891 (Tolstoj, *Perepiska* p. 534).

69. "Oskorblennaja Netèta; istoričeskaja povest'," ed. A. A. Izmajlov,

Nevskij al'manax, issue 2 (Petrograd, 1917), pp. 138-186; not reprinted.

70. *The Works of Flavius Josephus*, trans. William Whiston (London, 1906), p. 531.

71. Dec. 7, 1889 (11:444).

72. Unpublished preface to an early draft called "Idol'skaja Netèta"; quoted in Valentina Gebel', *N. S. Leskov: v tvorčeskoj laboratorii* (Moscow, 1945), p. 67.

73. Leskov to V. M. Lavrov, Dec. 7, 1889 (11:444).

74. Gebel', *Leskov*, p. 67.

75. Leskov to D. N. Tsertelev, Sept. 20, 1890 (11:461). Leskov did an enormous amount of reading for "Insulted Neteta," mostly in Russian translations of classical Latin authors. The story contains echoes, epigraphs, or quotations from Tacitus, Catullus, Tibullus, Ovid, Horace, and Martial. For Josephus Leskov used and cited a Russian edition of 1783. See esp. Leskov to E. M. Bem, June 20, 1891 (*Nevskij al'manax*, 2:142).

76. Leskov to D. N. Tsertelev, Oct. 23, 1890 (11:465).

77. Leskov to A. F. Marks, Sept. 25, 1890, in N. S. Pleščunov, ed., "Iz perepiski N. S. Leskova," in A. V. Bagrij, ed., "Literaturnyj seminarij," *Izvestija Azerbajdžanskogo gosudarstvennogo universiteta imeni V. I. Lenina*, 8-10 (Baku, 1927): 29. Unfortunately, the "reminiscences" remained unwritten.

78. Leskov to D. N. Tsertelev, Dec. 14, 1891 (11:505).

79. ANL, p. 449.

80. Grossman, *Leskov*, pp. 231-232.

37. John of Kronstadt

1. Leskov to Tolstoy, Jan. 23, 1891 (L. N. Tolstoj, *Perepiska s russkimi pisateljami* [Moscow, 1962], p. 534).

2. Leskov to D. N. Tsertelev, Oct. 23, 1890 (11:466). My translation is a feeble attempt to echo Leskov's rhyme: *ladon i kadilo očen' načadilo*, "smoked out by incense and the censer."

3. V. Mikulič, pseud. (Lidija Ivanovna Veselitskaja-Božidarovič), "Pis'ma N. S. Leskova," *Literaturnaja mysl'; al'manax*, 3 (Leningrad, 1925): 297. According to the memoirs of Tolstoy's cousin, Countess Aleksandra Tolstaya, Alexander III acknowledged that Tolstoy and Father John were the two "most remarkable and popular persons in Russia." See Ivan Zaxarin-Jakunin, "Grafinja A. A. Tolstaja; ličnye vpečatlenija i vospominanija," *Vestnik Evropy*, no. 4 (April 1905), p. 617. A somewhat fuller exposition of the material in this chapter is contained in my article, "Leskov and Ioann of Kronstadt: On the Origins of *Polunoščniki*," *American Slavic and East European Review*, no. 1 (Feb. 1953), pp. 93-108. See also L. G. Čudnova, "Satira N. S. Leskova 1890-x godov 'Polunoščniki'," *Učenye zapiski gos. pedagogičeskogo instituta imeni A. I. Gercena*, 245 (1963): 313-334.

Notes to Pages 597-600

4. On Sergiev, see *Otec Ioann Kronštadtskij (otkliki pečati po povodu ego končiny)* (Sergiev Posad, 1910); A. Semenov-Tjan-Šanskij, *Otec Ioann Kron-štadtskij* (New York, 1954); G. P. Fedotov, *A Treasury of Russian Spirituality* (New York, 1948), pp. 346-416; *Ènciklopedičeskij slovar'*, 29 (SPb. 1900): 647; *Ènciklopediceskij slovar'*, 37 (Granat, Moscow, n.d.): 614-616. His spiritual autobiography, *Moja žizn' vo Xriste*, has been translated into English: *My Life in Christ*, E. E. Goulaeff trans. (London, 1897).

5. *Obličenie lžeučenija grafa L'va Tolstogo: Apologetičeskij listok*; reprinted as a supplement to *Prixodskaja žizn'* (1912).

6. A. Černovskij, compiler, and V. P. Viktorov, ed., *Sojuz russkogo naroda po materialam črezvyčajnoj sledstvennoj komissii vremennogo pravitel'stva 1917 g.* (Moscow-Leningrad, 1929), p. 36.

7. Henry W. Nevinson, *The Dawn in Russia, or Scenes in the Russian Revolution* (London and New York, 1906), p. 253.

8. Jan. 12, 1891 (11:476). The hospital referred to was in the same building in Petersburg, Furshtadtskaya 50, where Leskov lived. V. Ya. Mikhailovsky was a priest at the Church of the Ascension in Petersburg and author of a book entitled *Drunkenness and Its Cure*.

9. Jan. 8, 1891 (11:475).

10. "Polunoščniki; pejzaž i žanr," *Vestnik Evropy*, no. 11-12 (Nov.-Dec. 1891), pp. 92-137, 537-576.

11. *Šestidesjatye gody: Materialy po istorii literatury i obščestvennomu dviženiju*, ed. N. K. Piksanov and O. V. Cexnovicer (Moscow-Leningrad, 1940), p. 356. Oral statement by Koni to Solomon Reiser in 1927.

12. On the circumstances of Leskov's reconciliation with Stasyulevich, see 11:765-766; and McLean, "Leskov and Ioann of Kronstadt," pp. 97-98n.

13. The rest of Khilkov's life is a curious study in the wheel come full circle. His "Tolstoyan" period lasted until about 1899; during that time he was administratively banished to the Caucasus for anticlerical propaganda among the peasants (1892), had his two children taken away from him by the police (1893)—at the instigation of his mother and "with the blessing of Ioann of Kronstadt"—so that they might be properly baptized in the Orthodox church (this incident made an enormous impression on both Leskov and Tolstoy), and accompanied the Dukhobors on their migration to Canada (1898). About this time he broke with the Tolstoyan doctrine of nonviolence, and, settling in western Europe, joined the Socialist Revolutionary party, for which he wrote several pamphlets (1900-1905). At the end of 1905 he returned to Russia, retired to his farm, and became a devout upholder of the Orthodox church. In 1914, he reentered the army, saying, "To die in this war would be the greatest blessing God could grant me." Khilkov was killed on a reconnaissance mission in the Carpathians in October 1914. See L. N. Tolstoj, *Polnoe sobranie sočinenij*, 85 (1935): 415-416; 87 (1937): 97.

14. "Printed from a copy preserved in the archives of N. S. Leskov," *L. N.*

Tolstoj, Letopisi: Gosudarstvennyj Literaturnyj Muzej, ed. N. N. Gusev (Moscow, 1938), pp. 114-117. In this publication the letter is erroneously dated August 1, 1891, which, if true, would invalidate my thesis about the genesis of *Polunoščniki*. However, this date is supplied by the editors; the end of the letter as they publish it bears the inscription "2 VIII 90 goda" (p. 117). The recently published volumes of Tolstoy's diaries and correspondence make the date 1890 certain beyond any doubt. The Tolstoy diary entry in which he speaks of receiving a "wonderful letter from Khilkov about Father John" is dated Aug. 3, 1890 (Tolstoj, *Polnoe*, 51 [1952]: 71). Tolstoy replied to the letter enthusiastically on the same day, Aug. 3, 1890 (ibid., 65 [1953]: 134-135).

15. A vivid contemporary picture of the crush and confusion during one of John of Kronstadt's visitations is quoted in 9:604, from *Nedelja*, 1885.

16. The saintly Klavdia had a living prototype in the niece of Savva Morozov, an enormously wealthy merchant. As Leskov wrote his stepson during the famine of 1891, "I once wrote you about the girl Morozova,—the niece of Savva Morozov, a beauty with a fortune of five to seven millions. I sketched something of her in *Polunoščniki*, [. . .] but in her there is an inexhaustible source for the ecstasies of a poet. A few days ago she came here [to Petersburg] to ask them to let her distribute a *million* to the hungry, but directly—without priests and officials. They say her request was refused. She is becoming a legend in her own lifetime. These are the angels one should look for—angels who have come down to earth and live in skins like ours, and not people who are somewhere off in the mists of fantasy." Leskov to B. M. Bubnov, Nov. 5, 1891 (*Šestidesjatye gody*, ed. Piksanov and Cexnovicer, pp. 368-369).

17. See Aleksandra Narcizova, *Pis'ma o putešestvijax s otcem Ioannom Kronštadtskim na ego rodinu i v drugie mesta* (SPb., 1894).

18. Nov. 30, 1890 (11:469).

19. According to A. N. Bogoslavsky in *Kratkaja literaturnaja ènciklopedija*, 6 (Moscow, 1971): 540.

20. 11:474. *Uvertjura* is one of the "slovečki" or trick words in the story—there is a pun on *uvertka*, "clever dodge."

21. Jan. 8, 1891 (11:475).

22. Jan. 20, 1891 (11:478).

23. Leskov to Tolstoy, 23, 1891 (Tolstoj, *Perepiska*, p. 534).

24. Feb. 26, 1891 (ibid., p. 538). What the censors missed was quickly picked up by the reactionary press, which lost no time in raising a hue and cry against Leskov for his "slander" of John of Kronstadt, adding, of course, that the story was in any case artistically worthless and unworthy of serious consideration. See, among others, Archimandrite Antonij, "Znamenie vremeni," *Bogoslovskij Vestnik*, Feb. 1892; Ju. Nikolaev, "Literaturnye zametki: Čto znamenuet 'znamenie'," *Moskovskie Vedomosti*, March 7, 1892; an anony-

mous review, "Literaturno-kritičeskij fel'eton," *Graždanin*, Dec. 3, 1891. A quotation from the last will serve for all of them.: " 'Night Owls' was written without any assistance from the Muse. . . . [It is] the most ordinary, vulgar, and vile 'women's chatter,' which no one on earth cares anything about."

25. Tolstoj, *Perepiska*, p. 538.

26. The first ten volumes of the collected works had been published by A. S. Suvorin in 1889-1890, but Leskov was displeased with Suvorin's business practices, and published the eleventh volume with Marks, who issued a twelfth, posthumous volume in 1896.

27. Jan. 23, 1891 (Tolstoj, *Perepiska*, p. 534).

28. It is entirely possible that some of the passages in the second, book version which are missing from the magazine text were not added later, but were included in the original manuscript, then eliminated for reasons of censorship, and subsequently restored. The English journalist E. J. Dillon recalls, "My friend Leskoff entertained the deepest contempt for John of Cronstadt and read me a tremendous attack on him wrapped up in literary form. *Part of it* appeared later in the *Messenger of Europe*" (*The Eclipse of Russia* [New York, 1918], p. 108n; italics mine). There are many passages that certainly could not have offended the censors, but nonetheless show stylistic revision in the second version of the story. It is thus clear that Leskov worked over the text between 1891 and 1893.

29. *Vestnik Evropy*, no. 11 (Nov. 1891), p. 121; italics mine.

30. Ibid., no. 12 (Dec. 1891), p. 555.

31. The phrase "It shall be unto you according to your faith" was a particular favorite of John of Kronstadt's. See Narcizova, *Pis'ma*, p. 34.

32. L. N. Tolstoj, "Otvet na opredelenie Sinoda ot 20-22 Fevralja i na polučennye mnoju po ètomu slučaju pis'ma," *Sobranie sočinenij*, 16 (Moscow, 1964): 548-549.

33. There is a fuller and more technical analysis of this performance in my article, "On the Style of a Leskovian *Skaz*," *Harvard Slavic Studies*, 2 (Cambridge and The Hague, 1954): 297-322. See also A. B. Ansberg, "Frame Story and First Person Story in N. S. Leskov," *Scando-Slavica*, 3 (Copenhagen, 1957): 49-73.

34. A. A. Slepcov, "Literatura 1891 goda," *Russkoe bogatstvo*, no. 1 (Jan. 1892), p. 115; quoted 9:606.

35. The word is explained below, note 37.

36. As I know from personal experience. But my despair was dispelled and my translation much improved by some brilliant suggestions from the editor of the volume where it appeared, William B. Edgerton. See *Satirical Stories of Nikolai Leskov* (New York; 1969), pp. 242-326.

37. My attempt to reproduce this effect was "expectension." I might point out for the statistical record that I counted 165 *different* examples in "Night Owls" of lexical distortions such as these.

38. Sodom and Gomorrah

1. *Proxvos.* On this word see above, chapter 35, note 56.
2. Leskov to L. N. Tolstoy, July 22, 1888 (11:392).
3. See above, chapter 35.
4. "Antukà; rasskaz," *Knižki Nedeli,* no. 10 (Oct. 1888), pp. 1-35.
5. Vsevolod Setchkarev (*N. S. Leskov,* [Wiesbaden, 1959], p. 123) thinks that it is a Czech revolt against Austria. The story's associations and atmosphere are all Polish rather than Czech; the only Czech connections are the locale of the author's original meeting with the first narrator and the fact that one set of oppressors of Poland are referred to as *rakušanskie švaby,* "Austrian Swabians," using the Czech word for "Austrian."
6. Leonid Grossman, *N. S. Leskov* (Moscow, 1945), p. 284.
7. "Improvizatory; kartinka s natury," *Knižki Nedeli,* no. 12 (Dec. 1892).
8. May 9, 1894; cited ANL, p. 563.
9. In his letter to V. A. Goltsev dated May 10, 1894 (11:582).
10. "Zimnij den'," *Russkaja mysl',* no. 9 (Sept. 1894).
11. *Satirical Stories of Nikolai Leskov* (New York, 1969), p. 353.
12. The translation provided by the Soviet editors for the French phrase *criminal conversations de Byzance* (9:448), with which the lady describes these incestuous relations, is "an improper conversation about crimes" (*neumestnyj razgovor o prestuplenijax*)!
13. Setchkareff, *Leskov,* pp. 153-154. Setchkarev rightly takes Leonid Grossman to task for his absurd misinterpretation of this last sentence as proclaiming the "unchanging domination of an elemental-materialistic worldview over all attempts to find moral meaning in life" (Grossman, *Leskov,* p. 245). Maria Goryachkina (*Satira Leskova* [Moscow, 1963], p. 132) also scolds Grossman for the same gaffe. While Leskov's indictment doubtless by implication applies universally, and not to Russia alone, the picture he draws of sexual depravity does bear striking resemblance to that found in a once famous article, "Sexual Morality in Russia," written by Leskov's friend, E. J. Dillon (E. B. Lanin, pseud.), and published in the Sept. 1890 issue of *The Fortnightly Review* (pp. 372-397). Dillon's article is reprinted in his book *Russian Characteristics* (London, 1891), *Russian Traits and Terrors* (Boston, 1891).
14. ANL, p. 557.
15. N. Makšeeva, "Pamjati N. S. Leskova," *Moskovskij eženedel'nik,* no. 42 (Oct. 25, 1908), p. 46. On "A. A. and Mlle L." see below, note 22.
16. Grossman, *Leskov,* p. 113.
17. Letter to M. O. Menshikov, Nov. 12, 1893; quoted ANL, p. 605.
18. Letter dated Oct. 11, 1894 (L. N. Tolstoj, *Perepiska s russkimi pisateljami* [Moscow, 1962], pp. 607-608).
19. Stasyulevich to Leskov, May 9, 1894; cited ANL, p. 563.
20. Leskov to V. A. Goltsev, May 10, 1894 (11:582). The evidence is thus

perfectly clear that "A Winter's Day" was not based on the Sollogub case, but only confirmed by it. The former assertion is carelessly repeated by some Leskov scholars: by Grossman (*Leskov*, p. 244); A. I. and S. I. Gruzdev (9:631). The Gruzdevs cite Andrei Leskov in support of their contention, but Andrei Leskov says clearly that the Sollogub trial "confirmed Leskov's picture of the disintegration of Russian society given in his story 'A Winter's Day,' then almost finished" (p. 563).

21. Leskov to V. A. Goltsev, Aug. 21, 1894; cited in B. M. Drugov, *N. S. Leskov* (Moscow, 1957), p. 140.

22. Maksheyeva may possibly be a relative (sister?) of Zakhar Andreevich Maksheyev, who married Leskov's stepdaughter, Vera Bubnova, and later served as executor of his will. She appears to be the "A. A."mentioned in the passage quoted above, the sister of N. Maksheyeva, the author of the article. She was studying nursing at the time N. Maksheyeva met Leskov, and Leskov expressed strong approval of such upperclass girls preparing themselves for careers of social service. He also stated his belief that, at least in that generation, the women were morally superior to the men, adding bitterly that the best girls do not get married, just as the best books do not get read. The "Mlle L." mentioned in the same passage is presumably Lörberg. See Makšeeva, "Pamjati N. S. Leskova."

23. *Pamjati V. A. Gol'ceva* (Moscow, 1910), p. 252; cited from Gorjačkina, *Satira Leskova*, p. 130. The "mirror" proverb is used as the epigraph to Gogol's *Inspector-General*.

24. ANL, p. 662.

25. Undated letter, assigned by Andrei Leskov (p. 661) to Feb. 14 or 15, 1895, first published in V. Mikulič, "Pis'ma N. S. Leskova," *Literaturnaja mysl'*, 3 (Leningrad, 1925); 299.

26. S. A. Tolstaja, *Pis'ma k Tolstomu, 1862-1910* (Moscow-Leningrad, 1936), p. 602.

27. A. I. Faresov, *Protiv tečenij* (SPb., 1904), p. 382.

28. A. I. Faresov, "Paradoksy N. S. Leskova," *Slovo*, no. 147, supp. (May 11, 1905); cited from ANL, p. 559.

39. The Rabbit Warren

1. "Zajačij remiz," *Niva*, no. 34-37 (Sept. 16, 1917), pp. 518-545; "Administrativnaja gracija," *God XVII*, book 4 (July 1934). It seems probable that both stories could have been published in the more liberal atmosphere that prevailed between 1905 and 1917, but there is no evidence that anyone tried to do so. Andrei Leskov reports (N. S. Leskov, *Izbrannye proizvedenija* [Moscow, 1945], p. 460) that "it was proposed in 1900 to publish 'Administrativnaja gracija' abroad, in a collection of forbidden Russian prose to be financed by S. Mamontov." He does not explain why this proposal was not carried out.

2. Andrei Leskov (ANL, p. 442) mistakenly identifies the professor as I. I.

Dityatin of Kharkov University. Ivan Dityatin (1847-1892) was a distinguished legal historian. He was dismissed from Kharkov University, but in 1887, not 1879; thus his case is another example of Delyanov's "graceless" repressions, not Dmitry Tolstoy's. I have not been able to identify the 1879 case, if there was one, on which Leskov's story is based.

3. *Satirical Stories of Nikolai Leskov* (New York, 1969), p. 343.

4. Prince D. N. Kropotkin, the governor of Kharkov Province, was assassinated on March 9, 1879, by a member of the Land and Liberty party, G. D. Goldenberg.

5. Leonid Grossman, *N. S. Leskov* (Moscow, 1945), p. 236.

6. Cited from ibid., p. 246n.

7. "Peregudinskij pustopljas," cited from Š. P. Sesterikov, "K bibliografii sočinenij N. S. Leskova," *Izvestija Otdelenija russkogo jazyka i slovesnosti Akademii Nauk SSSR*, 30 (1925): 302.

8. See Leskov to V. M. Lavrov, Dec. 14, 1891 (11:504).

9. Leskov to D. N. Tsertelev, Dec. 14, 1891 (11:505).

10. Ibid., Dec. 18, 1891 (11:507). Technically, *Russian Thought* was not subject to preliminary censorship. The editors therefore could publish anything they pleased; but if the censors found it reprehensible, the magazine could be first warned and then closed down.

11. The manuscript of this early "Rabbit Warren" does not seem to have survived among Leskov's papers.

12. Leskov to V. A. Goltsev, May 4, 1891 (11:485). Aleksandr Zhomini (1814-1888) was a prominent Russian diplomat and historian. Nikolai Ashinov was the Russian adventurer who, with Pobedonostsev's support, tried to stake out a Russian imperial claim to African territory. He is ridiculed in several other stories and articles by Leskov, notably "The Cattle-pen." M——v's daughter is probably the millionairess Morozova who may have served as the prototype for Klavdia in "Night Owls."

13. Ibid., May 10, 1891 (11:486-488).

14. This is the opinion of Boris Eikhenbaum: see his note in N. S. Leskov, *Izbrannye sočinenija* (Moscow-Leningrad, 1931), p. 751.

15. Cited in Andrei Leskov's note to the story in N. S. Leskov, *Izbrannye proizvedenija* (Moscow, 1945), p. 462.

16. Cited from ibid., p. 461.

17. This is the opinion of Andrei Leskov (ibid., pp. 461-462); and of I. Ya. Aizenshtok (11:767).

18. Leskov to V. A. Goltsev, Nov. 16, 1894 (11:599). The variant title of "A Game with a Dummy" (*Igra s bolvanom*) is also found, canceled, in the manuscript from which the 1917 text was printed. See note in 9:642. The meaning of "dummy" is, of course, punningly restored from its "card" sense to its "real" one—thus introducing yet another meaning for *bolvan*.

19. V. M. Lavrov to Leskov, Dec. 13, 1894; cited 9:643. The fact that in their 1894 correspondence neither Leskov nor Lavrov, who had read "An In-

vasion of Barbarians" in 1891, refers to any resemblance or genetic connection between them would appear to support Eikhenbaum's view that they are entirely different works. See also L. I. Levandovskij, "K tvorčeskoj istorii povesti N. S. Leskova 'Zajačij remiz'," *Russkaja literatura*, no. 4 (1971), 124-128.

20. I will defend here the zoological inaccuracy of my translation of the "obscure" title *Zajačij remiz.* The Russian word *zajac* properly means "hare," not "rabbit," and the correct translation would therefore be "Hare Warren." But in the first place, Americans customarily, though inaccurately, call all the leporids *rabbits;* for us the *hare* belongs more to English literature than to the kingdom of live animals. (By contrast, David Magarshack's translation of the title, "The March Hare," though ingenious, seems to me to invoke English literature illegitimately, with an allusion never intended by Leskov.) In the second place, in the biblical passage Leskov cites in explanation of his title, the Russian *hare* is in fact just as inaccurate as *rabbit.* In Psalm 104:18 (Orthodox numbering 103:18) the Authorized Version has *conies* where the Russian has *zajcy,* "hares": "The high hills are a refuge for the wild goats; and the rocks for the conies." This "coney," Hebrew *shāphān,* has been identified by some authorities as a "rock badger," *Hyrax syriacus,* and by others as the "daman," *Procavia syriaca,* a small hoofed mammal. It is neither a hare nor a rabbit; and I therefore felt free to use a translation that seemed more alliteratively and trochaically "sonorous and enticing."

21. Leskov to M. M. Stasyulevich, Jan. 8, 1895 (11:606). A variant of the Sternean alternative title was eventually used as a subtitle: "The Observations, Experiences, and Adventures of Onopry Peregud of Peregudy."

22. Cited from 9:643, but without date. Presumably written toward the end of Jan. 1895.

23. Leskov to M. M. Stasyulevich, Feb. 8, 1895 (11:607).

24. Ivan Shylapkin reports that Leskov told him "The Rabbit Warren" was the third part of a trilogy on the fate of Russian society in the nineteenth century, the first two parts of which were *No Way Out* and *Falcon Flight.* Apart from the fact that all three invoke the theme of nihilism and revolution, it is difficult to perceive any serious artistic connection linking these works. It seems likely that Leskov did not mean "trilogy" in the sense of a three-part work with a unifying design, but was simply citing examples of his long-term commitment as a social critic. Furthermore, the "Rabbit Warren" referred to may have been the early, "Invasion of Barbarians" version. See I. A. Šljapkin, "K biografii N. S. Leskova," *Russkaja starina*, 84 (Dec. 1895): 210.

25. On these late changes, with quotations from early and late variants, see Valentina Gebel', *N. S. Leskov; v tvorčeskoj laboratorii* (Moscow, 1945), pp. 152-154.

26. The name Ovechkin is incongruously derived from *ovečka,* "little sheep," though the man is very much a wolf. The prefixed *vek,* meaning "an age, century, one's whole life," besides implying the permanence of his non-ovine qualities, gives the impression of being derived by folk etymology from

the second syllable of Ovečkin.

27. 9:528. Besides the intrinsic pointlessness of memorizing such precise and totally unsubstantiated dates, Leskov also mocks Vekovechkin with the fact that even his senseless statistics do not work out arithmetically. If Mary was born in 22 B.C. (according to Byzantine tradition, the creation occurred in 5508 B.C.) and Jesus in 0, the Annunciation could not have occurred in 8 B.C. Moreover, if Mary was born in 22 B.C., she was not in the twelfth year and seventh month of her age in 8 B.C.

28. Andrei Leskov reports (ANL, p. 473) that "angry eelpouts" were a favorite delicacy of the writer Vsevolod Krestovsky.

29. In a letter to L. N. Tolstoy dated Dec. 15, 1893, Leskov reported his rediscovery of this article in Zhukovsky's collected works (11:572).

30. N. S. Pleščunov, "Zametki o stile povesti Leskova," *Literaturnyj seminarij*, ed. A. V. Bagrij, no. 6 (Baku, 1928), pp. 37-62; also in *Vostokovedenie*, 3 (Baku, 1928); P. Filippovič, "Ukrajins'kyj element v tvorax M. Leskova," in M. Leskov, *Vybrani tvory* (Kiev, 1929)—inaccessible to me, but cited in Boris Eikhenbaum's notes in N. S. Leskov, *Izbrannye sočinenija* (Moscow-Leningrad, 1931), pp. 752-753; a similar judgment was stated to me orally by Ḍmitry Čiževsky.

31. For example, *poza roži*, literally "the pose of the mug," for "facial expression"; *sicilisty* for *socialisty*, with possible associations both with "Sicily" and "syphilis"; [*v sadu*] *možno bludit' strašnej, čem v lesu*, "[in a garden] one can get lost [pun: fornicate] more terribly than in the woods"; *egalité i bratarnite*, the last, of course, for "fraternité," from Russian, *brat*, "brother"; and many others.

32. In his list of "great gentlemen" who have described the Ukraine, Onopry Peregud includes, along with Gogol and Kvitko-Osnovyanenko, the mysterious name of Dzyubaty (9:510). My own library research and inquiries among Ukrainian scholars have proved fruitless in identifying this figure. A. I. and S. I. Gruzdev, as well as other annotators of the story, are silent about Dzyubaty, although Eikhenbaum seems to believe in his reality (Leskov, *Izbrannye sočinenija*, p. 752). Donald Fanger, who assisted me in my pursuit of Dzyubaty, suggested that the name, which means "beaked," might be a second "Sternean" reference to the nose-obsessed Gogol, mentioned in the same passage by his proper name.

33. Grossman, *Leskov*, pp. 247-248.

34. Ibid., p. 203. The Russian title of the Chekhov story is "Peresolil." It has been—inaccurately—translated into English as "Overspiced."

40. A Winter's Night

1. ANL, p. 661. Most of the material on Leskov's death in this chapter is derived from ANL.

2. Leskov to A. S. Suvorin, Dec. 30, 1890, cited ANL, p. 649.

3. "Geroi Otečestvennoj vojny po gr. L. N. Tolstomu" (1869), 10:101.

4. Leskov to L. N. Tolstoy, May 18, 1894 (*Pis'ma Tolstogo i k Tolstomu* [Moscow, 1928], p. 167).

5. Leskov to A. S. Suvorin, Dec. 30, 1890; cited ANL, p. 649.

6. Leskov to N. P. Krokhin, April 6, 1889; cited ANL, p. 648.

7. Leskov to L. N. Tolstoy, May 18, 1894 (*Pis'ma Tolstogo*, p. 167).

8. ANL, p. 664.

9. Chekhov to A. S. Suvorin, Feb. 25, 1895 (A. P. Čexov, *Sobranie sočinenij*, 12 [Moscow, 1964]: 69).

10. The full text of Leskov's will, with the exception of the paragraph dealing with property, is published in ANL, pp. 671-672.

11. Lidija Veselitskaja (V. Mikulič), "Pis'ma N. S. Leskova," *Literaturnaja mysl'; al'manax*, 3 (Leningrad, 1925): 301.

Bibliographical Note

The following is a brief survey of works by and about Leskov.

Editions of Leskov's works

The "canonical" edition—the last one seen through the press by the author and thus containing final authoritative texts—is the following: N. S. Leskov, *Sobranie sočinenij* (SPb.: A. S. Suvorin, 1889-90), 10 vols. Two supplementary volumes were issued in Petersburg in 1893 and 1896 by a different publisher, A. F. Marks. Although the final, twelfth volume appeared after Leskov's death, he had prepared the material for it, and its texts are therefore likewise authoritative. This edition was reprinted, in twelve volumes, by Marks in 1897, with an introduction by Rostislav Sementkovsky. An expanded edition, in thirty-six volumes, was published by Marks in 1902-1903 as a supplement to his magazine *Ploughland;* and for many years this remained the most widely accessible multivolume edition of Leskov. The first large-scale Soviet edition came out in the Khrushchev era: N. S. Leskov, *Sobranie sočinenij,* ed. V. G. Bazanov and others (Moscow, 1956-1958), 11 vols. Besides an introduction by Boris Eikhenbaum and P. P. Gromov and extensive commentaries, it contains some fiction omitted from the last Marks edition, but it also omits several stories and the entire novel *At Daggers Drawn* included in that edition. The last two volumes (10 and 11) contain a small selection of Leskov's nonfiction and a large number of his letters, some published there for the first time.

Bibliographies of Leskov's works

Since many of Leskov's works, especially his articles, have never been reprinted, these bibliographies are of crucial importance. The fundamental one was compiled by P. V. Bykov: "Bibliografija sočinenij N. S. Leskova za tridcat' let (1860-1889)," included in vol. 10 (1890) of the first edition of the collected works. (It is considerably fuller than the separate edition published the previous year.) It was supplemented by S. P. Šesterikov, "K bibliografii sočinenij N. S. Leskova," *Izvestija otdelenija russkogo jazyka i slovesnosti Rossijskoj Akademii Nauk*, 30 (1925), 268-310. See also B. Ja. Buxštab, *N. S. Leskov; ukazatel' osnovnoj literatury* (Moscow, 1948).

English translations

The Sentry, and Other Stories, tr. A. E. Chamot (London, 1922; New York, 1923; rpt. Westport, Conn., 1977). *The Cathedral Folk*, tr. Isabel F. Hapgood (New York and London, 1924; rpt. Westport, Conn., 1971). *The Enchanted Wanderer*, tr. A. G. Paschkoff (New York, 1924; London, 1926). *The Musk-ox and Other Tales*, tr. R. Norman (London, 1944; rpt. Westport, Conn., 1977). *The Enchanted Pilgrim and Other Stories*, tr. David Magarshack (London, 1946; rpt. Westport, Conn., 1977). *The Amazon and Other Stories*, tr. David Magarshack (London, 1949; rpt. London, 1962, under the title *Sinners and Saints*, and under the original title in Westport, Conn., 1977). *Selected Tales*, tr. David Magarshack (New York, 1961). *Satirical Stories*, tr. William B. Edgerton (New York, 1968). *The Wild Beast*, tr. Guy Daniels (New York, 1968). Separate editions of "The Lefthander" have been published under various titles: *The Steel Flea*, tr. Isabel F. Hapgood (Boston, 1906); *The Steel Flea*, adapted by Babette Deutsch and Avrahm Yarmolinsky (New York, 1924); *Lefty; Being the Tale of Cross-eyed Lefty of Tula and the Steel Flea*, tr. George H. Hanna (Moscow, 1965). In addition, a larger selection of Leskov stories has been published in Moscow in English: *The Enchanted Wanderer and Other Stories*, tr. George H. Hanna (Moscow, n.d. [1958?]).

Leskov scholarship

The record of Russian scholarship on Leskov is lamentable. Before the Revolution only two monographs on him had appeared. The first was by the proto-Symbolist critic Akim Volynsky (Flekser), *N. S. Leskov* (SPb., 1898), also included in his *Carstvo Karamazovyx* (SPb., 1901); the Leskov chapters were reprinted without change in Petrograd in 1923. It marked the beginning of a revision of the traditional nineteenth-century underestimation of Leskov's stature and showed some appreciation of the aesthetic qualities of his work, but it is unsystematic and inaccurate and often uses Leskov merely as a pretext for long disquisitions on the critic's own pet ideas. The second was by the neopopulist critic and journalist Anatoly Faresov: *Protiv tečenij: N. S. Leskov; ego žizn', sočinenija, polemika i vospominanija o nem* (SPb., 1904). For all its many faults of conception and organization it has permanent scholarly value, primarily because it contains what purport to be transcriptions of numerous conversations Faresov had with Leskov in the 1890s.

In the Soviet period, apart from a few scattered articles, no new full-length study of Leskov was published until 1945. In that year the fiftieth anniversary of the writer's death was commemorated by the appearance of a comprehensive and well-written monograph by Leonid Grossman: *N. S. Leskov, žizn', tvorčestvo, poètika* (Moscow, 1945), only slightly marred by various exigencies of the Stalin period. In the same year appeared a less ambitious, but valuable work by Valentina Gebel: *N. S. Leskov; v tvorčeskoj laboratorii* (Moscow, 1945), which makes extensive use of unpublished materials. Finally, in 1954, it was at last possible to publish—posthumously, alas—the massive biography of Leskov by his son Andrei: *Žizn' Nikolaja Leskova po ego ličnym, semejnym i nesemejnym zapisjam i pamjatjam* (Moscow, 1954). This monumental work not only contains vast amounts of new material on the writer's private as well as public life, but is a work of art in its own right.

In more recent years, Soviet scholarship on Leskov has been more prolific than distinguished. Five monographs have appeared, none of which rises above the level of mediocrity: B. M. Drugov, *N. S. Leskov; očerk tvorčestva* (Moscow, 1957; 2nd ed., Moscow, 1961); M. S. Gorjačkina, *Satira Leskova* (Moscow, 1963); N. S. Pleščunov, *Romany Leskova "Nekuda" i "Soborjane"* (Baku, 1963); V. Ju. Troickij, *Leskov-xudožnik* (Moscow, 1974); L. G. Čudnova, *Leskov v Peterburge* (Leningrad, 1974). Even the warmest thaw temperatures did not unfreeze at least three manuscript books on Leskov held in Soviet archives, the most important of which is a detailed chronological account of his life and works by the late S. P. Shesterikov: "Trudy i dni Leskova." (Notes on this work were kindly made available to me by William B. Edgerton.) It has been extensively used by Shesterikov's widow, K. P. Bogaevskaya, in her much abbreviated chronology of Leskov's life and works appended to the eleventh volume of the 1956-1958 edition of Leskov's works (pp. 799-834). Other unpublished works are mentioned by Solomon Reisser in an article written in 1930:

a bibliography of works about Leskov also compiled by S. P. Shester-ikov: "Materialy dlja bibliografičeskogo ukazatelja russkoj literatury o Leskove" and a pre-Revolutionary biography by the critic and paro-dist A. Izmailov. See S. Reisser, "Die Leskov-Forschung in den letzten Jahren," *Zeitschrift für slavische Philologie*, vol. 6, nos. 3-4 (1930), 495-513.

Until the Second World War no significant research on Leskov had been done outside of Russia. Three monographs about him had ap-peared in Western languages, one in French, one in German, and one in Swedish; but they are all trivial and slipshod compilations: Pierre Kovalewsky, *Nikolai Leskov: peintre méconnu de la vie nationale russe* (Paris, 1925); Marie Luise Rössler, *Nikolai Leskov und seine Darstellung des religiösen Menschen* (Weimar, 1939); Fredrik Böök, *Det eviga Ryssland; en studie över Nikolaj Leskov* (Stockholm, 1942). Since 1945, however, the situation has improved. In the 1950s two ex-cellent dissertations on Leskov were written outside the Soviet Union, one in Germany and the other in the United States, both of which finally gave religion its due in Leskov's development: Brigitte Macher, "Nikolai Leskovs Verhältnis zur Orthodoxie" (Marburg, 1952); Wil-liam B. Edgerton, "Nikolai Leskov: The Intellectual Development of a Literary Nonconformist" (Columbia University, 1954). More recently, there has been quite a proliferation of Leskov dissertations in English, not all of which, unfortunately, could be used in the present work: Thomas Lee Aman, "Structural Features of Leskov's *Soborjane* and His Stories of the 1860s" (Toronto, 1968); Valentina Kompaniec Bar-som, "The Misunderstood Leskov: Leskov in Pre-Revolutionary and Soviet Literary Criticism" (Pittsburgh, 1969); Stephen S. Lottridge, "Nikolaj Semenovič Leskov's *Prolog* Tales" (Columbia, 1970); James George Kelso Russell, "Leskov and Folklore" (Princeton, 1971).

Three monographs on Leskov have appeared in German since the war: a compact and well-informed, though somewhat hostile, life and works by Vsevolod Setchkarev, *Nikolaj Leskov: sein Leben und sein Werk* (Wiesbaden, 1959); a rather pedantic study, relentlessly formal-istic, of some of Leskov's longer works by Bodo Zelinsky: *Roman und Romanchronik: Strukturuntersuchungen zur Erzählkunst Nikolaj Leskovs* (Cologne and Vienna, 1970); and a solid treatise on his lan-guage by Wolfgang Girke, *Studien zur Sprache N. S. Leskovs* (Munich, 1969). A popular, well-grounded collection of essays on Leskov has been published in Dutch: *Over Ljeskow* (Amsterdam, 1957); it contains original essays by Thomas Eekman and C. G.

Schwenke as well as selections from Andrei Leskov's biography, translated by Eekman.

Bibliographies of articles on Leskov are to be found in many of the monographs and dissertations listed above.

Leskov's Fiction

The following list of Leskov's fictional writings is arranged by date of publication (not composition). From it the reader can readily identify references to the Soviet edition of Leskov's collected works, which is also chronologically arranged (N. S. Leskov, *Sobranie sočinenij*, ed. V. G. Bazanov and others [Moscow, 1956-1958], 11 vols.). This edition is cited in the text by volume and page number only. For convenience, the list also includes the contents of the last pre-Revolutionary edition (N. S. Leskov, *Polnoe sobranie sočinenij* [St. Petersburg, 1902-1903], 36 vols.), identified in the notes as "P.s.s." A few stories not included in either of these editions have also been listed; these are starred, and full bibliographical references for them will be found in the notes. No attempt has been made to include here Leskov's uncollected nonfiction, lists of which will be found in the Bykov and Shesterikov bibliographies (see Bibliographical Note).

English title	Russian title	1902-1903	1956-1958
	1862		
*A Case That Was Dropped [= Drought]	Pogasšee delo [= Zasuxa]		
*In a Coach	V tarantase		
The Robber	Razbojnik		1:1-10
	1863		
*The Mind Takes Its Own and the Devil His Own	Um svoe, a čert svoe		
*A Short History of a Case of Private Derangement	Kratkaja istorija odnogo častnogo umopomeša- tel'stva		
*My Darling! What's the Use of Talking?	Kochanko moja! Na co nam rozmowa?		

English title	Russian title	1902-1903	1956-1958
The Musk-ox	Ovcebyk	14:3-69	1:31-95
The Mocker [= The Stinger]	Jazvitel'nyj	22:114-133	1:11-30
The Life of a Peasant Martyress	Žitie odnoj baby		1:263-385
	1864		
No Way Out	Nekuda	vols. 8-11 (complete)	vol. 2 (complete)
	1865		
Lady Macbeth of the Mtsensk District	Ledi Makbet Mcenskogo uezda	13:83-130	1:96-143
The Bypassed	Obojdennye	6 (complete) 7:3-102	
	1866		
*A Humble Petition [poem]	Čelobitnaja		
The Battle-axe	Voitel'nica	13:3-82	1:144-221
The Islanders	Ostrovitjane	12 (complete)	3:5-192
	1867		
*Waiting for the Moving of the Water	Čajuščie dviženija vody		
Kotin the He-Cow and Platonida	Kotin doilec i Platonida	16:86-125	1:222-262
The Spendthrift	Rastočitel'	36:65-166	1:386-489
*Dwellers in God's House	Božedomy		
	1869		
Old Times in the Village of Plodomasovo	Starye gody v sele Plodomasove	16:3-85	3:193-275
	1870		
An Enigmatic Man	Zagadočnyj čelovek	28:3-111	3:276-381
	1870-1871		
At Daggers Drawn	Na nožax	vols. 23-27 (complete)	
	1871		
Laughter and Grief	Smex i gore	15:5-193	3:382-570

English title	Russian title	1902-1903	1956-1958
	1872		
Cathedral Folk	Soborjane	1:67-188 2 (complete)	4:5-319
	1873		
The Sealed Angel	Zapečatlennyj angel	3:5-72	4:320-384
The Enchanted Pilgrim [= The Enchanted Wan- derer]	Očarovannyj strannik	5:3-135	4:385-513
	1874		
A Decrepit Clan	Zaxudalyj rod	17:5-215	5:5-211
Pavlin [The Peacock]	Pavlin	34:105-166	5:212-278
	1875		
Years of Childhood	Detskie gody [= Bluždajuščie ogon'ki]	32:3-170	5:279-450
At the Edge of the World	Na kraju sveta	7:101-172	5:451-517
	1876		
Iron Will	Železnaja volja		6:5-87
The Pygmy	Pigmej	3:108-121	
	1877		
Episcopal Justice	Vladyčnyj sud	22:55-113	6:88-145
The Cynic	Besstydnik	16:166-179	6:146-158
The Unbaptized Priest	Nekreščenyj pop	22:3-54	6:159-210
	1878		
*An Apparition	Javlenie duxa		
The Melamed of Österreich	Rakušanskij melamed	14:130-165	
	1878-1879		
The Little Things in a Bishop's Life	Meloči arxierejskoj žizni	35:3-140 (bowlderized)	6:398-538
Russian Cryptomatrimony	Russkoe tajnobračie		6:578-623
	1879		
The Monognome [= Singlethought]	Odnodum	3:76-107	6:211-243

English title	Russian title	1902-1903	1956-1958
Sheramur	Šeramur	5:136-192	6:244-301
Exorcism [= Devilchase]	Čertogon	14:187-199	6:302-314
A Bishop's Rounds	Arxierejskie ob"ezdy		6:539-557
1880			
Diocesan Justice	Eparxial'nyj sud	35:159-173	6:558-577
The Cadet Monastery	Kadetskij monastyr'	3:122-157	6:315-350
Deathless Golovan	Nesmertel'nyj Golovan	4:5-50	6:351-397
White Eagle	Belyj orel	14:166-186	7:5-25
A Russian Democrat in Poland	Russkij demokrat v Pol'še	3:158-175	
1881			
A Flaming Patriot	Plamennaja patriotka	16:157-165	
*Christ Visits a Muzhik	Xristos v gostjax u mužika		
The Lefthander [= Lefty; The Steel Flea]	Levša	4:109-141	7:26-59
Leon the Butler's Son	Leon dvoreckij syn		7:60-78
The Spirit of Mme Genlis	Dux gospoži Žanlis	18:169-182	7:79-92
1882			
The Darner	Štopal'ščik	18:124-139	7:93-109
An Apparition in the Engineers' Castle	Prividenie v inženernom zamke	18:51-64	7:110-124
Yid Somersault	Židovskaja kuvyrkalegija	18:140-168	
A Journey with a Nihilist	Putešestvie s nigilistom	19:12-19	7:125-131
*The Celestial Serpent	Rajskij zmej		
*A Struggle for Supremacy [= Personages of the Synod]	Bor'ba za preobladanie [= Sinodal'nye persony]		
*Vagabonds of the Cloth	Brodjagi duxovnogo čina		
1883			
*Falcon Flight	Sokolij perelet		
Deception	Obman	18:91-123	

English title	Russian title	1902-1903	1956-1958
*The Sensible Robber	Blagorazumnyj razbojnik		
The Magic Ruble	Nerazmennyj rubl'	18:22-30	
Pechersk Eccentrics	Pečerskie antiki	31:3-89	7:133-219
The Toupee Artist	Tupejnyj xudožnik	16:126-147	7:220-242
The Voice of Nature	Golos prirody	21:47-55	7:243-251
A Little Mistake	Malen'kaja ošibka	19:20-27	7:252-259
The Wild Beast	Zver'	18:31-50	7:260-279
*Philosopher of the Synod	Sinodal'nyj filosof		
*Senichka's Poison	Seničkin jad		
*An Adventure at the Church of the Savior in Nalivki [= Priestly Leapfrog and Parish Caprice]	Priključenie u Spasa na Nalivkax [= Popovskaja čexarda i prixodskaja prixot']		

1884

English title	Russian title	1902-1903	1956-1958
*New Testament Jews	Novozavetnye evrei		
An Enigmatic Event in a Madhouse	Zagadočnoe proisšestvie v sumasšedšem dome	20:105-118	
Choice Grain	Otbornoe zerno	18:65-90	7:280-304
Notes in an Unknown Hand	Zametki neizvestnogo		7:322-398
The Old Genius	Staryj genij	19:3-11	7:313-321
The Co-functionaries	Sovmestiteli	19:105-137	7:399-431
*Two Swineherds	Dva svinopasa		
*The Debauchers	Pagubniki		
*Unlimited Goodness	Bezgraničnaja dobrota		
*Sleepy Memories at the Trial of Sarah Becker	Dremotnye vospominanija na dele Sarry Bekker		
*A Faint Trace	Nezametnyj sled		

1885

English title	Russian title	1902-1903	1956-1958
The Alexandrite	Aleksandrit	20:91-104	
Pearl Necklace	Žemčužnoe ožerel'e	18:6-21	7:432-447
Ancient Psychopaths	Starinnye psixopaty	19:138-182	7:448-491

English title	Russian title	1902-1903	1956-1958
The Bugbear	Pugalo	19:28-78	8:5-54
Interesting Men	Interesnye mužčiny	20:3-60	8:55-111
Mysterious Omens	Tainstvennye predvestija	20:61-90	
	1886		
*An Aleutian Clairvoyant	Aleutskij duxovidec		
*Fish Soup without Fish	Uxa bez ryby		
The Tale of the God-favored Woodcutter	Povest' o bogougodnom drovokole	29:91-95	11:103-108
The Tale of Theodore the Christian and His Friend Abraham the Hebrew	Povest' o Fedore-xristianine i o druge ego Abrame-židovine	30:88-111	
	1887		
Domestic Bondmen	Domašnjaja čeljad'	22:150-163	
Pamphalon the Mountebank	Skomorox Pamfalon	29:108-165	8:174-231
The Sentry	Čelovek na časax	4:142-160	8:154-173
A Robbery	Grabež	13:131-172	8:112-153
The Unmercenary Engineers	Inženery-bessrebreniki	4:51-108	8:232-290
	1888		
The Legend of Conscience-stricken Daniel	Legenda o sovestnom Danile	30:3-20	
The Beauteous Aza	Prekrasnaja Aza	29:96-107	8:291-302
The Elder Jerome's Lion	Lev starca Gerasima	30:21-28	
The Dead Estate	Umeršee soslovie	20:119-131	8:450-462
Kolyvan Husband	Kolyvanskij muž	14:70-129	8:390-449
Antukà	Antukà	13:173-199	
	1889		
The Felon of Ashkelon	Askalonskij zlodej	30:29-87	
Figura	Figura	19:79-104	8:463-485
	1890		
Vexation of Spirit	Tomlenie duxa	16:148-156	
The Mountain	Gora	29:3-90	8:303-389

English title	Russian title	1902-1903	1956-1958
The Devil's Puppets	Čertovy kukly	31:90-167	8:487-564
The Hour of God's Will	Čas voli Božiej	29:166-191	9:5-49
*Offended before Christmas	Pod Roždestvo obideli		

1891

Innocent Prudentius	Nevinnyj Prudencij	30:112-178	9:50-116
Night Owls	Polunoščniki	34:3-102	9:117-217
The Little Fool	Duraček	33:118-125	

1892

Vale of Tears	Judol'	33:3-96	9:218-312
On Quakeresses	O "kvakerejax"	33:97-105	9:313-321
The Improvisers	Improvizatory	36:47-64	9:322-339
Legendary Characters	Legendarnye xaraktery	23:126-195	

1893

Siberian Scenes of the Eighteenth Century	Sibirskie kartinki XVIII veka	21:56-110	
A Product of Nature	Produkt prirody	22:134-149	9:340-355
The Pustoplyasians	Pustopljasy	33:106-117	
The Cattle-pen	Zagon	20:132-164	9:356-396

1894

Inspired Vagabonds	Vdoxnovennye brodjagi	21:111-145	
Descent into Hell	Sošestvie vo ad	21:146-163	
A Winter's Day	Zimnij den'	28:112-170	9:397-455
The Lady and the Wench	Dama i fefela	21:3-46	9:456-500

1899

Concerning "The Kreutzer Sonata"	Po povodu "Krejcerovoj sonaty"		9:32-49

1903

Brahmadatta and Radovan	Bramadata i Radovan	30:179-192	
Malanya Muttonhead	Malan'ja—golova baran'ja	33:196-201	

English title	Russian title	1902-1903	1956-1958
	1917		
The Rabbit Warren [= The March Hare]	Zajačij remiz		9:501-591
*Insulted Neteta	Oskorblennaja Netèta		
	1924		
*Amour in Bast Shoes	Amur v lapotočkax		
	1934		
Administrative Grace	Administrativnaja gracija		9:388-396
*A Wild Fantasy	Dikaja fantazija		
	1957		
Man of Darkness	Temnjak		5:552-573
	1958		
A Just Man	Spravedlivyj čelovek		7:305-312

∽ Index ∾

Index

Index

Leskov, Nikolai (*works, cont'd*):
221, 257-270, 273, 274, 275, 279, 290-291, 322, 353, 354, 388, 493, 547, 575, 680, 703; "Descent into Hell" ("Sošestvie vo ad"), 486-487, 715; *The Devil's Puppets* (*Čertovy kukly*), 503-512, 700, 717, 718, 719; "Devočka ili mal'čik?" 722; "Diocesan Justice" ("Eparxial'nyj sud"), 347, 350, 690; "Drought" ("Zasuxa"), *see* "A Case That Was Dropped"; "Dvorjanskij bunt v Dobrynskom prixode," 647, 650, 681, 694; "The Dwarfs of Plodomasovo" ("Plodomasovskie karliki"), 177, 185, 188-189, 289, 671; "Dwellers in God's House" ("Božedomy"), early version of *Cathedral Folk*, 152, 176-177, 192, 205, 207, 671, 673, 674

"The Elder Jerome's Lion" ("Lev starca Gerasima"), 577-579, 733-734; *The Enchanted Pilgrim* (*Očarovannyj strannik*), 221, 242-255, 280, 290, 353, 438, 619, 677; "Energetic Tactlessness" ("Energičnaja bestaktnost' "), 539, 684, 685, 723; "An Enigmatic Incident in an Insane Asylum" ("Zagadočnoe proisšestvie v sumasšedšem dome"), 473-474, 713; "An Enigmatic Man" ("Zagadočnyj čelovek"), 69, 78, 84, 130, 131, 214-217, 665, 675, 687; "Episcopal Justice" ("Vladyčnyj sud"), 37-39, 40, 299, 302, 309-313, 344, 410, 415, 418-419, 651, 685, 686-687, 698, 707; "Evrejskaja gracija" 704-705; "Exorcism" ("Čertogon"), revised version of "Christmas Eve with a Hypochondriac," 376, 383, 460, 696; "Explanation" ("Ob'jasnenie") 131, 665, 666

A Faint Trace (*Nezametnyj sled*), 471, 496, 497-503, 665, 716, 717; *Falcon Flight* (*Sokolij perelet*), 493-497, 498, 502, 503, 665, 716, 744; "The Featherbrains," *see* "Deception"; "The Felon of Ashkelon" ("Askalonskij zlodej"), 395, 579-582, 587, 734; "Figura," 353, 547-549, 692, 724, 725; "Fish Soup without Fish" ("Uxa bez

Leskov, Nikolai (*works, cont'd*):
ryby"), 428-429, 485, 706; "A Flaming Patriot" ("Plamennaja patriotka"), 326-327, 688; "From a Travel Diary" ("Iz odnogo dorožnogo dnevnika"), 86-87, 647, 651, 657, 678; "From You It Doesn't Hurt" ("Ot tebja ne bol'no"), 658, 661

"Gde vojuet vol'nyj kazak," 715; "Geroi otečestvennoj vojny po gr. L. N. Tolstomu," 720, 746; "A Ghostly Apparition" ("Javlenie duxa"), 693, 696; "A Ghostly Witness for Women" ("Zagrobnyj svidetel' za ženščin"), 526-527, 721; "Graf L. N. Tolstoj i F. M. Dostoevskij kak eresiarxi," 720

"Herod's Work" ("Irodova rabota"), 327, 328, 659, 687, 688; *A High-Society Schism* (*Velikosvetskij raskol*), 331, 333-337, 683, 689, 690 712; "The Hour of God's Will" ("Čas voli Božiej"), 550-553, 593, 725; "How I Learned to Celebrate" ("Kak ja učilsja prazdnovat' "), 29, 146, 649, 668; "How People Are Poisoned by Coal Fumes in Paris" ("Kak otravljajutsja ugol'nym čadom v Pariže"), 648, 658; "A Humble Petition" ("Čelobitnaja"), 211-212, 675

"Iezuit Gagarin v dele Puškina," 648, 684; "The Improvisers" ("Improvizatory"), 613-614, 741; "In a Coach" ("V tarantase"), 103-104, 152, 661; "Innocent Prudentius" ("Nevinnyj Prudentij"), 587-592, 736; "Inspired Vagabonds" ("Vdoxnovennye brodjagi"), 486, 715; "Insulted Neteta" ("Oskorblennaja Netèta"), 581, 592-595, 596, 736, 737; "Interesting Men" ("Interesnye mužčiny"), 475, 478-481, 714; "An Invasion of Barbarians," early verion of "Rabbit Warren," 626-627, 743-744; "Iron Will" ("Železnaja volja"), 53, 285, 322-326, 329, 389, 688; "Iskanie škol staroobrjadcami." 659, 687; *The Islanders* ("Ostrovitjane"), 161-163, 170, 321, 504, 669;

Index

Leskov, Nikolai (*works, cont'd*):
662; "Neulovimyj mnogoženec (Iz istorii bračnyx zatrudnenij)," 667; "Neskol'ko slov o policejskix vračax v Rossii," 653; "Neskol'ko slov o vračax rekrutskix prisutstvij," 650, 653, 705; "New Testament Jews" ("Novozavetnye evrei"), 472, 712; *Night Owls* ("Polunoščniki"), 152-153, 292, 301, 353, 358, 403, 460, 461, 483, 588, 593, 596, 598-609, 614, 615, 623, 697, 738, 739, 740; "Nikolaj Gavrilovič Černyševskij v ego romane 'Čto delat'?'" 665; *No Way Out* (*Nekuda*), 18, 49, 69, 71, 72-77, 109, 123-138, 141-143, 144, 145, 164, 173, 191, 207, 208, 216, 217, 231, 261, 348, 351, 399, 434, 455, 492, 494, 496-497, 511, 519, 533, 618, 619, 652, 662, 665, 666, 667-668, 671, 708, 716, 744; "A Note on Buildings" ("Zametka o zdanijax"), 60, 649, 653; "Note on Myself," 30; "Notes in an Unknown Hand" ("Zametki neizvestnogo"), 456-460, 466, 497, 709, 710; "Notes on Russian Society" ("Russkie obščestvennye zametki"), 208, 674, 720; "Novye brošjury, pripisyvaemye peru gr. L. N. Tolstogo," 721

"O dobrom grešnike," 731; "O krest'janskix vkusax," 709; "O naemnoj zavisimosti," 654; "O nekotoryx bumagax Pelikana," 713; *O raskol'nikax goroda Rigi, preimuščestvenno v otnošenii k školam*, 93, 659, 671; "O russkom rasselenii i o politiko-èkonomičeskom komitete," 653-654; "O šepotnikax i pečatnikax," 666; "O suščnosti i značenii raskola," 659; "O vol'nom kazake," 715; "O xoždenii Štandelja po Jasnoj Poljane," 722; "O xudožnom muže Nikite i o sovospitannyx emu," 680; "O zamečatel'nom, no ne blagotvornom napravlenii nekotoryx sovremennyx pisatelej," 654; "Ob Irodovoj temnice (Pis'mo v redakciju)," 700, 734; "Ob odnoj pračke," 695; "Ob jasnenie po

Leskov, Nikolai (*works, cont'd*):
trem punktam," 712; "Obrjady i sueverija evreev," 704-705; "Offended before Christmas" ("Pod Roždestvo obideli"), 391, 553-556, 558, 699, 722, 726; "The Old Genius" ("Staryj genij"), 389, 698; "Old Times in the Village of Plodomasovo" ("Starye gody v sele Plodomasove"), 177, 185-188, 257, 261, 457, 671; "On Quakeresses" ("O kvakerejax"), 446-447, 473, 486, 707; "On the Kitchen Muzhik, Etc." ("O kufel'nom mužike i proč."), 526, 661, 721; "On the Russian Lefthander (A Literary Explanation)," 395; "On the Working Class" ("O rabočem klasse"), 60-61, 653, 654; "Otkuda posla glagolemaja 'erunda' ili 'xirunda,'" 717

"Pamphalon the Mountebank" ("Skomorox Pamfalon"), 394-395, 566-570, 729, 732; "Pavlin," 183, 275-278, 279, 681; "Pearl Necklace" ("Žemčužnoe ožerel'e"), 373-375, 378, 385, 389-390, 475, 698; "Pechersk Eccentrics" ("Pečerskie antiki"), 44, 93, 179, 240, 408-416, 547, 651, 671, 679, 703, 704; "A Pedagogical Monstrosity" ("Pedagogičeskoe jurodstvo"), 539-540, 684, 723; "Personalities of the Synod" ("Sinodal'nye persony"), 25, 694, 711, 714; "Pervenec bogemy v Rossii," 700, 705; "Pis'mo iz Peterburga," 653, 654, 656; "Policejskie vrači v Rossii," 653; "Poslednee slovo o 'Meločax' (Pis'mo v redakciju)," 691; "Poslednjaja vstreča i poslednjaja razluka s Ševčenko," 654; "Possessed Salt" ("Obujannaja sol'"). 555, 722, 726; "Praktičeskaja zametka; ob iščuščix kommerčeskix mest v Rossii," 654; "Pribavlenie k rasskazu o Kadetskom monastyre," 690-691; "Priestly Leap-frog and Parish Caprice" ("Popovskaja čexarda i prixodskaja prixot'"), 369, 694; "A Product of Nature" ("Produkt prirody"), 53, 447-

Index

Index